# Foundations of Marketing
## Fourth Canadian Edition

# Foundations of Marketing

## Fourth Canadian Edition

M. DALE BECKMAN

DAVID L. KURTZ

LOUIS E. BOONE

HOLT, RINEHART AND WINSTON OF CANADA, LIMITED   TORONTO

**Canadian Cataloguing in Publication Data**
Beckman, M. Dale, 1934–
    Foundations of marketing

4th ed.
Includes bibliographical references and indexes.
ISBN 0-03-922577-1

1. Marketing.   I. Kurtz, David L.   II. Boone, Louis E.   III. Title.

HF5415.B42 1988      658.8      C88-093309-7

Publisher: Richard Kitowski
Editor: Rachel Campbell
Publishing Services Manager: Karen Eakin
Editorial Co-ordinator: Edie Franks
Copy Editor: Riça Night
Interior Design: Peter Maher
Cover Design: Pronk and Associates
Typesetting and Assembly: Compeer Typographic Services Limited
Printing and Binding: T. H. Best Printing Company Limited

Printed in Canada

2 3 4 5    92 91 90 89

# *Preface*

The late 1980s are both trying and exciting times in which to begin a study of marketing. Organizations — both profit and nonprofit — are engaged in intense competition for customers, audiences, and clients. The marketplace has grown rapidly. Rising costs and the increasing scarcity of energy and other needed resources have resulted in increasingly complex decision-making. Marketing will play an important role in the Canadian economy. Organizations ranging from the local symphony orchestra to the Federal Government are attempting to employ marketing concepts and techniques in their operations. Politicians, hospital administrators, accountants, financial institutions, and provincial tourism offices are studying — and applying — marketing knowledge in their attempts to identify their clients and provide them with needed services.

*Foundations of Marketing* is designed to be the textbook for such an environment. It provides the reader with the following features that we believe make it one of the most thorough and comprehensive textbooks available.

- Comprehensive coverage of marketing planning and strategy and of orthodox marketing subjects

*Foundations of Marketing* is written with a strong marketing planning/strategy orientation. Several chapters deal with the vital subjects of marketing planning, forecasting, evaluation, and control. Two chapters are devoted to market segmentation. Since planning occurs at the beginning of the marketing effort, coverage of marketing planning and forecasting begins in Chapter 3.

- Major emphasis on consumer behaviour and elements of the marketing mix

Although the text does emphasize the importance of marketing planning, this is not done at the expense of coverage of essential marketing concepts. The vital subjects of consumer behaviour and the elements of the marketing mix are stressed throughout the book. *Foundations* devotes two entire chapters to the critical subject of consumer behaviour, and a third chapter is devoted to industrial buyer behaviour. In addition, at least two chapters are devoted to each of the elements of the marketing mix, and separate chapter treatment of retailing, wholesaling, and physical distribution is provided.

• Separate chapter coverage of important marketing subjects

This textbook pays special attention to emerging areas of marketing. The areas of international marketing, marketing of services, industrial marketing, marketing and society, and marketing in non-profit settings are too important to ignore in the 1980s. *Foundations of Marketing* provides complete coverage of these subjects in the following chapters:

Chapter  9   Buyer Behaviour in Industrial and Government Markets
Chapter 12   Services
Chapter 22   International Marketing
Chapter 23   Marketing in Nonprofit Settings
Chapter 24   Marketing and Society

• Longer, more comprehensive cases in marketing

The authors have made a special effort to avoid simplistic, made-up cases that provide little possibility for class use. We thank the authors of the cases included at the end of the book for their assistance in obtaining them. This collection of thirty-one discussion-oriented cases makes it possible for instructors who use cases to choose from a good selection. Four more comprehensive cases are included for longer written assignments.

• Technical appendices

To provide instructors with more detailed, analytical material and additional reading assignments on several sections, the authors have included four technical appendices following appropriate chapters in *Foundations of Marketing*. The appendices are as follows:

Appendix A   Developing a Marketing Plan
Appendix B   Locating Secondary Data
Appendix C   Consumer Behaviour Models
Appendix D   Careers in Marketing

• Readable text with marketing concepts emphasized by real-world examples

*Foundations of Marketing* is comprehensive, systematic, and rigorous. We hope it is also both prctical and written in a lively, engaging manner that avoids tedious, boring prose. Readily identifiable cases and real-world examples are included to illustrate the application — correct and incorrect — of fundamental marketing concepts discussed in the text. Opening vignettes provide the reader with a flavour of the marketing concepts to be treated in each chapter. Examples following the explanation of each concept reinforce student learning. Comprehensive cases then require application of this knowledge. The book avoids sexist language and portrays women in realistic roles.

• The Marketing Disk

The study of marketing can be greatly enhanced by examining various problems using computer-assisted quantitative techniques. Accordingly, the exercises and software available with this book enhance the teaching and learning of such sophisticated concepts and analytical techniques.

Most chapters contain a section titled *Microcomputer Exercise,* where students are assigned quantitative problems focusing on a concept or technique discussed in the text. Additional computer-based problems are also included among the discussion questions and exercises at the end of the chapter.

Almost 100 computer problems are included in the text. Each of these computer problems can be solved with the use of a new software supplement available free to adopters for use with the IBM PC® microcomputer. *The Foundations of Marketing Disk* includes the following programs, presented in a user-friendly, menu-driven format for use in solving marketing problems:

1. Sales Forecasting
2. Engel's Laws
3. Sales Analysis
4. Evaluation of Alternatives
5. Competitive Bidding
6. Return on Investment
7. Breakeven Analysis
8. Decision Tree Analysis
9. Inventory Turnover
10. Markups
11. Markdowns
12. Economic Order Quantity (EOQ)
13. Promotional Budget Allocations
14. CPM
15. Sales Force Size Determination
16. ROAM
17. Ratio Analysis

Since full descriptions of each technique and sample worked-out problems are included in the text, the instructor can use these computer problems in a variety of formats. If students have ready access to microcomputers, problem assignments can be used as daily homework. If students do not have easy access to computers, the problems can be solved by using a hand calculator. When microcomputer access is difficult, instructors can integrate computer usage in their classes by making one or two assignments during the term and/or by spacing computer assignments for different groups of students throughout the course to relieve demand for computer access in the microcomputer lab. Each of these alternatives provides homework assignments involving quantitative problems for most chapters in the textbook.

• Comprehensive teaching-learning package

*Foundations of Marketing* is available in a complete educational package, designed for both instructor and student. The package includes:

*Study Guide:* a comprehensive aid for students. It includes review exercises to be done by the students as well as many study questions and cases that can be discussed in class. A special feature of the study guide is an extensive and comprehensive marketing project that unfolds with the textual materials. This provides a thread that requires students to tie theory and practice together. Experience has proven this to be a powerful learning aid.

*Chapter Organizer with Film Guide:* the most complete manual available with any basic marketing text. The *Chapter Organizer* includes lecture suggestions, a film guide, reference materials, and suggestions for using the transparency masters and acetates.

*Test Bank:* 2000 items organized into quiz-type and comprehensive exam-type questions. Written by Ann Walker of the Ryerson Polytechnical Institute, the *Test Bank* is available on floppy disk and in printed format.

*Transparencies:* a complete transparency package, prepared by Jim Forbes of The University of British Columbia, is available.

## *Publisher's Note to Instructors and Students*

This textbook is a key component of your course. If you are the instructor of this course, you undoubtedly considered a number of texts carefully before choosing this as the one that would work best for your students and you. The authors and publishers of this book spent considerable time and money to ensure its high quality, and we appreciate your recognition of this effort and accomplishment.

If you are a student we are confident that this text will help you to meet the objectives of your course. You will also find it helpful after the course is finished as a valuable addition to your personal library.

As well, please do not forget that photocopying copyright work means the authors lose royalties that are rightfully theirs. This loss will discourage them from writing another edition of this text or other books; doing so would simply not be worth their time and effort. If this happens we all lose — students, instructors, authors, and publishers.

Since we want to hear what you think about this book, please be sure to send up the stamped reply card at the end of the text. This will help us to continue publishing high-quality books for your course.

# Acknowledgements

The authors gratefully acknowledge the contributions of a large number of persons — colleagues, students, professional marketers in businesses and nonprofit organizations, and the fine professionals at Holt, Rinehart and Winston of Canada, Limited for their invaluable critiques, questions, and advice in making **Foundations of Marketing** a reality. In particular, our thanks go to Mike Roche, Ric Kitowski, and Edie Franks for their efforts. We would like to express our special appreciation to Professor Jim Forbes of the University of British Columbia for his comprehensive analysis and suggestions and Marvin Ryder of McMaster University for his cases. We would like to express our appreciation to the following instructors who have formally commented on this text over the years:

Padraig Cherry, British Columbia Institute of Technology
Byron Collins, Humber College
Knud Jenson, Ryerson Polytechnical Institute
Karen Karpuk, Southern Alberta Institute of Technology
William Lyon, Fanshawe College
David C. Mulder, Northern Alberta Institute of Technology
Lewis A. Presner, Durham College
Jay Rubinstein, Vanier College
J. Steen, Georgian College
Gordon Thomas, University of Manitoba
Don Yurchuk, Northern Alberta Institute of Technology
J.L. Zoellner, Seneca College

We would also like to thank Ron Scott of Scali, McCabe, Sloves (Canada) Ltd. for his cooperation and assistance in providing the full-colour Canadian advertisements that appear in this book. The specific advertisers — Volvo Canada Ltd., William Nielson Ltd., Labatts Brewing Company Limited, Chase Manhatten Bank of Canada — also deserve our appreciation.

M. Dale Beckman
Professor and Head
Dept. of Marketing
University of Manitoba
Winnipeg, Manitoba

David L. Kurtz
The Thomas F. Gleed Chair in Business Administration
Seattle University
Seattle, Washington

Louis E. Boone
Professor of Business Administration
University of South Alabama
Mobile, Alabama

January, 1988

# Contents

## Part 4   Products

## Part 5   Price

**Part 6   Distribution**

## Part 7   Promotion

Part 8   *Emerging Dimensions in Marketing*

## Cases

# PART

1

## The Marketing Envrionment

*CHAPTER 1*

## The Marketing Process

*CHAPTER 2*

## The Environment for Marketing Decisions

Marketing has been defined as the creation and delivery of a standard of living. Part One of Foundations of Marketing traces the evolution of marketing as a means of identifying and responding to the consumer's needs. Essential definitions and concepts are explained in order to define the relationship of marketing to society at large.

# The Marketing Process

1. *To explain the types of utility and the role played by marketing in their creation.*

2. *To relate the definition of marketing to the concept of the exchange process.*

3. *To contrast marketing activities in each of the three eras in the history of marketing.*

4. *To explain the concept of marketing myopia.*

5. *To identify the variables involved in marketing decision-making and the environments in which these decisions must be made.*

Would you predict success for a retailer with a fanatical dedication to quality of products offered to its customers? Marks and Spencer of Canada spends about $1 million a year in trying to achieve this. A staff of twenty technologists and quality control persons ensure that textiles used in their clothing are made to rigorous standards, monitoring all steps of the manufacturing process. Similarly, a staff of eight tastes every new item of food sold by the company, while senior technologists regularly visit food plants to make quality checks.

Marks and Spencer, Britain's most successful retailer discovered that quality products and methods that worked in Britain were not enough to make the firm successful in Canada. They ignored the fundamental fact that marketing success comes from finding out which products and services *customers* want, providing these, and then communicating the benefits offered to these customers.

After several years of financial losses, the company has finally added new and interesting styles and colours to its product assortment, and renovated stores to make them more interesting. It has also changed its no-advertising policy and allocated $1 million to an advertising campaign to inform people about the unique quality and values offered by this very interesting retail organization. Such an application of marketing thinking and practices augurs well for the future success of the company.[1]

---

[1] Based on James Walker, "New Look for Marks & Spencer," *Financial Times of Canada*, September 26, 1983, p. 3.

**The Conceptual Framework**

All business organizations perform two basic operating functions — they produce a good or a service, and they market it. This is true of all firms — from giant corporations such as Canada Packers and Canadian Pacific to the neighbourhood convenience store. Production and marketing are the very essence of economic life in any society.

**Production and Marketing Create Utility for the Consumer**

Through the production and marketing of desired goods and services, businesses fulfill the needs of society, their customers, and their owners. They create **utility**, which may be defined as *the want-satisfying power of a product or service*. There are four basic kinds of utility — form, time, place, and ownership.

*Form utility* is created when the firm converts raw materials and component inputs into finished products and services. Glass, steel, fabrics, rubber, and other components are combined to form a new Peugeot or Firebird. Cotton, thread, and buttons are converted into GWG jeans. Sheet music, musical instruments, musicians, a conductor, and the facilities of Roy Thomson Hall are converted into a performance by the Toronto Symphony. Although marketing inputs may be important in specifying consumer and audience preferences, the actual creation of form utility is the responsibility of the production function of the organization.

*Time, place,* and *ownership utility* are created by marketing. They are created when products and services are available to the consumer when the person wants to purchase them, at a convenient location, and where facilities are available whereby title to the product or service may be transferred at the time of purchase.

Chapter 1 sets the stage for the entire text by examining the meaning of marketing and its importance to organizations — both profit-seeking and nonprofit. The chapter examines the development of marketing in our society and its contributions. The marketing variables utilized in a marketing strategy are also introduced.

**What Is Marketing?**

All organizations must create utility if they are to survive. The design and marketing of want-satisfying products, services, and ideas is the foundation for the creation of utility. However, the role of marketing in the success of an organization has only recently been recognized. An expert on business management, Peter F. Drucker, emphasized the importance of marketing in his book, *The Practice of Management*.

If we want to know what a business is we have to start with its purpose. And its purpose must lie outside the business itself. In fact, it must lie in society since a business enterprise is an organ of society. There is one valid definition of business purpose: to create a customer.[2]

How does an organization "create" a customer? As Professors Guiltinan and Paul explain:

> Essentially, 'creating' a customer means identifying needs in the marketplace, finding out which needs the organization can profitably serve, and developing an offering to convert potential buyers into customers. Marketing managers are responsible for most of the activities necessary to create the customers the organization wants. These activities include:
> * identifying customer needs
> * designing products and services that meet those needs
> * communicating information about those products and services to prospective buyers
> * making the products or services available at times and places that meet customers' needs
> * pricing the products to reflect costs, competition, and customers' ability to buy
> * providing for the necessary service and follow-up to ensure customer satisfaction after the purchase.[3]

*Marketing Defined*   Ask five persons to define marketing and you are likely to get five definitions. Due to the continuing exposure to advertising and personal selling, most respondents are likely to link marketing and selling. The Definitions Committee of the American Marketing Association, the international professional association in the marketing discipline, has attempted to standardize marketing terminology by proposing the following definition: "Marketing is the process of planning and executing the conception, pricing, promotion, and distribution of ideas, goods, and services to create exchanges that satisfy individual and organizational objectives."[4]

This definition clearly indicates that marketing is much more than selling or advertising. It is a complete process of planning and organizing the market-linking activities of the organization. It is an organized behaviour system designed to generate outputs of value to consumers. Furthermore, it is not only concerned with products and services, but also ideas, and encompasses all types of organizations.

---

[2] Peter F. Drucker, *The Practice of Management* (New York: Harper & Row, 1954), p. 37.
[3] Joseph P. Guiltinan and Gordon W. Paul, *Marketing Management* (New York: McGraw-Hill, 1982), pp. 3–4.
[4] "AMA Board Approves New Marketing Definition," *The Marketing News* (March 1, 1985), p. 1.

Marketing is an important function for both profit and non-profit organizations. All have found that marketing is vital to their success. In profit-making organizations, profitability is achieved through creating customer satisfaction. In non-profit organizations, success in furthering the cause is the result of the same process of matching organizational offerings with target audience needs.

In a well-run organization, marketing activities do not begin with finished goods (or programs) ready for delivery. Instead, the first step is an analysis of how specific consumer needs might be better filled with products and services more precisely designed to meet those needs. Thus a properly oriented marketing system reflects consumer and societal needs.

This expanded concept of marketing activities should permeate all activities of an organization. It assumes that true marketing effort is in accordance with ethical business practices and that it is effective from the standpoint of both society and the individual firm. It also emphasizes the need for efficiency in distribution although the nature and degree of efficiency is dependent upon the kind of business environment within which the firm must operate. The final assumption included in the definition is that those consumer segments to be satisfied through production and marketing activities of the firm have already been selected and analysed *prior to* production. In other words, the customer, client, or public determines the marketing program.

However not all companies have a market orientation. In addition to market-oriented firms, there are still some which are *product-oriented* and/or *production-oriented*. In a product-oriented firm, the emphasis is on the product itself rather than the consumer's needs, while in the production-oriented firm, the dominant considerations in product design are those of ease or cheapness of production. In either case, market considerations are ignored or de-emphasized.[5]

## The Origins of Marketing

The essence of marketing is the **exchange process**. This is the process by which two or more parties give something of value to one another to satisfy felt needs.[6] In many cases, the item is a tangible

[5] M. Kubr, ed., *Management Consulting: A Guide to the Profession* (Geneva: International Labour Organization, 1977), pp. 188–189.

[6] Richard P. Bagozzi, "Marketing as an Organized Behavioral System of Exchange," *Journal of Marketing* (October 1974), p. 77. Further work by Bagozzi on this subject appears in "Marketing as Exchange," *Journal of Marketing* (October 1975), pp. 32–39, and "Marketing as Exchange: A Theory of Transactions in the Marketplace," *American Behavioral Scientist* (March–April 1978), pp. 535–536.

good, such as a newspaper, a hand calculator, or a pair of shoes. In other cases, intangible services, such as a car wash, transportation, or a concert performance, are exchanged for money. In still other instances, funds or time donations may be offered to political candidates, a Red Cross office, or a church or synagogue.

The marketing function is both simple and direct in subsistence-level economies. For example, assume that a primitive society consists solely of Person A and Person B. Assume also that the only elements of their standard of living are food, clothing, and shelter. The two live in adjoining caves on a mountainside. They weave their own clothes and tend their own fields independently. They are able to subsist even though their standard of living is minimal.

Person A is an excellent weaver but a poor farmer, while Person B is an excellent farmer but a poor weaver. In this situation, it would be wise for each to specialize in the line of work that he or she does best. The net result would then be a greater total production of both clothing and food. In other words, specialization and division of labour will lead to a production surplus. But neither A nor B is any better off until they *trade* the products of their individual labour, thereby creating the exchange process.

Exchange is the origin of marketing activity. In fact, marketing has been described as "the process of creating and resolving exchange relationships."[7] When there is a need to exchange goods, the natural result is marketing effort on the part of the people involved.

Wroe Alderson, a leading marketing theorist, said, "It seems altogether reasonable to describe the development of exchange as a great invention which helped to start primitive man on the road to civilization."[8]

While the cave dweller example is simplistic, it does point up the essence of the marketing function. Today's complex industrial society may have a more complicated exchange process, but the basic concept is the same: production is not meaningful until a system of marketing has been established. Perhaps the adage "Nothing happens until somebody sells something"[9] sums it up best.

---

**Three Eras in the History of Marketing**

Although marketing has always been present in businesses, its importance has varied greatly. Three historical eras can be identified: the production era, the sales era, and the marketing era.

---

7 *Ibid*.
8 Wroe Alderson, *Marketing Behavior and Executive Action* (Homewood, Ill.: Richard D. Irwin, 1962), p. 292.
9 T. G. Povey, "Spotting the Salesman Who Has What It Takes," *Nation's Business* (July 1972), p. 70.

The Production Era   One hundred years ago, most firms were production-oriented. Manufacturers stressed production of products and then looked for people to purchase them. The Pillsbury Company of this period is an excellent example of a production-oriented company. Here is how the company's board chairman, the late Robert J. Keith, described the Pillsbury of the early years:

> We are professional flour millers. Blessed with a supply of the finest North American wheat, plenty of water power, and excellent milling machinery, we produce flour of the highest quality. Our basic function is to mill high-quality flour, and, of course (and almost incidentally), we must hire salesmen to sell it, just as we hire accountants to keep our books.[10]

The prevailing attitude of this era was that a good product (defined in terms of physical quality) would sell itself. This production orientation dominated business philosophy for decades. Indeed, business success was often defined in terms of production victories.

Although marketing had emerged as a functional activity within the business organization prior to the twentieth century, management's orientation remained with production for quite some time. In fact, what might be called industry's production era did not reach its peak until the early part of this century. The apostle of this approach to business operations was Frederick W. Taylor, whose *Principles of Scientific Management* was widely read and accepted at that time. Taylor's approach reflected his engineering background by emphasizing efficiency in the production process. Later writers, such as Frank and Lillian Gilbreth, the originators of motion analysis, expanded on Taylor's basic concepts.

Henry Ford's mass production line serves as a good example of this orientation. Ford's slogan, "They [customers] can have any colour they want, as long as it's black," reflected a prevalent attitude toward marketing. Production shortages and intense consumer demand were the rule of the day. It is no wonder that production activities took precedence.

A production orientation still exists in many businesses today. Often a firm does not consider changing from this outdated approach until it runs into trouble.

The Sales Era   As production techniques became more sophisticated and as output grew, manufacturers began to increase the emphasis on an effective sales force to find customers for their output. This era saw firms attempting to match customers to their output.

---

10 Robert J. Keith, "The Marketing Revolution," *Journal of Marketing* (January 1960), p. 36.

A sales orientation assumes that customers will resist purchasing products and services not deemed essential, and that the task of personal selling and advertising is to convince them to buy. Marketing efforts were also aimed at wholesalers and retailers in an attempt to motivate them to stock greater quantities of the manufacturer's output.

Although marketing departments began to emerge during the sales era, they tended to remain in a subordinate position to production, finance, and engineering. Many chief marketing executives held the title of sales manager. Here is how Pillsbury was described during the sales era:

> We are a flour-milling company, manufacturing a number of products for the consumer market. We must have a first-rate sales organization which can dispose of all the products we can make at a favourable price. We must back up this sales force with consumer advertising and market intelligence. We want our sales representatives and our dealers to have all the tools they need for moving the output of our plants to the consumer.[11]

But selling is only one component of marketing. As marketing expert Theodore Levitt has pointed out: ". . . marketing is as different from selling as chemistry is from alchemy, astronomy from astrology, chess from checkers."[12]

The Marketing Era   As personal income and consumer demand for goods and services dropped rapidly during the Great Depression of the 1930s, marketing was thrust into a more important role. Organizational survival dictated that managers pay closer attention to the markets for their products. This trend was halted by the outbreak of World War II, when rationing and shortages of consumer goods were commonplace. The war years, however, were an atypical pause in an emerging trend that was resumed almost immediately after the hostilities ceased. An important new philosophy known as the marketing concept was about to emerge.

**Emergence of the Marketing Concept**

What was the setting for the crucial change in management philosophy? Perhaps it can best be explained by the shift from a **seller's market** (*one with a shortage of goods and services*) to a **buyer's**

---

[11]*Ibid*.
[12]Theodore Levitt, *Innovations in Marketing* (New York: McGraw-Hill, 1962), p. 7.

# "If You Build a Better Mousetrap . . ."

More than 100 years ago, the philosopher Ralph Waldo Emerson remarked, "If a man writes a better book, preaches a better sermon or makes a better mousetrap than his neighbour, though he builds his house in the woods, the world will make a beaten path to his door." The implications of this statement are that a quality product will sell itself and that an effective production function is the key to high profits. But don't tell this to Chester M. Woolworth. He knows better.

Woolworth is president of Woodstream Corporation, the nation's largest producer of mousetraps. After thoroughly researching the type of trap that would be most "appealing" to mice, Woodstream's new trap was introduced. The new model was a modern black plastic design, completely sanitary, and priced only a few cents more than the commonplace wood variety. Also, it never missed!

The better mousetrap also failed as a new product venture. While Woodstream had created a quality product, the company had forgotten the customer and the environment in which this purchase decision is made. The post-mortem analysis of this marketing disaster went something like this: men bought the majority of the newly

designed plastic mousetraps. In most instances, it was also the responsibility of the male member of the household to set the trap before the family retired for the night. But the problem occurred the next morning when he failed to check the trap before leaving for work. Even though most married women work, they are most likely to check the trap — during the morning in the case of wives who are not employed outside the home, or in the afternoon when they returned from work.

With the conventional wood trap, they would simply sweep both trap and mouse onto a dustpan and minimize the effort and time involved with this undesirable job. However, the new trap looked too expensive to throw away — even though it cost only a few cents more. Consequently, the wife was faced with ejecting the mouse and then cleaning the instrument. In a short time the new, improved mousetrap was replaced with the wooden version.

The moral of the mousetrap story is obvious: a quality product is not successful until it is effectively marketed. Mr. Woolworth expressed it most eloquently when he said, "Fortunately, Mr. Emerson made his living as a philosopher, not a company president."

Source: The Woodstream Corporation experience is described in Chester M. Woolworth, "So We Made A Better Mousetrap," *The President's Forum* (Fall 1962), pp. 26–27.

market (*one with an abundance of goods and services*). When World War II ended, factories stopped manufacturing tanks and jeeps and started turning out consumer goods again — an activity that had for all practical purposes stopped in 1940.

Once the pent-up demand created by the war had been satisfied, Canadian businesses found themselves operating in a buyer's market. It was no longer possible to sell just anything they chose to produce. In fact, it was not good enough to put special emphasis on selling or advertising. Buyers were becoming choosy, and purchased the products and services that *they* perceived would serve their needs.

Firms began to discover their principal task was to understand, and then make the business serve the interests of the customers rather than trying to make the customer buy what the business wanted to produce. A sincere customer orientation was required.

The realization that emerged has been identified as *the marketing concept*. The recognition of the marketing concept and its dominating role in business can be dated from 1952, when General Electric Company's annual report heralded a new management philosophy:

> [The concept] . . . introduces the marketing man at the beginning rather than at the end of the production cycle and integrates marketing into each phase of the business. Thus, marketing, through its studies and research, will establish for the engineer, the design and manufacturing man, what the customer wants in a given product, what price he is willing to pay, and where and when it will be wanted. Marketing will have authority in product planning, production scheduling, and inventory control, as well as in sales distribution and servicing of the product.[13]

In other words, marketing would no longer be regarded as a supplemental activity to be performed after the production process had been accomplished. For instance, the marketer would now play the lead role in product planning. Marketing and selling were no longer synonymous.

In a marketing-oriented firm, the decisions are based upon the analysis of market needs and demands. The objective is to take the opportunities the market offers. This approach can produce any of the good effects of the other two orientations, and avoids their drawbacks. More important, it can identify new opportunities.[14]

Optimal success for all products requires effective marketing based on a thorough understanding of what consumers want and need. Therefore, marketing is a primary function of any organization.

The **marketing concept** may be defined as *a company-wide consumer orientation with the objective of achieving long-run profits*. The key words are "company-wide consumer orientation." All facets of the business must be involved with assessing and then satisfying customer wants and needs. This is not something to be left just to the marketers. Accountants working in the credit office and the engineers employed in product design in the credit office and the engineers employed in product design also play important roles. Consumer orientation must indeed be company-wide.

---

13 *Annual Report* (New York: General Electric, 1952), p. 21.
14 Richard P. Bagozzi, "Marketing as an Organized Behavioral System of Exchange," *Journal of Marketing* (October 1974), p. 77. See also Richard P. Bagozzi, "Marketing as Exchange," *Journal of Marketing* (October 1975), pp. 32–39.

The words "with the objective of achieving long-run profits" are used in order to differentiate the marketing concept from policies of short-run profit maximization. The marketing concept is a modern philosophy for dynamic business growth. Since the continuity of the firm is an assumed part of the concept, such a company-wide consumer orientation will lead to greater long-run profits than would be the case for other managerial philosophies geared to reaching short-run goals.

## Avoiding Marketing Myopia

The emergence of the marketing concept has not been without setbacks. One troublesome situation has been what Theodore Levitt called "marketing myopia."[15] According to Levitt, **marketing myopia** is *the failure of management to recognize the scope of its business*. Future growth is endangered when management is product oriented rather than customer oriented. Levitt cited many service industries — dry cleaning, electric utilities, movies, and railways — as examples of companies which defined their business too narrowly. Railways thought of themselves as being in the "railway business" rather than the "transportation business," and thus lost much to the trucking industry.

Organizational goals must be broadly defined and oriented toward consumer needs. One air carrier, for example, has redefined its business from that of air transportation to travel. This allows the firm to offer complete travel services, such as hotel accommodations, credit, and ground transportation, as well as air travel. Texas Instruments, a firm known for its technological innovations, completely reorganized in 1982 in an attempt to mesh its capabilities with consumer needs instead of trying to *sell* what it could produce. As one observer noted, "The company has always developed products from a technology point of view, as opposed to what the market wanted. What we see happening now is a corporate determination to match technology prowess with what will sell."[16] Such efforts illustrate how firms may overcome marketing myopia.

## Broadening the Marketing Concept for the 1980s and 1990s

Industry has been responsive to the marketing concept as an improved method of doing business. Consideration of the consumer is now well accepted in many organizations. Today the relevant question

---

[15] Theodore Levitt, "Marketing Myopia," *Harvard Business Review* (July-August 1960), pp. 45–56.
[16] "An About-Face in TI's Culture," *Business Week* (July 5, 1982), p. 77.

is an inquiry into what the nature and extent of the concepts' parameters should be.[17]

Can nonbusiness organizations like art galleries, churches, and charities benefit from the application of marketing principles? Some marketers argue that the marketing discipline should be substantially broadened to include many areas formerly not concerned with marketing efforts. Others contend that the application of marketing has been extended too far.[18] Certainly, recent experience has shown that many nonprofit organizations have accepted the marketing concept. For instance, the Canadian government is Canada's leading advertiser and spends approximately $54.5 million in advertising annually.[19] The Canadian Forces advertise to recruit volunteers; the United Way and other charitable groups have developed considerable marketing expertise; some police departments have used marketing-inspired strategies to improve their image with the public; and we are all familiar with the marketing efforts employed in a political campaign.[20] Chapter 23 discusses marketing in nonprofit settings more fully.

It would be difficult to envisage business returning to an era

---

[17] The current status of the marketing concept is explored in such articles as Roger C. Bennett and Robert G. Cooper, "Beyond the Marketing Concept," *Business Horizons* (June 1979), pp. 76–83; David Carson, "Gotterdammerung for Marketing?" *Journal of Marketing* (July 1978), pp. 11–19; William S. Sachs and George Benson, "Is It Time to Discard the Marketing Concept?" *Business Horizons* (August 1978), pp. 68–74; Wayne Norvell, "Changing Attitudes toward Consumer Orientation in Making Marketing Decisions," *Pittsburgh Business Review* (June 1977), pp. 7–10; Jack L. Engledow, "Was Consumer Satisfaction a Pig in a Poke?" *Business Horizons* (April 1977), pp. 87–94; and William G. Nickels and Earnestine Hargrove, "A New Societal Marketing Concept," in *Contemporary Marketing Thought*, ed. Barnett A. Greenberg and Danny N. Bellenger (Chicago: American Marketing Association, 1977), p. 541.
[18] Definitive articles on the subject include Philip Kotler and Sidney J. Levy, "Broadening the Concept of Marketing," *Journal of Marketing* (January 1969), pp. 10–15; Leslie M. Dawson, "The Human Concept: New Philosophy for Business," *Business Horizons* (December 1969), pp. 29–38; and Sidney J. Levy and Philip Kotler, "Beyond Marketing: The Furthering Concept," *California Management Review* (Winter 1969), pp. 67–73. See also David J. Luck, "Broadening the Concept of Marketing—Too Far," *Journal of Marketing* (July 1969), pp. 53–55.
[19] *The Financial Post 500*, June 1983, p. 130.
[20] The use of marketing by nonprofit organizations is discussed in John D. Claxton, Thomas C. Kinnear, and J. R. Brent Ritchie, "Should Government Programs Have Marketing Managers?" *Michigan Business Review* (May 1978), pp. 10–16; Avraham Shama, "The Marketing of Political Candidates," *Journal of the Academy of Marketing Science* (Fall 1976), pp. 764–777; Leonard L. Berry and Bruce H. Allen, "Marketing's Crucial Role for Institutions of Higher Education," *Atlanta Economic Review* (July-August 1977), pp. 24–31; and Philip Kotler, "Strategies for Introducing Marketing into Nonprofit Organizations," *Journal of Marketing* (January 1979), pp. 37–44.

when engineering genius prevailed at the expense of consumer needs. It would be equally difficult for nonprofit organizations to return to a time when they lacked the marketing skills necessary to present a message of vital public importance. Marketing is a dynamic function, and it will no doubt be subject to continuous change. But in one form or another marketing is playing an ever more important role in all organizations and in our daily lives.

## Introduction to the Marketing Process

The starting place for effective marketing is the consumer. The marketer sets out to make profits by satisfying customer needs with a firm's products and services. (Consumer analysis is treated in detail in a later chapter.)

However, since people's wants and needs vary so greatly, it is unlikely that any particular product or service can adequately serve everyone. For this reason, one of the first tasks in marketing planning is to divide the market into relatively homogeneous segments. Once a particular customer group has been identified and analysed, the marketing manager can direct company activities to profitably satisfy this segment.

Figuratively speaking, management asks itself the following questions:

1. What problems do our customers or potential customers have that our products or services can solve better than those of other suppliers?
2. Who has these problems?
3. What are the particular circumstances, actual or potential, that would suggest modifications in our products, prices, distribution, or promotion?

The idea of thinking in terms of providing *solutions* to *problems* is a very useful one in marketing. It helps considerably in identifying new markets, finding new products for existing customers, finding new customers for existing products, and very importantly, discovering potential and possibly unsuspected competition.[21]

Although thousands of variables are involved, marketing decision-making can be conveniently classified into four strategy elements:

1. Product strategy          3. Distribution strategy
2. Pricing strategy          4. Promotional strategy

**Product strategy** includes *decisions about the product and its uses, package design, branding, trademarks, warranties, guarantees, product life cycles, and new product development.* The marketer's

21 Adapted from M. Kubr, ed., *Management Consulting: A Guide to the Profession* (Geneva: International Labour Organization, 1977).

concept of product strategy involves more than just the *physical* product. It also considers the satisfaction of all consumer needs in relation to a good or service.

**Pricing strategy**, one of the most difficult parts of marketing decision-making, deals with *the methods of setting profitable and justified prices*. Most prices are freely set in Canada. However some prices, such as those for public utilities, airlines, and some food products, are regulated and subject to public scrutiny.

**Distribution strategy** involves *the selection and management of marketing channels and the physical distribution of goods*. **Marketing channels** are *the steps or handling organizations that a good or service goes through from producer to final consumer*. Channel decision-making involves establishing and maintaining the institutional structure in marketing channels. This includes retailers, wholesalers, and other institutional middlemen.

**Promotional strategy** involves *personal selling, advertising, sales promotion tools, and publicity*. The various aspects of promotional strategy must be blended together in order to communicate effectively with the marketplace.

**Figure 1-1    Elements of the Marketing Mix**

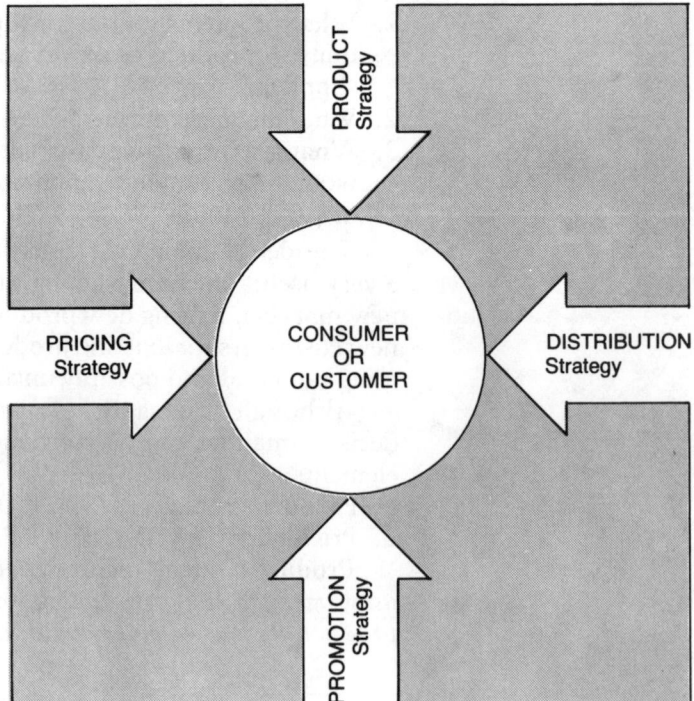

The total package forms the **marketing mix** — *the blending of the four strategy elements of marketing decision-making to satisfy chosen consumer segments.* Each of the strategies is a variable in the mix (see Figure 1–1). While that fourfold classification may be useful for the purpose of study and analysis, it is the total package (or mix) that determines the degree of marketing success.[22] As Figure 1-1 shows, the central focus of the marketing concept is the consumer. A closer examination of the variables in the marketing mix forms a major part of this text (Chapters 10 to 21).

---

[22] Some interesting perspectives of the marketing mix are offered in Peter M. Banting and Randolph E. Ross, "The Marketing Mix: A Canadian Perspective," *Journal of the Academy of Marketing Science* (Spring 1973), pp. 1–11; Adel I. El-Ansary, "Societal Marketing: A Strategic View of the Marketing Mix in the 1970's," *Journal of the Academy of Marketing Science* (Fall 1974), pp. 553–566.

# Neil H. Borden's Marketing Mix

The marketing decision-maker must actually make wise decisions about many subelements of the four categories in the marketing mix. This takes much skill and attention. In fact, this is basically what this book is about. Neil Borden, who first elaborated the concept of the marketing mix used the following list in his teaching and consulting:

Elements of the Marketing Mix of Manufacturers

1. *Product Planning*— policies and procedures relating to:
   a. Product lines to be offered— qualities, design, etc.
   b. Markets to sell— whom, where, when, and in what quantity.
   c. New product policy— research and development program.
2. *Pricing* — policies and procedures relating to:
   a. Price level to adopt.
   b. Specific prices to adopt — odd-even, etc.
   c. Price policy— one price or varying price, price maintenance, use of list prices, etc.
   d. Margins to adopt— for company, for the trade.
3. *Branding*— policies and procedures relating to:
   a. Selection of trade marks.
   b. Brand policy— individualized or family brand.
   c. Sale under private label or unbranded.

4. *Channels of Distribution*— policies and procedures relating to:
   a. Channels to use between plant and consumer.
   b. Degree of selectivity among wholesalers and retailers.
   c. Efforts to gain cooperation of the trade.
5. *Personal Selling*— policies and procedures relating to:
   a. Burden to be placed on personal selling and the methods to be employed in:
      1. Manufacturer's organization.
      2. Wholesale segment of the trade.
      3. Retail segment of the trade.
6. *Advertising*— policies and procedures relating to:
   a. Amount to spend— i.e., the burden to be placed on advertising.
   b. Copy platform to adopt:
      1. Product image desired.
      2. Corporate image desired.
   c. Mix of advertising— to the trade, through the trade, to consumers.
7. *Promotions*— policies and procedures relating to:
   a. Burden to place on special selling plans or devices directed at or through the trade.
   b. Form of these devices for consumer promotions, for trade promotions.

8. *Packaging*—policies and procedures relating
   to:
   a. Formulation of package and label.
9. *Display*—policies and procedures relating to:
   a. Burden to be put on display to help effect
      sale.
   b. Methods to adopt to secure display.
10. *Servicing*—policies and procedures relating
    to:
    a. Providing service needed.

11. *Physical Handling*—policies and procedures
    relating to:
    a. Warehousing.
    b. Transportation.
    c. Inventories.
12. *Fact Finding and Analysis*—policies and
    procedures relating to:
    a. Securing, analysis, and the use of facts in
       marketing operations.

Source: Neil H. Borden, "The Concept of the Marketing Mix," *Journal of Advertising Research* (Advertising Research
Foundation, Inc., June, 1964), pp. 2–7.

# Canadian Tire Corporation: Developing an Effective Marketing Mix

Canadian Tire provides a good example of a
company which has developed an effective marketing mix. From modest beginnings in Ontario,
Canadian Tire has become a household name in
virtually every part of Canada. Thousands of
Canadians make the local Canadian Tire store a
major port of call whenever they need automotive
parts, leisure products, household maintenance
products, or housewares.

Dean Muncaster, president of the company,
says, "Our merchandise mix and marketing policies are notably melded to provide the products
people want or need to buy, and at a price they
want to pay, almost regardless of the economic
outlook."[23] Muncaster makes this statement with
confidence because the firm has carefully developed a strategy that fits the needs of the consumer.

Consider how Canadian Tire has dealt with the
four elements of the marketing mix. First, they
selected a limited assortment of products in four
areas of long-term consumer need. Second, they

deliberately chose a pricing policy that would
produce a "more for the money" image. Third,
stores have been distributed across the country in
market areas of significant size, convenient to
customers with automobiles. Fourth, promotion is
handled by experts at headquarters and made
available in each market area through the stores as
well as in national advertising media. It informs
customers of the firm's offerings and reinforces
the Canadian Tire image.

The combination of these variables constitutes
the marketing mix for Canadian Tire. The effectiveness of the total marketing plan that is developed determines the long-term outlook for this
company as it does for other companies and
individual products.

Continued and growing acceptance illustrates
that Canadian Tire has been successful in creating
an organization and an assortment of products
that possess significant utility for their
customers.

**The Marketing
Environment**

Marketing decisions are not made in a vacuum. Marketers cannot
make changes to marketing mix variables without recognizing that
a change made to one variable will likely require an adjustment to

[23] Dean Muncaster, "A Perspective on Canadian Tire," *The Canadian Marketer*
(Winter 1975), p. 15.

one or more of the others to produce a balanced, effective marketing mix.

Furthermore, to be successful marketing decisions must take into account environmental factors over which the decision maker has little or no control — competition, political and legal considerations, the economy, technology, and the socio-cultural environment. These five environmental factors require a great deal of attention when making marketing decisions. They are examined in detail in Chapter 2.

## The Study of Marketing

Marketing is a pervasive element in contemporary life. In one form or another, it is close to every person. Three of its most important concerns for students are the following:

1. Marketing costs may be the largest item in the personal budget. Numerous attempts have been made to determine these costs, and most estimates have ranged between 40 and 60 percent. Regardless of the exact cost, however, marketing is obviously a key item in any consumer's budget.

   Cost alone, however, does not indicate the value of marketing. If someone says that marketing costs are too high, that person should be asked, "Relative to what?" The standard of living in Canada is in large part a function of the country's efficient marketing system. When considered in this perspective, the costs of the system seem reasonable. For example, marketing expands sales, thereby spreading fixed production costs over more units of output and reducing total output costs. Reduced production costs offset many marketing costs.

   Eight **marketing functions** occur in the marketing process: *buying, selling, transporting, storing, grading, financing, risk taking, and information collection and dissemination.* These are inherent to a greater or less degree in all marketing transactions. They may be shifted to various members of the channel, or to the customer, but they cannot be eliminated.

2. Marketing-related occupations account for 25 to 33 percent of the nation's jobs, so it is likely that many students will become marketers. Indeed, marketing opportunities remained quite strong even during recent periods when many graduates could not find jobs. History has shown that the demand for effective marketers is relatively unaffected by cyclical economic fluctuations.

3. Marketing provides an opportunity to contribute to society as well as to an individual company. Marketing decisions affect everyone's welfare. Furthermore, opportunities to advance to decision-making positions come sooner in marketing than in most occupations. (Social aspects of marketing will be covered in detail in later chapters.)

Why study marketing? The answer is simple: marketing affects numerous facets of daily life as well as individuals' future careers and economic well-being. The study of marketing is important because it is relevant to students today and tomorrow. It is little wonder that marketing is now one of the most popular fields of academic study.

**Summary**

This overview of the marketing process has pointed out that the two primary functions of a business organization are production and marketing. Traditionally, industry emphasized production efficiency, often at the expense of marketing. Sometime after World War II the marketing concept became the accepted business philosophy. The change was caused by the economy shifting from a seller's market to a buyer's market.

Marketing is the development and efficient distribution of goods, services, issues, and concepts for chosen consumer segments, and marketing decision-making has been classified into four strategy elements: 1) product strategy, 2) pricing strategy, 3) distribution strategy, and 4) promotional strategy. The combination of these four variables forms the total marketing mix. It has been stressed that marketing decisions must be made in a dynamic environment determined by competitive, legal, economic, and social functions.

Three basic reasons for studying marketing are:
1. Marketing costs may be the largest item in your personal budget.
2. There is a good chance you may become a marketer.
3. Marketing provides an opportunity to make a real contribution not only to your business, but to society as a whole.

**Key Terms**

| | |
|---|---|
| utility | marketing myopia |
| marketing | product strategy |
| exchange process | pricing strategy |
| seller's market | distribution strategy |
| buyer's market | marketing channels |
| marketing concept | promotional strategy |
| marketing functions | marketing mix |

**Review Questions**

1. What are the four types of utility? With which is marketing concerned?
2. How does the text definition of marketing differ from the definition proposed by the American Marketing Association?

3. Relate the definition of marketing to the concept of the exchange process.
4. Contrast the production era and the sales era.
5. In what ways does the marketing era differ from the previous eras?
6. Explain the concept of marketing myopia. Why is it likely to occur? What steps can be taken to reduce the likelihood of its occurrence?
7. What did the General Electric annual report mean when it said it was introducing the marketer at the beginning rather than at the end of the production cycle?
8. What are the parameters of the marketing concept?
9. Identify the major variables of the marketing mix.
10. What are the components of the marketing environment? Why are these factors not included as part of the marketing mix?

**Discussion Questions and Exercises**

1. What types of utility are being created in the following examples?
   a. One-hour cleaners
   b. 7-Eleven convenience food store
   c. Michelin Tire factory in Nova Scotia
   d. Annual boat and sports equipment show in local city auditorium
   e. Regional shopping mall
2. How would you explain marketing and its importance in the Canadian economy to someone not familiar with the subject?
3. Identify the product and the consumer market in each of the following:
   a. Local cable television firm
   b. Vancouver Canucks hockey team
   c. Planned Parenthood
   d. Milk Marketing Board
4. Suggest methods by which the following organizations might avoid marketing myopia by correctly defining their industries:
   a. Atari Computer Division
   b. First Choice (pay television)
   c. Northern Alberta Railway
   d. Petro-Canada
   e. Bank of Nova Scotia
5. Give two examples of firms you feel are in the following eras:
   a. Production era
   b. Sales era
   c. Marketing era
   Defend your answer.

## CHAPTER 2

# The Environment for Marketing Decisions

## CHAPTER OBJECTIVES

1. To identify the environmental factors that affect the consumer and the marketing mix.

2. To explain the types of competition faced by marketers and how an organization develops a competitive strategy.

3. To trace the legal framework within which marketing decisions are made.

4. To outline the economic factors that affect marketing strategy.

5. To explain the impact of the technological environment on a firm's marketing activities.

6. To explain how the socio-cultural environment influences marketing.

A changing environment, important political decisions and rapid advances in technology have created enormous challenges and opportunities for Canada's two major telecommunications companies. They have leapt ahead in a seven-year rush to the top of the telephone world. Northern Telecom Ltd. of Toronto and Mitel Corp. of Ottawa are currently ranked two and four respectively in North America in regard to the numbers of sales of private branch exchanges (PBXs), the internal switching systems that channel telephone calls within companies and to the outside world.

Recent political decisions in the United States introduced the most feverish marketing competition in history in this billion-dollar-a-year market. The U.S. government decided that one of the world's largest companies, American Telephone and Telegraph Co. was too large to assure real competition in the marketplace. Therefore, AT&T was forced to divest itself of 22 operating subsidiaries which were then grouped into seven regional operating companies. These were given freedom to buy and market telephone equipment as they pleased. The impact of this was phenomenal, considering that the average assets of each of the seven were about U.S. $17 billion, roughly 1.5 times the size of Bell Canada. Since it was expected that the new companies would try to establish a clean break with their former parent company, Northern Telecom and Mitel saw great potential for sales of their equipment in this new market.

Technology was a critical factor for Mitel. Mitel's founders, Michael Cowpland and Terry Matthews, had left Northern Telecom in 1973 to start their own company. As a result of their expertise, technological innovation and sound marketing pushed Mitel's sales to a staggering $255 million over a ten-year period. However, by 1983 technology was becoming a potential problem. Technical hitches forced the postponement of the introduction of the company's long-awaited SX-2000 switching system. This system, handling up to 10 000 lines and heralded by Mitel executives as the firm's entry into the big league of digital switching, was more than a year overdue. It was to allow Mitel to compete directly with Northern Telecom's SL1, which had similar capabilities.

Competition was another important concern. Despite its rapid growth, and large resource base, Mitel was still a modest firm compared with its chief Canadian rival. Sales of $255 million did not seem so large alongside Northern Telecom's $3 billion. Furthermore, Northern Telecom was shortly expected to announce an advanced version of its SL1.[1]

From 1982 to 1985 the company had cumulative losses of $224.7 million. The company lost business because of poor product positioning in the U.S. market, and lost customers because of doubts concerning the firm's financial strength. Finally, British Telecom purchased 51 percent of the company in 1986. It is now working to regain its earlier momentum.

---

**The Conceptual Framework**

The changing environment is constantly creating and destroying business opportunities. The battle between Northern Telecom and Mitel reveals the importance of environmental factors to the success of any organization. A combination of political, technological, and competitive forces has led to great opportunities in their industry. These forces must be identified and analyzed, and the marketing decision-makers must determine their impact upon a particular marketing situation. Although they cannot be controlled by the marketing manager, they must be considered in the development of marketing strategies together with the more controllable variables of the marketing mix.

Chapter 1 introduced marketing and the elements of the marketing mix used to satisfy chosen market targets. But the blending of a successful marketing mix must be based upon thorough analysis of environmental forces. The marketer's product, distribution,

---

[1] Adapted from Ian Anderson, "Switching Allegiances: Why the Breakup of US Telephone Markets is Wiring up Canadians," *Canadian Business*, Oct. 1983, pp. 15–20.

promotion, and pricing strategies must filter through these forces before they reach their goal: the consumers who represent the firm's market target. In this chapter we will examine how each of the environmental variables can affect a firm's marketing strategy.

As Figure 2-1 indicates, the environment for marketing decisions may be classified into five elements: the *competitive* environment, the *political and legal* environment, the *economic* environment, the *technological* environment, and the *social and cultural* environment. The forces are important because they provide the frame of reference within which marketing decisions are made. However, since they represent outside factors, they are *not* considered marketing mix components.

**Figure 2-1   Elements of the Marketing Mix as They Operate within an Environmental Framework**

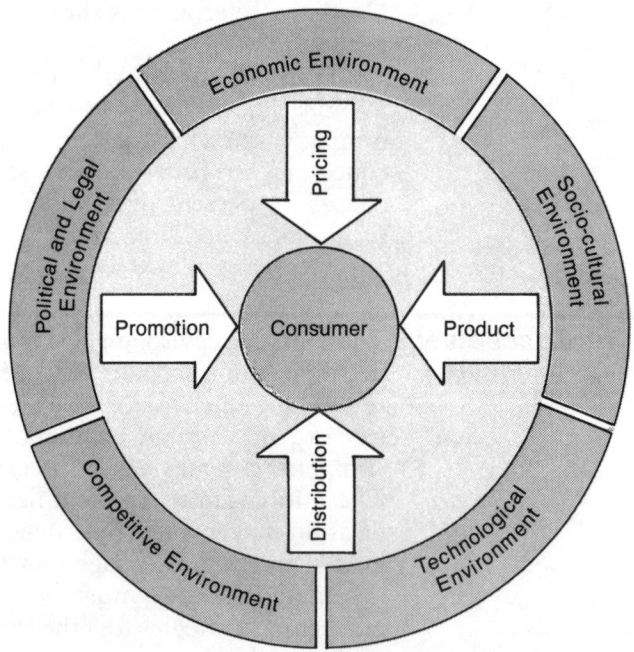

In addition to their importance in affecting current marketing decisions, their dynamic nature means that management at every level must continually reevaluate marketing decisions in response to changing environments. Even modest environmental shifts can alter the results of marketing decisions. Polaroid Corporation's failure to recognize the flexibility, ease of use, and rapidly declining prices of videocassette cameras and recorders contributed to disappointing sales for their Polavision instant movies that required users to purchase a display unit and lacked the re-recording features of the videocassette competition.

## The Competitive Environment

*The interactive process that occurs in the marketplace as competing organizations seek to satisfy markets* is known as the **competitive environment**. Marketing decisions by an individual firm influence consumer responses in the marketplace; they also affect the marketing strategies of competitors. As a consequence, marketers must continually monitor the marketing activities of competitors—their products, channels, prices, and promotional efforts.

In a few instances, organizations enjoy a monopoly position in the marketplace. Utilities, such as natural gas, electricity, water, and cable television service, accept considerable regulation from government in such marketing-related activities as rates, service levels, and geographic coverage in exchange for exclusive rights to serve a particular group of consumers. However, such instances are rare. In addition, portions of such traditional monopoly industries as telephone service have been deregulated in recent years, and telephone companies currently face competition in such areas as the sale of telephone receivers, some long distance services, and installation and maintenance of telephone systems in larger commercial and industrial firms.

Sporting goods provide an illustration of the importance of the competitive environment. Sports and recreation fads result in boom periods for the manufacturers of the equipment involved. Bowling boomed in the early 1960s, snowmobiles in 1971, skiing in 1973, tennis in 1975 and aerobic dancing in 1980. Each of these periods has been followed by a terrific expansion of the related segment of the sporting goods industry. Excess supply soon develops, and the net result is that some firms try to compete by cutting prices. Other firms are then forced to make similar reductions to remain competitive. Tensor sold its metal tennis racquets for $25 in 1968 and for $9 by the mid-1970s. Eventually, many of the marginal competitors are forced out of the industry, and production and marketing resume normal patterns, although the industry may be vastly restructured.

Jogging and racquetball are among the sports fads today that have given rise to industries serving the participants. Many companies now make running shoes or "training flats" for joggers. Racquetball courts dot the landscape of most suburban areas and smaller cities. Today, supplying racquetball equipment and accessories is a major industry. But the signs of change are already here. Joggers can choose from more than a hundred different models of jogging shoes. And racquetball courts face increased competition in many major metropolitan areas. The competitive environment is a fact of life even in recreation and leisure activities.

*Types of Competition*     Marketers actually face three types of competition. The most direct form of competition occurs between marketers of similar products. Xerox photocopiers compete with models offered by Canon, Sharp, and Olivetti. Massey-Ferguson tractors face competition from Ford Motor Company's farm equipment division, Case, and John Deere.

A second type of competition is competition between products that can be substituted for one another. In the construction industry and in manufacturing, steel products by Stelco may compete with similar products made of aluminum by Alcan. Cast-iron pipes compete with pipes made of such synthetic materials as polyvinyl chloride (PVC). In instances where a change such as a price increase or an improvement in the strength of a product occurs, demand for substitute products is directly affected.

The final type of competition involves all organizations that compete for the consumer's purchases. Traditional economic analysis views competition as a battle between companies in the same industry or between substitutable products and services. Marketers, however, accept the argument that *all* firms are competing for a limited amount of discretionary buying power. Restaurants compete with microwave ovens and gourmet delicatessens. The Mazda 323 competes with a vacation in the Bahamas and the local live theatre centre competes with pay television and the Leafs, Blue Bombers, or Expos for the consumer's entertainment dollars.

Since the competitive environment often determines the success or failure of the product, marketers must continually assess marketing strategies of competitors. New product offerings with technological advances, price reductions, special promotions, or other competitive actions must be monitored in order to adjust the firm's marketing mix in light of such changes. Among the first purchasers of any new product are the product's competitors. Careful analysis of its components — physical components, performance attributes, packaging, retail price, service requirements, and estimated production and marketing costs — allows the marketer to forecast its likely competitive impact. If necessary, adjustments to one or more marketing mix components may take place as a result of the new market entry.

*Developing a*     All marketers must develop an effective strategy for dealing with
*Competitive Strategy*   the competitive environment. Some will compete in a broad range of product markets in many areas of the world. Others prefer to specialize in particular market segments such as those determined by geographical, age, or income factors. Essentially, the determination of a competitive strategy involves three questions.
1. Should we compete?
2. If so, in what markets should we compete?
3. How should we compete?

The first question — should we compete? — should be answered based on the resources and objectives of the firm and expected profit potential for the firm. In some instances, potentially successful ventures are not considered due to a lack of a match between the venture and the overall organizational objectives. For example, a clothing manufacturer may reject an opportunity to diversify through the purchase of a profitable pump manufacturer. Or a producer of industrial chemicals might refrain from entering the consumer market and instead sell chemicals to another firm familiar with serving consumers at the retail level.

In other cases a critical issue is expected profit potential. If the expected profits are insufficient to pay an adequate return on the required investment, then the firm should consider other lines of business. Many organizations have switched from less profitable ventures quite efficiently. This decision should be subject to continual reevaluation so that the firm avoids being tied to traditional markets with declining profit margins. It is also important to anticipate competitive responses.

The second question concerns the markets in which to compete. This decision acknowledges that the firm has limited recources (engineering and productive capabilities, sales personnel, advertising budgets, research and development, and the like) and that these resources must be allocated to the areas of greatest opportunity. Too many firms have taken a "shotgun" approach to market selection and thus do an ineffective job in many markets rather than a good one in selected markets.

"How should we compete?" is the third question. It requires the firm's marketers to make the tactical decisions involved in setting up a comprehensive marketing strategy. Product, pricing, distribution, and promotion decisions, of course, are the major elements of this strategy.

---

**The Political and Legal Environment**

Before you play the game, learn the rules! It would be absurd to start playing a new game without first understanding the rules, yet some businesspeople exhibit a remarkable lack of knowledge about marketing's **political and legal environment** — *the laws and interpretation of laws that require firms to operate under competitive conditions and to protect consumer rights*.[2] Ignorance of laws, ordinances, and regulations could result in fines, embarrassing negative publicity, and possibly civil damage suits.

It requires considerable diligence to develop an understanding of the legal framework of marketing. Numerous laws, often vague

---

[2] M. Dale Beckman, "What Businessmen Know About Government and Legislative Intent," *The Canadian Marketer* (Fall 1973), pp. 13–17.

and legislated by a multitude of different authorities, characterize the legal environment for marketing decisions. Regulations affecting marketing have been enacted at the federal, provincial, and local levels as well as by independent regulatory agencies. Our existing legal framework was constructed on a piecemeal basis, often in response to a concern over current issues.

Canada has tended to follow a public policy of promoting a competitive marketing system. To maintain such a system, competitive practices within the system have been regulated. Traditionally, the pricing and promotion variables have received the most legislative attention.

*Society's Expectations Create the Framework*

We live in and desire a "free enterprise society" — or do we? The concept of free enterprise is not clear, and has been gradually changing. At the turn of the century the prevalent attitude was to let business act quite freely. As a result, it was expected that new products and jobs would be created and the economy would develop and prosper.

This provided great freedom for the scrupulous and the unscrupulous. Although most businesses sought to serve their market targets in an equitable fashion, abuses did occur. Figure 2-2 is an example of questionable marketing practices. Such advertisements were not unusual in the late 1800s and early 1900s. Advancing technology led to the creation of a multitude of products in many fields. Often the buying public did not possess the expertise needed to choose among them.

With the increasing complexity of products, the growth of big, impersonal business, as well as the unfair or careless treatment of

Figure 2-2   An Example of Questionable Advertising

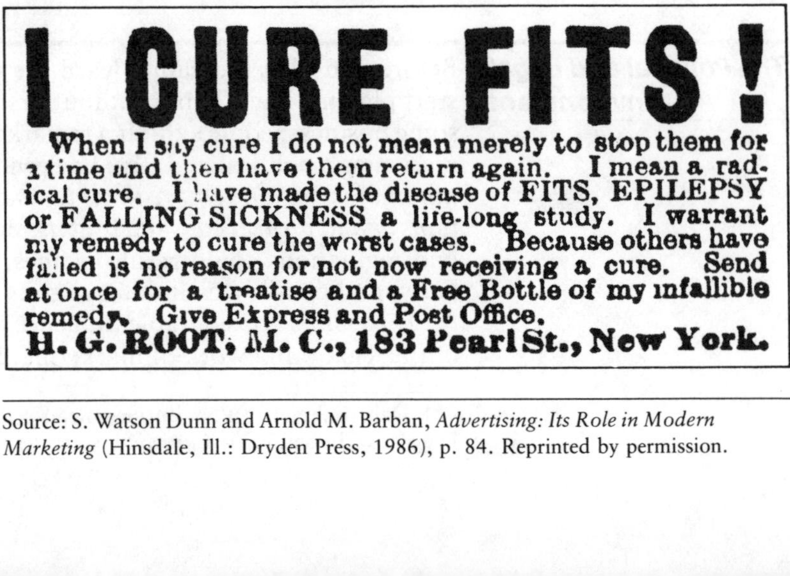

Source: S. Watson Dunn and Arnold M. Barban, *Advertising: Its Role in Modern Marketing* (Hinsdale, Ill.: Dryden Press, 1986), p. 84. Reprinted by permission.

consumers by a few, the values of society changed. "Government should regulate business more closely," we said. Over time, governments at the federal and provincial levels have responded until many laws have been passed to protect consumers, and to attempt to maintain a competitive environment for business. Large bureaucracies have grown with this increase in market regulation.

A significant development in the legal environment at the federal level was the consolidation in 1967 of consumer and business regulation programs into Consumer and Corporate Affairs Canada, and the appointment of a cabinet minister to represent these interests at the highest level. Previously these functions had been scattered among several different government departments. Following the lead of the federal government, most provinces have established consumer and corporate affairs branches and have generally streamlined the regulation of these sectors. Figure 2-3 lists some of

**Figure 2-3   Legislation Administered by Consumer and Corporate Affairs Canada**

**1. Fully Administered by CCA**
- Bankruptcy Act and Bankruptcy Rules
- Boards of Trade Act
- Canada Cooperative Associations Act
- Canada Corporations Act
- Combines Investigation Act
- Consumer Packaging and Labelling Act
- Copyright Act
- Department of Consumer and Corporate Affairs Act
- Electricity Inspection Act
- Farmer's Creditors Arrangement Act
- Gas Inspection Act
- Hazardous Products Act
- Industrial Design Act
- National Trade Mark and True Labelling Act
- Patent Act
- Precious Metals Marking Act
- Textile Labelling Act
- Timber Marking Act
- Trade Marks Act
- Weights and Measures Act

**2. Administered Jointly with Other Departments**
- Canada Agricultural Products Standards Act (with Agriculture)
- Canada Dairy Products Act (with Agriculture)
- Fish Inspection Act (with Environment)
- Food and Drugs Act (with Health and Welfare)
- Maple Products Industry Act (with Agriculture)
- Shipping Conferences Exemption Act (with Transport)
- Winding-up Act (with Finance)

the significant federal legislation that affects business today. The detailed study of provincial laws and regulations is beyond the scope of this text.

## The Competition Act Sets the Standards

Of all the legislation mentioned in Figure 2-3, the Competition Act (formerly the Combines Investigation Act) has the most significance in the legal environment for marketing decisions. The Act dates back to 1889, when it was enacted to protect the public interest in free competition.[3] Since then, various revisions have occurred in response to changes in social values and in business practices (Figure 2-4).

The Act prohibits rather than regulates. That is, it does not spell out in detail the activities that industry may undertake, but greatly discourages certain activities through the threat of penal consequences.

The provisions of the Act fall into three main classes. Generally speaking, they prohibit the following:

1. Combinations that prevent, or lessen unduly, competition in the production, purchase, sale, storage, rental, transportation, or supply of commodities, or in the price of insurance.
2. Mergers, monopolies, or abuses of dominant market position that may operate to the detriment of the public.
3. Deceptive trade practices including:
   - price discrimination
   - predatory pricing
   - certain promotional allowances
   - false or misleading representations, by any means whatever, to promote the sale of a product or to promote a business
   - unsubstantiated claims of performance
   - misleading warranties or guarantees
   - misrepresentation as to the ordinary price
   - misleading testimonials for a product or service
   - double ticketing
   - pyramid sales
   - referral selling
   - nonavailability of advertised specials
   - sale above advertised price
   - promotional contests

Despite the long history of the Combines Investigation Act, it proved remarkably powerless for prosecuting those who appeared to contravene either of the first two categories. The passage of the

[3] This section has been adapted and updated from a section in M. Dale Beckman and R.H. Evans, "Social Control of Business Through the Federal Department of Consumer and Corporate Affairs," by D. H. Henry, *Marketing: A Canadian Perspective* (Scarborough, Ont.: Prentice-Hall, 1972), pp. 102–129.

## Figure 2-4   Evolution of Major Combines Legislation

| Date | Legislation | Reason for Legislation |
|------|-------------|------------------------|
| 1888 | Combines Investigation Commission | To protect small businesses who suffered from monopolistic and collusive practices in restraint of trade by large manufacturers. |
| 1889 | Act for the Prevention and Suppression of Combinations Formed in Restraint of Trade | To declare illegal monopolies and combinations in restraint of trade. |
| 1892 | Above Act incorporated into the Criminal Code as Section 502 | To make the above a criminal offence. |
| 1900 | Above Act amended | To make the Act effective because as it stood, an individual would first have to commit an illegal act within the meaning of common law. Now, any undue restriction of competition became a criminal offence. |
| 1910 | Additional legislation passed to complement the Criminal Code and assist in the application of the Act | To stop a recent rush of mergers that had involved some 58 firms. |
| 1919 | The Combines and Fair Prices Act | To prohibit undue stockpiling of the "necessities of life" and prohibit the realization of exaggerated profits through "unreasonable prices." |
| 1923 | Combines Investigation Act | To consolidate combines legislation. |
| 1952, 1960 | Amendments to the above | |
| 1976 | Bill C-2; amendments | To include the service industry within the Act; to prohibit additional deceptive practices; to give persons the right to recover damages; to protect rights of small businesses. |
| 1986 | Competition Act replaces Combines Investigation Act | To facilitate prosecutions of illegal combinations, mergers, and monopolies. |

Competition Act to replace the Combines Investigation Act in June 1986 was an important change. Being classified as civil law it corrected many problems in the strictly criminal, proof-beyond-a-reasonable-doubt, approach of the old Combines Act. The new

Competition Act also created a quasi-judicial body, known as the Competition Tribunal, to deal with matters via the civil route, and to make certain rules.

**Combines and Restraint of Trade**

It is an offence to conspire, combine, agree, or arrange with another person to prevent or lessen competition unduly. The most common types of combination relate to price fixing, bid rigging, market sharing and group boycotting of competitors, suppliers, or customers.

While this covers much territory, it should be noted that in the following circumstances agreements between business persons are *not* unlawful.

1. The exchange of statistics.
2. Definition of product standards.
3. The exchange of credit information.
4. Definition of trade terms
5. Co-operation in research and development.
6. Restriction of advertising.

Consequently, it is possible to report statistics centrally for the purpose of providing analysis of factors relating to industrial operation and marketing, as long as competition is not lessened unduly.

**Mergers**

Until the passage of the Competition Act in 1986, the law regarding mergers was largely ineffective. Important provisions in the new Act changed the situation. The Competition Tribunal has the power to stop mergers that substantially lessen competition without offering offsetting efficiency gains. Furthermore, the Tribunal must be notified in advance of large mergers (transactions larger than $35 million in sales or assets, and/or companies with combined revenues or assets of more than $400 million). This will enable the review and modification of large, complex mergers that are difficult to reverse once consummated.

**Deceptive Trade Practices**

This is an extremely important section for marketing decision-makers, as it contains a number of directly related provisions. There are real teeth in the legislation which the marketer should be aware of. Many successful prosecutions have been made under this section.

Misleading Advertising   False statements of every kind (even in the picture on a package) made to the public about products or services are prohibited. For example on November 15, 1986, First Choice Canadian Communications Corporation was convicted of making

# How one company keeps a clean slate

Not many large advertisers can say they have never been caught under the misleading advertising provisions of the Combines Investigation Act, but Canada Safeway Ltd. appears to have a clean record. A 1979 study carried out for the federal combines branch showed that practically every large supermarket chain in Canada — except Calgary-based Safeway — had been convicted for an offence of selling above advertised prices. The overcharging reportedly totalled a whopping $15 million to $20 million a year during the 1970s.

Safeway's spotless record stems, according to the company, from its strict adherence to policies that ensure that any claims made on price reduction or quality are completely accurate.

Safeway's 297 Canadian stores are split into six divisions, each with its own advertising manager who is responsible for promotional strategy and claims in that division. The decentralized planning helps ensure greater control over claims made. In other companies, much of the advertising planning and co-ordination is carried out from head office. "By the time it gets out to a far-flung centre, if prices or products are substituted, the possibility of confusing or misleading results would be greater," says Jim Waters, Safeway's vice-president of public affairs.

The company also monitors charges and fines against competitors "and has expressed the strong desire (to senior operators) to see that Safeway would not become involved."

Source: *Financial Times of Canada* (July 18, 1983), p. 14.

statements designed to mislead the public.[4] The company, in promoting the sale of subscriptions to its pay television service, claimed in newspaper advertisements that it would offer "all new movies every month." It was established that all new movies were only provided for the first three months of the service. The company was convicted and fined $15 000.

Often carelessness has been seen as responsible for the offence, and over the years, numerous advertisers have been prosecuted under the misleading advertising provisions of the Combines Investigation Act. The fines meted out have been surprisingly small.

A greater level of determination to discourage deceptive advertising was signalled in 1983 when a fine levied against Simpsons-Sears sent shock waves through the entire advertising industry. Simpsons-Sears had been found guilty of advertising through its catalogues and through newspapers between 1975 and 1978 diamond rings that it claimed had been appraised at values significantly higher than those given by bona fide diamond appraisers consulted by Consumer and Corporate Affairs Canada. The fine imposed was a million

---

[4] Consumer and Corporate Affairs, *Misleading Advertising Bulletin*, January/March 1986, p. 7.

dollars! — the highest ever levied under the Act. This set a precedent for vigorous prosecution of violaters of the Act.[5]

It is an offence to make unsubstantiated claims. Therefore claims for a product are expected to be based on an adequate and proper test. Significantly, the onus is upon whoever is making the claim to prove its efficacy, rather than for someone to prove that the product is not as claimed. This reverse onus has been challenged before the courts under the Charter of Rights as being unconstitutional because it purports to put the onus on the accused to prove innocence, but the section was upheld. One example, and there are many, concerns Professional Technology of Canada, who were convicted in Edmonton on May 27, 1986 for promoting a gas-saving device that purported to offer 10 to 35 percent better mileage for cars. The company was convicted and fined $12 500.[6]

Another important facet of misleading advertising legislation concerns pricing. Many businesses seem to be unaware that much care needs to be taken when advertising comparative prices. It is, for example, considered misleading for a retailer to advertise a television set as follows:

| Manufacturer's suggested list price | $680.00 |
| On sale for | $500.00 |

if the manufacturer's suggested list price is not normally followed in this area of activity, and the usual price is normally around $600. Thus, while the retailer is offering a bargain, the magnitude of it is not indicated accurately.

Retailers may try to get around this provision by choosing different comparative expressions such as "regular price," "ordinarily $ . . . ," "list price," "hundreds sold at," "compare with," "regular value," and the like. For example, in Moncton, Best for Less (a division of Dominion Stores Ltd.) compared its price to a "why pay up to" price on in-store signs, and depicted the savings. It was established that items were available from competitors at lower prices than the "why pay up to" prices, and the firm was convicted and fined $7650.[7]

The business person who genuinely seeks to comply with this provision should ask two questions:

5 James Walker and Alan D. Gray, "$1 Million Ad Fine Signal to Retailers," *Financial Times*, July 1983, Vol. 72, no. 6, p. 14.
6 Consumer and Corporate Affairs, personal communication.
7 Consumer and Corporate Affairs, *Misleading Advertising Bulletin*, July/September 1986, p. 11.

1. Would a reasonable shopper draw the conclusion from the expression used that the figure named by way of comparison is a price at which goods have been, are, or will ordinarily be sold?
2. If the answer is yes, would such a representation be true?

Pricing Practices   It is an offence for a supplier to make a practice of discriminating in price among purchasers who are in competition with one another and who are purchasing like quantities of goods. Selling above the advertised price is also prohibited. Furthermore, the lowest of two or more prices must be used in the case of double-ticketed products. This latter provision has led to the development of easy-tear-off, two-price stickers, so that the sale price can readily be removed after a sale.

If you are a ski manufacturer and wish all ski shops to sell your skis at your suggested list price, can you force them to do so? No; it is an offence under the Act to deny supplies to an outlet that refuses

# The Cost of Resale Price Maintenance

An Ontario waterbed manufacturer, Andico Manufacturing Ltd., found that it couldn't make resale price maintenance work when it tried to pressure a Winnipeg dealer into raising the prices of its beds. The manufacturer was fined a total of $11 000 for cutting off supplies to its dealer, Burron Lumber of Winnipeg, when it refused to raise prices. Burron was charging considerably less for its waterbeds than other specialty waterbed stores in the city to which Andico also sold its products.

Andico was convicted of two offences under the Combines Investigation Act. A fine of $1000 was levied for attempting to influence Burron to raise prices, and another $10 000 fine was imposed for refusing to supply waterbeds and components to the lumber store.

According to trial evidence, Burron decided to enter the waterbed market in October 1981, and began buying waterbed kits and accessories from Andico. Burron president Ramond Burron testified that less than two weeks later, the company representative told him that other city waterbed retailers were pressuring him to stop selling to Burron because of its cut-rate pricing policy. He was told that he would either have to raise his prices or his supplies would be cut off. He refused, and the supplier stopped filling his orders.

Andico's representative contended that he stopped selling products to Burron because he did not regard it as a "bona fide" waterbed retailer. He said that he did not feel Burron had adequate waterbed display space at its lumber store, or qualified staff to sell and service waterbeds. He maintained that a manufacturer has a right to not sell products to an outlet which it feels is not a legitimate dealer.

The judge agreed that "there is nothing wrong with making sure the people [a firm] deals with have some financial stability." However, "In this case, the company did not have any such concerns. It exercised its decision solely on the basis that Burron should have been selling at higher prices than he was, and that if he didn't, he wouldn't get any more supplies."

Source: Adapted from Murray McNeill, "Waterbed Maker Fined $11 000," *Winnipeg Free Press* (November 23, 1983), p. 14.

to maintain the resale price. Thus, resale price maintenance is illegal, and a retailer is generally free to set whatever price is considered to be appropriate.

The Combines Investigation Act includes several other prohibitions, including ones against bait-and-switch selling, pyramid selling, and some types of referral selling and promotional contests.

**Other Provisions of the Competition Act**

**Protection Against Foreign Laws and Directives**   Foreign companies doing business in Canada sometimes have been constrained by laws or judgments in their home country to the detriment of competition in Canada, or of opportunities for Canadian international trade. For example, Canadian subsidiaries of American companies have felt constraints of American law against doing business with Cuba. This is theoretically no longer the case because the Restrictive Trade Practices Commission (established under the anti-combines provisions of the Combines Investigation Act) has been given power to rule against such interference in Canadian affairs.

**Civil Damages**   In some situations persons have the right to recover damages incurred as a result of a violation by others. This has profound implications. In some jurisdictions, not only can an individual sue for damages, but if the person wins, that judgment will apparently serve as evidence for anyone else who has experienced a similar loss. Would this mean that a company could face the possibility of virtually every purchaser of a product claiming damages? Consider the millions of dollars involved for an automobile manufacturer, for example. To our knowledge, there have been no such cases in Canada.

**Regulation, Regulation, and . . . More Regulation**

So far, only some of the provisions from the most important federal Act have been cited. Figure 2-3 shows that the federal government has a virtual sea of regulations that marketers must be aware of. Provincial governments are also very active in this area. Fortunately, each marketer need not be aware of all provisions, for many are specific to situation, time, place, and products.

In addition, provincial and municipal governments have other laws and by-laws that must be considered when developing marketing plans. For example, regulations vary from province to province concerning the amount and nature of advertising directed at children. Some other significant laws or regulations relate to bilingual specifications for packaging and labelling; there are special language requirements in Quebec.

From a broad point of view, the legal framework for relations between business and consumers is designed to encourage a competitive marketing system employing fair business practices. In many respects the action taken by the federal government in 1967 has resulted in more effective competition, although there are many who feel business is over-regulated and others who think that more regulations are needed. There is little doubt that consumers in Canada are protected as well as or better than consumers in any other country in their dealings with sellers, especially regarding truth in advertising. It is clear that governments will continue to act in response to society's expectations of a fair and honest market place.

## The Economic Environment

In addition to the competitive and political and legal environments, marketers must understand the economic environment and its impact upon their organizations. Three economic subjects of major concern to marketers in recent years have been recession, unemployment, and inflation.

Clearly, in a deteriorating economic environment many firms experience a decline. However, it is good news for some companies. As inflation and unemployment go up and production declines, consumer buying patterns shift. Flour millers note that flour sales go up. Automobile repairs and home improvements also increase. Greeting card firms report that consumers buy fewer gifts, but more expensive cards. Hardware stores show higher sales. The economic environment will considerably affect the way marketers operate.

### Stages of the Business Cycle

The **economic environment** is *a complex setting operating within which are dynamic business fluctuations that tend to follow a cyclical pattern* composed of four stages:

1. recession (sometimes involves such factors as inflation and unemployment)
2. depression[8]
3. recovery
4. prosperity

No marketer can disregard the economic climate in which a business functions, for the type, direction, and intensity of a firm's marketing strategy depends upon it. In addition, the marketer must be aware of the economy's relative position in the business cycle and

---

[8] Many economists argue that society is capable of preventing future depressions through intelligent use of various economic policies. Thus, a recession is followed by a period of recovery.

how it will affect the position of the particular firm. This requires the marketer to study forecasts of future economic activity.

Of necessity, marketing activity differs with each stage of the business cycle. During prosperous times, consumers are usually more willing to buy than when they feel economically threatened. For example, during the recent recession, personal savings climbed to high levels as consumers (fearing possible layoffs and other workforce reductions) cut back their expenditures for many products they considered nonessential. Marketers must pay close attention to the consumer's relative willingness to buy. The aggressiveness of one's marketing strategy and tactics is often dependent upon current buying intentions. More aggressive marketing may be called for in periods of lessened buying interest, as when automakers use cash rebate schemes to move inventories. Such activities, however, are unlikely to fully counteract cyclical periods of low demand.

While sales figures may experience cyclical variations, the successful firm has a rising sales trend line. This depends upon management's ability to foresee, correctly define, and reach new market opportunities. Effective forecasting and research is only a partial solution. Marketers must also develop an intuitive awareness of potential markets. This requires that one be able to correctly delineate opportunities.[9]

Inflation    Another economic factor that critically influences marketing strategy is **inflation**, which can occur during any stage in the business cycle. Inflation is *a rising price level resulting in reduced purchasing power for the consumer*. A person's money is devalued (in terms of what it can buy). Traditionally, this circumstance has been more prevalent in countries outside of North America. However, in the late 1970s and early 1980s Canada experienced "double digit inflation" (an inflation rate of over 10 percent a year). Although the rate of inflation has declined considerably during the mid-1980s, the recent experiences led to widespread concern over political approaches to controlling interest rates and stabilizing price levels, and over ways in which the individual can adjust to such reductions in the spending power of the dollar.

**Stagflation** is a word that has been coined to describe a peculiar brand of inflation that characterized some of the recent Canadian economic experience. It is a situation where an economy has *high unemployment and a rising price level at the same time*. Formulation of effective strategies is particularly difficult under these circumstances.

---

[9] The concept of environmental forecasting is examined in T. F. Mastri, "Environmental Forecasting," *Fairleigh Dickinson University Business Review* (Winter 1973), pp. 3–10.

**Unemployment**   Another significant economic problem that has affected the marketing environment in recent years is unemployment. The ranks of the unemployed — officially defined as people actively looking for work who do not have jobs — swelled to 12.4 percent of the Canadian labour force by January 1984. By contrast the unemployment rate was 5.9 percent in January 1965.

In the severe recession of the early 1980s, numerous businesses failed, production slowed, many factories ceased operation entirely, and thousands of workers found themselves out of work. The consequences of reduced income and uncertainty about future income were reflected in the marketplace in many ways.

**Government Tools for Combatting Inflation and Unemployment**
The government can attempt to deal with the twin economic problems of inflation and unemployment by using two basic approaches: fiscal policy and monetary policy. **Fiscal policy** concerns *the receipts and expenditures of government.* To combat inflation, an economy could reduce government expenditures, raise its revenue (primarily taxes), or do a combination of both. It could also use direct controls such as wage and price controls. **Monetary policy** refers to *the manipulation of the money supply and market rates of interest.* In periods of rising prices monetary policy may dictate that the government take actions to decrease the money supply and raise interest rates, thus restraining purchasing power.

Both fiscal and monetary policy have been used in our battles against inflation and unemployment. Their marketing implications are numerous and varied. Higher taxes mean less consumer purchasing power, which usually results in sales declines for nonessential goods and services. However, some taxes which have been collected may find their way into various job-creation programs. Income earned from these will tend to be spent on basic goods and services. Lower federal expenditure levels make the government a less attractive customer for many industries. A lowered money supply means less liquidity is available for potential conversion to purchasing power. High interest rates often lead to a significant slump in the construction and housing industry.

Both unemployment and inflation affect marketing by modifying consumer behaviour. Unless unemployment insurance, personal savings, and union supplementary unemployment benefits are sufficient to offset lost earnings, the unemployed individual has less income to spend in the marketplace. Even if the individual is completely compensated for lost earnings, his or her buying behaviour is likely to be affected. As consumers become more conscious of inflation, they are likely to become more price conscious in general. This can lead to three possible outcomes, all important to marketers. Consumers can (1) elect to buy now in the belief that prices will be higher later (automobile dealers often use this argument in their commercial messages); (2) decide to alter their purchasing patterns; or (3) postpone certain purchases.

## The Technological Environment

The **technological environment** consists of *the applications to marketing of knowledge based upon scientific discoveries, inventions, and innovations*. It results in new products for consumers and improves existing products. It is a frequent source of price reductions through the development of new production methods or new materials. It also can make existing products obsolete virtually overnight—as slide rule manufacturers would attest. Technological innovations are exemplified in the container industry, where glass and tinplate containers have faced intense competition from such innovations as aluminum, fiberfoil, and plastics.

Marketing decision makers must closely monitor the technological environment for a number of reasons. New technology may be the means by which they remain competitive in their industries. It may also be the vehicle for the creation of entirely new industries. For example, the development of the microchip and lasers has resulted in the development of major industries during the past 25 years.

In the case of high technology products such as computers and related items, marketers face real challenges in keeping up with the pace of change. They not only have to maintain an understanding of the industry, but must somehow try to communicate totally new concepts and ways of solving problems to potential customers. As Francis McInerney, president of Northern Business Information says, "The time it takes to explain a product may be longer than the time it takes to introduce a whole new generation of products."[10]

In addition, marketers must anticipate the effect such technological innovations are likely to have upon the lifestyles of consumers, the products of competitors, the demands of industrial users, and the regulatory actions of government. The advent of videocassette recorders, videodiscs, and lower cost satellite receiving stations may adversely affect concert attendance and movie ticket sales. A longer lasting engine may reduce industrial purchases. A new process may result in reduction of pollution and produce changes in local ordinances.

A major source of technological innovations has been the space program. Hundreds of industrial applications of space technology

---

[10] David Thompson, "Rising to The Challenge," *Marketing*, May 2, 1983, p. 13.

---

**Figure 2-5  Technological Spinoffs from the Space Program**

---

Orbiting satellites that can monitor the earth and provide valuable data on crops, weather, and earthquakes.

Carbon fibers used in jet aircraft, golf clubs, and tennis rackets. They are lighter than steel, but they are stronger and stiffer.

Advances in health and medical areas, such as improved splints for broken limbs and more effective cancer detection devices.

New alloys used in tools, kitchenware, and household appliances.

Trajectory and moon landing analyses have resulted in a fully computerized auto traffic control system for at least one city. The system calculates the best traffic light sequence during rush hour traffic. Mobility has been increased by 15 percent during tests, resulting in gas consumption savings and reduced air pollution.

Wind deflectors for trucks have been developed to reduce wind resistance by 24 percent, resulting in a 10 percent fuel savings.

Life rafts equipped with radar reflective canopies greatly increase their visibility from the air.

Orbiting satellites have been responsible for the virtual elimination of the screwworm. The worm destroys cattle, poultry, and wildlife.

Land surveying satellites can spot 99 percent of the fresh water sources currently not being used.

Aluminized plastic used to keep fluids cold in space programs is used in lightweight jackets, sleeping bags, and parkas.

Silicone plastic from airplane seats has been used in football helmet liners.

A computer image process used to enhance satellite photos can indicate missing chromosomes in fetuses, thus identifying possible inherited diseases before the infant is born.

---

Source: Richard T. Hise, Peter L. Gillett, and John K. Ryans, Jr., *Basic Marketing* (Boston, Mass.: Little, Brown & Co., 1979), p. 121. Reprinted by permission.

---

have been made, and private enterprise has been encouraged to make use of these innovations. Figure 2-5 reveals some applications, not all of them obvious, that have already been implemented.

**Demarketing — Dealing with Shortages**

Shortages — temporary or permanent — can be caused by several factors. A brisk demand may exceed manufacturing capacity or outpace the response time required to gear up a production line. Shortages may also be caused by a lack of raw materials, component parts, energy, or labour. Regardless of the cause, shortages require marketers to reorient their thinking.[11]

**Demarketing**, a term that has come into general use in recent years, refers to the process of *cutting consumer demand for a product, because the demand exceeds the level that can reasonably be supplied by the firm or because doing so will create a more favourable corporate image.* Some oil companies, for example, have publicized tips on how to cut gasoline consumption as a result of the gradual depletion of oil reserves. Utility companies have encouraged homeowners to install more insulation to lower heating bills. And many cities have discouraged central business district traffic by raising parking fees and violation penalties.

Shortages sometimes force marketers to be allocators of limited supplies. This is in sharp contrast to marketing's traditional objective of expanding sales volume. Shortages require marketers to decide whether to spread a limited supply over all customers so that none are satisfied, or to back-order some customers so that others may be completely supplied. Shortages certainly present marketers with a unique set of marketing problems.

## The Social Environment

The Chevalline Meat Company knows that the social environment works against them. When you try to get someone to eat somebody's pony, you've got trouble. Chevalline is trying to induce Canadians to eat more horsemeat, despite a social environment that views horses as pets and companions, not livestock for slaughter. Canadians consume virtually no horsemeat, although in France and other European countries the meat is highly thought of.

Chevalline even had some difficulty obtaining a licence to open a horsemeat market. The company wishes to sell to Canadians, rather than rely on overseas markets for its customers. Whether the firm will ever change Canadian opinion is a moot question. But its prob-

---

[11] Interesting articles related to this topic include Philip Kotler and Sidney J. Levy, "Demarketing, Yes, Demarketing," *Harvard Business Review* (November-December 1971), pp. 74–80; David W. Cravens, "Marketing Management in an Era of Shortages," *Business Horizons* (February 1974), pp. 79–85; A. B. Blankenship and John H. Holmes, "Will Shortages Bankrupt the Marketing Concept?" *MSU Business Topics* (Spring 1974), pp. 13–18; Philip Kotler, "Marketing During Periods of Shortages," *Journal of Marketing* (July 1974), pp. 20–29; Zohrab S. Demirdjian, "The Role of Marketing in an Economy of Affluence and Shortages," *Business and Society* (Spring 1975), pp. 15–21; Nessim Hanna, A. H. Kizilbash, and Albert Smart, "Marketing Strategy Under Conditions of Economic Scarcity," *Journal of Marketing* (January 1975), pp. 63–67; and Sunier C. Aggarwal, "Prepare for Continual Materials Shortages," *Harvard Business Review* (May-June 1982), pp. 6–10.

lems dramatize the importance of understanding and assessing the social environment when making marketing decisions.

The **socio-cultural environment** is *the marketer's relationship with the society and culture in which the company operates.* Obviously, there are many different facets of significance. One important category is the general readiness of society to accept a marketing idea, as discussed above.

Another important category is the trust and confidence of the public in business as a whole. Such relationships have been on the decline since the mid-1960s. Opinion polls suggest that people have lost confidence in major companies (although they maintain faith in the private enterprise system). These declines should, however, be viewed in perspective. All institutions have lost public confidence to some degree. In fact, some would argue that governments and labour unions are even less popular than business.

The socio-cultural environment for marketing decisions has both expanded in scope and increased in importance. Today no marketer can initiate a strategy without taking the social environment into account. Marketers must develop an awareness of the manner in which it affects their decisions.[12] The constant flux of social issues requires that marketing managers place more emphasis on solving these questions instead of merely concerning themselves with the standard marketing tools.[13] Some firms have created a new position — manager of public policy research — to study the changing social environment's future impact on the company.

One question facing contemporary marketing is how to measure the accomplishment of socially oriented objectives. A firm that is attuned to its social environment must develop new ways of evaluating its performance. Traditional income statements and balance sheets are no longer adequate. This issue will be further developed in a later chapter as one of the most important problems facing contemporary marketing.

### Importance in International Marketing Decisions

The societal context for marketing decision-making is often more crucial in the international sphere than in the domestic. Marketers must be cognizant of social differences in the way that business affairs are conducted abroad. Consider the following case:

---

[12] Laurence P. Feldman, "Societal Adaptation: A New Challenge for Marketing," *Journal of Marketing* (July 1971), pp. 54–60. See also Edward M. Mazze, "Current Marketing Practice: Some Societal Implications," *Marquette Business Review* (Summer 1971), pp. 86–89.

[13] This is suggested in Leslie M. Dawson, "Marketing Science in the Age of Aquarius," *Journal of Marketing* (July 1971), pp. 66–72. See also Leslie M. Dawson, "The Human Concept: New Philosophy for Business," *Business Horizons* (December 1969), pp. 29–38.

The stereotype of the North American male — hail-fellow-well-met, cordial, friendly, outgoing and gregarious — does not mesh with the discomfort he feels and often shows in his contacts with Latin Americans and Middle Easterners. These people crowd close to him to talk, and in Latin America his host is likely to greet him with a warm *abrazo*, suggesting unfamiliar intimacy. Anyone who has ever attended a party or a reception in Latin America must surely have observed the self-consciousness of the uninitiated . . . visitor, who keeps backing away from his native host, to whom it is natural to carry on a conversation separated by inches. Last year at a business-man's club in Brazil, where many receptions are held for newly arrived executives, the railings on the terrace had to be reinforced because so many businessmen fell into the garden as they backed away.[14]

Consumer behaviour and tastes also differ from place to place, as is suggested by these situations.[15]

1. In Thailand Helene Curtis sells black shampoo because Thai women feel it makes their hair look glossier.
2. Nestlé, a Swiss multinational company now brews more than 40 varieties of instant coffee to satisfy different national tastes.
3. General Foods Corp. entered the British market with its standard powdered Jell-O only to find that British cooks prefer the solid-wafer or cake form, even if it takes more time to prepare. After several frustrating years, the company gave up and pulled out of the market.
4. In Italy a United States company that set up a corn-processing plant found that its marketing effort failed because Italians think of corn as "pig food."

Many marketers recognize societal differences between countries, but assume that a homogeneous social environment exists domestically. Nothing could be farther from the truth! Canada is a mixed society composed of varied submarkets. These submarkets can be classified by age, place of residence, sex, ethnic background, and numerous other determinants.

For example, the Quebec market segment has historically been ignored by too many firms. In recent years, however, Quebec has been recognized as a distinct market within itself. The culture and

---

[14] Lawrence Stessin, "Incidents of Culture Shock Among American Businessmen Overseas," *Pittsburgh Business Review* (November-December 1971), p. 3. Reprinted by permission.
[15] These examples are from "Why a Global Market Doesn't Exist," *Business Week* (December 9, 1970), pp. 140, 142, 144. Reprinted by special permission; © 1970 by McGraw-Hill, Inc. All rights reserved.

values of this market require more careful treatment than merely translating English into French.

Sex is another increasingly important social factor. The feminist movement has had a decided effect on marketing, particularly promotion. Television commercials now feature women in less stereotyped roles than in previous years.

Since social variables change constantly, marketers must continually monitor their dynamic environment. What appears to be out-of-bounds today may be tomorrow's greatest market opportunity. Consider the way that previously taboo subjects such as feminine hygiene products are now commonly advertised.

The social variables must be recognized by modern business executives since they affect the way consumers react to different products and marketing practices. One of the most tragic — and avoidable — of all marketing mistakes is the failure to appreciate social differences within our own domestic market.

The rise of consumerism can be partially traced to the growing public concern with making business more responsible to its constituents. Consumerism, which is discussed in detail in a later chapter, is an evolving aspect of marketing's social environment.

**Figure 2-6   The Marketing Manager Controls Marketing Elements**

**Forces Bearing on a Firm's Marketing Mix**

1. The social environment and behaviour of consumers
2. The economic environment
3. The competitive environment
4. The legal environment
5. The technological environment

**External factors**

**Objectives and Resources of the Organization**

**MARKETING MANAGER**

**Marketing Program**
A unique blend of marketing elements related to each other and the forces bearing on the mix

**Elements of the Firm's Marketing Mix**

1. Product strategy
2. Pricing strategy
3. Distribution strategy
4. Promotion strategy

**Internal factors**

Certainly the advent of this movement has influenced the move toward more direct protection of consumer rights in such areas as product safety and false and misleading advertising. These concerns will undoubtedly be amplified and expanded in the years ahead.

**Role of the Marketing Manager**   As a conclusion to this look at the marketing environment, Figure 2-6 illustrates how the marketing manager works, controlling marketing elements in relation to the forces bearing on a firm's marketing mix. In light of the opportunities and constraints perceived in the environmental framework, as well as the objectives and resources of the firm, the manager develops a marketing program (marketing strategy). The elements or tools of the marketing strategy are product, pricing, distribution, and promotion strategies. These are blended together in a unique manner to make up the marketing mix. The result wins customers, sales, and profits for the firm.

While this concept is simple in itself, it is extremely complicated in practice and difficult to do well. The rest of this text will elaborate on the process. The next chapters start with marketing planning and discuss some important basic concepts that must be considered.

**Summary**   A consideration of several environmental variables is of paramount importance in making marketing decisions. Five specific environments should be considered: competitive, political and legal, economic, technological, and social and cultural. These are important to the study of marketing because they provide the framework within which marketing strategies are formulated. Environmental factors are among the most dynamic aspects of contemporary business.

The competitive environment is the interactive process that occurs in the marketplace. Marketing decisions influence the market and are, in turn, affected by the counterstrategies of competition. The legal segment attempts to maintain a competitive environment as well as regulate specific marketing practices. The economic environment often influences the manner in which consumers will behave toward varying marketing appeals. Socio-cultural aspects, however, may become the most important to marketers. The matter of adapting to a changing social environment, both domestically and internationally, has advanced to the forefront of marketing thought.

**Key Terms**   competitive environment
political and legal environment
economic environment

fiscal policy
monetary policy
technological environment

inflation                              demarketing
stagflation                            socio-cultural environment

---

**Review Questions**

1. Identify and briefly describe the five components of the marketing environment.
2. Explain the types of competition faced by marketers.
3. What are the steps involved in developing a competitive strategy?
4. How does inflation affect marketing activity?
5. How did the Great Depression influence marketing legislation?
6. Trace the evolution of Consumer and Corporate Affairs Canada into an "activist watchdog" of marketing practices. Then evaluate the department's degree of success.
7. What are the major economic factors affecting marketing decisions?
8. Distinguish between inflation and stagflation. In what ways do they affect marketing?
9. Indentify the ways in which the technological environment affects marketing activities.
10. Explain how the socio-cultural environment influences marketing.

---

**Discussion Questions and Exercises**

1. Give an example of how each of the environmental variables discussed in this chapter might affect the following firms:
   a. Eastern Provincial Airlines
   b. Local aerobics exercise centre
   c. Swiss Chalet franchise
   d. Avon Products
   e. Sears catalogue department
   f. Local television station
2. Comment on the following statement: The legal framework for marketing decisions is basically a positive one.
3. Can the consumerism movement be viewed as a rejection of the competitive marketing system? Defend your answer.
4. As a consumer, do you favour laws permitting resale price maintenance agreements? Would your answer vary if you were the producer of Sony television sets? If you were the retailer of Sony television sets? Why or why not?
5. Would a gas station that sold gasoline to a city's police department for one cent a litre less than its price for other customers be in violation of the Competition Act? Why? Explain your answer.

# PART

2

## Planning The Marketing Effort

The focus on the four chapters in part Two is planning—anticipating the future and determining the courses of action designed to achieve organizational objectives. The chapters treat such vital subjects as development of marketing strategies, sales forecasting, use of market segmentation in selecting market targets, and provision of needed, decision-relevant marketing information. This part provides a foundation for the development of appropriate marketing programs for profitably serving chosen market segments.

# CHAPTER 3

# Marketing Planning and Forecasting

## CHAPTER OBJECTIVES

1. To distinguish between strategic planning and tactical planning.

2. To explain how marketing planning differs at different levels of the organization.

3. To identify the steps in the marketing planning process.

4. To explain the portfolio and the BCG growth-market matrix approaches to marketing planning.

5. To identify the alternative marketing strategies available to marketers.

6. To identify the major types of forecasting methods.

7. To explain the steps involved in the forecasting process.

Rex Faithfull and Herman Herbst had a plan to break into the electric kettle market. However, given the tough competition from Canadian General Electric, Sunbeam, and others, many businesspeople would not have given them much of a chance. Careful marketing planning and aggressive marketing implementation resulted in their company, Creative Appliance Corp., growing from nothing to 24 percent of the Canadian market in four years. Today, the company is the largest manufacturer of kettles in Canada next to Black & Decker Canada Inc.

The Creative story started when industrial consultant Faithfull teamed up with Herbst, the former owner of a tool-and-die metal stamping business. Their new company began by turning out metal parts for small appliances. This put them in an ideal position to take advantage of a strategic window that soon appeared in the electric kettle market. In 1975 Consumer and Corporate Affairs Canada declared that kettles using lead solder were a health hazard and these kettles, most at the low end of the price range, were withdrawn from the Canadian market.

Faithfull and Herbst believed that they could design their own kettle, and make it better and cheaper. They felt this was an opportunity waiting for a marketing strategy. They decided to deal with large retailers directly, rather than marketing their product through middlemen.

Herbst designed a kettle using silver solder and an innovative plastic upper section. The plastic looked nice, and the design cost less than the traditional steel. This allowed the kettle to retail initially at what one competitor calls "the magic price-point of $9.99."

The partners took a wooden model of their proposed kettle to Canadian Tire and Woolco and got orders for more than 50 000 units. Tooling up for production cost $100 000, and as the company had sales of only $800 000 a year at the time, the partners went on what Faithfull calls "minimum wage." They put all the money they had or could borrow — mainly from the Federal Business Development Bank — into preparing steel dies and getting production established in order to fill the orders. In that first year they sold more than 100 000 units to Woolco, Canadian Tire, Zellers, and Towers stores.

In 1980 they added a second kettle to the product line. The first export order of this "international" model was shipped to Trinidad in 1981. Faithfull predicted the company's total export sales in 1983 to France, Trinidad, Jamaica, South Africa, Chile, Japan, Hong Kong, the United States, and Britain would be worth at least $800 000.

Creative's marketing and production have obviously been very successful. The biggest problem has been the generation of sufficient funds to finance their successful marketing venture. Rex Faithfull and Herman Herbst have found that sound marketing planning pays off![1]

---

**The Conceptual Framework**

"Should we grant a licence for our new liquid-crystal display watch to a Japanese firm or simply export our models to Japan?"

"Will changing the performance time and date affect concert attendance?"

"Should we use company sales personnel or independent agents in the new territory?"

"Should discounts be offered to cash customers? What impact would such a policy have on our credit customers?"

These questions are examples of thousands of both major and minor decisions that regularly face the marketing manager. Continual changes in the marketplace resulting from changing consumer expectations, competitive actions, economic trends, political and legal changes, as well as developments in such areas as product innovations or pressures from distribution channel members, are likely to have substantial impact on the operations of any organization. Although such changes are often beyond the control

[1] Adapted from Sandy Fife, "Creative Appliance Puts Kettle Sales on Boil," *Financial Times*, May 9, 1983, pp. 23–24.

of the marketing manager, effective planning can prepare the manager by anticipating many changes and focusing upon possible actions to take should such changes occur. Effective planning is often a major factor in the difference between success and failure. Figure 3-1 summarizes the major benefits of planning for an organization.

## Marketing Planning

Planning is *the process of anticipating the future and determining the courses of action to achieve organizational objectives*. In other words, planning is a continuous process that includes the specification of objectives and the actions required to achieve them. The planning process results in the creation of a blueprint that not only specifies the means of achieving organizational objectives but also includes checkpoints where actual performance can be compared with expectations in order to determine whether the organizational activities are moving the organization in the direction of its objectives. Such checkpoints are important means of *control* — another critical managerial function that is the subject of Chapter 25.

Marketing planning — *the implementation of planning activities as they relate to the achievement of marketing objectives* — is the basis for all marketing strategies. Product lines, pricing decisions, selection of appropriate distribution channels, and decisions relating to promotional campaigns all depend upon the plans that are formulated within the marketing organization.

## Strategic Planning vs. Tactical Planning

Planning is often classified on the basis of scope or breadth. Some plans are quite broad and long-range, focusing on major organizational objectives with major impact on the organization for a period of five or more years. Such plans are typically called strategic plans. Strategic planning can be defined as *the process of determining the primary objectives of an organization, and the adoption of courses of action and the allocation of resources necessary to achieve those objectives.*[2]

The word *strategy* is derived from a Greek term meaning "the general's art." Strategic planning has a critical impact on the destiny of the organization since it provides long-run direction for decision-makers. At K-Mart, the strategic plan calls for marketers to use low prices on commodity type items to attract customers who may also buy merchandise with higher margins.

By contrast, tactical planning focuses on *the implementation of those activities specified by the strategic plans*. Tactical plans typically have a shorter term than strategic plans, focusing more on current and near-term activities that must be executed in order to

---

[2] Alfred D. Chandler, Jr., *Strategy and Structure* (Cambridge, Mass.: MIT Press 1962), p. 13. See also Paul F. Anderson, "Marketing, Strategic Planning, and The Theory of the Firm," *Journal of Marketing* (Spring 1982), pp. 15-26.

implement overall strategies. Resource allocation is a common deci-sion area for tactical planning. The decision by a car-rental firm to counter special offers by a competitor would be the result of tacti-cal planning.

---

**Figure 3-1   What Planning Can Accomplish for a Firm**

1. It leads to a better position or standing for the organization.
2. It helps the organization progress in the ways that its management considers most suitable.
3. It helps every manager think, decide, and act more effectively for progress in the desired direction.
4. It helps keep the organization flexible.
5. It stimulates a co-operative, integrated, enthusiastic approach to organizational problems.
6. It indicates to management how to evaluate and check up on progress toward the planned objectives.
7. It leads to socially and economically useful results.

Source: Subhash, C. Jain, *Marketing Planning and Strategy* (Cincinnati: Southwestern Publishing Co., 1981), p. 5.

---

***Planning at Different Levels in the Organization***

Planning is a major responsibility for every manager. Although managers at all levels within an organization devote some of their workdays to planning, the relative proportion of time spent in plan-ning activities and the types of planning vary at different organiza-tion levels.

Top management of a corporation — the board of directors, president, and functional vice-presidents such as the chief market-ing officer — spend greater proportions of their time engaged in plan-ning than do middle- and supervisory-level managers. In fact, one company president recommends that 30 to 50 percent of a chief executive's time should be spent on strategic planning.[3] Also, top management are more likely to devote more of their planning activities to longer-range strategic planning, while middle-level managers (such as the director of the advertising department, re-gional sales managers, or the physical distribution manager) tend to focus on narrower, tactical plans for their departments, and supervisory management are more likely to engage in developing specific programs designed to meet the goals for their responsibility areas. Figure 3-2 indicates the types of planning engaged in at the various organizational levels.

---

[3] "Strategic Planning Should Occupy 30 to 50 Percent of CEO's Time: Schanck," *Marketing News* (June 1, 1979), p. 1.

**Figure 3-2   Types of Plans Prepared by Different Levels of Management**

| Management Level | Type of Plan | General Content |
|---|---|---|
| *Top*<br>board of directors, president, operating division vice-presidents including marketing | strategic planning | objectives of organization; fundamental strategies; total budget |
| *Middle*<br>general sales manager, marketing research director, head of advertising department | tactical planning | quarterly and semiannual plans; subdivision of budgets; policies and procedures for each individual's department |
| *Supervisory*<br>district sales manager, supervisors | tactical planning derived from planning at higher organization levels | daily and weekly plans; unit budgets |

Source: Adapted from William F. Glueck, *Management* (Hinsdale, Ill.: Dryden Press, 1980), p. 246. Copyright 1980 by Dryden Press, a division of Holt, Rinehart and Winston. Adapted by permission of Holt, Rinehart and Winston.

## Steps in the Planning Process

As Figure 3-3 indicates, the *objectives* of the organization are the starting point for marketing planning. These basic goals of the organization are the guideposts from which marketing objectives and plans are derived. They provide direction for all phases of the organization and serve as standards in evaluating performance. For Nike, Inc., the overall objective is to be the leading firm in the quality athletic-shoe market. Nike's marketing plans — both strategic and tactical — are based on this objective.

The planning process also requires a careful analysis of the firm's current *market position*. It is not enough to know that sales and profits are rising or falling. Sales movements *in relation to* competitors should also be known, and understood. Also, a realistic assessment of the relative current and long-term competitiveness of company products and services must be made.

Marketing *opportunities* arise from a number of circumstances. The dramatic increase in prices for oil and natural gas has given rise to new ventures such as firms which specialize in finding air leaks in your home so that you can reinsulate it. Other companies are marketing solar heating products or are developing a new breed of windmills for many different energy applications. Opportunities often arise from improved technology, for example, the digital record industry.

## Figure 3-3   Steps in the Marketing Planning Process

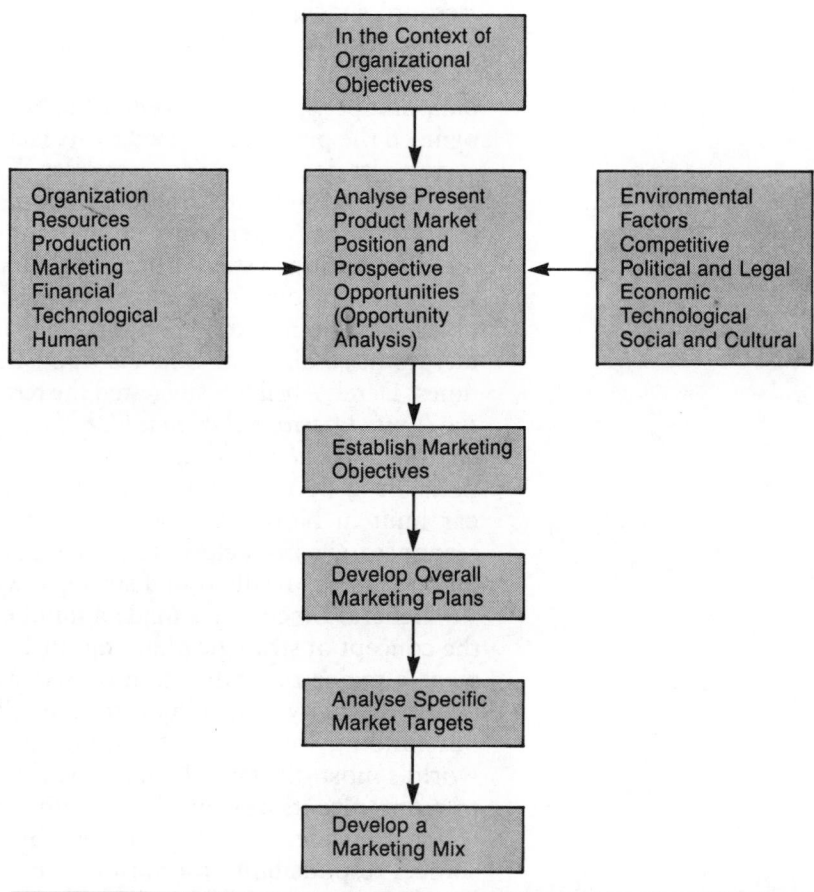

The *environmental forces* described in Chapter 2 — competitive, political and legal, economic, technological, and social and cultural — are forces which affect marketing opportunities. For instance, environmental factors have decreased the market for afternoon papers. Such papers, frequently called PMs, were very popular when people went to work in the predawn hours and returned home sometime in the afternoon. The PM environment has changed in recent times. The white-collar labour force now reports for work at 9 a.m. rather than 6 a.m. Approximately 60 percent of all married women now work, so that families are more likely to shop during the evening hours, when they used to read PMs. Furthermore, television is rapidly becoming the most popular source of news. The PMs are attempting to counter this trend by improving their suburban, entertainment, and special-interest sections. Some are even beginning to offer morning editions.

Another major influence on a firm's decision to take advantage of marketing opportunities is the *resources of the organization*. Resources include marketing strengths, production strengths, financial position, research and development capability, and quality of management. When Bic, a French manufacturer of inexpensive ballpoint pens, decided to enter the North American market, it recognized the problems caused by its lack of an effective distribution system. Its decision was to purchase Waterman, a firm that manufactured and marketed refillable fountain pens. Although Bic discontinued the Waterman pen line four years later, it had acquired the distribution system it previously lacked.

Marketing *objectives* and *plans* result from overall organizational objectives and marketing opportunity analysis. The environmental factors have different impacts upon the organization at different times. Derek Abell has suggested the term **strategic window** to define *the limited periods during which the key requirements of a market and the particular competencies of a firm best fit together.*[4] Pontiac's decision to develop and market the Fiero in 1983, the first sports car built in North America for more than two decades, was in response to its marketers' decision that organizational and environmental factors resulted in a strategic window.

General Electric has made a number of major contributions to the concept of strategic planning. In 1970, General Electric underwent a major reorganization by separating planning- and policy-oriented activity from administration. GE is now regarded as having outstanding long-range planning functions. Often labelled the world's most diversified company, the following year GE decided to reorganize its nine product groups and 48 divisions into a portfolio of businesses called **strategic business units** (SBUs). For instance, responsibility for various GE food preparation appliances had been scattered through three separate divisions; they were merged into a housewares SBU. The GE reorganization forced the firm's personnel to focus on customer needs, rather than on internal divisions.

The SBU concept of *related product groupings within a multiproduct firm* was quickly adopted by such major firms as Union Carbide and International Paper. Although such early experimenters as General Foods have already returned to traditional organizational structure, the SBU concept is utilized currently in about 20 percent of the largest manufacturing corporations.[5]

---

[4] Derek F. Abell, "Strategic Windows," *Journal of Marketing* (July 1978), pp. 21–26.
[5] Philippe Haspeslagh, "Portfolio Planning: Uses and Limitations," *Harvard Business Review* (January–February 1982), pp. 58–73.

# The Product Timing Window

It is sometimes helpful to think about the process of new product development as consisting of three stages: need identification, technical evaluation, and commercial implementation. And timing is the thread which holds them together.

In the need identification phase, we ask "What are the marketplace needs, when will the need be there, and how big is the market created by the need?" Technical evaluation includes such questions as "Is there a match with the company capabilities (marketing, manufacturing, technology)? Do we have all the pieces we need? If we don't, what's missing?" The final phase of the process, commercial implementation, involves the development of a successful business or product. This is the point at which large amounts of money will be spent.

Timing is the common denominator in each of these steps. The concept of the "product timing window" illustrates the relationship. The product timing window is analogous to the window in space at which a rocket is aimed in order to achieve a successful satellite launch. Just as the rocket team aims at a point in space and time, the product timing window combines the three steps of product development with time. Here are three examples to show the relationship: one involves a project that worked; in another the need changed; and the third might be termed a "technical success" that was too early for its time.

1. Our first example is the Phosgard story. Phosgard is Monsanto's registered trademark for a line of flame retardants for use with polyurethane foams. In the late 1950s, Monsanto recognized that the increasing use of urethane foams, which are highly flammable, would require the application of a flame-retardant in certain uses. After documenting the size of market a matching of capabilities and market need was done. A technical fit was found with a series of patented compounds invented by one of Monsanto's scientists.

   Following a period of product development in the laboratory and other trials, a commercial fit was confirmed. The product timing window was identified in the early 1970s. New regula-

tions decreed that materials in passenger compartments of automobiles should meet certain flame retardant specifications. Phosgard was a product which could help. It was off and running. The product cleared the window in 1974. Today it is widely used in polyurethane foams in cars and for many flame retardant applications.

2. The story of the Edsel has been told and retold; it exemplifies one of the pitfalls that must be avoided in the new product process. In the early 1950s Ford took great pains to determine the market needs of the public. The public was demanding large, well-appointed cars with generous amounts of chrome and other luxuries.

   Ford then set about to develop such a car. The technical fit was a cinch. When the Edsel was first introduced, things seemed to go well. Then sales began to fall off. Ford had correctly identified customer needs in the early 1950s, but by the time the product was introduced in the late 1950s the fickle car-buying public had changed its desires. It was interested in more economical cars and began buying large numbers of Volkswagens. The ready window had moved. The lesson here is that even if you correctly identify a need, due to the time period required to develop any product, you must continually monitor that need to make certain that your target has not moved.

3. A third example comes again from Monsanto's archives. In the late 1950s it was determined that it would be desirable to reduce the hydrocarbon and NOX emissions from internal combustion engines in some way.

   A technical fit was feasible since the company had considerable amounts of catalytic experience. However, monitoring the target market, auto manufacturers, showed that they were unlikely to install such a device unless they were required to do so. Since that did not seem to be in the offing, Monsanto dropped the project.

   The lesson is that a project must be stopped midstream if certain basic premises change. It takes a long time, usually a matter of years, to

## The Product Timing Window

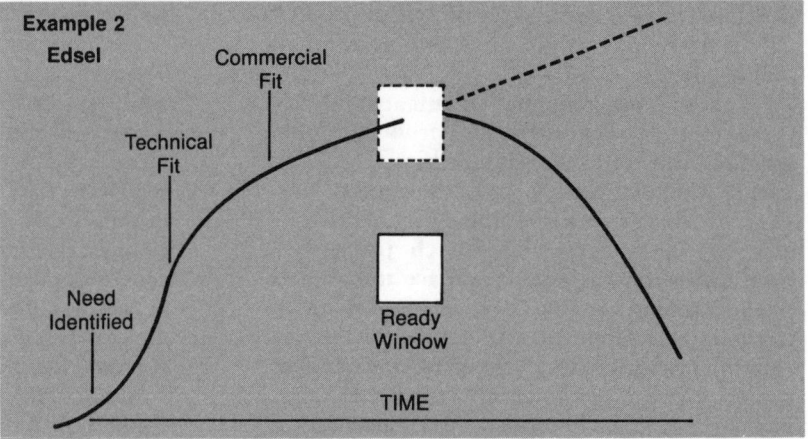

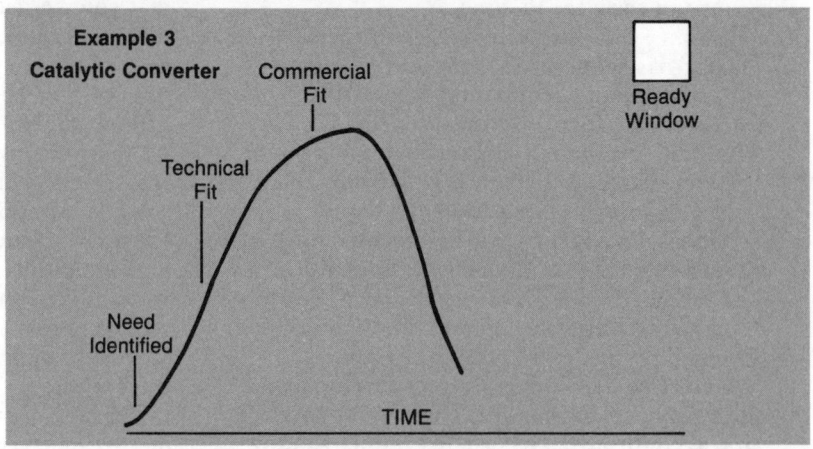

Adapted from Roger W. Bucknell, "The Product Timing 'Window'," *Industrial Marketing* (May 1982), pp. 62–64.

successful complete a new product or business development. During that period, a company must continue to monitor the identified

need and make any adjustments in goals and specifications required — including cancellation of the project, if necessary.

---

Source: Adapted from Roger W. Bucknell, "The Product Timing 'Window'," *Industrial Marketing* (May 1982), pp. 62-64.

---

### The Portfolio Approach to Marketing Planning

Portfolio analysis is a very useful tool in developing marketing plans. The criteria used can provide valuable insights into the effects of past planning and the needs for future decisions. Portfolio analysis across the entire range of products or product lines helps to assure that no marketing plan will be based solely on the merits of an individual item considered in isolation from others. Instead, the key elements of any marketing plan are likely to be pre-positioned within the portfolio framework of management's deliberations on how best to allocate resources between all of its product offerings.[6]

### The BCG Matrix

The work of the Boston Consulting Group (BCG) is widely known in industry. BCG has developed a four-quadrant matrix, shown in Figure 3-4, that is useful in understanding the strategic planning-marketing strategy interface. The **BCG growth-share matrix** *plots market share*, the percentage of a market controlled by a firm, *against market growth potential*. All of a firm's various businesses can be plotted in one of the four quadrants. The resulting quadrants are labeled cash cows, stars, dogs, and question marks, and each one has a unique marketing strategy. Marketers employ varying strategies for each category of business.

*Cash Cows* (dominant market share in a market with low growth): Cash cows are the main source of earnings and cash to support growth areas. Marketing planners want to maintain this situation for as long as possible since it produces a strong cash flow. The objective is to maximize cash flow while maintaining market share.

*Stars* (dominant market share in a market with high growth): While this type of business produces profits, it requires heavy cash consumption in order to maintain a leading market position. If this share can be maintained until growth of the market slows, stars may become high dollar earners. In the meantime stars may even

---

[6] David S. Hopkins, *The Marketing Plan* (New York: The Conference Board, Inc., 1981), p. 34.

### Figure 3-4   A Matrix for Marketing Planning

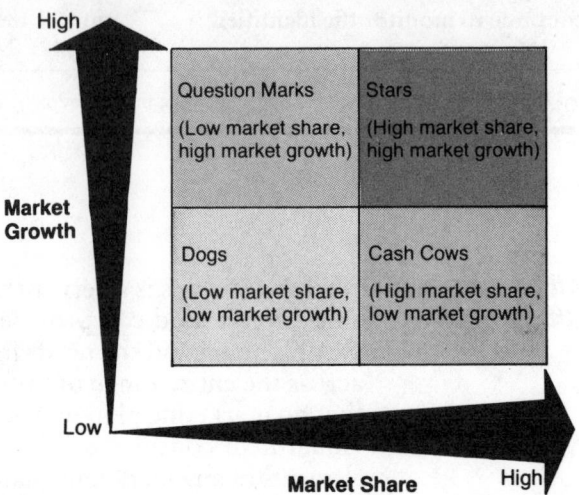

Source: "The Product Portfolio," Perspectives No. 66, The Boston Consulting Group, Inc. 1970.

produce a negative cash flow. Such products require considerable management attention.

*Dogs* (small market share in a market with low growth): This type of business generally consumes far more than an equitable amount of management attention. Usually, the company should minimize its position in this market area, pulling investment from it and withdrawing completely if possible.

*Question Marks* (small market share in a market with high growth): Question mark enterprises must achieve a dominant position before growth slows, or they will be frozen in a marginal position and become dogs. Because they demand a heavy commitment from limited financial and management resources, their number in the portfolio should be restricted. These situations require that marketers make a basic go/no go decision. Unless question marks can be converted to stars the firm should pull out of these markets.[7]

The BCG matrix highlights the importance of creating a mix that positions the firm to its best advantage. A portfolio approach to the setting of business strategies has won a growing number of adherents during recent years. Numerous variations of this basic

---

[7] Some of the ideas expressed here are from an address by D. D. Monieson published in "Effective Marketing Planning: An Overview," *Executive Bulletin No. 8.* (Ottawa: The Conference Board in Canada, 1978).

approach are now in use. The BCG matrix highlights the importance of creating a mix that positions the firm to best advantage. It is largely the result of the BCG's pioneering work with the experience curve first identified in 1966. The **experience curve** indicates that the highest market-share competitor will have a cost advantage over others. BCG reports that higher market shares reduce costs because of factors like learning advantages, increased specialization, higher investment, and economies of scale.[8] Doubling the experience factor can cut product costs by 25 to 30 percent. The consultants suggest that market share is a better measure of performance than profitability.

Critics of the BCG approach often point to the tendencies of some marketers to apply it in a largely mechanistic manner. In an attempt to develop a product line of stars, marketers may ignore possible methods of converting products and services labelled as dogs. Critics also suggest that the firm with no stars may successfully find means of expanding market and sales opportunities of an existing product regardless of the label attached to it. The advantages of following the matrix approach must be balanced against the potential shortcomings by each organization.[9]

## The Strategic Planning/ Marketing Strategy Interface

The net result of strategic planning is marketing planning designed to achieve corporate objectives. This transaction requires that marketing planning efforts be directed toward the establishment of marketing strategies that are resource-efficient, flexible, and adaptable. **Marketing strategy** describes *the overall company program for selecting a particular market segment and then satisfying the consumers in that segment through careful use of the elements of the marketing mix.* Planning is an integral part of marketing strategy formulation and is the basis of effective strategy.

## Need for a Comprehensive Marketing Program

A productive marketing strategy requires that all aspects of the marketing mix be considered. The components of an overall marketing strategy are product planning, pricing, distribution, and promotion. An advertising strategy by itself is not a marketing strategy. Marketing mix components are subsets of the overall marketing strategy.

---

[8] For a critical assessment of the experience curve, see Walter Kiechel III, "The Decline of the Experience Curve," *Fortune* (October 5, 1981), pp. 139–146.
[9] See Walter Kiechel III, "Corporate Strategies Under Fire," *Fortune* (December 27, 1982), pp. 34–39.

A strategy may emphasize one mix component more than others. For example, a discount store may depend primarily on its pricing strategy, but it must also maintain adequate product selection and efficient distribution and promotion. One industrial goods manufacturer may emphasize its advanced product technology, while a competitor may stress its superior field sales force. But neither can totally neglect the other elements of marketing strategy.

Marketers must also be prepared to alter their strategy. When S. C. Johnson introduced Pledge, the first aerosol furniture polish, most competitors felt certain that it would fail because its quality was believed lower than some competitive products, including Johnson's own Old English brand. But Pledge proved a major sales success when Johnson carefully positioned it as an easy-to-use dusting product rather than a furniture polish. Johnson succeeded because it adapted its marketing strategy with the "waxed beauty instantly as you dust" advertising theme.[10]

## Alternative Marketing Strategies

An essential first step in the marketing management decision process is an assessment of the marketing strategy positions already taken by the company, and an assessment of the new situations into which it might move. A firm entering a new market with a new product or service faces a substantially different marketing challenge than one operating in an existing market with a line of established products.

A number of alternative strategies are available for the marketing manager. The selection of any given strategy is based upon market and product factors, competition, and other environmental influences. In large, multiproduct firms, more than one strategy may be used for different products and services. The five alternative marketing strategies are: (1) balancing strategy, (2) market retention strategy, (3) market development strategy, (4) growth strategy, and (5) new venture strategy.[11] Examples of businesses employing the five strategy positions are given in Figure 3-5.

Balancing Strategy   A balancing strategy is used for mature products in established markets where the competition is well known. The strategy here is for the company to balance revenues and costs in

---

10 Robert S. Wheeler, "Marketing Tales with a Moral," *Product Marketing* (April 1977), p. 43.

11 The discussion of these strategies is based on David W. Cravens, "Marketing Strategy Positioning," *Business Horizons* (December 1975), pp. 53–61. Cravens notes that other arrays of strategy positions are presented in J. Igor Ansoff, *Corporate Strategy* (New York: McGraw-Hill, 1965), pp. 122–138; John W. Humble, *How to Manage by Objectives* (New York: American Management Association, 1973), p. 75; and David Kollat, Roger Blackwell, and James Robeson, *Strategic Marketing*, 2nd ed. (Hinsdale, Ill.: The Dryden Press, 1975), pp. 21–23.

### Figure 3-5   The Five Alternative Strategy Positions

| Strategy | Description | Example | Opportunity Risk | Profit |
|---|---|---|---|---|
| Balancing | Mature products: Conservative balance of revenues and costs. Fine-tuning strategy | Railways, electrical utilities; Mature industries | | |
| Market Retention | Modification extension of existing products to be more competitive | Annual model change of appliances, cars; add baked potatoes to Wendy's assortment | INCREASING RISK | INCREASING PROFIT POTENTIAL |
| Market Development | Extension beyond existing market/product capabilities | Aluminum company development of automotive and beverage can markets | | |
| Growth | Expansion of existing market/product plus new market/product entry | Texas Instruments' move into consumer electronic calculator market | | |
| New Venture | Development of an entirely new area | Xerox's pioneering development and marketing of copying equipment | | |

Source: Adapted from David W. Cravens, "Marketing Strategy Positioning," *Business Horizons* (December 1975). Copyright 1975 by the Foundation of the School of Business at Indiana University. Reprinted by permission.

order to generate profits. The emphasis for management is control rather than planning. A broad base of knowledge and experience about familiar markets and products exists, and the focus of environmental analysis is on monitoring external influences to identify possible opportunities and threats. Only modest changes are normally made to marketing programs.

**Market Retention Strategy**   Market retention is probably the most typical stratregy followed by established firms. It is based on the desire to improve corporate performance. Such a strategy relies on product modifications and adaptations and/or expansion of current markets. It is the next step beyond a balancing strategy.

**Market Development Strategy**   Pursuit of a market development strategy may extend an enterprise beyond existing market-product capabilities, and is likely to require realignments of resources, personnel, product lines, and organizational structure. It requires a major effort on the part of the organization. Caution is needed in undertaking such a venture.

**Growth Strategy**   A growth strategy is riskier than the alternatives already described. The company offers a new product or enters a new market while expanding its existing markets and adapting its products. Major new resources are needed to pursue this strategy. In this strategy position, design of the marketing program presents a major challenge to management. The growth strategy can probably not be launched from the firm's existing marketing program base. Texas Instruments' decision to move into consumer electronic calculators is an illustration of growth strategy.

**New-Venture Strategy**   When a firm decides to follow a new-venture strategy, it is making an effort in an entirely new area for the company. While risks are high, so are business opportunities. Competition is usually limited. The development of an effective marketing program is a difficult aspect of this strategy.

Firms often follow multiple marketing strategies. However, it is extremely useful to analyse the strategies followed because the characteristics and demands of widely separated strategies may vary significantly. Attempting to launch a growth strategy through marketing organization built around a balancing strategy is a clear mismatch of capabilities and needs. Furthermore, marketing decisions that lead an organization to try to use several strategies at once may require more resources and skills than the firm can muster. Thus, considerable insight into the marketing task can be gained by determining what a firm's marketing strategy is. Analysis of its current strategy and evaluation of possible shifts may lead to the development of a sound basis for making needed changes.

## The Importance of Flexibility

The need for adaptable marketing planning is evident in the abundant examples provided by a variety of industries and firms. Toyota's management recognizes the challenge faced by the company in the North American market. The highly profitable Japanese firm knows that several factors are working against further increases in automobile imports to North America. Slower sales have led North American firms to offer small cars to compete with the Japanese compacts. And the rising value of the yen relative to the Canadian dollar forced Toyota to raise its retail price by more than 20 percent in a recent year.

What has Toyota done to counter the possibility of a slowdown in new car sales? It has begun to produce and market prefabricated houses and commercial buildings through its strong domestic dealer network. Although the new products represent a very small percentage of total sales, the move into a completely different industry illustrates Toyota's marketing planning adaptability.[12]

When a Kentucky Fried Chicken franchise opened in Harlan, Kentucky (population 3300), some customers waited in line 1½ hours to purchase their chicken.[13] Over a ton of fried chicken was sold on the opening day despite the fact that the store did no advertising. Kentucky Fried Chicken's move to a community of 3300 people illustrates a dramatic change taking place in fast-food franchising. KFC Corporation once preferred *not* to operate in areas of under 35 000 population. Now, 890 of its 4000 units are located in towns with fewer than 10 000 residents.

Other fast-food franchisers are also revamping their distribution plans. Pizza Hut is considering areas of under 4000 population, and Burger King has plans for reduced-size units for smaller towns. These fast-food franchisers have found that smaller communities sometimes offer less competition than do larger areas. The franchise operators can benefit from changed consumer preferences and national advertising. The move to smaller towns illustrates how fast-food franchisers have modified their marketing planning to cope with the modern business environment.

**Potential Influences on Marketing Planning**

Various factors will influence marketing planning in the future. Some current trends will likely accelerate in the years ahead and will play a critical role in new marketing strategies. Other anticipated changes will take some factors out of marketing decision-making. Many potential influences cluster around a few basic areas: structural changes in the marketing system, public and legal pressures, market changes, and technological changes. Environmental forecasting is an integral component of good strategic marketing planning.

Structural Changes   Some structural changes in the marketing system have had a pronounced effect on marketing decisions. The franchise system has altered concepts of small-business ownership. Collective marketing organizations such as OPEC have certainly influenced the world markets for their products, as have Common

12 "Toyota Motor: Hedging Autos with a Move into Housing," *Business Week* (November 13, 1978), pp. 162–65.
13 The move of fast-food franchises to smaller communities is described in David P. Garino, "Fast Food Chains Deserve a Break Today, So They Are Moving into Smaller Towns," *Wall Street Journal* (April 21, 1976), p. 36.

Market trade practices, restricting access to historical sales outlets for Canadian exports. Executives must constantly evaluate the changes taking place in the marketing system. Even slight and gradual changes can have a profound effect on sales and profits.

**Public and Legal Pressures**   Future marketing planning is very subject to public and legal decisions. Actions such as the deregulation of the airline industry may shake many of the basic foundations upon which marketers in that industry have always operated. Legislative controls of business practices gradually increase as all levels of government strive to fill what some critics see as loopholes in the system. There is a real need for self-regulation in marketing if restrictive legislation is to be avoided.

**Market Changes**   Market changes are perhaps the most obvious potential influence on strategic plans. Market potentials for various goods and services shift with changes in geographical patterns of population and income. Lifestyle preferences also influence marketing. Record inflation rates affect marketers of recreational equipment, bank services, and real estate. Often this impact is negative. Monitoring market shifts is vital to successful marketing.

**Technological Changes**   The goods and services that are marketed in the relatively free competitive system of Canada are affected by technological changes. Since technological shifts can make a product obsolete overnight, marketers must be assured of a constant new-product development effort. Marketing planning requires that products and services be effectively matched with consumer desires.

Change is inevitable. A permanent part of contemporary marketing, it must be dealt with constantly. Marketers know that changes in the structure of the marketing system, the public and legal framework, markets, and technology can alter the very foundation of today's marketing discipline. Successful future marketers will be those who are best able to cope with these changes.

## Sales Forecasting

The basic building block of marketing planning is the **sales forecast** — *the estimate of company sales for a specified future period*. In addition to its use in marketing planning, the sales forecast also plays an instrumental role in production scheduling, financial planning, inventory planning and procurement, and in the determination of personnel needs. An inaccurate forecast will result in incorrect decisions in each of these areas. The sales forecast is also an important tool for marketing control because it produces standards against which actual performance can be measured. Without such standards, no comparisons can be made — if there exists no criterion of success, there is also no definition of failure.

Sales forecast periods vary in length. Short-run forecasts are usually for a period of up to one year, while long-run forecasts tend to look several years ahead. Since all forecasts are developed in basically the same manner, and since more firms forecast sales for the coming year, short-run forecasting will be discussed here.

## Types of Forecasting Methods

Although forecasters utilize dozens of techniques of divining the future (ranging from complex computer simulations to crystal-ball gazing by professional futurists), two broad categories exist. *Quantitative* forecasting methods employ such statistical techniques as trend extensions based upon past data; computer simulation; and econometrics to produce numerical forecasts of future events. The second type, *qualitative* forecasting techniques, are more subjective in nature. They include surveys of consumer attitudes and intentions, estimates by the field sales force, predictions of key executives in the firm and in the industry. Since each method has its advantages, most organizations use both in their attempts to predict future events and to provide a range into which they expect actual performance to fall.

A survey of forecasting techniques used in 175 firms revealed that qualitative measures such as estimates by the sales force and a jury of executives are most commonly used. The techniques used on a regular basis by the respondent firms are shown in Figure 3-6.

**Figure 3-6 Sales Forecasting Methods Used Regularly in 175 Firms**

| Method | Percentage |
|---|---|
| Jury of Executive Opinion | 52% |
| Sales Force Composite | 48% |
| Trend Projections | 28% |
| Industry Survey | 22% |
| Intention-to-Buy Survey | 15% |
| Simulation Models | 8% |
| Input-Output Models | 6% |

Source: Reported in Douglas J. Dalrymple, "Sales Forecasting Methods and Accuracy," *Business Horizons* (December 1975), p. 71.

**Qualitative Forecasting Techniques**[14]

Qualitative techniques include the jury of executive opinion and estimates by the sales force. Both rely upon experience and expectations. The **jury of executive opinion** method consists of *combining and averaging the forecasts of top executives from such areas as finance, production, marketing, and purchasing*. It is particularly effective when top management is experienced and knowledgeable about situations which influence sales, open-minded concerning the future, and aware of the bases for their judgments.

The **sales force composite** is *a forecast based on the combined estimates of the firm's salespeople* on the assumption that organizational members closest to the marketplace — those with specialized product, customer, and competitor knowledge — are likely to have better insight concerning short-term future sales than any other group. This approach is a *bottom-up method* since the salespeoples' estimates are usually combined at the district level, the regional level, and the national level to obtain an aggregate forecast of sales. Few firms rely upon the sales force composite solely, however. Since salespeople recognize the role of the sales forecast in determining expected performance in their territories, they are likely to estimate conservatively. Moreover, their narrow perspectives on their limited geographic territories may prevent them from being knowledgeable about developing trends in other territories, forthcoming technological innovations, or major changes in company marketing strategies. Consequently, the sales force composite is typically combined with other forecasting techniques in developing the final forecast.

A third method of forecasting is through **surveys of buyer intentions**. *Mail questionnaires, telephone polls, or personal interviews may be used in attempting to determine the intentions of a representative group of present and potential consumers*. This technique is obviously limited to situations where customers are willing to confide their buying intentions. Moreover, customer expectations do not necessarily result in actual purchases.

**Quantitative Forecasting Techniques**

Quantitative techniques, which make use of past data to predict future performance, attempt to eliminate the guesswork of the qualitative forecasting methods. They include such techniques as market tests, trend projections, and input-output models.

**Market tests** are frequently used in *assessing consumer response to new product offerings*. The procedure typically involves establishing a small number of test markets to gauge consumer responses

---

[14] This discussion is adapted from Arthur G. Bedeian, *Management* (Hinsdale, Ill.: The Dryden Press, 1986), pp. 212–218.

to a new product under actual conditions. Such tests also permit evaluation of different prices, different promotional strategies, and other marketing mix variations through comparisons in different test markets. The primary advantage of market tests is the realism it provides for the marketer. On the other hand, it is an expensive and time-consuming approach that communicates marketing plans to competitors before a product is introduced to the market. Test marketing is discussed in more detail in Chapter 11.

**Trend analysis** involves *forecasting future sales by analysing the historical relationship between sales and time*. It is based upon the assumption that the factors which collectively determined past sales will continue to exert similar influence in the future. If historical data is available, it can be performed quickly and inexpensively.

An example will make this clear. If sales were $X$ last year and have been increasing at $Y$ percent for the past several years, the sales forecast for next year would be calculated as follows:

$$\text{Sales Forecast} = X + XY.$$

In actual numbers, if last year's sales totalled 280 000 units and the average sales growth rate has been 5 percent, the sales forecast would be:

$$\begin{aligned} \text{Sales Forecast} &= 280\ 000 + (280\ 000 \times .05) \\ &= 294\ 000. \end{aligned}$$

The danger of trend analysis lies in its underlying assumption that the future is a continuation of the past. Any variations in the influences that affect sales will result in an incorrect forecast. In addition, historical data may not be readily available in some instances; in the case of new products it may not exist.

During periods of steady growth, the trend extension method of forecasting produces satisfactory results, but it implicitly assumes that the factors contributing to a certain level of output in the past will operate in the same manner in the future. When conditions change, the trend extension method often produces incorrect results. For this reason, forecasters are increasingly turning to more sophisticated techniques and more complex mathematical models.

**Input-output models,** *which depict the interactions of various industries in producing goods*, are being developed by the various government and private agencies. Since outputs (sales) of one industry are the inputs (purchases) of another, a change of inputs in one industry affects the outputs of other industries. Input-output models show the impact on supplier industries of changing production in a given industry and can be used to measure the impact of increasing or decreasing demand in any industry throughout the economy.

**Steps in Sales**    Although sales forecasting methods vary, the most typical method
**Forecasting**    begins with a forecast of general economic conditions which the
marketer uses to forecast industry sales and to develop a forecast of
company and product sales. This approach can be termed the *top-
down method*.

Forecasting General Economic Conditions   The most common measure of economic output is *gross national product* (GNP), the market value of all final products produced in a country in a given year.
Trend extension is the most frequently used method of forecasting
increases in GNP.

Since many federal agencies and other organizations develop
regular forecasts of the GNP, a firm may choose to use their estimates.
These forecasts are regularly reported in such publications as *The
Financial Post* and *The Globe & Mail*.

Developing the Industry Sales Forecast   Once the economic forecast has been produced, the next step is developing an industry sales
forecast. Since industry sales may be related to GNP or some other
measure of the national economy, a forecast may begin by measuring the degree of this relationship, then applying the trend
extension method to forecast industry sales. More sophisticated
techniques, such as input-output analysis or multiple regression
analysis, may also be used.

Forecasting Company and Product Sales   Once the industry forecast has been made, the company and product forecasts are developed. They begin with a detailed trend analysis. The firm's past
and present market shares are reviewed, and product managers and
regional and district sales managers are consulted to produce a sales
force composite. Since an accelerated promotional budget or the
introduction of new products may stimulate additional demand,
the marketing plan for the coming year is also considered.

The product and company forecast must evaluate many aspects
of company sales including sales of each product; future trends; sales
by customer, territory, salesperson, and order size; financial
arrangements; and other aspects. Once a preliminary sales forecast
has been developed, it is reviewed by the sales force and by district,
regional, and national sales managers.

New Product Sales Forecasting   Forecasting sales for new products
is an especially hazardous undertaking since no historical data is
available for analysis. Companies often ask consumer panels for
reactions to the products in order to assess probable purchase
behaviour. They may also use test market data.

Since few products are totally new, forecasts carefully analyse the sales of competing products that may be displaced by the new entry. A new type of fishing reel, for example, will compete in an established market with other reels. This substitute method provides the forecaster with an estimate of market size and potential demand.

# One Management's View of What Can and Cannot Be Expected from Planning

- Planning *will not* give you a "perfect crystal ball," nor will it enable you to predict the future with extreme accuracy.

- Planning *will not* necessarily prevent you from making mistakes.

- Planning *will* or should minimize the degree to which you are taken by surprise, and help you revise both programs and objectives whenever it is desirable to do so. In other words, planning *will* help you react creatively to change.

- Planning *will* result in the integration of all of the company's activities and maximize your efforts toward the attainment of corporate goals.

- Planning *does not* stifle creativity. Planning *enhances* creativity by creating orderly processes whereby viable objectives and plans can be reached.

Source: *Guide to Preparing Marketing Plans*, Publishing Group, Litton Industries, Inc.

**Summary**   Planning is the process of anticipating the future and determining the courses of action to achieve company objectives, and it is the basis for all strategy decisions. Strategic planning refers to the primary objectives of the organization and the ways they will be implemented. Marketing planning is the implementation of strategic planning as it relates to the achievement of marketing objectives.

The marketing planning process is based upon the overall organizational objectives. Opportunity analysis is a continual process of assessing environmental factors and comparing them with the objectives of the organization and its resources. Marketing objectives are based upon organizational objectives and result in the development of marketing plans. Market target analysis and the development of a marketing mix to position products and services to satisfy chosen targets make up the marketing strategy of the organization.

The strategic business unit (SBU) concept and the market/growth matrix developed by the Boston Consulting Group are frequently used by marketing planners.

Effective strategic planning is now regarded as a prerequisite to survival. It is an organization-wide responsibility involving chief executive officers, heads of operating units, and corporate strategic planning personnel. Strategic planning provides a basis for marketing planning, which is then translated into the development of marketing strategies.

Five marketing strategies can be identified: (1) balancing strategy, (2) market retention strategy, and (3) market development strategy, (4) growth strategy, and (5) new venture strategy. Potential future influences on the planning/strategy interface are the marketing system itself, public and legal pressures, market changes, and technological changes.

Sales forecasting is an important component of both planning and controlling marketing programs. Forecasting techniques may be categorized as quantitative or qualitative. The most common approach to sales forecasting is to begin with a forecast of the national economy and use it to develop an industry sales forecast, which is then used to develop a company and product forecast.

## Key Terms

| | |
|---|---|
| planning | marketing strategy |
| marketing planning | sales forecast |
| strategic planning | jury of executive opinion |
| tactical planning | sales force composite |
| strategic window | survey of buyer intentions |
| strategic business unit (SBU) | trend analysis |
| BCG growth-share matrix | input-output models |
| experience curve | |

## Review Questions

1. Distinguish between strategic planning and tactical planning.
2. Contrast marketing planning at different levels in the organization.
3. Identify the steps in the marketing planning process.
4. Explain the concept of the strategic window. Give an example.
5. Differentiate among *cash cows, dogs, stars,* and *question marks* in the BCG matrix.
6. Outline the five marketing strategies that can be employed by marketers.
7. Identify and discuss the major external and internal influences on marketing strategy.
8. Compare and contrast each of the major types of forecasting methods.
9. Explain the steps involved in the forecasting process.
10. Suggest methods for forecasting sales for newly introduced products.

## Discussion Questions and Exercises

1. Give two examples of products currently in each of the following quadrants of the BCG matrix:
   a. Cash cow

    b. Dog

    c. Star

    d. Question mark

    Suggest marketing strategies for each product.

2. Relate the discussion of the development of Creative Appliance Corp. to the model of the marketing planning process shown in Figure 3-3.

3. Discuss the advantages and shortcomings of basing sales forecasts exclusively on estimates developed by the firm's sales force.

4. Assume that growth in industry sales will remain constant for Year 6, the coming year. Forecast company sales for Year 6 based upon the following data:

    Year 1:   $320 000

    Year 2:   $350 000

    Year 3:   $340 000

    Year 4:   $380 000

    Year 5:   $580 000

    What assumptions have you made in developing your forecast?

5. Which forecasting technique do you feel is most appropriate for each of the following:

    a. Bayer aspirin

    b. Royal Winnipeg Ballet

    c. Office supplies retailer

    d. Fender guitars

**MICROCOMPUTER
EXERCISE:
Sales Forecasting**

Directions: Use the Menu Item titled "Sales Forecasting" on the Marketing disk to solve the following problems.

1. European sales are a major component of the total sales for United Brands. The European market has produced sustained growth since 1979. Annual European sales revenues for United Brands are shown below.

| Year | Annual Sales Revenue |
|------|---------------------|
| 1979 | $ 50 million |
| 1980 | 110 million |
| 1981 | 170 million |
| 1982 | 290 million |
| 1983 | 310 million |
| 1984 | 360 million |
| 1985 | 480 million |
| 1986 | 600 million |
| 1987 | 740 million |

Forecast European sales revenues for 1988 and 1989, using the trend-extension method.

2. Total annual sales for a videocassette-rental chain are shown below. Forecast 1988 sales, using the trend-extension method.

| Year | Annual Sales Revenue |
|------|---------------------|
| 1980 | 1 million |
| 1981 | 3 million |
| 1982 | 6 million |
| 1983 | 10 million |
| 1984 | 11 million |
| 1985 | 13 million |
| 1986 | 14 million |
| 1987 | 16 million |

3. During 1979, the first year of operation for Northland University, enrollment totaled 1200 students. The following year's enrollment grew to 2100 students, and in 1981 the growth continued as 2800 students attended the university. Enrollment for subsequent years was: 4200 in 1982; 4400 in 1983; 4500 in 1984; 4800 in 1985; 5400 in 1986; and 6000 in 1987. Use the trend-extension method to estimate Northland University enrollment in 1988 and 1989.

# Developing a Marketing Plan

The natural outgrowth of the marketing-planning process is a marketing plan, a detailed expression of resources and actions necessary to accomplish stated marketing objectives. Once this plan is formulated and implemented, it may be evaluated on a periodic basis to determine its success in moving the organization toward its stated objectives.

Although the format, length, and focus of marketing plans may vary, they typically focus upon identifying answers to the following three questions.

- Where are we now?
- Where do we want to go?
- How can we get there?

The following outline is illustrative of how marketing plans provide answers to each of these questions. The format may be used in a manufacturing, wholesale, retail, or service setting.[1]

## Components of the Marketing Plan

### I. SITUATION ANALYSIS
- Where are we now?

#### A. Historical Background
- Nature of the firm, its sales and profit history, and current situation.

#### B. Consumer Analysis
- Who are the customers this firm is attempting to serve?
- What segments exist?
- How many consumers are there?
- How much do they buy and why?

#### C. Competitive Analysis
- Given the nature of the markets — size, characteristics, competitive activities, and strategies — what marketing opportunities exist for this firm?

[1] The following sections are reprinted by permission of the publisher from Stephen K. Keiser, Robert E. Stevens, and Lynn J. Loudenback, *Contemporary Marketing Study Guide* (Hinsdale, IL: The Dryden Press, 1986), pp. 482–487. Two excellent sources on marketing plans are David S. Hopkins, *The Marketing Plan* (New York: The Conference Board, 1981); and W. Douglas Johnstone, *Planning for Corporate Growth: The Annual Marketing Plan* (Washington, DC: Direct Selling Association, n.d.).

## II.  MARKETING OBJECTIVES
● **Where do we want to go?**
A.  *Sales Objectives*
● What level of sales volume can we achieve during the next year?
B.  *Profit Objectives*
● Given the sales level and the cost structure of the firm, what level of profits should be achieved?
C.  *Consumer Objectives*
● How will we serve our market-target customers?
● What do we want consumers to think about our firm?

## III.  STRATEGY
● **How can we get there?**
A.  *Product/Service Strategy*
● What products/services should we offer to meet consumers' needs?
● What is their exact nature?
B.  *Pricing Strategy*
● What level of prices should be used?
● What specific prices and price concessions are appropriate?
C.  *Distribution Strategy*
● What channel(s) will be used in distributing our product/service offerings?
● What physical distribution facilities are needed?
●  Where should they be located?
● What should be their major characteristics?
D.  *Promotional Strategy*
● What mix of personal selling, advertising, and sales promotional activities is needed?
● How much should be spent using what themes and what media?
E.  *Financial Strategy*
● What will be the financial impact of this plan on a one-year pro forma (projected) income statement?
● How does this income statement compare with one without the plan?

---

**Sample Marketing Plan:**
**The Driftwood Inn**

The following excerpts from a marketing plan prepared for a large motel, the Driftwood Inn, illustrate the value of such a plan in directing the organization in pursuit of its objectives.

*Objectives*

## I.  SHORT TERM: 1988
*Sales Objectives:*
A.  To experience an increase in food sales of 100 percent through increased awareness of the Driftwood Inn restaurant and changing consumer attitudes toward motel restaurants — especially the Driftwood Inn restaurant.

*Basic Strategy Statement*

The basic strategy for the Driftwood Inn marketing campaign is as follows:

### I. LODGING
A. Increase occupancy during seasonal and weekend "slack" periods through development and promotion of special "holiday packages."

B. Attract participants and spectators for special events through direct mailing of promotional literature where names and addresses are available.

### II. FOOD
A. Develop an identity and image for the restaurant that are separate and distinct from the Driftwood Inn motel by (a) choosing a new name for the dining facilities, (b) developing a new menu, and (c) making minor changes in decor to create a distinctive dining atmosphere.

B. Create awareness of the changes in the restaurant among local residents as well as motel guests by developing a complete promotional campaign and improving in-house promotion (such as lobby signs and promotional "tents" in rooms).

C. Attract civic-group luncheon and wedding-rehearsal dinners through price dealing and personal selling.

*Situation Analysis*

### I. GENERAL MARKET — LODGING, FOOD, AND BEVERAGE
Figure A-1 shows the total sales for lodging and eating places between 1984 and 1987 in Anytown, and the Driftwood Inn's share of this market. The figures indicate that, while total city sales increased 20 percent, the Driftwood Inn's sales increased only 15 percent.

**Figure A-1   Driftwood Inn's Share of the Anytown Area Market for Lodging and Food by Year (1984–1987)**

| Year | Anytown | Driftwood Inn | Percentage Market Share |
|------|---------|---------------|-------------------------|
| 1984 | $12 088 017 | $620 740 | 5.14% |
| 1985 | 11 537 122 | 690 552 | 5.98 |
| 1986 | 12 471 294 | 711 921 | 5.70 |
| 1987 | 14 555 443 | 715 043 | 4.91 |

### II. LODGING
A breakdown of lodging sales for Anytown and Driftwood Inn is shown in Figure A-2. The last column indicates the Inn's market share. Although the Inn's lodging sales have increased substantially during the 1984–1987 period, its market share has fallen. This is due to an increase in total area lodging sales and increasing competition. It is worthwhile to note that the Inn's market share fell to

16 percent between 1986 and 1987. The Inn's sales fell slightly more than 2 percent in those two years, while area lodging sales rose more than 17 percent.

**Figure A-2  Driftwood Inn's Share of the Anytown Lodging Market by Year (1984–1987)**

| Year | Anytown | Driftwood Inn | Percentage Market Share |
|------|---------|---------------|------------------------|
| 1984 | $2 677 086 | $401 556 | 14.99% |
| 1985 | 2 604 772 | 467 829 | 17.96 |
| 1986 | 3 024 437 | 489 128 | 16.15 |
| 1987 | 3 547 427 | 476 604 | 13.44 |

## III. FOOD SALES

Figure A-3 presents a comparison of Northland County, Anytown, and Driftwood Inn food sales. The last two columns represent the Inn restaurant's respective market shares. During the 1984–1987 period, county sales increased almost 38 percent; city sales, 17 percent; and Inn food sales only 9 percent. New competitors are one possible explanation for these losses of market share.

**Figure A-3  Driftwood Inn's Share of Washington County and Anytown's Food Market by Year (1984–1987)**

| Year | Northland County | Anytown | Driftwood Inn | Market Percentage Northland County | Market Percentage Anytown |
|------|------------------|---------|---------------|-----------------------------------|---------------------------|
| 1984 | $10 172 610 | $ 9 410 931 | $219 184 | 2.1% | 2.3% |
| 1985 | 11 273 462 | 8 932 350 | 222 723 | 1.9 | 2.4 |
| 1986 | 12 215 053 | 9 446 857 | 222 793 | 1.8 | 2.3 |
| 1987 | 13 994 611 | 11 008 016 | 238 439 | 1.7 | 2.1 |

*Consumer Analysis*  **I. LODGING**

Generally, the lodging market can be broadly divided into the segments shown in the market grid in Figure A-4.

**Figure A-4  Driftwood Inn Lodging Market**

|  | Individuals or Couples | Groups |
|--|------------------------|--------|
| **Business** | Salespeople<br>Management Personnel<br>Special Events<br>On-Premise Business | Conventions<br>Seminars and Workshops<br>Union Negotiations<br>National Guard |
| **Nonbusiness** | Vacationers<br>Military<br>Moving Through, In,<br>or Out | Tour Groups<br>Party Groups<br>Sports Groups<br>Reunions |

These distinguishable groups of potential customers represent the market the Driftwood Inn must attract. The basic consumer characteristics that are most appropriate for analysing the lodging market are the nature of the person's stay (business or nonbusiness) and the number of persons staying (individuals and couples or groups). Individuals in business might include salespeople on regular routes, management personnel on special supervisory trips, or people who wish to do business on a temporary basis from their rooms. Groups whose stay might be of a business nature include conventions, company seminars, and the like (see Figure A-5).

**Figure A-5   Driftwood Inn Food-Service Market**

|  | Individuals or Couples | Groups |
|---|---|---|
| **Guests** | Vacationers<br>Salespeople<br>Family Visits<br>Relocation | Tour Groups<br>Conventions<br>Sports Groups<br>Military |
| **Nonguests** | "Night Out"<br>Special Occasion<br>Regular Buffet<br>Transients | Tour Groups<br>Business Meetings<br>Rehearsal Dinners<br>Receptions<br>Civic Groups |

Food sales may be derived from the public or private dining facilities. An analysis showed that although total food sales increased somewhat, this increase was not sufficient to maintain the Inn's market share. Revenues from private dining are derived from three basic sources: wedding-rehearsal dinners, wedding receptions, and civic-group luncheons. The potential revenues from these three sources are estimated as being over $50 000 annually. The Driftwood Inn appears to have captured a large share of this market, but it must be kept in mind that there are a limited number of competitors for the private-dining market. It is believed that little selling effort has been directed toward local civic organizations, which are important potential customers.

**Assignment**

1. Use the format described in this appendix to develop a marketing plan for one of the following.
   a. Local retailer
   b. Local service provider
   c. Local shopping centre
   d. Nonprofit organization
   e. College or university athletic program (generating fan support for intercollegiate sports events)

## CHAPTER 4

# Market Segmentation

1. *To relate market segmentation to the marketing mix.*
2. *To explain what is meant by a market.*
3. *To outline the role of market segmentation in the development of a marketing strategy.*
4. *To discuss the four bases for segmenting consumer markets.*
5. *To describe the three bases for segmenting industrial markets.*

The Canadian consumer magazine industry has gone through a number of changes in the past twenty years or so. In the 1960s the market was dominated by a few mass-market magazines such as *Maclean's*, *Time*, and *Reader's Digest*. However, the position of these products in the marketplace was gradually eroded by a number of specialty magazines which concentrated on specific market groups. This "vertical specialization" enabled publishers to produce a magazine product that was specially geared for a particular interest group. Thus magazines were developed which dealt with sports, hobbies, and other interests. Publishers discovered that they could serve smaller interest groups in depth, and therefore generate loyalty, circulation, and subscription and advertising revenues.

Now there is a "specialty, broad interest" magazine which is focussed on yet another market segment. This is the city magazine. While city magazines have been around for some years, they appear to be rapidly gaining in popularity. Examples of such magazines are *Toronto Life*, *Calgary*, and *Vancouver*. These provide superior graphics, full-colour presentation, and good paper quality, as well as well-written articles. Many deal with items of interest to each particular city. Readers relate to such magazines because they provide quality, in-depth coverage of their cities. Advertisers like them because of their popularity, and the ability to reach a specific geographical and income level-market, as well as the quality of advertisements such magazines can produce.

There are a remarkable number of different market segments for consumer magazines, and a similar number of magazines which have been specifically designed to serve the needs of each of these segments. The same type of specialization has also occurred to an extensive degree in the industrial market; there is a special trade magazine for virtually every industry segment in the country. The magazine industry is thus a good example of the concept of market segmentation.

| | |
|---|---|
| **The Conceptual Framework** | Although marketers may face hundreds of decisions in developing an effective plan for achieving organizational objectives, these decisions may be summarized as two fundamental tasks: |

1. They must identify, evaluate, and ultimately select a market target.
2. Once the market target has been selected, they must develop and implement a marketing mix designed to satisfy the chosen target group.

These two tasks reflect the philosophy of consumer orientation in action. The choice of a market target is based on recognition of differences among consumers and organizations within a heterogeneous market. The starting point is to understand what is meant by a *market*.

**What Is a Market?**    A market is *people*. It is also business, nonprofit organizations, and government — local, provincial, and federal purchasing agents who buy for their "firms." But people alone do not make a market. The local dealer for foreign automobiles is unimpressed by news that 60 percent of the marketing class raise their hands in response to the question, "Who wants to buy a new XKE?" The next question is, "How many of them are waving cheques in their outstretched hands?" A **market** *requires not only people and willingness to buy, but also purchasing power and the authority to buy.*

One of the first rules that the successful salesperson learns is to determine who in the organization or household has the authority to make particular purchasing decisions. Too much time has been wasted convincing the wrong person that a product or service should be bought.

**Types of Markets**    Products may be classified as consumer or industrial goods. **Consumer goods** are *those products and services purchased by the ultimate consumer for personal use.* **Industrial goods** are *those products purchased to be used, either directly or indirectly, in the production of the other goods or for resale.* Most of the products you buy — books, clothes, milk — are consumer goods. Refined nickel is an industrial good for the mint; rubber is a raw material for the B.F. Goodrich Company.

Sometimes the same product is destined for different uses. The new set of tires when purchased by your neighbour are clearly consumer goods; yet when bought by Chrysler Corporation, they become part of a new Horizon and are classified as industrial goods, since they become part of another good destined for resale. The key to the proper classification of goods lies in the purchaser and *the reasons for buying the good.*

## Market Segmentation

A country is too large and filled with too many diverse people and firms for any single marketing mix to satisfy everyone. Unless the product or service is an item such as an unbranded, descriptive-label detergent aimed at the mass market, an attempt to satisfy everyone may doom the marketer to failure. Even a seemingly functional product like toothpaste is aimed at a specific market segment. Stripe was developed for children; Crest focuses on tooth-decay prevention; Ultra Brite hints at enhanced sex appeal; and Aqua Fresh promises both protection and teeth whiteners.

The auto manufacturer who decides to produce and market a single automobile model to satisfy everyone will encounter seemingly endless decisions to be made about such variables as the number of doors, type of transmission, colour, styling, and engine size. In its attempt to satisfy everyone, the firm may be forced to compromise in each of these areas and, as a result, may discover that it does not satisfy anyone very well. Other firms appealing to particular segments — the youth market, the high-fuel-economy market, the large family market, and so on — may capture most of the total market by satisfying the specific needs of these smaller, more homogeneous market targets. *The process of dividing the total market into several homogeneous groups with similar interests in a particular product or service category* is called **market segmentation**.

Once a specific market segment has been identified, the marketer can design an appropriate marketing mix to match its needs, improving the chance of sales to that segment. Market segmentation can be used by both profit-oriented and nonprofit organizations.[1]

## Segmenting Consumer Markets

Market segmentation results from a determination of factors that distinguish a certain group of consumers from the overall market. These characteristics — such as age, sex, geographic location, income and expenditure patterns, and population size and mobility, among others — are vital factors in the success of the overall marketing

---

[1] See Scott M. Smith and Leland L. Beik, "Market Segmentation for Fund Raisers," *Journal of the Academy of Marketing Science* (Summer 1982), pp. 208–216.

strategy. Toy manufacturers such as Ideal, Hasbro, Mattel, and Kenner study not only birthrate trends, but also shifts in income and expenditure patterns. Colleges and universities are affected by such factors as the number of high school graduates, changing attitudes toward the value of college educations, and increasing enrolment of older adults. Figure 4-1 identifies four commonly used bases for segmenting consumer markets.

**Figure 4-1   Bases for Market Segmentation**

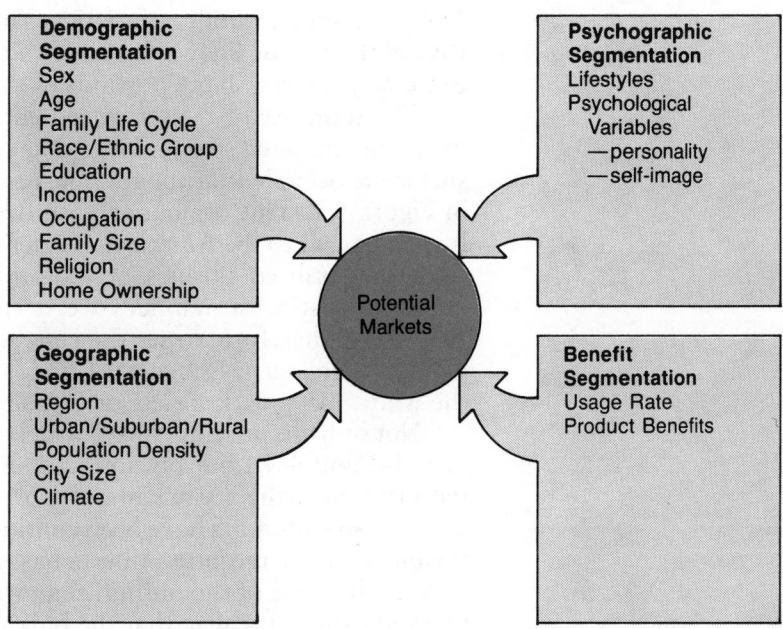

*Geographic segmentation*, the dividing of an overall market into homogeneous groups based on population location, has been used for hundreds of years. The second basis for segmenting markets is *demographic segmentation*—dividing an overall market on the basis of characteristics such as age, sex, and income level. Demographic segmentation is the most commonly used method of subdividing total markets.

The third and fourth bases represent relatively recent developments in market segmentation. *Psychographic segmentation* utilizes behavioural profiles developed from analyses of the activities, opinions, interests, and lifestyles of consumers in identifying market segments. The final basis, *benefit segmentation*, focuses on benefits the consumer expects to derive from a product or service. These segmentation bases can be important to marketing strategies provided they are significantly related to differences in buying behaviour.

## Geographic Segmentation

A logical starting point in market segmentation is to find out where buyers are. It is not surprising, therefore, that one of the earliest bases for segmentation was geographic. Regional variations in consumer tastes often exist. Per capita consumption of seafood, for example, is higher in the Maritimes than in Alberta. Brick and stone construction, a mainstay in many homes in Ontario, is much less common in the West.

### Geographic Location of the Canadian Population

Canada has grown tremendously from a population of 3 million in 1867 to about 25 million in 1985. The Canadian population, like that of the rest of the world, is not distributed evenly. In fact, it is extremely uneven; large portions of this country are uninhabited.[2]

The term used to describe settled areas is "ecumene," literally meaning inhabited space.[3] In Canada less than 8 percent of the land surface is occupied farmland. The ecumene in Canada is depicted in Figure 4-2. This dramatically shows that a relatively small strip lying adjacent to the American border is the land area most heavily settled and utilized. Business and social activities therefore must operate in an east–west manner, over tremendous distances. It is not surprising, therefore, to see the emergence of various distinct market segments, such as central Canada (Ontario and/or Quebec), the Maritimes, the Prairies, or British Columbia.

Not only do provinces vary widely in total population (see Figures 4-3 and 4-4), but pronounced shifts are also evident. People tend to move where work and opportunities exist. Thus, Ontario and British Columbia have been continuously attractive to those on the move. More recently, Alberta has experienced large population influxes because of the oil-induced prosperity there. However, the marketer should realize that the bulk of the country's sales potential is still in Ontario and Quebec. In fact, better than three-fifths, 62 percent, still lives in the two provinces.

Natural factors and immigration also influence population. Growth has occurred as a result of natural increase (births minus deaths) and net migration (immigration minus emigration). Overall, the rate of natural increase has been considerably higher than net migration. In fact, the Atlantic provinces and Saskatchewan depend on natural increase to restore population levels lost by emigration. On the other hand, Ontario, Alberta, and British Columbia have shown significant total population increases because they have received migration flows plus a natural increase. In recent years natural increases have been declining.

[2] This section relies heavily on Harry H. Hiller, *Canadian Society: A Sociological Analysis* (Scarborough, Ont.: Prentice-Hall of Canada Ltd., 1976), pp. 13–37.
[3] R. T. Gajda, "The Canadian Ecumene—Inhabited and Uninhabited Areas," *Geographical Bulletin*, 15 (1960), p. 6.

**Figure 4-2   The Canadian Ecumene, 1985**

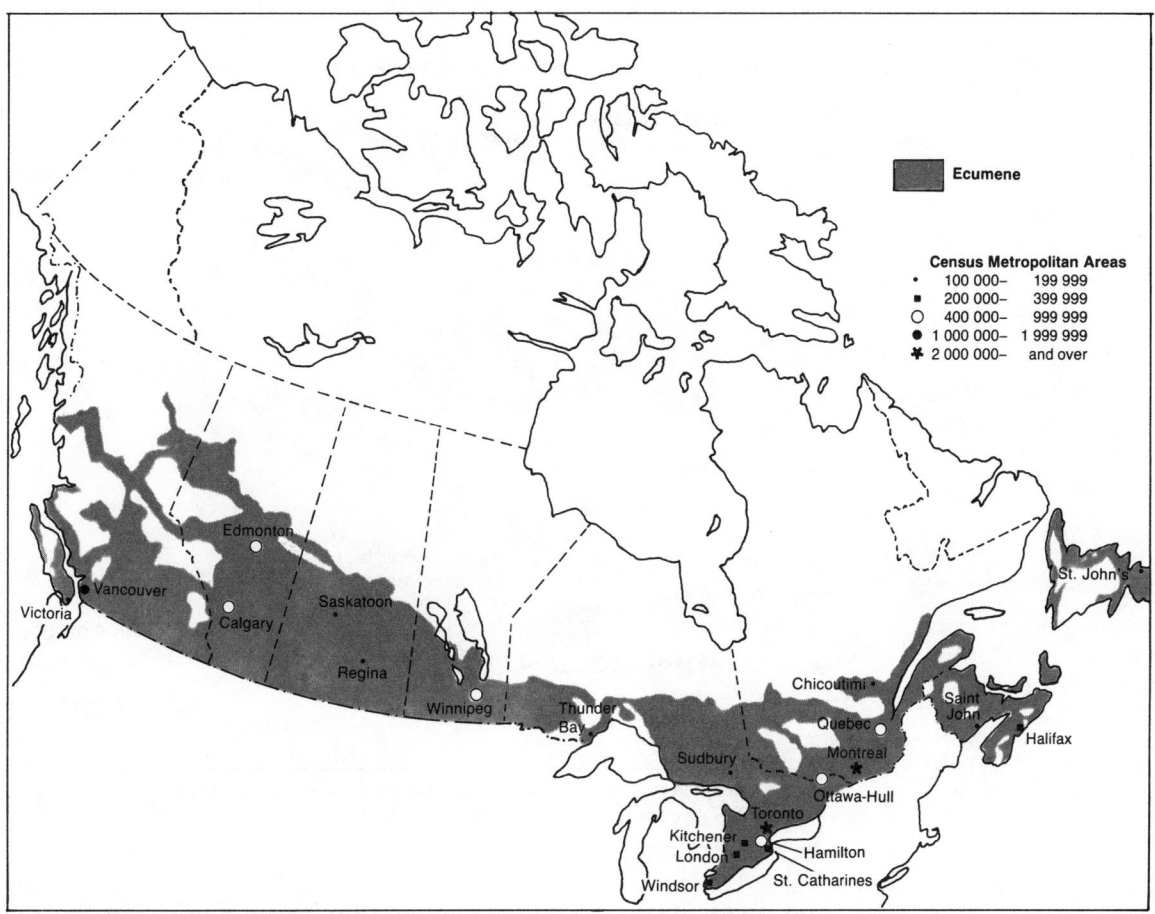

Source: *Perspective Canada: A Compendium of Social Statistics* (Ottawa: Information Canada, 1974). Reproduced by permission of the Minister of Supply and Services Canada. Updated.

Immigration has had a tremendous impact on Canadian society. The injection of a steady stream of British immigrants and short bursts of central, eastern, and southern Europeans and southeast Asians into the Canadian population have created immense social pressures in assimilation and citizenship. Some areas have attracted much more immigration. In fact, Ontario contains 51.8 percent of Canada's living foreign-born people. The western provinces contain the greatest percentages of foreign-born who are "old-timers" (immigrated prior to 1946).

Postwar immigration tended to be from European urban centres

**Figure 4-3    Percentage Distribution of the Population of Canada by Province as of January 1987**

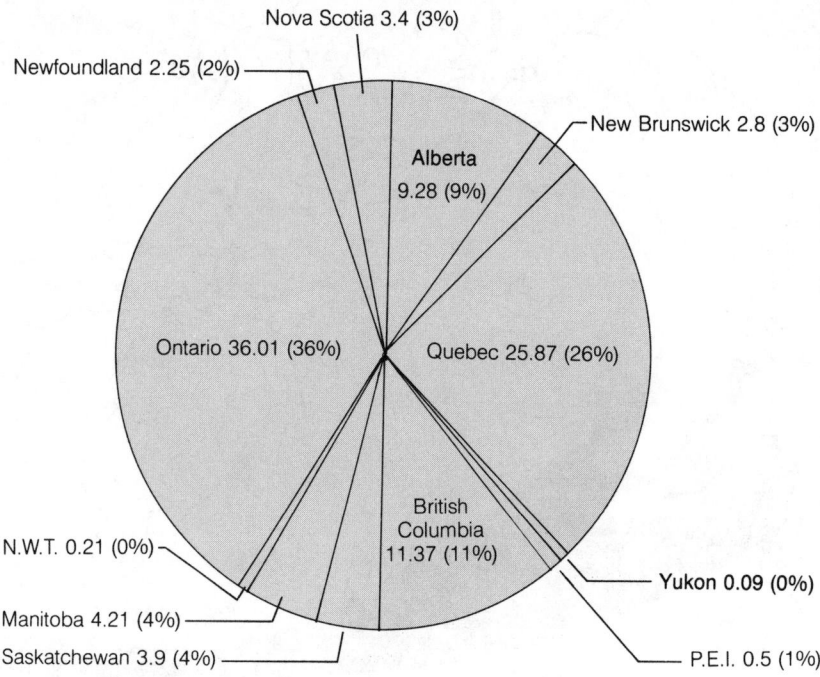

Source: Adapted from *1976 Census of Canada* (Ottawa: Statistics Canada), Cat. 92-807. By permission of the Minister of Supply and Services Canada.

to Canadian cities, whereas immigration before World War II was largely from European rural locations to Canadian rural areas.

A remarkable influence has been the immigration–emigration flow in Canada. Despite the fact that 8 million people entered the country through immigration between 1851 and 1961, it is estimated that more than 6 million *left*. From Confederation to 1967, Canada's growth was due largely to natural increase (14.5 million), whereas net migration produced only a 2.4-million increase.[4]

It is estimated that emigration has decreased in recent years. However, the tremendous immigration and emigration in proportion to the size of Canada's population has resulted in a somewhat unstable set of common goals and ends for society. The character of Canadian society has continually been pulled in various directions

[4] T. R. Weir, "Population Changes in Canada, 1867–1967," *The Canadian Geographer*, Vol. 2, No. 4 (1967), p. 198.

through the infusion of different ethnic groups at varying periods of history via immigration.

The large-scale migration flow from the East to Alberta and British Columbia in the late 1970s and 1980s is the latest significant population flow. In fact, its size rivals the immigration flows that occurred when the West was first settled.

These factors have traditionally affected the political outlook of Canada's geographic regions. Marketers also recognize that they must take geographical market segments into account.

**Figure 4-4   Provincial and Territorial Populations, 1971, 1980, 1987**

|                       | 1971       | 1980       | 1987       |
|-----------------------|------------|------------|------------|
| Newfoundland          | 522 105    | 582 900    | 579 500    |
| Prince Edward Island  | 111 640    | 124 000    | 128 200    |
| Nova Scotia           | 788 960    | 855 000    | 887 600    |
| New Brunswick         | 634 560    | 708 700    | 721 200    |
| Quebec                | 6 027 765  | 6 310 800  | 6 657 700  |
| Ontario               | 7 703 105  | 8 587 300  | 9 273 300  |
| Manitoba              | 988 245    | 1 028 000  | 1 082 500  |
| Saskatchewan          | 926 245    | 973 000    | 1 021 700  |
| Alberta               | 1 627 875  | 2 113 300  | 2 386 300  |
| British Columbia      | 2 184 620  | 2 662 000  | 2 926 200  |
| Yukon                 | 18 390     | 21 600     | 23 600     |
| Northwest Territories | 34 810     | 43 000     | 50 100     |
| TOTAL                 | 21 568 320 | 24 009 600 | 25 737 900 |

Source: Statistics Canada, *Canadian Statistical Review,* March 1987, No. 11-003E.
By permission of the Minister of Supply and Services Canada.

**People Are in the Cities**   It is a myth that Canada's population is rural and agricultural. People have been migrating to the cities for many years. Figure 4-5 shows that the percentage of farm dwellers has dropped to 4.5 percent, whereas 75.5 percent of the population is urban. Figure 4-6 shows population and growth rate for the 23 largest metropolitan areas. The three largest, Toronto, Montreal, and Vancouver, already contained approximately 28 percent of Canada's total population by 1983 and approximately 55 percent of Canada's population lived in cities of 100 000 and over.

The Canadian population, along with the American and the Australian, is one of the most mobile in the world. The average Canadian moves 12 times in a lifetime, as compared to eight times for the average English citizen and five for the typical Japanese.[5]

[5] Larry H. Long, "On Measuring Geographic Mobility," *Journal of the American Statistical Association* (September 1970).

However, this trend may be waning. The slowdown may be due to a number of factors: poor job prospects elsewhere; the tendency of wage earners in two-income families to refuse transfers; an aging population; a heightened concern for the quality of one's life.

**Figure 4-5   Urban-Rural Population Distribution 1871-1987**

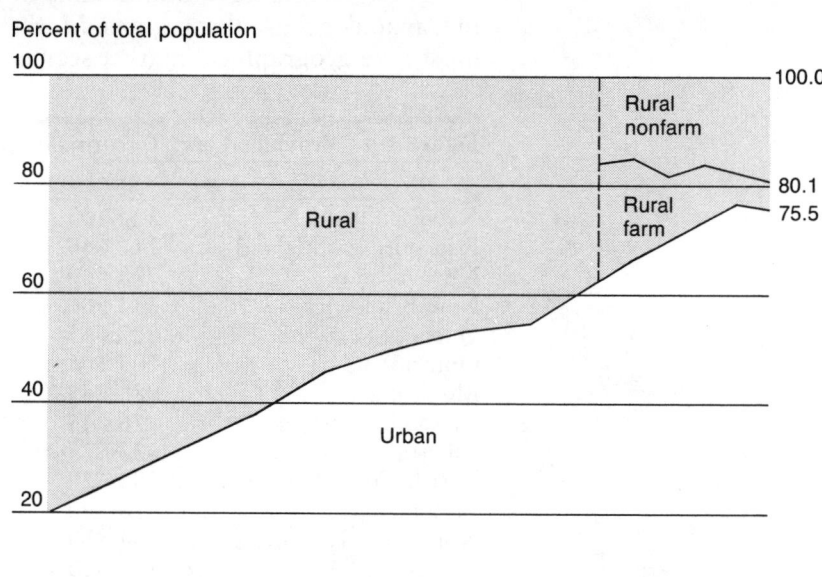

Source: Statistics Canada, *Perspectives Canada III*, 1983, p. 11. By permission of the Minister of Supply and Services Canada.

# The Dispersion of the Canadian Population

1. Most of the population lives adjacent to the American border, though climate and agriculture allow more northerly settlement in the prairie provinces.
2. History, climate, politics, and industry have favoured the population growth and dominance of Ontario and Quebec so that they possess almost two-thirds of the total Canadian population.
3. The smallest provinces with the most inhabit-

able territory have the highest population densities.
4. Contrary to an international myth, Canada's population is largely urban, with the lowest percentage of urbanization in the Maritimes and the highest in Ontario and Quebec.
5. Large urban areas possess a greater percentage distribution of the population in the younger and highly employable age group of 20 to 40 years.

Source: Reprinted with permission from Harry H. Miller, *Canadian Society: A Sociological Analysis* (Toronto: Prentice-Hall, 1976), p. 21.

### Figure 4-6   The 25 Largest Metropolitan Areas in 1986

| Rank | Area | 1986 Population (in thousands) | Ten-Year Growth Rate |
|---|---|---|---|
| 1 | Toronto | 3377 | 20.5% |
| 2 | Montreal | 2914 | 4.0 |
| 3 | Vancouver | 1392 | 19.3 |
| 4 | Ottawa-Hull | 809 | 16.6 |
| 5 | Edmonton | 703 | 26.4 |
| 6 | Calgary | 664 | 40.9 |
| 7 | Quebec | 615 | 13.4 |
| 8 | Winnipeg | 614 | 6.3 |
| 9 | Hamilton | 569 | 7.4 |
| 10 | Halifax | 309 | 15.4 |
| 11 | Kitchener | 308 | 13.2 |
| 12 | St. Catharines-Niagara | 306 | 1.2 |
| 13 | London | 286 | 5.7 |
| 14 | Windsor | 251 | 5.7 |
| 15 | Victoria | 238 | 9.2 |
| 16 | Regina | 177 | 16.7 |
| 17 | St. John's | 176 | 20.8 |
| 18 | Saskatoon | 170 | 27.3 |
| 19 | Oshawa | 166 | 22.9 |
| 20 | Chicoutimi-Jonquiere | 156 | 21.5 |
| 21 | Sudbury | 148 | −6.0 |
| 22 | Sherbrooke | 124 | 11.8 |
| 23 | Kingston | 123 | 7.6 |
| 24 | Saint John | 123 | 8.9 |
| 25 | Trois Rivieres | 120 | 13.3 |

Source: The *Financial Post Survey of Markets*, 1986, p. 24.

**Using Geographic Segmentation**

There are many instances where markets for products and services may be segmented on a geographic basis. Regional variations in taste often exist. Quebec has long been known for its interest in fine and varied foods.

Residence location within a geographic area is another important geographic variable. Urban dwellers may eat more meals in restaurants than their suburban and rural counterparts, while suburban dwellers spend proportionally more on lawn and garden care than do people in rural or urban areas. Both rural and suburban dwellers may spend more of their household income on gasoline and automobile needs than urban households.

Climate is another important factor. Snow blowers, snowmobiles, and sleds are popular products in many parts of Canada. Residents of southwestern British Columbia may spend proportionately less of their total income on heating and heating equipment than other Canadians. Climate also affects patterns of clothing purchases.

Geographic segmentation is useful only when true differences in preference and purchase patterns for a product emerge along regional lines. Geographic subdivisions of the overall market tend to be rather large and often too heterogeneous for effective segmentation without careful consideration of additional factors. In such cases, it may be necessary to use several segmentation variables.

## Demographic Segmentation

The most common approach to market segmentation is to divide consumer groups according to demographic variables. These variables—age, sex, income, occupation, education, household size, and others—are typically used to identify market segments and to develop appropriate market mixes. Demographic variables are often used in market segmentation for three reasons:

1. They are easy to identify and measure.
2. They are associated with the sale of many products and services.
3. They are typically referred to in describing the audiences of advertising media, so that media buyers and others can easily pinpoint the desired market target.[6]

Vast quantities of data are available to assist the marketing planner in segmenting potential markets on a demographic basis. Sex is an obvious variable for segmenting many markets, since many products are sex-specific. Electric razor manufacturers have utilized sex as a variable in the successful marketing of such brands as Lady Remington. Diet soft drinks have often been aimed at female markets. Even deodorants are targeted at males or females.

Age, household size, stage in the family life cycle, and income and expenditure patterns are important factors in determining buying decisions. The often distinct differences in purchase patterns based upon such demographic factors is justification for their frequent use as a basis for segmentation.

## Age — An Important Demographic Segmentation Variable

The population of Canada is expected to grow by 16 percent between 1981 and 2001, but this growth will be concentrated in two age groups—adults between 35 and 54, and persons aged 65 and older. Both of these markets represent potentially profitable market targets.

The young to middle-aged adult segment includes family households with demand for goods such as houses, furniture, recreation, clothes, toys and food. The older and senior middle-aged adult segment (45–64) includes households where the children have grown

---

[6]Kenneth Runyon, *Consumer Behavior* (Columbus, Ohio: Charles E. Merrill, 1980), p. 35.

up and most have left home. For many, housing costs are lower because mortgages are paid off. In general, this group finds itself with substantial disposable income because it is in a peak earning period, and many basic purchases for everyday living have been completed. This disposable income is often used for luxury goods, new furniture, and travel. While this segment currently represents 19 percent of the Canadian population, it will account for 50 percent of the growth in population between 1981 and 2001.

Not so many years ago, there was no such thing as a senior citizen market, since few people reached old age. Now, however, some 9 percent of the total population is 65 or older. Not only is it comforting for this year's retiree to learn that at age 65 his or her average life expectancy is at least another 13 years, but the trend also creates a unique and potentially profitable segment for the marketing manager.[7] The manager of course will not ignore the youth segment,

---

[7] See John A. Reinecke, "The 'Older' Market—Fact or Fiction?" *Journal of Marketing* (January 1964), pp. 60–64; and Sidney Goldstein, "The Aged Segment of the Market, 1950–1960," *Journal of Marketing* (April 1968), pp. 62–68.

**Figure 4-7  Population Projections by Age Groups**

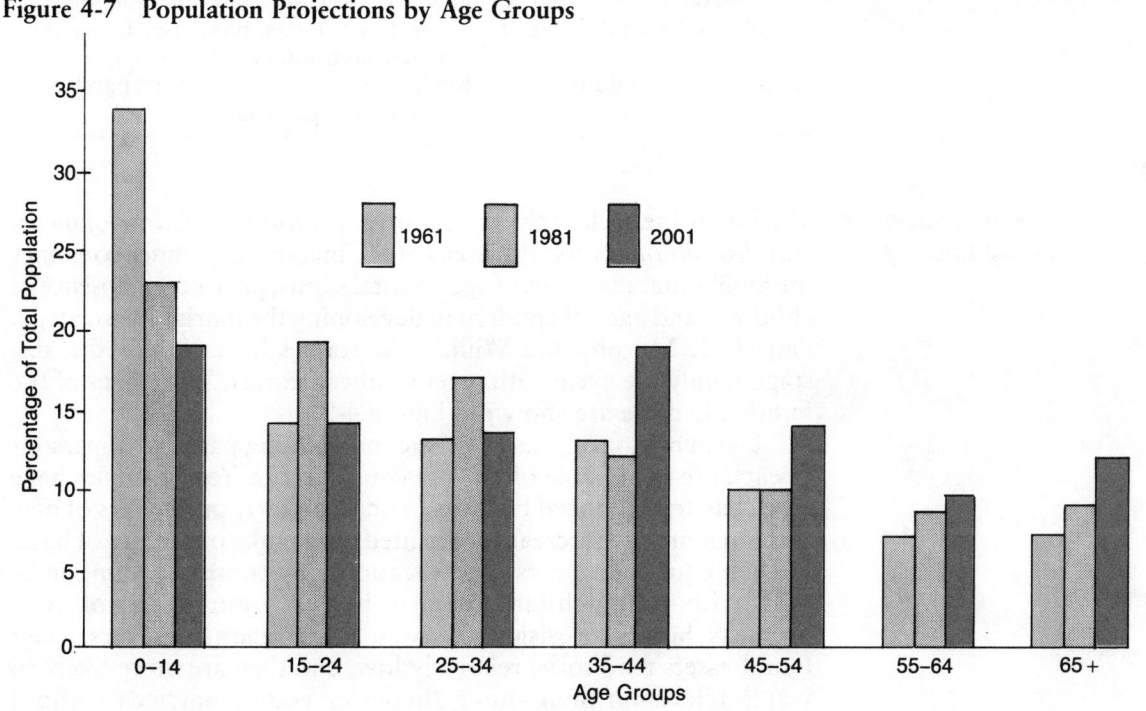

Source: For years 1981 and 2001 projection data from Series 4 Population Projections for Canada and the Provinces 1976–2001 Cat. No. 91520 Stats Canada.

which will decline in proportion to the whole population, but remain large. Figure 4-7 shows the changing profile of the Canadian population.

Each of the age groups in Figure 4-7 represents different consumption patterns and each serves as the market target for particular firms. For instance, Gerber Products Company has been extremely successful in aiming at the infant market and prepacked tours appeal to older consumers. Figure 4-8 lists some of the types of merchandise often purchased by the various age groups.

**Figure 4-8   Buying Patterns for Different Age Groups**

| Age | Name of Age Group | Merchandise |
|-----|-------------------|-------------|
| 0–5 | Young Children | Baby food, toys, nursery furniture children's wear |
| 6–19 | School Children (including teenagers) | Clothing, sports equipment, records, school supplies, food, cosmetics, used cars |
| 20–34 | Young Adult | Cars, furniture, houses, clothing, recreational equipment, purchases for younger age segments |
| 35–49 | Younger Middle-Aged | Larger homes, better cars, second cars, new furniture, recreational equipment |
| 50–64 | Older Middle-Aged | Recreational items, purchases for young marrieds and infants |
| 65 + | Senior Adults | Medical services, travel, drugs, purchases for younger age groups |

**Segmenting by Family Life Cycle**

The **family life cycle** *is the process of family formation, development, and dissolution.* Using this concept the marketing planner combines the family characteristics of age, marital status, presence or absence of children, and ages of children in developing the marketing strategy. Patrick E. Murphy and William A. Staples have proposed a six-stage family life cycle with several subcategories. The stages of the family life cycle are shown in Figure 4-9.

The behavioural characteristics and buying patterns of persons in each life cycle stage often vary considerably. Young singles have relatively few financial burdens; tend to be early purchasers of new fashion items; are recreation oriented; and make purchases of basic kitchen equipment, cars, and vacations. By contrast, young marrieds with young children tend to be heavy purchasers of baby products, homes, television sets, toys, and washers and dryers. Their liquid assets tend to be relatively low, and they are more likely to watch television than young singles or young marrieds without children. The empty-nest households in the middle-aged and older categories with no dependent children are more likely to have more disposable income; more time for recreation, self-education, and travel; and more than one member in the labour force than their full-nest counterparts with younger children. Similar differences in behavioural and buying patterns are evident in the other stages of the family life cycle as well.[8]

Analysis of life cycle stages often gives better results than reliance on single variables such as age. The buying patterns of a 25-year-old bachelor are very different from those of a father of the same age. The family of five headed by parents in their forties is a more likely prospect for the World Book Encyclopedia than the childless 40-year-old divorced person.

---

**Figure 4-9   Family Life Cycle Stages**

1. Young Single
2. Young Married without Children
3. Other Young
    a. Young divorced without children
    b. Young married with children
    c. Young divorced with children
4. Middle-Aged
    a. Middle-Aged married without children
    b. Middle-Aged divorced without children
    c. Middle-Aged married with children
    d. Middle-Aged divorced with children
    e. Middle-Aged married without dependent children
    f. Middle-Aged divorced without dependent children
5. Older
    a. Older married
    b. Older unmarried (divorced, widowed)
6. Other
    All adults and children not accounted for by family life cycle stages

Source: Adapted with permission from Patrick E. Murphy and William A. Staples, "A Modernized Family Life," *Journal of Consumer Research* (June 1979), p. 16.

---

Marketing planners can use published data such as census reports and divide their markets into more homogeneous segments than would be possible if they were analyzing single variables. Such data is available for each classification of the family life cycle.

---

[8] These examples are from an earlier life cycle study. See William D. Wells and George Gubar, "Life Cycle Concept in Marketing Research," *Journal of Marketing Research* (November 1966), p. 362. See also Frederick W. Derrick and Alane K. Lehfeld, "The Family Life Cycle: An Alternative Approach," *Journal of Consumer Research* (September 1980), pp. 214-217.

**The Changing
Household**

Half the households in Canada are composed of only one or two persons, and the average household size is 3.3 persons. This development is in marked contrast to households that averaged more than four persons before World War II. Married couples still form the largest segment of households, but in relative terms their numbers are decreasing.

There are several reasons for the trend toward smaller households. Among them are lower fertility rates; the tendency of young people to postpone marriage; the increasing desire among younger couples to limit the number of children; the ease and frequency of divorce; and the ability and desire of many young single adults and the elderly to live alone.

Over 1.6 million people live alone today — approximately 20 percent of all households. The single-person household has emerged as an important market segment with a special title: **SSWD** (*single, separated, widowed, and divorced*). SSWDs buy approximately 25 percent of all passenger cars, but a much higher proportion of specialty cars. They are also customers for single-serving food products, such as Campbell's Soup-for-One and Green Giant's single-serving casseroles.

**Segmenting Markets
on the Basis of Income
and Expenditure
Patterns**

Earlier, markets were defined as people and purchasing power. A very common method of segmenting consumer markets is on the basis of income. Fashionable specialty shops stocking designer label clothing obtain most of their sales from high-income shoppers.

Between 1971 and 1982 there continued to be a significant movement of families from lower to higher income groups. Income distribution has traditionally been depicted as a pyramid with a few families at the top and the majority at the base. This has gradually changed until the "pyramid" is now upside down. The changing pyramid is depicted in Figure 4-10.

Income statistics can be better understood by examining family structures more closely. Families can be divided into two groups: husband-wife families and lone-parent families. The latter can be further subdivided by sex of the parent. Significant changes have occurred in the structure of families over the decade. The number of husband-wife families increased by 22 percent, while that of male lone-parent families increased by 25 percent. However, the number of female lone-parent families increased by 59 percent. The three groups fared differently with respect to their incomes over the decade as can be seen in Figure 4-10a. The husband-wife families increased their average income by 30 percent and male lone-parent families by 35 percent. The average income of female lone-parent families increased by only 18 percent.[9]

---

[9] Based on Statistics Canada Catalogue 62-544, and the Conference Board of Canada *Statistics: Handbook of Consumer Markets*, current data bank.

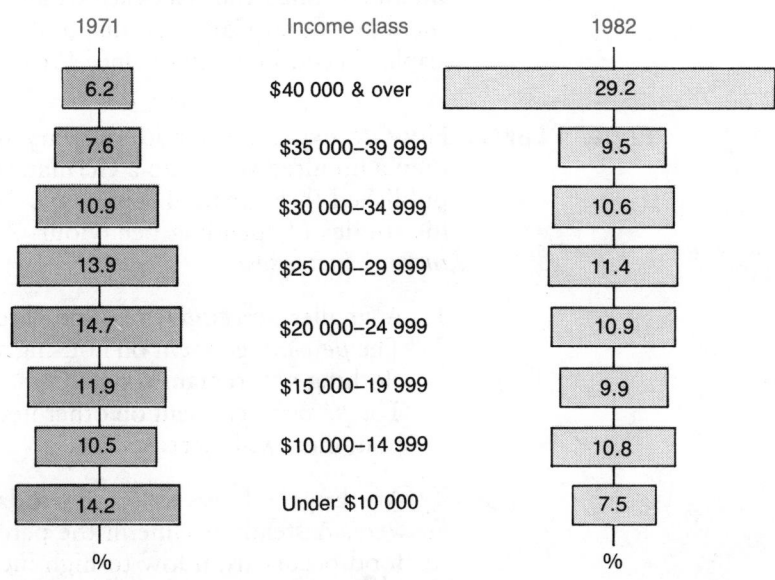

Figure 4-10   Changing Income Pyramid

(percentage distribution based on constant 1982 dollars)

| 1971 | Income class | 1982 |
|---|---|---|
| 6.2 | $40 000 & over | 29.2 |
| 7.6 | $35 000–39 999 | 9.5 |
| 10.9 | $30 000–34 999 | 10.6 |
| 13.9 | $25 000–29 999 | 11.4 |
| 14.7 | $20 000–24 999 | 10.9 |
| 11.9 | $15 000–19 999 | 9.9 |
| 10.5 | $10 000–14 999 | 10.8 |
| 14.2 | Under $10 000 | 7.5 |
| % | | % |

Source: Conference Board of Canada, *Handbook of Canadian Consumer Markets*
(Ottawa: 1984), p. 95.

Figure 4-10a   Percentage Distribution by 1970 and 1980 Family Income Groups of Families
by Family Structure, Canada

| Family income group (1980 dollars) | All families | | Husband-wife families | | Male lone-parent families | | Female lone-parent families | |
|---|---|---|---|---|---|---|---|---|
| | 1970 | 1980 | 1970 | 1980 | 1970 | 1980 | 1970 | 1980 |
| Under $5 000 | 7.1 | 4.8 | 5.5 | 3.1 | 13.3 | 7.6 | 26.2 | 19.9 |
| $ 5 000-$ 9 999 | 13.6 | 9.8 | 12.4 | 8.1 | 17.1 | 12.3 | 27.4 | 26.8 |
| 10 000- 14 999 | 16.0 | 11.7 | 15.7 | 11.0 | 19.6 | 13.0 | 19.0 | 17.5 |
| 15 000- 19 999 | 19.0 | 12.7 | 19.5 | 12.6 | 19.3 | 15.5 | 11.9 | 13.0 |
| 20 000- 24 999 | 16.0 | 14.1 | 16.8 | 14.6 | 12.4 | 15.4 | 6.6 | 8.7 |
| 25 000- 34 999 | 17.4 | 23.0 | 18.5 | 24.6 | 11.0 | 19.2 | 5.8 | 8.9 |
| 35 000- 44 999 | 6.1 | 12.6 | 6.5 | 13.6 | 3.8 | 9.1 | 1.8 | 3.2 |
| 45 000 and over | 4.8 | 11.3 | 5.2 | 12.4 | 3.5 | 7.9 | 1.3 | 2.1 |
| Total | 100.0 | 100.0 | 100.0 | 100.0 | 100.0 | 100.0 | 100.0 | 100.0 |
| Number          '000 | 5 055 | 6 325 | 4 585 | 5 612 | 99 | 124 | 370 | 589 |
| Average income  $ | 20 820 | 26 748 | 21 631 | 28 186 | 17 286 | 23 243 | 11 714 | 13 790 |
| Median income   $ | 18 447 | 23 894 | 1 210 | 25 250 | 15 002 | 20 468 | 9 246 | 10 890 |

Source: Statistics Canada, *Changes in Income in Canada*, 1970-1980.

A household's expenditures may be divided into the two categories: 1) basic purchase of essential household needs, and 2) other purchases that can be made at the discretion of the household members once the necessities have been purchased (disposable income). Total Canadian disposable income is estimated to have tripled in constant dollars since 1961.[10] This is a substantial increase.

**Engel's Laws**  How do expenditure patterns vary with increased income? More than a hundred years ago a German statistician named Ernst Engel published three general statements — **Engel's Laws** — based upon his studies of spending behaviour. According to Engel, *as family income increases*:

1. A smaller *percentage* of expenditures goes for food.
2. The *percentage* spent on housing and household operations and clothing will remain constant.
3. The *percentage* spent on other items (such as recreation, education, etc.) will increase.

Are Engel's Laws still valid today? Figure 4-11 supplies the answers. A steady decline in the percentage of total income spent for food occurs from low to high incomes. Note the emphasis on the word *percentage*. The high-income families will spend a greater absolute amount on food purchases, but their purchases will represent a smaller percentage of their total expenditures than will be true of low-income households. The second law also appears partially correct since percentage expenditures for housing and household operations are relatively unchanged in all but the very lowest income group.

The third law is also true with respect to recreation and education. However, there are notable exceptions to the original generalization, such as transportation. It has become a much greater part of family expenditures than Engel might have dreamed.

Engel's Laws provide the marketing manager with useful generalizations about types of consumer demand that will evolve with increased income. They may also be useful when evaluating a foreign country as a potential market target.[11]

---

10*Changes in Income in Canada, 1970–1980*, Statistics Canada, Catalogue 99-941.

11 Other countries may have different expenditure patterns, however. One study of European Common Market countries revealed that housing expenditures increased as a percentage of total spending with increased income. See J. Allison Barnhill, "The Application of Engel's Laws of Personal Consumption (1857) to the European Common Market (1957–1961)," *The Marketer* (Spring 1967), pp. 17–22.

## Figure 4-11   Percentage Annual Family Expenditures by Income Groups, 1982

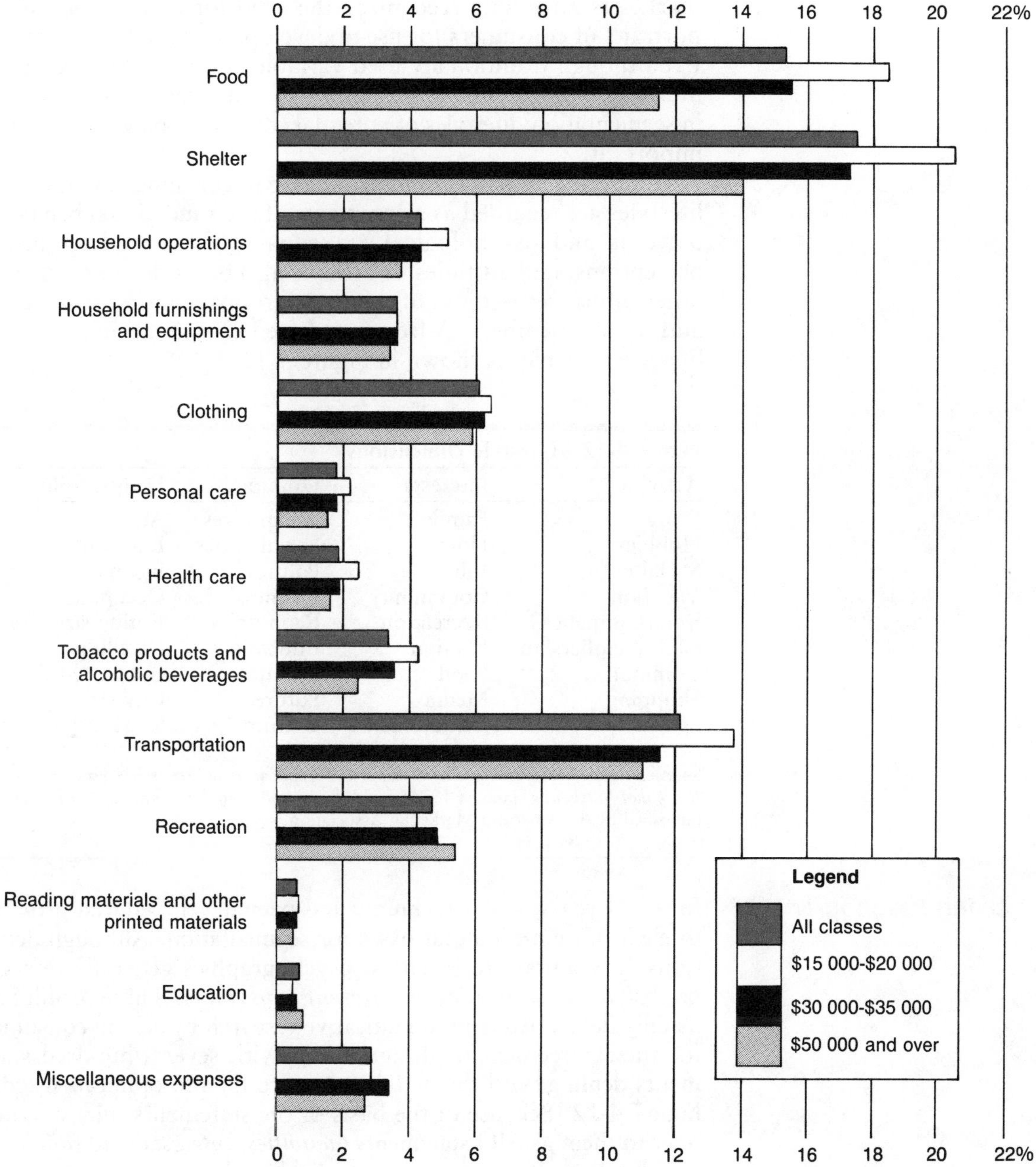

Source: Statistics Canada, *Market Research Handbook* (Ottawa, 1985-86) p. 349.

**Psychographic**
**Segmentation**

Although geographic and demographic segmentation traditionally have been the primary bases for dividing consumer and industrial markets into homogeneous segments to serve as market targets, marketers have long recognized the need for fuller, more lifelike portraits of consumers for use in developing marketing programs. Even though traditionally used variables such as age, sex, family life cycle, income, and population size and location are important in segmentation, lifestyles of potential consumers may prove equally important.

**Lifestyle** refers to *the mode of living* of consumers. Consumers' lifestyles are regarded as a composite of their individual behaviour patterns and psychological makeups — their needs, motives, perceptions, and attitudes. A lifestyle also bears the mark of many other influences — those of reference groups, culture, social class, and family members. A frequently used classification system for lifestyle variables is shown in Figure 4-12.

**Figure 4-12    Lifestyle Dimensions**

| Activities | Interests | Opinions | Demographics |
|---|---|---|---|
| Work | Family | Themselves | Age |
| Hobbies | Home | Social issues | Education |
| Social events | Job | Politics | Income |
| Vacation | Community | Business | Occupation |
| Entertainment | Recreation | Economics | Family size |
| Club membership | Fashion | Education | Dwelling |
| Community | Food | Products | Geography |
| Shopping | Media | Future | City size |
| Sports | Achievements | Culture | Stage in life cycle |

Source: Joseph T. Plummer, "The Concept and Application of Life-style Segmentation," *Journal of Marketing* (January 1974), p. 34. Reprinted from the *Journal of Marketing* published by the American Marketing Association.

*Using Psychographics*

In recent years, a new technique has been developed that promises to elicit more meaningful bases for segmentation. Although definitions vary among researchers, **psychographics** generally refers to *the behavioural profiles of different consumers.* These profiles are usually developed from quantitative research by asking consumers for their agreement or disagreement with several hundred statements dealing with the activities, interests, and opinions listed in Figure 4-12. Because of the basis of the statements, many writers refer to them as **AIO statements** *(activities, interests, and opinions).*

Hundreds of psychographic studies have been conducted on products and services ranging from soap to air travel. A study of household food buying identified four distinct segments based on psychographic research. Of the 1800 adults interviewed, 98 percent were categorized by the researcher as falling into one of the following groupings:

*Hedonists*, who represent 20 percent of the population, want the good life — foods that taste good, are convenient, and inexpensive. They aren't worried about sugar, fat, cholesterol, salt, calories, additives, or preservatives. They are most likely young, male, and child-free. Hedonists are above average consumers of regular soft drinks, beer, margarine, presweetened cereal, candy, and gum.

*Don't Wants*, another 20 percent of the population, are the opposite extreme from the Hedonists. They avoid all the "no-no" ingredients in some processed foods. They will sacrifice taste and convenience and will pay more to obtain foods without sugar, artificial ingredients, cholesterol, and fat. They are concerned about calories and nutrition. Their avoidance behaviour is more health oriented than diet conscious. This segment is older; more than half are over age 50. They tend to be better educated, live in large urban areas, and don't have children at home. The Don't Wants are major consumers of decaffeinated coffee, fruit juices, wine, unsalted butter, corn oil margarine, nutritionally fortified cereal, yogurt, and sugar-free foods and beverages.

*The Weight Conscious*, who comprise about one-third of the population, are primarily concerned about calories and fat. They like convenience foods, but try to avoid cholesterol, sugar, and salt. They're not particularly nutrition or taste conscious and don't avoid foods simply because they have artificial ingredients or preservatives. Members of this segment tend to have higher incomes and many are women employed full time. Given their concern for calories, the Weight Conscious are above average consumers of iced tea, diet soft drinks, diet margarine, and sugar-free candy and gum.

*The Moderates*, the final 25 percent of the population, are average in everything. They balance the trade-offs they make in food selection and don't exhibit strong concerns about the avoidance factors. Their profile closely fits that of the general population, and their consumption levels are average for the foods and beverages listed in the study.[12]

---

12 Reported in "Research on Food Consumption Values Identifies Four Market Segments: Finds 'Good Taste' Still Tops," *Marketing News* (May 15, 1981), p. 17. Used by permission of the American Marketing Association.

As the profiles of two very different market groups in Figure 4-13 suggest, the marketing implications of psychographic segmentation are considerable. Psychographic profiles produce a much richer description of a potential market target, and should assist promotional decision-makers in matching the image of the company and its product offerings with the type of consumer using the product.

Psychographic segmentation often serves as a component of an overall segmentation strategy in which markets are also segmented on the basis of demographic/geographic variables. These more traditional bases provide the marketer with accessibility to consumer segments through orthodox communications channels such as newspapers, radio and television advertising, and other promotional outlets. Psychographic studies may then be implemented to develop lifelike, three-demensional profiles of the lifestyles of the firm's market target. When combined with demographic/geographic characteristics, psychographics emerges as an important tool in understanding the behaviour of present and potential market targets.[13]

## Benefit Segmentation

A fourth approach to market segmentation is to focus on such attributes as product usage rates and the benefits derived from the product. These factors may reveal important bases for pinpointing prospective market targets. One analysis of 34 segmentation studies indicated that benefit analysis provided the best predictor of brand use, level of consumption, and product type selected in 51 percent of the cases.[14] Many marketers now consider benefit segmentation the most useful approach to classifying markets.

### Usage Rates

Marketing managers may divide potential segments into two categories: 1) users and 2) nonusers. Users may be further divided into heavy, moderate, and light users.

---

[13] For a thorough survey of previous psychographic studies and some case histories of the uses of psychographic research, see William D. Wells, "Psychographics: A Critical Review," *Journal of Marketing Research* (May 1975), pp. 196–213. See also John J. Burnett, "Psychographic and Demographic Characteristics of Blood Donors," *Journal of Consumer Research* (June 1981), pp. 62–86; Mary Ann Lederhaus and Ronald J. Adams, "A Psychographic Profile of the Cosmopolitan Consumers," Robert H. Ross, Frederic B. Kraft, and Charles H. Davis, eds., *Proceedings of the Southwestern Marketing Association* (Wichita, Kansas: Southwestern Marketing Assoc., 1981), pp. 142–145; and J. Paul Merenski, "Psychographics: Valid by Definition and Reliable by Technique," Venkatakrishna V. Bellur, ed., *Developments in Marketing Science* (Miami Beach: Academy of Marketing Science, 1981), pp. 161–166.
[14] See "Lifestyle Research: A Lot of Hype, Versus Little Performance," *Marketing News* (May 14, 1982), Section 2, p. 5.

## Figure 4-13   Profile of Heavy Users: Eye Makeup and Shortening

| Heavy User of Eye Makeup | Heavy User of Shortening |
| --- | --- |

### Demographic Characteristics

| | |
| --- | --- |
| Young, well-educated, lives in metropolitan areas | Middle-aged, medium to large family, lives outside metropolitan areas |

### Product Use

| | |
| --- | --- |
| Also a heavy user of liquid face makeup, lipstick, hair spray, perfume, cigarettes, gasoline | Also a heavy user of flour, sugar, canned lunch meat, cooked pudding, ketchup |

### Media Preferences
*Agrees more than average with*

| | |
| --- | --- |
| Fashion magazines, *The Tonight Show*, adventure programs | *Reader's Digest*, daytime TV serials, family-situation TV comedies |

### Activities, Interests, and Opinions
*Agrees more than average with*

| | |
| --- | --- |
| "I often try the latest hairdo styles when they change." | "I love to bake and frequently do." |
| "An important part of my life and activities is dressing smartly." | "I save recipes from newspapers and magazines." |
| "I like to feel attractive to all men." | "I love to eat." |
| "I want to look a little different from others." | "I enjoy most forms of housework." |
| "I like what I see when I look in the mirror." | "Usually I have regular days for washing, cleaning, etc., around the house." |
| "I take good care of my skin." | "I am uncomfortable when my house is not completely clean." |
| "I would like to spend a year in London or Paris." | "I try to arrange my home for my children's convenience." |
| "I like ballet." | "Our family is a close-knit group." |
| "I like to serve unusual dinners." | "Clothes should be dried in fresh air and out-of-doors." |
| "I really do believe that blondes have more fun." | "I would rather spend a quiet evening at home than go out to a party." |

*Disagrees more than average with*

| | |
| --- | --- |
| "I enjoy most forms of housework." | "My idea of housekeeping is once over lightly." |
| "I furnish my home for comfort, not for style." | "Classical music is more interesting than popular music." |
| "If it was good enough for my mother, it's good enough for me." | "I like ballet." |
| | "I'd like to spend a year in London or Paris." |

Source: William D. Wells and Arthur D. Beard, "Personality and Consumer Behavior," in Scott Ward and Thomas S. Robertson, eds., *Consumer Behavior*, © 1973, pp. 195–96. Reprinted by permission of Prentice-Hall, Inc. Englewood Cliffs, N.J.

In some product categories, such as air travel, car rentals, dog food, and hair colouring, less than 20 percent of the population accounts for more than 80 percent of the total purchases. Even for such widely used products as coffee and soft drinks, 50 percent of all households account for almost 90 percent of the total usage.[15]

An early study of usage patterns by Dik Warren Twedt divided users into two categories: 1) light and 2) heavy. Twedt's analysis of consumer-panel data revealed that 29 percent of the sample households could be characterized as heavy users of lemon-lime soft drinks. This group represented 91 percent of sales in the product category.[16] It is, therefore, not surprising that usage rates are important segmentation variables for Coca-Cola, Pepsi-Cola, and 7-Up.

Heavy users often can be identified through analysis of internal records. Retail stores and financial institutions have records of charge-card purchases and other transactions. Warranty records may also be used.[17]

**Product Benefits**  Market segments may also be identified by the *benefits* the buyer expects to derive from a product or brand. In a pioneering investigation, Daniel Yankelovich revealed that much of the watch industry operated with little understanding of the benefits watch buyers expect in their purchases. At the time of the study, most watch companies were marketing relatively expensive models through jewellery stores and using prestige appeals. However, Yankelovich's research revealed that less than one-third of the market was purchasing a watch as a symbol. In fact, 23 percent of his respondents reported they purchased the lowest-price watch and another 46 percent focused on durability and overall product quality. The Timex Company decided to focus its product benefits on those two categories and market its watches in drugstores, variety stores, and discount houses. Within a few years of adopting the new segmentation approach, it became the largest watch company in the world.[18]

Figure 4-14 illustrates how benefit segmentation might be applied to the toothpaste market. The table reveals that some consumers are primarily concerned with price; some with tooth decay, some

15 Reported in David T. Kollat, Roger D. Blackwell, and James F. Robeson, *Strategic Marketing* (New York: Holt, Rinehart and Winston, 1972), p. 192.
16 Dik Warren Twedt, "How Important to Marketing Strategy is the 'Heavy User'?" *Journal of Marketing* (January 1964), pp. 71–72.
17 These methods are suggested in Martin L. Bell, *Marketing: Concepts and Strategy* (Boston: Houghton Mifflin, 1979), p. 129.
18 Daniel Yankelovich, "New Criteria for Market Segmentation," *Harvard Business Review* (March–April 1964), p. 83–90.

**Figure 4-14    Benefit Segmentation of the Toothpaste Market**

| | Segment name | | | |
|---|---|---|---|---|
| | *The sensory segment* | *The sociables* | *The worriers* | *The in-dependent segment* |
| Principal benefit sought | Flavour, product appearance | Brightness of teeth | Decay prevention | Price |
| Demographic strengths | Children | Teens, young people | Large families | Men |
| Special behavioural characteristics | Users of spearmint-flavoured toothpaste | Smokers | Heavy users | Heavy users |
| Brands dis-proportionately favoured | Colgate, Stripe | MacLean's, Plus White, Ultra Brite | Crest | Brands on sale |
| Personality characteristics | High self-involvement | High sociability | High hypo-chondriasis | High autonomy |
| Lifestyle characteristics | Hedonistic | Active | Conserva-tive | Value-oriented |

Source: Reprinted by permission from Russell I. Haley, "Benefit Segmentation: A Decision-Oriented Research Tool," *Journal of Marketing* (July 1968), p. 33, published by the American Marketing Association.

with taste, and others with brightness. Also included are the demographic and other characteristics utilized in focusing on each subgrouping.[19]

**Segmenting Industrial Markets**

While the bulk of market segmentation research has concentrated on consumer markets, the concept can also be applied to the industrial sector. The overall process is similar. Three industrial market segmentation approaches have been identified: geographic segmentation, product segmentation, and segmentation by end-use application (see Figure 4-15).

**Geographic Segmentation**

Geographic segmentation is useful in industries where the bulk of the customers are concentrated in specific geographical locations. This approach can be used in such instances as the automobile

[19] See Russell I. Haley, "Benefit Segmentation: A Decision-Oriented Research Tool," *Journal of Marketing* (July 1968), pp. 30–35.

**Figure 4-15    Segmentation Bases for Industrial Markets**

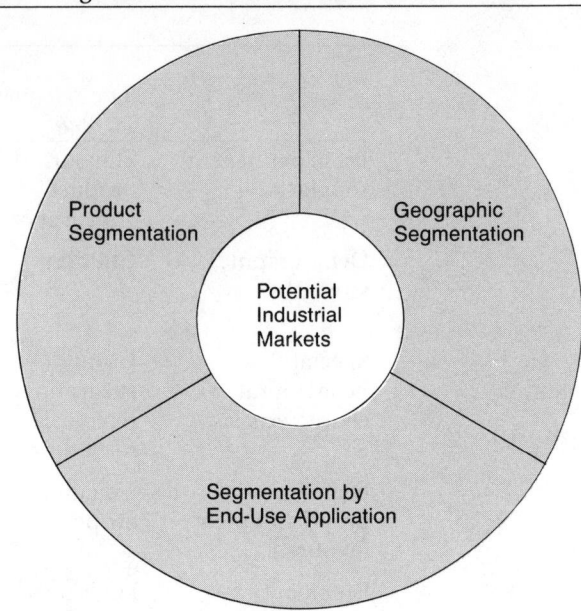

industry, concentrated in the central Ontario area, or the lumber industry, centred in British Columbia and Quebec. It might also be used in cases where the markets are limited to just a few locations. The oil-field equipment market, for example, is largely concentrated in cities like Calgary and Edmonton.

*Product Segmentation*    It is possible to segment some industrial markets in terms of their need for specialized products. Industrial users tend to have much more precise product specifications than do ultimate consumers, and such products often fit very narrow market segments. For example, special rivets for bridge building might be a market segment. Therefore, the design of an industrial good or service and the development of an associated marketing mix to meet specific buyer requirements is a form of market segmentation.

*Segmentation by*    A third segmentation base is end-use applications or precisely how
*End-Use Applications*    the industrial purchaser will use the product. (This is similar to benefits segmentation in consumer markets.) A manufacturer of, say, printing equipment may serve markets ranging from a local utility to a bicycle manufacturer to Agriculture Canada. Each end-use may dictate unique specifications of performance, design, and price. The market for desk-top computers provides a good example. Xerox is targeting its 820-II model to the office market, rather than the home market. Technology Group Inc.'s BMC computer is being offered

for end-use applications in accounting and blood diagnostics.[20] Regardless of how it is done, market segmentation is as vital to industrial marketing as it is in consumer markets.

**Summary**   A market consists of people or organizations with the necessary purchasing power and willingness to buy. The authority to buy must also exist. Markets can be classified by the type of products they handle. Consumer goods are products purchased by the ultimate consumer for personal use. Industrial goods are products purchased for use either directly or indirectly in the production of other goods and services for resale. Products are typically targeted at specific market segments. The process of dividing the total market into several homogeneous groups is called market segmentation.

Consumer markets can be divided on the bases of geographic, demographic, psychographic, or benefit segmentation. Geographic segmentation is the process of dividing the overall market into homogeneous groups on the basis of population location. It is one of the oldest forms of segmentation. The most commonly used form is demographic segmentation, which classifies the overall market into homogeneous groups based upon characteristics such as age, sex, and income levels. Psychographic segmentation is a relatively new approach. It uses behavioural profiles developed from analyses of the activities, opinions, interests, and lifestyles of consumers to identify market segments. The fourth approach, benefit segmentation, may be the most useful. It segments markets on the basis of the perceived benefits consumers expect to derive from a product or service.

Benefit segmentation is also useful in industrial markets. There are three bases for industrial market segmentation: geographic segmentation, product segmentation, and segmentation by end-use applications. Geographic segmentation is commonly used since many industries are concentrated in a few locations. A second industrial market segmentation base is by product. Industrial markets are characterized by precise product specifications, making this approach feasible. Segmentation by end-use applications is the final base. This approach is predicated upon the use that the industrial purchasers will make of the good or service.

This chapter has examined the various bases for segmenting both consumer and industrial markets. Chapter 5 examines how these concepts may be applied to market segmentation strategies. This section concludes with Chapter 6 on marketing research and information systems.

---

[20]Susan Chace, "Marketing Grows More Vital for Desktop Computer Sales," *The Wall Street Journal* (October 22, 1982), 27.

| Key Terms | market | family life cycle |
|---|---|---|
| | consumer goods | SSWD |
| | industrial goods | Engel's Law |
| | market segmentation | lifestyle |
| | psychographics | |
| | AIO statements | |

**Review Questions**

1. Explain why each of the four components of a market is needed for a market to exist.
2. Bicycles are consumer goods; iron ore is an industrial good. What about trucks — are they consumer goods or industrial goods? Defend your answer.
3. Identify and briefly explain the bases for segmenting consumer markets.
4. Identify the major population shifts that have occurred in recent years. How do you account for these shifts?
5. Explain and describe the use of AIO questions.
6. Why is demographic segmentation the most commonly used approach to marketing segmentation?
7. How can lifestyles be used in market segmentation?
8. Explain the use of product usage rates as a segmentation variable.
9. What market segmentation base would you recommend for the following:
   a. Professional soccer team
   b. Porsche sports car
   c. Capitol Records
   d. Scope mouthwash
10. Identify and briefly explain the bases of segmenting industrial markets.

**Discussion Questions and Exercises**

1. Match the following bases for market segmentation with the items below:
   a. Geographic segmentation
   b. Demographic segmentation
   c. Psychographic segmentation
   d. Benefit segmentation
   _____1. A government-financed study divided households into five categories of eating patterns: meat eaters; healthy eaters; conscientious eaters; "in a dither" eaters; and on the go eaters.

_____2. A department store chain decides to emphasize suburban rather than downtown outlets.

_____3. "7-Up, clear, crisp with no caffeine."

_____4. A catalogue retailer targets its catalogues at 25- to 54-year-old working women with household incomes of $34 000.

2. The 1988 Calgary Winter Olympics will be extensively televised. What types of products would most likely benefit from advertising associated with the games? Will they appeal to more than one market segment?

3. Prepare a brief report on the future growth prospects of the geographical area in which you live.

4. Explain why the household growth rate is more than double the increase in population.

5. Canadian census data reveal that a significant number of Canadians have a mother tongue other than English or French (mother tongue is defined as the language first learned and still understood). Some of the larger language groups are Italian (529 000 people), German (523 000), Ukrainian (292 000), and Chinese (224 000). How could a marketer use this demographic information?

**MICROCOMPUTER EXERCISE:**
**Engel's Laws**

Directions: Use the Menu Item titled "Engel's Laws" on the Marketing disk to solve the following problems.

1. The Martin family of Swift Current, Saskatchewan uses a budget to monitor and control household expenditures. The family just prepared this year's budget to reflect the salary increases that both spouses expect at the beginning of the year. The general categories of expenditures and savings and the amounts allocated to each category are shown in Table A.

Is the Martin budget for this year consistent with Engel's Laws? With which, if any, of the laws is the Martin budget in conflict?

**Table A   Budget of the Martin Family**

| Budget Category | Last Year's Expenditures | This Year's Budgeted Amount |
|---|---|---|
| Food | $18 000 | $19 500 |
| Clothing and Housing | 24 000 | 29 250 |
| Other | 18 000 | 16 250 |
| Total | $60 000 | $65 000 |

**2.** Julia Wiley is a single, 26-year-old marketing-research analyst at a major consumer-goods company in Toronto. Last year, Wiley saved $3200 and spent the remainder of her salary as follows: food, $6400; housing and clothing, $12 800; and miscellaneous (including entertainment and vacations), $9600. But a recent promotion and salary increase have prompted Wiley to reevaluate her personal budget. She has decided to use a payroll-deduction program to increase her savings to $4200, cut her food expenditures to $5600, increase her housing and clothing outlays slightly to $14 000, and spend the rest of next year's $35 000 salary on miscellaneous items (including a vacation).

Does Wiley's budget conflict with Engel's Laws? If so, how?

**3.** The Jacobs family of Abbotsford, B.C. uses the budget shown in Table B.

Do the Jacobs' financial plans conflict with Engel's Laws? If so, how?

| Table B   Budget of the Jacobs Family | | |
|---|---|---|
| Budget Category | Last Year's Expenditures | This Year's Budgeted Amount |
| Food | $ 8 000 | $ 9 000 |
| Housing | 15 000 | 19 500 |
| Other | 4 000 | 3 500 |
| Total | $27 000 | $32 000 |

# Market Segmentation Strategies

*1. To explain the rationale for and process of developing market matching strategies.*

*2. To outline the stages in the market segmentation process.*

*3. To present the concept of market positioning in developing market matching strategies.*

*4. To show how market target decision analysis can be used in market segmentation.*

*5. To show how market target decision analysis can be used to assess a product mix.*

Most major bakeries have been losing market share, but Corporate Foods Ltd. of Toronto has made its sales rise. Companies such as General Bakeries and Weston Bakeries have lost ground to in-store bakeries and to a growing list of specialized franchise bakeries. However, the strategy adopted by Corporate Foods has helped them to overcome such changes in the industry.

Corporate Foods' success lies in its ready willingness to recognize and cater to the growing fragmentation of the bread market through an intelligent market segmentation strategy. Corporate Foods delivers different types of fresh baked bread and rolls throughout Ontario under the brands Dempster's, Toastmaster, and Bamby, and under specialty labels such as Hollywood, Brownberry, and Sun-Maid Raisin Bread.

Through its Gainsborough division, it produces frozen pastry products for distribution across Canada. A 25 percent interest in the Quebec firm Unipain gives it a share of that market. This willingness to serve a variety of market segments has resulted in a 13 percent climb in sales over the past three years, compared with a 30 percent decline in market share by the major bakeries.

President Norman Currie concedes that "in-store bakeries do affect markets, as do neighbourhood bakeries and bakery franchises. On the other hand, we sell products they cannot and do not produce. It's a very segmented market; it isn't a mass market. You have to design the product to meet each of those segments."

The company also plans to continue serving market segments through specialty product lines such as the newly introduced Gainsborough frozen croissant. Corporate Foods last summer bought a 49 percent interest in the pita and croissant baker Dough Delight of Toronto.

"I don't think there has been any decline in consumption of bakery products," Currie says. "Bread consumption hasn't changed; the market just shifts . . ."[1]

Market targets that are viable under current economic and competitive conditions must be identified and monitored continuously. The marketing planner must be prepared to make dramatic switches when necessary.

## The Conceptual Framework

Chapter 5 takes the discussion of market segmentation further. Chapter 4 discussed the role of market segmentation in developing a marketing strategy and the bases for segmenting consumer markets (geographic, demographic, psychographic, and benefit segmentation) and industrial markets (geographic, product, and segmentation by end-use application). Here the emphasis shifts to the strategies associated with the concepts of market segmentation.

This chapter looks at the rationale for and process of matching product offerings to specific market segments. The selection of the appropriate market matching strategy is dependent upon a variety of internal and external variables facing the firm.

Next, the chapter outlines the various stages that exist in the segmentation process. The starting point is to identify the dimension that can be used to segment markets. The process ends with the decision on the actual market target segments. Chapter 5 concludes with a separate section on market target decision analysis, the procedure for selecting targeted market segments.

## Alternative Market Matching Strategies

Market segmentation may take many forms, theoretically ranging from treating the entire market as a single homogeneous entity to subdividing it into several segments and providing a separate product and marketing mix for each segment.

The very core of the firm's strategies is to match product offerings with the needs of particular market segments. To do so successfully the firm must take the following factors into consideration:

---

[1] Adapted from Tessa Wilmott, "Bread Company on the Rise," *The Financial Post*, November 26, 1983, p. 25.

1. *Company Resources* must be adequate to cover product development and other marketing mix costs.
2. *Differentiability of products.* Some products can be easily differentiated from others. Some can be produced in versions designed specially for individual segments.
3. *Stage in the product life cycle.* As a product matures, different marketing mix emphases are required to fit market needs.
4. *Competitors' strategies.* Strategies and product offerings must be continually adjusted in order to be competitive.

Essentially, the firm makes a number of product/service offerings to the market in light of these determinants. One firm may decide on a **single-offer strategy**. This defined as *the attempt to satisfy a large or a small market with one product and a single marketing mix.* Such a strategy may be adopted for different reasons. A small manufacturer of wheelbarrows might concentrate on marketing one product to retailers in one city only because it does not have the resources to serve a mass market. A large producer of drafting equipment might offer a single product line with a marketing mix aimed at draftspersons because it believes that only this limited segment would be interested in the product. A single-offer strategy aimed at one segment is often called *concentrated marketing*; aimed at mass

# A Single-Offer Strategy— Ford Motor Company in 1908

In 1908 Henry Ford introduced the Model T, and revolutionized the automobile business around the world. Until the late 1920s he sold only the Model T and Model T truck. Ford's strategy was based on the belief that if he could get the price of a serviceable, utilitarian automobile low enough, he could develop a large mass market. His competitors were several hundred manufacturers of automobiles who were producing vehicles that were virtually custom built, with short production runs and high costs. Ford's strategy generated unprecedented sales. A dealership organization evolved, which carried spare parts and service facilities to users across North America and through much of Europe. The marketing mix of product, price, promotion, and distribution and service network quickly made Henry Ford a multi-millionaire and contributed to economic development through improving the transportation system.

There are some dangers inherent in a single-offer strategy however. A firm that attempts to satisfy a very wide market with a single product or service *fairly well* is vulnerable to competition from those who choose to develop more specialized products that appeal to and serve segments of the larger market *very well*. Over time General Motors and Chrysler developed a wider variety of models, price ranges, styles, and colour options. What worked superbly in 1908 faltered in the 1920s and Ford had to move to a multi-offer strategy. The firm developed the Model A and the Model B, offering them with various options. The company differentiated the product line further in the 1930s by introducing the first mass-produced V-8 engine, which was a company hallmark for years.

markets it is often called *undifferentiated* or *mass marketing*. The marketing of Coca-Cola is an example of the latter.

On the other hand, another company with greater resources may recognize that there are several segments of the market that would respond well to specifically-designed products and marketing mixes. It adopts a **multi-offer strategy**. This is defined as *the attempt to satisfy several segments of the market very well with specialized products or services and unique marketing mixes aimed at each segment*. A bank designs particular services to fit the unique needs of different consumer and commercial market segments. A multi-offer strategy is also called *differentiated marketing*.

When these determinants are combined with markets segmented on the dimensions discussed in Chapter 4, the firm is able to develop a market matching strategy. A successful match of products to segments through the development of a marketing mix with appropriate product design, pricing strategy, distribution strategy, and promotion strategy is vital to the market success of the firm.

## An Extensive Multi-Offer Strategy — Ford Motor Company in 1985

The market matching strategy of the Ford Motor Company in 1985 is quite different from that of 1915. It has evolved with the changing environment that faces the automobile industry. Ford's product line is much expanded from the Model T days, but the company still does not produce products for *all* markets. Instead, it serves those markets where its resources, marketing skills, product strengths, and competitive offerings can be best exploited. Figure 5-1 provides a comparison of the product lines then and now.

## A Single-Offer Strategy for Different Reasons — Audi/Volkswagen/Porsche in 1955

When Volkswagen decided to enter the North American market they chose to do it with only the "beetle" for a variety of reasons. First, the company was strapped for funds and could not expand its production facilities, stretched to the limit in trying to supply automobile-short post-war Europe. It also recognized that a dealer-support system and spare parts inventory had to be developed from scratch if it was to compete successfully in North America. With these constraints in mind Volks- wagen marketers determined that the serviceable beetle was the answer. The beetle was relatively low priced, was supported by an imaginative promotional campaign, and become an immediate success with those who wanted a small, relatively basic car. Volkswagen sold a much wider variety of products in Europe (and continued to introduce new products in that market much earlier than in North America). They deliberately chose to make a single offer to this market.

# A Strategic Move to a Multi-Offer Strategy — Audi/Volkswagen/Porsche, 1985

Today, products under the Volkswagen parent company control compete for a much broader number of market segments than the Beetle. The changes are indicative of a major change in the segmentation strategies. They not only have the products, but also the resources, and the marketing infrastructure to serve more segments.

**Figure 5-1   Market Matching Strategies**

| | Product Offerings | | | |
|---|---|---|---|---|
| | *Ford Motor Company* | | *Audi/Volkswagen/Porsche* | |
| | 1908 | 1985 | 1955 | 1985 |
| Market Segment | Single-Offer Strategy | Multi-Offer Strategy | Single-Offer Strategy | Multi-Offer Strategy |
| General Purpose Cars | | | | |
| Small | Model T | Escort Lynx | "Beetle" | Jetta Rabbit |
| Medium | Model T | LTD Tempo Topaz | | Golf |
| Large | | LTD Crown Marquis | | |
| Sport Cars | | | | |
| Low-priced | | EXP | | |
| Medium-priced | | Mustang Capri | | Scirocco |
| High-priced | | Thunderbird Cougar | | Porsche 911, 944 |
| Luxury Cars | | | | |
| Medium-priced | | Lincoln | | Audi Quattro Audi 4000 |
| High-priced | | Continental | | Audi 5000 |
| Trucks | | | | |
| Small | Model T (truck) | Ford | | Vanagon |
| Medium | | Ford | | |

Source: Adapted from *Canadian Consumer*, Vol. 14, No. 4, April 1984, and *Consumer Reports*, Vol. 49, No. 4, April 1984.

Many firms, large and small, practise a multi-offer strategy in today's environment. Procter & Gamble markets Tide, Dash, Duz, Cheer, Bold, Gain, Oxydol, and Bonus among other detergents to meet the desires of specific groups of detergent buyers. Lever Brothers offers two brands of complexion soap (Dove and Lux) and two brands of deodorant soap (Lifebuoy and Phase III).

Generally speaking, the company with a multi-offer marketing strategy should produce more sales by providing increased satisfaction for each of several market targets than would be possible with only a single-offer strategy. However, whether a firm should choose a single- or multi-offer strategy depends on the economics of the situation — whether the company has the resources, and whether greater profits can be expected from the additional expense of a multi-offer strategy.

## The Market Segmentation Process

The marketer has a number of potential bases for determining the most appropriate market-matching strategy. Geographic, demographic, product attributes, and psychographic bases are often utilized in converting heterogeneous markets into specific segments that serve as market targets for the consumer-oriented marketer. The industrial marketer segments geographically, by product, or by end-use application. In either case, a systematic five-stage decision process is followed. This framework for market segmentation is shown in Figure 5-2.

Since no single base for segmentation is necessarily the best, the analyst should segment the market in a way that will make the marketing mix easy to apply and that will achieve results. For example, demographic segmentation may be used in planning a print advertising campaign because magazines are normally aimed at specific demographic segments. The analyst thus often experiments with segmenting markets in several ways in the process of discovering which of the mix elements can be changed for greatest effect. (Similarly, marketing opportunities are sometimes discovered by rating how well competitors have served segments differentiated on a particular dimension.) This is part of the interactive process of analysis. Figure 5-2 shows a systematic, five-stage decision process that lends form to what are otherwise often complex and unstructured problems.[2]

### Stage I: Select Market Segmentation Bases

The decision process begins when a firm seeks characteristics of potential buyers as bases that will allow the marketer to classify them into market segments. Segmentation bases should be selected

[2] This section is based on materials written by J. D. Forbes, University of British Columbia.

**Figure 5-2   The Market Segmentation Decision Process**

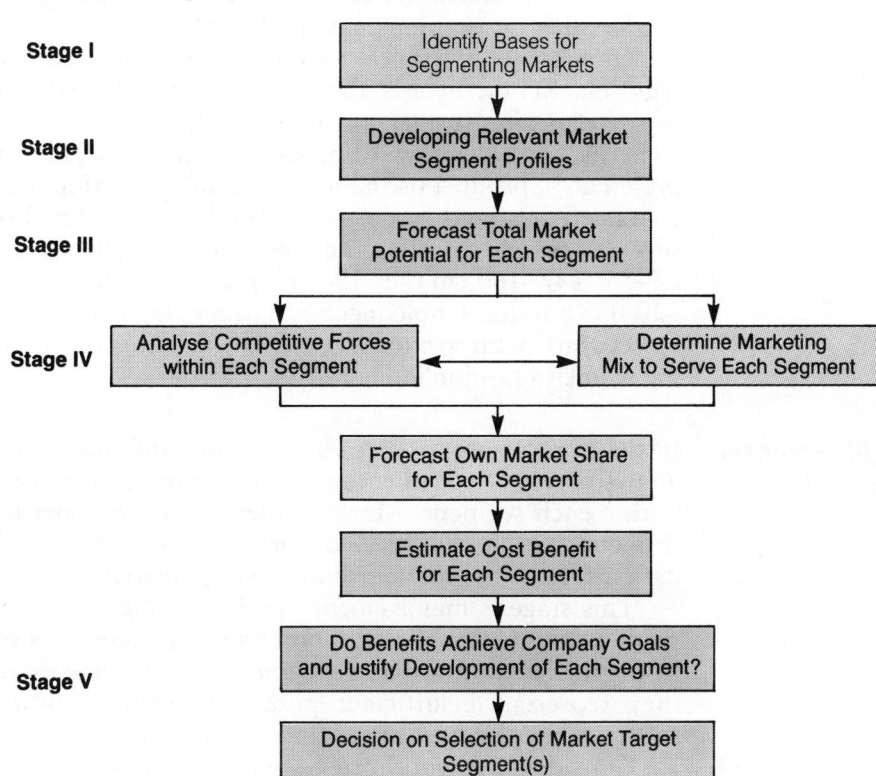

so that each segment contains customers who respond similarly to specific marketing mix alternatives. For example, before Procter & Gamble decides to market Crest to a segment made up of large families, management should be confident that most large families are interested in preventing tooth decay so they will be receptive to the Crest marketing offer. In some cases, this objective is difficult to achieve. Consider the marketer seeking to reach the consumer segment that is over 50 years of age. Saturday evening television commercials can reach this group, but much of the expenditure may be wasted since the other major viewer group is comprised of teenagers.[3]

*Stage II: Develop Relevant Profiles for Each Segment*

Once segments have been identified, marketers should seek to understand the customer in each segment.

Segmentation bases provide some insight into the nature of customers, but typically not enough for the kinds of decisions that

---

[3] Fred Rothenberg, "Saturday-Night Television Isn't What Is Used to Be," *The Seattle Times* (July 31, 1982), p. B 8.

marketing managers must make. Managers need more precise descriptions of customers in order to match marketing offers to their needs. Such descriptions can explain the similarities among customers within each segment as well as account for differences among segments. In other words, the task at this stage is to develop profiles of the typical customer in each segment with regard to lifestyle patterns, attitudes toward product attributes and brands, brand preferences, product use habits, geographic location, demographic characteristics, and so on. For example, one regional retail chain surveyed female customers and identified the following profile: age 25–55; 147–160 cm tall; 38–55 kg; career oriented, and having a $20 000 plus household income. The retailer used this profile to set up separate petite sections, one of the fastest growing segments of the women's fashion industry.[4]

**Stage III: Forecast Market Potentials**

In the third stage, market segmentation and market opportunity analysis are used together to produce a forecast of market potential within each segment. Market potential is the upper limit on the demand that can be expected from a segment and, combined with data on the firm's market share, sales potential.

This stage is management's preliminary go or no-go decision point as to whether the sales potential in a segment is sufficient to justify further analysis. Some segments will be screened out because they represent insufficient potential demand; others will be sufficiently attractive for the analysis to continue.

Consider the toothbrush part of the dental supply and mouthwash market — a multi-million dollar annual market. Dentists say that people should buy three of four toothbrushes a year for efficient brushing, but the current annual replacement rate is only 1.3.[5] If a marketer could convince the public to replace their toothbrushes when they should, market potential should almost triple.

**Stage IV: Forecast Probable Market Share**

Once market potential has been estimated, the share of that market that can be captured by the firm must be determined. This requires an analysis of competitors' positions in target segments. At the same time the specific marketing strategy and tactics should be designed for these segments. These two activities should lead to an analysis of the costs of tapping the potential demand in each segment.

---

[4] "Small Clothes Are Selling Big," *Business Week* (November 16, 1981), pp. 152, 156.
[5] Jennifer Alter, "Toothbrush Makers' Lament: Who Notices?" *Advertising Age* (October 4, 1982), p. 66.

Colgate once trailed Procter & Gamble nearly two to one in dishwashing liquids and also ran behind in heavy duty detergents and soaps. A realistic assessment indicated that for most directly competitive products they had little chance of overtaking P & G. So Colgate diversified its product line. Today, 75 percent of the firm's offerings do not face a directly competitive Procter & Gamble product, and those that do compete effectively.[6]

*Stage V: Select Specific Market Segments*

Finally the information, analyses, and forecasts accumulated through the process allow management to assess the potential for the achievement of company goals and justify the development of one or more market segments. Demand forecasts combined with cost projections are used to determine the profit and return on investment that can be expected from each segment. Analysis of marketing strategy and tactics will determine the degree of consistency with corporate image and reputation goals as well as with unique corporate capabilities that may be achieved by serving a segment. These assessments will, in turn, determine management's selection of specific segments as market targets.

At this point of the analysis the costs and benefits to be weighed are not just monetary, but include many difficult-to-measure but critical organizational and environmental factors. For example, the firm may not have enough experienced personnel to launch a successful attack on what clearly could be an almost certain monetary success. Similarly, a firm with 80 percent of the market may face legal problems with the federal Combines Branch if it increases its market concentration. The public utility may decide not to encourage higher electricity consumption because of environmental and political repercussions. The assessment of both financial and non-financial factors is a vital and final stage in the decision process.

There is not, and should not be, any simple answer to the market segmentation decision. The marketing concept's prescription to serve the customer's needs and to earn a profit while so doing implies that the marketer has to evaluate each possible marketing program on how it achieves this goal in the marketplace. By performing the detailed analysis outlined in Figure 5-2, the marketing manager can increase the probability of success in profitably serving consumers' needs.

---

6 Philip Kotler and Ravi Singh, "Basic Marketing Strategy for Winning Your Marketing War," *Marketing Times* (November/December 1982), pp. 23–24. This article is reprinted by permission from the *Journal of Business Strategy*, Vol. 1, No. 3, Winter 1981, Copyright © 1981, Warren, Gorham and Lamont, Inc., 210 South St., Boston, Mass. 02111. All rights reserved.

**Market Target**
**Decision Analysis**

Identifying specific market targets is an important aspect of overall marketing strategy. Clearly delineated market targets allow management to employ marketing efforts effectively like product development, distribution, pricing, and advertising to serve these markets.

**Market target decision analysis,** *the evaluation of potential market segments*, is a useful tool in the market segmentation process. Targets are chosen by segmenting the total market on the basis of any given characteristics (as described in Chapter 4). The example that follows illustrates how market target decision analysis can be applied.[7]

*A Useful Method of*
*Identifying Target*
*Markets*

One method of identifying target markets is simply to divide the total market into a number of boxes or cells. Each cell represents a potential target market. The definition of the cells can be based on consumer benefits desired, or geographic, demographic and psychographic characteristics, or some combination of these. While this concept is simple, it can be extremely complex in practice, and creativity is often required.

Consider the decisions of an airline company marketing manager wishing to analyse the market potential for various levels of passenger service. The company wants to delineate all possible market targets, and to assess the most profitable multi-offer strategy.

As a tool to outline the scope of the market, the marketing manager devises a grid like the one in Figure 5-3. This enables the company to match the possible types of service offerings with various customer classifications. The process of developing the target market grid forces the decision-maker to consider the entire range of possible market matching strategies. New or previously underserved segments may be uncovered. The framework also encourages an assessment of the sales potential in each of the possible segments, and aids in the proper allocation of marketing efforts to areas of greatest potential.

Having the cells of the grid identified helps the marketer to evaluate the wants, needs, and motivations of each market segment. For example, it appears that senior executives would be the appropriate targets for first-class service and extra-service categories. Further research could confirm or modify these evaluations and enable the marketer to determine whether the market size is worth developing a special offering for, and if so, what the marketing mix should

[7] A similar analysis is suggested in Robert M. Fulmer, *The New Marketing* (New York: Macmillan, 1976), pp. 34–37; Philip Kotler, *Marketing Management* (Englewood Cliffs, N.J.: Prentice-Hall, 1976), pp. 141–151; and E. Jerome McCarthy, *Basic Marketing* (Homewood, Ill.: Richard D. Irwin, 1975), pp. 111–126.

**Figure 5-3  Market for Airline Passenger Travel**

Type of Service

| Market | First Class | Extra Service Business Class | Regular Tourist Class | Seat Sale Class | Age Specials | Charter |
|---|---|---|---|---|---|---|
| Senior Executives | X | X | ? | | | X |
| Employees of large firms | | X | X | ? | | X |
| Employees of small business | | X | X | X | | |
| Wealthy Individuals | X | X | | | | ? |
| Other Individuals | | | X | X | | X |
| Senior Citizens | | | ? | X | X | X |
| Youth | | | X | X | X | X |

X = Probable demand for service
? = Uncertain or limited demand

**Figure 5-4  Employees of Large Firms Extra Service Class**

| Service Benefit Desired | Heavy Traffic Regions | Southern Canada | North. Canada |
|---|---|---|---|
| Schedules | X | | |
| Food | | | |
| Attendent service | | | |
| Leg Room | | | |

be. *Market segmentation thus enables appropriate marketing mix design.*

The cross-classification in Figure 5-4 shows that the matrix can be further subdivided to gather more specific data about the characteristics of the proposed market target and to accurately develop a suitable marketing mix. The potential bases for segmenting markets is virtually limitless. For example, the segments might have been based on psychographic data, or on the basis of benefits sought. In the latter instance, prestige, comfort, and basic transportation might be some benefits which would assist in designing market offerings. Such divisions are sometimes made intuitively in the first place, but the final decisions are usually supported by concrete data.[8]

**Using Market Target Decision Analysis in Assessing a Product Mix**

**Product mix,** a concept in Chapter 11, refers to *the assortment of product lines and individual offerings available from a marketer.* Market target decision analysis can be used to assess a firm's product mix and to point up needed modifications. For example, one telephone company has used the concept to evaluate its product offerings.[9] The company segments the total market by psychographic categories as shown in Figure 5-5. Two of these categories are "belongers," and "achievers." Belongers were defined in this instance as those who are motivated by emotional and group influences. Achievers were defined as those whose dominant characteristic is the need to get ahead.

**Figure 5-5   Using Market Target Decision Analysis to Evaluate a Product Mix**

|  | Belongers | Achievers | Etc. |
|---|---|---|---|
| Romantic | Phone M<br>Phone A<br>Phone C |  |  |
| Character |  | Phone R<br>Phone Y |  |
| Message-Centre | Phone T |  |  |
| Contemporary |  |  |  |

Source: Reprinted from "Properly Applied Psychographics Add Marketing Luster," *Marketing News* (November 12, 1982), p. 10.

The telephone company's rule is to offer two and only two types of telephone sets in a given market segment in order not to have too complicated a market offering. The belonger segment was thus offered a regular phone and a romantic-type telephone to appeal to their sentiments. Achievers were offered the regular phone plus one designed to conote the idea of efficiency and character. This analysis helped to select a product from the assortment shown in Figure 5-5.

---

[8] A good example of this systematic approach to identifying a precise market target appears in Richard P. Carr, Jr., "Developing a New Residential Market for Carpeting: Some Mistakes and Successes," *Journal of Marketing* (July 1977), pp. 101–2.

[9] "Properly Applied Psychographics Add Marketing Luster," *Marketing News* (November 12, 1982), p. 10.

# Try Your Hand at Selecting Market Targets

For each of the following situations or products, pick the market target cells for which you would aim. The actual customer profiles are shown overleaf.

*Exercise A: Gourmet Food Market*   A type of store that features higher-priced, top-of-the-line gourmet foods.

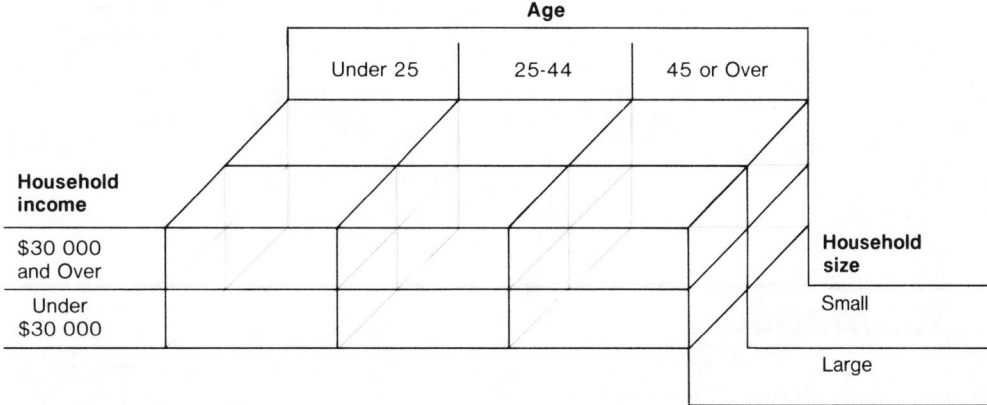

*Exercise B: Workbench*   A 700 000 circulation magazine that is aimed at those who consider craftsmanship their hobby.

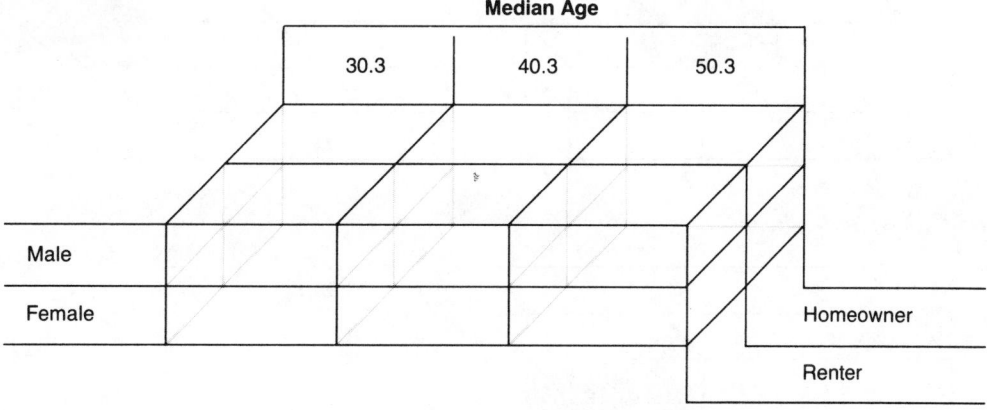

*Exercise C: Mercedes-Benz*
Some models run in the
$50 000 range. This
exercise refers to
American buyers only.

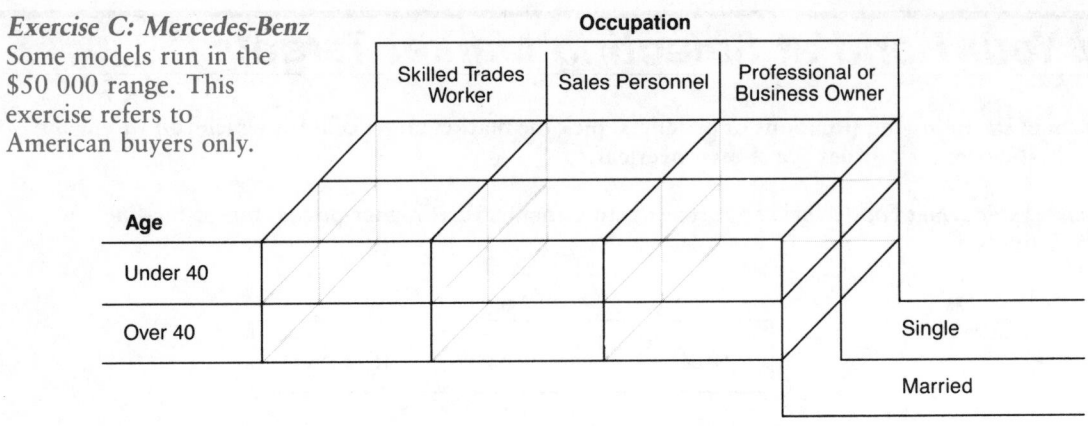

# *The Solutions*

The actual customer profiles of these items is as
follows.

*Exercise A: Gourmet Food Market*

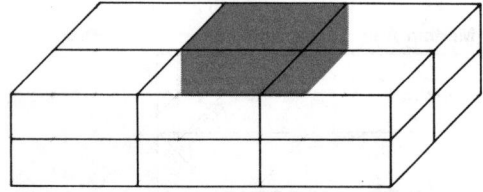

*Exercise B: Workbench Magazine*

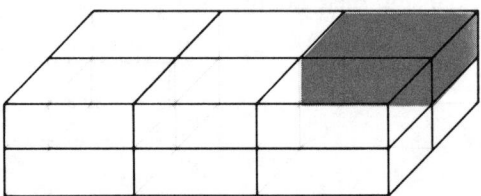

*Exercise C: Mercerdes-Benz*

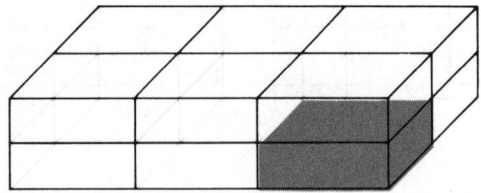

Source: Janet Guyon, "Gourmet-Food Market Grows as Affluent Shoppers Indulge," *The Wall Street Journal* (May 6, 1982), p. 31; "Magazine Publisher Advertisers' Target Growing, 'Overlooked' Empty Nest Market," *Marketing News* (October 2, 1981), pp. 1, 10; and "Rolling Along," *Fortune* (December 14, 1981), p. 13.

Market target decision analysis can go beyond merely identifying market targets. It can play a crucial role in actually developing marketing strategies such as product mixes.

## Product Positioning

After a target market has been selected, the next task is to develop a market mix that will enable your product to compete effectively against others which are already in that market segment. It is unlikely that success will be achieved with a mix that is virtually identical to competitors for they already have attained a place in the minds of individuals in the target market and are used by a portion of them. Since people have a variety of needs and tastes, market acceptance is more easily achieved by **positioning** — *shaping the product and developing a market mix in such a way that the product is perceived to be* (and actually is) *different from competitors' products.*

This process requires a careful analysis of the features and strengths of competitive offerings, as well as a good understanding of the needs and wants of the target market. From comparing the two, the marketer tries to find a significant sized niche which is presently poorly served, and develops a marketing mix to fit that opportunity. Positioning generally goes beyond the simple use of promotion to differentiate a product or service in the mind of the customer, although this is often an important aspect.

7-Up used promotion as the sole element in positioning. The firm discovered that its product was missing the primary market for soft drinks — children, teenagers and young adults — because 7-Up's image was a mixer for older people's drinks. The firm used its now well-known "Uncola" campaign, first to identify the product as a soft drink, and then to position it as an alternative to colas in the soft drink market.

Another classic positioning campaign was Avis positioning itself against Hertz with the theme, "Avis is only number two, so why go with us? Because we try harder." In this instance, the service was also adjusted to make the claim true.

An example of the use of a total marketing mix package in market positioning is the case of Digital Equipment Corporation (DEC). This firm successfully carved out a niche in the small computer marketplace by identifying a competitive gap in IBM's domination of the computer market. IBM had concentrated on large mainframe applications, and had paid little attention to smaller business applications. The computer giant had easily fended off the efforts of many other major marketers such as Xerox, General Electric, and Singer, to crack IBM's hold on computer sales. A major error by these firms was their attempt to position their products in direct competition to IBM's mainframe computers. However, IBM's image as "the major computer producer" was too strongly entrenched in the minds of potential purchasers. They were unwilling to risk a major expenditure on a large computer from a newcomer.

All of these new competitors eventually pulled out of the mainframe market. However, by designing a minicomputer to fit the market niche it had discovered, and supporting it with a complementary marketing mix, DEC was able to capture a portion of the small computer market. Whether it can remain in that market over the long run remains to be seen. However, the use of product positioning to evaluate and develop marketing strategies in light of competitive offerings in the market is a useful and basic concept. It should follow naturally from the market segmentation decision.

## Summary

This chapter continues the discussion of market segmentation introduced in Chapter 4. Various strategies associated with the market segmentation concept are considered here.

Correct strategy decisions are dependent upon a host of situational variables. The basic determinants of market matching strategy are: 1) company resources, 2) degree of product homogeneity, 3) stage in the product life cycle, and 4) competitors' strategies.

In light of an analysis of the market potential as well as these situational variables, the firm determines whether to adopt a single or multi-offer strategy. It then proceeds to position its offering(s) in the market with a marketing mix that will make it the most competitive.

The market segmentation process follows a sequential framework consisting of five stages. These stages can be outlined as follows:

- Stage 1. Determine the bases upon which markets can be segmented.
- Stage 2. Develop consumer profiles for the appropriate market segments.
- Stage 3. Assess the overall market potential for the relevant market segments.
- Stage 4. Estimate market share and cost benefit of each market segment given the existing competition and the marketing mix that is selected.
- Stage 5. Select the segments that will become the firm's market targets.

Market target decision analysis is a useful tool in the market segmentation process. A grid is developed that outlines the various market segments by their distinguishing characteristics. All bases for segmentation can be employed in market target decision analysis.

In addition to selecting the actual market target segments, the type of analysis can also be used for assessing the firm's current and planned product mix.

Part Two began with a chapter on marketing planning and forecasting. This chapter dealt with the concept of market segmentation. In the next chapter, attention shifts to the research procedures and techniques used to acquire information for building effective marketing strategies. Chapter 6 covers marketing research and information systems and concludes Part Two.

| **Key Terms** | single-offer strategy | positioning |
| --- | --- | --- |
| | multi-offer strategy | market target decision analysis |
| | product mix | |

**Review Questions**

1. Outline the basic features of a single-offer strategy.
2. Outline the basic features of a multi-offer strategy.
3. Outline the rationale of market matching strategies.
4. What are the primary determinants of product market strategy selection?
5. List and describe the five stages of the market segmentation process.
6. What is meant by market target decision analysis?
7. Show how market target decision analysis can help select market segments that the firm should attempt to reach.
8. Illustrate how the four consumer-oriented segmentation bases can be used in market target decision analysis.
9. Illustrate how the three industrial market segmentation bases can be used in market target decision analysis.
10. How can market target decision analysis be used to assess a product mix?

**Discussion Questions and Exercises**

1. What can be learned from the Corporate Foods example at the beginning of the chapter? Discuss.
2. Prepare a term paper on an actual firm employing marketing segmentation in the development of its marketing strategy.
3. Identify the conditions where a single-offer market matching strategy would be appropriate and those where a multi-offer would be.
4. Prepare a report that traces an actual company's experience as it moved through the various market segmentation stages.
5. Assess a firm's actual product mix using market target decision analysis.

# CHAPTER 6

# Marketing Research and Information Systems

## CHAPTER OBJECTIVES

1. To relate marketing research and information systems to the elements of the marketing mix.

2. To describe the development and current status of the marketing research function.

3. To list the steps in the marketing research process.

4. To differentiate the types and sources of primary and secondary data.

5. To identify the methods of collecting survey data.

6. To explain the various sampling techniques.

7. To distinguish between marketing research and marketing information systems.

8. To describe the current status of marketing information systems.

Marketing research played a vital role in the design, development, and marketing of Kodak's successful Disc Camera, says John J. Powers*, vice president–director of marketing communications, Eastman Kodak Co. Essentially, careful marketing research discovered a market segment that could be better served with new technology.

The photographic industry enjoys widespread consumer satisfaction with existing products. Simple-to-use, cartridge-loading cameras were extremely popular in the late 1970s. However, sales peaked in 1978 because the market was saturated. Consumers were generally very happy with the cameras they had already bought, and were willing to live with their limitations. Only those in the ranks of advanced amateurs invested significantly more time and money in the more complex world of 35 mm photography.

This situation challenged Kodak to restimulate the amateur photographic market. Kodak already knew that adding new features to its basic camera would not make it more attractive. After a point, more features interfered with an automatic camera's simplicity and

---

* John Powers, "Credit Success of Kodak Disc Camera to Research," *Marketing News*, January 21, 1983, pp. 8–9.

resulted in unwanted complexities for the picture-taker. So Kodak marketing researchers were given a two-fold objective: to determine under what conditions consumers were and more importantly *were not* taking pictures.

With the answers to the second part of the question, Kodak set out to develop a photographic system that could function well under the conditions that made photography unappealing to consumers. From a technical viewpoint they were looking at a total systems approach to solving a photographic problem uncovered by behavioural research. The result was the disc format and a number of breakthroughs in optics, electronics, and manufacturing technology, which Kodak utilized to produce its Disc Camera. The product is compact, easy to load and to use, and fits the picture-taking needs of a substantial segment of casual picture-takers.

From conception to introduction, marketing research played a key role in this innovative product line. Research findings were instrumental in determining the need for the products, in designing them to meet specific consumer wants and ultimately selling them. At later stages, research indicated a very high intent to purchase, and Kodak was able to set some high sales goals. Actual sales of film, cameras, and photofinishing equipment far exceeded the firm's most optimistic projections.

## The Conceptual Framework

It has been said that the recipe for effective decisions is 90 percent information and 10 percent inspiration. All marketing strategy decisions depend on the type, quantity, and quality of the information on which they are based. A variety of sources of marketing information are available to the decision-maker. Some are well-planned investigations designed to elicit specific information. Other valuable sources are sales force reports, accounting data, or published reports. Controlled experiments or computer simulations can elicit still more information.[1]

A major source of information takes the form of market research. **Marketing research** has been defined as "*the systematic gathering, recording, and analysing of data about problems relating to the marketing of goods and services.*"[2]

The critical task of the marketing manager is decision-making.

---

[1] An excellent article on knowledge needs is Calvin P. Duncan and Charles M. Lillis, "Directions for Marketing Knowledge Development: Opinions of Marketing Research Managers," *Journal of the Academy of Marketing Science* (Winter 1982), pp. 2a, 36.

[2] Committee on Definitions, *Marketing Definitions: A Glossary of Marketing Terms* (Chicago, American Marketing Association, 1960), p. 17. Italics added.

Managers earn their salaries by making effective decisions that enable their firms to solve problems as they arise, and by anticipating and preventing the occurrence of future problems. Many times though, they are forced to make decisions with limited information of uncertain accuracy and with inadequate facts. Marketing research aids the decision-maker by presenting pertinent facts, analysing them and suggesting possible action.

Chapter 6 deals with the marketing research function. Marketing research is closely linked with the other elements of the marketing planning process. All marketing research should be done within the framework of the organization's strategic plan. Research projects should be directed toward the resolution of marketing decisions that conform to an overall corporate strategy. Alfred S. Boote, the marketing research director for the Singer Company, estimates that research costs 50 to 60 percent more for firms that lack a strategic marketing plan because too much useless information is collected.[3]

Much of the material outlined in Chapters 4 and 5 on market segmentation and market target analysis is based on information collected through marketing research. Clearly, marketing research is the primary source of the information needed to make effective marketing decisions.

## An Overview of the Marketing Research Function

Before looking at how marketing research is actually done, it is important to get an overall perspective of the field. What activities are considered part of the marketing research function? How did the field develop? Who is involved in marketing research?

## Marketing Research Activities

All marketing decision areas are candidates for marketing research investigations. As Figure 6-1 indicates, marketing research efforts are commonly centred on developing sales forecasts for the firm's products, determining market and sales potential, designing new products and packages, analysing sales and marketing costs, evaluating the effectiveness of the firm's advertising, and determining consumer motives for buying products.

Marketing research in Canada may be said to have existed since there first were buyers and sellers. However, the day on which marketing research became a full-time profession was January 2, 1929. On that day, Henry King became the first full-time marketing

---

[3] "Include Marketing Research in Every Level of Corporate Strategic Planning," *Marketing News* (September 18, 1981), Section 2, p. 8.

**Figure 6-1   Marketing Research Activities of 798 Companies**

| Research Activity | Percentage of Companies Conducting the Activity |
|---|---|
| **Advertising Research** | |
| Motivation research | 48 |
| Copy research | 49 |
| Media research | 61 |
| Studies of advertising effectiveness | 67 |
| **Business Economic and Corporate Research** | |
| Short-range forecasting (up to a year) | 85 |
| Long-range forecasting (over a year) | 82 |
| Plant and warehouse location studies | 71 |
| Export and international studies | 51 |
| **Corporate Responsibility Research** | |
| Consumers' "right-to-know" studies | 26 |
| Ecological impact studies | 33 |
| Studies of legal constraints on advertising and promotion | 51 |
| Social values and policies studies | 40 |
| **Product Research** | |
| New-product acceptance and potential | 84 |
| Competitive product studies | 85 |
| Product testing | 75 |
| Packaging research | 60 |
| **Sales and Market Research** | |
| Measurement of market potentials | 93 |
| Market share analysis | 92 |
| Determination of market characteristics | 93 |
| Sales analyses | 89 |
| Establishment of sales quotas, territories | 75 |
| Distribution channel studies | 69 |
| Test markets, store audits | 54 |
| Consumer panel operations | 50 |

Source: Dik Warren Twedt, ed., *1978 Marketing Research* (Chicago: American Marketing Association, 1978), p. 41. Reprinted by permission.

researcher in Canada. His employer was an advertising agency, Cockfield Brown.[4]

In 1932, through the encouragement of Cockfield Brown, the first independent research company — Ethel Fulford and Associates — was founded in Toronto. In 1937, the Fulford company

[4] John A. Gonder, "Marketing Research in Canada," *Cases & Readings in Marketing* (Toronto: Holt, Rinehart and Winston, 1974), p. 221.

became known as Canadian Facts. By the end of World War II, four other major research companies had been established — Elliott-Haynes (now Elliott Research), the Canadian Institute of Public Opinion (Gallup Poll of Canada), A. C. Nielsen, and International Surveys. Since 1945, the number of research firms across Canada has grown dramatically.[5]

**Participants in the Marketing Research Function**

Many of the nation's leading manufacturing firms have established their own formal marketing research departments. Although such operations are found mostly in companies manufacturing consumer products, a substantial increase in marketing research departments has occurred recently in financial service firms, such as banks, trust companies, other lending institutions, insurance companies, and major nonprofit organizations.[6] Total expenditures for marketing research in 1985 are estimated at more than $70 million. Many smaller firms depend on independent marketing research firms to conduct their research studies. Even large firms typically rely on outside agencies to provide interviews, and they often farm out some research studies to independent agencies as well.[7] The decision whether to conduct a study internally or through an outside organization is usually based on cost and the reliability of the information collected by the agency.

Research is likely to be contracted to outside groups when:

1.  Problem areas can be defined in terms of specific research projects that can easily be delegated.
2.  There is a need for specialized know-how or equipment.
3.  Intellectual detachment is important.[8]
    A marketing research firm is often able to provide technical assistance and expertise not available within the firm. Also, the use of outside groups helps ensure that the researcher is not conducting the study only to validate the wisdom of a favourite theory or a preferred package design.

---

5 Jo Marney, "Beyond the 6 P's of Marketing Research," *Marketing*, April 25, 1983, p. 8.
6 Estimate based on Frances Phillips, "Why It Pays to be a Pollster," *The Financial Post*, June 4, 1983, p. 1.
7 Increased use of such groups in the future is predicted in Linden A. Davis, "What's Ahead in Marketing Research?" *Journal of Advertising Research* (June 1981), pp. 49–51.
8 Bertram Schoner and Kenneth P. Uhl, *Marketing Research: Information Systems and Decision Making* (New York: John Wiley & Sons, Inc., 1975), p.199.

Marketing research companies can be classified as either syndicated services, full-service suppliers, or limited-service suppliers depending upon the primary thrust of the organization.[9]

Syndicated Services   A **syndicated service** is *an organization that offers to provide a standardized set of data on a regular basis to all who wish to buy it.* The Consumer Panel of Canada gathers information on consumer purchases of food and other household items from 3400 households that periodically report a detailed list of all food and other household products purchased during a particular time. This information can be extremely useful in determining brand preferences, the effects of various promotional activities on retail sales in one region or among a particular age group, and the degree of brand switching that occurs with certain products.

## Marketing Research in Action

—Hershey Canada recently launched a line of milder-flavoured milk chocolate bars after surveys indicated that Canadians preferred a light, creamy chocolate. The company expects to pick up three extra market-share points within a year by developing a product, and marketing strategy based on continued marketing research.

—Canadian National Railways commissioned several research projects to find out what kind of new railway car might better serve the needs of CN customers. In one project, they hired students to count the number of tractor trailers travelling the Toronto–Montreal corridor. As a result of their findings, CN introduced the Laser piggy-back service on the Toronto–Montreal run.

—Marketing research showed the Ontario government that it had the wrong theme in its "Rally Round Ontario," advertising program. Tourists felt that they were being asked to rally round a sinking ship. The findings led to the much more successful theme, "Yours to Discover."

Source: Adapted from Frances Phillips, "Why It Pays To Be a Pollster," *The Financial Post*, June 14, 1983, p. 2.

Full-Service Research Suppliers   **Full-service research suppliers** *contract with a client to conduct the complete marketing research project.* Full-service research suppliers start at the problem definition or conceptualization stage; work through the research design, data collection, and analysis states; and prepare the final report to management. Full-service research suppliers literally become the client's marketing research arm.

---

[9] The classification and definitions of marketing research companies are based on William G. Zikmund, *Exploring Marketing Research* (Hinsdale Ill.: The Dryden Press, 1982), pp. 79–81.

**Limited-Service Research Suppliers**   **Limited-service research suppliers** are *organizations that specialize in a limited number of marketing research activities*. Companies that provide field interviews are the best example. Still others might provide data processing services. A syndicated service is a particular type of limited-service research supplier.

*The Marketing Research Process*

How is marketing research actually conducted? The starting point, of course, is the need for information on which to base a marketing decision, whether it be a specific question or an ongoing set of decisions. If need for information is perceived, the marketing research process can be invoked.

**Figure 6-2   The Marketing Research Process**

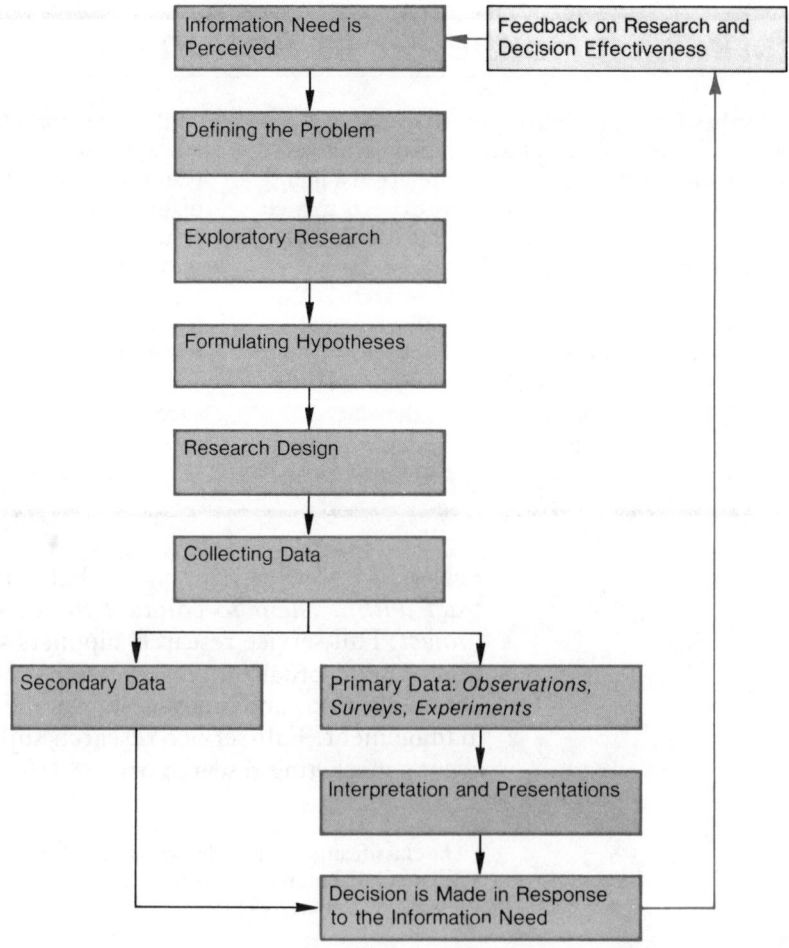

The marketing research process can be divided into six specific steps: 1) defining the problem; 2) exploratory research; 3) formulating a hypothesis; 4) research design; 5) collecting data; and 6) interpretation and presentation.

Figure 6-2 diagrams the marketing research process from information need to the research-based decision.

**Problem Definition**      Someone once remarked that well-defined problems are half solved. Problems are barriers that prevent the accomplishment of organizational goals. A clearly defined problem permits the researcher to focus the research process to secure the data necessary to solve the problem. Sometimes it is easy to pinpoint problems. Top executives at one airline company stood in airport line-ups in order to spot passenger complaints. The two most common gripes were inadequate flight information and cold in-flight coffee.[10] Once these problems were identified, they were corrected without further research.

However, it is often difficult to determine the specific problem, since what the researcher may be confronted with may be only symptoms of an underlying problem. In the late 1970s, Ciba-Geigy was stunned when its newly acquired Airwick Industries suffered $2 million loss on sales of such products as liquid room fresheners. When the parent firm investigated the problem, it recognized the losses as symptoms of a bitter price war in this market and that Airwick needed a more systematic method of developing and introducing product innovations to keep pace with competition. In order to solve the problems facing the firm, management had to look *beyond* the symptoms.

**Exploratory Research**   *In searching for the cause of a problem the researcher will learn about the problem area and begin to focus on specific areas for study.* This search, often called **exploratory research**, consists of discussing the problem with informed sources within the firm and with wholesalers, retailers, customers and others outside the firm, and examining secondary sources of information. Marketing researchers often refer to internal data collection as the *situation analysis* and to exploratory interviews with informed persons outside the firm as the *informal investigation.* Exploratory research also involves evaluating company records, such as sales and profit analyses of its own and its competitors' products. Figure 6-3 provides a checklist of topics to be considered in an exploratory analysis.

---

[10] Reported in Priscilla A. La Barbera and Larry J. Rosenberg, "How Marketers Can Better Understand Consumers," *MSU Business Topics* (Winter 1980), p. 29.

## Figure 6-3   Topics for the Exploratory Analysis

| | |
|---|---|
| **The Company and Industry** | 1. Company objectives<br>2. The companies in the industry (size, financial power) and industry trends<br>3. Geographic locations of the industry<br>4. The company's market share as compared with competitors'<br>5. Marketing policies of competitors |
| **The Market** | 1. Geographic location<br>2. Demographic characteristics of the market<br>3. Purchase motivations<br>4. Product use patterns<br>5. Nature of demand |
| **Products** | 1. Physical characteristics<br>2. Consumer acceptance — strengths and weaknesses<br>3. Package as a container and as a promotional device<br>4. Manufacturing processes, production capacity<br>5. Closeness and availability of substitute products |
| **Marketing Channels** | 1. Channels employed and recent trends<br>2. Channel policy<br>3. Margins for resellers |
| **Sales Organization** | 1. Market coverage<br>2. Sales analysis by number of accounts per salesperson, size of accounts, type of account, etc.<br>3. Expense ratios for various territories, product types, account size, etc.<br>4. Control procedures<br>5. Compensation methods |
| **Pricing** | 1. Elasticity<br>2. Season or special promotional price cuts<br>3. Profit margins of resellers<br>4. Legal restrictions<br>5. Price lines |
| **Advertising and Sales Promotion** | 1. Media employed<br>2. Dollar expenditures as compared with competitors<br>3. Timing of advertising<br>4. Sales promotional materials provided for resellers<br>5. Results from previous advertising and sales promotional campaigns |

**Formulating
Hypotheses**

After the problem has been defined and an exploratory investigation conducted, the marketer should be able to formulate a **hypothesis**, *a tentative explanation about the relationship between variables as a starting point for further testing.*

A marketer of industrial products might formulate the following hypothesis:

> *Failure to provide 36-hour delivery service will reduce our sales by 20 percent.*

Such a statement may prove correct or incorrect. The formulation of this hypothesis does, however, provide a basis for investigation and an eventual determination of its accuracy. It also allows the researcher to move to the next step: development of the research design.

Lever Brothers' Pepsodent toothpaste had been on the market since 1944, but by the mid-1960s surveys were indicating that young consumers were dissatisfied with current offerings in two areas: tooth whitening and breath freshening. Lever Brothers began to work on a hypothesis that a combination toothpaste and mouth-wash could become a successful market entry. The end result of the firm's hypothesis testing was Close-up toothpaste.[11]

**Research Design**

The research design should be a comprehensive plan for testing the hypotheses formulated about the problem. **Research design** refers to *a series of advance decisions that, taken together, make up a master plan or model for the conduct of the investigation.* Development of such a plan allows the researcher to control each step of the research process. Figure 6-4 lists the steps involved in the research design.

**Data Collection**

A major step in the research design is the determination of what data are needed to test the hypotheses. Two types of data are typically used: primary data and secondary data. **Primary data** refer to *data being collected for the first time* during a marketing research study, and for reasons that will become apparent will be discussed at length later in the chapter.

**Secondary data** are *previously published matter.* They serve as an extremely important source of information for the marketing researcher.

**Collecting
Secondary Data**

Not only are secondary data important, they are also abundant in many areas that the marketing researcher may need to investigate. In fact,

---

[11] "Marketing Oriented Lever Uses Research to Capture Bigger Dentifrice Market Shares," *Marketing News* (February 10, 1978), p. 9.

### Figure 6-4  Sixteen Steps in the Research Design

| Questions Faced | Steps to Take or Choices |
|---|---|
| 1. What is needed to measure the outcome of the alternative solutions? | 1. Decide the subjects on which data are needed.<br>2. Examine the time and cost considerations. |
| 2. What specific data are needed for that approach? | 3. Write exact statements of data to be sought. |
| 3. From whom are such data available? | 4. Search and examine relevant secondary data.<br>5. Determine remaining data gaps. |
| 4. How should primary data be obtained? | 6. Define the population from which primary data may be sought. |
|   a. What are the types of data? | 7. Determine the various needed facts, opinions, and motives. |
|   b. What general collection methods shall be used? | 8. Plan for obtaining data by survey, observational, or experimental methods. |
|   c. How shall the sources be contacted? | 9. If using a survey, decide whether to contact respondents by telephone, by mail, or in person. |
|   d. How may the data be secured from the sources? | 10. Consider the questions and forms needed to elicit and record the data. |
|   e. Shall there be a complete count of the population or a sample drawn from it? How chosen? | 11. Decide on the coverage of the population:<br>  a. Choose between a complete enumeration and a sampling.<br>  b. If sampling, decide whether to select from the whole population or restricted portions of it.<br>  c. Decide how to select sample members. |
|   f. How will the fieldwork be conducted? | 12. Map and schedule the fieldwork. |
| 5. How will the data be interpreted and presented? | 13. Plan the personnel requirements of the field study.<br>14. Consider editing and tabulating requirements.<br>15. Anticipate possible interpretation of the data, and be sure it can answer the research questions which need answering.<br>16. Consider the way the findings may be presented. |

Source: Adapted from David J. Luck, Hugh G. Wales, and Donald A. Taylor, *Marketing Research*, 3rd ed. (Englewood Cliffs, N.J.: Prentice-Hall, Inc., 1970), p. 87. Reprinted by permission.

the overwhelming quantity of secondary data available at little or no cost often challenges the researcher in the selection of only pertinent information.

Secondary data consists of two types: internal and external. *Internal secondary data* include records of sales, product performances, sales force activities, and marketing costs. *External data* are obtained from a variety of sources. Governments—local, provincial, and federal — provide a wide variety of secondary data. Private sources also supply secondary data for the marketing decision-maker. An appendix at the end of Part Two describes a wide range of data sources.

Government Sources   The federal government provides the country's most important sources of marketing data, the most frequently used being census data. Although the government spent millions of dollars in conducting the various Censuses of Canada, the information is available at no charge at local libraries and Statistics Canada offices, or it can be purchased at a nominal charge on computer tapes for instant electronic access. In fact, Statistics Canada produces several different censuses. Figure 6-5 briefly describes the main ones.

---

**Figure 6-5 Census Data Collected by Statistics Canada**

*Census of Canada.* Conducted once each decade, with certain categories checked every five years. It provides a count of all residents of Canada by province, city or town, county or other suitable division, and, in large cities, by census tract. Particularly useful to marketers is the data provided by economic rather than political boundaries, such as greater metropolitan areas. Data is also gathered on age, sex, race, citizenship, educational levels, occupation, employment status, income and family status of inhabitants. A less detailed census is conducted at the half-way point in the decade.

*Census of Housing.* Provides information regarding the housing conditions of Canadians, such as value of the dwelling, number of rooms, type of structure, ethnic origin of occupants, and year built.

*Census of Manufacturers.* Annual coverage of major industries revealing the value of products produced by industry, cost of materials and equipment, number of establishments, and wages paid.

*Census of Agriculture.* Conducted every five years. Data regarding the number of farms, number of persons residing on farms (by age and sex), value of farm products sold, area of each major crop, number of tractors, number of livestock, presence of electricity and running water.

*Census of Minerals.* Data on employees, wages, quantities produced, cost of materials and supplies, types of equipment used, and hours worked.

The 1981 data are so detailed for large cities that breakdowns of population characteristics are available for a few city blocks (census tracts). Thus local retailers or shopping centre developers can easily gather detailed information about the immediate neighbourhoods that will constitute their customers without spending time or money in conducting a comprehensive survey.

So much data is produced by the federal government that the marketing researcher often purchases summaries such as the *Canada Year Book* or *Market Research Handbook* or subscribes to *Statistics Canada Daily*. It is also possible to receive *Informat Weekly*, which provides a listing of new releases by Statistics Canada. A further source of Statistics Canada data is the *Statistics Canada Catalogue*, which lists major data published by the agency. Furthermore, the researcher can gain access to unpublished data through on-line terminals at Statistics Canada User Advisory Services Centres.

Provincial and city governments are other important sources of information on employment, production, and sales activities within a particular province.

---

**Figure 6-6    A Page From *Handbook of Canadian Consumer Markets*. It Provides Many Types of Data for the Marketing Researcher**

**Family Expenditures on Foods at Home and Away, 1982**
(average urban family[1] expenditures on food = 100%)

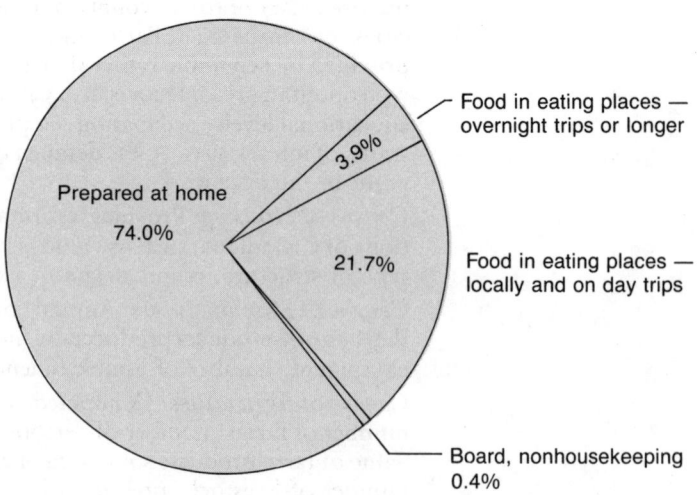

Note: Data are based on the 1982 16-city Survey of Urban Family Expenditure.
[1]Figures include all families and unattached individuals.

---

Source: Statistics Canada; The Conference Board of Canada.

**Family Expenditures on Food at Home and Away**
(average expenditures on food, urban families[1])

| Item | Expenditure (dollars) 1978 | Expenditure (dollars) 1982 | Percentage distribution 1978 | Percentage distribution 1982 |
|---|---|---|---|---|
| **Total, food** .............................. | **3063.8** | **4350.0** | **100.0** | **100.0** |
| Prepared at home ...................... | 2131.5 | 3219.5 | 69.6 | 74.0 |
|   Locally and on day trips ............ | n.a. | 3183.9 | n.a. | 73.2 |
|   Overnight trips or longer ........... | n.a. | 35.5 | n.a. | 0.8 |
| Board paid to private households ... | 8.3 | 18.8 | 0.3 | 0.4 |
| Food purchased in restaurants ....... | 893.9 | 1111.8 | 29.2 | 25.6 |
|   Locally and on day trips ............ | 694.7 | 941.7 | 22.7 | 21.6 |
|     At work ............................. | n.a. | 369.7 | n.a. | 8.5 |
|     At school .......................... | n.a. | 36.7 | n.a. | 0.8 |
|     Other ............................... | n.a. | 441.5 | n.a. | 10.1 |
|     Between-meal ...................... | n.a. | 93.7 | n.a. | 2.2 |
|   On overnight trips or longer ....... | 199.2 | 170.2 | 6.5 | 3.9 |
|     On a job ........................... | 8.8 | 16.3 | 0.3 | 0.4 |
|     At school .......................... | 25.0 | 9.2 | 0.8 | 0.2 |
|     On vacation ....................... | 165.4 | 144.6 | 5.4 | 3.3 |
| Meals prepared on a trip .............. | 28.1 | n.a. | 0.9 | n.a. |

Note: All 1982 data are preliminary. The 1982 data are based on the Survey of Urban
Family Expenditure carried out by Statistics Canada in 16 major cities across Canada.
The 1978 data are based on a similar survey.
n.a.: Not available/applicable.
[1]Figures include all families and unattached individuals.
Sources: Statistics Canada; The Conference Board of Canada.

Source: *Handbook of Canadian Consumer Markets*, 3rd ed. (Ottawa: The Conference
Board of Canada, 1984), p. 147.

Private Sources   Numerous private organizations provide information for the marketing executive. In the *Handbook of Canadian
Consumer Markets* published by The Conference Board of Canada
the marketer will find a wide range of illuminating and valuable
data. Figure 6-6 illustrates the type of information collected for each
of the provinces. Another excellent source is *Canadian Markets* published by *The Financial Post*. Other good summary data can be found
in the annual survey of buying power published by *Sales & Marketing Management* magazine. For activities in a particular industry,
trade associations are excellent resource sources. Advertising agencies continually collect information on the audiences reached by various media.

Several national firms offer information to business firms on a
subscription basis. The largest of these, A. C. Nielsen Company,

collects data every two months on product sales, retail prices, display space, inventories, and promotional activities of competing brands of food and drug products from a substantial sample of food stores and drugstores. The Consumer Panel of Canada (International Surveys), mentioned earlier, gathers information on consumer purchases.

*Advantages and Limitations of Secondary Data*

The use of secondary data offers two important advantages over that of primary data:
1. The assembly of previously collected data is almost always less expensive than the collection of primary data.
2. Less time is involved in locating and using secondary data. Figure 6-7 shows the estimated time involved in completing a research study requiring primary data. The time involved will naturally vary considerably depending on such factors as the research subject and the scope of the study.

The researcher must be aware of two potential limitations to the use of secondary data: 1) the data may be obsolete, or 2) the classifications of the secondary data may not be usable in the study. Published information has an unfortunate habit of rapidly going out of date. A marketing researcher analysing the population of the Calgary metropolitan market in 1985 discovers that much of the 1981 census data is already obsolete due to the influx of people attracted by the development of the oil and gas industry.

**Figure 6-7   Time Requirements for a Primary Data Research Project**

| Step | Estimated Time Required For Completion |
|---|---|
| Problem Definition | Several Days |
| Development of Methodology | One Week |
| Questionnaire Design | One Week |
| Questionnaire Pretest and Evaluation of Pretest Results | Two Weeks |
| Field Interviews | One to Six Weeks |
| Coding of Returned Questionnaires | One week |
| Data Transfer to Computer Tape | One Week |
| Data Processing and Statistical Analysis | Seven to Ten Days |
| Interpretation of Output | One Week |
| Written Report and Presentation of Findings | Two Weeks |
| **Total Elapsed Time** | **12 to 17 Weeks** |

Source: Estimates by Alfred S. Boote, Corporate Director of Market Research, The Singer Company. Quoted in "Everyone Benefits from Closer Planning, Research Ties," *Marketing News* (January 9, 1981), p. 30. Used by permission of the American Marketing Association.

Data may also have been collected previously on such bases as county or city boundaries, when the marketing manager requires it broken down by city blocks or census tracts. In such cases the marketing researcher may not be able to rearrange the secondary data in a usable form and must begin the collection of primary data.

**Collecting Primary Data**   When secondary data is incomplete or does not relate to the problem at hand, the research design must call for a direct test of a hypothesis. Producers at Paramount Pictures were fearful that the death of Mr. Spock in *Star Trek II — The Wrath of Khan* would turn "Trekkies" against it, so the movie was shown to participants at a science-fiction meeting. The audience loved the movie, and Paramount Pictures decided to leave Mr. Spock dead.[12]

As Figure 6-4 indicated, the marketing researcher has three alternative methods for collecting primary data: observation, survey, or controlled experiment. No one method is best in all circumstances.

**The Observation Method**   Observational studies are conducted by actually viewing (either by visual observation or through mechanical means such as hidden cameras) the overt actions of the respondent.[13] This may take the form of traffic counts at a potential location for a fast-food franchise, a check of licence plates at a shopping centre to determine the area from which shoppers are attracted, or the use of supermarket scanners to record sales of certain products viewed.

The observation method has both advantages and drawbacks. Merits are that observation is often more accurate than questioning techniques like surveys and interviews, and that it may be the only way to get information such as actual shopping behaviour in a supermarket. It may also be the easiest way to get specific data. Limitations include observer subjectivity and errors in interpretation. For instance, the researchers might incorrectly classify people's economic status because of the way they were dressed at the time of observation.[14]

Eastman Kodak used the observation method in evaluating advertisements it scheduled for the launch of the Ektra camera. Perception Research Service was hired to study patterns of viewer eye movements when looking at advertisements featuring television actor Michael Landon. The eye-tracking tests resulted in Eastman Kodak's

---

12 "Marquee," *The Seattle Times* (May 16, 1982), p. H 4.
13 See A. Coskun Samli, "Observation as a Method of Fact Gathering in Marketing Decisions," *Business Perspectives* (Fall 1967), pp. 19ff.
14 Zikmund, *Exploring Marketing Research*, pp. 216–217.

moving the headline "Kodak introduces the Ektra pocket camera" from the bottom of the ad to the top, since a majority of eye movements flowed to the top.[15]

**The Survey Method**   The amount and type of information that can be obtained through mere observation of overt consumer acts is limited; the researcher must ask questions to obtain information on attitudes, motives, and opinions. The survey method is the most widely used approach to collecting primary data. There are three kinds of surveys: telephone, mail, and personal interviews.

*Telephone interviews* are inexpensive and fast in obtaining small quantities of relatively impersonal information. Many firms have leased WATS services, which reduce considerably the cost of long-distance calls.[16]

Telephone interviews account for 55 to 60 percent of all primary marketing research.[17] They are limited to simple, clearly worded questions. Such interviews have two drawbacks: it is extremely difficult to obtain personal characteristics of the respondent, and the survey may be prejudiced since two groups will be omitted — those households without telephones and those with unlisted numbers. One survey reported that alphabetical listings in telephone directories excluded one-fourth of large-city dwellers, and that they underrepresented service workers and separated and divorced persons. In addition, the mobility of the population creates problems in choosing names from telephone directories. As a result, a number of telephone interviewers have resorted to using digits selected at random and matched to telephone prefixes in the geographic area to be sampled. This technique is designed to correct the problem of sampling those with new telephone listings and those with unlisted numbers.[18]

---

15 John F. Cooney, "In Their Quest for Sure Fire Ads, Marketers Use Psychological Tests to Find Out What Grabs You," *The Wall Street Journal* (April 12, 1979), p. 40.

16 *Wide Area Telephone Service*, a telephone company service that allows a business firm to make unlimited long-distance calls for a fixed rate per region. See also Douglas J. Tigert, James G. Barnes, and Jacques C. Bourgeois, "Research on Research: Mail Panel Versus Telephone Survey in Retail Image Analysis," *The Canadian Marketer* (Winter 1975), pp. 22–27.

17 "Many Researchers Prefer Interviewing by Phone," *Marketing News* (July 14, 1978), p. 8.

18 Reported in A. B. Blankenship, "Listed versus Unlisted Numbers in Telephone-Survey Samples," *Journal of Advertising Research* (February 1977), pp. 39–42. See also Roger Gates, Bob Brobst, and Paul Solomon, "Random Digit Dialing: A Review of Methods," in *Proceedings of the Southern Marketing Association*, New Orleans, La. (November 1978), pp. 163–65; and Donald S. Tull and Gerald S. Albaum, "Bias in Random Digit-Dialed Surveys," *Public Opinion Quarterly* (Fall 1977), pp. 389–95.

# TeloFacts: Telephone Interviewing with Your Personal Computer

It is now possible to design on your personal computer a questionnaire for a telephone survey and then have the machine guide you through each interview. TeloFacts is a software package that shows you how to design and automate custom questionnaires and to gather marketing survey data quickly and easily.

After you have developed your questionnaire, you can sit in front of your computer and start calling respondents. As they answer, a single key stroke records the response. Answers can be easily corrected, removed, or "restored." TeloFacts will do the rest. It automatically pages to the next question and simultaneously tabulates answers.

When you have finished the survey, you can select how you wish to analyse the data. If you want to know the number of people between the ages of 25 and 45 who prefer product X, TeloFacts will display the answer on the screen, or on a printer. The software package also allows the researcher to display results in report format, with ranks, lists, or scores of respondents.

Systems like this expedite marketing research, and make it possible for even the smallest businesses and organizations to do the marketing research that is necessary for sound decision-making.

Source: Deborah Smithy-Willis, Jerry Willis, and Merl Miller, *How to Use TeloFacts* (Beaverton, Oregon: Dilithium Press, 1982).

*Mail interviews* allow the marketing researcher to conduct national studies at a reasonable cost. While personal interviews with a national sample may be prohibitive, by using the mail, the researcher can reach each potential respondent for the price of a postage stamp. Costs may be misleading, however, since *returned* questionnaires for such a study may average only 40 to 50 percent, depending upon the length of the questionnaire and respondent interest. When returns are even lower, the question arises as to the opinions of the majority who did not respond. Also, some surveys use a coin or other device to gain the reader's attention which further increases costs. Unless additional information is obtained from nonrespondents, the results of the study are likely to be biased, since there may be important differences between the characteristics of these people and of those who took the time to complete and return the questionnaire. For this reason a follow-up questionnaire is sometimes mailed to nonrespondents, or telephone interviews may be used to gather additional information.[19]

*Personal interviews* are typically the best means of obtaining more detailed information since the interviewer has the opportunity to

---

[19] Douglas R. Berdie and John F. Anderson, "Mail Questionnaire Response Rates: Updating Outmoded Thinking," *Journal of Marketing* (January 1976), pp. 71–73; A. Marvin Roscoe, Dorothy Lang, and Jagdish N. Sheth, "Follow-up Methods, Questionnaire Length, and Market Differences in Mail Surveys," *Journal of Marketing* (April 1975), pp. 20–27; and Richard T. Hise and Michael A. McGinnis, "Evaluating the Effect of a Follow-up Request on Mail Survey Results," *Akron Business and Economic Review* (Winter 1974), pp. 19–21.

establish rapport with the respondent. The interviewer can also explain questions that might be confusing or vague to the respondent. Mail questionnaires must be carefully worded and pretested to eliminate any potential misunderstanding by respondents. But misunderstandings can occur with even the most clearly worded questions. When a truck operated by a government agency accidentally killed a cow, an official responded with an apology and a form to be filled out. It included a space for "disposition of the dead cow." The farmer responded "kind and gentle."[20]

Personal interviews are slow and the most expensive method of collecting data. However, their flexibility coupled with the detailed information that can be collected often offset these limitations. Recently marketing research firms have rented locations in shopping centres where they have greater access to potential buyers of the products in which they are interested. Downtown retail districts and airports are other on-site locations for marketing-research.

*Focus group interviews* have been widely used in recent years as a means of gathering preliminary research information. In a **focus group interview** eight to 12 people are brought together to discuss a subject of interest. Although the moderator typically explains the purpose of the meeting and suggests an opening discussion topic, he or she is interested in stimulating interaction among group members in order to develop the discussion of numerous points about the subject. Focus group sessions, which are often one to two hours long, are usually taped so the moderator can devote full attention to the discussion.[21] This process gives the researcher an idea of how consumers view a problem. Often it uncovers points of view that the researcher had not thought of.

**The Experimental Method**   The final and least-used method of collecting marketing information is through the use of *controlled experiments*.[22] An experiment is a scientific investigation in which the researcher controls or manipulates a test group that did not receive the controls or manipulations. Such experiments can be conducted in the field or in a laboratory setting.

Although a number of experiments have been conducted in the controlled environment of a laboratory, most have been conducted in the field. To date, the most common use of this method has been in **test marketing**.

---

20 *The Wall Street Journal* (June 28, 1972), p. 1.
21 See Fred D. Reynolds and Deborah K. Johnson, "Validity of Focus-Group Findings," *Journal of Advertising Research* (June 1978), pp. 21–24; and Bobby J. Calder, "Focus Groups and the Nature of Qualitative Marketing Research," *Journal of Marketing Research* (August 1977), pp. 353–64.
22 For a thorough discussion, see Seymour Banks, *Experimentation in Marketing* (New York: McGraw-Hill Book Company, 1965).

Marketers face great risks in introducing products to the Canadian market. They often attempt to reduce this risk by *introducing the new, untried product into a particular metropolitan area and then observing its degree of success*. Frequently used cities include Calgary, Lethbridge, and Winnipeg. Consumers in the test-market city view the product as they do any other new product since it is in retail outlets and is advertised in the local media. The test-market city becomes a small replica of the total market. The marketing manager can then compare actual sales with expected sales and can project them on a nationwide basis. If the test results are favourable, the risks of a large-scale failure are reduced. Many products fail at the test-market stage, and thus consumers who live in these cities may purchase products that no one else will ever buy.

The major problem with controlled experiments is the difficult task of controlling all variables in a real-life situation. The laboratory scientist can rigidly control temperature and humidity, but how can the marketing manager determine the effect of varying the retail price through refundable coupons when the competition decides to retaliate or deliberately confuse the experiment by also issuing competitive coupons?

In the future, experimentation will become more frequent as firms develop more sophisticated simulated competitive models requiring computer analysis. Simulation of market activities promises to be one of the great new developments in marketing.

## Sampling Techniques

Sampling[23] is one of the most important aspects of marketing research. *The total group that the researcher wants to study* is called the **population** or **universe**. For a political campaign, the population would be all eligible voters. For a new cosmetic line, it might be all women in a certain age bracket. If this total group is contacted, the results are known as a **census**. Unless the group is small, the cost will be overwhelming. Even the federal government only attempts a full census once every ten years.

Information, therefore, is rarely gathered from the total population during a survey. Instead, researchers select a representative group called a sample. Samples can be classified as either probability samples or nonprobability samples. A **probability sample** is *one in which every member of the population has an equal chance of being selected*. **Nonprobability samples** are *arbitrary*, and standard statistical tests cannot be applied. Marketing researchers usually base their studies on probability samples, but it is impor-

---

23 This discussion follows William G. Zikmund, *Exploring Marketing Research* (Hinsdale, Ill.: The Dryden Press, 1982), pp. 377–393. Used by permission.

tant to be able to identify all types of samples.[24] Some of the best known sampling plans are outlined below.

**A convenience sample** is *a nonprobability sample based on the selection of readily available respondents*. Broadcasting's "on-the-street" interviews are a good example. Marketing researchers sometimes use it in exploratory research, but not in definitive studies.

*Nonprobability samples of people with a specific attribute* are called **judgment samples**. Election-night predictions are usually based on polls of "swing voters" and are a type of judgment sample.

A **quota sample** is *a nonprobability sample that is divided so that different segments or groups are represented in the total sample*. An example would be a survey of auto import owners that included 33 Nissan owners, 31 Toyota owners, 7 BMW owners, and so on.

Sometimes called a snowball sample, a **referral sample** *is done in waves as more respondents with the characteristics are identified*. An industrial goods manufacturer might poll its customer list about a new cutting machine it will introduce. The survey might also ask respondents to identify other businesses who might use such a machine. The referrals would then be the target of a second stage of the research.

The basic type of probability sample is the **simple random sample** where *every item in the relevant universe has an equal opportunity of being selected*. Provincial lotteries are an example. Each number that appears on a ticket has an equal opportunity of being selected and each ticket holder an equal opportunity of winning. Using a computer to select 200 respondents randomly from a mailing list of 1000 would give every name on the list an equal opportunity of being selected.

*A probability sample that takes every Nth item on a list, after a random start*, is called a **systematic sample**. Sampling from a telephone directory is a common example.

---

**Interpreting Research Findings**

The actual design and execution of a survey seeking primary data are beyond the scope of this book. A number of marketing research books contain solutions to the many problems involved in survey-

---

[24] A recent article on sampling is Henry Assael and John Keon, "Nonsampling vs. Sampling Errors in Survey Research," *Journal of Marketing* (Spring 1982), pp. 114–123.

ing the public.[25] Among these problems are designing the questionnaires; selecting, training, and controlling the field interviewers; editing, coding, tabulating, and interpreting the data; presenting the results; and following up on the survey.

---

**Figure 6-8   Manager and Researcher Complaints**

**Management complaints about marketing reserachers:**
1. Research is not problem-oriented. It tends to provide a plethora of facts, not actionable results or direction.
2. Researchers are too involved with techniques. They tend to do research for research's sake and they appear to be reluctant to get involved in management "problems."
3. Research is slow, vague, and of questionable validity. It depends too much on clinical evidence.
4. Researchers can't communicate; they don't understand; and they don't talk the language of management. In many cases, researchers are inexperienced and not well rounded.

**Marketing researcher complaints about management:**
1. Management doesn't include research in discussions of basic fundamental problems. Management tends to ask only for specific information about parts of problems.
2. Management pays no more than lip service to research and doesn't really understand or appreciate its value. Research isn't given enough corporate status.
3. Management has a propensity to jump the gun — not allowing enough time for research. Management draws preliminary conclusions based on early or incomplete results.
4. Management relies more on intuition and judgement than on research. Research is used as a crutch, not a tool. Management tends to "typecast" the marketing researcher.

---

Source: Reprinted by permission from "Communication Gap Hinders Proper Use of Market Research," *Marketing Insights* (February 19, 1968), p. 7. Copyright 1968 by Crain Communications Inc.

---

It is crucial that marketing researchers and research users cooperate at every stage in the research design. Too many studies go unused because marketing management views the results as too restricted due to the lengthy discussion of research limitations that accompanies the data, or the use of unfamiliar terminology such as

---

[25] Two excellent marketing research texts are Gilbert A. Churchill, Jr., *Marketing Research* (Hinsdale, Ill.: Dryden Press, 1979); and Paul E. Green and Donald S. Tull, *Research for Marketing Decisions* (Englewood Cliffs, N.J.: Prentice-Hall, 1978).

"levels of confidence" and "Type 1 errors."[26] Occasional misunderstandings between researchers and the manager-user may lead to friction and failure to make effective use of the findings. Figure 6-8 lists several complaints that each party may express about the other.

These complaints reflect lack of understanding of the needs and capabilities of both parties. They can often be settled by involving both managers and researchers in specifying needed information, developing research designs, and evaluating the findings of the research. The research report should include recommendations and, whenever possible, an oral report should explain, expand upon, or clarify the written summary. These efforts increase the likelihood of management's utilizing the research findings.

## Marketing Information Systems

Many marketing managers discover that their information problems result from an overabundance—not a paucity—of marketing data. Their sophisticated computer facilities provide them daily with a deluge of printouts about sales in 30 different market areas, a hundred different products, and 6400 customers. A marketing manager may solve the crisis of too much information of the wrong kind in the wrong form each morning by gently sliding the ominous stack of computer printouts to the edge of the desk, where it quietly falls into the wastebasket. Data and information are not necessarily synonymous terms. *Data* refers to statistics, opinions, facts, or predictions categorized on some basis for storage and retrieval. *Information* is data relevant to the marketing manager in making decisions.

The solution to the problem of obtaining relevant information appears simple — establish a systematic approach to information management through the installation of a planned marketing information system. Establishment of an effective marketing information system (MIS) is, however, much easier said than done, as documented by the large number of firms who have attempted to develop an MIS and have only succeeded in increasing the amounts of irrelevant data.

The ideal **marketing information system** should be *a designed set of procedures and methods for generating an orderly flow of pertinent information for use in making decisions, providing management with the current and future states of the market with*

26 See Kenneth Gary McCain, "Business Decision Researchers Can't Afford to be 'Pure'," *Business and Economic Perspectives* (Spring 1979), pp. 41–46; Jeffrey Gandz and Thomas W. Whipple, "Making Marketing Research Accountable," *Journal of Marketing Research* (May 1977), pp. 202–8; and Dwight L. Gentry and John Hoftyzer, "The Misuse of Statistical Techniques in Evaluating Sample Data," *Journal of the Academy of Marketing Science* (Spring 1977), pp. 106–12.

*indications of market responses to company actions as well as to the actions of competitors.*[27]

Properly constructed, the MIS could serve as the nerve centre for the company, providing instantaneous information suitable for each level of management. It would act as a thermostat, monitoring the marketplace continuously so that management can adjust its actions as conditions change.

**Figure 6-9   The Decision — Turn the Furnace On or Off**

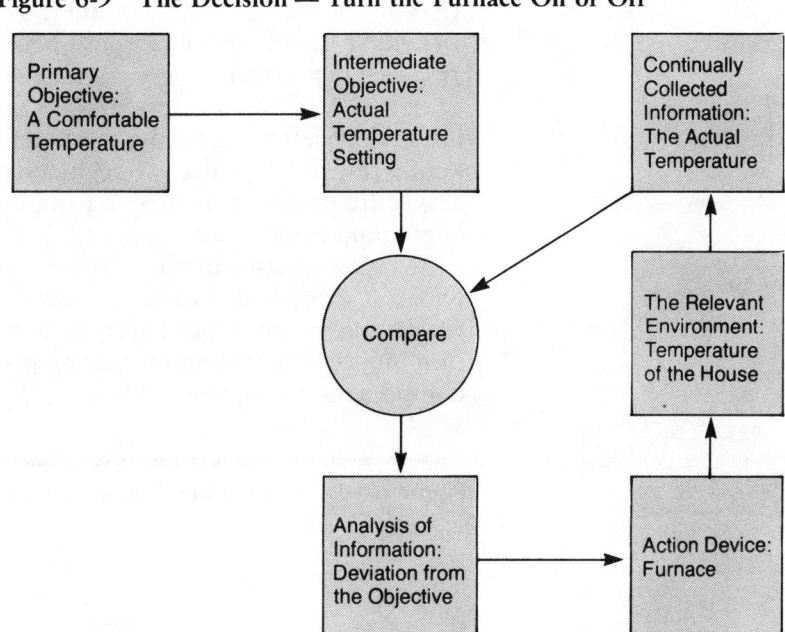

Source: Reprinted by permission from Bertram Schoner and Kenneth F. Uhl, *Marketing Research: Information Systems and Decision Making* (New York: Wiley, 1975), p. 10.

The analogy of an automatic heating system shows the role of marketing information in a firm's marketing system (see Figure 6-9). Once the objective of a temperature setting (perhaps 20°C) has been established, information about the actual temperature in the house is collected and compared with the objective, and a decision is made based upon this comparison. If the temperature drops below an established figure, the decision is made to activate the furnace until the temperature reaches some established amount. On the other hand, a high temperature may require a decision to turn off the furnace.

[27] Donald F. Cox and Robert E. Good, "How to Build a Marketing Information System," *Harvard Business Review* (May–June 1967), p. 147.

Deviation from the firm's goals of profitability, return on investment, or market share may necessitate changes in price structures, promotional expenditures, package design, or numerous marketing alternatives. The firm's MIS should be capable of revealing such deviations and possibly suggesting tactical changes that will result in attaining the established goals.

Many marketing executives feel that their company does not need a marketing information system, for various reasons. Two arguments are most often given: 1) the size of the company operations does not warrant such a complete system, and 2) the information provided by an MIS is already being supplied by the marketing research department.

These contentions arise from a misconception of services and functions performed by the marketing research department. Marketing research has already been described as typically focusing on a specific problem or project; the investigations have a definite beginning, middle, and end.

Marketing information systems, on the other hand, are much wider in scope and involve the continual collection and analysis of marketing information. Figure 6-10 indicates the various information inputs — including marketing research studies — that serve as components of the firm's MIS.

**Figure 6-10   Information Components of a Firm's MIS**

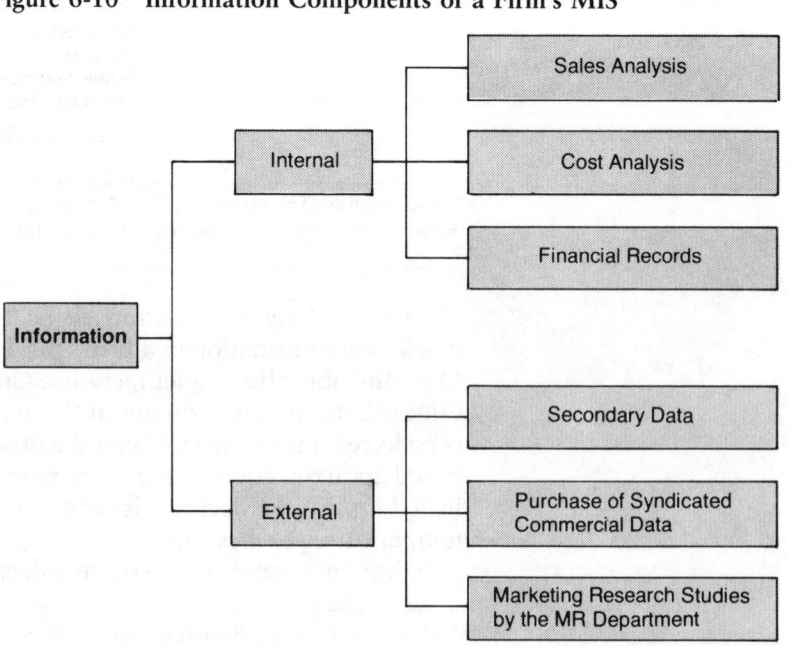

Robert J. Williams, creator of the first and still one of the most notable marketing information systems in 1961 at the Mead Johnson division of Edward Dalton Company explains the difference in this manner:

> The difference between marketing research and marketing intelligence is like the difference between a flash bulb and a candle. Let's say you are dancing in the dark. Every 90 seconds you're allowed to set off a flash bulb. You can use those brief intervals of intense light to chart a course, but remember everybody is moving, too. Hopefully, they'll accommodate themselves roughly to your predictions. You may get bumped and you may stumble every so often, but you can dance along.
>
> On the other hand, you can light a candle. It doesn't yield as much light, but it's a steady light. You are continually aware of the movements of the other bodies. You can adjust your own course to the courses of the others. The intelligence system is a kind of candle. It's no great flash on the immediate state of things, but it provides continuous light as situations shift and change.[28]

By focusing daily on the marketplace, the MIS provides a continuous systematic and comprehensive study of areas that indicate deviations from established goals. The up-to-the minute data allows problems to be corrected before they adversely affect company operations. Figure 6-11 summarizes many of the applications and possible benefits of a sophisticated information system.

*Current Status of Marketing Information Systems*

Marketing information systems have progressed a long way from the days when they were primarily responsible for clerical activities — and usually at an increased cost over the old method! Today, managers have available special computer programs, remote access consoles, better data banks, direct communication with the computer, and assignment of authority to the computer for periodic review and referral. In some instances, the computer simulates various market conditions and makes decisions based on the results of the model. But just how common are these computer-based marketing information systems in company offices?

Some larger Canadian companies have had well-developed MISs for several years. While statistics are lacking, it is thought that the use of *marketing* information systems is not widespread. It appears that finance and production currently receive most of the overall *management* system's resources. It is logical that a growing proportion of resources will be devoted to marketing systems during the next few years.

---

[28] "Marketing Intelligence Systems: A DEW Line for Marketing Men," *Business Management* (January 1966), p. 32.

**Figure 6-11   Benefits Possible With an Information Sytem**

| Typical Applications | Benefits | Examples |
|---|---|---|
| *Control Systems* | | |
| 1. Control of marketing costs | 1. More timely computerized reports | 1. Undesirable cost trends are spotted more quickly so that corrective action may be taken sooner. |
| 2. Diagnosis of poor sales performance | 2. Flexible on-line retrieval of data | 2. Executives can ask supplementary questions of the computer to help pinpoint reasons for a sales decline and reach an action decision more quickly. |
| 3. Management of fashion goods | 3. Automatic spotting of problems and opportunities | 3. Fast-moving fashion items are reported daily for quick reorder, and slow-moving items are also reported for fast price reductions. |
| 4. Flexible promotion strategy | 4. Cheaper, more detailed, and more frequent reports | 4. Ongoing evaluation of a promotional campaign permits reallocation of funds to areas behind target. |
| *Planning Systems* | | |
| 1. Forecasting | 1. Automatic translation of terms and classifications between departments | 1. Survey-based forecasts of demand for complex industrial goods can be automatically translated into parts requirements and production schedules. |
| 2. Promotional planning and corporate long-range planning | 2. Systematic testing of alternative promotional plans and compatibility testing of various divisional plans | 2. Complex simulation models, developed and operated with the help of data bank information, can be used for promotional planning by product managers and for strategic planning by top management. |
| 3. Credit manager | 3. Programmed executive decision rules can operate on data bank information | 3. Credit decisions are automatically made as each order is processed. |
| 4. Purchasing | 4. Detailed sales reporting permits automation of managment decisions | 4. Computer automatically repurchases standard items on the basis of correlation of sales data with programmed decision rules. |
| *Research Systems* | | |
| 1. Advertising strategy | 1. Additional manipulation of data is possible when stored for computers in an unaggregated file | 1. Sales analysis is possible by new market segment breakdowns. |
| 2. Pricing strategy | 2. Improved storage and retrieval capability allows new types of data to be collected and used. | 2. Systematic recording of information about past R & D contract bidding situations allows improved bidding strategies. |

**Figure 6-11   continued**

| Typical Applications | Benefits | Examples |
|---|---|---|
| 3. Evaluation of advertising expenditures | 3. Well-designed data banks permit integration and comparison of different sets of data. | 3. Advertising expenditures are compared to shipments by district to provide information about advertising effectiveness. |
| 4. Continuous experiments | 4. Comprehensive monitoring of input and performance variables yields information when changes are made. | 4. Changes in promotional strategy by type of customer are matched against sales results on a continuous basis. |

Source: Reprinted by permission of the *Harvard Business Review*. Exhibit from "How to Build a Marketing Information System," by Donald F. Cox and Robert E. Good, *Harvard Business Review* (May–June 1967), p. 146 Copyright © 1967 by the President and Fellows of Harvard College; all rights reserved.

## Successful Marketing Information Systems

Although only a few large companies have sophisticated, computer-based marketing information systems, considerable attention is being focused on their contributions. By the end of the decade many of the larger companies will establish their own information systems. The Monsanto Company and General Mills Incorporated are examples of firms with a successful MIS in operation.

Monsanto has designed one of the most advanced marketing information systems in operation. The system provides detailed sales analyses by product, sales, district, type of mill, and end use. Computer analyses are obtained from a continuing panel of households who represent a cross-section of the national market. Information is collected on purchase patterns by socio-economic group and is then analysed to determine current buying trends.

Monsanto also collects survey data to record the actions of competitors. In addition the system generates short-, medium-, and long-range forecasts for the company and industry. Short-term forecasts are developed for each of 400 individual products.

The General Mills computer supplies each zone, regional, and district manager with a daily teletype report on the previous day's orders by brand and a comparison of current projections of monthly sales with the monthly total projected the week before. Each of 1700 individual products is analysed in terms of current profitability and projected annual profitability as compared with target projections made at the beginning of the year. The "problem" products requiring management attention are then printed out on the daily reports. A similar report looks for problem areas in each region and breaks down the nature of the problem according to cause (for example, profit margins, over- or underspending on advertising and sales promotion).[29]

**Developing an MIS**

The first step in the construction of the MIS is obtaining the total support of top management. Management not only must be truly enthusiastic about the potential of the system, but also must maintain the belief that it is top management's place to oversee its development. Too often the technical staff are left to build such a system.

The next step involves a review and appraisal of the entire marketing organization and of the policies that direct it. The marketing managers' responsibilities must be clearly defined. If the system is to measure their performance against plans, then it is necessary to specify precisely each person's areas of accountability.

Once the organization is readied for the development of the system, the level of sophistication of the MIS must be determined. Before this can be done the company needs and the costs of meeting these needs must be carefully considered. The abilities of managers to develop and use a sophisticated system effectively must also be considered. Managers must be able to define their specific information needs. A questionnaire, such as the one in Figure 6-12, may be used to pinpoint specific information requirements.

**Figure 6-12   Sample Questionnaire for Determining Market Information Needs**

1. What types of decisions are you regularly called upon to make?
2. What types of information do you need to make the decision?
3. What types of information do you regularly get?
4. What types of special studies do you periodically request?
5. What types of information would you like to get but are not currently receiving?
6. What information would you like to receive daily? weekly? monthly? yearly?
7. What magazines and trade journals would you like to receive regularly?
8. What types of data analysis programs would you like to receive?
9. What are four improvements you would like to see made in the present marketing information stystem?

Source: Philip Kotler, "A Design for the Firm's Marketing Nerve Center," *Business Horizons* (Fall 1966), p. 70. Copyright 1966 by The Foundation for the School of Business at Indiana University. Reprinted by permission.

[29] "Marketing Management and the Computer," *Sales Management* (August 20, 1965), pp. 49–60. See also Leon Winer, "Putting the Computer to Work in Marketing," *Pittsburgh Business Review* (November–December 1972), pp. 1–5ff.

Management must also be able to state explicitly its planning, decision-making, and control processes and procedures. For example, an automated exception reporting system may be developed for the manager who is able to verbalize a specific set of decision rules, such as " I always like to know about all situations in which sales, profits, or market shares are running 4 percent or more behind plan. Furthermore, in any exceptional cases I also require the following diagnostic information: prices, distribution levels, advertising, and consumer attitude."[30]

---

[30] Donald F. Cox and Robert E. Good, "How to Build a Marketing Information System," *Harvard Business Review* (May–June 1967), p. 152.

# A Peek at the Future of Information Systems

The year is 1995. The place is the office of the marketing manager of a medium-sized consumer products manufacturer. The participants in the following discussion are John, the marketing manager; Anne, the director of marketing science; Rod, Anne's assistant, who specializes in marketing research; and Scott, the sales manager for the company. The scene opens as Anne, Rod, and Scott enter John's office.

John:   *Good morning. What's up for discussion this morning?*

Anne:   *We want to take a look at the prospects for our new beef substitute.*

John:   *What do we have on it?*

Rod:   *We test marketed the product late in 1994 in four cities, so we have that data from last quarter.*

John:   *Let's see how it did.*

(All four gather around the remote console video display unit. John activates the console and requests it to display the sales results from the most recent test market. The system retrieves the data and displays the information on the video device.)

John:   *That looks good! How does it compare to the first test?*

(The console retrieves and displays the data from the first test on command from John.)

Rod:   *Let me check the significance of the sales increase of the most recent test over last year's test.*

(Rod requests that the system test and display the

likelihood that the sales increase could be a chance occurrence.)

Rod:   *Looks like a solid sales increase.*

Anne:   *Good! How did the market respond to our change in price?*

(Anne commands the system to display the graph of the price-quantity response based on the most recent test data.)

John:   *Is that about what our other meat substitute products show?*

(John calls up past price-quantity response graphs for similar products.)

John:   *Just as I suspected. This new product is a bit more responsive to price. What's the profit estimate?*

(John calls for a profit estimate from the product-planning model within the system.)

John:   *Hmm . . . $5 500 000. Looks good. Is that based on the growth model I supplied to the model bank last week?*

Anne:   *No. This is based on the market-share progress other food substitutes have shown in the past as well as the information we have on the beef substitute from our test markets.*

John:   *Let's see what mine would do.*

(He reactivates the product-planning model, this time using his growth model. The profit implications are displayed on the console.)

John:   *Well, my model predicts $5 million. That's close. Looks like my feelings are close to* *the statistical results.*

Anne: *Let's see if there's a better marketing strategy for this product. We must remember that these profit estimates are based on the preliminary plan we developed two weeks ago.*

(Anne calls for the marketing mix generator to recommend a marketing program based upon the data and judgmental inputs on file for this product.)

John: *I'm a little worried about our advertising appeals. Can we improve in this area?*

Anne: *Let's see what the response to advertising is.*

(The video unit shows a graph of the predicted sales-advertising response function.)

Anne: *If we changed from a taste appeal to a convenience appeal, what would the results be, John?*

John: *I think it would look like this.*

(John takes a light pen and describes a new relationship on the video unit based upon his judgment of the effectiveness of the new appeal.)

Rod: *Let me check something.*

(Rod calls for a sample of past sales-advertising response curves of similar products using the convenience appeal.)

Rod: *I think you are underestimating the response on the basis of past data.*

John: *Well, this product is different. How much would it cost for a test of this appeal?*

(Rod calls a marketing research evaluation model from the console.)

Rod: *It looks like a meaningful test would cost about $5000.*

John: *I wonder what risk we'd run if we made a decision to go national with the product right now. What are the chances of a failure with this product as it stands if we include this morning's revisions to the marketing mix?*

(A risk-analysis model is called up on the system.)

John: *Looks like a 35 percent chance of failure. Maybe we'd best run further tests in order to reduce the risk. What's next on the agenda this morning?*

---

Source: David B. Montgomery and Glen L. Urban, *Management Science in Marketing* (Englewood Cliffs, N.J.: Prentice-Hall, 1969), pp. 1–3. Adapted by permission of Prentice-Hall, Inc. Englewood Cliffs, N.J.

As marketing research becomes increasingly scientific and is combined by a growing number of organizations into fully functional information systems, decision-makers benefit by making informed decisions about problems and opportunities. Sophisticated computer simulations make it possible to consider alternative courses of action by posing a number of "what if?" situations. These developments may convert the scenario we imagine in 1995 into reality in a much shorter time.

## Summary

Information is vital for marketing decision-making. No firm can operate without detailed information on its market. Information may take several forms: one-time marketing research studies, secondary data, internal data, subscriptions to commercial information sources, and the output of a marketing information system.

Marketing research, an important source of information, deals with studies that collect and analyse data relevant to marketing decisions. It involves the specific delineation of problems, research design, collection of secondary and primary data, interpretation of research findings, and presentation of results for management action.

The most common market research activities are determining market potential, developing sales forecasts for the firm's products and services, competitive product analysis, new product estimates, studies related to marketing mix decisions and international trade, and social and cultural research. Annual expenditures for marketing research now exceed $70 million and most large companies have internal market research departments. However, outside suppliers still remain vital to the research function. Some of these outside research suppliers perform the complete research task, while others specialize in limited areas or provide syndicated data services.

The marketing research process can be divided into six specific steps: 1) defining the problem; 2) exploratory research; 3) formulating hypotheses; 4) research design; 5) collecting data; and 6) interpretation and presentation. A clearly defined problem allows the researcher to obtain the relevant decision-oriented information. Exploratory research refers to information gained both outside and inside the firm. Hypotheses—tentative explanations of some specific event — allow the researcher to set out a specific research design, the series of decisions that, taken together, comprise a master plan or model for the conduct of the investigation. The data collection phase of the marketing research process can involve either or both primary data (original data) and secondary data (previously published data). Primary data can be collected by three alternative methods: observation, survey, or experimental. Once the data are collected, it is important that researchers interpret and present them in a way that is meaningful to management.

An increasing number of firms have installed planned marketing information systems. Properly designed, the MIS will generate an orderly flow of decision-oriented information as the marketing executive needs it. The number of firms with planned information systems will grow during the 1980s as more managers recognize their contribution to dealing with the information explosion.

Chapter 6 concludes the section on planning the marketing effort. Attention now shifts to the marketing mix variables: product, price, distribution, and promotion. The next section discusses products and services.

---

| *Key Terms* | | |
| --- | --- | --- |
| marketing research | population or universe |
| syndicated service | census |
| full-service research supplier | probability sample |
| limited-service research supplier | nonprobability sample |
| exploratory research | convenience sample |
| hypothesis | judgment sample |
| research design | quota sample |

primary data                             referral sample
secondary data                           simple random sample
focus group interview                    systematic sample
test marketing                           marketing information system

---

**Review Questions**

1. Outline the development and current status of the marketing research function.
2. Explain the services offered by different types of marketing research suppliers.
3. List and explain the various steps in the marketing research process.
4. Distinguish between primary and secondary data.
5. What advantages does the use of secondary data offer the marketing researcher? What potential limitations exist in using such data?
6. Distinguish among surveys, experiments, and observational methods of data collection.
7. Illustrate each of the three methods for gathering survey data. Under what circumstances should each be used?
8. Explain the differences between probability and nonprobability samples and the various types of each.
9. Distinguish between marketing research and marketing information systems.
10. What is the current status of marketing information systems?

---

**Discussion Questions and Exercises**

1. Prepare a brief two- to three-page report on a syndicated marketing research service. Explain how this data is used by marketing decision-makers.
2. Collect from secondary data the following information:
   a. retail sales in Windsor, Ontario
   b. number of persons over 65 in Moncton, New Brunswick
   c. earnings per share for International Business Machines Corporation last year
   d. bituminous coal production in Canada
   e. consumer price index for a given month
   f. number of households earning more than $35 000 in your home town or city
3. Look up the "Survey of Buying Power" data for your community or one nearby. What marketing implications can be drawn from these situations?
4. James Roe, the vice-president of Gadget Electronics, a medium-to-large Canadian company, refuses to involve himself with the activities of his marketing research staff. He explains that he has hired competent professionals for the research department, and he does not plan to meddle in their operation. Critically evaluate Roe's postion.
5. You have been asked to determine the effect on Gillette of Schick's

introduction of a revolutionary new blade that is guaranteed to give a hundred nick-free shaves. Outline your approach to the study.

**MICROCOMPUTER EXERCISE:**

**Sales Analysis**

**Directions:** Use the Menu Item titled "Sales Analysis" on the Marketing disk to solve each of the following problems.

1. A Saskatoon company organizes its sales force into three sales regions: A, B, and C. The average salaries in these regions are $32 000, $36 000, and $42 000, respectively. Region A sales personnel average $800 000 in sales; Region B sales representatives, $740 000; and Region C personnel, $985 000. Selling expenses average $15 000 in all regions. Calculate the cost/sales ratios for each of the three regions.

2. One of the first assignments given to Gordon Morgenstern following his employment in the marketing department of a Halifax-based firm was to develop a sales analysis for the company's five sales divisions. Morgenstern's supervisor indicated a particular concern with Division 2's average selling expenses of $27 700. Morgenstern collected the data shown in Table A on sales, sales compensation, and selling expenses. What should Morgenstern tell his supervisor concerning the firm's cost/sales ratios?

**Table A   Morgenstern's Sales Analysis**

| Division | Average Sales per Salesperson | Average Sales Compensation | Average Selling Expenses |
|---|---|---|---|
| 1 | $651 000 | $31 650 | $14 175 |
| 2 | 778 000 | 30 500 | 27 700 |
| 3 | 664 000 | 28 100 | 9 375 |
| 4 | 602 000 | 33 650 | 7 300 |
| 5 | 518 000 | 29 500 | 7 100 |

3. The Alberta Division of a Montreal firm employs five sales representatives. All were assigned sales quotas of $750 000. The division's manager, Eleanor Tomlinson, is now preparing an analysis of how her people performed in 1987. The actual sales results were as follows.

| Salesperson | Actual Sales |
|---|---|
| Fulgoni | $734 000 |
| Watson | 825 000 |
| Hwong | 675 000 |
| O'Connell | 725 000 |
| Mitchell | 785 000 |

a. Calculate the performance-to-quota ratio for each of the sales representatives in the Alberta Division.

b. What is the overall performance-to-quota ratio for the Alberta Division?

*A p p e n d i x   B*

# Locating Secondary Data

The publications listed in this appendix refer mainly to the Canadian market. Some international marketing sources are covered briefly in the final section.

These are by no means all the sources of secondary data available for Canada or international markets; however, it is hoped that they will serve as a starting point in your search for secondary sources of marketing data.[1]

**Canadian Government Publications**

Statistics Canada publishes extensive statistical information, gathered through various sources. The statistics generally cover the wide range of data on the economic and social activities of Canadians. There are too many publications to list and describe here, but detailed information can be obtained from these sources:

**Statistics Canada Local Reference Centres**

Statistics Canada has reference centres in:
- St. John's, Nfld.
- Halifax, N.S.
- Montreal, P.Q.
- Ottawa, Ont.
- Toronto, Ont.
- Winnipeg, Man.
- Regina, Sask.
- Edmonton, Alta.
- Vancouver, B.C.

  These centres provide assistance to users in a variety of ways.
1. Inquiry Service: provides statistical information by phone, letter, and personal request.
2. Professional Consultation Services: assist with data problems; also provide feedback to Statistics Canada on statistical needs and user problems.
3. Data Distribution and Promotion Services: take orders for all statistical publications and related material, such as microfiche and census maps.

---

[1] Written with the assistance of J. Scott McLeod and D. Felbel.

4. Education Services: provide booklet on finding and using statistics; also distribute the *Statistics Canada Current Publications Index* of publications (see below).

5. Data Collection Service: arranges for the design management and implementation of surveys for government, institutions, and private agencies.

**Statistics Canada Current Publications Index**

The *Index* replaces and updates the annual *Statistics Canada Catalogue*, and contains a listing of numbered publications released by Statistics Canada up to June 30 of any given year. Publications include statistical data on primary industries, manufacturing, transportation, communication, commerce, employment, population, and general topics. Section one lists publications by catalogue number and by subject; section two is an alphabetical title, subject, and commodity index.

Catalogued publications typically contain one or more of the following kinds of information:

- compilations of statistical information
- reference material to assist in the use and understanding of statistical data
- special studies
- descriptions of Statistics Canada's services and operations

Each of these major groupings is further divided into sub-groupings consisting of major classifications.

**Other Statistics Canada Data**

*CANSIM—Canadian Socio-economic Information Management System*   CANSIM is a computerized data base comprising two modules: the CANSIM Time Series module, which contains a wide range of current and historical information from socio-economic fields; and the CANSIM Cross-Classified module, which contains multidimensional data in the fields of demography, education, health, and justice.

1. Time Series: contains information from the following subject areas:
   - system of national accounts
   - prices and price indexes
   - labour
   - manufacturing and primary industry
   - capital and finance
   - construction
   - merchandising and services
   - external trade
   - transportation
   - agriculture and food

- population estimates and projections
- health and welfare

This module is available through a number of distributors, and the content is always growing as new sets of data are added.

2. Cross-Classified: currently consists of information gathered from the Agriculture, Health, Justice, Education, Science, and Culture divisions of Statistics Canada. This module allows for analysis and tabulation of data on social conditions.

The CANSIM Cross-Classified module is available only at the CANSIM host service bureau, Datacrown Inc., Ottawa. A list of secondary distributors may be obtained through Datacrown (650 McNicoll Ave., Willowdale, Ont. M2H 2E1).

*Data in Microform*   Statistics Canada makes available large blocks of data in microform, including the most recent census data and all current serial publications of the external trade division.

All publications ever published by Statistics Canada are available under an arrangement with Micromedia Ltd. This includes those listed in the Dominion Bureau of Statistics (1918–1960) and all subsequent catalogues. Inquiries concerning these sources should be directed to Micromedia Ltd. (144 Front St. W., Toronto, Ont. M5J 2L7).

*Machine-Readable Data*   Statistics Canada provides a selection of census data on magnetic tape, including:

1. User Summary Tapes: contain tabulated data, usually in more detail than in printed reports. They are available commencing with the 1961 census year.
2. Public Use Sample Tapes: provide the user with access to records of unidentifiable individual respondents commencing with the 1971 census.
3. Spatial Reference Tapes: contain supplementary geographical data commencing with the 1971 census.

**Listing of Supplementary Documents**   This is a list of documents such as technical papers and memoranda, discussion papers, and working papers. It should be noted that this information is often of a tentative, transitory, or speculative nature, its purpose being to report on progress and to invite further discussion, or to make available research findings that Statistics Canada does not wish to endorse officially. This document is set up using an author-title index.

Statistics Canada publications are available in libraries, including most provincial libraries and many public and university libraries.

**Provincial Government Publications**

The provincial governments publish thousands of documents through their departments and agencies. The information covered by these publications covers a variety of topics reflecting the many departments in which the documents originated. They cover the whole spectrum, from agriculture to urban affairs.

Because the documents available are too numerous to describe individually, we can only direct you to the major sources that list and describe all the documents published by the provincial governments. As an example, here is the way to find documents in Manitoba. Information for other provincial governments can be obtained in a similar way.

**The Province of Manitoba**

Like most provinces, Manitoba makes most of its publications available through a department of the government. In Manitoba, that department is Publications. (The name used in other provinces may vary slightly; in some provinces each ministry or department publishes its own material.)

Statistics on the following areas will normally be found in the publications department (or departments):

• agriculture
• ecology
• energy
• health
• industry
• mines
• Queen's Printer
• resources
• tourism and general information

The Province of Manitoba, like the federal government, prepares a book that lists all its publications. This publication is entitled *Looking for Manitoba Government Publications*. It is available at a variety of public and private libraries as well as the University of Manitoba, the University of Winnipeg, and other libraries across the province. The book can also be purchased from the Queen's Printer.

The guide is arranged alphabetically by the government department that prepared each document, and also by subject. A brief explanation of each publication helps the user to determine its suitability. Each document has been assigned a level, a broad designation to indicate the approximate audience for whom the publication was intended. The levels are: Elementary, Advanced, and All Levels.

**Chambers of Commerce**

Most cities and towns have a Chamber of Commerce. A Chamber of Commerce is an association established to further the business interests of its community. The Chambers in most metropolitan cities publish information about their cities. These groups are often very useful sources of information.

This is the sort of general information you can expect to find at most Chambers of Commerce.

1. Economic Facts: for instance, value added by sector or the sales figures of retail chain stores.
2. Employment: totals for the area, average weekly earnings, average hourly wage, etc.
3. Government: city administration, revenues and expenditures.
4. Population: distribution by sex and age, family size, migration estimates, etc.
5. Quality of Life: housing starts and completions, city climate, cultural facilities, etc.

The Chamber of Commerce publications can be obtained directly from the Chambers, or at public or university libraries located in the city that the Chamber services.

### Market Reports, Surveys, Directories, Special Issues, and Newsletters

Many of the documents listed in the remainder of this appendix are available through university and public libraries. As many of them can be fairly expensive — from about $5 to over $100 — you may wish to locate them in a library before deciding if you need to purchase them.

The publications are listed under major headings that describe the industry, trade, or sector to which the documents pertain. Some of these many appear in libraries under the magazine title. Furthermore, some of the following "annual" publications may not always be published.

### Advertising

1. *Report on Advertising Revenues in Canada*   Published annually. Provides media gross revenue totals and net revenues for broadcasting, newspapers, and other print media. Billings and gross revenue for agencies are also listed. *(Maclean Hunter Research Bureau)*

2. *Canadian Advertising Rates and Data*   Published monthly. The media authority for all the major Canadian broadcast and print media. Provides addresses, advertising rates, circulation, mechanical requirements, and personnel and ownership information as well as a very useful service feature section. *(Maclean Hunter)*

3. *Media Editorial Profile*   Published annually. Provides a brief statement on the editorial direction and subject matter of the articles within some 700 Canadian business, consumer, and farm magazines. *(Maclean Hunter)*

*4. National List of Advertisers*   Published annually. Lists over 3000 organizations involved in national advertising in Canada. Includes their key personnel, advertising budget, and media used. Also contains sections on brand names, advertising agencies and their accounts, and direct marketing. *(Maclean Hunter)*

**Automotive**

*1. Area Sales Guide to Canada's Automotive After Market* Includes data by county and census divisions for motor vehicle registrations as of the last census, with estimates for the current year. Special tabulation of general repair shops, specialized service shops, new car and truck dealers, automotive jobbers, and service stations. These data are gathered from the mailing lists of *Canadian Automotive Trade* and *Revenue Motor. (Maclean Hunter)*

*2. Automotive Service Data Book*   Published annually as an issue of *Canadian Automotive Trade.* Provides detailed specifications for the components of Canadian and imported automobiles for the current and five preceding years. *(Maclean Hunter Business Publications)*

*3. Canadian Special Truck Equipment Manual*   A complete listing of the sources of supply for special truck equipment. *(Maclean Hunter)*

**Aviation/Aerospace**

*1. Canadian Aviation Report*   Contains statistical information on most areas of aviation in Canada. It includes statistics on the aerospace industry, imports and exports, commercial airlines, passenger loads, freight, and licences. Also contains aircraft registrations by type, airport movements, etc. *(Maclean Hunter)*

*2. Aviation Directory of Canada*   Published annually as an issue of *Canadian Aviation.* Covers approximately 1800 Canadian companies active in the aviation and aerospace industry. Also carries information on associations, publications, academic institutions, and government departments involved in the industry. *(Maclean Hunter Business Publications)*

*3. Avionics Buyers Guide*   Annual listing of what is available in avionics in Canada. Also includes a list of distributors and dealers. *(Maclean Hunter)*

*4. Aerospace Directory of Canada*   Published annually. Lists all Canadian aerospace industrial companies with an interest in the export of products or services. *(Maclean Hunter)*

**Canadian Market, General**

*1. Report of Canada*   Published annually. Contains historical data on Canada and its population, income, GNP, construction, and manufacturing. Also provides forecasts and economic indicators. *(Maclean Hunter Research Bureau)*

*2. Canada*   Published quarterly. Intended for U.S. manufacturers interested in developing their business in Canada. Contains current economic data on the Canadian market. *(Maclean Hunter Research Bureau)*

*3. Handbook of Canadian Consumer Markets*   Published biennially. Draws together consumer market data from government, trade, and Conference Board sources. Includes tables and charts that provide detail on economic and demographic data and illustrate major trends, distributions, and projections for the Canadian consumer market. The six major subject areas covered are population (characteristics and growth), labour force and employment, income, expenditures, production and retail trade, and consumer and industry price indexes. *(Conference Board of Canada)*

*4. Canada Year Book*   Published irregularly. Records developments in Canada's economic, social, and political life. The 1985 edition is the latest in a series that began 80 years previously. *(Statistics Canada)*

*5. Bank of Canada Review*   Published monthly. Provides articles by leading members of the financial community, followed by charts and statistical tables on such subjects as monetary aggregates and fiscal policy, the chartered banks, interest rates, selected economic indicators, the labour market, prices, income and costs, external trade, and the Canadian balance of international payments. *(Bank of Canada)*

*6. Canadian Outlook: Economic Forecast*   Published quarterly. Features current forecasts on aspects of the Canadian economy such as consumer expenditures, housing, government investment, trade, employment, labour, costs, prices, markets, and budgets, followed by comparative tables. *(Conference Board of Canada)*

*7. Provincial Outlook: Economic Forecast*   Published quarterly. Similar to *Canadian Outlook*, but with separate sections on each of the Canadian provinces. *(Conference Board of Canada)*

*8. Canadian Statistical Review*   Published monthly. Contains current statistical information retrieved from CANSIM, the Statistics Canada computerized data bank. Topics include selected economic indicators, population statistics, national accounts, labour, prices, manufacturing, fuel, power, mining, construction, food and agriculture, domestic trade, external trade, transportation, and finance. *(Statistics Canada)*

*9. Canadian Markets*   Published annually. A very valuable source of data about Canadian markets. Provides estimates and forecasts that give current figures for population, households, personal disposable income, and retail sales for markets nationwide. Buying power index allows comparison of one market against another. Extensive provincial and municipal market data are given in geographical sequence from east to west. The 1987 edition will incorporate 1986 census data. *(Financial Post Information Service)*

10. *Market Guide*   Published annually. A compilation of marketing information for every city or community in the United States and Canada where a daily newspaper is published. Information includes geographic location, transportation features, population and household data, and retailing and industrial features. *(Editor & Publisher)*

11. *It's Your Business Guide to Marketing Research 1*   Intended to help owners or prospective owners of small businesses in dealing with daily business operations. The publication covers business organization, financial planning, accounting procedures, marketing research, etc. *(Small Business Assistance Centre, Manitoba Department of Industry, Trade and Commerce)*

12. *It's Your Business Guide to Basic Marketing Statistics*   This document is intended particularly for Winnipeg businesses and attempts to show how statistics can be used. The document covers general economic and social data; economic sectors of manufacturing, service, and agriculture; and wholesale and retail trade. Limited to four markets: Winnipeg, Manitoba, Saskatchewan, and Alberta. *(Small Business Assistance Centre, Manitoba Department of Industry, Trade and Commerce)*

**Clothing**

1. *Report on the Canadian Apparel Industry*   Published annually. A statistical report on consumer expenditures for men's, women's, and children's clothing in Canada. Also includes information on manufacturing, imports, and exports. *(Maclean Hunter)*

2. *Style Buyers Guide*   Published annually as a special issue of *Style*. A source of information for names, addresses, and merchandise classifications of women's clothing manufacturers and importers in Canada. *(Maclean Hunter Business Publications)*

**Construction, Public Works, Hardware**

1. *Building Material Sources*   The annual directory issue of *Building Supply Dealer* magazine. Contains information on buying groups, national distributors, hardware wholesalers, brand-name index, associations, and executives. *(Maclean Hunter)*

2. *Canada's Hardware Market*   Annual statistical report on the production and sale of items classed as hardware. Data include Canadian production, imports, exports, retail and department store sales, and family expenditures. *(Maclean Hunter)*

3. *Canada's Hardware Market for Power Driven Tools*   Published annually. Covers Canadian production, imports, and exports of power driven tools. Information on brand preferences and best-selling brands for related items. *(Maclean Hunter Research Bureau)*

4. *Canadian Survey of Building Materials Retailing*   Provides information on store operation among Canada's building supply stores. The document compares best-selling brand information for items in various years. *(Maclean Hunter)*

*5. Construction Canada*   Published annually. Describes the size of the Canadian construction industry and the market, and the challenges facing the industry in the immediate future. Includes work performed by the construction industry, expenditures and forecasted expenditures on machinery, distributors' and manufacturers' sales of construction equipment, domestic supply of construction equipment, U.S. construction, and exports to Canada and all countries. Discusses roads and streets, housing, structural steel, concrete products and asphalt, population, and GNP forecasts. *(Maclean Hunter)*

*6. Contractors Handbook*   Published annually as a special issue of *Heavy Construction News*. Provides the names of manufacturers and distributors of construction equipment and accessories. Also contains information on industry associations, auctioneers, and schools for heavy-equipment operators. *(Maclean Hunter Business Publications)*

*7. Public Works Reference Manual and Buyers Guide*   An annual directory and purchasing guide to more than 2000 items in five categories: roads and streets, water and sewage, waste management, parks and recreation, and public works operation. Also contains a listing of manufacturers and agents, consulting engineers by region and area of specialization, and a directory of municipal associations. *(Maclean Hunter)*

*8. Real Estate Development Annual*   Published annually as a special issue of *Canadian Building*. Provides information on Canadian public and private real estate developers, investors, and lenders, and development-related organizations. Also highlights major development projects. *(Maclean Hunter Business Publications)*

**Data Processing and Computers**

*1. Canada's Data Processing Market*   Published annually. Reports the market background, trends, and forecasts for computers. Statistical data available include the number of computers installed as of May 1980 by supplier and industry, and the imports of computers and related equipment. *(Maclean Hunter)*

*2. Canadian Datasystems User Preference Survey*   Annual report of a survey of EDP personnel to determine preferences for a wide variety of EDP products and services. The results are reported by geographical area and are compared to the results of prior surveys. *(Maclean Hunter)*

*3. Canadian Datasystems Reference Manual*   Published annually as a special issue of *Canadian Datasystems*. Provides information on Canadian EDP organizations, suppliers, and products. Also has an index to *Canadian Datasystems* and a calendar of major conferences in the field. *(Maclean Hunter Business Publications)*

*4. Canadian Datasystems Annual Review and Forecast*   An annual report that features comments by government officials and leaders in the industry. The document has general economic forecasts for the information industry. *(Maclean Hunter)*

*5. Canadian Computer Census*  Published annually. Provides information on computer installations in Canada. Organized by province, city, and computer type. *(Canadian Information Process Society)*

*6. Canadian Salary Survey*  Lists average salaries in data processing, by province and by city. *(Canadian Information Processing Society)*

**Drugs and Phamaceuticals**  *1. Annual Review of Drug Chains, Groups, and Wholesalers* Published annually as a special issue of *Drug Merchandising*. Reports on the Canadian pharmacy industry, giving information on sales, individual operations, and key personnel. *(Maclean Hunter Business Publications)*

*2. Canadian Drug Store Report*  Published annually. Reports the latest statistics on pharmaceutical sales by province, city, and major urban areas. Includes the number of pharmacies by province, plus sales of specific products. *(Maclean Hunter)*

*3. Drug Index*  An annual incorporating a brand-name directory of prescription drugs, self-medications, and personal care products, cross-referenced to manufacturer or distributors. *(Maclean Hunter)*

*4. A Survey on Prescriptions*  Published annually. Reviews Canadian prescription statistics: number of scripts, prices to patients, and most commonly prescribed drugs. Statistics are broken down by area, and are comparable to figures from past surveys. *(Maclean Hunter)*

**Electronics**  *1. Audioscene Canada's Annual Canadian Hi-Fi Buyers Catalogue* Provides a list of specifications on virtually every product available in Canada, and a directory of manufacturers and their representatives. *(Maclean Hunter)*

*2. Audioscene Canada Hi-Fi Equipment Brand Preference Studies* A survey conducted among subscribers to *Audioscene Canada* to determine brand awareness and preference by both consumers and retailers across Canada. *(Maclean Hunter)*

*3. Canadian Electronics Engineering Annual Buyers Guide* Published annually as the directory issue of *Canadian Electronics Engineering*. Lists products and services, Canadian sources, foreign manufacturers, and Canadian distributors. *(Maclean Hunter Business Publications)*

*4. Canada's Electronic Market*  A detailed look at the Canadian electronic-products market, including imports, exports, and net production. The document also reviews the imports of U.S. products. *(Maclean Hunter)*

**Financial and Insurance**

*1. Directory of Employee Benefit Consultants*   Contains information on all firms providing employee benefit consulting services. It also provides details on the types of services offered. *(Maclean Hunter)*

*2. Directory of Group Insurance*   Contains information on all group insurance companies in Canada, as well as the type of group insurance offered. Organized by province; provides an address, telephone number, and a contact person. *(Maclean Hunter)*

*3. Directory of Pension Fund Investment Services*   Contains information on all trust companies, insurance companies, and investment counsellors in Canada who provide investment counselling for corporations and institutions. Includes statistics on asset mix, number of clients, and size of pension fund assets managed by each. *(Maclean Hunter)*

**Food and Food Processing and Retailing**

*1. Attitudes of Food Service Operators towards Food Distributors* A survey to determine what the food service industry feels are the main factors involved in selecting a food wholesaler or distributor. This includes what they expect to receive from the distributors' salespeople and how they rate the salespeople. *(Maclean Hunter)*

*2. A Report on Frozen Foods*   A market report on Canadian production, imports and exports of, and expenditures on frozen products. *(Maclean Hunter Research Bureau)*

*3. Buyers Directory and Service Index*   Lists source information and a directory of supply and services necessary for efficient operation in the industry. Includes indexes of the food and beverage associations, food brokers, federal government officials, and personnel. *(Maclean Hunter)*

*4. Canadian Hotel & Restaurant Sources Directory*   Published annually. Lists food, service, and lodging suppliers in Canada. *(Maclean Hunter)*

*5. Directory of Restaurant and Fast Food Chains in Canada* Published annually. Provides information on over 600 restaurant and fast food chains in Canada that have three or more outlets. Includes head and regional office addresses, personnel listings, and advertising, franchise, and financial data. *(Monday Report on Retailers)*

*6. Food Industry Economic Review and Forecast*   Provides a forecast for many of the industries in the food and beverage sector. More than 80 tables are presented, exploring the historical performance of each industry's principal statistics. *(Maclean Hunter)*

*7. Frozen Food Survey*   Results of a survey performed to determine attitudes toward frozen foods in the food service industry. *(Maclean Hunter)*

*8. Survey of Food Brokers and Their Markets*   Published annually. Contains a listing of food brokers and the brands they sell, as well as food store sales by provinces and national, provincial, and city market statistics. *(Maclean Hunter)*

**Forestry**   *1. Canada's Pulp and Paper Industry Market*   Provides an insight into the largest segment of the Canadian forest industry. *(Maclean Hunter)*
*2. Canadian Pulp and Paper Industry 198__ Forecast*   Annual report on the capital spending of Canada's pulp and paper industry. *(Maclean Hunter)*
*3. Survey of Buying Influences*   The result of personal interviews at 10 mills in Canada. Discusses who influences the purchase of such items as conveyor belting, drive belts, dryer fabrics, electric motors, flow control valves, paper machine wires, pumps, chemicals, etc. *(Maclean Hunter)*

**Furniture, Furnishings, and Appliances**   *1. Canada's Furniture Market*   A statistical report on the furniture manufacturing industry in Canada. Includes imports, exports, and Canadian production data, and details the various furniture industries. Sales at the retail level and consumer expenditure are also covered. *(Maclean Hunter Research Bureau)*
*2. Canada's Home Appliance Market*   A statistical report on the size of the market (including data on retail sales), manufacturing industries in detail, apparent domestic consumption, imports, exports, and forecast of manufacturers' sales. Also covers consumer data such as home ownership, intentions, and preferences. *(Maclean Hunter Research Bureau)*
*3. Microwave Oven Chart*   Merchandising guide for microwave ovens, including a list of all microwave ovens available in Canada and their features. *(Maclean Hunter)*
*4. Sources*   Annual product directory of contract interior products available in Canada: furniture, floor covering, lighting, seating, wall covering, fabric, art, accessories, etc. *(Maclean Hunter)*
*5. Canadian Carpet Chart*   Lists all carpets produced in Canada by manufacturers, with subheadings to indicate carpet type and specifications. This issue of *Floor Covering News* has a report on Canadian carpet market trends. *(Maclean Hunter)*

**Industrial**   *1. Brand Preference Survey Steam Equipment and Supplies*   Documents brand preferences reported by 195 manufacturing plants and institutions for a variety of steam and steam-related equipment. *(Modern Power & Engineering)*
*2. The Canadian Market for Air-Conditioning, Heating and Ventilation Equipment*   A statistical report on apparent domestic consumption value of shipments, imports and exports of air-conditioning, heating, and ventilation equipment. *(Maclean Hunter Research Bureau)*

*3. Market/Media Portfolio*  A booklet with information on the Canadian manufacturing market, including value of shipments, materials and supplies used, capital and repair expenditures, the size of the market, and a circulation profile. *(Maclean Hunter)*

*4. Modern Power & Engineering's Plant and Power Service Profile*  A summary of a survey conducted of more than 354 plants. It indicates responsibility for plant and power services, major equipment installed, who handles plant expansion, and reader buying influence and actions taken. *(Maclean Hunter)*

*5. Profile of Canadian Plant and Its Management*  Provides information about plant size, number of employees, adequacy of present facilities. The report also addresses the plant from the employee standpoint, including years on the job, income, and publications read. *(Maclean Hunter)*

*6. Survey of Industrials*  Published annually. Covers all Canadian public industrial corporations with details for each on operations, management, financial data, and subsidiaries. *(Financial Post Corporation Service)*

**Materials Handling**  *1. Materials Handling & Distribution Market in Canada*  A statistical report on production and imports of materials-handling equipment. Information on capital expenditure and forecasts is also included. *(Maclean Hunter)*

*2. Materials Management & Distribution: Handbook and Directory of Buying Services*  Published annually as the directory issue of *Materials Management & Distribution.* Acts as a purchasing guide for materials handling equipment and supplies. It is divided into three sections: manufacturers, equipment listed alphabetically, and equipment in a classified list. *(Maclean Hunter Business Publications)*

**Metalworking**  *1. Canada's Metalworking Market*  A statistical report on the metalworking industry in Canada. Includes Canadian production, number of plants, cost of material used, and number of employees. Also includes imports of metalworking equipment and production of major products in this industry. *(Maclean Hunter)*

*2. Canadian Machinery and Metalworking: Metalworking Directory and Buying Guide*  Published annually as the directory issue of *Canadian Machinery and Metalworking.* Provides information on products, manufacturers, distributors, trade names, and government, industry, and association sources. *(Maclean Hunter Business Publications)*

**Office Equipment and Supplies**  *1. The Canadian Survey*  The results of a survey intended to obtain a profile of Canadian secretaries, to determine what influences them to purchase a broad range of office equipment and office supplies. *(Maclean Hunter)*

2. *The Office Equipment & Supplies Market in Canada*   Reports Canadian production, imports, exports, and apparent domestic consumption. The publication also forecasts the individual industries. *(Maclean Hunter)*

3. *Office Equipment & Methods: Buyer's Guide and Directory* Published annually as the directory issue of *Office Equipment & Methods*. Lists suppliers, associations, and trade shows for the office equipment and services sector. *(Maclean Hunter Business Publications)*

**Packaging**
1. *Canada's Packaging Market*   Contains statistics on all facets of Canada's packaging market, including production, imports, exports, etc. *(Maclean Hunter)*

2. *Canadian Packaging Buyers Guide*   A directory issue of *Canadian Packaging* that provides an index to materials, machinery, and services available to Canada's packaging industry. *(Maclean Hunter)*

**Petroleum and Mining**
1. *Petroleum Industry in Canada Report*   Published annually. Provides statistical breakdown of the petroleum market in Canada by segments of the industry. *(Maclean Hunter)*

2. *Survey of Mines and Energy Resources*   Published annually. Covers the mining and energy industries in Canada. Provides details on approximately 2900 companies, covering their operations, management, and financial status. *(Financial Post Corporation Service)*

**Photography**
1. *Canada's Photography Market*   The result of a study of photography sales in Canada. Includes an estimate of total sales, estimated retail sales of equipment, and imports by country. *(Maclean Hunter)*

2. *Canadian Photography Buyers Guide*   Lists photography equipment, brand names, and Canadian distributors and manufacturers. Also contains a listing of photography associations in Canada and official repair centres. *(Maclean Hunter)*

3. *Photo Canada Annual Buyers Guide*   Describes hundreds of pieces of photographic equipment available in Canada, including suggested retail prices. *(Maclean Hunter)*

**Printing, Publishing, Graphic Arts**
1. *Canadian Printer & Publisher's Buyer's Guide and Directory of Canadian Sources*   Lists 20 product classifications and more than 500 companies that serve the printing, publishing, and allied industries in the Canadian graphic arts market. *(Maclean Hunter)*

**Product Design and Engineering**
1. *Canadian Market for OEM (Original Equipment Manufacturers) Components and Materials*   A market report containing Canadian production and imports and exports of industrial products associated with the original equipment market. *(Maclean Hunter)*

*2. Fluid Power Handbook and Industry*   Published biennially. Provides information on over 950 manufacturers and distributors of fluid power products in Canada and the U.S. The directory has four sections: engineering data, manufacturers'/product/trade name directory, catalogues, and local source outlets. *(Penton/IPC Publications)*

**Retailing**   *1. Canadian Directory of Shopping Centres*   Published annually. Lists all shopping centres in Canada over 4600 m². Provides the names of retail tenants and managers/owners, and statistical data such as rent costs, traffic figures, and market population. *(Monday Report on Retailers)*

*2. Directory of Retail Chains in Canada*   Published annually. Lists all retail chains in Canada with more than three stores. Provides addresses for head and regional offices, listings of personnel, merchandise range, financial status, and lease and expansion information. *(Monday Report on Retailers)*

*3. Directory of Restaurant and Fast Food Chains in Canada*   Published annually. Provides information on over 600 restaurant and fast food chains in Canada that have three or more outlets. Includes head and regional office addresses, personnel listings, and advertising, franchise, and financial data. *(Monday Report on Retailers)*

*4. Monday Report on Retailing*   Weekly newsletter reporting on Canadian chain retailers, with emphasis on store expansion plans, merchandise and policy changes, financial data, etc. *(Maclean Hunter)*

*5. Shopping Centre Canada's Sources*   A directory for all Canadian shopping centre industries, which provides detail by category on all firms acting as suppliers to the Canadian shopping centre industry. This includes construction companies, building material suppliers, security equipment and services, financial and leasing services, etc. The companies are listed alphabetically and also by product categories. Manufacturers and distributors are also listed. *(Maclean Hunter)*

*6. The Top 100*   A prospectus on the emergence of larger hardware stores and consumer-oriented lumber and building materials stores into home centres. Contains the names and addresses of the top 100 chains, wholesalers, and mass merchandisers serving some 8000 retail stores. *(Maclean Hunter)*

**Business Guides, Directories, and Indexes**   *1. Canadian Trade Index*   Published annually. Contains a classified list of products manufactured in Canada, a geographical list of Canadian manufacturers, and an alphabetical list of Canadian manufacturers. Also included are sections on farm products, trademarks, and services *(Canadian Manufacturers' Association)*

*2. Fraser's Canadian Trade Directory*   Published annually. The main section of this directory is a list of manufacturers by product, followed by an alphabetical list of manufacturers. Also included are a list of trade names and their manufacturers, and a list of foreign firms with their agents or distributors. *(Fraser's)*

*3. The Blue Book of Canadian Business*   Provides information on Canadian companies and their social and economic impact. The document reviews some 2500 medium and large firms. Its three sections are profiles of the leading Canadian corporations; ranking of major Canadian corporations; and Canadian business index. *(Canadian Newspaper Services International Ltd.)*

*4. Moody's Industrial Manual*   Published annually with updates. Covers companies listed on the major American stock exchanges. Provides corporate histories, business and product descriptions, subsidiaries, a personnel listing, and financial statements for the companies listed. *(Moody's Investors Service)*

*5. Sales and Marketing Management*   Published monthly. An American magazine featuring articles on sales and marketing management. The magazine also reports data from other countries. Particularly interesting are its annual issues of market survey data: 1) Survey of Buying Power (July); 2) Survey of Industrial and Commercial Purchasing Power (April); and 3) Survey of Selling Costs (February). *(Bill Communications)*

*6. Canadian Urban Trends — National Perspective*   Provides a general orientation, giving the users a set of tables, charts, maps, and descriptive text outlining the social and economic ramifications of growing urbanization. The first section focuses on 137 urban areas of more than 10 000 people and discusses population growth, economy, manufacturing, income disparities, family life cycle, the cultural mosaic, housing, and patterns of interaction among urban areas. Section 2 focuses on the 22 census metropolitan areas, both as single entities and as agglomerations of neighbourhoods. It provides differences between metropolitan areas and neighbourhoods in terms of the family life cycle, income, and cultural characteristics. The third section provides much of the same information as the second one, for more than 2200 metropolitan areas. *(Copp Clark Pitman/Ministry of State for Urban Affairs)*

## International Marketing Publications

Most of these are available in university and public libraries.

*1. International Marketing Data and Statistics*   Published annually. Provides statistical information on all basic marketing parameters for 132 countries. The statistics are presented in four-page comparative tables for easy use and comparison between regions. Includes sections on consumer spending and households. *(Euromonitor)*

*2. European Marketing Data and Statistics*   Published annually. Provides current statistical market information on 30 countries of Western and Eastern Europe. Comparative tables include population, employment, production, trade, the economy, standard of living, market size, and health. Useful for planning and development studies. *(Euromonitor)*

*3. Statistical Year Book*   Provides information on some 200 countries and territories that are members of the United Nations. The book includes reference tables and covers education, science and technology, libraries, book production, cultural information, newspapers, radio broadcasting, and television. *(Office of Statistics of the United Nations and the National Commission for UNESCO)*

*4. Yearbook of International Trade Statistics*   An annual publication that provides basic information on external trade performances of 163 United Nations member countries in terms of the overall trends in current value as well as in volume and price, the importance of trading partners, and the significance of individual commodities imported and exported.

There are two volumes: Volume 1 contains the detailed data for individual countries with summary tables, value of market economies, index numbers by regions, value of market economies, etc., and provides the trends in world trade, population, and production; Volume 2 contains a chapter on price and price indexes, commodity tables showing the total economic world trade of certain commodities analysed by regions and countries, and commodity matrix tables. *(Gower Press)*

*5. World Index of Economic Forecasts*   A compendium of information about 370 organizations that provides forecasts, plans, and surveys for over 100 countries. Includes alphabetical profiles of the forecasting organizations, plus three other indexes (which analyse the organizations according to their coverage — such as commodity forecasters, exchange rate specialists, and business activity forecasters). *(Gower Publishing)*

*6. Year Book of Labour Statistics*   Published annually. Provides a summary of the principal labour statistics for some 180 countries. The data cover the most recent 10-year period and are obtained mainly from the respective national statistical services. *(International Labour Organization)*

*7. The World Economic Survey*   This survey is intended to provide the basis for a synthesized appraisal of the current trends in the world economy, particularly as they affect the progress of developing countries. *(Office for Development Research and Policy Analy-*

*sis, Department of International Economic and Social Affairs, the United Nations)*

**8. The World Tables**    A collection of tables of economic and social data for a large number of countries. The tables show three groups of indicators: basic economic data for individual countries, derived economic indicators suitable for making comparisons between countries and country groups, and demographic and social data. The economic data are presented in a continuous time series, whereas the derived indicators are shown for selected years only. *(World Bank)*

**9. Periodic Markets in Africa, Asia and Latin America**    This document discusses the importance of periodic markets — sites at which buyers and sellers converge on a regular schedule — in the development process, and the effect of development on the periodic markets. The bibliography is presented in four sections: general, Africa, Asia, and Latin America. *(Robert H.T. Smith, Department of Geography, Queen's University, Kingston, Ont.)*

**10. Demographic Trends 1970–1985 in OECD Member Countries**    The result of a study by the Organization for Economic Cooperation and Development on projections of population for the period 1970–1985. The projections for total population for some countries go up to the year 2000. *(Manpower and Social Affairs Committee, OECD)*

**11. Demographic Trends 1950–1990**    A study of demographic and labour force trends over the period 1950–1990, based on historical material and projections supplied to the OECD by member countries. The changes in population and labour markets are analysed in depth by age and sex, and a considerable number of graphs are included to facilitate comparison between countries. *(OECD)*

**12. World Studies from Predicasts Inc.**    *World Studies* provides information in the following areas:
- major producers
- growing markets
- plant expansion
- world price situation for a given product
- political factors affecting markets
- role of multinationals
- participation in the world market
- trend forecasts *(Predicasts Inc.)*

# *P A R T*

## Consumer Behaviour

*Understanding consumers and industrial buyers and their behaviour is essential to the correct application of the marketing concept. It is also the starting point in the development of an effective marketing strategy. The chapters in Part Three study the ways in which individuals, industries, and government make decisions and take actions designed to satisfy their needs. The chapters focus on the internal factors and external environmental influences that affect consumer decision-making and industrial purchase behaivour.*

## CHAPTER 7

# Interpersonal Influences on Consumer Behaviour

*1. To relate interpersonal influences on consumer behaviour to the variables of the marketing mix.*

*2. To explain the classification of behavioural influences.*

*3. To outline steps in the consumer decision process.*

*4. To identify the interpersonal determinants of consumer behaviour.*

*5. To explain the role of culture and subculture in consumer behaviour.*

*6. To describe the Asch phenomenon.*

*7. To know the impact of reference groups on consumer behaviour.*

*8. To explain the importance of social class in the study of consumer behaviour.*

*9. To describe family influences on consumer behaviour and how they are changing.*

Li Shuang, Ke Ming, Li Yong, and Tan Yun Wei from the People's Republic of China learned a lot about the "different" behaviour of American consumers in Cleveland. The four accountants were on a six-month assignment with Ernst & Whinney, a Cleveland-based accounting firm. Their visit was part of an agreement whereby one of the firm's partners would go to China, while two teams of Chinese accountants would study American accounting practices in Cleveland and Chicago. But the foursome were probably more struck by North American consumption behaviour than the way we treat our debits and credits.

Some of their experiences were perhaps more amusing than shocking: on the way from Peking to San Francisco, Li Shuang was puzzled by the cup of salad dressing and glass of water on his airplane tray. So he mixed them together and drank the concoction. Li later remarked in his limited English: "It wasn't very delicious." Similarly, his companion Tan Yun Wei was a bit surprised over the "sour oranges" he got when he ordered grapes — which he called grapefruit — for breakfast.

Li Yong admits he had heard a rumour that North Americans actually sell dog food in their supermarkets. He was amazed when told it was true: "It's unbelievable. The dogs and cats in America eat better than people in some Asian countries." Li points out that most Chinese do not keep dogs as pets; indeed dogs are more likely to be eaten than provided for by consumers. Li also did not understand the strange custom of a buyer tipping a seller of a service. He wanted to know why North Americans did not tip before rather than after the fact, if they wanted better service.

While Ernst was renting a suite for the men in a downtown high rise, the rental agent launched into a long discourse on the garbage disposal, dishwasher, and so on. The four clients were oblivious to her spiel because they had never felt the need for such features before.[1]

## The Conceptual Framework

**Consumer behaviour** consists of *the acts of individuals in obtaining and using goods and services, including the decision processes that precede and determine these acts.*[2] This definition includes both the ultimate consumer and the purchaser of industrial products. A major difference in the purchasing behaviour of industrial consumers and ultimate consumers is that additional influences from within the organization may be exerted on the industrial purchasing agent.

This chapter assesses interpersonal influences on consumer behaviour, while the next chapter explores personal influences. Chapter 9 deals with industrial and organizational buyer behaviour.

## Classifying Behavioural Influences: Personal and Interpersonal

The field of consumer behaviour borrows extensively from other areas like psychology and sociology.[3] The work of Kurt Lewin, for instance, provides an excellent classification of influences on buying behaviour. Lewin's proposition was:

$$B = f(P, E)$$

where behaviour ($B$) is a function ($f$) of the interactions of personal influences ($P$) and the pressures exerted upon them by outside forces in the environment ($E$).[4]

---

[1] Dean Rotbart, "Chinese Accountants Find that America Is Hard to Figure," *The Wall Street Journal* (June 5, 1981), pp. 1, 12.

[2] This definition is adapted from James F. Engel and Roger D. Blackwell, *Consumer Behaviour,* 4th ed. (Hinsdale, Ill.: The Dryden Press, 1982), p. 9.

[3] See Albert J. Della Bitta, "Consumer Behaviour: Some Thoughts on Sheth's Evaluation of the Discipline," *Journal of the Academy of Marketing Science* (Winter 1982), pp. 5–6.

[4] See Kurt Lewin, *Field Theory in Social Science* (New York: Harper & Row, 1951), p. 62. See also C. Glenn Walters, "Consumer Behavior: An Appraisal," *Journal of the Academy of Marketing Science* (Fall 1979), pp. 237–284.

This statement is usually rewritten for consumer behaviour as follows:

$$B = f(I,P)$$

where consumer behaviour ($B$) is a function ($f$) of the interaction of interpersonal determinants ($I$), like reference groups and culture, and personal determinants ($P$), like attitudes, on the consumer. Understanding consumer behaviour requires an understanding of both the individual's psychological makeup and the influences of others.

## The Consumer Decision Process

Consumer behaviour may be viewed as a decision process and the act of purchasing is merely one point in the process. To understand consumer behaviour, the events that precede and follow the purchase must be examined. Figure 7-1 identifies the steps in the consumer decision process: problem recognition, search, evaluation of alternatives, purchase decision, purchase act, and postpurchase evaluation. The consumer uses the decision process to solve problems and to take advantage of opportunities that arise. Through this process consumers correct differences between their actual and desired states. Feedback from each decision serves as additional experience to rely upon in subsequent decisions.

The process can be illustrated by the young couple whose only television set has been declared irreparable by the service representative. They clearly need to purchase a new set since television is a primary form of recreation for their young children (*problem recognition*). The couple questions their friends and acquaintances who have bought televisions recently. They pore over consumer-oriented reports on new models (*search*). Once they have collected all the necessary information the couple consider the various models on the basis of what is important to them — reliability and price (*evaluation*). They decide to buy a new set the next weekend (*purchase decision*). They do so at a local discount store the next Saturday (*purchase act*). The new set is hooked up, and the young family sits back to enjoy their purchase (*post purchase evaluation*) and check out its special features.

This process is common to consumer purchase decisions. It is introduced here to provide an advance perspective of the field of consumer behaviour. An expanded discussion of the model concludes Chapter 8, after the reader has an overview of the various factors that affect consumer behaviour.

**Figure 7-1   Steps in the Consumer Decision Process**

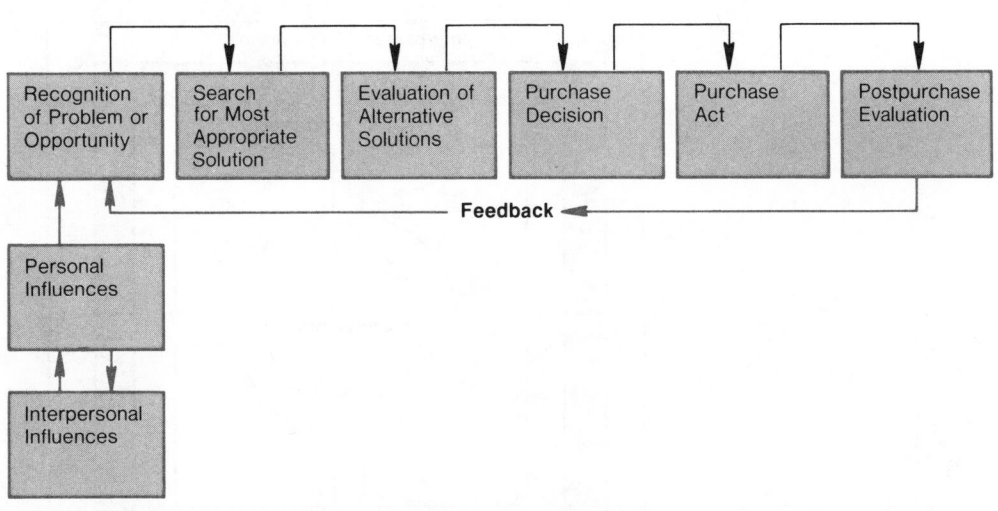

Source: Adapted from C. Glenn Walters and Gordon W. Paul, *Consumer Behavior: An Integrated Framework* (Homewood, Ill.: Richard D. Irwin, Inc., 1970), p. 18 © 1970 by Richard D. Irwin, Inc. and John Dewey, *How We Think* (Boston, Mass.: D. C. Heath, 1910), pp. 101-105. Similar steps are also discussed in Del I. Hawkins, Roger J. Best, and Kenneth A. Coney, *Consumer Behavior: Implications for Marketing Strategy*, revised ed. (Plano, Texas: Business Publications, Inc., 1983), pp. 447–606.

### *Interpersonal Determinants of Consumer Behaviour*

People are social animals. They often buy products and services that will enable them to project a favourable image to others. Cultural environment, membership of reference groups, and family may influence such purchase decisions. A general model of the interpersonal (or group) determinants of consumer behaviour is shown in Figure 7-2. It indicates that there are three categories of interpersonal determinants of consumer behaviour: cultural influences, social influences, and family influences. (The model will be expanded to include personal influences in Chapter 8.)

### *Cultural Influences*

Culture is the broadest environmental determinant of consumer behaviour. Sometimes it is a very elusive concept for marketers to handle. General Mills knew that few Japanese homes had ovens, so it designed a Betty Crocker cake mix that could be made in the electric rice cookers widely used in that country. The product failed because of a cultural factor. Japanese homemakers regard the purity of their rice as very important, so they were afraid that a cake flavour might be left in their cookers.[5]

---

[5] "Learning How to Please the Baffling Japanese," *Fortune* (October 5, 1981), p. 122.

Figure 7-2   Interpersonal Determinants of Consumer Behaviour

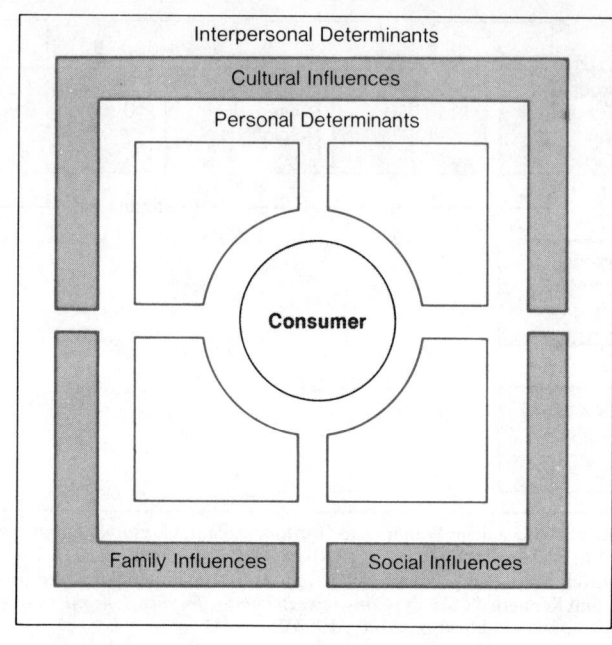

Source: Adapted with permission from C. Glenn Walters and Gordon W. Paul, *Consumer Behavior: An Integrated Framework* (Homewood Ill.: Richard D. Irwin, 1970), p. 16. © 1970 by Richard D. Irwin, Inc.

**Culture** can be defined as *"the complex of values, ideas, attitudes, institutions, and other meaningful symbols created by people to shape human behaviour and the artifacts of that behaviour, transmitted from one generation to the next."*[6] It is the way of life learned and handed down through generations that gives each society its own peculiar characteristics and values.

***Core Values in the Canadian Culture***
The list in Figure 7-3 provides a useful summary of characteristics significant to the Canadian culture today. There are trends and shifts in cultural values, yet traditionally these changes have been gradual, unlike the revolutionary 1960s when some people felt overwhelmed by the pace of change. Rapid technological shifts may alter the pace once again in the future, so marketers must constantly assess cultural norms.[7] One of the most recent cultural trends is the search

[6] Engel and Blackwell, *Consumer Behavior*, 4th ed., p. 72.
[7] Daniel Yankelovich, "New Rules," *The Seattle Times* (November 1, 1981), pp. F 1, F 4. Excerpted from the book, *New Rules: Searching for Self-Fulfillment in a World Turned Upside Down* by Daniel Yankelovich. Copyright 1981, Daniel Yankelovich. Distributed by Los Angeles Times Syndicate.

for more interpersonal relationships, rather than the self-centered orientation that characterized recent value structures. In other words, many people want greater friendship.[8] This trend has been noted by marketers who now feature more family and friendship groups in their scenarios for commercials. Restaurant and soft drink commercials often provide good examples.

---

**Figure 7-3  Summary of Significant Canadian Characteristics**

As a function of being a part of the North American reality:

Modern orientation
Openness to new ideas
Egalitarianism
A rich developing society with many needs and high materialistic
   expectations
Growing, more diffuse "middle class"

In relation to the United States:

Conservative tendencies
Traditional bias
Greater confidence in bureaucratic institutions
Collectivity orientation — reliance on institutions such as state, big
   business, and the church vs. personal risk-taking
Less achievement-oriented
Lower optimism — less willing to take risks
Greater acceptance of hierarchical order and stratification
Tolerance for diversity — acceptance of cultural mosaic
Family stability
Selective emulation of the United States — resistance to some American
   characteristics and dominance, yet willingness to emulate
Elitist and ascriptive tendencies

---

**Cultural Influences: An International Perspective**

An awareness of cultural differences is particularly important for international marketers. Different attitudes, mores, and folkways all have an impact on marketing strategy. Examples of cultural influences on marketing strategy are abundant in the international environment. Look at the marketing implications of the following situations:

• Because of inept translation, Schweppes Tonic Water was advertised in Italy as "bathroom water," and in South America, Parker Pen Company unwittingly indicated that its product would prevent unwanted pregnancies.[9]

---

[8] This is noted in Engel and Blackwell, *Consumer Behavior*, 4th ed., p. 75.
[9] Robert Linn, "Americans Turn Deaf Ear to Foreign Tongues," *Orlando Sentinel Star* (November 1, 1981).

- A Goodyear advertisement demonstrated the strength of its "3T" tire cord by showing a steel chain breaking. When the commercial was shown in West Germany, however, it was perceived as an insult to steel chain manufacturers.[10]
- The headline for a series of advertisements shown in Japan to introduce Seiko's new line of coloured dial watches read as follows: "Like a Wind, I am the Colour of a Bird." To people in North America it was meaningless. But to Japanese consumers it meant something like: "This watch is light and delicate. It floats on your hand like a seedpod on the wind. Or a bird. A hummingbird with its jewel-like colours, the colours of the watch itself."[11]
- Deodorant usage among men ranges from 80 percent in the United States to 55 percent in Sweden, 28 percent in Italy, and 8 percent in the Philippines.[12]
- White is the colour of mourning in Japan. The colour purple is associated with death in many Latin American countries.
- Feet are regarded as despicable in Thailand. Athlete's-foot remedies with packages featuring a picture of feet will not be well received.[13]
- In Ethiopia the time required for a decision is directly proportional to its importance. This is so much the case that the low-level bureaucrats there attempt to elevate the prestige of their work by taking a long time to make decisions. North Americans there are innocently prone to downgrade their work in the local people's eyes by trying to speed things up.[14]

Often a marketing program that has been proven successful in Canada cannot be applied directly in international markets because of cultural differences. Real differences exist among different countries, and the differences must be known and evaluated by the international firm. When Helene Curtis introduced its Every Night shampoo line in Sweden, it renamed the product Every Day, since Swedes usually wash their hair in the morning.[15]

Denture makers are aware of the impact of cultural difference on tastes in false teeth. The people of Thailand are extremely fond of betel nuts, which stain their teeth black. For many years, once

---

10 *Wall Street Journal* (March 9, 1977), p. 1.

11 Leon G. Schiffman and Leslie Lazar Kanuk, *Consumer Behavior* (Englewood Cliffs, N.J.: Prentice-Hall, 1978), p. 390.

12 *Advertising Age* (April 1, 1974).

13 Charles Winich, "Anthropology's Contributions to Marketing," *Journal of Marketing* (July 1961), p. 59.

14 Edward T. Hall, "The Silent Language in Overseas Business," *Harvard Business Review* (May–June 1960), p. 89.

15 Patricia L. Layman, "In Any Language, the Beauty Business Spells Success," *Chemical Week* (September 17, 1975), p. 26.

their original teeth wore out, they were replaced with black dentures. After World War II, however, fashions changed, and the Thais began using abrasives to scrub off the black stains. Abrasives are now popular items in Thailand. Scandinavians like greyish false teeth, mostly because nature has blessed them with naturally grey teeth. The Japanese select false teeth noticeably longer than their natural ones.[16]

World marketers face competition from firms in Germany, France, the Soviet Union, Japan, and a dozen other countries as well as firms in the host nation, and they must become intimately familiar with all aspects of the local population — including their cultural heritage. The local market segments in each country must be thoroughly analysed prior to the development of a marketing plan just as they are at home. The topic of cultural influences in international marketing is explored more fully in Chapter 22.

**Subcultures**      Within each culture are numerous **subcultures** — *subgroups with their own distinguishing modes of behaviour.* Any culture as heterogeneous as that existing in Canada is composed of significant subcultures based on such factors as race, nationality, age, rural-urban location, religion, and geographic distribution. The size of such subculture groups can be very significant. For example, the Italian population in the Toronto area is about 500 000 — larger than most Canadian cities.

Many people on the West Coast display a lifestyle emphasizing casual dress, outdoor entertaining, and water recreation. Mormons refrain from purchasing tobacco and liquor; orthodox Jews purchase kosher or other traditional foods; Chinese may exhibit more interest in products and symbols of their Chinese heritage.

The French-Canadian Market   Although Canada has many subcultures, in fact, the two founding cultures — English and French — are the most influential through sheer force of numbers. The francophone population is a significant market in Canada.[17] Twenty-

---

[16] N. R. Kleinsfield, "This is One Story with Teeth in It — False Ones, That Is," *The Wall Street Journal* (August 18, 1975), p. 1; see also Joseph F. Hair, Jr., and Rolph E. Anderson, "Culture, Acculturation and Consumer Behavior: An Empirical Study," in Boris W. Becker and Helmut Becker (eds.), *Dynamic Marketing in a Changing World* (Chicago: American Marketing Association, 1973), pp. 423–428.

[17] See Jean-Charles Chebat and Georges Henault, "The Cultural Behavior of Canadian Consumers," in *Cases and Readings in Marketing* by R. H. Rotenberg (Toronto: Holt, Rinehart and Winston, 1974), pp. 176–180. This material also appeared in *Revue Commerce*, September 1971. Also see M. Brisebois, "Industrial Advertising and Marketing in Quebec," *The Marketer* (Spring-Summer 1966), p. 11.

five percent of the Canadian population identify French as their mother tongue. While most of this population is in Quebec, there are significant French segments in other provinces. Proportionately, the largest is in New Brunswick where 33.6 percent of the population, or 224 000, have French as their mother tongue.[18] Numerically, Ontario has the larger group with 462 000.

The Quebec market is large enough and different enough to create an entire advertising industry of its own. Quebec constitutes about 27 percent of the total Canadian market for goods and services, and is the second largest market in Canada.[19] Personal disposable income in 1982 was over $48 billion, and retail sales were estimated at $23.5 billion.[20]

While there is no doubt that the Quebec market is substantially different from the rest of Canada, it is difficult to define those differences precisely. Considerable research over the years has pointed out many characteristics specific to the area — French Canadians, for example, are more fond of sweets than other Canadians. However, other data can usually be found to contest any such finding or show that it is at least not true any longer.

Such statements only reflect measurement of traits in the Quebec culture at one particular period. These measurements may be legitimate and necessary for a firm wishing to market a product in that segment at a particular point in time. However, similar differences can probably be detected between consumers in Nova Scotia and British Columbia, if you look for them.

Attention should not be concentrated on *specific* differences between the Quebec market and the rest of Canada, but rather on the fact that there is a basic cultural difference between the two markets. "Culture is a way of being, thinking and feeling. It is a driving force animating a significant group of individuals united by a common tongue, and sharing the same customs, habits and experiences."[21] Because of this cultural difference, some marketing programs may be distinctly different in Quebec than in the rest of Canada.

In the French-Canadian market, it is not the products that are

---

[18] Gail Chaisson, "The French Market Today," *Marketing* (June 1, 1981), pp. 11, 14.

[19] Eleine Saint-Jacques and Bruce Mallen, "The French Market under the Microscope," *Marketing* (May 11, 1981), p. 10.

[20] Gail Chaisson, "The French Market Today," *Marketing* (June 1, 1981), p. 11. And Statistics Canada, catalogue # 63-005, and 13-201.

[21] Canadian Royal Commission on Bilingualism and Biculturalism.

different, it is the state of mind.[22] For example, Renault achieved a Quebec market penetration 10 times greater than in the rest of Canada. Since the product and price is the same, the difference must lie in the marketing program attuned to the Quebec market. In English Canada, Renault used the same campaign theme as in the U.S.: "Le Car." That was considered unsuitable for Quebec, where "Le Car" would have created negative feelings. The image of Renault was not good enough to be called the tops, the absolute Number One, which is what "Le Car" would mean in French. It would not be credible. Therefore, the Quebec agency for Renault chose "le chameau," a theme that humorously emphasized economy and fitted the needs of Quebec consumers (see Figure 7-4).

**Current characteristics of the Quebec market**   Nevertheless there are current differences between the Quebec market and the English-Canadian market.[23] First, except for Atlantic Canada, income levels are somewhat lower in Quebec, although the differences are being quite rapidly eliminated.

Second, food consumption patterns differ significantly. French Canadians spend substantially more on food than English Canadians. These cultural patterns are reflected in the type and quantities of food and ancillary items purchased.

French Canadians use their leisure differently also. More go to the movies and attend plays, concerts, opera, or ballet. However, more anglophones read books. Francophones spend less on travel than anglophones, although this is changing rapidly.

French Canadians watch slightly more television per week than English Canadians. Naturally they watch mainly French-language television, which has stimulated a large television and cinema industry in the province.

Michel Cloutier argues that many differences between French- and English-Canadian cultures are the result of education and income.[24] As the gap between these factors narrows, and as cultures are affected by similar political and technological influences, so will the differences in values and consumption patterns narrow. Nevertheless, it appears that frames of reference and significant cues will continue to be different, requiring the marketer to be astute in

---

22 Based on Jan Morin and Michel Ostiguy, "View From the Top," *Marketing* (June 1, 1981), p. 28.
23 Adapted from Eleine Saint-Jacques and Bruce Mallen, "The French Market under the Microscope," *Marketing* (May 11, 1981), pp. 12–13.
24 M. Cloutier, "Marketing in Quebec," Industrial Marketing Research Association Conference, Toronto, March 1978.

**Figure 7-4   Taking Cultural Differences into Consideration in Advertising**

Advertisement used in French Canada.

dealing with these market segments. This is shown in Figure 7-5.

The key to success in this important Canadian market is having marketing specialists who understand people, and understand how to deal in that specific market. Sophisticated marketers now realize this. That is why there are so many Quebec advertising agencies.

A final unique aspect of the Quebec market is the influence of the provincial government. Numerous special laws have been passed

**Figure 7-4   Continued**

Advertisement used in English Canada.

# *Introducing the new 5-door Renault Le Car. Advantage, yours!*

*Renault has just made Europe's number one car even better. And the advantages of this newest Renault Le Car are all yours!*

### *Easy access and passenger comfort.*
*Advantage, yours! Four wide opening doors for easy entry and exit, reclining front bucket seats, plus a large rear hatch that opens to 9.1 cubic feet of covered cargo space. (The rear seat folded more than triples the capacity to 31.5 cu. ft.!)*

### *Remarkable fuel economy. Advantage, yours!*
*A responsive 1.4 litre 4-cylinder engine and all-synchromesh 4-speed manual transmission deliver a Transport Canada rating of 6.5 L/100 km or 43 mpg with a highway fuel consumption of 53 mpg\*. That's performance you'll feel in your wallet!*

### *Front-wheel drive. Advantage, yours! On the*
*open road the 5-door Renault Le Car is uncommonly quick, smooth and maneuverable, thanks to front-wheel drive, rack-and-pinion steering, 4-wheel independent torsion bar suspension and Michelin radial tires.*

### *Built by Renault. Advantage, yours!*
*Renault is one of the largest automobile manufacturers in the world and has been developing and building front-wheel drive automobiles for more than 20 years. In fact, over 18 million front-wheel drive Renault cars have been sold around the world. The new 5-door Renault Le Car. Spirited performance, precise handling, remarkable fuel economy and now the extra advantage of five doors.*

*and Renault are trade marks of Regie Nationale des Usines Renault*

*\* Transport Canada Fuel Consumption Guide, February 1981. (Fuel consumption rating 6.5 L/100 km, Highway 5.3 L/100 km, Urban 8.1 L/100 km). Ratings are only for comparison between various makes and models. Your actual fuel consumption may vary depending on road conditions, driving habits, road, weather and vehicle condition.*

Le Car

**At over 200 Renault and American Motors Dealers across Canada.**

Source: Courtesy of American Motors (Canada) Inc.

or are being proposed. Most notable is Bill 101, which makes French the official language of the province. The marketing communications implications of this appear in the design of signs and billboards, where it is illegal to use any language but French. The Quebec government is also probably more protective of the consumer than any other provincial government. For example, advertising to children is strictly regulated and restricted.

Figure 7-5   Cultural Characteristics of English- and French-speaking
             Canadians

|  | English-speaking | French-speaking |
|---|---|---|
| Ethnic origin | Anglo-Saxon | Latin |
| Religion | Protestant | Catholic |
| Intellectual attitude | Pragmatic | Theoretical |
| Family | Matriarchy | Patriarchy |
| Leisure time | In function of the professional class | In function of the family circle |
| Individual vis-à-vis the environment | More social | More individualistic |
| Business management | Administrator | Innovator |
| Political tendencies | Conservative | Liberal |
| Consumption attitudes | Propensity to save; conformist; financier more than financed | Propensity to spend; innovator; financed more than a financier |

Note: These cultural characteristics are very general and there will be many variations within each culture.

Source: Georges Hénault, "Les conséquences du biculturalisme sur la consommation,"
*Commerce* (septembre 1971).

# The Right Words for the Right Market

In advertising, language plays a key role. Misuse of language can be, and often is, a source of confusion and misunderstanding. Since language is more than just a sequence of words without reference to cultural context, the problem of translation is never as simple as the mere mechanical use of a dictionary. Occasionally, a literal translation may be acceptable. However, there are serious pitfalls. The following "gems" illustrate the point:

1. Car wash: Lavement d'auto (car enema).
2. Fresh milk used: Lait frais usagé (used fresh milk).
3. They are terrific: Elles sont terrifiantes (they are terrifying).
4. Big John: Gros Jos (large breast).

5. Chicken to take out: Poulet pour sortir (chicken to go out with).

   The same observation applies to literal translations from French to English. Here are the literal English translations of a few extremely successful French Canadian slogans:

1. He there knows that: Lui y connaît ça (he really knows what he's talking about)!
2. There is in it: Y en a dedans (there's a lot to it)!
3. That — that walks: Ça, ça marche (that really works)!
4. One chance out of thirteen: Une chance sur treize (thirteen to one)!
5. That's all a number: C'est tout un numéro (He's a [terrific] guy)!

Source: Eleine Saint-Jacques and Bruce Mallen, "The French Market Under the Microscope," *Marketing* (May 11, 1981), p. 14.

**Social Influences**   The earliest awareness of children confirms that they are members of a very important group — the family — from whom they seek total satisfaction of their physiological and social needs. As they grow older, they join other groups — neighbourhood play groups, school groups, the Cub Scouts, Brownies, minor hockey — as well as groups of friends. From these groups they acquire both status and role. **Status** refers to their *relative position in the group.* **Role** refers to the *rights and duties expected by other members of the group of the individual in a certain position in the group.* Some of these are formal groups (the Cub Scouts) and others are quite informal (the friendship groups). But both types supply their members with status and roles and, in doing so, influence the activities, including the consumer behaviour, of each member.

**The Asch**   Although most persons view themselves as individuals, groups are
**Phenomenon:**   often highly influential in purchase decisions. In situations where
**Group Influence**   individuals feel that a particular group or groups are important,
**Effects on Conformity**   they tend to adhere in varying degrees to the general expectations of that group.

The surprising *impact that groups and group norms can exhibit on individual behaviour* has been called the **Asch phenomenon.** The phenomenon was first documented in the following study conducted by the psychologist S. E. Asch:

> Eight subjects are brought into a room and asked to determine which of a set of three unequal lines is closest to the length of a fourth line shown some distance from the other three. The subjects are to announce their judgments publicly. Seven of the subjects are working for the experimenter and they announce incorrect matches. The order of announcement is arranged such that the naive subject responds last. In a control situation, 37 naive subjects performed the task 18 times each without any information about others' choices. Two of the 37 subjects made a total of 3 mistakes. However, when another group of 50 naive subjects responded *after* hearing the unanimous but *incorrect* judgment of the other group members, 37 made a total of 194 errors, all of which were in agreement with the mistake made by the group.[25]

This widely replicated study illustrates the role of groups upon

---

[25] Del I. Hawkins, Kenneth A. Coney, and Roger J. Best, *Consumer Behaviour: Implications for Marketing Strategy* (Dallas: Business Publications, 1980), pp. 181–82. The quotation is adapted from S. E. Asch, "Effects of Group Pressure upon the Modification and Distortion of Judgments," in *Readings in Social Psychology,* eds. E. E. MacCoby et al. (New York: Holt, Rinehart and Winston, 1958), pp. 174–83.

individual choice-making. Marketing applications range from the choice of automobile models and residential locations to the decision to purchase at least one item at a Tupperware party.

**Reference Groups**     In order for groups to exert such influence on individuals, they must be categorized as **reference groups,** or groups whose *value structures and standards influence a person's behaviour.* Consumers usually try to keep their purchase behaviour in line with what they perceive to be the values of their reference group.

The status of the individual within the reference group produces three subcategories: **membership group,** where *the person actually belongs* to, say, a country club; **aspirational group,** a situation where *a person desires to associate with a group*; and a **disassociative group,** one *with which the individual does not want to be identified by*

**Figure 7-6    Extent of Reference Group Influence on Product and Brand Decision**

**Influence on Product Selected**

|  | **Influence on Brand Selected** |
|---|---|

| Magazines<br>Furniture<br>Clothing<br>Instant Coffee<br>Aspirin<br>Air Conditioners<br>Stereos<br>Laundry Detergent<br>Microwave Ovens<br><br>**Weak Product**<br>**Strong Brand** | Automobiles<br>Color TV<br><br><br><br><br><br><br><br><br>**Strong Product**<br>**Strong Brand** |
| **Weak Product**<br>**Weak Brand**<br><br>Canned Peaches<br>Toilet Soap<br>Beer<br>Cigarettes<br>Small Cigars | **Strong Product**<br>**Weak Brand** |

Source: Reprinted from Donald W. Hendon, "A New and Empirical Look at the Influence of Reference Groups on Generic Product Category and Brand Choice: Evidence from Two Nations," *Proceedings of the Academy of International Business: Asia-Pacific Dimensions of International Business* (Honolulu: College of Business Administration, University of Hawaii, December 18–20, 1979), pp. 752–761. Based on Francis S. Bourne, *Group Influence in Marketing and Public Relations* (Foundation for Research on Human Behavior, 1956), p. 8.

*others.* For example, teenagers are unlikely to enjoy the middle-of-the-road music played on radio stations catering to their parents' generation.

It is obviously not essential that the individual be a member in order for the group to serve as a point of reference. This partially explains the use of athletes in advertisements. Even though few possess the skills necessary to pilot a racer, all racing fans can identify with the Mosport winner by injecting their engines with STP.

The extent of reference-group influence varies widely among purchases. For reference-group influence to be great, two factors must be present:

1. The item must be one that can be seen and identified by others.
2. The item must also be conspicuous in the sense that it stands out, is unusual, and is a brand or product that not everyone owns.

Figure 7-6 shows the influence of reference groups on both the basic decision to purchase a product and the decision to purchase a particular brand. The figure shows that reference groups had a significant impact on both the decision to purchase an automobile and the type of brand that was actually selected. By contrast, reference groups had little impact on the decision to purchase canned peaches or the brand that was chosen. Figure 7-6 was derived from a survey which updated a widely cited 1956 study. A comparison with the earlier study shows that over time the extent of reference group influence can vary for both types of decisions.[26]

**Social Classes**   Although North Americans prefer to think of their society as open with equality for all, a well-structured class system exists on this continent as it does in all parts of the world. Research conducted during the 1940s by W. Lloyd Warner and during the late 1950s in Chicago by Pierre Martineau identified a six-class system within the social structure of both small and large cities. A description of the members of each class and an estimate of the population percentage in each class is shown in Figure 7-7. John Porter performed a similar analysis of social class in Canada and reported comparable findings in his classic book, *The Vertical Mosaic.*

Membership in a **social class** is determined by *occupation, source of income (not amount), education, family background, and dwelling areas.* Income is not the main determinant, and the view that "A rich person is a poor person with more money" is incorrect. Pipe-fitters paid at union scale will earn more money than many college professors, but their purchase behaviour may be quite different.

Richard Coleman illustrates the behaviour of three families, all

---

26 Francis S. Bourne, *Group Influence in Marketing and Public Relations* (Ann Arbor, Mich.: Foundation for Research on Human Behavior, 1956).

**Figure 7-7    The Warner Social Class Hierarchy**

| Social Class | Membership | Population Percentage (Estimated) |
|---|---|---|
| Upper-upper | Locally prominent families, third- or fourth-generation wealth. Merchants, financiers, or higher professionals. Wealth is inherited. Do a great amount of travelling. | 1.5 |
| Lower-upper | Newly arrived in upper class; "nouveau riche." Not accepted by upper class. Executive elite, founders of large businesses, doctors, lawyers. | 1.5 |
| Upper-middle | Moderately successful professionals, owners of medium-sized businesses, and middle management. Status conscious. Child- and home-centred. | 10.0 |
| Lower-middle | Top of the average world. Nonmanagerial office workers, small-business owners, and blue-collar families. Described as "striving and respectable." Conservative. | 33.0 |
| Upper-lower | Ordinary working class. Semiskilled workers. Income often as high as the next two classes above. Enjoy life. Live from day to day. | 38.0 |
| Lower-lower | Unskilled, umemployed, and unassimilated groups. Fatalistic. Apathetic. | 16.0 |
| Total | | 100.0 |

Source: Adapted from Charles B. McCann, *Women and Department Store Newspaper Advertising* (Chicago: Social Research, Inc., 1957). Reprinted by permission. (The estimates are based on Warner and Hollings's distributions in rather small communities. However, an estimate of social class structure for the U.S. and Canada approximates these percentages.)

earning less than $25 000 a year (in the mid 1970s), but each decidedly in a different social class. An upper-middle-class family in this income bracket — a young lawyer or a college professor and his or her family — is likely to spend its income to live in a prestige neighbourhood, buy expensive furniture from "quality stores," and join social clubs.

The lower-middle-class family — headed by a grocery store owner or a sales representative — buys a good house in a less expensive neighbourhood. They buy more furniture from less expensive stores and typically have a savings account at the local bank.

The lower-class family — headed by a truck driver or welder — spends less money on the house but buys one of the first new cars sold each year and owns one of the largest colour television sets in

# A New Look at Social Class Hierarchy

Analysis of people's lifestyle can be a revealing thing. It can tell you where they live, how they live, where they travel, what motivates them. More important, it can tell you the kinds of things they purchase. Because it is lifestyle, not just income, that determines what a person buys!

Without knowledge of a person's lifestyle you cannot intelligently target a product or service. With that knowledge you have the means to accurately profile your consumer base. You will know where to market a new product, where to best locate a new store, where to promote with direct mail, where to spend your advertising budget wisely. In fact, you will have the answers to every important marketing question!

In order to meet marketers' needs for better information, Compusearch has developed a system that groups all the neighbourhoods in Canada into unique clusters. A total of 70 different lifestyles has been identified (48 in urban centres and 22 in rural or nonurban areas). Following is a description of the major categories and a sample target market profile.

Who can use these new insights?
• Direct response advertisers can profile test mailings, target unaddressed mail, or boost name list response.
• Publishers can profile their subscription lists, know who their readers are, and acquire more.
• Banks, credit card companies, retailers—anyone with a list of customers who buy more than one product or service—can attach the codes to each customer record, find their own areas of strength, and cross-sell products to those most likely to buy.
• Manufacturers can put their products in the right hands or test new products in the right place.
• Retailers can find the best areas to expand into, or they can better customize merchandise mix in existing locations.

Source: © 'Lifestyles' is a trademark of Compusearch Market and Social Research Limited. Reprinted with the permission of Compusearch Market and Social Research Limited, 1987.

### Figure 1   Major Categories — Lifestyles™

| Code | Lifestyle Category | No. of Lifestyles | % All 1987 Households |
|------|--------------------|-------------------|------------------------|
| | **Urban** | | |
| A | Affluent | 4 | 1.29% |
| U | Upscale | 4 | 6.95% |
| M | Middle & Upper-Middle Class | 7 | 17.68% |
| W | Working (Lower-Middle) Class | 6 | 15.34% |
| L | Lower Class | 5 | 7.01% |
| S | Young Singles | 5 | 4.25% |
| C | Young Couples | 3 | 3.46% |
| N | Empty Nesters | 5 | 8.58% |
| O | Old & Retired | 5 | 3.92% |
| E | Ethnic | 4 | 3.32% |
| | **Nonurban** | | |
| X | Upscale & Middle Class | 8 | 10.38% |
| Y | Working & Lower Class | 9 | 15.14% |
| Z | Farming | 5 | 2.70% |

**Figure 2**

LIFESTYLES
SAMPLE TARGET MARKET PROFILE
PENETRATION ANALYSIS

| Lifestyle Descriptor | # Clients | % Clients | %HHDS Toronto | Index |
|---|---|---|---|---|
| A1 Wealthiest, highest education, large families in very expensive houses, age 45-54 | 2 539 | 1.03% | 0.59% | 175 |
| A2 Wealthy, well-educated families in expensive houses, age 45-64 | 6 732 | 2.73% | 1.08% | 253 |
| A3 Older, wealthy, well-educated couples and widow(er)s in apartments and condominiums | 1 388 | 0.56% | 0.28% | 200 |
| A4 Younger wealthy, well-educated, larger families with young teenagers in high-value houses | 3 651 | 1.48% | 0.99% | 149 |
| Total: Affluent | 14 310 | 5.80% | 2.94% | 197 |
| | | | | |
| U1 High income, older families with teenagers in higher-value houses; stable neighbourhoods | 12 665 | 5.13% | 3.08% | 167 |
| U2 High income, very well-educated, small mixed and older households in old, expensive mixed housing | 7 648 | 3.10% | 1.98% | 157 |
| U3 Younger professional families with young children in new houses; both spouses work | 12 797 | 5.18% | 4.46% | 116 |
| U4 Middle-aged to older families with older children in modest housing | 11 741 | 4.76% | 4.85% | 98 |
| Total: Upscale | 44 851 | 18.17% | 14.37% | 126 |

town. The working-class family stocks its kitchen with appliances — its symbols of security. The husband spends relatively more money on tickets to sporting events and more time hunting and bowling.[27]

Usage of the same product or service may vary among social classes. A study of commercial bank credit-card holders uncovered

---

[27] See Richard P. Coleman, "The Significance of Social Stratification in Selling," and "Retrospective Comment," in (ed.) Louis E. Boone, *Classics in Consumer Behaviour* (Tulsa, Okla.: PPC Books, 1977), pp. 288–302; and Richard P. Coleman and Lee Rainwater, *Social Standing in America: New Dimensions of Class* (New York: Basic Books, 1978).

social class variations in how the cards were used. Lower-class families were more likely to use their credit cards for instalment purchases, while upper-class families used them mainly for convenience as a cash substitute.[28]

The role of social class in determining consumer behaviour continues to be a source of debate in the field of marketing.[29] Some have argued against using social class as a market segmentation variable. Others disagree as to whether income or social class is the best base for market segmentation. The findings tend to be mixed. One recent study found that social class was the superior segmentation variable for food and nonsoft drink/nonalcoholic beverage markets. Social class also influenced shopping behaviour and evening television watching. Income was the superior segmentation variable for major appliances, soft drinks, mixes, and alcoholic beverages. For other categories, like clothing, a combination of the two variables was the best approach.[30]

*Opinion Leaders*     Each group usually contains a few members who can be considered **opinion leaders** or trend setters. These individuals are more likely to purchase new products early and to serve as information sources for others in the group.[31] Their opinions are respected, and they are often sought out for advice.

Generalized opinion leaders are rare. Individuals tend to be opinion leaders in specific areas. Their considerable knowledge and interest in a particular product or service motivates them to seek out further information from mass media, manufacturers, and other supply sources; and, in turn, they transmit this information

---

28 John W. Slocum, Jr., and H. Lee Mathews, "Social Class and Income as Indicators of Consumer Credit Behaviour," *Journal of Marketing* (April 1970), pp. 69–74. See also Gillian Garcia, "Credit Cards: An Interdisciplinary Survey," *Journal of Consumer Research* (May 1980), pp. 327–337; Patrick E. Murphy, "The Effect of Social Class on Brand and Price Consciousness for Supermarket Products," *Journal of Retailing* (Summer 1978), pp. 33–45; and Harold W. Berkman and Christopher C. Gilson, "Social Class and Consumer Behaviour: A Review for the 70s," *Journal of the Academy of Marketing Science* (Summer 1976), pp. 644–657.

29 See, for example, Luiz V. Dominquiz and Albert L. Page, "Stratification in Consumer Research: A Re-Examination," *Journal of the Academy of Marketing Science* (Summer 1981), pp. 250–271; Paul S. Hugstad, "A Re-Examination of the Concept of Privilege Groups," *Journal of the Academy of Marketing Science* (Fall 1981), pp. 399–408.

30 Charles M. Schaninger, "Social Class Versus Income Revisited: An Empirical Investigation," *Journal of Marketing Research* (May 1981), pp. 192–208.

31 See Danny N. Bellenger and Elizabeth C. Hirschman, "Identifying Opinion Leaders by Self-Report," in *Contemporary Marketing Thought* (eds.) Barnett A. Greenberg and Danny N. Bellenger (Chicago: American Marketing Association, 1977), pp. 341–344.

**Figure 7-8   Direct, Two-Step, and Multi-Step Communication Flows**

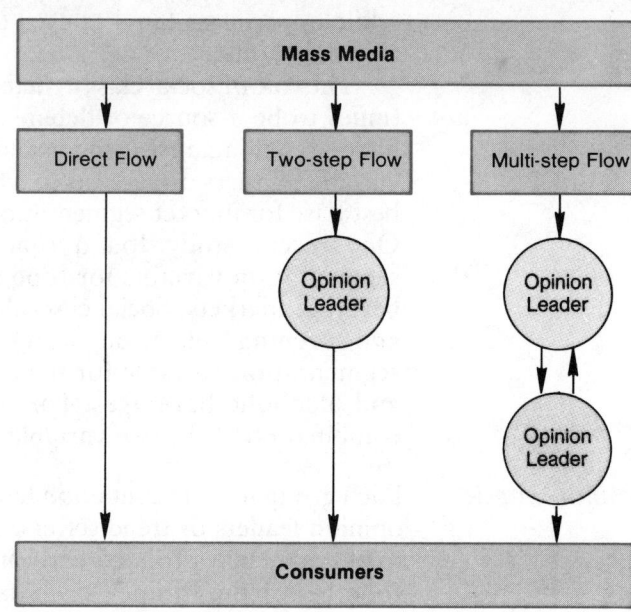

to their associates through interpersonal communications. Opinion leaders are found within all segments of the population.

Communication Flows   Information about products, retail outlets and ideas flow through a number of channels. In some instances, the information flow is direct. Continuing access to radio, television and other mass media allows much information to be transmitted directly to individuals who represent the organization's market target with no intermediaries. Preliminary findings indicating some success in the use of the experimental drug Interferon, in treating certain types of cancer, were quickly disseminated to the general public by the mass media. Researchers were forced to utilize the same channels in an attempt to dispel the general public's belief that the new drug was a miracle cure.

In some cases, the flows are from the media to opinion leaders, and then from opinion leaders to the masses of the population. Elihu Katz and Paul Lazarfeld referred to this channel as the *two-step process* of communication.[32]

---

[32]Elihu Katz and Paul F. Lazarsfeld, *Personal Influence* (New York: Free Press, 1957), p. 32.

Another possible channel for information flows is a multi-step flow. In this case, the flows are from mass media to opinion leaders and then on to other opinion leaders before being disseminated to the general public. Figure 7-8 illustrates the types of communication flows.

**Applying the Opinion Leadership Concept**    Opinion leaders play a crucial role in interpersonal communication. The fact that they distribute information and advice to others indicates their potential importance to marketing strategy. Opinion leaders can be particularly useful in the launching of new products.

General Motors once provided Chevettes to college marketing classes as a basis for a course project. Rock stations have painted teenagers' cars for them. Of course, the paint job includes the stations' call letters and slogans. Politicians sometimes hold issues forums for community leaders. All of these efforts are directed at the opinion leaders in a particular marketplace. These people play an important role in how successful a new or established product, idea, or political candidacy is communicated to consumers.

## Family Influences

The family is an important interpersonal determinant of consumer behaviour. The close, continuing interactions among family members are the strongest group influences for the individual consumer.

Most people in our society are members of two families during their lifetime: the family into which they are born, and the family they eventually form as they marry and have children. With divorce an increasingly common phenomenon, many people become involved with three or more families.

The establishment of a new household upon marriage produces marketing opportunities. A new household means a new home and accompanying furniture. The need for refrigerators, vacuum cleaners, and an original oil painting for the living room is dependent not upon the number of persons in the household but upon the number of *households* themselves.

As children are added to the household, sizes of products purchased naturally increase. Two litres of milk will be purchased instead of one. Some larger families will purchase station wagons, or larger cars. Many other child-related purchases will be made over the period of time they remain in the home. Marketers find many opportunities in this market segment. For example, Nissan Motors was able to expand the market for its Datsun Z-cars greatly by adding a four-seat "2 + 2" series to meet the needs of family purchasers who are sports car enthusiasts.

Another market evolves as parents are left alone when the children move away from home. These parents find themselves with a four-bedroom "empty nest" and a sizeable lawn to maintain each week. Lacking assistance from their children and no longer needing the extra space, they become customers for town houses, condominiums, and high-rise luxury apartments in the larger cities. This market segment also eventually purchases bifocals, and is a good target for organized tour packages.

**Figure 7-9   Marital Roles in 25 Decisions**

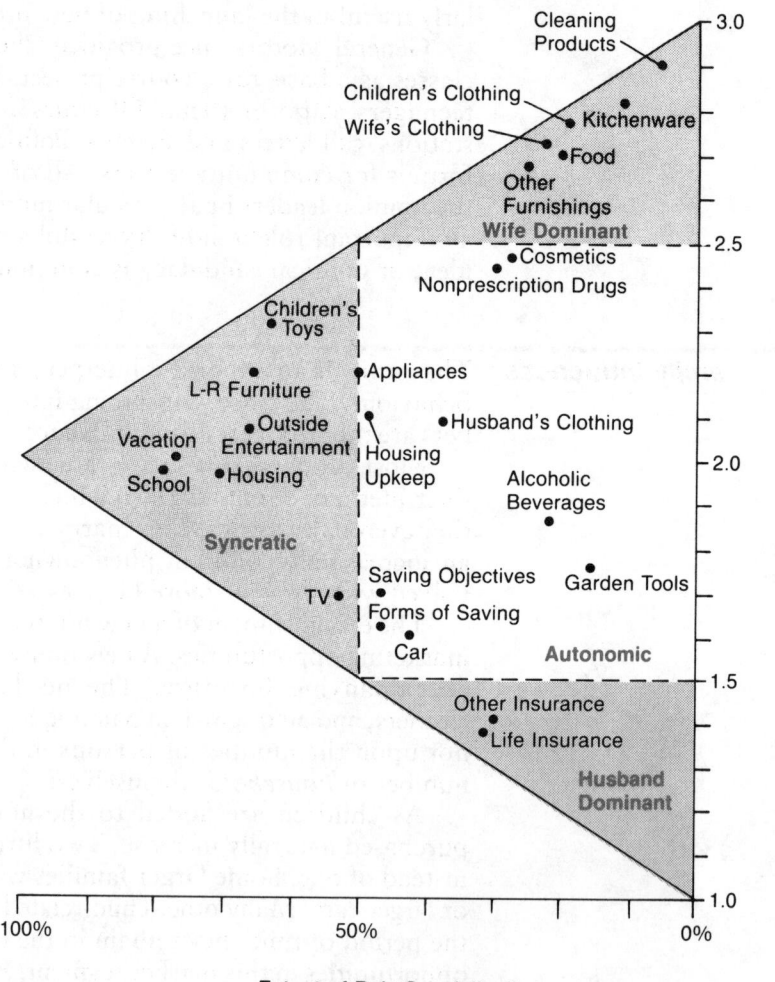

Source: Harry L. Davis and Benny P. Rigaux, "Perception of Marital Roles in Decision Processes," *Journal of Consumer Research* (June 1974), p. 57. Reprinted by permission from the *Journal of Consumer Research*, published by the Journal of Consumer Research, Inc.

**Traditional Household Roles**

Although an infinite variety of roles are played in household decision-making, four role categories are often used: 1) *autonomic* — situations where an equal number of decisions is made by each partner, but each decision is made individually by one partner or the other; 2) *male-dominant*; 3) *female-dominant*; and 4) *syncratic* — situations where decisions are made jointly by male and female.[33] Figure 7-9 shows the roles commonly played by household members in the purchase of a number of products.

**Changing Family Roles**

Two forces have changed the female's role as sole purchasing agent for most household items. First, a shorter work week provides each wage-earning household member with more time for shopping. Second, a large number of women are now in the work force. In 1950, only about a quarter of married women were also employed outside the home; by 1981 that figure had doubled. Currently, over half of all married women with school-age children hold jobs outside the home. Studies of family decision-making have shown that working wives tend to exert more influence than nonworking wives. Households with two wage earners also exhibit a larger number of joint decisions and an increase in night and weekend shopping.

These changing roles of household members have led many marketers to adjust their marketing programs. Men's clothing stores, such as Stollery's in Toronto, now offer suits and accessories for the career woman. Although demand for men's suits has been sluggish in recent years, sales of women's suits increased 70 percent in 1980. Meanwhile a survey of 1000 married men revealed that 77 percent participate in grocery shopping and 70 percent cook. A Del Monte promotional campaign recognized these changes and de-emphasized women as the sole meal preparer. Its theme, "Good things happen when you bring Del Monte home," is applicable to both male and female food shoppers.[34]

**Children's Roles in Household Purchasing**

The role of the children evolves as they grow older. Their early influence is generally centred on toys to be recommended to Santa Claus and the choice of brands of cereals. Younger children are important to marketers of fast-food restaurants. Even though the parents may

---

33 James F. Engel and Roger D. Blackwell, *Consumer Behavior*, 4th ed., pp. 176–182. See also Wilson Brown, "The Family and Consumer Decision Making," *Journal of the Academy of Marketing Science* (Fall 1979), pp. 335–343.
34 "Business Shifts Its Sales Pitch for Women," *U.S. News & World Report* (July 9, 1981), p. 46; and Margaret LeRoux, "Exec Claims Most Ads to Women Miss the Mark," *Advertising Age* (May 21, 1979), p. 24.

decide when to eat out, the children often select the restaurant.[35] As they gain maturity, they increasingly influence their clothing purchases.

One study revealed that thirteen- to fifteen-year-old teenage boys spend most of their money on food, snacks, movies, and entertainment. Girls in this same age group buy clothing, food and snacks, tickets for movies and entertainment, and cosmetics and fragrances. Sixteen- to nineteen-year-old boys spend most of their money on entertainment, dating, movies, automobiles and gasoline, clothing, food, and snacks while girls of the same age buy clothing, cosmetics, fragrances, automobiles and gasoline, and movie and entertainment tickets.[36]

**Summary**     Consumer behaviour refers to the way people select, obtain, and use goods and services. Both interpersonal and personal factors determine patterns of consumer behaviour, but the consumer decision process itself can be divided into six steps: problem recognition, search, evaluation, purchase decision, purchase act, and post purchase evaluation. The consumer decision process has been introduced here to provide an overall perspective. It is explained in detail at the end of Chapter 8.

There are three interpersonal determinants of consumer behaviour: cultural influences, social influences, and family influences. Culture is the broadest of these three influences. Culture refers to behavioural values that are created and inherited by a society. Cultural norms can change over time, although traditionally the pace of change is slow. However, it may occur at a faster pace in the future.

Cultural influences are particularly significant in international marketing, but they are also a crucial factor in domestic marketing. Increased attention is being devoted to the consumption behaviour patterns of subcultures. Canada's two founding cultures, English and French, have a significant effect on the design of marketing programs in various regions, as do the presence of other cultural groups.

Social influences are described as the nonfamily group influences on consumer behaviour. The role that groups play in individual decision making was demonstrated by research conducted by S. E. Asch. If a group's values or standards influence an individual's behaviour, the group may be called a reference group for that person. The importance of reference groups in specific product and brand decisions varies.

---

[35] George J. Szybillo, Arlene K. Sosanie, and Aaron Tenebein, "Should Children Be Seen but Not Heard?" *Journal of Advertising Research* (December 1977), pp.7–13.
[36] Lester Rand, *The Rand Youth Poll*, 1981.

Social class ranking also influences consumer behaviour. The existence of a class structure was demonstrated by W. Lloyd Warner more than 40 years ago. The reaction of opinion leaders or trend setters to new products is highly influential in the future success of the good or service. Marketers must make special efforts to appeal to these bellwethers of consumer behaviour.

Family influences are the third major interpersonal determinant of consumer behaviour. Family purchasing patterns vary. In some cases, the female is dominant; in others, the male. Some purchase decisions are made jointly, while in other situations, the decisions are made separately, but the number of such decisions is roughly equal between male and female. The traditional role for the female as the family's purchasing agent is now in flux.

## Key Terms

| | |
|---|---|
| consumer behaviour | reference group |
| culture | membership group |
| subculture | aspirational group |
| status | disassociative group |
| role | social class |
| Asch phenomenon | opinion leader |

## Review Questions

1. What are the two primary determinants of behaviour according to Lewin?
2. List the steps in the consumer behaviour process.
3. Explain the interpersonal determinants of consumer behaviour.
4. How does culture influence buying patterns?
5. Identify the two major cultures in Canada. How do their consumption patterns differ?
6. Describe the Asch phenomenon.
7. Why are reference groups important in the study of consumer behaviour?
8. Relate social class to consumer behaviour.
9. Why are opinion leaders important to marketers?
10. Describe family influences on consumer behaviour and how they are changing.

## Discussion Questions and Exercises

1. Relate a recent purchase you made to the consumer decision process shown in Figure 7-1.
2. Discuss the cultural values or norms that have had the greatest effect on your purchase behaviour.

3. For which of the following products is reference-group influence likely to be strong?
   a. Rolex watch          e. Portable radio
   b. Skis                 f. Personal computer
   c. Shaving lather       g. Electric blanket
   d. 10-speed bicycle     h. Contact lenses
4. Identify the opinion leaders in a group to which you belong. Why are these people the group's opinion leaders?
5. List two product purchases for which the influence of the following family members might be most important:
   a. Mother               d. Teenage son
   b. 6-year-old child     e. Teenage daughter
   c. Father               f. 2-year-old child

## CHAPTER 8

# Personal Influences on Consumer Behaviour

### CHAPTER OBJECTIVES

1. *To relate personal influences on consumer behaviour to the variables of the marketing mix.*

2. *To identify the personal determinants of consumer behaviour.*

3. *To distinguish between needs and motives.*

4. *To explain perception.*

5. *To describe how attitudes influence consumer behaviour.*

6. *To demonstrate how learning theory can be applied to marketing strategy.*

7. *To explain the self-concept.*

8. *To outline the steps in the consumer decision process.*

9. *To differentiate among routinized response behaviour, limited problem solving, and extended problem solving.*

At Paul Magder Furs in Toronto it was business as usual one recent Sunday. As it does most Sundays the store racked up more than a quarter of the week's sales, and for the 34th time in the past two years, the furrier was charged with violating Ontario's Retail Business Holidays Act.

Even retailers strongly opposed to the idea of Sunday shopping concede that pressure to change Canada's so-called blue laws may win out in the end. However, retailers are divided on the advantages, if any, of opening Sunday. Those in favour argue that business is now lost because retailers have failed to adapt to changing lifestyles and shopping patterns to fit consumer shopping preferences. The additional sales generated by opening on Sunday combined with revamping shopping hours on Monday to Friday will, they say, more than offset costs. "Traditional shopping habits and patterns are changing and whenever that happens, everything has to change," says Rubin Stahl, executive vice-president of Edmonton-based Triple Five Corp., owners of the giant 426 West Edmonton Mall. "Retailers must find all sorts of ways to retail—be it on a Sunday, or a Saturday, or evenings, or whatever."

Opponents deny that opening an extra day will mean a corresponding increase in sales. "It's been proven as you open up more nights that that is not the case," argues Grant MacLaren, president of Woodward Stores Ltd. of Vancouver.

Until now, there has been little firm evidence to support either side of the debate. Even the experience in the U.S. where shopping seven days a week is widespread, has been less than conclusive. There are more sales on Sunday, but whether the sales are new ones is questionable. It is clear however, that the behaviour of consumers is changing, and the issue is how marketers should adjust given the social considerations that surround the decision.[1]

### The Conceptual Framework

Chapter 7 defined consumer behaviour as the acts of individuals in obtaining and using goods and services, including the decision processes that precede and determine these acts. The chapter introduced the concept of the consumer decision process and explained the interpersonal determinants of consumer behaviour.

This chapter is a continuation of the discussion of consumer behaviour. It concentrates on the personal determinants of consumer behaviour such as needs and motives which are affecting retail shopping behaviour, for example. The chapter concludes by reintroducing and expanding the discussion of the consumer decision process.

### Personal Determinants of Consumer Behaviour

Consumer behaviour is a function of both interpersonal and personal influences. The personal determinants of consumer behaviour include the individual's needs, motives, perceptions and attitudes, and self-concept. Figure 8-1 shows how these determinants operate within the framework of interpersonal influences discussed in Chapter 7, and that together these factors cause the individual to act.

### Needs and Motives

The starting point in the purchase decision process is the recognition of a felt need. A **need** is simply *the lack of something useful*. The consumer is typically confronted with numerous unsatisfied needs. It is important to note that a need must be sufficiently aroused before it may serve as a motive.

**Motives** are *inner states that direct us toward the goal of satisfying a felt need*. The individual is *moved* (the root word of motive) to take action to reduce a state of tension and to return to a condition of equilibrium.

---

[1] Adapted from James Walker, "Changing Consumer Patterns Fuel Sunday Debate," *Financial Times of Canada*, November 14, 1983, pp. 4–5.

**Figure 8-1   Personal and Interpersonal Determinants of Consumer Behaviour**

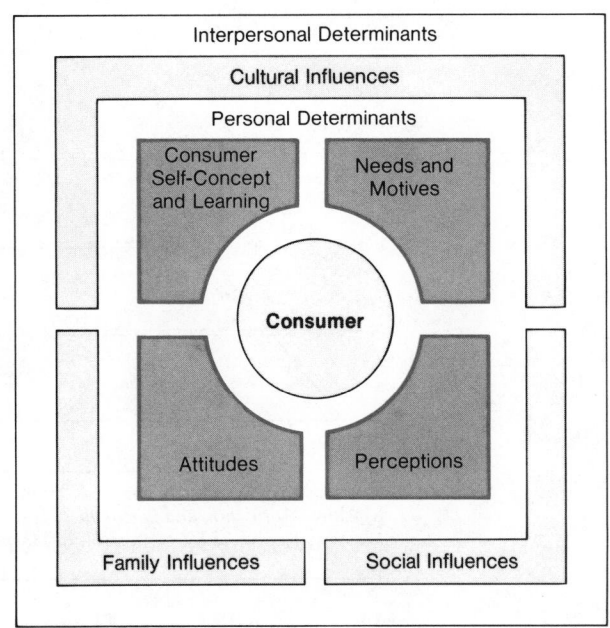

Source: C. Glenn Walters and Gordon W. Paul, *Consumer Behavior: An Integrated Framework* (Homewood, Ill.: Richard D. Irwin, 1970), p. 14 © by Richard D. Irwin, Inc. Reprinted by permission.

*Hierarchy of Needs*   Although psychologists disagree on specific classifications of needs, a useful theory that may apply to consumers in general has been developed by A. H. Maslow.[2] He proposes a classification of needs (sometimes referred to as a hierarchy), as shown in Figure 8-2. It is important to recognize that Maslow's hierarchy may not apply to each individual, but seems to be true of groups in general. His list is based upon two important assumptions:

1. People are wanting animals, whose needs depend upon what they already possess. A satisfied need is not a motivator; only those needs that have not been satisfied can influence behaviour.
2. Once one need has been largely satisfied, another emerges and demands satisfaction.

---

[2] A. H. Maslow, *Motivation and Personality* (New York: Harper & Row, Publishers, 1954), pp. 370–396.

**Figure 8-2   Need Classification Structure**

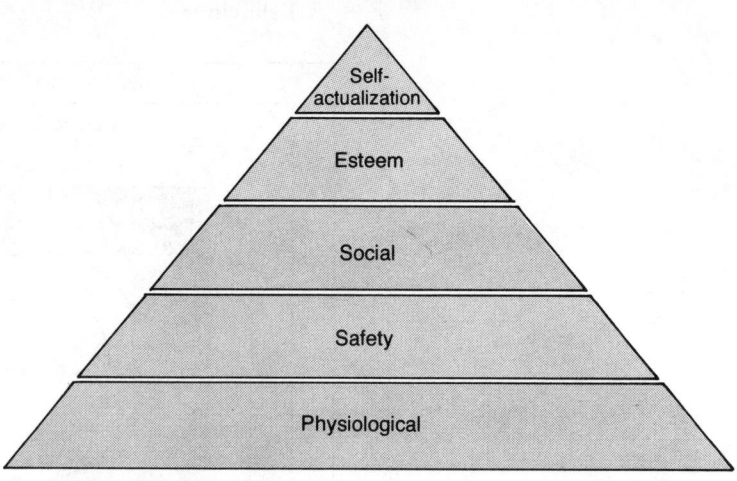

Source: Adapted from "A Theory of Human Motivation," in Abraham H.
Maslow, *Motivation and Personality*, 2nd ed. Copyright © 1970 by Abraham H.
Maslow. Reprinted by permission of Harper & Row, Publishers, Inc.

**Physiological Needs**   The primary needs for food, shelter, and clothing normally must be satisfied before the higher-order needs are
considered. A hungry person is possessed by the need to obtain food.
Other needs are ignored. Once the physiological needs are at least
partially satisfied, other needs come into the picture.

**Safety Needs**   Safety needs include protection from physical harm,
the need for security, and avoidance of the unexpected. Gratifica-
tion of these needs may take the form of a savings account, life
insurance, the purchase of radial tires, or membership in the local
health club. American Express advertisements target this need.

**Social Needs**   Satisfaction of physiological and safety needs may
be followed by the desire to be accepted by members of the family
and other individuals and groups — that is, the social needs. Individuals may be motivated to join various groups, to conform to
their standards of dress, purchases, and behaviour, and become interested in obtaining status as a means of fulfilling these social needs.
Chapter 7 pointed out that social needs seem to be becoming a more
important cultural value.

**Esteem Needs**   The higher-order needs are prevalent in the developed countries where a sufficiently high per capita income has
allowed most families to satisfy the basic needs and to concentrate

on the desire for status, esteem, and self-actualization.[3] These needs are more difficult to satisfy. At the esteem level is the need to feel a sense of accomplishment, achievement, and respect from others. The competitive need to excel—to better the performance of others and "stand out" from the crowd — is an almost universal human trait.

Esteem needs are closely related to social needs. At this level, however, the individual desires not just acceptance but also recognition and respect in some way.

### Self-Actualization — The Need for Fulfilment

Source: © 1970 United Feature Syndicate, Inc.

**Self-Actualization Needs**   Self-actualization needs are the desire for fulfilment, for realizing one's own potential, for using one's talents and capabilities totally. Maslow defines self-actualization this way: "The healthy man is primarily motivated by his needs to develop and actualize his fullest potentialities and capacities. What man can be, he must be."[4] The author Robert Louis Stevenson was describing self-actualization when he wrote, "To be what we are, and to become what we are capable of becoming, is the only end of life."

---

[3] See B. Curtis Hamm and Edward W. Cundiff, "Self-Actualization and Product Perception," *Journal of Marketing Research* (November 1969), pp. 470–472.
[4] A. H. Maslow, *Motivation and Personality* (New York: Harper & Row, 1954), p. 382. See also George Brooker, "The Self-Actualizing Socially Conscious Consumer," *Journal of Consumer Research* (September 1976), pp. 107–12.

Maslow argues that a satisfied need is no longer a motivator. Once the physiological needs are satiated, the individual moves on to the higher-order needs. Consumers are periodically motivated by the need to relieve thirst or hunger, but their interests are most often directed toward satisfaction of safety, social, and other needs.

Caution must be used in applying Maslow's theory. Empirical research shows little support for a universal hierarchical ordering of needs in *specific individuals*.[5] It would therefore be unsafe to use the theory to explain a particular purchase. The need hierarchy and motive strength concept may be useful in considering the behaviour of consumers *in general*, however. It has been verified that in consumer buying, previously ignored desires often surface only after a purchase has satisfied a predominant (and *perhaps* lower-order) motive.[6]

## Perceptions

Several years ago, a pharmaceutical firm developed Analoze, a cherry-flavoured combination pain killer and stomach sweetener that could be taken without water. The product failed because consumers associated the ritual of taking pills and a glass of water with pain relief.[7] Analoze was not perceived as an effective remedy because it violated their experience with other pain killers. Individual behaviour resulting from motivation is affected by how we perceive stimuli. **Perception** is *the meaning that each person attributes to incoming stimuli received through the five senses.*

Psychologists previously assumed that perception was an objective phenomenon, that is, that the individual perceived what was there to be perceived. Only recently have researchers recognized that what we perceive is as much a result of what we *want* to perceive as of what is actually there. This does not mean that people view dogs as pigeons. We can distinguish shopping centres from churches, but a retail store stocked with well-known brand names and staffed with helpful, knowledgeable sales personnel is perceived differently from a largely self-serve discount store. The Dodge Colt and the BMW 320 are both important automobiles, but they carry quite different images.

---

[5] E. E. Lawlor and J. L. Suttle, "A Causal Correlational Test of the Need Hierarchy Concept," *Organizational Behaviour and Human Performance* 3 (1968), pp. 12–35. See also Jerry L. Gray and Fredrick A. Starke, *Organizational Behaviour Concepts and Applications* (Columbus, Ohio: Charles E. Merrill Publishing Co., 1977), pp. 27–29.

[6] George Katona, *The Powerful Consumer* (New York: McGraw-Hill, 1960), p. 132. See also James F. Engel, Roger D. Blackwell and David T. Kollat, *Consumer Behaviour*, 3rd edition (Hinsdale, Ill.: The Dryden Press, 1978), pp. 223–225.

[7] Burt Schorr, "The Mistakes: Many New Products Fail Despite Careful Planning, Publicity," *The Wall Street Journal* (April 5, 1961), pp. 1, 22.

Our perception of an object or event is the result of the inter-action of two types of factors:

1. Stimulus factors, which are characteristics of the physical object such as size, colour, weight, or shape.
2. Individual factors, which are characteristics of the perceiver. These factors include not only sensory processes but also past experiences with similar items and basic motivations and expectations.

**Perceptual Screens**   The individual is continually bombarded with a myriad of stimuli, but most are ignored. In order to have time to function, each of us must respond selectively to stimuli. What stimuli we respond to, then, is the problem of all marketers. How can they gain the atten-tion of the individual so that he or she will read the advertisement, listen to the sales representative, react to a point-of-purchase display?

Even though studies have shown that the average consumer is exposed to more than a thousand ads daily, most of them never break through our **perceptual screen**, *the filter through which messages must pass*. Sometimes breakthroughs may be accomplished in the printed media through larger ads, since doubling the size of the ad increases the attention value by approximately 50 percent. Colour ads in the newspaper, in contrast with the usual black and white ads, are another device to break the reader's perceptual screen. However, the colour ad must produce enough additional readers to justify the extra cost, which is considerable. Another method of using contrast is to include a large amount of white space to draw atten-tion to the ad, or to use white type on a black background.

In general, the marketer seeks to make the message stand out, to be sufficiently different from other methods in order to gain the attention of the prospective customer. Menley & James Labora-tories followed the practice of running hay-fever radio commercials for their Contac capsules only on days when the pollen count was above specified minimum levels. Each commercial was preceded by live announcements of the local pollen count.

Piercing the perceptual screen can be a frustrating task. Con-sider the problem of getting consumers to try a product for the first time. The manufacturer bombards people with television and magazine advertising, sales promotion discounts and premiums, and point-of-purchase displays, often with little change in sales. Follow-up research shows that many consumers have no knowledge of the product or promotion. Why? Because this information sim-ply never penetrated their perceptual screens.

With such selectivity at work, it is easy to see the importance of the marketer's efforts to obtain a "consumer franchise" in the form

# Poison Labels — A Case of Misconception

Marketers of potentially dangerous products take numerous precautions to keep consumers from accidentally swallowing them—from child-resistant closures to warning labels. Yet it is estimated that 2 million poisonings and more than 400 deaths occur annually in the United States among children under 5 years of age.[8]

The skull and crossbones shown in the first box is the traditional symbol for poisonous products. But studies indicate that this symbol has lost most of its meaning. In fact, a group of nursery schoolchildren interpreted the label to mean "pirate food."

A proposed new warning symbol is shown in the second box. Mr. Yuk avoids the relationship of the skull and crossbones with pirates while denoting an unpleasant taste. Symbolic representations of danger are especially important in the case of young children, who cannot read written warnings.

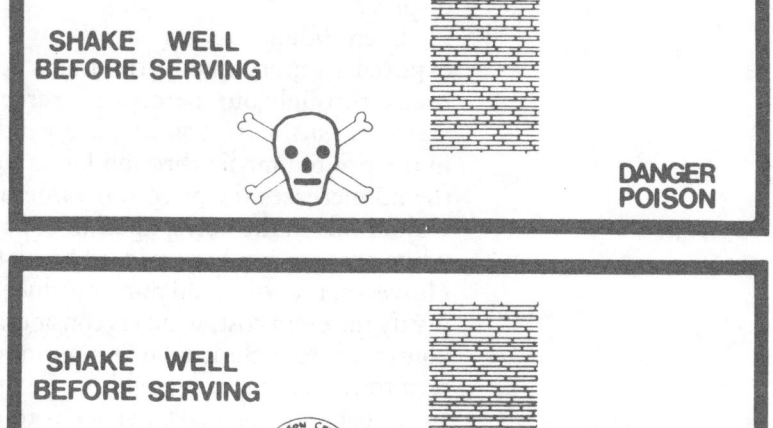

Source: Information from Kenneth C. Schneider, "Prevention of Accidental Poisoning through Package and Label Design," *Journal of Consumer Research* (September 1977), pp. 67–74. Labels courtesy of the journal. Reprinted with permission.

of brand loyalty to a product. Satisfied customers are less likely to seek information about competing products. Even when it is forced on them, they are not as likely as others to allow it to pass through their perceptual screens. They simply tune out information that is not in accord with their existing beliefs and expectations.

---

[8] T. M. Deeths and J. T. Breeden, "Poisoning in Children—A Statistical Study of 1967 Cases," *Journal of Pediatrics* (February 1971), pp. 299–305.

**Weber's Law**   The relationship between the actual physical stimulus such as size, loudness, or texture, and the corresponding sensation produced in the individual is known as *psychophysics*, which can be expressed as a mathematical equation:

$$\frac{\Delta I}{I} = k$$

where $\Delta I$ = the smallest increase in stimulus that will be noticeably different from the previous intensity

$I$ = the intensity of the stimulus at the point where the increase takes place

$k$ = a constant (that varies from one sense to the next)

In other words, *the higher the initial intensity of a stimulus, the greater the amount of the change in intensity that is necessary in order for a difference to be noticed.*

This relationship, known as **Weber's Law**, has some obvious implications in marketing. A price increase of $300 for a Chevette is readily apparent for prospective buyers; the same $300 increase on a $45 000 Mercedes seems insignificant. A large package requires a much greater increase in size to be noticeable than a smaller-sized package requires. People perceive *by exception*, and the change in stimuli must be sufficiently great to gain the individual's attention.[9]

**Subliminal Perception**   Is it possible to communicate with persons without their being aware of the communication? In other words, is there **subliminal perception** — *a subconscious level of awareness*? In 1957 the words "Eat popcorn" and "Drink Coca-Cola," were flashed upon the screen of a New Jersey movie theatre every five seconds for 1/300th of a second. Researchers then reported that these messages, although too short to be recognizable at the conscious level, resulted in a 58 percent increase in popcorn sales and an 18 percent increase in the sale of Coca-Cola. After the publication of these findings, advertising agencies and consumer protection groups became intensely interested in subliminal perception.[10] Later attempts to duplicate the test findings have, however, invariably been unsuccessful.

Subliminal advertising is aimed at the subconscious level of

---

9 Steuart Henderson Britt, "How Weber's Law Can Be Applied to Marketing," *Business Horizons* (February 1975), pp. 21–29.

10 John Brooks, "The Little Ad That Isn't There," *Consumer Reports* (January 1958), pp. 7–10. See also Del Hawkins, "The Effects of Subliminal Stimulation on Drive Level and Brand Preference," *Journal of Marketing Research* (August 1970), pp. 322–326.

awareness to avoid the perceptual screens of viewers. The goal of the original research was to induce consumers to purchase without being aware of the source of the motivation. Although subliminal advertising has been universally condemned (and declared illegal in Canada and California), it is exceedingly unlikely that such advertising can induce purchases anyway. There are several reasons for this: 1) strong stimulus factors are required to even gain attention, as discussed earlier; 2) only a very short message can be transmitted; 3) individuals vary greatly in their thresholds of consciousness[11] (message transmitted at the threshold of consciousness for one person will not be perceived at all by some people and will be all too apparent for others: when exposed subliminally, the message "Drink Coca-Cola" might go unseen by some viewers while others read it as "Drink Pepsi-Cola," "Drink Cocoa," or even "Drive Slowly");[12] 4) perceptual defences *also* work at the subconscious level.

Contrary to earlier fears, research has shown that subliminal messages cannot force the receiver to purchase goods that he or she would not consciously want.[13]

---

**Attitudes**

Perception of incoming stimuli is greatly affected by attitudes regarding these stimuli. In fact, decisions to purchase products are based upon currently held attitudes about the product, the store, or the salesperson.

**Attitudes** may be defined as *a person's enduring favourable or unfavourable evaluations, emotional feelings, or pro or con action tendencies toward some object or idea.*[14] Attitudes are formed over a period of time through individual experiences and group contacts and are highly resistant to change.

**Components of an Attitude**

Attitudes consist of three related components: cognitive, affective, and behavioural. The *cognitive* component is the information and knowledge one has about an object or concept. The *affective* component is one's feelings or emotional reactions. The *behavioural* com-

---

11 See James H. Myers and William H. Reynolds, *Consumer Behavior and Marketing Management* (Boston: Houghton Mifflin Company, 1967), p. 14.
12 Richard P. Barthol and Michael J. Goldstein, "Psychology and the Invisible Sell," *California Management Review* (Winter 1959), p. 34.
13 One researcher reports that some overt behaviour in pathologically prone individuals can be influenced if they appeal to the appropriate unconscious wish. See Joel Saegert, "Another Look at Subliminal Perception," *Journal of Advertising Research* (February 1979), pp. 55–57.
14 David Krech, Richard S. Crutchfield, and Egerton L. Ballachey, *Individual in Society* (New York: McGraw-Hill Book Company, 1962), Chapter 2.

ponent is the way one tends to act or to behave. In considering the decision to shop at a warehouse-type food store, a person obtains information from advertising, trial visits, and input from family, friends, and associates (cognitive). A consumer also receives inputs from others about their acceptance of shopping at this new type of store, as well as impressions about the type of people who shop there (affective). The shopper may ultimately decide to make some purchases of canned goods, cereal, and bakery products there, but continue to rely upon a regular supermarket for major food purchases (behavioural).

As Figure 8-3 illustrates, the three components exist in a relatively stable and balanced relationship to one another and combine to form an overall attitude about an object or idea.

Figure 8-3   Three Components of an Attitude

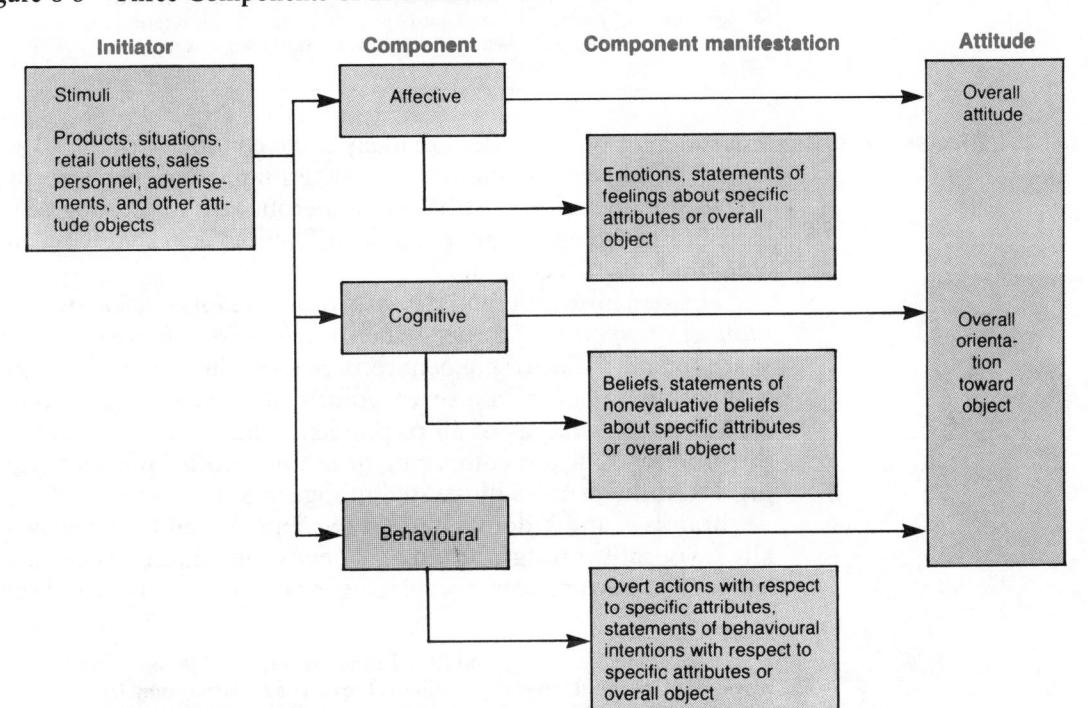

Source: Del I. Hawkins, Kenneth A. Coney, and Roger J. Best, *Consumer Behaviour: Implications for Marketing Strategy* (Dallas, Tex.: Business Publications, Inc. 1980), p. 334. The figure is adapted from M. J. Rosenberg and C. I. Hovland, *Attitude Organization and Change* (New Haven, Conn.: Yale University Press, 1960), p. 3. Reprinted by permission.

Figure 8-4   Product Images of Brands X, Y, and Z

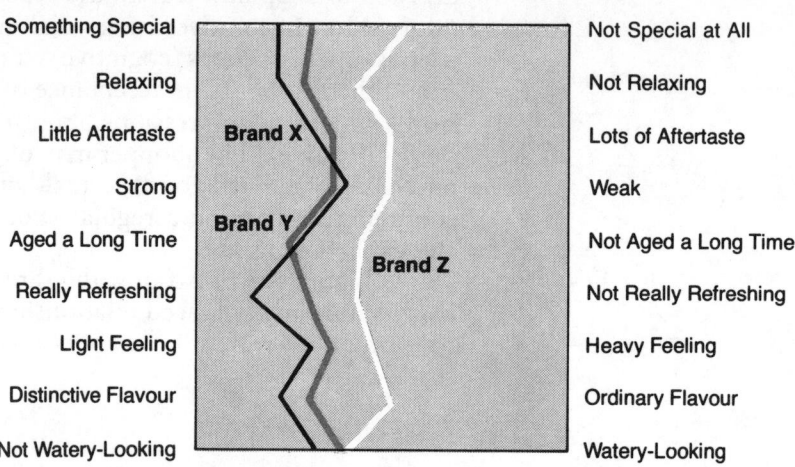

Source: Adapted from William A. Mindak, "Fitting the Semantic Differential to the Market Problem," *Journal of Marketing* (April 1961), pp. 28–33. Reprinted from *Journal of Marketing*, published by the American Marketing Association.

*Attitude Measurement*

Since favourable attitudes are likely to be conducive to brand preference, marketers are interested in determining consumer attitudes toward their products. Although numerous attitude scaling devices have been developed, the **semantic differential** is probably the most commonly used technique.[15]

The semantic differential is *an attitude scaling device that uses a number of bipolar adjectives* — such as new–old, reliable–unreliable, sharp–bland.[16] The respondent records an evaluation of the product by checking a point on a seven-point scale between the extremes. The average rankings of all respondents then become a profile of the product. One test comparing three unidentified product brands produced the profiles illustrated in Figure 8-4.

Brands X and Y dominated the local market and enjoyed generally favourable ratings. Brand Z, a newly introduced product, was less well known and was reacted to neutrally. A comparison of Brands

[15] C. E. Osgood, G. J. Suci, and P.H. Tannenbaum, *The Measurement of Meaning* (Urbana: University of Illinois Press, 1957). For a comparison of the semantic differential with the Likert Scale and the Stapel Scale, two other widely used attitude scaling formats, see Dennis Menezes and Norbert F. Elbert, "Alternative Semantic Scaling Formats for Measuring Store Image: An Evaluation," *Journal of Marketing Research* (February 1979), pp. 80–87.
[16] See Irwin Weinstock and Monroe M. Bird, Jr., "Scoring the Semantic Differential: Attacking the Response-Set Problem," *Business Ideas and Facts* 4 (Winter 1971), pp. 3–13.

X and Y can be made, and weak areas in the brand image can be noted for possible remedial action. The semantic differential scale provides management with a more detailed picture of the direction and intensity of opinions and attitudes about a product than could be obtained through a typical research questionnaire. It supplies a comprehensive multidimensional portrait of brand images and is often used in deciding how to position or reposition a brand in the market.

## Producing Attitude Change

Given that a favourable consumer attitude is a prerequisite to market success, how can a firm lead prospective buyers to adopt a more favourable attitude toward its products? The marketer has two choices: either attempt to change attitudes to make them consonant with the product or determine consumer attitudes and then change the product to match them.[17]

If consumers view the product unfavourably, the firm may choose to redesign the product to better conform with their desires. To accommodate the consumer, the firm may make styling changes, variations in ingredients, changes in package size, and changes in retail stores handling the product.

The other course of action—changing consumer attitudes toward the product without changing the product—is much more difficult. A famous study using two imaginary shopping lists (see Figure 8-5) revealed surprisingly negative attitudes toward homemakers who served instant coffee. Half of a sample of 100 homemakers were shown List 1 and the other half were shown List 2. Each respondent was asked to describe the hypothetical shopper.

The only difference in the lists was in the form of coffee, but the shopper who bought instant coffee was described as lazy by 48 percent of those evaluating List 1; only 24 percent of those evaluating List 2 described the shopper as lazy. Forty-eight percent described the instant coffee purchaser as failing to plan household purchases and schedules well; only 12 percent described the homemaker who purchased regular coffee this way.

But consumer attitudes often change with time. The shopping

---

[17] George S. Day, "Using Attitude Change Measures to Evaluate New Product Introductions," *Journal of Marketing Research* (November 1970), pp. 474–482; see also Stephen J. Miller, Michael B. Mazis, and Peter L. Wright, "The Influence of Brand Ambiguity on Brand Attitude Development," *Journal of Marketing Research* (November 1971), pp. 455–459; Frank Schuhmann, "Consumer Cognitive Systems: A Study of the Relationship Between Consumer Attitudes and Values," *Idaho Business and Economic Journal* (January 1975), pp. 1–15; and Kent B. Monroe, "The Influence of Price Differences and Brand Familiarity on Brand Preferences," *The Journal of Consumer Research* (June 1976), pp. 42–49.

### Figure 8-5   Shopping Lists Used in the Haire Study

| Shopping List 1 | Shopping List 2 |
| --- | --- |
| 1 kg of hamburger | 1 kg of hamburger |
| 2 loaves of Wonder bread | 2 loaves of Wonder Bread |
| Bunch of carrots | Bunch of carrots |
| 1 can Rumford's Baking Powder | 1 can Rumford's Baking Powder |
| Nescafé Instant Coffee | 500 g Maxwell House coffee (drip grind) |
| 2 cans Del Monte peaches | 2 cans Del Monte peaches |
| 2 kg potatoes | 2 kg potatoes |

Source: Mason Haire, "Projective Techniques in Marketing Research," *Journal of Marketing* (April 1950), pp. 649–656. Reprinted from *Journal of Marketing*, published by the American Marketing Association.

list study was repeated 20 years later, and this time revealed that much of the stigma attached to buying and using instant coffee had disappeared. Instead of describing the instant coffee purchaser as lazy and a poor planner, most respondents felt that the writer of List 1 was a working woman.[18] Nonetheless General Foods took no chances when it introduced its new freeze-dried Maxim as a coffee that "tastes like *regular* and has the convenience of *instant*."

***Modifying the Attitudinal Components***

Attitude change frequently occurs when inconsistencies are introduced among the three attitudinal components. The most common examples of such inconsistencies are changes to the cognitive component of an attitude as a result of new information.

The Pepsi Challenge showed consumers that a larger-than-expected group would prefer Pepsi if they tried it. This new information was expected to lead to increased sales. A recent Life Savers advertising campaign was built around the theme that a Life Saver contains only ten calories, in order to correct misconceptions in the minds of many consumers about the candy's high caloric content.

The affective component may be altered by relating the use of the new product or service to desirable consequences for the user. The growth of health clubs can be attributed to the successful promotion of the benefits of being trim and physically fit.

The third alternative in attempting to change attitudes is to focus upon the behavioural component by inducing someone to engage

[18] Frederick E. Webster, Jr., and Frederick Von Pechmann, "A Replication of the 'Shopping List' Study," *Journal of Marketing* (April 1970), pp. 61–63. See also Johan Arndt, "Haire's Shopping List Revisited," *Journal of Advertising Research* (October 1973), pp. 25–32.

in behaviour that is contradictory to the person's currently held attitudes. Attitude-discrepant behaviour of this type may occur if the consumer is given a free sample of a product. Such trials may lead to attitude change.

## Self-Concept Theory

Self-concept plays an important role in consumer behaviour. An individual is both a physical and mental entity. Each of us possesses a multifaceted picture of ourselves. We may view ourselves as intellectual, self-assured, moderately talented athletes, and rising young business executives. Our actions, including purchase decisions, are dependent upon our actual or desired *mental conception of self.* This is our **self-concept.** For example, the response to such direct questions as "Why do you buy Pierre Cardin cologne?" is likely to reflect our desired self-image.[19] Personal needs, motives, perception, attitudes, and learning lie at the core of an individual's conception of self. So too do the environmental interpersonal factors of family, social, and cultural influences.

As Figure 8-6 indicates, the self may be regarded as having four components: real self, self-image, looking-glass self, and ideal self. The *real self* is an objective view of the total person as he or she actually is. This image is partially distorted into the *self-image* — the way individuals view themselves. The *looking-glass self* — the way individuals think others see them — may also be quite different from their self-image since they may choose to project a different image to others. A person's *ideal self* serves as a personal set of objectives since it is the image to which he or she aspires. All of these affect self-concept.

In purchasing goods and services, people are likely to choose those products that will move them closer to their ideal selves. Persons who possess images of themselves as scholars are more likely to join the literary book club. The young woman who sees herself as a budding tennis star may become engrossed in evaluating the merits of graphite versus steel racquets and may view with disdain the cheaply made imports. The college graduate on the way up the organization ladder at the bank may hide a love for bowling and instead take up golf — believing that this is the typical sport for a banker.

---

[19] See Corbett Gaulden, "Self and Ideal Self Images and Purchase Intentions," in *Proceedings of the Southern Marketing Association,* (eds.) Robert S. Franz, Robert M. Hopkins and Alfred G. Toma (New Orleans, La., November 1978); and Terrence V. O'Brien, Humberto S. Tapia, and Thomas L. Brown, "The Self-Concept in Buyer Behavior," *Business Horizons* (October 1977), pp. 65–74.

Figure 8-6   Components of Self

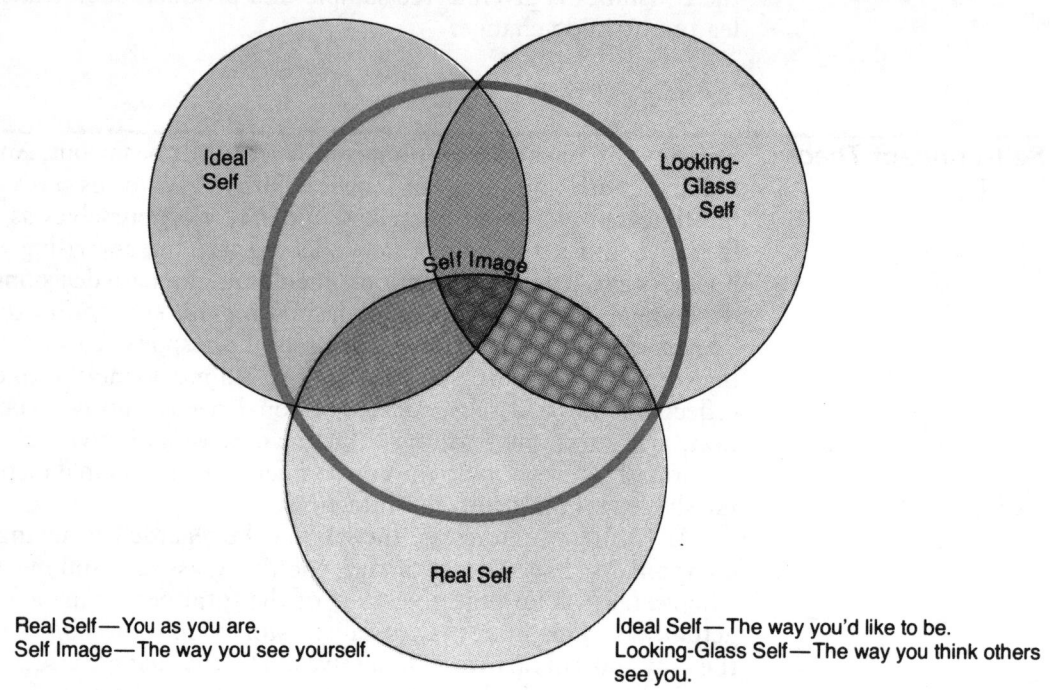

Real Self—You as you are.
Self Image—The way you see yourself.

Ideal Self—The way you'd like to be.
Looking-Glass Self—The way you think others
see you.

Source: John Douglas, George A. Field, and Lawrence S. Tarpey, *Human Behavior in Marketing* (Columbus, Ohio: Charles E. Merrill Publishing, 1967), p. 65. Reprinted by permission.

**Learning**     Since marketing is as concerned with the process by which consumer decisions change over time as with describing those decisions at one point in time, the study of how learning takes place is important. A useful definition of **learning** is *changes in behaviour, immediate or expected, as a result of experience.*[20]

The learning process includes several components. The first component, **drive**, refers to any strong stimulus that impels action. Examples of drives include fear, pride, desire for money, thirst, pain avoidance, and rivalry.

---

[20] Learning is perhaps the most thoroughly researched field in psychology, and several learning theories have been developed. For a discussion of these theories, see James Engel, Roger Kollat, and Roger Blackwell, *Consumer Behavior*, 3d ed. (Hinsdale: Dryden Press, 1978), pp. 227–246.

**Cues**, the second component of the learning process, are any objects existing in the environment that determine the nature of the response to a drive. Cues might include a newspaper advertisement for a new French restaurant, an in-store display, or a Petrocan sign on a major highway. For the hungry person, the shopper seeking a particular item, or the motorist needing gasoline, these cues may result in a specific response to satisfy a drive.

A **response** is the individual's reaction to the cues and drive, such as purchasing a package of Gillette Trac II blades, dining at a Burger King, or deciding to enroll at a particular university or community college.

**Reinforcement** is the reduction in drive that results from a proper response. The more rewarding the response, the stronger the bond between the drive and the purchase of that particular item becomes. Should Trac II blades result in closer shaves through repeated use, the likelihood of their purchase in the future is increased.

*Applying Learning Theory to Marketing Decisions*

Learning theory has some important implications for marketing strategists.[21] A desired outcome such as repeat purchase behaviour has to be developed gradually. **Shaping** is *the process of applying a series of rewards and reinforcement so that more complex behaviour* (such as the development of a brand preference) *can evolve over time*. Both promotional strategy and the product itself play a role in the shaping process.

Figure 8-7 shows the application of learning theory and shaping procedures to a typical marketing scenario in which marketers attempt to motivate consumers to become regular buyers of a certain product. An initial product trial is induced by a free sample package that includes a substantial discount coupon on a subsequent purchase. This illustrates the use of a cue as a shaping procedure. The purchase response is reinforced by satisfactory product performance and a coupon for the next purchase.

The second stage is to entice the consumer to buy the product with little financial risk. The large discount coupon enclosed in the free sample prompts such an action. The package that is purchased has a smaller discount coupon enclosed. Again, the reinforcement is satisfactory product performance and the second coupon.

The third step would be to motivate the person to buy the item again at a moderate cost. The discount coupon accomplishes this objective, but this time there is no additional coupon in the package.

---

21 This section is based on Michael L. Rothschild and William C. Gaidis, "Behavioral Learning Theory: Its Relevance to Marketing and Promotion," *Journal of Marketing* (Spring 1981), pp. 70–78.

**Figure 8-7    Application of Learning Theory and Shaping Procedure to Marketing**

| Approximation Sequence | Shaping Procedure | Reinforcement Applied |
|---|---|---|
| Induce product trial. | Free samples distributed, large discount coupons enclosed. | Product performance and coupon. |
| Induce purchase with little financial obligation. | Discount coupon prompts purchase with little cost. Coupon good for small discount on next purchase enclosed. | Product performance and coupon. |
| Induce purchase with moderate financial obligation. | Small discount coupon prompts purchase with moderate cost. | Product performance |
| Induce purchase with full financial obligation. | Purchase occurs without coupon association. | Product performance |

| Terminal Goal: Repeat Purchase Behaviour |
|---|

Source: Adapted from Michael L. Rothschild and William C. Gaidis, "Behavioral Learning Theory: Its Relevance to Marketing and Promotions," *Journal of Marketing* (Spring 1981), p. 72.

The only reinforcement is satisfactory product performance.

The final test comes when the consumer is asked to buy the product at its true price without a discount coupon. Satisfaction with product performance is the only continuing reinforcement. Thus, repeat purchase behaviour has been literally shaped.

Kellogg used learning theory and shaping when it introduced its Nutri-Grain brand sugarless whole grain cereal. Coupons worth 40 cents off—about a third of the product's cost—were distributed to elicit trial purchases by consumers. Inside boxes of the new cereal were additional cents-off coupons of lesser value.[22] Kellogg was clearly trying to shape future purchase behaviour by effective application of learning theory within a marketing strategy context.

-----
[22] John Koten, "For Kellogg, the Hardest Part is Getting People Out of Bed," *The Wall Street Journal* (May 27, 1982), p. 27.

**The Consumer Decision Process**

Chapter 7 began with a discussion of the consumer decision process, using a schematic model showing six stages: problem recognition, search, evaluation of alternatives, the purchase decision, the purchase act, and postpurchase evaluation. For convenience, it is reproduced here as Figure 8-8.

Consumer behaviour research traditionally has focused on such specific areas as attitudes, personality, and the influence of reference groups on the individual. These fragments, however, should be seen in their proper perspective. This model allows us to integrate the various components of consumer behaviour and assists us in understanding the complex relationships among them. It also provides a means of integrating new research findings in the search for a more complete explanation of why consumers behave as they do. The total model approach can be used in major buying situations, such as a first-time purchase of a new product or the purchase of a high-priced, long-lived article. It can also be applied to routine purchases handled in a largely habitual manner, such as buying a newspaper or a particular brand of chewing gum.

The discussion that follows presents one generalized model of consumer behaviour. A more detailed description of the technical elements of the two most widely accepted models of consumer behaviour is presented in Appendix C at the end of Part Three.

**Figure 8-8   Steps in the Consumer Decision Process**

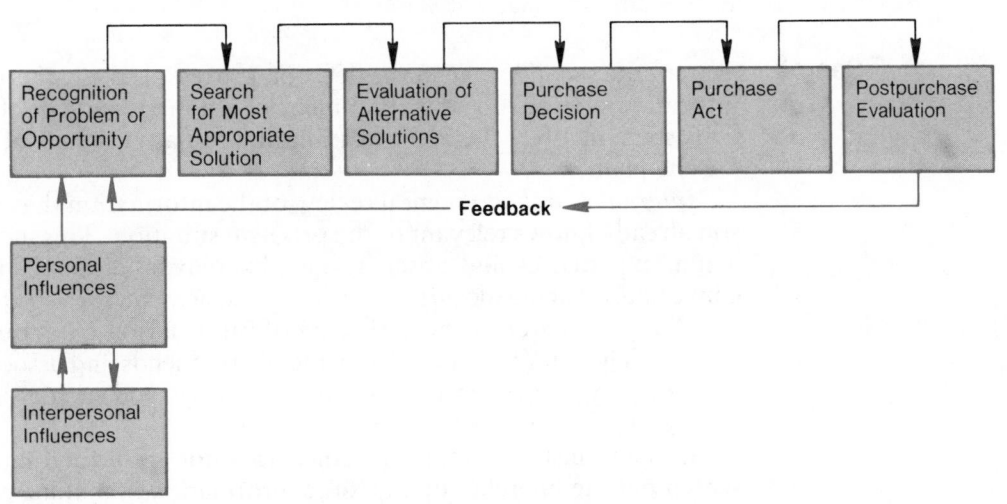

Source: Adapted from C. Glenn Walters and Gordon W. Paul, *Consumer Behavior: An Integrated Framework* (Homewood, Ill.: Richard D. Irwin, Inc., 1970), p. 18 © 1970 by Richard D. Irwin, Inc. and John Dewey, *How We Think* (Boston, Mass.: D. C. Heath, 1910), pp. 101–105. Similar steps are also discussed in Del I. Hawkins, Roger J. Best, and Kenneth A. Coney, *Consumer Behavior: Implications for Marketing Strategy*, revised ed. (Plano, Texas: Business Publications, Inc., 1983), pp. 447–606.

**Problem Recognition**    This first stage in the decision process occurs when the consumer becomes aware of a discrepancy of sufficient magnitude between the existing state of affairs and a desired state of affairs. Once the problem has been recognized, it must be defined in order that the consumer may seek out methods for its solution. Having recognized the problem, the individual is motivated to achieve the desired state.

What sort of problems might a person recognize? Perhaps the most common is a routine depletion of the stock of products. A large number of consumer purchases involve the replenishment of items ranging from gasoline to groceries. In other instances, the consumer may possess an inadequate assortment of products. The individual whose hobby is gardening may make regular purchases of different kinds of fertilizers, seeds, or gardening tools as the size of the garden grows.

A consumer may also be dissatisfied with a present brand or product type. This situation is a common factor in the purchase of a new automobile, new furniture, or a new fall wardrobe. In many instances, boredom with current products and a desire for novelty may be the underlying rationale for the decision process leading to new-product purchases.

Another important factor is changed financial status. The infusion of added financial resources from such sources as a salary increase, a second job, or an inheritance may permit the consumer to recognize desires and make purchases that previously had been postponed due to their cost.[23]

**Search**    Search, the second stage in the decision process, is the gathering of information related to the attainment of a desired state of affairs. This stage involves the identification of alternative means of solving the problem.

*Internal search* is a mental review of the information that a person already knows relevant to the problem situation. This includes actual experiences and observations plus remembered reading or conversations and exposures to various persuasive marketing efforts.

*External search* is the gathering of information from outside sources. These may include family members, friends and associates, store displays, sales representatives, brochures, and such product-testing publications as *Canadian Consumer*.

In many instances, the consumer does not go beyond internal search but merely relies upon stored information in making a purchase decision. Achieving favourable results using Du Pont's Rain Dance car polish may sufficiently motivate a consumer to repurchase

---

[23] See J. P. Liefeld, "Problem Recognition," in *Consumer Decision-Making: An Annotated Bibliography* (Ottawa: Consumer and Corporate Affairs, 1979).

this brand rather than consider possible alternatives. Since external search involves both time and effort, the consumer will rely upon it only in instances in which for some reason information remembered is inadequate.

The search process will identify alternative brands for consideration and possible purchase. *The number of brands that a consumer actually considers in making a purchase decision* is known as the **evoked set.** In some instances, the consumer will already be aware of the brands worthy of further consideration; in others the external search process will permit the consumer to identify those brands. Not all brands will be included in the evoked set. The consumer may remain unaware of certain brands and others will be rejected as too costly or as having been tried previously and considered unsatisfactory. In other instances, unfavourable word-of-mouth communication or negative reactions to advertising or other marketing efforts will lead to the elimination of some brands from the evoked set. While the number of brands in the evoked set will vary by product categories, research indicates that the number is likely to be as few as four or five brands.[24]

**Evaluation of Alternatives**

The third step in the consumer decision process involves the evaluation of alternatives identified during the search process. Actually, it is difficult to completely separate the second and third steps since some evaluation takes place simultaneously with the search process as consumers accept, discount, distort, or reject some incoming information as they receive it.

Since the outcome of the evaluation stage is the choice of a brand or product in the evoked set (or, possibly, the search for additional alternatives should all those identified during the search process prove unsatisfactory), the consumer must develop a set of **evaluative criteria,** *features the consumer considers in making a choice among alternatives.* These criteria can either be *objective* (federal government automobile fuel consumption tests in litres per 100 kilometres, or comparison of retail prices) or *subjective* (favourable image of Calvin Klein sportswear). Commonly used evaluative criteria include price, reputation of the brand, perceived quality, packaging, size, performance, durability, and colour. Most research studies indicate that consumers seldom use more than six criteria in the evaluation process. Evaluative criteria for detergents include suds level and smell as indicators of cleaning power. High quality and potential

---

[24] B. M. Campbell, "The Existence of Evoked Set and Determinants of its Magnitude in Brand Choice Behavior," in *Buyer Behavior: Theoretical and Empirical Foundations*, eds. John A. Howard and Lonnie Ostrom (New York: Alfred A. Knopf, Inc., 1973), pp. 243–44.

for long wear were the underlying criteria in the choice of nylon stockings, according to one research study.[25]

**The Purchase Decision and the Purchase Act**

When the consumer has evaluated each of the alternatives in the evoked set, utilizing his or her personal set of evaluative criteria, and narrowed the alternatives to one, the end result is the purchase decision and the act of making the purchase.

The consumer must decide not only to purchase a product but also where to buy it. Consumers tend to choose the purchase location by considering such factors as ease of access, prices, assortment, store personnel, store image, physical design, and services provided. The product category will also influence the store selected. Some consumers will choose the convenience of in-home shopping by telephone or mail order rather than complete the transaction in a retail store.[26]

**Postpurchase Evaluation**

The purchase act results in the removal of the discrepancy between the existing state and the desired state. Logically, it should result in satisfaction to the buyer. However, even in many purchase decisions where the buyer is ultimately satisfied, it is common for that person to experience some initial postpurchase anxieties. He or she often wonders if the right decision has been made. Leon Festinger refers to this postpurchase doubt as **cognitive dissonance**.[27]

Cognitive dissonance is a psychologically unpleasant state that occurs after a purchase when there exists a discrepancy among a person's knowledge and beliefs (cognitions) about certain attributes of the final products under consideration. This occurs because several of the final product choice candidates have desirable characteristics, making the final decision difficult. Consumers may, for example, experience dissonance after choosing a particular automobile over several alternative models, when one or more of the rejected models have some desired features that the purchased automobile does not.

Dissonance is likely to increase 1) as the dollar value of the purchase increases, 2) when the rejected alternatives have desirable features not present in the chosen alternative, and 3) when the decision is a major one. The consumer may attempt to reduce dissonance in a variety of ways. He or she may seek out advertisements and other

[25] James Engel, David Kollat, and Roger Blackwell, *Consumer Behavior*, 3d ed. (Hinsdale: Dryden Press, 1978), p. 369.

[26] For a thorough discussion of purchase location, see David L. Loudon and Albert J. Della Bitta, *Consumer Behavior: Concepts and Applications* (New York: McGraw-Hill, 1979), pp. 483–511.

[27] Leon Festinger, *A Theory of Cognitive Dissonance* (Stanford, Calif.: Stanford University Press, 1958), p. 3.

information supporting the chosen alternative or seek reassurance from acquaintances who are satisfied purchasers of the product. At the same time the individual will avoid information favouring un-chosen alternatives. The Toyata purchaser is more likely to read Toyota advertisements and to avoid Datsun and Volkswagen ads. The cigarette smoker may ignore the magazine articles reporting links between smoking and cancer.

Marketers should try to reduce cognitive dissonance by providing informational support for the chosen alternative. Automobile dealers recognize "buyer's remorse" and often follow up purchases with a warm letter from the president of the dealership, offering personal handling of any customer problems and including a description of the quality of the product and the availability of convenient, top quality service.

The consumer may ultimately deal with cognitive dissonance by changing opinions, deciding that one of the rejected alternatives would have been the best choice, and forming the intention of purchasing it in the future.[28]

Should the purchase prove unsatisfactory, the consumer will revise purchase strategy to obtain need satisfaction. Feedback from the results of the decision process, whether satisfactory or not, will be called upon in the search and evaluation stages of similar buying situations.

## Classifying Consumer Problem-Solving Processes

The consumer decision process is dependent on the type of problem-solving effort required. Problem-solving behaviour has been divided into three categories: routinized response, limited problem solving, and extended problem solving.[29]

**Routinized Response**   Many purchases are made as a routine response to a need. The selection is a preferred brand or from a limited group of acceptable brands. The consumer has set the evaluative

---

[28] See Robert J. Connole, James D. Benson, and Inder P. Khera, "Cognitive Dissonance among Innovators," *Journal of the Academy of Marketing Science* (Winter 1977), pp. 9–20; David R. Lambert, Ronald J. Dornoff, and Jerome B. Kernan, "The Industrial Buyer and the Postchoice Evaluation Process," *Journal of Marketing Research* (May 1977), pp. 246–51; and William H. Cummings and M. Venkatesan, "Cognitive Dissonance and Consumer Behavior: A Review of the Evidence," *Journal of Marketing Research* (August 1976), pp. 303–8.

[29] These categories were originally suggested in John A. Howard, *Marketing Management: Analysis and Planning* (Homewood, Ill.: Richard D. Irwin, 1963). The discussion here is based on Donald R. Lehmann, William L. Moore, and Terry Elrod, "The Development of Distinct Choice Process Segments over Time: A Stochastic Modelling Approach," *Journal of Marketing* (Spring 1982), pp. 48–50.

criteria and identified the available options. The routine purchase of a particular newspaper or regular brands of soft drinks or toilet soap would be examples.

**Limited Problem Solving**   Consider the situation where the consumer has set evaluative criteria but encounters a new, unknown brand. The introduction of a new fragrance line might create a limited problem-solving situation. The consumer knows the evaluative criteria but has not assessed the new brand on the basis of these criteria. A certain amount of time and external search will be required. Limited problem solving is affected by the multitude of evaluative criteria and brands, the extent of external search, and the process by which preferences are determined.

**Extended Problem Solving**   Extended problem solving occurs in important purchase decisions when evaluative criteria have not been established for a product category, or where the individual wishes to review such criteria. Today many individuals are in the process of purchasing personal computers. Since most have never owned one before, they generally engage in an extensive search process. The main aspect of this is the determination of appropriate evaluative criteria which are relevant to the needs of the decision maker. How much computing power is required? Is portability important? What will be its main uses? What special features are required? As the criteria are being set, an evoked set of brands is also established. Most extended problem-solving efforts are lengthy, involving considerable external search.

Regardless of the type of problem solving, the steps in the basic model of the consumer decision process remain valid. The problem-solving categories described here relate only to the time and effort that is devoted to each step in the process.

**Summary**   Consumer behaviour is a function of both interpersonal and personal influences. The personal determinants of consumer behaviour have been identified as needs, motives, perception, attitudes, and self-concept. Learning theory also plays a role in consumer buying processes.

A need is the lack of something useful, while motives are the inner states that direct individuals to satisfy such needs. A. H. Maslow proposed a need classification structure that started with basic physiological needs and proceeded to progressively higher levels of needs — safety, social, esteem and self-actualization. Perception is the meaning that people assign to incoming stimuli received through the five senses. Most of these stimuli are screened or filtered out, so that the marketer must break through these screens to present the sales message effectively. Attitudes are a person's evaluations and feelings toward an object or idea. There are three components of attitudes: cognitive (what the person knows), affective (what the person feels about something), and behavioural (how the person tends to act). Learning refers to changes in behaviour, immediate or expected, as a result of experience. The learning theory concept can be useful in building a consumer franchise for a particular brand. Self-concept refers to an individual's conception of him- or herself. Self-concept theory has important implications for marketing tactics such as in targeting advertising messages.

The consumer decision process consists of six stages: problem recognition, search, evaluation of alternatives, the purchase decision, the purchase act, and postpurchase evaluation. Various types of problem-solving effort are required in the decision process. Routinized response, limited problem solving, and extended problem solving are the three categories of problem-solving behaviour.

| **Key Terms** | need | learning |
|---|---|---|
| | motive | drive |
| | perception | cue |
| | perceptual screen | response |
| | Weber's Law | reinforcement |
| | subliminal perception | shaping |
| | attitudes | evoked set |
| | semantic differential | evaluative criteria |
| | self-concept | cognitive dissonance |

**Review Questions**

1. What are the personal determinants of consumer behaviour?
2. How do needs and motives influence consumer behaviour?
3. Explain the concept of perception. Consider perceptual screens, selective perception, Weber's Law, and subliminal perception in your explanation.
4. How do attitudes influence consumer behaviour? How can negative attitudes be changed?
5. Describe the steps that occur in learning.
6. How can learning theory be applied to marketing strategy?
7. Differentiate among the four components of the self-concept: ideal self, looking-glass self, self-image, and real self.
8. Outline the steps in the consumer decision process.
9. Describe internal and external research.
10. Differentiate among routinized response behaviour, limited problem solving, and extended problem solving.

**Discussion Questions and Exercises**

1. Using Maslow's classification system, which needs are being referred to in the following advertising slogans:
   - No caffeine. Never had it. Never will. (7-Up)
   - Swedish engineering. Depend on it. (SAAB)
   - A blending of art and machine. (Jaguar)
   - The best bed a body can buy. (Simmons)
   - Don't leave home without it. (American Express Card)
2. Poll your friends about subliminal perception. How many believe that marketers can control consumers at a subconscious level? Report the results of this survey to your marketing class.
3. Find examples of shaping procedures being used in marketing applications.
4. Outline your own ideal self, looking-glass self, self-image, and real self.
5. Taking a recent shopping experience, analyse your attitudes as related to your consumer behaviour. Be sure your assessment considers all three components of an attitude.

**MICROCOMPUTER EXERCISE: Evaluation of Alternatives**

Consumers develop various methods for making purchase choices from alternative products or brands. For major purchases and cases where considerable risk is present, potential buyers may score or rank the brands that comprise their evoked set on the basis of various evaluative criteria. Then the question becomes how to best make the actual purchase decision. Approaches to this problem include 1) the overall-scoring method, 2) the weighted-scoring method, and 3) the minimum-score method.

• *Overall-Scoring Method.* This approach to ranking alternative purchase possibilities uses the highest total score to select a brand from among the evoked set. All of the evaluative criteria are considered of equal importance, and the brand with the highest overall score is chosen.

• *Weighted-Scoring Method.* The second approach involves assigning different weights to the various evaluative criteria in accordance with the consumer's perception of their relative importance. Once the variables are assigned their weighted scores, they are totaled, and the brand with the highest score is selected.

• *Minimum-Score Method.* This approach sets a floor for one or more of the evaluative criteria below which a brand will not be selected. For example, should the consumer decide that a brand must receive a ranking of 4 or more on the "service availability," a brand ranked 3 for this criterion would be rejected, even though it might receive the highest overall score. The minimum-score method is frequently used in conjunction with either the overall-scoring method or the weighted-scoring method.

It should be noted that these methods are representative of quantitative approaches to a typically qualitatively oriented subject. Not all consumers behave in such a fashion. Moreover, those who do may differ significantly in their scoring evaluations. The problems that follow refer to a specific situation in which the individual has already determined the evaluative criteria and the evoked set.

**Directions:** Use Menu Item titled "Evaluation of Alternatives" on the *Foundations of Marketing* disk to solve the following problems.

**1.** A Hamilton consumer is considering four brands of washing machine (the evoked set). The consumer has decided to evaluate the brands on the bases of price, quality, warranty, and service availability (the evaluative criteria). The consumer has also decided to give each model a score of 1 (poor) to 5 (best) on each of the evaluative criteria. These scores are shown in Table A.

**Table A   A Consumer Evaluation of Washing Machines**

| Evoked Set | Evaluative Criteria: Decision Factors | | | |
|---|---|---|---|---|
| | (A) | (B) | (C) | (D) Service |
| Alternatives | Price | Quality | Warranty | Availability |
| 1. Washmaster | 4 | 3 | 4 | 4 |
| 2. Magic Washer | 4 | 4 | 4 | 4 |
| 3. Wonder Machine | 2 | 5 | 5 | 5 |
| 4. The Marvel | 5 | 5 | 4 | 2 |

**a.** Which model would the consumer select, using the overall-scoring method?

**b.** Suppose the consumer considers price 50 percent more important than any of the other evaluative criteria. Which model would be selected?

**c.** Suppose the consumer, using the overall-scoring method, also decides that any model that scores lower than 3 on any variable is not acceptable. Which model would be selected?

**d.** Would your response to Question C change if the consumer used the weighted-scoring method?

**2.** Pierre Rousseau, of Saint John, N.B., is attempting to select a new car based on the following criteria: price, trade-in allowance, styling, riding comfort, and fuel economy. Rousseau had earlier narrowed his decision to four models: Elegance, Standard, Speedo, and Majestic. He then decided to rate each model on each of the specified evaluative criteria. Rousseau used a 3 to represent "excellent," 2 for "good," and 1 for "fair." His rankings are shown in Table B.

**a.** Which model would the consumer select, using the overall-scoring method?

**b.** Suppose that the consumer considers that fuel economy, price, and trade-in allowance are each 50 percent more important than the other two evaluative criteria. Which model would he select?

c. Suppose that Rousseau, using the overall-scoring method, also decides he will not accept any model that is rated lower than good on fuel economy, price, and trade-in allowance. Which model would he prefer?

d. Would Rousseau's decision in Question C change if he decides to use the weighted-scoring method?

### Table B   A Consumer Evaluation of Cars: Example 1

| Evoked Set | Evaluative Criteria: Decision Factors | | | | |
|---|---|---|---|---|---|
| | (A) | (B) Trade-in | (C) | (D) Riding | (E) Fuel |
| Alternatives | Price | Allowance | Styling | Comfort | Economy |
| 1. Elegance | 2 | 2 | 3 | 3 | 2 |
| 2. Standard | 2 | 2 | 2 | 2 | 3 |
| 3. Speedo | 3 | 3 | 3 | 3 | 1 |
| 4. Majestic | 3 | 3 | 1 | 1 | 3 |

3. Like Pierre Rousseau in Problem 2, Judy Krantz is also contemplating the purchase of a new car. In fact, she and Rousseau conferred before assigning the ratings for the Elegance, Standard, Speedo, and Majestic. However, Krantz also considers another auto model, the Olympic, to be viable option. Her rankings are shown in Table C.

a. Which model would the consumer select, using the overall-scoring method?

b. Suppose Krantz considers riding comfort and fuel economy 100 percent more important than styling and price, and trade-in allowance 200 percent more important than styling. Which model would she select?

c. Suppose that Krantz, using the overall-scoring method, also decides that she will not accept a car that is rated lower than good on any variable. Which model would she select?

d. Would Krantz's decision in Question C change if she decides to use the weighted-scoring method?

### Table C   A Consumer Evaluation of Cars: Example 2

| Evoked Set | Evaluative Criteria: Decision Factors | | | | |
|---|---|---|---|---|---|
| | (A) | (B) Trade-in | (C) | (D) Riding | (E) Fuel |
| Alternatives | Price | Allowance | Styling | Comfort | Economy |
| 1. Elegance | 2 | 2 | 3 | 3 | 2 |
| 2. Standard | 2 | 2 | 2 | 2 | 3 |
| 3. Speedo | 3 | 3 | 3 | 3 | 1 |
| 4. Majestic | 3 | 3 | 1 | 1 | 3 |
| 5. Olympic | 3 | 2 | 2 | 2 | 2 |

## CHAPTER 9

# Buyer Behaviour in Industrial and Government Markets

1. To relate buying behaviour in industrial and government markets to the variables of the marketing mix.

2. To differentiate among the three types of industrial markets.

3. To identify the three distinctive features of industrial markets.

4. To explain the characteristics of industrial market demand.

5. To identify the basic categories of industrial products.

6. To discuss the nature of the industrial purchase.

7. To outline the classification system for industrial purchasing situations: straight rebuy; modified rebuy; and new task buying.

8. To explain the buying centre concept.

9. To explain the steps in the industrial purchasing process.

10. To explain how government markets differ from other markets.

Through its Univac computers, Unisys has a long history of involvement in the computer industry. The company also has a well-established reputation in the defence industry. Yet in spite of its size and its success in business, many people have never heard of Unisys because it has concentrated on providing products and services for the industrial rather than the consumer market.

Unisys has now developed a personal computer, a product that would be suitable for both businesses and individual consumers. Should Unisys enter the consumer market? The firm has decided not to do so — at least, not directly. Recognizing that its marketing skills are in the industrial field, Unisys has chosen to turn over the retail marketing of its personal computers to a distributor who knows the consumer market.

**The Conceptual Framework**

Unisys is a good example of a firm that operates in the industrial market, and that realizes that successful marketing practices in one will not necessarily produce success in the other. While the consumer market consists of individuals who purchase goods and services for personal use, the **industrial market** consists of *those individuals and organizations who acquire goods and services to be used, directly or indirectly, in the production of other goods and services or to be resold.* Although industrial marketers face decisions very similar to those of their consumer-market counterparts, important differences exist in the characteristics of market targets and in the development of appropriate marketing mixes. As James D. Hlavacek noted, "Overall, the strategic and tactical emphasis and elements in the industrial and consumer marketing mixes are as different as silicon chips and potato chips."[1]

The first two chapters in Part Three have dealt with the buying behaviours that exist in consumer markets. Attention now shifts to the industrial and government markets. The next part of the text considers the product aspect of the marketing mix including a comprehensive classification system for industrial products.

## Types of Industrial Markets

The industrial market can be divided into three categories: producers, trade industries (wholesalers and retailers), and governments. **Producers** are *industrial customers who purchase goods and services for the production of other goods and services.* A Canadian Airlines International purchase of a new fuel-efficient Boeing 767 plane, a wheat purchase by General Mills for its cereals, and the purchase of light bulbs and cleaning materials for a Dominion Steel manufacturing facility all represent industrial purchases by producers. Some products aid in producing another product or service (the new plane provides transportation); others are physically used up in the production of a product (the wheat becomes part of the cereal); and still others are routinely used in the day-to-day operations of the firm (light bulbs and cleaning materials are maintenance items). Producers including manufacturing firms, farmers and other resource industries, construction contractors, providers of such services as transportation, public utilities, and banks.

**Trade industries** are *organizations such as retailers and wholesalers that purchase for resale to others.* In most instances, resale products, such as clothing, applicances, sports equipment, and automobile parts, are finished goods that are marketed to customers. In other instances, some processing or repackaging may take place. Retail meat markets may make bulk purchases of sides of beef and convert them into individual cuts for their customers. Lumber deal-

---

[1] James D. Hlavacek, "Business Schools Need More Industrial Marketing," *Marketing News* (April 4, 1980), p. 1.

ers and carpet retailers may purchase in bulk, then provide quantities and sizes to meet customers' specifications. In addition to resale products, trade industries also buy cash registers, computers, display equipment, and other products required to operate their business. These products (as well as maintenance items and the purchase of such specialized services as marketing research studies, accounting services, and consulting) all represent industrial purchases. Retailing and wholesaling activities are discussed in separate chapters later in the text.

Governments at the federal, provincial, and local level represent the final category of industrial purchasers. This important component of the industrial market purchases a wide variety of products, ranging from highways to education to F–16 fighter aircraft. The primary motivation of government purchasing is to provide some form of public benefit such as national defence, education, or health services. Buying behaviour in government markets is discussed separately in this chapter because of its immense size and importance.

**Figure 9-1   Summary of Manufacturers by Province, 1982**

| Province or Territory | Number of Establishments | Total Employees | Materials and Supplies Used | Total Value Added ($000) |
|---|---|---|---|---|
| Ontario | 14 822 | 589 649 | 56 027 076 | 35 188 820 |
| Quebec | 10 753 | 348 333 | 28 208 448 | 18 745 836 |
| British Columbia | 3 919 | 103 653 | 9 073 549 | 5 917 997 |
| Alberta | 2 490 | 54 834 | 9 058 291 | 3 801 812 |
| Manitoba | 1 279 | 39 130 | 2 863 844 | 1 859 175 |
| Nova Scotia | 781 | 24 967 | 2 248 815 | 1 123 255 |
| Saskatchewan | 749 | 14 075 | 1 640 905 | 777 615 |
| New Brunswick | 591 | 21 479 | 2 140 961 | 938 432 |
| Newfoundland | 295 | 13 764 | 661 468 | 549 475 |
| Prince Edward Island | 127 | 2 253 | 169 569 | 75 559 |
| Northwest Territories and Yukon | 19 | 219 | 23 651 | 9 761 |
| Total | 35 834 | 1 212 424 | 112 120 148 | 68 990 447 |

Source: 1982 Census of Manufacturers, Catalogue 11-001E ISSN 0380-612X Statistics Canada Daily, Tues., May 1, 1984, p. 6.

**Scope of the Industrial Market**

The scope of the industrial market is illustrated in Figure 9-1. In the manufacturing sector alone there are nearly 36 000 establishments, and they employ over 1.2 million people. The significance of this market is dramatized in the amount of materials and supplies used in their operations — over $112 billion worth! In total, the industrial market accounts for some 50 percent of purchases of manufactured goods in Canada.

One measure of industrial output is the **value added** by manufacturing, *the increase in value of input material when transformed into semi-finished or finished goods*. For example, value is added to a tonne of iron ore when it is made into steel plate, and more value is added when the plate is stamped into refrigerator bodies. In 1982, the value added by manufacturing in Canada totalled approximately $73.3 billion.

## Distinctive Features of the Industrial Market

The industrial market has three distinctive features: geographic market concentration, a relatively small number of buyers, and systematic buying procedures.

### Geographic Market Concentration

The market for industrial goods in Canada is much more concentrated geographically than that for consumer goods. The largest markets are in Ontario and Quebec. However, industrial markets for specific items often do not follow the general pattern. As an example, the market for marine engines and fishing gear is concentrated on the Atlantic and Pacific coasts, and oil drilling equipment in Alberta, British Columbia, and to a lesser extent Saskatchewan. New finds on the East Coast mean that this market is now expanding eastward.

### Small Number of Buyers

The industrial market is concentrated not only on a geographical basis, but also by a limited number of buyers. Although the 1984 Census of Manufacturers revealed a total of approximately 36 000[2] firms in Canada, a small proportion of firms — those with 500 or more employees — were responsible for approximately half of the total dollar value added by manufacturing.

The concentration of the industrial market greatly influences the strategy used in serving this market. The industrial marketer can usually make more profitable use of a sales force to provide regular personal contacts with a small, geographically concentrated market than consumer goods companies can provide with ultimate consumers. Wholesalers are less frequently used, and the marketing channel for industrial goods is typically much shorter than for consumer goods. Advertising plays a much smaller role in the industrial goods market, as funds may be more effectively spent on the sales force and other means of promotion than with consumer goods.

---

[2] *Statistics Canada Daily*, Tues., May 1, 1984, p. 6

**Standard Industrial Classifications**

The marketer focusing on the industrial market is aided by a wealth of information collected by the federal government, including number of firms, sales volumes, and the number of employees for firms in each industry broken down by province. This data is broken down by **Standard Industrial Classifications** (SIC codes). The SIC codes begin with 12 divisions, and under each division is a list of major groups into which all types of businesses are divided.

| Division | | Major Groups | Number of Groups |
|---|---|---|---|
| 1 | Agriculture | 001-021 | 8 |
| 2 | Forestry | 031-039 | 2 |
| 3 | Fishing and Trapping | 041-047 | 3 |
| 4 | Mines, Quarries, and Oil Wells | 051-099 | 5 |
| 5 | Manufacturing Industries | 101-391 | 20 |
| 6 | Construction Industry | 404-421 | 2 |
| 7 | Transportation, Communication, and Other Utilities | 501-579 | 4 |
| 8 | Trade | 602-699 | 2 |
| 9 | Finance, Insurance, and Real Estate | 701-737 | 3 |
| 10 | Community, Business, and Personal Service Industries | 801-899 | 8 |
| 11 | Public Administration and Defence | 902-991 | 4 |
| 12 | Industry Unspecified or Undefined | 999-000 | — |

Each major industry within these broad groups is assigned a separate two-digit number, and three- and four-digit numbers are used to subdivide the industry into smaller segments. For example, the forestry and kindred products group (Division 2) can be further subdivided into such segments as wood products (code 08) and furniture (code 09). The furniture segment can then be further refined to office furniture and other related products (code 264).

The SIC code breakdowns can aid greatly in analysing the industrial market. The detailed information for each market segment is an invaluable secondary source, providing industrial marketers with a comprehensive description of the activities of their potential customers on both a geographical and an industrial basis.[3]

Beyond the SIC data, trade associations and business publica-

---

[3] *Standard Industrial Classification Manual, Revised 1970*, Statistics Canada Catalogue 12-501, pp. 17–20.

tions provide additional information on the industrial market. Private firms such as Dun & Bradstreet publish detailed reports on individual firms. These secondary sources serve as useful starting points for analysing industrial markets.

## Industrial Market Demand

Gillette's Paper Mate division had long been a successful provider of medium-priced ballpoint pens to consumer markets. But this market was becoming increasingly divided into low- and premium-priced segments. So Paper Mate decided to come out with new offerings at both ends of the price spectrum.

The firm also decided to enter the office supplies field — an industrial market. The Gillette division clearly recognized that the industrial marketplace was different from the consumer markets in which they had traditionally competed. The unique characteristics of industrial settings require that marketing strategies be tailored to the special requirements of this marketplace. It established a special commercial sales force to promote its pens to industrial buyers. Paper Mate also acquired Liquid Paper, an established name in office supplies. Liquid Paper's industrial marketing strengths were seen as complementing the consumer marketing in which Paper Mate had specialized.[4]

What are the primary characteristics of industrial market demand? Most lists would include the following:[5]

### Derived Demand

The demand for an industrial product is typically **derived demand**, *derived from (or linked to) demand for a consumer good*. The demand for cash registers (an industrial good) is partially derived from demand at the retail level (consumer products). Lower retail sales may ultimately result in lower demand for cash registers.

The "down-sizing" of automobile engines by auto manufacturers in an attempt to develop smaller, fuel-efficient cars adversely affects spark-plug manufacturers like Champion. Since four-cylinder engines use half as many plugs as V-8s, Champion's total sales may decline drastically unless total auto sales increase dramatically, or unless Champion can increase its share of the total market.

### Joint Demand

The demand for some industrial products is *related to the demand for other industrial goods*. There is a **joint demand** for coke and

---

[4] "Paper Mate's Broader Outlook," *Business Week* (January 28, 1980), p. 69.
[5] These characteristics are suggested in Robert W. Haas, *Industrial Marketing Management* (New York: Petrocelli/Charter, 1976), pp. 21–26; H. Robert Dodge, *Industrial Marketing* (New York: McGraw-Hill, 1970), pp. 21–25; and Richard M. Hill, Ralph S. Alexander, and James S. Cross, *Industrial Marketing*, Fourth Edition (Homewood, Ilinois: Richard D. Irwin, Inc., 1975), pp. 46–47.

iron ore in the manufacture of pig iron. If the coke supply is reduced, there will be an accompanying reduction in the demand for iron ore.

**Inventory Adjustments**
*Changes in the amounts of materials a manufacturer keeps on hand* can have an impact on industrial demand. A two-month supply of raw materials is often considered the optimal inventory in some manufacturing industries.[6] But suppose economic conditions or other factors dictate that this level be increased to a 90-day supply. The raw materials supplier would then be bombarded with a tremendous increase in new orders. Thus, **inventory adjustments** can be a major determinant of industrial demand.

**Demand Variability**
Derived demand in the industrial market is related to and often creates immense variability in industrial demand. Assume the demand for industrial product A is derived from the demand for consumer product B — an item whose sales volume has been growing at an annual rate of 10 percent. Now suppose that the demand for product B slowed to a 5 percent annual increase. Management might decide to delay further purchases of product A, using existing inventory until the market conditions were clarified. Therefore, product A's **demand variability** becomes significantly affected by even modest shifts in the demand for product B. *The disproportionate impact that changes in consumer demand have upon industrial market demand* is called the **accelerator principle.**

---

**Basic Categories of Industrial Products**
There are two general categories of industrial products: capital items and expense items. **Capital items** are *long-lived business assets that must be depreciated over time.* **Depreciation** is *the accounting concept of charging a portion of a capital item as a deduction against the company's annual revenue for purposes of determining its net income.* Examples of capital items include major installations like new plants and office buildings as well as equipment.

**Expense items,** by contrast, *are products and services that are used within a short period of time.* For the most part, they are charged against income in the year of purchase. Examples of expense items include the supplies that are used in operating the business, ranging from raw materials and fabricated parts to paper clips and machine lubricants.

Chapter 10 presents a comprehensive classification of industrial products. This initial breakdown into capital and expense items is useful because buying behaviour varies significantly depending upon

---

6 The 60-day figure is suggested in Bob Luke, "Purchasing Agents: Supply Sergeants to the Business World," *Detroit News* (May 20, 1979), p. 2-E.

how a purchase is treated from an accounting viewpoint. Expense items may be bought routinely and with minimal delay, while capital items involve major fund commitments and are thus subject to considerable review by the purchaser's personnel. Differences in industrial purchasing behaviour are discussed in the sections that follow.

## The Nature of the Industrial Purchase: Systematic and Complex

Industrial purchase behaviour tends to be more complex than the consumer decision process described in Chapters 7 and 8. There are several reasons for this increased complexity:

1. Many persons may exert influence in industrial purchases, and considerable time may be spent in obtaining the input and approval of various organizational members.
2. Organizational purchasing may be handled by committees with greater time requirements for majority or unanimous approval.
3. Many organizations attempt to utilize several sources of supply as a type of insurance against shortages.

Most industrial firms have attempted to systematize their purchases by employing a professional consumer — the industrial purchasing manager who is responsible for handling most of the organization's purchases and for securing needed products at the best possible price. Unlike the ultimate consumer who makes periodic purchase decisions, a firm's purchasing department devotes all its time and effort to determining needs, locating and evaluating alternative sources of supply, and making purchase decisions.

## The Complexity of Industrial Purchases

Where major purchases are involved, negotiations may take several weeks or even months, and the buying decisions may rest with a number of persons in the organization. The choice of a supplier for industrial drill presses, for example, may be made jointly by the purchasing agent and the company's production, engineering, and maintenance departments. Each of these principals has a different point of view and they must all be reconciled in making a purchase decision. As a result, representatives of the selling firm must be well versed in all aspects of the product or service and be capable of interacting with managers of the various departments involved. In the transportation equipment industry, for instance, it takes an average of 4.9 face-to-face presentations to make a sale. The average cost of closing the sale — including salesperson compensation and travel and entertainment expenses — is $1121.02. Figure 9-2 shows the average number of sales calls required to complete a sale in several industries and the average cost of each sale.

Many industrial goods are purchased over long periods of time on a contractual basis. A manufacturing operation requires a continual supply of materials, and a one- or two-year contract with a supplier ensures a steady supply of raw materials as they are needed. Other industrial goods, such as conveyors, typewriters, and forklifts, generally last several years before replacement is necessary.

Purchase decisions are frequently made on the bases of service, certainty of supply, and the efficiency of the products. These factors may be even more important than the prices quoted for the products. Automobile manufacturers purchase steel, glass windows, spark plugs, and batteries as ingredients for their output. Since demand for these parts is derived entirely from the demand for consumer goods, price changes do not substantially affect their sale. Price increases for paint will have little effect on auto sales at General Motors since paint represents a minute portion of the total costs of the automobile.

**Figure 9-2   Calls and Costs Needed to Close a Sale**

| Industry | Average Number of Calls to Close a Sale | Average Cost to Close a Sale[a] |
|---|---|---|
| Food and Kindred Products | 2.6 | $ 229.16 |
| Furniture and Fixtures | 3.8 | 388.20 |
| Paper and Allied Products | 4.7 | 597.22 |
| Petroleum/Retailing and Related Industries | 4.0 | 360.56 |
| Primary Metal Industries | 3.9 | 465.89 |
| Transportation Equipment | 4.9 | 1 121.02 |
| Transportation by Air | 4.1 | 265.68 |
| Business Services | 5.6 | 800.01 |
| Automotive Repair, Services and Garages | 5.0 | 488.00 |

[a]Determined by multiplying the average number of calls to close a sale by the average cost per sales call for each industry.
Source: "Industrial Sales Call Tops $137, but New 'Cost to Close' Hits $589," *Marketing News* (May 1, 1981), p. 1. Used by permission of the American Marketing Association.

***Purchase of a Capital Item***   A utility company's decision to buy a reinforced Fiberglas utility pole faced a complicated process. The sales representative dealt with the members of several departments of the utility company and went through months of negotiations before a purchase was made. The new pole had several advantages over the traditional steel, wood, or aluminum post: it was lightweight; had nonelectrical conducting and noncorrosive properties; never needed painting; and met all strength requirements. Its major disadvantage, other than its unfamiliarity to the purchaser, was its high initial purchase price compared to the alternatives. The decision process began when the manager of the utility consulted the engineering head who, in turn, brought in the purchasing department manager. Purchasing then prepared a list of alternative suppliers and materials, which was approved by engineering, and the purchasing manager discussed the organization's needs in detail with the sales representatives of three suppliers. The salespeople met with the managers of the stores department, the marketing department, and the engineering department. After a series of meetings with the salespeople and numerous discussions among the utility's department heads, the utility decided to submit the new Fiberglas pole to a test conducted by the engineering department. The results of the test were reported to the various department heads, and bids were then requested from suppliers A, B, and C. These bids were reviewed by the department heads, who ultimately decided to select the Fiberglas pole offered by supplier B. This complex decision process is diagrammed in Figure 9-3.[7]

## Classifying Industrial Purchasing Situations

Industrial buying behaviour is affected by the degree of effort and involvement by different levels within the organization. There are three generally recognized industrial purchasing situations: straight rebuy, modified rebuy, and new task buying.[8]

### Straight Rebuy

A **straight rebuy** is *a recurring purchase decision where an item that has performed satisfactorily is purchased again by a customer.* This industrial buying situation occurs when a purchaser is pleased with the good or service and the terms of sale are acceptable. Seeing little reason to assess other options, the purchaser follows some routine buying format.

Low-cost items like paper clips and HB pencils are typically rebought. If the purchaser is pleased with the products and their prices and terms, future purchases will probably be treated as a straight rebuy from the current vendor. Even expensive items especially designed for a customer's needs can be treated as a straight rebuy in some cases. For example, a manufacturer might be virtually committed to buying additional lathes from a certain company because they purchased them before, and want to keep a standardized production situation.

---

[7] The development of the new type of pole and the problems involved in its adoption are described in Arch G. Woodside, "Marketing Anatomy of Buying Process Can Help Improve Industrial Strategy," *Marketing News* (May 1, 1981), Section 2, p. 11.

[8] These are suggested in Patrick J. Robinson, Charles W. Farris, and Yoram Wind, *Industrial Buying and Creative Marketing* (Boston: Allyn and Bacon, 1967), Chapter 1. The discussion here follows Hutt and Speh, *Industrial Marketing Management*, pp. 51–55.

Figure 9-3   The Decision to Purchase a New Type of Utility Pole

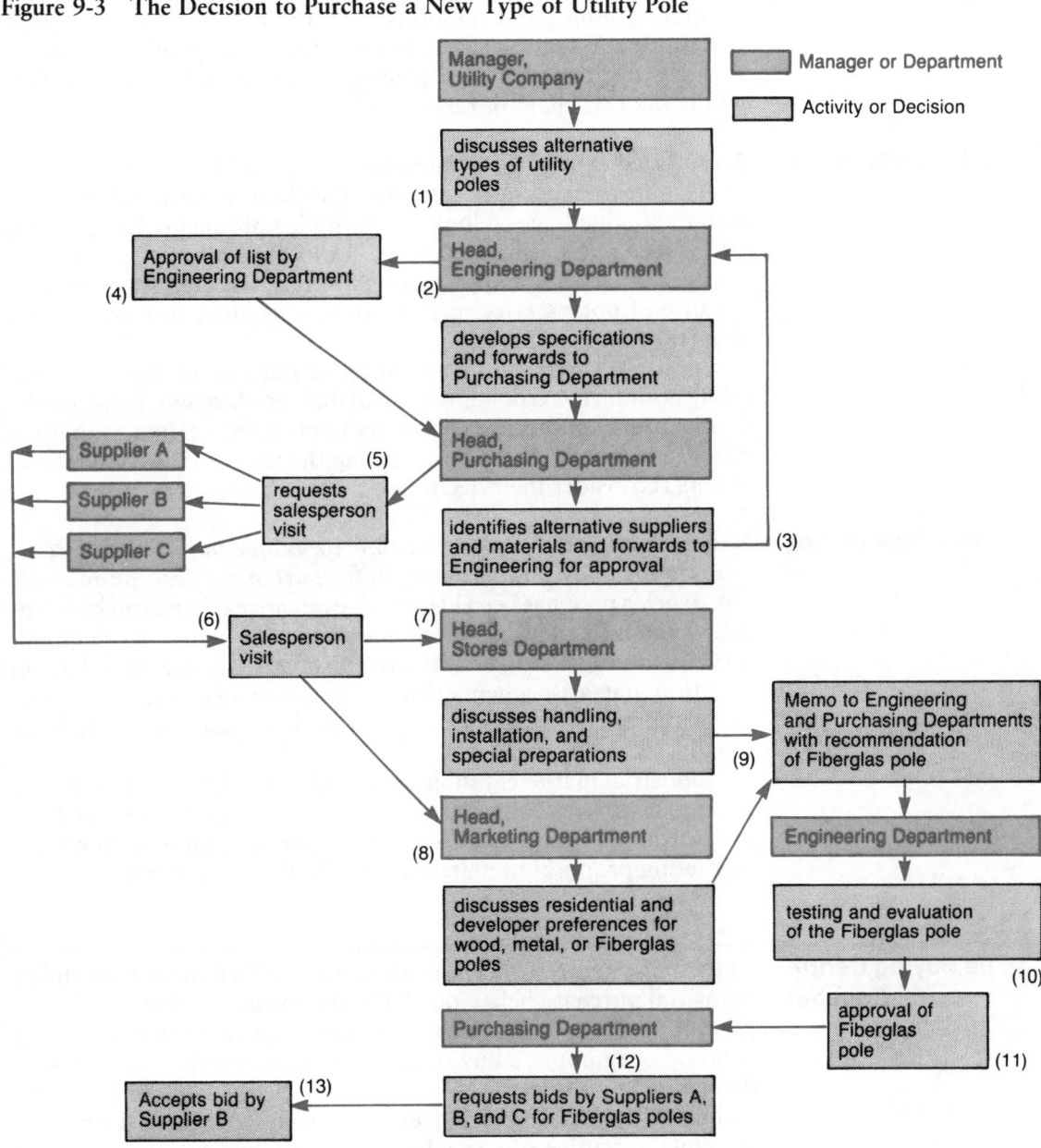

Source: Adapted from Arch G. Woodside, "Marketing Anatomy of Buying Process Can Help Improve Industrial Strategy," *Marketing News* (May 1, 1981), Section 2, p. 11. Used by permission of the American Marketing Association.

Marketers facing straight rebuy situations should concentrate on maintaining good relations with the buyer through prompt attention, adequate service, and the like. Competitors are faced with the difficult task of presenting a unique sales proposal that will break this chain of repurchases.

**Modified Rebuy**

A **modified rebuy** is *a situation where purchasers are willing to re-evaluate their available options.* The decision-makers feel that it is to their advantage to look at alternative product offerings using established purchasing guidelines. A modified rebuy situation may occur if a marketer allows a straight rebuy situation to deteriorate because of poor service or delivery or if quality, cost and service differences are perceived.

Industrial marketers want to move purchasers into a straight rebuy position by responding to all of their product and service needs. Competitors, on the other hand, try to move buyers into a modified rebuy situation by correctly assessing the factors that would make buyers reconsider their decisions.

**New Task Buying**

New **task buying** *refers to first-time or unique purchase situations that require considerable effort on the part of the decision-makers.* Once such a need has been identified, evaluative criteria can be established and an extensive search launched. Alternative product and service offerings and vendors are considered. A new task buying situation may arise when a firm enters a new field and has to seek out suppliers of component parts that have not previously been purchased.

Industrial marketers should work closely with the purchaser in the case of new task buying situations. This will allow them to study the factors the purchaser considers important and to design their marketing proposal to match the needs of the purchaser.

**The Buying Centre Concept**

The buying centre concept is an important key to understanding industrial purchase behaviour.[9] The **buying centre** simply *refers to everyone who participates in some fashion in an industrial buying action.* For example, a buying centre may include the architect who designs a new research laboratory; the scientist who will use the facility; the purchasing manager who screens contractor proposals; the chief executive officer who makes the final decision; and the

---

[9] This section is based on Hutt and Speh, *Industrial Marketing Management*, pp. 80–85.

**Figure 9-4   Definitions of Buying Centre Roles**

| Role | Description |
|---|---|
| *Users* | As the role name implies, these are the personnel who will be using the product in question. Users may have anywhere from inconsequential to an extremely important influence on the purchase decision. In some cases, the users initiate the purchase action by requesting the product. They may even develop the product specifications. |
| *Gatekeepers* | Gatekeepers control information to be reviewed by other members of the buying centre either by the ways they disseminate printed information or advertisements or by controlling which salesperson will speak to which individuals in the buying centre. The purchasing agent might perform this screening role by opening the gate to the buying centre for some sales personnel and closing it to others. |
| *Influencers* | These individuals affect the purchasing decision by supplying information for the evaluation of alternatives or by setting buying specifications. Typically, technical personnel such as engineers, quality control personnel, and research and development personnel are significant influences to the purchase decision. Sometimes individuals outside of the buying organization can assume this role (e.g., an engineering consultant or an architect who writes very tight building specifications). |
| *Deciders* | Deciders are the individuals who actually make the buying decision, whether or not they have the formal authority to do so. The identity of the decider is the most difficult role to determine: buyers may have formal authority to buy, but the president of the firm may actually make the decision. A decider could be a design engineer who develops a set of specifications that only one vendor can meet. |
| *Buyers* | The buyer has *formal* authority for selecting a supplier and implementing all procedures connected with securing the product. The power of the buyer is often usurped by more powerful members of the organization. Often the buyer's role is assumed by the purchasing agent, who executes the clerical functions associated with a purchase order. |

Source: Adapted from Frederick E. Webster, Jr. and Yoram Wind, *Organizational Buying Behavior* (Englewood Cliffs, N. J.: Prentice-Hall, 1972), pp. 77–80. This adaptation is reprinted from Michael D. Hutt and Thomas W. Speh, *Industrial Marketing Management* (Hinsdale, Ill.: The Dryden Press, 1981), p. 83.

vice-president for research who signs the formal contracts for the project.[10]

Buying centres are not part of a firm's formal organizational structure. They are informal groups whose composition will vary from one purchase situation to another and from one firm to the next. Buying centres typically include anywhere from 4 to 20 participants,[11] and tend to evolve as the purchasing process moves through its various stages.

Buying centre participants play the roles of users, gatekeepers, influencers, deciders and buyers in the purchasing decision process. Each of these roles is described in Figure 9-4.

A critical task for the industrial marketer is to determine the specific role and the relative buying influence of each buying centre participant. Sales presentations and information can then be tailored to the role that the individual plays at each step in the purchase process. Industrial marketers have also found that while their initial, and in many cases most extensive, contacts are with the purchasing department, the buying centre participants having the greatest influence are often elsewhere in the company.[12]

## The Process of Buying Industrial Goods and Services

The exact procedures that are used in buying industrial goods and services vary according to the buying situation confronted: straight

[10] Buying centres are discussed in two articles in the July 1982 issue of the *Journal of Business Research*. See Gloria P. Thomas and John F. Grashof, "Impact of Internal and External Environments' Stability on the Existence of Determinant Buying Roles," pp. 159–168; and Yoram Wind and Thomas S. Robertson, "The Linking Pin Role in Organizational Buying Centers," pp. 169–184. Also see Earl Naumann, Robert McWilliams, and Douglas J. Lincoln, "How Different Buying Center Members Influence Different Purchasing Phases," in *Development in Marketing Science*, (eds.) Vinay Kothari, Danny R. Arnold, James Cavusgil, Jay D. Lindquist, Jay Nathan, and Stan Reid (*Proceedings of the Academy of Marketing Science*, 1982), pp. 186–190.
[11] Hutt and Speh, *Industrial Marketing Management*, p. 80, cite the following sources for their statistics: "Industrial Salespeople Report 4.1 Buying Influences in Average Company," *LAP Report* 1042.2 (McGraw-Hill Research, October 1977); and G. van der Most, "Purchasing Process: Researching Influences Is Basic to Marketing Plan," *Industrial Marketing* (October 1976), p. 120.
[12] An interesting discussion of influences is found in Robert J. Thomas, "Correlates of Interpersonal Purchase Influence in Organizations," *Journal of Consumer Research* (September 1982), pp. 171–182. Also see Robert E. Krapfel, Jr., "An Extended Influence Model of Organizational Buyer Behavior," *Journal of Business Research* (June 1982), pp. 147–157.

rebuy, modified rebuy, or new task buying.[13] Most industrial purchases follow the same general process. Research by Agarwal, Burger, and Venkatesh suggested the model presented in Figure 9-5. While this model was formulated for industrial machinery purchases, it has general application to the industrial buying process.

**Dissecting the Model**   The specific steps as shown in Figure 9-5 are outlined below.

*Need Recognition*   A triggering event such as an equipment failure stimulates recognition of a perceived need for an industrial purchase.

*Information Search*   Buying centre members begin to collect information on potential suppliers from sales personnel, advertisements, word of mouth, pamphlets, and other sources. The net result is to delineate the technical nature of the purchase.

*Delineation of Suppliers*   Given the specifications established in the previous step, potential suppliers are then determined. Budget considerations may also be a factor in this step.

*Sales Demonstration/Proposal*   Vendor sales representatives are then invited to provide demonstrations and sales proposals. These proposals typically include technical and economic options as well as prices.

*Word of Mouth*   Buying centre members may then contact current users of the product for their evaluation of its performance. Reliability, costs, and operational abilities are explored. Some vendors are eliminated because of negative information.

*Final Decision*   Eventually a purchase decision is made. In many cases, this extensive process leads to a consensus decision, but some buying centre members have more influence than others in this final decision stage.

**Reciprocity**   A highly controversial practice in a number of industrial purchasing situations is **reciprocity**, *the extension of purchasing preference to suppliers who are also customers.* For example, an office-equipment manufacturer may favour a particular supplier of component parts if the supplier has recently made a major purchase of the manufacturer's products. Reciprocal arrangements were

---

13 This section is based on Manoj K. Agarwal, Philip C. Burger, and Alladi Venkatesh, "Industrial Consumer Behavior: Toward An Improved Model," in *Developments in Marketing Science*, (eds.) Venkatakrishna V. Bellur, Thomas R. Baird, Paul T. Hertz, Roger L. Jenkins, Jay D. Lindquist, and Stephen W. Miller (Miami Beach: Academy of Marketing Science, 1981), pp. 68–73.

**Figure 9-5   A Model of the Industrial Buying Process**

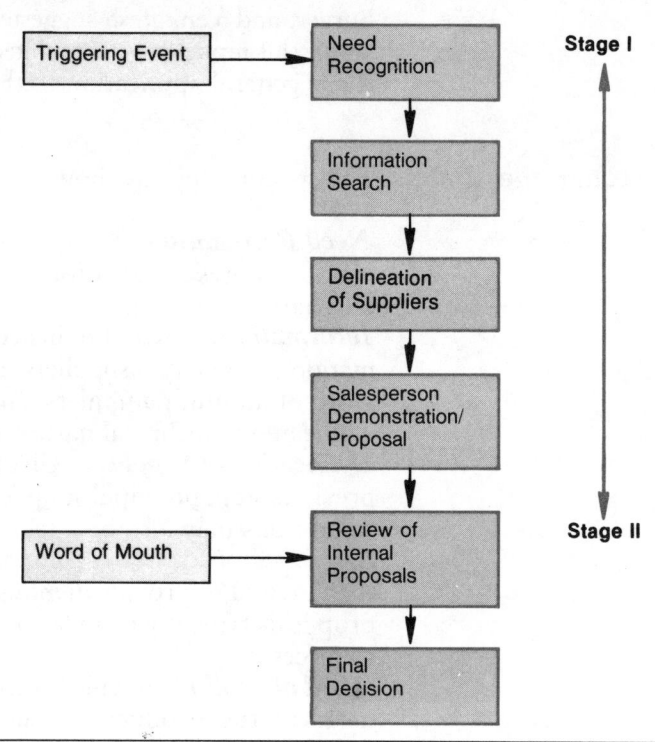

Source: Reprinted from Manoj K. Agarwal, Philip C. Burger, and Alladi Venkatesh, "Industrial Consumer Behavior: Toward an Improved Model," in *Developments in Marketing Science*, (eds.) Venkatakrishna V. Bellur, Thomas R. Baird, Paul T. Hertz, Roger L. Jenkins, Jay D. Lindquist, and Stephen W. Miller (Miami Beach: Academy of Marketing Science, 1981), p. 72.

traditionally used in industries with homogeneous products with similar prices, such as the chemical, paint, petroleum, rubber, and steel industries.

Two other forms of reciprocity have been used. *Reverse reciprocity* is the practice of supplying parts and raw materials in short supply to firms who can provide other needed supplies in return. In times of shortages, reverse reciprocity occasionally emerges as firms attempt to obtain raw materials and parts to continue operations. A more recent reciprocity spinoff is the *voluntary price roll-back*, where purchasers request vendors to agree to temporary price cuts or freezes. While no threats are made, it is difficult for a supplier to refuse a request from a major purchaser. This sometimes forces the vendor to ask for concessions from its own work-force and/or suppliers.[14] The various forms of reciprocity are evidence of the close links that exist between the various elements of the industrial marketplace.[15]

| **Government Markets** | The various levels of government make up a sizeable segment of the market for industrial products. There are many similarities between the government market and other industrial markets, for they seek to purchase many similar goods and services. However, the numerous regulations that affect government purchases create differences in the way items are procured. |

The various levels of government make up a sizeable segment of the market for industrial products. There are many similarities between the government market and other industrial markets, for they seek to purchase many similar goods and services. However, the numerous regulations that affect government purchases create differences in the way items are procured.

Government expenditures represent nearly 52 percent of Canada's gross national product. More than 60 000 firms supply close to 20 000 items and services to the various levels of government, whose total spending in 1982 amounted to approximately $213 billion. The federal government accounted for approximately 42 percent of that total. Figure 9-6 indicates the major categories of government expenditures.

**How Governments Buy**

Since most government purchases must, by law, be made on the basis of **bids** (*price quotations from potential suppliers*), the government buyer must develop **specifications**, *specific descriptions of needed items* for prospective bidders (this is often done in the industrial market also). For the federal government most of the branded items, such as general-purpose supplies, are purchased for all federal agencies by the Department of Supply and Services. Each province generally has a comparable office for such items.

**Bidding on Government Contracts**

All Canadian business and industrial operations are eligible to bid on federal government contracts.[16] The only requirement is that the firm must indicate interest and be prepared to provide evidence that

---

[14] These price cuts are described in Thomas F. O'Boyle, "Price Cutting Being Forced on Suppliers," *The Wall Street Journal* (May 14, 1982), p. 27.

[15] The history and current status of reciprocal agreements is summarized in E. Robert Finney, "Reciprocity: Gone but Not Forgotten," *Journal of Marketing* (January 1978), pp. 54–59. See also William J. Kehoe and Byron D. Hewett, "Reciprocity and Reverse Reciprocity: A Literature Review and Research Design," in *Proceedings of the Southern Marketing Association*, (eds.) Robert S. Franz, Robert M. Hopkins, and Al Toma (New Orleans, La., November 1978), pp. 481–483; and Monroe M. Bird, "Reverse Reciprocity: A New Twist to Industrial Buyers," *Atlanta Economic Review* (January–February 1976), pp. 11–13.

[16] Adapted from *How to Do Business with the Department of Supply and Services* (Ottawa: Department of Supply and Services, 1980), pp. 1–11.

**Figure 9-6   Gross General Expenditures, All Levels of Government, for 1982**

| Function | $(thousands) |
|---|---:|
| Total general services | 11 122 143 |
| Protection of persons and property | 14 104 777 |
| Transportation and communications | 12 804 294 |
| Health | 27 581 940 |
| Social security | 13 874 081 |
| Labour force plans | 12 266 112 |
| Family allowances | 2 417 060 |
| Veterans' benefits | 1 265 485 |
| Social welfare | 12 804 062 |
| Tax credits and rebates | 2 443 372 |
| Social services | 45 639 883 |
| Education | 34 747 121 |
| Resource conservation and industrial development | 16 070 506 |
| Environment | 4 199 187 |
| Recreation and culture | 4 046 707 |
| Labour, employment, and immigration | 1 372 008 |
| Housing | 2 603 486 |
| Foreign affairs and international assistance | 1 542 973 |
| Regional planning and development | 1 310 628 |
| Research establishments | 1 203 102 |
| General-purpose transfers to other levels of government | 7 819 544 |
| Transfers to own enterprises | 4 280 692 |
| Debt charges | 22 515 621 |
| Other expenditures | 425 530 |
| **TOTAL GROSS GENERAL EXPENDITURE** | 213 390 142 |

Source: *Consolidated Government Finance, 1982* (Ottawa: Statistics Canada, 1986), Catalogue 68-202, pp. 24-26. By permission of the Minister of Supply and Services Canada.

it can supply needed goods or services in accordance with the time, cost, quality, performance, and other terms and conditions.

There are three ways of obtaining bids:

1. An *invitation to tender* is normally used for all purchases of more than $5000. Two or more bids are requested and the contract award is to be based on the lowest responsive bid. To ensure fairness, unclassified tenders are opened publicly.
2. *Requests for quotations* may be used for all purchases of less than $5000. They are not opened publicly.
3. *Requests for proposals* are used for all noncompetitive purchases valued at more than $5000, and for competitive purchases where the selection of the supplier cannot be made solely on the basis

of the lowest-priced responsive bid. The evaluation of proposals is based on schedule, price, and the relevant technical, scientific, financial, managerial, and socio-economic factors identified in the solicitation. Requests for proposals are not opened publicly.

In addition to the head office in Hull, Quebec, there are 19 regional or district suboffices throughout the country that also purchase for the federal government. Although the details are not exactly the same, there are similar types of procedures used by provincial and municipal governments.

**Source Lists**    The Department of Supply and Services keeps extensive records of thousands of commodity groupings purchased. Matched against these are the names of companies that have indicated they want to be considered as suppliers, and that the department considers capable of carrying out a contract. These records are referred to when requirements arise. A firm wishing to be listed should write to the Executive Secretary for Supply Administration in Hull, or to the regional or district office in its area. Separate lists are maintained at head office and in each regional or district office.

**Selling to Government Markets**    Sometimes it is difficult for government to obtain bidders, even for relatively large contracts. Despite its immense size, the government market is often viewed as too complex and unprofitable by many suppliers. A survey conducted by *Sales and Marketing Management* reported that industrial marketers registered a variety of complaints about government purchasing procedures. These included excessive paperwork, bureaucracy, needless regulations, emphasis on low bid prices, decision-making delays, frequent shifts in procurement personnel, and excessive policy changes.[17]

On the other hand, marketers generally credit the government with being a relatively stable market. Once an item is purchased from a firm by the government, the probability of more sales is good. Other marketers cite such advantages as the instant credibility established by sales to the federal government, timely payment, excise and sales tax exemptions, acceptance of new ideas, and reduced competition.

Only a few industrial firms maintain a separate government sales manager or sales force. But many firms have experienced success with specialized government marketing efforts. It is expected that a growing number of large companies will organize for dealing with government purchasers.

---

17 Based on "Out of the Maze," *Sales and Marketing Management* (April 9, 1979), pp. 44–52.

***Summary***   The industrial goods market consists of all entities that buy goods and services for use in producing other products for resale. The market has three distinctive characteristics: 1) geographical market concentration, 2) a relatively small number of buyers, and 3) systematic buying procedures.

The industrial market is heavily concentrated in Ontario and Quebec. A large portion of the value added by manufacturing is accounted for by these provinces. The number of buyers is quite small in the industrial market, as compared with the consumer market. Industrial marketers often find the Standard Industrial Classification (SIC) codes — the categorization of all businesses into 12 broadly defined groups — to be a useful tool in analysing the industrial market.

There are four major characteristics of industrial market demand. Derived demand means that the demand for industrial goods is linked to the demand for consumer goods. Joint demand refers to demand for some industrial products that is related to the demand for other products used jointly with the first. Changes in inventory policy can also have a significant effect on industrial demand. The fourth characteristic of industrial market demand involves the accelerator principle, which indicates that even modest changes in consumer demand can have a disproportionate impact on industrial demand.

There are two basic categories of industrial products: capital items and expense items. Capital items are long-lived business assets that must be depreciated for a period ranging from 3 to 15 years. Depreciation is the accounting concept of charging a portion of a capital item as a deduction against the company's annual revenue for purposes of determining its net income. Expense items, by contrast, are products and services that are used within a short period of time. For the most part, they are charged against income in the year of purchase.

Industrial buyer behaviour tends to be more complex than the consumer behaviour of individuals. More people and time are involved, and buyers often seek several supply sources. There are three generally recognized industrial purchasing situations: straight rebuy, modified rebuy, and new task buying. A straight rebuy is a recurring purchase decision where an item that has performed satisfactorily is purchased again. A modified rebuy is a situation where purchasers are willing to re-evaluate their available options. New task buying refers to first-time or unique purchase situations that require considerable effort on the part of the decision-makers.

Industrial buying behaviour may also be illustrated by the concept of the buying centre. The buying centre simply refers to everyone that participates in some fashion in an industrial buying action.

Buying centres include users, decision makers, influencers, gatekeepers who control information, and buyers who actually consummate the transaction. The actual process of buying an industrial product or service consists of need recognition, a search for information, delineation of vendors, solicitation of sales proposals, review of proposals, and the actual purchase decision. A controversial practice that comes into play for some industrial purchasing situations is reciprocity, the extension of purchasing preference to suppliers who are also customers.

Government markets are a sizeable segment of the economy. Government differs from other industrial markets because of the numerous regulations that bear on procurement practices. For instance, most government purchases are made on the basis of bids or written sales proposals from vendors. Government buyers usually develop detailed descriptions of needed items for prospective buyers, called specifications. Industrial buying often is similar in this respect.

## Key Terms

| | |
|---|---|
| industrial market | capital item |
| producers | expense item |
| trade industries | straight rebuy |
| value added | modified rebuy |
| Standard Industrial Classification (SIC) | new task buying |
| derived demand | buying centre |
| joint demand | reciprocity |
| inventory adjustments | bids |
| demand variability | specifications |
| accelerator principle | |

## Review Questions

1. What are the three major types of industrial markets?
2. Describe the three distinctive features of industrial markets.
3. Explain the characteristics of industrial market demand.
4. Differentiate between capital items and expense items.
5. Why is industrial purchase behaviour so complex?
6. Differentiate among straight rebuy, modified rebuy, and new task buying.
7. Explain the concept of a buying centre.
8. Outline the general process for buying goods and services.
9. Discuss the issue of reciprocity.
10. Explain how government markets differ from other industrial markets.

**Discussion Questions and Exercises**

1. Prepare a brief report on the market opportunity that exists in some specific industrial market. Be sure to consult all of the standard reference sources on the industrial marketplace.
2. How could an industrial marketer use the SIC codes?
3. Find some actual examples of where derived demand, joint demand, inventory adjustments, and the accelerator principle affected industrial market demand. Report your findings to the class.
4. Prepare a report on a recent purchase by a local organizational buyer. What can be learned from this exercise?
5. Prepare a brief report on the market opportunity that exists in a specific government market. Identify all of the information sources that are available for such an assessment.

**MICROCOMPUTER EXERCISE: Competitive Bidding**

**Developing a Bidding Strategy**   Because many government and other organizational purchasers make buying decisions on the basis of competitive bids from alternative suppliers, determination of the most appropriate bid is an imporant assignment for industrial marketers. One method of quantifying this task is to use the concept of expected net profit (ENP). The formula for calculating ENP is as follows.

Expected Net Profit = P(Bid − Cost)

where

P    = the probability of the buyer accepting the bid
Bid  = the bid price of the product or project
Cost = the estimated total cost of the product or project

**Directions:**   Use the Menu Item titled "Competitive Bidding" on the *Foundations of Marketing* disk to solve each of the following problems.

1. Esta Morgenroth, marketing manager of Ottawa-based Electronic Industries, wants to submit a bid for a government project that she estimates will cost $23 000. She has prepared two preliminary proposals: 1) a bid for $60 000, and 2) a bid for $50 000. If Morgenroth estimates that there is a 40 percent chance of her first bid being accepted, and a 60 percent chance of her second bid being accepted, which of the two bids would yield the best expected net profit?

2. Product-development engineers at Hamilton Industries have developed a new industrial scrubber. Marketing executives at the Ontario firm are actively working on a large sale to the leading firm in its market target, a firm whose purchase decisions are frequently imitated by other companies in the industry. One of Hamilton's executives has proposed a price of $60 000 per unit, while another has suggested $70 000. Total costs of the scrubber average $45 000 per unit. Hamilton's marketing-research department has assigned a 55 percent probability of the buyer accepting the lower price, and a 45 percent probability of purchase at the higher price. Use the ENP formula to recommend a bid price for the scrubber.

3. Erie Industries, Inc. has been supplying Milwaukee Manufacturing with a certain rivet for years. Milwaukee Manufacturing treats these purchases from Erie as what is referred to in this chapter as a straight rebuy. Erie's price of $400 per thousand rivets has remained unchanged for the past three years. But the cost of producing the rivet has recently risen from $300 to $325 per thousand. Erie's national sales manager would like to pass the $25 cost increase along to Milwaukee Manufacturing in the form of a price increase. However, Erie's president feels that a 20 percent chance exists that Milwaukee Manufacturing would locate a different supplier. At $400 per thousand, the president is 95 percent confident that the Milwaukee firm will continue to be an Erie Industries customer. What should Erie's management do in this case?

# Appendix C

# Consumer Behaviour Models

Following World War II, consumer behaviour began to be studied more extensively by two distinct groups: marketing practitioners and social scientists. Marketing researchers were, of course, more pragmatic in their study; and it is only in the last two decades that real progress has been made in developing theories about consumer behaviour.

## Modelling Consumer Behaviour

A *model* is a visual representation of a phenomenon, for it specifies the elements and demonstrates the nature of the relationships among them. As such, it provides a testable "map" of reality, and its utility lies in the extent to which successful prediction or outcome is possible.[1] There are various types of models, but of special interest to this study is the *systems model*. It is in this model that the human being is analysed as a *system* with outputs (behaviour) in response to inputs. This model is used to study the human being as a *system of action*, analysing relationships among inputs, motivational determinants, and goal-oriented behaviour.

Basically, there are two ways to study consumer behaviour empirically: 1) the distributive approach, which focuses on behaviour outcomes; and 2) the decision-process method, which describes the way consumers actually make decisions. Research using the distributive method is fairly simple and comparatively inexpensive, but it can provide only a partial or incomplete explanation of consumer behaviour. The decision-process approach is more useful for marketing managers because it examines the processes preceding the purchase decision, the decision itself, and the actions following the decision, giving the manager very relevant information.

Decision-process models encompassing many variables, however, cannot explain the details of consumer behaviour in every situation. Indeed, a workable model should delineate 1) the variables associ-

---

[1] James Engel, Roger Blackwell, and Paul Miniard, *Consumer Behavior*, 5th ed. (Hinsdale: Dryden Press, 1986), p. 559.

ated with consumer decision processes; 2) the general relationships existing among variables; and 3) the general principles that express the model's applicability in particular purchase occasions.

**The Engel, Blackwell, and Miniard Model**   The Consumer Decision Process of Engel, Blackwell, and Miniard is examined here as one workable consumer behaviour model. The model adheres to the following criteria: 1) it conforms to the rules of logic; 2) it is internally consistent; 3) it encompasses relevant theories; 4) it can be used empirically; 5) it functions as a basis to derive new propositions; 6) it is consistent with existing knowledge; and 7) it offers new directions for research.[2]

The model is based on five decision process steps: problem recognition, search, alternative evaluation, choice (purchase), and outcomes. These have already been discussed using similar terminology in Chapter 8 (see Figure 8-8).

Figure C-1, which depicts the Engel, Blackwell, and Miniard model of consumer behaviour, suggests that an understanding of consumer behaviour can be gained by considering four different areas: 1) information input, 2) information processing, 3) decision process stages, and 4) variables influencing the decision process. A complete development of the model and each of these factors would require an entire book, so only a few general comments can be provided here. The reader should find it useful to see how the factors discussed in Chapters 7 and 8 fit into this comprehensive model.

Information Input   Many types of information enter into a consumer's decision to purchase a product. Stimuli come from the mass media, personal influences, and the general cultural environment. Some stimuli can be influenced or controlled by the marketer, but most cannot.

Information Processing   An individual screens out most of the many stimuli present through a mechanism known as *selective processes*: selective exposure, selective attention, and selective reception. These processes occur sequentially. Some factor in the active memory determines whether the mind will process the stimulus at each stage. The criteria used are based on previously gained information and experience.

Decision Process Stages   These factors have already been discussed in Chapter 8.

---

2 Carl E. Block and Kenneth J. Roering, *Essentials of Consumer Behaviour: Concepts and Applications,* 2nd ed. (Hinsdale: Dryden Press, 1979), p. 45.

## Figure C-1   A Complete Decision Process Model

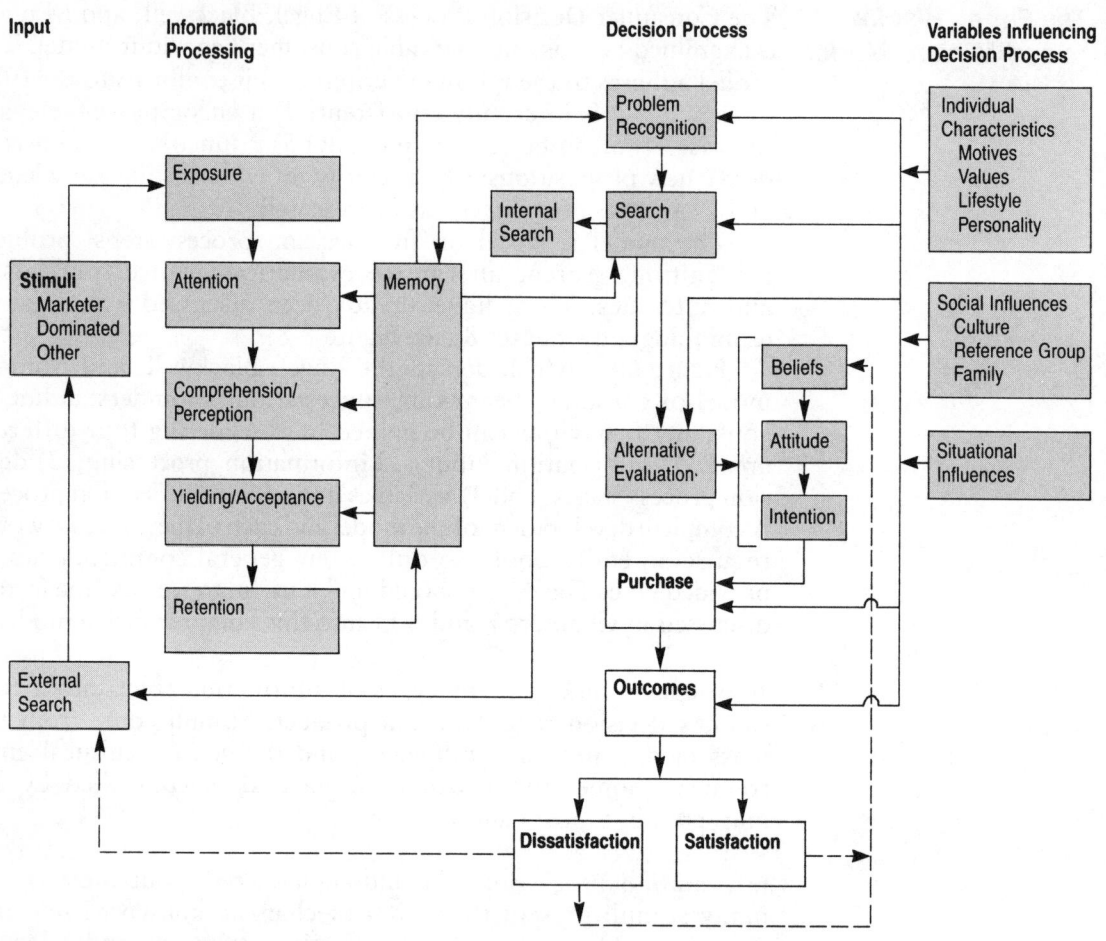

Source: James Engel, Roger D. Blackwell, and Paul Miniard, *Consumer Behavior*, 5th ed., p. 35. Copyright © 1986 by the Dryden Press, a division of CBS College Publishing. Reprinted by permission.

**Variables Influencing the Decision Process**   The decision process is influenced in varying ways by individual characteristics such as motives, values, lifestyle, and personality. Social influences such as culture, reference group, and family are also important, as discussed previously. Furthermore, situational influences, such as atmosphere, urgency of purchase, and availability have an effect on the final purchase decision.

**The Howard-Sheth Model**   Another widely known model of consumer behaviour is the Howard-Sheth Model shown in Figure C-2. The theory states that buyer behaviour consists of four sets of variables or constructs:

**Input Variables**   These are realistic, objective stimuli from the buyer's environment and can be divided into three categories: social, symbolic, and significative.

**Output Variables**   These include the following five types: attention, brand comprehension, attitude, intention (including the plan to buy a product), and purchase.

**Hypothetical Constructs**   These abstract variables describe the buyer's mental state related to a buying decision and therefore "map" it by identifying, classifying, and labelling conditions. There are two major types of hypothetical constructs:

1) Perceptual constructs: These include attention (the opening and closing of receptors controlling the intake of information), stimulus ambiguity (uncertainty about information gathered), perceptual bias (distortion of information in buyer's mind), and overt search (the seeking of information).
2) Learning constructs: These include motives, brand comprehension, choice criteria, attitude toward the brands, intention to buy, confidence in judging, and satisfaction.

**Exogenous Variables**   These are the contexts in which buying behaviour occurs. They are not integral to the decision-making process itself, but are powerful influences that affect the foregoing construct categories, and therefore, consumer behaviour.

This general model again shows that many variables affect the decision process. Consumers are aware that a wrong decision will have undesirable consequences; hence with certain products, buyers may resort to extended problem-solving in hopes of reducing the risk factor. Ultimately, the extent of decision-making will vary depending upon the individual, the social environment, and specific product characteristics.

**Other Consumer Behaviour Models**   No model is perfect. Models are, however, extremely helpful in analysing consumer behaviour and making better marketing decisions. Any lack of empirical verification does not invalidate them "if the constructs and hypotheses, taken by themselves, are consistent with present knowledge of the behaviour process."[3] No one now has or will have *the* model of consumer behaviour. A useful model will change as knowledge changes, and we should expect modifications as time passes.

---

[3] James Engel, Roger Blackwell, and Paul Miniard, *Consumer Behavior*, 5th ed. (Hinsdale: Dryden Press, 1986), p. 559.

Figure C-2    Simplified Description of the Howard-Sheth Model of Buyer Behaviour

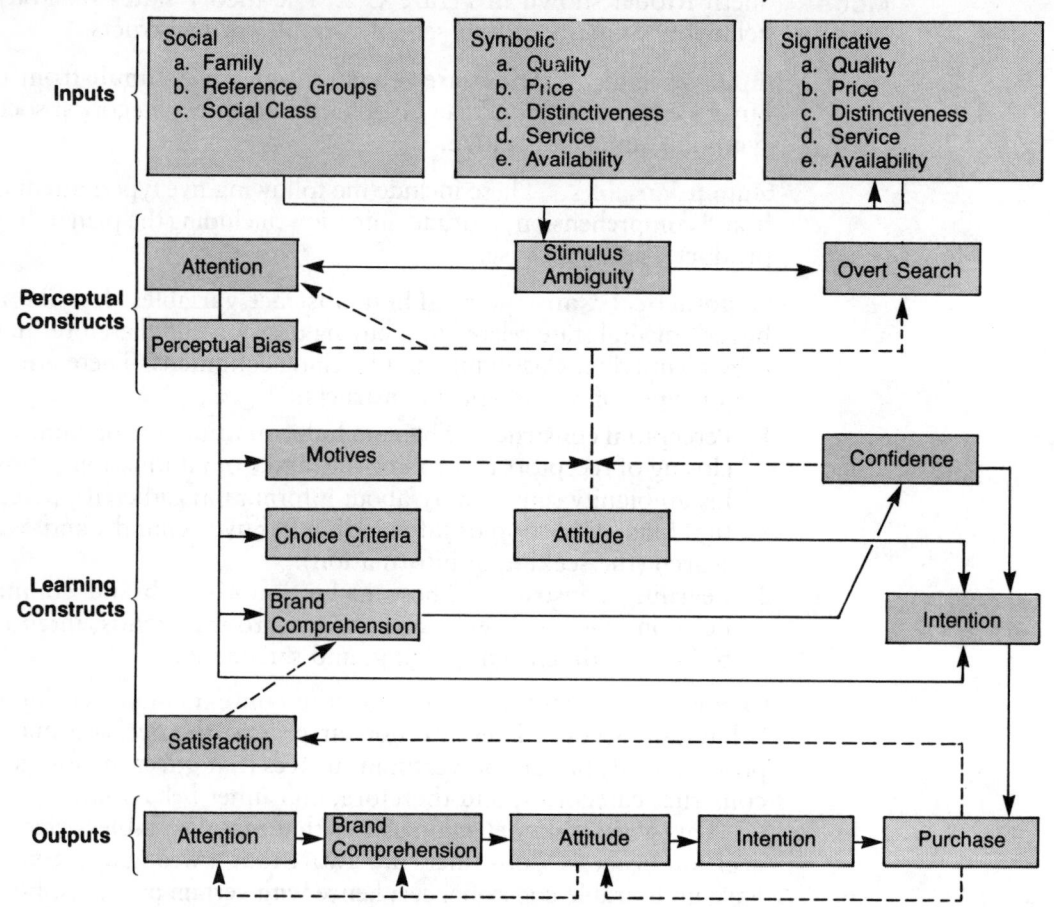

Source: J.A. Howard and J.N. Sheth, *The Theory of Buyer Behavior* (New York: John Wiley and Sons, Inc., 1969). Reprinted by permission of the publisher.

Significant contributions to the development of consumer behaviour models have been made by a number of writers. A short list of useful reference works follows.

1) Francesco M. Nicosia, *Consumer Decision Process: Marketing and Advertising Implications* (Englewood Cliffs, N.J.: Prentice-Hall), 1966.

2) Alan R. Andreason, "Attitudes and Customer Behavior: A Decision Model," in Lee E. Preston, ed., *New Research in Marketing* (Berkeley, Calif.: Institute of Business and Economic Research, 1965), pp. 1–16.

3) Flemming Hansen, *Consumer Choice Behavior* (New York: The Free Press, 1972).
4) Rom J. Markin, *The Psychology of Consumer Choice* (Englewood Cliffs, N.J.: Prentice-Hall), 1969.

**Sources**   Block, Carl E., and Kenneth J. Roering, *Essentials of Consumer Behaviour: Concepts and Applications*, 2nd ed. (Hinsdale: Dryden Press, 1979).

Engel, James, Roger Blackwell, and Paul Miniard, *Consumer Behavior*, 5th ed. (Hinsdale: Dryden Press, 1986).

Howard, John A., and Jagdish N. Sheth, *The Theory of Buyer Behaviour* (New York: John Wiley and Sons, 1969).

Newman, Joseph W., ed., *On Knowing the Consumer* (New York: John Wiley and Sons, 1966).

# PART

# 4

## Products

*CHAPTER 10*

# Product Strategy

*CHAPTER OBJECTIVES*

1. *To relate product strategy to the other variables of the marketing mix.*

2. *To explain the concept of the product life cycle, as well as its uses and limitations.*

3. *To identify the determinants of the speed of the adoption process.*

4. *To explain the methods for accelerating the speed of adoption.*

5. *To identify the classifications for consumer goods and to briefly describe each category.*

6. *To classify the types of industrial goods.*

Product managers in the photocopier business are both excited and apprehensive these days. The separate technologies of copiers, printers and computers are merging into a new generation of supermachines complete with microprocessors and disk drives.[1] The managers are wondering whether their current lines of photocopy machines will soon be obsolete, and whether the technological path that they are following in developing new machines will produce winning products among the new generation of copiers.

When they arrive, these new "intelligent" machines may not even be called copiers, because they will be able to do so much — print, copy *and* transmit material.[2] However, a great deal of market segmentation exists in this field. It will be a real challenge to develop the right mix of products to fit existing and potential segments. Current market needs range from small offices which require less than 2000 copies per day, to those which require two or more copiers, each capable of volumes of 20 000 to 50 000 copies a month. Will the new copiers be chosen on the basis of number and speed of copies produced, or will the new information transmission technology be more important? What combinations, number, speed and transmission capabilities will serve which market segments? How will the ready availability of computers from micros to mainframe in virtually every office affect the demand for compatible copiers?

---

[1] Bruce Gates, "Smart 'Super Machines' to Invade Copier Market," *The Financial Post*, November 5, 1983, p. s10.

[2] Ibid.

Marketing managers will not only face such decisions about designing and positioning new products, but will have to decide how to manage existing ones. Over the life of each product they will have to determine whether prices should be lowered or raised, whether money should be spent on redeveloping such older products, and how they should be promoted and distributed. Establishing strategies for new products, and managing older ones is a major aspect of marketing management.

## The Conceptual Framework

Chapter 10 looks at product concepts, and Chapter 11 covers the product mix and new product planning. Planning efforts begin with the choice of products to offer the market target. Pricing structures, marketing channels, and promotional plans — the other variables of the marketing strategy — are all based on product planning. In a very real sense, the sole economic justification of the firm's existence is the production and marketing of want-satisfying products.

Designing services is similar to designing physical products. However, because some characteristics of services are unique, Chapter 12 is devoted exclusively to this class of want-satisfying items.

## Products: A Definition

A narrow definition of the word *product* would focus on the physical or functional characteristics of a good offered to consumers. For example, a Sony videocassette recorder is a rectangular container of metal and plastic wires connecting it to a television set, accompanied by a series of special tapes for recording and viewing. This is the core product. But purchasers have a much broader view of the recorder. They have bought the convenience of viewing television programs at their leisure; the warranty and service that Sony, the manufacturer, provides; the prestige of owning this relatively new product innovation; and the ability to rent or purchase recently released movies for home viewing. Thus the brand product image, warranty and service are also all parts of the product as seen by the consumer.

Marketing decision-makers must have this broader concept in mind and realize that people purchase more than just the physical features of products. *They are buying want satisfaction.* Most drivers know very little about the gasoline they so regularly purchase. If they bother to analyse it, they discover that it is almost colourless and emits a peculiar odour. However, most of them do not think of gasoline as a product at all — to them, gasoline is a tax. It is a payment that they must periodically make for the privilege of driving their cars on the streets and highways. And the friendly service station attendant is a tax collector. Petroleum retailers should be aware of this image in the minds of many customers before spending huge

**Figure 10-1   The Total Product Concept**

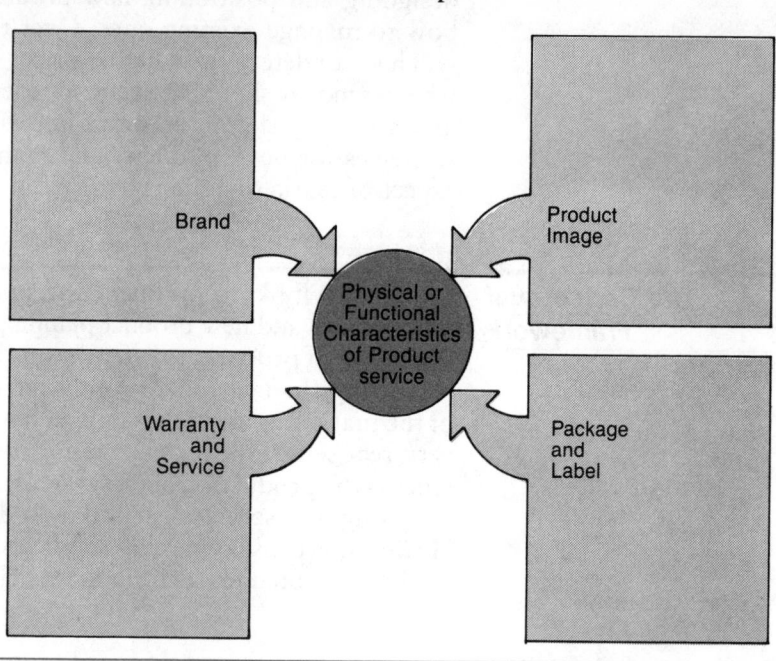

sums to promote dozens of secret ingredients designed to please the motorist.

The shopper's conception of a product may be altered by such features as packaging, labelling, or the retail outlets in which the product may be purchased. An image of high quality has been created for Maytag appliances, whose television commercials describe the Maytag repairer as "the loneliest person in town." Twenty-five years ago, the firm's president set a standard of "10 years of trouble-free operation" for automatic clothes washers. The company's success in achieving a reputation for high product quality is evident in Maytag's continued sales growth record, even though the washer's retail price is about $70 higher than the nearest competitor's.

Some products have no physical ingredients. A haircut and blow-dry at the local hair stylist produces only well-groomed hair. A tax counsellor produces only advice. Thus, a broader view of product must also include services.

A **product**, then, may be defined as *a total bundle of physical, service, and symbolic characteristics designed to produce consumer want satisfaction.*[3] Figure 10-1 reflects this broader definition by

---

[3] For a provocative discussion of this broader conception of products, see Sidney J. Levy, "Symbols for Sale," *Harvard Business Review* (July–August 1959), pp. 117–124. See also Jerome B. Kernan and Montrose S. Sommers, "Dimensions of Product Perception," *Journal of Business Research* (April 1967), pp. 94–102.

identifying the various components of the total product.

An important feature of many products is a product **warranty**. The warranty is *a guarantee to the buyer that the manufacturer will replace a defective product (or part of a product) or refund its purchase price during a specified period of time*. Such warranties serve to increase consumer purchase confidence and can prove to be an important means of stimulating demand. Zippo lighters used a warranty as one of the most important features of the firm's marketing strategy. The manufacturer agreed to a lifetime guarantee, promising to repair or replace any damaged or defective Zippo lighter regardless of age. Many retailers have a broad, unwritten but frequently honoured warranty of satisfaction or your money back.

**Figure 10-2  Stages in the Product Life Cycle**

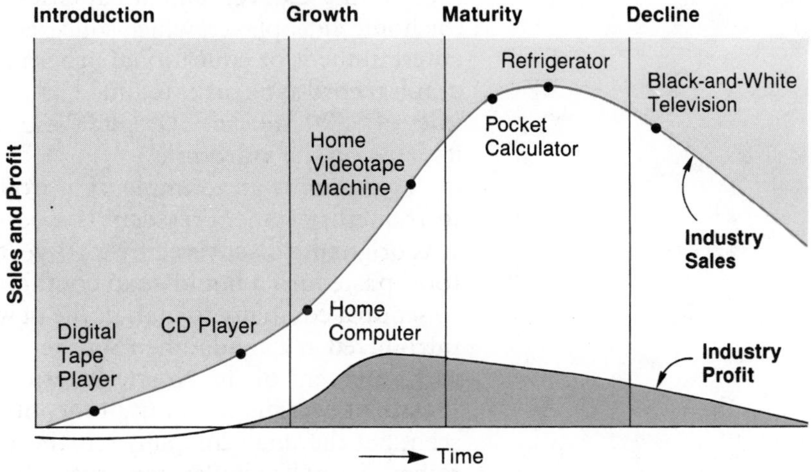

**The Product Life Cycle**  Product types, like individuals, pass through a series of stages. As humans progress from infancy to childhood to adulthood to retirement to death, successful products also progress through stages before their death. This progression of *introduction, growth, maturity, and decline* is known as the **product life cycle**. The cycle is depicted in Figure 10-2, with examples of products currently at each stage of development.[4]

[4] A good summary of the product life-cycle concept is contained in George S. Day, "The Product Life Cycle: Analysis and Applications Issues," *Journal of Marketing* (Fall 1981), pp. 60–67. Also see Gerald J. Tellis and C. Merle Crawford, "An Evolutionary Approach to Product Growth Theory," *Journal of Marketing* (Fall 1981), pp. 125–132.

**Stages of the Cycle**   Introductory Stage   The firm's objective in the early stages of the product life cycle is to stimulate demand for the new market entry. Since the product is not known to the public, promotional campaigns stress information about its features. Promotion may also be directed toward middlemen in the channel to induce them to carry the product. In this initial phase the public is being acquainted with the merits of the new product and acceptance is being gained.

As Figure 10-2 indicates, losses are common during the introductory stage due to heavy promotion and extensive research and development expenditures. But the groundwork is being laid for future profits. Firms expect to recover their costs and to begin earning profits when the new product moves into the second phase of the cycle — the growth stage.

In the case of the videodisk, RCA Corporation and a joint team of the Dutch-based Philips and MCA, Inc., spent more than $200 million in the development expenses prior to its introduction. But the home videoplayer, which squeezes 30 minutes of movies or other entertainment or educational programs onto each side of a phonograph record-type disk, is aimed at a market with estimated annual sales of $500 million.[5] Despite these efforts, the market has turned its back on the videodisk.

Pressdent is an example of a product that recently entered the introductory stage. Pressdent is a pump-dispensed toothpaste that was originally discovered by a 10-year-old who dumped water and toothpaste into a liquid-soap container. The child's father decided to set up a company to market the new product. Pressdent was first introduced in Canada, then Southern California. The eventual goal is 3.5 percent of the North America dentifrice market. Whether Pressdent ever makes it out of the introductory stage remains to be seen, but the small company remains confident. The entrepreneurial father, Nathalie Goulet, remarked, "Eventually toothpaste in a tube will go the way of shaving cream in a tube."[6]

Growth Stage   Sales volume rises rapidly during the growth stage as new customers make initial purchases and repurchases are made by the early users of the product. Word-of-mouth and mass advertising induce hesitant buyers to make trial purchases. Videotape machines now seem to have entered this phase of the cycle.

As the firm begins to realize substantial profits from its investment during the growth stage, it attracts competitors. Success breeds imitation, and firms rush into the market with competitive products in search of profit during the growth stage. As soon as the

---

5 "Videodiscs: The Expensive Race to Be First," *Business Week* (September 15, 1975), pp. 58–66.
6 Alan Freeman, "Will People Buy Toothpaste that Doesn't Come in a Tube?" *The Wall Street Journal* (June 3, 1982) p. 25.

dramatic market acceptance of the IBM personal computer was realized, many other manufacturers jumped into the market with "IBM compatible" versions of the IBM PC.

**Maturity Stage**   Industry sales continue to grow during the early portion of the maturity stage but eventually reach a plateau as the backlog of potential customers is exhausted. By this time a large number of competitors have entered the market, and profits decline as competition intensifies.

In the maturity stage differences among competing products have diminished as competitors have discovered the product and promotional characteristics most desired by the market. Heavy promotional outlays emphasize subtle differences among competing products, and brand competition intensifies.

For the first time, available products exceed industry demand. Companies attempting to increase sales and market share must do so at the expense of competitors. As competition intensifies, the tendency grows among competitors to cut prices in an attempt to attract new buyers. Even though a price reduction may be the easiest method of inducing additional purchases, it is also one of the simplest moves for competitors to duplicate. Reduced prices will result in decreased revenues for all firms in the industry unless the price cuts produce enough increased purchases to offset the loss in revenue on each product sold.[7]

**Figure 10-3   Overlap of Life Cycle for Products A and B**

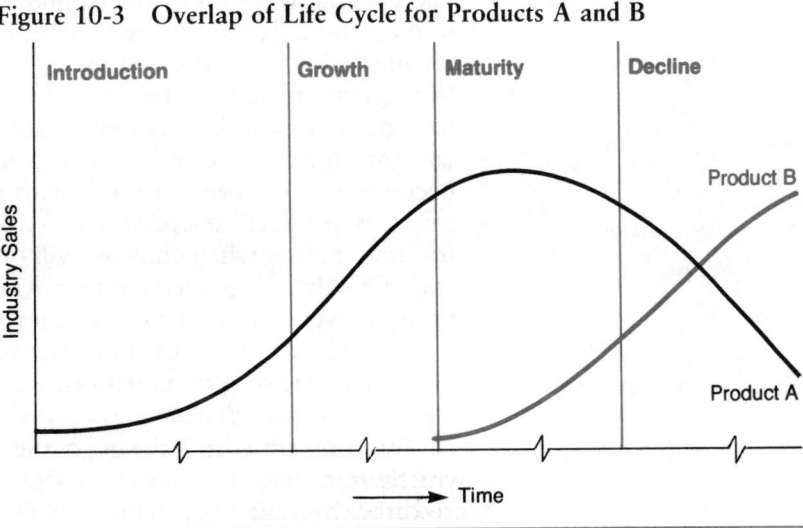

7 Students of economics will recognize this as elasticity of demand. For a discussion of the concept of elasticity, see Edwin G. Dolan and Roy Vogt, *Basic Economics, Second Canadian Edition*. Toronto: Holt, Rinehart and Winston, 1984. pp. 377–384.

Decline Stage   In the final stage of the product's life, new innovations or shifting consumer preferences bring about an absolute decline in total industry sales. The safety razor and electric shavers replace the straight razor, *Pac-Man* replaces *Rubik's Cube* as the latest fad, and the black and white television is exchanged for a colour set. As Figure 10-3 indicates, the decline stage of the old product is also the growth stage for the new market entry.

Industry profits decline and in some cases actually become negative as sales fall and firms cut prices in a bid for the dwindling market. Manufacturers gradually begin to leave the industry in search of more profitable products.

## Departures from the Traditional Product Life-Cycle Model

The preceding discussion has examined what is considered the traditional product life cycle with its four clearly delineated stages. Some marketing theorists divide the life cycle into additional stages, but these four, identified in Figure 10-2, are generally accepted within the marketing discipline.

Yet despite the vast body of material written on the subject, considerable controversy surrounds the format and usefulness of product life-cycle theory. On the one hand, the concept has an enduring appeal because of the intuitive logic of the birth-to-decline biological analogy.[8] As such, it has considerable descriptive value when used as a systematic framework for explaining market dynamics.

However, the simplicity of the concept has led to simplistic uses and expectations for the model, and this has called the concept itself into question. Part of the problem lies in failing to distinguish between the life cycle of a *product type* and that of an *individual brand* within that generic product category. Life-cycle theory is most applicable to product types. A truly new brand is obviously also the generic category for a while, but as competing brands are introduced, it becomes one of several brands within that category. The greatest misuse of product life-cycle theory is to consider it a predictive model for anticipating when changes will occur and to presume that one stage will always succeed another. Managers can make grave errors if they naively interpret a particular rise or fall in sales as a sign that a product has moved from one stage to another. Such an interpretation could lead to serious errors in strategy, such as concluding that a product was in decline and removing it from the market.

A second criticism is the use of the life cycle as a *normative* model which *prescribes* the alternative strategies which should be considered at each stage. As will be shown later, there are strategies which are generally appropriate at various stages of the life cycle of a product

---

[8] This section relies on George S. Day, "The Product Life Cycle: Analysis and Applications Issues," *Journal of Marketing.* (Fall 1981), pp. 60–65.

*category.* In the case of an individual brand *within* a product category, however, as Enis, LaGarce, and Prell argue, "the product life cycle [of a brand] is a *dependent* variable. . . . That is, the brand's stage in the product life cycle depends primarily upon the marketing strategy implemented for that product at a particular time."[9]

A more realistic view is that life cycle analysis serves several different roles in the formulation of strategy. In the case of both generic product type and individual brand the life cycle serves as an *enabling condition* in the sense that the underlying forces that inhibit or facilitate growth create opportunities and threats having strategic implications. The stage of the life cycle also acts as a *moderating variable* through its influence on the value of market share position and the profitability consequences of strategic decisions. In the case of an individual brand a stage in the life cycle is partially a *consequence* of managerial decisions. Its position is not necessarily

### Figure 10-4    Alternative Product Life Cycles

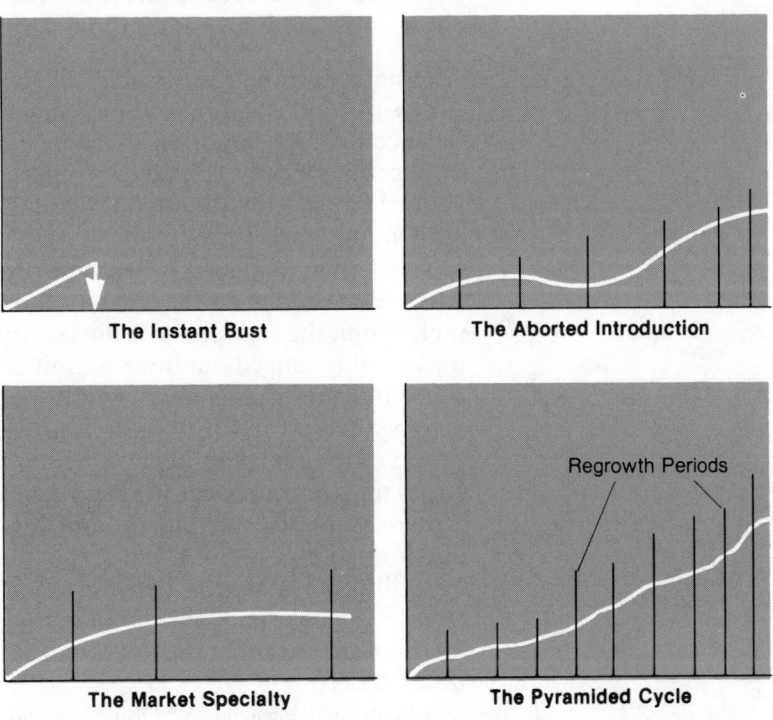

The Instant Bust

The Aborted Introduction

The Market Specialty

Regrowth Periods

The Pyramided Cycle

Source: Reprinted from Chester R. Wasson, *Dynamic Competitive Strategy and Product Life Cycle*, 3rd ed. (Austin, Texas: Austin Press, 1978), p. 13.

---

[9] Ben M. Enis, Raymond LaGarce, and Arthur E. Prell "Extending the Product Life Cycle," *Business Horizons*, (June 1977), pp. 46–56.

a *fait accompli*, which can only be reacted to, but instead is only one of several scenarios that are conditional on the life cycle of the product category, competitive actions and managerial decisions.

***Other Life-Cycle Issues***    Three other issues that modify the original life-cycle concept are 1) the length of each product life-cycle stage; 2) the existence of product life-cycle variants; and 3) the current role of product and service fashions and fads.

**Length of Cycle Stages**    Professor John O. King has argued that product life-cycle models should reflect the reality that products and services move through cycles at varying speeds. He suggests that the model should be drawn to show a broken horizontal axis to reflect that the stages may be of varying lengths, as we did in Figures 10-2 and 10-3. Research now suggests that product life cycles may be getting shorter, especially in the introductory and growth stages.[10]   While definitive conclusions are not yet available, most marketers do accept the fact that product life cycles and their stages show considerable variation in length.

**Alternative Product Life Cycles**    In a study dealing with 100 categories of food, health, and personal care products, the Marketing Science Institute reported that the traditional life-cycle model was applicable for only 17 percent of the general categories and 20 percent of the specific brands.[11]   Variants to the traditional model are shown in Figure 10-4.

As shown in Figure 10-4, some products simply do not make it. These can be labeled the "instant busts"; a failure simply does not go through the four steps of the traditional model. Still other products are introduced but information derived from test market situations indicates that changes will be necessary if the product launch is to be successful. (Test markets are described in Chapter 11.) The products then have to be modified in some way, such as in design, packaging, promotional strategy, before they are reintroduced. This type of start-up, start-again launch is labeled the "aborted introduction" in Figure 10-4.

Still other products become market specialty items (discussed later in the chapter), and provide long and stable maturity stages. A common variant is the "pyramided cycle," where the product is

---

10 William Qualls, Richard W. Olshavsky, and Ronald E. Michaels, "Shortening the PLC — An Empirical Test," *Journal of Marketing* (Fall 1981), pp. 76–80.
11 Rolando Pilli and Victor J. Cook, "A Test of the Product Life Cycle as a Model of Sales Behavior," *Marketing Science Institute Working Paper* (November 1967) and "Validity of the Product Life Cycle," *The Journal of Business* (October 1969), pp. 385–400. This research is reviewed in William S. Sachs and George Benson, *Product Planning and Management* (Tulsa, Okla.: PennWell Books, 1981), p. 80.

adapted through new technology or a revised marketing strategy. The pyramided cycle (also discussed later in the chapter) is characterized by a series of regrowth periods.

Fashions and Fads   Fashions and fads are also important to marketers. **Fashions** are *currently popular products that tend to follow recurring life cycles.*[12] Women's apparel fashions provide the best examples. The miniskirt was reintroduced in 1982 after being out of fashion for over a decade.

By contrast, **fads** are *fashions with abbreviated life cycles.* Consider the case of popular music for teenagers. Disco gave way to punk and new wave, which has since been replaced by the *new music,* a take-off on rock and roll.[13] Most fads experience short-lived popularity and then fade quickly. However, there are some that maintain a residual market among certain market segments. Both of these fad cycles are shown in Figure 10-5.

**Figure 10-5   Fad Cycles**

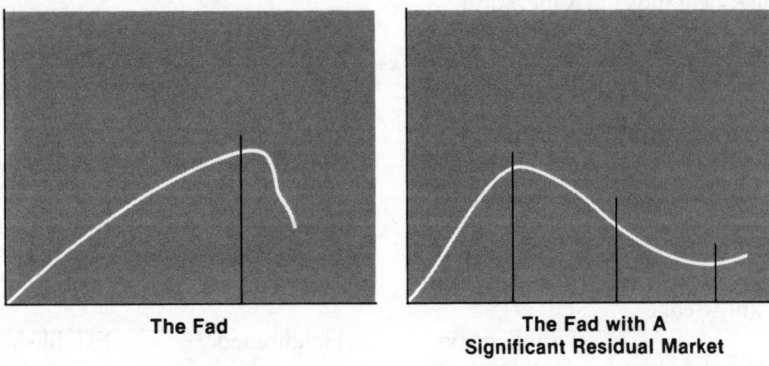

The Fad

The Fad with A
Significant Residual Market

Source: Reprinted from Chester R. Wasson, *Dynamic Competitive Strategy and Product Life Cycle*, 3rd ed. (Austin, Texas: Austin Press, 1978), p. 13.

***Product Life Cycle Considerations in Marketing Strategy***   Marketing strategy related to the product life cycle is most useful when carried out on an individual *brand* basis rather than a generic product category basis.[14] There are too many uncontrollable vari-

---

[12] Fashion cycles are discussed in Raymond A. Marquardt, James C. Makens, and Robert G. Roe, *Retail Management*, 3rd ed. (Hinsdale, Ill.: The Dryden Press, 1983), pp. 98–99. Also see George B. Sproles, "Analyzing Fashion Life Cycles—Principles and Perspectives," *Journal of Marketing* (Fall 1981), pp. 116–124.

[13] Stephen Grover, "Record Business Slumps as Taping and Video Games Take Away Sales," *The Wall Street Journal* (February 18, 1982), p. 25.

[14] Enis et al., op. cit.

ables at the generic level. The product life cycle—with all its variants —is a useful tool in marketing strategy decision making. The knowledge that profits assume a predictable pattern through the stages and that promotional emphasis must shift from product information in the early stages to brand promotion in the later ones allows the marketing decision-maker to take advantage of conditions that

**Figure 10-6  Organizational Conditions, Marketing Efforts, and Environmental Conditions at Each Stage of the Product Life Cycle**

| | | Maturity | | |
| Introduction | Growth | Early Maturity | Late Maturity | Decline |
|---|---|---|---|---|
| **Organizational Conditions** | | | | |
| High costs | Smoothing production | Efficient scale of operation | Low profits | |
| Inefficient production levels | Lowering costs | Product modification work | Standardized production | |
| Cash demands | Operation efficiencies Product improvement work | Decreasing profits | | |
| **Environmental Conditions** | | | | |
| Few or no competitors | Expanding markets | Slowing growth | Faltering demand | Permanently declining demand |
| | | Strong competition | Fierce competition | |
| Limited product awareness and knowledge | Expanded distribution | Expanded market | Shrinking number of competitors | Reduction of competitors |
| Limited demand | Competition strengthens Prices soften a bit | Heightened competition | Established distribution patterns | Limited product offerings Price stabilization |
| **Marketing Efforts** | | | | |
| Stimulate demand | Cultivate selective demand | Emphasize market segmentation | Ultimate in market segmentation | Increase primary demand |
| Establish high price | Product improvement | Improve service and warranty | Competitive pricing | Profit opportunity pricing |
| Offer limited product variety | Strengthen distribution | Reduce prices | Retain distribution | Prune and strengthen distribution |
| Increase distribution | Price flexibility | | | |

Source: Adapted from Burton H. Marcus and Edward M. Tauber, *Marketing Analysis and Decision Making* (Boston: Little, Brown 1979), pp. 115–16. Copyright © 1979 by Burton H. Marcus and Edward M. Tauber. Reprinted by permission of Little, Brown and Company.

exist in each stage of the product life cycle through appropriate marketing efforts.

A firm's marketing efforts should emphasize stimulating demand at the introductory stage. The emphasis shifts to cultivating selective demand in the growth period. Market segmentation should be used extensively in the maturity period. During the decline, the emphasis again shifts to increasing primary demand. Figure 10-6 suggests possibilities for appropriate pricing, distribution, product development, and service and warranty strategies for each life-cycle stage. The reader is again cautioned that the life cycle does not determine the strategy. The market matching process suggested in chapter 5 is applicable for analysis in each situation.

## Extending the Product Life Cycle

A good example of the concept that the product life cycle is often subject to managerial strategy is the practice of extending the cycle as long as possible. Marketing managers can accomplish this objective if they take action early in the maturity stage. Product life cycles can sometimes be extended indefinitely by actions designed to:

1. Increase the frequency of use by present customers.
2. Add new users.
3. Find new uses for the product.
4. Change package sizes, labels, or product quality.[15]

Examples of such actions are cited below.

Increase the Frequency of Use   Noxzema was orginally intended as an occasional-use skin medicine but it was repositioned as a routine-use, beauty-care item. This substantially increased the rate of use — and amount purchased.

Add New Users   Cadillac introduced its Cimarron to attract non-Cadillac buyers who usually purchased cars like BMW. Crest and Colgate were reintroduced as sweeter-tasting gels to appeal to younger consumers, further extending the life cycles of these well-known brands.[16] Finding new users is sometimes difficult. Gerber Products failed in attempts to sell its products to the 15 to 22 age group as desserts and snacks. Many still regarded Gerber as baby food.[17]

---

[15] See David R. Rink and John E. Swan, "Product Life Cycle Research: A Literature Review," *Journal of Business Research* (September 1979), pp. 219–242.

[16] Bill Abrams, "Warring Toothpaste Makers Spend Millions Luring Buyers to Slightly Altered Products," *The Wall Street Journal* (September 9, 1981), p. 33.

[17] Gail Bronson, "Baby Food It Is, but Gerber Wants Teen-Agers to Think of It as Dessert," *The Wall Street Journal* (July 17, 1981), p. 29.

Find New Uses   Q-tips cotton swabs were originally sold as a baby-care item, but Chesebrough-Pond's Inc.'s marketers found a new use for them as makeup applicators. Cow Brand baking soda was used primarily in cooking until its product life cycle was extended by finding new uses as a denture cleaner, swimming pool pH adjuster, cleaning agent, flame extinguisher, first-aid remedy, and refrigerator freshener.[18]

Change the Package Size, Label, or Product Quality   Levi Strauss Canada Inc. has introduced a limited edition jean called 555. The straight-leg jean uses details of the original jean that Levi Strauss made during the California Gold Rush of 1849. Each pair carries a five-digit serial number. A postage-paid card is used to register each pair of the $33.95 jeans.[19] One of the best examples of a product that has been managed well and avoided the decline stage is Tide. This synthetic detergent, introduced nationally in 1947, continues to sell well in 1985. But more than 50 modifications of packaging, cleaning performance, sudsing characteristics, aesthetics, and physical properties have been made during its lifetime.[20]

| **Consumer Adoption** | Once the product is launched, consumers begin a process of evaluat- |
| **Process** | ing the new item. This evaluation is known as the **adoption pro-** |

**Consumer Adoption Process**   Once the product is launched, consumers begin a process of evaluating the new item. This evaluation is known as the **adoption process**, whereby potential consumers go through *a series of stages from learning of the new product to trying it and deciding to purchase it regularly or to reject it.* The process has some similarities to the consumer decision process discussed in chapters 7 and 8. These stages in the consumer adoption process can be classified as:

1. *Awareness:* individuals first learn of the new product but lack information about it.
2. *Interest:* they begin to seek out information about it.
3. *Evaluation:* they consider whether the product is beneficial.
4. *Trial:* they make a trial purchase in order to determine its usefulness.
5. *Adoption/Rejection:* if the trial purchase is satisfactory, they decide to make regular use of the product.[21] Of course, rejection may take place at any stage of the process.

[18] Karger, "5 Ways to Find New Uses — Re-Evaluate Your Old Products," p. 18
[19] Alan Freeman, "Levi Unit Tries to Give Jeans Limited Appeal," *The Wall Street Journal* (August 11, 1981). p. 25.
[20] "Good Products Don't Die, P&G Chairman Declares," *Advertising Age* (November 1, 1976) p. 8.
[21] Everett M. Rogers and F. Floyd Shoemaker, *Communication of Innovations* (New York: The Free Press, 1971), pp. 135–157.

The marketing managers need to understand the adoption process so that they can move potential consumers to the adoption stage. Once the manager is aware of a large number of consumers at the interest stage, steps can be taken to stimulate sales. For example, Gillette introduced Aapri Apricot Facial Scrub by mailing 15 million samples to households in Canada and the United States. Total sample costs for the new skin product, designed to compete with Noxzema, Ponds, and Oil of Olay, were $4.1 million.[22] Sampling, if it is successful, is a technique that reduces the risk of evaluation and trial, moving the consumer quickly to the adoption stage.

**Adopter Categories**

Some people will purchase a new product almost as soon as it is placed on the market. Others wait for additional information and rely on the experiences of the first purchasers before making trial purchases. **Consumer innovators** are the *first purchasers* at the beginning of a product's life cycle. Some families are first in the community to buy colour television sets.[23] Some doctors are the first to prescribe new drugs,[24] and some farmers will use new hybrid seeds much earlier than their neighbours.[25] Some people are quick to adopt new fashions,[26] while some drivers are early users of automobile diagnostic centres.[27]

A number of investigations analysing the adoption of new products has resulted in the identification of five categories of purchasers based upon relative time of adoption, which are shown in Figure 10-7.

The **diffusion process** refers to this *acceptance of new products and services by the members of a community or social system.* Figure 10-7 shows this process as following a normal distribution. A

[22] Gillette Spends $17.4 Million to Introduce Aapri, Gain Foothold in Skin Care Market," *Marketing News* (May 29, 1981), p. 6. For a discussion of the use of marketing techniques to facilitate trial purchases, see James W. Taylor and Paul S. Hugstad, "Add-On Purchasing: Consumer Behavior in the Trial of New Products," *Journal of the Academy of Marketing Science* (Winter 1980), pp. 294–299.
[23] Walter P. Gorman III and Charles T. Moore, "The Early Diffusion of Color Television Receivers into a Fringe Market Area," *Journal of Retailing* (Fall 1968), pp. 46–56.
[24] James Coleman, Elihu Katz, and Herbert Menzel, "The Diffusion of an Innovation Among Physicians," *Sociometry* (December 1957), pp. 253–270.
[25] Bryce Ryan and Neal Gross, "The Diffusion of Hybrid Seed Corn in Two Iowa Communities," *Rural Sociology* (March 1943), pp. 15–24.
[26] Joseph Barry Mason and Danny Bellenger, "Analyzing High-Fashion Acceptance," *Journal of Retailing* (Winter 1974), pp. 79–88.
[27] See James F. Engel, Robert J. Kegerreis, and Roger D. Blackwell, "Word-of-Mouth Communication by the Innovator," *Journal of Marketing* (July 1969), pp. 15–19.

few people adopt at first, and then the number of adopters increases rapidly as the value of the innovation is apparent. The rate finally diminishes as fewer potential consumers remain in the nonadopter category.

Since the categories are based on the normal distribution, standard deviations are used to partition each category. Innovators are defined as the first 2.5 percent of the individuals to adopt the new product; laggards are the final 16 percent to adopt. Excluded from the figure are the nonadopters, persons who never adopt the innovation.

*Identifying the First Adopters*   Locating first buyers of new products represents a challenge for the marketing manager. If the right people can be reached early in the product's development or introduction, they may serve as a test market, evaluating the products and possibly making suggestions for modifications. Since early purchasers are frequently opinion leaders, from whom others seek advice, their attitudes toward new products are communicated in their neighbourhood and in clubs and organizations. Acceptance or rejection of the innovation by these purchasers may serve as a kind of signal for the marketing manager, indicating the probable success or failure of the new product.[28]

Unfortunately, persons who are first adopters of one new product may not necessarily be innovators for other products or services. A large number of research studies have, however, established some general characteristics possessed by most first adopters.

In general, first adopters tend to be younger, have a higher social status, be better educated, and enjoy a higher income. They are more mobile than later adopters and change both their jobs and their home addresses more often. They are more likely to rely upon impersonal information sources than later adopters who depend

---

[28] For a discussion of characteristics of first adopters, see William E. Bell, "Consumer Innovators: A Unique Market for Newness," in Stephen A. Greyser (ed.), *Toward Scientific Marketing* (Chicago: American Marketing Association, 1964), pp. 89–95. See also Louis E. Boone, "The Search for the Consumer Innovator," *The Journal of Business* (April 1970), pp. 135–140; David W. Cravens, James C. Cotham, Ill, and James R. Felix, "Identifying Innovator and Non-Innovator Firms," *Journal of Business Research* (April 1971), pp. 45–51; Lyman E. Ostland, "Identifying Early Buyers," *Journal of Advertising Research* (April 1972), pp. 29–34; Robert A. Peterson, "Diffusion and Adoption of a Consumer Durable," *Marquette Business Review* (Spring 1974), pp. 1–4; Steven A. Baumgarten, "The Innovative Communicator in the Diffusion Process," *Journal of Marketing Research* (February 1975), pp. 12–18; Laurence P. Feldman and Gary M. Armstrong, "Identifying Buyers of a Major Automobile Innovation," *Journal of Marketing* (January 1975), pp. 47–53; and Robert T. Green and Eric Langeard, "A Cross-National Comparison of Consumer Habits and Innovator Characteristics," *Journal of Marketing* (July 1975), pp. 34–41.

**Figure 10-7    Categories of Adopters on the Basis of Relative Time of Adoption**

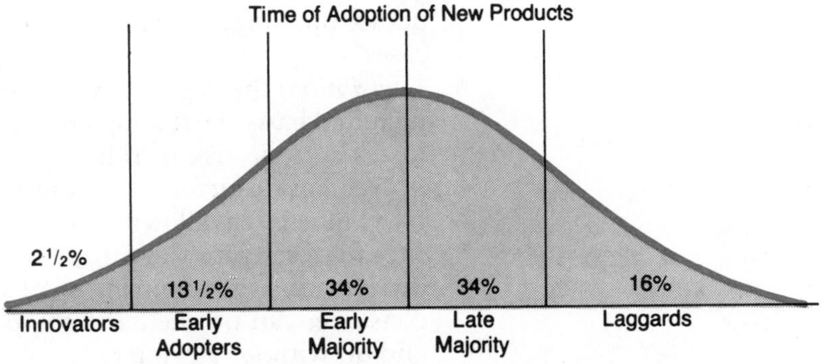

Time of Adoption of New Products

2½%        13½%        34%        34%        16%

Innovators    Early        Early        Late        Laggards
              Adopters     Majority     Majority

Source: Everett M. Rogers and F. Floyd Shoemaker, *Communication of Innovations* (New York: Free Press, 1971), p. 182. Copyright © 1971 by the Free Press of Glencoe. Reprinted by permission.

more on promotional information from the company and word-of-mouth communications.[29]

**What Determines the Rate of Adoption?**

The electronic calculator replaced the slide-rule as the engineering student's friend as soon as prices came within range of the student budget because of its versatility and ease of use. It took 13 years to convince most corn farmers to use hybrid seed corn — an innovation capable of doubling corn yields — even though some progressive farmers adopted it at once. The adoption rate is influenced by five characteristics of the innovation.[30]

1. *Relative advantage:* the degree to which the innovation appears superior to previous ideas. The greater the relative advantage, whether manifested in terms of lower price, physical improvements, or ease of use, the faster the adoption rate.

2. *Compatibility:* the degree to which the innovation is compatible with existing facilities or consistent with the values and experiences of potential adopters. The business student who purchases a personal computer will likely buy one that is compatible with

[29] Ronald Marks and Eugene Hughes, "Profiling the Consumer Innovator", in *Evolving Marketing Thought for 1980*, (eds.) John H. Summey and Ronald D. Taylor (New Orleans: Southern Marketing Association, 1980), pp. 115–118; Elizabeth Hirschman, "Innovativeness, Novelty Seeking and Consumer Creativity," *Journal of Consumer Research* (December 1980), pp. 283–295; and Richard W. Olshavsky, "Time and the Rate of Adoption of Innovations," *Journal of Consumer Research* (March 1980), pp. 425–428.

[30] For a more thorough discussion of speed of the adoption process, see Everett Rogers and Floyd Shoemaker, *Communication of Innovations* (New York: Free Press, 1971), pp. 135–57.

those at the school he or she attends or with those of his or her friends.

3. *Complexity:* the more difficult to understand or use the new product is, the longer it will take to be generally accepted in most cases.

4. *Divisibility:* the degree to which the innovation may be used on a limited basis. First adopters face two types of risk — financial losses and the risk of ridicule by others — if the new product proves unsatisfactory. The option of sampling the innovation on a limited basis allows these risks to be reduced and, in general, should accelerate the rate of adoption.[31] Computers can be divisible; instead of buying all of a new system on the market, a consumer can try the basic components using a home TV set, and do without a printer.

5. *Communicability:* the degree to which the results of the product may be observable or communicated to others. If the superiority of the innovation may be displayed in a tangible form, it will increase the adoption rate.

These five characteristics can be used, to some extent, by the marketing manager in accelerating the rate of adoption. First, will consumers perceive the product as complex, or will its use necessitate a significant change in typical behaviour patterns? Product complexity must be overcome by promotional messages of an informational nature. Products should be designed to emphasize their relative advantages and, whenever possible, be divisible for sample purchases. If divisibility is physically impossible, in-home demonstrations or trial placements in the home may be used. Positive attempts must also be made to ensure compatibility of the innovation with the adopters' value systems.

These actions are based on extensive research studies of innovators in agriculture, medicine, and consumer goods. They should pay off in increased sales by accelerating the rate of adoption in each of the adopter categories.

---

[31] See Raymond A. Bauer, "Consumer Behavior as Risk Taking," in Robert S. Hancock (ed.), *Dynamic Marketing for a Changing World* (Chicago: American Marketing Association, 1960), pp. 389–398. See also James R. Bettman, "Perceived Risk and Its Components: A Model and Empirical Test," *Journal of Marketing Research* (May 1973), pp. 184–190; Arch G. Woodside, "Informal Group Influence in Risk Taking," *Journal of Marketing Research* (May 1972), pp. 223–225; Robert D. Hisrich, Ronald J. Dornoff, and Jerome B. Kernan, "Perceived Risk in Store Selection," *Journal of Marketing Research* (November 1972), pp. 435–439; and James W. Taylor, "The Role of Risk in Consumer Behavior," *Journal of Marketing* (April 1974), pp. 54–60.

## Consumer Goods and Industrial Goods: A Definition

How a firm markets its product depends largely on the product itself. For example, a perfume manufacturer stresses subtle promotions in prestige media such as *Chatelaine* and *Vogue* magazines, and markets the firm's products through exclusive department stores and specialty shops. Cadbury Schweppes Powell Ltd. markets its candy products through candy wholesalers to thousands of supermarkets, variety stores, discount houses, and vending machines. Its marketing objective is to saturate the market and to make its candy as convenient as possible for potential buyers. A firm manufacturing and marketing fork-lifts may use sales representatives to call on purchasing agents and ship its product either directly from the factory or from regional warehouses.

Product strategy differs for consumer goods and industrial goods. As defined earlier, consumer goods are products destined for use by the ultimate consumer, and industrial goods are products used directly or indirectly in producing other goods for resale. These two major categories can be broken down further.

## Characteristics of Consumer Goods

Although a number of classification systems have been suggested, the system most often used is based on consumer buying habits. The three categories of consumer goods are convenience goods, shopping goods, and specialty goods.[32]

*Convenience Goods* The *products that the consumer wants to purchase frequently, immediately, and with a minimum of effort* are called **convenience goods**. Consumers substitute if their desired brand is not available, or forego consumption. They do not make up lost consumption. Milk, bread, butter, and eggs (the staples of the 24-hour convenience food stores) are all convenience goods. So are newspapers, chewing gum, magazines, chocolate bars, and items found in most vending machines.

Convenience goods are usually branded and are low-priced. Many of them are staple items, such as bread, milk, and gasoline, and the consumer's supply must be constantly replenished. In most cases the buyer has already made a decision on a particular brand of gasoline or candy or a particular store and spends little time in conscious deliberation in making a purchase decision. The buyer has already decided on a specific gas station or brand of soft drink and makes a purchase of an item *through habit when supply is low.*

---

[32] This three-way classification of consumer goods was first proposed by Melvin T. Copeland. See his book, *Principles of Merchandising* (New York: McGraw-Hill Book Company, 1924), Chapters 2–4. For a more recent discussion of this classification scheme, see Richard H. Holton, "The Distinction between Convenience Goods, Shopping Goods and Specialty Goods," *Journal of Marketing* (July 1958), pp. 55–56.

Those *products often purchased on the spur of the moment* are referred to as **impulse goods**.

The consumer rarely visits competing stores or compares price and quality in purchasing convenience goods. The possible gains from such comparisons are outweighed by the costs of gaining the additional information. This does not mean, however, that the consumer is destined to remain permanently loyal to one brand of detergent, pop, or candy. The consumer is continually receiving new information inputs through radio and television advertisements, billboards, and word-of-mouth communications. Since the price of most convenience goods is low, trial purchases of competing brands or products can be made with little financial risk and can sometimes lead to new habits.

Since the consumer is unwilling to expend much effort in purchasing convenience goods, the manufacturer must strive to make them as convenient as possible. Newspapers, soft drinks, and candy are sold in almost every supermarket, variety store, service station, and restaurant. Where retail outlets are physically separated from a large number of consumers, the manufacturer constructs small "stores" in the form of vending machines and places them in office buildings and factories for the convenience of its customers. Coca-Cola distributors know that most of their customers will not leave the building in search of a Coke if the vending machine is completely stocked with Pepsi. They must protect this fragile brand loyalty by ensuring that their product is easily available.

Retailers usually carry several competing brands of convenience products and are unlikely to promote any particular brand. The promotional burden, therefore, falls on the *manufacturer.* The firm must advertise extensively to develop consumer acceptance for its product. The Coca-Cola promotional program, consisting of radio and television commercials, magazine ads, billboards, and point-of-purchase displays in the store designed to motivate the consumer to choose Coke over competing brands, is a good example of promotion by the manufacturer designed to stimulate consumer demand.

*Shopping Goods*   In contrast with convenience goods, **shopping goods** are usually purchased only *after the consumer has made comparisons of competing goods* on such bases as price, quality, style, and colour in competing stores. The consumer is willing to forego consumption for a period in order to evaluate product offerings because he or she anticipates monetary savings and/or greater satisfaction of needs by evaluating alternatives.

The purchaser of shopping goods lacks complete information prior to the actual purchase and gathers additional information during the shopping trip. A woman intent on adding a new dress to her wardrobe may visit many stores, try on perhaps 30 dresses, and may spend days in making the final decision. She may follow a regular route from store to store in surveying competing offerings and ultimately selects the dress that most appeals to her. New stores carrying assortments of shopping goods must ensure that they are located near other shopping goods stores so that they will be included in shopping expeditions.

Shopping goods are typically more expensive than convenience goods and are most often purchased by women. In addition to women's apparel, shopping goods include such items as jewellery, furniture, appliances, shoes, and used automobiles.

Some shopping goods, such as children's shoes, may be classed as *homogeneous* — that is, the consumer views them as essentially the same — while others, such as furniture and clothing, are *heterogeneous*—essentially different. Price is a more important factor in the purchase of homogeneous shopping goods while quality and styling are more important in the purchase of heterogeneous goods.[33]

Brands are often less important for shopping than for convenience goods. Although some furniture brands may come to mind, they are typically less important than the physical attributes of the product, its price, styling, and even the retail store that handles the brand. Even though apparel companies have spent large amounts of money in promoting their brands, the dress buyer knows that the brand is inside the dress, and is more impressed with how the dress looks on her and its fit than with the hidden label.

Manufacturers of shopping goods utilize fewer retail stores than is common for convenience goods since purchasers can be expected to expend some effort in finding what they want to buy, and retailers will expend more effort on selling an exclusively distributed good. Thinness of the market may also affect the number of outlets. Retailers often purchase directly from the manufacturer or its representative rather than going through wholesalers. Fashion merchandise buyers for department stores and specialty shops make regular visits to Toronto, Montreal, New York, and Winnipeg on buying trips. Manufacturers often visit regional centres such as Vancouver, Edmonton, or Moncton to meet retailers there. Buyers for furniture retailers often go directly to the factories of furniture manufacturers or visit major furniture trade shows.

*Specialty Goods*    The specialty goods purchaser is well aware of what he or she wants and is willing to make a special effort to obtain it. The nearest Leica camera dealer may be 20 km away, but the camera enthusiast will go to that store to obtain what he or she may

---

33 For an early discussion of the distinctions between homogeneous and heterogeneous shopping goods, see E. J. McCarthy, *Basic Marketing* (Homewood, Ill.: Richard D. Irwin, 1964), pp. 398–400. See also Harry A. Lipson and John R. Darling, *Marketing Fundamentals* (New York: John Wiley & Sons, 1974), p. 244.

consider to be the ultimate in cameras. The Chicoutimi collector who longs for a $2500 *objet d'art* of Steuben glassware is willing to journey to Montreal to find the nearest Steuben dealer.

**Specialty goods** possess *some unique characteristics that cause the buyer to prize that particular brand.* The buyer possesses relatively complete information about the product prior to the shopping trip and is unwilling to accept substitutes.

Specialty goods are typically high-priced and frequently are branded. Since consumers are willing to exert a considerable effort in obtaining the good, fewer retail outlets are needed. Mercury outboard motors and Porsche sports cars may be handled by only one or two retailers for each 100 000 population.

**Applying the Consumer Goods Classification System**

The three-way classification system gives the marketing manager additional information for use in developing a marketing strategy. For example, if the new food product sells well in a test market as a convenience good, this provides insights about marketing needs in branding, promotion, pricing, and distribution methods. The impact of the goods classifications on their associated consumer factors and to marketing mix variables is shown in Figure 10-8.

**Figure 10-8   The Marketing Impact of the Consumer Goods Classification**

| Factor | Convenience Goods | Shopping Goods | Specialty Goods |
|---|---|---|---|
| *Consumer Factors* | | | |
| Planning time involved in purchase | Very little | Considerable | Extensive |
| Purchase frequency | Frequent | Less frequent | Infrequent |
| Importance of convenient location | Critical importance | Important | Unimportant |
| Comparison of price and quality | Very little | Considerable | Very little |
| *Marketing Mix Factors* | | | |
| Price | Low | Relatively high | High |
| Advertising | By manufacturer | By manufacturer and retailer | By manufacturer and retailer |
| Channel length | Long | Relatively short | Very short |
| Number of retail outlets | Many | Few | Very small number; often one per market area |
| Store image | Unimportant | Very important | Important |

But the classification system also poses problems of which the marketing manager must be aware. One pitfall is that it suggests a neat, three-way series of demarcations into which all products can easily be fitted. Some products do fit neatly into one of the three classifications, but others fall into the grey areas between categories.

How should a new automobile be classified? It is expensive, is branded, and is handled by a few exclusive dealers in each city. But before it is classified as a specialty good, other characteristics must be considered. Most new-car buyers shop extensively among competing models and auto dealers before deciding on the best "deal." A more effective method of utilizing the classification system, therefore, is to consider it as a continuum representing degrees of effort expended by the consumer.[34] The new-car purchase can then be located between the categories of shopping and specialty goods, but nearer the specialty-goods end of the continuum.

A second problem with the classification system is that consumers differ in their buying patterns. One person will make an unplanned purchase of a new Pontiac Firebird, while others will shop extensively before purchasing a car. One buyer's impulse purchase does not make the Firebird a convenience good. Goods are classified by the purchase patterns of the *majority* of buyers.

**Classifying Industrial Goods**

Industrial goods can be subdivided into five categories: installations, accessory equipment, fabricated parts and materials, raw materials, and industrial supplies. Industrial buyers are professional customers; their job is to make effective purchase decisions. Although details may vary, the purchase decision process involved in buying supplies of flour for General Mills, for example, is much the same as that used in buying the same commodity for Robin Hood. Thus the classification system for industrial goods must be based on product uses rather than on consumer buying patterns.

Installations **Installations** are *major capital assets like factories and heavy machinery used to produce products and services.* Installations are the specialty goods of the industrial market. New aircraft for Canadian Airlines International, locomotives for Canadian National, or a new pulp mill for Macmillian Bloedel, are examples of installations.

---

[34] A similar classification scheme has been proposed by Leo Aspinwall, who considers five product characteristics in classifying consumer goods — *replacement rate, gross margin* (the difference between cost and selling price), *adjustment* (the necessary changes made in a goal to satisfy precisely the consumer's needs), *time of consumption* (the time interval during which the product provides satisfaction), and length of consumer *searching time.* See Leo V. Aspinwall, "The Characteristics of Goods Theory," in *Four Marketing Theories* (Boulder: Bureau of Business Research, University of Colorado, 1961).

Since installations are relatively long-lived and involve large sums of money, their purchase represents a major decision for an organization. Sales negotiations often extend over a period of several months and involve the participation of numerous decision-makers. In many cases, the selling company must provide technical expertise. When custom-made equipment is involved, representatives of the selling firm work closely with the buyer's engineers and production personnel to design the most feasible product.

Price is almost never the deciding factor in the purchase of installations. The purchasing firm is interested in the product's efficiency and performance over its useful life. The firm also wants a minimum of breakdowns. "Down time" is expensive because employees are nonproductive (but still are paid) while the machinery is repaired.

Since most of the factories of firms purchasing installations are geographically concentrated, the selling firm places its promotional emphasis on well-trained salespeople who often have a technical background. Most installations are marketed directly on a manufacturer-to-user basis. Even though a sale may be a one-time transaction, contracts often call for regular product servicing. In the case of extremely expensive installations, such as computer and electronic equipment, some firms lease the installations rather than sell them outright and assign personnel directly to the lessee to operate or to maintain the equipment.

**Accessory Equipment**   Fewer decision-makers are usually involved in purchasing **accessory equipment** — *second-level capital items that are used in the production of products and services but are usually less expensive and shorter-lived than installations.* Although quality and service still remain important criteria in purchasing accessory equipment, the firm is likely to be much more price conscious. Accessory equipment includes such products as desk calculators, hand tools, portable drills, small lathes, and typewriters. Although these goods are considered capital items and are depreciated over several years, their useful life is generally much shorter than that of an installation.

Because of the need for continuous representation and the more widespread geographic dispersion of accessory equipment purchasers, a *wholesaler*, often called an **industrial distributor**, may be used to contact potential customers in each geographic area. Technical assistance is usually not necessary, and the manufacturer of accessory equipment often can effectively utilize such wholesalers in marketing the firm's products. Advertising is more important for accessory manufacturers then it is for installation producers.

**Component Parts and Materials**   While installations and accessory equipment are used in producing the final product, **component**

**parts and materials** are the *finished industrial goods that actually become part of the final product*. Champion spark plugs make a new Chevrolet complete; nuts and bolts are part of a Peugot bicycle; tires are included with a Dodge pickup truck. Some materials, such as flour, undergo further processing before producing a finished product.

Purchasers of component parts and materials need a regular continuous supply of uniform quality goods. These goods are generally purchased on contract for a period of one year or more. Direct sale is common, and satisfied customers often become permanent buyers. Wholesalers sometimes are used for fill-in purchases and in handling sales to smaller purchasers.

# The Ordeal of Becoming a McDonald's French Fry

French fries are a big deal at McDonald's. They account for about one fifth of total sales. Leaving out breakfast sales, 70 percent of McDonald's customers order them. As a result, McDonald's pays particular attention to the raw materials used in their popular product.

McDonald's uses only russet Burbanks which have a unique taste and make crispier french fries because of a high solid to water ratio. McDonald's has exacting standards for its fries. McDonald's fries are:

- Steamed, not blanched or quick-scalded
- Dried at higher than normal heat levels, and
- Sprayed with sugar, not dipped.

The company believes this process produces better fries. Even the length has to be just right. Only 20 percent of McDonald's fries can be less than 2 inches long; 40 percent have to be 2 to 3 inches long; and another 40 percent must exceed 3 inches.

McDonald's ran into some problems with its raw materials standards when it expanded overseas. Russet Burbanks are not grown in Europe, and potato imports are prohibited. McDonald's considers European-grown potatoes unacceptable, so it tried some unique approaches to getting russet Burbanks into Europe. The Dutch agreed to admit five potatoes after an eight-month quarantine, but they were destroyed by a potato virus. McDonald's planted russet Burbanks in Spain under the theory that they would be acceptable throughout Europe when Spain joined the Common Market in 1983, but this effort also failed. However, McDonald's did get its potatoes to grow in Tasmania, so they can now supply Australian outlets with the proper type of french fries. In any case, it is clear that McDonald's regards russet Burbanks as an important raw material in their business.

Source: Meg Cox, "A French-Fry Diary: From the Idaho Furrow to Golden Arches," *The Wall Street Journal* (February 8, 1982), pp. 1, 23.

Raw Materials   *Farm products, such as cattle, wool, eggs, milk, pigs, and canola, and natural products, such as coal, copper, iron ore, and lumber*, constitute **raw materials**. They are similar to component parts and materials in that they become part of the final products.

Since most raw materials are graded, the purchaser is assured of standardized products with uniform quality. As with component parts and materials, direct sale of raw materials is common, and sales are typically made on a contractual basis. Wholesalers are increasingly involved in the purchase of raw materials from foreign suppliers.

Price is seldom a *controllable* factor in the purchase of raw materials, since it is often quoted at a central market and is virtually identical among competing sellers. Purchasers buy raw materials from the firms they consider most able to deliver in the quantity and the quality required.

Supplies    If installations represent the specialty goods of the industrial market, then operating supplies are the convenience goods. **Supplies** are *regular expense items necessary in the daily operation of the firm, but not part of the final product.*

Supplies are sometimes called **MRO items** because they can be divided into three categories: 1) *maintenance items*, such as brooms, floor-cleaning compounds, and light bulbs; 2) *repair items*, such as nuts and bolts used in repairing equipment; and 3) *operating supplies*, such as heating fuel, lubricating oil, and office stationery.

The regular purchase of operating supplies is a routine aspect of the purchasing agent's job. Wholesalers are very often used in the sale of supplies due to the items' low unit prices, small sales, and large number of potential buyers. Since supplies are relatively standardized, price competition is frequently heavy. However, the purchasing agent spends little time in making purchase decisions. He or she frequently places telephone orders or mail orders, or makes regular purchases from the sales representative of the local office-supply wholesaler.

**Summary**    A critical variable in the firm's marketing mix is the product it plans to offer its market target. The best price, most efficient distribution channel, and most effective promotional campaign cannot maintain continuing purchases of an inferior product.

Consumers view products not only in physical terms but more often in terms of expected want satisfaction. The broad marketing conception of a product encompasses a bundle of physical, service, and symbolic attributes designed to produce this want satisfaction. The total product concept consists of the product image, brand, package and label, and warranty and service.

Most successful products pass through the four stages of the product life cycle: introduction, growth, maturity and decline. The rate at which they pass through the cycle is affected partially by many external uncontrollable factors. It can also be affected in many instances by managerial decisions. Therefore, marketers should not simply view the product life cycle as a deterministic phenomenon to which they can only react.

Several departures from the traditional product life-cycle are noted. First there is evidence that product life cycles may be getting shorter, particularly in the introductory and growth stages. Second, research shows that a number of products do not actually conform to the standard product life cycle model, and several alternative product life cycles are outlined. Finally, there is the matter of fashions and fads. Fashions are currently popular products that tend to have recurring life cycles. By contrast, fads are fashions with abbreviated life cycles.

The product life-cycle concept provides significant opportunities to adjust marketing strategy. Pricing, distribution, and promotion strategies, as well as product strategy, may affect the life-cycle stage, and should also be appropriate to it. Marketers should also attempt to extend the life cycles of successful individual products. Of course, they generally have little control over the life cycle of a product *category*.

Consumers go through a series of stages in adopting new product offerings: initial product awareness, interest, evaluation, trial purchase, and adoption or rejection of the new product.

Although first adopters of new products vary among product classes, several common characteristics have been isolated. First adopters are often younger, better educated, and more mobile, and they have higher incomes and higher social status than later adopters.

The rate of adoption for new products depends on five characteristics: 1) relative advantage, the degree of superiority of the innovation over the previous product; 2) compatibility, the degree to which the new product or idea is consistent with existing operations or the value system of potential purchasers; 3) complexity of the new product; 4) divisibility, the degree to which trial purchases on a small scale are possible; and 5) communicability, the degree to which the superiority of the innovation can be transmitted to other potential buyers.

Products are classified as either consumer or industrial goods. Consumer goods are used by the ultimate consumer and are not intended for resale or further use in producing other products. Industrial goods are used either directly or indirectly in producing other products for resale.

Differences in consumer buying habits can be used to further classify consumer goods into three categories: convenience goods, shopping goods, and specialty goods. Industrial goods are classified on the basis of product uses. The five categories in the industrial goods classification are installations, accessory equipment, component parts and materials, raw materials, and industrial supplies.

| **Key Terms** | product | shopping goods |
|---|---|---|
| | warranty | specialty goods |
| | product life cycle | installations |
| | fashions | accessory equipment |
| | fads | industrial distributor |
| | adoption process | component parts and materials |
| | consumer innovator | raw materials |
| | diffusion process | supplies |
| | convenience goods | MRO items |
| | impulse goods | |

**Review Questions**

1. Describe the total product concept.
2. Draw and explain the product life-cycle concept.
3. Outline the various forms that the traditional product life cycle might take.
4. Suggest several means by which the life cycle of a product (such as Scotch tape) can be extended.
5. Identify and briefly explain the stages in the consumer adoption process.
6. Describe each of the determinants of the rate of adoption.
7. Why is the basis used for categorizing industrial goods different from that used for categorizing consumer goods?
8. Compare a typical marketing mix for convenience goods with a mix for specialty goods.
9. Outline the typical marketing mix for a shopping good.
10. Discuss the marketing mix for the various types of industrial goods.

**Discussion Questions and Exercises**

1. Select a specific product in each stage of the product life cycle (other than those shown in the text). Explain how the marketing strategies might vary by life-cycle stage for each product.
2. Trace the life cycle of a recent fad. What marketing strategy implications can you draw from your study?
3. Home burglar alarm systems using microwaves are the fastest-growing product in the home-security market. Such systems operate by filling rooms with microwave beams, which set off alarms when an intruder intercepts one of them. What suggestions can you make to accelerate the rate of adoption for this product?
4. Classify the following consumer goods:
   a. Furniture
   b. Puma running shoes
   c. Felt-tip pen
   d. Swimsuit
   e. Nissan sports car
   f. Binaca breath freshener
   g. *Hockey News* magazine
   h. Original oil painting

5. Classify the following products into the appropriate industrial goods category. Briefly explain your choice for each product.
   a. Calculators
   b. Land
   c. Light bulbs
   d. Wool
   e. Paper towels
   f. Nylon
   g. Airplanes
   h. Tires

**MICROCOMPUTER EXERCISE: Return on Investment**

Directions: Use the Menu Item titled "Return on Investment" on the *Foundations of Marketing* disk to solve each of the following problems.

1. The management of Blue Grass Ind. of Vancouver is considering the development of a new product. Total development costs are estimated at $2 million, with forecasted sales of $12 million and profits of $1 million. Calculate the ROI for the new product.

2. Simpson Manufacturing Co. of Guelph, Ont. has marketed an industrial grinder for years. Current sales are $10 million annually, but last year Simpson Manufacturing earned only $450 000 on the product due to the rapidly rising cost of component parts. A recent proposal for a new version of the grinder using less expensive components would increase profits to $900 000 while maintaining sales at $14 million. However, this would require several plant-layout changes costing $2.8 million. What is the ROI of the proposed new product?

3. MotorSports of Penticton, B.C., has developed a new type of ski boat. Special placement tests at ski-instruction schools on Lake Okanagan proved highly successful. The firm's top management estimates that it would be able to generate $7 million in revenue from the sale of the boat at wholesale prices. However, development expenses for the boat are estimated at $3 million. Management believes that the new boat would add $800 000 to the firm's annual profits. What is the ROI of the proposed ski boat?

# *Product Management Decisions and New-Product Planning*

## *C H A P T E R    O B J E C T I V E S*

*1. To relate product-mix decisions and new-product planning to the other variables of the marketing mix.*

*2. To explain the various product-mix decisions that must be made by marketers.*

*3. To explain why most firms develop a line of related products rather than a single product.*

*4. To outline alternative new-product strategies and the determinants of their success.*

*5. To identify and explain the various organizational arrangements for new-product development.*

*6. To list the stages in the product development process.*

*7. To explain the role of brands, brand names, and trademarks.*

*8. To define the package and its major functions.*

New-product management decisions are much more complex than many managers realize. Here is the description of a new-product decision made in 1983. Approximately a year later this large successful company was in receivership:

> "We felt we had to get into it because that's our market, our business — home entertainment," says Philip Kives, president of K-Tel International Ltd. A continent-wide decline in the record industry has helped push K-Tel into the tough home video game business. With 1000 new games expected in the current year, the market is crowded and the fight for retail shelf space is ferocious.
>
> Despite the competition, Mr. Kives believed that K-Tel's experience in mass distribution would enable the company to enter the market successfully. "Basically, we are distributing the merchandise in the same manner as we would records. And we can probably distribute merchandise better than any company that I know of," he said.
>
> Kives, 54, has some unusual and extensive experience. A former door-to-door salesman of vacuum cleaners and cookware, he and his brother started K-Tel in 1962 and carved an empire out of gadgets

such as the Veg-O-Matic, Hair Magician, and Miracle Lint Brush. The company now has subsidiaries in 16 countries and franchises in 31 others.

Since the mid-1970s, K-Tel has concentrated mostly on musical recordings, selling established hits performed by little-known artists and repackaged into theme albums. Supported by a barrage of television advertising, the company has sold 150 million albums in the past six years.

The video game industry is expected to be tough. A hit game often depends on the finicky whims of 12-year-olds. It will be tougher to forecast a popular video game than a popular record, at least until K-Tel gains more experience in the market. To be successful, the company must select the right products for the right market and then use its expertise to advertise in the right media.

Obtaining shelf space is another critical variable, but K-Tel will likely have little problem here since they have a proven track record for moving products. Furthermore, the company has developed a reputation for dependable delivery of merchandise. It appears that the key to K-Tel's success in this new venture will be the selection of appropriate products for the chosen target markets.[1]

There are many interrelated reasons for the quick demise of K-Tel. The company leaped headlong into the oil and gas exploration business about the time when the bottom began to fall out of energy prices. And it also got into the real estate business just as interest rates began to take off. These were businesses in which it had no experience.

Soon after, the video game began to go the way of the hula hoop. Following this, the company introduced an unsuccessful line of TV screen toys just when it could least afford to. Other unfortunate investments compounded the problems.

Finally, losses of $37 million (U.S.) in 1982 and 1983 led five U.S. banks to demand repayment of the company's loans. After this, others got jumpy. Soon the company was deluged with merchandise returned from retailers whose proprietors feared that K-Tel would collapse, leaving them with goods they could not sell. Finally, the Bank of Montreal placed K-Tel's Canadian subsidiary into receivership.[2]

Product management requires continual diligence in assessing the changing needs of the market. Among other failures, K-Tel missed the fact that the product life cycle for video games was near its end.

---

[1] Adapted from Edward Greenspon, "K-Tel Moves on From Records to Video Games," *The Financial Post* (June 25, 1983), pp. 1–2.

[2] Roger Newman, "Death [and Rebirth] of a Salesman," *Report on Business Magazine* (May 1986), pp. 75–78.

**The Conceptual
Framework**

Chapter 11 expands the discussion of products and services by examining the product mix and new product planning. A starting point is to consider the concept of a product mix.

A **product mix** is the *assortment of product lines and individual offerings available from a marketer.* Its two components are the **product line**, *a series of related products*, and the **individual offerings** or *single products* within those lines.

---

**Figure 11-1   The Canada Packers Product Mix**

|  | | Width of Assortment | |
|---|---|---|---|
| | **Meats** | **Groceries** | **Nonedible** |
| | Fresh meats | Peanut butter | By-products |
| | Bacon | Mincemeat | Soap |
| Depth | Pepperoni | Canned pumpkin | Hides |
| of | Wieners | Cheese | Pharmaceutical raw |
| Assortment | Bologna | Lard | materials |
| | Canned ham | Shortening | |
| | Poultry | | |
| | Kolbassa | | |
| | Garlic sausage | | |

---

Product mixes are typically measured by width and depth of assortment. Width of assortment refers to the number of product lines that the firm offers, while depth of assortment refers to the extension of a particular product line.[3] Canada Packers offers an assortment of consumer product lines — meats, and several unrelated grocery items such as peanut butter. These product lines would be considered the width of the Canada Packers product mix. The depth is determined by the number of individual offerings within each product line. For example, their meat line consists of fresh meats, smoked and processed meats, and the grocery line is represented by York peanut butter and several types of canned vegetables. The company also sells a non-edible line of by-products.

**The Existing Product
Mix**

The starting point in any product planning effort is to assess the firm's current product mix. What product line does it now offer? How deep are the offerings within each of the product lines? The marketer wants to look for gaps in the assortment that can be filled by new products or modified versions of existing products.

---

[3] The width and depth of assortment is described in Raymond A. Marquardt, James C. Makens, and Robert G. Roe, *Retail Management*, 3d ed. (Hinsdale, Ill.: The Dryden Press, 1983), pp. 95–96.

**Cannibalization**    The firm wants to avoid a costly new-product introduction that will adversely affect sales of one of its existing products. *A product that takes sales from another offering in a product line* is said to be **cannibalizing** the line. Marketing research should ensure that cannibalization effects are minimized or at least anticipated. When Coke introduced Diet Coke they were resigned to the fact that the sales of their existing diet brand, Tab, would be negatively affected.

**Line Extension**    An important rationale for assessing the current product mix is to determine whether line extension is feasible. A **line extension** refers to *the development of individual offerings that appeal to different market segments, but are closely related to the existing product line.* If cannibalization can be minimized, line extension provides a relatively cheap way of increasing sales revenues at minimal risk. Oh Henry chocolate bars can now be purchased in ice cream bar format, in addition to their traditional form.[4] This illustrates the line extension of an existing product.

Once the assessment of the existing product mix has been made and the appropriate line extensions considered, marketing decision makers must turn their attention to product line planning and the development of new products.

## The Importance of Product Lines

Firms that market only one product are rare today. Most offer their customers a product line — a series of related products. Polaroid Corporation, for example, began operations with a single product, a polarized screen for sunglasses and other products. Then, in 1948, it introduced the world's first instant camera. For the next 30 years, these products proved to be sufficient for annual sales and profit growth. By 1983, however, instant cameras accounted for only about two thirds of Polaroid's sales. The company had added hundreds of products in both industrial and consumer markets, ranging from nearly 40 different types of instant films for various industrial, medical, and other technical operations, to batteries, sonar devices, and machine tools.[5] Several factors account for the inclination of firms such as Polaroid to develop a complete line rather than concentrate on a single product.

**Desire to Grow**    A company places definite limitations on its growth potential when it concentrates on a single product. In a single 12-month period,

---

[4] Nancy Giges, "Nestle's Chief's Mission: Pick Winners, Ax Losers," *Advertising Age* (September 7, 1981), p. 64.

[5] Polaroid's product development strategies are described in "Polaroid: Turning Away from Land's One Product Strategy," *Business Week* (March 2, 1981), pp. 108–112.

Lever Brothers introduced 21 new products in its search for market growth and increased profits. A study by a group of management consultants revealed that firms expect newly developed products to account for 37 percent of their sales and 51 percent of their profits over the next five years.[6]

Firms often introduce new products to offset seasonal variations in the sales of their current products. Since the majority of soup purchases are made during the winter months, Campbell Soup Company has made attempts to tap the warm-weather soup market. A line of fruit soups to be served chilled was test-marketed, but results showed that consumers were not yet ready for fruit soups. The firm continued to search for warm-weather soups, however, and in some markets in the early 1980s, it added gazpacho and other varieties to be served chilled, to its product line.

## Optimal Use of Company Resources

By spreading the costs of company operations over a series of products, it may be possible to reduce the average costs of all products. Texize Chemicals Company started with a single household cleaner and learned painful lessons about marketing costs when a firm has only one major product. Management rapidly added the products K2r and Fantastik to the line. The company's sales representatives can now call on middlemen with a series of products at little more than the cost for marketing a single product. In addition, Texize's advertising produces benefits for all products in the line. Similarly, production facilities can be used economically in producing related products. For example, Chrysler has produced a convertible, van, and sports car from the basic K car design.[7] Finally, the expertise of all the firm's personnel can be applied more widely to a line of products than to a single one.

## Increasing Company Importance in the Market

Consumers and middlemen often expect a firm that manufactures and markets small appliances to also offer related products under its brand name. The Maytag Company offers not only washing machines but also dryers, since consumers often demand matching appliances. Gillette markets not only razors and blades but also a full range of grooming aids, including Foamy shave cream, Right Guard deodorant, Gillette Dry Look hair spray and Super Max hair dryers.

The company with a line of products is often more important to both the consumer and the retailer than the company with only one product. Shoppers who purchase a tent often buy related items, such

---

[6] Bill Abrams, "Despite Mixed Record, Firms Still Pushing for New Products," *The Wall Street Journal* (November 12, 1981), p. 25.

[7] Douglas R. Scase, "Chrysler Is Upbeat as Market Share Rises, but Some Doubt It Can Maintain Success," *The Wall Street Journal* (April 22, 1982), p. 33.

as tent heaters, sleeping bags and air mattresses, camping stoves, and special cookware. Recognizing this tendency, the Coleman Company now includes in its product line dozens of items associated with camping. The firm would be little known if its only product were lanterns. Similarly, new cameras from Eastman Kodak help the firm sell more film — a product that carries a 60 percent profit margin.[8]

**Exploiting the Product Life Cycle**

As its output enters the maturity and decline stages of the life cycle of a product category, the firm must add new products if it is to prosper. The regular addition of new products to the firm's line helps ensure that it will not become a victim of product obsolescence. The development of stereophonic sound in the 1950s shifted single-speaker high-fidelity phonographs from the maturity stage to the decline stage, and companies such as RCA and Zenith began to develop new products incorporating stereo.[9]

**New-Product Planning**

The product development effort requires considerable advance planning. New products are the lifeblood of any business firm, and a steady flow of new entries must be available if the firm is to survive. Some new products are major technological breakthroughs. For instance, Procter & Gamble has filed patent applications for a male baldness cure, a margarine that cuts cholesterol in the blood, and a plaque-eliminating dental product.[10] Other new products are simple product-line extensions. In other words a new product is simply a product new to either the company or the customer. One survey found that for products introduced between 1976 and 1981, about 85 percent were line extensions, and only 15 percent were truly new products.[11]

**The Product Decay Curve**

New-product development is risky and expensive. A Conference Board study of 148 medium and large North-American manufacturing companies revealed that one out of three new industrial and consumer products introduced within the past five years has failed.

---

8 Howard Rudnitakey, "Snap Judgments Can Be Wrong," *Forbes* (April 12, 1982).

9 Roger Leigh Lawton and A. Parasuraman, "So You Want Your New Product Planning to Be Productive," *Business Horizons* (December 1980), pp. 29–34; and Roger Calantone and Robert G. Cooper, "New Product Scenarios: Prospects for Success," *Journal of Marketing* (Spring 1981), pp. 48–60.

10 Carol J. Loomis, "P & G Up Against Its Wall," *Fortune* (February 23, 1981), pp. 49–54.

11 Abrams, "Despite Mixed Record, Firms Still Pushing for Products," p. 25.

**Figure 11-2    Decay Curve of New-Product Ideas**

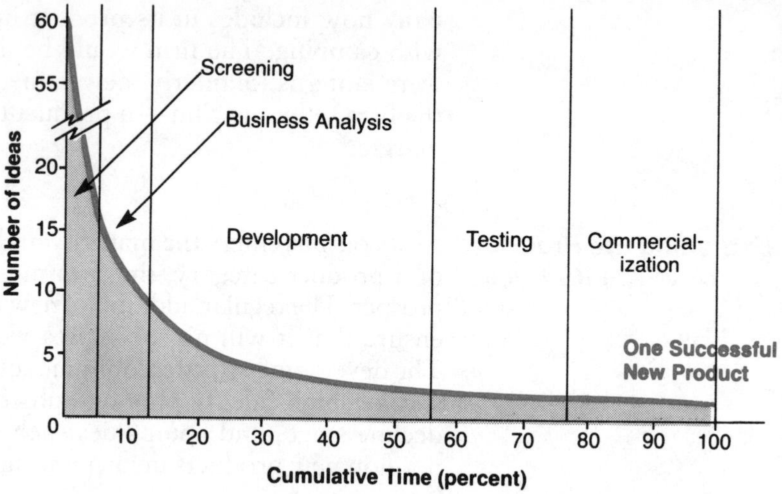

Source: Reprinted by permission from *New Products Management for the 1980s* (New York: Booz, Allen & Hamilton, 1982), p. 3.

***Characteristics of the Superior Product***

The leading cause of new product failure was insufficient and poor marketing research.[12]

Dozens of new-product ideas are required to produce even one successful product. Figure 11-2 depicts the product decay curve in a 1968 survey of 51 companies. Of every 58 ideas produced in these firms, only 12 passed the preliminary screening test designed to determine whether they were compatible with company resources and objectives. Of these 12, only 7 showed sufficient profit potential in the business analysis phase. Three survived the development phase, two made it through the test marketing stage, and only one, on the average, was commercially successful. Thus, less than 2 percent of new ideas resulted in a successful product.

A 1981 follow-up study reported that while the success rate may be no better today, new product development is becoming more cost effective. According to the new data, some 54 percent of total new product expenditures are going to successes, compared with 30 percent in 1968. Capital investment in new products has fallen from 46 percent to 26 percent of total new-product spending.[13] These figures suggest that new-product development is now more efficient.

---

[12] David S. Hopkins, *New Product Winners and Losers* (New York: The Conference Board, Inc., 1980). See also "Booz Allen Looks at New Products' Role," *The Wall Street Journal* (March 26, 1981), p. 25.

[13] Abrams, "Despite Mixed Record, Firms Still Pushing for Products," p. 25.

**Determinants of Success for New Products**

What determines the success or failure of a new product? A research effort known as Project New Product suggests the following six categories as determinants of new-product outcomes:[14]

1. the relative strengths of the new product and its marketplace launch
2. the nature and quality of the information available during the product development process
3. the relative proficiency of new product development efforts
4. the characteristics of the marketplace at which the new product is aimed
5. the fit or compatibility of the new product and the firm's resource base
6. the specific characteristics of the new product effort

These hypothetical variables allowed Robert Cooper of McGill University to classify various types of new products. Cooper contends that the most important key to new-product success lies in the product strategy itself. In his research he found that in the cases he studied, the best 20 percent of the products had an astounding success rate of 82 percent. In contrast, the 20 percent at the other end of the scale (the "me-too" products) suffered a *failure* rate of 78 percent.

What then is a superior product? Cooper found that a number of characteristics comprised the superior product dimension. In descending order of importance these critical characteristics are:

1. a product that meets customers' needs better than competing products
2. a product that offers features or attributes to the customer that competing products do not
3. a higher quality product than competitive products (one that has tighter specifications, is stronger, lasts longer, or is more reliable)
4. a product that does a special task or job for the customer — something that cannot be done with existing products
5. a product that is highly innovative, totally new to the market
6. a product that permits the customer to reduce costs.[15]

Products with these characteristics supported by creative marketing strategies will greatly contribute to a profitable product line.

---

14 This list is adapted from Roger Calantone and Robert G. Cooper, "New Product Scenarios: Prospects for Success," *Journal of Marketing* (Spring 1981), p. 49.

15 Robert G. Cooper, "The Myth of the Better Mousetrap: What Makes a New Product a Success?" *The Business Quarterly* (Spring, 1981), pp. 71, 72; and Robert G. Cooper, *Winning at New Products* (Toronto: Holt, Rinehart and Winston of Canada, 1986), p. 33.

Figure 11-3    Forms of Product Development

|  | Old Product | New Product |
|---|---|---|
| **Old Market** | Product Improvement | Product Development |
| **New Market** | Market Development | Product Diversification |

Source: Charles E. Meisch, "Marketers, Engineers Should Work Together in 'New Product' Development Departments," *Marketing News* (November 13, 1981), p. 10. Earlier discussion of these strategies is credited to H. Igor Ansoff, "Strategies for Diversification," *Harvard Business Review* (September-October 1957), pp. 113–124. See Philip Kotler, *Principles of Marketing*, 2nd ed. (Englewood Cliffs, N.J.: Prentice-Hall, Inc. 1983), pp. 34, 52.

**Product Development Strategies**

The firm's strategy for new-product development should vary in accordance with the existing product mix and the determinants cited above. Marketing decision-makers also need to look at the firm's present market position. Figure 11-3 provides a means for looking at overall product development strategy. Four forms of product development are suggested: product improvement, market development, product development, and product diversification.

A *product improvement strategy* refers to modification in existing products. Product positioning often plays a major role in such strategy. **Product positioning** (discussed in Chapter 5) refers to *the consumer's perception of a product's attributes, use, quality, and advantages and disadvantages in relation to competing brands.* Good examples are the recent effort to reposition 7-Up as a caffeine-free soft drink[16] and Canadian Airlines International's effort to get travellers to consider the airline as an alternative when planning a flight. To achieve this they positioned themselves as "the competition," in an extensive advertising campaign.

A *market development strategy* concentrates on finding new markets for existing products. Market segmentation (discussed in Chapters 4 and 5) is a useful tool in such an effort. The penetration of new markets with Cow Brand baking soda, an established product, is illustrative of this strategy.

*Product development strategy*, as defined here, refers to the introduction of new products into identifiable or established markets.

[16] "Seven-Up Uncaps a Cola—And an Industry Feud," *Business Week* (March 22, 1982), pp. 98, 100. Also see "Seven-Up's Caffeine War," *Newsweek* (April 9, 1982), p. 73.

Sometimes, the new product is the firm's first entry in this particular marketplace. In other cases, firms choose to introduce new products into markets in which they have already established positions in an attempt to increase overall market share. These new offerings are called *flanker brands*.

*Product diversification strategy* refers to the development of new products for new markets. In some cases, the new market targets are complementary to existing markets; in others, they are not.

New products should be consistent with the firm's overall strategic orientation. Assume that a beverage firm has set four strategic requirements for a new product:

1. It must appeal to the under-21 age segment.
2. It must utilize off-season or excess capacity.
3. It must successfully penetrate a new product category for the firm.
4. It could simply be a cash cow that funds other new products.[17]

Each of these criteria would fit in well with the orientation, skills, and resources of the firm. As the above section indicates, new-product planning is a complex area. The critical nature of product planning decisions requires an effective organizational structure to make them.

## The Organizational Structure for New-Product Development

A prerequisite for efficient product innovation is an organizational structure designed to stimulate and co-ordinate new-product development. New-product development is a specialized task and requires the expertise of many departments.[18] A company that delegates new-product development responsibility to the engineering department often discovers that engineers sometimes design good products from a structural standpoint but poor ones in terms of consumer needs. Many successful medium and large companies assign new-product development to one or more of the following: 1) new-product committees, 2) new-product departments, 3) product managers, or 4) venture teams.

## New-Product Committees

The most common organizational arrangement for new-product development is the *new-product committee*. Such a committee is typically composed of representatives of top management in areas such as marketing, finance, manufacturing, engineering, research,

---

17 Abrams, "Despite Mixed Record Firms Still Pushing for Products," p. 25.
18 David Gordon and E. Edward Blevins, "Organizing for Effective New-Product Development," *Journal of Business* (December 1978), pp. 21–26; and James Rothe, Michael Harvey, and Walden Rhines, "New Product Development under Conditions of Scarcity and Inflation," *Michigan Business Review* (May 1977), pp. 16–22.

# Does the World Really Want a . . .?

Here are some new products and services that may or may not make it in today's competitive marketplace. What do you think about their chances of success?

- *Career Guard.* John Lorriman was a $40 000-a-year executive who fought with his boss constantly. Eventually he was fired, and a new product idea was generated. Lorriman began developing an insurance policy that pays a person's salary for two years if they are laid off or fired because of personality conflicts, takeover, or bankruptcy. Career Guard, which is designed for executives earning $25 000 or more, also provides legal help and employment assistance. The cost is 1.3 percent of the person's salary.
- *Pick Point Enterprises.* A small firm, Pick Point Enterprises, is now offering lighted tennis balls. This new product is made of translucent plastic and contains a chemical that radiates light, much like a firefly.
- *Juicie Treat.* Rosebud Products has introduced just the thing for Fido. Juicie Treat is a drink for dogs that is made of vitamin-enriched sugar water but has the smell of beef bouillon. It can also be mixed with dog food and sells for 99 cents per quart.

Source: Peggy Berkowitz, "These Days, You Don't Have to Be the Boss's Kid to Get Job Insurance," *The Wall Street Journal* (April 7, 1982), Section 2, p. 29; "Business Bulletin," *The Wall Street Journal* (January 28, 1982), p. 1; and, "Arf! Gimme a Virgin Bullshot," *Newsweek* (April 12, 1982), p. 64.

and accounting. Committee members are less concerned with conception and development of new product ideas than with reviewing and approving new product plans.

Since key executives in the functional areas are committee members, their support for a new-product plan is likely to result in its approval for further development. However, new-product committees tend to be slow, are generally conservative, and sometimes compromise in order to expedite decisions so that members may get back to their regular company responsibilities.

**New-Product Departments**   To overcome the limitations of the new-product committee, a number of firms have established a separate, formally organized department responsible for all phases of the product's development within the firm, including making screening decisions, development of product specifications, and co-ordinating product testing. The head of the department is given substantial authority and usually reports to the president or to the top marketing officer.

**Product Managers**   **Product managers** (also called **brand managers**) are *individuals assigned one product or product line and given responsibility for determining its objectives and marketing strategies.* Procter & Gamble assigned the first product manager back in 1927 when they

# A Typical Product Manager Under 30

Joe Antonelli graduated from Dalhousie University eight years ago with a major in political science. He then transferred to York University's MBA program. After graduating with good marks two years later, he accepted a position with a large consumer goods manufacturer.

Joe's first assignment was brand manager of a liquid sugar substitute. Although he reported directly to the marketing vice-president, Joe was completely in charge of the product and made the decision for an optimal promotional mix of the product, its price, its distribution channels, and even its chemical content.

Joe found it difficult at first, but his marketing efforts resulted in a market share increase of more than two percentage points in a 15-month period. He also averaged 50 hours per week on the job.

Joe's salary increased steadily. In less than a year he had been promoted to product manager for a more important part of the firm's business. His new job involved the responsibility for all of the firm's cake mixes and the frosting line. Another raise accompanied this promotion.

This job is both stimulating and challenging. In effect, Joe runs a miniature company within the larger firm, with all of the problems and decisions of a one-product firm. His next promotion will place him in charge of a group of four to six product managers.

made one person responsible for Camay soap.[19] The role of product manager is now widely accepted by marketers. Johnson & Johnson, Canada Packers and General Mills are examples of firms employing product managers.

Product managers are deeply involved in setting prices, developing advertising and sales promotion programs, and working to provide assistance to sales representatives in the field. Although product managers have no line authority over the field sales force, they share the objective of increasing sales for the brand, and managers try to help salespeople accomplish their task. In multiproduct companies, product managers are key people in the marketing department. They provide individual attention to each product, while the firm as a whole has a single sales force, marketing research department, and advertising department that all product managers can utilize.

In addition to product analysis and planning, the product manager uses interpersonal skills and salesmanship to gain the cooperation of people over which he has no authority. This occurs with levels above the manager, as well as with those in sales and advertising.

---

19 Reported in Ann M. Morrison, "The General Mills Brand of Manager," *Fortune* (January 12, 1981), pp. 99–107. Another interesting discussion appears in "Brand Management System Is Best, but Refinements Needed," *Marketing News* (July 9, 1982), p. 12.

In addition to having primary responsibility for marketing a particular product or product line, the product manager is often responsible for new-product development, the creation of new-product ideas, and recommendations for improving existing products. These suggestions become the basis for proposals submitted to top management.

The product manager system is open to one of the same criticisms as the new-product committee: new-product development may get secondary treatment because of the manager's time commitments for existing products. Although a number of extremely successful new products have resulted from ideas submitted by product managers, it cannot be assumed that the skills required for marketing an existing product line are the same as those required for successfully developing new products.[20]

**Venture Teams**    An increasingly common technique for organizing new-product development is the use of **venture teams**.[21]

The venture-team concept is an organizational strategy to develop new-product areas through *the combination of the management resources of technological innovations, capital, management, and marketing expertise.*[22] Like new-product committees, venture teams are composed of specialists from different functions in the organization: engineering representatives for expertise in product design and the development of prototypes; marketing staff members for development of product-concept tests, test marketing, sales forecasts, pricing, and promotion; and financial accounting representatives for detail cost analyses and decisions concerning the concept's probable return on investment.

---

[20] Jacob M. Duker and Michael V. Laric, "The Product Manager: No Longer on Trial," in *The Changing Marketing Environment: New Theories and Applications*, (eds.) Kenneth Bernhardt, Ira Dolich, Michael Etzel, William Kehoe, Thomas Kinnear, William Perrault, Jr., and Kenneth Roering (Chicago: American Marketing Association, 1981), pp. 93–96; and Peter S. Howsam and G. David Hughes, "Product Management System Suffers from Insufficient Experience, Poor Communication," *Marketing News* (June 26, 1981), Section 2, p. 8.

[21] This discussion is based on Richard M. Hill and James D. Hlavacek, "The Venture Team: A New Concept in Marketing," *Journal of Marketing* (July 1972) pp. 44–50.

[22] See D. W. Karger and Robert G. Murdick, *New-Product Venture Management* (New York: Gordon and Breach, Science Publishers, 1972); Frederick W. Cook, "Venture Management Organizations — An Overview," in Fred C. Allvine (ed.), *Relevance in Marketing* (Chicago: American Marketing Association, 1972), p. 129; and James D. Hlavacek, "Toward More Successfull Venture Management," *Journal of Marketing* (October 1974), pp. 56–60. See also Dan T. Dunn, Jr., "The Rise and Fall of Ten Venture Groups," *Business Horizons* (October 1977), pp. 32–41; and William W. George, "Task Teams for Rapid Growth," *Harvard Business Review* (March–April 1977), pp. 71–80.

Unlike representatives on new-product committees, venture-team members do not disband after every meeting. They are assigned to the project as a major responsibility, and the team possesses the necessary authority to both plan and carry out a course of action.

As a means of stimulating product innovation, the team is typically separated from the permanent organization and is also linked directly with top management. One company moved its three-member venture team from its divisional headquarters to the corporate head office. Since the venture-team manager reports to the division head or to the chief administrative officer, communications problems are minimized and high-level support is assured.

The venture team usually begins as a loosely organized group of members with common interest in a new-product idea. Team members are frequently given released time during the workday to devote to the venture. If viable product proposals are developed, the venture team is formally organized as a task force within a venture department or as a task force reporting to a vice-president or the chief executive officer.

The venture team must meet such criteria as prospective return on investment, uniqueness of the product, existence of a well-defined need, degree of the product's compatibility with existing technology, and strength of patent protection. Although the organization is considered temporary, the actual life span of the venture team is extremely flexible and often extends over a number of years. When the commercial potential of new products has been demonstrated, the products may be assigned to an existing division, may become a division within the company, or may serve as the nucleus of a new company.

The flexibility and authority of the venture team allows the large firm to operate with the manoeuvrability of smaller companies. Venture teams established by Colgate-Palmolive Company have already broadened the base of the toiletries and detergents manufacturer into such products as freeze-dried flowers. Such teams also serve as an outlet for innovative marketing by providing a mechanism for translating research and development ideas into viable products.

> The venture team with its single mission, unstructured relationships, insulation from the daily routine, and entrepreneurial thrust is an organizational concept uniquely suited to the task of product innovation. For many companies whose future depends as much on the successful launching of new products as the successful marketing of existing ones, the venture team concept offers a promising mechanism for more innovative marketing and the growth which it makes possible.[23]

23 Richard M. Hill and James D. Hlavacek, "The Venture Team: A New Concept in Marketing," *Journal of Marketing* (July 1972), p. 50.

Figure 11-4   Seven Stages of the New Product Process

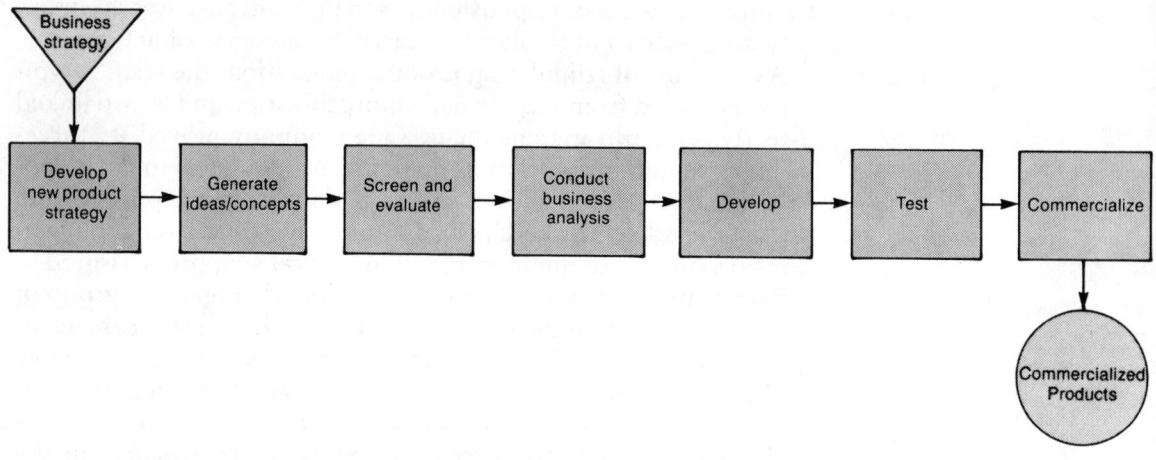

Business strategy

Develop new product strategy → Generate ideas/concepts → Screen and evaluate → Conduct business analysis → Develop → Test → Commercialize

Commercialized Products

**Stages in the New-Product Development Process**

New-product development strategy should be built upon the existing business strategy of the company. Companies that have successfully launched new products are more likely to have had a formal new-product process in place for some time. They are also more likely to have a strategic plan, and be committed to growth through internally developed new products.[24]

Once the firm is organized for new-product development, it can establish procedures for evaluating new-product ideas. The product development process may be thought of as involving seven stages: 1) development of overall new-product strategy, 2) new-product idea generation, 3) screening, 4) business analysis, 5) final product development, 6) test marketing, and 7) commercialization. At each stage, management faces the decision to abandon the project, continue to the next stage, or seek additional information before proceeding further.[25] The process is illustrated in Figure 11-4.

**New-Product Strategy**

New-product strategy links corporate objectives to the new-product effort, provides direction for the new-product process, and identi-

---

[24] Adapted from John R. Rockwell and Marc C. Particelli, "New Product Strategy: How the Pros Do It," *Industrial Marketing* (May 1982), p. 50.

[25] For an excellent treatment of the product development process, see Robert D. Hisrich and Michael P. Peters, *Marketing a New Product* (Menlo Park, Calif.: Benjamin Cummings Publishing, 1978); Richard T. Hise, *Product/Service Strategy* (New York: Mason/Charter Publishers, 1977); A. Edward Spitz, *Product Planning*, 2d ed. (New York: Mason/Charter Publishers, 1977); and Chester R. Wasson, *Dynamic Competitive Strategy and Product Life Cycles* (Austin, Tex.: Austin Press, 1978).

fies the strategic roles in the product line that the new products should play. It also helps set the formal financial criteria to be used in measuring new-product performance and in screening and evaluating new-product ideas.[26]

**Idea Generation**   New-product development begins with an idea. Ideas emanate from many sources: the sales force, marketing employees, research and development (R & D) specialists, competitive products, retailers, inventors outside the company, and customers who write letters asking "Why don't you . . . ?" It is extremely important for the firm to develop a system of stimulating new ideas and for rewarding persons who develop them.[27]

**Screening**   This crucial stage involves separating ideas with potential from those incapable of meeting company objectives. Some organizations use checklists to determine whether product ideas should be eliminated or subjected to further consideration. These checklists typically include such factors as product uniqueness; availability of raw materials; and compatibility of the proposed product with current product offerings, existing facilities, and capabilities. In other instances, the screening stage consists of open discussions of new-product ideas among representatives of different functional areas in the organization. This is an important point in the product development process since any product ideas that go beyond this point will cost the firm valuable time and money.[28] Figure 11-5 presents some basic criteria used in the screening process.

**Business Analysis**   Product ideas surviving the initial screening are then subjected to a thorough business analysis. This involves an assessment of the potential market, its growth rate, and the likely competitive strength of the new product. Decisions must be made in determining the compatibility of the proposed product with such company resources as financial support for necessary promotion, production capabilities and distribution facilities.

Concept testing, or the consideration of the product idea prior to its actual development, is an important aspect of the business analysis stage. **Concept testing** is *a marketing research project that*

---

26 Rockwell, op. cit.

27 See Eric von Hippel, "Successful Industrial Products from Customer Ideas," *Journal of Marketing* (January 1978), pp. 39–49; and James L. Ginter and W. Wayne Talarzyk, "Applying the Marketing Concept to Design New Products," *Journal of Business Research* (January 1978), pp. 51–66.

28 See William B. Locander and Richard W. Scamell, "Screening New Product Ideas — A Two-Phase Approach," *Research Management* (March 1976), pp. 14–18.

---

**Figure 11-5   Basic Criteria for Preliminary Screening**

1. The item should be in a field of activity in which the corporation is engaged.
2. If the idea involves a companion product to others already being manufactured, it should be made from materials to which the corporation is accustomed.
3. The item should be capable of being produced on the type and kind of equipment that the corporation normally operates.
4. The item should be easily handled by the corporation's existing sales force through the established distribution pattern.
5. The potential market for the product should be at least $_____.
6. The market over the next five years should be expected to grow at a faster rate than the GNP.
7. Return on investment, after taxes, must reach a minimum level of _____ percent.

Source: Reprinted from Willam S. Sachs and George Benson, *Product Planning and Management* (Tulsa, Okla.: PennWell Books, 1981), p. 231.

---

*attempts to measure consumer attitudes and perceptions relevant to the new product idea.* Focus groups (see Chapter 6) and in-store polling can be effective methods for assessing a new-product concept.

*Product Development*   Those product ideas with profit potential are then converted into a physical product. The conversion process becomes the joint responsibility of development engineering, which is responsible for developing the original concept into a product, and the marketing department, which provides feedback on consumer reactions to alternative product designs, packages, features, colours, and other physical appeals. Numerous changes may be necessary before the original mock-up is converted into the final product.

The series of revisions, tests, and refinements should result in the ultimate introduction of a product with a greater likelihood of success. Some firms use their own employees as a sounding board and obtain their reactions to proposed new-product offerings. Employees at Levi Strauss & Company test new styles by wearing them and providing feedback. A shoe manufacturer asks its workers to report regularly over an eight-week testing period on shoe wear and fit.[29]

But occasionally attempts to be first with a new product result in the premature introduction of new products. Kellogg and several other cereal-makers experienced this several years ago when they all failed in attempts to introduce freeze-dried fruit cereal. In their

---

[29] *Wall Street Journal* (March 26, 1974), p. 1.

rush to be first on the market with the new offering, they failed to perfect the product. The small, hard pellets of real fruit took too long to reconstitute in the bowl. Millions of bowls of cereal went into garbage cans.[30]

**Test Marketing**    To determine consumer reactions to their products under normal shopping conditions, a number of firms test-market their new offerings. Up to this point, consumer information has been obtained by submitting free products to consumers who then gave their reactions. Other information may have been gathered by asking shoppers to evaluate competitive products, but test marketing is the first point where the product must perform in a "real life" environment.

*Test marketing* involves selecting usually one to three cities or television-coverage areas considered reasonably typical of the total market, and introducing the product in this area with a total marketing campaign. A carefully designed and controlled test allows management to develop estimates of the effectiveness of marketing-mix decisions and of sales on full scale introduction.[31]

Some firms omit the test-marketing stage and move directly from product development to full-scale production. They cite three problems with test marketing:

1. Test marketing is expensive. As one marketing executive pointed out:

   It's very difficult to run a little [test market] for six months or a year in three or four markets across the [country] and then project what your sales volume is going to be two or three years in the future, mainly because you're testing in such small localities, generally to keep your costs down.

   You simply can't afford to test your product in markets like [Toronto or Montreal]. So you run your test in [smaller cities]. And your test costs are over $1 million even in places like that.[32]

2. Competitors who learn about the test market many disrupt the findings by reducing the price of their products in the test area, distributing cents-off coupons, installing attractive in-store displays, or giving additional discounts to retailers to induce them to display more of their products.

   Test marketing a new product also communicates company plans to competitors prior to the product's introduction. The

---

[30] Reported in Edward Buxton, *Promise Them Anything* (New York: Stein and Day, 1972), p. 101.

[31] See N. D. Cadbury, "When, Where, and How to Test Market," *Harvard Business Review* (May-June 1975), pp. 96–105.

[32] Quoted in Mary McCabe English, "Marketers: Better than a Coin Flip," *Advertising Age* (February 9, 1981), p. S–15. Copyright 1981 by Crain Communications, Inc. Reprinted by permission.

Kellogg Company discovered a new product with suspected sales potential by learning of a test marketing of a new fruit-filled tart designed to be heated in the toaster and served hot for breakfast. Kellogg rushed a similar product into full-scale production and became the first national marketer of the product they named Pop Tarts.

3. Long-lived durable goods, such as dishwashers, hair dryers, and VCRs, are seldom test marketed due to the major financial investment required for the development, the need to develop a network of dealers to distribute the products, and the parts and servicing required. A company such as Whirlpool invests from $1 million to $33 million in the development of a new refrigerator. To develop each silicon chip in an Apple microcomputer costs approximately $1 million and takes from one to 15 months. Producing a prototype for a test market is simply too expensive, so the "go/no go" decision for the new durable product is typically made without the benefit of test-market results.[33]

A decision to skip the test-marketing stage should be based on a very high likelihood of the product's success. The costs of developing a new detergent from idea generation to national marketing have been estimated at *$10 million*. Even though a firm will experience losses on any product that passes the initial screening process but is not introduced, it will still be much better off by stopping as soon as it discovers that the product cannot succeed, rather than being faced with a failure such as Corfam, an artificial leather that DuPont introduced and suffered losses of more than *$100 million* over the lengthy period they tried to make it a success.

**Commercialization**  The few product ideas that will survive all of the steps in the development process are now ready for full-scale marketing. Marketing programs must be established, outlays for necessary production facilities may be necessary, and the sales force, middlemen, and potential customers must become acquainted with the new product.

New product development should follow the step-by-step approach previously outlined in Figure 11-4. Systematic planning and control of all phases of development and introduction can be accomplished through the use of such scheduling methods as the Program Evaluation and Review Technique (PERT)[34] and the Critical Path Method (CPM). These techniques map out the sequence

---

[33] Dylan Landis, "Durable Goods for a Test?" *Advertising Age* (February 9, 1981), pp. S-18, S-19.

[34] For a description of how Diamond Alkali Company uses these techniques, see Warren Dusenburg, "CPM for New-Product Introductions," *Harvard Business Review* (July–August 1967), pp. 124–139.

**Figure 11-6    Elapsed Time Between Initial Development and Full-Scale Introduction**

| Product | Years |
|---|---|
| Strained baby foods | 1 |
| Frozen orange juice | 2 |
| Filter cigarettes | 2 |
| Polaroid Land Camera | 2 |
| Dry dog food | 4 |
| Electric toothbrush | 4 |
| Stripe toothpaste | 6 |
| Roll-on deodorant | 6 |
| Plastic tile | 6 |
| Liquid shampoo | 8 |
| Freeze-dried instant coffee | 10 |
| Fluoride toothpaste | 10 |
| Penicillin | 15 |
| Xerox electrostatic copier | 15 |
| Polaroid Color-pack Camera | 15 |
| Transistors | 16 |
| Minute rice | 18 |
| Instant coffee | 22 |
| Zippers | 30 |
| Television | 55 |

Source: Lee Adler, "Time Lag in New Product Development," *Journal of Marketing* (January 1966), pp. 17–21. Reprinted from *Journal of Marketing*, published by the American Marketing Association.

in which each step must be taken and show the time allotments for each activity. Detailed PERT and CP flow charts will not only assist in coordinating all activities in the development and introduction of new products, but they can also highlight the sequence of events which will be the most critical in scheduling.

As Figure 11-6 indicates, new-product development and introduction can take many years. A study of the elapsed time between initial development and full-scale introduction of 42 products revealed a time lag ranging from six months for a new heavy-duty oil to 55 years for television. Since the time needed for orderly development of new products is longer than might be expected, the planning horizon for new-product ideas may have to be extended five to ten years into the future.[35]

[35] Lee Adler, "Time Lag in New-Product Development," *Journal of Marketing* (January 1966), p. 17.

**Product Deletion Decisions**

While many firms devote a great deal of time and resources to the development of new products, the thought of eliminating old products from the firm's line is painful for many executives. Often sentimental attachments to marginal products prevent objective decisions to drop products with declining sales. Management finds it difficult to bury an old friend.

If waste is to be avoided, product lines must be pruned, and old products must eventually be eliminated from the firm's line. This decision is typically faced in the late maturity and early decline stages of the product life cycle. Periodic reviews of weak products should be conducted in order to prune weak products or to justify their retention.

In some instances a firm will continue to carry an unprofitable product so as to provide a complete line of goods for its customers. Even though most supermarkets lose money on such bulky, low-unit-value items as salt, they continue to carry it to meet shopper demands.

Shortages of raw materials have prompted some companies to discontinue the production and marketing of previously profitable items. Du Pont dropped an antifreeze from its product line due to raw material shortages.

Other cases arise where profitable products are dropped because of failure to fit into the firm's existing product line. The development of automatic washing machines necessitated the developing of a low-sudsing detergent. The Monsanto Company produced the world's first low-sudsing detergent in the 1950s and named it All. All was an instant success, and Monsanto was swamped with orders from supermarkets throughout the nation. But the Monsanto sales force was primarily involved with the marketing of industrial chemicals to large-scale buyers. A completely new sales force was required to handle a single product. Nine months after the introduction of All, Procter & Gamble introduced the world's second low-sudsing detergent and named it Dash. The Procter & Gamble sales force handled hundreds of products and could spread the cost of contacting dealers over all of these products. Monsanto had only All. Rather than attempting to compete, Monsanto sold All in 1958 to Lever Brothers, a Procter & Gamble competitor with a marketing organization capable of handling it.[36]

**Product Identification**

Manufacturers identify their products through the use of brand names, symbols, and distinctive packaging. So also do large retailers such as Canadian Tire, with its line of Mastercraft products,

---

[36] Spencer Klaw, "The Soap Wars: A Strategic Analysis," *Fortune* (June 1963), pp. 122ff.

and Simpsons and The Bay with their Beaumark Brand. Almost every product distinguishable from another contains a means of identification for the buyer. Even a 5-year-old can distinguish a Chiquita banana from other ones. And the California Fruit Growers Exchange literally brands its oranges with the name Sunkist. The purchasing agent for a construction firm can turn over an ordinary sheet of roofing and find the name and symbol for Domtar. The choice of means of identification for the firm's output is often a major decision area for the marketing manager.

## Brands, Brand Names, and Trademarks

A **brand** is *a name, term, sign, symbol, design, or some combination used to identify the products of one firm and to differentiate them from competitive offerings.* A **brand name** is that part of the brand consisting of *words, letters or symbols making up a name used to identify and distinguish the firm's offerings from those of competitors.*[37] The brand name is, therefore, that part of the brand that may be vocalized. A **trademark** is *a brand that has been given legal protection and has been granted solely to its owner.* Thus, the term trademark includes not only pictorial design but also the brand name.[38] Many thousands of trademarks are currently registered in Canada.

For the consumer, brands allow repeat purchases of satisfactory products. The brand assures a uniform quality and identifies the firm producing the product. The purchaser associates the satisfaction derived from a carbonated soft drink with the brand name Pepsi-Cola.

For the marketing manager, the brand serves as the cornerstone around which the product's image is developed. Once consumers have been made aware of a particular brand, its appearance becomes further advertising for the firm. The Shell Oil Company symbol is instant advertising to motorists who view it while driving. Well-known brands also allow the firm to escape some of the rigours of price competition. Although any chemist will confirm that all ASA tablets contain the same amount of the chemical acetylsalicylic acid, Bayer has developed so strong a reputation that it can successfully market its Aspirin at a higher price than competitive products. Similarly, McDonald's "golden arches" attract customers to their outlets.

---

[37] Committee on Definitions, *Marketing Definitions: A Glossary of Marketing Terms* (Chicago: American Marketing Association, 1960), pp. 9–10.
[38] See Keith K. Cox, "Consumer Perception of Company Trademarks," *Journal of Business Research* (October 1970), pp. 128–131; and Sidney A. Diamond, "Trademark No. 1,000,000 Goes to 'Sweet 'N Low,' " *Advertising Age* (February 3, 1975), p. 39.

**What Constitutes a
Good Brand Name?**

Good brand names are easy to pronounce, recognize and remember.[39] Short names like Coke, Gleem, Dash, and Kodak meet these requirements. Multinational marketing firms face a particularly acute problem in selecting brand names in that an excellent brand name in one country may prove disastrous in another.

For 21 years, Nissan Motor Corporation marketers struggled with an easily mispronounced brand name for Datsun cars and trucks. Nissan found that in English-speaking nations some people pronounced the *a* like the *a* in *hat*, while others pronounced it like the *o* in *got*, and the difference hindered brand recogition. Finally, Nissan marketers decided to change the name of all of its automobile products to Nissan beginning with its Stanza model in 1982. Total costs of the change — to be effected in more than 135 countries — are estimated as high as $150 million.[40]

Every language has "O" and "K" sounds, and "okay" has become an international word. Every language also has a short "a," so that Coca-Cola and Texaco are good in any tongue. An American advertising campaign for E-Z washing machines failed in the United Kingdom because the British pronounce "Z" as "zed," as we do in Canada.

The brand name should give the buyer the right connotation. Mercury Marine presents favourable images of boating pleasures. The Craftsman name used on the Sears line of quality tools also produces the correct image. Accutron suggests the quality of the high-priced and accurate timepiece by the Bulova Watch Company. But what can the marketing manager do if the brand name is based on a strange-sounding company name? Sometimes the decision may be to poke fun at this improbable name in a promotional campaign built around the theme "With a name like Koogle, it has to be good!"

**The Brand Name
Should Be Legally
Protectable**

S. C. Johnson and Son, makers of OFF, lost a court case against Bug Off since it was held that OFF was an improper trademark, because it was not unusual enough to distinguish it from other similar products.[41]

*When all offerings in a class of products become generally known by the brand name of the first or leading brand in that product class,* the brand name may be ruled a descriptive **generic name**, and the original owner loses exclusive claim to it. Generic names like cola, nylon, zipper, kerosene, linoleum, escalator, and shredded wheat were once brand names.

---

[39] See Kenneth Uhl and Carl Block, "Some Findings Regarding Recall of Brand Marks: Descriptive Marks vs. Non-Descriptive Marks," *Journal of Business Research* (October 1969), pp. 1–10.

[40] "A Worldwide Brand for Nissan," *Business Week* (August 24, 1981), p. 104.

[41] See " 'OFF' Row ON Again," *Marketing* (May 8, 1978), p. 1.

Bayer's Aspirin is the only ASA tablet permitted to carry that protected trademark in Canada. All other acetylsalicylic acid tablets are called ASA. In the United States, because Bayer did not protect its trade name, the generic name "aspirin" is given to all acetylsalicylic acid tablets. Most drug purchasers there would not know what an ASA tablet is.

There is a difference between brand names that are legally generic and those that are generic in the eyes of many consumers. Jell-O is a brand name owned exclusively by General Foods. But to most grocery purchasers the name Jell-O is the descriptive generic name for gelatin dessert. Legal brand names, such as Formica, Xerox,

**From Brand Name to Generic Name**

# Nylon
# Aspirin
# Escalator
# Kerosene
# Zipper
# Addressograph

### Sometimes a company's product becomes so well known that its name becomes generic.

It's not going to happen to Addressograph, no sir. Even though some of our competitors have lately fallen into the unfortunate habit of using variations of our trademark to describe their equipment.

For 82 years, no one's beat us in offering you the broadest best line of addressing equipment. We make the addresser you need. We always will. And now we've added folders and inserters, too.

So the next time their salesman tells you he's got something that's "just like Addressograph", please help us protect our good name. Tell him that as far as you're

concerned "there's nothing like Addressograph."

Then call your nearby AM Representative. He'll show you why you're right. Or write: Dept. M., 1800 W. Central Rd., Mt. Prospect, Ill. 60056.

**We make you look better on paper.**

 **ADDRESSOGRAPH MULTIGRAPH**
MULTIGRAPHICS DIVISION

NOTE: Nylon, Aspirin, Escalator, Kerosene, and Zipper—all once registered trademarks—are now generic dictionary words. "Addressograph" remains a registered and protected trademark of Addressograph Multigraph Corp., as it has been since 1906.

Source: Courtesy of Addressograph Farrington Inc.

Frigidaire, Kodak, Frisbee, Styrofoam, Coke, Kleenex, Scotch Tape, Fiberglas, Band-Aid, and Jeep, are often used by consumers as descriptive names. Xerox is such a well-known brand name that it is frequently used as a verb. British and Australian consumers often use the brand name Hoover as a verb for vacuuming.

To prevent their brand names from being ruled descriptive and available for general use, companies must take deliberate steps to inform the public of their exclusive ownership of brand names. They may resort to legal action in cases of infringement. The Eastman Kodak Company developed a series of advertisements around the theme "If it isn't an Eastman, it isn't a Kodak." The Coca-Cola Company uses the ® symbol for registration immediately after the names Coca-Cola and Coke and sends letters to newspapers, novelists, and other writers who use the name Coke with a lower-case first letter, informing them that the name is owned by Coca-Cola.[42] These companies face the pleasant dilemma of attempting to retain the exclusive rights to a brand name that is generic to a large part of the market.

Since any dictionary word may eventually be ruled to be a generic name, some companies create new words to use for brand names. Brand names such as Keds, Rinso, and Kodak have obviously been created by their owners.

**Measuring Brand Loyalty**

Brands vary widely in consumer familiarity and acceptance.[43] While a boating enthusiast may insist on a Mercury outboard motor, one study revealed that 40 percent of homemakers could not identify the brands of furniture in their own homes.[44]

Brand loyalty may be measured in three stages: brand recognition, brand preference, and brand insistence.

**Brand recognition** is a company's first objective for newly introduced products — *to make them familiar to the consuming public.* Often the company achieves this through advertising. Sometimes it uses free samples or coupons offering discounts for purchases. Several new brands of toothpaste have been introduced on college campuses through free samples contained in Campus Pacs. Once the consumer has used the product, it moves from the "unknown" to the "known" category, and provided the consumer was satisfied with the trial sample, he or she is more likely to repurchase it.

---

42 John Koten, "Mixing with Coke over Trademarks is Always a Fizzle," *The Wall Street Journal* (March 9, 1978). For a thorough discussion of the brand
43 The question of brand choice is pursued in articles like J. Morgan Jones and Fred S. Ziefryden, "An Approach for Assessing Demographic and Price Influences on Brand Purchase Behavior," *Journal of Marketing* (Winter 1982), pp. 36–46.
44 *Business Week* (February 20, 1960), p. 71.

# What's in a Name Change?

For five years, executives at Alberta Gas Trunk Line Co. Ltd. toyed with the idea of changing the company's name. Alberta Gas Trunk, with its connotations of bewhiskered Victorians in frock coats tending rusted pipe, was hardly suitable for a company with more than $1 billion in annual revenues, diversified energy interests, and a mandate to build the Canadian portion of the Alaska Highway gas pipeline. But at an executive meeting in March 1980, they hit on an obvious choice, a name that connotes newness or life in a host of languages.

The formal changeover to "Nova, An Alberta Corporation" cost $2 million in media and regulatory expenses, equivalent to about half a day's revenues. "Nobody could ever get the old name right; it was old-fashioned and far too long," says Nova senior vice-president Dianne Hall. "We also felt it was time to tell all Canadians just how multifaceted we are."

If the change helps preserve Nova's share price from day-to-day stock market shocks, the three-month campaign will have been worthwhile. Not only that, the company is sure that the $1 million spent on advertising alone — including five television commercials and print ads in everything from rural weeklies to *Time* magazines — will erase forever any popular impression that the company is either a Crown corporation or a foreign-controlled resource monger.

Vancouver-based Intercorp Marketing Ltd. retained the Alberta Gas Trunk logo but came up with the six-part interlocking puzzle block — representing Nova's manufacturing, gas transmission, research, oil, petrochemical, and pipeline development interests — as a visual symbol of strength and diversity. Hall says that in general the feedback from shareholders and investment dealers has lived up to expectations. The francophone version of the campaign even elicited congratulations from Hydro-Quebec.

Source: Adapted from Martin Keeley, "What's in a Name Change? For Nova, a Cool $2 Million," *Canadian Business* (February 1981), pp. 22–23.

**Brand preference** is the second stage of brand loyalty. Because of previous experience with the product, *consumers will choose it rather than competitors — if it is available.* Even if students in a classroom prefer Coca-Cola as a means of quenching their thirst, almost all of them will quickly switch to Pepsi-Cola or 7-Up when they discover the vending machine has no Coke and the nearest supply is two buildings away. Companies with products at the brand-preference stage are in a favourable position in competing in their industries.

The ultimate stage in brand loyalty is **brand insistence** when *consumers will accept no alternatives and will search extensively for the product.* Such a product has achieved a monopoly position with this group of consumers. Even though brand insistence may be the goal of many firms, it is seldom achieved. Only the most exclusive specialty goods attain this position with a large segment of the total market.

*The Importance of Brand Loyalty*   A study of 12 patented drugs including well-known drugs like Librium and Darvon illustrates the importance of brand loyalty. The research indicated that patent expiration had minimal effect on the drugs' market shares or price levels, a resiliency credited to the brand loyalty for the pioneer product in the field.[45] Another measure of the importance of brand loyalty is found in the Brand Utility Yardstick used by the J. Walter Thompson advertising agency. These ratings measure the percentage of buyers who remain brand loyal even if a 50-percent cost savings was available from generic products. Beer consumers were very loyal with 48 percent refusing to switch. Sinus-remedy buyers were also brand loyal with a 44 percent rating. By contrast, only 13 percent of the aluminum-foil buyers would not switch to the generic product.[46]

Some brands are so popular that they are carried over to unrelated products because of their marketing advantages. *The decision to use a popular brand name for a new product entry in an unrelated product category* is known as **brand extension**. This should not be confused with line extension, which refers to new sizes, styles, or related products. Brand extension, by contrast, refers only to carrying over the brand name.

Examples of brand extension are abundant in contemporary marketing. Deere & Co.'s insurance line prominently features the John Deere brand made famous in the farm machinery business. In fact, John Deere Insurance proudly notes: "Our name is the best insurance you can buy." Similarly, General Foods is extending its Jell-O brand. In some markets the company now has Jell-O Pudding Pops, Jell-O Slice Creme, and Jell-O Gelatin Pops.[47]

*Choosing a Brand Strategy*

Brands may be classified as family brands or individual brands. A **family brand** is *one brand name used for several related products.* E. D. Smith markets dozens of food products under the E. D. Smith brand. Black & Decker Canada Inc. now has small appliances as well as power tools under the brand name Black & Decker. Johnson & Johnson offers parents a line of baby powder, lotions, plastic pants, and baby shampoo under one name.

On the other hand, manufacturers such as Procter & Gamble market hundreds of products with **individual brands**, such as Tide, Cheer, Crest, Gleem, Oxydol, and Dash. The item is *known by its own brand name rather than by the name of the company producing it or an umbrella name covering similar items.* Individual brands are more expensive to market since a new promotional program must be developed to introduce each new product to its market target.

---

[45] Meir Statman and Tyzoon T. Tyebjee, "Trademarks, Patents, and Innovation in the Ethical Drug Industry," *Journal of Marketing* (Summer 1981), pp. 71–81.
[46] Bill Abrams, "Brand Loyalty Rises Slightly, but Increase Could Be Fluke," *The Wall Street Journal* (February 7, 1982), p. 21.
[47] "Name Game," *Time* (August 31, 1981), p. 41.

The use of family brands allows promotional outlays to benefit all products in the line. The effect of the promotion is spread over each of the products. A new addition to the H. J. Heinz Company gains immediate recognition due to the well-known family brand. Use of family brands also facilitates the task of introducing the product—for both the customer and the retailer. Since supermarkets carry an average of nearly 10 000 items in stock, they are reluctant to add new products unless they are convinced of potential demand. A marketer of a new brand of turtle soup would have to promise the supermarket chain buyer huge advertising outlays for promotion and evidence of consumer buying intent before getting the product into the stores. The Campbell Soup Company, with approximately 85 percent of the market, would merely add the new flavour to its existing line and could secure store placements much more easily than could a company using individual brand names.

Family brands should be used only when the products are of similar quality—or the firm risks the danger of harming its product image. Use of the Mercedes brand name on a new, less expensive auto model might severely tarnish the image of the other models in the Mercedes product line.

Individual brand names should be used for dissimilar products. Campbell Soup once marketed a line of dry soups under the brand name Red Kettle. Large marketers of grocery products, such as Procter & Gamble, General Foods, and Lever Brothers, employ individual brands to appeal to unique market segments. Unique brands also allow the firm to stimulate competition within the organization and to increase total company sales. Product managers are also freer to try different merchandising techniques with individual brands. Homemakers who do not prefer Tide may choose Dash or Oxydol rather than purchase a competitor's brand.

## National Brands or Private Brands?

Most of the brands mentioned in this chapter have been *manufacturers' brands*, commonly termed **national brands**. But, to an increasing extent, *large wholesalers and retailers operating over a regional or national market are placing their own brands on the products that they market*. These brands offered by wholesalers and retailers are usually called **private brands**. Eaton's carries its own brands such as Viking, Birkdale, Haddon Hall, Eatonia, and Teco. Safeway store shelves are filled with such company brands as Edwards, Town House, Empress, and Taste Tells. Safeway brands represent a large percentage of all products in an average Safeway supermarket.

For a large retailer such as Eaton's, The Bay, or Canadian Tire, private brands allow the firm to establish an image and to attain greater control over the products that it handles. Quality levels, prices, and availability of the products become the responsibility of the retailer or wholesaler who develops a line of private brands.

Even though the manufacturers' brands are largely presold through national promotional efforts, the wholesaler and retailer may easily lose customers since the same products may be available in competing stores. But only Eaton's handles the Viking line of appliances. By eliminating the promotional costs of the manufacturers' brands, the dealer can often offer a private brand at a lower price than the competing national brands or make higher margins. Both consumers and the company benefit. As private brands achieve increasing brand loyalty they may even enable a retailer to avoid some price competition since the brand can only be sold by the brand owner.

**Battle of the Brands**   Competition between manufacturers' brands and the private brands offered by wholesalers and large retailers has been called the "battle of the brands." Although the battle appears to be intensifying, the marketing impact varies widely among industries. One survey showed that private brands represented 36 percent of the market in replacement tires but only 7 percent in portable appliances. Fifty-two percent of shoe sales are by private brands. For example, Agnew Surpass and Bata stores distribute their own private brands. Department stores capture about 53 percent of heavy appliance sales, most of which are private brands.[48]

The growh of private brands has paralleled the growth of chain stores in Canada. Most of the growth for both has occurred since the 1930s. The chains with their own brands become customers of the manufacturer, who will place the chains' private brands on the products that the firm produces. Such leading corporations as Westinghouse, Armstrong Rubber, and Heinz obtain an increasingly larger percentage of total sales through private labels.

Even though the battle of the brands is far from over, it is clear that great inroads have been made on the dominance of the manufacturers' national brands. Private brands have proven that they can compete with the national brands and have often succeeded in causing price reductions on the national brands to make them more competitive.

**Generic Products**   *Food and household staples characterized by plain labels, little or no advertising, and no brand names* are called **generic products**. Generic products were first sold in Europe, where their prices were as much as 30 percent below brand name products. By 1979, they had captured 40 percent of total volume in European supermarkets.

---

[48] Frances Phillips, "Private Label Appliances Vie with National Brands," *The Financial Post*, Aug. 13, 1983, p. 12.

This new version of private brands has received significant acceptance in Canada. Surveys indicate that both professional, college-educated consumers and lower-income, blue-collar consumers are heavy purchasers of generics. Canned vegetables are the most commonly purchased generic product, followed by fruits and paper goods. Shoppers are indicating some willingness to forgo the known quality levels of regular brands in exchange for the lower prices of the generics.[49]

For all food categories in Ontario food chain stores generics represented 10.4 percent, private brands 10.8 percent, and national brands 78.8 percent of the volume. The proportion held by generics remained about constant over three years, but private labels lost about three points to national brands.[50] Thus in the retail food industry, private brands seem to be caught between the success of generic products and the continuing influence of national brands. According to Dominion Stores' director of advertising, Craig Hemming, private brands seem to have slipped from the minds of consumers. Since they are unique to each retail chain, firms like Dominion are beginning to develop special advertising campaigns to re-emphasize them.[51]

---

**Packaging**    In a very real sense the package is a vital part of the total product. Indeed, in an overcrowded supermarket, packaging very often *is* the significant difference between one product and another. Take Nabob, for example. Nabob coffee was packaged in a new type of tough, vacuum-seal package which gave the coffee greater freshness. "Five years ago our market share [of the ground coffee market] was 5%," says John Bell, vice-president of marketing. "Today we have 26%."[52]

---

[49] See Norman Seigle, "Generic Foods—A Further Report," *Nargus Merchandising Letter* (May 1980); Robert Dietrich, "Still Rooted in the Basics, Generics Sprout New Buds Too," *Progressive Grocer* (May 1980), p. 119. Generics are also discussed in Robert H. Ross and Frederic B. Kraft, "Creating Low Consumer Product Expectations," *Journal of Business Research* (March, 1983), pp. 1–9; Betsy Gelb, " 'No-Name' Products: A Step towards 'No-Name' Retailing," *Business Horizons* (June 1980), pp. 9–13; and Joseph A. Bellizzi, Harry F. Krueckelbert, and John R. Hamilton, "A Factor Analysis of National, Private, and Generic Brand Attributes," in *1981 Proceedings of the Southwestern Marketing Association*, (eds.) Robert H. Ross, Frederic B. Kraft, and Charles H. Davis, pp. 208–210.

[50] Osama Al-Zand and Joseph Bitton, "Development of Performance of Generic Foods in Canada," *Food Market Commentary*, Vol. 5, No. 1, March 1983, p. 23.

[51] "Private Brands Get More Public Attention," *Marketing* (August 29, 1983), p. 1.

[52] Frances Phillips, "New Packaging Looks are Making Some Products Winners," *The Financial Post* (June 4, 1983), p. 24.

# The Story Behind Generic Food Products

What really lurks behind those mystery products wrapped in plain, no-name packages? Each generic product has its own story, says David Nichol, president of the Ontario division of Toronto-based Loblaws Ltd. Some items are produced by the same people who make the leading name brands. In fact, sometimes the products are the same as the national brands because the manufacturers often sell their extra stock to supermarkets.

But in most cases, generic products are made for the supermarket chains to their specifications — the supermarkets decide everything from the quality of the product to the packaging. Usually generic products are a lower quality than the national brands and that is why they cost less. Supermarket executives make no secret about this fact. They simply say they are providing customers with a choice that is not offered by the major manufacturers.

Generics provide the minimum standards to get the job done. A bleach, for example, will have a lower acid content or a chocolate chip cookie will have fewer chips. Almost all of the major grocery manufacturers make no-frill, generic products — even those that have a chunk of the market grabbed by the generics. It is one way to make use of otherwise surplus capacity. No-frills are also produced by custom manufacturers that will make almost anything if the price is right.

Mr. Nichol said the no-frill pancake mix carried by Loblaws comes from Robin Hood Multifoods Ltd. of Montreal. Robin Hood developed the product some time ago, but found it could not compete with the more popular Aunt Jemima brand, produced by Quaker Oats Co. of Canada Ltd. of Peterborough, Ont. So Robin Hood has been content to make the mix for Loblaws as a generic. This is one generic product that has a quality comparable to the national brand, Mr. Nichol said.

Source: Paul Taylor, "Chains Decide Grade of Generic Produced to Their Specifications," Toronto *Globe and Mail* (April 14, 1980), p. B2.

Packaging represents a vital component of the total product concept. Its importance can be inferred from the size of the packaging industry. Approximately $50 billion is spent annually on packaging in Canada. A study of packaging costs in the food industry[53] found that total packaging costs as a percentage of net processed food sales range from 4 to 59 percent, averaging about 22 percent. In the cases where packaging costs appear disproportionately high, ingredient costs were found to be very low (e.g. salt).

The package has several objectives that can be grouped into three general categories: 1) protection against damage, spoilage, and pilferage; 2) assisting to market the product; and 3) cost effectiveness.

**Protection Against Damage, Spoilage, and Pilferage**
The original purpose of packaging was to offer physical protection. The typical product is handled several times between manufacture and consumer purchase, and its package must protect the contents

---

[53] See M. Dale Beckman, "An Analysis of Food Packaging Costs: Does Packaging Cost Too Much?" in *ASAC 1978 Conference Proceedings* (London, Ont.: University of Western Ontario, 1978).

against damage. Perishable products must also be protected against spoilage in transit, in storage, or while awaiting selection by the consumer.

Another important role provided by many packages for the retailer is in preventing pilferage, which at the retail level, is very costly. Many products are packaged with oversized cardboard backings too large to fit into a shoplifter's pocket or purse. Large plastic packages are used in a similar manner on such products as eight-track and cassette tapes.

***Assisting to Market the Product***  Package designers frequently use marketing research in testing alternative designs. Increasingly scientific approaches are utilized in designing a package that is attractive, safe, and esthetically appealing. Kellogg's, for instance, tested the package for a new product as well as the product itself.[54]

In a grocery store containing as many as 15 000 different items, a product must capture the shopper's attention. Walter Margulies, chairman of Lippincott & Margulies advertising, summarizes the importance of first impressions in the retail store: "Consumers are more intelligent, but they don't read as much. They relate to pictures." Margulies also cites another factor: one of every six shoppers who needs eyeglasses does not wear them while shopping. Consequently, many marketers offering product lines are adopting similar package designs throughout the line in order to create more visual impact in the store. The adoption of common package designs by such product lines as Weight Watchers foods and Planter's nuts represent attempts to dominate larger sections of retail stores as Campbell's does.[55]

Packages can also offer the consumer convenience. Pump dispenser cans facilitate the use of products ranging from mustard to insect repellent. Pop-top cans provide added convenience for soft drinks, and other food products. The six-pack carton, first introduced by Coca-Cola in the 1930s, can be carried with minimal effort by the food shopper.

A growing number of firms provide increased consumer utility with packages designed for reuse. Peanut butter jars and jelly jars have long been used as drinking glasses. Bubble bath can be purchased in plastic bottles shaped like animals and suitable for bathtub play. Packaging is a major component in Avon's overall marketing strategy. The firm's decorative reusable bottles have even become collectibles.

---

[54] "Packaging Linked to Ad's Effect," *Advertising Age* (May 3, 1982), p. 63.
[55] Bill Abrams and David P. Garino, "Package Design Gains Stature as Visual Competition Grows," *The Wall Street Journal* (August 6, 1981).

**Cost Effective** Although packaging must perform a number of functions for the
**Packaging** producer, marketer, and consumer, it must accomplish them at a
reasonable cost. Packaging currently represents the single largest
item in the cost of producing numerous products. For example, it
accounts for 70 percent of the total cost of the single-serving pack-
ets of sugar found in restaurants. However, restaurants continue to
use the packs because of the saving in wastage and washing and
refilling sugar containers.

An excellent illustration of how packaging can be cost effective
is provided by the large Swedish firm. Tetra-Pak. They pioneered
aseptic packaging for products like milk and juice. Aseptic packaging wraps a laminated paper around a sterilized product and seals it
off. The big advantage of the packaging technology is that products
can be kept unrefrigerated for months. Aseptically packed sterilized
milk, for instance, will keep its nutritional qualities and flavour for
six months. With 60 percent of a supermarket's energy bill going
for refrigeration, aseptic packaging is certainly cost effective. The
paper packaging is also cheaper and lighter than the cans and bottles used for unrefrigerated fruit juices. Handling cost can also be
reduced in many cases.[56]

**Labelling** Although in the past the label was often a separate item applied to
the package, most of today's plastic packages contain the label as
an integral part of the package. Labels perform both a promotional
and an informational function. A **label** in most instances *contains
1) brand name or symbol, 2) name and address of the manufacturer
or distributor, 3) product composition and size, and 4) recommended
uses of the product.*

Government-set and voluntary packaging and label standards
have been developed in most industries. The law requires a listing
of food ingredients, in descending order of the amounts used, and
labels of such companies as Del Monte Corporation now show
specific food values and include a calorie count and a list of vitamins
and minerals. In other industries, such as drugs, fur, and clothing,
federal legislation requires the provision of various information and
prevents false branding. The marketing manager in such industries
must be fully acquainted with these laws and must design the package and label in compliance with these requirements.

The informational aspect of a label is particularly noteworthy.
Figure 11-7 depicts the results of a study of consumer expectations
for drug labels. People who condemn all types of elaborate or fancy
packaging fail to realize that the information on the label and the
nature of the container enhance the product itself. In some cases,

---

[56] Robert Ball, "Warm Milk Wakes Up the Packaging Industry," *Fortune*
(August 7, 1982), pp. 78–82.

Figure 11-7 What Consumers Want on Drug Labels

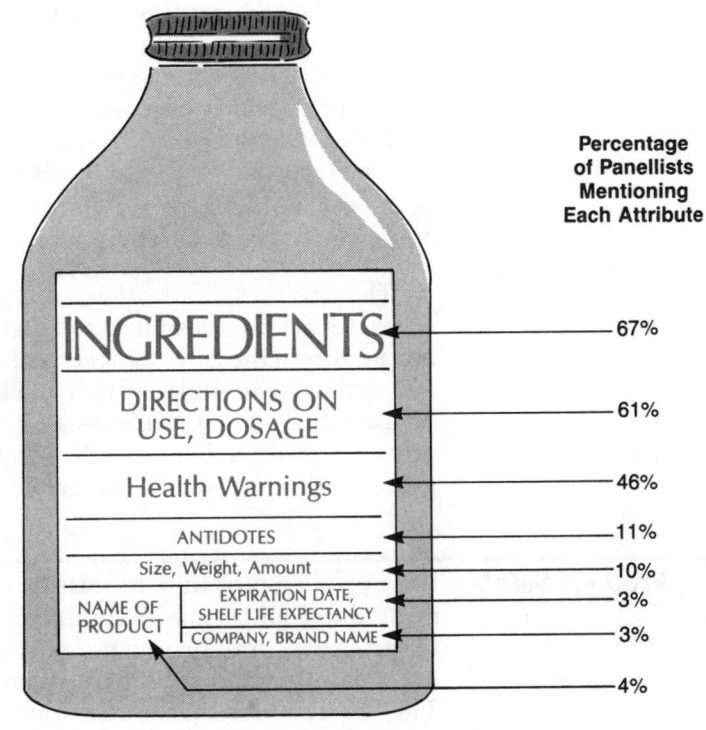

**Percentage of Panellists Mentioning Each Attribute**

INGREDIENTS — 67%

DIRECTIONS ON USE, DOSAGE — 61%

Health Warnings — 46%

ANTIDOTES — 11%

Size, Weight, Amount — 10%

NAME OF PRODUCT

EXPIRATION DATE, SHELF LIFE EXPECTANCY — 3%

COMPANY, BRAND NAME — 3%

— 4%

Source: *Sales Management* (September 15, 1970), p. 46. Reprinted by permission from *Sales Management, The Marketing Magazine*, copyright 1970.

the dispenser is almost as important as the contents and is really an integral part of the total "product." Furthermore, with the advent of self-service nearly everywhere, the information on the label takes the place of a salesperson. Self-service improves marketing efficiency and lowers costs.

**Universal Product Code (UPC)** The Universal Product Code (UPC) designation is another very important point of a label or package. A great number of packages now display the zebra-stripe UPC on the label. In other cases, the code lines are printed right into the package, such as on a can of Tab.

The **Universal Product Code**, introduced as an attempt to cut expenses in the supermarket industry, is *a code read by optical scanners that can print the name of the item and the price on the cash register receipt.* Some 95 percent of all packaged grocery items contain the UPC lines.

While the initial cost of UPC scanners is high — about $125 000 for a four-lane supermarket — they do permit considerable cost savings. The advantages include:

1. Labour saving because products are no longer individually priced.
2. Faster customer check-out.
3. Better inventory control since the scanners can be tied to inventory records.
4. Easier marketing research for the industries involved with it.
5. Fewer errors in entering purchases at the check-out counter.

Despite these and other advantages, UPC still faces several obstacles. Many consumers still do not understand the purpose and advantages of the UPC scanners. In some localities, regulations specifically require items to be individually priced, thus negating much of the labour savings advantage of UPC scanners. It is obvious, however, that the Universal Product Code is going to play an even greater role in product management over the next few years.

## Product Safety

If the product is to fulfil its mission of satisfying consumer needs, it must above all be safe. Manufacturers must design their products in such a way as to protect not only children but all consumers who use them. Packaging can play an important role in product safety. The law requires that bottle tops of dangerous products such as pharmaceuticals be child-proof (some are virtually parent-proof). This safety feature has reduced by two-thirds the number of children under five years of age who swallow dangerous doses of ASA. Prominent safety warnings on the labels of such potentially hazardous products as cleaning fluids and drain cleaners inform users of the dangers of these products and urge purchasers to store them out of the reach of children. Changes in product design have reduced the dangers involved in the use of such products as lawn mowers, hedge trimmers, and toys.

The need for fire-retardant fabrics for children's sleepwear was recognized long before federal regulations were established. While fire-retardant fabrics were available, the problems lay in how to produce them to meet consumer requirements in the areas of softness, colour, texture, durability, and reasonable cost. Monsanto spent seven years and millions of dollars in research before introducing a satisfactory fabric in 1972. Today government flame-retardancy standards are strictly enforced.

Federal and provincial legislation has long played a major role in promoting product safety. The **Hazardous Products Act**, passed in 1969, was a major piece of legislation, consolidating previous legislation and setting significant new standards for product safety.

---

**Figure 11-8    Some Hazardous Products Act Regulations**

Bedding may not be highly flammable.

Children's sleepwear, dressing gowns, and robes must meet flammability standards.

Children's toys or equipment may not contain toxic substances, such as lead pigments beyond a prescribed limit.

Two plastic balloon-blowing kits containing organic solvents are banned.

Certain household chemical products must be labelled with appropriate symbols to alert consumers to their hazards.

Hockey helmets must meet safety standards to protect young hockey players.

Pencils and artists' brushes are regulated to limit lead in their decorative coating.

Matches must meet safety standards for strength and packaging.

Safety glass is mandatory in domestic doors and shower enclosures.

Liquid drain cleaners and furniture polishes containing petroleum solvents must be sold in child-proof packaging.

Toys and children's playthings must comply with safety standards.

Crib regulations provide for increased child safety.

---

The Act defines a hazardous product as any product that is included in a list called a schedule compiled by Consumer and Corporate Affairs Canada or Health and Welfare Canada. Any consumer product considered to be a hazard to public health or safety may be listed in the schedule. Figure 11-8 lists some of the main items and outlines the regulations that affect them.

The Act itself consists of just 15 clauses. Those relating to criminal penalties and seizure put sharp teeth in the law. Inspectors designated under the Act have powers of search and seizure. Hazardous products inspectors may enter, at any reasonable time, any place where they reasonably believe a hazardous product is manufactured, prepared, packaged, sold, or stored for sale. They may examine the product, take samples, and examine any records believed to contain information relevant to enforcement of the Act. Products that an inspector has reasonable grounds to believe are in contravention of the Act may be seized.

These regulatory activities have prompted companies voluntarily to improve safety standards for their products. For many companies, safety has become a very important ingredient in the broader definition of product.

---

**Summary**    A product mix is the assortment of product lines and individual offerings available from a marketer. A product line is a series of related products, and an individual offering is a single product offered within that line. Product mixes are assessed in terms of width and depth of assortment. Width of assortment refers to the variety of product lines offered, while depth refers to the extent of the line. Firms usually produce several related products rather than a single product in order to achieve the objectives of growth, optimal use of company resources, and increased company importance in the market.

New products experience a decay curve from idea generation to commercialization. Only one of 58 new product ideas typically makes it all the way to commercialization. The success of a new product depends on a host of factors and can be the result of four alternative product development strategies: product improvement, market development, product development, and product diversification.

The organizational responsibility for new products in most large firms is assigned to new-product committees, new-product departments, product managers, or venture teams. New product ideas evolve through seven stages before their market introduction: 1) development of new product strategy, 2) idea generation, 3) screening, 4) business analysis, 5) product development, 6) test marketing, and 7) commercialization.

While new products are added to the line, old ones may face deletion from it. The typical causes for product eliminations are unprofitable sales and failure to fit into the existing product line.

Product identification may take the form of brand names, symbols, distinctive packaging, and labelling. Effective brand names should be easy to pronounce, recognize, and remember; they should give the right connotation to the buyer; and they should be legally protectable. Brand loyalty can be measured in three stages: brand recognition, brand preference, and finally, band insistence. Marketing managers must decide whether to use a single family brand for their product line or to use an individual brand for each product. Retailers have to decide the relative mix of national and private brands as well as generic products that they will carry.

Modern packaging is designed to: 1) protect against damage, spoilage, and pilferage; 2) assist in marketing the product; and 3) be cost effective. Labels identify the product, producer, content, size, and uses of a packaged product. Most products also contain a Universal Product Code designation so that optical check-out scanners can be used.

Product safety has become an increasingly important component of the total product concept. This change has occurred through voluntary attempts by product designers to reduce hazards and through strict requirements established by Consumer and Corporate Affairs Canada.

**Key Terms**

product mix
product line
individual offering
cannibalizing
line extension
product positioning
product managers
venture teams
concept testing
brand
brand name
trademark
generic names

brand recognition
brand preference
brand insistence
brand extension
family brand
individual brand
national brand
private brand
generic product
label
Universal Product Code
Hazardous Products Act

**Review Questions**

1. What is meant by a product mix? How is the concept used in making effective marketing decisions?
2. Why do most business firms market a line of related products rather than a single product?
3. Explain the new-product decay curve.
4. Outline the alternative organizational structures for new-product development.
5. Identify the steps in the new-product development process.
6. What is the chief purpose of test marketing? What potential problems are involved in it?
7. List the characteristics of an effective brand name. Illustrate each characteristic with an appropriate brand name.
8. Identify and briefly explain each of the three stages of brand loyalty.
9. What are the objectives of modern packaging?
10. Explain the chief elements of the Hazardous Products Act.

**Discussion Questions and Exercises**

1. General Foods gave up on Lean Strips, a textured vegetable protein strip designed as a bacon substitute, after eight years of test marketing. Lean Strips sold well when bacon prices were high but poorly when they were low. General Foods hoped to offer a protein analogue product line that also included Crispy Strips, a snack and salad dressing item. Consumers liked the taste of Crispy Strips but felt it was too expensive for repeat purchases, and the product was abandoned before Lean Strips' demise. General Foods decided to concentrate on new product categories instead of on individual items like Lean Strips. What can be learned from General Food's experience with Lean Strips?

2. A firm's new-product idea suggestion program has produced a design for a portable car washer that can be attached to a domestic garden hose. Outline a program for deciding whether the product should be marketed by the firm.

3. Campbell Soup Company's Belgian candy company, Godiva Chocolates, introduced a designer line called "Bill Blass Chocolates." The premium chocolates sold for $14 per pound. Relate this action to the material discussed in Chapter 11.

4. Exxene, a $1 million manufacturer of antifog coatings for goggles, was sued for trademark infringement by Exxon Corp. The oil company giant claimed that it had nearly exclusive rights to the letters *EXX* regardless of what followed it. Four and a half years later, a jury awarded Exxene $250 000 in damages instead. Exxon filed an appeal. Relate this case to the discussion of trademarks.

# CHAPTER 12

# Services

Suppose that you live in Victoria, and must have a meeting with several people in St. John's. A new service greatly expands your alternatives for holding that meeting. Traditionally, one would expect to take several days to fly to Newfoundland, hold the meeting and return. Conference 600 is a nation-wide, fully interactive, two-way videoconferencing service which can save direct costs of travel and hotels in addition to the time taken to travel.

Telecom Canada suggests that the benefits can be substantial. For example, for a meeting of six people in St. John's conferring with six others from Victoria, airfares and hotel bills alone would cost about $7600. A four-hour meeting on Conference 600 would come to about $4000.

The secret of Conference 600 is an advanced picture processor that converts the video signal to digital form and enables the signal to be compressed by as much as 60 times. The signal is transferred by Anik C, but the compression reduces demand on capacity of the satellite and thus on earthly costs.

The name of the company providing the service is also new. Telecom Canada used to be known as the TransCanada Telephone System. The advent of technology that goes beyond that of the telephone and the potential of a huge market has led to the change in name.[1]

---

[1] Adapted from Robert L. Perry, "Telecom Takes to The Airwaves for Business," *The Financial Post*, (Sept. 17, 1983), p. 39.

A tremendous amount of economic activity is accounted for by service industries. These range from communications enterprises like Telecom Canada to life insurance, pizza restaurants, and cleaning services for office buildings. Marketing planning for services is similar to that for products, yet there are some important differences.

## The Conceptual Framework

The first two chapters in this section on product/service strategy dealt with the basic concepts of this aspect of marketing. Product lines, product life cycles, branding, and classification systems are examples of some of these concepts.

Chapter 12 deals with services. In a fundamental sense, marketers approach the development of marketing programs for both products and services in the same manner. Such programs begin with an investigation, analysis, and selection of a particular market target and follow with the development of a marketing mix designed to satisfy the chosen target. Although tangible products and intangible services are similar in that both provide consumer benefits, there are significant differences in the marketing of the two. Both the similarities and differences are examined in this chapter. Services are treated in a special chapter because of two factors:

1) the immense size of the service industry market sector; and
2) the differences between marketing strategies for services and for tangible products.[2]

## Services: A Definition

Services are troublesome to define. It is difficult to distinguish between certain kinds of goods and services. Personal services, such as hair styling and dry cleaning, are easily recognized as services, but these are only a small portion of the total service industry.

Some firms provide both goods and services. A protection specialist may market alarms and closed-circuit TVs (goods) as well as uniformed guards (a service). A dentist's business may also be divided into goods and service components. A bridge, crown, or filling is a good, while the dentist's professional skills are a service. Some services are an integral part of the marketing of physical goods. Thus, a computer sales representative may emphasize his or her firm's *service* capabilities to minimize machine down-time. These illustrations suggest that business needs some method to alleviate the problems of definition in the marketing of services.

One useful approach is a products spectrum, which shows most products to have both goods and services segments. Figure 12-1

---

[2] Some of the material in this chapter is adapted from Eugene M. Johnson, "The Selling of Services" in Victor P. Buell (ed.), *Handbook of Modern Marketing* (New York: McGraw-Hill, 1970), pp. 12–110 to 12–120.

presents a **goods-services continuum**, a method that is *useful in visualizing the differences and similarities among goods and services.*[3] A tire is relatively a pure good, although services like balancing may be sold along with the product (or included in the total price). Hair styling, at the other end of the spectrum, is relatively a pure service. The middle of the continuum consists of products with both goods and services components. The satisfaction that comes from dining in an exclusive restaurant is derived not only from the food and drink but also from the services rendered by the establishment's personnel.

While it is difficult, if not impossible, to describe in one definition all of the services that are available to consumers, a general definition can be developed. *A* **service** *is a product with no physical characteristics; it is a bundle of performance and symbolic attributes designed to produce consumer want satisfaction.*

Figure 12-1   Goods-Services Continuum

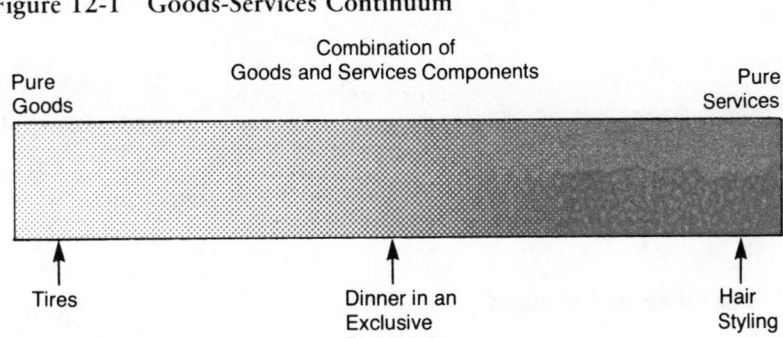

Source: After John M. Rathmell, "What Is Meant by Services?" in *Journal of Marketing* (October, 1966), published by the American Marketing Association.

**The Nature of the Service Sector**

There has been a considerable increase in expenditure for consumer services over the past decade. Services—ranging from such necessities as electric power and dry cleaning to such luxuries as foreign travel, backpacking guides, ski resorts, and hockey schools—now account for over 40 percent of the average consumer's total expenditures. Services also provide about two-thirds of all jobs. In fact, total employment in the Canadian economy more than doubled from 1950 to 1980 and nearly 90 percent of this increase took

[3] A goods-services continuum is suggested in G. Lynn Shostock, "Breaking Free from Product Marketing," *Journal of Marketing* (April 1977), p. 77. See also John M. Rathmell, "What Is Meant by Services?" *Journal of Marketing* (October 1966), pp. 32–36.

place in the service-producing sector. The distribution of persona consumption expenditures for goods and services is shown in Fig ure 12-2.

The increasing complexity of modern business has also provided substantial opportunities for business service firms such as Deloitt Haskins & Sells (public accountants), A. C. Nielsen (marketing research), and Brinks, Inc. (protection). For most consumer and business service firms, marketing is an emerging activity for two reasons: 1) the growth potential of the service market represents a vast marketing opportunity, and 2) increased competition is forc ing traditional service industries to emphasize marketing in order to compete in the marketplace.

**Figure 12-2   Personal Consumption Expenditures for Selected Years**

| | Percent Distribution | | | | | | |
|---|---|---|---|---|---|---|---|
| | Actual | | | | | Forecast | |
| | 1955 | 1960 | 1970 | 1981 | 1982 | 1985 | 1987 |
| Durable Goods | 14.1 | 11.6 | 13.2 | 13.8 | 12.3 | 15.0 | 15.2 |
| Semidurable Goods | 55.8 | 55.1 | 13.1 | 11.8 | 11.0 | 11.0 | 10.9 |
| Nondurable Goods | | | 31.8 | 31.1 | 32.0 | 31.8 | 32.0 |
| Services | 30.1 | 37.3 | 42.0 | 43.3 | 44.7 | 42.2 | 41.9 |

Source: Statistics Canada, *National Income and Expenditure Accounts*, Catalogue 13-001, 1983, pp. 42–43. Forecast adapted from *Market Research Handbook, 1983*, Catalogue 63-224, p. 344.

**Features of Services**

The preceding discussion suggests that services are varied and complex. Following are the four key features of services that have major marketing implications:
1. Services are intangible.
2. Services are perishable.
3. Services are often not standardized.
4. Buyers are often involved in the development and distribution of services.

*Intangibility*   Services do not have tangible features that appeal to consumers' senses of sight, hearing, smell, taste, and touch. They are therefore difficult to demonstrate at trade fairs, to display in retail stores, to illustrate in magazine advertisements, and to sample. Consequently, imaginative personal selling is usually an essential ingredient in the marketing of services.

Furthermore, buyers are often unable to judge the quality of a service before buying it. Because of this, the reputation of the service's vendor is often a key factor in the buying decision. Consumers are literally buying a promise, so it is important to "tangibilize" services. A good example is an architect's rendering of an office building that shows contented workers enjoying a casual lunch in a beautiful courtyard.[4]

Service marketers are sometimes perceived as more personal, friendlier, and more co-operative than goods marketers. These and other distinctive personal elements are a main component of interservice competition. Personal contact between salespeople and customers occurs in the marketing of goods as well as services; however, for service representatives it plays an even more important role. One writer described it in this way:

> With service retailing there is a change in the sequence of events that occur—the sale must be made before production and consumption take place. Thus the truism that all customer contact employees are engaged in personal selling is much more real for the service firm than for the goods firm. With goods, the physical object can carry some of the selling burden. With services, contact personnel *are* the service. Customers, in effect, perceive them to be "the product." They become the physical representation of the offering. The service firm employees are both factory workers *and* salespersons because of the simultaneous production and consumption of most services.

*Perishability*   The utility of most services is short-lived; therefore, they cannot be produced ahead of time and stored for periods of peak demand. Vacant seats on an airplane, idle dance instructors, and unused electrical generating capacity represent economic losses that can never be recovered. Sometimes, however, idle facilities during slack periods must be tolerated so the firm will have sufficient capacity for peak periods. Electric and natural gas utilities, resort hotels, telephone companies, and airlines all face the problem of perishability.

Some service firms are able to overcome this problem with off-peak pricing. Resorts feature high and low season pricing schemes, the telephone company grants reduced rates on Sunday, and baseball teams offer low-priced general admission seats.

*Difficulty of Standardization*   Services are often dissimilar since it is frequently impossible to standardize offerings among sellers of the same service, or even to assure consistency in the services provided by one seller. For instance, no two hair styles from the same hairdresser are identical. Although the standardization of services is often desirable, it occurs only in the case of equipment-based firms, such as those offering automated banking services, car washes, and computer time-sharing. Creative marketing is needed to adapt

---

4 Theodore Levitt, "Marketing Intangible Products and Product Intangibles," *Harvard Business Review* (May–June 1981), pp. 94–102. The example is from pp. 96–97.

satisfactorily a nonstandardized service to the needs of individual customers.

*Involvement of Buyers*   Buyers often play major roles in the marketing and production of services. The hair stylist's customer may describe the desired style and make suggestions at several stages during the styling process. Different firms often require unique blends of insurance coverage, and the final policy may be developed after several meetings between the purchaser and the insurance agent. Although purchaser specifications also play a role in the creation of major products such as installations, the interaction of buyer and seller at both the production and the distribution stages is a common feature of services.

**Classifying Consumer and Industrial Services**   Literally thousands of services are available to consumer and industrial users. In some instances, they are provided by specialized machinery with almost no personal assistance (such as an automated car wash). In other cases, the services are provided by skilled professionals with little reliance on specialized equipment (such as accountants and management consultants). Figure 12-3 provides a means of classifying services based on the following factors: the degree of reliance on equipment in providing the service, and the degree of skill possessed by the people who provide the service.

**Buyer Behaviour**   Important elements of buyer behaviour were discussed in Chapters 7 and 8. There are many similarities between buyer behaviour for goods and for services, yet some important differences exist. These differences may be grouped into three categories — 1) attitudes, 2) needs and motives, and 3) purchase behaviour. In most of these the personal element of the services is the key to the consumer's decision of which services to purchase.[5]

---

[5] This section is based on Eugene M. Johnson, "Are Goods and Services Different? — An Exercise in Marketing Theory," unpublished DBA dissertation, Washington University, 1969, pp. 83–205. Used by permission. See also Leonard L. Berry, "Services Marketing Is Different," *Business* (May–June 1980), pp. 24–29; Joseph L. Orsini, "Strategic Implications of Differences between Goods and Services: An Empirical Analysis of Information Source Importance," in *Proceedings of the 1982 Conference of the Western Marketing Educators*, (ed.) Stephen H. Achtenhagen, pp. 61–62; and Duane L. Davis and Robert M. Cosenza, "Identifying Search Prone Segments in the Service Sector: A Test of Taxonometric Research," in *Developments in Marketing Science*, (eds.) Vinay Kothari, Danny R. Arnold, Tamer Cavusgil, Jay D. Lindquist, Jay Nathan, and Stan Reid (Las Vegas, Nevada: Proceedings of the Sixth Annual Conference of the Academy of Marketing Science, 1982), pp. 301–305.

**Figure 12-3   Types of Service Businesses**

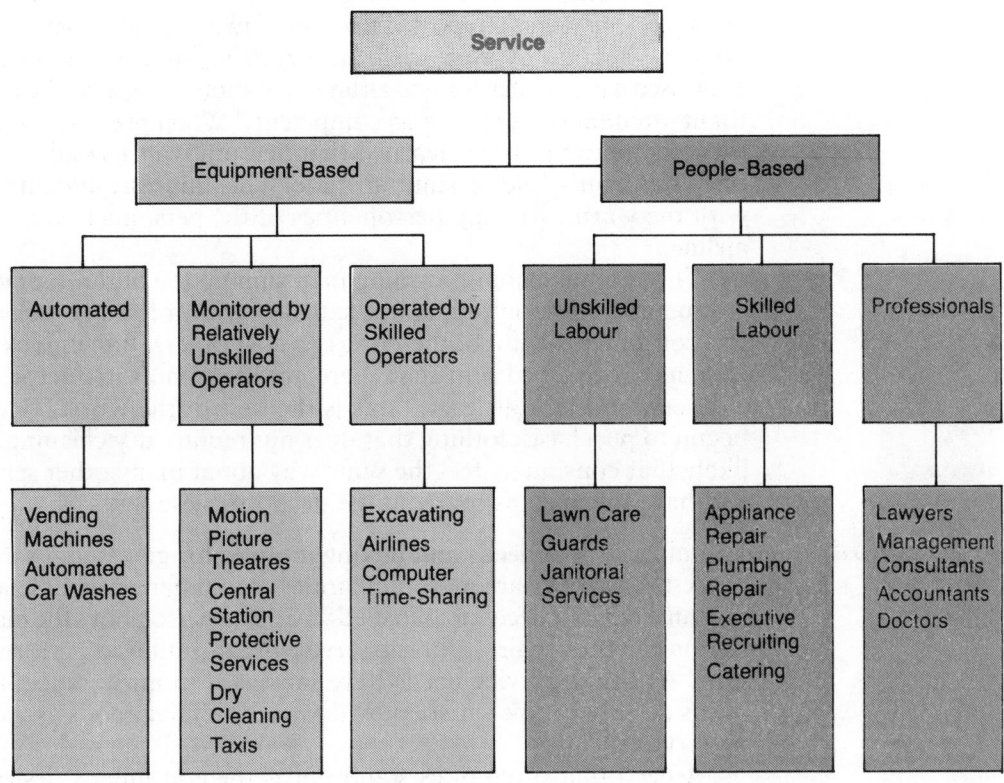

**Attitudes**   For almost any product or service a consumer's attitudes will directly influence his or her buying decision. Attitudes seem to be especially pertinent to the marketing of services since services are intangible. This probably causes buyers to emphasize their subjective impressions of a service and its seller when buying a service. This is less true in the purchase of tangible goods. Two attributes appear to represent important distinctions between goods and services: 1) services are perceived as being more personal than goods, and 2) consumers are sometimes less satisfied with purchases of services.[6]

Dissatisfaction with the personal elements of a service, such as

[6] William R. George, "The Retailing of Services — A Challenging Future," *Journal of Retailing* (Fall 1977), pp. 89–90. See also Richard B. Chase, "Where Does the Customer Fit in a Service Operation?" *Harvard Business Review* (November–December 1978), pp. 137–142.

an unfriendly flight attendant or impolite bank teller, is likely to lead to an attitude of dissatisfaction with the entire service. For example, one woman reported that her Hawaii vacation was marred only by her annoyance with an airline's flight attendant. She expressed a preference for one airline over another because the latter's flight attendants "were not as competent." When pressed for a further explanation, it was learned that her annoyance resulted from one attendant's cold, distant attitude. This impression contrasted with the warm, friendly personalities of the personnel on another airline.

The comments of one young man sum up the outlook of many consumers. Although he is not satisfied with a local dry cleaner, this consumer has not bothered to consider others. Previous experience has convinced him that there are really no satisfactory dry cleaners, and that at least, "this is the best of the worst." He has begun to purchase clothing that does not require dry cleaning. It is likely that consumers feel the same way about many other services and have taken steps to avoid the need for these services.

## Needs and Motives

A comparison of needs and buying motives for goods and services suggests that there are more similarities than differences. Essentially the same types of needs are satisfied whether a person buys the materials for a home repair or hires a service organization to perform the task. Although service needs have increased in importance, these needs usually can be satisfied by new or modified goods as well as by services.

A need that often does stand out is the consumer's desire for personal attention. By appealing to this need, the hair stylist, the banker, or the insurance agent provides a form of satisfaction that the seller of a good cannot easily match. The desire for personal attention is often the dominant need satisfied by a service.

## Purchase Behaviour

Research suggests that differences between goods and services are most noticeable in the case of purchase behaviour. Goods-selection decisions are normally concerned more with the question of whether to purchase, while service-selection decisions emphasize proper timing and selection of a source.[7] This situation suggests several dis-

---

[7] Sidney P. Feldman and Merline C. Spencer, "The Effect of Personal Influence in the Selection of Consumer Services," in *Marketing and Economic Development*, (ed.) Peter D. Bennett (Chicago: American Marketing Association, 1967), p. 440. See also Richard B. Chase, "Where Does the Customer Fit in a Service Organization?" *Harvard Business Review* (November–December 1978), pp. 137–142; and Duane Davis, "Alternative Predictors of Consumer Search Propensities in the Service Sector," in *Marketing in the 80s*, (eds.) Richard P. Bagozzi, Kenneth L. Bernhardt, Paul S. Busch, David W. Cravens, Joseph F. Hair, Jr., and Carol A. Scott (Chicago: American Marketing Association, 1980), pp. 160–163.

tinctions between purchase behaviour for goods and for services. In particular, the degree of prepurchase planning may differ, influences on the buyer may differ, and the buyer may be more personally involved in a service purchase.

Consumers are influenced more by others — friends, neighbours, and salespeople — when buying services than when buying goods. Since services are intangible, it is difficult for the service buyer to judge quality and value. Buyers are usually unable to inspect or try out a service prior to purchase, so they may depend on the experiences and observations of others.

The dominant role of personal influence in the selection of services has two principal implications for services marketing: 1) added emphasis must be placed upon developing a professional relationship between service suppliers and their customers, and 2) promotional efforts must be aimed toward exploiting word-of-mouth promotion.

The service sector has traditionally been a cottage-type industry consisting of many small, independent firms. Some aspects still are, for example, the local hairdresser. Other service firms have become giant organizations. Scott's Restaurants started as a working-man's diner. When Colonel Harland Saunders walked into one of their outlets carrying a bag of chicken, another carrying a mixture of herbs and spices and a special cooking pot, management saw potential. They opened the world's first take-out location devoted exclusively to Kentucky Fried Chicken in northeastern Toronto. Scott's has opened other food chains and now owns Commonwealth Hospitality Inns of Canada.

## The Status of Marketing in Service Firms

Although spending for services has grown substantially, the development of marketing as a major business activity has come slowly to most service industries. This is largely due to what Theodore Levitt has called *marketing myopia* (described in Chapter 1), the thesis that top executives in many industries have failed to recognize the scope of their businesses.[8] Future growth is endangered because management is product-oriented rather than customer-oriented. Levitt specifically mentions several service industries, including dry cleaning, motion pictures, railways, and electric utilities. The film studio president, for example, who defines the firm's activities as "making movies" instead of as "marketing entertainment" is suffering from marketing myopia, in Levitt's view.

Indicative of the low status of marketing in many service industries are the findings of a survey of manufacturing and service firms

8 Theodore Levitt, "Marketing Myopia," *Harvard Business Review* (July–August 1961), pp. 45–56.

that concluded that "the marketing function appears to be less structured in service companies than in manufacturing firms."[9] The following major findings were reported:

> In comparison to manufacturing firms, service firms appear to be
> 1) generally less likely to have marketing mix activities carried out in
> the marketing department, 2) less likely to perform analysis in the
> offering area, 3) more likely to handle their advertising internally
> rather than go to outside agencies, 4) less likely to have an overall sales
> plan, 5) less likely to develop sales training programs, 6) less likely to
> use marketing research firms and marketing consultants, and 7) less
> likely to spend as much on marketing when expressed as a percentage
> of gross sales.[10]

For many service industries the shift to a marketing orientation
will require a change from traditional ways of doing business.
Fortunately, this change is already taking place in some of the leading service industries. Airlines have shifted their emphasis from the
technical aspects of operation to marketing considerations. Long-
range, high-capacity jets forced airline managements to think in terms
of marketing as practised in goods industries. Banking and insurance are other service industries that have begun to emphasize marketing co-ordination.[11]

## The Marketing Environment for Service Industries

The environmental framework for marketing decisions was discussed
in Chapter 2. In many ways the economic, social, legal, and competitive forces exert the same type of pressures on service firms as
they exert on goods producers. However, certain features of the
environment for service marketing should be highlighted.

### Economic Environment

The growth of consumer expenditures for services has been accompanied by the further expansion of business and government services
to keep pace with the increasing complexity of the Canadian
economy. The sharp increase in spending for services and the
development of the service industries as the major employer of labour

---

[9] William R. George and Hiram C. Barksdale, "Marketing Activities in the
Service Industries," *Journal of Marketing* (October 1974), p. 69.
[10] *Ibid.*, p. 65.
[11] Discussions of the application of the marketing concept to banking are
included in Richard B. Stall, "Marketing in a Service Industry," *Atlanta
Economic Review* (May–June 1978), pp. 15–18; Donald E. Vinson and Wayne
McVandon, "Developing a Market for a New E.F.T.S. Bank Service," *Journal of
Marketing* (April 1978), pp. 83–86; and Bruce Seaton and Ronald H. Vogel, "A
Replication Study of Innovation in the Service Sector," in Barnett A. Greenberg
and Danny N. Bellenger, eds., *Contemporary Marketing Thought* (Chicago:
American Marketing Association, 1977), p. 517.

is one of the most significant economic trends in our post-World War II economy. Most explanations of this trend are based upon changes associated with a maturing economy and the by-products of rapid economic growth. A theory developed by economist Colin Clark describes the growth of service industries.[12] In the first, most primitive, stage, the vast majority of an economy's population is engaged in farming, grazing, hunting, fishing, and forestry. As an economy becomes more advanced, emphasis shifts from agriculture to manufacturing activity. The final and most advanced stage occurs when the majority of labour is engaged in the so-called **tertiary industries** — industries engaged in *the production of services*.

Technological advances, population shifts, and changing consumer needs also contribute to increased spending for consumer services. The evolution of science and technology has altered productivity trends, and higher productivity in the manufacturing industries brought about the shift of workers to service industries. Technological advances have created a higher standard of living for the average person, who spends a larger portion of his or her increased discretionary income for services. In addition, population changes, particularly increased urbanization resulting from advanced technology, have widened the demand for personal and public services. Psychological and sociological factors are also relevant. The consumer's growing desire for personal service, for convenience, and for a wider range of services is an important economic trend.

Perhaps even more spectacular than the growth of consumer expenditures for services has been the increased spending for business services. Servicing other business has become big business, and companies in this field range from suppliers of temporary help to highly specialized consultation services.

Business services have grown rapidly for two reasons. First, business service firms are frequently able to perform a specialized function more cheaply than the purchasing company can do it itself. Enterprises providing maintenance, cleaning, and protection services to office buildings and industrial plants are common examples. For instance, the decorative plants in Ottawa's many federal buildings are cared for and maintained by a firm specializing in such services. Second, many companies are unable to perform certain services for themselves. Marketing research studies, for example, often require outside specialists.

***Socio-cultural Environment***

The socio-cultural environment has a significant impact on the marketing of services. Consumers are offered a wide array of services;

---

12 Colin Clark, *The Conditions of Economic Progress*, 3rd ed. (London: Macmillan, 1957), pp. 490–491.

some are accepted, others rejected. Tastes can also shift over time. For instance, the increased use of counsellors and consultants influences many aspects of modern personal, family, and work lives. A few years ago some of these services were not even available, let alone influential. Now there are even leisure consultants to advise consumers on what to do with their spare time.

Various social trends are relevant. For example, there is evidence that the Canadian consumer's tastes are shifting to a preference for services as status symbols. Travel, culture, health and beauty, and higher education have partially replaced durable goods as status symbols in the minds of many consumers. Other trends include a growing emphasis on financial security, which has expanded the market for insurance, banking, and investment services; greater stress on health, which has led to a greater demand for exercise programs, dental, medical, and hospital services; and the changing attitude toward credit, which has expanded the demand for the services of banks and other lending agencies.

**The Greenskeeper Inc., a Service Specialist**

PLANT LEASING
AND MAINTENANCE
PROGRAMMES

**Greenskeeper Sales, Leasing & Maintenance** is THE strategic answer to those sad, dusty plastic replicas of foliage that follow so many failures. It is specifically designed for the commercial or industrial environment and will, with the intelligent use of refreshingly alive greenery, give you more relaxed, impressive surroundings.

Here at the Greenskeeper we understand the problems of owning and maintaining healthy plants. The Greenskeeper staff has years of experience and success in creating indoor plant arrangements that rival nature's own settings.

the Greenskeeper Inc.

Source: The Greenskeeper Inc.

Attitudes toward some services change slowly, however. One study of the attitudes of homemakers toward the use of personal services such as home cleaning and window washing observed that homemakers resisted using some services because they felt that purchasing personal services violated the virtues of hard work and self-reliance which are part of the homemaker's traditional image, although they recognized the time and effort using these services would save.[13]

**Political and Legal Environment**

Service businesses are more closely regulated than most other forms of private enterprise. There are few service firms that are not subject to some special form of government regulation in addition to the usual taxes and anti-combines legislation. For example, many services are subject to restrictions on promotion and price discrimination. Airline fares are subject to the approval of the Canadian Transport Commission; a railway must ensure that its rates do not contravene federal legislation, and adding or dropping a route is subject to hearings. Even hair stylists must be licensed in most provinces.

Marketers of services must recognize the impact of government on their competitive strategies. Regulation affects the marketing of services in at least three significant ways:

1. It typically reduces the range of competition; as this occurs, the intensity of competition is typically reduced.
2. It reduces a marketer's array of options and introduces certain rigidities into the marketing process.
3. Because the decisions of the regulatory agency are binding, part of the marketing decision process must be to predict the actions of the regulatory agency and to influence these actions in regulatory hearings and through lobbying.[14]

Many service industries are regulated at the national level by special government agencies such as the National Energy Board, the Canadian Radio-television and Telecommunications Commission, and the Canada Deposit Insurance Corporation, to name a few. Other services — insurance and real estate — are traditionally regulated at provincial and local levels. In addition, many personal and business services are restricted at provincial and local levels by special fees or taxes, certification, and licensing. Often included in this category are the legal and medical professions, barbers and beauticians, funeral directors, accountants, engineers, and other professions.

**Technological Environment: Productivity Remains a Problem**

Historically, a large proportion of the economic growth in Canada has resulted from increases in **productivity** — *the output produced by each worker*. Technological developments accounted for significant increases in productivity in the past. The invention of the com-

---

13 William R. Darden and Warren A. French, "Selected Personal Services: Consumer Reactions," *Journal of Retailing* (Fall 1972), pp. 42–48.
14 Blaine Cooke, "Analyzing Markets for Services," in Victor P. Buell (ed.), *Handbook of Modern Marketing* (New York: McGraw-Hill Book Company, 1970), pp. 2–44.

bine harvester almost tripled the output of the average wheat farmer, and Henry Ford's innovations made it possible to reduce the cost of an average car by 50 percent. How are increases in productivity accomplished in a service economy?

Theodore Levitt argues that service marketers should assume a "manufacturing" attitude. "Instead of looking to the service workers to improve results by greater exertion of animal energy, managers must see what kinds of organizations, incentives, technology, and skills could improve overall productivity.[15]

Levitt cites McDonald's as the ultimate example of how service can be industrialized:

> Each variety of McDonald's hamburger is in a colour-coded wrapper. Parking lots are sprinkled with brightly painted, omnivorous trash cans that even the most chronic litterer finds difficult to ignore. A special scoop has been devised for French fries so that each customer will believe he is getting an over-flowing portion, while actually receiving a uniform ration. Employee discretion is eliminated; everything is organized so that nothing can go wrong.[16]

The manufacturing attitude is already evident in many service firms. Conversion of such businesses as dry cleaners and car washes from hand labour to automatic equipment has increased output per worker. The introduction of wide-bodied jets by the airlines enables them to fly twice as many passengers with the same number of high-salaried pilots and flight engineers. The development of multiple-unit motion picture theatres with a single refreshment stand, ticket-selling booth, and projection room reduced necessary floor space and the number of people needed to operate them.[17] For small personal loans, some banks have shifted from analysis by loan officers to a simple "scorecard" to evaluate prospective borrowers (one point for having a telephone, five points for home ownership, five points for several years of steady employment, and so on). The challenge to service marketers is to produce gains in productivity without sacrificing the quality of service.

---

[15] "The 'Big Mac' Theory of Economic Progress," *Forbes* (April 15, 1977), p. 137. See also Theodore Levitt, "The Industrialization of Service," *Harvard Business Review* (September-October 1976), pp. 63–75.

[16] Levitt, "The Industrialization of Service," p. 70.

[17] Dan R. E. Thomas, "Strategy Is Different in Service Business," *Harvard Business Review* (July–August 1978), p. 160. See also Donald J. Hempel and Michael V. Laric, "A Total Performance System for Evaluating Marketing Productivity in Service Industries," in *Marketing Looks Outward*, (ed.) William Locander (Chicago: American Marketing Association, 1977), pp. 73–79.

**Competitive Environment**   The competitive environment for services is a paradox. For many service industries, competition comes not from other services but from goods manufacturers or government services. Internal competition is almost nonexistent in some service industries. Price competition is severely limited in such areas as transportation, communication, and legal and medical services. Moreover, many important service producers like hospitals, educational institutions, and religious and welfare agencies are not even operating for a profit in the business sense. Finally, many service industries are difficult to enter; they may require a major financial investment or special education or training or may be restricted by government regulations.

*Competition from Goods*   Direct competition between goods and services is inevitable since competing goods and services often provide the same basic satisfactions. Consumers may satisfy their service requirements by substituting goods. Competition has become greater because manufacturers, recognizing the changing desires of consumers, are building services and added conveniences into their products. Wash-and-wear clothing has replaced some laundry and dry cleaning services; improved appliances have reduced the need for domestic employees; and television competes with motion pictures and other forms of entertainment. Consumers often have a choice between goods and services that perform the same general function.

*Competition from Retailers and Manufacturers*   The entry of retailers and manufacturers into consumer and service markets is also increasing the intensity of competition for the service dollar. Large retailers such as Eaton's, Woodwards, and The Bay are providing services such as optical centres and automobile repair facilities that go far beyond traditional department store offerings. Sears has been a leader in the trend to diversify into services with its entry into insurance (Allstate). Eaton's and others have travel agencies and provide financial services. These large retailers have apparently decided that the mass merchandising of consumer services is possible and profitable.

*Competition from Government*   An expanded number of services are now provided by all levels of government. Some services can only be provided by government agencies, but others compete with privately produced goods and services. Often, the consumption of government services is mandatory, such as contributions to Canada Pension Plan, unemployment insurance, and compulsory education. Private auto insurance companies have been pushed out of some provinces. Current public debates concern how far government should be involved, and how the consumer should pay for such government services.

**The Marketing Mix for Service Firms**

Satisfying the service needs of buyers requires the development of an effective marketing mix. Service policies and distribution, promotional, and pricing strategies must be combined in an integrated marketing program. This section introduces the marketing mix for service firms.

**Service Policies**

Like tangible products, services may be classified according to their intended use. Thus all are either consumer services or industrial services. Even when the same service (telephone, gas, and electric services) is sold to both consumer and industrial buyers, a service firm will often have separate marketing groups for each market segment.

Consumer services may also be classified as convenience, shopping, and specialty services. Dry cleaning, shoe repairs, and similar personal services are commonly purchased on a convenience basis. Auto repairs and insurance are services that can involve considerable shopping to compare price and quality. Specialty services, where the consumer will accept no alternatives, may include professional services, such as financial, legal, and medical assistance.

Some service firms have developed new services or diversified their service mix in an attempt to boost sales. Insurance policies for homeowners, vacation package tours, and air-travel family plans

**Figure 12-4   Examples of Service Product Innovations**

| Nature of Service | New Service Product | or | Service Product Improvement |
|---|---|---|---|
| *Communications* | Communication satellite | | Free-standing public telephone |
| *Consulting and business facilitating* | Equipment leasing | | Overnight TV rating service |
| *Educational* | Ecology-management major | | New curricula |
| *Financial* | Automated bank tellers | | Extended banking hours |
| *Health* | Treatment with lasers | | Intensive care |
| *Household operations* | Laundromat | | Fuel budget accounts |
| *Housing* | Housing for the elderly | | Motel swimming pool |
| *Insurance* | National health insurance | | No-fault insurance |
| *Personal* | Physical fitness facilities | | |
| *Recreational* | Dual cinema | | New play |
| *Transportation* | Unit train | | Flight reservation system |

Source: Adapted from *Marketing in the Service Sector* by John Rathmell. Copyright © 1974 by Winthrop Publishers Inc. Reprinted by permission of the publisher.

all represent examples of expanded service offerings that have received favourable consumer response.

A new service may often be an improved method of delivering an existing service.[18] Figure 12-4 presents a list of service product innovations.

Some important differences between service policies and product policies should be noted. First, because services are intangible, packaging and labelling decisions are very limited. Service marketers are rarely able to use the package to promote their services. Second, the lack of a tangible product limits sampling by service marketers as a means of introducing a new service to the market.

*Pricing Strategy*

In service industries, pricing practices are not substantially different from those in goods industries. The service marketer must consider the demand for the service, production, marketing, and administrative costs, and the influence of competition when developing pricing strategies.[19] However, for many services price competition has been limited. Until recently, prices of transportation, communications, and other utilities been closely regulated by federal, provincial, and local agencies. Business and the public are watching to see how recent deregulation activities will affect pricing in these industries. For many other service firms, such as advertising agencies, there is a traditional pricing structure that is closely followed within the industry.

Price negotiation is an important part of many professional service transactions. Consumer services that sometimes involve price negotiation include auto repairs, foreign travel, and financial and legal assistance. Specialized business services, such as equipment rental, market research, insurance, and maintenance and protection services, are also priced through direct negotiation.

Many firms use variable pricing to overcome the problems associated with the perishable nature of services. The Canadian telephone system is one service organization that has used this approach. Lower rates for long-distance calls are in effect during evening hours and on weekends. Off-season rates at resort hotels and motels are another example.

*Distribution Strategy*

Channels of distribution for services are usually simpler and more direct than channels of distribution of goods. In part, this is due to the intangibility of services. The marketer of services is often less

18 John M. Rathmell, *Marketing in the Service Sector* (Cambridge, Mass.: Winthrop Publishers, 1974), p. 61.
19 See Martin R. Schlissel, "Pricing in a Service Industry," *MSU Business Topics* (Spring 1977), pp. 37–48.

concerned with storage, transportation, and inventory control, so shorter channels may be employed.[20]

Another consideration is the need for continuing personal relationships between performers and users of many services. Consumers will remain with the same insurance agent, bank, or travel agent if they are reasonably satisfied. Likewise, public accounting firms and lawyers are retained on a relatively permanent basis by industrial buyers.

When marketing intermediaries are used by service firms they are usually agents or brokers. Common examples include insurance agents, securities brokers, travel agents, and entertainment agents.

**Promotional Strategy**  Promotion is an important aspect of the marketing mix for most services. As with goods, the importance of each particular form of promotion varies for different services.

The *advertising* of services is somewhat more challenging than the advertising of goods since it is more difficult to illustrate intangible services. Several strategies may be used. One is to make the service seem more tangible by personalizing it. This may be done by featuring employees or recognizable entertainment or sports personalities.

A second strategy is to attempt to create a favourable image for the service or the service company.[21] Some of the themes used by service organizations are efficiency, progressiveness, status, and friendliness. For example, advertisements for American Express show its card being used by well-known personalities.

A third advertising strategy is to show the tangible benefits of purchasing an intangible service. An airline shows grandparents greeting a granddaughter as she arrives for a visit; a local bank shows a young couple enjoying a new home purchased through a home mortgage or a retired couple relaxing in Victoria because of a savings plan they had established years ago. These and many similar themes help buyers relate to the benefits of the particular service that they may be unable to visualize.

The desire of many service buyers for a personal relationship with a service seller increases the importance of *personal selling*. In

---

[20] Some insights into the distribution of services are offered in James H. Donnelly, Jr., "Marketing Intermediaries in Channels of Distribution for Services," *Journal of Marketing* (January 1976), pp. 55–57; and Dean E. Allmon and Michael T. Troncalli, "Concepts of a Channel of Distribution for Services," in *Proceedings of the Southern Marketing Association*, (eds.) Robert S. Franz, Robert M. Hopkins, and Alfred G. Toma (New Orleans, La., November 1978), pp. 209–210.

[21] See Eugene M. Johnson, *An Introduction to the Problems of Service Marketing Management* (Newark: University of Delaware, 1964), pp. 61–87.

fact, except for a very simple or highly standardized service, personal selling is usually the backbone of service marketing.

Life insurance marketing provides a good illustration of the sales representative's key role. Because insurance is a confusing, complex subject for the average buyer, the agent must be a professional financial adviser who develops a close personal relationship with the client. Life insurance companies and other service firms must develop well-trained, highly motivated sales forces to provide the high-quality, personalized service that customers require. Their success is closely related to their ability to develop such salespeople.

*Sales promotion* is difficult because services are intangible. Sampling, demonstrations, and physical displays are limited, but service firms often do use premiums and contests. Publicity is also important for many services, especially for entertainment and sports events. Television and radio reports, newspaper articles, and magazine features inform the public of events and stimulate interest. Contributions to charitable causes, employees' service to nonprofit organizations, sponsorship of public events, and similar activities are publicized to influence the public's opinion of the service firm.[22]

## Organizational Responsibility for Marketing

In many service firms, the organizational responsibility for marketing may be considerably different than in manufacturing companies. In any company there may be confusion about what marketing is. It is frequently considered to be what the *marketing department does*. Marketing is, however, often carried out by others in the company to some degree. This confusion may be much more acute for service firms than for manufacturing firms and may constitute an organizational dilemma. In many professional service organizations, the marketing department's role may be limited to handling advertising, sales promotion, and some public relations. The "sales force" are those people in direct contact with customers, for example, the branch managers and the tellers in a bank. With the exception of the members of the marketing department, however, the staff is not hired for its marketing know-how but for its ability to produce services. *Yet the person who produces a service must also be able to market that service.* In most cases, what is needed is not professional salespeople but service workers who sell.

The dilemma arises when service firms are insufficiently aware of the need to have personnel who are able to perform adequately both marketing and service-production functions. Furthermore, when the workload is high, too little time may be spent on market-

22 The use of promotions in service industries is discussed in Christopher H. Lovelock and John A. Quelch, "Consumer Promotions in Service Marketing," *Business Horizons* (May–June 1983), pp. 66–75.

ing, which may have very serious long-term consequences for the organization.

**Summary**   Approximately 40 percent of all personal consumption expenditures go to the purchase of services. Services can be defined as intangible efforts that satisfy consumer needs when efficiently developed and distributed to chosen consumer segments.

The marketing of services has many similarities to the marketing of goods, but there are also some significant differences. Key features of services have implications for marketing:
1. Services are intangible.
2. Services are perishable.
3. Services are often not standardized.
4. Buyers are often involved in the development and distribution of services.

Important aspects of buyer behaviour are different for services as contrasted to goods. These differences may be grouped into three categories: attitudes, needs and motives, and purchase behaviour.

Although service industries have grown substantially, their development of effective marketing programs has been slow. Many service firms have not adopted the marketing concept, while others, such as the insurance companies, are very efficient marketers.

Environmental factors affect service industries the same way they influence goods producers. Marketers of services must be continuously aware of changes in the economic, socio-cultural, political and legal, and competitive environments.

An effective marketing mix is mandatory in the sale of services. Service policies (service industries' versions of product planning) and pricing, distribution, and promotional strategies must all be combined into a co-ordinated marketing mix if the service marketer is to succeed.

Service industries will need to increase their marketing function in order to increase productivity and to attain the maximum profit from the growing demands for their varied services.

**Key Terms**   goods-services continuum          tertiary industries
service                           productivity

**Review Questions**   1. Explain why services are difficult to define.
2. How is a goods-services continuum useful in defining the term *service*?
3. Outline the proportions of the consumer dollar spent on products and services.

4. Describe the evolution of the service sector.
5. Explain the classification of services on the bases of reliance on equipment and relative skills of service personnel.
6. Identify and outline the key features of services.
7. How does Levitt's marketing myopia thesis relate to service industries?
8. What is the status of the marketing concept in service industries?
9. Explain how Colin Clark's concept describes the growth of service industries.
10. Cite major differences in the marketing strategies of firms producing goods and firms producing services.

**Discussion Questions and Exercises**

1. Prepare a brief report on the marketing activities conducted by a local lawyer, and a local insurance broker. In addition, compare and contrast the two. What generalizations can be reached from your study?
2. Describe the last service you purchased. What was your impression of the way in which the service was marketed? How could the firm's marketing effort have been improved?
3. Commonwealth Holiday Inns of Canada has tried to overcome the problems of a service industry by stressing consistency in their product offering. The slogan "The best surprise is no surprise" is an illustration of Holiday Inn's effort to provide a service of consistently reliable quality. What is your opinion of Holiday Inns' approach to the consistency problem faced by all varieties of services?
4. Outline a marketing mix for the following service firms:
   a. local radio station
   b. independent insurance agency
   c. janitorial service
   d. funeral home
5. Identify three or four service firms and propose methods by which their productivity can be improved. Point out any potential problems with your proposal.

# PART

# 5

## *Price*

*CHAPTER 13*

## Price Determination

*CHAPTER 14*

## Managing the Pricing Function

*Recent empirical data indicate that pricing strategy plays an important role in marketing. Part Five consists of two chapters on this critical element of the marketing mix. Chapter 13 examines the role of pricing as well as price determination in both theory and practice. Chapter 14 examines how the pricing structure is set and the overall management of this function.*

# Price Determination

Steinberg, Quebec's third largest food retailer, developed a new marketing strategy which had quite unintended effects — it led to a price war. The strategy was to offer coupons worth 5 percent off future purchases.

Metro-Richelieu, holding second place in the Quebec market, with 900 stores, reacted with a speed that surprised market analysts. It countered with its own offer — stamped cash register bills that allowed a 5 percent rebate on future orders.

IGA Boniprix joined the fray by announcing that its 122 stores would close for a day to allow substantial lowering of prices. And the chain with the largest market share, Provigo, topped them all with an offer of an immediate cash refund of 6 percent on sales in its 250 corporate and privately-owned stores.

All stores supported their strategies with expensive multimedia advertising campaigns. Increased sales would not help in the short-run because the discounts offered were apparently greater than margins on sales. Profits on food products are usually around one to two percent and industry analysts doubted that the competitors could offer discounts of 5 percent or more for any length of time without substantial losses. If the price war lasted for one month, based on normal profits and current market share, Steinberg alone could lose between $3 million and $3.5 million. However, despite the unintended effects of its strategy, Steinberg was optimistic that in the long-term the strategy would result in more customers and increased profits.[1]

Marketers must carefully consider the effects of pricing decisions, because such decisions are usually very visible in the marketplace. In addition, competitors can counter them with amazing speed, and this may be very costly to an entire industry. Consumers may benefit at first but perhaps not in the long-run, as marketers will eventually try to recoup their losses.

| | |
|---|---|
| ***The Conceptual Framework*** | Part Four examined the first critical element of a firm's marketing mix: the determination of the products and services to offer the market target. Part Five focuses upon price—the second element of the marketing mix. Determination of profitable and justified prices is the result of pricing objectives and various approaches to setting prices. These topics are discussed in this chapter. The following chapter focuses upon management of the pricing function and discusses pricing strategies, price-quality relationships, and both industrial pricing and the pricing of public services. The starting place for examining pricing strategy is to understand the meaning of the term *price*. |

**Price** is *the exchange value of a good or service, the value of an item being what it can be exchanged for in the marketplace*. In earlier times, the price of an acre might have been twenty bushels of wheat, three cattle, or a boat. Price is a measure of what one must exchange in order to obtain a desired good or service. When the barter process was abandoned in favour of a monetary system, price became the amount of money required to purchase an item. As David Schwartz has pointed out, contemporary society uses a number of terms to refer to price:

> Price is all around us. You pay *rent* for your apartment, *tuition* for your education, and a *fee* to your physician or dentist.
>
> The airline, railway, taxi, and bus companies charge you a *fare*; the local utilities call their price a *rate*; and the local bank charges you *interest* for the money you borrow.
>
> The price for taking your car on the ferry to Prince Edward Island or Vancouver Island is a *toll*, and the company that insures your car charges you a *premium*.
>
> Clubs or societies to which you belong may make a special *assessment* to pay unusual expenses. Your regular lawyer may ask for a *retainer* to cover her services.
>
> The "price" of an executive is a *salary*; the price of a salesperson may be a *commission*; and the price of a worker is a *wage*.
>
> Finally, although economists would disagree, many of us feel that *income taxes* are the price we pay for the privilege of making money![2]

---

1 Adapted from "Steinberg Strategy Starts Price War," *Marketing* (March 21, 1983), p. 15.

2 Adapted from *Marketing Today* by David J. Schwartz, copyright © 1981 by Harcourt Brace Jovanovich, Inc. Reprinted by permission of the publisher.

All products have some degree of *utility*, or want-satisfying power. While one individual might be willing to exchange the utility derived from a colour television for a vacation, another may not be willing to make that exchange. Prices are a mechanism that allows the consumer to make a decision. In contemporary society, of course, prices are translated into monetary terms. The consumer evaluates the utility derived from a range of possible purchases and then allocates his or her exchange power (in monetary terms) so as to maximize satisfaction. Pricing may be the most complicated aspect of the marketing manager's job. It is difficult to determine the price needed to realize a profit. But an even greater problem is that of determining the meaning of price and its role in society.

## The Importance of Price as an Element of the Marketing Mix

Ancient philosophers recognized the importance of price to the functioning of the economic system. Early written accounts refer to attempts to develop a fair, or just, price. Their limited understanding of time, place, and possession utilities, however, thwarted such efforts.

Today, price still serves as a means of regulating economic activity. The employment of any or all of the four factors of production (land, labour, capital, and entrepreneurship) is dependent upon the prices received by each. For an individual firm, prices (along with the corresponding quantity that will be sold) represent the revenue to be received. Prices, therefore, influence a company's profit as well as its use of the factors of production.

A widely cited 1964 study by Jon G. Udell found that executives ranked pricing as the sixth in a long list of factors in achieving marketing success.[3] When Udell's factors were reorganized into the four major marketing mix variables, price ranked third — ahead only of distribution.

But times have changed. When Udell conducted his study, prices were relatively constant. A 1979 study of marketing executives, conducted when inflation was high, concluded that pricing ranked as the single most important marketing mix variable.[4] Product planning and management was a close second, while distribution strategy and promotional decisions ranked third and fourth respectively.

---

[3] Jon G. Udell, "How Important Is Pricing in Competitive Strategy?" *Journal of Marketing* (January 1964), pp. 44–48.

[4] "Pricing Objectives and Practices in American Industry: A Research Report," © 1979 by Louis E. Boone and David L. Kurtz; all rights reserved. These findings were also consistent with a study by Robert A. Robicheaux; see "How Important is Pricing in Competitive Strategy? Circa 1975," in *Proceedings of the Southern Marketing Association*, Henry W. Nash and Donald P. Robin, eds. (Atlanta, November 1976), pp. 55–57.

Figure 13-1 compares the Udell findings to those of the later study by Boone and Kurtz.

**Figure 13-1   Relative Importance of Marketing Variables: A Comparison of the Udell Study and the Boone and Kurtz Study**

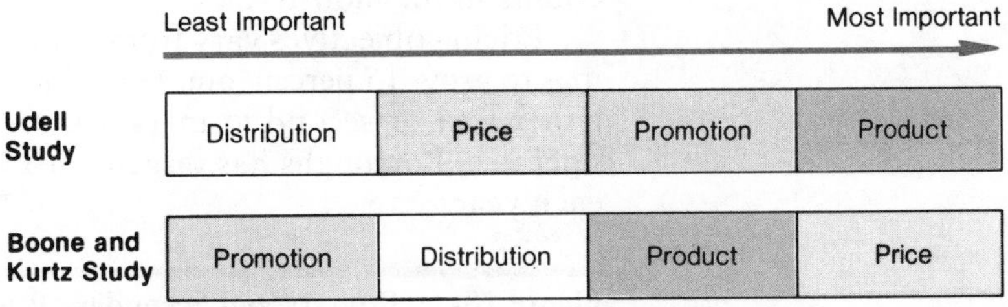

Least Important ────────────────────────────────► Most Important

| **Udell Study** | Distribution | Price | Promotion | Product |
| --- | --- | --- | --- | --- |
| **Boone and Kurtz Study** | Promotion | Distribution | Product | Price |

Source: Udell rankings from Jon G. Udell, "How Important Is Pricing in Competitive Strategy?" *Journal of Marketing* (January 1964), pp. 44–48. Boone and Kurtz rankings from Louis E. Boone and David L. Kurtz, *Pricing Objectives and Practices in American Industry: A Research Report*. All rights reserved.

**Pricing Objectives**   Pricing objectives are a crucial part of a means–end chain from overall company objectives to specific pricing policies and procedures (see Figure 13-2). The goals of the firm and the marketing organization provide the basis for the development of pricing objectives, which must be clearly established before pricing policies and procedures are implemented.

**Figure 13-2   The Role of Pricing Objectives in Contemporary Marketing**

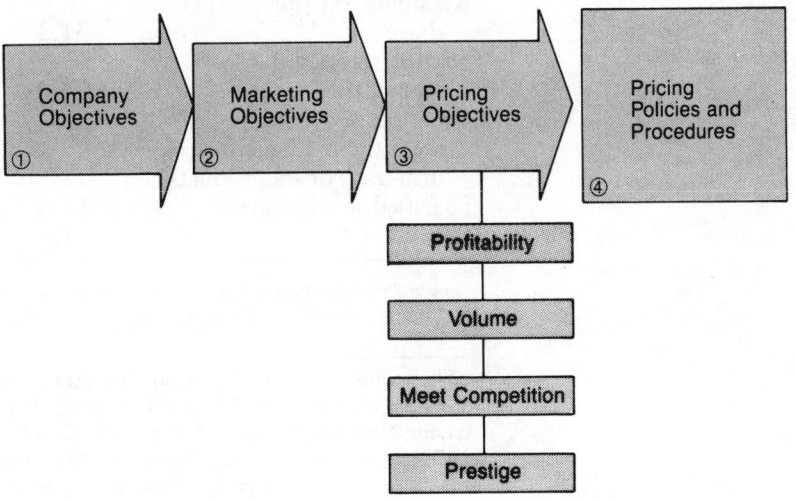

A firm may have as its primary objective the goal of becoming the dominant supplier in the domestic market. Its marketing objective might then be to achieve maximum sales penetration in all sales regions. The related pricing goal would be sales maximization. This means–end chain might lead to the adoption of a low price policy implemented through provision of the highest cash and trade discounts in the industry.

Pricing objectives vary from firm to firm. Xerox wants its earnings to grow 15 percent annually. Eaton Corporation aspires to rank either first or second in market share in each market in which it operates. Burroughs has targeted a 15 percent increase in revenue each year.[5]

**Figure 13-3  Primary and Secondary Pricing Objectives of Firms**

| Pricing Objective | Percentage of Respondents Ranking the Item | | |
|---|---|---|---|
| | As Primary Objective | As Secondary Objective | As Either Primary or Secondary Objective |
| Meeting competitive price level | 38.3 | 43.0 | 81.3 |
| Specified rate of return on investment | 60.9 | 17.2 | 78.1 |
| Specified total profit level | 60.2 | 17.2 | 77.4 |
| Increased market share | 31.3 | 42.2 | 73.5 |
| Increased total profits above previous levels | 34.4 | 37.5 | 71.9 |
| Specified rate of return on sales | 47.7 | 23.4 | 71.1 |
| Retaining existing market share | 31.3 | 35.9 | 67.2 |
| Serving selected market segments | 26.6 | 39.1 | 65.7 |
| Creation of a readily identifiable image for the firm and/or its products | 21.9 | 41.4 | 63.3 |
| Specified market share | 15.6 | 40.6 | 56.2 |
| Other | 5.5 | — | 5.5 |

Source: *Pricing Objectives and Practices in American Industry: A Research Paper.* ©1979 by Louis E. Boone and David L. Kurtz; all rights reserved.

[5] These objectives are reported in Bro Uttal, "Xerox Is Trying Too Hard," *Fortune* (March 13, 1978), p. 84; Ralph E. Winter, "Corporate Strategists Giving New Emphasis to Market Share, Rank," *Wall Street Journal* (February 3, 1978), p. 1; and Bro Uttal, "How Ray MacDonald's Growth Theory Created IBM's Toughest Competitor," *Fortune* (January 1977), p. 96.

In a recent U.S. study, marketers were to identify the primary and secondary pricing objectives of their companies. Meeting competitive prices was most often mentioned, but many marketers ranked two profitability-oriented objectives higher: a specified rate of return on investment and specified total profit levels. These two objectives ranked first and second as *primary* pricing objectives.[6] The findings are shown in Figure 13-3.

Pricing objectives can be classified into four major groups: 1) profitability objectives; 2) volume objectives; 3) meeting competition objectives; and 4) prestige objectives. Profitability objectives include profit maximization and target return goals.

***Profitability Objectives***      In classical economic theory, the traditional pricing objective has been to *maximize profits*.[7] The study of microeconomics is based upon certain assumptions: that buyers and sellers are rational, and that rational behaviour is an effort to maximize gains and minimize losses. In terms of actual business practice, this means that profit maximization is the basic objective of individual firms.

Profits, in turn, are a function of revenue and expenses:

$$\text{Profits} = \text{Total Revenues} - \text{Total Costs}$$

And revenue is determined by the selling price and the quantity sold:

$$\text{Total Revenue} = \text{Price} \times \text{Quantity Sold}$$

Price, therefore, should be increased up to the point where it causes a disproportionate decrease in the number of units sold. A 10 percent price increase that results in only an 8 percent cut in volume adds to the firm's revenue. However, a 10 percent hike that causes an 11 percent sales decline reduces total revenue.

Economists refer to this approach as *marginal analysis*. They identify the point of **profit maximization** as where *the addition to total revenue is just balanced by an increase in total cost*. The basic problem centres on the difficulty in achieving this delicate balance between marginal revenue and marginal cost. As a result, relatively few firms actually achieve an objective of profit maximization. A significantly larger number prefer to direct their efforts toward goals that are more easily implemented and measured.

---

[6] Research by Saeed Samiee ranked "satisfactory return on investment" first among a similar list of objectives. Samiee correctly points out the difficulties in making the "meeting competition" objectives operational. See "Pricing Objectives of U.S. Manufacturing Firms," *Proceedings of the Southern Marketing Association*, (eds.) Robert S. Franz, Robert M. Hopkins, and Alfred G. Toma (New Orleans, Louisiana, November 1978), pp. 445–47.
[7] An alternative to the profit maximization concept is suggested in Bruce Gunn, "Profit Optimization, A Paradigm for Risk Reduction," *Akron Business and Economic Review* (Spring 1977), pp. 14–22.

Consequently, target return objectives have become quite common in industry, particularly among the larger firms where public pressure may limit consideration of the profit maximization objective.[8] Automobile companies are an example of this phenomenon.[9] **Target return objectives** may be *either short-run or long-run goals and usually are stated as a percentage of sales or investment.* A company, for instance, may seek a 15 percent annual rate of return on investment or an 8 percent rate of return on sales. A specified return on investment was the most commonly reported pricing objective in Figure 13-3. Goals of this nature also serve as useful guidelines in evaluating corporate activity. One writer has aptly expressed it: "For management consciously accepting less than maximum profits, the target rate can provide a measure of the amount of restraint. For firms making very low profits, the target rate can serve as a standard for judging improvement."[10] Furthermore, they are more likely to result in a more stable and planned profit pattern for the company. This contrasts with a profit maximization approach, which can be very unstable.

Target return objectives offer several benefits to the marketer. As noted above, they serve as a means for evaluating performance. They also are designed to generate a "fair" profit, as judged by management, stockholders, and the general public as well.

***Volume Objectives***

Some writers argue that a better explanation of actual pricing behaviour is William J. Baumol's belief that firms attempt to **maximize sales** within a given profit constraint.[11] In other words, they set *a minimum floor at what they consider the lowest acceptable profit level* and then seek to maximize sales (subject to this profit constraint) in the belief that *increased sales are more important to*

[8] Target rate-of-return pricing is discussed in Douglas G. Brooks, "Cost-Oriented Pricing: A Realistic Solution to a Complicated Problem," *Journal of Marketing* (April 1975), pp. 72–74.

[9] See James E. Hansz and Kenneth P. Sinclair, "Target Return Pricing: Panacea or Paradox," in Franz, Hopkins, and Toma, eds., *Proceedings of the Southern Marketing Association* (1978), pp. 441–444.

[10] Robert A. Lynn, *Price Policies and Marketing Management* (Homewood, Ill.: Richard D. Irwin, 1967), p. 99. See also Stuart U. Rich, "Firms in Some Industries Should Use Both Target Return and Marginal Cost Pricing," *Marketing News* (June 25, 1982), Section 2, p. 11.

[11] See William J. Baumol, "On the Theory of Oligopoly," *Economica* (August 1958), pp. 187–198. See also William J. Baumol, *Business Behavior, Value, and Growth* (New York: The Macmillan Company, 1959).

*the long-run competitive picture.*[12] The company will continue to expand sales as long as their total profits do not drop below the minimum return acceptable to management.

Another volume-related pricing objective is the **market share** objective — that is, the goal set as *the control of a specific portion of the market for the firm's product.* The company's specific goal can be to maintain or increase its share of a particular market. For example, a firm may desire to increase its 10 percent share of a particular market to 20 percent.[13] As Figure 13-3 indicates, almost two-thirds of all responding firms list retaining existing market share as either a primary or secondary pricing objective.

Some firms with high market shares may even prefer to reduce their share at times because the possibility of government action in the area of monopoly control has become more important in recent years. Courts have used market share figures in their evaluation of cases involving alleged monopolistic practices.

The PIMS Studies   Market share objectives can be critical to the achievement of other objectives. High sales, for example, may mean more profit. The extensive *Profit Impact of Market Strategies (PIMS)* project conducted by the Marketing Science Institute analysed more than 2000 firms and revealed that two of the most important factors influencing profitability were product quality and market share.

The link between market share and profitability is dramatically demonstrated in Figure 13-4. Firms enjoying more than 40 percent of a market achieved a pre-tax return on investment averaging 32.3 percent. By contrast, firms with a minor market share of less than 10 percent generate pre-tax investment returns of 13.2 percent. The underlying factor in this relationship appears to be the operating experience and lower overall costs of high-market-share firms as compared with competitors who possess smaller shares of the market.[14] However, there remains some question: Does profitability come from market share per se, or are both profitability and market share related to a sound marketing strategy over time?

Henry Allesio has warned marketers not to place too much stress on market share because of the foregoing findings. He correctly

---

12 The importance of volume objectives is pointed out in Robert A. Lynn, "Unit Volume as a Goal for Pricing," *Journal of Marketing* (October 1968), pp. 34–39.
13 An interesting discussion appears in Carl R. Frear and John E. Swan, "Marketing Managers' Motivation to Revise Their Market Share Goals: An Expectancy Theory Analysis," in *1981 Southwestern Marketing Proceedings*, (eds.) Robert H. Ross, Frederic B. Kraft, and Charles H. Davis (Wichita, Kansas), pp. 13–16.
14 Robert D. Buzzell and Frederick D. Wiersema, "Successful Share-Building Strategies," *Harvard Business Review* (January–February 1981), pp. 135–144.

**Figure 13-4    Relationship of Market Share to Return on Investment (ROI)**

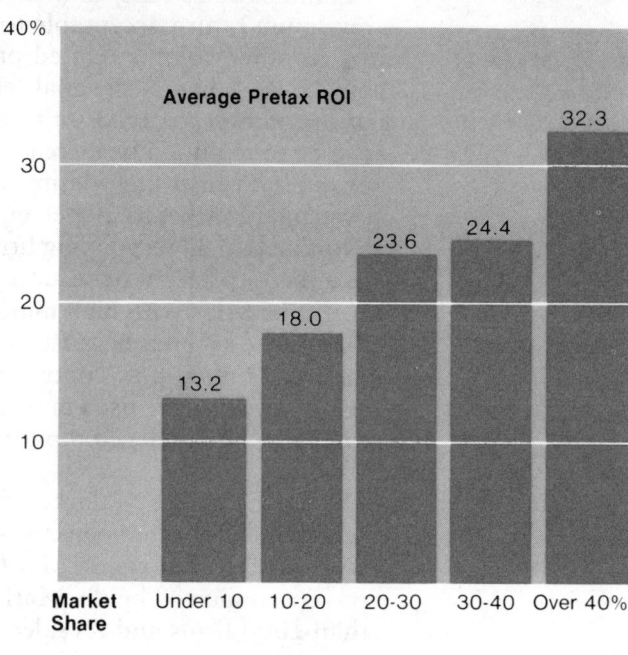

Source: Reprinted by permission from Robert D. Buzzell and Frederik D. Wiersema, "Successful Share-Building Strategies," *Harvard Business Review* (January–February 1981), p. 137.

points out that marketing strategy should include a conscious recognition of what a firm's real source of comparative advantage is, as well as the delivered cost (not just manufactured cost) of products.[15] Not everyone can obtain market share predominance, but most can still do very well in the market.

*Meeting Competition as a Pricing Objective*

**Status quo objectives** — *objectives based on the maintenance of stable prices* — are the basis of the pricing philosophy for many enterprises. This philosophy usually stems from a desire to minimize competitive pricing action. The maintenance of stable prices allows the firm to concentrate its efforts on non-price elements of the marketing mix such as product improvement or promotion. For a long time the automobile producers de-emphasized price competition in their advertisements in favour of developing product features that differentiated their products from the competition. Even today, status quo objectives remain a significant factor in pricing.

[15] Henry Allesio, "Market Share Madness," *Strategic Marketing* (Fall 1982), p. 76.

| | |
|---|---|
| ***Prestige Objectives*** | Another category of pricing objectives unrelated to either profitability or sales volume is that of prestige objectives. **Prestige objectives** involve *the establishment of relatively high prices in order to develop and maintain an image of quality and exclusiveness.* Such objectives reflect marketers' recognition of the role of price in the creation of an overall image for the firm and its products and services. It appears that Birks and Holt Renfrew follow this strategy. And Rolls-Royce has opted for a higher price image with its Cabriolet convertible model, priced at approximately $150 000. While some marketers set relatively high prices in order to maintain a prestige image with their consumers, others prefer the opposite approach of developing a low-price image among customers. |

| | |
|---|---|
| ***Price Determination*** | There are two general ways to look at the determination of price. One is theoretical price derivation; the other is the cost-plus type of approach, which in numerous variations and combined with an eye on demand and the competition, characterizes actual business practice. |
| | During the first part of this century most formal discussion of price determination emphasized the classical concepts of supply and demand. (Whether actual business practice followed this is another question.) Since World War II the emphasis has shifted to a cost-oriented approach to pricing. The advantage of hindsight allows us to see that both concepts have certain flaws in practice. Most firms use a combination of both in their pricing decisions. |
| | There is, however, another aspect that is often overlooked. *Custom, tradition, and social habit* also play an important role in price determination. Numerous examples of **customary pricing** exist. The candy-makers' attempt to hold the line on the traditional 5-cent candy bar led to considerable reductions in the size of the product. Eventually almost all vending machines were supplied with larger 10-cent bars, and the shrinking process began again. Similar practices have prevailed in the marketing of soft drinks. |
| | At some point, someone had to set the *initial* price. Sustained inflation has also created a need for periodically reviewing the firm's price structures. |
| | The remainder of this chapter will discuss the traditional and current concepts of price determination. Finally, we shall deal with the question of how best to tie these concepts together so as to develop a more realistic approach to pricing. |

| | |
|---|---|
| ***Price Determination in Economic Theory*** | The microeconomic approach, or price theory, assumes a profit maximization objective and leads to the derivation of correct equilibrium prices in the marketplace. Price theory considers both |

supply and demand factors and thus is a more complete analysis than what is typically found in practice.

*Demand* refers to a schedule of the amounts of a firm's product or service that consumers will purchase at different prices during a specific period. *Supply* refers to a schedule of the amounts of a product or service that will be offered for sale at different prices during a specified time period. These schedules may vary for different types of market structures.

**Market Structures**

There are four types of market structures; pure competition, monopolistic competition, oligopoly, and monopoly. Very briefly, **pure competition** is *a market structure where there is such a large number of buyers and sellers that no one of them has a significant influence on price.* Other characteristics of pure competition include a homogeneous product and ease of entry for sellers, and complete and instantaneous information.

This marketing structure is largely theoretical in contemporary society; however, some uncontrolled sectors of the agricultural commodity sector exhibit many of the characteristics of such a market, and provide the closest example of it.

**Monopolistic competition** is also *a market structure with a large number of buyers and sellers.* However, in this market there is *some degree of heterogeneity in product and/or service and usually geographical differentiation.* The existence of differentiation allows the marketer some degree of control over price. Most retail stores fall into this category, which partially explains why small retailers can exist with 5 to 10 percent higher prices than their larger competitors.

An **oligopoly** is *a market structure in which there are relatively few sellers.* Each seller may affect the market, but no one seller controls it. Examples are the automobile, steel, tobacco, and petroleum-refining industries. Because of high start-up costs, new competitors encounter significant entry barriers. **Oligopsony** is the other side of the coin: *a market where there are only a few buyers.*

A **monopoly** is *a market structure with only one seller of a product with no close substitutes.* Anti-combines legislation has tended to eliminate all but *temporary* monopolies, such as those provided by patent protection, and *regulated* monopolies, such as the public utilities (telephone, electricity, gas). Regulated monopolies are granted by government in markets where competition would lead to an uneconomic duplication of services. In return for this monopoly, government regulates the monopoly rate of return through regulatory bodies such as the Canadian Transport Commission, the Canadian Radio-television and Telecommunications Commission, the National Farm Products Marketing Council, and provincial public utility regulatory commissions.

**Revenue, Cost, and** Within each of these market structures the elements of demand, costs,
**Supply Curves** and supply must be considered. The demand side of price theory is
concerned with **revenue curves**. *Average revenue* (AR) is obtained
by dividing *total revenue* (TR) by the *quantity* (Q) associated with
these revenues:

$$AR = \frac{TR}{Q}$$

The average revenue line is actually the demand curve facing
the firm. *Marginal revenue* (MR) is the change in total revenue ($\Delta$TR)
that results from selling an additional unit of output ($\Delta$Q). This can
be shown as:

$$MR = \frac{\Delta TR}{\Delta Q}$$

In order to complete the analysis, the supply curves must be determined for each of these market situations. A firm's cost structure
determines its supply curves. Let us examine each of the cost curves
applicable to price determination.

**Average cost** (AC) is obtained by dividing total cost by the quantity (Q) associated with these costs. *Total cost* (TC) is composed of
both fixed and variable components. *Fixed costs* are those costs that
do not vary with differences in output, while *variable costs* are those
that change when the level of production is altered. Examples of
fixed costs include executive compensation, depreciation, and
insurance. Variable costs include raw materials and the wages paid
production workers.

**Average variable cost** (AVC) is simply the total variable cost
(TVC) divided by the related quantity. Similarly, *average fixed cost*
(AFC) is determined by dividing total fixed costs (TFC) by the related
quantity. **Marginal cost** (MC) is the change in total cost ($\Delta$TC) that
results from producing an additional unit of output ($\Delta$Q). Thus, it
is similar to *marginal revenue*, which is the change in total revenue
resulting from the production of an incremental unit. The point of
profit maximization is where marginal costs are equal to marginal
revenues.

These cost derivations are shown in the following formulas:

$$AC = \frac{TC}{Q} \qquad AFC = \frac{TFC}{Q}$$

$$AVC = \frac{TVC}{Q} \qquad MC = \frac{\Delta TC}{\Delta Q}$$

The resulting *cost curves* are shown in Figure 13-5. The marginal cost curve (MC) intersects the average variable cost curve (AVC)
and average cost curve (AC) at the minimum points.

In the short run a firm will continue to operate even if the price falls below AC, provided it remains above AVC. Why is this rational market behaviour? If the firm were to cease operations after the price fell below AC, it would still have some fixed costs, but no revenue. Any amount received above AVC can be used to cover fixed costs. The manager is acting rationally by continuing to produce as long as price exceeds AVC since this is minimizing losses. If price falls below AVC the manager would cease operation because continued operation would result in real losses from out-of-pocket costs per unit, with no control of fixed costs. The **supply curve**, therefore, is *the marginal cost curve above its intersection with AVC since this* is the area of rational pricing behaviour for the firm.

**Figure 13-5    Cost Curves**

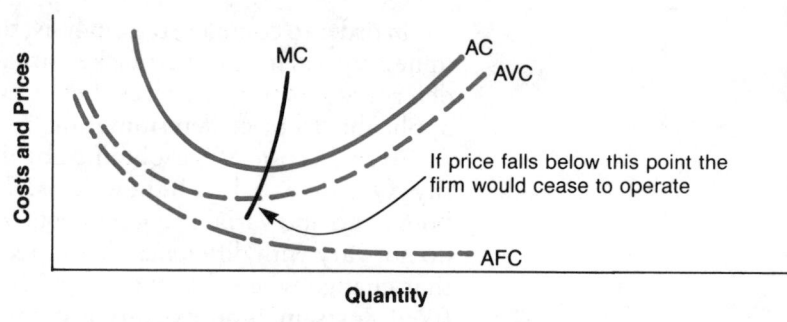

How, then, are prices set in each of the product market situations? Figure 13-6 shows how prices are determined in each of the four product markets. The point of profit maximization (MC = MR) sets the equilibrium output (Point A), which is extended to the AR line to set the equilibrium price (Point B). In the case of pure competition, AR = MR, so price is a predetermined variable in this product market.

**The Concept of Elasticity in Pricing Strategy**

Although the intersection of demand and supply curves determines the equilibrium price for each of the market structures, the specific curves vary. To understand why, it is necessary to understand the concept of elasticity.[16]

**Elasticity** is *a measure of responsiveness of purchasers and suppliers to changes in price.* The *price elasticity of demand* is the percentage change in the quantity of a product or service demanded,

---

[16] This section is adapted from Edwin G. Dolan, *Basic Economics*, 3d ed. (Hinsdale, Ill.: The Dryden Press, 1983); and Richard H. Leftwich, *The Price System and Resource Allocation* (Hinsdale, Ill.: The Dryden Press, 1979), pp. 55–56. Reprinted by permission of Holt, Rinehart & Winston.

Figure 13-6   Price Determination in the Four Product Markets

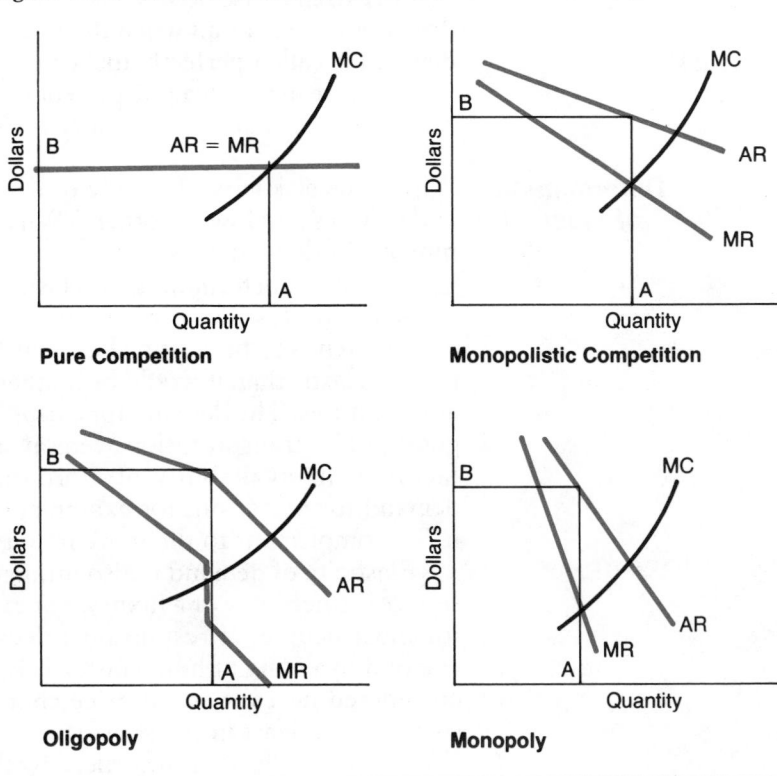

divided by the percentage change in its price. A 10 percent increase in the price of eggs that results in a 5 percent decrease in the quantity of eggs demanded yields a price elasticity of demand for eggs of 0.5.

The *price elasticity of supply* of a good is the percentage change in the quantity of a product or service supplied, divided by the percentage change in its price. If a 10 percent increase in the price of milk brings about a 22 percent increase in the quantity supplied, the change yields a price elasticity of supply for milk of 2.2.

*Elasticity Terminology*   Consider a case in which a one percent change in price causes more than a one percent change in the quantity supplied or demanded. Numerically, that means an elasticity greater than one. When the elasticity of demand or supply is greater than one, it is termed *elastic*.

If a one percent change in price results in less than a one percent change in quantity, a good's elasticity of supply or demand will be numerically less than one and is called *inelastic*. The demand for eggs in the example above is inelastic. The demand for gasoline is relatively inelastic. During 1979, retail gasoline prices rose

50 percent, but gasoline sales fell by only about 8 percent.

An extreme case occurs when the quantity supplied or demanded does not change at all when the price changes. Then the supply or demand is called perfectly inelastic.

The case in which a one percent change in price results in exactly a one percent change in quantity is called *unit* (or *unitary*) *elastic*.

**Determinants of Elasticity**

Why is the elasticity of supply or demand high for some products and services and low for others? What constitute the specific determinants of demand elasticity?[17]

One factor determining the elasticity of demand is the availability of substitutes. If a product or service has close substitutes, the demand tends to be elastic. The demand for olive oil, for instance, is more elastic than it would be if other salad oils were not available as substitutes. The demand for cars is less elastic than it would be if good public transportation were available everywhere. A related factor is the availability of more important complements. The demand for motor oil, for example, tends to be inelastic, because it is a complement to the more important good, gasoline.

Elasticity of demand is also influenced by whether a product or service is a necessity or a luxury. For example, dining out is a luxury for most people. If restaurant prices increase, most people can respond by eating at home instead. By contrast, eggs and milk are considered necessities, so price changes have less effect on consumption, at least in the short run.

Elasticity is further influenced by the portion of a person's budget that is spent on a product or service. Matches, for example, are no longer really a necessity, and good substitutes exist. Nonetheless, the demand for matches is thought to be very inelastic because people spend so little on them that they hardly notice a price change. However, the demand for housing and transportation is not perfectly inelastic even though they are necessities. Both occupy a large part of people's budgets, so a change in price cannot be ignored.

Elasticity of demand is also affected by the time perspective under consideration. Demand is often less elastic in the short run than in the long run. Consider the demand for home heating fuel. In the short run, when the price goes up, people find it difficult to cut back on the quantity they use. They are accustomed to living at a certain temperature, dressing a certain way, and so forth. Given time, though, they may find ways to economize. They can better insulate their homes, form new habits of dressing more warmly, or even move to a warmer climate.

---

[17] For a discussion of the application of price elasticity to a consumer service, see Steven J. Skinner, Terry L. Childers, and Wesley H. Jones, "Consumer Responsiveness to Price Differentials: A Case for Insurance Industry Deregulation," *Journal of Business Research* (December 1981), pp. 381–396.

All the factors mentioned here are only tendencies; yet often the tendencies reinforce one another. The classic case of inelastic demand is salt, which has no good substitute, is a nutritional necessity, and uses a very small part of one's budget. Sometimes, though, the rules just do not seem to fit. Alcohol and tobacco, which are not necessities and do occupy a large share of some personal budgets, also are subject to notoriously inelastic demand.

**Elasticity and Revenue**

There is an important relationship between the elasticity of demand and the way that total revenue changes as the price of a product or service changes. Suppose Montreal wants to find a way to raise more money for the public transportation system. One possible fund-raising method is to change the transit fare, but should it be raised or lowered? The correct answer depends on the elasticity of demand for subway rides. A 10 percent decrease in fares is sure to attract more riders, but unless there is more than a 10 percent increase in riders, total revenue will fall. A 10 percent increase in fares will bring in more money per rider, but if more than 10 percent of the riders are lost, revenue will fall. A price cut will increase revenue only if demand is elastic, and a price increase will raise revenue only if demand is inelastic.

**Practical Problems in Applying Price Theory**

From the viewpoint of the marketer, price theory concepts are sometimes difficult to apply in practice. What are their practical limitations?

1.  Many firms do not attempt to profit-maximize. Economic analysis is subject to the same limitations as the assumptions upon which it is based — for example, the proposition that all firms attempt to maximize profits.
2.  It is difficult to estimate demand curves. Modern accounting procedures provide the manager with a clear understanding of his or her cost structure. The manager, therefore, can readily comprehend the supply side of the price equation. But it is difficult to estimate demand at various price levels. Demand curves must be based upon market research estimates that are often not as exact as cost figures. Although the demand element can be identified, it is often difficult to measure in the real-world setting.[18]

---

[18] Experimental methods for estimating demand curves are discussed in Edgar A. Pessemier, *Experimental Methods of Analyzing Demand for Branded Consumer Goods* (Pullman: Bureau of Economic and Business Research, Washington State University, 1963). See also William J. Kehoe, "Demand Curve Estimation and the Small Business Managers," *Journal of Small Business Management* (July 1972), pp. 29–31.

3. Inadequate training and communications hinder price theory in the real world. Many businesspersons lack the formal training in economics to be able to apply its concepts to their own pricing decisions. On the other hand, many economists remain essentially theorists devoting little interest or effort to real-world pricing situations. This dual problem significantly hinders the use of economic theory in actual pricing practice.[19]

### Price Setting in Practice

The practical limitations inherent in price theory have forced practitioners to turn to other techniques. Actual price determination tends to be based upon some form of the cost-plus approach. For many years government contracts with suppliers called for payments of all expenses plus a set profit, usually stated as a percentage of the cost of the project. (These cost-plus contracts, as they were known, have now been abandoned in favour of competitive bidding or specifically negotiated prices.)

**Cost-plus pricing** uses some *base cost figure per unit to which is added a markup to cover unassigned costs and to provide a profit.*[20] The only real difference in the multitude of cost-plus techniques is the relative sophistication of the costing procedures employed. For example, the local clothing store may set prices by adding a 40 percent markup to the invoice price charged by the supplier. This markup is expected to cover all other expenses, as well as permit the owner to earn a reasonable return on the sale of the garments.

In contrast to this rather simple pricing mechanism, a large manufacturer may employ a pricing formula that requires a computer to handle the necessary calculations for a sophisticated costing procedure. But in the end the formula still requires someone to make a decision about the markup. The clothing store and the large manufacturer may be vastly different with respect to the *cost* aspect, but they are remarkably similar when it comes to the *markup* side of the equation.

---

[19] Some problems of using economic models in practice are discussed in Kent B. Monroe and Albert J. Della Bitta, "Models of Pricing Decisions," *Journal of Marketing Research* (August 1978), pp. 413–428. Also see Robert J. Dolan and Abel P. Jeuland, "Experience Curves and Dynamic Models: Implications for Optional Pricing Strategies," *Journal of Marketing* (Winter 1981), pp. 52–62. (Winter 1981), pp. 52–62.

[20] Interesting discussions of how costs may be used in pricing appear in David R. Rink, "What Every Businessman Should Know About the Direct Costing Approach," *IN-Sights* (Ball State University: November 1973), pp. 1–8; Len F. Minars, "Management Accounting and Product Costs for Pricing Decisions," *Baylor Business Studies* (July 1975), pp. 55–66; and Joseph P. Guiltinan, "Risk-Aversion Pricing Policies; Problems and Alternatives," *Journal of Marketing* (January 1976), pp. 10–15.

The above discussion demonstrates one of the problems associated with cost-oriented pricing. "Costs do not determine prices, since the proper function of cost in pricing is to determine the profit consequences of pricing alternatives."[21] Unfortunately, this is not always understood by some marketers.

**Full-Cost Pricing**   The two most common cost-oriented pricing procedures are the full-cost method and the incremental-cost method. *Full-cost pricing* uses all relevant variable costs in setting a product's price. In addition, it considers an allocation of the fixed costs that cannot be directly attributed to the production of the specific item being priced. Under the full-cost method, if job order 515 in a printing plant amounts to 0.000127 percent of the plant's total output, then 0.000127 percent of the firm's overhead expenses are allocated to this job. This approach, therefore, allows the pricer to recover all costs plus the amount added as a profit margin.

The full-cost approach has two basic deficiencies. First, there is no consideration of the demand for the item or its competition. Perhaps no one wants to pay the price that the firm has calculated. Second, any method of allocating overhead, or fixed expenses, is arbitrary and may be unrealistic. In manufacturing, overhead allocations are often tied to direct labour hours. In retailing, the mechanism is sometimes floor area in each profit centre. Regardless of the technique, it is difficult to show a cause-and-effect relationship between the allocated cost and most products.

**Incremental-Cost Pricing**   One way to overcome the arbitrary allocation of fixed expenses is by *incremental-cost pricing*, which attempts to use only those costs directly attributable to a specific output in setting prices. For example, consider a small manufacturer with the following income statement:

| | | |
|---|---:|---:|
| Sales (10 000 units at $10) | | $100 000 |
| Expenses | | |
| Variable | $50 000 | |
| Fixed | 40 000 | 90 000 |
| Net Profit | | $ 10 000 |

Suppose that the firm is offered a contract for an additional 5000 units. Since the peak season is over, these items can be produced at the same average variable cost. Assume that the labour force would be idle otherwise. In order to get the contract, how low could the firm price its product?

Under the full-cost approach the lowest price would be $9 each. This is obtained by dividing the $90 000 in expenses by an output

21 Theodore E. Wentz, "Realism in Pricing Analysis," *Journal of Marketing* (April 1966), p. 26.

of 10 000 units. The full-cost pricer would consider this a profitless situation. One study indicated that this method of calculation and the subsequent decision was typical of many small businesses: "A common practice is to use full costs, not as a flexible point at which the price is to be set, but as a floor below which the price will not be allowed to fall — a reference point to which flexible markups are added."[22]

The incremental approach, on the other hand, would permit a price of anywhere from $5.01 upwards depending on the competition.[22] If competition was strong, a price of $5.10 would be competitive. This price would be composed of the $5 variable cost related to each unit of production, plus a 10 cents per unit contribution to fixed expenses and overhead. With these conditions of sale, note the revised income statement:

| | | |
|---|---|---|
| Sales (10 000 at $10 plus | | |
|     5 000 at $5.10) | | $125 500 |
| Expenses | | |
|   Variable (15 000 × $5) | $75 000 | |
|   Fixed | 40 000 | 115 000 |
| Net Profit | | $ 10 500 |

Profits were increased under the incremental approach. Admittedly, the illustration is based on two assumptions: 1) the ability to isolate markets so that selling at the lower price would not affect the price received in other markets; and 2) the absence of certain legal restrictions on the firm. The example, however, does show that profits can sometimes be enhanced by using the incremental approach.

**Limitations of Cost-Oriented Pricing**

While the incremental method eliminates one of the problems associated with full-cost pricing, it fails to deal effectively with the basic malady: *cost-oriented pricing does not adequately account for product demand.*

The problem of estimating demand is as critical to these approaches as it is to classical price theory. To the marketer, the challenge is to find some way of introducing demand analysis into cost-plus pricing. It has also been pointed out that:

A well-reasoned approach to pricing is, in effect, a comparison of the impact of a decision on total sales receipts, or revenue, and on total costs. It involves the increase or decrease in revenue and costs, not just of the product under consideration, but of the business enterprise as a whole.[23]

[22] W. Warren Haynes, "Pricing Decisions in Small Business," *Management Research Summary* (Washington, D.C.: Small Business Administration, 1966), p. 1.
[23] *Ibid.*, p. 2.

# Why the Big Three Can't Cut Prices

Probably nothing the North American auto industry does today makes less sense to consumers than the way it sets car prices. If the industry persists in its contention that its pricing structure is a function of the need to calculate costs five years before production, it is unlikely that the Byzantine pricing structure will change much. However, consumer rebellion is forcing auto makers to take a new look at their manufacturing costs and marketing assumptions before affixing a price to a model. Two factors complicate the search for a solution to the problem of reducing car prices: persistent inflation and the domestic auto makers' need to pay for an $80 billion retooling switch to small vehicles.

Traditionally, the domestic auto makers keyed their prices to General Motors Corporation, because that company controls more than 60 percent of the market for North American–built cars. The process got more complicated when imports, mainly from Japan, began infiltrating North America. Foreign auto makers pay different labour rates, have different levels of productivity, make different assumptions about investment paybacks for new tooling, and even manage their factories differently. Several studies say the difference in production costs between domestic and Japanese auto makers is at least $1500 per car. That

difference would give Japanese companies a huge cushion from which to react to permanent price cuts from the Big Three. Robert J. Orsini, vice-president for strategic management consulting with William C. Roney & Co., estimates that domestic car makers must find a way to cut production costs a staggering $2200 per car if they expect to compete fully with the Japanese. Analysts suggest North American producers could give up their determination to break even on a new car model within four or five years and stretch the payback period to perhaps eight years as the Japanese do. This would reduce costs per year by altering the way the auto makers account for such expenses.

But LeRoy H. Lindgren, a vice-president and industrial cost consultant with Rath & Strong, Inc., believes that much of the $1500 difference comes from the production snags that accompany the conversion to front-wheel drive and brand-new body designs. "We're going through a tremendous conversion, and the Japanese aren't," he says. Lindgren figures it takes a plant about two years after such sweeping changes in tooling and manufacturing methods to achieve output efficiencies. In the meantime, he says, many North American auto plants are running up costs per car two or three times their eventual levels.

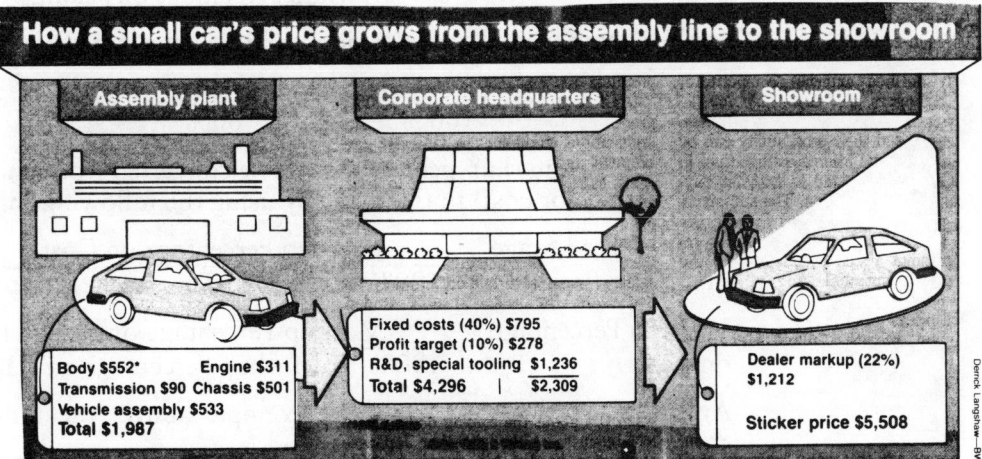

Source: Adapted from "Why Detroit Can't Cut Prices," *Business Week* (March 1, 1982), pp. 110–111. Drawing by Derrick Langshaw. Reprinted by permission.

**Markups, Markdowns,
and Turnover**

A frequent criticism of pricing practices is that decision-makers have consistently attempted to develop rigid procedures by which prices can be derived in a largely mechanical fashion. These efforts often produce inappropriate prices for specific market situations because they ignore the creative aspects of pricing.

**Markups**   Markup policies are an example of this problem. A **markup** is *the amount a producer or channel member adds to cost in order to determine the selling price.* It is typically stated as either a percentage of the selling price or of cost. The formulas used in calculating markup percentages are as follows:

$$\text{Markup Percentage on Selling Price} = \frac{\text{Amount Added to Cost (the Markup)}}{\text{Price}}$$

$$\text{Markup Percentage on Cost} = \frac{\text{Amount Added to Cost (the Markup)}}{\text{Cost}}$$

Consider an example from retailing. Suppose an item selling for $1.00 has an invoice cost of $0.60. The total markup is $0.40. The markup percentages would be calculated as follows:

$$\text{Markup Percentage on Selling Price} = \frac{\$0.40}{\$1.00} = 40\%$$

$$\text{Markup Percentage on Cost} = \frac{\$0.40}{\$0.60} = 67\%$$

To determine selling price when only cost and markup percentage on selling price are known, the following formula is utilized:

$$\text{Price} = \frac{\text{Cost in Dollars}}{100\% - \text{Markup Percentage on Selling Price}}$$

In the example cited above, price could be determined as $1.00:

$$\text{Price} = \frac{\$.60}{100\% - 40\%} = \frac{.60}{60\%} = \$1.00.$$

Similarly, the markup percentage can be converted from one basis (selling price or cost) to the other by using the following formula:

$$\text{Markup Percentage on Selling Price} = \frac{\text{Markup Percentage on Cost}}{100\% + \text{Markup Percentage on Cost}}$$

$$\text{Markup Percentage on Cost} = \frac{\text{Markup Percentage on Selling Price}}{100\% - \text{Markup Percentage on Selling Price}}$$

Again, using the data from the example above, the following conversions can be made:

$$\text{Markup Percentage on Selling Price} = \frac{67\%}{100\% + 67\%} = \frac{67\%}{167\%} = 40\%$$

$$\text{Markup Percentage on} \atop \text{Cost} = \frac{40\%}{100\% - 40\%} = \frac{40\%}{60\%} = 67\%$$

**Markdowns**   A related pricing issue that is particularly important to retailers is markdowns. Markups are based partially on executive judgements about the prices consumers are likely to pay for a given product or service. If buyers refuse to pay the price, however, the marketer must take a **markdown**, a reduction in the price of the item. For purposes of internal control and analysis, the markdown percentage is computed as follows:

$$\text{Markdown Percentage} = \frac{\text{Markdown}}{\text{"Sale" (New) Price}}$$

Suppose no one was willing to pay $1.00 for an item and the marketer decided to reduce the price to $.75. The markdown percentage would be:

$$\text{Markdown Percentage} = \frac{\$.25}{\$.75} = 33\frac{1}{3}\%$$

From a customer's viewpoint, this is only a 25% reduction, and is known as the "off-retail percentage." This is the percentage which should be quoted in advertisements. Markdowns are also used for evaluative purposes. For instance, department managers or buyers in a large department store could be evaluated partially on the basis of the average markdown percentage on the product lines for which they are responsible.

**Turnover**   All too often, traditional markup and markdown percentages lead to competitive inertia within an industry. Standard percentages are too frequently applied to all items in a given category regardless of factors such as demand.

A method for avoiding competitive inertia is to use flexible markups that vary with **stock turnover** — *the number of times the average inventory is sold annually*. The figure can be calculated by one of the following formulas. When inventory is recorded at retail:

$$\text{Stock Turnover} = \frac{\text{Sales}}{\text{Average Inventory}}$$

When inventory is recorded at cost:

$$\text{Stock Turnover} = \frac{\text{Cost of Goods Sold}}{\text{Average Inventory}}$$

Store A, with $100 000 in sales and an average inventory at $20 000 (at retail), would have a stock turnover of 5. Store B, with $200 000 in sales, a 40 percent markup rate, and an average inventory of $30 000 (at cost), would have a stock turnover of 4.

| Store A | | Store B |
|---|---|---|
| $\dfrac{\text{Stock}}{\text{Turnover}} = \dfrac{\$100\ 000}{\$20\ 000} = 5$ | | $\$200\ 000$ Sales |
| | | $-80\ 000$ Markup (40 percent) |
| | | $\$120\ 000$ Cost of Goods Sold |
| | | $\dfrac{\text{Stock}}{\text{Turnover}} = \dfrac{\$120\ 000}{\$30\ 000} = 4$ |

While most marketers recognize the importance of turnover, they often use it more as a measure of sales effectiveness than as a pricing tool. However, it can be particularly useful in setting markup percentages if some consideration is given to consumer demand.

Figure 13-7 indicates the relationship between stock turnover and markup. Above-average turnover, such as for grocery products, are generally associated with relatively low markup percentages. On the other hand, higher markup percentages typically exist in such product lines as jewellery and furniture where relatively lower annual stock turnover is common and inventory and overhead costs must be covered through higher margins.

**Figure 13-7    Relationship between Markup Percentage and Stock Turnover**

| Stock Turnover Rate in Relation to the Industry Average | Markup Percentage in Relation to the Industry Average | Product Example |
|---|---|---|
| High | Low | Soft Drinks |
| Average | Average | Motor Oil |
| Low | High | Sports Cars |

**Break-even Analysis**

**Break-even analysis** is *a means of determining the number of products or services that must be sold at a given price in order to generate sufficient revenue to cover total costs.* Figure 13-8 shows calculation of the break-even point graphically. The total cost curve includes both fixed and variable segments, and total fixed cost is represented by a horizontal line. Average variable cost is assumed to be constant per unit as it was in the example used for incremental pricing.

The break-even point is the point at which total revenue ($TR$) just equals total cost ($TC$). It can be found by using the following formulas:

$$\text{Break-even Point (in Units)} = \frac{\text{Total Fixed Cost}}{\text{Per Unit Selling Price} - \text{Average variable cost}}$$

$$= \frac{\text{Total Fixed Cost}}{\text{Per Unit Contribution to Fixed Cost}}$$

$$\text{Break-even Point (in Dollars)} = \frac{\text{Total Fixed Cost}}{1 - \dfrac{\text{Variable Cost per Unit}}{\text{Selling Price}}}$$

In our earlier example, a selling price of $10 and an average variable cost of $5 resulted in a per unit contribution to fixed costs of $5. This figure can be divided into total fixed costs of $40 000 to obtain a break-even point of 8000 units, or $80 000 in total sales revenue:

$$\text{Break-even Point (in Units)} = \frac{\$40\ 000}{\$10 - \$5} = \frac{\$40\ 000}{\$5} = 8000 \text{ units}$$

$$\text{Break-even Point (in Dollars)} = \frac{\$40\ 000}{1 - \dfrac{\$5}{\$10}} = \frac{\$40\ 000}{0.5} = \$80\ 000$$

$$\text{Break-even Profit Point (in Dollars)} = \frac{\$40\ 000 + 10\% \text{ on Sales } (\$8000)}{1 - \dfrac{\$5}{\$10}} = \frac{\$48\ 000}{.5} = \$96\ 000$$

Break-even analysis is an effective tool for marketers in assessing the required sales in order to cover costs and achieve specified profit levels. It is easily understood by both marketing and nonmarketing

**Figure 13-8   Break-even Chart**

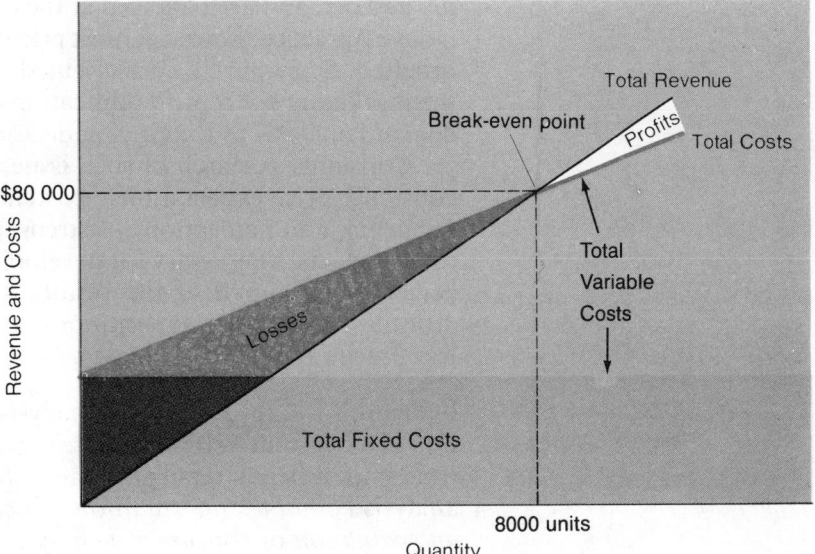

executives and may assist in deciding whether required sales levels for a certain price are in fact realistic goals. Extending this analysis a bit further, a simple profit breakdown is also shown in the example. If a 10 percent profit on sales were desired, sales of $96 000 would be required. More data would be needed if a return on investment, or some other measure was used as a profitability target. However, it is not without shortcomings.

First, the model assumes that costs can be divided into fixed and variable categories. Some costs, such as salaries and advertising outlays, may be either fixed or variable depending upon the particular situation. In addition, the model assumes that per unit variable costs do not change at different levels of operation. However, these may vary as a result of quantity discounts, more efficient utilization of the work force, or other economies resulting from increased levels of production and sales. Finally, the basic break-even model does not consider demand. It is a cost-based model and does not directly address the crucial question of whether consumers will actually purchase the product at the specified price and in the required quantities to break even or to generate profits. The challenge of the marketer is to modify break-even analysis and the other cost-oriented approaches to pricing in order to introduce demand analysis. Pricing must be examined from the buyer's perspective. Such decisions cannot be made in a management vacuum in which only cost factors are considered.

### Toward Realistic Pricing

Traditional economic theory considers both costs and demand in the determination of an equilibrium price. The dual elements of supply and demand are balanced at the point of equilibrium. In actual industry practice, however, most pricing approaches are largely cost-oriented. Since purely cost-oriented approaches to pricing violate the marketing concept, modifications are required in order to add demand analysis to the pricing decision.

Consumer research of such issues as degree of price elasticity, consumer price expectations, existence and size of specific market segments, and perceptions of strengths and weaknesses of substitute products is necessary for developing sales estimates at different prices. Since much of the resultant data involves perceptions, attitudes, and future expectations, such estimates are likely to be less precise than cost estimates.

### The Dynamic Break-even Concept

In Figure 13-8, the break-even analysis was based upon the assumption of a constant $10 retail price regardless of quantity. What happens when different retail prices are considered? **Dynamic break-even analysis** *combines the traditional break-even analysis model with an evaluation of consumer demand.*

Figure 13-9 summarizes both the cost and revenue aspects of a number of alternative retail prices. The cost data are based upon the costs utilized earlier in the basic break-even model. The expected unit sales for each specified retail price are obtained from consumer research. The data in the first two columns of Figure 13-9 represent a demand schedule by indicating the number of units consumers are expected to purchase at each of a series of retail prices. This data can be superimposed onto a break-even chart in order to identify the range of feasible prices for consideration by the marketing decision-maker. This is shown in Figure 13-10.

**Figure 13-9   Revenue and Cost Data for Dynamic Break-even Analysis**

| | Revenues | | | Costs | | |
|---|---|---|---|---|---|---|
| Price | Quantity Demanded | Total Revenue | Total Fixed Cost | Total Variable Cost | Total Cost | Total Profit (or Loss) |
| $14 | 3 000 | $ 42 000 | $40 000 | $ 15 000 | $ 55 000 | ($13 000) |
| 12 | 6 000 | 72 000 | 40 000 | 30 000 | 70 000 | 2 000 |
| 10 | 10 000 | 100 000 | 40 000 | 50 000 | 90 000 | 10 000 |
| 8 | 14 000 | 112 000 | 40 000 | 70 000 | 110 000 | 2 000 |
| 6 | 26 000 | 156 000 | 40 000 | 130 000 | 170 000 | (14 000) |

As Figure 13-10 indicates, the range of profitable prices exists from a low of approximately $8 ($TR_4$) to a high of $12 ($TR_2$), with a price of $10 ($TR_3$) generating the greatest projected profits. Changing the retail price produces a new break-even point. At a relatively high $14 retail price, the break-even point is 4445 units; at a $10 retail price the break-even point is 8000 units; and at a $6 price, 40 000 units must be sold in order to break even.

The contribution of dynamic break-even analysis is that it forces the pricing decision-maker to consider whether the consumer is likely to purchase the required number of units of a product or service that will achieve break-even at a given price. It demonstrates that a larger number of units sold does not necessarily produce added profits, since — other things equal — lower prices are necessary to stimulate added sales. Consequently, it necessitates careful consideration of both costs and consumer demand in determining the most appropriate price.

*A Pricing Decision Procedure*   A product which is new to the world, as opposed to being merely new to the company, passes through distinctive stages in its life cycle. The appropriate pricing policy is likely to be different at each stage.[24] Perhaps the most difficult task is establishing an initial price for the

[24] Joel Dean, "Techniques for Pricing New Products and Services," in Victor P. Buell and Carl Heyel, eds., *Handbook of Modern Marketing*, (McGraw-Hill Book Company, 1970), pp. 5–51.

product. In later stages of the product life cycle, pricing is complicated enough, but strategic decisions hinge largely on decisions to
meet or beat competition in various ways.

G. David Hughes has suggested a pricing procedure that is especially appropriate for new products but which can be used for new-
to-the-company market entries as well (see Figure 13-11). It takes

**Figure 13-10   Dynamic Break-even Chart Reflecting Costs and Consumer Demand**

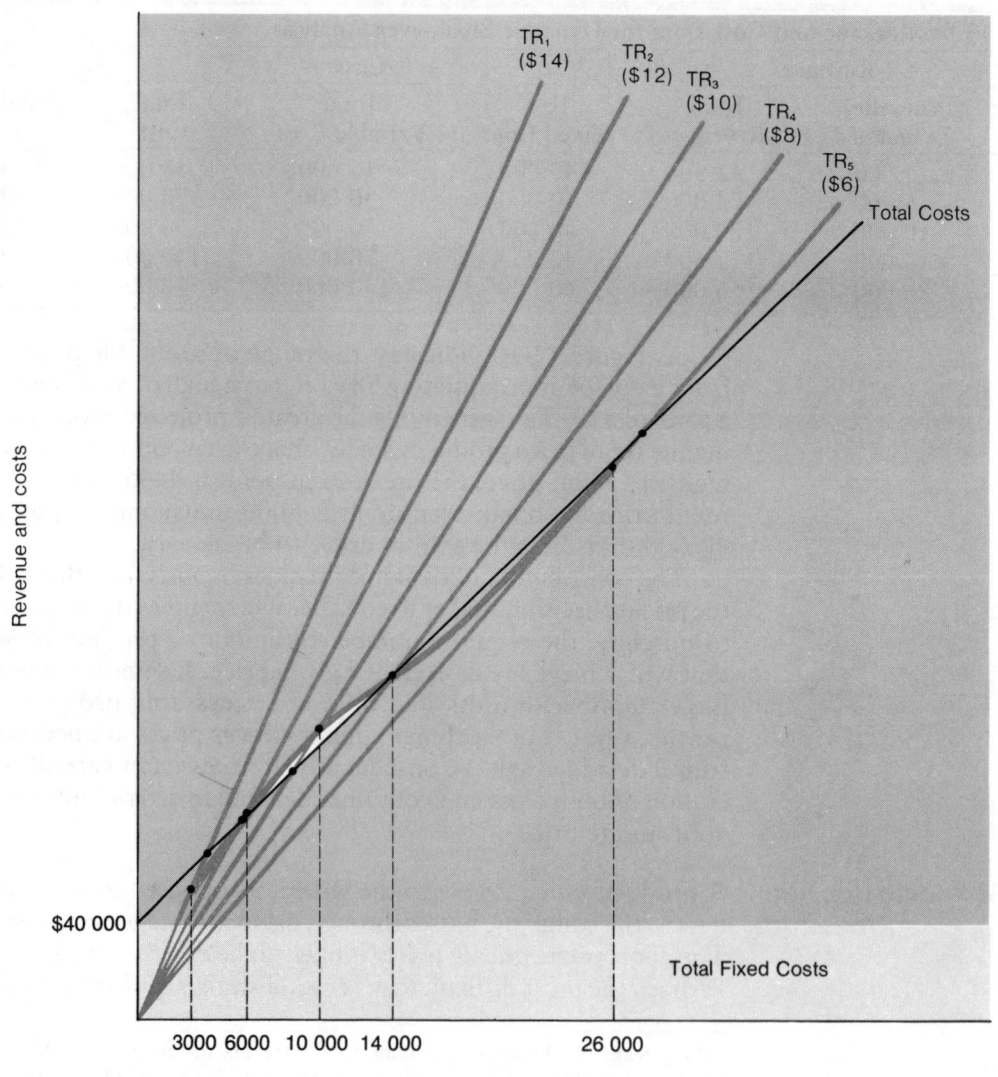

into account many of the points considered in this chapter.[25]

**Establish the range of acceptable prices.** The first step is to establish a price range that is consistent with corporate values, objectives, and policies. The pricing policies of top executives who are risk-takers may be different from those of risk-averters. The range of prices will be predicated on the company's desire to establish a discount image or a quality image. Similarly, a decision to use a prestige channel of distribution will determine channel discount structures, which in turn will be reflected in a final price.

**Set price for a planned target market.** As with virtually all marketing mix decisions, the pricing process has to be developed with a specific market target in mind. Given some estimate of the demand curve for the target segment, the price strategist attempts to identify the price that will maximize sales or profits.

**Estimate demand for the brand.** This price is then positioned against competitive prices to determine expected market share. If this share is too small, the strategist will go back to the generic demand (i.e., primary demand, or those needs which can be met by a product category) and select a new price.

**Estimate competitor's reactions.** Once a price is selected which provides what seems to be an acceptable sales volume, the next task is to estimate how competitors will react. A very low price may cause a price war in an oligopoly. An exceptionally high price may attract lower priced competition. If either of these responses would destroy the basic marketing strategy, the strategist must go back and select a new price.

**Consider public policy implications.** Unfavourable reactions from the public may take many forms. Provincial or federal authorities may look on a given price strategy in a monopoly-type situation as unconscionable and therefore subject to legislation or regulation. Consumerists may regard a price as excessive and boycott all of the company's products. Labour unions may regard a price increase as an indication that the company can now afford to raise wages.

**Test the price against financial goals.** The next test is to see if the pricing strategy will meet financial goals such as return on investment (ROI), target rate of return on sales, or a payback period. Failure to meet financial goals sends the pricing strategist back to the generic-demand curve to select a new price for analysis. In actual practice, the strategist will probably have tested the price against the financial goals before proceeding to the positioning of the price among other brands, because rough calculations can be based on previous experience. In fact, it is desirable to make profit plans as

---

25 This section has been adapted from G. David Hughes, *Marketing Management: A Planning Approach* (Menlo Park: Addison-Wesley Publishing Company, 1978), pp. 324–326.

**Figure 13-11    Pricing Decision
                  Flow Chart**

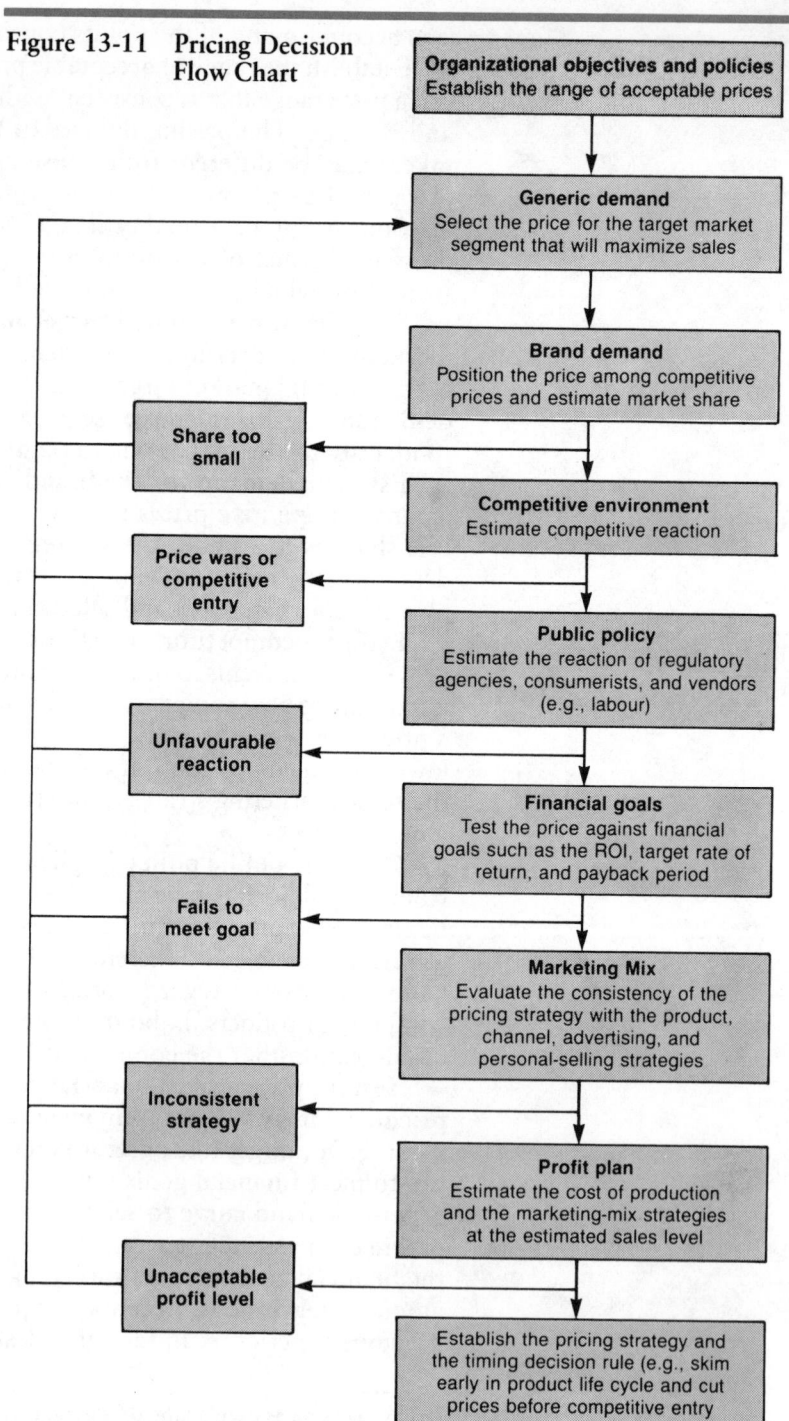

Source: Adapted from G. David Hughes, *Marketing Management: A Planning Approach*
(Menlo Park: Addison-Wesley Publishing Company, 1978), p. 325.

early as the concept stage during new-product development. These plans can be continually updated as the product passes through the development stages.

**Evaluate its congruence in the mix.** The selected price must be evaluated in terms of the product, channel, advertising, and personal-selling strategies that will be used in the market segment in question. The role of price in the marketing mix should be specifically identified, and all elements of the mix must blend together. Any inconsistencies must be reconciled by altering the price or one of the other elements of the mix.

A low price is appropriate when the product category is at the mature stage in its cycle. A low price may also be appropriate when there is little promotion, the product is mass-produced, market coverage is intense, production is capital intensive, technological change is slow, the product is needed to complete the product line, few services are offered, the product is disposable, or the life cycle is short.[26]

**Develop a profit plan.** The cost of production and the cost of the marketing-mix strategy at the estimated sales level provide inputs for the profit plan. An inadequate profit may send the strategist back to the setting of a new price or to the reduction of the cost of other elements in the marketing mix.

**Finalize actual price and timing.** The last stage in the process is to establish the final price. This is done in light of the preceding steps, but it also takes into specific consideration the actual prices of competing products. For example, the profit plan calculation might indicate a price of $71.87, but the final price offered to the market might be $69.95. This might be chosen for psychological reasons (it sounds less expensive), or better to meet the prices of competitors. If a high-priced skimming strategy (described in Chapter 14) has been chosen, a timing decision should also be reached in order to be ready to cut prices when predetermined conditions occur.

---

[26] W. J. E. Crissy and R. Boewadt, "Pricing in Perspective," *Sales Management* (June 15, 1971).

# The Multistage Approach to Pricing

Alfred R. Oxenfeldt's research into pricing led to the development of a decision model commonly identified as the multistage approach to pricing.[27]

This model provides a sequential process for making improved pricing decisions. The various steps in the Oxenfeldt approach are as follows:

1. *Select specific target markets.* The target groups should be explicitly identified, to provide a basis for the price decision.
2. *Select appropriate brand image.* The image should have a strong positive appeal to target customers.
3. *Determine the best marketing mix.* Allocate specific attention to the relative emphasis given to the price variable.
4. *Set a pricing policy that will provide a consistent response to recurring pricing questions.*
5. *Choose a price strategy for existing market conditions.*
6. *Set the actual price.* The price should be a logical consequence of the earlier steps.

## The Multistage Approach at Humbolt Electric

The management of Humbolt Electric Company, the world's third largest manufacturer of small appliances, had been considering the introduction of its newest product — a battery-driven household blender. One of the company's greatest concerns was how to price the blender. Here is how Humbolt went about solving its pricing quandary.

With the help of the market research department, the blender's target market was defined as younger couples who the firm believed were more inclined to purchase a new appliance innovation. Management decided to retain its existing brand image as a quality, higher-priced product line. The composition of the marketing mix was announced by Allan R. Ferzacurri, the director of marketing, after consultation with market research, sales, and advertising personnel in the organization. It was decided that the blender would be custom-packaged and distributed through leading department stores in line with Humbolt's existing brand image. Since the battery blender would carry a price tag somewhat higher than conventional blenders, Ferzacurri decided to employ substantial promotional expenditures to support the new appliance entry.

Humbolt elected to follow its existing price policy of maintaining its suggested retail price. The firm did not offer discounts, promotional allowances, or other price reductions to its dealers. Ferzacurri's pricing strategy was one of skimming the cream off the market rather than trying to gain consumer acceptance through low introductory prices. Finally, the specific price of the new item was set at 15 percent above that of standard plug-in blenders. This price was set after the marketing staff had compared profit consequences of alternative prices by using break-even analysis and had evaluated varying markup percentages in relationship to expected stock turnover.

Humboldt's pricing of the new blender is an excellent example of how the multistage approach should be employed.

---

[27] Alfred R. Oxenfeldt, "Multi-Stage Approach to Pricing," *Harvard Business Review* (July–August 1960), pp. 125–133. See also Alfred R. Oxenfeldt, *Pricing for Marketing Executives* (Belmont, Calif.: Wadsworth Publishing Company, 1961), pp. 72–76, and "A Decision-Making Structure for Price Decisions," *Journal of Marketing* (January 1973), pp. 48–53.

**Summary**    Price—the exchange value of a good or service—is important because it regulates economic activity as well as determines the revenue to be received by an individual firm. As a marketing mix element, pricing is one of those grey areas where marketers struggle to develop a theory, technique, or rule of thumb on which they can depend. It is a complex variable because it contains both objective and subjective aspects. It is an area where precise decision-making tools and executive judgement meet.

Pricing objectives should be the natural consequence of overall organizational goals and more specific marketing goals. They can be classified into four major groupings: 1) profitability objectives, including profit maximization and target return; 2) volume objectives, including sales maximization and market share; 3) meeting competition objectives; and 4) prestige objectives.

Prices can be determined by theoretical or cost-oriented approaches. Economic theorists attempt to equate marginal revenue and marginal cost. Elasticity is an important element in price determination. The degree of consumer responsiveness to changes in price is affected directly by the availability of substitutes and inversely to the availability of complementary goods. It is also affected by whether a product or service is a necessity or a luxury, the portion of a person's budget being spent, and the time perspective under consideration.

Price determination in practice frequently emphasizes costs. Break-even analysis and the use of markups are essentially cost-plus approaches to pricing.

A more realistic approach to effective price decisions is to integrate both buyer demand and costs. Dynamic break-even analysis is a method for accomplishing this task.

**Key Terms**

| | |
|---|---|
| price | revenue curves |
| profit maximization | average cost |
| target return objectives | average variable cost |
| sales maximization | marginal cost |
| market share | supply curve |
| status quo objectives | elasticity |
| prestige objectives | cost-plus pricing |
| customary prices | markup |
| pure competition | markdown |
| monopolistic competition | stock turnover |
| oligopoly | break-even analysis |
| oligopsony | dynamic break-even analysis |
| monopoly | |

1. Identify the four major categories of pricing objectives.
2. Categorize each of the following into a specific type of pricing objective:
   a. 8 percent increase in market share
   b. 5 percent increase in profits over previous year
   c. prices no more than 5 percent higher than prices quoted by independent dealers
   d. 20 percent return on investment (before taxes)
   e. highest prices in product category to maintain favourable brand image
   f. follow price of most important competitor in each market segment
3. What are the major price implications of the PIMS studies? Suggest possible explanations for the relationships discovered by the studies.
4. What market situations exist for the pricing of the following products:
   a. telephone service       e. potatoes
   b. Candu nuclear reactors  f. dishwashers
   c. golf clubs              g. tape recorders
   d. steel                   h. skis
5. Explain the concept of elasticity. What are the determinants of the degree of price elasticity for a product or service?
6. What are the practical problems involved in attempting to apply price theory concepts to actual pricing decisions?
7. Explain the advantages of using incremental cost pricing rather than full cost pricing. What potential drawbacks exist?
8. Explain the relationship between markups and stock turnover rates.
9. Explain the primary benefits of using break-even analysis in price determination. What are the shortcomings of the basic break-even model?
10. In what ways is dynamic break-even analysis superior to the basic model?

**Discussion Questions**
**and Exercises**  1. A retailer has just received a new kitchen appliance invoiced at $28. The retailer decides to follow industry practice for such items and adds a 40 percent markup percentage on selling price. What retail price should the retailer assign to the appliance?
2. If a product has a markup percentage on selling price of 28 percent, what is its markup percentage on cost?
3. An economic downturn in the local area has seriously affected sales of a retailer's line of $150 dresses. The store manager decides to mark these dresses down to $125. What markdown percentage should be featured in advertising this sale item?

4. A store with an average inventory of $50 000 (at cost) operates on a 40 percent markup percentage on selling price. Annual sales total $750 000. What is the stock turnover rate?

5. What is the break-even point in dollars and units for a product with a selling price of $25, related fixed costs of $126 000, and per unit variable costs of $16?

**MICROCOMPUTER EXERCISE: Markups**

As noted in this chapter, markup policies play a significant role in real-world pricing. Markups can be defined as the amounts a producer or channel member adds to costs in order to determine the selling prices. Markups are stated as a percentage of the selling price or cost.

Directions:   Use the Menu Item titled "Markups" on the *Foundations of Marketing* disk to solve the following problems.

1. An art boutique in downtown Toronto sells a native carving for $180. The carving actually costs the boutique $60. What are the boutique's markup percentages on selling price and on cost?

2. The gift shops at the Dorval airport use a markup percentage based on selling price of 60 percent for a line of T-shirts. What would be the markup percentage on cost for the T-shirts?

3. A shoe store in Windsor, Ont., adds a 50 percent markup (based on selling price) to its shoes. A shipment has just arrived, carrying an invoice price of $50 per pair. What should the retail selling price be for each pair of shoes?

**MICROCOMPUTER EXERCISE: Break-even Analysis**

Break-even analysis is a useful tool in pricing strategy. It can be used to determine the sales volume (either in dollars or units) that must be achieved at a specified price to generate sufficient revenues to cover total production and marketing costs. Target-profit returns, either in absolute dollar amounts or in percentages of sales, can also be included in the break-even model. Modified break-even analysis is a technique for including assessments of consumer demand into the basic break-even model. By considering estimated sales at several different possible prices, modified break-even analysis aids the marketing decision-maker in determining the required volume needed to break even at various prices. It also shows whether such sales can be achieved.

Directions:   Use the Menu Item titled "Break-even Analysis" on the *Foundations of Marketing* disk to solve the following problems.

1. Federated Manufacturing of Burnaby, B.C., is considering the possible introduction of a new product. The marketing-research staff

estimates that the product could be marketed at a price of $20. Total fixed costs are $120 000 and the average variable costs are calculated to be $14.

a. What is the break-even point in units for the proposed product?

b. Federated's controller has suggested a target-profit return of $90 000 for the proposed product. How many units must be sold to break even and achieve this target return?

c. The national sales manager at Federated made a counter-proposal of a 10 percent return on sales as a realistic expectation for the proposed new product. How many units must be sold to break even and achieve the return specified by the national sales manager?

d. How would your answers to Questions A, B, and C change if the proposed price were increased to $23?

2. Sunshine Industries of Edmonton, Alta., has developed the following sales estimates for a proposed new gag gift designed to be marketed through direct-mail sales.

| Proposed Selling Price | Sales Estimates, in Units |
|---|---|
| $4.00 | 27 500 |
| $5.00 | 11 000 |
| $7.50 | 7 500 |
| $10.00 | 2 500 |
| $12.00 | 1 400 |

The new product has total fixed costs of $30 000, and a $3.50 variable cost per unit.

a. Which of the prices listed above would be profitable to Sunshine Industries?

b. The marketing-research director also estimates that an additional $0.25-per-unit promotion allocation would produce the following increases in sales estimates: 34 500 units at a $4.00 selling price; 14 000 units at $5.00; 8 500 units at $7.50; 3 000 units at $10.00; and 1 750 units at $12.00. Indicate the feasible range of prices if this proposal is implemented and it results in the predicted sales increases.

c. Indicate the feasible price or prices if the $0.25-per-unit additional proposal is not implemented, but management insists upon a $12 500 target return.

## CHAPTER 14

# Managing the Pricing Function

1. To explain how pricing decisions are organized.

2. To describe how prices are quoted.

3. To identify the various pricing policy decisions that must be made by the marketer.

4. To compare skimming and penetration pricing.

5. To explain the relationship between price levels, advertising expenditures, and profitability.

6. To contrast negotiated prices and competitive bidding.

7. To explain the importance of transfer pricing.

8. To describe pricing in the public sector.

---

**The Conceptual Framework**

Chapter 13 introduced the concept of price and its role in the economic system and in marketing strategy. It concluded with a discussion of useful decision models for pricing strategy. There are, however, several other important aspects of pricing.

This chapter will consider who should be responsible for the pricing decision and how prices are quoted, and will discuss various aspects of pricing policies. Finally, other pricing practices such as negotiated prices, competitive bidding, and the pricing of public services are considered.

---

**Organization for Pricing Decisions**

In translating pricing objectives into pricing decisions, there are two major steps to follow. First some person or group must be assigned responsibility for making pricing decisions and administering the pricing structure. Then that person or group must set the overall pricing structure — that is, the selected price and the appropriate discounts for channel members as well as for various quantities and for geographic and promotional considerations.[1]

---

[1] The delegation of pricing responsibility is discussed in P. Ronald Stephenson, William L. Cron, and Gary L. Frazier, "Delegating Pricing Authority to the Sales Force: The Effects on Sales and Profit Performance," *Journal of Marketing* (Spring 1979), pp. 21–28.

A recent survey of marketing executives found that the people or groups most commonly chosen to *set* price structures were 1) a pricing committee composed of top executives, 2) the president of the company, and 3) the chief marketing officer. According to the same survey, the pricing structure is *administered* most often by marketers. As Figure 14-1 indicates, the chief marketing officer was the responsible person in 51 percent of the firms surveyed. In all, marketers administered the pricing structure in over 68 percent of

**Figure 14-1    Executives Responsible for Setting and Administering Price Structures**

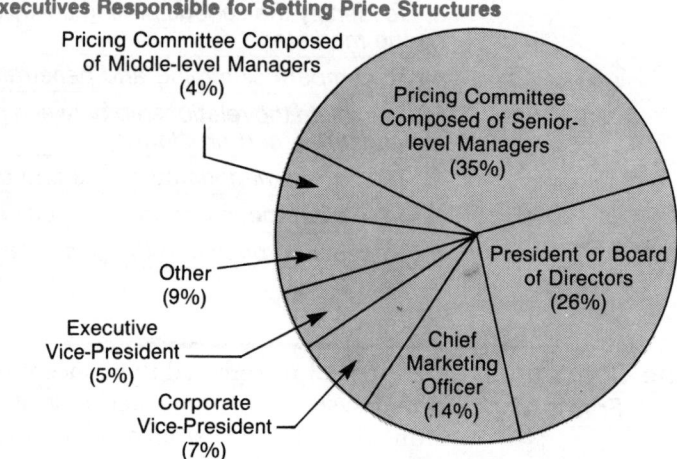

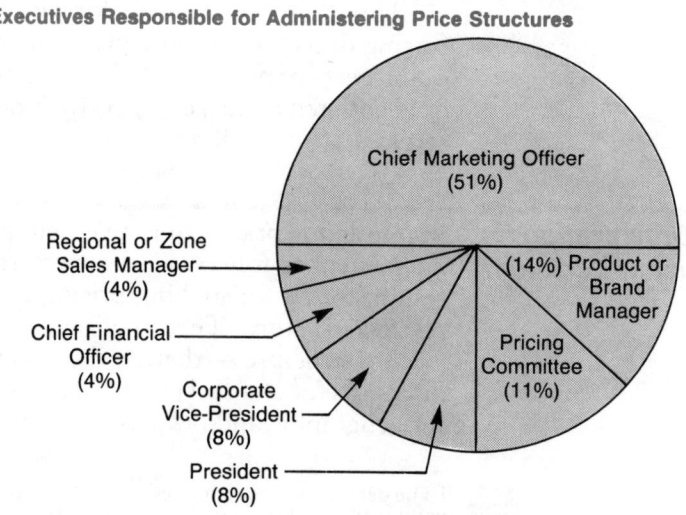

the companies, a result that is consistent with industry's attempt to implement the marketing concept.

**Price Quotations**

How prices are quoted depends on many factors, such as cost structures, traditional practice in the particular industry, and the policies of individual firms. In this section we shall examine the reasoning and methodology behind price quotations.

The basis upon which most price structures is built is the **list price**, *the rate normally quoted to potential buyers.* List price is usually determined by one or a combination of the methods discussed in Chapter 13. The sticker prices on new automobiles are good examples. They show the list price for the basic model, then add the list price for the options that have been included.

**Discounts, Allowances, and Rebates**

*The amount that a consumer pays* — the **market price** — may or may not be the same as the list price. In some cases discounts or allowances reduce the list price. List price is often used as the starting point from which discounts that set the market price are derived. Discounts can be classified as cash, quantity, or trade.

**Cash discounts** are those *reductions in price that are given for prompt payment of a bill.* They are probably the most commonly used variety. Cash discounts usually specify an exact time period, such as "2/10, net 30." This would mean that the bill is due within 30 days, but if it is paid in 10 days, the customer may subtract 2 percent from the amount due. Cash discounts have become a traditional pricing practice in many industries. They are legal provided that they are granted all customers on the same terms. Such discounts were originally instituted to improve the liquidity position of sellers, lower bad-debt losses, and reduce the expenses associated with the collection of bills. Whether these advantages outweigh the relatively high cost of capital involved in cash discounts depends upon the buyer's need for liquidity as well as alternative sources (and costs) of funds.

**Trade discounts**, which are also called *functional discounts*, are *payments to channel members or buyers for performing some marketing function normally required of the manufacturer.* These are legitimate as long as all buyers in the same category, such as wholesalers and retailers, receive the same discount privilege. Trade discounts were initially based on the operating expenses of each trade category, but have now become more of a matter of custom in some industries. An example of a trade discount would be "40 percent, 10 percent off list price" for wholesalers. In other words, the wholesaler passes the 40 percent on to his or her customers (retailers) and keeps the 10 percent discount as payment for activities such as storing and transporting. The price to the wholesaler on a $100 000 order would be $54 000 ($100 000 less 40% = $60 000 less 10%).

**Quantity discounts** are *price reductions granted because of large purchases*. These discounts are justified on the grounds that large-volume purchases reduce selling expenses and may shift a part of the storing, transporting, and financing functions to the buyer. Quantity discounts are lawful provided they are offered on the same basis to all customers.

| Figure 14-2   A Noncumulative Quantity Discount Schedule | |
|---|---|
| Units Purchased | Price |
| 1 | List price |
| 2–5 | List price less 10 percent |
| 6–10 | List price less 20 percent |
| over 10 | List price less 25 percent |

Quantity discounts may be either noncumulative or cumulative. *Noncumulative quantity discounts* are one-time reductions in list price. For instance, a firm might offer the discount schedule in Figure 14-2. *Cumulative quantity discounts* are reductions determined by purchases over a stated time period. Annual purchases of $25 000 might entitle the buyer to an 8 percent rebate, while purchases exceeding $50 000 would mean a 15 percent refund. These reductions are really patronage discounts since they tend to bind the customer to one source of supply.

Allowances are similar to discounts in that they are deductions from the price the purchaser must pay. The major categories of allowances are trade-ins and promotional allowances. **Trade-ins** are often used in the sale of durable goods such as automobiles. They *permit a reduction without altering the basic list price* by deducting from the item's price an amount for the customer's old item that is being replaced. **Promotional allowances** are *attempts to integrate promotional strategy in the channel*. For example, manufacturers often provide advertising and sales-support allowances for other channel members. Automobile manufacturers have offered allowances to retail dealers several times in recent years to permit dealers to lower prices while maintaining their margins.

**Rebates** are *refunds by the seller of a portion of the purchase price*. They have been used most prominently by automobile manufacturers eager to move models during periods of slow sales. Wardair has also used rebates. Wardair promised warm weather for its Florida charter customers and backed the promise with a $5 rebate for each day of less than 22°C weather.[2] Manufacturers' rebates are sometimes used to stimulate sales of small appliances such as coffee brewers.

---

[2] Katrinka W. Leefmans, "Business Bulletin," *Wall Street Journal* (December 20, 1979), p. 1.

**Geographic Considerations**

Geographic considerations are important in pricing when the shipment of heavy, bulky, low unit-cost materials is involved. Prices may be quoted with either the buyer or seller paying all transportation charges or with some type of expense sharing.

> The way in which this problem is handled can greatly influence the success of a firm's marketing program by helping to determine the scope of the geographic market area the firm is able to serve, the vulnerability of the firm to price competition in areas located near its production facilities, the net margins earned on individual sales of the product, the ability of the firm to control or influence resale prices of distributors, and how difficult it is for salesmen in the field to quote accurate prices and delivery terms to their potential customers.[3]

The seller has several alternatives in handling transportation costs.

**F.O.B. plant** or *F.O.B. origin* pricing provides a price that does not include any shipping charges. *The buyer must pay all the freight charges.* The seller pays only the cost of loading the merchandise aboard the carrier selected by the buyer. The abbreviation F.O.B. means *Free on Board*. Legal title and responsibility pass to the buyer once the purchase is loaded and a receipt is obtained from the representative of the common carrier.

Prices may also be shown as F.O.B. origin — freight allowed. *The seller permits the buyer to subtract transportation expenses from the bill.* The amount the seller receives varies with the freight charges charged against the invoice. This alternative, called **freight absorption**, is commonly used by firms with high fixed costs (who need to maintain high volume) because it permits a considerable expansion of their market, since a competitive price is quoted regardless of shipping expenses.

*The same price (including transportation expenses) is quoted to all buyers* when a **uniform delivered price** is the firm's policy. Such pricing is the exact opposite of F.O.B. prices. This system is often compared to the pricing of a first-class letter, which is the same across the country. Hence, it is sometimes called *postage-stamp pricing*. The price that is quoted includes an *average* transportation charge per customer, which means that distant customers are actually paying a lesser share of selling costs while customers near the supply source pay what is known as *phantom freight* (the average transporation charge exceeds the actual cost of shipping).

In **zone pricing**, which is simply a modification of a uniform delivered pricing system, *the market is divided into different zones and a price is established within each.* Canadian parcel post rates depend

---

[3] Donald V. Harper, *Price Policy and Procedure* (New York: Harcourt Brace Jovanovich, 1966), p. 204. By permission of the author.

upon zone pricing. The primary advantage of this pricing policy is that it is easy to administer and enables the seller to be more competitive in distant markets. Figure 14-3 shows how a marketer in Winnipeg might divide its market into geographic segments. All customers in zone 1 would be charged $10 per unit freight, while more distant customers would pay freight costs based on the zone in which they are located.

**Figure 14-3   Zone Pricing For a Winnipeg Firm**

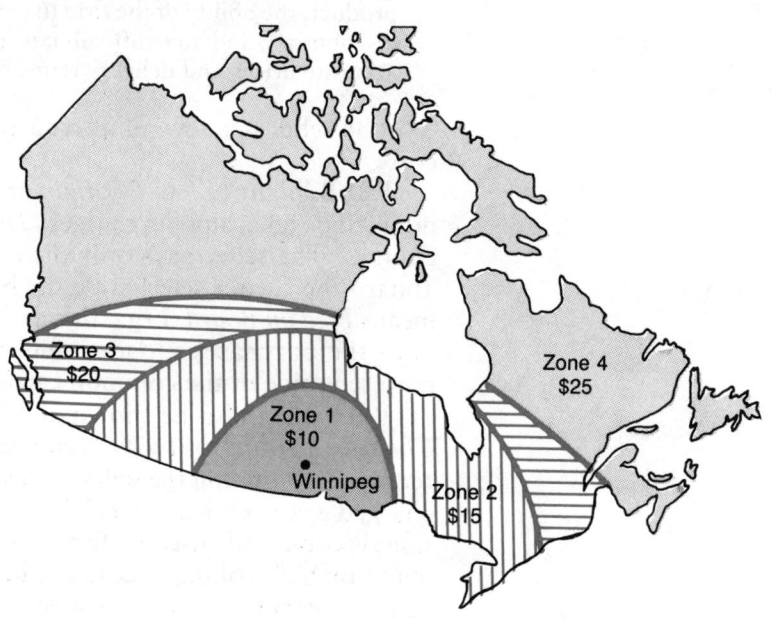

Pricing policies are an important ingredient in the firm's total image. They provide the overall framework and consistency needed in pricing decisions. A **pricing policy** is a *general guideline based upon pricing objectives that is intended for use in specific pricing decisions*. Decisions concerning price structure generally tend to be more technical in nature than those concerning price policies. Price structure decisions take the selected price policy as a given, and specify the discount structure details. Price policies have a greater strategic importance, particularly in relation to competitive considerations. They are the bases on which pricing decisions are made.

Many businesses would be well advised to spend more managerial effort in the establishment and periodic review of their pricing policies. Some years ago, a top executive aptly referred to the study and determination of prices as "creative pricing":

Few businessmen, I am sure, would deny that every well-run business should have a price policy. We give a great deal of thought and planning to our engineering, manufacturing, advertising, and sales promotion policies. Certainly the same kind of careful study and planning should be directed toward the formulation of those price policies that will best serve the various long-run objectives of our businesses. I call pricing based on such a well-formulated policy "creative pricing." There are probably better ways of saying it, but this term comes pretty close to describing what I believe to be the true function of pricing.[4]

Pricing policies must deal with varied competitive situations. The type of policy is dependent upon the environment within which the pricing decision must be made. The types of policies to be considered are new-product pricing, price flexibility, relative price levels, price lining, and promotional prices. They should all be arrived at through the use of a pricing procedure similar to those described in Chapter 13.

**Psychological Pricing**    **Psychological pricing** is based upon *the belief that certain prices or price ranges are more appealing to buyers than others*. There is, however, no consistent research foundation for such thinking. Studies often report mixed findings.[5] Prestige pricing, mentioned in Chapter 13, is one of many forms of psychological pricing.

# The High-Class Nickel Discount

When the proprietor of a restaurant runs a newspaper ad for a meal costing less than $7, the price usually ends in 9 — $5.99, for example — to imply a discount. A price in the $7 to $10 range usually ends in 5.

We owe the discovery of these facts of restaurant life to Lee Kreul, a professor at Purdue's School of Consumer and Family Sciences, who analyzed 467 prices from 242 restaurants advertised in 24 newspapers around the country. Restaurateurs switch from 9 to 5 as prices go up, he thinks, because at higher price levels "it takes more than 1 cent to create the discount illusion" and because patrons interested in paying more than $7 for a meal might think a price ending in 9 suggests "discounts, low quality, or hurried service."

Source: Jack C. Horn, "The High-Class Nickel Discount," *Psychology Today Magazine* (September 1982). Reprinted by permission.

---

[4] Fred C. Foy, "Management's Part in Achieving Price Respectability," *Competitive Pricing* (New York: American Management Association, 1958), pp. 7–8.

[5] See for example Zarrel V. Lambert, "Perceived Prices as Related to Odd and Even Price Findings," *Journal of Retailing* (Fall 1975), pp. 13–22, 78.

**Odd pricing** is a good example of the application of psychological pricing. *Prices are set ending in numbers not commonly used for price quotations.* A price of $16.99 is assumed to be more appealing than $17 (supposedly because it is a lower figure).

Originally odd pricing was used to force clerks to make change, thus serving as a cash control device within the firm.[6] Now it has become a customary feature of contemporary price quotations. For instance, one discounter uses prices ending in 3 and 7 rather than 5, 8, or 9, because of a belief that customers regard price tags of $5.95, $6.98, $7.99 as *regular* retail prices, while $5.97 and $6.93 are considered *discount* prices.

**Unit Pricing**      Consumer advocates have often pointed out the difficulty of comparing consumer products that are available in different-size packages or containers. Is an 800 g can selling for 75 cents a better buy than two 450 g cans priced at 81 cents or another brand that sells three 450 g cans for 89 cents? The critics argue that there should be a common way to price consumer products.

**Unit pricing** is a response to this problem. Under unit pricing all prices are stated *in terms of some recognized unit of measurement* (such as grams and litres) *or a standard numerical count.* There has been considerable discussion about legislating mandatory unit pricing. The Consumers' Association of Canada has endorsed unit pricing, and many of the major food chains have adopted it.[7]

Some supermarket chains have come to regard the adoption of unit pricing as a competitive tool upon which to base extensive advertising. However, unit pricing has not been particularly effective in improving the shopping habits of the urban poor. Others argue that unit pricing significantly increases retail operating costs.

The real question, of course, is whether unit pricing improves consumer decisions.[8] One study found that the availability of unit prices resulted in consumer savings and that retailers also benefitted

---

[6] See David M. Georgoff, "Price Illusion and the Effect of Odd-Even Retail Pricing," *Southern Journal of Business* (April 1969), pp. 95–103. See also Dik W. Twedt, "Does the '9 Fixation in Retailing Really Promote Sales?" *Journal of Marketing* (October 1965), pp. 54–55; Benson P. Shapiro, "The Psychology of Pricing," *Harvard Business Review* (July-August, 1968), pp. 14–16; and David M. Georgoff, *Odd-Even Retail Price Endings: Their Effects on Value Determination, Product Perception, and Buying Propensities* (East Lansing: Michigan State University, 1972).

[7] Victor Grostern, "Unit Pricing: A Case for Adoption and Use," *Canadian Consumer* (December 1975), p. 28–29.

[8] Two excellent articles appeared in the July 1972 issue of the *Journal of Marketing*: Kent B. Monroe and Peter J. La Placa, "What Are the Benefits of Unit Pricing?" pp. 16–22; and Michael J. Houston, "The Effect of Unit Pricing on Choices of Brand and Size in Economic Shopping," pp. 51–54. See also Carl E. Block, Robert Schooler, and David Erickson, "Consumer Reaction to Unit

when unit pricing led to greater purchases of store brands. The study concluded that unit pricing was valuable to both buyer and seller and that it merited full-scale usage.[9] Unit pricing is a major pricing policy issue that must be faced by many firms.

**New-Product Pricing**     The pricing of new products is a crucial question for marketers.[10] The initial price that is quoted for an item may determine whether or not the product will eventually be accepted in the marketplace. The initial price also may affect the amount of competition that will emerge.

Consider the options available to a company pricing a new product. While many choose to price at the *level of comparable products*, some select other alternatives (see Figure 14-4). A **skimming pricing** policy chooses *a relatively high entry price*. The name is derived from the expression "skimming the cream." One purpose

**Figure 14-4  The Market for Product X**

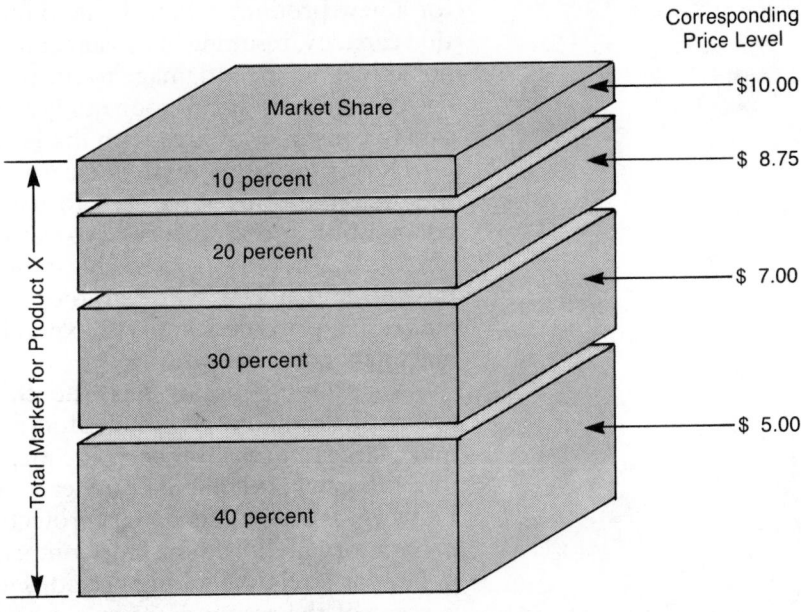

Corresponding Price Level

- $10.00
- $ 8.75
- $ 7.00
- $ 5.00

Market Share

- 10 percent
- 20 percent
- 30 percent
- 40 percent

Total Market for Product X

Pricing: An Empirical Study," *Mississippi Valley Journal of Business and Economics* (Winter 1971–72), pp. 36–46; William E. Kilbourne, "A Factorial Experiment on the Imact of Unit Pricing," *Journal of Marketing Research* (November 1974), pp. 453–455; and J. Edward Russo, Gene Krieser, and Sally Miyashita, "An Effective Display of Unit Price Information," *Journal of Marketing* (April 1975), pp. 11–19.

9 J. Edward Russo, "The Value of Unit Price Information," *Journal of Marketing Research* (May 1977), pp. 193–201.

10 See for example G. Clark Thompson and Morgan B. MacDonald, Jr., "Pricing New Products," *The Conference Board* (January 1964), pp. 7–9.

of this strategy is to allow the firm to recover its development cost quickly. The assumption is that competition will eventually driv the price to a lower level, as was the case, for example, with electri toothbrushes.

A skimming policy, therefore, attempts to maximize the reve nue received from the sale of a new product before the entry o competition. Ballpoint pens were introduced shortly after Worl War II at a price of about $20. Today the best-selling ballpoint pen are priced at less than $1. Other examples of products that hav been introduced using a skimming policy include television sets Polaroid cameras, videocassette recorders, home computers, an pocket calculators. Subsequent price reductions allowed the mar keters of these products to appeal to additional market segment that are more price sensitive.

A skimming strategy permits the marketer to control demand i the introductory stages of the product's life cycle and to adjust it productive capacity to match demand. A danger of low initial pric for a new product is that demand may outstrip the firm's produc tion capacity, resulting in consumer and intermediary complaints an possibly permanent damage to the product's image. Excess deman occasionally results in poor quality products as the firm strives t satisfy consumer desires with inadequate production facilities.

During the late growth and early maturity stages of the produc life cycle the price is reduced for two reasons: 1) the pressure o competition and 2) the desire to expand the product's market. Fig ure 14-4 shows that 10 percent of the market for Product X woul buy the item at $10, while another 20 percent would buy at $8.75 Successive price declines will expand the firm's market as well a meet new competition.

A skimming policy has one chief disadvantage: it attract competition. Potential competitors, who see the innovating firm make large returns, also enter the market. This forces the price eve lower than where it might be under a sequential skimming procedure However if a firm has patent protection — as Polaroid had — or proprietory ability to exclude competition, it may use a skimming policy for a relatively long period. Figure 14-5 indicates that 14. percent of the respondents in a recent pricing study used a skim ming policy. Skimming also appears to be more common in indus trial markets than in consumer markets.

**Penetration pricing** is the opposite policy in new-product pricing It results in *an entry price for a product lower than what is believe to be the long-term price.* The pricing study shown in Figure 14- suggests that penetration pricing is used more often in consume markets. Soaps and toothpastes are often good examples of this kin of pricing.

The premise is that an initially lower price will help secure mar

### Figure 14-5   Use of New-Product Pricing Strategies

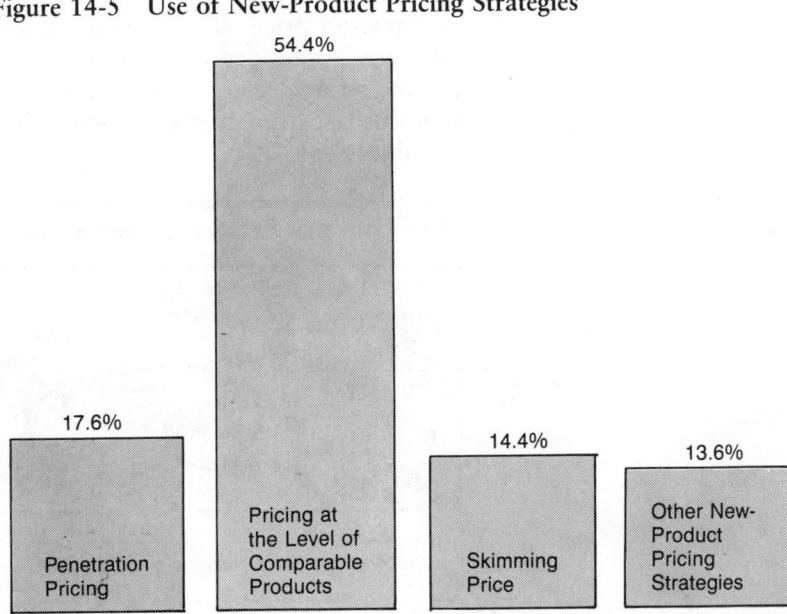

ket acceptance. Since the firm later intends to increase the price, brand popularity is crucial to the success of a penetration policy. One advantage of such a policy is that it discourages competition from entering since the prevailing low price does not suggest the attractive returns associated with a skimming policy.

Penetration pricing is likely to be used in instances where demand for the new product or service is highly elastic and large numbers of consumers are highly price sensitive. It is also likely to be used in instances where large-scale operations and long production runs result in substantial reductions in production and marketing costs. Finally, penetration pricing may be appropriate in instances where the new product is likely to attract strong competitors when it is introduced. Such a strategy may allow it to reach the mass market quickly and capture a large share of the market before the entry by competitors.

The key decision, of course, is when to move the price to its intended level. Consumers tend to resist price increases; therefore, correct timing is essential. The solution depends upon the degree of brand loyalty that has been achieved. Brand loyalty must be at the point where a price increase would not cause a disproportionate decrease in customers. A series of modest price changes, rather than a single large hike, also can retain customers.

A firm may, of course, decide to use neither a skimming nor a penetration price. It may try to price a new product at the point where it is intended to sell in the long run. All three new-product pricing strategies are common, but it can be seen from Figure 14-5 that this last strategy was chosen in 54 percent of new-product pricing situations.

**Most Canadian Retailers Follow a One-Price Policy**

Source: Reprinted by permission of Newspaper Enterprise Association.

**Price Flexibility**

Marketing executives must also determine company policy with respect to **flexible pricing**. Is the firm going to have just one price or pursue *a variable price policy in the market*? As a generalization, *one-price policies* characterize situations where mass selling is employed, and *variable pricing* is more common where individual bargaining typifies market transactions, for example, the purchase of a car.

A one-price policy is common in Canadian retailing since it facilitates mass merchandising. For the most part, once the price is set, the manager can direct his or her attention to other aspects of the marketing mix. Flexible prices, by contrast, are found more in wholesaling and industrial markets. This does not mean that price flexibility exists only in manufacturing industries. A study of the retail home appliance market concluded that persons who had purchased identical products from the same dealer had often paid different prices for them. The primary reasons for the differences were customer knowledge and bargaining strength.[11]

While variable pricing has the advantage of flexibility in selling situations, it may result in conflict with Competition Act provisions.

---

[11] Walter J. Primeaux, Jr., "The Effect of Consumer Knowledge and Bargaining Strength on Final Selling Price: A Case Study," *Journal of Business* (October 1970), pp. 419–426. Another excellent article is James R. Krum, "Variable Pricing as a Promotional Tool," *Atlanta Economic Review* (November–December), 1977, pp. 47–50

It may also lead to retaliatory pricing on the part of competitors, and it is not well received by those who have paid the higher prices.

**Relative Price Levels** Another important pricing policy decision concerns the relative price level. Are the firm's prices to be set above, below, or at the prevailing market price? In economic theory this question would be answered by supply and demand analysis. However, from a practical viewpoint, marketing managers *administer* prices. In other words, cost-oriented pricing allows them the option of subjectively setting the markup percentages.[12] Chapter 13 provided a framework for determining markups, but the decision-maker must still develop a basic policy in regard to relative price levels.

*Following the competition* is one method of negating the price variable in marketing strategy, since it forces competition to concen-

---

**Some Marketers Set Their Prices above the Prevailing Market Price**

"All I need is one good customer."

---

Source: Reprinted with permission. © 1974 The Saturday Evening Post Company.

---

12 A survey technique for testing price levels above and below current levels is described in D. Frank Jones, "A Survey Technique to Measure Demand under Various Pricing Strategies," *Journal of Marketing* (July 1975), pp. 75–77.

trate on other factors. Some firms choose to price below or above competition. These decisions are usually based on a firm's cost structure, overall marketing strategy, and pricing objectives.

**Price Lining**     Most companies sell a varied line of products. An effective pricing strategy should consider the relationship among the firm's products rather than viewing each in isolation. Specifically, **price lining** is *the practice of marketing merchandise at a limited number of prices.*[13] For example, a clothier might have a $150 line of men's suits and a $225 line. Price lining is used extensively in retail selling; the old five-and-ten-cent stores were run this way. It can be an advantage to both retailer and customer. Customers can choose the price range they wish to pay, then concentrate on all the other variables, such as colour, style, and material. The retailer can purchase and offer specific lines rather than a more generalized assortment.

Price lining requires that one identify the market segment or segments to which the firm is appealing. For example, "Samsonite sees its market not as all luggage, but as the 'medium-priced, hard-side' portion of the luggage trade."[14] The firm must decide how to *line* its product prices. A dress manufacturer might have lines priced at $39.95, $59.95, and $89.95. Price lining not only simplifies the administration of the pricing structure, but also alleviates the confusion of a situation where all products are priced separately. Price lining is really a combined product/price strategy.

One problem with a price-line decision is that once it is made, retailers and manufacturers have difficulty in adjusting it. Rising costs, therefore, put the seller in the position of either changing the price lines, with the resulting confusion, or reducing costs by production adjustments, which opens the firm to the complaint that "XYZ Company's merchandise certainly isn't what it used to be!"

**Promotional Prices**     A **promotional price** is *a lower-than-normal price used as an ingredient in a firm's selling strategy.* In some cases promotional prices are recurrent, such as the annual shoe store sale: "Buy one pair of shoes, get the second for one cent." Or a new pizza restaurant may have an opening special to attract customers. In other situations a firm may introduce a promotional model or brand to allow it to compete in another market.

---

13 See Alfred R. Oxenfeldt, "Product Line Pricing," *Harvard Business Review* (July–August 1966), pp. 137–144. Also, a recent article by Kent B. Monroe and Andris A. Zoltners discusses some other interesting aspects of product line pricing. See "Pricing the Product Line During Periods of Scarcity," *Journal of Marketing* (Summer 1979), pp. 49–59.

14 Robert A. Lynn, *Price Policies and Marketing Management* (Homewood, Ill.: Richard D. Irwin, 1967), p. 143.

Most promotional pricing is done at the retail level.[15] One type is **loss leaders**, *goods priced below cost to attract customers* who, the retailer hopes, will then buy other regularly priced merchandise. The use of loss leaders can be effective.

> Probably one of the best innovators of this pricing method was Cal Mayne. He was one of the first men to systematically price specials and to evaluate their effect on gross margins and sales. Mayne increased sales substantially by featuring coffee, butter, and margarine at 10 percent below cost. Ten other demand items were priced competitively and at a loss when necessary to undersell competition. Still another group of so-called secondary demand items were priced in line with competition. Mayne based his pricing policy on the theory that a customer can only remember about 30 prices. Keep prices down on these items and the customer will stay with you.[16]

The ethical or moral implications of this practice are not being considered here. Some studies have indeed reported considerable price confusion on the part of consumers. One study of consumer price recall reported that average shoppers misquoted the price they last paid for coffee by over 12 percent, toothpaste by over 20 percent, and green beans by 24 percent. While some people hit the prices exactly, others missed by several hundred percent.[17]

Three potential pitfalls should be considered when one faces a promotional pricing decision:
1. The Competition Act may prohibit some types of promotional pricing practices. (See Chapter 2.)
2. Some consumers are little influenced by price appeals, so promotional pricing will have little effect on them.[18]
3. Continuous use of an artificially low rate may result in it being accepted as customary for the product. For example, poultry, which was used as a loss leader during the 1930s and 1940s, later suffered from this phenomenon.

---

[15] An interesting study of consumer response to promotion prices is outlined in Norman D. French and Robert A. Lynn, "Consumer Income and Response to Price Charges: A Shopping Simulation," *Journal of Retailing* (Winter 1971–72), pp. 21–23.

[16] Bernie Faust, William Gorman, Eric Oesterle, and Larry Buchta, "Effective Retail Pricing Policy," *Purdue Retailer* (Lafayette, Indiana: Department of Agricultural Economics, 1963), p. 2.

[17] Karl A. Shilliff, "Determinants of Consumer Price Sensitivity for Selected Supermarket Products: An Empirical Investigation," *Akron Business & Economic Review* (Spring 1975), pp. 26–32.

[18] John F. Willenborg and Robert E. Pitts, "Perceived Situational Effects on Price Sensitivity," *Journal of Business Research* (March 1977), pp. 27–38.

**The Price–Quality**
**Concept**

One of the most researched aspects of pricing is the relationship between price and the consumer's perception of the product's quality.[19] In the absence of other cues, price is an important indication for the consumer in the perception of the product's quality.[20] The higher the price, the better the buyer believes the quality of the product to be. One study asked 400 people what terms they associated with the word *expensive*. Two-thirds of the replies were related to high quality, such as *best* and *superior*.[21] The relationship between price and perceived quality is a well-documented fact in contemporary marketing.

Probably the most useful concept in explaining price–quality relationships is the idea of **price limits.**[22] It is argued that consumers have *limits within which product quality perception varies directly with price*. A price below the lower limit is regarded as too cheap, while one above the higher limit means it is too expensive. Most consumers do tend to set an acceptable price range when purchasing goods and services. The range, of course, varies, depending upon consumers' socio-economic characteristics and buying dispositions. Consumers, nonetheless, should be aware that price is not necessarily an indicator of quality. Alberta Consumer and Corporate Affairs summarized seven price-quality research studies, six covering *Consumer Reports* analyses of 932 products between 1940 and 1977, and one for 43 products tested by *Canadian Consumer* between 1973 and 1977. It found that while there was a positive relationship

---

19 See, for instance, I. Robert Andrews and Enzo R. Valenzi, "The Relationship Between Price and Blind-Rated Quality for Margarines and Butter," *Journal of Marketing Research* (August 1970), pp. 393–395; Robert A. Peterson, "The Price-Perceived Quality Relationship: Experimental Evidence," *Journal of Marketing Research* (November 1970), pp. 525–528; David M. Gardner, "An Experimental Investigation of the Price/Quality Relationship," *Journal of Retailing* (Fall 1970), pp. 25–41; and Arthur G. Bedelan, "Consumer Perception as an Indicator of Product Quality," *MSU Business Topics* (Summer 1971), pp. 59–65; and R. S. Mason, "Price and Product Quality Assessment," *European Journal of Marketing* (Spring 1974), pp. 29–41.
20 J. Douglass McConnell, "An Experimental Examination of the Price-Quality Relationship," *Journal of Business* (October 1968), pp. 439–444. See also J. Douglass McConnell, "The Alphabet and Price as Independent Variables: A Note on the Price-Quality Question," *Journal of Business* (October 1970), pp. 448–451.
21 James H. Myers and William H. Reynolds, *Consumer Behavior and Marketing Management* (Boston: Houghton-Mifflin Company, 1967), p. 47.
22 See Kent B. Monroe and M. Venkatesan, "The Concepts of Price Limits and Psychophysical Measurement: A Laboratory Experiment," in Phillip R. McDonald (ed.), *Marketing Involvement in Society and the Economy* (Cincinnati: Proceedings of the American Marketing Association, 1969), pp. 345–351.

between price and quality, the correlation was low (Spearman rank correlation = .25). In addition, about 25 percent of products tested had a negative price-quality relation. That is, products ranked lower in performance had higher prices than products deemed superior by the Canadian and U.S. consumer testing organizations.[23]

---

**Negotiated Prices and Competitive Bidding**

Many situations involving government and industrial procurement are not characterized by set prices, particularly for nonrecurring purchases such as a defence system for the armed forces. Markets such as these are growing at a fast pace. Governmental units now spend nearly half of Canada's GNP!

*Competitive bidding* is a process by which buyers request potential suppliers to make price quotations on a proposed purchase or contract.[24] *Specifications* give a description of the item (or job) that the government or industrial firm wishes to acquire. One of the most important tasks in modern purchasing management is to describe adequately what the organization seeks to buy. This generally requires the assistance of the firm's technical personnel, such as engineers, designers, and chemists.

Competitive bidding strategy should employ the concept of *expected net profit*, which can be stated as:

$$\text{Expected Net Profit} = P\,(\text{Bid} - \text{Costs})$$

where P = the probability of the buyer accepting the bid.

Consider the following example. A firm is contemplating the submission of a bid for a job that is estimated to cost $23 000. One executive has proposed a bid of $60 000; another, $50 000. It is estimated that there is a 40 percent chance of the buyer accepting bid 1 ($60 000) and a 60 percent chance that bid 2 ($50 000) will be accepted. The expected net profit formula indicates that bid 2 would be best since its expected net profit is the higher.

Bid 1
ENP = 0.40 ($60 000 − $23 000)
    = 0.40 ($37 000)
    = $14 800

---

23 *Market Spotlight* (Edmonton: Alberta Consumer and Corporate Affairs, March 1979).
24 See for example Stephen Paranka, "Competitive Bidding Strategy," *Business Horizons* (June 1971), pp. 39–43. See also Richard C. Newman, "A Game Theory Approach to Competitive Bidding," *Journal of Purchasing* (February 1972), pp. 50–57; James E. Reinmuth and Jim D. Barnes, "A Strategic Competitive Bidding Approach to Pricing Decisions for Petroleum Industry Drilling Contractors," *Journal of Marketing Research* (August 1975), pp. 362–365.

Bid 2
ENP = 0.60 ($50 000 − $23 000)
    = 0.60 ($27 000)
    = $16 200

The most difficult task in applying this concept is in the estimation of the probability as to the likelihood a certain bid will be accepted. But this is not a valid reason for failing to quantify one's estimate. Prior experience can often provide the foundation for such estimates.

In some cases industrial and governmental purchasers use *negotiated contracts* instead of inviting competitive bidding for a project. In these situations, the terms of the contract are set through talks between the buyer and a seller. Where there is only one available supplier or where contracts require extensive research and development work, negotiated contracts are likely to be employed.

Some provincial and local governments permit their agencies to negotiate purchases under a certain limit, say, $500 or $1000. This policy is an attempt to reduce cost since obtaining bids for relatively minor purchases is expensive and there is little prospect of large savings to the agency involved.

The fear that inflation may have unknown effects on the economic viability of prices has become a major deterrent to companies bidding for or negotiating contracts. One response has been to include an **escalator clause**[25] that allows the seller *to adjust the final price based upon changes in the costs of the product's ingredients between the placement of the order and the completion of construction or delivery of the product.* Such clauses typically base the adjustment calculation on the cost-of-living index or a similar indicator. While an estimated one-third of all industrial marketers use escalator clauses in some of their bids, they are most commonly used with major projects involving long time periods and complex operations.

## *The Transfer Pricing Problem*

One pricing problem peculiar to large-scale enterprises is that of determining an internal **transfer price** — that is, *the price for sending goods from one company profit centre to another.*[26] As a com-

---

[25] See Mary Louise Hatten, "Don't Get Caught with Your Prices Down: Pricing in Inflationary Times," *Business Horizons* (March/April 1982), pp. 23–28.

[26] See Paul E. Dascher, "Some Transfer Pricing Standards," *Pittsburg Business Review* (November–December 1971), pp. 14–21; Thomas S. Goho, "Intracompany Pricing Strategy for International Corporations," *Business Studies* (Spring 1972), pp. 5–9; David Granick, "National Differences in the Use of Internal Transfer Prices," *California Management Review* (Summer 1975), pp. 28–40; and Peter Mailandt, "An Alternative to Transfer Pricing," *Business Horizons* (October 1975), pp. 81–86. Interesting discussions of transfer pricing

pany expands, it usually needs to decentralize management. Profit centres are then set up as a control device in the new decentralized operation. **Profit centres** are *any part of the organization to which revenue and controllable costs can be assigned, such as a department.*

In large companies the centres can secure many of their resource requirements from within the corporate structure. The pricing problem becomes what rate should Profit Centre A (maintenance department) charge Profit Centre B (sales department) for the cleaning compound used on B's floors? Should the price be the same as it would be if A did the work for an outside party? Should B receive a discount? The answer to these questions depends upon the philosophy of the firm involved.

The transfer pricing dilemma is an example of the variations that a firm's pricing policy must deal with. Consider the case of UDC-Europe, a Universal Data Corporation subsidiary that itself has 10 subsidiaries. Each of the 10 is organized on a geographic basis, and each is treated as a separate profit centre. Intercompany transfer prices are set at the annual budget meeting. Special situations, like unexpected volume, are handled through negotiations by the subsidiary managers. If complex tax problems arise, UDC-Europe's top management may set the transfer price.[27]

## Pricing in the Public Sector

The pricing of public services has also become an interesting, and sometimes troublesome, aspect of contemporary marketing.[28]

Traditionally, government services either were very low-cost or were priced using the full-cost approach: users paid all costs associated with the service. In more recent years there has been a tendency to move toward incremental or marginal pricing, which considers only those expenses specifically associated with a particular activity. However, it is often difficult to determine the costs that should be assigned to a particular activity or service. Governmental accounting problems are often more complex than those of private enterprise.

Another problem in pricing public services is that taxes act as an *indirect* price of a public service. Someone must decide the relative relationship between the direct and indirect prices of such a

appear in Sylvain R. F. Plasschaert, *Transfer Pricing and Multinational Corporations* (New York: Praeger, 1979), and Roger Y. W. Tang, *Transfer Pricing Practices in the United States and Japan* (New York: Praeger, 1979).

[27] M. Edgar Barret, "Case of the Tangled Transfer Price," *Harvard Business Review* (May–June 1977), p. 22.

[28] See, for example, Marvin Brame, "Pricing Problems of the Water Industry: A Case Study of Northern New Castle County, Delaware," *Economic and Business Bulletin* (Spring–Summer 1971), pp. 37–42.

service. A shift toward indirect tax charges (where an income or earnings tax exists) is generally a movement toward charging on the *ability-to-pay* rather than the *use* principle.

The pricing of any public service involves a basic policy decision as to whether the price is an instrument to recover costs or a technique for accomplishing some other social or civic objective. For example, public health services may be priced near zero so as to encourage their use. On the other hand, parking fines in some cities are high so as to discourage use of private automobiles in the central business district. Pricing decisions in the public sector are difficult because political and social considerations often outweigh the economic aspects.

**Summary**   The main elements to consider in setting a pricing strategy are the organization for pricing decisions, pricing policies, price-quality relationships, negotiated prices, competitive bidding, transfer pricing, and pricing in the public sector. Methods for quoting prices depend on factors such as cost structures, traditional practices in a particular industry, and politics of individual firms. Prices quoted can involve list prices, market prices, cash discounts, trade discounts, quantity discounts, and allowances such as trade-ins, promotional allowances, and rebates.

Shipping costs often figure heavily in the pricing of goods. A number of alternatives exist for dealing with these costs: F.O.B. plant, when the price does not include any shipping charges; freight absorption, when the buyer can deduct transportation expenses from the bill; uniform delivered price, when the same price — including shipping expenses—is charged to all buyers; and zone pricing, when a set price exists within each region.

Pricing policies vary among firms. Among the most common are psychological pricing; unit pricing; new-product pricing, which includes skimming pricing and penetration pricing; price flexibility; relative pricing; price lining; and promotional pricing.

The relationship between price and consumer perception of quality has been the subject of much research. A well-known and accepted concept is that of price limits — limits within which the perception of product quality varies directly with price.

Sometimes, prices are negotiated through competitive bidding, a situation in which several buyers quote prices on the same service or good. At other times, prices depend on negotiated contracts, a situation in which the terms of the contract are set through talks between a particular buyer and seller.

A phenomenon of large corporations is transfer pricing, in which a company sets prices for transferring goods or services from one company profit centre to another.

The pricing of public services has become a troublesome aspect of marketing. It involves decisions on whether the price of a public service serves as an instrument to recover costs or as a technique for accomplishing some other social or civic purpose.

| **Key Terms** | | |
|---|---|---|
| list price | psychological pricing |
| market price | odd pricing |
| cash discount | unit pricing |
| trade discount | skimming pricing |
| quantity discount | penetration pricing |
| trade-in | flexible pricing |
| promotional allowance | price lining |
| rebate | promotional pricing |
| F.O.B. plant | loss leader |
| freight absorption | price limits |
| uniform delivered price | escalator clause |
| zone pricing | transfer price |
| pricing policy | profit centre |

**Review Questions**

1. Who in the organization is most likely to be responsible for setting a price structure? Who is most likely to administer a price structure?
2. How are prices likely to be quoted?
3. Contrast the freight absorption and uniform delivered pricing systems.
4. List and discuss the reasons for establishing price policies.
5. What are the benefits derived from utilizing a skimming approach to pricing?
6. Under what circumstances is penetration pricing most likely to be used?
7. When does a price become a promotional price? What are the pitfalls in promotional pricing?
8. What is the relationship between prices and consumer perceptions of quality?
9. Contrast negotiated prices and competitive bidding.
10. What types of decisions must be made in the pricing of public services? What role could escalator clauses play in this area?

**Discussion Questions and Exercises**

1. What type of new-product pricing would be appropriate for the following items:
   a. a new deodorant
   b. a fuel additive that increases fuel efficiency by 50 percent
   c. a new pattern of fine china

    d. a new ultrasensitive burglar, smoke, and fire alarm
    e. a new video game
2. How are prices quoted for each of the following:
    a. a CP Air ticket to Montreal
    b. an aluminum siding installation by a local contractor
    c. a new jogging suit from a sportswear retailer
    d. a new Nissan pick-up truck
3. Comment on the following statement: Unit pricing is ridiculous because everyone ignores it.
4. Prepare a list of arguments that might be used in justifying a negotiated contract instead of requiring competitive bids.
5. What criteria should be considered for transfer pricing in a large corporation like Westinghouse Electric?

---

**MICROCOMPUTER EXERCISE:**
**Competitive Bidding**

Expected net profit is a very useful concept in a competitive-bidding situation. Expected net profit is equal to the probability of the buyer accepting the bid times the residual of the bid minus the costs.

Directions:  Use the Menu Item titled "Competitive Bidding" on the *Foundations of Marketing* disk to solve the following problems.

**1.** Nancy Terry, the sales manager for Winnipeg Editorial Advisors, wishes to submit a bid on a freelance writing project. She estimates that her firm would actually spend $15 000 completing the project. Terry has prepared two alternative proposals, one for $20 000 and the other for $25 000. Assume she estimates that there is a 70 percent chance of the publisher accepting the $20 000 bid, but only a 40 percent chance of acceptance of the higher bid. Use expected-net-profit analysis to determine which bid Terry should submit to the publisher.

**2.** The president of Red Deer Industries would like to earn an expected net profit of $15 000 on a project for the province of Alberta. The estimated cost of completing the project is $10 000.

    **a.** What probability of acceptance is being assigned if the president submits a bid of $35 000?

    **b.** What probability of acceptance is being assigned if the president submits a bid of $40 000?

# P A R T

## Distribution

*This section deals with the third element of the marketing mix, focusing on the activities and institutions involved in moving the products and services to the firm's chosen market target. Channel selection and strategy are the subject of Chapter 15, while Chapters 16 and 17 analyse wholesalers and retailers — the marketing institutions that comprise many marketing channels. Chapter 18 focuses on physical distribution — the physical movement of products from producer to consumer or industrial user.*

# Channel Strategy

1. *To relate channel strategy to the other variables of the marketing mix.*
2. *To explain the role of distribution channels in marketing strategy.*
3. *To describe the various types of distribution channels.*
4. *To explain the concept of power in the distribution channel.*
5. *To outline the major channel strategy decisions.*
6. *To discuss conflict and co-operation in the distribution channel*

How can a firm with an 80 percent market share have problems? That was exactly the situation for Binney & Smith, the makers of Crayola crayons. The firm had continued to show sales increases over the years because of a strong market position and population growth. Binney & Smith remained complacent even after its market target — children — began to decline in numbers.

The company continued to concentrate on its traditional channel — selling to the education market through school-supply distributors. It largely ignored mass merchandisers like K-mart, Woolworth, and Zellers, spending 60 percent of its marketing dollars on their traditional market. Yet the education market was only yielding 30 percent of sales.

The manufacturer acquired a poor reputation with mass merchandisers. It turned down requests for extended payment terms which were common practice among toy manufacturers selling to these large retailers. In addition, promotions were timed wrong for the consumer market because Binney & Smith had traditionally regarded its product as nonseasonal.

Since then, new management has drastically altered the crayon producer's distribution strategy. Binney & Smith now concentrates on mass merchandisers. Its sales force has distributed Crayola Fun Centres, an in-store display for 37 of its products. The company also puts substantial monies into a co-operating advertising program, whereby it shares promotional costs with retailers.

The success of their new distribution strategy is quite evident. Their plant is running three shifts a day. In fact, the company has decided to expand its capacity.

**The Conceptual Framework**

Basic channel strategy—such as the decisions reached by Binney & Smith—is the starting point for a discussion of the distribution function and its role in the marketing mix. This chapter covers such basic issues as the role and types of distribution channels; power in the distribution channel; channel strategy decisions; and conflict and co-operation in the channel of distribution. Chapters 16 and 17 deal with wholesaling and retailing, the marketing institutions in the distribution channel. Chapter 18 ends Part 6 with a discussion of physical distribution. The starting point of this section is to look at what marketers call distribution channels.[1]

Carson luggage is made in Ottawa, Staedtler pens and erasers come from Germany, plywood is produced in British Columbia, and Timex watches are assembled in Toronto. All are sold throughout Canada. In each case, some method must be devised to bridge the gap between producer and consumer. Distribution channels provide the purchaser with a convenient means of obtaining the products that he or she wishes to buy. **Distribution channels** (also called **marketing channels**) are *the paths goods—and title to these goods —follow from producer to consumer.*[2] Specifically, the term *channels* refers to the various marketing institutions and the interrelationships responsible for the flow of goods and services from producer to consumer or industrial user. Intermediaries are the marketing institutions in the distribution channel. A **marketing intermediary**, or **middleman**, is *a business firm operating between the producer and the consumer or industrial purchaser.* The term therefore *includes both wholesalers and retailers.*

**Wholesaling** is *the activities of persons or firms who sell to retailers, other wholesalers, and industrial users but not significant amounts to ultimate consumers.* The terms *jobber* and *distributor* are considered synonymous with wholesaler in this book.

Confusion can result from the practices of some firms that operate both wholesaling and retailing operations. Sporting goods stores, for example, often maintain a wholesaling operation in marketing a line of goods to high schools and colleges as well as operating retail stores. For the purposes of this book, we will treat such operations as two separate institutions.

A second source of confusion is the misleading practice of some retailers who claim to be wholesalers. Such stores may actually sell

---

1 An interesting discussion appears in Michael M. Pearson, "Ten Distribution Myths," *Business Horizons* (May–June 1981), pp. 17–23.
2 Committee on Definitions, *Marketing Definitions: A Glossary of Marketing Terms* (Chicago: American Marketing Association, 1960), p. 10. Some authors limit the definition to the route taken by the *title* to the goods, but this definition also includes agent wholesaling intermediaries who do not take title but who do serve as an important component of many channels.

at wholesale prices and can validly claim to do so. However, *stores that sell products purchased by individuals for their own use and not for resale* are by definition **retailers**, not wholesalers.

## The Role of Distribution Channels in Marketing Strategy

Distribution channels play a key role in marketing strategy since they provide the means by which goods and services are conveyed from their producers to consumers and users. The importance of distribution channels can be explained in terms of the utility that is created and the functions that are performed.

### Utility Created by Marketing Channels

Marketing channels create three types of utility: time, place, and ownership (or possession). *Time* utility is created when marketing channels have products and services available for sale when the consumer wants to purchase them. *Place* utility is created when products and services are available where consumers want to buy them. *Ownership* utility is created when title to the goods passes from the manufacturer or intermediary channel member to the purchaser.

Swimwear provides a good illustration of how the distribution channel can create time utility. Swimwear for the coming spring and summer has already been produced in the months of December and January and is en route to retail stores throughout the nation. Swimwear manufacturers' success or failure depends on consumer reactions to new colours, styles, and fabrics that are decided on months earlier. But the swimsuits are ready in the store for the first warm day in April that customers decide to shop for them. Similarly, this textbook is available before the beginning of classes.

The provision of place utility is illustrated by flight insurance vending machines in airport terminals, a stock of *TV Guides* near a supermarket checkout counter — or this book in your bookstore rather than in the publisher's warehouse in suburban Toronto.

The offices of a real estate broker or lending institution are often used to create ownership utility. Legal title and possession of a new home is often transferred to a buyer in these settings.

### The Functions Performed by Distribution Channels

The distribution channel performs several functions in the overall marketing system.[3] These include facilitating the exchange process; sorting to alleviate discrepancies in assortment; standardizing transactions; holding inventories; and the search process.[4]

---

[3] This section is adapted by permission from Louis W. Stern and Adel I. El-Ansary, *Marketing Channels*, 2d ed. (Englewood Cliffs, N.J.: Prentice-Hall, Inc., 1982) pp. 6–11.
[4] These functions were developed in Wroe Alderson, "Factors Governing the Development of Marketing Channels," in *Marketing Channels for Manufactured Products*, (ed.) Richard M. Clewitt (Homewod, Ill.: Richard D. Irwin, 1954), pp. 5–22.

Facilitating the Exchange Process   The evolution of distribution channels began with the exchange process described in Chapter 1. As market economies grew, the exchange process itself became complicated. With more producers and more potential buyers, intermediaries came into existence to facilitate transactions by cutting the number of marketplace contacts. For example, if ten orchards in the Okanagan valley each sell to six supermarket chains, there are a total of 60 transactions. If the producers set up and market their apples through a co-operative, the number of contacts declines to 16. This process is described in detail in Chapter 16.

**Figure 15-1   The Sorting Process**

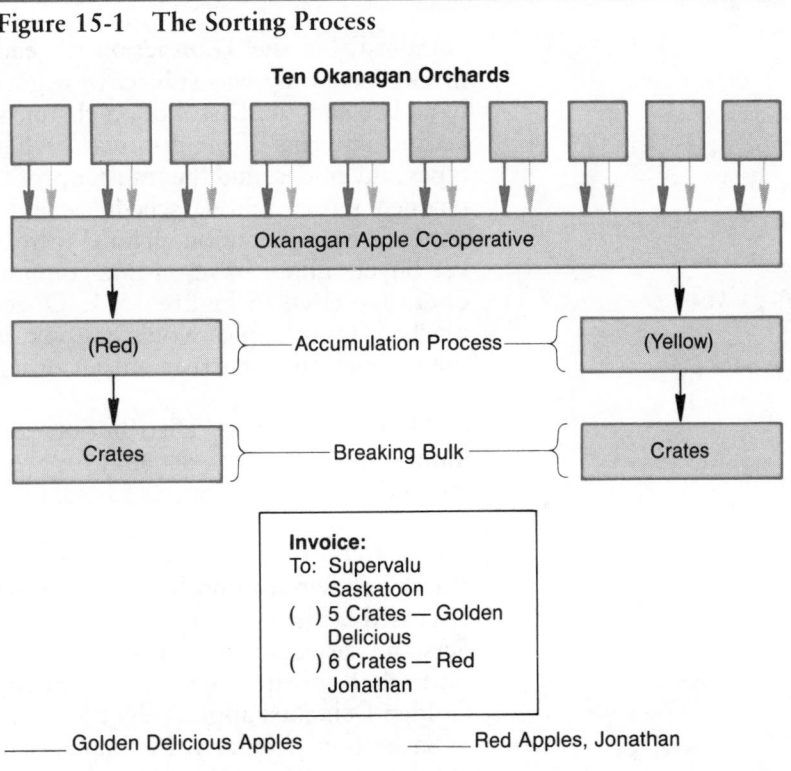

Sorting to Alleviate Discrepancies in Assortment   Another essential function of the distribution channel is to adjust discrepancies in assortment. For economic reasons, a producer tends to maximize the quantity of a limited line of products, while the buyer needs a minimum quantity of a wide selection of alternatives. Thus, there is a discrepancy between what the producer has to offer and what the customers want. **Sorting** is *the process that alleviates discrepancies in assortment by re-allocating the outputs of various producers into assortments desired by individual purchasers.*

Figure 15-1 shows an example of the sorting process. First, an individual producer's output is divided into separate homogeneous categories such as the various types and grades of apples. These apples are then combined with the similar crops of other orchards, a process known as *accumulation*. These accumulations are broken down into smaller units or divisions, such as crates of apples. This is often called *breaking bulk* in marketing literature. Finally, an assortment is built for the next level in the distribution channel. For example, the Okanagan co-operative might prepare an assortment of four crates of Golden Delicious and six crates of Red Johnathan apples for Supervalu supermarket in Saskatoon.

**Standardizing the Transaction**   If each transaction in a complex market economy was subject to negotiation, the exchange process would be chaotic. Distribution channels standardize exchange transactions in terms of the product, such as the grading of apples into types and grades, and the transfer process itself. Order points, prices, payment terms, delivery schedules, and purchase lots tend to be standardized by distribution channel members. For example, supermarket buyers might have on-line communicaitons links with the co-operative cited in Figure 15-1. Once a certain stock position is reached, more apples would automatically be ordered from either the co-operative's current output or its cold storage.

**Holding Inventories**   Distribution channel members hold a minimum of inventories to account for economies of scale in transporting and to provide a buffer for small changes in demand.

**The Search Process**   Distribution channels also accommodate the search behaviour of both buyers and sellers. (Search behaviour was discussed earlier in Chapter 7). Buyers are searching for specific products and services to fill their needs, while sellers are attempting to find what consumers want. A college student looking for some Golden Delicious apples might go to the fruit section of Supervalu in Saskatoon. Similarly, the manager of that department would be able to provide the Okanagan co-operative with information about sales trends in his or her marketplace.

---

**Types of Distribution**   Literally hundreds of marketing channels exist today; however, there is no one marketing channel that is superior to all others. "Best" for Electrolux vacuum cleaners may be direct from manufacturer to consumer through a sales force of 1000 men and women. The "best" channel for frozen French fries may be from food processor to agent intermediary to *merchant wholesaler* (a wholesaler who takes title) to supermarket to consumer. Instead of searching for a "best" channel for all products, the marketing manager must analyse alternative channels in the light of consumer needs and competitive restraints to determine the optimum channel or channels for the firm's products.[5]

Even when the proper channels have been chosen and established, the marketing manager's channel decisions are not ended. Channels, like so many of the other marketing variables, change, and today's ideal channel may prove obsolete in a few years.

For example, the typical channel for motor oil until the 1960s was from oil company to company-owned service stations, because most oil was installed there. But a significant number of oil purchases are now made by motorists in automotive supply stores, discount department stores, and even supermarkets, as today many motorists install motor oil themselves. Others use rapid oil-change specialty shops. And the channel for Shell, Esso, Texaco, Quaker State, and Castrol must change to reflect these changes in consumer buying patterns.

Figure 15-2 depicts the major channels available for marketers of consumer and industrial products. In general, industrial products channels tend to be shorter than consumer goods channels due to geographic concentrations of industrial buyers, a relatively limited number of purchasers, and the absence of retailers from the chain. The term retailer refers to consumer goods purchases. Service channels also tend to be short because of the intangibility of services and the need to maintain personal relationships in the channel.

*Direct Channel*    The simplest, most direct marketing channel is not necessarily the best, as is indicated by the relatively small percentage of the dollar volume of sales that moves *directly from the producer to the consumer.* Less than 5 percent of all consumer goods are candidates for the producer to consumer channel. Dairies, Tupperware, Avon cosmetics, and numerous mail-order houses are examples of firms whose marketing moves directly from manufacturer to the ultimate consumer.

Direct channels are much more important in the industrial goods market, where most major installations and accessory equipment — and many of the fabricated parts and raw materials — are marketed through *direct contacts between producer and user.*

---

[5] Wilke English, Dale M. Lewison, and M. Wayne DeLozier, "Evolution in Channel Management: What Will Be Next?" in *Proceedings of the Southwestern Marketing Association*, (eds.) Robert H. Ross, Frederic B. Kraft, and Charles H. Davis (Wichita, Kansas: 1981), pp. 78–81.

## Figure 15-2   Alternative Distribution Channels

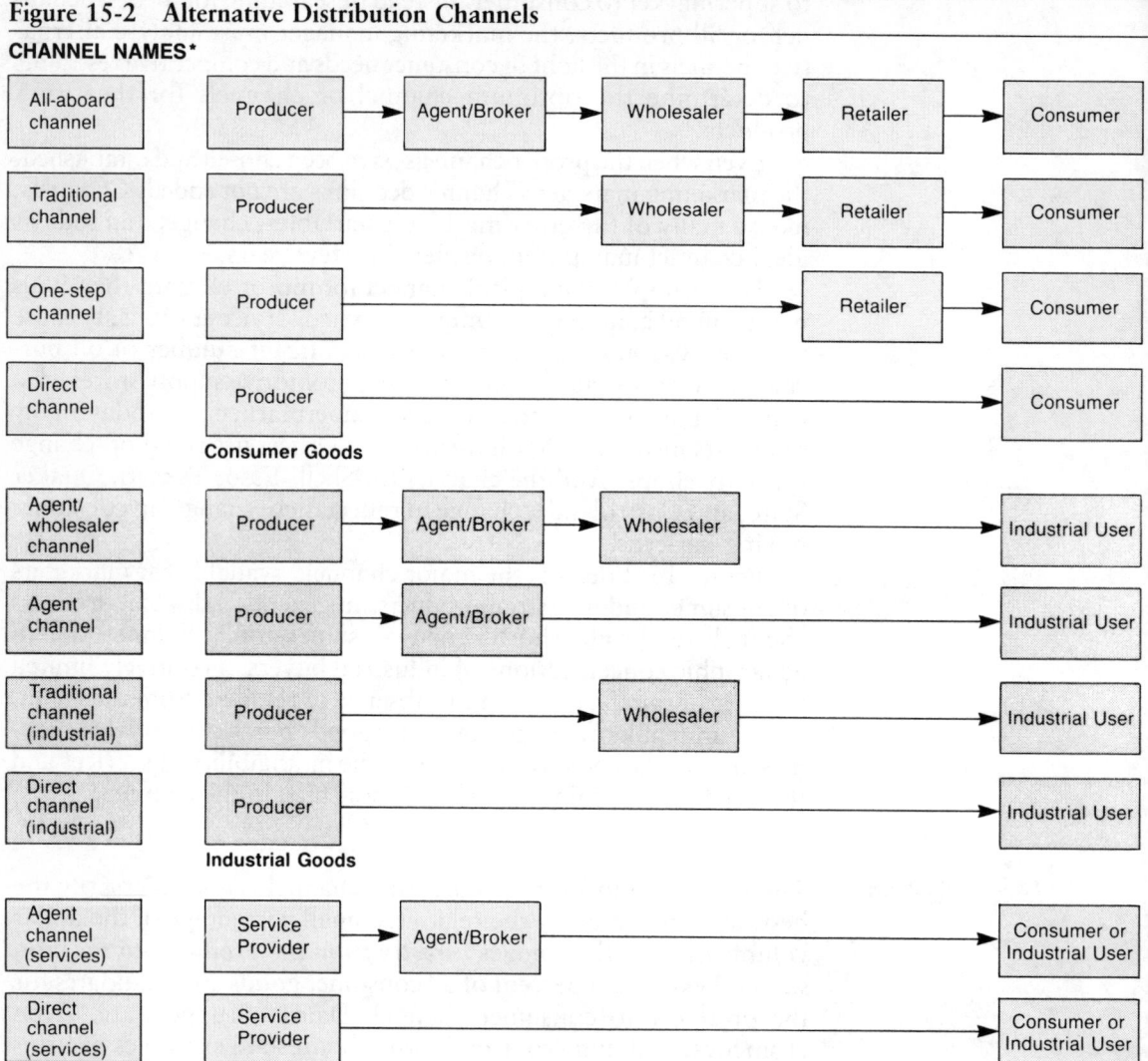

*These descriptive terms were suggested by Lewis Presner, Durham College, Oshawa, Ontario.

**All-Aboard Channel**   Probably the longest channel is *from producer to agent to whole-saler to retailer to consumer.* Where products are produced by a large number of small companies, a unique intermediary appears to perform the basic function of bringing buyer and seller together — the agent, or broker. **Agents** are, in fact, *wholesaling intermediaries, but they differ from the typical wholesaler in that they do not take title to the goods.*

They merely represent the producer or the regular wholesaler (who does take title to the goods) in seeking a market for the producer's output or in locating a source of supply for the buyer. A canner of vegetables in Ontario has 6000 cases of string beans to sell. The firm informs the food brokers (agents) regularly used in various provinces of this fact. A broker in the Maritimes ascertains that the Maritime supermarket chain Sobey's will buy 800 cases. The broker takes the order, informs the canner, and if the price is acceptable, the canner ships the order to Sobey's. The canner bills Sobey's and sends a commission cheque (approximately 3 percent of the sale price) to the food broker for the service of bringing buyer and seller together.

**One-Step Channel**  This channel is being used more and more, and in many instances it has taken the place of the traditional channel. When large retailers are involved, they are willing to take on many functions performed by the wholesaler — consequently, goods move *from producer to retailer to consumer.*

**Traditional Channel (Consumer)**  The traditional marketing channel for consumer goods is *from producer to wholesaler to retailer to user.* It is the method used by literally thousands of small manufacturers or companies producing limited lines of products and by as many or more small retailers. Small companies with limited financial resources utilize wholesalers as immediate sources of funds and as a marketing arm to reach the hundreds of retailers who will stock their products. Smaller retailers rely on wholesalers as *buying specialists* to ensure a balanced inventory of goods produced in various regions of the world.

The wholesaler's sales force is responsible for reaching the market with the producer's output. Many manufacturers also use sales representatives to call on the retailers to assist in merchandising the line. These representatives serve the manufacturer as sources of market information and influence, but will generally not make the sales transaction. If they do initiate a sale, they give it to a wholesaler to complete.

**Agent/Wholesaler Channel**  *Producer to agent to wholesaler to industrial user.* Similar conditions often exist in the industrial market, where small producers often use a channel to market their offerings. The agent wholesaling intermediary, often called a manufacturer's representative or manufacturer's agent, serves as an independent sales force in contacting large, scattered wholesalers and some key industrial buyers. For example, a manufacturer of specialty industrial tapes might use agents to sell to industrial wholesalers and to encourage the wholesaler's sales force to push the product to industrial users.

**Agent Channel**   Where the unit sale is small, merchant wholesalers must be used to cover the market economically. By maintaining regional inventories, they can achieve transportation economies by stockpiling goods and making the final small shipment over a small distance. But where the unit sale is large and transportation costs account for a small percentage of the total product costs, the *producer to agent to industrial user* channel may be employed. The agent wholesaling intermediaries become, in effect, the company's sales force. For example, a producer of special castings might engage agents who are already calling on potential customers with other lines to represent them as well.

**Traditional Channel**   Similar characteristics in the industrial market often lead to the
**(Industrial)**   utilization of *wholesalers between the manufacturer and industrial purchaser*. The term **industrial distributor** is commonly used in the industrial market to refer to those *wholesalers who take title to the goods they handle*. These wholesalers are involved in the marketing of small accessory equipment and operating supplies, such as building supplies, office supplies, small hand tools, and office equipment.[6] For example, in an effort to orient its own sales force toward high-priority computer products, IBM has turned to industrial distributors. The IBM industrial distributors sell only two products: a moderately priced display terminal and a desk-top printer. IBM continues to sell its entire product line, but it concentrates on items with higher priority.[7]

**Direct Channel**   Distribution of services to both consumers and industrial users is
**(Services)**   usually simpler and more direct than for industrial and consumer goods. In part, this is due to the intangibility of services; the marketer of services does not often have to worry about storage, transportation, and inventory control; shorter channels, often direct *from service provider to consumer or industrial user*, are typically used.

Many services can only be performed on a direct basis, and personal relationships between performers and users are very important. Consumers will remain clients of the same bank, automobile repair shop, or hair stylist as long as they are reasonably satisfied. Likewise, public accounting firms and attorneys are retained on a relatively permanent basis by industrial buyers.

---

6 See Frederick E. Webster, Jr., "The Role of the Industrial Distributor in Marketing Strategy," *Journal of Marketing* (July 1976), pp. 10–16.
7 James A. White, "IBM Expands Outside Its Sales Channel," *The Wall Street Journal* (October 7, 1981), p. 2. Industrial distributors are also discussed in James D. Hlavacek and Tommy J. McCusition, "Industrial Distributors—When, Who, and How?" *Harvard Business Review* (March-April 1983), pp. 96–101.

**Agent Channel (Services)**    When *service providers use marketing intermediaries to reach consumers or industrial users*, these are usually *agents* or *brokers*. Common examples include insurance agents, securities brokers, travel agents, and entertainment agents.

For instance, travel and hotel packages are sometimes created by intermediaries and then marketed at the retail level by travel agents to both vacationers and firms wanting to offer employee incentive awards.

**A Special Note on Channel Strategy for Consumer Services**    A dominant reason for patronage of many consumer services, such as banks, motels, and auto rental agencies, is convenient location. It is absolutely essential that careful consideration be given to selecting the retail site. For example, banks are being sensitive to consumers' needs when they locate branches in suburban shopping centres and malls. The installation of automated electronic tellers that enable customers to withdraw funds and to make deposits when a bank's offices are closed is a further example of attempts to provide convenience.

**Multiple Channels**    An increasingly common phenomenon is the use of more than one marketing channel for similar products. These *multiple channels* (or dual distribution) are utilized when the same product is marketed both to the ultimate consumer and industrial users. Dial soap is distributed through the traditional grocery wholesaler to food stores to the consumer, but a second channel also exists, from the manufacturer to large retail chains and motels that buy direct from the manufacturer. Competition among retailers and other intermediaries striving to expand lines, profitability, and customer service has created these multiple channels.

In other cases, the same product is marketed through a variety of types of retail outlets. A basic product such as a paintbrush is carried in inventory by the traditional hardware store; it is also handled by such nontraditional retail outlets as auto accessory stores, building supply outlets, department stores, discount houses, mail-order houses, supermarkets, and variety stores. Each retail store may utilize a different marketing channel.

Firestone automobile tires are marketed:
1. directly to General Motors, where they serve as a fabricated part for new Chevrolets;
2. through Firestone stores, company-owned retail outlets;
3. through franchised Firestone outlets;
4. from the factory to tire jobbers to retail gas stations.

Each channel enables the manufacturer to serve a different market.

**Reverse Channels**    While the traditional concept of marketing channels involves movement of products and services from producer to consumer or indus-

# A Multiple Channel Problem in the Miniblind Business

Rainbow Window Fashions, Inc., a successful small manufacturer of venetian blinds, was organized by Louis Sterner when he realized that the growing market for one-inch miniblinds was not being satisfied. About 90 percent of miniblind sales were custom-made orders, which typically took up to five weeks to fill.

Sterner decided to produce and stock quality miniblinds that would be available for immediate installation. However, his new enterprise had a distribution problem. Small, independent stores sold the most miniblinds, but brand recognition came from acceptance by department stores. Sterner felt he needed this recognition to establish Rainbow's position in the marketplace. His dilemma was complicated by the fact that department store buyers were reluctant to accept brands sold by the smaller stores.

Sterner decided to offer two brands: the Rainbow label went to department stores, while smaller retailers got stripped-down versions of the miniblind under the Streamline brand. The firm's small sales force was able to penetrate both of these distribution channels successfully. Today, Rainbow Window Fashions is growing by about $2 to $3 million annually.

Source: Sanford L. Jacobs, "How Enterpreneur Exploited Chance the Big Firms Ignored," *The Wall Street Journal* (March 1, 1982), p. 23.

trial user, there is increasing interest in reverse channels. **Reverse channels** are *the paths goods follow from consumer to manufacturer or to marketing intermediaries.* William G. Zikmund and William J. Stanton point out several problems in developing reverse channels in the *recycling* process.

> The recycling of solid wastes is a major ecological goal. Although recycling is technologically feasible, reversing the flow of materials in the channel of distribution — marketing trash through a "backward" channel — presents a challenge. Existing backward channels are primitive, and financial incentives are inadequate. The consumer must be motivated to undergo a role change and become a producer — the initiating force in the reverse distribution process. [8]

Reverse channels will increase in importance as raw materials become more expensive, and as additional laws are passed to control litter and the disposal of packaging materials such as soft-drink bottles. In order for recycling to succeed, four basic conditions must be satisfied:

1. a technology must be available that can efficiently process the material being recycled;
2. a market must be available for the end product — the reclaimed material;

[8] William G. Zikmund and William J. Stanton, "Recycling Solid Wastes: A Channels-of-Distribution Problem," *Journal of Marketing* (July 1971), p. 34.

3. a substantial and continuing quantity of secondary product (recycled aluminum, reclaimed steel from automobiles, recycled paper) must be available;
4. a marketing system must be developed that can bridge the gap between suppliers of secondary products and end users on a profitable basis.[9]

In some instances, the reverse channel consists of traditional marketing intermediaries. In the soft-drink industry, retailers and local bottlers perform these functions. In other cases, manufacturers take the initiative by establishing redemption centres. A concentrated attempt by the Reynolds Metals Company in one area permitted the company to recycle an amount of aluminum equivalent to 60 percent of the total containers marketed in the area. Other reverse-channel participants may include community groups, which organize "clean-up" days and develop systems for rechannelling paper products for recycling, and specialized organizations developed for waste disposal and recycling.

*Reverse Channels for Product Recalls and Repairs*   Reverse channels are also used for product recalls and repairs. Ownership of some products (like tires) is registered so that proper notification can be sent if there is a product recall. In the case of automobile recalls, owners are advised to have the problem corrected at their dealership. Similarly, reverse channels have been used for repairs to some products. The warranty for a small appliance may specify that if repairs are needed in the first 90 days, the item should be returned to the dealer. After that period, the product should be returned to the factory. Such reverse channels are a vital element of product recalls and repair procedures.

## Facilitating Agencies in the Distribution Channel

A **facilitating agency** *provides specialized assistance for regular channel members (such as producers, wholesalers, and retailers) in moving products from producer to consumer.* Included in the definition of facilitating agencies are transportation companies, warehousing firms, financial institutions, insurance companies, and marketing research companies.

## Power in the Distribution Channel

Some marketing institutions must exercise leadership in the distribution channel if it is to be an effective aspect of marketing strategy. Decisions must be made and conflicts among channel members

[9] Donald A. Fuller, "Aluminum Beverage Container Recycling in Florida: A Commentary," *Atlanta Economic Review* (January–February 1977), p. 41.

resolved. Channel leadership is a function of one's power within the distribution channel.[10]

**Bases of Power**

Researchers have identified five bases of power: reward power, coercive power, legitimate power, referent power, and expert power.[11] All of these bases can be used to establish a position of channel leadership.[12]

*Reward Power*   If channel members can offer some type of reward, such as the granting of an exclusive sales territory or franchise, to another member, then they possess reward power.

*Coercive Power*   The threat of economic punishment is known as coercive power. A manufacturer might threaten an unco-operative retailer with loss of its dealership, or a giant retailer like Eaton's might use its market size as a significant base of power against its suppliers in its distribution channel.

*Legitimate Power*   Distribution channels that are linked contractually provide examples of legitimate power. A franchise might be contractually required to perform such activities as maintaining a common type of outlet, contributing to general advertising, and remaining open during specified time periods.

*Referent Power*   Referent power stems from an agreement among channel members as to what is in their mutual best interests. For instance, many manufacturers maintain dealer councils to help resolve potential problems in distribution of a product or service. Both parties have a mutual interest in maintaining effective channel relationships.

*Expert Power*   Knowledge is the determinant of expert power. A manufacturer might assist a retailer with store layout or advertising based on its marketing expertise with the product line.

**Channel Leadership**

Leadership in the marketing channel typically falls to the most powerful member. At various times and under certain circumstances channel members will utilize one or more of the foregoing bases of power to influence relationships and channel procedures. The *dominant and controlling member of the channel* is called the **channel cap-**

10 Interesting discussions of power appear in F. Robert Dwyer and Orville C. Walker, Jr., "Bargaining in an Asymmetrical Power Structure," *Journal of Marketing* (Winter 1981), pp. 104–115.
11 These bases were identified in John R. P. French, Jr., and Bertram Raven, "The Bases of Social Power," in *Group Dynamics: Research and Theory*, 2d ed., (eds.) Darwin Cartwright and Alvin Zandler (Evanston, Ill.: Row, Putnam, 1960), pp. 607–623. The list originally came from *Studies in Social Power* (ed.) Darwin Cartwright (Ann Arbor: University of Michigan, 1959), pp. 612–613.
12 The discussion that follows is based on Bert Rosenbloom, *Marketing Channels: A Management Overview*, 2d ed. (Hinsdale, Ill.: The Dryden Press, 1983).

**tain.**[13] Historically, the role of channel captain belonged to the manufacturer or wholesaler, since retailers tended to be both small and localized. However, retailers are increasingly taking on the role of channel captain as large chains assume traditional wholesaling functions and even dictate product design specifications to the manufacturer.

*Manufacturers as Channel Captains*   Since manufacturers typically create new-product and service offerings and enjoy the benefits of large-scale operations, they fill the role of channel captain in many marketing channels. Examples of such manufacturers include Armstrong Cork, General Electric, Sealy Mattress Co., and Black & Decker.

*Retailers as Channel Captains*   Retailers are often powerful enough to serve as channel captains in many industries. Larger chain operations may bypass independent wholesalers and utilize manufacturers as suppliers in producing the retailers' private brands at quality levels specified by the chains. Major retailers such as The Bay, Eaton's, Woodward's, Canadian Tire, Sears, and Provigo serve as leaders in many of the marketing channels with which they are associated.[14]

*Wholesalers as Channel Captains*   Although the relative influence of wholesalers has declined since 1900, they continue to serve as vital members of many marketing channels. Large-scale wholesalers, such as the Independent Grocers' Association (IGA), serve as channel captains as they assist independent retailers in competing with chain outlets.

---

**Channel Strategy Decisions**   Marketers face several channel strategy decisions. The selection of a specific distribution channel is the most basic of these, but the level of distribution intensity and the issue of vertical marketing systems must also be addressed.

---

[13] Bruce J. Walker and Donald W. Jackson, Jr., "The Channels Manager: A Needed New Position," in *Proceedings of the Southern Marketing Association*, (eds.) Robert S. Franz, Robert M. Hopkins, and Al Toma (New Orleans, La.: November 1978), pp. 325–328. See also R.K. Teas and Stanley D. Sibley, "An Examination of the Moderating Effect on Channel Member Size of Perceptions of Preferred Channel Linkages," *Journal of the Academy of Marketing Science* (Summer 1980), pp. 277–293.

[14] See Bert Rosenbloom, "The Retailer's Changing Role in the Marketing Channel," in *1979 Educator's Conference Proceedings*, eds. Neil Beckwith, Michael Houston, Robert Mittelstaedt, Kent B. Monroe, and Scott Ward (Chicago: American Marketing Association, 1979), pp. 392–395; and Ian F. Wilkinson, "Power and Satisfaction in Channels of Distribution," *Journal of Retailing* (Summer 1979), pp. 79–84.

**Selection of a
Distribution Channel**
What makes a direct channel (manufacturer to consumer) best for
the Fuller Brush Company? Why do operating supplies often go
through both agents and merchant wholesalers before being purchased by the industrial firm? Why do some firms employ multiple
channels for the same product? The firm must answer many such
questions when it determines its choice of marketing channels. The
choice is based upon an analysis of the market, the product and the
producer, and various competitive factors. Each is often of critical
importance, and all are often interrelated.

Market Factors   A major determinant of channel structure i
whether the product is intended for the consumer or the industria
market. Industrial purchasers usually prefer to deal directly with
the manufacturer (except for supplies or small accessory items), bu
most consumers make their purchases from retail stores. Product
sold to both industrial users and the consumer market usually requir
more than one channel.

The geographic location and the needs of the firm's potential
market will also affect channel choice. Direct sales are possible where
the firm's potential market is concentrated in a few regions. Industrial production tends to be concentrated in a relatively small
geographic region, making direct contact possible. The small number
of potential buyers also increases the feasibility of direct channels.
Consumer goods are purchased by every household everywhere.
Since consumers are numerous and geographically dispersed, and
purchase a small volume at a given time, intermediaries must be
employed to market products to them efficiently.

In Canada, population distribution is an extremely influential
factor in channel decisions. For example, the markets for fishing
nets are on the two coasts, with smaller markets on the Great Lakes,
Lake Winnipeg, and a few other large lakes. The Rockies and the
Canadian Shield effectively divide markets and strongly offset channels of distribution. Our relatively smaller and widely dispersed centres of population tend to result in less specialized wholesaling and
retailing institutions than in the United States and other developed,
heavily populated countries. This, of course, may limit the range of
channel opportunities available to the marketing manager.

Order size will also affect the marketing channel decision.
Manufacturers are likely to employ shorter, more direct channels in
cases where retail customers or industrial buyers place relatively small
numbers of large orders. Retail chains often employ buying offices
to negotiate directly with manufacturers for large-scale purchases.
Wholesalers may be used to contact smaller retailers.

Shifts in consumer buying patterns also influence channel
decisions. The desire for credit, the growth of self-service, the
increased use of mail-order houses, and the greater willingness to

purchase from door-to-door salespeople all affect a firm's marketing channel.[15]

Product Factors   Product characteristics also play a role in determining optimum marketing channels. *Perishable products*, such as fresh produce and fruit, and fashion products with short life cycles, *typically move through relatively short channels* direct to the retailer or to the ultimate consumer. Old Dutch Potato Chips are distributed by company salespeople-truck drivers direct to the retail shelves. Each year Hines & Smart Corporation ships over 2 million kg of live lobsters by air, in specially designed insulating containers, directly to restaurants and hotels throughout North America.

Complex products, such as custom-made installations or computer equipment, are typically sold direct from the manufacturer to the buyer. As a general rule, *the more standardized a product, the longer the channel will be.* Such items will usually be marketed by wholesalers. Also, products requiring regular service or specialized repair services usually avoid channels employing independent wholesalers. Automobiles are marketed through a franchised network of regular dealers whose employees receive regular training on how to service their cars properly.

Another generalization concerning marketing channels is that *the lower the unit value of the product, the longer the channel.* Convenience goods and industrial supplies with typically low unit prices are frequently marketed through relatively long channels. Installations and more expensive industrial and consumer goods go through shorter, more direct channels.

Producer Factors   Companies with adequate resources — financial, marketing, and managerial — will be less compelled to utilize intermediaries in marketing their products.[16] A financially strong manufacturer can hire its own sales force, warehouse its products, and grant credit to the retailer or consumer. A weaker firm relies on intermediaries for these services (although some large retail chains may purchase all of the manufacturer's output, making it possible to bypass the independent wholesaler). Production-oriented firms may be forced to utilize the marketing expertise of intermediaries to replace the lack of finances and management in their organization.

---

15 See Fred D. Reynolds, "An Analysis of Catalog Buying Behavior," *Journal of Marketing* (July 1974), pp. 47–51; Marvin A. Jolson, "Direct Selling: Consumer vs. Salesman," *Business Horizons* (October 1972), pp. 87–95; and Patrick Dunne, "Some Demographic Characteristics of Direct Mail Purchasers," *Baylor Business Studies* (May–July 1975), pp. 67–72.

16 Robert E. Weigand, "The Marketing Organization, Channels, and Firm Size," *The Journal of Business* (April 1963), pp. 228–236.

A firm with a broad product line is better able to market it
products directly to retailers or industrial users since its sales forc
can offer a variety of products to the customers. Larger total sale
allow the selling costs to be spread over a number of products an
make direct sales more feasible. The single-product firm (remembe
the discussion in Chapter 11 of Monsanto and its single consume
good, All?) often discovers that direct selling is an unaffordabl
luxury.

The manufacturer's need for control over the product will als
influence channel selection. If aggressive promotion for the firm'
products at the retail level is desired, the manufacturer will choos
the shortest available channel. For new products the manufacture

**Figure 15-3   Factors Affecting Choice of Marketing Channels**

| Factor | Channels Tend to Be Shorter When: |
|---|---|
| *Market Factors* | |
| Consumer market or industrial market | Users are in industrial market |
| Geographic location of market target | Customers are geographically concentrated |
| Customer service needs | Specialized knowledge, technical know-how, and regular service need are present |
| Order size | Customers place relatively small number of large orders |
| *Product Factors* | |
| Perishability | Products are perishable, either because of fashion changes or physical perishability |
| Technical complexity of product | Products are highly technical |
| Unit value | Products have high unit value |
| *Producer Factors* | |
| Producer resources — financial, managerial, and marketing | Manufacturer possesses adequate resources to perform channel functions |
| Product line | Manufacturer has broad product line to spread distribution costs |
| Need for control over the channel | Manufacturer desires to control the channel |
| *Competitive Factors* | |
| Need for promotion to channel members | Manufacturer feels that independent intermediaries are inadequately promoting products |

may be forced to implement an introductory advertising campaign before independent wholesalers will handle the item.

Competitive Factors   Some firms are forced to develop unique marketing channels because of inadequate promotion of their products by independent intermediaries. Avon concentrated on house-to-house selling rather than being directly involved in the intense competition among similar lines of cosmetics in traditional channels. This radical departure from the traditional channel resulted in tremendous sales by the firm's thousands of neighbourhood salespeople. Similarly, Honeywell discovered about 15 years ago that its $700 home security system, Concept 70, was being inadequately marketed by the traditional wholesaler-to-retailer channel and switched to a direct-to-home sales force.

Figure 15-3 summarizes the factors affecting the choice of optimal marketing channels and shows the effect of each characteristic upon the overall length of the channel.

**Determining Distribution Intensity**   Adequate market coverage for some products could mean one dealer for each 50 000 people. On the other hand, Procter & Gamble defines adequate coverage for Crest toothpaste as almost every supermarket, discount store, drugstore, and variety store plus many vending machines.

Intensive Distribution   *Producers of convenience goods who attempt to provide saturation coverage of their potential markets* are the prime users of **intensive distribution**. Soft drinks, cigarettes, candy, and chewing gum are available in convenient locations to enable the purchaser to buy with a minimum of effort.

Bic pens can be purchased in thousands of retail outlets in Canada. TMX Watches of Canada Ltd. uses an intensive distribution strategy for its Timex watches. Consumers may buy a Timex in many jewellery stores, the traditional retail outlet for watches. In addition, they may find Timex in discount houses, variety stores, department stores, hardware stores, and drugstores.

Mass coverage and low unit prices make the use of wholesalers almost mandatory for such distribution. An important exception to this generalization is Avon Products, which operates direct to the consumer through a nationwide network of neighbourhood salespeople who purchase directly from the manufacturer, at 60 percent of the retail price, and service a limited area with cosmetics, toiletries, jewellery, and toys.

It must be remembered that while a firm may wish intensive distribution, the retailer or industrial distributor will only carry products that make a profit. If demand is low the producer may have to settle for less than complete market coverage.

**Selective Distribution**    As the name implies, **selective distribution** involves *the selection of a small number of retailers to handle the firm's product line*. By limiting its retailers, the firm may reduce its total marketing costs, such as those for sales force and shipping while establishing better working relationships within the channel. This practice may also be necessary to give the retailers an incentive (through having a product available to a limited number of sellers) to carry the product and promote it properly against many competing brands. Co-operative advertising (where the manufacturer pays a percentage of the retailer's advertising expenditures and the retailer prominently displays the firm's products) can be utilized to mutual benefit. Marginal retailers can be avoided. Where product service is important, dealer training and assistance is usually forthcoming from the manufacturer. Finally, price-cutting is less likely since fewer dealers are handling the firm's line.

**Exclusive Distribution**    When *manufacturers grant exclusive rights to a wholesaler or retailer to sell in a geographic region*, they are practising **exclusive distribution**, which is an extreme form of selective distribution. The best example of exclusive dealership is the automobile industry. For example, a city of 100 000 might have a single Toyota dealer or one Cadillac agency. Exclusive dealership arrangements are also found in the marketing of some major appliances and in fashion apparel. Powerful retailers may also negotiate to acquire excusive distribution.

Some market coverage may be sacrificed through a policy of exclusive distribution, but this is often offset through the development and maintenance of an image of quality and prestige for the products, with more active attention by the retailer to promote them, and the reduced marketing costs associated with a small number of accounts. Producers and retailers co-operate closely in decisions concerning advertising and promotion, inventory to be carried by the retailers, and prices.

**The Legal Problems of Exclusive Distribution**    The use of exclusive distribution presents a number of potential legal problems. Three problem areas exist — exclusive dealing, tied selling, and market restriction. Each will be examined briefly.

**Exclusive dealing** *prohibits a marketing intermediary* (either a wholesaler or, more typically, a retailer) *from handling competing products*. Through such a contract the manufacturer is assured of total concentration on the firm's product line by the intermediaries. For example, an oil company may consider requiring all dealers to sign a contract agreeing to purchase all of their accessories from that company.

The legal question is covered in Part IV of the Competition Act, which prohibits exclusive dealing by a major supplier if it is likely to:

1. impede entry into or expansion of a firm in the market;
2. impede introduction of a product into or expansion of sales of a product in the market; or
3. have any other exclusionary effect in the market, with the result that competition is or is likely to be lessened substantially.[17]

A second problem area is **tied selling**. In this case *a supplier might force a dealer who wishes to handle a product to also carry other products from the supplier or to refrain from using or distributing someone else's product.* Tied selling is controlled by the same provision as exclusive dealing.

The third legal issue of exclusive distribution is the use of **market restriction**. In this case *suppliers restrict the geographic territories for each of their distributors.* The key issue is whether such restrictions substantially lessen competition. If so, the Restrictive Trade Practices Commission had power to order the prohibition of such practices. For example, a *horizontal territorial restriction*, where retailers or wholesalers agree to avoid competition in products from the same manufacturer, would likely be declared unlawful.

## Vertical Marketing Systems

The traditional marketing channel has been described as a "highly fragmented network in which vertically aligned firms bargain with each other at arm's length, terminate relationships with impunity, and otherwise behave autonomously."[18] This potentially inefficient system of distributing goods in some industries   is gradually being replaced by **vertical marketing systems** — *"professionally managed and centrally programmed networks preengineered to achieve operating economies and maximum impact."*[19] In other words, a vertical marketing system (VMS) is the use of various types of economic

---

[17] Combines Investigation Act, Part IV. 1, 31.4, 1976.

[18] Bert C. McCammon, Jr., "The Emergence and Growth of Contractually Integrated Channels in the American Economy," in Peter D. Bennett (ed.), *Marketing and Economic Development* (Chicago: American Marketing Association, 1965), p. 496. This section is based on material in this paper, pp. 496–515.

[19] See Bert C. McCammon, Jr., "Perspectives for Distribution Programming," in Louis P. Bucklin (ed.), *Vertical Marketing Systems* (Glenview, Ill.: Scott, Foresman and Company, 1970, pp. 32–51 (italics added.) These are also described by William J. Hannaford, "Contractually Integrated Systems for the Marketing of Industrial Supplies," *Journal of the Academy of Marketing Science* (Fall 1974), pp. 567–581.

**Figure 15-4   Three Types of Vertical Marketing Systems**

| Type of System | Description | Examples |
|---|---|---|
| Corporate | Channel owned and operated by a single organization | Bata Shoes<br>Firestone<br>Sherwin-Williams<br>Singer<br>McDonald's (partial) |
| Administered | Channel dominated by one powerful member who acts as channel captain | Kodak<br>General Electric<br>Corning Glass |
| Contractual | Channel co-ordinated through contractual agreements among channel members | *Wholesaler-Sponsored Voluntary Chain:*<br>IGA<br>Canadian Tire<br>Independent Druggists Alliance (IDA)<br>Allied Hardware<br><br>*Retail Co-operative:*<br>Associated Grocers<br><br>*Franchise Systems:*<br>McDonald's (partial)<br>Century 21 Real Estate<br>AAMCO Transmissions<br>Coca-Cola bottlers<br>Ford dealers |

power to attain maximum operating efficiencies, deep market penetration, and sustained profits. Vertical marketing systems produce economies of scale through their size and elimination of duplicated services. Three types prevail: corporate, administered, and contractual. They are depicted in Figure 15-4.

**Corporate System**   When there is single ownership of each stage of the marketing channel, a *corporate vertical marketing system* exists. Holiday Inn owns a furniture manufacturer and a carpet mill. Bata Shoes owns a retail chain of shoe stores. Many McDonald's food outlets are corporate-owned.

**Administered System**   Channel co-ordination is achieved through the exercise of economic and "political" power by a dominant channel member in an *administered vertical marketing system.*[20] Camco Inc. (an affiliate

---

[20] See Robert E. Weigand and Hilda C. Wasson, "Arbitration in the Marketing Channel," *Business Horizons* (October 1974), pp. 39–47; and John H. Holmes, "Leverage: A Key Factor in Marketing Channel Negotiation," *Pittsburgh Business Review* (May–June 1974), pp. 1–5.

of General Electric Canada, Inc.) has a network of major appliance dealers who aggressively display and promote the line because of its strong reputation and brand. Although independently owned and operated, these dealers co-operate with the manufacturer because of the effective working relationships enjoyed over the years and the profits to be realized from selling the widely known, well-designed, broad range of merchandise.

**Contractual System**   The most significant form of vertical marketing is the *contractual vertical marketing system*. It accounts for nearly 40 percent of all retail sales. Instead of the common ownership of channel components that characterizes the corporate VMS or the relative power relationships of an administered system, the contractual VMS is characterized by formal agreements between channel members. In practice there are three types of agreements: the wholesaler-sponsored voluntary chain, the retail co-operative, and the franchise.[21]

Wholesaler-Sponsored Voluntary Chain   The wholesaler-sponsored voluntary chain represents an attempt by the independent wholesaler to preserve a market for the firm's products through the strengthening of the firm's retailer customers. In order to enable the independent retailers to compete with the chains, the wholesaler enters into a formal agreement with a group of retailers, whereby the retailers agree to use a common name, have standardized facilities, and purchase the wholesaler's products. The wholesaler often develops a line of private brands to be stocked by the members of the voluntary chain. A common store name and similar inventories allow the retailers to achieve cost savings on advertising, since a single newspaper advertisement promotes all retailers in the trading area. IGA, with a membership of approximately 800 food stores, is a good example of a voluntary chain.

Retail Co-operatives   A second type of contractual VMS is the retail co-operative, which is established by a group of retailers who set up a wholesaling operation better to compete with the chains. A group of retailers purchase shares of stock in a wholesaling operation and agree to purchase a minimum percentage of their inventory from the firm. The members may also choose to use a common store name, such as Home Hardware, and devleop their own private brands in order to carry out co-operative advertising.

Buying groups like wholesaler-sponsored chains and retail co-operatives are not a new phenomenon in the Canadian distribution industry. They date back at least 50 years, some having evolved

---

21 See Michael Etgar, "Differences in the Use of Manufacturer Power in Conventional and Contractual Channels," *Journal of Retailing* (Winter 1978), pp. 49–62.

from the co-operative movement of the early years of the century. Under the Combines Investigation Act, suppliers could charge different prices for different volumes of purchases, so long as these prices are available to all competing purchasers of articles of like quantity and quality. And suppliers have done so; it is common practice to offer volume rebates. Thus buying groups improved the small retailers' bargaining position with their suppliers, thus increasing competition for their large rivals.

A phenomenon is now occurring in the retail food industry. Buying groups which originally existed to enable small retailers and wholesalers to compete on a more equitable basis with the large chains have now themselves become as large as the chains. At the same time the chains have been coming together to form their own even larger groups. The result is that there are now five groups representing some 14 000 stores, and accounting for about 85 percent of all retail food sales in Canada: Foodwide of Canada (Loblaws and Provigo), Volume 1 (Dominion and Steinberg), IGA-Safeway, United Grocery Wholesales, and Independent Wholesale Grocers. This recent development leads to the concern that while buying groups may improve the balance of market power in some areas, there is a possibility of abuse of this power in others.[22]

**Franchising**   A third type of contractual VMS is the **franchise**. A franchise is *an agreement whereby dealers (franchisees) agree to meet the operating requirements of a manufacturer or other franchiser*. The dealer typically receives a variety of marketing, management, technical, and financial services in exchange for a specified fee.

Although franchising attracted considerable interest beginning in the late 1960s, the concept actually began 100 years earlier when the Singer Company established franchised sewing machine outlets. Early impetus for the franchising concept came after 1900 in the automobile industry.[23] The soft-drink industry is another example of franchising, but in this case the contractual arrangement is between the syrup manufacturer and the wholesale bottler.

The franchising form that created most of the excitement both in retailing and on Wall Street in the late 1960s was the retailer franchise system sponsored by the service firm.[24] McDonald's Corporation is an excellent example of such a franchise operation.

[22] Adapted from Lawson A. W. Hunter, "Buying Groups," *Agriculture Canada: Food Market Commentary*, Vol. 5, No. 4, p. 15.
[23] Thomas G. Marx, "Distribution Efficiency in Franchising," *MSU Business Topics* (Winter 1980), p. 5.
[24] See Aaron M. Rothenberg, "A Fresh Look at Franchising," *Journal of Marketing* (July 1967), pp. 52–54; P. Ronald Stephenson and Robert G. House, "A Perspective of Franchising," *Business Horizons* (August 1971), pp. 35–42; and Jack M. Starling, "Franchising," *Business Studies* (Fall 1970), pp.10–16.

McDonald's brought together suppliers and a chain of hamburger outlets. It provided a proven system of retail operation (the operations manual for each outlet weighs over a kilogram) with a standardized product and ingenious promotional campaigns. This enabled the offering of lower prices through the franchiser's purchasing power on meat, buns, potatoes, napkins, and other supplies. In return the franchisee pays a fee for the use of the name (over $150 000 for McDonald's) and a percentage of gross sales. Other familiar examples include Hertz, Avis, Kentucky Fried Chicken, Pizza Hut, and Weight Watchers.

McDonald's has several stores in operation in every major centre and has expanded its menu to include such items as Egg McMuffin, hotcakes, scrambled eggs, and McChicken. These efforts are aimed at obtaining even more of the millions of dollars Canadians spend annually in restaurants. Almost one-third of all meals are eaten in restaurants, and the rate is expected to grow to 50 percent within the next five to ten years.[25]

Fast-food franchising has already proven itself in the international market. In Tokyo, London, Rome, and Paris, McDonald's hamburgers are consumed daily. Kentucky Fried Chicken has opened nearly 500 restaurants in Canada and in such locations as Manila and Munich, Nice and Nairobi. In some countries adjustments to the North American marketing plans have been made to match local needs. Although their menu is rigidly standardized in Canada, McDonald's executives approved changes to the menu in outlets in France. Kentucky Fried chicken replaced French fries with mashed potatoes to satisfy their Japanese customers.[26]

Although many franchises have proven extremely profitable, the infatuation with the franchising concept and the market performance of franchise stocks have lured dozens of newcomers into the market. Lacking experience and often with a well-known celebrity's name as their sole asset, many of these firms have disappeared almost as quickly as they entered the market.[27]

---

[25] See Walter Margulies, "Fast-Food Chains Push Revamp to Stand Out from the Crowd," *Advertising Age* (September 15, 1975), pp. 33–34; and "Broader Menus for Fast Foods," *Business Week* (July 14, 1975), pp. 118–122.

[26] See "The Finger Lickin' Fast-Food Fad," *Newsweek* (October 23, 1972), pp. 32–35; Bruce J. Walker and Michael J. Etzel, "The Internationalization of U.S. Franchise Systems: Progress and Procedures," *Journal of Marketing* (April 1973), pp. 38–46.

[27] Leonard L. Berry, "Is It Time to Be Wary about Franchising?" *Arizona Business Bulletin* (October 1970), pp. 3–9. See also Donald F. Dixon, "Impact of Recent Antitrust Decisions upon Franchise Marketing," *MSU Business Topics* (Spring 1969), pp. 68–79; "A Changing Pattern for the Franchise Boom," *U.S. News & World Report* (April 24, 1972), pp. 88–89; and Shelby D. Hunt and John R. Nevin, "Full Disclosure Laws in Franchising: An Empirical Investigation," *Journal of Marketing* (April 1976), pp. 53–62.

The median investment for a franchise varies tremendously from one business area to another. A pet-sitting franchise might sell for as low as $9500, whereas a restaurant franchise will likely average over $250 000. The great bulk of the nation's franchises are in the "traditional" franchise areas such as auto dealers, service stations, and soft-drink bottlers. Figure 15-5 shows the proportion of sales accounted for by the various franchise categories.

Despite the many franchise opportunities available, there are few specific regulations with respect to the proper disclosure of information to prospective franchisees. It is worthwhile to carefully evaluate the opportunity before investing.

VMS—whether in the form of corporate, administered, or contractual systems — are already becoming a dominant factor in the consumer goods sector of the Canadian economy. Over 60 percent of the available market is currently in the hands of retail components of VMS.

**Typical Franchise Advertisements**

Source: *The Financial Post Special Report on Franchising*, October 8, 1983, p. S15.

# "Welcome to Hamburger University!"

Since the typical McDonald's outlet generates annual sales of approximately $500 000 a year and produces earnings before taxes of around $70 000, it is not surprising that the main offices in Canada and the United States receive thousands of requests for franchises each year. Only about 10 percent of them are accepted, and many of the outlets are corporately owned and operated.

McDonald's guards its leading position in the fast-food business carefully and takes every possible step to ensure the success of each new outlet.

The McDonald's sales success story is being repeated in Australia, Germany, and Japan. One of the first requirements for new Canadian franchisees is a series of courses in Toronto, in order to earn a "Bachelor of Hamburgerology, with a minor in french fries." The franchisee must take courses covering everything from how to scrape a grill to how to keep books. Thorough grounding in the McDonald's system allows each new franchisee to apply techniques that have been proven successful in more than 3000 instances.

Source: Max Boas and Steve Chain, *Big Mac: The Unauthorized Story of McDonald's* (New York: E. P. Dutton, 1976).

Figure 15-5   How Franchising Branches Out

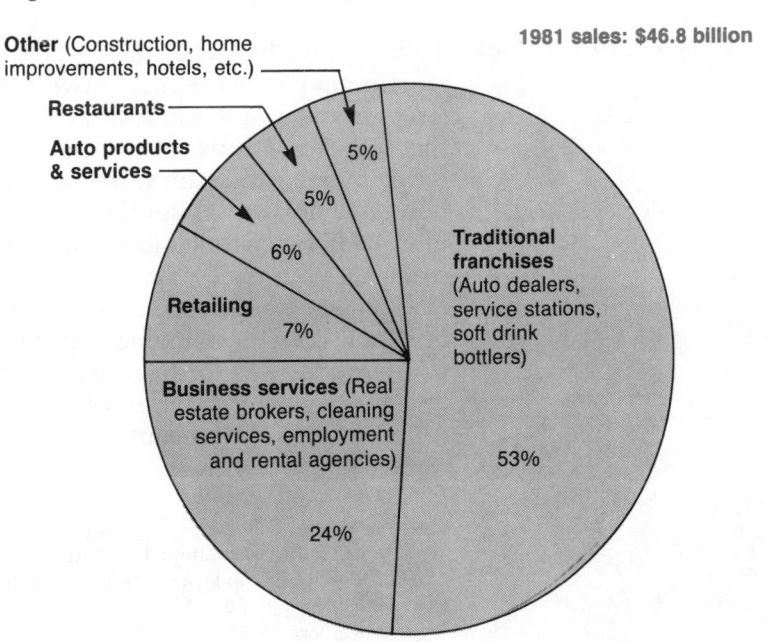

Source: *The Financial Post Report on Franchising*, October 8, 1983, p. S1, from information provided by Statistics Canada, Merchandising & Services Division.

**The Distribution Channel: Conflict and Co-operation**

Distribution channels must be organized and regarded as a systematic co-operative effort if operating efficiencies are to be achieved. Yet channel members often perform as separate, independent, and even competitive forces. Too often, marketing institutions within the channel believe it extends only one step forward or backward. They think in terms of suppliers and customers rather than of vital links in the total channel.[28]

Channel conflict can evolve from a number of sources:

A manufacturer may wish to promote a product in one manner . . . while his retailers oppose this. Another manufacturer may wish to get information from his retailers on a certain aspect relating to his product, but his retailers may refuse to provide this information. A producer may want to distribute his product extensively, but his retailers may demand exclusives. A supplier may force a product onto its retailers, who dare not oppose, but who retaliate in other ways, such as using it as a loss leader. Large manufacturers may try to dictate the resale price of their merchandise; this may be less or more than the price at which the retailers wish to sell it. Occasionally a local market may be more competitive for a retailer than is true nationally. The manufacturer may not recognize the difference in competition and refuse to help this channel member. There is also conflict because of the desire of both manufacturers and retailers to eliminate the wholesaler.[29]

**Types of Conflict**

Two types of **channel conflict**—horizontal or vertical—may occur. *Horizontal* conflict occurs between channel members at the same level—two or more wholesalers or two or more retailers. Such conflict may occur between intermediaries of the same type, such as two competing discount stores or several retail florists. More often, however, horizontal conflict occurs between different types of intermediaries who handle similar products. The retail druggist competes with variety stores, discount houses, department stores, convenience food stores, and mail-order houses, all of which may be supplied by the manufacturer with identical branded products. Consumer desires for convenient, one-stop shopping have led to multiple channels and the use of numerous outlets for many products. A major function of manufacturers' sales personnel is to attempt to resolve horizontal conflict and to maintain distribution. Some such

[28] Channel conflict is examined in James R. Brown and Ralph L. Day, "Measures of Manifest Conflict in Distribution Channels," *Journal of Marketing Research* (August 1981), pp. 263–274.
[29] Bruce Mallen, "A Theory of Retailer-Supplier Conflict, Control, and Cooperation," *Journal of Retailing* (Summer 1963), p. 26. Reprinted with permission. See also F. Robert Dwyer, "Channel-Member Satisfaction: Laboratory Insights," *Journal of Retailing* (Summer 1980), pp. 45–65.

conflict is inevitable since the retail or wholesale firms are competing for one or more market segments.

*Vertical* conflict occurs between channel members at different levels—between wholesalers and retailers or between manufacturers and wholesalers or retailers. Vertical conflict occurs frequently and is often the more severe form of conflict in the channel. Conflict may occur between manufacturers and retailers when retailers develop private brands to compete with the manufacturers' brands, or when manufacturers establish their own retail stores or create a mail-order operation in competition with retailers. Conflict between manufacturers and wholesalers may occur in cases where the manufacturer attempts to bypass the wholesaler and make direct sales to retailers or industrial users. In other instances, wholesalers may promote competitive products.

A third type of vertical conflict may occur between wholesalers and retailers. Retailers may believe that wholesalers are failing to offer credit or to allow returns on the same basis as is being provided for other types of retail outlets. Wholesalers may complain that retailers are making sales to institutions that previously dealt directly with the wholesaler. A wholesaler in the sporting goods field may argue that sales by retail sporting goods outlets directly to local school systems are unfairly competing with its own sales force.[30]

**Achieving Co-operation among Channel Members**

The basic antidote to channel conflict is effective co-operation among channel members. In general, channels have more harmonious relationships than conflicting ones; if they did not, the channels would have ceased to exist long ago. Co-operation is best achieved by considering all channel members as part of the same organization. Achievement of this co-operation is the prime responsibility of the channel captain, who must provide the leadership necessary to ensure efficient functioning of the channel. However, complete harmony is almost never achieved, nor will it be in a competitive system.

**Summary**

Distribution channels refer to the various marketing institutions and the interrelationships responsible for the physical and title flow of goods and services from producer to consumer or industrial user. Wholesaling and retailing intermediaries (or middlemen) are the marketing institutions in the distribution channel.

---

30 *Educators Conference Proceedings*, (eds.) Neil Beckwith, Michael Houston, Robert Mittelstaedt, Kent B. Monroe, and Scott Ward (Chicago: American Marketing Association, 1970), pp. 495–499; Michael Etgar, "Sources and Types of Intra Channel Conflict," *Journal of Retailing* (Spring 1979), pp. 61–78; and Louis W. Stern and Torger Reve, "Distribution Channels as Political Economies," *Journal of Marketing* (Summer 1980), pp. 52–64.

Distribution channels bridge the gap between producer and consumer. By making products and services available when and where the consumer wants to buy, and by arranging for transfer of title, marketing channels create time, place, and possession utility.

Distribution channels also perform such specific functions as 1) facilitating the exchange process; 2) sorting to alleviate discrepancies in assortment; 3) standardizing the transaction; 4) holding inventories; and 5) accommodating the search process.

A host of alternative distribution channels are available for makers of consumer products, industrial products, and services. They range from contacting the consumer or industrial user directly to using a variety of intermediaries. Multiple channels are also increasingly commonplace today. A unique distribution system—the reverse channel—is used in recycling, product recalls, and in some service situations.

Channel leadership is primarily a matter of relative power within the channel. There are five bases for power: reward power, coercive power, legitimate power, referent power, and expert power. The channel leader that emerges is called the channel captain.

Basic channel strategy decisions involve channel selection, the level of distribution intensity, and the use of vertical marketing systems. The selection of a distribution channel is based on market, product, producer, and competitive factors. The decision on distribution intensity involves choosing from among intensive distribution, selective distribution, or exclusive distribution. The issue of vertical marketing systems also has to be explored by the marketing manager. There are three major types of vertical marketing systems: corporate, administered, and contractual, this third including wholesaler-sponsored chains, retail co-operatives, and franchises.

Channel conflict is a problem in distribution channels. There are two types of conflict: horizontal, between channel members at the same level; and vertical, between channel members at different levels. Marketers should work toward co-operation among all channel members as the remedy for channel conflict.

---

**Key Terms**

| | |
|---|---|
| distribution channel | intensive distribution |
| marketing intermediaries | selective distribution |
| wholesaling | exclusive distribution |
| retailer | exclusive dealing |
| sorting | tied selling |
| agent | market restriction |
| industrial distributor | vertical marketing systems |
| reverse channels | (VMS) |
| facilitating agencies | franchise |
| channel captain | channel conflict |

**Review Questions**

1. What types of products are most likely to be distributed through direct channels?
2. Which marketing channel is the traditional channel? Give some reasons for its frequent use.
3. Why would manufacturers choose more than one channel for their products?
4. Explain the concept of power in the distribution channel.
5. Under what circumstances is the retailer likely to assume a channel leadership role?
6. Explain and illustrate the major factors affecting distribution channel selection.
7. Why would any manufacturer deliberately choose to limit market coverage through a policy of exclusive coverage?
8. Explain and illustrate each type of vertical marketing system.
9. What advantages does franchising offer the small retailer?
10. In what ways could the use of multiple channels produce channel conflict?

**Discussion Questions and Exercises**

1. Chipwich, an ice cream and chocolate-chip cookie snack, is marketed via vendor carts as well as supermarkets. Relate Chipwich's distribution strategy to the material presented in this chapter.
2. Which degree of distribution intensity is appropriate for each of the following:
   a. *Maclean's*
   b. Catalina swim wear
   c. Irish Spring soap
   d. Johnson outboard motors
   e. Cuisinart food processors
   f. Kawasaki motorcycles
   g. Waterford crystal
3. Outline the distribution channels used by a local firm. Why were these particular channels selected by the company?
4. Prepare a brief report on the dealer requirements for a franchise that has units in your area.
5. One generalization of channel selection mentioned in the chapter was that low unit value products require long channels. How can you explain the success of a firm (such as Avon) that has a direct channel for its relatively low unit value products?

**MICROCOMPUTER EXERCISE: Decision Tree Analysis**

A useful method for making decisions in an uncertain marketing environment is *decision tree analysis*. This is a quantitative technique used in identifying alternative courses of action, assigning probability estimates for the profits or sales associated with each alternative, and indicating the course of action with the highest profit or sales. In order to use this the marketer must be able to estimate the likelihood of occurrence of each alternative. In addition, he or she must assign financial payoffs (sales, profits, or losses) for the various alternative courses of action.

The following example illustrates how decision tree analysis works. A Montreal-based firm is in the process of choosing one of two possible wholesalers to distribute its Christmas novelty items. A marketing research consultant retained by the firm has prepared both a best-case and worst-case forecast for each wholesaler. The researcher estimates a probability of 50/50 for occurrence of the "best" and "worst" cases. The potential sales volumes for the two wholesalers are shown in Table A.

The problem can be illustrated as a type of decision tree lying on its side, as shown in Table B. Each branch represents a different possible course of action. In this example, the expected revenue from a decision to use the first wholesaler in the firm's distribution channel is $2.5 million. This determination is made by first multiplying

**Table A**

| Forecast | First Wholesaler | Second Wholesaler |
|---|---|---|
| Best Case | $3 million | $5 million |
| Worst Case | $2 million | $1 million |

**Table B**

| Decision to Analyze | Courses of Action | Possible Outcomes | Expected Revenue or Profit | |
|---|---|---|---|---|
| | Yes | "Best Case" Occurs | .5(3,000,000) = | 1,500,000 |
| | | No "Best Case" Occurs | .5(2,000,000) = | 1,000,000 |
| | | | | $2,500,000 |
| Use the First Wholesaler? | | | | |
| | No | "Best Case" Occurs | .5(5,000,000) = | 2,500,000 |
| | | No "Best Case" Occurs | .5(1,000,000) = | 500,000 |
| | | | | $3,000,000 |

expected revenue from the occurrence of the "best case" forecast by the .5 probability of such a forecast being realized. Next the expected revenue is multiplied by the .5 probability that the "worst case" forecast will occur. Finally, the expected values of the two outcomes are combined for a total of $2.5 million ($1.5 million plus $1 million). A similar series of calculations is made for the possible use of the second wholesaler, producing a total expected revenue of $3 million.

In this example, the decision to utilize the second wholesaler as a component of the firm's distribution channel produces a slightly larger net expected value of revenues. Unless the firm's marketers feel that the data being used in the forecast are incorrect, they should begin serious negotiations with the second wholesaler.

Directions:  Use the Menu Item titled "Decision Tree Analysis" on the Foundations of Marketing disk to solve each of the following problems.

**1.** A consumer-goods company headquartered in Mississauga, Ont., believes that it can increase its current $60 million annual sales volume to as much as $73 million if it replaces its current selective distribution with a strategy of intensive distribution. While the firm's vice-president of marketing believes that the probability of such a sales increase is only 30 percent, she is also convinced that no possibility exists for sales to fall below $60 million if the firm converts to an intensive distribution. If the firm elects to continue its selective distribution, there is a 90/90 chance that sales will rise to $65 million. Recommend a course of action for the firm, based upon the decision tree analysis model.

**2.** A Regina firm with $20 million in annual sales is considering bypassing its independent wholesaling intermediaries and setting up its own retail outlets. If the new distribution arrangement is successful, the firm's management estimates that next year's sales will increase to $23 million. The likelihood of sucess is calculated to be 60 percent. Management estimates that sales will decline to $17 million if the new distribution system is unsuccessful. If the firm chooses to continue its current distribution channel, sales volume is given a 60/90 chance to remain at $20 million and a 40/90 chance to drop to $19 million. Should the Regina firm set up its own retail outlets?

**3.** A Kingston-based industrial-supplies firm is seriously considering the replacement of its current network of industrial distribution with its own sales force. The firm's marketing vice-president believes that the establishment of a quality sales force could increase next year's sales to $50 million — $10 million more than the "best case" scenario of $40 million in sales expected under the current distribution system. In addition, he feels that this sales increase can be achieved with no increase in selling costs. But the vice-president also believes that the conversion to a new distribution channel could cause next year's sales to decline to $20 million unless the firm is successful in attracting, training, and motivating high-quality sales representatives. This compares to $35 million that he feels is the minimum the current system will provide. Since management is confident of its ability to create an effective selling organization, it assigns a 70-percent probability of success for the new sales force. If the current system is retained, management projects a 50 percent chance for earning $40 million in sales and an equal chance for dropping to $35 million. Use the decision tree analysis to suggest a course of action for the firm.

## CHAPTER 16

# Wholesaling

1. *To relate wholesaling to the other variables of the marketing mix.*

2. *To identify the functions performed by wholesaling intermediaries.*

3. *To explain the channel options available to a manufacturer who desires to bypass independent wholesaling intermediaries.*

4. *To identify the conditions under which a manufacturer is likely to assume wholesaling functions rather than use independents.*

5. *To distinguish between merchant wholesalers and agents and brokers.*

6. *To identify the major types of merchant wholesalers and instances where each type might be used.*

7. *To describe the major types of agents and brokers.*

At 9:15 a.m. George Martin enters the Save-Easy supermarket in Miramichi Mall on King George Highway, in Newcastle, New Brunswick. He introduces himself to the store manager, and registers in a sign-in book kept near the loading dock. Martin goes first to the deli section where he finds that a label from a brand of cheese his company represents has fallen off. He heats it with a lighter and sticks it back on the package. Martin then deals with the problem of a damaged package of shrimp cocktail and notes that the brands of onion dip and orange juice he is responsible for are out of stock.

The rest of Martin's day is similar. He issues a credit for a spoiled package of ham at the IGA on Chaplin Island Road. At Sobey's on Pleasant Street, the dairy manager complains that the meat company that Martin represents has been shipping its frankfurters, salami, and knockwurst too near the "best before" date when they will have to be removed from sale. Later, he meets the manager of a dairy section at a supermarket in Chatham where there is limited refrigerated space. The manager is upset with him because some fruit punch was shipped with defective seals, and Martin promises to look into the situation.

What does George Martin do for a living? He is a retail sales supervisor for a large food broker that represents many national brands. Food brokers, who account for about 50 percent of all food items sold to food retailers, are classified as wholesaling intermediaries. And wholesaling is the focus of this chapter.

**The Conceptual Framework**

Wholesaling is the initial marketing institution in most channels of distribution from manufacturers to consumer or industrial user. Chapter 15 introduced the basic concepts of channel strategy, primarily from the point of view of the manufacturer. Attention now shifts to the institutions within the distribution channel.

Wholesaling intermediaries are a critical element of the marketing mixes of many products, but many intermediaries are also separate business entities with their own marketing mixes. A good starting point for the discussion is to look at the terminology used in wholesaling.

**Wholesaling Activities**

Wholesaling involves the activities of persons or firms who sell to retailers and other wholesalers or to industrial users, but not in significant amounts to ultimate consumers. The term **wholesaler** (or **merchant intermediary**) is applied only to *those wholesaling intermediaries who take title to the products they handle*. **Wholesaling intermediaries** (or wholesaling middlemen) is a broader term that describes not only *intermediaries who assume title*, but also *agents and brokers who perform important wholesaling activities without taking title to the goods*. Under this definition, then, a wholesaler is a *merchant intermediary*.

**Wholesaling Functions**

The route that goods follow on the way to the consumer or industrial user is actually a chain of marketing institutions—wholesalers and retailers. Only 3 percent of the dollar volume of all goods sold to the ultimate consumer is purchased directly from the manufacturer. The bulk of all products sold passes through these marketing institutions.

An increasing number of consumer complaints about high prices is heard each year. The finger of guilt is often pointed at wholesalers and retailers, the intermediaries who allegedly drive prices up by taking "high profits." Discount stores often advertise that their prices are lower since they buy direct and eliminate the intermediaries and their profits. Chain stores often assume wholesaling functions and bypass the independent wholesalers.

Are these complaints and claims valid? Are wholesaling intermediaries anachronisms doomed to a swift demise? Answers to these questions can be formulated by considering the functions and costs of these marketing intermediaries.

**Wholesaling Intermediaries Provide a Variety of Services**

A marketing institution will continue to exist only so long as it fulfils a need by performing a required service. Its death may be slow, but it is inevitable if other channel members discover that they can survive without it. Figure 16-1 examines a number of possible ser-

Figure 16-1    Possible Wholesaling Services for Customers and
Producers-Suppliers

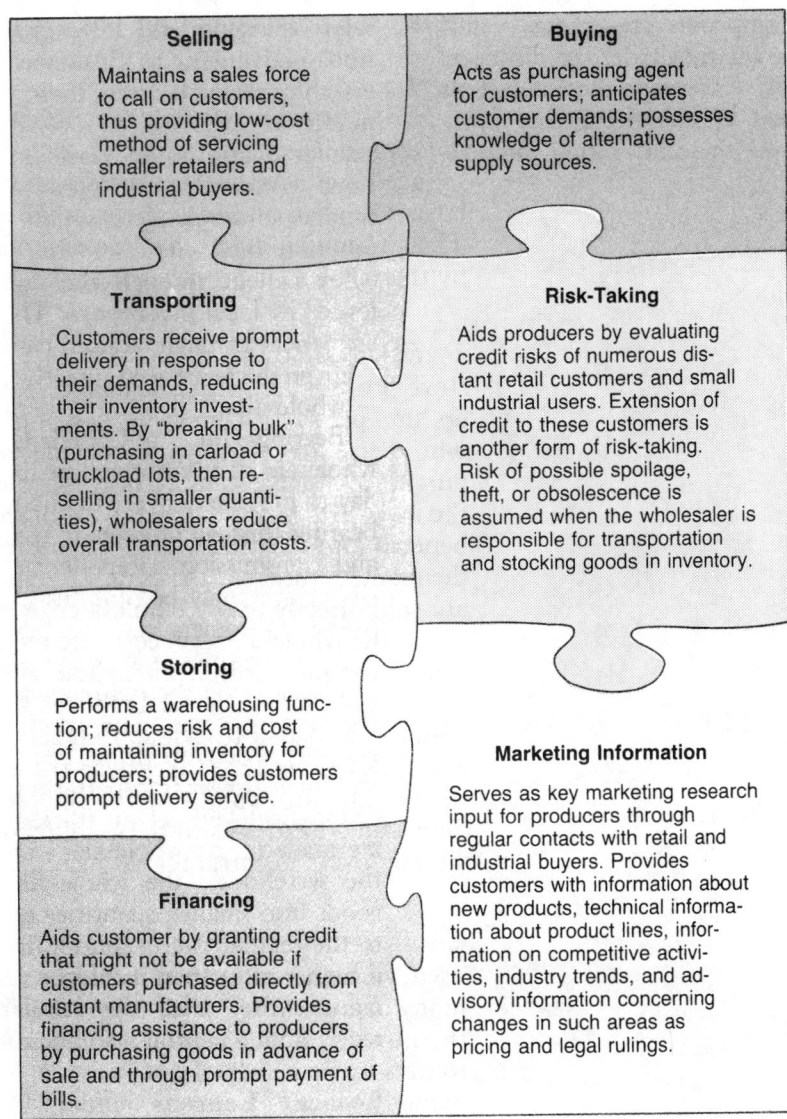

**Selling**

Maintains a sales force
to call on customers,
thus providing low-cost
method of servicing
smaller retailers and
industrial buyers.

**Buying**

Acts as purchasing agent
for customers; anticipates
customer demands; possesses
knowledge of alternative
supply sources.

**Transporting**

Customers receive prompt
delivery in response to
their demands, reducing
their inventory invest-
ments. By "breaking bulk"
(purchasing in carload or
truckload lots, then re-
selling in smaller quantities), wholesalers reduce
overall transportation costs.

**Risk-Taking**

Aids producers by evaluating
credit risks of numerous distant retail customers and small
industrial users. Extension of
credit to these customers is
another form of risk-taking.
Risk of possible spoilage,
theft, or obsolescence is
assumed when the wholesaler is
responsible for transportation
and stocking goods in inventory.

**Storing**

Performs a warehousing function; reduces risk and cost
of maintaining inventory for
producers; provides customers
prompt delivery service.

**Marketing Information**

Serves as key marketing research
input for producers through
regular contacts with retail and
industrial buyers. Provides
customers with information about
new products, technical information about product lines, information on competitive activities, industry trends, and advisory information concerning
changes in such areas as
pricing and legal rulings.

**Financing**

Aids customer by granting credit
that might not be available if
customers purchased directly from
distant manufacturers. Provides
financing assistance to producers
by purchasing goods in advance of
sale and through prompt payment of
bills.

vices provided by wholesaling intermediaries. It is important to note
that numerous types of wholesaling intermediaries exist and that
not all of them provide every service listed in Figure 16-1. Producer-
suppliers and their customers, who rely on wholesaling intermediaries for distribution, select those intermediaries providing the
desired combination of services.

The listing of possible services provided by wholesaling intermediaries clearly indicates the provision of marketing utility — time, place, and ownership — by these intermediaries. The services also reflect the provision of the basic marketing functions of buying, selling, storing, transportation, risk-taking, financing, and market information.

The critical marketing functions — transportation and convenient product storage; reduced costs of buying and selling through reduced contacts; market information; and financing — form the basis of evaluating the efficiency of any marketing intermediary. The risk-taking function is present in each of the services provided by the wholesaling intermediary.

Transportation and Product Storage   Wholesalers transport and store products at locations convenient to customers. Manufacturers ship products from their warehouses to numerous wholesalers, who then ship smaller quantities to retail outlets convenient to the purchaser. A large number of wholesalers and most retailers assume the inventory function (and cost) for the manufacturer. The retailer benefits through the convenience afforded by local inventories, and the manufacturer's cash needs are reduced since the firm's products are sold directly to the wholesaler or retailer.

At the wholesale level costs are reduced through large purchases from the manufacturer. The wholesaler receives quantity discounts from the manufacturer and reduced transportation rates since economical carload or truckload shipments are made to the wholesaler's warehouses. At the warehouse the wholesaler breaks bulk into smaller quantities and ships to the retailer over a shorter distance than would be the case if the manufacturer filled the retailer's order directly from a central warehouse.

Cost Reductions   Costs are often lowered when intermediaries are used, since the sales force of the retailer or wholesaler can represent many manufacturers to a single customer. As Figure 16-2 indicates, the number of transactions between manufacturers and their customers are markedly reduced through the introduction of an intermediary (a wholesaler or retailer). Reduced market contacts can lead to lowered marketing costs. By adding a wholesaling intermediary, the number of transactions in this illustration is reduced from 16 to 8, thereby creating economies of scale by providing an assortment of goods with greater utility and at lower cost than without such an intermediary.

Source of Information   Because of their central position between the manufacturer and retailers or industrial buyers, wholesalers serve

Figure 16-2   Achieving Transaction Economy with Wholesaling
Intermediaries

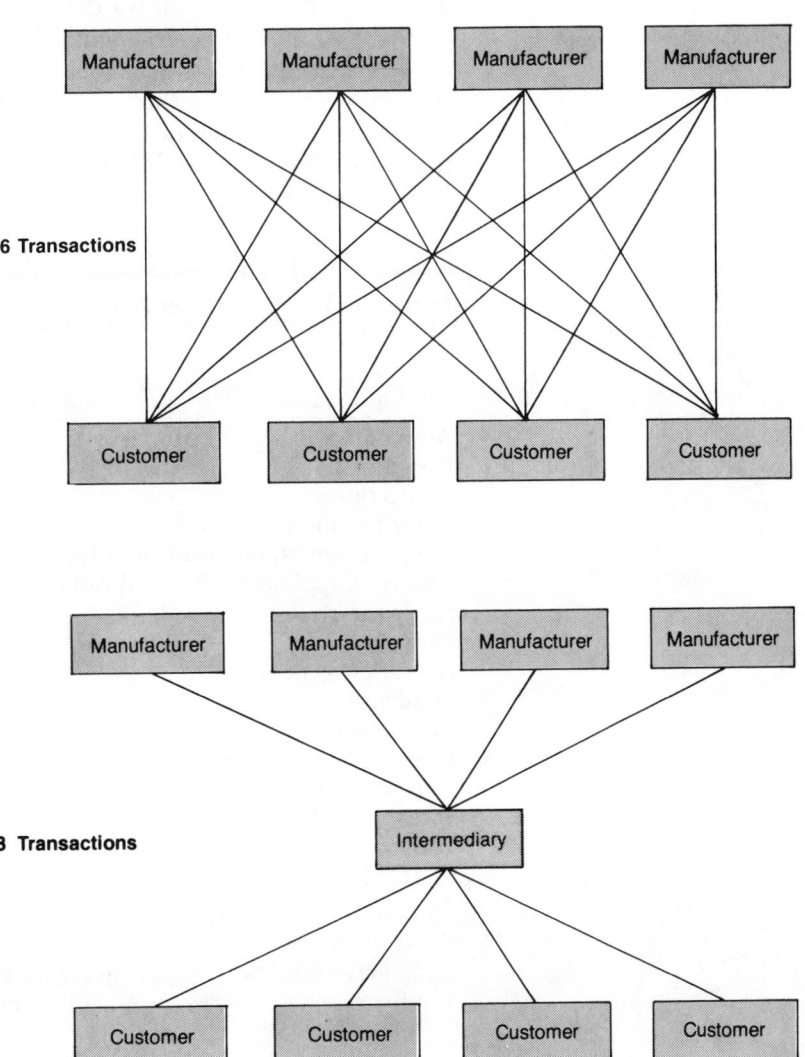

as important information links. Wholesalers provide their retail customers with useful information about new products. In addition
they supply manufacturers with information concerning market
reception of their product offerings.

Source of Financing   Wholesalers also provide a financing function.
Wholesalers often provide retailers with goods on credit. By pur-

chasing products on credit, retailers can minimize their cash invest-ments in inventory and pay for most of their purchases as the goods are being sold. This allows them to benefit from the principle of *leverage*; a minimum investment inflates their return on investment. A retailer with an investment of $1 million and profits of $100 000 will realize a return on investment (ROI) of 10 percent. But if the necessary invested capital can be reduced to $800 000 through credit from the wholesaler, and if the $100 000 profits can be maintained, the retailer's ROI increases to 12.5 percent.

**Figure 16-3   Median Net Profits of Selected Wholesalers**

| Kind of Business | Net Profit as a Percentage of Net Sales* | Annual Turnover Rate** |
|---|---|---|
| Automotive parts and supplies | 3.7 | 4.2 |
| Beer and ale | 2.5 | 14.3 |
| Confectionery | 1.4 | 13.0 |
| Dairy products | 1.4 | 43.1 |
| Drugs, proprietaries, and sundries | 1.9 | 7.6 |
| Electrical appliances, TV and radio sets | 1.9 | 7.4 |
| Footwear | 2.7 | 6.5 |
| Furniture | 3.7 | 8.6 |
| Groceries, general line | 1.5 | 6.2 |
| Hardware | 3.8 | 5.9 |
| Meat products | 0.9 | 39.6 |
| Paper and paper products | 3.1 | 10.3 |
| Petroleum and petroleum products | 1.5 | 32.0 |
| Tires and tubes | 2.2 | 6.7 |
| Tobacco and tobacco products | .9 | 17.5 |

\* After provision for federal income taxes
\*\* Net sales to inventory

Source: "The Ratios," *Dun's Business Month* (Feb. 1983), pp. 116–17. Reprinted with the special permission of *Dun's Business Month*, Feb. 1983. Copyright 1983, Dun & Bradstreet Publications Corporation.

Wholesalers of industrial goods provide similar services for the purchasers of their goods. In the steel industry, intermediaries called metal service centres currently market approximately one-fifth of the steel shipped by Canadian mills. Such a centre may stock as many as 6500 items for sale to many of the thousands of major metal users who buy their heavy usage items in large quantities directly from the steel mills, but who turn to service centres for quick delivery of special orders and other items used in small quantities.

While an order from the mills may take 90 days for delivery, a service centre can usually deliver locally within 24 to 48 hours. Such service reduces the investment needed in stock.

## Who Should Perform Distribution Channel Functions?

While wholesaling intermediaries often perform a variety of valuable functions for their producer, retailer, and other wholesale clients, these functions could be performed by other channel members. Manufacturers may choose to bypass independent wholesaling intermediaries by establishing networks of regional warehouses, maintaining large sales forces to provide market coverage, serving as sources of information for their retail customers, and assuming the financing function. In some instances, they may decide to push the responsibility for some of these functions through the channel on to the retailer or the ultimate purchaser. Large retailers who choose to perform their own wholesaling operations face the same choices.

A fundamental marketing principle is that marketing functions must be performed by some member of the channel; they may be shifted, but they cannot be eliminated. Either the larger retailers who bypass the wholesaler and deal directly with the manufacturer will assume the functions previously performed by wholesaling intermediaries, or these functions will be performed by the manufacturer. Similarly, a manufacturer who deals directly with the ultimate consumer or with industrial buyers will assume the functions of storage, delivery, and market information previously performed by marketing intermediaries. Intermediaries themselves can be eliminated from the channel, but the channel functions must be performed by someone.

The potential gain for the manufacturer or retailer who might be considering bypassing wholesaling intermediaries is reflected in Figure 16-3. The table shows the potential savings that could be realized *if* channel members performed the wholesale functions as efficiently as the independent wholesaling intermediary. Such savings, indicated in the net profit column, could be used to reduce retail prices, to increase the profits of the manufacturer or retailers, or both. Note, however, the low profit rates on sales earned by most wholesalers. High turnover is necessary to provide adequate returns on investment.

## Types of Wholesaling Intermediaries

As mentioned previously, various types of wholesaling intermediaries are present in different marketing channels. Some provide a wide range of services or handle a broad line of products, while others specialize in a single service, product, or industry. Figure 16-4 classifies wholesaling intermediaries based on two characteristics: *ownership*, whether the wholesaling intermediary is independent, manufacturer-owned, or retailer-owned; and *title flows*, whether

**Figure 16-4   Major Types of Wholesaling Intermediaries**

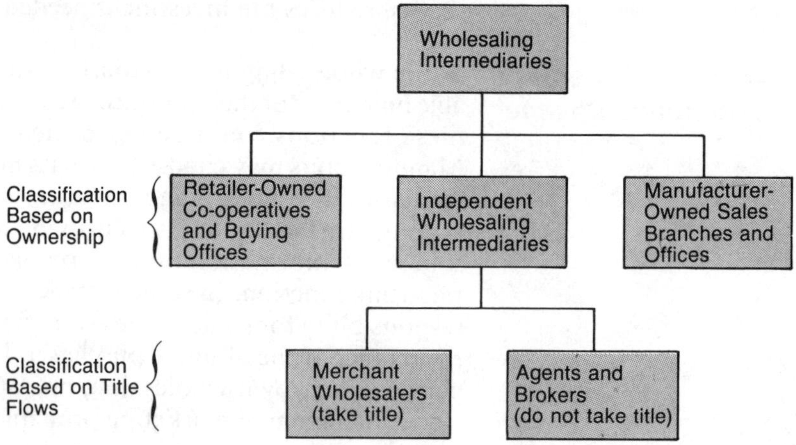

title passes from the manufacturer to the wholesaling intermediary or not. There are, in turn, three basic types of ownership: 1) independent wholesaling, which can be merchant wholesalers who do take title to goods or agents and brokers who do not,[1] 2) manufacturer-owned sales branches and offices, and 3) retailer-owned co-operatives and buying offices.

***Manufacturer-Owned Facilities***

Increasing volumes of products are being marketed directly by manufacturers through company-owned facilities. There are several reasons for this trend. Some products are perishable; some require complex installation or servicing; others need more aggressive promotion; still others are high unit-value goods that the manufacturer wishes to control through the channel directly to the purchaser. Among the industries that have largely shifted from the use of independent wholesaling intermediaries to company-owned channels are paper, paint, lumber, construction materials, piece goods, and apparel manufacturers.[2] More than 50 percent of all industrial goods are sold directly to users by the manufacturer, and slightly more than one-third of *all* products are marketed through manufacturer-owned channels.[3]

[1] An interesting discussion of types of wholesaling appears in J. Howard Westing, "Wholesale Indifference," *The Courier* (Spring, 1982), pp. 3, 8.
[2] James R. Moore and Kendell A. Adams, "Functional Wholesaler Sales Trends and Analysis," Edward M. Mazze (ed.), *Combined Proceedings* (Chicago: American Marketing Association, 1976), pp. 402–405.
[3] Louis P. Bucklin, *Competition and Evolution in the Distributive Trades* (Englewood Cliffs, N.J.: Prentice-Hall, 1972), p. 214.

This does not mean that independent wholesalers are being squeezed out. Their numbers are in the thousands, and their volume of trade in the billions of dollars.

*Sales Branches and Offices*   The basic distinction between sales branches and sales offices is that the **sales branch** of a company *carries inventory, and orders are processed to customers from available stock*. The branch duplicates the storage function of the independent wholesaler and serves as an office for sales representatives in the territory. Sales branches are prevalent in the marketing of commercial machinery and equipment, petroleum products, motor vehicles, and chemicals.

A **sales office**, by contrast, *does not carry stock but serves as a regional office for the firm's sales personnel*. Maintenance of sales offices in close proximity to the firm's customers assists in reducing selling costs and in improving customer service. The listing of the firm in the local telephone directory and yellow pages may result in sales for the local representative. Many buyers will choose to telephone the office of a supplier of a needed product rather than take the time to write letters to distant suppliers.

Since warehouses represent a substantial investment in real estate, smaller manufacturers and even larger firms developing new sales territories may choose to use **public warehouses**. They are *independently owned storage facilities*. For a rental fee the manufacturer may arrange to store its inventory in one of the nation's many public warehouses for shipment by the warehouse to customers in the area. The warehouse owner will break bulk (divide up a carload or truckload), package inventory into smaller quantities to fill orders, and will even bill the purchaser for the manufacturer. The public warehouse can even provide a financial service for the manufacturer by issuing a warehouse receipt for the inventory. The receipt can then be used as collateral for a bank loan.

*Other Outlets for the Manufacturer's Products*   In addition to the use of a sales force and regionally distributed sales branches, manufacturers will often market their products through trade fairs and exhibitions and merchandise marts. **Trade fairs** or **trade exhibitions** are *periodic shows where manufacturers in a particular industry display their wares for visiting retail and wholesale buyers*. The Montreal toy show and the Toronto, Montreal, and Calgary furniture shows are annual events for both manufacturers and purchasers of toys and furniture.

A **merchandise mart** provides space for *permanent exhibitions where manufacturers rent showcases for their product offerings*. One of the largest is Place Bonaventure in Montreal, which is approximately a block square and is several storeys high. Thousands of items are on display there. A retail buyer can compare the offerings of dozens of competing manufacturers and make many purchase decisions in a single visit to a trade fair or merchandise mart.

***Independent Wholesaling Intermediaries***

As has been mentioned earlier, there are many independent wholesaling intermediaries. Figure 16-5 shows that they are flourishing. They perform vital functions in the marketing of goods and services, and their role and categorization should be understood clearly. These intermediaries may be divided into two categories: **merchant wholesalers,** who *take title to the goods*, and **agents and brokers,** who *may take possession of the goods, but who do not take title.* Merchant wholesalers account for 82.9 percent of all sales handled by independent wholesalers. As Figure 16-6 indicates, they can be further classified as full- or limited-function wholesalers.

**Figure 16-5   Wholesale Trade by Type of Operation 1983**

| Type of Operation | Number of Establishments | Volume of Trade (billions of $) | Percentage of Volume of Trade |
|---|---|---|---|
| Merchant Wholesalers | 47 482 | 148.34 | 83.2 |
| Agents and Brokers | 4 806 | 29.98 | 16.8 |
| Total | 52 288 | 179.32 | 100.0 |

Source: Statistics Canada, *Market Research Handbook*, 1985–86 (cat. 63-224). By permission of the Minister of Supply and Services Canada.

**Figure 16-6   Classification of Independent Wholesaling Intermediaries**

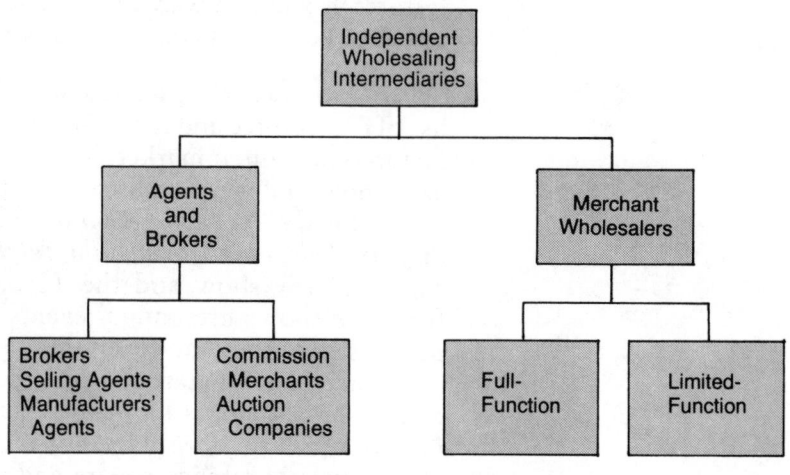

*Full-function merchant wholesalers* provide a complete assortment of services for the retailers or industrial purchasers. They store merchandise in convenient locations, thus allowing their customers to make purchases on short notice. To minimize their inventory requirements, they usually maintain a sales force who regularly call on retailers, make deliveries, and extend credit to qualified buyers. In the industrial goods market the full-function merchant wholesaler (often called an *industrial distributor*) usually markets machinery, less expensive accessory equipment, and supplies.

Full-function merchant wholesalers prevail in industries where retailers are small and carry large numbers of relatively inexpensive items, none of which is stocked in depth. The hardware, drug, and grocery industries have traditionally been serviced by them.

A unique type of service wholesaler emerged after World War II as supermarkets began to stock high-margin nonfood items. Since the supermarket manager possessed no knowledge of such products as toys, housewares, paperback books, records, and health and beauty items, the **rack jobber** provided the necessary expertise. This wholesaler *provides the racks, stocks the merchandise, prices the goods, and makes regular visits to refill the shelves.* In essence, the rack jobber rents space from the retailer on a commission basis. Rack jobbers have expanded into drug, hardware, variety, and discount stores.

## A Wholesaler Must Be Versatile

National Drugs is a typical merchant wholesaler and offers its drugstore customers a range of services. These include accounting, merchandising, site location, store design, and financing. For a fee that seldom exceeds a few hundred dollars, National will assist a retail customer in analysing everything from market share, cash flow, and current profit position to evaluations of proposed store locations. Retail stores can even obtain a daily printout of individual department performance as compared with expectations. National has developed standards of performance through experience and can use them to point out trouble spots. For instance, paper goods such as paper towels and toilet paper take up a substantial amount of selling space, yet average a gross profit of only 13 percent. By comparison, toothpaste chalks up gross profits of 25 percent and pocket novels deliver 30 percent. Magazines produce only 20 percent, but the great volume sold makes it worthwhile to stock them.

National Drugs not only serves many independent drugstores, but has diversified through the direct ownership of large drugstores. These are directly competing with franchise chain stores such as Shoppers Drug Mart, who have bypassed the independent wholesaler by establishing their own wholesaling operations across Canada.

Since full-function merchant wholesalers perform a large number of services, their costs are sometimes as high as 20 percent of sales. Attempts to reduce the costs associated with dealing with the full-function wholesaler have led to the development of a number of *limited-function* intermediaries.

Four types of limited-function merchant wholesalers are: cash-and-carry wholesalers, truck wholesalers, drop shippers, and direct-response wholesalers.

**Cash-and-carry wholesalers** perform most wholesaling functions except financing and delivery. They first appeared on the marketing stage in the grocery industry during the Depression era of the 1930s. In an attempt to reduce costs, retailers drove to the wholesaler's warehouse, paid cash for their purchases, and made their own deliveries. By eliminating the delivery and financing functions, cash-and-carry wholesalers were able to reduce operating costs to approximately 9 percent of sales.

Although feasible in servicing small stores, such wholesalers have generally proven unworkable for the large-scale operation. The chain store manager is unwilling to perform the delivery function, and the cash-and-carry operation typically operates today as one department of a regular full-service wholesaler. This type of wholesaler, however, has proven quite successful in the United Kingdom; 600 cash-and-carry operations produce over $1 billlion in sales a year. However, as the U.K. grocery industry moves toward large supermarkets such as Tesco and Sainsbury's in the 1980s, the volume of cash-and-carry operations is expected to diminish.

**Truck wholesalers**, or *truck jobbers, market perishable food items*, such as bread, tobacco, potato chips, candy, and dairy products. They make regular deliveries to retail stores and simultaneously perform the sales, delivery, and collection functions. The relatively high cost of operating a delivery truck and the low dollar volume per sale account for relatively high operation costs of 15 percent. The truck wholesaler does provide aggressive promotion for these product lines.

The **drop shipper** *takes orders from customers and places them with producers who ship directly to the customer.* Although drop shippers take title to the products, they never physically handle — or even see — the goods. Since they perform no storage or handling function, their operating costs are a relatively low 4 to 5 percent of sales.

The drop shipper operates in fields where the product is bulky and customers make purchases in carload lots. Since transportation and handling costs represent a substantial percentage of the total cost of such products as coal and lumber, the drop shipper does not maintain an inventory and thereby eliminates the expenses of loading and unloading carload shipments. Their major service is in developing a complete assortment for customers. For example, drop shippers constitute a highly skilled group of sellers of lumber products out of British Columbia. While the major forest product firms, such as MacMillan-Bloedel and British Columbia Forest Products, have their in-house lumber traders, independent drop shippers compete head-to-head with them in selling the output of independent sawmills to eastern Canada and the United States.

The **direct-response wholesaler** is a limited-function merchant wholesaler who *relies on catalogues rather than a sales force to contact retail, industrial, and institutional customers.* Purchases are made by mail or telephone by relatively small customers in outlying areas. Mail-order operations are found in the hardware, cosmetics, jewellery, sporting goods, and specialty food lines, as well as in general merchandise.

Figure 16-7 compares the various types of merchant wholesalers in terms of services provided. Full-function merchant wholesalers and truck wholesalers are relatively high-cost intermediaries because of the number of services they perform, while cash-and-carry wholesalers, drop shippers, and direct-response wholesalers provide fewer services and have relatively low operating costs.

**Figure 16-7    Services Provided by Merchant Wholesalers**

| Services | Full-Function Wholesalers | Limited-Function Wholesalers | | | |
| --- | --- | --- | --- | --- | --- |
| | | Cash-and-Carry Wholesalers | Truck Wholesalers | Drop Shippers | Direct-response Wholealers |
| Anticipates customer needs | Yes | Yes | Yes | No | Yes |
| Carries inventory | Yes | Yes | Yes | No | Yes |
| Delivers | Yes | No | Yes | No | Yes (by mail) |
| Provides market information | Yes | Rarely | Yes | Yes | No |
| Provides credit | Yes | No | No | Yes | Sometimes |
| Assumes ownership risk by taking title | Yes | Yes | Yes | Yes | Yes |

*Agents and Brokers*    A second group of independent wholesaling intermediaries — the agents and brokers — may or may not take possession of the goods but they *never take title* to them. They normally perform fewer services than the merchant wholesalers and are typically involved in bringing together buyers and sellers. Agent wholesaling intermediaries may be classified into five categories — commission merchants, auction companies, brokers, selling agents, and manufacturers' agents.

Commission merchants predominate in the marketing of agricultural products. The **commission merchant** *takes possession when the producer ships goods to a central market for sale.* The commission merchant acts as the producer's agent and receives an agreed-upon fee when a sale is made. Since customers will make inspections of the products and prices may fluctuate, the commission merchant is given considerable latitude in making decisions. The owner of the goods may specify a minimum price, but the commission merchant will sell them on a "best price" basis. The commission merchant deducts the appropriate fee from the price and the balance is remitted to the original seller.

A valuable service in such markets as used cars, livestock, antiques, works of art, fur, flowers, and fruit is performed by agent wholesaling intermediaries known as **auction houses**. They *bring buyers and sellers together in one location and allow potential buyers to inspect the merchandise before purchasing*. A commission, often based on the sale price, is charged by the auction company for its services. Auction houses tend to specialize in merchandise categories such as agricultural products and art. Sotheby's is a world-famous auction house specializing in arts and related products.

The task of **brokers** is to *bring buyers and sellers together*. They operate in industries characterized by a large number of small suppliers and purchasers—real estate, frozen foods, and used machinery, for example. They may represent either buyer or seller in a given transaction, but not both. The broker receives a fee from the client when the transaction is completed. The service performed is finding buyers or sellers and negotiating for exchange of title. The operating expense ratio for the broker may be as low as 2 percent and rises depending on the services performed.

Because brokers operate on a one-time basis for sellers or buyers, they cannot serve as an effective marketing channel for manufacturers seeking regular, continuing services. A manufacturer who seeks to develop a more permanent channel utilizing agent wholesaling intermediaries must evaluate the use of the selling agent or the manufacturers' agent.

For small, poorly financed, production-oriented manufacturers, the **selling agent** may prove an ideal marketing channel. These wholesaling intermediaries have even been referred to as independent marketing departments, since they are *responsible for the total marketing program for the firm's product line*. They typically have full authority over pricing decisions and promotional outlays, and they often provide financial assistance for the manufacturer. The manufacturer can concentrate on production and rely on the expertise of the selling agent for all marketing activities.

Selling agents are common in the textile, coal, sulphur and lumber industries. Their operating expenses average about 3 percent of sales.

Instead of a single selling agent, a manufacturer may use a number of manufacturers' agents. A **manufacturers' agent** is essentially *an independent salesperson who works for a number of manufacturers of related but noncompeting products* and receives a commission based on a specified percentage of sales. Manufacturers' agents can be thought of as an independent sales force. Although some commissions may be as high as 20 percent of sales, they usually average between 6 and 7 percent. Unlike the selling agent, who may be given exclusive world rights to *market* a manufacturer's product, the manufacturers' agent *sells* in a specified territory.[4]

Manufacturers' agents reduce their selling costs by spreading the cost per sales call over a number of different products. An agent in the plumbing supplies industry may represent a dozen different manufacturers.

Producers may develop their marketing channels through the use of manufacturers' agents for several reasons. First, when they are developing new sales territories the costs of adding new salespersons to "pioneer" new territories may be prohibitive. The agents, who are paid on a commission basis, can perform the sales function in the new territories at a much lower cost to the manufacturer.

Second, firms with unrelated lines may need to employ more than one channel. One line of products may be marketed through the company's sales force. A second, unrelated line might be marketed through independent manufacturers' agents. This is particularly common where the unrelated product line is a recent addition and the regular sales force has no experience with the products.

Finally, small firms with no existing sales force may turn to manufacturers' agents in order to have access to the market. A newly organized firm producing pencil sharpeners may use office equipment and supplies manufacturers' agents to reach retail outlets and industrial purchasers.

Although the importance of selling agents is now very limited

**Figure 16-8   Services Provided by Agents and Brokers**

| Services | Commission Merchants | Auction Houses | Brokers | Manufacturers' Agents | Selling Agents |
|---|---|---|---|---|---|
| Anticipates customer needs | Yes | Some | Some | Yes | Yes |
| Carries inventory | Yes | Yes | No | No | No |
| Delivers | Yes | No | No | Infrequently | No |
| Provides market information | Yes | Yes | Yes | Yes | Yes |
| Provides credit | Some | No | No | No | Some |
| Assumes ownership risk by taking title | No | No | No | No | No |

---

[4] For a profile of the typical manufacturers' agent, see Stanely D. Sibley and R.K. Teas, "Agent Marketing Channel Intermediaries' Perceptions of Marketing Channel Performance," in Robert S. Franz, Robert M. Hopkins, and Al Toma, *eds., Proceedings of the Southern Marketing Association* (New Orleans, November 1978), pp. 336–39.

because of the desire of manufacturers to have better control of their marketing programs, the volume of sales by manufacturers' agents has increased substantially since that date.

**Retailer-Owned Facilities**   Retailers have also assumed numerous wholesaling functions in attempts to reduce costs or to provide special service. Independent retailers have occasionally banded together to form buying groups

# Why Airwick Closed Its Sales Offices

Airwick Industries is a well-known manufacturer and marketer of household cleaners and de-odorizers. Its product line, led by Carpet Fresh and Stick-Ups products, generated approximately $220 million in sales internationally in 1980.

Success in the consumer market led Airwick to establish a professional product division to market a variety of disinfectants, cleaning agents, odour counteractants, insecticides, and environmental sanitation products for airports, government installations, hospitals, hotels/motels, industrial plants, nursing homes, office complexes, restaurants, and retail stores. Airwick's original distribution network consisted entirely of independent wholesaling intermediaries. In the 1970s, the firm began purchasing many of the independents with the idea of eventually converting entirely to company-owned distribution facilities. By 1980, a network consisting of independent wholesaling operations and company-owned offices had been developed.

But Airwick managers were unable to detect improved performance in those areas where company-owned facilities operated. In addition, independent wholesalers were expressing growing dissatisfaction with what they considered at least the potential of unfair competition from Airwick's sales offices. At that point, Airwick decided to close the sales offices and establish new independent distributors. John Updegraph, division president, summed up the decision this way: "We felt it was better to ride one horse successfully rather than risk falling on our faces riding two horses at the same time."

Updegraph recognized that the new distribution

structure meant that Airwick was relinquishing some control, but he felt that the advantages outweighed the limitations. "In some ways, it is actually better to have the sales of your products handled by private entrepreneurs. These independent distributors run their own businesses and if anyone wants to turn a profit, they do. The more they push our products, the more money they make.

"Also, when you market your products through distributors you eliminate numerous management headaches. In fact, we found that Airwick is even stronger now because the distributors know we are behind them 100 percent."

Supporting the change are programs that help distributors hire and train salespersons, manage time and territories, control inventory and receivables, increase sales effectiveness, install better accounting systems, and make computer records conversions.

"Before the phase-out we were not able to do very much in the way of advertising and promotion support for the distributors. But now we can direct more attention to those areas," Updegraph said.

"What's important is that you maintain good marketing and sales efforts and continue to cultivate good management. It doesn't really matter what type of distribution channel you use. . . . I think with the current inflation situation, high interest rates, high labour costs, high rents and construction prices, and energy costs, many firms will have to re-examine their distribution and service systems."

Source: Adapted with permission from Bernard F. Whalen," Airwick Drops Sales Offices to Increase Sales," *Marketing News* (February 8, 1980), p. 6, published by the American Marketing Association.

in order to achieve cost savings through quantity purchases. Other groups of retailers have established retailer-owned wholesale facilities as a result of the formation of a co-operative chain. Larger chain retailers often establish centralized buying offices to negotiate large-scale purchases directly with manufacturers for the members of the chain. This was discussed in Chapter 15. The various types of agents and brokers are compared in Figure 16-8.

## Independent Wholesaling Intermediaries — A Durable Marketing Institution

Many marketing observers of the 1920s felt that the end had come for the independent wholesaling intermediaries as chain stores grew in importance and attempted to bypass them. From 1929 to 1939 the independents' sales volume dropped, but it has increased again since then.

Figure 16-5 shows how the relative numbers and shares of total independent wholesale trade volumes have changed over two recent years. While this period has seen a more important role for company-owned channels, it is also true that independent wholesaling intermediaries are far from obsolete. Their continued importance is evidence of the ability of independent wholesaling intermediaries to adjust to changing conditions and changing needs. Their market size proves their ability to continue to fill a need in many marketing channels.

## Summary

Wholesaling is one of the two major institutions that make up many firms' marketing channels. (The second is retailing.) Wholesaling includes the activities of persons or firms selling to retailers and other wholesalers or to industrial users but who do not sell in significant amounts to ultimate consumers.

Three types of wholesaling intermediaries are manufacturer-owned facilities, independent wholesaling intermediaries, and retailer-owned co-operatives. In this last category are merchant wholesalers and agents and brokers. Merchant wholesalers take title to goods they handle. Agents and brokers may take possession, but do not take title to the goods. Merchant wholesalers include full-function wholesalers, cash-and-carry wholesalers, rack jobbers, truck jobbers, drop shippers, and mail-order wholesalers. Since they do not take title, commission merchants, auction companies, brokers, selling agents, and manufacturers' agents are classified as agent wholesaling intermediaries.

The operating expenses of wholesaling intermediaries vary considerably, depending on the number of services provided and the costs involved. These services may include storage facilities in conveniently located warehouses, market coverage by a sales force, financing for retailers and sometimes manufacturers, market information for retailers and manufacturers, transportation, and management services, sales training, and merchandising assistance and advice for retailers.

While the percentage of wholesale trade by manufacturer-owned facilities has increased since 1958, independent wholesaling intermediaries continue to account for a significant proportion of total wholesale trade. They accomplish this by continuing to provide desired services to manufacturers and retailers.

## Key Terms

| | |
|---|---|
| wholesaler | cash-and-carry wholesaler |
| wholesaling intermediary | truck wholesaler |
| sales branch | drop shipper |
| sales office | direct-response wholesaler |
| public warehouse | commission merchant |
| trade fair | auction house |
| merchandise mart | broker |
| merchant wholesaler | selling agent |
| rack jobber | manufacturers' agent |

## Review Questions

1. Distinguish between a wholesaler and a retailer.
2. In what ways do wholesaling intermediaries assist manufacturers? How do they assist retailers?
3. Explain how wholesaling intermediaries can assist retailers in increasing their return on investment.
4. Distinguish between sales offices and sales branches. Under what conditions might each type be used?
5. What role does the public warehouse play in distribution channels?
6. Distinguish merchant wholesalers from agents and brokers.
7. Why is the operating expense ratio of the merchant wholesaler higher than that of the typical agent or broker?
8. In what ways are commission merchants and brokers different?
9. Distinguish between a manufacturers' agent and a selling agent.
10. Under what conditions would a manufacturer utilize manufacturers' agents for a distribution channel?

## Discussion Questions and Exercises

1. Match each of the following industries with the most appropriate wholesaling intermediary:

| | |
|---|---|
| _____ Groceries | a. Drop shipper |
| _____ Potato chips | b. Truck wholesaler |
| _____ Coal | c. Auction house |
| _____ Grain | d. Manufacturers' agent |
| _____ Antiques | e. Full-function merchant wholesaler |
| | f. Commission merchant |

2. Comment on the following statements: Drop shippers are good candidates for elimination. All they do is process orders. They don't even handle the goods.

3. Prepare a brief five-page report on a wholesaler in your local area.

4. The term *broker* also appears in the real estate and securities fields. Are these brokers identical to the agent wholesaling intermediaries described in this chapter?

5. Interview someone who works at a local wholesaling firm. Report to the class on this person's job within the wholesaling sector.

---

**MICROCOMPUTER EXERCISE:**
*Inventory Turnover*

**Directions:**   Use the Menu Item titled "Inventory Turnover" on the Foundations of Marketing disk to solve each of the following problems.

**1.** A Brandon, Manitoba wholesaling intermediary carries an average inventory recorded at cost of $5 million. Its total cost of goods sold is $27.5 million. What is the firm's inventory-turnover rate?

**2.** A Lethbridge, Alberta wholesaler started 1987 with an inventory of $4 million at retail. During the year, the wholesaler decided to reduce its overall inventory position. The firm ended 1987 with a $3 million inventory (at retail). Sales in 1987 were $36 million. What was the wholesaler's inventory-turnover rate for the year?

**3.** A wholesaler in Quebec City had a $22 million cost-based inventory on January 1, 1987, but was able to reduce it to $20 million by the end of the year. The firm has a 20-percent markup percentage on selling price. In 1987, sales volume totaled $90 million. Calculate the wholesaler's 1987 inventory-turnover rate.

# CHAPTER 17

# *Retailing*

## CHAPTER OBJECTIVES

1. *To relate retailing to the other variables of the marketing mix.*

2. *To outline the decision framework for retailing.*

3. *To distinguish between limited-line retailers and general merchandise retailers.*

4. *To identify and explain each of the five bases for categorizing retailers.*

5. *To identify the major types of mass merchandisers.*

6. *To explain the types of nonstore retailing.*

7. *To distinguish between chain and independent retailers and to identify several industries dominated by chains.*

8. *To contrast the three types of planned shopping centres.*

They are as ubiquitous as fast-food outlets. Indeed, they may become to retailing in the 1980s what fast food was in the 1970s — a high growth area where entrepreneurs big and small can cash in on the changing tastes and needs of consumers. In the making is nothing short of a revolution. Some 500 home-video stores are now in business in Toronto where two years ago there were virtually none. And the revolution has found its way into all major centres and smaller cities across the country as the consumer appetite for video-cassette recorders and the movies and entertainment that they can provide grows more voracious.

Yet even as future home-video kings are opening up business for as little investment as $30 000, many operators are finding the fledgling business a minefield of risks. Some home-video stores are out of the picture within several months, their owner-managers left to wonder what went wrong.

Plenty can go wrong. Along with the usual start-up problems of undercapitalization, poor location and the like, the home-video entrepreneur is faced with the challenge of identifying just what business he or she is in. Is it a cassette-machine renting business? Should there be an emphasis on sales of equipment?

Competition is growing because franchise operators are entering the home-video market, as are the big mass merchandisers. The Bay, Eaton's, Simpson's, Loblaws, Dominion Stores, Consumers

Distributing, and K-mart are all feeling out the home-video market.

In addition to the growing competition, there is still high uncertainty as to which VCR technology will be popular in the future. The retailer who will make it in the long run will have to be very sensitive to the current market needs as well as the many cross-currents of change which are becoming evident in this retailing business.[1]

**The Conceptual Framework**

Retailing is the third aspect of distribution to be considered here. Chapter 15 introduced basic concepts in channel strategy. Wholesaling intermediaries were discussed in Chapter 16. This chapter explores retailing, which often links the consumer with the rest of the distribution channel.

In a very real sense, retailers *are* the marketing channel for most consumers, since consumers have little contact with manufacturers and almost none with the wholesaling intermediaries. As a result, the services provided—location, store hours, quality of salespeople, store layout, selection, and returns, among others—often figure even more importantly than the physical product in developing consumer images of the products and services offered.

Retailers are both customers and marketers in the channel. They market products and services to ultimate consumers, and also are the consumers for wholesalers and manufacturers. Because of their critical location in the channel, retailers may perform an important feedback role in obtaining information from customers and transmitting it to manufacturers and other channel members.

Retailing is the "last step of the marketing channel" for the consumer goods manufacturer. Whether the manufacturer has established a company-owned chain of retail stores or uses several of the thousands of retail stores in Canada, the success of the entire marketing strategy rides with the decisions of consumers in the retail store.

**Retailing** may be defined as *all the activities involved in the sale of products and services to the ultimate consumer.* Retailing involves not only sales in retail stores, but also several forms of nonstore retailing. These include telephone and direct-response sales, automatic merchandising, and direct house-to-house solicitations by salespersons.

**Evolution of Retailing**

Early retailing can be traced to the voyageurs, to the establishment of trading posts by the Hudson's Bay Company and others, and to pack peddlers who literally carried their wares to outlying settle-

[1] Adapted from Susan Hoeschen, "Selling the Home Video Revolution," *The Financial Times of Canada* (January 24, 1983), p. 2.

ments. After the trading post days, the Hudson's Bay and other retailers evolved into the institution known as the *general store*. The
general store was stocked with general merchandise to meet the needs
of a small community or rural area. Here customers could buy
clothing, groceries, feed, seed, farm equipment, drugs, spectacles,
and candy. The following account provides a good description of
this early retail institution:

> The country store was in many respects a departmental store on a
> small scale, for a well-equipped store contained a little of everything.
> On one side were to be seen shelves well filled with groceries,
> crockery-ware, and a few patent medicines, such as blood purifiers,
> painkillers, and liniments; on the other side, a well assorted stock of
> dry goods, including prints, woollens, muslins, calico, cottons, etc.
> At the back, a lot of hardware, comprising nails, paints, oils, putty,
> glass, and garden tools, as well as an assortment of boots and shoes
> — from the tiny copper-toe to the farmer's big cowhide. In the back
> room, at the rear end of the store, were to be found barrels of sugar
> and New Orleans molasses, crates of eggs, and tubs of butter and
> lard. With this miscellaneous mixture — tea, coffee, dry goods,
> codfish, and boots and shoes — the odour of the country store was
> truly a composite one, and trying to the olfactory organs of the
> visitor. The country merchant was usually a man in good circum-
> stances, for he was obliged in most cases to give a year's credit, the
> farmers paying their bills in the fall of the year, after the "threshing"
> or the "killing"; their only source of revenue at any other time being
> from butter and eggs, which their wives took to the country store,
> usually once a week, and exchanged for store goods. Perhaps there
> was no more popular place of meeting than the country store. After
> the day's work was over, it was customary for many of the men in the
> neighbourhood, especially the farmers' hired men, who had no other
> place of amusement to go to, to gather here. Even if they did not have
> occasion to buy anything, they would drop in for a few minutes to
> while away the time; have a chat, see someone they wished, hear
> politics discussed, and generally learn all the latest news. The society
> of the country store had a peculiar fascination for many of them, for
> there generally happened to be some one there who was gifted with
> the faculty of cracking jokes, telling funny yarns, or interesting
> stories; besides it was a comfortable place, especially on the long
> winter evenings, when they would gather around the big box stove,
> lounge on the counters, sit on the boxes and barrels, puff away at
> their pipes, chew tobacco, and chaff one another to their heart's
> content.[2]

The basic needs that caused the general store to develop also
doomed this institution to a limited existence. Since the general store-

[2] *Pen Pictures of Early Pioneer Life in Upper Canada* by a "Canuck," Coles
Canadiana Collection (Toronto: Coles Publishing Company, 1972), pp. 80–82.

keepers attempted to satisfy the needs of customers for all types of "store-bought" goods, they carried a small assortment of each good. As the villages grew, the size of the market was large enough to support stores specializing in specific product lines, such as groceries, hardware, dry goods, and drugs. Most general stores either converted into more specialized limited-line stores or closed. But the general store did, and in some rural areas still does, fill a need for its customers. General stores are still operated profitably in less developed countries where income levels cannot support more specialized retailers, and in some isolated parts of Canada as well.

**Innovation in Retailing**

Retailing operations are remarkable illustrations of the marketing concept in operation. The development of new retail innovations can be traced to attempts to better satisfy particular consumer needs.

As consumers demand different bundles of satisfactions from retailers, new institutions emerge to meet this demand. The supermarket appeared in the early 1930s to meet consumer desires for lower prices. Convenience food stores today meet the consumer's desire for convenience in purchasing and after-hours availability. Discount houses and catalogue stores reflect consumer demands for lower prices and a willingness to give up services. Department stores provide a wide variety of products and services to meet the demands of their clientele. Vending machines, door-to-door retailers, and mail-order retailing offer buyer convenience. Planned shopping centres provide a balanced array of consumer goods and services and include parking facilities for their customers. Canada's 162 000 retailing establishments are involved in developing specific marketing mixes designed to satisfy chosen market targets.[3]

**The Framework for Decisions in Retailing**

The retailer's decision-making process, like the producer's and wholesaler's, centres upon the two fundamental steps of 1) analysing, evaluating, and ultimately selecting a *market target*, and 2) development of a *marketing mix* designed to satisfy the chosen market target profitably. In other words, the retailer must develop a product or service offering to appeal to the chosen consumer group, set prices, and choose a location and method of distribution. Finally, the retailer has to develop a promotional strategy.[4]

---

3 Gerald Albaum, Roger Best, and Del Hawkins, "Retailing Strategy for Customer Growth and New Customer Attraction," *Journal of Business Research* (March 1980), pp. 7–19; and Bert Rosenbloom, "Strategic Planning in Retailing: Prospects and Problems," *Journal of Retailing* (Spring 1980), pp. 107–120.
4 Interesting discussions include Sak Onkvisit and John J. Shaw, "Modifying the Retail Classification System for More Timely Marketing Strategies," *Journal of the Academy of Marketing Science* (Fall 1981), pp. 436–453; and Bobby C. Vaught, L. Lyn Judd, and Jack M. Starling, "The Perceived Importance of

**The Market Target**  Like other marketers, retailers must start by selecting the market target to which they wish to appeal. Marketing research is often used in this aspect of retail decision-making. For example, retailers entering new countries, or even new markets in the same country, have been surprised that the same target market as in the home location apparently does not exist. Canadian Tire expanded to the larger U.S. market with the purchase of White Stores, Inc.,[5] but found that U.S. market acceptance of virtual carbon copies of the successful Canadian stores was so limited that they abandoned that market after significant losses. Marketing research can help a company adjust to a new environment faster.

Sometimes a retailer finds it necessary to shift market targets. For example, stores established to serve specialty markets such as skiers or snowmobilers have found that lack of snow or changes in consumer recreation habits have forced them to expand or change their offerings to serve more viable target markets. Market selection is as vital an aspect of retailers' marketing strategy as it is for any other marketer.[6]

**Product/Service Strategy**  Retailers must also determine and evaluate their offerings with respect to:

1. general product/service categories
2. specific lines
3. specific products
4. inventory depth
5. width of assortment

The starting point is to assess their positions in the product/service matrix (shown in Figure 17-2, which appears later in this chapter), which relates convenience, shopping, and specialty retailers to convenience, shopping, and specialty goods. Other marketing factors can influence product and/or service offerings. For instance, the discount-price policies of warehouse supermarkets forces these retailers to restrict their product offerings to 1500 to 1700 items, compared to the 15 000 found in traditional supermarkets.[7]

Retailing Strategies and Their Relationships to Four Indexes of Retailing Success," in *Progress in Marketing: Theory and Practice*, (eds.) Ronald D. Taylor, John J. Bennen, and John H. Summey (Carbondale, Ill.: Southern Marketing Association, 1981), pp. 25–28.

[5] Frances Phillips, "Canadian Tire Finds Texas Trail a Bit Bumpy," *The Financial Post* (March 26, 1983), p. 18.

[6] A good discussion appears in Mary Carolyn Harrison and Alvin C. Burns, "A Case for Departmentalizing Target Market Strategy in Department Stores," in *Progress in Marketing: Theory and Practice*, (eds.) Ronald D. Taylor, John J. Bennen, and John H. Summey (Carbondale, Ill.: Southern Marketing Association, 1981), pp. 21–24.

[7] Bill Abrams, "New Worry for Manufacturers: Growth of Warehouse Outlets," *The Wall Street Journal* (May 28, 1981), p. 29.

Product strategy evolves to meet competition as well as changing consumer needs. Smaller specialty food stores developed an intriguing version of the old-time bulk-food grocery store. The new version offered quality products that could be purchased in exactly the amount desired by consumers. Furthermore, it was a novel idea. It combined the concept of self-service within a relatively intimate store atmosphere, *and* was economical.

Many supermarkets have now added similar bulk food facilities. They have done so to be competitive with the smaller shops, as well as to try to differentiate themselves from their larger rivals. Competition, as well as demand, has forced such modifications to product strategy despite the fact that it is more inconvenient for a large mass retailer to handle bulk foods.

**Retail Pricing Strategy**

Pricing is another critical element of the retailing mix. The essential decisions concern relative price levels. Does the store want to offer higher-priced merchandise (as Holt Renfrew does) or lower-priced items (like Zellers)? Some of the larger department stores such as Eaton's have clearly opted for a higher-price strategy, but try simultaneously to serve some of the lower-priced market targets with basement and warehouse outlets.

Other pricing decisions concern markups, markdowns, loss leaders, odd pricing, and promotional pricing. The retailer is the channel member with direct responsibility for the prices paid by consumers. As Chapters 13 and 14 pointed out, the prices that are set play a major role in buyer perceptions of the retail market.

**Location and Distribution Decisions**

Real estate professionals often point out that location may be the determining factor in the success or failure of a retail business. A store must be in an appropriate location for the type and price of merchandise carried. Small service outlets such as dry cleaners have discovered that there is a difference between being on the "going to work" side of a busy street and the "going home" side. Other retailers have found success in small strip neighbourhood shopping centres that are close to where people live. These centres continue to flourish despite the advent of larger suburban community shopping centres.[8]

**Retail Trade Area Analysis**

**Retail trade area analysis** refers to *studies that assess the relative drawing power of alternative retail locations.* For example, shoppers might be polled as to where they live, how they get to the stores they shop at, how long it takes, how often they shop, and the like. Similarly, the credit charges of an existing store might be plotted to show what its service area is.

[8] Clayton Sinclair, "The New Priorities for Shopping Centres," *Financial Times of Canada* (March 21, 1983), p. 12.

Another technique to use is the law of retail gravitation, sometimes called Reilly's law after its originator, William J. Reilly.[9] The **law of retail gravitation**, originally formulated in the 1920s, *delineates the retail trade area of a potential site on the basis of distance between alternative locations and relative populations.* The formula is:

$$\text{Breaking Point in km from A} = \frac{\text{km between A and B}}{1 + \sqrt{\dfrac{\text{Population of B}}{\text{Population of A}}}}$$

Assume a retailer is considering locating a new outlet in Town A or Town B, which are located 60 km from each other. The population of A is 80 000 and the population of B, 20 000. One of the questions that concerns the retailer is where people living in a small rural community located on the highway between the two towns 25 km from B are likely to shop.

According to the law of retail gravitation, these rural shoppers would most likely shop in A even though it was 10 km further away than B. The retail trade area of A extends 40 km toward B, and the rural community was located only 35 km away.

$$\text{Breaking Point in km from A} = \frac{60}{1 + \sqrt{\dfrac{20\ 000}{80\ 000}}} = \frac{60}{1 + \sqrt{.25}} = \frac{60}{1.5} = 40$$

The formula can be applied inversely to find B's trade area, yielding a figure of 20 km, which falls 5 km short of the rural community.

$$\text{Breaking Point in km from B} = \frac{60}{1 + \sqrt{\dfrac{80\ 000}{20\ 000}}} = \frac{60}{1 + \sqrt{4}} = \frac{60}{3} = 20 \text{ km}$$

The complete trade area for A or B could be found by similar calculations with other communities.

The application of this technique is limited in an area of urban sprawl, regional shopping centres, and consumers who measure distances in terms of travel time. As a result, a contemporary version of retail trade analysis has been offered by David Huff.

Huff's work is an interurban model that assesses the likelihood that a consumer will patronize a specific shopping centre. Trading areas are expressed in terms of a series of probability contours. The probability that a consumer will patronize a specific shopping centre is viewed as a function of centre size, travel time, and the type of

---

[9] The following discussion of Reilly and Huff's work is adapted from Joseph Barry Mason and Morris Lehman Mayer, *Modern Retailing: Theory and Practice* (Plano, Tex.: Business Publications, Inc., 1978), pp. 486–489.

merchandise sought.[10] Practical application of such models, however, are difficult. They are more often used for structuring decision-making than as a precise, predictive tool.

*Other Distribution Decisions* Retailers are faced with a variety of other distribution decisions, largely in order to ensure that adequate quantities of stock are available when consumers want to buy. The definition of "adequate" will vary with the service strategy of the retailer. Since the cost of carrying inventory is high, a high-margin full-service retailer will likely have a greater depth and range of merchandise than a low-margin, limited-line, high-volume outlet.

**Retail Image and Promotional Strategy**

**Retail image** refers to *the consumer's perception of a store and of the shopping experience it provides.*[11] Promotional strategy is a key element in determining the store's image with the consumer. Another important element is the amenities provided by the retailer — the so-called "atmospherics."

Promoting a store with screaming headlines about fantastic once-in-a-lifetime sale prices creates a substantially different image than using a subdued, tasteful illustration of clothing of obvious style and elegance. Similarly, walking into a discount store redolent of caramel popcorn produces an image dramatically different from that of entering a beautifully carpeted boutique.

Regardless of how it is accomplished, the objective of retailer promotional strategy should be to position the consumer's perception of the store in line with other elements of the retailing mix: retail image should match the market target that is selected.

**Categorizing Retailers by Retailing Strategy**

The nation's retailers come in a variety of forms. Since new types of retail operations continue to evolve in response to changing demands of their markets, no universal classification has been devised. The following characteristics or bases can be used in categorizing them:
1. shopping effort expended by customers
2. services provided to customers
3. product lines

---

10 Huff's work is described in David Huff, "A Probabilistic Analysis of Consumer Spatial Behavior," *Emerging Concepts in Marketing*, (ed.) William S. Decker (Chicago: American Marketing Assocaiton, 1972), pp. 443–461. Shopping Centre trade areas are also discussed in Edward Blair, "Sampling Issues in Trade Area Maps Drawn from Shopper Surveys," *Journal of Marketing* (Winter 1983), pp. 98–106.

11 Retail images are discussed in a variety of articles. See, for example, Pradeep K. Korgaonbar and Kamal M. El Sheshai, "Assessing Retail Competition with Multidimensional Scaling," *Business* (April–June, 1982), pp. 30–33; Jack K. Kasulis and Robert F. Lush, "Validating the Retail Store Image Concept," *Journal of the Academy of Marketing Science* (Fall 1981), pp. 419–435.

4. location of retail transactions
5. form of ownership.

Any retailing operation can be classified using each of these five bases. A 7–11 food store may be classified as a convenience store (category 1); self-service (category 2); relatively narrow product lines (category 3); in-store retailing (category 4); and a member of a corporate chain (category 5). Figure 17-1 illustrates the bases for classifying retail operations.

**Figure 17-1   Bases for Classifying Retailers**

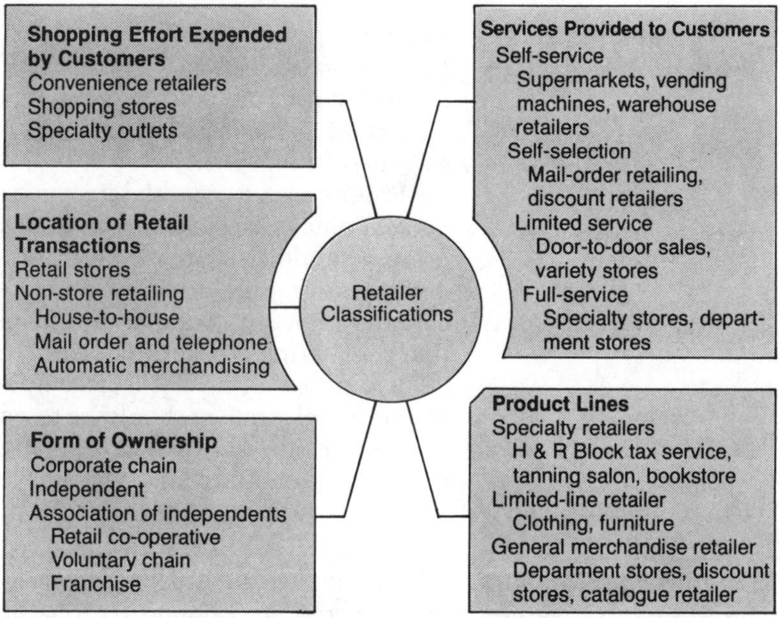

**Shopping Effort Expended by Customers**
Convenience retailers
Shopping stores
Specialty outlets

**Location of Retail Transactions**
Retail stores
Non-store retailing
   House-to-house
   Mail order and telephone
   Automatic merchandising

**Form of Ownership**
Corporate chain
Independent
Association of independents
   Retail co-operative
   Voluntary chain
   Franchise

Retailer Classifications

**Services Provided to Customers**
Self-service
   Supermarkets, vending machines, warehouse retailers
Self-selection
   Mail-order retailing, discount retailers
Limited service
   Door-to-door sales, variety stores
Full-service
   Specialty stores, department stores

**Product Lines**
Specialty retailers
   H & R Block tax service, tanning salon, bookstore
Limited-line retailer
   Clothing, furniture
General merchandise retailer
   Department stores, discount stores, catalogue retailer

**Retailers Classified by Shopping Effort**

A three-way classification of consumer goods based on consumer purchase patterns in securing a particular product or service was presented in Chapter 10. This system can be extended to retailers by considering the reasons consumers shop at a particular retail outlet. The result is a classification scheme in which retail outlets, like consumer goods, are categorized as convenience, shopping, or specialty.[12] The type of retail outlet has a significant influence on the marketing strategies the retailer should select. *Convenience retailers* focus on convenient locations, long store hours, rapid

---

[12] This section is adapted from Louis P. Bucklin, "Retail Strategy and the Classification of Consumer Goods," *Journal of Marketing* (January 1963), pp. 50–55, published by the American Marketing Association.

checkout service, and adequate parking facilities. Small food stores, gasoline retailers, and some barber shops may be included in this category.

*Shopping stores* typically include furniture stores, appliance retailers, clothing outlets, and sporting goods stores. Consumers will compare prices, assortments, and quality levels of competing outlets before making a purchase decision. Managers of shopping stores attempt to differentiate their outlets through advertising, window displays and in-store layouts, knowledgeable salespeople, and appropriate merchandise assortments.

*Specialty retailers* provide some combination of product lines, service, and reputation that results in consumers' willingness to expend considerable effort to shop there. Holt Renfrew and Birks have developed a sufficient degree of preference among many shoppers to be categorized as specialty retailers.

**Figure 17-2   Matrix of Consumer Purchase Behaviour**

| Goods | Retailers | | |
|---|---|---|---|
| | Convenience | Shopping | Specialty |
| Convenience | 1 | 4 | 7 |
| Shopping | 2 | 5 | 8 |
| Specialty | 3 | 6 | 9 |

**A Product/Retailer Matrix**

By cross-classifying the product and retailer classifications, a matrix is created representing nine possible types of consumer purchase behaviour. This matrix is shown in Figure 17-2.

Behaviour patterns in each numbered cell can be described as:

1. *Convenience store–convenience good.* The consumer purchases the most readily available brand of the product at the nearest store.
2. *Convenience store–shopping good.* The consumer chooses a product from among the assortment carried by the most accessible store.
3. *Convenience store–specialty good.* The consumer purchases a favoured brand from the nearest store carrying it.
4. *Shopping store–convenience good.* The consumer is indifferent to the brand purchased; shopping is done among competing stores to secure the best service or price.
5. *Shopping store–shopping good.* The consumer makes compari-

sons among store-controlled factors and factors associated with the product or brand.

6. *Shopping store–specialty good*. The consumer purchases only a favourite brand but shops among a number of stores to obtain the best service or price for it.

7. *Specialty store–convenience good*. The consumer trades only at a specific store and is indifferent to the brand purchased.

8. *Specialty store–shopping good*. The consumer trades only at a specific store and chooses a product from among the assortment carried by it.

9. *Specialty store–specialty good*. The consumer has a strong preference for both a particular store and a specific brand.

This matrix gives a realistic picture of how people buy. The most exclusive specialty store carries handkerchiefs, and many supermarkets have gourmet food departments. The cross-classification system should help the retailer develop appropriate marketing strategies to satisfy particular market segments. The retailer who chooses cells 8 and 9 must seek to develop an image of exclusivity and a good selection of widely accepted competing brands. The same retailer must also carry an assortment of specialty goods, such as high-fashion clothing and expensive perfumes.

### Retailers Classified by Services Provided

Some retailers seek a differential advantage by developing a unique combination of service offerings for the customers who compose

Figure 17-3   Classification of Retailers on the Basis of Customer Service Levels

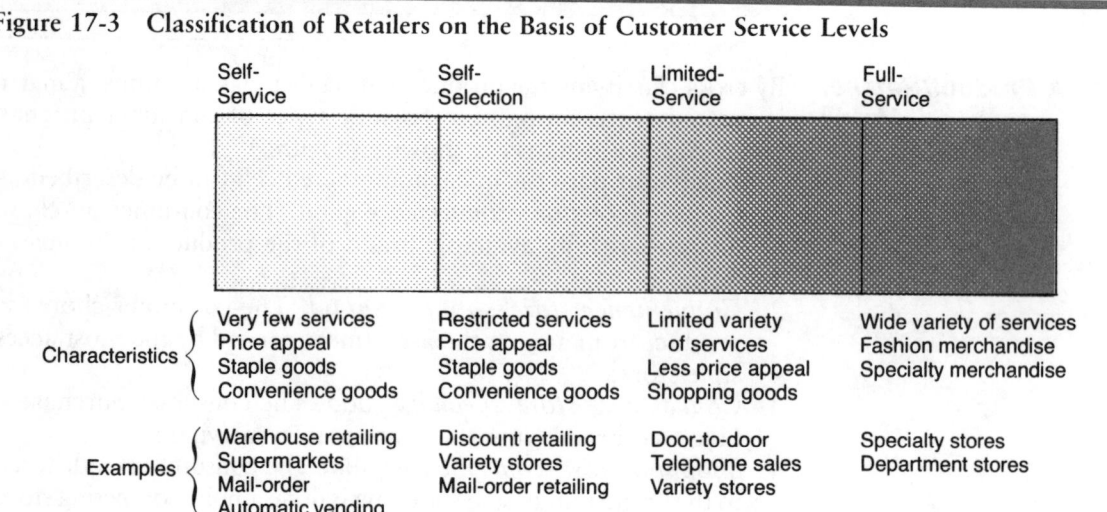

|  | Self-Service | Self-Selection | Limited-Service | Full-Service |
|---|---|---|---|---|
| Characteristics | Very few services<br>Price appeal<br>Staple goods<br>Convenience goods | Restricted services<br>Price appeal<br>Staple goods<br>Convenience goods | Limited variety<br> of services<br>Less price appeal<br>Shopping goods | Wide variety of services<br>Fashion merchandise<br>Specialty merchandise |
| Examples | Warehouse retailing<br>Supermarkets<br>Mail-order<br>Automatic vending | Discount retailing<br>Variety stores<br>Mail-order retailing | Door-to-door<br>Telephone sales<br>Variety stores | Specialty stores<br>Department stores |

Source: Adapted from *Retailing Management: A Planning Approach*, p. 12, by Larry D. Redinbaugh. Copyright © 1976 McGraw-Hill Book Company. Used with the permission of McGraw-Hill Book Company.

their market target. Retailing operations may be classified according to the extent of the services they offer. Figure 17-3 indicates the spectrum of retailer services from virtually no services (self-service) to a full range of customer services (full-service retailers).

Since the self-service and self-selection retailers provide few services to their customers, retailer location and price are important factors. These retailers tend to specialize in staple and convenience goods that are purchased frequently by customers and require little product service or advice from retail personnel.

The full-service retail establishments focus more on fashion-oriented shopping goods and specialty items and offer a wide variety of services for their clientele. As a result, their prices tend to be higher than those of self-service retailers due to the higher operating costs associated with the services.

## Retailers Classified by Product Lines

A commonly used method of categorizing retailers is to consider the product lines they handle. Grouping retailers by product lines produces three major categories: limited-line stores, specialty stores, and general merchandise retailers. Figure 17-4 shows changing shopping patterns by comparing retail trade for type of outlet in 1975 and 1980.

### Limited-Line Retailers

*A large assortment of a single line of products or a few related lines of goods* are offered in **limited-line stores**. Their development paralleled the growth of towns when the population grew sufficiently to support them. These operations include such retailers as furniture stores, hardware stores, grocery stores and supermarkets, appliance stores, and sporting goods stores. Examples of limited-line stores include Sherwin-Williams (paints), Leon's and House of Teak (furniture), Radio Shack (home electronics), Agnew Surpass and Bata (shoes), Calculator World (electronic calculators), D'Allaird's (ready-to-wear), and Coles (books).

These retailers choose to cater to the needs of a specific market target—people who want to select from a complete line in purchasing a particular product. The marketing vice-president of one limited-line firm summarized the limited-line retailer's strategy this way: "Sears can show customers three types of football, but we can show them 40.[13] Most retailers are in the limited-line category.

*The Supermarket*  Until the 1920s, food purchases were made at full-service grocery stores. Store personnel filled orders (often from a shopping list presented to them), provided delivery services, and often granted credit to their customers. The supermarket eliminated

---

13 "Sears' Identity Crisis," *Business Week* (December 8, 1975), p. 54.

## Figure 17-4    Retail Chain and Independent Store Trade, by Selected Kind of Business, 1984

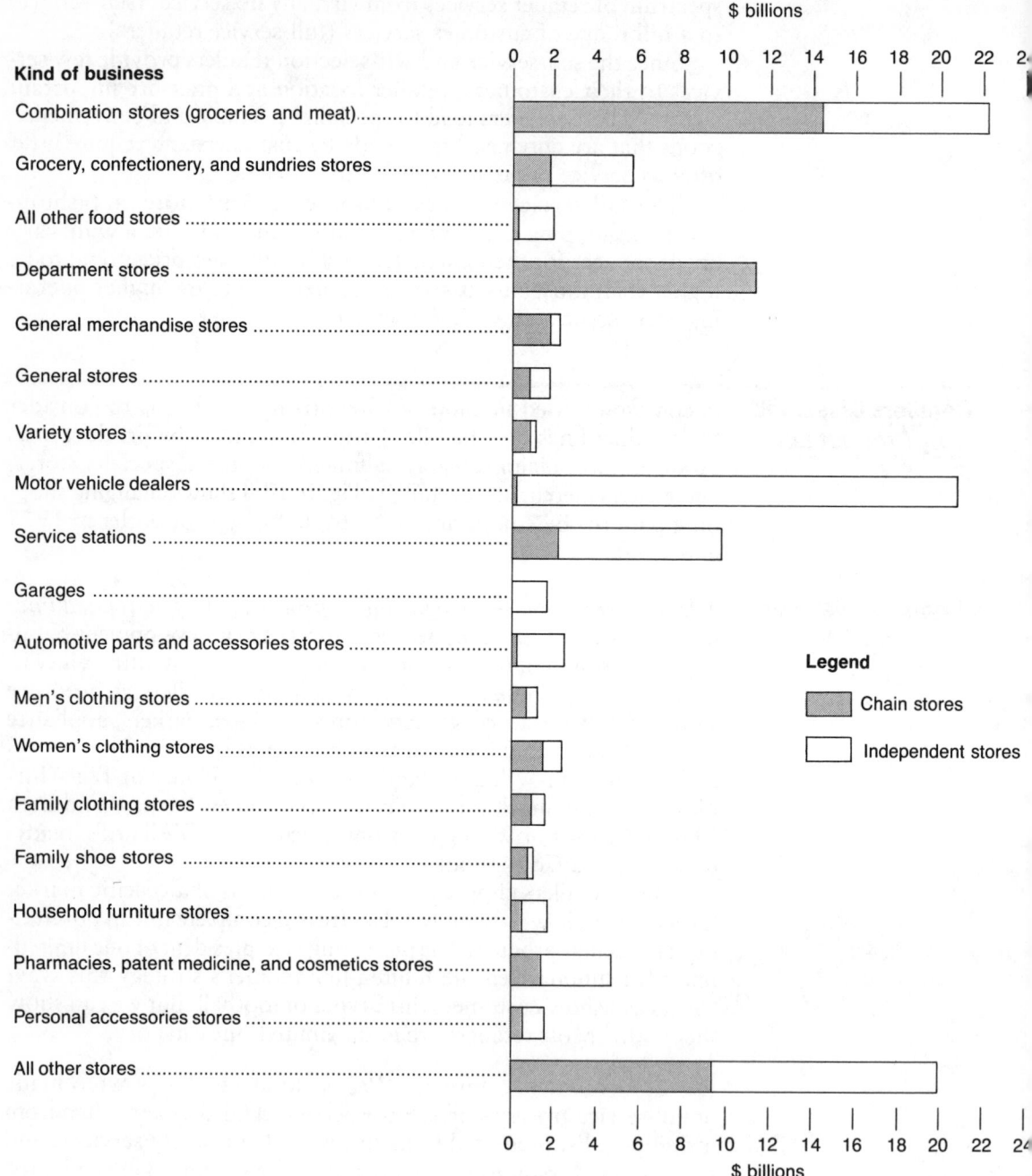

Source: *Market Research Handbook* (Ottawa: Statistics Canada, 1986), Cat. No. 63-224, p. 157.

these services in exchange for lower prices, and it quickly revolutionized food shopping in Canada and much of the world.[14]

A **supermarket** can be defined as *a large-scale, departmentalized retail store offering a large variety of food products* such as meats, produce, dairy products, canned goods, and frozen foods in addition to various nonfood items. It operates on a *self-service* basis and emphasizes price and adequate parking facilities. Supermarket customers typically shop once or twice a week and make fill-in purchases between each major shopping trip. Although supermarkets account for only 1546 of the 31 310 food stores in Canada (1977 figures), they have a large percentage of total food sales. In combination with the convenience stores (Becker's, Mac's Milk, etc.) their sales reached nearly 60 percent of all food sales in 1977. The largest supermarket chains in Canada are Provigo, Canada Safeway, stores owned by George Weston Ltd. (Loblaws, Super Valu, and Westfair Foods) and Dominion Stores.[15]

In recent years supermarkets have become increasingly competitive. One Ontario supermarket attempted to increase its share of the market through a well-publicized price-cutting program. The ramifications were quickly felt in other areas of the country where branches of competing chains operate. Retaliation by other supermarkets was swift, and temporary price cuts ensued — as well as reductions in profits. Supermarket profits average only about 1 percent of sales after taxes. However, a high turnover of 20–26 times per year provides attractive returns on investment.

With a razor-thin profit margin, supermarkets compete through careful planning of retail displays in order to sell more merchandise per week and reduce the amount of investment in inventory. Product location is studied carefully in order to expose the consumer to as much merchandise as possible (and increase impulse purchases). In an attempt to fight the fast-food threat — the tendency of consumers to eat many of their meals outside the home — supermarkets have begun to feature their own delicatessens and bakeries, and to devote ever increasing portions of their stores to nonfood items. Nonfood products such as toys, toiletries, magazines, records, over-the-counter drugs, and small kitchen utensils are carried for two reasons: 1) consumers have displayed a willingness to buy such items in supermarkets, and 2) supermarket managers like them because they have a higher profit margin than the food products.

---

14 See Thomas J. Stanley and Murphy A. Sewell, "Predicting Supermarket Trade: Implications for Marketing Management," *Journal of Retailing* (Summer 1978), pp. 13–22. See also Danny N. Bellenger, Thomas J. Stanley, and John W. Allen, "Trends in Food Retailing," *Atlantic Economic Review* (May–June 1978), pp. 11–14.
15 *The Financial Post 500* (June 1983), p. 110.

Non-food sales have grown substantially as a percentage of super-market sales.

Another change is an increased emphasis on warehouse stores, box stores (carrying a very limited line of high-volume items which customers carry out in discarded boxes), and food barns. All of these provide fewer items within a narrower range of size and brand options than conventional supermarkets.[16]

**Specialty Stores**    A **specialty store** typically *handles only part of a single line of products*. However, this narrow line is stocked in considerable depth. Such stores include meat markets, shoe stores, bakeries, furriers, and luggage shops. Although some of these stores are operated by chains, most are run as independent small-scale operations. The specialty store is perhaps the greatest stronghold of the independent retailer, who can develop expertise in providing a very narrow line of products for his or her local market.

Specialty stores should not be confused with specialty goods, for the specialty store typically carries convenience and shopping goods. The label "specialty" comes from the practice of handling a specific, narrow line of merchandise.

# Developing a Retail Product Mix

Retailers, like manufacturers and wholesalers, develop a product mix designed to attract the customers who make up their market target. In analysing retail product mixes, it is useful to consider three dimensions of retailers' merchandise assortments: variety, width, and depth.

*Variety* refers to the number of product lines carried by the retailer. Department stores, discount houses, drug retailers, and catalogue stores all handle a wide number of lines. The typical catalogue retailer carries lines of jewellery, small appliances, toys, sporting goods, sound systems, household accessories, records, luggage, candy, toiletries, and even clothing. Such a retailer appeals to a larger potential market than a competitor who specializes in, say, leather goods. In addition, the potential for unplanned purchases in other merchandise lines is increased for the retailer offering a variety of lines.

*Width* (or breadth) refers to complementary products within a merchandise line. Bakeries, jewellery stores, meat markets, and shoe stores typically carry a number of complementary items in their respective product lines. Customers are attracted to such stores because of the wide assortment of goods available.

*Depth* refers to the number of sizes, colours, and other features of a single product line. A men's clothing store stocking Izod sweaters in 12 colours, five sizes, and V-neck and crew neck offers its customers considerable depth in this product line.

Most retailers compete on the bases of the variety, width, and depth of their merchandise. Some retailers, such as department stores, feature all three dimensions in their merchandise assortments. Discount houses tend to offer a variety of merchandise lines, but they often stock only the popular sizes and best-selling complementary items. Limited-line retailers such as Sam the Record Man (record stores) and Floating Ecstasy (waterbeds) specialize in a narrow line of products stocked in considerable depth.

---

[16] D. Richard and G. Hewston, "More on Canadian Food Retailers: Some Recent Observations," *Food Market Commentary* (March 1983), p. 18.

**General Merchandise Retailers**

**Department Stores**   The department store is actually a series of limited-line and specialty stores under one roof. A *department store*, by definition, is *a large retail firm handling a variety of merchandise* that includes men's and boy's wear, women's wear and accessories, household linens and dry goods, home furnishings, appliances, and furniture. It serves the consumer by acting as a one-stop shopping centre for almost all personal and household items.

A distinguishing feature of the department store is indicated by its name. The entire store is *organized around departments* for the purposes of service, promotion, and control. A general merchandising manager is responsible for the entire store's product planning. Reporting to the merchandising manager are the buyers who manage each department. The buyers typically run the departments almost as independent businesses and are given considerable discretion in merchandising and layout decisions. Acceptance of the retailing axiom that "well-purchased goods are half sold" is indicated in the department manager's title of *buyer*. The buyers, particularly those in charge of high-fashion departments, spend a considerable portion of their time making decisions concerning the inventory to be carried in their departments.[17]

The department store has been the symbol of retailing since the turn of the century. It started in Canada with Timothy Eaton in 1869, when he purchased the 4 m-wide dry-goods store and stock of William Jennings for $6500. Eaton established a one-price, cash policy (instead of bargaining and paying in produce) and formulated the famous "goods satisfactory or money refunded" guarantee. By 1929, half the retail sales in Canada were made at Eaton's.[18]

Today, almost every urban area in Canada has one or more department stores associated with its downtown area and its major shopping areas. Department stores have had a major impact in many cities. For example, as recently as 1969, Eaton's received 40 percent of every retail dollar (except groceries) in Winnipeg.[19]

The impact of department stores on urban life is not confined to Canada. Such stores are, of course, widespread in the United States. European shoppers associate London with Harrod's, Paris with Au Printemps, and Moscow with GUM. Myer is the dominant department store in both Melbourne and Sydney.

Department stores are known for offering their customers a wide variety of services such as charge accounts, delivery, gift wrapping, and liberal return privileges. In addition, approximately 50 percent of their employees and some 40 percent of their floor space are

---

[17] See Claude R. Martin Jr., "The Contribution of the Professional Buyer to a Store's Success or Failure," *Journal of Retailing* (Summer 1973), pp. 69–80.
[18] See Ian Brown, "The Empire that Timothy Built," *The Financial Post Magazine* (May 1978), pp. 16–47.
[19] *Ibid.*, p. 20.

devoted to nonselling activities. As a result, department stores have relatively high operating costs, averaging between 45 and 60 percent of sales.

Department stores have faced intense competition in the past 30 years. Their relatively high operating costs make them vulnerable to such new retailing innovations as discount stores, catalogue merchandisers, and hypermarkets (discussed later in this section). In addition, department stores are typically located in downtown business districts and experience the problems associated with limited parking, traffic congestion, and urban migration to the suburbs.

Department stores have displayed a willingness to adapt to changing consumer desires. Addition of bargain basements and expansion of parking facilities were attempts to compete with discount operations and suburban retailers. Also, department stores have followed the movement of the population to the suburbs by opening major branches in outlying shopping centres. Canadian department stores have led other retailers in maintaining a vital and dynamic downtown through modernization of their stores, extended store hours, emphasis on attracting the trade of tourists and people attending conventions, and focusing on the residents of the central cities. For example, the first new major downtown department store in more than 20 years in North America was opened by Eaton's in Vancouver in 1973, followed in 1977 by the 108 500 $m^2$ Eaton Centre in downtown Toronto. The complex has over 300 boutiques, restaurants, and stores along a three-level 260 m long shopping mall, in addition to Eaton's and nearby Simpsons anchor stores.

*Variety Stores*    Retail firms that offer an extensive range and assortment of low-priced merchandise are called variety stores. Some examples are Woolworth and Stedmans. The nation's variety stores account for only about 1.2 percent of all retail sales.[20] Variety stores are not as popular as they once were. Many have evolved into or been replaced by other retailing categories such as discounting.

*Mass Merchandisers*    Mass merchandising has made major inroads on department store sales during the past two decades by emphasizing lower prices for well-known brand-name products, high turnover of goods, and reduced services. **Mass merchandisers** often stock a *wider line of products than department stores*, but they usually do not offer the depth of assortment in each line. Major types of mass merchandisers are discount houses, hypermarkets, and catalogue retailers.

---

[20] Statistics Canada; The Conference Board of Canada, *Handbook of Canadian Consumer Markets, 1982*, p. 190.

*Discount Houses*— Limited Services and Lower Prices.   The birth of the modern **discount house** came at the end of World War II when a New York operation named Masters discovered that a very large number of customers were willing to shop at a store that *did not offer such traditional retail services* as credit, sales assistance by clerks, and delivery, *in exchange for reduced prices*. Within a very brief period retailers throughout the country followed the Masters formula and either changed over from their traditional operations or opened new stores dedicated to discounting. At first the discount stores were primarily involved with the sale of appliances, but they have spread into furniture, soft goods, drugs, and even food.

Discount operations had existed in previous years, but the early discounters usually operated from manufacturers' catalogues, with no stock on display and often a limited number of potential customers. The new discounters operated large stores, advertised heavily, emphasized low prices on well-known brands, and were open to the public. Elimination of many of the "free" services provided by traditional retailers allowed the discount operations to reduce their markups to 10 to 25 percent below their competitors. And consumers, who had become accustomed to self-service by shopping at supermarkets, responded in great numbers to this retailing innovation. Conventional retailers such as Kresge and Woolworth joined the discounting practice by opening their own K-mart and Woolco stores.

As the discount houses move into new product areas, a noticeable increase in the number of services offered as well as a corresponding decrease in the discount margin is evident. Carpets are beginning to appear in discounters' stores, credit is increasingly available, and many discounters are even quietly dropping the term *discount* from their name. Even though they still offer fewer services, their operating costs are increasing as they become similar to the traditional department stores. Some have even moved into the "best" shopping areas, and now offer such name brands as Seiko watches, Puma running shoes, and Pentax cameras.

*Hypermarkets*—Shopping Centres in a Single Store. A relatively recent retailing development has been the introduction of **hypermarkets** — giant *mass merchandisers who operate on a low-price, self-service basis and carry lines of soft goods, hard goods, and groceries*. Hypermarkets are sometimes called superstores, although this latter term has also been used to describe a variety of large retail operations.[21] The *hypermarché*, or hypermarket, began in France and has

---

21 Superstores are discussed in Myron Gable and Ronald D. Michman, "Superstores—Revolutionizing Distribution," *Business* (March–April 1981), pp. 14–18.

since spread to Canada and the United States to a limited degree. The Hypermarché Laval outside Montreal was the first to open and had 19 500 m² of selling space (11 to 15 times the size of the average supermarket) and 40 checkouts. A typical hypermarket is like a shopping centre in a single store. It sells food, hardware, soft goods, building materials, auto supplies, appliances, and prescription drugs, and has a restaurant, a beauty salon, a barber shop, a bank branch, and a bakery. More than 1000 of these superstores are currently in operation throughout the world.[22] It appears that they are more popular in Europe than in North America. This is likely because North America already had many large, well-developed shopping centres before the hypermarket concept arrived.

*Catalogue Retailers*   One of the major growth areas in retailing in the past decade has been that of catalogue retailing. **Catalogue retailers** *mail catalogues to their customers and operate from a showroom* displaying samples of their products. Orders are filled from a backroom warehouse. Price is an important factor for catalogue store customers, and low prices are made possible by few services, storage of most of the inventory in the warehouse, reduced shoplifting losses, and handling products that are unlikely to become obsolete, such as luggage, small appliances, gift items, sporting equipment, toys, and jewellery. The largest catalogue retailer in Canada is Consumers Distributing. (Mail-order catalogue retailing is discussed later in this chapter.)

| Retailers Classified by Location of Retail Transaction | A fourth method of categorizing retailers is by determining whether the transaction takes place in a store. While the overwhelming majority of retail sales occur in retail stores, non-store retailing is important for many products. Non-store retailing includes direct house-to-house sales, mail-order retailing, and automatic merchandising machines. These kinds of sales account for about 2.5 percent of all retail sales. |
|---|---|
| **House-to-House Retailing** | One of the oldest marketing channels was built around direct contact between the retailer seller and the customer at the home of the |

---

[22] See E. B. Weiss, "The Hypermarché Marches into U.S. Mass Retailing," *Advertising Age* (December 30, 1974), p. 20; "A 'Hypermarketer' Takes over Fed-Mart," *Business Week* (June 9, 1975), pp. 35–36; "New Superstores Change Packaging, Increase Research Needs," *Marketing News* (October 10, 1975), p. 1; Eric Langeard and Robert A. Peterson, "Diffusion of Large-Scale Food Retailing in France: *Supermarché et Hypermarché*," *Journal of Retailing* (Fall 1975), pp. 43–63, 80; David L. Loudon, "Reversing the Flow of Retailing Technology: The Hypermarket Example," *Proceedings: The Southern Marketing Association*, edited by Henry W. Nash and Donald P. Robin (1976), p. 120.

customer — *house-to-house retailing*. It provides maximum convenience for the consumer and allows the manufacturer to control the firm's marketing channel. House-to-house retailing is a minor part of the retailing picture with less than 1 percent of all retail sales.

House-to-house retailing is conducted by a number of different merchandisers. Manufacturers of such products as bakery and dairy products and newspapers utilize this channel. Firms whose products require emphasis on personal selling and product demonstrations may also use it. Such products and services would include, for example, cosmetics (Avon), vacuum cleaners (Electrolux), household brushes (Fuller Brush Company), encyclopedias (World Book), and insurance.

Some firms, such as Tupperware, and Stanley Home Products, use a variation called *party-plan selling* where a customer gives a party and invites several neighbours and friends. During the party a company representative makes a presentation of the products, and the host or hostess receives a commission based on the amount of products sold. Another version depends heavily on the *personal influence network* and "positive thinking" techniques — for example, Amway and Shaklee. Friends and acquaintances are recruited to recruit others and sell merchandise. A commission scheme on sales made by recruits makes it generally more profitable for sponsors to aggressively solicit recruits than sell themselves.

The house-to-house method of retailing would appear to be a low-cost method of distribution. No plush retail facilities are required; no investment in inventory is necessary; and most house-to-house salespersons operate on a commission basis. In fact, this method is an extremely high-cost approach to distribution. Often the distribution cost of a product marketed through retail stores is half that of the same product retailed house-to-house. High travel costs, the problems involved in recruiting and training a huge sales force that generally has a high turnover, nonproductive calls, several layers of commissions, and the limited number of contracts per day result in high operating expenses. Figure 17-5 shows the relative sales of selected commodities by direct selling.

**Mail-Order Retailing**   The customers of *mail-order merchandisers* can order merchandise by mail, by telephone, or by visiting the mail-order desk of a retail store. Goods are then shipped to the customer's home or to the local retail store.

Figure 17-6 identifies a number of socio-economic, external, and competitive factors that have contributed to the growing consumer acceptance of catalogue retailing.

Many department stores and specialty stores issue catalogues to seek telephone and mail-order sales and to promote in-store purchases of items featured in the catalogues. Among typical depart-

## Figure 17-5   Sales of Direct Selling Organizations, by Selected Commodities, 1978–1983

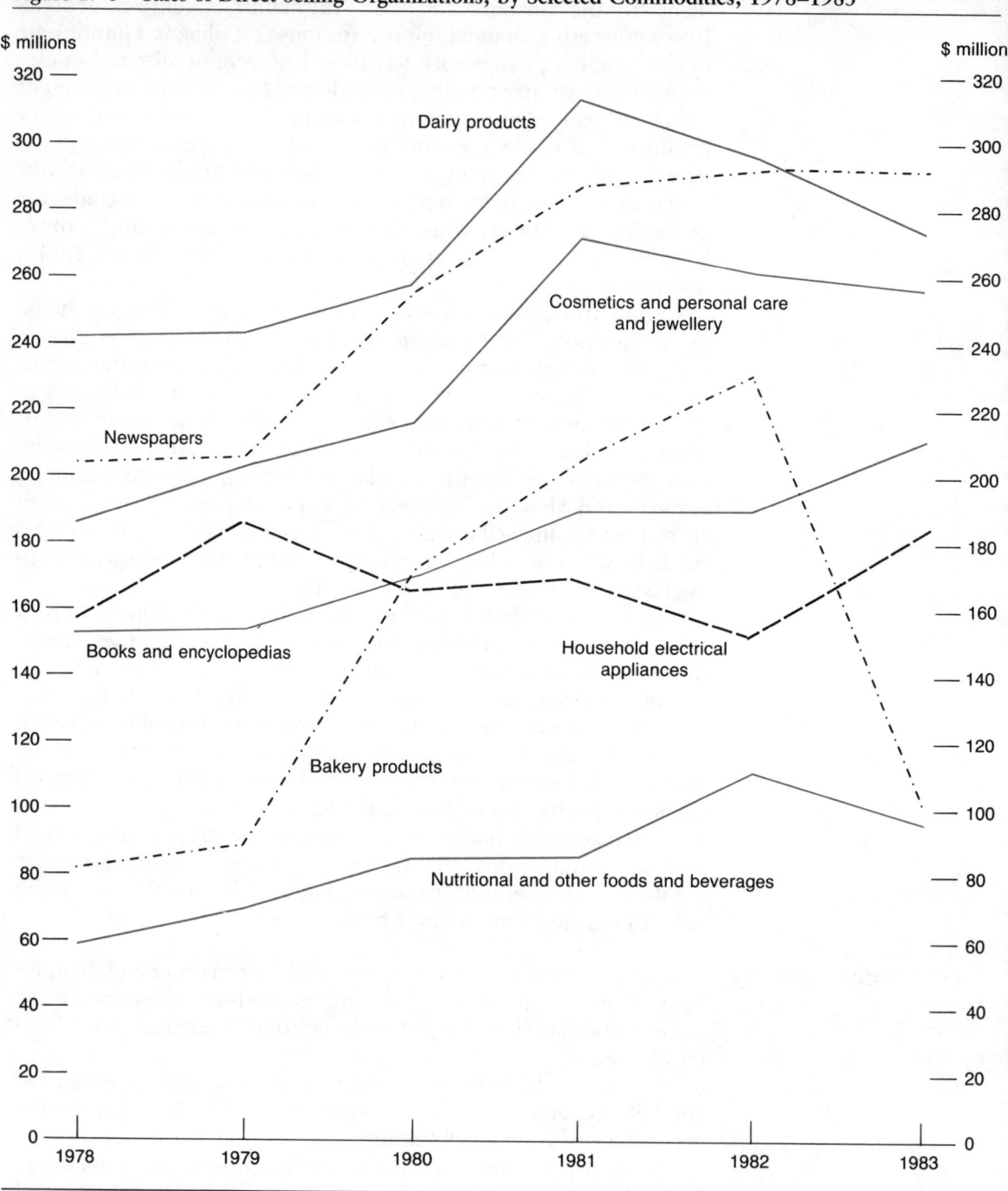

## Figure 17-6  Factors Contributing to the Success of Mail-Order Catalogues

| Socio-economic Factors | External Factors | Competitive Factors |
|---|---|---|
| More women joining the work force<br>Population growing older<br>Rising discretionary income<br>More single households<br>Growth of the "me generation" | Rising costs of gasoline<br>Availability of WATS (800) lines<br>Expanded use of credit cards<br>Low-cost data processing<br>Availability of mailing lists | Inconvenient store hours<br>Unsatisfactory service in stores<br>Difficulty of parking, especially near downtown stores<br>"If you can't beat 'em join 'em" approach of traditional retailers |

Source: John A. Quelch and Hirotaka Takeuchi, "Nonstore Marketing: Fast Track or Slow?" *Harvard Business Review* (July–August 1981), p. 77. Reprinted by permission of the *Harvard Business Review*. Copyright © 1981 by the President and Fellows of Harvard College; all rights reserved.

ment stores, telephone, and mail-generated orders account for 15 percent of total volume during the Christmas season.[23]

Mail-order selling began in Canada in 1894 when Eaton's distributed a slim 32-page booklet to rural visitors at the Canadian National Exposition in Toronto. That first catalogue contained only a few items, mostly clothing and farm supplies. Simpsons soon followed, and mail-order retailing became an important source of products in isolated Canadian settlements.

Even though mail-order sales represent only a small percentage of all retail sales, it is an important channel for many consumers who desire convenience and a large selection of colours and sizes.

With the demise of the Eaton's catalogue sales operations in 1976, apparently due to a failure to introduce effective cost and inventory control measures, Simpsons-Sears became the one major mail-order catalogue marketer left in Canada. Sales have been strong. Catalogue sales contributed at least a third to Simpsons-Sears' $3.1 billion in sales in 1982. Simpsons-Sears now has nearly 1300 catalogue sales offices across Canada and produces 11 catalogues a year, with a combined distribution of 45 million.[24]

Mail-order houses offer a wide range of products—from novelty items (Regal Gifts) to sporting equipment (S.I.R.). The growing number of working women, increasing time pressures, and a decline in customer service in some department stores augur well for catalogue sales.

---

23 John A. Quelch and Hirotaka Takeuchi, "Nonstore Marketing: Fast Track or Slow?" *Harvard Business Review* (July–August 1981), p. 75.
24 Quoted by a Sears executive in Toronto (Mr. Knox).

**Automatic**    *Automatic vending machines* — the true robot stores — are a good
**Merchandising**    way to purchase a wide range of convenience goods. These machines
accounted for over $363 million in sales in Canada.[25] Approximately
122 000 vending machines are currently in operation throughout
the country.

While automatic merchandising is important in the retailing of
some products, it represents less than 1 percent of all retail sales. Its
future growth is limited by such factors as the cost of machines and
the necessity for regular maintenance and repair. In addition, automatically vended products are confined to convenience goods that
are standardized in size and weight with a high rate of turnover.
Prices for some products purchased in vending machines are higher
than store prices for the same products.

## Retailers Classified by Form of Ownership

The fifth method of classifying retailers is by ownership. The two
major types are corporate chain stores and independent retailers. In
addition, independent retailers may join a wholesaler-sponsored voluntary chain, band together to form a retail co-operative, or enter
into a franchise arrangement through contractual agreements with
a manufacturer, wholesaler, or service organization. Each type has
its special characteristics.

**Chain Stores**    **Chain stores** are *groups of retail stores that are centrally owned and
managed and handle the same lines of products*. The concept of
chain stores is certainly not new; the Mitsui chain was operating in
Japan in the 1600s. Woolworth's, Zellers, The Bay, and Reitman's
have operated in Canada for many years.

The major advantage possessed by chain operations over independent retailers is economies of scale. Volume purchases through
a central buying office allow such chains as Safeway and Dominion
to obtain lower prices than independents. Since a chain such as
Safeway has hundreds of retail stores, specialists in layout, sales
training, and accounting systems may be used to increase efficiency.
And advertising can be effectively used. An advertisement in a national magazine for Eaton's promotes every Eaton's store in Canada.

Chains account for approximately one-third of all retail stores and
their dollar volume of sales amounts to 44 percent of all retail sales.
At the present time, chains dominate four fields: department stores,
with virtually 100 percent of department store sales; variety stores,
with 82.6 percent of all variety sales; shoe stores, with 68 percent
of all retail shoes sales; and food stores, with 55 percent of all retail
food sales.[26] Figure 17-7 lists the 25 largest retailers in Canada.

[25] *Vending Machine Operators* (Ottawa: Statistics Canada, 1982), Catalogue
63–213.
[26] *Department Store Sales by Regions* (Ottawa: Statistics Canada) Catalogue
63–005 1982).

## Figure 17-7  Canada's Largest Retailers

| RETAILERS | Operating revenue per store ($000) | Operating revenue ($000) | % change | Oper. margin (%) current | previous | Inventory turnover |
|---|---|---|---|---|---|---|
| *Department stores* | | | | | | |
| Gendis | 1 288 | 588 536 | 13 | 8.0 | 9.3 | 4.4 |
| Sears Canada | 2 395 | 3 891 817 | 3 | 7.2 | 6.5 | 5.7 |
| K mart Canada | 11 740 | 1 385 323 | 12 | na | na | na |
| Hudson's Bay Co. | 14 069 | 5 669 733 | 8 | 5.5 | 4.3 | 5.4 |
| Woodward's | 41 928 | 1 132 069 | 2 | −0.4 | 0.9 | 6.3 |
| *Clothing stores* | | | | | | |
| Grafton Group | 603 | 605 192 | 18 | 6.2 | 8.9 | 7.1 |
| Mark's Work Wearhouse | 1 729 | 159 054 | 8 | 4.3 | 3.9 | 5.9 |
| Marks & Spencer (Canada) | 1 384 | 336 274 | 14 | 6.0 | 5.0 | 5.6 |
| Dalmys (Canada) | 570 | 131 054 | 18 | 4.1 | −3.4 | 7.3 |
| Reitmans (Canada) | 470 | 349 346 | 4 | 5.4 | 8.3 | 11.8 |
| Dylex | 428 | 1 208 600 | 12 | 7.7 | 8.8 | 8.6 |
| *Specialty stores* | | | | | | |
| Leon's Furniture | 12 121 | 193 942 | 22 | 11.5 | 8.7 | 6.1 |
| Canadian Tire | 5 801 | 2 326 002 | 12 | 8.7 | 8.8 | 7.8 |
| Computer Innovations Dist. | 3 236 | 255 614 | 103 | 5.1 | 4.0 | na |
| Consumers Distributing | 3 021 | 933 382 | 6 | 2.6 | 1.5 | 3.7 |
| Groupe Ro-Na | 787 | 398 961 | 17 | 2.6 | 2.1 | 13.7 |
| Peoples Jewellers | 624 | 184 837 | 4 | 9.4 | 7.7 | 1.5 |
| Revelstoke | 3 690 | 140 206 | 6 | 1.2 | 1.6 | 3.8 |

*na = not available*

**FOOD DISTRIBUTION**

| Company | Operating revenue ($000) | Oper. margin (%) current | previous | Inventory turnover | Interest coverage |
|---|---|---|---|---|---|
| Westfair Foods | 1 408 091 | 3.2 | 3.2 | 14.2 | 8.7 |
| Provigo | 5 401 600 | 2.4 | 2.3 | 16.8 | 6.2 |
| Oshawa Group | 3 526 098 | 2.4 | 2.4 | 15.7 | 13.5 |
| Kelly Douglas & Co. | 2 041 083 | 2.8 | 2.3 | 14.2 | 17.2 |
| Becker Milk | 312 959 | 3.8 | 4.4 | 12.2 | 14.1 |
| Sobeys Stores | 918 456 | 2.1 | 1.9 | 17.5 | 2.8 |
| Aligro | 276 464 | 2.6 | 2.8 | 12.8 | 6.4 |
| George Weston | 10 026 100 | 3.1 | 2.9 | 11.6 | 3.8 |
| Canada Safeway | 3 489 488 | 3.0 | 2.9 | 9.5 | 4.8 |
| Empire | 1 041 861 | 4.3 | 3.9 | 16.2 | 1.9 |
| Loblaw Cos. | 7 838 900 | 2.1 | 2.2 | 14.0 | 3.5 |
| Silcorp | 651 534 | 1.9 | 1.5 | 14.9 | 2.0 |
| Metro-Richelieu | 1 659 413 | 1.3 | 0.9 | 22.6 | 1.9 |
| Steinberg | 4 045 615 | 2.3 | 2.2 | 11.8 | 2.3 |

*na = not available.*

Source: *Report on Business Magazine*, (July 1987), p. 76.

Many of the larger chains have expanded their operations to the rest of the world. Sears now has branch stores in Spain, Mexico, and several countries in South America. Safeway operates supermarkets in Germany, the United Kingdom, and Australia. Bowring's has expanded internationally, as has Marks & Spencer. Direct

retailers such as Avon and Tupperware have sales representatives
in Europe, South America, and Southeast Asia.[27]

**Independent Retailers**   Even though most retailers are small independent operators, the
large chains dominate a number of fields. As Figure 17-8 indicates,

**Figure 17-8   Retail Trade in Canada by Sales Size of Establishments**

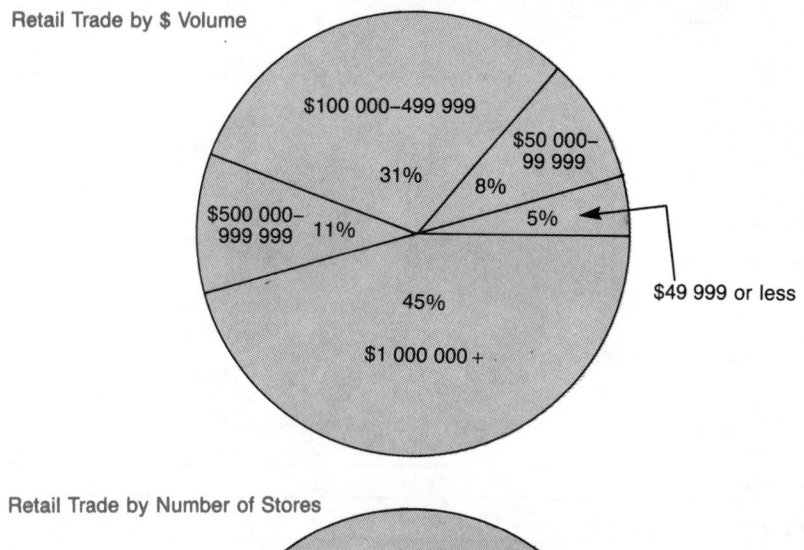

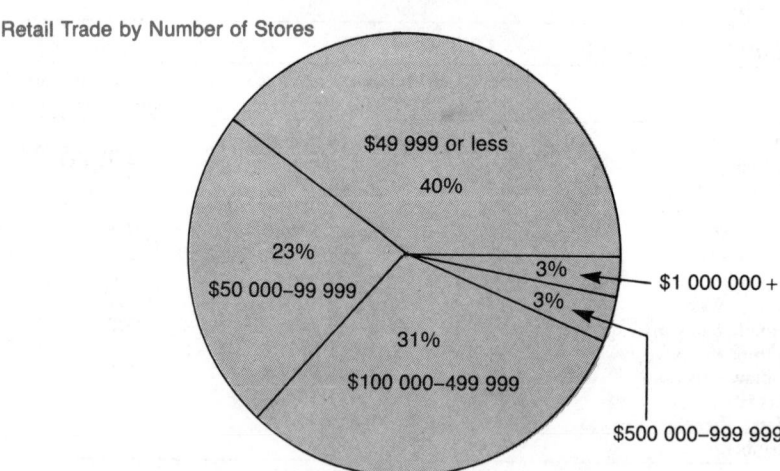

Source: *Market Research Handbook*, CS 63-224 (Ottawa: Statistics Canada, 1977),
pp. 146–147. By permission of the Minister of Supply and Services Canada.

[27]See Michael Y. Yoshino, "International Opportunities for American Retailers,"
*Journal of Retailing* (Fall 1966), pp. 1–10ff; and Stanley C. Hollander, "The
International Retailers," Fred C. Alvine (ed.), *Relevance in Marketing* (Chicago:
American Marketing Association, 1972), pp. 271–274.

about 13 percent of all stores in Canada have sales of less than $100 000 each year. The Canadian retailing structure can be characterized as a very large number of small stores, a sizeable number of medium-size stores, and a very small number of large stores. Even though only about 3 percent of all stores have annual sales of $1 million or more, they account for nearly one-half of all retail sales in Canada.

Independents have attempted to compete with chains in a number of ways. Some independents were unable to do so efficiently and went out of business. Others have joined retail co-operatives, wholesaler-sponsored voluntary chains, or franchise operations as described in Chapter 15. Still others have remained in business by exploiting their advantages of flexibility in operation and knowledge of local market conditions. The independents continue to represent a major part of Canadian retailing. (See Figure 17-9.)

## Significant Developments Affecting Retailing Strategy

Two developments that have significantly altered retailing strategy in recent decades are the development of the planned shopping centre and the practice of scrambled merchandising. Both have a significant impact on the retail environment in Canada.

17–9   Sales of Retail Stores, Independent, Chain and Department Stores, 1981 and 1984

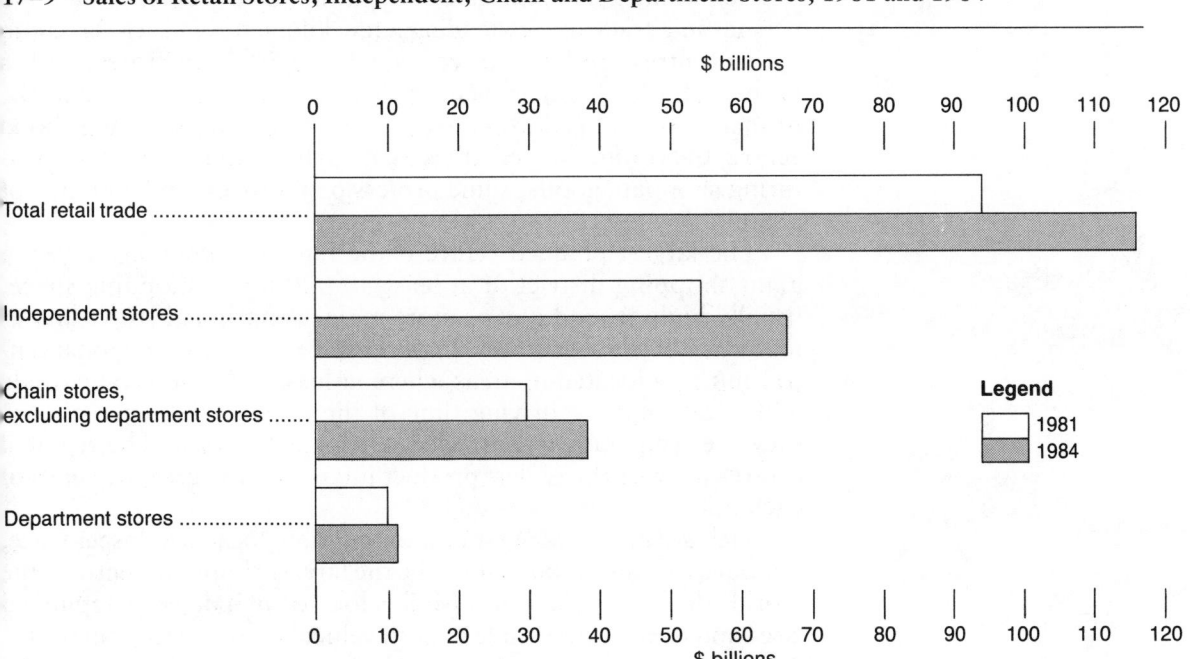

Source: *Market Research Handbook* (Ottawa: Statistics Canada, 1986), Cat. No. 63-224, p. 159.

**Planned
Shopping Centres**

A pronounced shift of retail trade has been developing since 1950 away from the traditional downtown retailing districts and toward suburban shopping centres. A **planned shopping centre** is a *group of retail stores planned, co-ordinated, and marketed as a unit* to shoppers in a particular geographic trade area. These centres have followed population shifts to the suburbs and have focused on correcting many of the problems involved in shopping in the downtown business districts. Ample parking and locations away from the downtown traffic congestion appeal to the suburban shopper. Additional hours for shopping during the evenings and on weekends facilitate family shopping.

Types of Shopping Centres    There are three types of planned shopping centres. The smallest and most common is the *neighbourhood shopping centre*, which is most often composed of a supermarket and a group of smaller stores such as a drugstore, a laundry and dry cleaner, a small appliance store, and perhaps a beauty shop and barbershop. Such centres provide convenient shopping for perhaps 5000 to 15 000 shoppers who live within a few minutes' commuting time of the centre. Such centres typically contain five to 15 stores whose product mix is usually confined to convenience goods and some shopping goods.

*Community shopping centres* typically serve 20 000 to 100 000 persons in a trade area extending a few kilometres in each direction. These centres are likely to contain 15 to 50 retail stores, with a branch of a local department store or a large variety store as the primary tenant. In addition to the stores found in a neighbourhood centre, the community centre is likely to have additional stores featuring shopping goods, some professional offices, and a branch of a bank.

The largest planned centre is the *regional shopping centre*, a giant shopping district of at least 30 000 m$^2$ of shopping space usually built around one or more major department stores and as many as 300 smaller stores. In order to be successful, regional centres must be located in areas where at least 150 000 people reside within 30 minutes' driving time of the centre. Characteristically they are temperature-controlled, enclosed facilities. The regional centres provide the widest product mixes and the greatest depth of each line.

Such a centre is the West Edmonton Mall, located in Jasper Place, a suburb of Edmonton. Said to be the largest shopping centre in the world, the West Edmonton Mall is located in a densely populated area and is easily accessible to both vehicular and pedestrian traffic. Catering to a relatively affluent suburban clientele, the stores at this mall offer a variety of quality merchandise to their customers.

Planned shopping centres account for approximately 40 percent of all retail sales in Canada. Their growth has slowed in recent years, however, as the most lucrative locations are occupied and the market for such centres appears to have been saturated in many regions. Recent trends have developed toward the building of smaller centres in smaller cities and towns.

**Scrambled Merchandising**

A second fundamental change in retailing has been the steady deterioration of clear-cut delineations of retailer types. Anyone who has attempted to fill a prescription recently has been exposed to the concept of **scrambled merchandising** — *the retail practice of carrying dissimilar lines to generate added sales volume.* The large mass-merchandising drugstore carries not only prescription and proprietary drugs, but also gifts, hardware, housewares, records, magazines, grocery products, garden supplies, even small appliances. Gasoline retailers now sell bread and milk; supermarkets carry antifreeze, televisions, cameras, and stereo equipment. Two-thirds of all toothpaste purchases are made in supermarkets. It has been estimated that fully one-fourth of all retail stores are at least par-

**Scrambled Merchandising Is Common in Modern Retailing**

"No used cars? What kind of a drugstore is this anyway?"

Source: Masters Agency

tially involved in selling tires, batteries, and other automobile part
and accessories.[28]

Scrambled merchandising was born out of retailers' willingnes
to add dissimilar merchandise lines in order to offer additional highe
profit lines as well as to satisfy consumer demands for one-sto
shopping. It complicates manufacturers' channel decisions becaus
attempts to maintain or increase the firm's market share mean, i
most instances, that the firm will have to develop multiple channe
to reach the diverse retailers handling its products.

# The Power of A Large Well-Planned Shopping Centre

There were few oases in Toronto's retail wasteland last year but merchants in the glass and greenery of the Eaton Centre felt the slump less than others.

Sales per square foot among ancillary tenants increased 10.2% in 1982, to $443, the highest average in North America. (Eaton's department store, which occupies two-thirds of the centre's almost 150 000 m² of gross leasable area, doesn't report figures.) J. A. "Buzz" Golightly, general manager of the centre, says that 60% of tenants reached "break-through" during the year—the sales level where a merchant crosses over from minimum to percentage rent.

But sales patterns in Toronto's flagship shopping mall—total sales last year were estimated at $500 million—showed the kind of wide swings that make retailers nervous. At the end of the first half, business was up 13%, and for most merchants the recession was only a rumour. Then the bottom fell out. The third quarter was extremely weak and only unusually strong volume in November and December allowed the centre to record a respectable year-over-year gain.

The spotty pattern has continued into 1983. Sales were soft in January and February, but came back strongly in March and April. Over-all, Golightly estimates the first quarter was up about 5% from 1982.

The centre's recession-resistance has come as a relief to its 305 retailers who pay premium prices for the privilege of doing business in what, with the floor space of the adjoining Simpsons Ltd. department store taken into account, is one of the world's largest shopping complexes. A store of 100 to 200 m² located in a high-traffic area will pay $700 to $1000/m² minimum rent, plus occupancy costs in the range of $280-$290/m².

Despite the high cost, the centre has a vacancy rate of only 2%, none of that in prime locations. There is a waiting list for new space that opens up.

Part of the reason for the centre's success is its surprise emergence as Toronto's No. 1 tourist attraction. Of the more than 50 million visits the Centre receives annually, an estimated 19.2 million are made by people from outside the metropolitan area. More importantly, they don't come just to gawk. They spend money. Surveys show that more than 75% of the people who come to the centre actually buy non-food merchandise.

*Financial Times of Canada* (June 13, 1983), p. 17.

### The Wheel-of-Retailing Hypothesis

M. P. McNair attempted to explain the patterns of change in retailing through what has been termed the **wheel of retailing**. Accordin

---

[28] William R. Davidson, "Changes in Distributive Institutions," *Journal of Marketing* (January 1970), p. 8. See also William R. Davidson, "Changes in Distributive Institutions: A Reexamination," *The Canadian Marketer* (Winter 1975), pp. 7–13.

to this hypothesis, new types of retailers gain a competitive foothold by offering lower prices to their customers through the reduction or elimination of services. Once they are established, however, they evolve by adding more services and their prices gradually rise. Then they become vulnerable to a new low-price retailer who enters with minimum services — and the wheel turns.

Most of the major developments in retailing appear to fit the wheel pattern. Early department stores, chain stores, supermarkets, and discount stores all emphasized limited service and low prices. In most of these instances price levels have gradually increased as services have been added.

There have been some exceptions, however. The development of suburban shopping centres, convenience food stores, and vending machines were not built around low-price appeals. However, the wheel pattern has been present often enough in the past that it should serve as a general indicator of future developments in retailing.[29]

**The Retail Life Cycle**      Closely related to the wheel hypothesis is the concept of the **retail life cycle**. The notion of "life cycle" was applied earlier to households and to products. It is also possible to apply the concept of "introduction–growth–maturity–decline" to retail institutions. Figure 17-10 applies the retail life cycle concept to a number of institutions and identifies the approximate stage in the life cycle of each institution.

Retailers have demonstrated that it is possible to extend the length of their life cycles through adaptation to changing environments. Such institutions as supermarkets and variety stores reached the maturity stage in their life cycles several decades ago, but have continued to function as important marketing institutions by adapting to changing consumer demands and by adjusting to meet changing competitive situations. Variety stores have countered the sales inroads of discount houses by becoming more price-competitive and by providing greater depth in their product lines. Supermarkets have taken such steps as offering generic brands at lower prices, developing departments of gourmet foods to counter the competition of specialty food retailers, and adding non-food items to meet the demand for one-stop shopping convenience.[30]

---

[29] For a complete discussion of the "wheel-of-retailing" hypothesis, see Stanley C. Hollander, "The Wheel of Retailing" and "Retrospective Comment," in Howard A. Thompson (ed.), *The Great Writings in Marketing* (Plymouth, Mich.: The Commerce Press, 1976), pp. 358–369. See also Dillard B. Tinsley, John R. Brooks Jr., and Michael d'Amico, "Will The Wheel Stop Turning?" *Akron Business and Economic Review* (Summer 1978), pp. 26–29.

[30] See William R. Davidson, Albert D. Bates, and Stephen J. Bass, "The Retail Life Cycle," *Harvard Business Review* (November–December 1976), pp. 89–96.

Figure 17-10   Life Cycles of Selected Retail Institutions

| Institutional Type | Period of Fastest Growth | Period from Inception to Maturity (Years) | Stage of Life Cycle |
|---|---|---|---|
| General store | 1800–1840 | 100 | Decline |
| Specialty store | 1820–1840 | 100 | Maturity |
| Variety store | 1870–1930 | 50 | Decline |
| Mail-order house | 1915–1950 | 50 | Maturity |
| Corporate chain | 1920–1930 | 50 | Maturity |
| Discount store | 1955–1975 | 20 | Maturity |
| Supermarket | 1935–1965 | 35 | Maturity |
| Shopping centre | 1950–1965 | 40 | Maturity |
| Gasoline station | 1930–1950 | 45 | Maturity |
| Convenience store | 1965–1975 | 20 | Maturity |
| Fast-food store | 1960–1975 | 15 | Maturity |
| Hypermarket | 1973– | – | Early growth |
| Warehouse retailer | 1970–1980 | 10 | Late growth |
| Catalogue showroom | 1970–1980 | 10 | Late growth |

Source: Joseph Barry Mason and Morris L. Mayer, *Modern Retailing: Theory and Practice* (Dallas: Business Publications, 1978), p. 58. © 1978 by Business Publications, Inc. Adapted with permission.

*The Future of Retailing*    A number of trends are currently emerging that may greatly affect tomorrow's retailer. One is the possibility of **teleshopping**—*ordering merchandise that has been displayed on home television sets or computers*. Cable television currently reaches 57 percent of Canadian homes, and as it grows it has the potential of revolutionizing many retail practices by the early 1990s, when interactive teleshopping through cable television should be possible. A similar concept is shopping through an interactive personal computer. In Manitoba the Grassroots system, which uses Telidon technology, enables farmers to obtain precise weather reports for their farm locality. This same system is linked with several retailers including the Bay, Sears, Sports Mart, and Compu store. Selected items are listed, along with prices, and orders can be placed through the computer network. Sears and S.I.R., a sporting goods catalogue retailer, both offer customers the opportunity of placing a catalogue order through the Grassroots system after browsing through the printed catalogue. Similarly, patrons may use the system to order tickets for the Jets hockey games.

Teleshopping obviously offers an exciting new dimension for retailing, but it is not without its drawbacks. A survey conducted for *Marketing News* found that only 10 percent of 2163 respondents expressed positive attitudes about teleshopping. Reasons for the low acceptance varied, but included a desire to inspect the product personally, preference for going out to shop, and the fear of being tempted to purchase unneeded items.[31]

Teleshopping via an interactive cable system is likely to be most effective for products where sight, feel, smell, and personal service are not important in the purchase decision.[32] Consumer resistance is not the only problem for the future development of teleshopping. There are also cable operator barriers and cost barriers.[33]

**Consumer Barriers**   Teleshopping faces several consumer barriers. The *Marketing News* survey reported little interest in shopping via interactive cable television. Several other consumer-related questions have been raised:

1. Given the range of other programming, will consumers watch catalogue programs?
2. How can catalogue programs overcome the advantages of printed catalogues?
3. What can be done about the impersonal nature of teleshopping?
4. How can consumer perceptions of higher prices be handled?
5. Will consumers be willing to use an electronic funds transfer system?

All of these questions must be resolved if teleshopping is to be a successful retail innovation.

**Technical Barriers**   Few cable operators now have interactive capability and many of the remaining ones cannot be converted. One system that does seem to be working is the Tella Digest of the Toronto Real Estate Board. This is an on-line, interactive system for user-friendly communications. There are also two significant operator-related obstacles to the development of teleshopping. Cable operators may resist catalogue programming because of their perception of consumer resistance to advertising. Cable operators have concentrated on subscription revenue rather than advertising revenues in the past.

**Cost Barriers**   Teleshopping also faces significant cost barriers. Catalogue marketers would have to absorb production costs, but would not have the ability to divide it over as many viewers as television, for example. Since the programming would be essentially advertising, a method of paying the cable operator, either by buying air time or giving the

---

31 "Only 10% of Consumers Interested in Shopping at Home Via 2-Way TV," *Marketing News* (May 29, 1981), pp. 1, 3.

32 Malcolm P. McNair and Eleanor G. May, "The Next Revolution of the Retailing Wheel," *Harvard Business Review* (September-October 1978), pp. 81–91. Another interesting article is Larry J. Rosenberg and Elizabeth C. Hirschman, "Retailing without Stores," *Harvard Business Review* (July–August 1980), pp. 103–112.

33 The discussion that follows is adapted from Quelch and Takeuchi, "Nonstore Marketing: Fast Track or Slow?" pp. 80–83.

operators a commission on the orders received through the interactive cable setup, would have to be arranged. These costs are expected to be significant when compared to other forms of retailing.

Regardless of the barriers, teleshopping will become a regular part of the retailing environment in the next decade, where it is cost efficient. In fact, the wheel of retailing seems to be rolling again.

**Other Growth Areas**

In the future, retail executives believe that catalogue stores, direct mail, discount houses, and telephone selling are likely to offer growth opportunities. Medium-size discount stores may be giving way to extremely large hypermarket discounters on one hand and specialty stores on the other.[34] The furniture warehouse retailer (such as Leon's) is regarded as a major threat to established furniture outlets. In addition, grocery, drug, and other limited-line retailers are likely to generate new competition for the consumers' general merchandise business.

A renewed emphasis upon the pleasurable aspects of shopping is another trend that should accelerate in the next few years. Department stores are placing increased emphasis on boutiques and specialty shops within the department store itself. This will allow them to provide more individualized service and to appeal to specific kinds of customers.

The future of specialty stores appears bright. They accounted for 40 percent of the general merchandise market in the 1970s, and their share is expected to increase to 48 percent by the mid-1980s. However, the *number* of small, independent specialty stores is expected to continue to decline. Those that survive will become stronger and will generate the increase in sales volume.

**Summary**

Retailers are vital members of the distribution channel for consumer products. They play a major role in the creation of time, place, and ownership utility. Retailers can be categorized on five bases: 1) shopping effort expended by customers; 2) services provided to customers; 3) product lines; 4) location of retail transactions; and 5) form of ownership.

Retailers — like consumer goods — may be divided into convenience, shopping, and specialty categories based upon the efforts shoppers are willing to expend in purchasing products. A second method of classification categorizes retailers on a spectrum ranging from self-service to full-service. The third method divides retailers into three categories: limited-line stores, which compete

34 See Douglas J. Tigert and George H. Haines, Jr., "The Death of the Discount Store: An Analysis of the Changing Structure of Retailing in Canada," in Donald N. Thompson, *Problems in Canadian Marketing* (Chicago: American Marketing Association, 1977), pp. 57–60.

by carrying a large assortment of one or two lines of products; specialty stores, which carry a very large assortment of only part of a single line of products; and general merchandise retailers, such as department stores, variety stores, and such mass merchandisers as discount houses, hypermarkets, and catalogue retailers — all handling a wide variety of products.

A fourth classification method distinguishes between retail stores and non-store retailing. While more than 97 percent of total retail sales in Canada takes place in retail stores, such non-store retailing as house-to-house retailing, mail-order establishments, and automatic merchandising machines are important in marketing many types of products.

A fifth method of classification categorizes retailers by form of ownership. The major types include corporate chain stores, independent retailers, and independents who have banded together to form retail co-operatives or to join wholesaler-sponsored voluntary chains or franchises.

Chains are groups of retail stores that are centrally owned and managed and that handle the same lines of products. Chain stores dominate retailing in four fields: department stores, variety stores, food stores and shoe stores. They account for more than a third of all retail sales.

Retailing has been affected by the development of planned shopping centres and the practice of scrambled merchandising. Planned shopping centres are a group of retail stores planned, co-ordinated, and marketed as a unit to shoppers in their geographic trade area. Shopping centres can be classified as neighbourhood, community, and regional centres. Another significant development is scrambled merchandising, the practice of carrying dissimilar lines in an attempt to generate additional sales volume.

The evolution of retail institutions has generally been in accordance with the wheel of retailing, which holds that new types of retailers gain a competitive foothold by offering lower prices to their customers through the reduction or elimination of services. Once they are established, however, they add more services and their prices generally rise. Then they become vulnerable to the next low-price retailer. The evolution of retail institutions can also be explained in terms of a retail life cycle. One form of retailing that is at the introductory stage or beginning growth stage is teleshopping conducted through interactive cable television.

| **_Key Terms_** | retailing | mass merchandiser |
| --- | --- | --- |
| | retail trade area analysis | discount house |
| | law of retail gravitation | hypermarket |
| | retail image | catalogue retailer |

limited-line store                    chain store
supermarket                           planned shopping centre
specialty store                       scrambled merchandising
general merchandise retailer          wheel of retailing
department store                      teleshopping

---

**Review Questions**

1. Discuss the evolution of retailing.
2. Outline the framework for decisions in retailing.
3. Outline the five bases for categorizing retailers.
4. How are limited-line and specialty stores able to compete with such general merchandise retailers as department stores and discount houses?
5. Identify the major types of general merchandise retailers.
6. Give reasons for the success of discount retailing in Canada.
7. Identify and briefly explain each of the types of non-store retailing operations.
8. Why has the practice of scrambled merchandising become so common in retailing?
9. Compare the retail life cycle concept with the wheel-of-retailing hypothesis.
10. Discuss the current development and potential for teleshopping.

---

**Discussion Questions and Exercises**

1. Computers are one of the fastest growing aspects of retailing. Computer outlets include Radio Shack, Computerland, Computer Connection, MicroAge, and Computer Innovations. Relate this growth to the concepts discussed in Chapter 17.
2. Xerox and IBM have recently opened stores to serve small businesses and professionals like attorneys, physicians, dentists, and chartered accountants. How would you classify these stores?
3. Assume that a retailer was considering opening an outlet in Town A, population 144 000. The retailer wanted to know how far his trade area would extend toward Town B (population 16 000), 72 km away. Apply the law of retail gravitation to the retailer's problem.
4. List several examples of the wheel of retailing in operation. List examples that do not conform to the wheel hypothesis. What generalizations can be drawn from this exercise?
5. What is your assessment of the future of teleshopping through interactive cable television?

**MICROCOMPUTER
EXERCISE: Markups
and Markdowns**

Directions:  Use the Menu Item titled "Markups" on the Foundations of Marketing disk to solve Problems 1 through 3. Use the Menu
Item titled "Markdowns" to solve Problems 4 through 6.

1. A Chatham, Ontario music store sells compact-disk recordings
for $19 each. The retailer purchases the disks for $13 each. What
are the music store's markup percentage on selling price and markup
percentage on cost?

2. A Thunder Bay children's clothing store always adds a 40-percent
markup (based on selling price) for its children's jeans. A shipment
of jeans just arrived, carrying an invoice cost of $11 per pair. What
should be the retail selling price for the new jeans?

3. A Banff art dealer uses a markup percentage on selling price of
50 percent for its art prints. What would be the markup percentage
on cost for the prints?

4. A period of growing unemployment has adversely affected the
sales of $350 suits in a local men's clothing store. The manager
decides to mark down these suits to $280. What markdown per-
centage should be featured in advertising for the sale items?

5. An Oshawa retailer paid $120 per dozen for a particular brand
of men's ties. The store attempted to sell these ties at $21 each, but
sales have been disappointing. In an attempt to stimulate additional
sales, the store manager decides to mark down the ties to $15. Deter-
mine the store's markdown percentage on the ties.

6. A Squamish, B.C. furniture dealer has reduced the price on a
dining-room suite from $1600 to $1200. What markdown percentage should be featured in advertising for the item?

# CHAPTER 18

# Management of Physical Distribution

## CHAPTER OBJECTIVES

1. *To relate physical distribution to the other variables of the marketing mix.*

2. *To explain the role of physical distribution in an effective marketing strategy.*

3. *To describe the objectives of physical distribution.*

4. *To discuss the problem of suboptimization in physical distribution.*

5. *To identify and compare the major components of a physical distribution system.*

6. *To relate the major transportation alternatives to such factors as energy efficiency, speed, dependability, and cost.*

While other companies struggled to stay afloat in the economic recession of the early 1980s, Canadian Tire has continued to rack up healthy sales. On top of that, the firm has actually increased inventory turnover by 40 percent since 1977 — during a period when inventory turnover in the retail industry was dropping steadily.

One of the major reasons for the firm's enviable financial position is its sophisticated physical distribution (PD) system. Says former Canadian Tire president Dean Muncaster: "PD represents a major opportunity for cost savings. In order to maintain a competitive position in the market and keep profits up, it is important to have the most cost-effective PD system."

As soon as a clerk rings up a sale on the electronic cash register in a Canadian Tire store, the inventory number is automatically routed through an on-line computer network to the store's order sheet at the company's Toronto distribution centre. As the orders come in, warehouse stock is automatically allocated, ensuring that in-store inventory is kept at the proper levels. Price tags, scheduling sheets, and routing stickers are also printed at this time. Merchandise is replaced within three to four days of being sold and emergency orders can be filled in half a day.

Each morning, pre-planned loads based on data on volume and mass are obtained from the computer. The scheduling staff goes through all of the orders until they have enough volume to fill 62 m³, the equivalent of a truckload, in order to "maximize the cube" — use the available volume to its full capacity. Canadian Tire's two PD centres work together to consolidate orders going to the same area or store.

The company also wishes to maximize equipment usage — it has more than 80 tractors and 650 trailers which move goods all over the country. Therefore, when Canadian Tire is delivering it tries to pick up its own supplies, creating a backhaul situation for greater efficiency.

In addition to maximizing cube in Canadian Tire's trucks, the computer also improves warehouse productivity. A warehouse employee who must locate a particular product asks the computer to find the shortest route to the goods. The computer allows the company to control its labour costs, which account for about 80 percent of the company's PD expenses.

The company recognizes that while a sophisticated PD program is important, a competent manager is needed to make the system work. Canadian Tire's experience demonstrates the benefits of a well-designed and sophisticated physical distribution system under the direction of a competent PD manager.[1]

## The Conceptual Framework

Chapters 15 through 17 dealt with the basic concepts of distribution channels and the marketing institutions within them. Yet there is another side to the distribution function. Effective marketing requires that products be physically moved within the channel of distribution. This chapter focuses specifically on the physical flow of goods. Improving customer service through more efficient physical distribution remains an important aspect of any organization's marketing strategy. In addition, this efficiency improvement means substantial cost savings.

**Physical distribution** or **logistics** is one of marketing's most innovative and dynamic areas. It involves a broad range of activities concerned with *efficient movement of finished products from the end of the production line to the consumer*. Physical distribution activities include such crucial decision areas as customer service, inventory control, materials handling, protective packaging, order processing, transportation, warehouse site selection, and warehousing.

## Importance of Physical Distribution

Increased attention has been focused in recent years on physical distribution activities, largely because these activities represent a major portion — almost half — of total marketing *costs*.

[1] Adapted from Michelle Ramsay, "Boosting Inventory Turns the Canadian Tire Way," *Canadian Transportation and Distribution Management* (November 1983), p. 33–34.

Management's traditional focal point for cost-cutting has been production. Historically, this began with the industrial revolution of the 1700s and 1800s, when businesses emphasized efficient production, stressing their ability to decrease production costs and improve the output levels of production facilities and workers. But managers have begun to recognize that production efficiency has reached a point at which it is difficult to achieve further cost savings. More and more managers are turning to physical distribution activities as a possible area for cost savings.

In a recent year, Canadian industry spent about $39 billion on transportation, $23 billion on warehousing, $23 billion on the costs of maintaining inventory, and $6 billion on administering and managing these aspects of physical distribution. Physical distribution now accounts for more than 24.5 percent of the nation's gross national product and is the second largest cost item for most companies.[2]

## Physical Distribution and Consumer Satisfaction

A second—and equally important—reason for the increased attention on physical distribution activities is the role they play in providing *customer service.* By storing products in convenient locations for shipment to wholesale and retail customers, firms create time utility. Place utility is created primarily by transportation. These major contributions indicate the importance of the physical distribution component of marketing.[3]

Customer satisfaction is heavily dependent upon reliable movement of products to ensure availability. Eastman Kodak Company committed a major marketing error in the late 1970s when it launched a multimillion-dollar advertising campaign for its new instant camera before adequate quantities had been delivered to retail outlets. Many would-be purchasers visited the stores and, when they discovered that the new camera was not available, bought a Polaroid camera instead.

By providing consumers with time and place utility, physical distribution contributes to implementing the marketing concept. Robert Woodruff, former president of Coca-Cola, emphasized the role of physical distribution in his firm's success when he stated that his organization's policy is to "put Coke within an arm's length of desire."

[2] Andrew M. Schell and Jim Heur, "Creating a PD Strategy for a Rebounding Economy,"*Canadian Transportation and Distribution Management* (November 1983), p. 79.
[3] See Douglas M. Lambert and James R. Stock, "Physical Distribution and Consumer Demands," *MSU Business Topics* (Spring 1978), pp. 49–56; and Bert Rosenbloom, "Using Physical Distribution Strategy for Better Channel Management," *Journal of the Academy of Marketing Science* (Winter 1979), pp. 61–69.

## Components of the Physical Distribution System

The study of physical distribution is one of the classic examples of the systems approach to business problems. The basic notion of a system is that it is a set of interrelated parts. The word is derived from the Greek word *systema*, which means an organized relationship among components. The firm's components include such interrelated areas as production, finance, and marketing. Each component must function properly if the system is to be effective and if organizational objectives are to be achieved.

A **system** may be defined as *an organized group of parts or components linked together according to a plan to achieve specific objectives*. The physical distribution system contains the following elements:

1. Customer service: What level of customer service should be provided?
2. Transportation: How will the products be shipped?
3. Inventory control: How much inventory should be maintained at each location?
4. Materials handling: How do we develop efficient methods of handling products in the factory, warehouse, and transport terminals?
5. Order processing: How should orders be handled?
6. Warehousing: Where will the products be located? How many warehouses should be utilized?

These components are interrelated, and decisions made in one area affect the relative efficiency of other areas. Attempts to reduce transportation costs by utilizing low-cost, relatively slow water transportation will probably reduce customer service and may increase inventory costs, since the firm may be required to maintain larger inventory levels to compensate for longer delivery times. The physical distribution manager must balance each component so that no single aspect is stressed to the detriment of the overall functioning of the distribution system.[4]

## The Objective of Physical Distribution

The objective of a firm's physical distribution system is *to produce a specified level of customer service while minimizing the costs involved in physically moving and storing the product* from its production point to the point where it is ultimately purchased. To achieve this, the physical distribution manager makes use of three basic concepts that are vital to effective logistics management: 1) the total-cost approach, 2) the avoidance of suboptimization, and 3) the use of cost trade-offs.

---

[4] David P. Herron, "Managing Physical Distribution for Profits," *Harvard Business Review* (May–June 1979), pp. 121–32.

**Total-Cost Approach**

The premise that *all relevant factors in physically moving and storing products should be considered as a whole and not individually* forms the basis of the **total-cost approach**. Thus, the following business functions should be included: 1) transportation, 2) warehousing, 3) warehouse location, 4) inventory control systems, 5) materials handling, 6) internal information flows, 7) customer service standards, and 8) packaging. All these cost items are considered as a whole when attempting to meet customer service levels at minimum cost.[5]

**The Problem of Suboptimization**

The total-cost approach requires that all physical distribution elements must be considered as a whole rather than individually. Sometimes this does not happen. **Suboptimization** is a condition in which *the manager of each physical distribution function attempts to minimize costs, but, due to the impact of one physical distribution task on the others, the results are less than optimal.* One writer explains suboptimization using the analogy of a football team made up of numerous talented individuals who seldom win games. Team members hold league records in a variety of skills: pass completions, average distance gained per rush, blocked kicks, and average gains on punt returns. Unfortunately, however, the overall ability of the team to accomplish the organizational goal — scoring more points than the opponents — is rarely achieved.[6]

Why does suboptimization occur frequently in physical distribution? The answer lies in the fact that each separate logistics activity is often judged by its ability to achieve certain management objectives, some of which are at cross-purposes with other objectives. Sometimes, departments in other functional areas take actions that cause the physical distribution area to operate at less than full efficiency. Psychological factors often come into play here. For example, a product manager might think to herself, "cartons are bought out of my department's budget, so we'll only buy standard, non-reinforced ones. We don't care if the warehouse staff complain — breakages are their problem, not ours. We'll look good because this department kept costs down." Counteracting this type of attitude is the responsibility of top management who must convince junior management that they are serious about total cost (which means not complaining about the cost of cartons to one department head and about breakages to the other).

[5] See Raymond LeKachman and John F. Stolle, "The Total Cost Approach to Distribution," *Business Horizons* (Winter 1965), pp. 33–46. See also Marvin Flaks, "Total Cost Approach to Physical Distribution," *Business Management* (August 1963), pp. 55–61.
[6] Warren Rose, *Logistics Management* (Dubuque, Iowa: Wm. C. Brown, 1979), p. 4.

Effective management of the physical distribution function requires some cost trade-offs. Some functional areas of the firm will experience cost increases while others will have cost decreases resulting in the minimization of total physical distribution costs. Of course, the reduction of any physical distribution cost assumes that the level of customer service will not be sacrificed.[7]

**Cost Trade-offs**   The third fundamental concept of physical distribution is the use of **cost trade-offs**. This approach assumes that *some functional areas of the firm will experience cost increases while others will have cost decreases*. The result will be that total physical distribution costs will be minimized. At no time will the established level of customer service be sacrified. By thinking in terms of the cost trade-offs shown in Figure 18-1, management should minimize the total of these costs rather than attempt to minimize the cost of each component.

For example, the Gillette Company, the world's largest producer of safety razors, was faced with an ever expanding assortment of products due to its expansion into a broad range of toiletry products. To produce good customer service, Gillette shipped by air freight, but this proved to be very expensive. Through a detailed study of its distribution system, Gillette discovered that its problem was inefficient order processing. By simplifying the paperwork involved, it was able to reduce the time required to process new orders. Gillette was then able to return to lower-cost surface transportation and still meet previous delivery schedules. The cost trade-off here was that the order-processing costs *increased* and transportation costs *decreased*, and the net result was that total logistics costs decreased.

*The integration of these three basic concepts — the total-cost approach, the avoidance of suboptimization, and the use of cost tradeoffs—forms what is commonly referred to as the physical distribution concept.* It should be noted that the real uniqueness of the physical distribution concept is not in the individual functions, since each function is performed anyway. Rather, it stems from the integration of all of these functions into a unified whole, the objective of which is providing an established level of customer service at the lowest possible distribution costs.

---

**Organizational Considerations**   The integration of these functions into a unified system is a very difficult organizational problem. In most companies that have not yet recognized the physical distribution concept, logistics functions are dispersed throughout the company. Figure 18-2 illustrates how physical distribution objectives might conflict in a typical company.

[7] James M. Daley and Zarrell V. Lambert, "Toward Assessing Trade-Offs by Shippers in Carrier Selection Decisions," *Journal of Business Logistics*, vol. 2, no. 1 (1980), pp. 35–54.

**Figure 18-1   Cost Trade-offs Required in a Physical Distribution System**

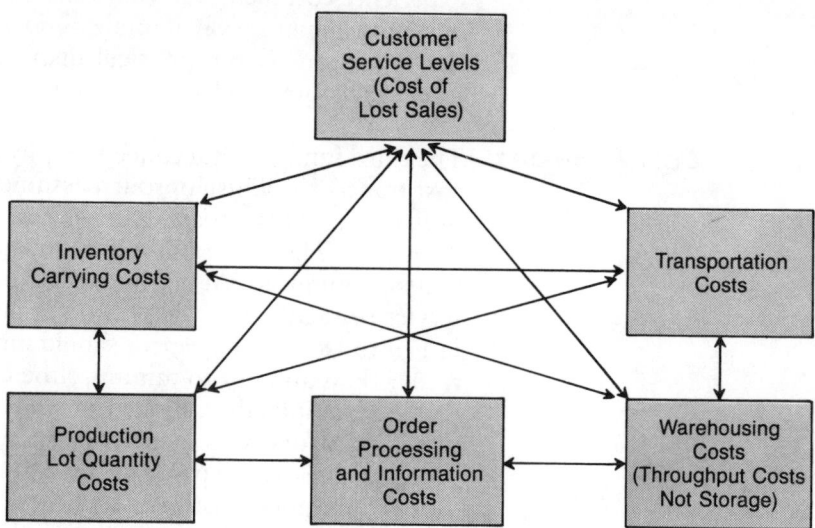

Objective:   Minimize Total Costs

Total Costs =   Transportation Costs + Warehousing Costs + Order Processing and
Information Costs + Production Lot Quantity Costs + Inventory
Carrying Costs + Cost of Lost Sales

Source: Douglas Lambert and Robert Quinn, "Increase Profitability by Managing the
Distribution Function," *Business Quarterly*, Spring 1981, p. 59.

Adapted from: Douglas M. Lambert, *The Development of an Inventory Costing
Methodology: A Study of the Cost Associated with Holding Inventory* (Chicago, Illinois:
The National Council of Physical Distribution Management, 1976), p. 7.

# A Case of Suboptimization

The traffic manager of a consumer goods producing company in eastern Canada was determined to reduce transport costs. Trucks were used to haul the product from the Toronto plant to a branch warehouse at a rate of 65 cents per 100 kg. By negotiating with a railroad, the traffic manager was able to get a rate of 56.1 cents per 100 kg. This 8.9 cents per 100 kg amounted to a savings of $4150 annually. The rail movement took three days, while the truck transport time was eight hours. The difference required an additional $112 500 in inventory, sufficient to cover the three additional days of lead time before an order arrived. The firm valued inventory holding costs at 15 percent per year, or an increased inventory cost of $16 900 per year. Thus, the reduced freight costs ended up costing the firm $12 750 in increased overall distribution costs. As soon as general management became aware of this situation, the firm's products were back in trucks.

Source: F. R. Denham, "Making the Physical Distribution Concept Pay Off," *Handling and Shipping* (October 1967).

**Figure 18-2   Physical Distribution Organization in a Typical Manufacturing Company**

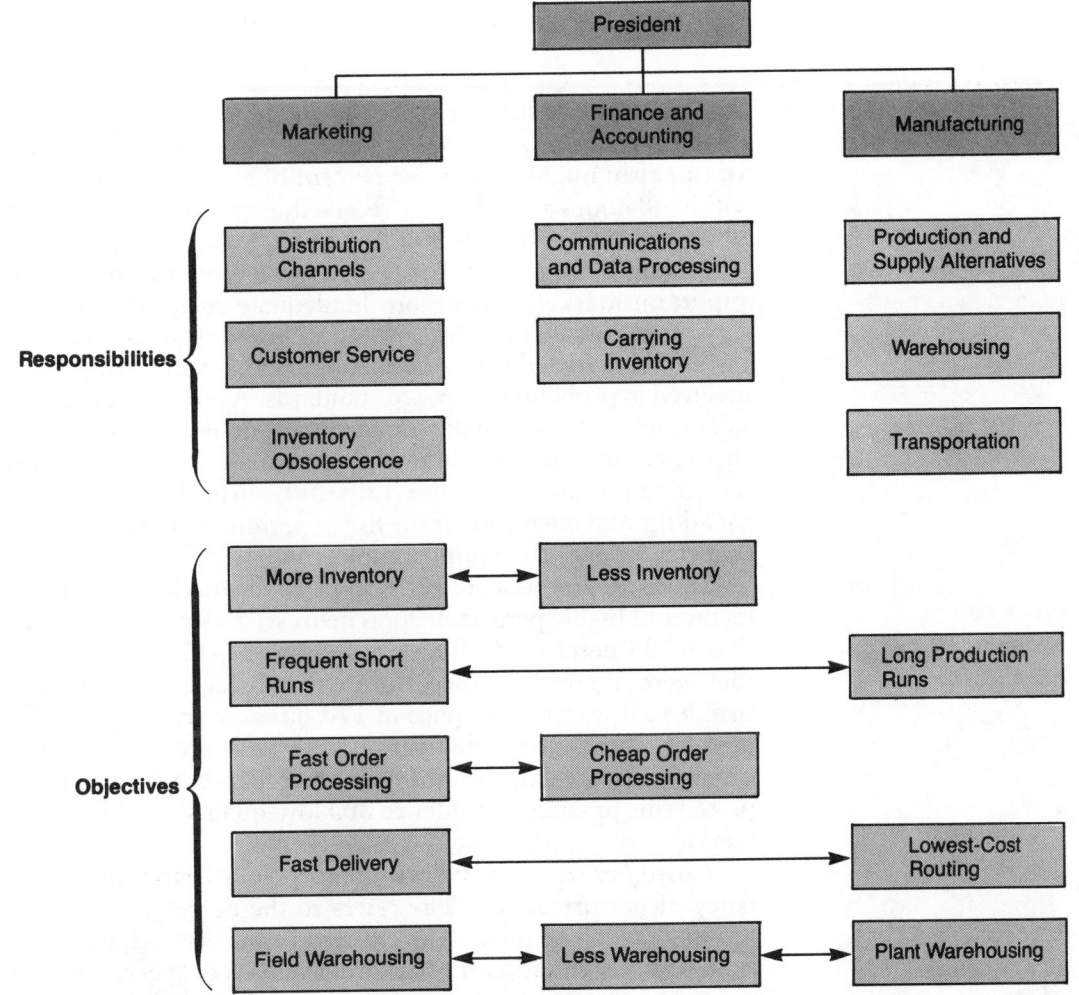

Unifying the physical distribution activities involves shifting functions from the other departments to form the new logistics division. Departments are reluctant to give up their jurisdiction over procedures. Too often when a new physical distribution department is finally established, the traffic manager receives the new title of director of physical distribution but in effect does little more than he or she previously did. Senior management must take the necessary or-

ganizational steps to see that enough power is given to the physica
distribution manager to make the appropriate changes within th
system. It must be clearly recognized that *some* costs may increas
in order to decrease the cost of physical distribution in total.

## Customer Service Standards

Customer service standards are *the quality of service that the firm'
customers will receive*. For example, a customer service standard
for one firm might be that 60 percent of all orders will be shipped
within 48 hours after they are received, 90 percent in 72 hours, and
all orders within 96 hours.

Setting the standards for customer service to be provided is an
important marketing decision. Inadequate customer service levels
may mean dissatisfied customers and loss of future sales.

Physical distribution departments must delineate the costs
involved in providing proposed standards. A conflict may arise when
sales representatives make unreasonable delivery promises to their
customers in order to obtain sales. In many cases such customer
service requirements are so costly to the firm, because of the need
for additional inventory or the use of premium-cost transportation,
that the orders prove unprofitable.

In an attempt to increase its share of the market, a major manufacturer of highly perishable food items set a 98 percent service level;
that is, 98 percent of all orders were to be shipped the same day
they were received. To meet this extremely high level of service, the
firm leased warehouse space in 170 different towns and cities and
kept large stocks in each location. The large inventories, however,
often meant the shipment of dated merchandise. Customers interpreted this practice as evidence of a low-quality product — or poor
"service."[8]

Customer service standards must include both time and consistency of performance. *Time* refers to the percentage of customer
orders that can be filled from existing inventory and the amount of
time between the receipt of an order and its delivery. *Performance
consistency* refers to the organization's dependability in meeting
delivery schedules; in shipping the right amount and type of
merchandise, damage-free; and in following special instructions.[9]
Figure 18-3 indicates specific objectives that might be developed
for each factor involved in customer service. It also illustrates the
importance of co-ordinating order processing, transportation, in-

---

[8] Robert E. Sabath, "How Much Service Do Customers Really Want?" *Business
Horizons* (April 1978), pp. 26–32. See also Philip B. Schary and Martin
Christopher, "The Anatomy of a Stock-Out," *Journal of Retailing* (Summer
1979), pp. 59–70.

[9] David T. Kollat, Roger D. Blackwell, and James F. Robeson, *Strategic
Marketing* (New York: Holt, Rinehart and Winston, 1972), p. 315.

**Figure 18-3 Customer Service Standards**

| Service Factor | Objectives |
| --- | --- |
| Order-Cycle Time | To develop a physical distribution system capable of effecting delivery of the product within eight days from the initiation of a customer order:<br>• transmission of order — one day<br>• order processing (order entry, credit verification, picking, and packing) — three days<br>• delivery — four days. |
| Dependability of Delivery | To ensure that 95 percent of all deliveries will be made within the eight-day standard and that under no circumstances will deliveries be made earlier than six days nor later than nine days from the initiation of an order. |
| Inventory Levels | To maintain inventories of finished goods at levels that will permit:<br>• 97 percent of all incoming orders for class A items to be filled<br>• 85 percent of all incoming orders for class B items to be filled<br>• 70 percent of all incoming orders for class C items to be filled. |
| Accuracy in Order Filling | To be capable of filling customer orders with 99 percent accuracy. |
| Damage in Transit | To ensure that damage to merchandise in transit does not exceed 1 percent. |
| Communications | To maintain a communication system that permits salespersons to transmit orders on a daily basis and that is capable of accurately responding to customer inquiries on order status within four hours. |

Source: David T. Kollat, Roger D. Blackwell, and James F. Robeson, *Strategic Marketing* (New York: Holt, Rinehart and Winston, 1972), p. 316. Copyright © 1972 by Holt, Rinehart and Winston, Inc. Reprinted by permission of Holt, Rinehart and Winston, Inc.

ventory control, and the other components of the physical distribution system in achieving these service standards.

**Physical Distribution System Components**

The establishment of acceptable levels of customer service provides the physical distribution department with a standard by which actual operations may be compared. The physical distribution system should be designed to achieve these standards by minimizing the total costs of the following components: 1) transportation, 2) warehouses and their location, 3) order processing, 4) inventory control, and 5) materials handling. Relative costs for major components are illustrated in Figure 18-4.

Figure 18-4   Relative Costs of Physical Distribution Components

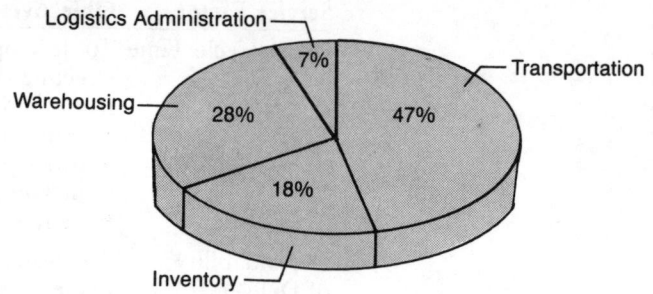

Source: Andrew M. Schell and Jim Heuer, "Creating a PD Strategy For a Rebounding Economy," *Canadian Transportation and Distribution Management* (November 1983), p. 79.

## Transportation Considerations[10]

The transportation system of Canada is a regulated industry, much like the phone and electricity industries. In fact, the courts have often referred to the transport modes as public utilities. The federal government plays a twofold role in affecting transportation services. One is promotional, to ensure growth and development of the transportation appropriate to need; the other is regulatory. This includes economic regulation of rates and services and the application of technical regulations to meet safety requirements. The National Transportation Act defines a national transportation policy for Canada with a view to achieving maximum efficiency in all available modes of transportation at the lowest cost. (Whether this is being accomplished is highly arguable.) The Act established the Canadian Transport Commission (CTC) to be responsible for the air, rail, pipeline, and inland water components of the transportation industry. In the case of road transport, the federal government establishes motor vehicle safety standards, and other regulation of motor vehicle activities is controlled by provincial and territorial governments.

In general, the purpose of the Act is to develop the industry while protecting the public against excessive or discriminatory charges.

## Rate Determination

One of the most difficult problems facing the physical distribution manager when choosing a transportation service is determining the correct rate or cost of the service. The complexity is related to **tariffs** — the *price lists that are used to determine shipping charges*. There are hundreds of these tariff books. Rate regulation in Canada provides only formulas for minimum and maximum rates. The wide range inside these limits is left to the private managements of the

[10] *Canada Year Book 1976/77* (Ottawa: Statistics Canada, 1977), pp. 731–732.

modal carriers. The manager must find the proper mixture of value of service and cost of service considerations, a mixture that recognizes all the varying conditions that can be found in the operation of the competing modal carriers.[11] Fortunately, physical distribution managers only have to master the rate system for the range of goods handled by their own firms. Consequently, they may avoid wading through the total tariff maze.

There are two basic freight rates: class and commodity. Of the two rates, the class rate is the higher. The **class non-carload rate** is *the standard rate that is found for every commodity moving between any two destinations*. The **commodity rate** is sometimes called a special rate, since it is *given by carriers to shippers as a reward for either regular use or large-quantity shipments*. It is used extensively by the railways and the inland water carriers.

*Classes of Carriers*     Freight carriers are classified as common, contract, and private. **Common carriers** have been called the "backbone" of the transportation industry. They are *for-hire carriers that serve the general public*. Their rates and services are regulated, and they cannot conduct their operations without the appropriate regulatory authority's permission. Common carriers exist for all the modes of transport.

**Contract carriers** are *for-hire transporters that do not offer their services to the general public*. Instead they establish specific contracts with certain customers and operate exclusively for the industry. Most contract carriers operate in the motor freight industry. These carriers are subject to much less regulation than the common carriers.

**Private carriers** are not for-hire carriers. *The operators only transport products for a particular firm* and may not solicit other transportation business. Since transportation is solely for the carrier's own use, there is no rate-of-service regulation.

*Transportation Alternatives*     The physical distribution manager has five major transportation alternatives. These are railways, trucking, water carriers, pipelines, and air freight. Figure 18-5 compares the major modes according to their operating revenues and freight tonnage shares of major bulk carriers. Trucking has gradually gained in share of tonnage at the expense of both water and rail.

Railways — The Backbone of the Industry     The largest transporter (as measured by tonne-kilometres of freight[12]) continues to be the railways. They are one of the most efficient modes for the movem,ent of bulk commodities over long distances.

---

11 See H. L. Purdy, *Transport Competition and Public Policy in Canada* (Vancouver: University of British Columbia Press, 1972), p. 95.
12 A tonne-kilometre is defined as 1 t of freight moving 1 km. Thus a 3 t shipment moved 8 km would be 24 t/k.

## Figure 18-5   The Major Modes of Transportation

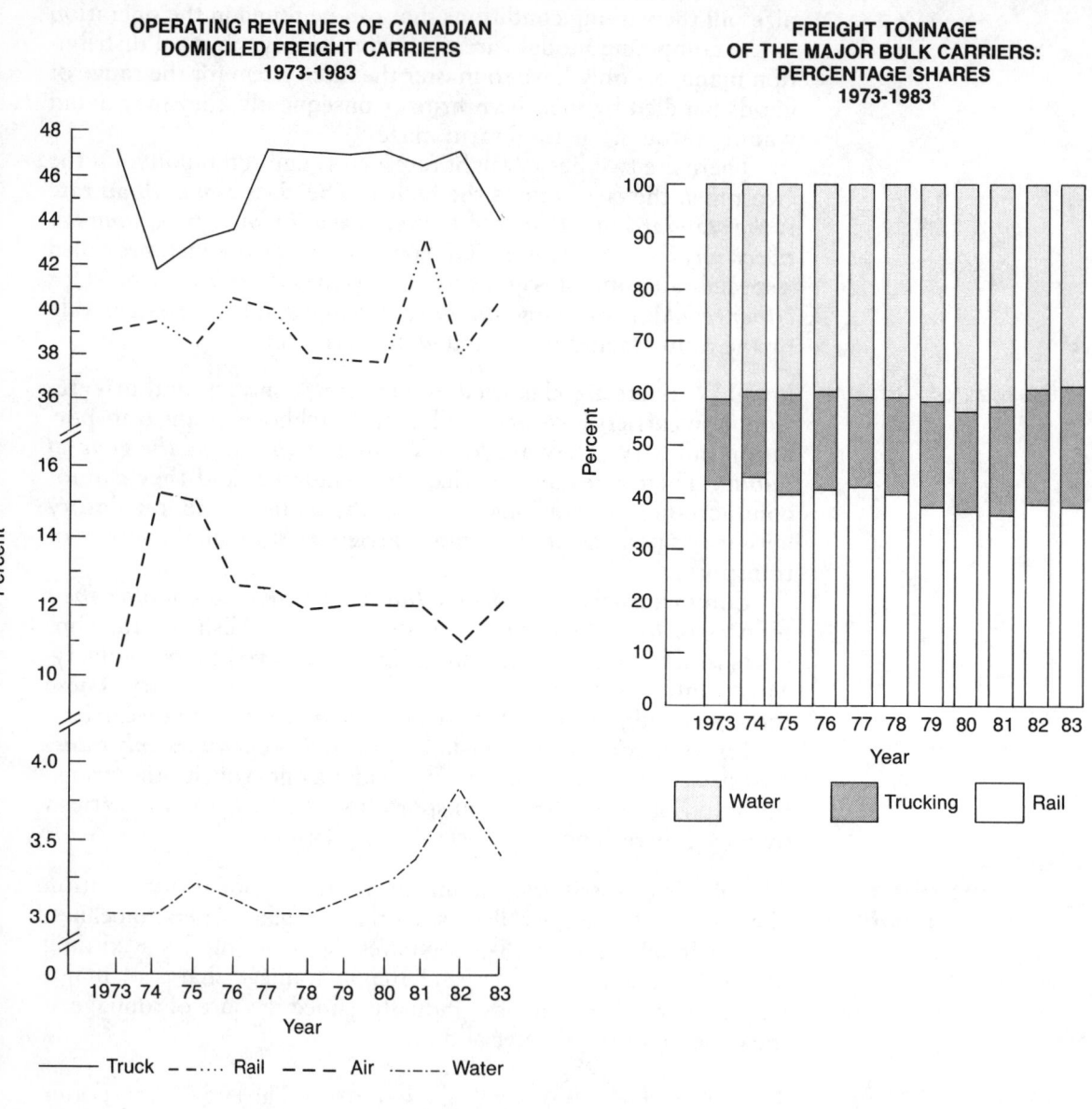

Source: *Transport Review* (Ottawa: Canadian Transport Commission, 1985), pp. 9, 10.

The railways have launched a drive in recent years to improve their service standards and capture a larger percentage of manufactured and other higher-value products. To reach their improved service standards, they have introduced a number of innovations. One is called *ACI (Automatic Car Identification)*. All rail cars and locomotives are equipped with a 13-line reflective label. The railway companies have positioned hundreds of scanners throughout Canada that can interpret these labels as they pass by at speeds as high as 130 km/h. These scanners "read" the labels and report to a central computer the car number and the name of the railway, allowing each railway to tell its customers at all times the exact location and status of their shipments.

Railways are also making extensive use of unit trains to provide time and cost savings for their customers. A unit train is used exclusively by a single customer who negotiates lower rates for its shipments. Specially designed single-usage unit trains are operated by Canadian National to haul coal for Japanese steel companies. The railway hauls a trainload of coal from interior British Columbia to the Roberts Bank Seaport, Vancouver, and then returns empty for another run, providing rapid low-cost transport. In Ontario, a unit train carries iron ore pellets from Temagami to a Hamilton steel mill, with cars loading from silos in 30 seconds and unloading over furnace bins in 60 seconds.

The Canadian railway system is showing transporters how to apply the marketing concept. It is stressing improved service to its shippers. In response to the need for a more efficient method of transporting various commodities, specialized new rail cars of different configurations have been designed. Most of us recognize the yellow and brown tubular cars used to haul the millions of tonnes of grain Canada exports annually. The new car has lowered the shipping costs significantly, since fewer steps in loading and unloading are required.

Motor Carriers — Flexible and Growing   The trucking industry has shown dramatic growth over recent decades. Its prime advantage over other modes is relatively fast, consistent service, for both large and small shipments. For this reason truckers concentrate on manufactured products, as opposed to the railways, which haul more bulk products and raw materials. Truckers, therefore, receive greater revenue per tonne shipped as compared to the railways (9 cents per tonne-kilometre to the railway's 3.3 cents in a recent year). In 1983, for-hire motor carriers accounted for 44 percent of the total operating revenues of all Canadian domiciled freight carriers (Figure 18-5).

Trucking's primary appeal to shippers is superior service, and the industry is working diligently to maintain this advantage. The Kwikasair trucking company is currently running schedules that just a few years ago would have seemed impossible. At one time it took seven to 10 days for a coast-to-coast truckload shipment. Kwikasair Express now offers three-day service between Montreal or Toronto and Vancouver.

Water Carriers — Slow but Cheap   There are basically two types of water carriers — the inland or barge lines and the ocean deep-water ships. Barge lines are very efficient transporters of bulk commodities.

Ocean-going ships operate on the Great Lakes, between Canadian port cities, and in international commerce. The international water freight bill for 1981 was $633 million, with domestic water transport billings totalling $634 million.[13]

Pipelines — One-Way Transporters   Even though the pipeline industry is second only to the railways in number of tonne-kilometres transported, many people are barely aware of its existence. Pipelines serve one-way traffic, making them extremely efficient transporters of natural gas and oil products. They are highly automated and involve low labour costs, as is demonstrated by the fact that they can turn a profit on an average revenue per tonne-kilometre of a little less than 0.2 cents. Oil pipelines haul two types of commodities: crude (unprocessed) oil and refined products, such as gasoline and kerosene. A second generation of pipeline is the "slurry" pipeline, where a product such as coal is ground up into a powder, mixed with water, and transported in suspension. A third generation will carry capsules that could contain a variety of products in a liquid medium.

Air Freight — Fast but Expensive   The use of air freight has been growing significantly. In 1973 Canadian airlines carried about 0.78 billion tonne-kilometres. By 1983, this figure had increased to 1.1 billion tonne-kilometres. However, air freight is still a relatively small percentage of the total tonne-kilometres shipped.

Because of air freight's relatively high cost, it is used primarily for very valuable or highly perishable products. Typical products include watches, computers, furs, fresh flowers, high-fashion clothing, and live lobsters. Air carriers market their services effectively by stressing that firms can offset the higher transportation costs with reduced inventory holding costs and faster customer service.

Figure 18-6 ranks the five transport modes on several bases.[14]

---

[13] *Water Transportation* (Ottawa: Statistics Canada, 1981), Catalogue 54-205.
[14] For a discussion of how alternative transportation methods are evaluated, see Michael A. McGinnis, "Segmenting Freight Markets," *Transportation Journal* (Fall 1978), pp. 58–68. See also Michael A. McGinnis and Thomas M. Carsi, "Are the Modes Really Competitive?" *Distribution Worldwide* (September 1979), pp. 39–41.

Figure 18-6    Comparing the Transport Modes

| Factor | Rank | | | | |
|---|---|---|---|---|---|
| | 1 | 2 | 3 | 4 | 5 |
| Speed | Air carriers | Motor carriers | Railways | Water carriers | Pipelines |
| Dependability in meeting schedules | Pipelines | Motor carriers | Railways | Water carriers | Air carriers |
| Cost | Water carriers | Pipelines | Railways | Motor carriers | Air carriers |
| Frequency of shipments | Pipelines | Motor carriers | Air carriers | Railways | Water carriers |
| Availability in different locations | Motor carriers | Railways | Air carriers | Water carriers | Pipelines |
| Flexibility in handling products | Water carriers | Railways | Motor carriers | Air carriers | Pipelines |

Source: Based on a discussion in James L. Heskitt, Nicholas A. Glaskowsky, Jr., and Robert M. Ivie, *Business Logistics* (New York: Ronald Press, 1973), pp. 113-118. Used with permission.

**Freight Forwarders — Transportation Intermediaries**    Since their function is to *consolidate shipments*, **freight forwarders** can be considered *transportation intermediaries*. They do this because the transport rates on LTL (less than truckload) and LCL (less than carload) shipments are significantly higher, on a per-unit basis, than on TL (truckload) and CL (carload) shipments. Freight forwarders consolidate shipments and charge their customers a rate per unit that is less than the LTL or LCL rate but greater than the TL or CL. They receive their profits by paying the TL or CL rate to the carriers. The advantage to the shipper, in addition to lower costs on small shipments, is faster delivery service than LTL and LCL shipments receive.[15]

**Supplemental Carriers**    The physical distribution manager also has available a number of auxiliary or supplemental carriers that specialize in the transportation of relatively small shipments. These include bus freight service and the post office.

**Intermodal Co-ordination**    Transport modes often combine their services to give the shipper the service and cost advantages of each mode. The most widely accepted form of intermodal co-ordination is *piggyback*. This technique involves placing the entire highway

---

15 For an interesting discussion of the current state of the art in freight forwarding, see Jim Dixon, "Which Way for Forwarders?" *Distribution Worldwide* (June 1975), pp. 39–42.

trailer on a rail flatcar and performing the majority of the intercity movement via the railway. The pickup and delivery of the shipment is performed by the motor carrier involved.

The combination of truck and rail service generally provides the shipper with both faster service and lower rates, since trucks are used where they are most efficient, for pickup and delivery, and the rails are used where they are best suited, as high-volume transporters of bulk shipments. Shipper acceptance of piggybacking has been tremendous. In 1960 fewer than 11 000 piggyback rail cars were shipped. By 1977 more than 240 000 cars were involved.

Another form of intermodal co-ordination is motor carriers with air carriers, called *birdyback*. Again, the truckers perform the pickup and delivery and the air carriers perform the long haul. In addition, truckers, railways, and water carriers have developed a form of intermodal co-ordination called *fishyback*. In fact, ferries are used for most goods moving to and from Newfoundland, Prince Edward Island, and Vancouver Island.

---

**Warehousing**

Two types of warehouses exist: storage warehouses and distribution warehouses. **Storage warehouses** store products for moderate to long periods of time in an attempt *to balance supply and demand* for producers and purchasers. They are used most often by firms whose products are seasonal in supply or demand.

**Distribution warehouses** are designed *to assemble and then redistribute products*. The object is to keep the products on the move as much as possible. Many distribution warehouses or centres achieve their operational objective of having the goods in the warehouse less than one day.

To save transportation costs, manufacturers have developed central distribution centres. A manufacturer in Kitchener, Ontario, with customers in Manitoba, Saskatchewan, and Alberta could send each customer a direct shipment. But since each places small orders, the transportation charges for the individual shipments are relatively high. A feasible solution is to use a "break-bulk" centre, probably Regina in this case. (See Figure 18-7.) A *consolidated shipment may be sent to such a central distribution centre, and then smaller shipments made* for delivery to the individual customers in the area. Such centres are known as **break-bulk warehouses**.

Another type of distribution centre *brings together shipments from various points or sources going to one point and consolidates these into one shipment* — the **make-bulk centre**. For example, a giant retailer such as Safeway Stores may have several satellite production facilities in a given area. Each production plant can send shipments to a storage warehouse in Calgary. However, this again would result in an excessive number of small, expensive shipments.

**Figure 18-7  Break-Bulk and Make-Bulk Centres**

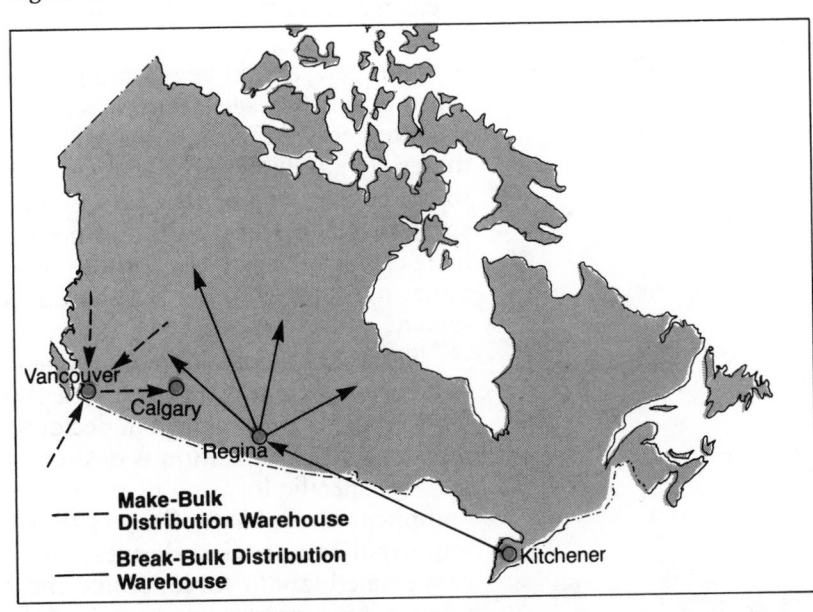

Therefore, a make-bulk distribution centre is created in Vancouver, as illustrated in Figure 18-7. Each supplier sends its shipment to the Vancouver make-bulk point, and all shipments bound for Calgary are consolidated into more economical shipments.

**Automated Warehouses**  Warehouses lend themselves exceptionally well to automation, with the computer as the heart of the operation. An outstanding example of the automated warehouse of the future is the Aerojet-General Industrial Systems Division warehouse in Frederick, Maryland. This huge warehouse is operated entirely by a single employee who gives instructions to the facility's governing computer. The computer operates the fully automated materials handling system and also generates all the necessary forms.[16]

Although automated warehouses may cost as much as $10 million, they can provide major savings to such high-volume distributors as grocery chains. Some current systems can select 10 000 to 300 000 cases per day of up to 3000 different items. They can "read" computerized store orders, choose the correct number of cases, then move them in the desired sequence to loading docks. Such ware-

---

16 The Ultimate in Automation," *Transportation and Distribution Management* (January 1970), p. 38. See also Kenneth B. Ackerman and Bernard J. Lalonde, "Making Warehousing More Efficient," *Harvard Business Review* (March–April 1980), pp. 94–102.

houses reduce labour costs, worker injuries, pilferage, fires, and breakage and assist in inventory control.

**Location Factors**   A major decision that each company must make is the number and location of its storage facilities. While this is a very complex question, the two general factors involved are the costs of warehousing and materials handling and the costs of delivery from the warehouse to the customer. The first set of costs are subject to economies of scale; therefore, their cost, on a per-unit basis, decreases as volume increases. Delivery costs, on the other hand, increase as the distance increases from the warehouse location to the customer to be served.

These cost items are diagrammed in Figure 18-8. The asterisk in Figure 18-8 marks the ideal area of coverage for each warehouse. This model is a useful tool in deciding the proper number of warehouses if decentralization is desired.

The specific location of the firm's warehouses is another very complicated problem. Factors that must be considered include municipal and provincial taxes; laws and regulations; availability of a trained labour force; police and fire protection; access to the various transport modes; attitude of the community toward the proposed warehouse; and the cost and availability of public utilities such as electricity and natural gas.

**Figure 18-8   Factors Influencing the Number of Warehouses**

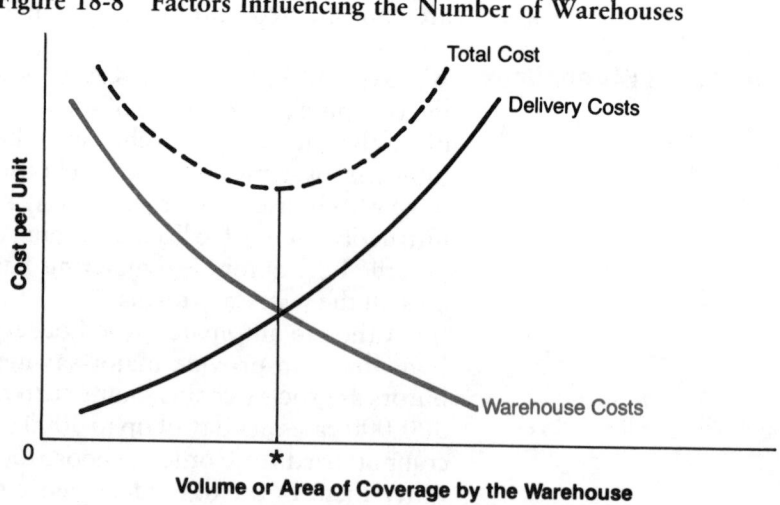

**Order Processing**   Like customer service standards, order processing is a logistics-type function. The physical distribution manager is concerned with order

# The Japanese View Inventory as "SIN"

The Japanese have perhaps come to grips with the true costs of inventory better than other industrial nations. Their view of inventory as "sin" reflects the pervasiveness and high cost of inventories. As a result, they have developed the Kan-ban or "just-in-time" method of distribution and inventory management. In essence, the system reduces stock levels to peak efficiency minimums through careful control of inbound materials. Here is an example of the effects of a reduction in inventories by a Japanese firm.

A Strategic Plan to Reduce Inventories.
Example of Operations Strategy in Japan:
Tokyo Sanyo Electric (Household Refrigerators)

1. Direction set by top management (1975)
   "Inventory covers many sins—inventory levels must be reduced significantly"
2. Actions taken
   Standardization of parts and components by marketing and engineering

Vendor deliveries 1–4 times/day, not 1–4 times/month
Development of mixed model assembly line for lower volume models
Reduction of setup/changeover times through equipment and procedures modifications
Smaller lot sizes/more frequent runs (daily or every other day)
Elimination of warehouse space
Discipline and commitment to the policy throughout operations and over time

3. Results achieved

|                               | 1975      | 1980    |
|-------------------------------|-----------|---------|
| WAREHOUSE SPACE (m²)          | 7500      | 1850    |
| INVENTORY LEVELS              |           |         |
| (raw and in-process)          | 10 DAYS   | 1.5 DAYS |
| PRODUCTION LOT SIZES          | 2–3 DAYS  | 1 DAY   |
| PRODUCTION QUANTITIES         |           |         |
| (index)                       | 100       | 300     |
| PRODUCTION MODELS             | 120       | 350     |
| PRODUCTION                    |           |         |
| COMPONENTS (index)            | 100       | 50      |

Source: Adapted from Robert Britney, "Productivity and Inventory Turnover: How High is High Enough?" *Business Quarterly* (Spring, 1982), and Steven Wheelwright, "Operations As Strategy Lessons From Japan," *Stanford Graduate School of Business* (Fall, 1981–82).

processing because it directly affects the firm's ability to meet its customer service standards. If a firm's order processing system is inefficient, the company may have to compensate by using costly premium transportation or increasing the number of field warehouses in all major markets.

Order processing typically consists of four major activities: a credit check; recording the sale, such as crediting a sales representative's commission account; making the appropriate accounting entries; and locating the item, shipping, and adjusting inventory records. *An item that is not available for shipment* is known as a **stock-out**, which requires the order-processing unit to advise the customer of the situation and of the action the company plans to take.[17]

[17]Based on James C. Johnson and Donald F. Wood, *Contemporary Physical Distribution and Logistics*, 2nd ed. (Tulsa, Okla.: Penn Well Books, 1982), p. 66.

**Inventory Control**    Inventories have been referred to as the "graveyard of Canadian
**Systems**    businesses." This title is earned because this aspect of business is
often regarded as unimportant, and therefore it is basically ignored
— *with deadly results*.

What many managers fail to realize is the significant expense
involved in holding inventory over a period of time. Most current
estimates of inventory holding costs are 25 percent per year. This
means that $1000 of inventory held for a single year costs the com-
pany $250. Inventory costs include such expenses as storage facilities,
insurance, taxes, transportation, handling costs, depreciation, lost
interest opportunities, and possible obsolescence of the goods in
inventory.[18]

**Figure 18-9   The EOQ Model**

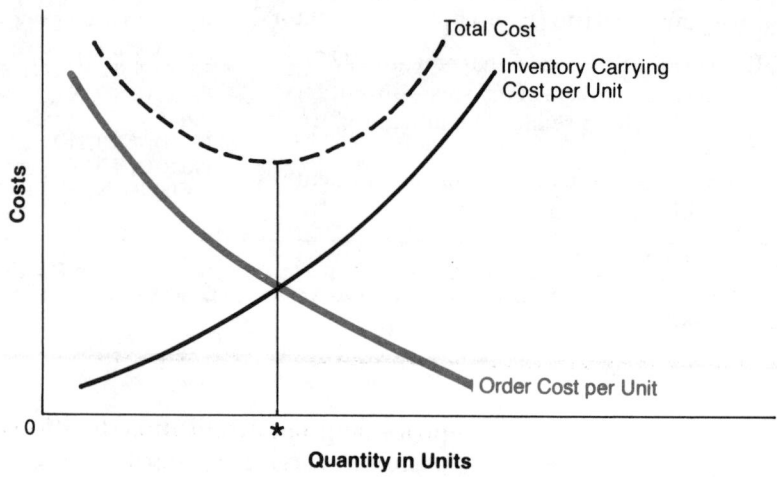

Inventory control analysts have developed a number of techniques that aid the physical distribution manager in effectively controlling inventory. The most basic is the **EOQ** (**economic order
quantity**) **model**. This technique *emphasizes a cost trade-off between
two fundamental costs involved with inventory. Inventory holding
costs* increase with the addition of more inventory. *Order costs*, those
involved in placing an order, decrease as the quantity ordered
increases. As Figure 18-9 indicates, these two cost items are then
"traded off" to determine the optimum order quantity of each
product.

---

[18] The impact of effective inventory control systems on company profitability is
discussed in Lewis Beman, "A Big Payoff from Inventory Controls," *Fortune*
(July 27, 1981), pp. 76–80.

The EOQ point in Figure 18-9 is the point at which total cost is minimized. By placing an order for this amount as needed, firms can minimize inventory cost.

**How the EOQ Is Calculated**   The size of the investment in inventory has prompted managers to develop scientific methods of determining the correct balance between the costs of holding goods available in inventory and order costs. The following formula has been developed for determining the economic order quantity:

$$EOQ = \sqrt{\frac{2RS}{1C}}$$

where EOQ = the economic order quantity (in units)
       R = the annual rate of usage
       S = the cost of placing an order
       I = the annual inventory carrying cost percentage
       C = the cost per unit

In the above formula, R is an estimate based upon the demand forecast for the item. S is calculated from the firm's cost records. I is also an estimate, based upon the costs of such items as depreciation, handling, insurance, interest, storage, and taxes. Since the costs of the item may vary over time, C is also likely to be an estimate. By inserting specific data into the formula, the EOQ can be determined. Consider, for example, the following data:

$$R = 5500 \text{ units}$$
$$S = \$7.50$$
$$I = 20 \text{ percent}$$
$$C = \$12.90$$

$$EOQ = \sqrt{\frac{(2)\,(5500)\,(7.50)}{(.20)\,(12.90)}}$$
$$= 178.82$$

Although the EOQ has been calculated at approximately 179 units, other factors should be taken into account. Truckload or railway carload shipments may consist of 200 units. In certain instances, the purchasing firm may discover that the units are shipped in special containers consisting of 175 units. In such cases, the EOQ may be adjusted to match these conditions and an order for 175 or 200 units, rather than the calculated 179 units, may be placed.

Once the EOQ has been determined, specific re-order points are determined by considering such factors as the lead time required for receiving an order once it has been placed and the average daily demand. If the necessary lead time is seven days and average daily sales consist of five units, orders must be placed when the available inventory reaches 35 units. Since demand may fluctuate, most organizations add a certain amount of inventory called *safety stock* to compensate for such demand fluctuations. In the above instance, a predetermined safety stock of five units would mean that new orders would be placed when the inventory level drops to 40 units.

Managers use the EOQ as a powerful tool in making rational decisions about inventory. Additionally, the EOQ has become a widely used technique as managers attempt to minimize the costs of ordering and maintaining inventory.

## Materials Handling Systems

All of the activities associated in *moving products among the manufacturer's plants, warehouses, and transportation company terminals* are called **materials handling**. The materials handling system must be thoroughly co-ordinated, for both intra- and intercompany activities. The efficiency of plants and warehouses is dependent on an effective system.[19]

Two important innovations have developed in the area of materials handling. One is known as **unitizing** — *combining as many packages as possible into one load*, preferably on a pallet. A pallet is a standard-size platform, generally made of wood, on which products are transported. It is designed to be lifted by forklift trucks. Utilizing can be done by using steel bands to hold the unit in place or by shrink packaging. Shrink packages are constructed by placing a sheet of plastic over the unit and then heating it so that when it cools, the plastic shrinks and holds the individual packages securely together. Unitizing has the advantages of requiring less labour per package, promoting faster movements, and reducing damage and pilferage.

The second innovation is **containerization**, the *combination of several unitized loads*. A container is typically a box 2.4 m wide, 2.4 m high, and 3, 6, 9, or 12 m in length. Such containers allow ease of intertransport mode changes. Thus, a container of oil rig parts could be loaded in Edmonton, sent by high-speed through-train to Montreal, and then on to Saudi Arabia by sea.

Containerization markedly reduces the time involved in loading and unloading ships. Container ships can often be unloaded in less than 24 hours — a task otherwise requiring up to two weeks. In-transit damage has also been reduced since individual packages are not handled en route to the purchaser, and pilferage is greatly reduced.

---

[19] For a discussion of materials handling innovations, see "Materials Handling Trends: One Expert's Viewpoint," *Traffic Management* (March 1981), pp. 36–38.

**International Physical
Distribution**

Canada has experienced rapid growth in international trade since World War II. In 1982 Canadian merchandise exports totalled approximately $81.4 billion, of which manufactured goods accounted for $56.7 billion, crude products and fuels another $14.8 billion, and food, beverages, and tobacco approximately $9.9 billion. Total imports for 1981 amounted to 67.4 billion.[20] This unparalleled growth of international commerce has placed new responsibilities on many firms' physical distribution departments.

A major problem facing international marketers is the pile of paperwork involved in exporting products. Over a hundred different international trade documents representing more than a thousand separate forms must be completed for each international shipment. As a result, documentation for the average export shipment requires approximately 36 employee-hours; for the average import shipment, it is 27 employee-hours. Paperwork alone now accounts for approximately 7 percent of the total value of Canadian international trade.[21] Many physical distribution departments are not large enough to employ international specialists to deal with these complexities, so this work is subcontracted to *foreign freight forwarders*, wholesaling intermediaries who specialize in physical distribution outside Canada.

A significant facilitating factor for the export business has been the advent of containerization and container ships. Shipping companies now use container ships that can make a round trip between Halifax, Bremerhaven, and Rotterdam in 14 days. Only four days are needed for each crossing of the Atlantic, and another six for the three port calls.[22] This speed allows Canadian exporters to provide competitive delivery schedules to European markets.

The largest volume of our shipments, however, still comprises agricultural products and raw materials (lumber and minerals). The importance of these basic commodities to Canada has resulted in specialized, complex systems at various ports for handling them.

**Summary**

Physical distribution, as a system, consists of six elements: 1) customer service, 2) transportation, 3) inventory control, 4) materials handling, 5) order processing, and 6) warehousing. These elements are interrelated and must be balanced for a smoothly functioning distribution system. The physical distribution department is one of the classic examples of the systems approach to business problems. Three basic concepts of the systems approach — the total-cost

20 *Summary of External Trade*, Statistics Canada Catalogue 65-001, 1982.
21 "Reducing Paperwork," *Transportation and Distribution Management* (November 1971), p. 15.
22 Robert L. Dausend, "Containerization—Stimulus to World Trade," *Transportation and Distribution Management* (January 1972), pp. 15–16.

approach, the avoidance of suboptimization, and cost trade-offs—combine to form the physical distribution concept.

The goal of a physical distribution department is to produce a specified level of customer service while minimizing the costs involved in physically moving and storing the product from its production point to the point where it is ultimately purchased.

The physical distribution manager has available five transportation alternatives: railways, motor carriers, water carriers, pipelines, and air freight. In addition, intermodal transport systems are available and increasingly used.

Other elements of the physical distribution department include warehousing and warehouse location, inventory control systems, materials handling systems, customer service standards, and order processing. Efficient international physical distribution allows a firm to compete more effectively in foreign markets.

Physical distribution, by its very nature, involves keeping track of thousands of details, such as transport rates, inventory locations, and customer locations. The computer is a necessary and invaluable tool for the logistics manager.

### Key Terms

| | |
|---|---|
| physical distribution | freight forwarder |
| total-cost approach | storage warehouse |
| suboptimization | distribution warehouse |
| cost trade-offs | break-bulk centre |
| customer service standards | make-bulk centre |
| tariffs | stock-out |
| class rate | EOQ (economic order quantity) model |
| commodity rate | |
| common carrier | materials handling |
| contract carrier | unitizing |
| private carrier | containerization |

### Review Questions

1. Why was physical distribution one of the last areas in most companies to be carefully studied and improved?
2. Outline the basic reasons for the increased attention to physical distribution management.
3. What are the basic objectives of physical distribution?
4. What is the most effective organization for physical distribution management? Explain.
5. What factors should be considered in locating a new distribution warehouse?
6. Who should be ultimately responsible for determining the level of customer service standards? Explain.

7. Outline the basic strengths and weaknesses of each mode of transport.
8. Under what circumstances are freight forwarders used?
9. Identify the major forms of intermodal co-ordination and give an example of a product that is likely to use each type.
10. Determine the EOQ (economic order quantity) for the following situation:
    A firm has calculated the cost of placing orders at $4.60 per order. The annual cost of carrying the product in inventory is estimated to be 22 percent. Cost per unit estimates for the next 12 months are $8.40. Annual usage rates are estimated to be 11 500.

---

**Discussion Questions and Exercises**

1. Comment on the following statement: The popularity of physical distribution management is a fad; ten years from now it will be considered a relatively unimportant function of the firm.
2. Prepare a brief report on career opportunities in physical distribution.
3. Suggest the most appropriate method of transportation for each of the following products and defend your choices:
   a.  Iron ore                                d.  Crude oil
   b.  Dash detergent                          e.  Orchids
   c.  Heavy earth-moving equipment            f.  Lumber
4. Develop an argument for the increased use of intermodal co-ordination. Present your argument to the class.
5. Which mode of transport do you believe will experience the greatest tonne-kilometre percentage growth during the 1980s? Why?

---

**MICROCOMPUTER EXERCISE: Economic Order Quantity**

Directions:   Use the menu item titled "Economic Order Quantity (EOQ)" on the Foundations of Marketing disk to solve the following problems.

1. A Niagara Falls vendor pays $1.80 for each of the 30 000 souvenir hats he sells annually. Inventory-carrying costs are a modest 8 percent, and placing an order costs only $10. Calculate the EOQ for the vendor.

2. Space Systems Inc. of St. Catharines sells 220 home satellite-television-signal systems annually. The retailer pays an average of $600 for these units, with each order costing $25 to place. The annual inventory-carrying-cost percentage is 10 percent. What is the appropriate EOQ for Space Systems Inc.?

**3.** The owner of a Langley, B.C. sporting-goods retail store wants to calculate the EOQ for a certain line of golf clubs. The clubs cost the store $180 per set and have an average inventory-carrying cost of 12 percent. Each order costs $35. The retail store sells 200 sets of this golf-club line each year.

**a.** Determine the economic order quantity for the golf clubs.

**b.** Suggest the most appropriate order size if the manufacturer insists that orders be placed in multiples of 10 sets of clubs.

# PART

# 7

## Promotion

# Promotional Strategy

1. *To relate the communications process to promotional strategy.*

2. *To explain the concept of the promotional mix and its relationship to the marketing mix.*

3. *To indentify the primary determinants of a promotional mix.*

4. *To contrast the two major alternative promotional strategies.*

5. *To list the objectives of promotion.*

6. *To explain the primary methods of developing a promotional budget.*

7. *To defend promotion against the public criticisms that are sometimes raised.*

Effective advertising programs stake out places in our memories and can be considered as signs of the times. The slogan, "Only in Canada — pity" is an advertising theme which helped to make Red Rose tea famous. The theme was the work of John Cronin and Peter Matthews from the advertising agency J. Walter Thompson, Ltd.

Brooke Bond, the tea company whose Red Rose brew is now inextricably linked with the "only in Canada" slogan, used the Cronin-Matthews brainchild from 1970 to 1982. This is one of the longest-running campaigns in Canadian television advertising history.

Marlene Hore, JWT's Toronto-based national creative director and a Red Rose ad writer from 1975 to 1981, says the ads, comparing Red Rose to highly respected British tea, were among the first of their kind.

"Consumer research showed British tea was the gold standard, so a number of campaigns were developed to tap the Britishness of the tea," Hore says. "At the same time, we knew that Canadians did not want to be lectured about the merits of tea by David Niven or Terry Thomas."

Instead, the 1970 ads borrowed characters from the then-popular British serial, *The Forsyte Saga*, and had them test the upstart Canadian blend. Throughout the duration of the "Only in Canada" series, Hore says, the ads played on the stereotype of the stiff-upper-lipped British tea snob.

The much-lauded Red Rose ads garnered the advertising world's top prizes. Among them were Canada's Clio and Cannes' bronze advertising awards. In spite of this success, Brooke Bond have finally adopted a new slogan, "the perfect cup of tea," instead of the long-lived "pity" slogan. Explains Hore: "Times change."[1]

**The Conceptual Framework**

Red Rose tea benefited from a well-designed advertising strategy that was brought to life through ingenuity and creativity. This is the essence of successful promotion. **Promotion,** the fourth variable in the marketing mix, can be defined as *the function of informing, persuading, and influencing the consumer's purchase decision.* Figure 19-1 depicts the relationship between the firm's promotional strategy and the other elements of the overall marketing strategy in accomplishing organizational objectives and producing utility for the consumer.

The marketing manager sets the goals and objectives of the firm's promotional strategy in accordance with overall organizational objectives and the goals of the marketing organization. Then, based on these goals, the various elements of the strategy—personal selling, advertising, sales promotion, publicity, and public relations—are formulated in a co-ordinated promotion plan. This becomes an integral part of the total marketing strategy for reaching selected consumer segments. Finally, the feedback mechanism, in such forms as marketing research and field reports, closes the system by identifying any deviations from the plan and by suggesting modifications for improvement.

Promotional strategy is closely related to the process of communications. A standard definition of *communications* is the transmission of a message from a sender to a receiver. **Marketing**

**Figure 19-1   Integrating the Promotional Plan into the Total Marketing Mix**

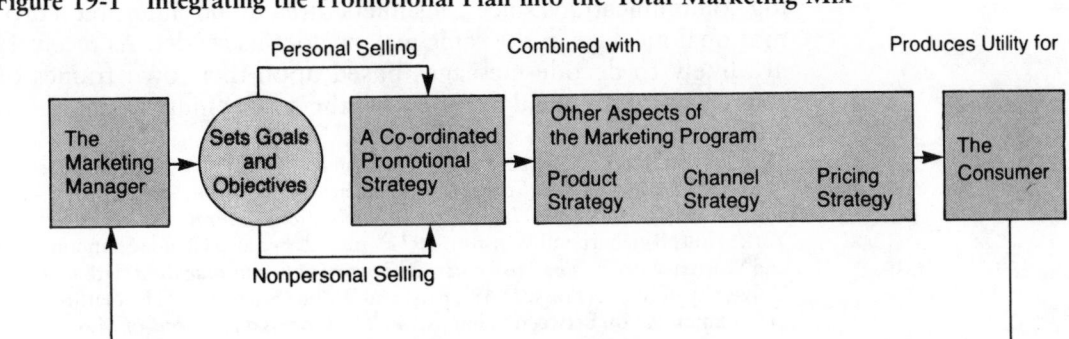

---

[1] Adapted from, "What Makes an Ad Package Stand Test of Time," *The Financial Post,* January 28, 1984, p. A13.

**communications**, then, are *those messages that deal with buyer-seller relationships*. Marketing communications is a broader term than promotional strategy since it includes word-of-mouth and other forms of unsystematic communication. A planned promotional strategy, however, is certainly the most important part of marketing communications.

| | |
|---|---|
| ***The Communications*** *** Process*** | Figure 19-2 shows a generalized communications process using terminology borrowed from radio and telecommunications.[2] The sender is the *source* of the communications system since he or she seeks to convey a *message* (a communication of information or advice or a request) to a *receiver* (the recipient of the communication). The message must accomplish three tasks in order to be effective: |

1. It must *gain the attention* of the receiver.
2. It must *be understood* by both the receiver and the sender.
3. It must *stimulate* the needs of the receiver and *suggest* an appropriate method of satisfying these needs.[3]

The message must be *encoded*, or translated into understandable terms, and transmitted through a communications medium. *Decoding* is the receiver's interpretation of the message. The receiver's response, known as *feedback*, completes the system. Throughout the process, *noise* can interfere with the transmission of the message and reduce its effectiveness.

In Figure 19-3 the marketing communications process is applied to promotional strategy. The marketing manager is the sender in the system. The message is encoded in the form of sales presentations, advertisements, displays, or publicity releases. The *transfer mechanism* for delivering the message may be a salesperson, the advertising media, or public relations channel.

The decoding step involves the consumer's interpretation of the sender's message. This is the most troublesome aspect of marketing communications since consumers often do not interpret a promotional message in the same way as does its sender. As receivers are likely to decode messages based upon their own frames of reference or individual experiences, the sender must be careful to

---

[2] Similar communication processes are suggested in David K. Berlo, *The Process of Communications* (New York: Holt, Rinehart and Winston, 1960), pp. 23–38; and Thomas S. Robertson, *Innovative Behaviour and Communication* (New York: Holt, Rinehart and Winston, 1971), p. 122. See also Claude Shannon and Warren Weaver, *The Mathematical Theory of Communication* (Urbana: University of Illinois Press, 1949), p. 5; and Wilbur Schramm, "The Nature of Communication Between Humans," in *The Process and Effects of Mass Communication*, rev. ed. (Urbana: University of Illinois Press, 1971), pp. 3–53.

[3] Wilbur Schramm, "The Nature of Communication Between Humans," in *The Process and Effects of Mass Communication*, rev. ed. (Urbana: University of Ilinois Press, 1971), pp. 3–53.

**Figure 19-2   A Generalized Communications Process**

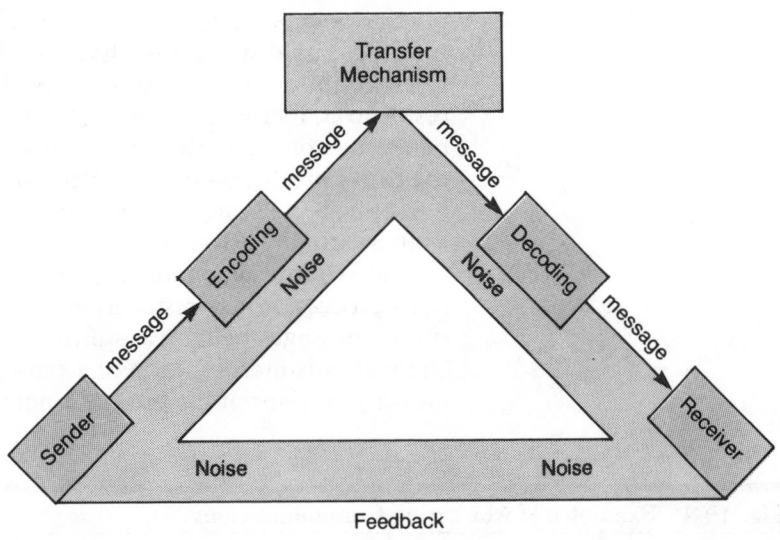

**Figure 19-3   The Process of Marketing Communications**

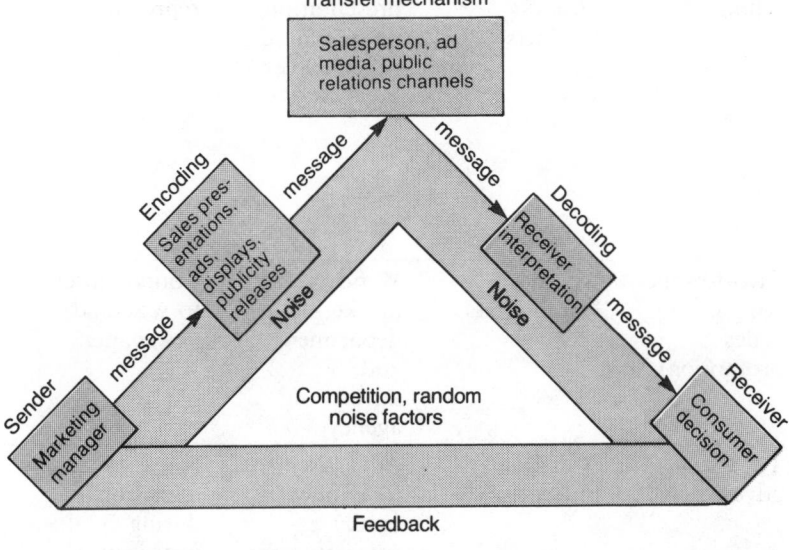

ensure that the message is encoded to match the target audience.

*Feedback* is the receiver's response to the message. It may take the form of attitude change, purchase, or nonpurchase. In some instances, firms may use promotion to create a favourable attitude toward its new products or services. Such attitude changes may result in future purchases. In other instances, the objective of the promotional communication is to stimulate consumer purchases. Such purchases indicate positive responses to the firm, its product/service offerings, its distribution channels, its prices, and its promotion. Even nonpurchases can serve as feedback to the sender. They may result from ineffective communication in that the message was not believed, not remembered, or failed to persuade the receiver that the firm's products or services are superior to its competitors. Feedback can be obtained from field sales reports and such techniques as marketing research studies.

*Noise* represents interference at some stage in the communications process. It may result from such factors as competitive promotional messages being transmitted over the same communications channel, misinterpretation of a sales presentation or an advertising message, receipt of the promotional message by the wrong person,

**Fig. 19-4   Examples of Marketing Communications**

| Type of Promotion | Sender | Encoding | Transfer Mechanism | Decoding by Receiver | Feedback |
|---|---|---|---|---|---|
| Personal selling | Sharp Business Products | Sales presentation on new model office copier | Sharp sales representative | Office manager and employees in local firm discuss Sharp sales presentation and those of competing suppliers. | Order placed for the Sharp copier |
| Two-for-one coupon (sales promotion) | Wendy's Hamburgers | Wendy's marketing department and advertising agency | Coupon insert to weekend newspaper | Newspaper reader sees coupon for hamburger and saves it. | Hamburgers purchased by consumers using the coupon |
| Television advertising | Walt Disney Enterprises | Advertisement for a new family entertainment animated movie is developed by Disney's advertising agency | Network television during programs with high percentage of viewers under 12 years old | Children see ad and ask their parents to take them; parents see ad and decide to take children. | Movie ticket purchased |

or random noise factors, such as people conversing during a television commercial or leaving the room.

Figure 19-4 illustrates the steps in the communications process with several examples of promotional messages. Although the types of promotion vary from a highly personalized sales presentation to such nonpersonal promotion as television advertising and two-for-one coupons, each form of promotion goes through each stage in the communications model.

## Components of the Promotional Mix

The promotional mix, like the marketing mix, involves the proper blending of numerous variables in order to satisfy the needs of the firm's market target and achieve organizational objectives. While the marketing mix is comprised of product, price, promotion, and distribution elements, the promotional mix is a subset of the overall marketing mix. In the case of the promotional mix, the marketing manager is attempting to achieve the optimal blending of various promotional elements in order to accomplish promotional objectives. The components of the **promotional mix** are *personal selling and nonpersonal selling (including advertising, sales promotion, and public relations).*[4]

Personal selling and advertising are the most significant elements since they usually account for the bulk of a firm's promotional expenditures. However, all factors contribute to efficient marketing communications. A detailed discussion of each of these elements is presented in the chapters that follow. Here only a brief definition will be given in order to set the framework for the overall discussion of promotion.

### Personal Selling

**Personal selling** may be defined as *a seller's promotional presentation conducted on a person-to-person basis with the buyer.* It is a direct face-to-face form of promotion. Personal selling was also the original form of promotion. Today it is estimated that 600 000 people in Canada are engaged in this activity.

### Nonpersonal Selling

Nonpersonal selling is divided into advertising, sales promotion, and public relations. Advertising is usually regarded as the most important of these forms.

**Advertising** may be defined as *paid nonpersonal communication through various media by business firms, nonprofit organizations, and individuals who are in some way identified with the advertising message and who hope to inform or persuade mem-*

---

[4] See William Dommermuth, "Promoting Your Product: Managing the Mix," *Business* (July–August 1980), pp. 18–21.

*bers of a particular audience.*[5] It involves the mass media, such as newspapers, television, radio, magazines, and billboards. Business has come to realize the tremendous potential of this form of promotion, and during recent decades advertising has become increasingly important in marketing. Mass consumption makes advertising particularly appropriate for products that rely on sending the same promotional message to large audiences.

**Sales promotion** includes *"those marketing activities other than personal selling and mass media advertising, and publicity, that stimulate consumer purchasing and dealer effectiveness*, such as displays, shows and expositions, demonstrations, and various nonrecurrent selling efforts not in the ordinary routine."*[6] Sales promotion is usually practised together with other forms of advertising to emphasize, assist, supplement, or otherwise support the objectives of the promotional program.

**Public relations** is *a firm's communications and relationships with its various publics.* These publics include the organization's customers, suppliers, shareholders, employees, the government, the general public, and the society in which the organization operates. Public relations programs can be either formal or informal. The critical point is that every organization, whether or not it has a formalized, organized program, needs to be concerned about its public relations.

In comparison to personal selling, advertising, and even sales promotion, expenditures for public relations are usually low in most firms. Therefore, *publicity* concerning a company's products or affairs is an important part of an effective public relations effort. It is information disseminated through the public media at no cost. It is generally achieved by placing commercially significant news or obtaining favourable presentation of company or product in a published medium. Since they don't pay for it, companies have little control over the publication by the press of "good" or "bad" company news. But for this very reason, a consumer may find this type of news source more believable than if the news were disseminated directly by the sponsor.

As Figure 19-5 indicates, each type of promotion has both advantages and disadvantages. Even though personal selling has a relatively high cost per contact, there is less wasted effort than in such nonpersonal forms of promotion as advertising. In addition, it is often more flexible than the other forms, since the salesperson can

[5] S. Watson Dunn and Arnold M. Barban, *Advertising: Its Role in Modern Marketing* (Hinsdale, Ill.: The Dryden Press, 1982), p. 7.
[6] Committee on Definitions, *Marketing Definitions: A Glossary of Marketing Terms* (Chicago: American Marketing Association, 1960), p. 20. Italics added.

tailor the sales message to meet the unique needs—or objections—of each potential customer.

On the other hand, advertising is an effective means of reaching mass audiences with the marketer's message. Sales promotion techniques are effective in gaining attention, and public relations efforts such as publicity frequently have a high degree of believability compared to other promotional techniques. The task confronting the marketer is to determine the appropriate blend of each of these techniques in marketing the firm's products and services.

**Figure 19-5   Comparing Alternative Promotional Techniques**

| Type of Promotion | Personal or Nonpersonal | Cost | Advantages | Disadvantages |
|---|---|---|---|---|
| Advertising | Nonpersonal | Relatively inexpensive per contact | Appropriate in reaching mass audiences; allows expressiveness and control over message | Considerable waste; difficult to demonstrate product; difficult to close sales; difficult to measure results |
| Personal selling | Personal | Expensive per contact | Permits flexible presentation and gains immediate response | Costs more than all other forms per contact; difficult to attract qualified salespeople |
| Sales promotion | Nonpersonal | Can be costly | Gains attention and has immediate effect | Easy for others to imitate |
| Public relations | Nonpersonal | Relatively inexpensive; publicity is free | Has high degree of believability | Not as easily controlled as other forms |

Source: Adapted from David J. Rachman and Elaine Romano, *Modern Marketing* (Hinsdale, Ill.: The Dryden Press, 1980), p. 450. Adapted by permission of the publisher.

### Factors Affecting the Promotional Mix

Since quantitative measures to determine the effectiveness of each component of the promotional mix in a given market segment are not available, the choice of a proper mix of promotional elements is one of the most difficult tasks facing the marketing manager. Factors affecting the promotional mix are: 1) nature of the market; 2) nature of the product; 3) stage in the product life cycle; 4) price; and 5) funds available for promotion.

### Nature of the Market

The marketer's target audience has a major impact upon the type of promotion to use. In cases where there is a limited number of buyers,

personal selling may prove highly effective. However, marke
characterized by a large number of potential customers scattere
over a large geographic area may make the cost of contact by per
sonal salespeople prohibitive, and in such instances, advertising ma
be extensively used. The type of customer also affects the promo
tional mix. A market target made up of industrial purchasers or retai
and wholesale buyers is more likely to require personal selling tha
one consisting of ultimate consumers.

*Nature of the Product*   A second important factor in determining an effective promotiona
mix is the product itself. Highly standardized products with mini
mal servicing requirements are less likely to depend upon persona
selling than higher priced custom products that are technically com
plex and require servicing. Consumer goods are more likely to rel

**Figure 19-6   A Reminder Advertisement Used in the
Maturity Stage of the Product Life Cycle**

Source: Reproduced by permission of General Foods Corporation, © 1981.

heavily upon advertising than industrial goods. Within each product category, promotional mixes vary.

For instance, installations typically involve heavy reliance upon personal selling compared to the marketing of operating supplies. Convenience goods rely heavily upon manufacturer advertising, and personal selling plays a small role. On the other hand, personal selling is often more important in the marketing of shopping goods, and both personal selling and nonpersonal selling are important in the marketing of specialty goods. Finally, personal selling is likely to be more important in the marketing of products characterized by trade-ins.

**Stage in the Product Life Cycle**  The promotional mix must also be tailored to the stage in the product life cycle. In the introductory stage, heavy emphasis is placed on personal selling to inform the marketplace of the merits of the new product or service. Salespeople contact marketing intermediaries to secure interest and commitment to handle the new product. Trade shows and exhibitions are frequently used to inform and educate prospective dealers and ultimate consumers. Any advertising at this stage is largely informative, and sales promotional techniques, such as samples and cents-off coupons, are designed to influence consumer attitudes and stimulate initial purchases.

As the product or service moves into the growth and maturity stages, advertising becomes more important in attempting to persuade consumers to make purchases. Personal-selling efforts continue to be directed at intermediaries in an attempt to expand distribution. As more competitors enter the marketplace, advertising stresses product differences in an attempt to persuade consumers to purchase the firm's brand. Reminder advertisements begin to appear in the maturity and early decline stages. Figure 19-6 is an example of a reminder ad used for Kool-Aid.

**Price**  Price of the product or service is a fourth factor in the choice of promotional mixes. Advertising is a dominant mix component for low unit value products due to the high costs per contact for personal selling. The cost of an industrial sales call, for example, is now estimated at over $105.[7] As a result, it has become unprofitable to promote lower value products and services through personal selling. Advertising, by contrast, permits a low promotional expenditure per sales unit, since it reaches mass audiences. For low value consumer products, such as chewing gum, colas, and snack foods, advertising is the only feasible means of promotion.

-----

7 "Market Research Facts and Trends" (Maclean-Hunter Research Bureau, 1981), p. 1.

**Funds Available for** A very real barrier to implementing any promotional strategy is th
**Promotion** size of the promotional budget. A 30-second television commerci
costs an average packaged goods company $86 000[8] to shoot, an
one showing during a Grey Cup game can cost $6000 or more
Even though the message is received by millions of viewers and th
cost per contact is relatively low, such an expenditure would excee
the entire promotional budget of thousands of firms. For many new
smaller firms, the cost of mass advertising is prohibitive, and the
are forced to seek less expensive, less efficient methods. Neighbour
hood retailers may not be able to advertise in metropolitan news
papers or on local radio and television stations; apart from per
sonal selling, their limited promotional budgets may be allocated t
an eye-catching sign, one of the most valuable promotional device
of a small retailer.

Figure 19-7 summarizes the factors influencing the determinatio
of an appropriate promotional mix.

**Figure 19-7   Factors Influencing the Promotional Mix**

| | Emphasis on | |
|---|---|---|
| Factor | Personal Selling | Advertising |
| *Nature of the Market* | | |
| Number of buyers | Limited number | Large number |
| Geographic concentration | Concentrated | Dispersed |
| Type of customer | Industrial purchaser | Ultimate consumer |
| *Nature of the Product* | | |
| Complexity | Custom-made, complex | Standardized |
| Service requirements | Considerable | Minimal |
| Type of good | Industrial | Consumer |
| Use of trade-ins | Trade-ins common | Trade-ins uncommo |
| *Stage in the Product Life Cycle* | | |
| | Introductory and early growth stages | Latter part of growth stages and maturity and early decline stages |
| Price | High unit value | Low unit value |

**Promotional** Essentially, there are two promotional policies that may be employed:
**Strategy—Pull** a pulling strategy and a pushing strategy. A **pulling strategy** is *a*
**or Push** *promotional effort by the seller to stimulate final-user demand*, which
then exerts pressure on the distribution channel. The plan is to build

[8] Frances Phillips, "Advertisers Seek Ways to Curb the Cost of TV Ads," *The Financial Post* (May 19, 1984), p. 14.

consumer demand for the product by means of advertising so that channel members will have to stock the product to meet that demand. If a manufacturer's promotional efforts result in shoppers requesting the retailer to stock an item, they will usually succeed in getting that item on the retailer's shelves, since most retailers want to stimulate repeat purchases by satisfied customers. A pulling strategy may be required to motivate marketing intermediaries to handle a product when they already stock a large number of competing products. When a manufacturer decides to use a pulling strategy, personal selling is often largely limited to contacting intermediaries, providing requested information about the product, and taking orders. Advertising and sales promotion are the most commonly used elements of promotion in a pulling strategy.

**Figure 19-8   Relative Importance of Advertising and Selling**

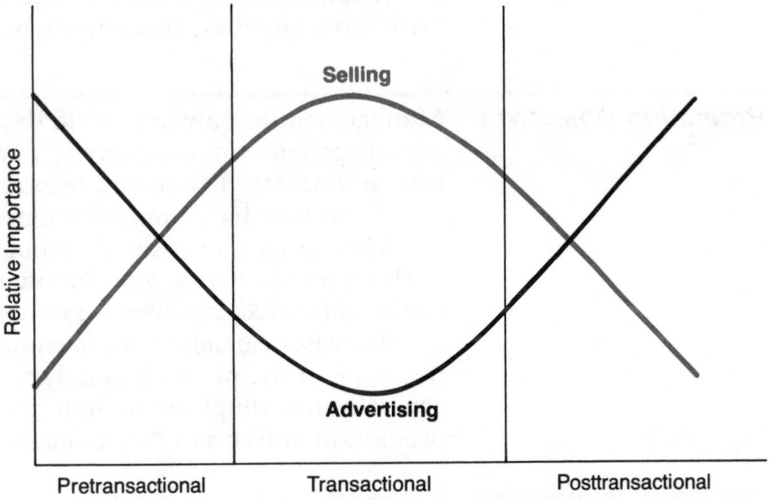

Source: Harold C. Cash and W.J.E. Crissy, "The Salesman's Role in Marketing," *The Psychology of Selling*, Vol. 12 (Personnel Development Associates, Box 3005, Roosevelt Field Station, Garden City, NY 11530). Reprinted by permission.

By contrast, a **pushing strategy** relies more heavily on personal selling. Here, the objective is the *promotion of the product to the members of the marketing channel rather than to the final user.* This can be done through co-operative advertising allowances, trade discounts, personal selling efforts by the firm's sales force, and other dealer supports. Such a strategy is designed to produce marketing success for the firm's products by motivating representatives of wholesalers and/or retailers to spend a disproportionate amount of time and effort in promoting these products to customers.

While these are presented as alternative policies, it is unlikel that very many companies will depend entirely upon either strateg In most cases a mixture of the two is employed.

Timing is another factor to consider in the development of promotional strategy. Figure 19-8 shows the relative importance o advertising and selling in different periods of the purchase process During the pretransactional period (before the actual sale) advertis ing is usually more important than personal selling. It is often argue that one of the primary advantages of a successful advertising pro gram is that it assists the salesperson in approaching the prospect Personal selling becomes more important than advertising durin; the transactional phase of the process. In most situations persona selling is the actual mechanism of closing the sale. In the post transactional stage advertising regains primacy in the promotiona effort. It serves as an affirmation of the customer's decision to bu; a particular good or service as well as a reminder of the product' favourable qualities, characteristics, and performance.

## Promotion Objectives

Management has always found that determining exactly what i expects promotion to achieve is a perplexing problem. Generally promotional strategy should be oriented toward achieving clearl; stated, measurable communications objectives.

What specific tasks should promotion accomplish? The answe: to this question varies with the situation. However, the followin; can be considered objectives of promotion: 1) to provide information 2) to increase demand; 3) to differentiate the product; 4) to accentuat the value of the product; and 5) to stabilize sales. Note that it i generally too simplistic to state the objective of advertising an promotion in terms of "increasing sales."

## Providing Information

The traditional function of promotion was to inform the marke about the availability of a particular product. Indeed, a large par of modern promotional effort is still directed at providing produc information to potential customers. An example of this is the typi cal university or college extension course program advertisemen appearing in the newspaper. Its content emphasizes informative features, such as the availability of different courses. Southam Busi ness Publications has employed an interesting idea in advertising tc potential business advertisers. It shows the back of a station wagon covered with bumper stickers, then makes the point: "To commu nicate effectively, deal with one idea at a time." By doing this, it educates potential advertisers, as well as showing how Southam can help.

The informative function often requires repeated customer exposures. For instance, "in a . . . study concerning customer acceptance of a new durable good, it was found that . . . at least several months were required after introduction (and accompanying promotion) before consumers became generally aware of the item and somewhat familiar with its characteristics."[9]

**Stimulating Demand**   The primary objective of most promotional efforts is to increase the demand for a specific brand of product or service. This can be shown by using the familiar demand curves of basic economics (see Figure 19-9). Successful promotion can shift demand from schedule 1 to schedule 2, which means that greater quantities can be sold at each possible price level. Cadbury Schweppes Powell accomplished this

**Figure 19-9   Promotion Can Help Marketers Achieve Demand Objectives**

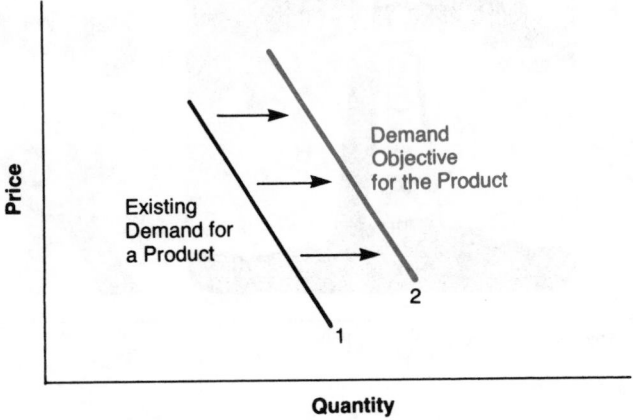

Source: *Principles of Marketing: The Management View*, 3d ed., by Richard H. Buskirk. Copyright © 1961, 1966, 1970, by Holt, Rinehart and Winston, Inc. Adapted and reprinted by permission of Holt, Rinehart and Winston, Inc.

with its "Thick" bars (see Figure 19-10), in a campaign that brought the chocolate bar to a position among the top five brands in the Canadian market.[10] The Thick bars were introduced in test markets in Vancouver, then in Ontario. The advertising series used such slogans as "Birds of a Feather Thick Together," "Great Minds Thick Alike," and "Chop Thicks." The ads have been very successful in the three years since they were first run. They not only won an award, but their success in influencing the market spawned a number of

9 Terrence V. O'Brien, "Psychologists Take a New Look at Today's Consumer," *Arizona Review* (August–September 1970), p. 2.
10 "Cadbury Gets Back in the Thick of the Action," *Marketing* (June 1, 1981), p. 1.

Figure 19-10   Using Advertising to Stimulate Demand

Source: Courtesy of Cadbury Schweppes Powell.

'thick' competitors. Cadbury's latest slogan, therefore, is "the thick of the crop."

**Differentiating the
Product**

*Product differentiation* is often an objective of the firm's promotional effort. Homogeneous demand, represented by the horizontal line in Figure 19-11, means that consumers regard the firm's output as no different from that of its competitors. In such cases the individual firm has no control over such marketing variables as price. A differentiated demand schedule, by contrast, permits more flexibility in marketing strategy, such as price changes.

For example, McCain's, a producer of high-quality frozen vegetables, advertises the dependable high quality and good taste of its products. This differentiates these products from others. Consequently some consumers wanting these attributes are willing to pay a higher price for McCain's than they would for other brands. Similarly, the high quality and distinctiveness of Cross pens are advertised, resulting in Cross's ability to ask and obtain a price 100 times that of some disposable pens. With the exception of commodities, most products have some degree of differentiation, resulting in a downward-sloping demand curve. The angle of the slope varies somewhat according to the degree of product differentiation.

**Accentuating the Value of the Product**

Promotion can point out more ownership utility to buyers, thereby accentuating the value of a product. The good or service might then be able to command a higher price in the marketplace. For example, status-oriented advertising may allow some retail clothing stores to command higher prices than others. The demand curve facing a prestige store may be less responsible to price differences than that of a competitor without a quality reputation. The responsiveness to price differences is shown in Figure 19-12.

Figure 19-11   Product Differentiation

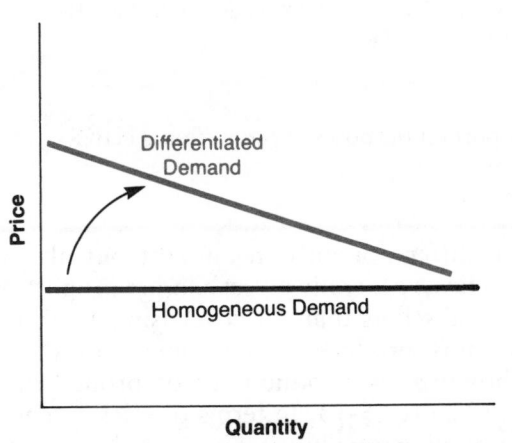

Figure 19-12   Promotion Can Accentuate the Value of the Product

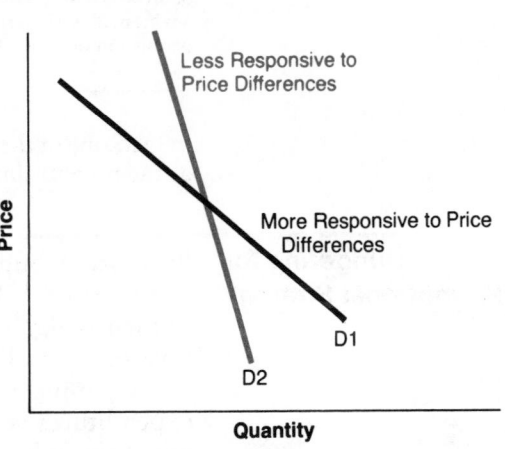

Source: *Markets and Marketing: An Orientation*, by Lee E. Preston (Glenview, Ill.: Scott, Foresman, 1970), p. 196. Copyright © 1970 by Scott, Foresman and Company. Adapted by permission.

**Stabilizing Sales**

A company's sales are not uniform throughout the year. Fluctuations can be caused by cyclical, seasonal, or other reasons. Reducing these variations is often an objective of the firm's promotional strategy. Lee E. Preston states:

> Advertising that is focused on such attitudinal goals as "brand loyalty" and such specific sales goals as "increasing repeat purchases" is essentially aimed at stabilizing demand. The prominence of such goals in the current literature and in advertising planning discussions suggests that stabilizing demand and insulating the market position of an individual firm and product against unfavourable developments is,

Figure 19-13    Promotion–Sales Curve

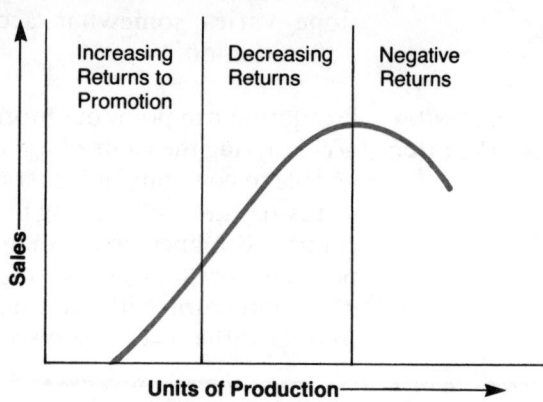

Source: *The Marketing Economy: An Analytical Approach*, by John C. Narver and Ronald Savitt, p. 294. Copyright © 1971 by Holt, Rinehart and Winston, Inc. Reprinted by permission of Holt, Rinehart and Winston, Inc.

in fact, one of the most important purposes of promotional activity at the present time.[11]

## Budgeting for Promotional Strategy

Promotion budgets can differ not only in amount but also in composition.[12] Industrial firms generally invest a larger proportion of their budgets for personal selling than for advertising, while the reverse is usually true of most producers of consumer goods.

A simple model showing the productivity of promotional expenditures is shown in Figure 19-13. In terms of sales revenue, initial expenditures on promotion usually result in increasing returns. There appear to be some economies associated with larger promotional expenditures. These economies result from such factors as the cumulative effects of promotion and repeat sales.

Evidence suggests that sales initially lag behind promotion for structural reasons (filling up the retail shelves, low initial production, lack of buyer knowledge). This produces a threshold effect, where there are no sales but lots of initial investment in promotion. A second phase might produce returns (sales) proportional to a given promotion expenditure; this would be the most predictable range.

---

[11] From *Markets and Marketing: An Orientation* by Lee E. Preston (Glenview, Ill.: Scott, Foresman and Company, 1970), p. 198. Copyright © 1970 by Scott, Foresman and Company. Reprinted by permission of the publisher.
[12] One writer has argued that promotional expenditures should be included in the capital budget and treated as investments. See Joel Dean, "Does Advertising Belong in the Capital Budget?" *Journal of Marketing* (October 1966), pp. 15–21.

Finally, the area of diminishing returns is reached when an increase in promotional expenditure does not produce a proportional increase in sales.[13]

For example, an initial expenditure of $40 000 may result in the sale of 100 000 product units for a consumer goods manufacturer. An additional $10 000 expenditure may then sell 30 000 more units of the item. And a further $10 000 may produce another 35 000-unit sale. The cumulative effect of the expenditures and repeat sales have resulted in increasing returns to the promotional outlays. However, as the advertising budget moves from $60 000 to $70 000, the marginal productivity of the additional expenditure may fall to 28 000 units. At some later point, no increase, or an actual decrease in units, may occur with additional expenditures. As competition intensifies, markets become saturated, and media effectiveness decreases because of increased noise in communications channels.

To test the thesis that there is a saturation point for advertising, Anheuser-Busch once quadrupled its advertising budget in several markets. After three months the company's distributors demanded an advertising cut. Many claimed that beer consumers came into their stores saying, "Give me anything *but* Bud."[14]

**Establishing a Budget**  Theoretically, the optimal method of allocating a promotion budget is to expand it until the cost of each additional increment equals the additional incremental revenue received. In other words, the most effective allocation procedure is to increase promotional expenditures until each dollar of promotion expense is matched by an additional dollar of profit (see Figure 19-13). This procedure—called *marginal analysis* — results in the maximization of the input's productivity. The difficulty arises in identification of this optimal point. It requires a precise balancing of marginal expenses for promotion and the resulting marginal receipts.

The more traditional methods of allocating a promotional budget are by percentage of sales, fixed sum per unit, meeting competition, and task-objective methods.[15]

---

[13] Determination of the correct advertising frequency is examined in Herbert E. Krugman, "What Makes Advertising Effective?" *Harvard Business Review* (March–April 1975), pp. 96–103.

[14] Charles G. Burch, "While the Big Brewers Quaff, the Little Ones Thirst," *Fortune* (November 1972), p. 107.

[15] An excellent discussion of budgeting for promotion is included in S. Watson Dunn and Arnold M. Barban, *Advertising: Its Role in Modern Marketing*, 4th ed. (Hinsdale, Ill.: Dryden Press, 1978), pp. 266–285. See also Gary L. Lilien, Alvin J. Silk, Jean-Marie Chaffray, and Murdidhar Rao, "Industrial Advertising Effects and Budgeting Practices," *Journal of Marketing* (January 1976), pp. 16–24; William A. Staples and Robert W. Sweadlow, "A Zero Base Approach to Advertising Planning," in *Proceedings of the Southern Marketing Association*,

*Percentage of sales* is a very common way of allocating promotion budgets. The percentage can be based on either past (such as the previous year) or forecasted (current year) sales. While the simplicity of this plan is appealing, it is not an effective way of achieving the basic promotional objectives. Arbitrary percentage allocations (whether applied to historical or future sales figures) fail to allow the flexibility that is required. Furthermore, such reasoning is circular, for the advertising allocation is made dependent upon sales, rather than vice versa, as it should be. Consider, for example, the implications of a decline in sales.

The *fixed sum per unit* approach differs from percentage of sales in only one respect: it applies a predetermined allocation to each sales or production unit. This also can be set on either a historical or a forecasted basis. Producers of high-value consumer durable goods, such as automobiles, often use this budgeting method.

Another traditional approach is simply to match competitors' outlays—in other words, *meet competition*—on either an absolute or a relative basis. However, this kind of approach usually leads to a status quo situation at best, with each company retaining its percentage of total sales. Meeting the competition's budget does not necessarily relate to the objectives of promotion and, therefore, seems inappropriate for most contemporary marketing programs.

The **task-objective method** of developing a promotional budget is based upon a sound evaluation of the firm's promotional objectives, and is thus better attuned to modern marketing practices. It involves two sequential steps.

1. The organization must *define the realistic communication goals* the firm wants the promotional mix to accomplish — for example, a 25 percent increase in brand awareness, or a 10 percent rise in consumers who realize that the product has certain specific differentiating features. The key is to specify quantitatively the objectives to be accomplished. They then become an integral part of the promotional plan.

2. The organization must *determine the amount (as well as type) of promotional activity required to accomplish each of the objectives* that have been set. These units combined become the firm's promotion budget.

---

eds. Robert S. Franz, Robert M. Hopkins, and Al Toma (New Orleans, La., November 1978), pp. 315–317; Michael Etgar and Meir Schneller, "Advertising in a Multiproduct Firm," in *Contemporary Marketing Thought*, eds. Barnett A. Greenberg and Danny N. Bellenger (Chicago: American Marketing Association, 1977), p. 527; and Joseph A. Bellizzi, A. Frank Thompson, and Lynn J. Loudenback, "Promotional Activity and the U.S. Business Cycle," in *Proceedings of the Southwestern Marketing Association*, eds. Robert C. Haring, G. Edward Kiser, and Ronnie D. Whitt (Houston, Texas, 1979), pp. 27–28.

A crucial assumption underlies the task-objective approach: that the productivity of each promotional dollar is measurable. That is why the objectives must be carefully chosen, quantified, and accomplished through promotional efforts. Generally, an objective like "We wish to achieve a 5 percent increase in sales" is an ill-conceived marketing objective because a sale is the culmination of the effects of *all* elements of the marketing mix. Therefore, an appropriate promotional objective might be "To make 30 percent of the target market aware of the facilities available at the health spa."

A study by the Marketing Science Institute found that many firms do not keep adequate records of promotional expenditures, nor do they attempt to test alternative promotional efforts.[16]

While promotional budgeting is always difficult, recent research studies, and more frequent use of computer-based models, make it less of a problem than it has been in the past.

### Measuring the Effectiveness of Promotion

It is widely recognized that part of a firm's promotional effort is ineffective. John Wanamaker, a successful nineteenth-century retailer, once observed: "I know half the money I spend on advertising is wasted; but I can never find out which half."

Measuring the effectiveness of promotional expenditures has become an extremely important research question, particularly among advertisers. Studies aimed at this measurement dilemma face several major obstacles, among them the difficulty of isolating the effect of the promotion variable.

Most marketers would prefer to use a **direct-sales results test** to measure the effectiveness of promotion. This test attempts to *ascertain for each dollar of promotional outlay the corresponding increase in revenue.* The primary difficulty is controlling the other variables operating in the marketplace. A $1.5-million advertising campaign may be followed by an increase in sales of $20 million. However, this may be more because of a sudden price hike by the leading competitor than because of the advertising expenditure. Therefore, advertisers are turning to establishing and assessing achievable, measurable objectives.

With the increasing sophistication of marketing analysts, analytical techniques, and computer-based marketing information systems, banks of historical data on promotional expenditures and their effects are being subjected to ever more scrutiny. More and more is being learned about measuring and evaluating the effects of promotional activity. While the technical literature in marketing

---

[16] Reported in *Marketing Science Institute Research Briefs* (December 1975), p. 1.

reveals much of what is happening in this critical area, firms are reluctant to release much of this information. Not only do they wish to keep their proprietary (privately held) information about how the market works to themselves for competitive reasons, but they do not want competitors knowing the methods and decision routines used in planning promotional activity.

Other methods of assessing promotion effectiveness include inquiries about the product, determination of change in attitudes toward the product, and improvement in public knowledge and awareness. One indicator of probable advertising effectiveness would be the elasticity or sensitivity of sales to promotion based on historical data concerning price, sales volume, and advertising expenditures.

It is difficult for the marketer to conduct research in a controlled environment like that which can be set up in other disciplines. The difficulty in isolating the effects of promotion causes many to abandon all attempts at measurement. Others, however, turn to indirect evaluation. These researchers concentrate on the factors that are quantifiable, such as recall (how much is remembered about specific products or advertisements) and readership (the size and composition of the audience). The basic problem here is that it is difficult to relate these variables to sales. Does extensive ad readership actually lead to increased sales? Another problem is the high cost of research in promotion. To assess the effectiveness of promotional expenditures correctly may require a significant investment.

## The Value of Promotion

Promotion has often been the target of criticism. A selection of these would include the following:

"Promotion contributes nothing to society."
"Most advertisements and sales presentations insult my intelligence."
"Promotion 'forces' consumers to buy products they cannot afford and do not need."
"Advertising and selling are economic wastes."
"Salespersons and advertisers are usually unethical."

Consumers, public officials, and marketers agree that all too often many of these complaints are true.[17] Some salespersons do use unethical sales tactics. Some product advertising is directed at consumer groups that can least afford to purchase the particular item. Many television commercials do contribute to the growing problem of cultural pollution.

While promotion can certainly be criticized on many counts, it

---

[17] See J. Edward Russo, Barbara L. Metcalf, and Debra Stephens, "Identifying Misleading Advertising," *Journal of Consumer Research* (September 1981), pp. 119–131.

is important to remember that it plays a crucial role in modern society. This point is best explained by looking at the importance of promotion on the business, economic, and social levels.

**Business Importance**  Promotional strategy has become increasingly important to business enterprises — both large and small. The long-term rise in outlays for promotion is well documented and certainly attests to management's faith in the ability of promotional efforts to produce additional sales. It is difficult to conceive of an enterprise that does not attempt to promote its product or service in some manner or another. Most modern institutions simply cannot survive in the long run without promotion. Business must communicate with the public.

Nonbusiness enterprises have also recognized the importance of this variable. The Canadian government is now the largest advertiser in Canada, promoting many programs and concepts. Religious organizations have acknowledged the importance of promoting what they do. Even labour organizations have used promotional channels to make their viewpoints known to the public at large. In fact, promotion now plays a larger role in the functioning of non-profit organizations than it ever has in the past. Figure 19-14 effectively points out the power of advertising in the case of a public appeal.

**Economic Importance**  Promotion has assumed a degree of economic importance, if for no other reason than that it is an activity that employs thousands of people.[18] More importantly, however, effective promotion has allowed society to derive benefits not otherwise available. For example, the criticism that "promotion costs too much" views an individual expense item in isolation. It fails to consider the possible effect of promotion on other categories of expenditures.

Promotion strategies that increase the number of units sold permit economies in the production process, thereby lowering the production costs assigned to each unit of output. Lower consumer prices then allow these products to become available to more people. Similarly, researchers have found that advertising subsidizes the informational content of newspapers and the broadcast media.[19] In short, promotion pays for many of the enjoyable entertainment and educational aspects of contemporary life, as well as lowering product costs.

**Social Importance**  Criticisms such as "most promotional messages are tasteless" and "promotion contributes nothing to society" sometimes ignore the

---

18 The economic effects of advertising are explored in Jean-Jacques Lambin, "What Is the Real Impact of Advertising?" *Harvard Business Review* (May–June 1975), pp. 139–147.
19 Francis X. Callahan, "Does Advertising Subsidize Information?" *Journal of Advertising Research* (August 1978), pp. 19–22.

Figure 19-14    Brian has a Serious Drinking Problem

# Brian has a serious drinking problem.

Brian has kidney failure. It bloats his small body with harmful fluids and poisons. It's robbed him of energy.

For Brian, life depends on routine dialysis treatments to cleanse his blood. Someday he may receive a successful kidney transplant

But preventing kidney disease and making successful transplants requires research which costs money... a lot of money.

Buddy, can you spare a donation? To donate call toll-free 1-800-268-7742, operator #77.

 THE KIDNEY FOUNDATION OF CANADA

Help put us out of business

fact that there is no commonly accepted set of standards or priorities existing within our social framework. We live in a varied economy characterized by consumer segments with differing needs, wants, and aspirations. What is tasteless to one group may be quite informative to another. Promotional strategy is faced with an "averaging" problem that escapes many of its critics. The one generally accepted standard in a market society is freedom of choice for the consumer. Customer buying decisions will eventually determine what is acceptable practice in the marketplace.

Promotion has become an important factor in the campaigns to achieve such socially oriented objectives as stopping smoking, family planning, physical fitness, and the elimination of drug abuse. Promotion performs an informative and educational task that makes it extremely important in the functioning of modern society. As with everything else in life, it is how one uses promotion, not the using itself, that is critical.

**Summary**      This chapter has provided an introduction to promotion, the fourth variable in the marketing mix (product, pricing, distribution, and promotional strategies). Promotional strategy is closely related to the marketing communications system, which includes the elements of sender, message, encoding, transfer mechanism, decoding, receiver, feedback, and noise. The major components of promotional strategy are personal selling and nonpersonal selling (advertising, sales promotion, and public relations). These elements are discussed in the two chapters that follow.

Developing an effective promotional strategy is a complex matter. The elements of promotion are related to the type and value of the product being promoted, the nature of the market, the stage of the product life cycle, and the funds available for promotion, as well as to the timing of the promotional effort. Personal selling is used primarily for industrial goods, for higher-value items, and during the transactional phase of the purchase decision process. Advertising, by contrast, is used primarily for consumer goods, for lower-value items, and during the pretransactional and posttransactional phases.

A pushing strategy, which relies on personal selling, attempts to promote the product to the members of the marketing channel rather than the final user. A pulling strategy concentrates on stimulating final-user demand, primarily in the mass media through advertising and sales promotion.

The five basic objectives of promotion are to 1) provide information, 2) stimulate demand, 3) differentiate the product, 4) accentuate the value of the product, and 5) stabilize sales.

There are several methods used in establishing promotional budgets. However, the task-objective method makes the most sense and promises best management of promotional resources.

Although the target of much criticism, promotion plays an important role in the business, economic, and social activity of the country.

| *Key Terms* | promotion | sales promotion |
|---|---|---|
| | marketing communications | public relations |
| | promotional mix | pulling strategy |
| | personal selling | pushing strategy |
| | advertising | task-objective method |
| | | direct-sales results test |

*Review Questions*

1. Relate the steps in the communications process to promotional strategy.
2. Explain the concept of the promotional mix and its relationship to the marketing mix.
3. Identify the major determinants of a promotional mix and describe how they affect the selection of an appropriate blending of promotional techniques.
4. Compare the five basic objectives of promotion. Cite specific examples.
5. Explain the concept of noise in marketing communications and its causes.
6. Under what circumstances should a pushing strategy be used in promotion? When would a pulling strategy be effective?
7. What are the primary objectives of promotion?
8. Identify and briefly explain the alternative methods for developing a promotional budget.
9. How should a firm attempt to measure the effectiveness of its promotional efforts?
10. Identify the major public criticisms sometimes directed toward promotion. Prepare a defence for each criticism.

*Discussion Questions and Exercises*

1. "Perhaps the most critical promotional question facing the marketing manager concerns when to use each of the components of promotion." Comment on this statement, and relate your response to the goods classification, product value, marketing channels, price, and the timing of the promotional effort.
2. What mix of promotional variables would you use for each of the following?
   a. Champion spark plugs
   b. Weedeater lawn edgers
   c. a management consulting service
   d. industrial drilling equipment
   e. women's sports outfits
   f. customized business forms
3. Develop a hypothetical promotion budget for the following firms. Ignore dollar amounts by using percentage allocations to the various promotional variables (such as 30 percent to personal selling,

60 percent to advertising, and 10 percent to public relations).

   a.  Tilden Rent-A-Car

   b.  Commonwealth Holiday Inns

   c.  a manufacturer of industrial chemicals

   d.  Great West Life Insurance Company

4.  Should doctors, dentists, and lawyers be prohibited from promoting their services through media like direct mail and newspaper advertisements? How do these professionals currently promote their services?

5.  When paperback book sales suffered a downturn, several of the major publishers adopted new promotional strategies. One firm began using 30-cents-off coupons to promote its romance series. Another company, on the other hand, established a returns policy that rewarded dealers with high sales. The new policy also contained penalties to discourage low volume by retail book outlets. Relate these promotional strategies to the material discussed in this chapter.

---

**MICROCOMPUTER EXERCISE: Promotional Budget Allocations**

While promotional budgeting is always difficult, the development of computer-based models has made it less of a problem than it has been in the past. The problems that follow focus on the promotional budgeting methods discussed in the preceding sections.

Directions: Use the Menu Item titled "Promotional Budget Allocations" on the Foundations of marketing disk to solve each of the following problems.

1.  Medicine Hat Enterprises (MHE) was founded in 1983 in Medicine Hat, Alberta. As indicated in Table A, both the firm's sales and promotional expenditures grew considerably during a five-year period. The 1988 sales forecast is $7 000 000. Table B shows the annual sales and promotional expenditures of the firm's four major competitors.

   a.  What percentage of 1988 sales should MHE include in its 1988 promotional budget if the budget is based on the percentage allocated for 1987 sales? How many dollars would be allocated to promotion?

   b.  Suppose the firm's marketers decide to use the average percentage allocated for promotion over the past five years. They determine this average by calculating total sales and total promotional outlays since 1983 and then dividing total promotional outlays by total sales. What percentage would be included in the 1988 promotional budget? How many dollars would be allocated to promotion?

c. MHE's marketers are also considering basing their promotional budget on the average promotional outlays of their major competitors. What percentage would be used for promotion if this approach is implemented?

**Table A   Growth of Sales and Promotional Expenditures for Medicine Hat Enterprises**

| Year | Annual Sales | Promotional Expenditures |
|------|--------------|--------------------------|
| 1983 | $   500 000  | $  24 000                |
| 1984 | 900 000      | 40 000                   |
| 1985 | 2 200 000    | 80 000                   |
| 1986 | 3 500 000    | 150 000                  |
| 1987 | 4 900 000    | 196 000                  |

**Table B   Annual Sales and Promotional Expenditures of Medicine Hat Industries' Major Competitors**

| Competitor | Annual Sales | Promotional Expenditures |
|------------|--------------|--------------------------|
| Drumheller Manufacturing | $1 200 000 | $725 000 |
| Landin Corp. | 4 500 000 | 250 000 |
| Grandin Consolidated | 8 000 000 | 500 000 |
| Swift Current | 6 500 000 | 425 000 |

# Advertising, Sales Promotion, and Public Relations

## C H A P T E R   O B J E C T I V E S

1. *To explain the current status and historical development of advertising.*
2. *To identify the major types of advertising.*
3. *To list and discuss the various advertising media.*
4. *To explain how advertising effectiveness is determined.*
5. *To outline the organization of the advertising function.*
6. *To describe the process of creating an advertisement.*
7. *To identify the methods of sales promotion.*
8. *To explain the role of public relations and publicity.*

When developing an advertising strategy, firms sometimes choose not to put much emphasis on individual products. Honda has chosen this strategy, and will emphasize its corporate image rather than details about products for at least the next year.

The first of Honda's magazine ads was purely corporate in emphasis. It featured a blank piece of graph paper, with the headline: "This is how a Honda engineer starts his day." On television, the Civics are described in a general way — only the silhouettes of the cars are shown — to emphasize the new look. The 30-second spot, called "The new car" is designed to convey the message that Honda has "taken another innovative step, established the benchmark again." That is why the shapes are shown, rather than individual features.

Coupled with this general image-building strategy, the company will also carry some detailed advertisements on each car. This will be done through the efforts of its dealers, as well as other magazine advertisements and outdoor billboards. Honda has clearly developed a strategy which they feel will best serve them in the market position in which they find themselves. The execution of the various elements of the advertising program seems to be well-balanced, and to fit in well with their overall strategy.[1]

### The Conceptual Framework

As explained in Chapter 19, promotion consists of both personal and nonpersonal elements. In this chapter the nonpersonal elements of promotion — advertising, sales promotion, and public relations — are examined. These elements play a critical role in the promotional mixes of thousands of organizations.

For most organizations, advertising represents the most important type of nonpersonal promotion. This chapter examines advertising objectives and the importance of planning for advertising. Also discussed are the different types of advertisements and media choices. Both retail advertising and manufacturer (national) advertising are discussed and the alternative methods of assessing the effectiveness of an advertisement are examined. Sales promotion and public relations — including publicity — are also discussed.

### Advertising

If you sought to be the next prime minister of Canada, you would need to communicate with every possible voting Canadian. If you had invented a new calculator and went into business to sell it, your chances of success would be slim without informing and persuading students and businesses of the usefulness of your calculator. In these situations you would discover, as have countless others, that you would need to use *advertising* — to communicate to buyers or voters. In the previous chapter, advertising was defined as a paid, nonpersonal communication through various media by business firms, nonprofit organizations, and individuals who are in some way identified in the advertising message and who hope to inform or persuade members of a particular audience.

Today's widespread markets make advertising an important part of business. Since the end of World War II, advertising and related expenditures have risen faster than gross national product and most other economic indicators. Furthermore, about 8500 people are employed in advertising, according to Statistics Canada.[2]

Three advertisers — the Government of Canada, Procter & Gamble, and Labatt's — spent over $35 million each for advertising in 1986. Figure 20-1 ranks the top advertisers in Canada. It is particularly noteworthy that governments, both federal and provincial, are such a major force in Canadian advertising. The government

---

[1] Rob Wilson, "Honda's Corporate Drive," *Marketing* (October 17, 1983), p. 1.
[2] *A Report on Advertising Revenues in Canada* (Toronto: Maclean-Hunter Research Bureau, 1978), p. 3.

| Figure 20-1   The Top 10 Advertisers in Canada, 1986 | | |
|---|---|---|
| Rank | Name (head office) | 1986 |
| 1 | Government of Canada (Ottawa) | 63.7 |
| 2 | Proctor & Gamble Inc. (Toronto) | 51.1 |
| 3 | John Labatt Ltd. (London, Ont.) | 37.6 |
| 4 | Molson Cos. (Montreal) | 32.0 |
| 5 | General Motors of Canada Ltd. (Toronto) | 27.3 |
| 6 | Unilever (Toronto) | 27.1 |
| 7 | Ontario Government (Toronto) | 26.0 |
| 8 | Thompson Group (Toronto) | 23.8 |
| 9 | RJR (Toronto) | 22.4 |
| 10 | McDonalds (Toronto) | 21.0 |

Figures were compiled by Media Measurement Services, Toronto, and represent expenditures in broadcast, print, and out-of-home media. They do not reflect retail advertising or production costs.

Source: *Marketing* (March 23, 1987), p. 2.

is still the nation's largest advertising spender. It spent $12.6 million more than the number two spender, Procter & Gamble. Total 1983 advertising expenditures were about $5.6 billion. This means that about $224 is spent on advertising each year for every person in Canada.[3]

Advertising expenditures vary among industries and companies. Cosmetics companies are often cited as an example of firms that spend a high percentage of their funds on advertising and promotion. Management consultants Schonfeld & Associates studied more than 4000 firms and calculated their average advertising expenditures as a percentage of both sales and gross profit margin. Estimates for selected industries are given in Figure 20-2. Wide differences exist among industries. Advertising spending can range from one fifth of one percent in an industry like iron and steel foundries to more than 7 percent of sales in the detergent industry.

Industry in general has become somewhat advertising-oriented as other elements of promotion have grown relatively more expensive. But advertising's future potential remains a matter of conjecture, although it may be determined by the environmental framework within which it operates. The role of advertising in Canadian society attracts considerable public interest today.

---

[3] Francis Phillips, "Bring Back The Good Old Days," *The Financial Post 500* (Summer, 1984), p. 200.

**Historical Development**   Some form of advertising products has probably existed since the development of the exchange process.[4] Most of the early advertising was vocal. Criers and hawkers sold various products, made public announcements, and chanted advertising slogans like the now familiar:

> One-a-penny, two-a-penny, hot-cross buns
> One-a-penny, two for tuppence, hot-cross buns

Signs were also used in early advertising. Most were symbolic and used to identify products or services. In Rome a goat signified a dairy; a mule driving a mill, a bakery; a boy being whipped, a school.

Later the development of the printing press greatly expanded advertising's capability. A 1710 advertisement in the *Spectator* billed one dentifrice as "the Incomparable Powder for cleaning of Teeth, which has given great satisfaction to most of the Nobility and Gentry in England."

**Figure 20-2   Estimates of Average Advertising to Sales in Ten Industries**

| Industry | Advertising and Promotion as Percentage of Sales, 1982 |
|---|---|
| Soap, detergent | 7.1% |
| Beer, ale | 6.9% |
| Toy, sporting goods | 6.9% |
| Cigarette | 6.4% |
| Restaurant | 3.1% |
| Photographic equipment and supply | 2.7% |
| Household furniture | 1.9% |
| Chemicals, allied industries | 1.3% |
| General building contractor | 0.6% |
| Iron and steel foundry | 0.2% |

Source: Schonfeld & Associates, Inc., 120 S. La Salle St., Chicago 60603, (312) 236-5846.

[4] This section follows in part the discussion in S. Watson Dunn and Arnold Barban, *Advertising: Its Role in Modern Marketing*, 3rd ed. (Hinsdale, Ill.: The Dryden Press, 1974), p. 5.

Many early newspapers carried advertising on their first page. Most of the advertisements would be called classified ads today — spouses looking for wandering partners, householders looking for servants, and the like. However, some future national advertisers also began to use newspaper advertising at this time.

The first advertising agency was organized in the United States in 1841. Originally, these agencies were simply brokers who sold advertising space. In their competition for business they gradually began to offer additional services like advertising research, copywriting, and advertising planning.

Claude C. Hopkins used a large-scale consumer survey concerning home-baked beans before launching a campaign for Van Camp's Pork and Beans in the early 1900s. Hopkins claimed that home-baked beans were difficult to digest, and suggested that consumers should try Van Camp's beans. He used "reason-why copy" to show the reasons why someone should buy the product.

Some of the early advertising promoted products of questionable value, such as patent medicines. As a result, a reformist movement developed in advertising during the early 1900s, and some newspapers began to screen their advertisements. Magazine publisher Cyrus Curtis began rejecting certain types of advertising, such as medical copy that claimed cures and advertisements for alcoholic beverages. These improvements established the springboard for the further growth in advertising that many of the industry's forefathers thought impossible.

**THE BORN LOSER**

Copyright © 1983, Newspaper Enterprise Association

One identifying feature of advertising in the last half of the twentieth century is its concern for researching the markets that it attempts to reach. Originally, advertising research dealt primarily with media selection and the product. Then, advertisers became increasingly concerned with aiming their messages more specifically through determining the appropriate *demographics* (such characteristics as the age, sex, and income level of potential buyers). Now, understanding consumer behaviour has become an important aspect of advertising strategy. Psychological influences on purchase decisions — often called *psychographics* — can be useful in describing potential markets for advertising appeals. As described in Chapter 4, these influences include such factors as lifestyle and personal attitudes. Increased knowledge in these areas has led to improved advertising decisions.

The emergence of the marketing concept, with its emphasis on a company-wide consumer orientation, saw advertising take on an expanded role as marketing communications assumed greater importance in business. Advertising provides an efficient, inexpensive, and fast method of reaching the much sought-after consumer. Its extensive use now rivals that of personal selling. Advertising has become a key ingredient in the effective implementation of the marketing concept.

## Advertising Objectives

Traditionally the objectives of advertising were stated in terms of direct sales goals. A more realistic approach, however, is to view advertising as having communications objectives that seek *to inform, persuade, and remind* potential customers of the product. Advertising seeks to condition the consumer so that he or she has a favourable viewpoint toward the promotional message. The goal is to improve the likelihood that the customer will buy a particular product. In this sense, advertising illustrates the close relationship between marketing communications and promotional strategy.

In instances where personal selling is the primary component of a firm's marketing mix, advertising may be used in a support role to assist the salespeople. Much of Avon's advertising is aimed at assisting the neighbourhood salesperson by strengthening the image of Avon, its products, and its salespeople. The well-known advertisement for McGraw-Hill Magazines, shown in Figure 20-3 illustrates the important role advertising can play in opening doors for the sales force by preparing customers for the sales call.

## Advertising Planning

Advertising planning begins with effective research. Research results allow management to make strategic decisions, which are then translated into tactical execution such as budgeting, copywriting, scheduling, and the like. Finally, there must be some feedback mechanism for measuring the effectiveness of the advertising. The elements of advertising planning are shown in Figure 20-4.

There is a real need for following a sequential process in advertising decisions. Novice advertisers are often guilty of being overly concerned with the technical aspects of advertisement construction,

**Figure 20-3   Use of Advertising to Assist Personal Selling**

"I don't know who you are.
I don't know your company.
I don't know your company's product.
I don't know what your company stands for.
I don't know your company's customers.
I don't know your company's record.
I don't know your company's reputation.
Now—what was it you wanted to sell me?"

MORAL: Sales start **before** your salesman calls—with business publication advertising.

McGRAW-HILL MAGAZINES
BUSINESS • PROFESSIONAL • TECHNICAL

Source: Reprinted with permission of McGraw-Hill Publications Company.

while ignoring the more basic steps such as market analysis. The type of advertisement that is employed in any particular situation is related in large part to the planning phase of this process.

## Positioning

The concept of positioning was discussed in Chapter 5. It involves the development of a marketing strategy aimed at a particular segment of the market in order to achieve a desired position in the mind of the prospective buyer. As Professors David A. Aaker and J. Gary Shansby point out, a variety of positioning strategies is available to the advertiser. An object can be positioned:

1. By attributes. (Crest is a cavity fighter.)
2. By price/quality. (Sears is a value store.)

## Figure 20-4   Elements of Advertising Planning

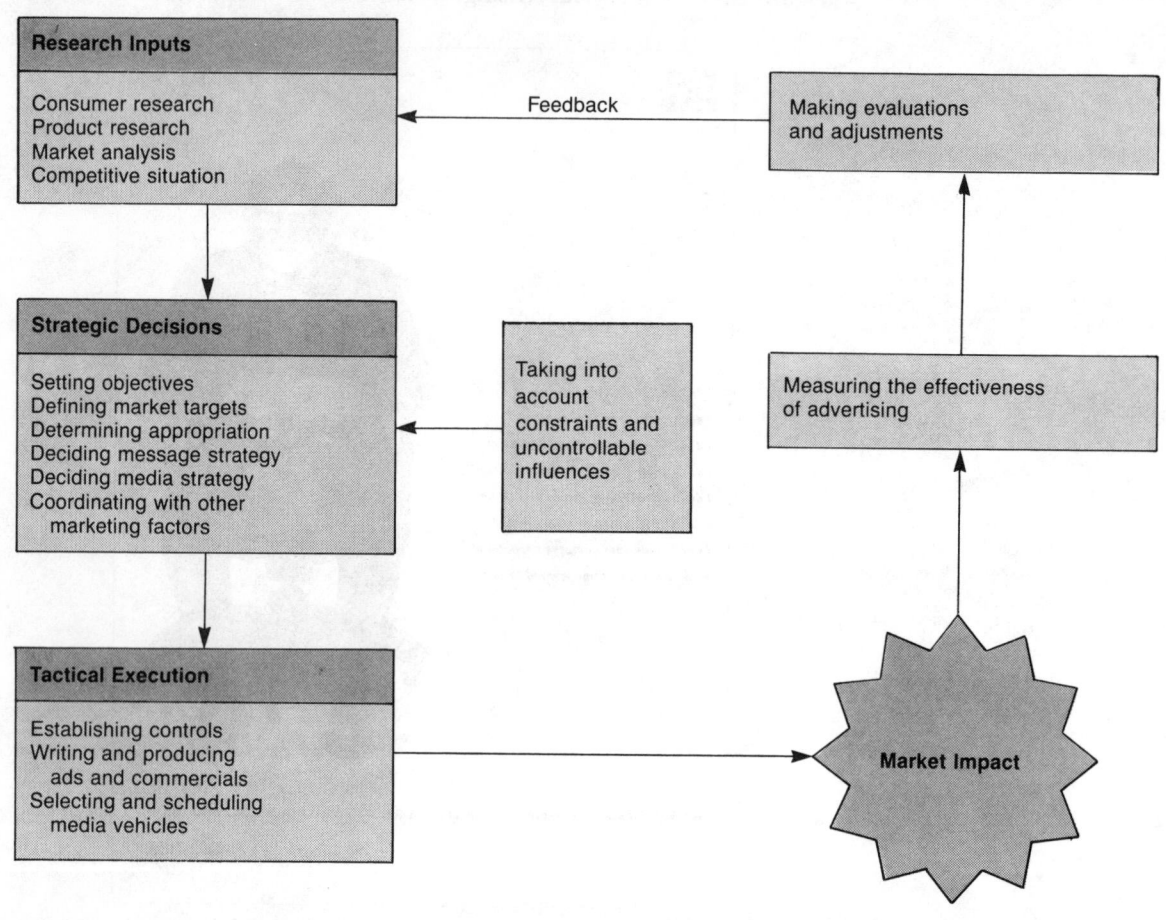

Source: Adapted from *Advertising: Its Role in Modern Marketing*, p. 202, by S. Watson Dunn and Arnold M. Barban. Copyright © 1982 by CBS College Publishing. Reprinted by permission.

3. By competitor. ("Avis is only number two in rent-a-cars, so why go with us? We try harder.")
4. By application. (Gatorade is for quick, healthful energy after exercise and other forms of physical exertion.)
5. By product user. (Mercedes-Benz automobiles are for discriminating executives.)
6. By product class. (Carnation Instant Breakfast is a breakfast food.)[5]

[5] David A. Aaker and J. Gary Shansby, "Positioning Your Product," *Business Horizons* (May/June 1982), p. 62. Reprinted by permission of the publisher. See also Jack Trout and Al Ries, "Positioning: Ten Years Later," *Industrial Marketing* (July 1979), pp. 32–44.

Figure 20-5   An Example of Institutional Advertising

"50,000 Canadian jobs
– a big responsibility."

Alcan's Jean Minville

As the world's leading international aluminum company, Canada's Alcan provides employment to almost 20,000 people across the country.

This, in turn, causes a 'ripple' effect that creates an additional 30,000 jobs in related sectors of the economy.

Major new projects under consideration will ensure Canada's leadership in the world's aluminum markets and secure long term employment opportunities for Canadians.

Productivity and the level of employment are of concern to everyone and, at Alcan, we make them prime considerations within our total planning process.

ALCAN

Source: *Maclean's* (May 7, 1984), Inside-back Cover.

## Types of Advertisements

Essentially, there are two basic types of advertisements: product and institutional. These can each be subdivided into informative, persuasive, and reminder categories.

**Product advertising** deals with *the nonpersonal selling of a particular good or service.* It is the type we normally think of when the subject of advertising comes up in a conversation. **Institutional advertising,** by contrast, is concerned with *promoting a concept, idea, or philosophy, or the goodwill of an industry, company, or* *organization*. It is often closely related to the public relations function of the enterprise.[6] An example of institutional advertising by Alcan appears in Figure 20-5.

**Informative Product Advertising**

All advertising seeks to influence the audience, as does any type of communication. **Informative product advertising** *seeks to develop*

**Figure 20.6   An Example of Informative Product Advertising**

6 See Thomas F. Garbett, "When to Advertise Your Company," *Harvard Business Review* (March-April 1982), pp. 100–106.

*demand through presenting factual information on the attributes of the product and/or service.* For example, an advertisement for a new type of photocopy machine would attempt to persuade through citing the various unique product and/or service features of that copier. Informative product advertising tends to be used in the promotion of new products since a major requirement in such cases is to announce availability and characteristics which will satisfy needs. Thus it is often seen in the introductory stages of the product life cycle. Figure 20-6 shows an advertisement for Mastercard which uses a factual approach to persuade people to use that service.

**Persuasive Product Advertising**

In **persuasive product advertising** *the emphasis is on the use of words and/or images to try to create an image for a product and to influ-*

**Figure 20-7   An Example of Persuasive Product Advertising**

BIG QUAKER COOKIES
FOR LITTLE COOKIE CRUMBLERS.

Store bought cookies, no matter how good they taste, just can't compare to cookies that you've baked yourself. Quaker Cookie Mix. Hot from the oven. Warmth from your heart.

*ence attitudes about it.* In contrast to informative product advertising, this type of advertising contains little objective information. Figure 20-7 shows an advertisement for Quaker cookie mix. While it gives a little objective information, the main thrust is persuasion. Coke and Pepsi use persuasive techniques in their lifestyle advertisements featuring a group of happy people enjoying the product. Persuasive advertising is generally used more in the growth period and to some extent in the maturity period of the product life cycle.

Figure 20-8   Relationship Between Advertising and the Product Life Cycle

| Reminder-Oriented Product Advertising | The goal of **reminder-oriented product advertising** is *to reinforce previous promotional activity by keeping the name in front of the public.* It is used in the maturity period as well as throughout the decline phase of the product life cycle. An example of a reminder-oriented slogan is Esso's well-known "we help to make you better." The general relationship between the type of advertising and the stage of the life cycle is illustrated in Figure 20-8. |

**Informative Institutional Advertising**

This approach seeks to increase public knowledge of a concept, idea, philosophy, industry, or company. In the early 1980s the oil industry was experiencing a degree of unfavourable publicity. Gulf Oil's communications director said, "We decided we had a story to tell."[7] Consequently, the company tripled its corporate advertising

---

[7]"Gulf to Tell a $3-Million Story," *Marketing* (May 25, 1981), p. 1. See also G.H.G. McDougall, "Comparative Advertising in Canada: Practices and Consumer Relations," *The Canadian Marketer* (1978), pp. 14–20.

budget to $3 million and undertook an extensive program to edu-
cate the public about the contributions of the company to society.
Other firms, such as Volkswagen have continuously advertised their
innovativeness and reliability. An example of a recent Volkswagen
institutional advertisement is shown in Figure 20-9.

**Figure 20-9    An Example of Informative Institutional Advertising**

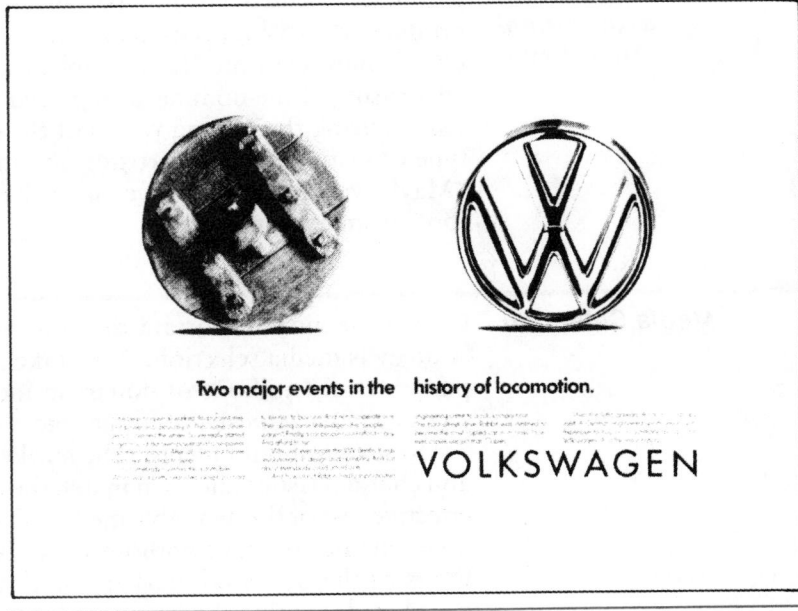

Two major events in the   history of locomotion.

VOLKSWAGEN

**Persuasive Institutional**    When a firm or advertising agency wishes *to advance the interests*
**Advertising**    *of a particular institution within a competitive environment*, it often
uses **persuasive institutional advertising**. Examples of persuasive institutional advertising include the efforts of Canada and others to
increase their shares of the intensely competitive tourism market.

*Advocacy Advertising*    One form of persuasive institutional
advertising that has grown in use during the past decade is advocacy advertising. **Advocacy advertising**, sometimes referred to as
*cause advertising*, can be defined as *any kind of paid public communication or message, from an identified source and in a conventional medium of public advertising, which presents information
or a point of view bearing on a publicly recognized controversial
issue.*[8] Such advertising is designed to influence public opinion, to
affect current and pending legislation, and to gain a following.

---

[8] *Controversy Advertising: How Advertisers Present Points of View in Public
Affairs; A Worldwide Study by the International Advertising Association*
(New York: Communication Arts Books, 1977), p. 18.

Advocacy advertising has long been utilized by such nonprofit organizations as Mothers Against Drunk Driving (MADD), Planned Parenthood, "right to life" anti-abortion groups, and the National Citizen's Coalition. (Such use of advocacy advertising will be examined in Chapter 23).

**Reminder-Oriented Institutional Advertising**

**Reminder-oriented institutional advertising**, like reminder-oriented product advertising, is used *to reinforce previous promotional activity*. In most elections, for example, early persuasive (issue-directed) advertising of the nominee is replaced by reminder-oriented advertising during the closing weeks of the campaign. Examples of this type of institutional advertising abound in the media. The 3M ad "Maybe you didn't know we made all these products. There's more too!" is an example.

## Media Selection

One of the most important decisions in developing an advertising strategy is media selection. A mistake at this point can cost a company literally millions of dollars in ineffectual advertising. Media strategy must achieve the communications goals mentioned earlier.

Research should identify the market target to determine its size and characteristics and then match the target with the audience and effectiveness of the available media. The objective is to achieve adequate media coverage without advertising beyond the identifiable limits of the potential market. Finally, alternative costs are compared to determine the best possible media purchase.

These are numerous types of advertising media, and the characteristics of some of the more important ones will be considered here.[9] The advantages and disadvantages of each are shown in Figure 20-10.

**Newspapers**

About 30 percent of Canada's total advertising revenues, the largest share received by any of the media, is spent on advertising in newspapers (including weekend supplements).[10] The primary advantages of newspapers are flexibility (advertising can be varied from one locality to the next), community prestige (newspapers have a deep impact on the community), intense coverage (in most places about nine out of ten homes can be reached by a single newspaper),

---

[9] The discussion of various advertising media is adapted from material in S. Watson Dunn and Arnold Barban, *Advertising: Its Role in Modern Marketing*, 5th ed. (Hinsdale, Ill.: Dryden Press, 1982), pp. 512–591.
[10] The 1985 advertising volume percentages for the four major media (newspapers, television, magazines, and radio) are etimated by Maclean-Hunter Research Bureau, Toronto.

**Fig. 20-10   Advantages and Disadvantages of the Various Advertising Media**

| Media | Advantages | Disadvantages |
|---|---|---|
| Newspapers | Flexibility<br>Community prestige<br>Intense coverage<br>Reader control of exposure<br>Co-ordination with<br>national advertising<br>Merchandising service | Short lifespan<br>Hasty reading<br>Poor reproduction |
| Magazines | Selectivity<br>Quality reproduction<br>Long life<br>Prestige associated with<br>some magazines<br>Extra services | Lack of flexibility |
| Television | Great impact<br>Mass coverage<br>Repetition<br>Flexibility<br>Prestige | Temporary nature of<br>message<br>High cost<br>High mortality rate for<br>commercials<br>Evidence of public lack of<br>selectivity |
| Radio | Immediacy<br>Low cost<br>Practical audience selection<br>Mobility | Fragmentation<br>Temporary nature of<br>message<br>Little research information |
| Outdoor Advertising | Communication of quick<br>and simple ideas<br>Repetition<br>Ability to promote products<br>available for sale nearby | Brevity of the message<br>Public concern over<br>aesthetics |
| Direct Mail | Selectivity<br>Intense coverage<br>Speed<br>Flexibility of format<br>Complete information<br>Personalization | High cost per person<br>Dependency on quality of<br>mailing list<br>Consumer resistance |

Source: Based on S. Watson Dunn and Arnold M. Barban, *Advertising: Its Role in Modern Marketing*, 5th ed. (Hinsdale, Ill.: The Dryden Press, 1982), pp. 513–577.

and reader control of exposure to the advertising message (unlike audiences of electronic media, readers can refer back to newspapers). The disadvantages are a short lifespan, hasty reading (the typical reader spends only 20–30 minutes on the newspaper), and poor reproduction.

**Magazines**   Magazines are divided into such diverse categories as consumer maga
zines, farm and business publications, and directories. They accoun
for about 12 percent of all advertising. The primary advantages o
periodical advertising are: selectivity of market targets; quality repro
duction; long life; the prestige associated with some magazines
and the extra services offered by many publications. Canadian con
sumer magazines have pioneered many controlled distribution tech
niques. Our Postal Code system, with its six-digit Forward Sortatior
Area (FSA) and Local Delivery Unit (LDU), can be linked with Cen
sus Data at the Enumeration Area (EA) level to produce well-defined
circulation clusters based on demographics, life-cycles, or other
interest-activity profiles.[11] The primary disadvantage is that period
icals lack the flexibility of newspapers, radio, and television. The
leading magazines in Canada are shown in Figure 20-11.

**Television**   Television is the second largest advertising medium. It now accounts
for about 18 percent of the total advertising volume. Television adver
tising can be divided into three categories: network, national spot
and local spot. The Canadian Broadcasting Corporation, the Cana
dian Television Network, and Global Television are the three nationa
networks. Network advertising usually accounts for over two-third
of the total television advertising expenditures. A national "spot"
refers to non-network broadcasting used by a general advertiser (fo
example, Black & Decker might choose to place an advertisemen
in several cities across the country, without buying time from a total
television network). Local spots, primarily used by retailers, consist
of locally developed and sponsored commercials. Television adver
tising offers the following advantages: impact, mass coverage,
repetition, flexibility, and prestige. The disadvantages include high
costs, high mortality rates for commercials, some evidence of pub
lic distrust, and lack of selectivity.

**Radio**   Advertisers using the medium of radio can also be classified as net
work or local advertisers. Radio accounts for about 10 percent of
total advertising volume. The advantages of radio advertising are
immediacy (studies show most people regard radio as the best source
for up-to-date news); low cost; flexibility; practical, low-cost audi
ence selection; and mobility (radio is an extremely mobile broad
cast medium). Radio's disadvantages include fragmentation (for
instance, Montreal has about 19 AM and FM stations), the unavail
ability of the advertising message for future reference, and less
research information than for television.

---

[11] Leonard Kubas, "Magazines Need it Razor Sharp," *Marketing* (April 6,
1987), p. 24.

## 0-11   Leading English Consumer Magazines in Canada

| Magazine | Circ. | Men 18 + Primary (000) | Men 18 + Total (000) | Women 18 + Primary (000) | Women 18 + Total (000) | Rate per page 4/C | Rate per page B/W |
|---|---|---|---|---|---|---|---|
| lberta Report ................. | 55 700 | 50 | 212* | 43 | 122* | $ 3 270 | 2 365 |
| tlantic Insight ................. | 35 600 | 59 | 114 | 31 | 77 | 3 475 | 2 610 |
| algary Magazine .............. | 49 700 | 23 | 41 | 26 | 32 | 2 630 | 1 805 |
| anadian Geographic ......... | 122 400 | 111 | 296 | 103 | 272 | 5 600 | 4 200 |
| anadian Living ................ | 503 600 | 164 | 388 | 642 | 1 516 | 14 105 | 11 990 |
| hatelaine ....................... | 1 105 600 | 379 | 575 | 1 288 | 2 005 | 23 410 | 18 260 |
| ity & Country Home ........ | 94 100 | 55 | 255 | 103 | 363 | 6 590 | 5 030 |
| dmonton Magazine .......... | 50 300 | 14 | 31 | 25 | 30 | 2 630 | 1 805 |
| quinox ......................... | 152 700 | 130 | 265 | 133 | 244 | 7 775 | 5 560 |
| inancial Post Magazine ...... | 211 800 | 189 | 319 | 78 | 167 | 10 266 | 7 548 |
| are ............................. | 221 000 | 50 | 114 | 289 | 566 | 8 220 | 6 140 |
| larrowsmith .................... | 148 800 | 167 | 287 | 129 | 224 | 5 910 | 4 370 |
| omemakers .................... | 1 382 300 | 386 | 450 | 1 067 | 1 230 | 19 725 | 16 766 |
| eisure Ways ................... | 503 900 | 240 | 274 | 222 | 243 | 5 940 | 4 620 |
| laclean's ....................... | 640 700 | 571 | 1 271 | 533 | 1 042 | 19 010 | 14 020 |
| lontreal Magazine ............ | 77 000 | 35 | 44 | 43 | 46 | 2 900 | 2 400 |
| lewsweek ...................... | 102 220 | 93 | 405 | 95 | 351 | 4 560 | 2 925 |
| eader's Digest ................. | 1 355 100 | 985 | 1 371 | 1 336 | 1 815 | 20 315 | 15 740 |
| aturday Night ................. | 143 200 | 88 | 182 | 86 | 162 | 6 640 | 4 640 |
| tarweek ......................... | 824 300 | 657 | 702 | 777 | 821 | 12 095 | 9 676 |
| ime ............................. | 362 600 | 355 | 1 060 | 320 | 798 | 9 900 | 6 285 |
| oronto Life .................... | 94 200 | 65 | 141 | 73 | 147 | 5 778 | 4 322 |
| V Guide ........................ | 822 500 | 746 | 1 007 | 829 | 1 091 | 13 440 | 10 750 |
| V Times ........................ | 1 903 100 | 1 410 | 1 520 | 1 392 | 1 476 | 25 116 | 20 093 |
| V Week Van/Vic .............. | 75 700 | 57 | 83 | 79 | 104 | 2 800 | 2 100 |
| ancouver Magazine ........... | 92 300 | 75 | 121 | 62 | 102 | 3 825 | 2 620 |
| Vestern Living .................. | 256 600 | 131 | 155 | 157 | 196 | 11 160 | 7 645 |
| Vestworld Magazine .......... | 288 900 | 169 | 209 | 179 | 211 | 15 000 | 12 000 |

Note the difference between paid circulation and total circulation. Cost per thousand is based on paid circulation.

ource: *The Canadian Media Directors' Council Media Digest* 1986/87, p. 45.

***Direct Mail***   Sales letters, postcards, leaflets, folders, broadsides (larger than folders), booklets, catalogues, and house organs (periodical publications issued by an organization) are all forms of direct mail advertising. The advantages of direct mail include selectivity, intensive coverage, speed, format flexibility, complete information, and the personalization of each mailing piece. Direct mail purchasers also tend to be consistent buyers by mail.[12] A disadvantage of direct

---

12 Patrick Dunne, "Some Demographic Characteristics of Direct Mail Purchasers," *Baylor Business Studies* (July 1975), pp. 67–72.

mail is its high cost per reader. Direct mail advertising is also dependent upon the quality of the mailing list.[13] Often those unfamiliar
with the efficacy of direct mail condemn it all as "junk mail." The
are very surprised to find that many people respond positively to
direct mail. In fact, marketing research surveys consistently show
majority who say they prefer to receive it. Effectively used, direct
mail is a successful and lucrative marketing tool. Figure 20-12 shows
an advertisement used by the Canadian Direct Mail/Marketing
Association.

---

**Figure 20-12    An Advertisement Used by the Canadian Direct
Mail/Marketing Association**

---

*This symbol assures you
there is order in the
mail order business*

When you see it printed on advertising mail or in mail order ads in publications, you know that it's from someone you can trust. So when you shop by mail, you know you'll receive exactly what you ordered.

The symbol shows that the seller is a member of the Canadian Direct Mail/Marketing Association. We insist that members abide by a tough 14-point code of ethics and follow the highest standards of practice or they get kicked out.

Our members work for publishers, mail order catalogues, book clubs, fund raisers, department stores, financial institutions, insurance firms, schools, government, etc. They represent about 80% of the direct marketing industry.

But we know that there are some mail order people who don't always treat customers properly. That's why the CDM/MA has set up a Task Force to investigate customer complaints.

If you've had poor treatment from a mail order seller, after trying to resolve the problem with the seller, write us about your experience. Give us as much information as possible. We'll get after them for you, member or non-member and we will do our best to resolve the problem for you.

Or, write us if you want your name taken off (or added on to) the mailing lists of our members; we call this our Mail Preference Service. It's been in operation since 1975. The score to date is 3,274 people wanted off and 1,440 wanted on.

Write us, too, if you'd like a free copy of our highly informative brochure "Direct Mail and You". It discusses some controversial points about advertising mail.

For copies, write to:
CDM/MA,
130 Merton Street,
Toronto, Ontario M4S 1A4.

**Canadian
Direct Mail/Marketing
Association**

---

[13] Mailing lists are discussed in Jeffrey A. Tannenbaum, "Mailing List Brokers
Sell More Than Names to Their Many Clients," *The Wall Street Journal*
(February 19, 1974), pp. 1–16.

# Who Ever Heard of Bonnie Herman?

onnie Herman is rumoured to make over 200 000 a year as a singer. Her voice is heard by illions of people daily, and her songs are hummed d whistled by many people. But you say you ave never heard of Bonnie Herman? This is not urprising because Bonnie Herman is a jingle nger. She has been the voice of commercials for rlines, Coca-Cola, McDonald's, Cheerios, and umerous other products. Jingle singers must be able to change pitch, tune, and rhythm quickly as they sometimes do several different commercials in a single day. Bonnie and her counterparts must also learn to cope with the lack of recognition accorded them. But most jingle singers feel that the security and high earnings are well worth the price. Despite their obscurity, people like Bonnie Herman are vital parts of the advertising industry.

urce: Philip Revzin, "For Jingle Vocalists, There Isn't Any Fame—But There Is Money," *The Wall Street Journal* (August 13, 175), pp. 1, 6. Reprinted with permission of *The Wall Street Journal*, © Dow Jones & Company, Inc., 1974. All rights reserved.

**Outdoor Advertising**   Posters (commonly called billboards), painted bulletins or displays (such as those that appear on building walls), and electric spectaculars (large illuminated, sometimes animated, signs and displays) make up outdoor advertising. Accounting for 6 percent of advertising volume, this form of advertising has the advantages of quickly communicating simple ideas, repetition, and the ability to promote products that are available for sale nearby. Outdoor advertising is particularly effective in metropolitan and other high-traffic areas. Disadvantages of the medium are the brevity of its message and public concern over aesthetics; however, a simple message can be extremely powerful, as seen in Figure 20-13.

**Organizing the**
**Advertising Function**   While the ultimate responsibility for advertising decisions often rests with top marketing management, the organization of the advertising function varies among companies. A producer of a technical industrial product may be served by a one-person operation primarily concerned with writing copy for trade publications. A consumer goods company, on the other hand, may have a large department staffed with advertising specialists.[14]

The advertising function is usually organized as a staff department reporting to the vice-president (or director) of marketing. The *director of advertising* is an executive position heading the functional activity of advertising. The individual filling this slot

---

[14] Employment in various types of advertising organizations is explored in Jack A. Gottschalk, "Industrial Advertising Management: The Gloomy Side of the 'Glamour' Business," *Fairleigh Dickinson University Business Review* (Summer 1975), pp. 20–25.

Figure 20-13   An Award-Winning Billboard

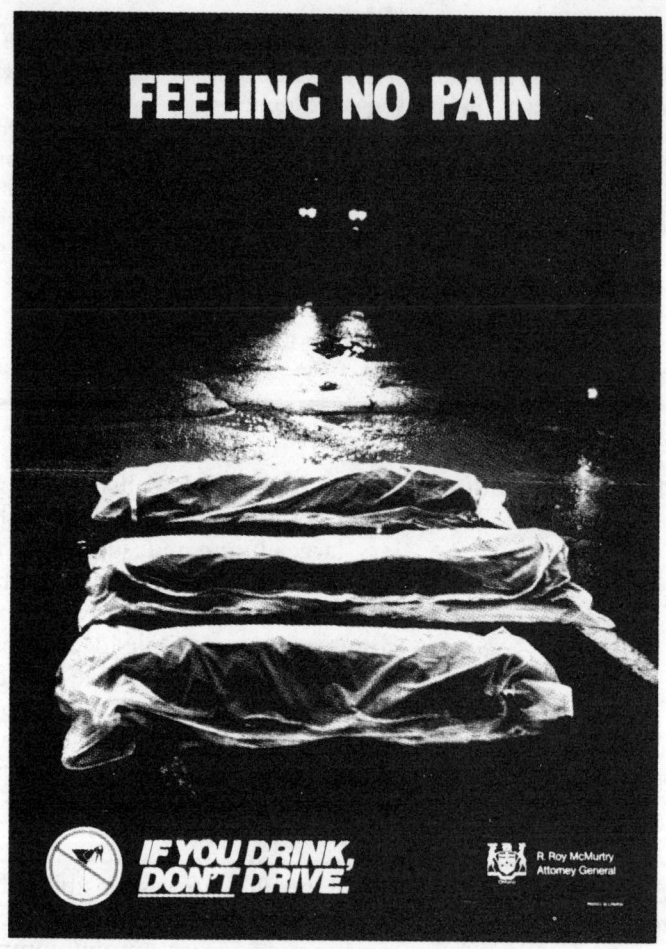

should be not only a skilled and experienced advertiser; he or she must also be able to communicate effectively within the organization. The success of a firm's promotional strategy depends upon the advertising director's willingness and ability to communicate both vertically and horizontally. The major tasks typically organized under advertising include advertising research, art, copywriting, media analysis, and, in some cases, sales promotion.

**Advertising Agencies**   Many advertisers also make use of an independent advertising agency. The **advertising agency** is *a marketing specialist firm that*

Figure 20-14   Organization Chart for a Large Advertising Agency

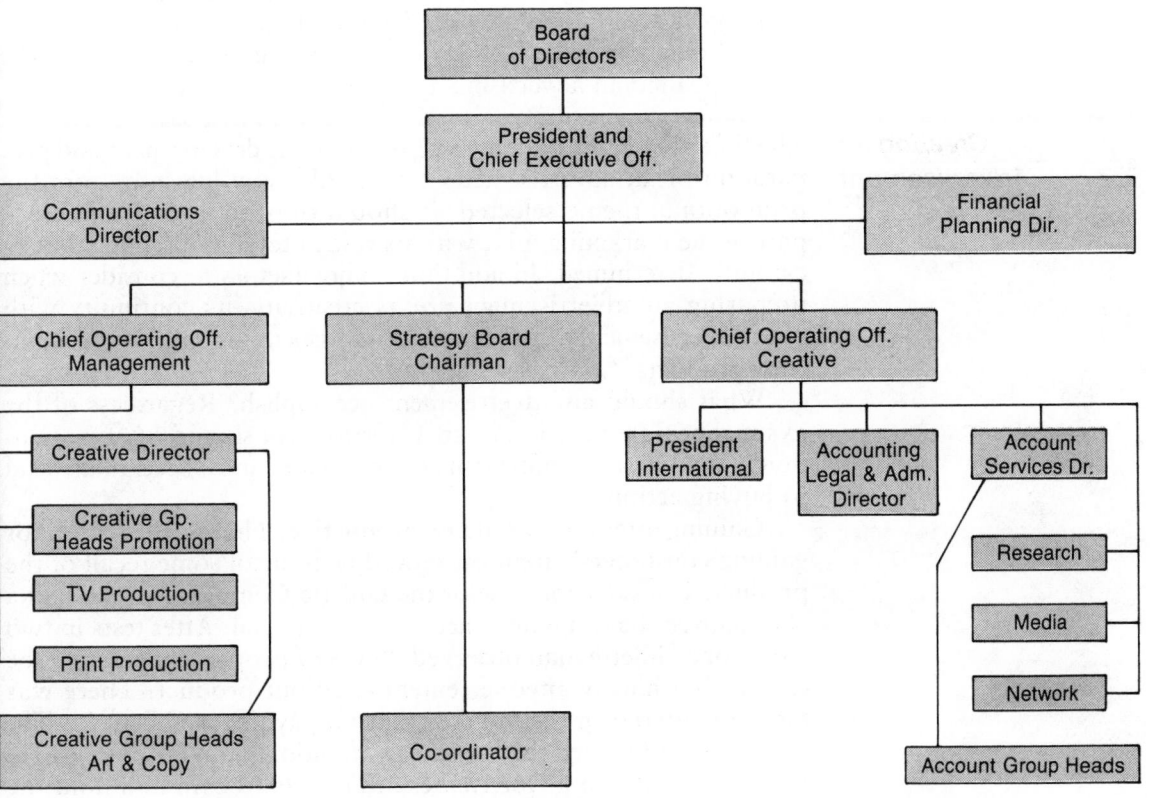

Source: Copyright © 1981 by Marsteller, Inc. Used by permission.

*assists the advertiser in planning and preparing its advertisements.*
There are several reasons why advertisers use an agency for at least
a portion of their advertising. Agencies are typically staffed with
highly qualified specialists who provide a degree of creativity and
objectivity that is difficult to maintain in a corporate advertising
department. In some cases the use of an agency reduces the cost of
advertising since the agency does not require many of the fixed expenses associated with internal advertising departments. Effective
use of an advertising agency requires a close relationship between
advertiser and agency.

Figure 20-14 shows the organization chart for a large advertising agency. While the titles may vary from agency to agency, the

major operational responsibilities can be classified as creative services, account management, research, and promotional services.[15]

J. Walter Thompson Company is the largest advertising agency with worldwide billings of over $900 million. Seven agencies have world billings in excess of $500 million. Figure 20-15 shows the leading Canadian advertising agencies.

## Creating an Advertisement

The final step in the advertising process is the development and preparation of an advertisement that should flow logically from the promotional theme selected. It should thus be a complementary part of the marketing mix, with its role in total marketing strategy carefully determined. In addition, major factors to consider when preparing an advertisement are its creativity, its continuity with past advertisements, and possibly its association with other company products.[16]

What should an advertisement accomplish? Regardless of the exact appeal that is chosen, an advertisement should 1) gain attention and interest, 2) inform and/or persuade, and 3) eventually lead to buying action.

Gaining attention should be productive. That is, the reason for gaining consumers' attention should be to instil some recall of the product. Consider the case of the Gillette Company, which had a chimpanzee shave a man's face in a commercial. After tests in two cities, one Gillette man observed, "Lots of people remembered the chimp, but hardly anyone remembered our product. There was fantastic interest in the monkey, but no payoff for Gillette."[17] The advertisement gained the audience's attention but it failed to lead to buying action. An advertisement that fails to gain and hold the receiver's attention is ineffectual.

Information and persuasion is the second factor to consider when creating an advertisement. For example, insurance advertisements typically specify the features of the policy and may use testimonials in attempting to persuade prospects.

Stimulating buying action, however, is often difficult since an advertisement cannot actually close a sale. Nevertheless, if the first two steps have been accomplished, the advertising has likely been

---

15 For an informative discussion of account management positions, See William V. Muse, "Recruiting and Training Practices of Advertising for Account Executive Positions: Some Survey Results," *Marquette Business Review* (Summer 1970), pp. 78–82.

16 An interesting discussion of the evaluation of advertising copy appears in James U. McNeal, "Advertising in the 'Age of Me'," *Business Horizons* (August 1979), pp. 34–38.

17 William M. Carley, "Gillette Co. Struggles as Its Rivals Slice at Fat Profit Margin," *The Wall Street Journal* (February 2, 1972), p. 1. Reprinted by permission.

**Figure 20-15    Canada's Top 15 Advertising Agencies**

TOP 15 ADVERTISING AGENCIES

| Rank | Company (head office) | Revenue ($ million)[1] 1986 | 1985 | Number of Offices | Number of employees |
|------|----------------------|------------------------------|------|-------------------|---------------------|
| 1 | MacLaren Advertising (Toronto) | 25.8 | 23.9 | 3 | 325 |
| 2 | J. Walter Thompson Co. (Toronto) | 24.6 | 26.6 | 7 | 415 |
| 3 | McKim Advertising Ltd. (Toronto) | 24.0[2] | 23.8 | 5 | 350 |
| 4 | Ogilvy & Mather (Canada) Ltd. (Toronto) | 21.4 | 21.1 | 9 | 273 |
| 5 | Vickers & Benson Cos. (Toronto) | 18.2 | 16.7 | 3 | 320 |
| 6 | Baker Lovick Ltd. (Toronto) | 17.1 | 15.6 | 6 | 241 |
| 7 | Cossette Communication-Marketing (Montreal)[3] | 15.6 | 13.5 | 4 | 252 |
| 8 | Foster Advertising Ltd. (Toronto) | 15.5 | 15.2 | 4 | 220 |
| 9 | Young & Rubicam Ltd. (Toronto) | 14.2 | 12.0 | 3 | 211 |
| 10 | Saffer Advertising Inc. (Toronto) | 14.0 | 13.5 | 2 | 200 |
| 11 | Ronalds-Reynolds & Co. (Toronto) | 14.0[2] | 12.9 | 2 | 201 |
| 12 | Grey Advertising Ltd. (Toronto) | 13.8 | 11.0 | 5 | 179 |
| 13 | McCann-Erickson Advertising of Canada Ltd. (Toronto) | 12.7 | 13.3 | 2 | 190 |
| 14 | Saatchi & Saatchi Compton Hayhurst Ltd. (Toronto)[3] | 12.1[2] | 11.2[2] | 1 | 129 |
| 15 | Ted Bates Advertising Inc. (Toronto) | 12.0 | 10.5 | 2 | 158 |

[1] Revenue is generally comprised of revenue from commissionable media (usually 15%) and fees negotiated with clients. Nine of the 15 agencies included figures from subsidiary or associated companies (public relations firms, graphic design shops, retail boutiques, direct marketing houses, radio and television production, and print operations). Foster, Y&R, Ronalds-Reynolds, McCann, Saatchi, and Ted Bates did not.
[2] Financial Post estimate based on 15% of reported billings.
[3] Yearend Sept. 30, 1986.

Source: *The Financial Post 500* (Summer, 1987), p. 196.

well worthwhile. Too many advertisers fail to suggest how the receiver of the message can buy the product if he or she so desires. This is a shortcoming that should be eliminated.

**Celebrity Testimonials: Advantages and Disadvantages**    In their attempts to improve the effectiveness of their advertising, a number of marketers utilize celebrities to present their advertising messages.[18] Well-known current examples include Wayne Gretzky for 7-Up, Gary Carter for Chrysler, James Garner and Mariette Hartley for Polaroid, and Bill Cosby for Jell-O pudding.

[18] Hershey H. Friedman and Linda W. Friedman, "Does the Celebrity Endorser's Image Spill Over to the Product?" *The Journal of Business* (May 1980), pp. 31–36.

The primary advantage of using big-name personalities is that they may improve product recognition in a promotional environment filled with hundreds of competing 20- and 30-second commercials. (Advertisers use the term *clutter* to describe this situation.) In order for this technique to succeed, the celebrity must be a credible source of information for the item being sold. Most advertisers believe that celebrity advertisements are ineffective where there is no reasonable relationship between the celebrity and the advertised product or service.

Canada is currently very sports- and celebrity-oriented.[19] Therefore, there is opportunity for firms profitably to sponsor athletes or sporting events. However, such promotion should clearly be an adjunct to existing promotional programs. There are several principles that corporate sponsors should consider before getting involved. First, they must be selective and specific. A market target should be pinpointed, and a sport or celebrity carefully matched to that target and objective. Second, sports interest trends should be followed carefully. Too often firms get involved without assessing the strength of the trend. Third, they must be original, looking for a special focus. Is it possible to come up with a unique concept? Fourth, firms should analyse the result, short- and long-term. Sponsorship is a business decision that should pay off in profits.

**Comparative Advertising**

Comparative advertising *makes direct promotional comparisons with leading competitive brands.* The strategy is best employed by firms that do not lead the market. Most market leaders prefer not to acknowledge that there are competitive products. Procter & Gamble and General Foods, for instance, traditionally have devoted little of their huge promotional budgets for comparative advertising. But many firms do use it extensively. An estimated 23 percent of all radio and television commercials make comparisons to competitive products. Here are some examples:

- Scope mouthwash prevents "medicine breath," but Listerine is never mentioned.

- Minute Maid lemonade is better than the "no-lemon lemonade," a reference to General Foods' Country Time brand.

- Suave antiperspirant will keep you just as dry as Ban Ultra Dry does and for a lot less.

- Nationwide, more Coca-Cola drinkers prefer the taste of Pepsi.

---

[19] This section is based on Jamie Wayne, "No Easy Way To Sports Promotion," *Financial Post* (February, 7, 1981), p. 15.

Marketers who contemplate using comparative advertising in their promotional strategies should take precautions to assure that they can substantiate their claims, because comparison advertising has the potential of producing lawsuits. Advertising experts disagree about this practice's long-term effects. The conclusion is likely to be that comparative advertising is a useful strategy in a limited number of circumstances.[20]

**Retail Advertising**   Retail advertising is all advertising by stores that sell goods or services directly to the consuming public. While accounting for a sizeable portion of total advertising expenditures, retail advertising varies widely in its effectiveness. One study showed that consumers were often suspicious of retail price advertisements. Responses to such advertisements were affected by perceptions of the source, nature of the message, and shopping experience.[21]

The basic problem is that advertising is often treated as a secondary activity, particularly in smaller retail stores. Store managers in these stores are usually given the responsibility of advertising as an added task to be performed along with their normal functions. Advertising agencies have traditionally been used rarely by retailers.

More recently, however, larger retailers have been spending more than ever on advertising, and they are going to agencies to buy the needed expertise.[22] One reason for this is that Canadians spend 42 percent of their consumer dollars in chain stores. Consequently, there is great incentive to promote a chain store nationally, as well as to stress its private brands.

**Co-operative advertising** is *a sharing of advertising costs between the retailer and the manufacturer or wholesaler.* For example, General Mills may pay 50 percent of the cost of the 50 cm$^2$ of a chain's weekly newspaper ad that features a Betty Crocker cake mix special.

Co-operative advertising resulted initially from the newspapers' practice of offering lower rates to local advertisers than to national advertisers. Later, co-operative advertising was seen as a method of

---

20 Bill Abrams, "Comparative Ads Are Getting More Popular, Harder Hitting," *The Wall Street Journal* (March 11, 1982), p. 27. See also Linda E. Swayne and Thomas H. Stevenson, "The Nature and Frequency of Comparative Advertising in Industrial Print Media," in *A Spectrum of Contemporary Marketing Ideas*, (eds.) John H. Summey, Blaise J. Bergiel, and Carol H. Anderson (New Orleans: Southern Marketing Association, 1982), pp. 9–12.
21 Joseph N. Fry and gordon H. McDougall, "Consumer Appraisal of Retail Price Advertisements," *Journal of Marketing* (July 1974), pp. 64–67.
22 This section is based on Tony Thompson, "Retail Advertisers 'Enter 20th Century,'" *Advertising Age* (October 13, 1980), p. 51.

improving dealer relations. From the retailer's viewpoint, co-op advertising permits a store to secure additional advertising that it would not otherwise have.

## Assessing the Effectiveness of an Advertisement

For many firms, advertising represents a major expenditure, so it is imperative to determine whether a campaign is accomplishing its promotional objectives. The determination of advertising effectiveness, however, is one of the most difficult undertakings in marketing. It consists of two primary elements — pre-testing and post-testing.[23]

### Pre-testing

Pre-testing is *the assessment of an advertisement's effectiveness before it is actually used*. It includes a variety of evaluative methods. To test magazine advertisements, the ad agency Batten, Barton, Durstine & Osborn cuts ads out of advance copies of magazines and then "strips in" the ads it wants to test. Interviewers later check the impact of the advertisements on the readers who receive free copies of the revised magazine.

Another ad agency, McCann-Erickson, uses a "sales conviction test" to evaluate magazine advertisements. Interviewers ask heavy users of a particular item to pick which of two alternative advertisements would "convince" them to purchase it.

Potential radio and television advertisements are often screened by consumers who sit in a studio and press two buttons — one for a positive reaction to the commercial, the other for a negative one. Sometimes, proposed ad copy is printed on a postcard that also offers a free product; the number of cards returned is viewed as an indication of the copy's effectiveness. "Blind product tests" are also often used, in which people are asked to select unidentified products on the basis of available advertising copy. Mechanical means of assessing how people read advertising copy are yet another method. One mechanical test uses a camera that photographs eye movement to see how people read ads; the results help determine headline placement and advertising copy length. These are but a few examples of the many methods of pre-testing developed by advertisers.

### Post-testing

Post-testing is *the assessment of advertising copy after it has been used*. Pre-testing is geneally a more desirable testing method than post-testing because of its potential cost savings. But post-testing

───────────
23 This section is based on S. Watson Dunn and Arnold Barban, *Advertising: Its Role in Modern Marketing*, 4th ed. (Hinsdale, Ill.: Dryden Press, 1978), pp. 287–310. An interesting article is Carlton A. Maile, "Predicting Changes in Advertising Effectiveness," *University of Michigan Business Review* (July 1979), pp. 18–22.

# The 24-Second Commercial

Recall is a standard way to measure advertising effectiveness. And according to Professor James MacLachlan, one way to improve recall is to cut the 30-second commercial to 24 seconds by electrically deleting blank space in the promotional message. MacLachlan's tests indicate a 36 percent improvement in an audience's ability to remember a product's name. He says that the faster pace makes personalities in the commercial more believable.

Source: "Commercials That Go Zip," *Newsweek* (June 25, 1979), p. 946.

can be helpful in planning future advertisements and in making adjustments to current advertising programs.

In one of the most popular post-tests, the *Starch Readership Report*, interviewers ask people who have read selected magazines whether they have read various ads in them. A copy of the magazine is used as an interviewing aid, and each interviewer starts at a different point in the magazine. For larger ads, respondents are also asked about specifics such as headlines and copy. All readership or recognition tests assume that future sales are related to advertising readership.

Unaided recall tests are another method of post-testing advertisements. Here, respondents are not given copies of the magazine but must recall the ads from memory. Interviewers for the Gallup and Robinson market-research firm require people to prove they have read a magazine by recalling one or more of its feature articles. The people who remember particular articles are given cards with the names of products advertised in the issue. They then list the ads they remember and explain what they remember about them. Finally, the respondents are asked about their potential purchase of the products. A readership test similar to the Starch test concludes the Gallup and Robinson interview. Other firms use telephone interviews the day after a commercial appears on television in order to test brand recognition and the effectiveness of the advertisement.

Inquiry tests are another popular form of post-test. Advertisements sometimes offer a free gift, generally a sample of the product, to people who respond to the advertisement. The number of inquiries relative to the cost of the advertisement is then used as a measure of effectiveness. Split runs allow advertisers to test two or more ads at the same time. Under this method, a publication's production run is split in two; half the magazines use Advertisement A, and half use Advertisement B. The relative pull of the alternatives is then determined by inquiries.

Regardless of the exact method used, marketers must realize that pre-testing and post-testing are expensive and must, therefore, plan to use them as effectively as possible.

## Sales Promotion Methods

The second type of nonpersonal selling is sales promotion. **Sales promotion** may be defined as *those marketing activities, other than personal selling, advertising, and publicity, that stimulate consumer purchasing and dealer effectiveness*. It includes such activities as displays, shows and exhibitions, demonstrations, and various non-recurrent promotional efforts not in the ordinary routine.[24]

Sales promotional techniques may be used by all members of a marketing channel: manufacturers, wholesalers, and retailers and are typically targeted at specific markets. For example, a manufacturer such as Texize Corporation might combine trial sample mailings of a new spot remover to consumers with a sales contest for wholesalers and retailers who handle the new product. In both instances, the sales promotion techniques are designed to supplement and extend the other elements of the firm's promotional mix.

Firms that wish to use sales promotion can choose from various methods—point-of-purchase advertising, specialty advertising, trade shows, samples, coupons and premiums, contests, and trading stamps. More than one of these options may be used in a single promotional strategy, but probably no promotional strategy has ever used all of the options in a single program. While they are not mutually exclusive, promotions are generally employed on a selective basis.

## Point-of-Purchase Advertising

*Displays and demonstrations that seek to promote the product at a time and place closely associated with the actual decision to buy* are called **point-of-purchasing advertising**. The in-store promotion of consumer goods is a common example. Such advertising can be extremely useful in carrying forward a theme developed in another element of promotional strategy. A life-size display of a celebrity used in television advertising, for instance, can become a realistic in-store display. Another example is the L'eggs store displays that completely altered the pantyhose industry.

## Specialty Advertising

**Specialty advertising** is a sales promotion medium that *utilizes useful articles to carry the advertiser's name, address, and advertising message* to reach the target customers.[25] The origin of specialty advertising has been traced to the Middle Ages, when wooden pegs bearing the names of artisans "were given to prospects to be driven into their walls and to serve as a convenient place upon which to hang armor."[26]

Examples of contemporary advertising specialties carrying a firm's name include calendars, pencils, pens, paperweights, match-

---

[24] Committee on Definitions, *Marketing Definitions: A Glossary of Marketing Terms* (Chicago: American Marketing Association, 1960), p. 20.
[25] This definition is adapted from "How to Play Championship Specialty Advertising," (Chicago: Specialty Advertising Association International, 1978).
[26] Walter A. Gaw, *Specialty Advertising* (Chicago: Specialty Advertising Association, 1970), p. 7.

# THE THICK OF THE CROP.

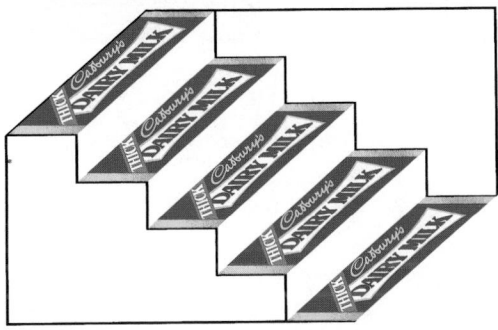

1983 Toronto Art Directors Club — Certificate of Merit • 1984 Toronto Art Directors Club — Certificate of Merit
1984 Billie Awards — Gold Billie Statue — Outdoor Advert.
Source: William Neilson Ltd. • Agency: Scali, McCabe, Sloves (Canada) Ltd.

# OPTHICKAL ILLUSION.

1983 Toronto Art Directors Club — Merit Award • 1984 CLIO Awards — Certificate of Recognition
Source: William Neilson Ltd. • Agency: Scali, McCabe, Sloves (Canada) Ltd.

# THICKELANGELO.

1983 Toronto Art Directors Club — Certificate of Merit • 1984 CLIO Awards — Certificate of Recognition
Source: William Neilson Ltd. • Agency: Scali, McCabe, Sloves (Canada) Ltd.

London  Paris  New York  Hong Kong

Frankfurt  Toronto  Zurich  Tokyo

# It's 11:00 p.m.
# Do you know where
# your money is?

Your order was clear.

Yen to Canadian at 5 points below the market to convert the proceeds of a Samurai issue. Well, the best deal going was in Tokyo at 12:00 noon.

That's 11:00 p.m. Toronto time. And the people who are supposed to be looking out for your best interests are, instead, checking out the late night news.

After all, who conducts trading activities at this hour? We do.

We're The Chase Manhattan Bank of Canada, part of the Chase worldwide network with trading offices around the globe open to serve you 24 hours a day.

It's the most efficient and only way we know to get you the best the world has to offer.

If it has to do with foreign exchange, domestic, or international securities, you owe it to yourself and your money to talk to Chase.

Talk to Jim Snook, V.P. and Manager, Foreign Exchange Trading or Peter Sacks, V.P. and Manager, Securities Trading. They can be reached at (416) 585-3300.

They've got everything required to help you take on the world. And win. Regardless of the hour.

 CHASE

# SOME OUTDATED IMPRESSIONS OF VOLVO ARE ABOUT TO GO UP IN SMOKE.

For more than 58 years, Volvo has pursued relentlessly, the challenge of producing automobiles of unparalleled comfort, safety and durability. As would be expected, this has resulted in enormously powerful and positive impressions of our automobiles.

We are however, about to generate some new perceptions of Volvo. Perceptions based upon performance.

Enter the new Volvo 700 Series with its most awesome member being the 760 Turbo. The latter being capable of launching you to 100 km/h in a time

that could prove more than a little embarrassing to most Autobahn hardware. Equally important, this staggering performance is being presented along with an even greater commitment to our more traditional virtues of safety, luxury, comfort and durability.

Experience the new Volvo 700 Series. And discover why it's causing more than a few outdated impressions of Volvo to vanish in a cloud of smoke. With considerable haste we might add.

**VOLVO**
A car you can believe in.

# HOW MUCH DOES THIS KIND OF LUXURY COST? MAYBE YOU HAD BETTER SIT DOWN.

In attempts to seduce the upwardly mobile, many automakers have served up an endless array of meaningless bells and whistles. The inference being that this is indeed the stuff of which true luxury is made.

At Volvo, we see things a little differently. Examine, if you will, the new Volvo 760 Turbo.

Observe the premium calf skin, deep pile carpeting, automatic control over ambient temperature, an audio system of the highest order and other amenities too plentiful to list.

There is, however, more to Volvo's concept of luxury than these trappings and the abundance of space in which they are to be found.

There is also performance. The likes of which is on par with some of Europe's more exotic two seat rockets.

What is more, the 760 Turbo, like all Volvos has been engineered to deliver this glittering performance long after other so called luxury cars have lost their lustre, which considering the

$29,680* price tag affixed to the 760 Turbo, may prove to be its most luxurious quality.

The new Volvo 760 Turbo.

Please be seated. And discover why it may prove extremely difficult to stand for anything less.

**VOLVO**
A car you can believe in.

*Manufacturer's suggested retail price for the Volvo 760 Turbo, exclusive of taxes, options, dealer prep, registration and other fees. Dealer may sell for less. Prices may change without notice.

# THEY SHOULD BE THERE TOO.

Every 4 years, when athletes go off to represent their country, there is a pride shared by everyone—that final step in the long journey towards excellence.

The competition itself is a test to be met by the athlete alone. But the opportunity to compete is a moment too precious not to be shared with those who matter most.

At Labatt's, we feel nothing should stand in the way of the sharing of this moment.

That's why we're sending every parent of every Canadian Olympic athlete to the Calgary Olympic Winter Games, through the Labatt's Olympic Parents Program.

Because, after all, they should be there too.

## THE LABATT'S OLYMPIC PARENTS PROGRAM.

 Proud Sponsor Calgary '88.

© ℗ COA 1979

Source: Labatt's Brewing Company Limited  •  Agency: Scali, McCabe, Sloves (Canada) Ltd.

books, personalized business gifts of modest value, pocket diaries, shopping bags, memo pads, ash trays, balloons, measuring sticks, key rings, glasses, and hundreds of other items.

Advertising specialties help reinforce previous or future advertising and sales messages. An A. C. Nielsen survey found that both the general public and business were more likely to purchase from firms using specialty advertising.[27]

When Gulf Metals Industries added aluminum and copper drill bits to its vast existing selection of products, the sales department sought an effective way to bring the new products to the attention of purchasing agents in the foundry industry. The challenge was to highlight the bits, thus allowing them to stand out from the rest of the company's products — as well as those of competitors — during the introduction period. The sales department turned to specialty advertising to accomplish their mission.

Playing on the idea of "two bits," Gulf Metals embedded two clusters of the new copper and aluminum bits alongside a quarter in a clear paperweight. The highly distinctive gift-reminders were delivered either in person by the salespeople or through the mail. Once in the purchasing agents' offices, these conversation piece specialties served to remind the recipients again and again of the Gulf Metals sales message. An entire year's production capacity of the new metal bits was sold during the first two months of the campaign.[28]

**Trade Shows**   To influence channel members and resellers in the distribution channel, it has become a common practice for a seller to participate in a *trade show*, exposition, or convention. These shows are often organized by an industry's trade association and may be part of the association's annual meeting or convention. Vendors serving the particular industry are invited to the show to display and demonstrate their products for the association's membership. An example would be the professional meetings attended by college professors in a given discipline where the major textbook publishers exhibit their offerings to the channel members in their marketing system. Shows are also used to reach the ultimate consumer. Home and recreation shows, for instance, allow businesses to display and demonstrate home-care, recreation, and other consumer products to the entire community.[29] Originally such shows were used for demonstration purposes only, but now many go beyond the display format and sell merchandise to the public.

---

27 *Specialty Advertising Report* (Second Quarter 1979), pp. 1–2.
28 "Gulf Metals Finds Little Bits Count," *Specialty Advertising Report*, Vol. VII. No. 3, p. 2, published by the Specialty Advertising Information Bureau, Chicago, Ill.
29 Thomas V. Bonoma, "Get More Out of Your Trade Shows," *Harvard Business Review* (January–February 1983), pp. 75–83.

**Samples, Coupons, and Premiums**

The distribution of samples, coupons, and premiums is probably the best-known sales promotion technique. *Sampling* is a free distribution of an item in an attempt to obtain consumer acceptance. This may be done on a door-to-door basis, by mail, through demonstrations, or insertion into packages containing other products. Sampling is especially useful in promoting new products.

*Coupons* offer a discount, usually some specified price reduction, from the next purchase of a product. Coupons are readily redeemable with retailers, who also receive an additional handling fee. Mail, magazine, newspaper, or package insertion are standard methods of distributing coupons.[30]

**Figure 20-16   Coupon Redemption Rates by Method of Distribution**

| Method of Distribution | Redemption Rate (percent) |
|---|---|
| Newspapers | 39.6 |
| In/on pack | 30.0 |
| Magazines | 14.0 |
| Direct mail | 10.8 |
| Sunday supplements | 7.9 |
| Free-standing inserts | 7.7 |

Source: Adapted from Richard H. Aycrigg, "A New Look at Coupons," *The Nielsen Researcher* (November 1, 1976), p. 6. Reprinted by permission.

*Premiums*, bonus items given free with the purchase of another product, have proved to be effective in getting consumers to try a new product or a different brand.[31] Service stations, for example, use glassware, ice scrapers, and beach balls to convince noncustomers to try their brand. Premiums are also used to obtain direct mail purchases. The value of premium giveaways runs into millions of dollars each year.

**Contests**

Firms may sponsor contests to attract additional customers, offering substantial cash or merchandise prizes to call attention to their products. A company might consider employing a specialist in developing this type of sales promotion because of the variety and complexity of schemes available.

**Trading Stamps**

Trading stamps are a sales promotion technique, similar to premiums, that offer additional value in the product being purchased. Whether the consumer benefits depends upon the relative price levels.

---

30 See David J. Reibstein and Phyllis A. Traver, "Factors Affecting Coupon Redemption Rates," *Journal of Marketing* (Fall 1982), pp. 102–113.
31 See, for example, Carl-Magnus Seipel, "Premiums—Forgotten by Theory," *Journal of Marketing* (April 1971), pp. 26–34.

In Canada the use of trading stamps is almost nonexistent, mainly for legal reasons.

**Public Relations**   The previous chapter defined *public relations* as the firm's communications and relationships with its various publics, including customers, suppliers, stockholders, employees, the government, and the society in which it operates. While public relations expenditures are small relative to those for personal selling, advertising, and even sales promotion, public relations does provide an efficient indirect communications channel for promoting a company's products.[32]

Modern public relations efforts were preceded by the publicity releases of the early entertainment promoters such as P. T. Barnum. Later, industry recognized the need to provide public information as well as to develop public understanding and goodwill. Companies began to develop internal public relations departments to improve their public image. Today, all of these objectives have merged into current public relations practice.

The public relations program has broader objectives than the other aspects of promotional strategy. It is concerned with the prestige and image of all parts of the organization. An example of a nonmarketing-oriented public relations objective would be a company's attempt to gain favourable public opinion during a long strike, or a "Don't sell your shares" plea to stockholders during a financial acquisition attempt by another firm. As a result, the public relations department is not usually placed within the structure of the marketing organization. In fact, many writers advocate having it report directly to the president. However, public relations activities invariably have an impact on promotional strategy.

**Publicity**   The part of public relations that is most directly related to promoting a firm's products or services is publicity. **Publicity** can be defined as *the nonpersonal stimulation of demand by placing commercially significant news about it in a published medium or obtaining favourable presentation of it upon radio, television, or stage that is not paid for by an identified sponsor.*[33] Designed to familiarize the general public with the characteristics, services, and advantages of a product, service, or organization, publicity is an information activity of public relations. Publicity is not entirely cost-free: while expenses are minimal in comparison to other forms of promotion, they include the salaries of marketing personnel assigned to creating and submitting publicity releases, printing and mailing, and other related items.

Some publicity is done to promote a company's image or

[32] The role of public relations is reviewed in Daniel S. Roher, "10 Ways (in Plain English) That Public Relations can Help Sales," *Marketing News* (April 11, 1975), pp. 4–5.
[33] Committee on Definitions, *Marketing Definitions: A Glossary of Marketing Terms* (Chicago: American Marketing Association, 1960), p. 18.

viewpoint, but a significant part is to provide information about products, particularly new ones. Since many consumers tend to accept the authenticity of a news story more readily than they do an advertisement's, publicity releases covering products are often sent to media editors for possible inclusion in newspapers, magazines, and the like. In many cases, such information is valuable to a newspaper or magazine writer, and is eventually published. Some of these releases are used almost word for word to fill voids in the publication, while others are incorporated into regular features. In either case, the use of publicity releases is a valuable supplement to advertising.

Public relations is now considered to be in a period of major growth as a result of increased environmental pressure for better communication between industry and the public. Many top executives are becoming involved. Lee Iacocca's efforts to publicize the justification for federal loan guarantees for Chrysler Corporation are an illustration. A survey of 185 chief executives concluded that 92 percent of them spend more time on public relations now than they did five years ago. And nearly 40 percent of the respondents reported that public relations accounted for 25 to 50 percent of their time.[34]

Some critics assert that the publication of product publicity is directly related to the amount of advertising revenue coming from a firm. But this is not the case at most respected newspapers and periodicals. The story is told that some years ago a bus company executive was enraged at a cartoon appearing in a newspaper that told of a character having numerous problems on a bus trip. The executive threatened to cancel future advertisements in the newspaper unless the cartoon strip was stopped or changed immediately. The newspaper's curt reply was, "One more such communication from you and the alternative of withdrawing your advertising will no longer rest with . . . your company. . . ."[35]

Today, public relations has to be considered an integral part of promotional strategy even though its basic objectives extend far beyond just attempting to influence the purchase of a particular good. While this is difficult to measure, public relations programs, especially their publicity aspects, make a significant contribution to the achievement of promotional goals.[36]

[34] The data in this section is from Alvin P. Sanoff, "Image Makers Worry about their Own Images," *U.S. News & World Report* (August 13, 1979), pp. 57–59; "The Corporate Image: PR to the Rescue," *Business Week* (January 22, 1979), pp. 46–50, 54, 56, 60–61; and Fred Kirsch, "No Slick Tricks in One-Man P.R. Firm," *Detroit News* (April 17, 1978), pp. 1-C, 3-C.

[35] Gene Harlan and Alan Scott, *Contemporary Public Relations: Principles and Cases* (Englewood Cliffs, N.J.: Prentice-Hall, 1955), p. 36.

[36] The measurement question is considered in William M. Domin and Jack Freymuller, "Can Industrial Product Publicity Be Measured?" *Journal of Marketing* (July 1965), pp. 54–57.

***Summary***   Advertising, sales promotion, public relations, and publicity — the nonpersonal selling elements of promotion — are not merely twentieth-century phenomena. Advertising, for instance, can trace its origin to very early times. Today, these elements of promotion have gained professional status and are vital policies of most organizations, both profit and nonprofit.

Advertising (a nonpersonal sales presentation usually directed to a large number of potential customers) should generally seek to achieve communications goals rather than direct sales objectives. It strives to inform, persuade, and remind the potential consumer of the product or service being promoted.

Advertising planning starts with effective research, which permits the development of a strategy. Tactical decisions about copy and scheduling are then made. Finally, advertisements are evaluated, and appropriate feedback is provided to management. There are six basic types of advertisements:
1. informative product advertising
2. persuasive product advertising
3. reminder-oriented product advertising
4. informative institutional advertising
5. persuasive institutional advertising
6. reminder-oriented institutional advertising

One of the most vital decisions in developing an advertising strategy is the selection of the mix of newspapers, periodicals, television, radio, outdoor advertising, and direct mail to be employed to attract the attention of the target market.

The major tasks of advertising departments are advertising research, art, copywriting, media analysis, and sales promotion. Many advertisers use independent advertising agencies to provide them with the creativity and objectivity missing in their own organizations and to reduce the cost of advertising. The final step in the advertising process is developing and preparing the advertisement.

The principal methods of sales promotion are point-of-purchase advertising; specialty advertising; trade shows; samples, coupons, and premiums; contests; and trading stamps. Public relations and publicity also play major roles in developing promotional strategies.

***Key Terms***

product advertising
institutional advertising
informative advertising
persuasive advertising
reminder-oriented advertising
advocacy advertising
advertising agency
comparative advertising

retail advertising
co-operative advertising
pre-testing
post-testing
sales promotion
point-of-purchase advertising
specialty advertising

**Review Questions**

1. Explain the wide variation in advertising expenditures as a percentage of sales in the industries shown in Figure 20-1.
2. Trace the historical development of advertising.
3. Describe the primary objectives of advertising.
4. List and discuss the six basic types of advertising. Cite an example of each type.
5. Discuss the relationship between advertising and the product life cycle.
6. What are the advantages and disadvantages associated with using each of the advertising media?
7. Describe the advertising planning process.
8. Under what circumstances are celebrity spokespeople in advertising likely to be effective?
9. Why is retail advertising so important today? Relate co-operative advertising to the discussion of alternative promotional strategies in Chapter 19.
10. List and discuss the principal methods of sales promotion.

**Discussion Questions and Exercises**

1. Develop an argument favouring the use of comparative advertising by a marketer who is currently preparing an advertising plan. Make any assumptions necessary.
2. Discuss the organization of the advertising function. Consider all of the major activities associated with company advertising.
3. What specialty advertising would be appropriate for the following?
   a. an independent insurance agent
   b. a retail furniture store
   c. Stelco
   d. a local radio station
4. Co-operative advertising results in a sharing of advertising costs between the retailer and the manufacturer or vendor. From society's viewpoint, should this kind of advertising be prohibited on the grounds that it leads to manufacturer domination of the distribution channel? Defend your answer.
5. Sweden's business practices court ordered an advertising agency and its client, a Swedish insurance company, to stop using models and incidents identified in their commercials as if the incidents and people were authentic. The court ruled that this practice misled buyers. Do you agree? Why or why not?

**MICROCOMPUTER EXERCISE: Cost per Thousand (CPM)**

CPM, or the cost per thousand, is an important media-selection tool. It allows advertisers to evaluate options within a specific advertising media.

**Directions:** Use the Menu Item titled "CPM" on the Foundations of Marketing disk to solve the following problems.

1. Aubrey Edwards has decided to use radio advertising to promote his Winnipeg sporting-goods store. He is targeting his advertising at people between 18 and 49 years of age. Edwards has decided to run his commercials during the morning and afternoon hours — the so-called drive time when people are commuting to and from work. He has assembled the data shown in Table A about the stations that offer the blend of programming designed to attact his market-target listeners.

    a. Which of the four radio stations has the lowest overall CPM? Which is the most expensive in terms of overall CPMs?

    b. Which of the four stations has the lowest CPM for listeners between the ages of 18 and 34? Which is the most expensive for this age category?

    c. Which of the four stations will reach the total audience at the lowest CPM?

**Table A Market-Target Members in Radio Audience**

| Radio Station | Total Audience | Listeners Aged 18–34 | Listeners Aged 35–49 | Cost of 30-Second Commercial |
|---|---|---|---|---|
| CFND | 22 500 | 7 000 | 5 000 | $ 90 |
| CFAM | 36 000 | 6 000 | 8 000 | $120 |
| CFOX | 50 000 | 35 500 | 11 500 | $200 |
| CJUB | 75 000 | 17 000 | 20 000 | $225 |

2. Linda Morrison is the product manager for Model 101, a sophisticated new microcomputer specifically designed for business applications. Model 101's programs assume the user is knowledgeable about business and finance and has some hands-on computer experience. Morrison is evaluating six magazines to use in advertising Model 101. She has collected the data shown in Table B.

    a. Which magazine has the lowest overall CPM? Which is more expensive in terms of overall CPMs?

    b. If Morrison defines her market target as consisting only of college graduates, which of the six magazines would offer her the lowest CPM?

    c. If Morrison decides to focus solely on persons holding managerial or administrative positions, which magazine would allow her to reach this target at the lowest CPM? Which would be most expensive in terms of CPMs?

## Table B   Market-Target Members in Magazines

| Magazine | Total Readers | Managerial/ Administrative | College Graduates | Black & White Page Rates |
|---|---|---|---|---|
| Computer Pro | 2 000 000 | 1 000 000 | 750 000 | $20 000 |
| Top Byte | 1 150 000 | 525 000 | 390 000 | $15 000 |
| Office Today | 2 575 000 | 1 500 000 | 425 000 | $17 500 |
| The Micro Manager | 600 000 | 400 000 | 250 000 | $10 000 |
| Today's Computer | 4 250 000 | 1 100 000 | 850 000 | $35 000 |
| Future Computer | 2 500 000 | 750 000 | 500 000 | $13 500 |

## CHAPTER 21

# Personal Selling and Sales Management

## CHAPTER OBJECTIVES

1. *To explain the factors affecting the importance of personal selling in the promotional mix.*

2. *To identify the three basic sales tasks.*

3. *To list the characteristics of successful salespersons.*

4. *To outline the steps in the sales process.*

5. *To describe the major problems faced by sales managers.*

6. *To list the functions of sales management.*

**The Conceptual Framework**

Personal selling was defined in Chapter 19 as a seller's promotional presentation conducted on a person-to-person basis with the buyer. Selling is an inherent function of any business enterprise. Accounting, engineering, personnel management, and other organizational activities are useless unless the firm's product can be sold to someone. Thousands of sales employees bear witness to selling's importance in the Canadian economy. While advertising expenses in the average firm may represent from 1 to 3 percent of total sales, selling expenses are likely to equal 10 to 15 percent of sales. In many firms, personal selling is the single largest marketing expense.

As Chapter 19 pointed out, personal selling is likely to be the primary component of a firm's promotional mix when customers are concentrated geographically; when orders are large; when the products or services are expensive, technically complex, and require special handling; when trade-ins are involved; when channels are short; and when the number of potential customers is relatively small. Figure 21-1 summarizes the factors affecting personal selling's importance in the overall promotional mix.

Selling has been a standard part of business for thousands of years.[1] The earliest peddlers were traders who had some type of

---

1 The remainder of this section is based on David L. Kurtz, "The Historical Development of Selling," *Business and Economic Dimensions* (August 1970), pp. 12–18. A good historical account of personal selling is contained in Henry W. Nash, "Origin and Development of Personal Selling," *Mississippi Business Review* (January 1977), pp. 6–8. See also A. Emerson Belcher, "What I Know About Commercial Travelling" (Toronto: Hunter-Rose, 1883).

ownership interest in the goods they sold after manufacturing or importing them. In many cases, these people viewed selling as a secondary activity.

Selling later became a separate function. The peddlers of the eighteenth century sold to the farmers and settlers of the vast North American continent. In the nineteenth century, salespeople called "drummers" sold to both consumers and marketing intermediaries. These early settlers sometimes employed questionable sales practices and techniques and earned an undesirable reputation for themselves and their firms. Some of this negative stereotype remains today.[2] But for the most part, selling is far different from what it was in earlier years.

**Figure 21-1    Factors Affecting the Importance of Personal Selling in the Promotional Mix**

|                | *Personal Selling* is likely to be more important when: | *Advertising* is likely to be more important when: |
|----------------|-----------------------------------------------|--------------------------------------------|
| consumer is:   | geographically concentrated, relatively small numbers; | geographically dispersed, relatively large numbers; |
| product is:    | expensive, technically complex, custom-made, special handling required, trade-ins frequently involved; | inexpensive, simple to understand, standardized, no special handling, no trade-ins; |
| price is:      | relatively high;                              | relatively low;                            |
| channels are:  | relatively short.                             | relatively long.                           |

**Sales Tasks**    The sales job has evolved into a professional occupation. Today's salesperson is more concerned with helping customers select the correct product to meet their needs than with simply selling whatever is available. Modern professional salespeople advise and assist customers in their purchase decisions. Where repeat purchases are common, the salesperson must be certain that the buyer's purchases are in his or her best interest or else no future sales will be made. The interests of the seller are tied to those of the buyer.

Not all selling activities are alike. While all sales activities assist the customer in some manner, the exact tasks that are performed

[2] See Alan J. Dubinsky, "Perceptions of the Sales Job: How Students Compare with Industrial Salespeople," *Journal of the Academy of Marketing Science* (Fall 1981), pp. 352–367.

vary from one position to another.[3] Three basic sales tasks can be identified: 1) order processing, 2) creative selling, and 3) missionary sales.

These tasks can form the basis for a sales classification system. It should be observed, however, that most sales personnel do not fall into any single category. Instead, we often find salespersons performing all three tasks to a certain extent. A sales engineer for a computer firm may be doing 50 percent missionary sales, 45 percent creative selling, and 5 percent order processing. In other words, most sales jobs require their incumbents to engage in a variety of sales activities. However, most selling jobs are classified on the basis of the primary selling task that is performed. We shall examine each of these selling tasks.

**Order Processing**

**Order processing** is most often typified by selling at the wholesale and retail levels. Salespeople who handle this task must do the following:

1. *Identify customer needs:* for instance, a soft-drink route salesperson determines that a store that carries a normal inventory of 40 cases has only seven cases left in stock.
2. *Point out the need* to the customer: the route salesperson informs the store manager of the inventory situation.
3. *Complete (or write up) the order:* the store manager acknowledges the situation; the driver unloads 33 cases; the manager signs the delivery slip.

Order processing is part of most selling jobs and becomes the primary task where needs can be readily identified and are acknowledged by the customer. Selling life insurance is usually not simple order processing. However, one insurance company reported that during a period of civil unrest in Belfast, Northern Ireland, one of their representatives, Danny McNaughton, sold 208 new personal accident income-protection policies in a week. McNaughton averaged one sale every 12 minutes of his working day.[4] Apparently, the need for insurance was readily recognized in Belfast.

**Creative Selling**

When a considerable degree of analytical decision-making on the part of the consumer is involved in purchasing a product, the salesperson must skilfully solicit an order from a prospect. To do so, creative selling techniques must be used. New products often require

---

[3] Interesting discussions of selling are presented in H. Robert Dodge, "The Role of the Industrial Salesman," *Mid-South Quarterly Business Review* (January 1972), pp. 11–15; and Benson P. Shapiro and Ronald S. Posner, "Making the Major Sale," *Harvard Business Review* (March–April 1976), pp. 68–78.

[4] Reported in "Sell, Sell, Sell," *The Wall Street Journal* (September 14, 1971), p. 1.

a high degree of **creative selling**. The seller *must make the buyer see the worth of the item*. Creative selling may be the most demanding of the three tasks.

**Missionary Sales**

**Missionary sales** are an indirect type of selling; people *sell the goodwill* of a firm and provide the customers with technical or operational assistance. For example, a toiletries company salesperson may call on retailers to look after special promotions and overall stock movement, although a wholesaler is used to take orders and deliver merchandise. In more recent times, technical and operational assistance, such as that provided by a systems specialist, have also become a critical part of missionary selling.

---

**Characteristics
of Successful
Salespeople**

The saying "Salespeople are born, not made" is untrue. Most people have some degree of sales ability. Each of us is called upon to sell others his or her ideas, philosophy, or personality at some time. However, while some individuals adapt to selling more easily than others, selling is not an easy job; it involves a great deal of practice and hard work.

Effective salespersons are self-motivated individuals who are well prepared to meet the demands of the competitive marketplace. The continuing pressure to solve buyers' problems requires that salespeople develop good work habits and exhibit considerable initiative.

Successful sales representatives are not only self-starters, they are knowledgeable businesspersons. Sales personnel are also in the peculiar position of having their knowledge tested almost continually. Sales success is often a function of how well a salesperson can handle questions. Salespeople must know their company, products, competition, customers, and themselves. They must also be able to analyse customer needs and fit them with products and services which satisfy those requirements.

**Feedback: The
Responsibility of Every
Salesperson**

There is *one function that all sales personnel perform* — providing sales intelligence to the marketing organization.[5] Chapter 19 noted that field sales reports are a part of the feedback generated within the marketing system. Since the sales force is close to the market, it is often the best (and most reliable) source of current marketing information, upon which management decisions are made.

The marketing intelligence provided by field sales personnel is copious and varied. Sales personnel can provide timely, current assessments of competitive efforts, new product launches, customer reactions, and the like. Marketing executives should nurture and implement this valuable information source.

---

[5] Joel Saegert and Robert J. Hoover, "Sales Managers and Sales Force Feedback: Information Left in the Pipeline," *Journal of the Academy of Marketing Science* (Winter/Spring 1980), pp. 33–39.

**The Sales Process**   What, then, are the steps involved in selling? While the terminology may vary, most authorities agree on the following sequence:
1. prospecting and qualifying
2. approach
3. presentation
4. demonstration
5. handling objections
6. closing
7. follow-up

# The Changing Face of Selling

The term *salesperson* all too often conjures up unpleasant visions of Arthur Miller's antihero Willy Loman in *Death of a Salesman*:

*You don't understand: Willy was a salesman . . . He don't put a bolt to a nut. He don't tell you the law or give you medicine. He's a man way out there in the blue, riding on a smile and a shoeshine. And when they start not smiling back — that's an earthquake.*

But the tasks of the modern salesperson are so different and so complex. Take, for example, the case of Louis J. Manara, a superb salesperson employed by American Cyanamid. The changes that have occurred in Manara's job over the past decade were depicted in a recent *Fortune* article as follows:

When Manara began selling chemicals for Cyanamid in 1971, the job was relatively straightforward. As in the days of Willy Loman, the salesman was assigned a territory and dispatched to tap every possible customer. He was told little about his division's goals, nothing about the profitability of his bag of products. His marching orders were uncomplicated: sell all you can, as fast as you can.

Back then, most industrial salespersons succeeded by nurturing close personal relationships with the customers — always a company, usually represented by a poorly paid purchasing agent who was wooed with long lunches, evening entertainment, and golf or fishing weekends. If the purchasing agent proved recalcitrant, the salesper-

son could try the "back door" approach of going directly to end users of the product, such as plant managers. On days when calls were finished early, the salesperson might try his luck "smokestacking," — that is, dropping in on potential customers whose factory smokestacks were spotted while driving down the highway.

But in the past decade the salesperson's job has become vastly more complex — so much so that a number of executives believe a new job title is required. "Salesman is just too narrow a word," says one marketing manager. Gordon Sterling, Manara's division president, pinpoints the basic change. "Ten years ago, it was sales, sales, sales," he says. "Now we tell our salespeople: don't just sell — we need information. What do our customers need? What is the competition doing? What sort of financial package do we need to win the order?"

The probing for market intelligence is not the only new duty. Manara also is expected to mediate disputes between Cyanamid's credit department, newly vigilant in these times of costly money, and slow-paying customers. He has to sort out customer complaints concerning Cyanamid products. He must keep abreast of fast changes in both government regulations and world chemical markets. "Ten years ago," he sighs, "we had back-up people to handle all this. But most of them have been let go. We have to be far better informed than we were then."

Source: Hugh D. Menzies, "The New Life of a Salesman," *Fortune* (August 11, 1980), p. 173. Reprinted by permission. Quote from Arthur Miller, *Death of a Salesman* (New York: Viking, 1949).

**Prospecting and**
**Qualifying**

**Prospecting,** *the identification of potential customers*, is difficult work involving many hours of diligent effort. Prospects may come from many sources: previous customers, friends and neighbours, other vendors, nonsales employees in the firm, suppliers, and social and professional contacts. New sales personnel often find prospecting frustrating, since there is usually no immediate payback. But without prospecting there are no future sales. For example, in the marketing of various types of adhesive tapes for industrial use, a representative of a tape manufacturing company, perhaps a manufacturers' agent, must seek out potential users of these specialty tapes. Prospecting is a continuous process because there will always be a loss of some customers over time, which must be compensated for by the emergence of new customers or the discovery of potential customers who have never been contacted before. Many sales management experts consider prospecting to be the very essence of the sales process.

**Qualifying** — *determining that the prospect is really a potential customer* — is another important sales task. Not all prospects are qualified to become customers. Qualified customers are people with both the money and the authority to make purchase decisions. A person with an annual income of $10 000[6] may wish to own a $75 000 house, but this person's ability to actually become a customer has to be questioned. Similarly, a parent with six children may strongly desire a two-seater sports car, but this would probably not be a practical purchase as the sole family vehicle.

**Approach**

Once the salesperson has identified a qualified prospect, he or she collects all available information relative to the potential buyer and plans an **approach** — *the initial contact of the salesperson with the prospective customer*. Figure 21-2 suggests that the relative aggressiveness of a sales approach usually varies inversely with the repeat-sale potential of the prospect. In other words, the lower the repeat-sale potential, the harder the approach is likely to be and vice versa. All approaches should be based on comprehensive research. The salesperson should find out as much as possible about the prospect. Retail salespeople often cannot do this in advance, but they can compensate by asking leading questions to learn more about the prospect's purchase preferences. Industrial marketers have far more data available, and they should make use of it before scheduling the first interview.

---

[6] For an analysis of problems involved in identifying specific decision makers in an industrial setting, see Thomas V. Bonoma, "Major Sales: Who *Really* Does the Buying?" *Harvard Business Review* (May–June 1982), pp. 111–119.

**Figure 21-2   The Sales Aggression Spectrum with Ecological Determinants**

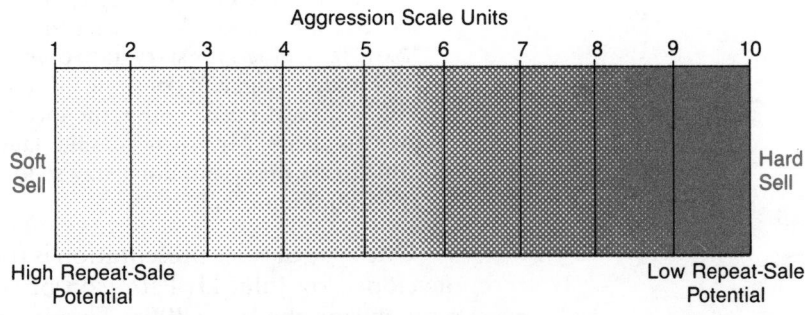

*Source:* Adapted from Barry J. Hersker, "The Ecology of Personal Selling," *Southern Journal of Business* (July 1970), p. 44. Reprinted by permission.

**Presentation**   When the salesperson *gives the sales message to a prospective customer*, he or she makes a **presentation**. The seller describes the product's major features, points out its strengths, and concludes by citing illustrative successes.[7] The seller's objective is to talk about the product or service in terms meaningful to the buyer — benefits, rather than technical specifications. Thus the presentation is the stage where the salesperson relates product features to customer needs.

The presentation should be clear and concise, and should emphasize the positive. For example, consider how, many years ago, a young college president presented an *idea* to industrialist Andrew Carnegie:

> One of the buildings of Wooster University burned down one night. On the following day the youthful, boyish-looking president, Louis E. Holden, started to New York City to see Andrew Carnegie. Without wasting a minute in preliminaries he began: "Mr. Carnegie, you are a busy man and so am I. I won't take up more than five minutes of your time. The main building of Wooster University burned down night before last, and I want you to give us $100 000 for a new one." "Young man," replied the philanthropist, "I don't believe in giving money to colleges." "But you believe in helping young men, don't you?" urged President Holden. "I'm a young man, Mr. Carnegie, and I'm in an awful hole. I've gone into the business of manufacturing college men from the raw material and now the best part of my plant is gone. You know how you would feel if one of your

---

[7] For an interesting discussion of promotional appeals, see Walter Gross, "Rational and Nonrational Appeals in Selling to Businessmen," *Georgia Business* (February 1970), pp. 1–3.

big steel mills were destroyed right in the busy season." "Young man,"
responded Mr. Carnegie, "raise $100 000 in thirty days and I'll give
you another." "Make it sixty days and I'll go you," replied Dr. Holden.
"Done," assented Mr. Carnegie. Dr. Holden picked up his hat and
started for the door. As he reached it, Mr. Carnegie called after him,
"Now remember, it's sixty days only." "All right, sir, I understand."
Dr. Holden's call had consumed just four minutes. The required
$100 000 was raised within the specified time, and when handing
over his check, Mr. Carnegie said, laughing, "Young man, if you ever
come to see me again, don't stay so long. Your call cost me just
$25 000 a minute."[8]

One type of sales presentation is the **canned approach** originally
developed by John H. Patterson of National Cash Register Company during the late 1800s. This is *a memorized sales talk* used to
ensure uniform coverage of the points deemed important by management.[9] While canned presentations are still used in such areas
as door-to-door **cold canvassing**, most professional sales forces have
long since abandoned their use.[10] The prevailing attitude is that flexible presentations allow the salesperson to account for motivational
differences among prospects. Proper planning, of course, is an important part of tailoring a presentation to each particular customer.

*Demonstration*     Demonstrations can play a critical role in a sales presentation. A
demonstration ride in a new automobile allows the prospect to
become involved in the presentation. It awakens customer interest
in a manner that no amount of verbal presentation can achieve.
Demonstrations supplement, support, and reinforce what the sales
representative has already told the prospect. The key to a good
demonstration is planning. A unique demonstration is more likely
to gain a customer's attention than a "usual" sales presentation. But
such a demonstration must be well planned and executed if a favourable impression is to be made. One cannot overemphasize that the
salesperson should check and recheck all aspects of the demonstration prior to its delivery.

*Handling Objections*     A vital part of selling involves handling objections. It is reasonable
to expect a customer to say, "Well, I really should check with my
family," or "Perhaps I'll stop back next week," or "I like everything

8 Quoted in James Samuel Knox, *Salesmanship and Business Efficiency* (New
York: The Gregg Publishing Company, 1922), pp. 243–244.
9 This approach is discussed in Marvin A. Jolson, "The Underestimated Potential
of the Canned Sales Presentation," *Journal of Marketing* (January 1975),
pp. 75–78.
10 *Cold canvassing* refers to unsolicited sales calls upon a random group of
people; that is, the prospecting and qualifying effort is minimal.

except the colour." A good salesperson, however, should use each objection as a cue to provide additional information to the prospect. In most cases an objection such as "I don't like the bucket seats" is really the prospect's way of asking what other choices or product features are available. A customer's question reveals an interest in the product. It allows the seller an opportunity to expand a presentation by providing additional information.

**Closing**   The moment of truth in selling is the **closing,** for this is when *the salesperson asks the prospect for an order.* A sales representative should not hesitate during the closing. If he or she has made an effective presentation, based on applying the product to the customer's needs, the closing should be the natural conclusion.

A surprising number of sales personnel have difficulty in actually asking for an order. But to be effective they must overcome the difficulty. Methods of closing a sale include the following:

1. The *alternative-decision technique* poses choices to a prospect where either alternative is favourable to the salesperson. "Will you take this sweater or that one?"
2. The *SRO (standing room only) technique* is used when a prospect is told that a sales agreement should be concluded now, because the product may not be available later.
3. *Emotional closes* attempt to get a person to buy through appeal to such factors as fear, pride, romance, or social acceptance.
4. *Silence* can be used as a closing technique since a discontinuance of a sales presentation forces the prospect to take some type of action (either positive or negative).
5. *Extra-inducement closes* are special incentives designed to motivate a favourable buyer response. Extra inducements may include quantity discounts, special servicing arrangements, or a layaway option.[11]

**Follow-up**   The *postsales activities* that often determine whether a person will become a repeat customer constitute the sales **follow-up.** To the maximum extent possible, representatives should contact their customers to find out if they are satisfied with their purchases. This step allows the salesperson to reinforce psychologically the person's original decision to buy. It gives the seller an opportunity, in addition to correcting any sources of discontent with the purchase, to secure important market information, and to make additional sales.[12] Auto-

---

11 These and other closing techniques are outlined in David L. Kurtz, H. Robert Dodge, and Jay E. Klompmaker, *Professional Selling* (Dallas: Business Publications, 1976), pp. 220–227.

12 Buyers, for instance, will often attempt to reduce their dissonance by promoting their purchases to friends and associates. See John R. Stuteville, "The Buyer as a Salesman," *Journal of Marketing* (July 1968), pp. 14–18.

mobile dealers often keep elaborate records on their previous customers. This allows them to remind individuals when they might be due for a new car. One successful travel agency never fails to telephone customers upon their return from a trip. Proper follow-up is a logical part of the selling sequence.

Effective follow-up also means that the salesperson should conduct a critical review of every call that is made. One should ask, "What was it that allowed me to close that sale?" or "What caused me to lose that sale?" Such continual review results in significant sales dividends.

### Retail Selling

For the most part, the public is more aware of retail selling than of any other form of personal selling. In fact, many writers have argued that a person's basic attitude toward the sales function is determined by his or her impression of retail sales personnel.[13]

Retail selling has some distinctive features that require its consideration as a separate subject. The most significant difference between it and its counterparts is that the customer *comes to* the retail salesperson. This requires that the retailer effectively combine selling with a good advertising and sales promotion program that draws the customer into the store. Another difference is that while store employees are sales personnel in one sense, they are also retailers in the broader dimension. Selling is not their only responsibility.

Retail sales personnel should be well versed in store policy and procedures. Credit, discounts, special sales, delivery, layaway, and return policies are examples of the type of information that the salesperson should know. *Uninformed sales personnel* are one of the major complaints voiced by today's customer.

The area of retail selling exhibiting the greatest potential for improvement is the greeting. The standard "May I help you?" seems totally out of place in contemporary marketing, and yet it is interesting to observe the number of retail salespeople who still use this outdated approach. "May I help you?" invites customer rejection in the form of the standard reply, "No thanks, I'm just looking." A better method is to use a merchandise-oriented greeting such as "The fashion editors say that this will be the most popular colour this fall." The positive approach helps to orient the customer toward the merchandise or display.

Two selling techniques particularly applicable to retailing are

---

[13] An interesting discussion is contained in Gilbert A. Churchill, Robert H. Collins, and William A. Strang, "Should Retail Salespersons Be Similar to Their Customers?" *Journal of Retailing* (Fall 1975), pp. 29–42, 79.

selling up and suggestion selling. **Selling up** is the technique of *convincing the customer to buy a higher-priced item than he or she originally intended.* An automobile salesperson may convince a consumer to buy a more expensive model than the person intended to buy. An important point is that the practice of selling up should always be used within the constraints of the customer's real needs. If the salesperson sells the customer something that he or she really does not need, the potential for repeat sales by that seller is substantially diminished.

**Suggestion selling** *seeks to broaden the customer's original purchase* with related items, special promotions, and/or holiday and seasonal merchandise. Suggestion selling, too, should be based upon the idea of helping the customer recognize true needs rather than selling the person unwanted merchandise. Suggestion selling is one of the best methods of increasing retail sales and should be practised by all sales personnel.

**Figure 21-3   Operational and Administrative Abilities Required for Sales Organization Jobs**

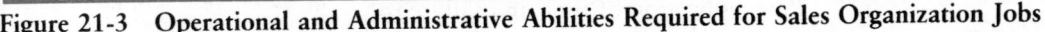
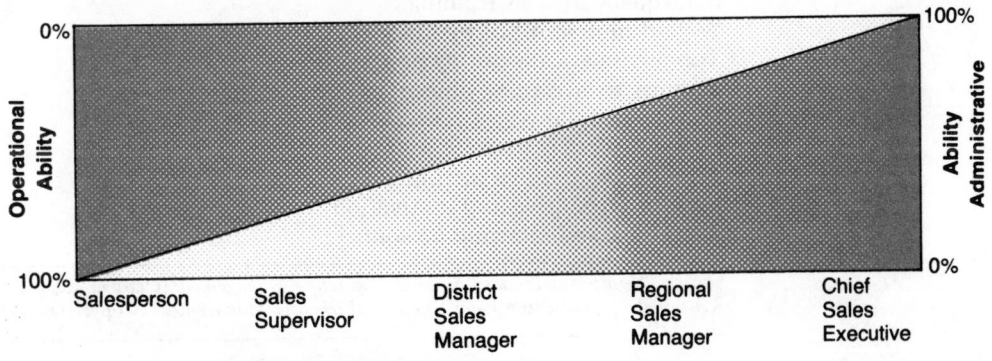

Source: Thomas R. Wotruba, *Sales Management Planning, Accomplishment, and Evaluation* (New York: Holt, Rinehart and Winston, 1971). Reprinted by permission of the author.

**Managing the Sales Effort**

Contemporary selling requires that **sales management** effort be exerted in the direction of *securing, maintaining, motivating, supervising, evaluating, and controlling an effective field sales force.* The sales manager is the link between the salesperson, customers and prospects, and the firm's management.[14] The sales manager has

14 See, for example, Robert F. Gwinner, "Coordinating Strategy and Tactics in Sales Administration," *MSU Business Topics* (Summer 1970), pp. 56–62. See also Hollister Spencer, "Salesmen and Sales Managers Look at the District Manager," *California Management Review* (Fall 1972), pp. 98–105.

professional responsibilities in both directions. Most sales management jobs require some degree of both operational (or sales-oriented) ability and administrative (or managerial) ability. The higher one rises in the sales management hierarchy, the more administrative ability and the less operational ability is required to perform the job. Figure 21-3 diagrams this relationship.[15]

## Problems Faced by Sales Management

Sales executives face a variety of management problems. However, with few exceptions, these problems have remained largely the same over the years. Poor utilization of time and failure to plan sales effort were reported as the leading problems in both the 1959 and the 1979 surveys cited earlier in this chapter. Other current major problem areas and their 1959 rankings are shown in Figure 21-4.

**Figure 21-4    Major Sales Management Problems**

| Problem Area | 1979 Ranking | 1959 Ranking |
|---|---|---|
| Poor utilization of time and failure to plan sales effort | 1 | 1 |
| Inadequacy in sales training | 2 | 21 |
| Wasted time in office by salespeople | 3 | 6 |
| Too few sales calls during hours | 4 | 3 |
| Inability to overcome objections | 5 | 5 |
| Indifferent follow-up | 6 | 7 |
| Lack of sales creativity | 7 | 2 |
| Meeting competitive pricing | 8 | 15 |
| Lack of sales drive and motivation | 9 | 8 |
| Recruiting and selecting personnel | 10 | 11 |

Source: "Significant Trends," *Sales & Marketing Management* (October 15, 1979), p. 102. Reprinted by permission from *Sales & Marketing Management*. Copyright 1979.

## Sales Management: Functions

The sales manager performs seven basic managerial functions: 1) recruitment and selection, 2) training, 3) organization, 4) supervision, 5) motivation, 6) compensation, and 7) evaluation and control.

### Recruitment and Selection

The initial step in building an effective sales force involves recruiting and selecting good personnel. Sources of new salespeople include community colleges, trade and business schools, colleges and universities, sales personnel in other firms, and people at present

[15] See Albert H. Dunn, "Should You Get Your Field Sales Manager Out of Selling?" *Sales Management* (October 1, 1966), pp. 37–40; and John J. McCarthy, "Sales Manager: Manager of Sales? or Manager of Salesmen?" *Sales Management* (April 15, 1967), pp. 69–76.

employed in nonsales occupations, including a company's own nonsales employees.

Not all of these areas are equally productive. One of the problem areas seems to be the reluctance of high school guidance counsellors to convey to the students the advantages of a selling career.[16] A successful career in sales offers satisfaction in all the five areas that a person generally looks for when deciding on a profession:

1. Opportunity for advancement: Studies have shown that successful sales representatives advance rapidly in most companies. Advancement can come either within the sales organization or laterally (to a more responsible position in some other functional area of the firm).

2. High earnings: The earnings of successful salespersons compare favourably to the earnings of successful people in other professions. In fact, over the long run, sales earnings often exceed those of most other professional occupations.

3. Personal satisfaction: One derives satisfaction in sales from achieving success in a competitive environment and from helping people satisfy their wants and needs.

4. Security: Contrary to what many students believe, selling provides a high degree of job security. Experience has shown that economic downturns affect personnel in sales less than those in most other employment areas. In addition, there is a continuing need for good sales personnel. Figure 21-5 shows the median employment situation for some sales occupations.

**Figure 21-5   Employment in Sales**

|  | Persons Employed in 1975 | Annual Average Job Openings 1975 to 1982 |
|---|---|---|
| Manufacturers' and Wholesale Salespersons | 70 000 | 1 400 |
| Retail Salespersons | 304 000 | 11 000 |

Source: Department of Manpower and Immigration, *Careers in Sales*, 1976, p. 30.

5. Independence and variety: Most often salespersons really operate as "independent" businesspeople (or as managers of sales territories). Their work is also quite varied and provides an opportunity for involvement in numerous business functions.

---

16 For discussions of this problem, see Gordon W. Paul and Parker Worthing, "A Student Assessment of Selling: Some Exploratory Findings," *Southern Journal of Business* (July 1970), pp. 57–65; David L. Kurtz, "An Evaluation of the Sales Recruiting Programs of Michigan Manufacturers," *Business Ideas and Facts* (Winter 1970), pp. 3–8; and Raymond L. Hilgert, "College Students and Their Attitudes Toward Selling," *Marquette Business Review* (Winter 1968), pp. 145–149.

Figure 21-6   Steps in the Sales Personnel Selection Process

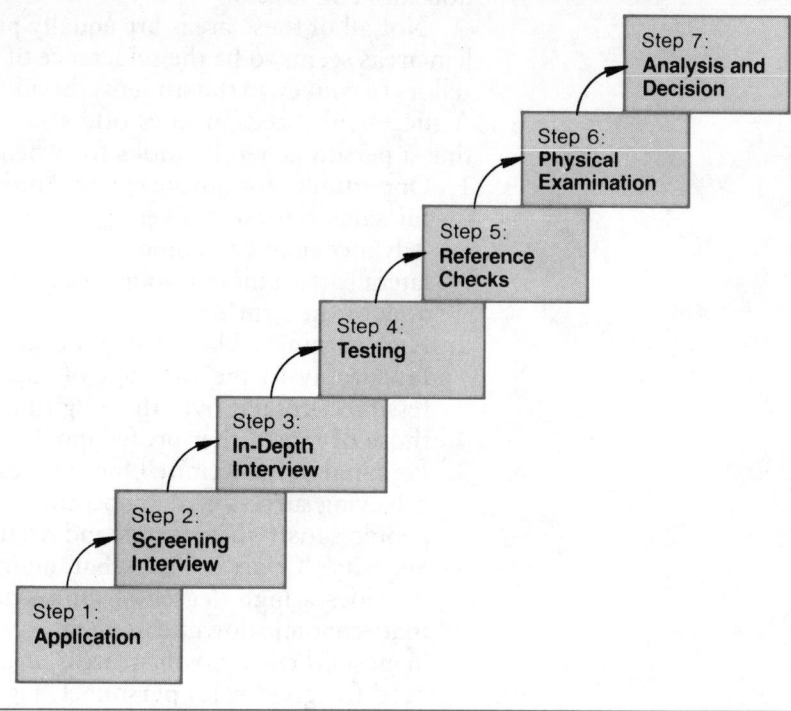

Salesperson selection is important because 1) it requires a substantial investment in money and management time, and 2) selection mistakes are detrimental to customer relations and performance of the sales force as a whole, as well as being costly to correct.

Selection of salespeople is more than a set of procedural steps. It is a *process*, in which the several steps are interrelated and independent. Each of the steps must be considered as a further refinement of a matching and screening process, a hurdle to be overcome.

The selection process for sales personnel is outlined in Figure 21-6. An application screening is followed by an initial interview. If there is sufficient interest, in-depth interviewing is conducted. Next, the company may use testing in their procedure. This step could include aptitude, intelligence, interest, knowledge, or personality tests. References are then checked to guarantee that job candidates have represented themselves correctly. A physical examination is usually included before a final hiring decision is made.[17]

[17] See Wesley J. Johnston and Martha Cooper, "Industrial Sales Force Selection: Current Knowledge and Needed Research," *Journal of Personal Selling & Sales Management* (Spring/Summer 1981), pp. 49–57.

This process indicates that sales managers use several types of *tools* in selecting new sales personnel. Interviews are considered the most helpful selection tool, although they are the most costly. In contrast, experienced managers rate intelligence, aptitude, and personality tests considerably lower.

**Training**   To shape new sales recruits into an efficient sales organization, management must conduct an effective training program. The principal methods used in sales training are lectures, role-playing, and on-the-job traning.

Sales training is also important for veteran salespeople. Most of this type of training is done in an informal manner by sales managers. A standard format is for the sales manager to travel with a field sales representative periodically, then compose a critique of his or her work afterward. Sales meetings are also an important part of training for experienced personnel.

**Organization**   Sales managers are responsible for the organization of the field sales force. General organizational alignments, which are usually made by top marketing management, can be based upon geography, products, types of customers, or some combination of these factors. Figure 21-7 presents simplified organization charts showing these alignments.

A product sales organization would have specialized sales forces for each major category of products offered by the firm. A customer organization would use different sales forces for each major type of customer served. For instance, a plastics manufacturer selling to the automobile, small appliance, and defence industries might decide that each type of customer requires a separate sales force.

The individual sales manager then has the task of organizing the sales territories within his or her area of responsibility. Generally, the territory allocation decision should be based upon company objectives, personnel qualifications, work-load considerations, and territory potential.[18]

**Supervision**   A source of constant debate among sales managers is the supervision of the sales force. It is impossible to pinpoint the exact amount of supervision that is correct in each situation since this varies with the individuals involved. However, there is probably a curvilinear relationship between the amount of supervision and organizational performance (see Figure 21-8). The amount of supervision input increases sales output to some point, after which additional supervision tends to retard further sales growth.

---

[18] Territory decisions are discussed in Michael S. Heschel, "Effective Sales Territory Development," *Journal of Marketing* (April 1977), pp. 39–43.

**Figure 21-7   Basic Approaches to Organizing the Sales Force**

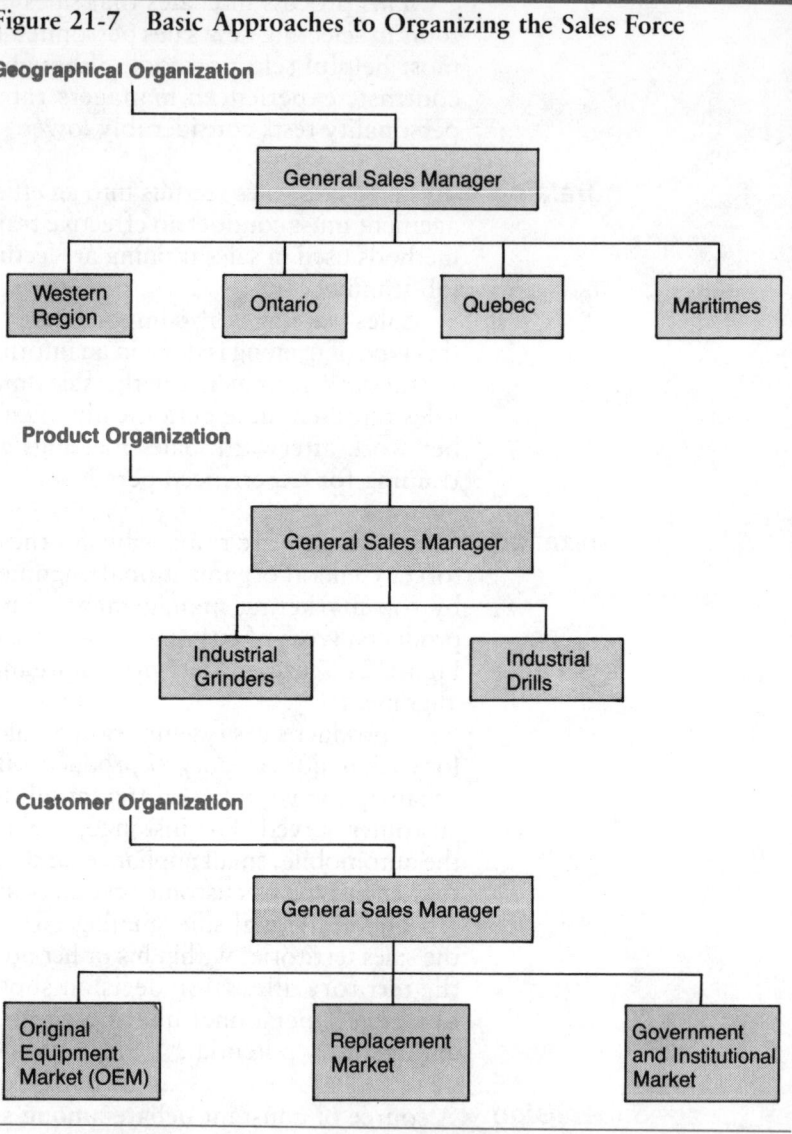

The key to effective supervision is clear communications with the sales force. This, of course, involves effective listening on the part of the sales manager. Sales personnel who clearly understand messages from management and who have an opportunity to express their concerns and opinions to their supervisors are usually easier to supervise and motivate.[19]

[19] The need for positive reinforcement is pointed out in Rom J. Markin and Charles M. Lillis, "Sales Managers Get What They Expect," *Business Horizons* (June 1975), pp. 51–58.

**Figure 21-8  Relationship Between Amount of Supervision and Organizational Performance**

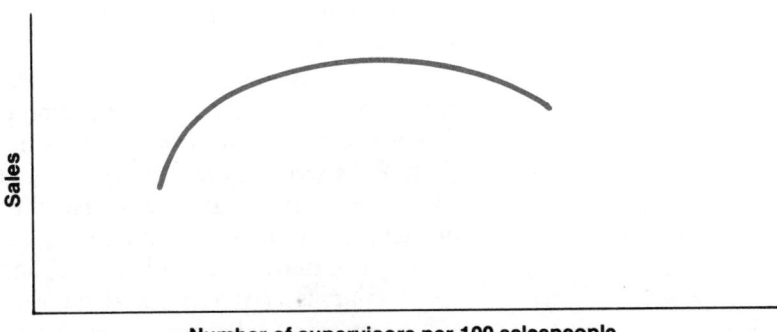

Number of supervisors per 100 salespeople

Source: *Management of the Personal Selling Function* by Charles S. Goodman. Copyright © 1971 by Holt, Rinehart and Winston, Inc. Reprinted by permission of Holt, Rinehart and Winston.

In fact, it has been argued that sales management has now entered a new era with the new emphasis being placed upon total human resource development. All personnel should be developed to their full abilities. One writer states, "In the long run, the total development approach may be desirable not only for humanistic reasons but also from a profit standpoint."[20]

**Motivation** The sales manager's responsibility for motivating the sales force cannot be glossed over.[21] Because the sales process is a problem-solving one, it often leads to considerable mental pressures and frustrations. Sales are often achieved only after repeated calls on customers and may, especially with new customers and complex technical products, occur over long periods of time. Motivation of salespeople usually takes the form of debriefing, information sharing, and both psychological and financial encouragement. Appeal to emotional needs, such as ego needs, recognition, and peer acceptance are examples of psychological encouragement. Monetary rewards, bonuses, club memberships, paid travel arrangements, and so forth are financial incentives.

[20] Leslie M. Dawson, "Toward a New Concept of Sales Management," *Journal of Marketing* (April 1970), p. 38.
[21] See Richard C. Becherer, Fred W. Morgan, and Lawrence M. Richard, "The Job Characteristics of Industrial Salespersons: Relationship to Motivation and Satisfaction," *Journal of Marketing* (Fall 1982), pp. 125–135; and Panos Apostolides, "Looking at the Age of Salespersons," *Journal of the Academy of Marketing Science* (Fall 1980), pp. 322–331.

**Compensation**     Monetary rewards are an important factor in human motivation, and, not surprisingly, the compensation of sales personnel is a critical matter to managers.[22] Basically, sales compensation can be determined on a commission plan, a straight salary plan, or some combination.[23]

A **commission** is *a payment directly tied to the sales or profits achieved by a salesperson.* For example, a salesperson might receive a 5 percent commission on all sales up to a specified quota, then 7 percent on sales beyond the quota. Commissions provide maximum selling incentive but may cause the sales force to short-change nonselling activities such as completing sales reports, delivering sales promotion materials, and normal account servicing.

A **salary** is *a fixed payment made on a periodic basis* to employees, including some sales personnel. A firm that has decided to use salaries rather than commissions might pay a salesperson a set amount every week, for example. Benefits of using salaries exist for both management and sales personnel. A straight salary plan allows management to have more control over how sales personnel allocate their efforts, but it reduces the incentive to expand sales. As a result, compensation programs combining features of both salary and commission plans have been accepted in many industries.

**Evaluation and Control**     Perhaps the most difficult of the tasks required of sales managers are evaluation and control.[24] The basic problems are setting standards and finding an instrument to measure sales performance. Sales volume, profitability, and investment return are the usual means of evaluating sales effectiveness. They typically involve the use of a **sales quota**—*a specified sales or profit target a salesperson is expected to achieve.* A particular sales representative might be expected to sell $300 000 in Territory 414 during a given year, for example. In many cases, the quota is tied to the compensation system.

---

[22] An interesting discussion appears in Gilbert A. Churchill, Jr., Neil M. Ford, and Orville C. Walker, Jr., "Personal Characteristics of Salespeople and the Attractiveness of Alternative Rewards," *Journal of Business Research* (7: 1979), pp. 25–50.

[23] The advantages and disadvantages of the commission, salary, and combination plans are adapted by permission from John P. Steinbrink, "How to Pay Your Sales Force," *Harvard Business Review* (July–August 1978), p. 113. Copyright © 1978 by the President and Fellows of Harvard College; all rights reserved.

[24] The need for careful evaluation is suggested in William P. Hall, "Improving Sales Force Productivity," *Business Horizons* (August 1975), pp. 32–42. See also Donald W. Jackson, Jr., and Ramon J. Aldag, "Managing the Sales Force by Objectives," *MSU Business Topics* (Spring 1974), pp. 53–59; and Porter Henry, "Manage Your Sales Force as a System," *Harvard Business Review* (March–April 1975), pp. 85–95.

Regardless of the key elements in the program for evaluating salespeople, the sales manager needs to follow a formalized system of decision rules.[25] The purpose of this system is to supply information to the sales manager as a basis for action.

What the sales manager needs to know are the answers to three general questions. First, what are the rankings of the salesperson's performance relative to the predetermined standards? In determining this ranking, full consideration should be given to the effect of uncontrollable variables on sales performance. It is preferable that each adjusted ranking be stated in terms of a percentage of the standard. This simplifies evaluation and makes it easier to convert the various rankings into a composite index of performance.

Second, what are the strong points of the salesperson? One way to answer this question is to list areas of the salesperson's performance where he or she has surpassed the respective standard. Another way is to categorize a salesperson's strong points under three aspects of the work environment.[26]

1. *Task*, or the technical ability of the salesperson. This is manifested in knowledge of the product (end uses), customer, and company, as well as selling skills.
2. *Process*, or the sequence of work flow. This pertains to the actual sales transaction — the salesperson's application of technical ability, and his or her interaction with customers. Personal observation is a frequently used technique for measuring process performance. Other measures are sales calls, expenses, and invoice lines.
3. *Goal*, or end results or output of sales performance. Usually this aspect of the salesperson's work environment will be stated in terms of sales volume and profits.

The third and final question is, what are the weaknesses or negatives in the performance of the salesperson in question? These should be listed or categorized as much as the salesperson's strong points. An evaluation summary for a hypothetical salesperson appears in Figure 21-9.

In making the evaluation summary the sales manager should follow a set procedure.

1. Each aspect of sales performance for which there is a standard should be measured separately. This helps to avoid the *halo effect*, whereby the rating given on one aspect is carried over to other aspects.

---

25 This section is adapted from H. Robert Dodge, *Field Sales Management* (Dallas: Business Publications, Inc., 1973), pp. 337–38.
26 Fremont A. Shull, Jr., Andre L. Delbecq, and L. L. Cummings, *Organizational Decision Making* (New York: McGraw-Hill, 1970), p. 215.

---

**Figure 21-9   An Evaluation Summary**

**Performance evaluation summary**

*Name:*   J. D. Martin
*Territory:*   Northern Saskatchewan
*Time period covered:*   1st Quarter 198__

| | |
|---|---|
| **Salesperson's ability** | |
| *Strong points* | 1. Has extensive product knowledge, knows end uses. |
| | 2. Keeps up to date on company pricing policies. |
| *Weaknesses* | 1. Does not have in-depth knowledge of customer requirements. |

| | |
|---|---|
| **Selling proficiency** | |
| *Strong points* | 1. Exceeded by 20 percent the standard for sales/call. |
| | 2. Exceeded by 12 percent the standard for sales calls/day. |
| | 3. Exceeded by 8 percent the standard for invoice lines/order. |
| *Weaknesses* | 1. Overspending of expense monies (14 percent). |
| | 2. Overaggressive in selling tactics. |

| | |
|---|---|
| **Sales results** | |
| *Strong points* | 1. Exceeded sales quota by 3 percent. |
| | 2. Exceeded new account quota by 6 percent. |
| *Weaknesses* | 1. Turnover of customers amounted to 5 percent. |
| | 2. Repeated delay in report submission. |

Source: H. Robert Dodge, *Field Sales Management* (Dallas: Business Publications, Inc., 1973), pp. 337–38.

---

2. Each salesperson should be judged on the basis of actual sales performance rather than potential ability. This emphasizes the importance of rankings in evaluation.

3. Each salesperson should be judged on the basis of sales performance for the entire period under consideration rather than particular incidents. The sales manager as the rater should avoid reliance on isolated examples of the salesperson's prowess or failure.

4. Each salesperson's evaluation should be reviewed for completeness and evidence of possible bias. Ideally this review should be made by the immediate superior of the sales manager.

While the evaluation step includes both revision and correction, the attention of the sales manager must necessarily focus on correction. This is defined as the adjustment of actual performance to predetermined standards. Corrective action with its obvious negative connotations poses a substantial challenge to the typical sales manager.

---

**Summary**   Personal selling is the seller's promotional presentation conducted on a person-to-person basis with the buyer. It is inherent in all business enterprises. The earliest sellers were known as peddlers, and some of the negative stereotyping associated with them remains today.

Three basic selling tasks exist: order processing, creative selling, and missionary selling. The successful salesperson is self-motivated and prepared to meet the demands of the competitive marketplace.

The basic steps involved in selling are 1) prospecting and qualifying, 2) approach, 3) presentation, 4) demonstration, 5) handling of objections, 6) closing, and 7) follow-up.

Retail selling is different from other kinds of selling, primarily in that the customer comes to the salesperson. Also, salespeople in stores are concerned with responsibilities other than selling. Two selling techniques particularly applicable to retailing are selling up and suggestion selling.

Sales management involves seven basic functions: 1) recruitment and selection, 2) training, 3) organization, 4) supervision, 5) motivation, 6) compensation, and 7) evaluation and control. Poor utilization of time and lack of planned sales effort rank as the leading problems faced by sales management today.

---

**Key Terms**

| | |
|---|---|
| order processing | closing |
| creative selling | follow-up |
| missionary sales | selling up |
| prospecting | suggestion selling |
| qualifying | sales management |
| approach | commission |
| presentation | salary |
| canned approach | sales quota |

---

**Review Questions**

1. Identify the factors affecting the importance of personal selling in the promotional mix.
2. Identify the three basic sales tasks and give an example of each.
3. Identify the characteristics of successful salespersons.
4. What are the steps in the sales process? Which step would take the most time?
5. Under what conditions is the canned approach to selling likely to be used? What are the major problems with this approach?

6. How is retail selling different from field selling?
7. Discuss the benefits of a sales career.
8. Describe the major problems faced by sales managers.
9. What are the primary functions of sales management?
10. Compare the alternative sales compensation plans. Point out the advantages and disadvantages of each.

---

**Discussion Questions and Exercises**

1. What sales tasks are involved in selling the following products?
   a. Lanier dictating machines and office equipment
   b. support for Easter Seals to a local Rotary Club
   c. a fast-food franchise
   d. used automobiles
   e. cleaning compounds to be used in plant maintenance
2. How would you describe the job of each of the following salespersons?
   a. a salesperson in a retail record store
   b. Century 21 real estate sales representative
   c. a route driver for Frito-Lay (sells and delivers to local food retailers)
   d. a sales engineer for Wang Computers
3. Who was the best salesperson you ever encountered? What made this person stand out in your thinking?
4. Suppose that you are the local sales manager for the telephone company's Yellow Pages and you employ six representatives who call upon local firms. What type of compensation system would you employ?
5. How would you evaluate the sales personnel described in Question 4?

---

**MICROCOMPUTER EXERCISE: Sales Force Size Determination**

The determination of the optimal number of salespeople is a crucial decision for sales management. The workload approach is a common method of accomplishing this objective.* The following steps are involved:

**1.** *Classify the firm's customers into categories.* Because customers vary greatly in terms of sales, servicing costs, and profitability, they should be divided into categories. One writer estimates that the top 15 percent of a firm's customers will account for 65 percent of its sales, the next 20 percent will account for 20 percent, and the remaining 65 percent will yield only 15 percent of sales.** The first

---

*The workload method was first described in Walter J. Talley, Jr., "How to Design Sales Territories," *Journal of Marketing* (January 1961), pp. 7–13. The steps are described in Richard R. Still, Edward W. Cundiff, and Norman A. Govoni, *Sales Management* (Englewood Cliffs, NJ: Prentice-Hall, 1981), pp. 99–101; and Gilbert A. Churchill, Jr., Neil M. Ford, and Orville C. Walker, Jr., *Sales Force Management* (Homewood, IL: Richard D. Irwin, 1985), pp. 181–183.

**Porter Henry, "The Important Few—The Unimportant Many," *1980 Portfolio of Sales and Marketing* (New York: Sales and Marketing Management, 1980), pp. 34–37.

group might be labelled A accounts, the second group B accounts, and the third group C accounts. A firm with 5200 accounts might categorize them as follows: 800 Type A accounts (high sales, high profitability), 1400 Type B accounts (medium sales, moderate profitability), and 3000 Type C accounts (low sales, low profitability).

2. *Specify the desired number of annual calls for each account type and the average length of each call.* These specifications can be based upon analysis of sales-call reports submitted by the field sales force. In addition, it is likely to involve the judgement and experience of sales management. Suppose that sales management decides upon weekly contacts for Type A accounts, biweekly contacts for Type B accounts, and monthly contacts for Type C accounts. In addition, the desired length of an average sales call is set at 40 minutes for Type A accounts, 30 minutes for Type B accounts, and 20 minutes for Type C accounts. Finally, an additional 10 percent is calculated for emergency or other unplanned calls in each account category. The number of hours required for each type of account can be calculated as in Table A.

**Table A   Determination of the Total Number of Hours Required for Each Type of Account**

| Type of Account | Number of Contacts per Year | × | Minutes per Sales Call | = | Time Required for Planned Call | + | Time Required for Unplanned Emergency Calls* | = | Total Minutes | = | Total Hours |
|---|---|---|---|---|---|---|---|---|---|---|---|
| A | 52 | | 40 | | 2080 | | 208 | · | 2288 | | 38.13 |
| B | 26 | | 30 | | 780 | | 78 | | 858 | | 14.30 |
| C | 12 | | 20 | | 240 | | 24 | | 264 | | 4.40 |

*Estimated by management at 10 percent of total time required for planned calls.

3. *Calculate the total hours required to contact all accounts.* This step is accomplished by multiplying the total number of hours required to service each account type by the number of customers in each category. In this example, the calculation would be as follows.

$$
\begin{aligned}
800 \text{ Type A accounts} \times 38.13 \text{ hours} &= 30\ 504 \\
1400 \text{ Type B accounts} \times 14.30 \text{ hours} &= 20\ 020 \\
3000 \text{ Type C accounts} \times\ \ 4.40 \text{ hours} &= \underline{13\ 200} \\
\text{Total} &= 63\ 724
\end{aligned}
$$

4. *Calculate the time available for each salesperson.* This step is accomplished by multiplying the number of hours the typical salesperson works each week by the average number of weeks worked per year. If the typical salesperson works 40 hours per week for 46 weeks, the average number of hours per year is 1840 (40 × 46).

5. *Allocate each salesperson's time to assigned tasks.* A considerable percentage of the typical salesperson's time is spent on activities other than making calls on established accounts. Some time is involved in travelling between accounts. In addition, the typical representative is responsible for such nonselling activities as preparing reports and attending sales meetings. Finally, time may be devoted to contacting potential customers to generate additional sales. For example, the salesperson working an average of 1840 hours per year may divide his or her hours as shown in Table B.

**Table B   Allocation of One Salesperson's Time to Assigned Tasks**

| *Activity* | *Percentage of Available Time* | *Number of Hours per Year* |
|---|---|---|
| Sales/service calls on established accounts | 40% | 736 |
| Sales calls on potential accounts | 10 | 184 |
| Travel | 30 | 552 |
| Other nonselling activities | 20 | 368 |
| TOTAL | 100% | 1840 |

6. *Determine the required number of salespersons.* The final step can be accomplished by dividing the total number of hours required to service all accounts by the average number of hours each salesperson devotes to sales and service of established accounts. The formula is as follows.

$$\text{Required Number of Salespeople} = \frac{\text{Total Number of Hours Required to Service Accounts}}{\text{Total Number of Hours Each Salesperson Devotes to Calling on Established Accounts}}$$

$$= \frac{63\,724}{736 \text{ hours}}$$

$$= 86.6, \text{ or } 87 \text{ salespeople}$$

Directions: Use the Menu Items titled "Sales Force Size Determination" on the Foundations of Marketing disk to solve the following problems.

1. Fred Filipchuk is the national sales manager for Consolidated Industries of Peterborough. Filipchuk uses three classifications for his firm's 1500 accounts: 200 Type A firms; 600 Type B firms, and

700 Type C firms. He estimates that Type A accounts should be called on 20 times a year, while Type B and C accounts should be called on 15 and 10 times per year, respectively. The length of time for each sales call should be 40 minutes for Type A and 20 minutes for Type B and C accounts. Another 10 percent is to be added to each type of account for unplanned or emergency calls. The typical Consolidated sales representative works a 40-hour week for 48 weeks each year. The salespeople spend 60 percent of their time calling on established accounts, 10 percent on potential accounts, 20 percent on travel, and 10 percent on nonselling activities. How many sales representatives does Filipchuk need to cover his market share?

**2.** Kwan-Li Parker is a Kitchener-based manufacturer's agent in the children's clothing industry. Over the years, the number of salespeople who work for her organization has grown to match the increase in the number of her firm's retail accounts. Parker divides her 550 retail-store accounts as follows: 82 Type A, 120 Type B, and 348 Type C. She expects each Type A account to be contacted once a month and the sales call to last 60 minutes. Type B accounts should be contacted every other month, with the average call lasting 40 minutes. The less profitable Type C accounts should be contacted once in the spring, summer, autumn, and winter, with each call lasting an average of 30 minutes. Unplanned or emergency calls add another 5 percent to the total. Parker estimates that her average sales representative works 40 hours each week and 45 weeks each year. Approximately 50 percent of a sales representative's time is spent in contacting established accounts, 20 percent on potential accounts, 15 percent on travel, and 15 percent on nonselling activities. How many salespeople should Parker employ?

---

**MICROCOMPUTER EXERCISE: Return on Assets Managed (ROAM)**

ROAM refers to return on assests managed or used. It is a useful evaluative tool in a variety of sales-management objectives.

Directions: Use of the Menu Item titled "ROAM" on the Foundation of Marketing disk to solve the following problems.

**1.** Charles Fulmer, national sales manager of Princess Products, is in the process of evaluating how well his sales force has sold the firm's three product lines. Year-end sales show the following sales volume: Product Line A, $5 000 000; Product Line B, $8 000 000; and Product Line C, $10 000 000. Accounts receivable are 20 percent for all product lines. Net profits are 10 percent of A's sales, 5 percent of B's, and 4 percent of C's. Average inventory levels are $1.5 million, $2.4 million, and $2 million for A, B, and C, respectively. Use ROAM to evaluate the firm's product-line sales performance.

**2.** Ellen Braum, National Industries division manager in Saskatoon, is studying a printout of sales and net-profit figures for her five sales representatives. Braum knows that both accounts receivable and inventory run at about 25 percent of sales for her division. She decides to calculate each sales representative's ROAM. What will she conclude from the following information?

| Representative | Sales | Net Profit |
|----------------|-------|------------|
| Debra Thomas | $700 000 | $35 000 |
| Steve Fedun | $800 000 | $32 000 |
| Brenda Levine | $500 000 | $40 000 |
| Fred Palmer | $900 000. | $54 000 |
| Kim Young | $1 000 000 | $30 000 |

# P A R T

**8**

## Emerging Dimensions in Marketing

*The final part of* Foundations of Marketing *explores important emerging dimensions in the discipline. The vital importance of the international marketplace is examined in Chapter 22. Chapter 23 discusses the increasingly important role of marketing in the realm of nonprofit organizations, and Chapter 24 the relationship of marketing and society. The final chapter focuses upon the evauation and control of the marketing process.*

# International Marketing

1. To explain the role that exporting, importing, balance of trade, balance of payments, exchange rate adjustments, and bartering play in international marketing.

2. To contrast the concepts of absolute advantage and comparative advantage.

3. To identify aspects of marketing strategy specially important in the international marketplace.

4. To identify the levels of involvement in international marketing.

5. To outline the environment for international marketing.

6. To list the various forms of multinational economic integration.

7. To show how Canada is an attractive market target for marketers in other nations.

Imagine that you are a home insulation salesperson. You have arrived on the doorstep of a prospective customer at the agreed-upon hour. Invited into the living room, you lay out your wares and make your standard presentation, but just at the moment when you think you have persuaded the householder to buy, he dashes into the kitchen where, through a half-opened door, you see a rival about to make *her* pitch. Twenty minutes later, you hear yet another bargaining session going on upstairs.

Your fears are confirmed when the householder reappears. Someone whom you had thought to be rather easy to sell to now becomes a hard-nosed bargainer. If he buys your insulation, he also wants free installation, weatherstripping for all exterior doors, and a guarantee that the job will reduce heating costs by 8.5 percent.

Suburban householders may not do business that way, but it is the sort of situation that Byron Cavadias, president of CAE Electronic Ltd. in St. Laurent, a Montreal suburb, often encounters when trying to sell $10-million flight simulators to airlines. He recalls one bidding game in particular.

"We flew down to this hotel in the U.S. where we had to sit around for two weeks haggling with airline executives. There were three potential suppliers in separate suites and they [the executives] went from one to another playing an auction game. Theoretically, you'd think they would simply choose the best deal for their requirements, but, in fact, it always turns out to be a price, as well as a technical, auction. Our range of simulators may have a feature that they want for nothing or they may demand easier financing. It's an extremely tough business."

Despite such obstacles, most companies, large and small, who work at it find that the international marketplace is extremely rewarding if the firm plans carefully and has the patience to persist. Here a Canadian firm can find markets of a size rarely encountered in this country. CAE is a good example. The electronics firm has about 30 percent of the world civil-aviation market in flight simulators. It exports 75 percent of its production and has boosted its work force from 460 in 1972 to 1700 in 1982.[1]

## The Conceptual Framework

Although international examples have been included in discussions in earlier chapters of such concepts as marketing planning, segmentation, and elements of the marketing mix, most of the previous material has focused upon domestic marketing. Increasingly, Canadian organizations are crossing national boundaries in search of markets and profits.

Coca-Cola is one of the most readily identifiable products in the world. This firm is one of the world's most successful international marketers. Coca-Cola operates in 135 foreign countries, receiving approximately 65 percent of its sales and profits from abroad.[2]

Everywhere one looks there is evidence of the growth of world marketing. Canada is both a seller and a purchaser in the world marketplace. Many Canadian firms, like their counterparts elsewhere, view the globe as their market. Hundreds of them are engaged in some type of international business activity. Canada needs even more firms to participate internationally.

International trade is vital to a nation and its marketers for several reasons. International business expands the market for a country's or firm's products and thus makes possible further production and distribution economies. An added benefit to an exporting firm is that it can compete more effectively with foreign competitors who enter this market because of added experience. World marketing can also mean more jobs at home. It is estimated that some 30 000 to 40 000 new jobs are supported by every billion export dollars.

---

1 Adapted from Mark Budgen, "Breadth of a Salesman," *The Financial Post Magazine* (September 1, 1983), pp. 16–17.
2 Thomas N. Troxell, Jr., "Smiles at Coke," *Barron's* (November 5, 1979), pp. 47–48.

## Figure 22-1   Importance of Foreign Markets to Some Canadian Companies

| Rank by exports 1986 | Total Canadian exports $'000 | Company | Rank in FP 500 | Exports as % of total sales | % change in exports vs 1982 |
|---|---|---|---|---|---|
| 1 | 10 895 372 | General Motors of Canada | 1 | 59 | −7 |
| 2 | 7 968 200 | Ford Motor Co. of Canada | 3 | 56 | +10 |
| 3 | 4 854 200 | Chrysler Canada | 7 | 66 | +9 |
| 4 | 3 169 200 | Canadian Wheat Board | 22 | 84 | −15 |
| 5 | 2 675 266 | Canadian Pacific | 2 | 18 | nil |
| 6 | 2 022 641[1] | Alcan Aluminium | 6 | 24 | +14 |
| 7 | 1 755 500 | MacMillan Bloedel | 36 | 70 | +1 |
| 8 | 1 235 000 | Gulf Canada | 20 | 31 | +36 |
| 9 | 1 180 000 | Sumitomo Canada | 60 | 82 | +56 |
| 10 | 1 037 798 | Mitsui & Co. (Canada) | 35 | 40 | +2 |
| 11 | 1 011 576 | Mitsubishi Canada | 67 | 74 | +3 |
| 12 | 1 008 704[1] | Inco | 46 | 50 | nil |
| 13 | 963 000 | Imperial Oil | 8 | 14 | +2 |
| 14 | 889 000 | Shell Canada | 14 | 19 | −40 |
| 15 | 881 000 | Falconbridge | 84 | 77 | +27 |
| 16 | 828 000 | IBM Canada | 31 | 28 | −11 |
| 17 | 817 000 | Noranda | 24 | 23 | −5 |
| 18 | 771 468 | Alberta & Southern Gas | 98 | 78 | −68 |
| 19 | 763 453 | Canadian Commercial Corp. | 128 | 100 | +6 |
| 20 | 748 274 | Royal Canadian Mint | 107 | 82 | −9 |
| 21 | 669 600 | British Columbia Resources Investment | 122 | 84 | −22 |
| 22 | 648 000 | Magna International | 95 | 63 | +30 |
| 23 | 633 230 | Pratt & Whitney Canada | 118 | 78 | +12 |
| 24 | 625 144 | Consolidated-Bathurst | 45 | 31 | +12 |
| 25 | 618 000 | Cominco | 71 | 47 | −9 |
| 26 | 582 300 | British Columbia Forest Products | 86 | 53 | −3 |
| 27 | 558 000 | Marubeni Canada | 116 | 68 | +51 |
| 28 | 554 000 | Cansulex | 165 | 100 | −14 |
| 29 | 542 000 | PetroCanada | 11 | 10 | −67 |
| 30 | 540 026 | Mobile Oil Canada | 55 | 33 | −69 |
| 31 | 527 000 | Canfor | 89 | 50 | +11 |
| 32 | 501 100 | TransCanada PipeLines | 18 | 12 | −65 |
| 33 | 483 811 | Rio Algom | 68 | 36 | −5 |
| 34 | 479 459 | Navistar International Canada | 105 | 52 | +2 |
| 35 | 472 130 | Cargill | 77 | 39 | −36 |
| 36 | 467 000 | Stelco | 38 | 19 | −7 |
| 37 | 428 386 | McDonnell Douglas Canada | 188 | 100 | +23 |
| 38 | 416 500 | Crown Forest Industries | 112 | 48 | +5 |
| 39 | 416 200 | Domtar | 39 | 18 | +11 |
| 40 | 414 577 | American Motors (Canada) | 130 | 55 | +45 |

[1]Converted from US$

| Rank by exports 1986 | Total Canadian exports $'000 | Company | Rank in FP 500 | Exports as % of total sales | % change in exports vs 1982 |
|---|---|---|---|---|---|
| 41 | 400 000 | George Weston | 5 | 4 | + 25 |
| 42 | 388 104 | Bombardier | 146 | 59 | + 44 |
| 43 | 377 728 | Hydro-Québec | 15 | 8 | + 12 |
| 44 | 349 932 | Ivaco | 47 | 18 | + 27 |
| 45 | 348 000 | Suncor | 83 | 30 | − 24 |
| 46 | 347 000 | Premetalco | 203 | 85 | − 14 |
| 47 | 340 000 | Boise Cascade Canada | 227 | 93 | + 4 |
| 48 | 337 550 | Canpotex | 241 | 100 | + 1 |
| 49 | 319 190 | Dofasco | 48 | 16 | + 21 |
| 50 | 317 049 | Westcoast Transmission | 100 | 33 | − 60 |

Source: *The Financial Post 500* (Summer 1987), p. 117.

Some Canadian companies are heavily dependent on their ability to sell their products abroad. For manufacturers like General Motors, MacMillan Bloedel, Alberta and Southern Gas, and others, the majority of sales dollars come from customers in other countries. The importance of international marketing to a number of companies is shown in Figure 22-1.

Some two million Canadians — one in five of the labour market — work in areas directly or indirectly related to export trade. Thus, there is a good chance that every single Canadian has a close connection with export trade through family or friend. Thirty cents of every dollar of our Gross National Product comes from our exports.

Our exports pay for the things we import that our high standard of living expects — our morning orange juice, fresh vegetables in winter, wool and cotton clothes, TV sets, cars, and computers. On another level, exports also pay for the interest and dividends on foreign investment, for the deficit on tourism, for access to foreign technologies, and for the borrowing which different levels of government use to finance our economic development.[3]

In other words, foreign trade is important to Canada from both the **exporting** (*selling goods abroad*) and **importing** (*buying foreign goods and raw materials*) viewpoints. Countries such as the United Kingdom, Belgium, the Scandinavian countries, and New Zealand are also heavily dependent upon international trade. However, participation in and dependence upon foreign trade varies tremendously. For example, although the U.S. is both the largest exporter and the largest importer in the world, exports only account for about 7.7 percent of its gross national product (GNP). Compare this to the percentages for Belgium (46 percent) and West Germany (23 percent). Canadian exports account for about 30 percent of our GNP. The

---

[3] Government of Canada, *Export Trade Month Information Kit*, Oct. 1983.

leading trade partners of Canada are shown in Figure 22-2. The United States is clearly our chief trading partner, supplying about 77 percent of our imports and buying about 68 percent of our exports.

Although international marketing strategies involve the same processes of identification of market targets, analyses of environmental influences, and development of marketing mixes, there are both similarities and differences between international and domestic marketing. This chapter examines characteristics of the international marketplace, environmental influences on marketing, and the development of an international marketing mix. It also discusses the sequential steps used by most firms in entering the international marketplace.

**Figure 22-2   Canada's Major Trading Partners**

| Total Canadian Imports $112.68 billion | | Total Canadian Exports $120.50 billion | |
|---|---|---|---|
| *Top Sellers to Canada* | 1986 | *Top Buyers of Our Products* | 1986 |
| United States | 77.34 | United States | 93.18 |
| Japan | 7.63 | Japan | 5.93 |
| Other Asia | 13.86 | Other Asia | 10.27 |
| United Kingdom | 3.72 | United Kingdom | 2.72 |
| West Germany | 3.45 | West Germany | 1.32 |
| France | 1.59 | France | 1.01 |
| Italy | 1.67 | Italy | 0.71 |
| Western Europe | 14.84 | Western Europe | 9.23 |
| Eastern Europe | 0.34 | Eastern Europe | 1.60 |
| Saudi Arabia | 0.19 | Saudi Arabia | 2.15 |
| Middle East | 0.63 | Middle East | 1.11 |
| Other Africa | 1.01 | Other Africa | 0.89 |
| Australia | 0.51 | Australia | 0.65 |
| Oceania | 0.69 | Oceania | 0.83 |
| Venezuela | 0.52 | Venezuela | 0.42 |
| South America | 1.89 | South America | 1.78 |
| Mexico | 1.18 | Mexico | 0.40 |
| Central America | 2.08 | Central America | 1.56 |
| TOTAL | 112.68 | TOTAL | 120.50 |

Source: *Canadian Statistical Review*, Statistics Canada, Pub. No. 11-003E (July 1987) pp. 120–121.

## Measuring International Marketing

Since imports and exports are important contributors to a country's economic welfare, governments and other organizations are concerned about the status of various components of international marketing. The concepts of balance of trade and balance of payments are a good starting point for understanding international business.

**Balance of Trade**

A nation's **balance of trade** is determined by *the relationship between a country's exports and imports*. A favourable balance of trade (trade surplus) occurs when the value of a nation's exports exceeds its imports. This means that, other things being equal, new money would come into the country's economic system via the sales abroad of the country's products. An unfavourable balance of trade (trade deficit), by contrast, results when imports are in excess of exports. The net money flow then would be outward, other things being equal. On the whole, Canada has maintained a favourable balance of trade.

**Balance of Payments**

A country's balance of trade plays a vital role in determining its **balance of payments**, *the flow of money into or out of a country*. However, other factors are also important. A favourable balance of payments indicates that there is a net money inflow; while an unfavourable balance of payments means a net money flow out of the country.

The balance of payments is also affected by such factors as tourism, military expenditures abroad, investment abroad, and foreign aid. A money outflow caused by these factors may exceed the money inflow from a favourable balance of trade and leave a nation with an unfavourable balance of payments.

In recent years Canada has had an unfavourable balance of payments, even when the nation had a favourable balance of trade. Foreign travel and interest on foreign borrowings have contributed to this situation.

**Exchange Rate Adjustments**

When the real value of a currency is out of line with international currencies in terms of relative buying power, the **exchange rate**, *the rate at which a nation's currency can be exchanged for other currencies or gold*, may change. Some countries try to fix the exchange rate. In Canada we have a floating rate. Fluctuations in the exchange rate have a significant impact on both the balance of trade and balance of payments. Because of this, government policy may lead to efforts to stem significant fluctuations by buying or selling foreign — i.e., U.S. — currency.

Foreign claims on Canadian currency led to the devaluation of the Canadian dollar in the late 1970s and early 1980s. **Devaluation** occurs *when a nation reduces the value of its currency in relation to gold or some other currency*. Devaluation of the dollar has the effect of making Canadian products less expensive abroad, and trips to Canada cheaper for foreign visitors. On the other hand, imports are more expensive. **Revaluation**, a less typical case, occurs *when a* *country adjusts the value of its currency upward.* Either of these actions may force firms to modify their world marketing strategies.

## International Marketing: Some Basic Concepts

The Pacific island republic of Nauru has only a few thousand people but has one of the richest deposits of phosphate in the world.[4] Australia has vast grazing lands, while Hong Kong's 4.1 million people are crowded into a small area that has become one of the most urbanized territories in the world. Hong Kong is a world trader in its own right as well as a source of foreign exchange for the People's Republic of China through handling many of China's goods. Kuwait has rich oil fields but few other industries or resources.

These situations lead to arguments that nations are usually better off if they specialize in certain products or marketing activities. By doing what they do best, nations are able to exchange the products not needed domestically for foreign-made goods that are needed. Nauru could attempt to develop a tourist trade, but it has opted for specializing in phosphate mining. This allows a higher standard of living than would be possible through diversified business enterprises.

On the other hand, if "specialization" means sale of nonrenewable resources, a country could find itself without a specialty and have a devastating balance of trade when these resources diminish. Specialization by countries sometimes produces odd situations. A classic example was when Britain's Conservative Party issued T-shirts with the party slogan "Put Britain First." Later, it was discovered that the T-shirts were made in Portugal.[5] Similarly, a number of "Buy Canadian" stickers can be found on the rear bumpers of Subarus and Toyotas.

An understanding of the concepts of absolute and comparative advantage is vital to the study of world marketing. These explain why countries specialize in the marketing of certain products. A nation has an **absolute advantage** in the marketing of a product if the country *is the sole producer or can produce the product for less than anyone else.* Since few nations are sole producers and economic conditions rapidly altar production costs, examples of absolute advantage are rare.

The concept of **comparative advantage** is a more practical approach to international trade specialization. A nation has a comparative advantage in an item *if it can produce it more efficiently than other products.* Nations will usually produce and export those goods in which they have the greatest comparative advantage (or

---

[4] An interesting description of Nauru's status as a provider of phosphate appears in Walter McQuade, "The Smallest, Richest Republic in the World," *Fortune* (December 1975), pp. 132–140.

[5] *The Age* (October 4, 1974), p. 1.

least comparative disadvantage) and import those items in which they have the least comparative advantage (or the greatest comparative disadvantage).

---

**Figure 22-3   Leading Commodities in Canadian Foreign Trade, 1986**

| Exports | $ millions |
|---|---|
| Total exports | 120 494.9 |
| Motor vehicles | 23 178.3 |
| Pulp and paper products | 11 279.8 |
| Energy products | 6 423.7 |
| Primary metals | 3 311.6 |
| Motor vehicle parts | 11 072.1 |
| Food, feed, beverages, and tobacco | 9 510.6 |
| Wheat | 2 835.8 |
| Lumber | 4 949.9 |
| Machinery, industrial and agricultural | 3 891.4 |
| Metal ores | 2 285.0 |

| Imports | $ millions |
|---|---|
| Total imports | 112 678.0 |
| Machinery, industrial and agricultural | 10 910.6 |
| Motor vehicles | 15 608.7 |
| Motor vehicle parts | 18 059.0 |
| Energy products | 5 252.0 |
| Food, feed, beverages, and tobacco | 6 541.0 |
| Communications and related equipment | 5 080.0 |
| Office machines and equipment | 4 446.0 |
| Personal apparel and accessories | 2 859.4 |
| Chemical and related products | 2 139.5 |

Source: *Canadian Statistical Review*, Statistics Canada, Pub. No. 11-003E (July 1987) pp. 122–125.

---

Figure 22-3 suggests how the comparative advantage concept is applied in Canada. The export commodities tend to be those in which there is a comparative advantage over the trading partners. Being an industrialized nation, with ample natural resources, Canada tends to export manufactured items, such as cars and machinery, and natural resources, such as grain, wood, and ores. By contrast, countries with lower-cost labour tend to specialize in products that require a significant labour content, such as textiles, shoes, and clothing.

Of course, there are also noneconomic reasons for not specializing in certain items. Some countries refuse to specialize their productive efforts because they want to be self-sufficient. The Communist nations have typically followed this pattern. Israel is another example. South Africa was forced into this position because of world reaction to its domestic policies. Still other nations adopt the self-sufficiency viewpoint only for certain commodities that they regard as important to their long-run development. Canada, for instance, has taken steps to reduce its dependency on foreign oil.

## Competing in the International Market

Many Canadian firms never venture outside their own domestic market. Why they do not is somewhat of a mystery because our market is not large. Even today only about 10 percent of domestic manufacturing firms export their products. If they do venture abroad, Canadian firms find that the world marketplace can be far different from the one to which they are accustomed. Market sizes, buyer behaviour, and marketing practices will all vary. This requires that the company involved in international marketing carefully evaluate all market segments in which it expects to compete.

### Market Size

A prime ingredient of market size is population growth. And every day the world's population increases by about 200 000 people. It is estimated that by the year 2000 the world's population is expected to be 6.3 billion. A review of these projections produces some important contrasts. Average birth rates are dropping, but death rates have been declining faster. Population growth has fallen in industrialized nations, but it has increased in the less developed countries. Nearly 80 percent of the population in 2000 will live in less developed nations.

Many of the world's new inhabitants will end up living in large cities. By the year 2000, urban dwellers are expected to account for 50 percent of the world population, contrasted with the current 39 percent. Today 21 cities have a population of 5 million or more. In 2000 there will be 60 such cities. Mexico City, which now ranks third among world cities, is forecasted to grow to 31.5 million, making it the world's largest city in the year 2000.[6]

Statistical data indicate that the world marketplace will continue to grow in size and that it will become increasingly urbanized. This does not mean, however, that all foreign markets have the same potential. Income differences, for instance, vitally affect a nation's market potential. India has a huge population of about 700 million, but its per capita income is very low. Canada, on the other hand, has only a small fraction of India's population, yet its per capita income is higher than the United States'. Figure 22-4 compares population and per capita incomes for a number of the world's nations.

---

[6] World population growth is traced in Jonathan Spivak, "Population of a World Growing Faster Than Experts Anticipated," *The Wall Street Journal* (April 12, 1976), pp. 1, 15.

**Figure 22-4    Per Capita Income for Selected Countries and Populations**

| Country | Per Capita Income | Population (in Millions) |
|---|---|---|
| *North America* | | |
| Canada | $10 296 | 24.0 |
| Cuba | 840 | 9.9 |
| Dominican Republic | 841 | 5.5 |
| Haiti | 260 | 5.7 |
| Mexico | 1 800 | 71.9 |
| United States | 8 612 | 226.5 |
| *South America* | | |
| Argentina | 2 331 | 27.3 |
| Bolivia | 477 | 5.6 |
| Brazil | 1 523 | 123.0 |
| Guyana | 437 | 0.8 |
| Venezuela | 2 772 | 14.5 |
| *Europe* | | |
| Denmark | 9 869 | 5.1 |
| France | 7 908 | 53.7 |
| Italy | 3 076 | 57.0 |
| Portugal | 2 000 | 9.9 |
| Soviet Union | 2 600 | 266.6 |
| Sweden | 9 274 | 8.3 |
| Turkey | 1 140 | 45.3 |
| West Germany | 11 142 | 61.7 |
| *Near East* | | |
| Egypt | 448 | 41.9 |
| Iran | 1 986 | 38.0 |
| Israel | 3 332 | 3.8 |
| Kuwait | 11 431 | 1.3 |
| Saudi Arabia | 11 500 | 9.2 |
| *Asia* | | |
| Afghanistan | 168 | 15.8 |
| Cambodia (Kampuchea) | 90 | 8.8 |
| People's Republic of China | 232 | 1 000.0 |
| India | 162 | 667.3 |
| Japan | 8 460 | 116.7 |
| *Australia* | 7 720 | 14.6 |
| *Africa* | | |
| Angola | 500 | 7.0 |
| Chad | 73 | 4.5 |
| Liberia | 453 | 1.8 |
| Morocco | 555 | 20.3 |
| Mozambique | 170 | 10.4 |

Source: *The World Almanac and Book of Facts 1982 (New York: Newspaper Enterprise Association, Inc., 1982), pp. 514–599. Reprinted by permission. Copyright 1982 NEA, Inc.*

*Buyer Behaviour*   Buyer behaviour differs from one country to another. Therefore, marketers should carefully study each market before implementing a marketing strategy. Too many companies try to export a marketing strategy that proved successful at home. A U.S. manufacturer introduced its mouthwash in Thailand with an advertising campaign portraying a boy and a girl, overtly fond of each other, one telling the other to use the mouthwash to fight bad breath. Such an open display of boy-girl relationships was considered improper by the Thai people. Sales increased only when two girls appeared in the same scene.[7]

Marketers must be careful that their marketing strategies comply with local customs, tastes, and buying practices. In some cases even the product has to be modified. General Foods, for instance, offers different blends of coffee to each of its overseas markets. One variety goes to British consumers, who prefer to use a lot of milk with their coffee, another to the French, who usually drink coffee black, and still another mix to Latin Americans, who prefer a chicory taste.[8]

Differing buying patterns mean that marketing executives should do considerable marketing research before entering a foreign market. Sometimes the research can be done by the marketer's own organization or a Canadian-based research firm. In other cases a foreign-based marketing research organization should be used. (See Figure 22-5.) Foreign research firms often better understand how to get the desired information from the target population. For example, Audits, Ltd., of Great Britain, was an innovator in the field of home audits of packaged goods. The British firm provides its respondents with a special trash container rather than relying on a diary of purchases. Discarded packages are then studied to determine consumer buying behaviour patterns.[9]

Various environmental factors can influence international marketing strategy. Marketers should be as aware of these influences as they are of those in domestic markets.

*Cultural, Economic,*   International marketing is normally affected and influenced by
*and Societal Factors*   cultural, economic, and societal factors. The economic status of some countries makes them less (or more) likely candidates for

---

[7] Jonathan Slater, "The Hazards of Cross-Cultural Advertising," *Business America* (April 2, 1984), p. 23.

[8] David A. Ricks, Marilyn Y. C. Fu, and Jeffrey S. Arpan, *International Business Blunders* (Columbus, Ohio: Grid, 1974), pp. 17–18.

[9] Ralph Z. Sorenson II, "U.S. Marketers Can Learn from European Innovators," *Harvard Business Review* (September-October 1972), p. 97.

**Figure 22-5    Using a Foreign-based Market Research Organization**

# These days building a better mousetrap isn't enough.

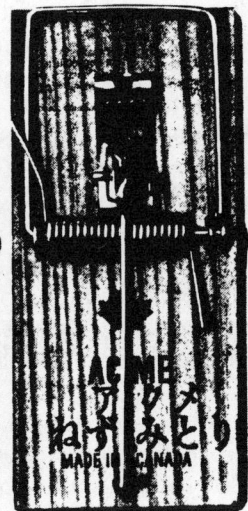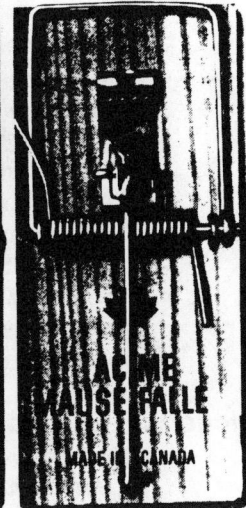

# You also have to beat a path to the world.

Gone are the days when people would line up at your door to buy innovative new products. To be successful in today's business world, you've got to fight for every dollar you earn. You've got to explore every possible avenue that could lead to new opportunities.

One of the best roads to success is often one of the least travelled by Canadian companies. It's the export market. Exporting opens new horizons that can increase volume, lower unit production costs and raise profits. In fact, giving your mousetrap more exposure could be one of the best ways to improve your competitiveness at home.

If you've never exported before, we have a new brochure that will make it seem a little less foreign. It will help answer your initial questions and provide information that could save you costly time and effort. By simply reviewing the services and programs available, you can make your preliminary groundwork a lot easier.

To get your free copy of the booklet, simply complete the coupon and mail it today. It could take some of the bumps and curves out of your path to the world.

**Ministry of Industry and Trade**

Please send me your "Trade Service brochure

Name _____

Title _____

Company _____

Address _____

City _____

Postal Code _____

GM02/08/84

Ministry of Industry and Trade,
Export Consulting Services,
Hearst Block, 8th Floor,
900 Bay St., Toronto, Ontario
M7A 2E1

**ⵣ Ontario**

Hon. Frank S. Miller, Minister

international business expansion. Nations with lower per capita income cannot afford the technical equipment necessary in an industrialized society so they may be poor markets for expensive industrial machinery but good markets for agricultural hand tools. Wealthier countries can prove to be prime markets for the products of many Canadian industries, particularly those involved with consumer goods and advanced industrial products.

Many products have failed abroad simply because the producing firm tried to use the same marketing strategy that was successful at home. Consider an advertising strategy based primarily on the use of print media and featuring testimonials. Such a campaign would offer dim prospects in a less developed nation with a high degree of illiteracy.

North American products do not always meet the needs of foreign consumers. Some products of North American automobile manufacturers have traditionally been rejected by European drivers, who complain of poor handling, high fuel consumption, and poor styling. Since an understanding of local, cultural, economic, and societal variables is not obvious to one used to the Canadian situation, international marketers must carefully monitor these factors in all of the markets in which they operate.

**Trade Restrictions**   Assorted trade restrictions also affect world trade. These restrictions are most commonly expressed through tariffs. A **tariff** is *a tax levied against products imported from abroad*. Some tariffs are based on a set tax per unit. Others are figured on the value of the imported product. Tariffs may be classified as either revenue or protective tariffs. *Revenue tariffs* are designed to raise funds for the government. Most of the revenue of the Canadian government in the early years of Confederation came from this source. *Protective tariffs* are designed to raise the retail price of imported goods to that of similar domestic products or higher. In the past it was believed that a country should protect its infant industries by using tariffs to keep out foreign-made products. Some foreign goods would still enter, but the addition of a high tariff payment would make the domestic products competitive. Protective tariffs are usually higher than revenue tariffs. Different interest groups argue whether or not tariffs should be raised to protect employment and profits in domestic Canadian industry. It is debatable whether, in the long run, such a goal is obtainable through tariff protection.

The **General Agreement on Tariffs and Trade (GATT)**, *an international trade accord*, has sponsored seven major tariff negotiations that have reduced the overall level of tariffs throughout the world. The latest series, the so-called Tokyo Round, began in 1974 and concluded in 1979. The Tokyo Round reduced tariffs by about 33 percent over an eight-year period. The agreement also lessened

# GATT: The Tokyo Round

The Tokyo Round was named for the city where it was decided to start the talks, but the negotiations actually took place in Geneva. Ninety-nine nations participated in this complex debate.

The Tokyo Round will result in considerable tariff reductions throughout the world. These cuts, expected to average 33 percent by the late 1980s, will affect about 5700 products.

Numerous nontariff barriers have also been reduced. With the exception of Japan, the participating governments agreed to change their pro-curement regulations to allow foreign marketers to bid on government purchases. The new pact reduced each nation's ability to use custom valuations or product standard regulations to discriminate against foreign goods. It also reduced restrictions on the international sale of civil aircraft and restricted government subsidies to exporters. Early assessments of the Tokyo Round suggest that it could lead to a considerable increase in international trade.

Sources: Information from Peter Nulty, "Why the 'Tokyo Round' Was a U.S. Victory," *Fortune* (May 21, 1979), pp. 130–132, 134–135; "A Smooth End to the Tokyo Round," *Business Week* (April 9, 1979), pp. 32–33; "How the U.S. Scored on Trade," *Business Week* (May 7, 1979), pp. 34–35; "Can World Head Off a Trade War?" *U.S. News & World Report* (April 23, 1979), pp. 43–44; and "Significant Trends," *Sales & Marketing Management* (May 14, 1979), p. 82.

nontariff barriers, such as government procurement regulations, that discriminated against foreign producers.

There are other forms of trade restrictions. An **import quota** *sets limits on the amount of products in certain categories that may be imported.* The objective of import quotas is to protect local industry and employment and preserve foreign exchange. The ultimate form of a quota is an **embargo**, *a complete ban on importing certain products.*

Foreign trade can also be regulated by exchange control through a central bank or government agency. **Exchange control** means that *firms gaining foreign exchange by exporting must sell their foreign exchange to the central bank or agency, and importers must buy foreign exchange from the same organization.* The exchange control authority can then allocate, expand, or restrict foreign exchange according to existing national policy.

**Dumping—A Marketing Problem**

The term **dumping** is applied to situations where *products are sold at significantly lower prices in a foreign market than in a nation's own domestic market.* If foreign goods sell in Canada for substantially lower prices than Canadian products, the likely consequence is a loss of jobs here. National Revenue, Canada Customs and Excise Branch, investigates alleged cases of dumping. If there is a preliminary determination of dumping, the Deputy Minister submits the finding to the Anti-Dumping Tribunal. The tribunal must make an inquiry within 90 days and issue a finding as to whether dumping is causing or likely to cause national injury to the production in Canada of like goods. This may lead to the imposition of anti-dumping

duties by Customs and Excise. The tariff charge is designed to protect Canadian employment by raising the product's price up to what it
sells for in its home market.

Some critics have argued that fear of the dumping procedure
and its tariff causes many foreign markets to keep their export prices
higher than would normally be the case. The result, it is argued, is
higher prices for the Canadian consumer. It is likely that dumping
will remain a controversial topic in international trade for some time.

**Political and Legal
Factors**

Political factors greatly influence international marketing. For
instance, Colgate's popular Irish Spring soap was introduced in
England with a political name change. The British know the product as Nordic Spring.[10] India once told Coca-Cola that it could not
continue to operate unless it gave the government its syrup formula.
The company declined, and the government began marketing a drink
called "77," using the same bottlers.[11]

Many nations try to achieve political objectives through international business activities. Like it or not, firms operating abroad
often end up involved in, or influenced by, international relations. A
dynamic political environment is a fact of life in world business.

Legal requirements complicate world marketing. Indonesia has
banned commercial advertisements from the nation's only television channel. It was feared that the advertisements would cause the
80 percent of the population living in rural areas to envy those who
resided in cities. All commercials in the United Kingdom and Australia must be cleared in advance. In the Netherlands, ads for candy
must also show a toothbrush. Some nations have **local content laws**
that *specify the portion of a product that must come from domestic
sources*. These examples suggest that managers involved in international marketing must be well versed in legislation affecting their
specific industry.

The legal environment for Canadian firms operating abroad can
be divided into three dimensions:
1. Canadian law
2. International law
3. Legal requirements of host nations

Canadian Law   International marketing is subject to various trade
regulations, tax laws, and import/export requirements. One significant provision in the Combines Investigation Act exempted from
anticombines laws groups of Canadian firms acting together to
develop foreign markets. An example is the cartel of Canadian ura-

10 *The Detroit News* (February 28, 1975), p. 1.
11 Richard Manville, "33 Caveats for the Overseas Marketer," *Marketing News*
(March 10, 1978), p. 6.

nium producers, which was designed to increase prices received in international markets. The intent is to give Canadian industry economic power equal to that possessed by foreign cartels. A **cartel** is *the monopolistic organization of a group of firms*. Companies operating under this provision must not reduce competition within Canada and must not use "unfair methods of competition." It is hard to say whether companies can co-operate internationally and remain competitive without collusion in the domestic market.

International Law   International law can be found in the treaties, conventions, and agreements that exist among nations. Canada has many **friendship, commerce, and navigation (FCN) treaties**. These treaties *include many aspects of commercial relations with other countries*, such as the right to conduct business in the treaty partner's domestic market.

Other international business agreements concern international standards for various products, patents, trademarks, reciprocal tax treaties, export control, international air travel, and international communications. The International Monetary Fund has been set up to lend foreign exchange to nations that require it to conduct international trade. This facilitates the whole process of international marketing.

Laws of the Host Nation   The legal requirements of host nations affect foreign marketers. For example, some nations limit foreign ownership in their business sectors. World marketers in general recognize the critical importance of obeying the laws and regulations of the countries within which they operate. Even the slightest violations of these legal requirements are setbacks for the future of international trade.

**Canadian Government Assistance to Exporters**   The Export Development Corporation (EDC) is a Canadian Crown corporation that provides financial services to Canadian exporters and foreign buyers in order to facilitate and develop export trade.[12] It does this through a wide range of insurance, guarantee, and loan services not normally provided by the private sector.

EDC services are provided for Canadian exporters who are offering competitive products in terms of price, quality, delivery, and service, to help them compete internationally. Exporters in other countries have access to similar support facilities from their governments.

Canadian firms of any size can insure their export sales against nonpayment by foreign buyers. EDC normally assumes 90 percent of the commercial and political risks involving insolvency or default

[12]Adapted from *The Financial Post* (May 3, 1980), supplement pp. 1–2.

by the buyer, as well as blockage of funds in a foreign country. EDC will also make long-term loans to foreign buyers of Canadian capital goods and services. Funds are paid direct to Canadian suppliers on behalf of the borrower, in effect providing the exporters with cash sales. EDC policy is to achieve maximum private-sector involvement in export financing; therefore it provides 100 percent guarantees to banks and financial institutions to facilitate the exporters' banking arrangements.

EDC is sensitive to the needs of the smaller exporter. There is no minimum value of export business required to qualify for support. The corporation continually reviews its programs and is prepared to consider tailoring its facilities — within the limits prescribed by legislation — to meet the specific needs of exporters with high potential for growth and competitiveness. Canada also has a network of trade commissioners in most major countries of the world. These commissioners seek new markets and facilitate the efforts of potential exporters. Such government involvement in international trade dramatizes the importance of this activity to Canada.

External Affairs Canada has trade officers in most major cities around the world. These officers seek out opportunities for Canadian companies and assist them in entering foreign markets.

Both federal and provincial governments actively encourage and assist firms at home to get involved in international marketing.

## The Marketing Mix in Foreign Markets

There is considerable variation in marketing practices in countries the world over.[13] These must be taken into consideration when an "outside" firm decides to launch a marketing campaign in a country. On the one hand, some European countries may have more advanced distribution systems than ours. On the other, high illiteracy rates in other world areas may substantially limit the types of advertising campaigns employed. Aggressive sales efforts may be regarded negatively in some foreign cultures. Business customs and traditions may restrict a firm's distribution strategy to certain marketing channels. A brief consideration of each marketing strategy compo-

---

[13] Some interesting viewpoints on varied marketing practices and environments abroad are presented in Dean M. Peebles, John K. Ryans, and Ivan R. Vernon, "Coordinating International Advertising," *Journal of Marketing* (January 1978), pp. 28–34; James Kilbough, "Improved Payoffs from Transnational Advertising," *Harvard Business Review* (July-August 1978), pp. 102–110; Jack G. Kaikati, "How Multinational Corporations Handle the Arab Boycott," *Columbia Journal of World Business* (Spring 1978), pp. 98–111; and Susan Douglas and Bernard Dubois, "Looking at the Cultural Environment for International Marketing Opportunities," *Columbia Journal of World Business* (Winter 1977), pp. 102–109.

nent will illustrate the differences that exist in marketing practices overseas.

**Product Strategy**

A power tool manufacturer had to change its products so that they could be sold in Australia, New Zealand, and South Africa. Those nations require that all power tools have equipment to prevent them from interfering with radio and television transmissions.[14] Packing modifications were necessary for an electric motor exporter before the firm could sell its product in Mexico because Mexican regulations do not permit packaging of parts and motors together.[15] According to one report, Holiday Inn decided to make its European hotels look less American and more European so as to compete better in the European marketplace.[16]

All of these examples illustrate that it is often necessary to adapt products to foreign markets. But it is often worthwhile to do so, for successful adaptation can significantly extend the market for a product. Sometimes the product itself has to be modified; in other cases it is the packaging; and in still others it is the product's identification. Consider the many products that might use the word "mist" as part of their names. But imagine the difficulty of marketing a consumer product using this name in Germany, where "mist" means "manure."[17]

**Pricing Strategy**

Pricing in foreign markets can be a very critical ingredient in overall marketing strategy. Pricing practices in overseas markets are subject to considerable competitive, economic, political, and legal pressures. International marketing managers must clearly understand these requirements if they are to succeed. Chapters 13 and 14 showed how complex the pricing decision is in Canadian markets. The international setting adds to that complexity because of different cultures, trade practices, and the added dimension of foreign laws and regulations.

**Distribution Strategy**

Distribution is a vital aspect of overseas marketing. Proper channels must be set up, and extensive physical distribution problems handled. Transportation systems, highways, and warehousing facili-

---

14 Lindley H. Clark, Jr. "Multinational Firms Under Fire All Over, Face a Changed Future," *The Wall Street Journal* (December 3, 1975), p. 25.
15 J. Donald Weinrauch and C. P. Rao, "The Export Marketing Mix: An Examination of Company Experiences and Perceptions," *Journal of Business Research* (October 1974), p. 451.
16 "An Idea That Didn't Travel Well," *Forbes* (February 15, 1976), pp. 26–27.
17 William Mathewson, "Trademarks Are a Global Business These Days, But Finding Registerable Ones is a Big Problem," *The Wall Street Journal* (September 4, 1975), p. 26.

ties may be unavailable or of inferior quality. International marketers must adapt speedily and efficiently to these situations if they are to profit from overseas sales.

Sears, one of the world's most effective retailers, has found its match in Seibu, a large Japanese retailer with 600 outlets. So Sears turned to Seibu to sell its catalogue merchandise in Japan. The venture was so successful that the Sears subsidiary Allstate Insurance has now begun to market its life insurance policies through Seibu's retail locations.[18]

Nissan is the leading automobile seller in oil-rich Saudi Arabia (where gasoline sells at 5.5 cents per litre). Nissan's Saudi Arabian market share is credited to an excellent organization of local distributors who were recruited in the early 1960s. The Japanese firm sought out Saudi entrepreneurs with sufficient investment capital who were skilled managers and marketers.[19] A sound distribution strategy has assisted greatly in the company's success.

**Promotional Strategy**    While effective personal selling continues to be vital in foreign markets, advertising has gained in importance. The wider availability of media such as radio and television has enhanced advertising's contribution to the overall promotional effort. However, many Canadian advertising approaches are not readily adaptable in some international markets where promotional practices are strictly regulated. Germany, for example, permits only 20 minutes a day for commercials and runs them bunched together between 6 and 8 p.m. daily, except Sundays and holidays.

Bribery, payoffs, and the sometimes dubious use of sales agents in foreign markets has received considerable publicity in recent years. Numerous executives claim that product quality and price must be supplemented by various types of bribes. Canadians are usually shocked by a firm that violates our accepted business customs and laws. All overseas marketing practices must be evaluated in terms of existing standards and practices here and abroad, as well as by ideal standards. Many organizations struggle with the decision as to what should be their practice.

**Levels of Involvement in International Marketing**    Several levels of involvement in international marketing can be identified — casual or accidental exporting, active exporting, foreign licensing, foreign marketing by the firm, and foreign production and marketing.[20]

---

18 "Sears Adds Insurance to Its Line of Exports," *Business Week* (August 4, 1975), p. 39.
19 "Nissan Competes with the Camel," *Business Week* (May 26, 1975), p. 44.
20 This section on international marketing involvement is based on Vern Terpstra, *International Marketing* (New York: Holt, Rinehart and Winston, 1972), pp. 11–14.

# Advertising in the Soviet Union

Who ever would have thought that more than 100 advertising agencies would be plying their trade today in the Soviet Union? Certainly not Marx! According to traditional Marxist-Leninist doctrine, advertising is a tool of capitalistic exploitation. It siphons off the surplus value belonging to underpaid workers and puts it in the hands of overpaid white-collar workers who are nonproductively employed writing jingles.

Yet there has been an impressive growth of advertising agencies in the Soviet Union. The initial argument was that these agencies exist to develop advertising to support Soviet goods in export markets where it is necessary to compete against other nations. But many advertisements also appear in print and broadcast media reaching Soviet consumers. Another rationale was established at the 1957 Prague Conference of Advertising Workers of Socialist Countries, which made three points as to how advertising was to be used: 1) to educate people's tastes, develop their requirements, and thus actively form demand; 2) to help the consumer by providing information about the most rational means of consumption; and 3) to help to raise the culture of trade. Furthermore, Soviet advertising is to be ideological, truthful, concrete, and functional. The Soviets claim that their advertising does not indulge in devices used in the West. Their ads will not use celebrities — only experts will be used to promote a product. They will not use mood advertising. They will not create brand differentiation when none exists.

Experts think that the main use of Soviet advertising is to help industry move products that come into excess supply where economic managers do not want to do the logical thing, cut prices.

Source: Courtland L. Bovee and William F. Arens, *Contemporary Advertising* (Homewood, Ill.: Richard D. Irwin, 1982), p. 119. Reprinted by permission. Photograph courtesy of Pepsico.

*Casual or accidental exporting* is a passive level of involvement in international marketing. A Canadian company may export goods without even knowing it, if its goods are bought by resident buyers for foreign companies. In other cases a firm may export only occasionally when surplus or obsolete inventory is available.

When the firm actually makes a commitment to seek export

business, it engages in *active exporting*. While the exact extent of the commitment may vary, active exporting implies that the firm is making a continuing effort to sell its merchandise abroad.

*Foreign licensing* occurs when a firm permits a foreign company under a formal agreement to produce and distribute its merchandise. For example, Matthews Conveyor Co. of Port Hope, Ontario, pioneered the airport luggage carousels and licenses firms around the world to manufacture them.[21] Licensing has several advantages over exporting, such as the availability of local marketing information and distribution channels and protection from various legal barriers. However, conflicts between the parties involved cause three of every 10 licensing agreements to fail. Another two or more are unsatisfactory to at least one of the participants.[22]

A firm that maintains a separate marketing or selling operation in a foreign country is involved in *foreign marketing*. Examples include foreign sales offices or overseas marketing subsidiaries. The product may come from various sources—domestic factories, foreign licensees, or contract manufacturers. In any case, the company directly controls foreign sales in this level of world business involvement.

*Foreign production and marketing*, the ultimate degree of company involvement in the international market arena, may be accomplished in several ways:

1. The firm may set up its own production and marketing operation in the foreign country.
2. The firm may acquire an existing company in the country in which it will do business.
3. The firm may form a *joint venture*, in which risks, costs, and management of the foreign operation are shared with a partner who is usually a national of the host nation.

---

**Multinational Marketing**   Switzerland's Nestlé now operates in 65 national markets with 146 000 employees and 300 plants. Sales total approximately $14 billion. Nestlé gets 41 percent of its revenue from Europe, 24 percent from Third World nations, and the remainder primarily from the United States and Japan.[23]

---

21 "Company Bagged International Market for Luggage Carrier Systems," *Financial Post* (March 4, 1978), p. 17.

22 These failure rates are reported in Erwin H. Klause, "How to Negotiate International Licensing Agreements and Keep Smiling," *Marketing News* (December 5, 1975), p. 8.

23 Robert Ball, "Nestlé Revs Up Its U.S. Campaign," *Fortune* (February 13, 1978), pp. 80–83.

**Multinational corporations** *operate in several countries* and literally view the world as their market. Nestlé is an example of an effective multinational corporation. The company is thoroughly international in perspective. The board chairman is French, the president is Swiss, one executive vice-president is French, and another is Italian. The senior vice-presidents include a U.S. and a Spanish citizen. Nestlé executives are regularly rotated to different assignments between the "centre" (company headquarters at Vevey on Lake Geneva) and the "markets" (as foreign operations are known). In Canada, Nestlé brands and acquisitions include Nescafé, Nestea, Taster's Choice, Crosse & Blackwell, and Libby, McNeill, & Libby.

Multinational corporations have become so dominant in some foreign markets that they are now the object of close political and economic scrutiny. Research studies have shown that multinationals usually make higher profits abroad than do their local competitors.[24] Canada and Australia — among others — have shown concern over the dominance of the multinationals. These firms will probably come in for even closer observation in the years ahead.

It seems likely that the multinational corporation will continue to be criticized in several areas.[25] Some criticism may be justified; other criticism certainly is not. Companies operating abroad must be sure that they act as fairly and responsibly in other countries as they do at home. It is obvious that multinational corporations have become fixtures in the international marketplace.

## Multinational Economic Integration and World Marketing

A noticeable trend toward multinational economic integration has developed since the end of World War II.[26] The Common Market, or European Economic Community (EEC), is the best known of these multinational economic communities. It unites the economies of 10 countries: Belgium, Britain, Denmark, France, West Germany, Ireland, Italy, Luxemburg, The Netherlands, and Greece. Goods move freely among all member states.

Multinational economic integration can be set up in several ways. The simplest approach is a *free trade area*, where the participants agree to free trade of goods among themselves in a particular area. All tariffs and trade restrictions are abolished between the nations involved. A *customs union* establishes a free trade area, plus a uniform tariff for trade with nonmember nations. The EEC is the best

---

24 William T. Ryan, "Multinationals Moving in While Africans Seek Capital, Know-How," *Marketing News* (September 1, 1974), p. 4.
25 An interesting discussion appears in James R. Wills, Jr., "The Misunderstood Multinational Corporation," *Carroll Business Bulletin* (Winter 1976), pp. 9–12.
26 Based on Vern Terpstra, *International Marketing* (New York: Holt, Rinehart and Winston, 1972), pp. 42–48.

example of a customs union, but it has been moving in the direction of an economic union. A true *common market*, or *economic union*, involves a customs union and also seeks to bring into agreement all government regulations affecting trade. Economic unions tend to erect barriers to imports from nations outside the union. For example, the percentage of Canadian trade in agricultural products with EEC countries has declined since the Market was formed.[27]

It seems certain that multinational economic communities will play a significant part in world business until the end of the century. North American firms invested heavily in Western Europe in the 1960s basically because of the attraction of larger markets offered by the EEC. Multinational economic integration is forcing management to adapt its operations abroad, and it is likely that the pace will accelerate. It may lead to less freedom in trade than in the past and may present marketers with certain challenges.

## Canada—An Attractive Market Target

Canada has become an increasingly inviting target for foreign marketers. Although our country does not have a large population, it has high levels of discretionary income, political stability, an attitude generally favourable to foreign investment, and economic ills that are relatively under control, in comparison with many other countries.

In 1976, foreign-controlled manufacturing establishments accounted for 51 percent of shipments of goods manufactured in Canada. There are some significant differences among the 20 major manufacturing groups. The level of foreign control was highest in the tobacco products industries (99.7 percent), petroleum and coal products industries (92.3 percent), and transportation equipment industries (84.6 percent). Canadian-controlled establishments accounted for more than 80 percent of shipments in the following major groups: printing, publishing, and allied industries; clothing industries; furniture and fixtures industries; knitting mills and leather industries.

Establishments controlled in the United States accounted for 41 percent of shipments, with those controlled in other foreign countries accounting for 10 percent. Those in the latter category were relatively important in the tobacco products industries.[28]

---

[27] Soe Lin and G. Labrosse, "Canada's Agricultural and Food Trade in the 1970's," *Canadian Farm Economics* (August 1980), pp. 1–8.
[28] Adapted from *Market Research Facts and Trends* (Maclean Hunter, June 1980) and *Domestic and Foreign Control of Manufacturing, Mining and Logging Establishments in Canada, 1976,* Statistics Canada, Catalogue 31-401.

Foreign control of the service sector is not large, however. Only 13 percent of assets in this sector were foreign-controlled. Foreign control is lowest in transportation, communications, and other utilities (7 percent). Financial services are estimated at 12 percent, and control is highest in wholesale trade, at 23 percent.[29]

The magnitude of foreign ownership in Canada is viewed by this country as a problem. In mining and manufacturing, a substantial majority of all assets are under foreign control. From a national point of view, it is considered undesirable to have such a substantial proportion of our economy that is not Canadian-owned because policies for these segments may be set by non-Canadians who do not have the same interests as we. Consequently, in 1974 the federal government established the Foreign Investment Review Agency to screen all new foreign investment in Canadian business. Only those investments that, in the opinion of the Agency, offered significant benefit to Canada were allowed. A large number of cases were considered each year. In 1980–81, 883 applications were received and 73% of these were approved.[30] FIRA processed more than 3500 applications between 1974 and 1981.[31]

The work of FIRA was extremely controversial. Few disagreed with its purpose, but many complained about the length of time FIRA took to make its decisions, and about the apparently arbitrary nature of those decisions.

Shortly after the Conservatives won the federal election in September, 1984, the name of the agency was changed to Investment Canada. Part of its new mandate was to make desirable investment in Canada easier.

Canadian marketers must expect to face substantial foreign competition in the years ahead. Canada is an attractive market target for many foreign firms, and our high levels of buying power are sure to have considerable appeal abroad. Until recently, continued reduction of trade barriers and expanded world marketing seemed to be the long-run trend. Only time will tell if this trend will continue.

*Free Trade with the United States*

On October 5, 1987, the political leaders of Canada and the United States signed a historic agreement to open the borders of their two countries to virtually unrestricted flows of goods. At the time of writing this book, this agreement had still not been ratified by the

---

29 Frank Swedlove, "Foreign Investment in the Service Sector" (Ottawa: Foreign Investment Review Agency, 1980).

30 *Foreign Investment Review Act, Annual Report 1980–81* (Government of Canada, Foreign Investment Review Agency), p. 1.

31 Wayne Lilley, "FIRA and Loathing on the Rideau," *Canadian Business* (September 1981), p. 49.

governments in each country. If ratified, the opportunities and challenges of becoming directly involved in an unrestricted North American market appear to be immense. No longer will marketers on either side of the border be able to compete from behind carefully managed tariff and nontariff walls. This could affect scale economies in production, distribution flows, pricing, and promotion strategies.

**Summary**        International marketing has become increasingly important. Many Canadian firms are now engaged in some type of international marketing activity. Foreign trade is important to Canada from both the exporting (selling abroad) and importing (buying foreign goods and raw materials) viewpoints.

International marketing is often considered in terms of a nation's balance of trade (the relationship between its exports and imports) and balance of payments (the flow of money into or out of the country). It is sometimes necessary for a nation to adjust its exchange rate, the rate at which its currency can be exchanged for other currencies or gold, because the real value of a domestic currency is out of line with international currencies in terms of relative buying power.

Basic concepts in world trade include those of absolute advantage and comparative advantage. These concepts as well as non-economic considerations, such as the political aim of self sufficiency, determine the products in which a nation specializes.

Competing in foreign markets is often considerably different from competing at home. Market size, buying behaviour, and marketing practices all differ. International marketers must often make significant adaptations in their product, distribution, promotion, and pricing strategies to fit different markets abroad.

Several levels of involvement in international marketing can be identified — casual or accidental exporting, active exporting, foreign licensing, foreign marketing by the firm, and foreign production and marketing.

The world's largest firms are usually multinational in their orientation. A multinational company operates in several countries and literally views the world as its market.

Various environmental factors can influence international marketing strategy. Cultural, economical, and societal factors can hinder international marketing. So can assorted trade restrictions and political and legal factors.

Since the end of World War II there has been a noticeable trend toward multinational economic integration. Three basic formats for economic integration exist: a free trade area, a customs union, and a common market.

Canada is now viewed as an attractive market target for world marketers. Today Canadian firms can expect to face stiff foreign competition in the Canadian domestic market.

| | | |
|---|---|---|
| **Key Terms** | exporting | tariff |
| | importing | GATT |
| | balance of trade | import quota |
| | balance of payments | embargo |
| | exchange rate | exchange control |
| | devaluation | dumping |
| | revaluation | local content laws |
| | absolute advantage | cartels |
| | comparative advantage | FCN treaties |
| | | multinational corporation |

**Review Questions**

1. Why is international marketing important to Canadian firms? To the Canadian economy?
2. What types of products are most often marketed abroad by Canadian firms?
3. In what ways is the international marketing mix likely to be different from a marketing mix used in the domestic country?
4. Describe the methods of measuring international marketing.
5. Identify the various levels of involvement in international marketing.
6. Explain how trade restrictions may be employed to restrict or to stimulate international marketing activities.
7. Distinguish between import quotas and embargoes.
8. Explain the international marketing practice of dumping. Why does dumping sometimes occur?
9. Identify and briefly explain the three basic formats for economic integration.
10. Why is Canada such an attractive market target for foreign marketers? What does this mean for Canadian firms?

**Discussion Questions and Exercises**

1. Comment on the following statement: It is sometimes dangerous for a firm to attempt to export its marketing strategy.
2. Outline the basic premises behind the operation of a multinational corporation. Do you think the term has a negative connotation?
3. The Foreign Investment Review Agency (FIRA) controlled foreign investment in Canada. Do you agree with such a restriction on firms entering our market, even though this brings in new money and products? Explain.
4. Give an example — hypothetical or actual — of a firm operating at each level of international marketing:
   a. casual or accidental exporting
   b. active exporting

    c. foreign licensing

    d. overseas marketing

    e. foreign production and foreign marketing

5. Relate specific international environmental considerations to each of the following aspects of a firm's marketing mix:

    a. brands and warranties

    b. advertising

    c. distribution channels

    d. discounts to intermediaries

    e. use of comparative advertising

# Marketing in Nonprofit Settings

1. To outline the primary characteristics of nonprofit organizations that distinguish them from profit-seeking organizations.

2. To describe the evolution of the broadening concept.

3. To identify types of marketing used by nonprofit organizations.

4. To explain how a marketing mix might be developed in a nonprofit setting.

5. To identify the variables that might be used in the evaluation and control of a nonprofit marketing program.

The marketing challenge for the Canadian Heart Foundation is multifaceted. This well-known organization provides information on heart disease, funds research into cures for this killer, and raises money to support these efforts. Where does marketing come in to the picture?

Too often people look at the advertising done by nonprofit organizations and equate that with marketing. By now, the reader of this book will realize that marketing is much more than advertising or sales. Marketing involves the application of the entire marketing mix in accordance with a well-planned marketing strategy.

For the Heart Foundation, the product/service is education about heart disease and research into its prevention and cure. Both education and research are attuned to the information and physical needs of the population. If support for those efforts is to continue, the public must perceive that the Foundation's output is valuable.

Potential donor segments must be identified in order to appeal to the various motivations in the population. For those who have heart disease, fear of the disease might be a motivation. Others may simply recognize that this is a worthy cause. Corporate donors may have less obvious motivations to which the Foundation should appeal. Marketing research may be necessary to develop a complete picture of the factors which would create a favourable response to an appeal for funds.

Marketing research may also be needed in order to learn how best to communicate current findings and advice concerning heart disease and to distribute appeal literature.

Another task for the Foundation is to find, manage, and motivate the thousands of volunteers who collect funds for its work. This has some similarities to sales management in a profit organization, but is broader in scope, especially since the motivation of volunteers is different from that of paid employees.

Above all, proper marketing planning will greatly improve the direction and effectiveness of this nonprofit organization. Not only the Heart Foundation has discovered this, but many other nonprofit organizations have successfully applied marketing thinking to their efforts.

| **The Conceptual Framework** | In Chapter 1, marketing was defined as the development and efficient distribution of goods, services, ideas, issues, and concepts for chosen consumer segments. Although much of the text concentrated on organizations that operate for profit, the activities of the Heart Foundation are as representative of modern marketing activities as the marketing programs of Burger King, Wendy's, and McDonald's. Our definition of marketing is sufficiently comprehensive to encompass nonprofit as well as profit-seeking organizations. |

A substantial portion of our economy is composed of **nonprofit organizations** — *those whose primary objective is something other than returning a profit to owners.* As estimated one out of every ten service workers and one of six professionals are employed in the nonprofit sector. The nonprofit sector includes thousands of religious organizations, human service organizations, museums, libraries, colleges and universities, symphony orchestras and other music organizations, and organizations such as government agencies, political parties, and labour unions. Figure 23-1 depicts one portion of the marketing efforts of one nonprofit organization — Foster Parents Plan of Canada.

Nonprofit organizations can be found in both public and private sectors of society. Federal, provincial, and local governmental units and agencies whose revenues are derived from tax collection have service objectives not keyed to profitability targets. The Department of National Defence provides protection. A provincial department of natural resources regulates conservation and environmental programs. And the local animal control officer enforces ordinances that protect both persons and animals.

Some public-sector agencies may be given revenue or behaviour goals. An urban transit system might be expected to pay a great deal of its costs out of revenues, for example. But society does not expect these units to routinely produce a surplus that is returned to the taxpayers.

The private sector offers an even more diverse array of non-

**Figure 23-1   Example of Advertising by a Nonprofit Organization**

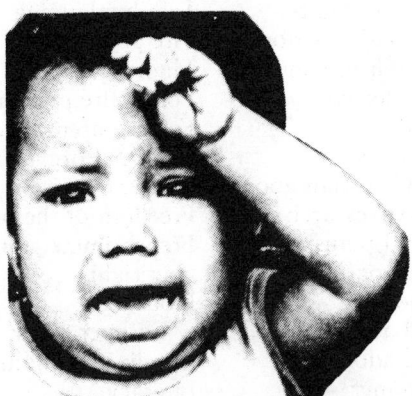

# Desperate for your help

For a boy of the developing world, every day is a desperate fight for survival. There's nowhere for him to turn. His family has no skills, no hopes. His community has no resources. But can't he turn to you? Foster Parents Plan can show you how to help him—and his community. Fill in the coupon below, or:

**Call toll-free right now at: 1-800-268-7174**

**PLAN**   **FOSTER PARENTS PLAN OF CANADA**
*(An international human development agency)*
153 ST. CLAIR AVENUE WEST, TORONTO, CANADA M4V 1P8

I want to be a Foster Parent of a boy ☐   girl ☐   age _____
country _____ or where the need is greatest ☐
I enclose my first payment of $23.00 Monthly ☐   $69.00 Quarterly ☐
$138.00 Semi-Annually ☐   $276.00 Annually ☐
I can't become a Foster Parent right now, however I enclose my contribution of
$_____ Please send me more information ☐ Tel. No. _____
Mr. ☐  Mrs. ☐  Miss ☐ _____
Address _____
City _____ Prov. _____ Code _____
I wish communication with PLAN to be in English ☐   French ☐

PLAN operates in Bolivia, Colombia, Ecuador, Egypt, El Salvador, Guatemala, Haiti, Honduras, India, Indonesia, Kenya, Liberia, Mali, Nicaragua, Nepal, the Philippines, Senegal, Sierra Leone, Sri Lanka, the Sudan, Thailand and Upper Volta. Foster Parents Plan of Canada is officially registered as a Canadian Charitable Organization by the Federal Government. Contributions are tax deductible.                                                    MA233 5144

Source: *Maclean's* (May 14, 1984).

profit settings. Art institutes, churches, labour unions, private schools, the United Way, the Rotary Club, and the local country club all serve as examples of private-sector, nonprofit organizations. The diversity of these settings suggests how pervasive organizational objectives other than profitability really are in a modern economy.

The market offering of the nonprofit organization is frequently more nebulous than the tangible goods or service provisions of profit-seeking firms. Figure 23-2 lists social issues and ideas ranging from gay rights to the use of motorcycle helmets that represent the offerings made by some nonprofit organizations to their publics.

The diversity of these issues suggests the size of the nonprofit sector and the marketing activities involved in accomplishing their

**Figure 23-2   Social Issues Marketed by Nonprofit Organizations**

| | | |
|---|---|---|
| Abortion rights | Family planning | Physical fitness |
| Affirmative action | Fire prevention | Police, support of |
| Alcoholism control | Fluoridation | Pollution control |
| Birth defects | Forest fire prevention | Population control |
| Blood | Foster parenthood | Prison reform |
| Blue laws | Fraternal organizations | Religion |
| Buy Canadian goods | Free enterprise | Right to Life |
| Cancer research | Freedom of the press | Save the whales |
| Capital punishment | French immersion | Seat belt use |
| CARE packages | Gay rights | Solar energy |
| Carpooling | Housing | Suicide hot line |
| Child abuse |    Co-operatives | Tax reform |
| Child adoption | Legalized gambling | UNICEF |
| Consumer | Literacy | United Way |
|   co-operatives | Littering prevention | VD hotline |
| Crime prevention | Mass transportation | 911-emergency number |
| Drunk driving | Mental health | |
| Energy conservation | Metric system | |
| Euthanasia | Military recruiting | |
| | Motorcycle helmets | |
| | Museums | |
| | Nonsmokers' rights | |
| | Nuclear energy | |

Source: Most of these issues are listed in Seymour H. Fine, *The Marketing of Ideas and Social Issues* (New York: Praeger, 1981), pp. 13–14.

objectives. What makes them different from their profit-seeking counterparts?

**Characteristics of Nonprofit Organizations**

Nonprofit organizations have a special set of characteristics that affects their marketing activities. Like the profit-oriented service offerings discussed in Chapter 12, the product offered by a nonprofit organization is often intangible. A hospital's diagnostic services exhibit marketing problems similar to those inherent in marketing a life insurance policy.

A second feature of nonprofit organizations involves multiple publics. As Professor Philip Kotler points out:

Nonprofit organizations normally have at least two major publics to work with from a marketing point of view: their clients and their funders. The former pose the problem of *resource allocation* and the latter, the problem of *resource attraction*. Besides these two publics, many other publics surround the nonprofit organization and call for marketing programs. Thus a college can direct marketing programs toward prospective students, current students, parents of students, alumni, faculty, staff, local business firms, and local government agencies. It turns out that business organizations also deal with a multitude of publics but their tendency is to think about marketing only in connection with one of these publics, namely their customers.[1]

A customer or service user may lack control over the organization's destiny. A government employee may be far more concerned with the opinion of a member of the Cabinet than that of a service user. Furthermore, nonprofit organizations often possess some degree of monopoly power in a given geographical area. An individual might object to the United Way's inclusion of a crisis centre among its beneficiary agencies. But a contributor who accepts the merits of the United Way appeal recognizes that a portion of total contributions will go to the agency in question.

Another problem involves the resource contributor, such as a legislator or a financial backer, who interferes with the marketing program. It is easy to imagine a political candidate harassed by financial supporters who want to replace an unpopular campaign manager (the primary marketing position in a political campaign).

Perhaps the most commonly noted feature of the nonprofit organization is its lack of a **bottom line** (business jargon referring to *the overall profitability measure of performance*). While a nonprofit organization may attempt to maximize its return from a specific service, less measurable goals such as service level standards are the usual substitute for an overall evaluation. The net result is that it is often difficult to set marketing objectives that are in line with overall organizational goals.

A final characteristic is the lack of a clear organizational structure. Nonprofit organizations often refer to constituencies that they serve, but these are often considerably less exact than, for example, the stockholders of a profit-oriented corporation. Nonprofit organizations often have multiple organizational structures. A hospital might have an administrative structure, a professional organization consisting of medical personnel, and a volunteer organization that dominates the board of trustees. These people may sometimes work at cross-purposes, and not be totally in line with the marketing strategy that has been devised.[2]

---

[1] Philip Kotler, *Marketing for Nonprofit Organizations* (Englewood Cliffs, N.J.: Prentice-Hall, 1982), p. 9.

[2] These differences and others are outlined in Harvey W. Wallender, III, "Managing Not-For-Profit Enterprises," *Academy of Management Review* (January 1978), p. 26; and Cecily Cannon Selby, "Better Performance for 'Nonprofits,' " *Harvard Business Review* (September-October 1978), pp. 93–95. Used by permission.

While the above factors may also characterize some profit-oriented organizations, they are certainly prevalent in nonprofit settings. These characteristics affect the implementation of marketing efforts in such organizations, and must be considered in the development of an overall strategy.

## The Broadening Concept

The current status of nonprofit marketing is largely the result of an evolutionary process that began in the early 1960s, when several writers suggested that marketing could be useful in situations beyond the traditional profit-oriented domain. Marketing was beginning to be seen as having wider application than had normally been the case.[3]

In 1969 Kotler and Levy argued that the marketing concept should be broadened to include the nonprofit sector of society.[4] The theoretical justification for this view was that marketing is a generic activity for all organizations.[5] In other words, marketing is a function that is performed by any type of organization. Thus, the **broadening concept** was *an extension of the marketing concept to nontraditional exchange processes*. In fact, of course, these organizations had experienced marketing-type problems all along, and these had been articulated at various times by marketing researchers.

The broadening concept was not unanimously accepted by marketers. Luck argued that it was an unwarranted extension of the marketing concept.[6] And more recently, Laczniak and Michie argued that a broadened marketing concept could be responsible for undesirable social changes and disorder.[7] Despite some dissent, the broadening concept is enjoying wide acceptance among nonprofit organizations and various students of marketing.

---

[3] This evolution is described in Philip D. Cooper and William J. Kehoe, "Marketing's Status, Dimensions, and Directions," *Business* (July-August 1979), pp. 14–15. Another interesting discussion of marketing's evolution appears in the same issue of *Business*. See Robert Bartels, "Upward Mobility in Marketing Management," pp. 9–13.

[4] Philip Kotler and Sidney J. Levy, "Broadening the Concept of Marketing" *Journal of Marketing* (January 1969), pp. 10–15.

[5] Philip Kotler, "A Generic Concept of Marketing" *Journal of Marketing* (April 1972), pp. 46–54.

[6] David J. Luck, "Broadening the Concept of Marketing—Too Far," *Journal of Marketing* (July 1969), pp. 53–55.

[7] This interesting series of exchanges appears in the *Journal of the Academy of Marketing Science* (Summer 1979). See Gene R. Laczniak and Donald A. Michie, "The Social Disorder of the Broadened Concept of Marketing," pp. 214–232; Sidney J. Levy and Philip Kotler, "Toward a Broader Concept of Marketing's Role in Social Order," pp. 232–238; and Laczniak and Michie, "Broadened Marketing and Social Order: A Reply," pp. 239–242.

## Types of Nonprofit Organizations

Although nonprofit organizations are at least as varied as profit-seeking organizations, it is possible to categorize them based upon the type of marketing each requires. The three major types of marketing among nonprofits are person marketing, idea marketing, and organization marketing.

### Person Marketing

**Person marketing** refers to *efforts designed to cultivate the attention, interest, and preference of a market target toward a person.*[8] This type of marketing is typically employed by political candidates and celebrities.

The leadership campaigns for the Conservative and Liberal parties in 1983 and 1984 and the federal election campaign of 1984 are good examples of person marketing. The serious contenders did considerable research into the various voter segments and developed strategies to reach them. Attention was given to those geographic areas that were the most promising, and those that required special treatment. Similarly, in a profit-seeking setting, various musicians are carefully marketed to subsegments of the total market. The marketing mix for marketing Anne Murray is different from that for Maureen Forrester.

### Idea Marketing

The second type of nonprofit marketing deals with causes and social issues rather than an individual. **Idea marketing** refers to *the identification and marketing of a cause to chosen consumer segments.*[9] A highly visible marketing mix element frequently associated with idea marketing is the use of *advocacy advertising*, discussed earlier in Chapter 20. The importance of wearing seat belts and motorcycle helmets is currently being marketed in several provinces.

Similar to profit organizations, nonprofit organizations may use marketing to advocate different viewpoints on the same social issue. For example, pro-choice and right-to-life groups espouse radically different perspectives on abortion.

### Organization Marketing

The third type of nonprofit marketing, **organization marketing**, attempts *to influence others to accept the goals of, receive the services of, or contribute in some way to an organization.* Included in this category are *mutual benefit* organizations, such as churches, labour unions, and political parties; *service* organizations, such as colleges and universities, hospitals, and museums; and *government* organizations such as military services, police and fire departments,

---

[8] Philip Kotler, *Marketing for Nonprofit Organizations* (Englewood Cliffs, N.J.: Prentice-Hall, 1982), p. 482.

[9] An excellent discussion of idea marketing appears in Jagdish N. Sheth and Gary L. Frazier, "A Model of Strategy Mix Choice for Planned Social Change," *Journal of Marketing* (Winter 1982), pp. 15–26.

the post office, and local communities.[10] Figure 23-3 illustrates the efforts of the town of High River to attract businesses to settle in that community. If successful, this advertising effort, along with other marketing mix elements, will create new jobs and stimulate the economic base of the community.

**Defining Marketing in Nonprofit Settings**

One of the most pervasive problems in nonprofit marketing is the way in which marketing is defined.[11] In many cases, marketing is taken to mean simply promotion. The development of well thought-out marketing strategy, as well as consideration of other components of the marketing mix — product development, distribution, and pricing strategies — have too often been largely ignored. Marketing, considered and practised merely as aggressive promotion, is a short-lived, surface-level solution for a variety of organizational problems and objectives. For instance, one university decided to "adopt marketing" and thought it was doing so by planning to release balloons containing scholarship offers. And "marketing planning" conference for a private school consisted mainly of the development of new slogans for advertisements.

Professor Seymour H. Fine recently conducted a survey of nonprofit organizations to assess the degree of marketing sophistication present. His findings, illustrated in Figure 23-4, revealed that many respondents were unaware of, or at least reluctant to admit, the presence of marketing efforts in their organizations.

Few nonprofit organizations take the time to develop a comprehensive marketing approach. Of course, there are exceptions. One university, for example, conducted a comprehensive marketing audit that designated strong and weak areas in its product mix (program offerings). Strategies should be devised only after the basic parameters of market, resources, and mission have been identified and analysed.

**The Importance of Marketing to Nonprofit Organizations**

Marketing is a late arrival to the management of nonprofit organizations. The practices of improved accounting, financial control, personnel selection, and strategic planning were all implemented before marketing.[12] Nevertheless, nonprofit organizations

---

10 David J. Rachman and Elaine Romano, *Modern Marketing* (Hinsdale, Ill.: The Dryden Press, 1980), p. 576. The delineation of person, idea, and organization marketing are proposed by Professors Rachman and Romano.
11 This section is based on and used with permission from Philip Kotler, "Strategies for Introducing Marketing into Nonprofit Organizations," *Journal of Marketing* (January 1979), pp. 37, 44, published by the American Marketing Association. See also Kotler, *Marketing for Nonprofit Organizations* (Englewood Cliffs, N.J.: Prentice-Hall, 1975).
12 *Ibid*, p. 38.

## Figure 23-3   An Advertisement for a Community

**5 Good reasons why you should choose HIGH RIVER for your home and business!**

**1. LOCATION**

Situated on the banks of the scenic Highwood River, 41 Km (26 mi) south of Calgary, the town of High River offers a small town attractiveness. High River is in close proximity to the majestic Rocky Mountains and to Alberta's major centres.

**2. COMMUNITY**

High River is a friendly community that has a commitment to quality of life in a rural setting. People of diverse backgrounds are involved in progressive service clubs, active churches, a wide variety of sports teams, talented theatre and musical groups, and organizations dedicated to preserving the area's history and enhancing its future.

**3. ECONOMY**

As regional and administration centre for a trading area in excess of 18,000, strong in agriculture. High River has achieved economic success with light industry and manufacturing as well as an impressive commercial sector.

**4. RECREATION**

High River summers often feature balloonists perched in clear blue skies, watching horse races on the track, ball games in the parks, or neighbours fishing or playing a leisurely game of golf. Comfortable winters are filled with sleigh rides, skiing, and curling. Annual spectacular events such as the Little Britches Rodeo draw visitors from around the world.

**5. SERVICES**

Complete retail, commercial and educational services are available and a unique new hospital offers the latest in medical technology. Access to road and rail systems and airport facilities is excellent.

A place to work    A place to play
High River is an ideal place to live

*For further information, contact:*
Town Office
P.O. Bag 10, High River, Alberta T0L 1B0
(403) 652-2307

**HIGH RIVER**

"The Town with a Past and Future"

**Figure 23-4   Responses of Selected Nonprofit Organization Representatives**

| Nonprofit Organization | Reponse to the Question: "Do you have a marketing department or equivalent?" |
| --- | --- |
| Public health service official | "Marketing fluoridation is not a function of government — promotion and public awareness is." |
| Administrator of regional women's rights group | "We have never thought of ourselves as marketing a product. We have people who are assigned equal pay for work of equal value as their 'item.'" |
| Group crusading for the rights of the left-handed | "Don't understand the term (marketing); we do lobbying, letter writing to appropriate government and commercial concerns. |
| A national centre for the prevention of child abuse | "We disseminate information without the marketing connotation. Besides, demand is too great to justify marketing. |
| Recruiting officer | "Not applicable." |

Source: Adapted from Seymour H. Fine, *The Marketing of Ideas and Social Issues* (New York: Praeger, 1981), p. 53.

have accepted it enthusiastically. Dozens of articles and speeches attest to marketing's popularity. Some colleges and universities now offer courses in nonprofit marketing. Meanwhile, university administrators attend seminars and conferences to learn how better to market their own institutions.

Marketing's rise in the nonprofit sector could not be continued without a successful track record. While it is often more difficult to measure results in nonprofit settings, marketing can already point to examples of success. Participaction is one example. Presbyterian-affiliated Church of the Covenant credits a 10 percent increase in average attendance to a series of radio commercials.[13] And one art gallery's marketing analysis resulted in a definition of two distinct market segments which it should serve. Marketing is now an accepted part of the operational environment of most successful nonprofit organizations. Figure 23-5 is a hypothetical job description for a marketing director at a college or university.

---

[13] Margaret Yao, "Big Pitch for God: Moore Churches Try Advertising in Media," *Wall Street Journal* (December 31, 1979), pp. 1, 7.

## Figure 23-5   Job Description: Director of Marketing for a University

**Position Title:** Director of Marketing

**Reports to:** A vice-president designated by the president

**Scope:** University-wide

**Position Concept:** The director of marketing is responsible for providing marketing guidance and services to university officers, school deans, department chairpersons, and other agents of the university.

**Functions:** The director of marketing will:
1. Contribute a marketing perspective to the deliberations of the top administration in its planning of the university's future
2. Prepare data that might be needed by any officer of the university on a particular market's size, segments, trends, and behavioural dynamics
3. Conduct studies of the needs, perceptions, preferences, and satisfactions of particular markets
4. Assist in the planning, promotion, and launching of new programs
5. Assist in the development of communication and promotion campaigns and materials
6. Analyse and advise on pricing questions
7. Appraise the workability of new academic proposals from a marketing point of view
8. Advise on new student recruitment
9. Advise on current student satisfaction
10. Advise on university fundraising

**Responsibilities:** The director of marketing will:
1. Contact individual officers and small groups at the university to explain services and to solicit problems
2. Rank the various requests for services according to their long-run impact, cost-saving potential, time requirements, ease of accomplishment, cost, and urgency
3. Select projects of high priority and set accomplishment goals for the year
4. Prepare a budget request to support the anticipated work
5. Prepare an annual report on the main accomplishments of the office

**Major Liaisons:** The director of marketing will:
1. Relate most closely with the president's office, admissions office, development office, planning office, and public relations department
2. Relate secondarily with the deans of various schools and chairpersons of various departments

Source: Reprinted with permission from Philip Kotler, "Strategies for Introducing Marketing into Nonprofit Organizations," *Journal of Marketing* (January 1979), p. 42, published by the American Marketing Association.

## Developing a Marketing Strategy

The need for a comprehensive marketing strategy rather than merely increasing promotion expenditures has already been noted. Substantial opportunities exist for effective, innovative strategies since there has been little previous marketing effort in most nonprofit settings.

### Marketing Research

Many decisions in nonprofit settings are based on little if any research. Numerous Canadian art galleries arbitrarily establish programs and schedules with little or no reference to audience marketing research.

Adequate marketing research can be extremely important in a variety of nonprofit settings. Resident opinion surveys in some cities have proven valuable to public officials.[14] Consumer surveys have the potential to play an important role in product-liability lawsuits.[15] And the analysis of projected population trends has led to tentative decisions to close obstetric units at some hospitals.[16]

### Product Strategy

Nonprofit organizations face the same product decisions as profit-seeking firms. They must choose a product, service, person, idea, or social issue to be offered to their market target. They must decide whether to offer a single product or a mix of related products. They must make product identification decisions. The fact that the United Way symbol and the Red Cross trademark are as familiar as McDonald's golden arches or the Shell symbol illustrates the similarity in the use of product identification methods.

A common failure among nonprofit organizations is the assumption that heavy promotional efforts can overcome a poor product strategy or marketing mix. Consider the number of liberal arts colleges that tried to use promotion to overcome their product mix deficiences when students became increasingly career-oriented. Successful institutions adjust their product offerings to reflect customer demand.

Boris Brott, of the Hamilton Symphony Orchestra, recognizes the importance of product strategy in a nonprofit setting. The orchestra's ticket sales and donations were on the decline when Brott took over as conductor. While the maestro is known as an aggressive promoter, he also is a very adept product manager.

---

[14] James M. Stearns, John R. Kerr, and Roger R. McGrath, "Advances of Marketing for Functional Public Policy Administration," *Proceedings of the Southern Marketing Association* (Atlanta, Ga.: November 1979), eds. Robert S. Franz, Robert M. Hopkins, and Alfred G. Toma, pp. 140–143.
[15] Fred W. Morgan, "The Admissibility of Consumer Surveys as Legal Evidence in Courts," *Journal of Marketing* (Fall 1979), pp. 33–40.
[16] Daniel J. Fink, "Marketing the Hospital," *MBA* (December 1978/January 1979), p. 56.

Brott took a small, little-known amateur orchestra in 1969 and made it into the 43rd largest (of 700) in North America. The orchestra now has considerable class and prestige. He hired a number of professional musicians to form the core of the orchestra, and they played together in small chamber groups in schools throughout the Hamilton region. They taught, trained, and convinced young people that music is a worthwhile pursuit. He also took to the streets, literally selling the orchestra. He offered wine and cheese concerts at the local Holiday Inn, and acted in crazy television commercials where he appeared in a surgeon's gown and talked about "classical gas." He also took the orchestra into the city's steel plants, garnering maximum media attention.

The marketing of the Hamilton Symphony has worked. The orchestra now sells 93 percent of ticket capacity. It outdraws cities of comparable size for grants and donations and has a budget of $1.5 million, with a surplus of $73 000. Brott understands the importance of developing an appropriate marketing mix.[17] Similarly, Charles Duboit and his orchestra manager, Marin Mehta, have led the Montreal Symphony Orchestra to a ranking of one of the finest in the world through producing a product of superior quality largely through its recordings aimed at and promoted to the selected target market.[18]

*Pricing Strategy*   Pricing is typically a very important element of the marketing mix for nonprofit organizations. Pricing strategy can be used to accomplish a variety of organizational goals in nonprofit settings. These include:

1. *Profit maximization.* While nonprofit organizations by definition do not cite profitability as a primary goal, there are numerous instances in which they do try to maximize their return on a single event or a series of events. The $1000-a-plate political fund-raiser is an example.

2. *Cost recovery.* Some nonprofit organizations attempt only to recover the actual cost of operating the unit. Mass transit, colleges, and bridges are common examples. The amount of recovered costs is often dictated by tradition, competition, and/or public opinion.

3. *Providing market incentives.* Other nonprofit groups follow a penetration pricing policy or offer a free service to encourage increased usage of the product or service. Winnipeg's bus system policy of very low fares on special buses in the downtown

---

[17] Janet Enright, "Maestro in Mickey Mouse Ears," *The Financial Post Magazine* (November 29, 1980), pp. 65–66.
[18] Anthony Wilson-Smith, "The Sweet, Heady Music of International Success," *Maclean's* (April 23, 1984), pp. 62–63.

area reduces traffic congestion, encourages retail sales, and minimizes the effort required to use downtown public services.

4. *Market suppression.* Price is sometimes used to discourage consumption. In other words, high prices are used to accomplish social objectives and are not directly related to the costs of providing the product or service. Illustrations of suppression include tobacco and alcohol taxes, parking fines, tolls, and gasoline excise taxes.[19]

## Distribution Strategy

The Canadian post office has introduced an innovative distribution strategy. It is now possible to take letters or documents to central post offices in major cities and have them relayed by satellite to various destinations, including London, England. There they are printed, put into envelopes, and addressed for next-day delivery.

Distribution channels for nonprofit organizations tend to be short, simple, and direct. If intermediaries are present in the channel, they are usually agents such as an independent ticket agency or a specialist in fund raising.

Nonprofit organizations often fail to exercise caution in the planning and execution of the distribution strategy. Organizers of recycling centres sometimes complain about lack of public interest, when their real problem is an inconvenient location or lack of adequate drop-off points. By contrast, some public agencies, like health and social welfare departments, have set up branches in neighbourhood shopping centres to be more accessible to their clientele. Nonprofit marketers must carefully evaluate the available distribution options if they are to be successful in delivering their products or in serving their intended consumers.

## Promotional Strategy

It is common to see or hear advertisements from nonprofit organizations such as educational institutions, churches, and public service organizations. A striking example of nonprofit advertising is Figure 23-6, a newspaper advertisement for the United Way.

Marketing communications and promotional strategy are affected by a variety of factors including relative involvement in the nonprofit setting, pricing, and perceived benefits.[20] But overall

[19] This section is based on Philip Kotler, *Marketing for Nonprofit Organizations*, 1982, pp. 306–309. Adapted by permission of Prentice-Hall, Inc., Englewood Cliffs, New Jersey. See also Chris T. Allen, "Self-Perception Based Strategies for Stimulating Energy Conservation," *Journal of Consumer Research* (March 1982), pp. 381–390.
[20] Michael L. Rothschild, "Marketing Communications in Nonbusiness Situations or Why It's So Hard to Sell Brotherhood Like Soap," *Journal of Marketing* (Spring 1979), pp. 11–20.

Figure 23-6   A Promotional Strategy for the United Way

# IF YOU WON'T GIVE, PICK THE ONE WHO WON'T GET.

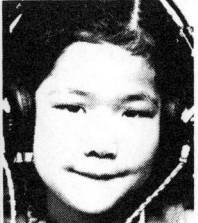

Who would you like to leave out?

The elderly? The Down's Syndrome children? The battered wives? The deaf? Who needs your help least?

It's not an easy decision to make, is it?

But it's the kind of decision you force to be made when you decide not to give to the United Way.

The United Way funds more than 100 agencies in Toronto. They're listed below.

When you give your dollars to the United Way, $88.00 of every $100.00 go directly to helping the people in those agencies help all the people just like the ones in this advertisement.

If you've given to the United Way before, we'd like you to give more this year.

If you've never given to the United Way, this is the year to start. There's never been a better time.

Because if United Way donations are up only 9% this year, there will have to be cutbacks, no new agencies admitted and limits put on innovative programs to meet new needs.

A 10% increase in 1980 would merely meet inflation and maintain the current level of service with no new agency admissions.

Even with a 12% increase in donations, only one third of the currently unmet needs would be met. And with a 20% increase, just two thirds of the unmet needs could be taken care of.

For all existing and new United Way member agencies to be successfully accommodated, it would take a 30% donation increase over last year.

So please think about the responsibility we all have. Please think about the kind of Toronto you'd like to live in. And help us help more this year.

Even a little will make life better for the entire community, for all of us.

And that way, no one will be left out.

United Way
OF GREATER TORONTO

IT'S YOU. IT'S ME. IT'S EVERYONE.

Source: United Way of Greater Toronto (1980 campaign).

promotion is seen by many nonprofit managers as the primary solution to their marketing problems. As noted earlier, this view is often naive, but it does not diminish the importance of promotion in a nonprofit setting.

All types of promotional strategy components have been utilized. The Canadian Forces have used television advertising to attract enlistments. University development officers rely on personal selling to build endowments. Fund-raising drives often rely on publicity and public relations efforts like TV talk shows to promote their product; charitable groups have used badges, paper flowers, and other specialty advertising items to identify donors or contributions, and to promote their particular cause. Promotion is likely to remain a key ingredient of most marketing strategies devised within nonprofit settings.

**Evaluation and Control of Nonprofit Marketing**

A comprehensive discussion of the evaluation and control of marketing activities is presented in Chapter 25. Several variables can be used to measure the effectiveness of nonprofit marketing efforts. Some of these are total market response, market share, cost per dollar of market response, efficiency measures, and market attitudes.[21]

*Total market response* is a measurement of numbers; examples of this measurement could be enrolment applications at a university or season ticket sales to the ballet. The actual market response can then be compared to forecasted response. The data can also be broken down into categories, like "first year," "transfer," and "first-time season ticket purchasers."

*Market share* is a comparative measure that allows a nonprofit agency to assess its performance against the competition. Symphony, ballet, and live theatre season ticket sales could be measured on a market-share basis.

*Cost per dollar of market response* is an evaluation measure often used in charitable fund-raising. Solicitation costs are cited as a percentage of each dollar collected in such efforts. *Efficiency measures* are also common in the evaluation and control of nonprofit marketing activities. Number of donor contacts per day, percentage of lost contributions, acceptance rates, and other measures are common in nonprofit settings.

*Market attitudes* can be evaluated by conducting consumer surveys among those whom the agency serves. A hospital, for example, might attempt to assess patients' attitudes toward its services, food, and personnel by sending them a questionnaire after their release. Colleges and universities often gauge student attitudes toward services like the dining halls, health centre, intramural facilities, parking, and placement office.

Regardless of how the evaluation is stated and conducted, it is essential that nonprofit agencies be subject to a degree of control similar to that found in profit-oriented institutions. An evaluation and control system forms an integral part of an effective marketing program.

---

[21] These variables are outlined in Philip Kootler, *Marketing for Nonprofit Organizations*, © 1975, pp. 250–251. Adapted by permission of Prentice-Hall, Inc., Englewood Cliffs, New Jersey.

**The Future of Nonprofit Marketing**

While marketing has gained increasing acceptance in the nonprofit sector of society, it is still viewed with suspicion by many of the people involved. The heavy emphasis on promotion is one reason. But in a broader sense, marketing efforts in nonprofit organizations often lack the sophistication and integration found in the marketing of profit-oriented industries. Marketing is too often seen as the "quick-fix" solution to a more basic problem. To combat this, marketers must market their own discipline in a realistic and socially responsible manner. The client must be made to understand the opportunities, benefits, behaviour modifications, and commitment involved in the adoption of the marketing concept in a nonprofit setting.

**Summary**

Nonprofit organizations are those enterprises whose primary objective is something other than returning profits to their owners. Nonprofit organizations are often characterized by the intangible nature of many of their services; multiple publics; minimal control by customers; professional rather than organizational orientation of their employees; involvement of resource contributors; lack of an overall bottom line; and the lack of a clear organizational structure. The three types of nonprofit marketing are person, idea, and organization marketing.

The introduction of marketing into nonprofit settings has been associated with the broadening concept, which extends the marketing concept to nontraditional exchange processes.

Marketing is now viewed as integral to many nonprofit settings, although it is too often defined merely in terms of promotional strategy.

Nonprofit agencies require a comprehensive marketing mix strategy based on accurate marketing research. An effective evaluation and control system must be set up to monitor the marketing strategy. This system might be based on one or more of the following variables: total market response; market share; cost per dollar of market response; efficiency measures; and market attitudes.

**Key Terms**

| | |
|---|---|
| nonprofit organization | person marketing |
| bottom line | idea marketing |
| broadening concept | organization marketing |

**Review Questions**

1. What are the primary characteristics of nonprofit organizations that distinguish them from profit-seeking organizations?
2. Describe the evolution of the broadening concept.

3.  What is person marketing? Contrast it with marketing of a consumer good such as magazines.
4.  Why is idea marketing more difficult than organization marketing?
5.  Identify the types of organization marketing and give examples of each.
6.  Why is marketing sometimes defined inaccurately in a nonprofit organization?
7.  Contrast the product strategy of nonprofit marketing with that of marketing for profit.
8.  Identify the pricing goals that are commonly found in nonprofit enterprises.
9.  Compare distribution and promotional strategies of nonprofit organizations with profit-seeking enterprises.
10. Explain the variables used in evaluating and controlling a nonprofit marketing program.

---

**Discussion Questions and Exercises**

1.  What type of nonprofit organization does each of the following represent:
    a.  United Auto Workers
    b.  Mulroney-for-leader committee
    c.  St. John's Public Library
    d.  Stanley Park Zoo (Vancouver)
    e.  Save the Whales Foundation
    f.  Girl Guides
    g.  Easter Seals
2.  Figure 23-4 reveals that many nonprofit organization executives have negative attitudes toward marketing. What needs to be done if this is to change?
3.  Cite several examples of circumstances when penetrating pricing might be practised by public utilities.
4.  How would you assess the marketing performance of the following:
    a.  your college or university
    b.  War Amps
    c.  Canadian Postal Workers Union
    d.  Planned Parenthood
    e.  re-election committee of a local M.P.
5.  Outline the marketing program of your college or university. Make any reasonable assumptions necessary. Where are the major strengths and weaknesses of the current program? What recommendations would you make for improving it?

## CHAPTER 24

# Marketing and Society

1. *To describe the contemporary social and ethical environment of marketing.*

2. *To outline the need for measuring social performance.*

3. *To identify the three major current issues in marketing.*

4. *To suggest how the contemporary issues in marketing might be resolved.*

"Friends," an advertisement sponsored by the Alberta Human Rights Commission, was developed to tackle the sensitive issue of bigotry and racism. It focuses on two young boys. One of them refuses to play with the other because "My mom says I have to play with my own kind." The advertisement points out that racism is not natural but learned behaviour, and that the attitudes of parents are picked up by their children.

With the ethnic origin of the boys obscured by shadowing their faces, the commercial has the effect of forcing viewers to determine each boy's race. Said David Hayward, Hayhurst creative director, "It's amazing how people relate that commercial to their own environment. One man told us he was sure one boy was Canadian Indian, although he wasn't sure why he felt that way. It turned out that he was raised next to an Indian reservation. Another person, who was raised in the United States, was equally certain one boy was Hispanic, and the other Black."

The campaign also includes two other versions of the advertisement. One is headed: "Racism means you're judged before you can stand up for yourself." It shows three babies of different races as the central graphic. The other ad shows a young boy in a dejected pose, under a heading, "My dad says I can't play with your kind." The ad program attracted national attention, including coverage on CBC's *The National*. The print ads were translated into 10 languages.[1]

Marketing functions can be used directly in helping to alleviate various social problems. On the other hand, since marketing is a

---

[1] Adapted from Randy Scotland, "Alberta Tackles Racism With Ads," *Marketing* (November 23, 1983), p. 1.

business activity which tries to affect behaviour, there are some concerns as to whether the social effects of certain practices themselves are desirable.

## The Conceptual Framework

It should be clear by now that the marketing decision-maker develops a marketing mix based on an analysis of the target *and* the environmental factors that affect the consumer and the marketing mix. Chapter 2 outlined the key environmental considerations from that perspective.

There is a further environmental dimension that goes beyond the previous considerations. This is the role that marketing plays in society itself, and the consequent effects and responsibilities of marketing activities. Since marketing is such a visible force in society, the issue is important to all.

General Motors, Royal Bank, and Air Canada have all set up committees from their boards of directors to decide in which social programs the companies should engage.[2] W. Michael Blumenthal, former chairman and president of Bendix Corporation, and others have advocated a code of professional ethics for business executives.[3]

What do these firms and executives have in common? All are attempting to act responsibly in regard to contemporary business and social issues. And marketing has a key role to play in the resolution of these matters.

This text has consistently stressed that marketing is a most dynamic business activity. Marketing's relationship to society in general and to various issues of concern is subject to constant scrutiny by the public. It may, in fact, be reasonably argued that marketing typically mirrors changes in the entire business environment. Since marketing is the final interface between the business enterprise and the society in which it operates, it is understandable that marketers often carry much of the responsibility for dealing with the various social issues affecting their firms.

The purpose of this chapter is to provide a framework within which you can constructively evaluate the marketing system. As you will see, the question "Does the marketing system serve Canadians well?" cannot easily be answered. You will, however, be helped to evaluate the marketing system for yourself.

## The Contemporary Environment of Marketing

Marketing operates in an environment external to the firm. It reacts to its environment and is, in turn, acted upon. These environmental relationships include relationships with customers, employees,

[2] George A. Steiner, "Institutionalizing Social Decisions," *Business Horizons* (December 1975), pp. 12–18.
[3] Terry P. Brown, "Profit-Minded Chief at Bendix Tries to Set a Businessmen's Code," *The Wall Street Journal* (November 18, 1975), pp. 1, 14.

the government, vendors, and society as a whole. While they are often a product of the exchange process, these relationships are coincidental to the primary sales and distribution functions of marketing.

External relationships form the basis of the social issues confronting contemporary marketing. Marketing's relationship to its external environment has a significant effect on the relative degree of success achieved by the firm. Marketing must continually find new ways to deal with the social issues facing our competitive system.

Historically, marketing has neglected the social issues raised by some environmental relationships. Various regulations and licence requirements have been enacted to limit door-to-door selling, which had become excessive in some areas. Numerous firms have been convicted for false or misleading advertising, and Consumer and Corporate Affairs Canada publishes quarterly announcements naming firms that have been convicted for offences under various consumer protection acts. The government has had to ban some children's toys because of their dangerous and harmful qualities.

The competitive marketing system, as we know it, is a product of our drive for material possessions. But it is important to note that materialism developed from society itself. Most facets of the Canadian culture, with their acceptance of the work ethic, have viewed the acquisition of wealth favourably. The motto of this philosophy seems to be "more equals better." A *better* life has been defined in terms of *more* physical possessions, although that may be changing.

Another example of the interaction between social trends and values is the toy, "GI Joe," which was reintroduced to the toy market in 1982 after being withdrawn because of low sales. Warrior toys like GI Joe and videogames that carry violent overtones trouble many child specialists who worry that they encourage aggressive and violent behaviour. Some retailers are surprised at the high demand for such toys in Canada, where militarism is not generally applauded.[4] Some condemn marketers for making profits from sales of toys that help make violence part of the consciousness of children. Others argue that business merely responds to the mood of the marketplace and to the values already in the social system, and therefore has no responsibility to worry about the effects of its offerings.

**Evaluating the Quality of Life**   One theme runs through the arguments of marketing's critics: materialism (as exemplified by the competitive marketing system) is concerned only with the *quantities* of life and ignores the *quality* aspect.

[4] Patricia Hluchy, "War and a Little Peace for Christmas," *Maclean's* (Nov. 28, 1983), p. 54.

# "Too Much Reality"

The fact is, few of us actually need all that we have or want. But once we've had our fill of simple food and shelter, can it honestly be said that everything else, including especially music, art, poetry, breathtaking cathedrals built at great expense to glorify God and humble man before Him, is unnecessary and perhaps even self-indulgent? Few of us in the more "advanced" nations will be satisfied to live ... in sackcloth and sandals. Nor, it seems, is anybody else who has a better choice. When T. S. Eliot said "Humankind cannot stand too much reality," he meant to explain why in so many ways we try to escape nature's rude animality with manufactured shelter, man-made possessions, entertainments, arts and fantasies. It's what we call "civilization."

Source: Theodore Levitt, "Marketing and Its Discontents," *Across the Board* (February 1984), p. 44.

Traditionally, a firm was considered socially responsible in the community if it provided employment to its residents, thereby contributing to its economic base. Employment, wages, bank deposits, and profits, the traditional measures of social contribution, are quantity indicators. But what of air, water, and cultural pollution? The boredom and isolation of mass assembly lines? The depletion of natural resources? The charges of neglect in these areas go largely unanswered simply because we have not developed reliable indices by which to measure a firm's contribution to the quality of life.

## An Indictment of the Competitive Marketing System

An indictment of the competitive marketing system would contain at least the following:

1. Marketing costs are too high.[5]
2. The marketing system is inefficient.
3. Marketers (the business system) are guilty of collusion and price-fixing.
4. Product quality and service are poor.
5. Consumers receive incomplete and/or false and misleading information.
6. The marketing system has produced health and safety hazards.
7. Unwanted and unnecessary products are promoted to those who least need them.

---

[5] This issue has been debated in such works as Paul M. Mazur, "Does Distribution Cost Enough?," *Fortune* (November 1947), pp. 138–139, 192, 194, 197–198, 200; R. S. Vaile, E. T. Grether, and Reavis Cox, *Marketing in the American Economy* (New York: Ronald Press Company, 1952); Stanley C. Hollander, "Measuring the Cost and Value of Marketing," *MSU Business Topics* (Summer 1961), pp. 17–27; and Reavis Cox, *Distribution in a High-Level Economy* (Englewood Cliffs, N.J.: Prentice-Hall, 1965).

One widely cited study of marketing costs concluded that high distribution costs should be blamed on consumers as well as marketers. See Paul W. Steward and J. Frederick Dewhurst with Louise Field, *Does Distribution Cost Too Much?* (New York: The Twentieth Century Fund, 1939), p. 348.

Almost anyone could cite specific examples where these charges have been proven. But each of us has a somewhat different set of values, so it should be recognized that we all evaluate the performance of the marketing system we experience *within our own frames of reference.*

Bearing this in mind, and taking the system as a whole, we can then evaluate the success or failure of the competitive marketing system in serving the needs of Canadians. Most of us will likely arrive at the uncomfortable and not terribly satisfying conclusion that the system usually works quite adequately, although there are some aspects of it that we would like to see changed.

How then can we change and regulate the system so that it is more in line with what we want for our society? What is the consumer interest? How much change do we really want?

## Current Issues in Marketing

Marketing faces numerous and diverse social issues. The current issues in marketing can be divided into three major subjects: consumerism, marketing ethics, and social responsibility. While the overlap and classification problems are obvious, the framework provides a foundation for systematically studying the issues.

## Consumerism

Despite factors that tend to inhibit the development of strong consumer groups, business practices and changing social values have led to the consumerism movement. Today everyone — marketers, industry, government, the public — is acutely aware of the impact of consumerism on the nation's economy and general well-being. **Consumerism** has been defined as *a social force within the environment designed to aid and protect the consumer by exerting legal, moral, and economic pressure on business.*[6] Professors George Day and David Aaker argue that consumerism includes "the widening range of activities of government, business, and independent or-

---

6 David W. Cravens and Gerald G. Hills, "Consumerism: A Perspective for Business," *Business Horizons* (August 1970), p. 21. See also Rom J. Markin, "Consumerism: Militant Consumer Behavior: A Social and Behavioral Analysis," *Business and Society* (Fall 1971), pp. 5–17; Bernard A. Morin, "Some Negativisms About Consumerism," *Journal of Small Business Management* (July 1972), pp. 6–10; Borris W. Becker, "Consumerism, a Challenge or a Threat?" *Journal of Retailing* (Summer 1972), pp. 16–28; Leonard L. Berry, "Consumerism, Marketing, and the Small Businessman," *Journal of Small Business Management* (July 1972), pp. 14–19; Hiram C. Barksdale and William R. Darden, "Consumer Attitudes Toward Marketing and Consumerism," *Journal of Marketing* (October 1972), pp. 28–35; Philip Kotler, "What Consumerism Means for Marketers," *Harvard Business Review* (May-June 1972), pp. 48–57; John O. King, "Rising Consumerism Restoring Competitive Nature to Markets," *Marketing News* (December 1, 1974), p. 5; Gary M. Grikscheit and Kent L. Granzin, "Who Are the Consumerists?" *Journal of Business Research* (January 1975), pp. 1–12; D. Wayne Norvell, Thomas L.

ganizations that are designed to protect individuals from practices that infringe upon their rights as consumers."[7] It is the demand of society that organizations apply the marketing concept in its fullest sense.

**The Consumer Interest**

The consumer interest lies in the development of a system that represents the interests of individuals in their role as consumers as well as in their role as suppliers of labour and owners of capital.[8] The emergence of groups such as the Consumers' Association of Canada and the Automobile Protection Association is the result of frustration by consumers who felt that business and other interest groups were not serving their interests as well as they might.

Businesses do not overtly try to displease consumers. In fact, since most business activities take place in the relatively free market system, those firms that do not satisfy consumers often go out of business eventually or are less profitable than they could be. Yet one need only refer to the many regulatory laws that have been introduced to recognize that there are areas where society has felt that the system needed improvement. Consumer groups have succeeded in strengthening consumer rights.[9]

**The Consumer's Rights**

Not all consumer demands are met. A competitive marketing system is based upon the behaviour of competing firms. Our economic system requires that reasonable profit objectives be achieved. Busi-

Brown, and John C. Cox, "Consumerism and the Marketing Concept: Some Empirical Evidence," *Arkansas Business and Economic Review* (Spring 1975), pp. 6–13; Norman Kangum, Keith K. Cox, James Higginbotham, and John Burton, "Consumerism and Marketing Management," *Journal of Marketing* (April 1975), pp. 3–10; Donald W. Hendon, "Toward a Theory of Consumerism," *Business Horizons* (August 1975), pp. 16–24; and William P. Anthony and Joel B. Haynes, "Consumerism: A Three-Generation Paradigm," *University of Michigan Business Review* (November 1975), pp. 21–26. See also two interesting papers in *Proceedings: Southern Marketing Association*, edited by Henry W. Nash and Donald P. Robin (January 1976): James M. Clapper, John F. Willenborg, and Robert E. Pitts, "Perceptions of Consumer Protection Issues and Their Relationship to Community Satisfaction," pp. 228–230; and Bruce L. Stern, O. C. Ferrell, and Gregory M. Gazda, "Social Class Differences in Consumers' Attitudes Toward Consumerism Issues," pp. 231–233.
[7] George S. Day and David A. Aaker, "A Guide to Consumerism," *Journal of Marketing* (July 1970), p. 12.
[8] J. D. Forbes and S. M. Oberg, "The Consumer Interest" (Faculty of Commerce and Business Administration, University of British Columbia, mimeo, 1981).
[9] See Helen Jones Dawson, "The Consumers' Association of Canada," *Canadian Public Administration* (March 1963), pp. 92–118; Helen J. Morningstar, "The Consumers' Association of Canada—An Effective Organization," *The Canadian Business Review*, Vol. 4, No. 4 (1977); and Ellen Roseman and Phil Edmonston, *Canadian Consumers' Survival Book* (Don Mills, Ont.: General Publishing Company, 1977).

ness cannot meet all consumer demands if it is to generate the profits necessary to remain viable[10] This selection process is one of the most difficult questions facing society and business today.

What should the consumer have the right to expect from the competitive marketing system?

The most frequently quoted statement of consumer rights was made by U.S. President John F. Kennedy on March 15, 1962. While it was not a definitive statement, it has proven to be a good rule of thumb to explain basic **consumer rights:**

1. The right to choose freely
2. The right to be informed
3. The right to be heard
4. The right to be safe

These rights have formed the conceptual framework of much of the consumer legislation passed since then. However, the question of how best to guarantee these rights remains unanswered.

**The Right to Choose Freely**    The first consumer right is the right to *free choice in the marketplace and to a range of products and services that best suit the individual consumer.* To exercise this right and to be a responsible consumer, everyone should know how to make decisions by being able to evaluate products rationally and make choices from which they derive maximum satisfaction. Consumer policies of industry and governments should provide education and information to enable individuals to be responsible consumers as well as to maintain markets that allow for an adequate range of goods and services from which choices can be made. In those cases where freedom of choice is restricted, for example where monopolies are given to privately or publicly owned utilities, governments should establish regulatory bodies to ensure that these monopolies do not misuse their power. There is much criticism of such controls, and of their major impact on consumers.

**The Right to Be Informed**    The second consumer right is *to be provided with adequate product/service information to be able to make an informed choice.* Controversy often surrounds government imposition of rules specifying information that sellers must provide to consumers.

Some consumer advocates work on the principle that more information is better. Others are sceptical of this point of view. While more may be better, consumers have difficulty processing masses of information unless they understand the relationships between the

---

10 An excellent discussion appears in Y. Hugh Furuhashi and E. Jerome McCarthy, *Social Issues of Marketing in the American Economy* (Columbus, Ohio: GRID, 1971), pp. 102–117.

various product/service attributes and are able to analyse information in a rational way.

There is much we do not know about how to assist consumers in exercising their right to be informed. A great deal of research by marketers about information, its form, the importance of format, and its availability during the buying process is now under way. Packaging and labelling regulations and "false and misleading advertising" provisions of federal, provincial, and local laws have contributed to increased information and decreased deception in recent years. With the research in progress, more effective information for consumers should be available in the future.

**The Right to Be Heard**

The third consumer right is that of *being able to express legitimate displeasure over one's inability to obtain goods and services, as well as the terms of trade under which they are purchased.* While the marketplace *may* produce the quality of product in the place and the time desired by the consumer, there is no guarantee that this will happen. In addition, products may not perform as the consumer or the manufacturer may have intended. In the vast majority of cases where the consumer is dissatisfied, one need only discuss the matter with the provider of the goods or service to obtain satisfaction. The concern and frustration evolve in those infrequent but often important situations where an effective system for redress is not available even though the complaint is valid.

While it is the consumer's responsibility to do what is possible on an individual level to make sure that his or her rights are exercised and to "sound off," the system for redress may not be available or only available at a cost out of proportion to the damage involved.[11] A faulty cabinet on a television set may involve only $100 damage, but to collect that amount may involve the costs of a lawyer and personal time of $300. A few firms have produced faulty products knowing that consumers would not press the matter. In the province of Quebec, *consumers who have been similarly damaged in such cases may join together and sue* in a **class action**. This strategy has not been used as much as might be expected. One reason is that if the group loses its case, it is liable to pay a penalty of one percent of the amount claimed in the suit. There is no pending legislation similar to this in other provinces.

Systems of handling complaints in large consumer-products organizations, ombudsmen's offices, departments of consumer and corporate affairs at the federal, provincial, and municipal levels of government, and several consumer assistance groups such as the Consumers' Association of Canada and the Automobile Protection

---

[11] See also Alan A. Shapiro, *An Economic Analysis of Consumer Redress Mechanisms* (Ottawa: Consumer and Corporate Affairs Canada, 1980).

Association have been set up to assist and expand the consumer's right to be heard. Even so, the systems do not work as well as desired by many consumers.

**The Right to Be Safe**   The fourth basic consumer right is the right to have *a high degree of assurance that a product will neither be injurious to health nor present undue risks of injury through normal use.* This means that products for general consumption should be designed so that the average consumer can use them safely.

Enlightened design by manufacturers, coupled with safety and health regulations and inspection by governments, has made consumers in the 1980s significantly better protected in matters of health

**Figure 24-1   Consumer Policy and Consumer Rights and Responsibilities**

| | CHOOSE FREELY / CHOOSE WISELY | BE INFORMED / KEEP INFORMED | BE HEARD / SOUND OFF | BE SAFE / SAFETY FIRST |
|---|---|---|---|---|
| **A. Education** | decision-making, budgeting; nature of market economy, rights and responsibilities | generic products and materials data, information sources | how to assert consumer rights | importance of health and safety, user manual, and training |
| **B. Information** | buying criteria buying advice | models and brands data, independent consumer info programs | market research, two-way market dialogue | safety certification, care and maintenance data |
| **C. Protection** | maintain open markets, antitrust; stop high-pressure and deceptive tactics | truly informative advertising, product claims substantiation | complaints-handling machinery | minimize health and accident risks |

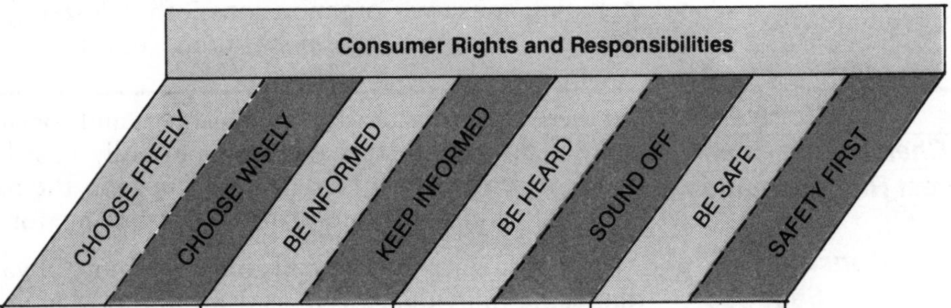

Source: Hans B. Thorelli, "Improving Policies Affecting Marketers, Consumer Groups, Universities and Governments," in Mel S. Moyer, *Marketers and Their Publics: A Dialogue* (Toronto: Faculty of Administrative Studies, York University, 1978), p. 22.

and safety than they were even 15 or 20 years ago. However, some people believe that there are so many regulations that the costs to minimize the risks of health and safety significantly exceed any benefits to the consumer that these regulations provide. This latter point is understandably a contentious issue and difficult to prove on either side of the argument.

A further specification of the four consumer rights has been made by Professor Hans Thorelli (Figure 24-1). Thorelli suggests that companies, consumer groups, and governments can develop useful consumer policies of education, information, and protection related to each consumer right. Such a scheme may focus the efforts of those concerned. Consumers also have some responsibility to provide feedback to companies, government, and others; to encourage useful change. Consumer apathy does little to improve the system. A third dimension of the matrix would show the makers of consumer policy, including consumer organizations, other citizen groups, business, government, educational institutions, and the mass media.

## Consumer Characteristics and Interest Representation

But there are characteristics of consumers and consumer groups that make it difficult to represent their broadly based interests in the political process.[12] It is easier to look after the narrower *special* interests (of business and professional groups, for example).

### Consumer Role Secondary

An individual's role as a consumer is almost always secondary to that same individual's role as a producer. It is in the individual's interest to devote more time to furthering the producer role than the consuming role. Members of a labour union devote much more time and receive much more immediate returns from activities affecting them as workers than from attempting to have producers improve the labelling on food products. In the role of a lawyer, a consumer would receive greater personal benefits from participating in the local law society than from participating in a study to determine the quality of fabrics and apparel construction.

### Diffuse Nature of Consumerism

The consumer purchases a wide range of products, few of which constitute a large proportion of his or her total budget. Goods and services are purchased from firms and individuals who have much greater product knowledge than the consumer. This usually puts the consumer at a disadvantage. The automobile salesperson who sells several cars a week is obviously more expert than the individual who purchases a car once every five years.

### Expertise and Information Costs

The relative benefits to an individual consumer of becoming expert on all he or she consumes are low, given the diffuse nature of the

12 The extensive contribution of Professor J. D. Forbes to the balance of the chapter is gratefully acknowledged.

consumer interest. Just as our lawyer finds it relatively unproductive to become expert in fabrics and apparel construction, so each of us can ill afford the time required to become expert in all fields. Individually we have neither the resources nor the time to investigate all products.

These three consumer characteristics — the consumer role being secondary, diffusion resulting from buying many products, and problems of expertise and information costs — have led to demands for more effective consumer representation in public policy-making to improve the consumer's position vis-à-vis producers.

Consumers periodically feel that their interests and rights are under attack and being eroded in the political process by special interest groups. Governments sometimes are less than vigorous in husbanding the consumer interest. Sometimes there is no effective advocate of the consumer interest to counteract the lobbying activities of special interest groups, and public policy can insidiously and incrementally drift away from the optimum for the consumer.[13] This is not a nefarious plot but results from characteristics of the groups being represented in the political process.[14]

**Special Interests**

Special interest groups such as unions, professional associations, and teachers' federations all compete with general interests such as those of consumers. Governments are organized along special interest lines: the various ministries such as Health, Industry, Trade and Commerce, Transportation, and Agriculture are concerned with specific issues and usually represent the interests of specific segments of the population. Special interest groups have fewer, more specific goals and generally can obtain resources more easily than consumer groups.[15]

**"Public Goods" and Consumer Interest**

There is little personal incentive for individuals to join ad hoc consumer groups since any gains by those groups are distributed to all consumers rather than just to members of the particular consumer

13 Anthony Downs, *An Economic Theory of Democracy* (New York: Harper and Row, 1957). See Robert Presthus, *Elite Accommodation in Canadian Politics* (Toronto: Macmillan, 1973); J. D. Forbes and S. M. Oberg, "The Consumer Interest" (Faculty of Commerce and Business Administration, University of British Columbia, mimeo, 1981); and Ben W. Lewis, "The 'Consumer' and 'Public' Interests under Public Regulation," *Journal of Political Economy* (February 1938), pp. 137–146, as reprinted in Donald Grunewald and Henry L. Bass, eds., *Public Policy and the Modern Corporation* (New York: Appleton-Century-Crofts, 1966).

14 See Anthony Downs, *An Economic Theory of Democracy* (New York: Harper and Row, 1957); Mancur Olson, *The Logic of Collective Action* (Cambridge, Mass.: Harvard University Press, 1965), 1971 printing.

15 Mancur Olson, *The Logic of Collective Action* (Cambridge, Mass.: Harvard University Press, 1965), 1971 printing.

group. This characteristic is not unique to consumer groups bu illustrates the "public goods" nature of large, mass-oriented, laten interest groups including groups such as women, the poor, the elderly and the young, to name some of the more prominent ones.[16]

Contrast the consumer group to the manufacturers of clothing. for example, who benefit directly from import restrictions that protect them from foreign competition. They receive direct benefits from contributing and participating in industry associations representing their interests to government.

| **Consumerism in Canada** | Only since 1967 has there been in Canada a federal Department of Consumer and Corporate Affairs. Similar provincial ministries are even more recent. These consumer ministries are the result of, among other things, organized pressure from ad hoc consumer groups who recognized that special interest groups were being overrepresented in the political system as compared to consumers. |

The Consumers' Association of Canada (CAC) is the national organization representing consumers of Canada.[17] Its present membership is about 100 000. Local groups exist throughout the country. Most of the national funding comes from subscriptions to *Canadian Consumer*. A significant amount comes from federal funds (between 27 and 44 percent in recent years), which are used to support the national organization. Each of the provinces usually contributes a majority of the funding for local CAC groups.[18]

The activities of the CAC are mainly carried out by volunteers, although there are several paid professionals and a small clerical and research staff working at the national level, and usually a small staff at provincial offices. Unpaid association officers and members dispense information to consumers, help consumers help themselves in redressing problems encountered in the marketplace, interact with concerned business and government representatives in designing and changing legislation affecting consumers, and represent the consumer interest in the political process.

A significant amount of volunteer aid comes in the form of technical advice from lawyers, economists, businesspeople, and other interested parties who assist in the preparation of briefs and position papers to present to government and business groups.

Recent activities by the CAC have led the way toward telephone deregulation, which is in the process of being introduced by the

---

16 *Ibid.*

17 Dawson and Morningstar; see footnote 7.

18 J. D. Forbes and S. M. Oberg, "The Consumer Interest" (Faculty of Commerce and Business Administration, University of British Columbia, mimeo, 1981), Chapter 7.

CRTC. In addition to the CAC, there are some smaller and more specialized interest groups such as the Automobile Protection Association, which has been highly successful in pointing our deficiencies in automobiles and automotive accessories.

## Marketing Ethics

Environmental considerations have led to increased attention to the subject of marketing ethics. **Marketing ethics** are *the marketer's standards of conduct and moral values.* They are concerned with the decision to do what is morally right or what is morally wrong. A discussion of marketing ethics highlights the types of problems faced by individuals in their role as marketers.[19] Such problems must be considered before we suggest possible improvements in the marketing system.

---

**Figure 24-2   A Marketing Code of Ethics**

**Our Code of Ethics**

As a member of the American Marketing Association, I recognize the significance of my professional conduct and my responsibilities to society and to the other members of my profession:

1. By acknowledging my accountability to society as a whole as well as to the organization for which I work.
2. By pledging my efforts to assure that all presentations of goods, services, and concepts be made honestly and clearly.
3. By striving to improve marketing knowledge and practice in order to better serve society.
4. By supporting free consumer choice in circumstances that are legal and are consistent with generally accepted community standards.
5. By pledging to use the highest professional standards in my work and in competitive activity.
6. By acknowledging the right of the American Marketing Association, through established procedure, to withdraw my membership if I am found to be in violation of ethical standards of professional conduct.

Source: American Marketing Association, *Constitution and Bylaws*, rev. ed. (Chicago: American Marketing Association, 1977), p. 20. Reprinted by permission.

---

People develop standards of ethical behaviour based upon their own systems of values. Their "individual ethics" help them deal with the various ethical questions in their personal lives. However, when

---

19 Excellent discussions of ethics appear in Douglas J. Lincoln, Milton M. Pressley, and Taylor Little, "Ethical Beliefs and Personal Values of Top Level Executives," *Journal of Business Research* (December 1982), pp. 475–487; Gene R. Laczniak, Robert F. Busch, and William A. Strang, "Ethical Marketing: Perception of Economic Goods and Social Problems," *Journal of Macromarketing* (Spring 1981), pp. 49–57; and James Weber, "Institutionalizing Ethics into the Corporation," *MSU Business Topics* (Spring 1981), pp. 47–52.

they are inserted into a work situation, a serious conflict may materialize. Individual ethics may differ from the "organizational ethic" of the employer. An individual may personally believe that industry participation in developing a recycling program for industial waste is highly desirable, but the person's firm takes the position that such a venture would be unprofitable. Similar conflicts are not difficult to imagine.

How can these conflicts be resolved? The development of an adherence to a professional ethic may provide a third basis of authority.[20] This ethic should be based on a concept of professionalism that transcends both organizational and individual ethics. It depends on the existence of a professional peer association that can exercise collective sanctions over a marketer's professional behaviour. The American Marketing Association (the major international association of marketers to which many Canadian marketers belong), for example, has developed a code of ethics that includes a provision to expel members who violate its tenets. This code is shown in Figure 24-2.

A variety of ethical problems faces the marketer every day. While promotional matters have received the greatest attention recently, ethical questions concerning the research function, product management, channel strategy, and pricing also arise.

**Ethical Problems in Marketing Research**

Marketing research has been castigated because of its alleged invasion of personal privacy. Citizens of today's urbanized, mechanized society seek individual identity to a degree not common in the past. Personal privacy is important to Canadians, and has therefore become a public issue for some.

**Ethical Problems in Product Management**

A few years ago Chevrolet motors were installed in 128 000 new Oldsmobiles, Buicks, and Pontiacs, as a result of unexpected demand for the medium-priced models. General Motors reasoned that the Chevrolet engines were the same size and horsepower and that a switch of this nature was an acceptable marketing practice. But buyers were not informed of the switch, and consumer complaints and legal cases resulted. General Motors was ordered by the court to make restitution in what the media labelled the "Chevymobile" case.[21] This incident suggests the changing nature and growing importance of ethical decisions in product management. Accepted marketing practice in this case was no longer acceptable to consumers.

---

[20] The discussion of individual, organizational, and professional ethics is based on Henry O. Pruden, "Which Ethic for Marketers?" in *Marketing and Social Issues: An Action Reader*, eds. John R. Wish and Stephen H. Gamble (New York: Wiley, 1971), pp. 98–104.

[21] Terry P. Brown, "GM, State Aides Due to Disclose Accord for $200 Rebates in 'Chevymobile' Case," *Wall Street Journal* (December 19, 1977), p. 16.

Product quality, planned obsolescence, brand similarity, and packaging all present ethical problems to product management. The packaging question represents a significant concern on the part of consumers, management, and governments. Competitive pressures have forced marketers into packaging practices that may be considered misleading, deceptive, and/or unethical in some quarters. Larger-than-necessary packages of an inconvenient shape are used to gain shelf space and customer exposure in the supermarket. Odd-sized packages make price comparisons difficult. Bottles with concave bottoms are used to give the impression that they contain more liquid than is actually the case.

Even though such practices may seem to be justified in the name of competition, consumers and legislators will eventually react against them.

**Ethical Problems in Pricing**

Pricing is probably the most regulated aspect of a firm's marketing strategy. Accordingly, most unethical price behaviour is also illegal. When asked to identify unethical practices they wanted eliminated, fewer executives specified issues such as price collusion, price discrimination, and unfair pricing in a 1976 survey than a similar group had in a 1961 study. This suggests that tighter government regulations exist in these areas now than in the past.[22]

There are, however, some grey areas in the matter of pricing ethics. For example, should some customers pay more for merchandise if distribution costs are higher in their areas? Do marketers have an obligation to warn customers of impending price, discount, or returns policy changes? All these questions must be dealt with in developing a professional ethic for marketing.

# Some Hypothetical Situations Involving Ethical Questions

A study conducted by the Bureau of Business Research at the University of Michigan posed a series of "action" situations to a sample of 401 marketing research directors and chief marketing executives. The respondents were told that the marketing research director of a company had taken some particular action. The participants were then asked, "Do you approve or disapprove of the action taken?" A sample of these situations and the resulting responses are shown below. How would you have replied?

*One-Way Mirrors*  One product of the X Company is brassieres, and the firm has recently been having difficulty making some decisions on a new line. Information was critically needed concerning the manner in which women put on their brassieres.

---

[22] See Steven N. Brenner and Earl A. Mollander, "Is the Ethics of Business Changing?" *Harvard Business Review* (January-February 1977), pp. 61–62; and Jeffrey Sonnenfeld and Paul R. Lawrence, "Why do Companies Succumb to Price Fixing?" *Harvard Business Review* (July-August 1978), pp. 145–157.

So the marketing research director designed a study in which two local stores co-operated in putting one-way mirrors in their dressing rooms. Observers behind these mirrors successfully gathered the necessary information.

|                    | Approve | Disapprove |
|--------------------|---------|------------|
| Research directors | 20%     | 78%        |
| Line marketers     | 18      | 82         |

*Advertising and Product Misuse*   Some recent research showed that many customers of X Company are misusing Product B. There's no danger; they are simply wasting their money by using too much of it at a time. But yesterday, the marketing research director saw proofs on Product B's new ad campaign, and the ads not only ignored the problem of misuse but actually seemed to encourage it. The director quietly referred the advertising manager to the research results, well known to all people involved with B's advertising, and let it go at that.

|                    | Approve | Disapprove |
|--------------------|---------|------------|
| Research directors | 41%     | 58%        |
| Line marketers     | 33      | 66         |

*General Trade Data to Citizens' Group*   The marketing research department of X Company frequently makes extensive studies of its retail customers. A citizens' group working to get a shopping centre in their low-income area wanted to know if they could have access to this trade information. But since the firm had always refused to share this information with trade organizations the marketing research director declined the request.

|                    | Approve | Disapprove |
|--------------------|---------|------------|
| Research directors | 64%     | 34%        |
| Line marketers     | 74      | 25         |

Source: Based on and quotes with permission from C. Merle Crawford, "Attitudes of Marketing Executives toward Ethics in Marketing Research," *Journal of Marketing* (April 1970), pp. 46–52, published by the American Marketing Association. Reprinted from the *Journal of Marketing* published by the American Marketing Association. Another excellent discussion of marketing research ethics is found in Robert Bezilla, Joel B. Haynes, and Clifford Elliot, "Ethics in Marketing Research," *Busines Horizons* (April 1976), pp. 83–86.

### Ethical Problems in Distribution Strategy

A firm's channel strategy is required to deal with two kinds of ethical questions:

1. What is the appropriate degree of control over the channel?
2. Should a company distribute its products in marginally profitable outlets that have no alternative source of supply?

The question of control typically arises in the relationship between a manufacturer and franchised dealers. Should an automobile dealership, a gas station, or a fast-food outlet be required to purchase parts, materials, and supplementary services from the parent organization? What is the proper degree of control in the channel of distribution?

Furthermore, should marketers serve unsatisfied market segments even if the profit potential is slight? What is marketing's ethical responsibility to provide retail services in low-income areas, users of limited amounts of the firm's product, or the declining rural market?

These problems are difficult to resolve because they often involve individuals rather than broad segments of the general public. An important first step would be to ensure that policies with respect to channels of distribution are enforced on a consistent basis.

Ethical distribution practices usually return a dividend but often the returns are not readily measurable and are seen only in the long run.

***Ethical Problems in Promotional Strategy***

Promotion is the component of the marketing mix where the majority of ethical questions arise. Personal selling has always been the target of criticism on ethical grounds.[23] Early traders, pack peddlers, greeters, drummers, and the twentieth-century used car salesperson, for example, have all been accused of marketing malpractices ranging from excessive puffing (exaggerating product merits) to outright deceit. Gifts, bribes, and the like were identified in studies done in 1961 and 1976.[24]

**WIZARD OF ID**

Source: Field Enterprises, Inc.

Advertising, however, is even more maligned than the salesperson. It is impersonal and, hence, easier to criticize. In fact, a study by the American Association of Advertising Agencies showed that it tied second (along with clothing and fashion) in a list of "Things in life that we enjoy complaining about but we may not really be serious about our complaints."[25]

While these studies may suggest that much of the criticism of advertising is overstated, there is ample evidence and legitimate concern regarding advertising.[26] In the year 1985–86, 10 668 complaints

23 For an interesting account of unethical sales practices, see "Flimflam, the 10 Most Deceptive Sales Practices of 1968 — So Far," *Sales Management* (September 15, 1968), pp. 33–36.
24 Steven N. Brenner and Earl A. Mollander, "Is the Ethics of Business Changing?" *Harvard Business Review* (January-February 1977), p. 62. See also Alan J. Dubinsky, Eric N. Berkowitz, and William Rudelius, "Ethical Problems of Field Sales Personnel," *MSU Business Topics*, (Summer 1980), pp. 11–16.
25 *Rebuttal To Some Unfounded Assertions About Advertising* (New York: American Advertising Foundation, 1967), p. 13.
26 Advertising ethics are examined in John A. Howard and Spencer F. Tinkham, "A Framework for Understanding Social Criticism of Advertising," *Journal of Marketing* (October 1971), pp. 2–7; Theodore Levitt, "The Morality (?) of Advertising," *Harvard Business Review* (July-August 1970), pp. 84–92; E. John Kottman, "Truth and Image of Advertising," *Journal of Marketing* (October 1969), pp. 64–66; Norman H. Strouse, "Advertising: The Most Public Kind of Responsibility," in *A New Measure of Responsibility for Marketing* (Chicago: Proceedings of the American Marketing Association, 1968), pp. 9–13; and Thomas S. Petit and Alan Zakon, "Advertising and Social Welfare," *Journal of Marketing* (October 1962), pp. 15–17.

were received. Of 2151 investigations completed by the Marketing Practices Branch, 109 resulted in convictions.[27] Charges of over-selling, uses of fear-based advertising messages (of social rejection, of growing old), sexism, and the like are common.

The portrayal of women in advertising has been of particular concern to marketers. Too often, it is argued, women have been portrayed as frivolous individuals or assigned stereotyped house-wife roles in radio and television commercials and in other media. Advertisers are now making a concerted effort to show women in varied situations, especially in nontraditional work roles such as bus drivers, bank officers, and heavy-equipment handlers.

Another ethical concern surrounds advertising to children. Some critics fear that television advertising exerts an undue influence on children.[28] They believe that children are easily influenced by toy, cereal, and snack-food commercials. Correspondingly, there is the assumption that children then exert "substantial" pressure on their parents to acquire these items. In recognition of this concern, the Canadian Association of Broadcasters has formulated a comprehensive Broadcast Code for Advertising to Children. (No similar code exists in the United States.)[29] The code, which applies to advertising directed at children 12 or under, states:

> The purpose of the Code is to serve as a guide to advertisers and agencies in preparing messages which adequately recognize the special characteristics of the children's audience. Children, especially the very young, live in a world that is part imaginary, part real, and sometimes do not distinguish clearly between the two. Advertisements should respect and not abuse the power of the child's imagination.[30]

---

[27] *Annual Report, Director of Investigations and Research, Competition Act* (Ottawa: Consumer and Corporate Affairs Canada, 1986), pp. 87–88.
[28] Recent discussions of advertising aimed at children are found in Bruce L. Stern and Alan J. Resnik, "Children's Understanding of a Televised Commercial Disclaimer," in *Research Frontiers in Marketing*, ed. Subhash C. Jain (Chicago: American Marketing Association, 1978), pp. 332–336; and John R. Rossiter, "Does TV Advertising Affect Children?" *Journal of Advertising Research* (February 1979), pp. 53–57.
[29] The issue of children's television advertising is traced in Scott Ward, "Kids' TV — Marketers on Hot Seat," *Harvard Business Review* (July-August 1972), pp. 16–18, 20, 22–23, 26, 28, 146, 150–151. Ward suggests that marketers should pretest children's commercials with samples of mothers. Additional suggestions are contained in James W. Cagley, "Relative Preferences of Print Appeals Among Children," a paper presented to the Southern Marketing Association, Washington, D.C., November 10, 1972.
[30] *Broadcast Code for Advertising to Children* (Ottawa: The Canadian Association of Broadcasters, 1982), pp. 1–5.

Some specific clauses of the Code are:

1. No commercial may employ any device or technique that attempts to transmit messages below the threshold of normal awareness.
2. To clearly establish relative size, something from the child's actual world, e.g., a child, coins, marbles — must appear with the product itself.
3. Drugs, proprietary medicines, and vitamins . . . must not be advertised to children.
4. Commercials must not directly urge children to purchase, or urge them to ask their parents to make inquiries or purchases.
5. Any single product, premium or service must not be promoted more than once during any half-hour period, except in the event of full program sponsorship.
6. Puppets, persons, and characters (including cartoon characters) well known to children or featured on children's programs must not be used to endorse or personally promote products, premiums, or services. This promotion does not apply to characters created by an advertiser for promotional purposes, to professional actors or announcers who are not featured on children's programs, or to factual statements about nutritional or educational benefits.
7. Price and purchase terms, when used, must be clear and complete. When parts or accessories, that a child might reasonably suppose to be part of the normal purchase, are available only at extra cost, this must be made clear, both orally and visually. The cost must not be minimized as by the use of "only," "just," "bargain price," etc.
8. Toy advertisements shall not make direct comparisons with the previous year's model, or with competitive makes even when the statements or claims are valid — because such references may undermine the child's enjoyment of present possessions or those that may be received as gifts.
9. Advertising must not imply that possession or use of a product makes the owner superior, or that without it the child will be open to ridicule or contempt.

## Social Responsibility

Another major issue affecting marketing is the question of social responsibility.[31] In a general sense, **social responsibility** is *the marketer's acceptance of the obligation to consider profit, consumer satisfaction, and the well-being of society of equal value in evalua-*

31 Social responsibility issues are examined in Ed Timmerman, "The Concept of Marketing's Corporate Social Responsibility," in *1981 Southwestern Marketing Proceedings*, (eds.) Robert H. Ross, Frederic B. Kraft, and Charles H. Davis (Wichita, Kan.: The Southwestern Marketing Association), pp. 188–191.

*ting the performance of the firm*. It is the recognition that marketers must be concerned with the more qualitative dimensions of consumer and social benefits as well as the quantitative measures of sales, revenue, and profits by which marketing performance is traditionally measured.

As Professors Engel and Blackwell point out, social responsibility is a more easily measured concept than marketing ethics:

> Actions alone determine social responsibility, and a firm can be socially responsible even when doing so under coercion. For example, the government may enact rules that *force* firms to be socially responsible in matters of the environment, deception, and so forth. Also, consumers, through their power to repeat or withhold purchasing, may *force* marketers to provide honest and relevant information, fair prices, and so forth. To be ethically responsible, on the other hand, it is not sufficient to act correctly; ethical intent is also necessary.[32]

The locus for social decision-making within the organization has always been an important question. Who should be specifically accountable for the social considerations involved in marketing decisions? The district sales manager? The marketing vice-president? The firm's president? The board of directors? Probably the most valid assessment is to say that *all marketers*, regardless of their stations in the organization, are accountable for the effects on society of their decisions.

A related aspect to this question is, how should socially responsible decisions be made? Figure 24-3 presents a decision-making flow chart. This chart illustrates the types and levels of social responsibility decision-making. It also provides a framework for dealing with these critical issues.

**Marketing's Responsibilities**

The concept of business responsibility has traditionally concerned the relationships between the manager and customers, employees, and stockholders. Management had the responsibility of providing customers with a quality product at a reasonable price, the responsibility of providing adequate wages and a decent working environment for employees, and the responsibility for providing an acceptable profit level for stockholders. Only on occasion did the concept involve relations with the government, and rarely with the general public.

Today, the responsibility concept has been extended to the entire societal framework. A decision to continue operation of a profitable

---

[32] James F. Engel and Roger D. Blackwell, *Consumer Behavior*, 4th ed. (Hinsdale, Ill.: The Dryden Press, 1982), p. 668.

## Figure 24-3 Decision-Making Flow Chart

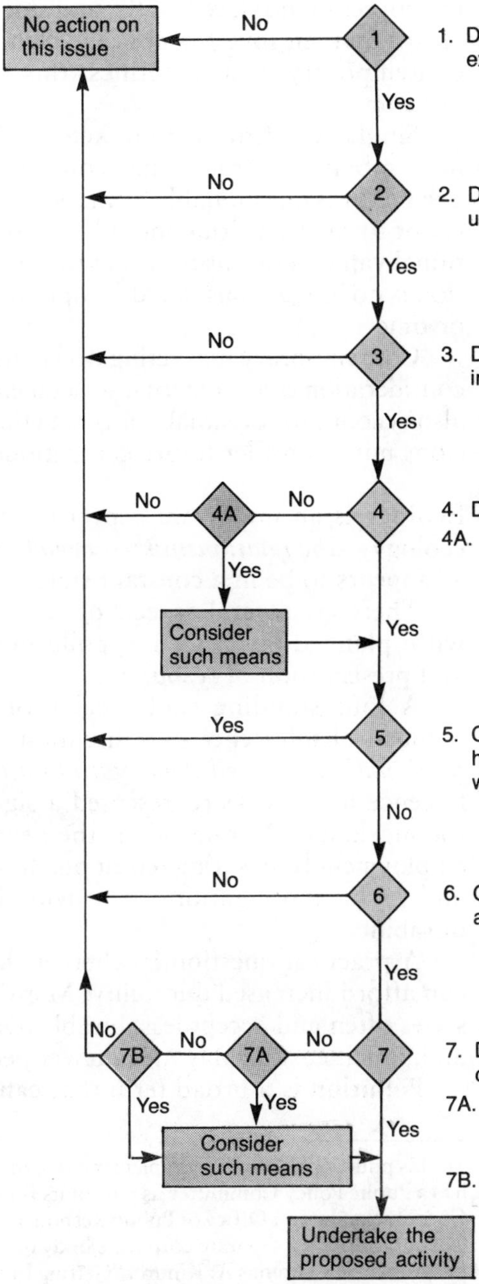


1. Does a social responsibility really exist in this case?
2. Does the firm have a right to undertake this action?
3. Does an assessment of all interests indicate that the act is desirable?
4. Do benefits outweigh costs?

4A. Can subcontracting or other means reduce the cost to a net beneficial level?

5. Could this action be better handled by other parties who are willing to undertake the task?
6. Can we bear the cost of this action?
7. Do we possess the managerial competence to do the job?

7A. Can we acquire needed competence through training or recruitment?

7B. Can we subcontract the activity to parties possessing the required competence?

Source: Ramon J. Aldag and Donald W. Jackson, Jr., "A Managerial Framework for Social Decision-Making," *MSU Business Topics* (Spring 1975), p. 34. Reprinted by permission of the publisher, Division of Research, Graduate School of Business Administration, Michigan State University.

but air-polluting plant may be responsible in the traditional sense; customers receive an uninterrupted supply of the plant's products, employees do not face layoffs, and stockholders receive a reasonable return on their investment in the plant. But from the standpoint of contemporary business ethics, this is not a socially responsible decision.

Similarly, a firm that markets foods with low nutritional value may satisfy the traditional concept of responsibility, but such behaviour is questionable from the contemporary perspective. This is not to say that firms should distribute only foods of high nutritional value; it means only that the previous framework for evaluation is no longer considered comprehensive in terms of either scope or time.

Contemporary marketing decisions must now regularly involve consideration of the external societal environment.[33] Decisions must also account for eventual, long-run effects. Socially responsible decisions must consider future generations as well as existing society.

## Marketing and Ecology

Ecology is an important aspect of marketing.[34] The concept of **ecology** — *the relationship between humanity and the environment* — appears to be in a constant state of evolution.

There are several aspects of ecology that marketers must deal with: planned obsolescence, pollution, recycling waste materials, and preservation of resources.

A long-standing ecological problem facing marketing was **planned obsolescence** — a situation where the *manufacturer intentionally produced items with limited durability*. Planned obsolescence has always represented a significant ethical question for the marketer. On one side is the need for maintaining sales and employment by ensuring repeat purchases; on the other is the ability, and perhaps obligation, to provide better levels of quality and durability.

A practical question is whether the consumer really wants or can afford increased durability. Many consumers prefer to change styles often and accept less durable items. Increased durability has an implicit cost. It may mean fewer people can afford the product.

**Pollution** is a broad term that can be applied to a number of

---

33 This philosophy has been implemented in many companies: General Motors has a Public Policy Committee as part of its Board of Directors; Chrysler Corporation has an Office of Public Responsibility; and Thiokel Chemical Corporation has a separate corporate body to administer its various social programs. See Thomas A. Kindre, "Getting Involved," *Marathon World* (No. 4, 1972), pp. 2–5.

34 Ecological aspects of marketing are discussed in Patrick E. Murphy and Gene R. Laczniak, "Marketing and Ecology: Retrospect and Prospect," *Business and Society* (Fall 1977), pp. 26–34.

circumstances. It usually means *"making unclean."* Pollution of such natural resources as the water and the air is of critical proportions in some areas.

**Recycling** — *the reprocessing of used materials for reuse* — is another important aspect of ecology. The marketing system annually generates billions of tonnes of packaging materials, such as glass, metal, paper, and plastics, adding to the nation's growing piles of trash and waste. The theory behind recycling is that if these materials can be processed so as to be reusable, they can benefit society by saving natural resources and energy as well as by alleviating a major factor in environmental pollution.

Tire manufacturers have built artificial fish reefs out of used tires.[35] Minnesota Mining and Manufacturing Company has printed outlines for splints on the corrugated shipping cartons destined for hospitals. The cartons are then used by emergency and rescue teams for temporary splints.[36] The beverage industry is using more aluminum cans because of the relative ease of recycling aluminum.[37]

Recovery rates for reusable materials vary by industry. For instance, the rate for copper is 50 percent, for iron and steel 30 percent, for paper and paper products 20 percent, and for glass only 4 percent. In many instances, the recovery rates are now less than they were in the mid-1950s. Yet it is estimated that extensive recycling could produce 40 percent of the materials needed by manufacturers.[38]

The biggest problem in recycling is getting the used materials from the consumer back to the manufacturer who will handle the technological aspects of recovery. These reverse channels are limited, and those that do exist are primitive and lack adequate financial incentives.[39] Marketing can play an important role by designing appropriate channel structures.

Another ecological problem concerns the preservation of natural resources. The natural gas and fuel oil shortages during the 1970s

35 Ralph E. Winter, "The Tiremakers Try All Sorts of Methods to Destroy Old Tires but Not Environment," *Wall Street Journal* (April 27, 1972), p. 30.
36 "Business Bulletin," *Wall Street Journal* (December 11, 1975), p. 1.
37 Amal Nag, "Recycling Ease Gives Aluminum an Edge over Steel in Beverage-Can Market Battle," *Wall Street Journal* (January 2, 1980), p. 28.
38 Edward M. Syring, "Realizing Recycling's Potential," *Nation's Business* (February 1976), pp. 68, 70.
39 William G. Zikmund and William J. Stanton, "Recycling Solid Wastes: A Channels-of-Distribution Problem," *Journal of Marketing* (July 1971), pp. 34–39. Also see Donald A. Fuller, "Recycling Consumer Solid Waste: A Commentary on Selected Channel Alternatives," *Journal of Business Research* (January 1978), pp. 17–31; and Peter M. Ginter and Jack M. Starling, "Reverse Distribution Channels: Concept and Structure," in *Proceedings of the Southern Marketing Association*, eds. Robert S. Franz, Robert M. Hopkins, and Al Toma (New Orleans, La.: November 1978), pp. 206–208.

illustrate the urgent need for effective policies for both conserving and finding new sources of these resources.

Some critics claim that business spends more money publicizing its ecological expenditures than it does meeting specific ecological problems. In many cases, the criticism is valid; but experience has shown that consumers are also at fault in that they sometimes fail to support ecology-inspired products or contribute to pollution in their own way, as the debris along the highways of the country attests.

### Controlling the Marketing System

When the marketing-economic system does not perform as well as we would like, we attempt to change it. We hope to make it serve us better by producing and distributing goods and services in a fairer way.

Most people in Canada appear to believe that the system is working sufficiently well not to require major changes, and that relatively minor adjustments can achieve a "fair" distribution.

Four ways in which we control or influence the direction of the marketing system and try to rid it of imperfections are: 1) assisting the competitive market system to operate in a self-correcting manner, as Adam Smith suggested; 2) consumer education; 3) regulation; and 4) political action.

The *competitive market system* operates to allocate resources and provide for our needs for most of the products we purchase. While we may hear many complaints against the system, most of the goods and services we purchase or use flow through the system with little difficulty. Competition works if the conditions of many buyers and sellers and other technical requirements of the free-market economic model are operative. We have attempted, albeit with limited success, to restore competition in instances where monopolies have reduced it.

Combined with the free market system, *consumer education* can lead to wise choices. As products become more complex, diverse, and plentiful, the consumer's ability to make wise decisions must also expand. Educational programs and efforts by parents, schools, business, government, and consumer organizations all contribute to a better system.

When the free market and consumer education have been insufficient to make the system work as we would like, we have attempted to introduce *regulatory procedures* to direct the economy. At present there is a great hue and cry about the need to deregulate Canadian society. Those who favour deregulation want to try to restore the competitive market system to a perceived level of original purity that probably never existed. Although there are many facts and philosophical arguments on both sides of the question, we can predict with certainty that regulation of monopolies such as public utilities will continue. Outside these realms it is difficult to predict whether we will see more regulation, or less. But the regulatory activities of agricultural marketing boards, the Canadian Radio-television and Telecommunications Commission, the Canadian Transport Commission, the National Energy Board, and others indicate that *more* rather than *less* regulation may be in store for the future.

One function of government is the satisfaction of the desires of society. Therefore, all regulation is the consequence of *political action*. The effectiveness of business lobbies in directing the economic system is an often-noted fact of Canadian life. But the political activities of groups representing consumers and their interests are becoming increasingly visible and effective, too. These groups are attempting to make the system more responsive to consumers. Since marketers are at the interface between business and consumers, a knowledge of how these consumer groups view the consumer interest and consumer rights can be quite helpful in circumventing confrontation. As citizens we should have an understanding of interest-group participation in the political process, and how large, broadly based interest groups such as consumers differ from smaller, narrowly based special interest groups in having their points of view adequately represented in the political process.

## Ethics and Values— The Enemy Is Us

In previous chapters on consumer behaviour and marketing segmentation, you became aware that there is a wide range of individual attitudes and desires to be satisfied by our marketing system. Walk through apparel shops in any large metropolitan area and you can see the wide diversity of products offered to satisfy individual needs.

The ethics and values that we hold as a society also have a wide range of diversity. Why else would we elect members of the New Democratic, Liberal, Progressive Conservative, and other political parties if we did not have a wide range of values that we want to be represented within our system of government?

Some values, such as the sanctity of human life and a desire for the rule of law, are common to almost all of us. At the other end of the scale are areas where we disagree widely as to what is normal product promotion and what is false and misleading advertising about a product. For example, is saying that your product is the best in the world a statement that has to be supported by a researched fact? Or can you reasonably expect consumers to take such a statement with a grain of salt?

In the very broadest sense the function of a government is to express the collective values of the citizenry through laws under which it wishes to be governed. Marketing is only one of a number of systems that reflect society's desires. If marketing as a system is to be indicted then we must all be defendants, since we find it impossible to differentiate among ourselves as members of society, as consumers, and as elements in the business system that serves us.

Adam Smith, the champion of capitalism, argued that the human desire to serve our own best interests would act as an "invisible hand" in guiding the economy. The resulting maximization of output would improve life and society by improving the standard of living. Smith saw competition as the watchdog that kept the economy on the correct course. He also observed that any time two or more business people got together there was a tendency to co-operate to use the system to their advantage. For this reason competition was necessary so that no individual or group could misuse the system to personal advantage.

Little could Adam Smith foresee our present-day economic systems with large international businesses, large governments, and large labour unions, all of which have the potential to abuse the system for their own advantage. As society has become more complex, we have tried to develop control mechanisms so that the interests of the members of society are well reflected in the way it operates.

## Consumerism, the Individual, and the Marketer

In our daily lives we are mainly consumers. Only when participating directly in the role of producers of goods and services do we switch into a situation of possible conflict. The wide range and diversity of values discussed earlier in the chapter explain why some of us may not fully subscribe to some particular stand of such broadly based interest groups as consumer groups. However, it is not surprising that most people agree in large degree with such activities.

As marketers, we should see that the reactions of consumers and the various consumer groups are an indication of how well our views fit with generally held views and of the appropriateness of our marketing activities in the marketplace. Businesses that could not or would not change some of their actions have been the root cause of legislation and regulation to change that behaviour. Conflicts between individual, organizational, and industry values and ethics will continue, as they have through history. The individual will still be required to resolve these conflicts within his or her value system. It is small consolation to know that we are not alone in the difficult choices each of us has to face. It is for just these reasons that we may find disagreement in answer to the question, "Does marketing serve Canada well?"

## The Paradox of the Marketing Concept

Very often, marketing is maligned for its pushy, noisy, manipulative intrusions into our lives; its corruptive teachings of greed and hedonism; its relentless pursuit of the consumer's cash, regardless of consequence, save the profit of the seller.[40]

Paradoxically, these complaints seem to rise in direct proportion to the rising practice of the marketing concept. Thus it appears that the more carefully companies try to give people what they want, the more surely they are attacked for trying to get people to buy what they don't want, what they don't need, and what they can't afford — and doing it with wanton waste, noise, abrasiveness, and vulgarity. In comparison, there is surprisingly little complaining about product failure or deliberate excesses, such as shoddy products, tricky warranties, deceptive advertising, misleading packaging, or questionable selling practices — and what there is is rarely addressed at the big, visible companies, which sell their products the hardest and research their consumers the most. What seems to bug people most is the charge of generalized wastefulness, offensiveness, and annoyance incident to so much marketing activity.

This paradox can be partly explained by considering how the concept of market segmentation is implemented. Many companies have faithfully produced products aimed at specific subsegments of the market and then, especially in the case of consumer goods, have used a mass marketing approach to communicate with and persuade their chosen segments. This means that many others are exposed to the marketing effort even though they have no interest in it and it is not intended for them.

The hemorrhoid ad may not be particularly offensive to the afflicted viewer, reader, or listener. But most people exposed to the message are not afflicted. Most likely they are either indifferent or offended. And there are always too many gasoline stations, except for the person who is running low or has actually run out of gas. Nor should we be surprised that laundry soap and detergent ads irritated 2500 executives, according to one study. How many of them do that household chore? A study by Stephen Greyser showed that only 7 percent of the ads for one's favourite brand were disliked, as compared with 76 percent of the ads for competing brands. Thus, if marketing efforts relate to what *we* are interested in, we generally find them acceptable.

There is often an incongruity between the intended and actual audience for marketing efforts, a poor fit between the sophisticated practice of the marketing concept and the media and institutions that facilitate marketing. Even where there is a proper fit, the receiver may have already purchased some brand, or cannot afford it now, and thus may still feel badgered. On the other hand, humanity's

---

[40] This section is adapted from Theodore Levitt, "Marketing and Its Discontents," *Across the Board* (February 1984), pp. 42–45.

relatively insatiable desire for possessions makes many ready for the product and the message over time.

### Resolving Contemporary Issues in Marketing

The resolution of the contemporary issues of consumerism, social responsibility, and marketing ethics is probably the most crucial task facing marketing in the years ahead.

Three courses of action are available to resolve these vital questions: increased regulation, better public information, and a more responsible marketing philosophy. Progress in these areas is essential if the competitive marketing system is to survive at all.

Few marketers doubt that increased regulation will become a reality in the marketplace unless reforms are instituted. History has shown that government, responding to consumer pressures, has always moved to fill voids created by business apathy and neglect. Expanded and improved self-regulation by marketers is needed if stricter governmental controls are to be avoided.[41]

Better public information is a solution that is applicable to many contemporary issues. In many cases these issues arise simply because the public was not informed or was mistakenly misinformed. Package labelling is a good example of where improvement has now taken place.

Unit pricing, explained in Chapter 14, was a widely debated method of providing better information, before it was adopted by major food chains. **Open dating**, which *sets the last date a perishable or semiperishable food can be sold*, involves similar discussion.[42] To what type of information should consumers be entitled? Is better public information worth the cost? How can marketers improve the information consumers receive? Many of these questions will have to be answered in the decades ahead.

A more responsible marketing philosophy is also needed in contemporary society. Incidents like the following one reflect badly on marketers and their firms:

> One unhappy patron who discovered bedbugs in his hotel bed and complained bitterly in writing to the company received a mollifying reply to which had been attached, accidentally, a scribbled note from

---

41 The marketing/government interface is examined in Andrew Tokas, "Societal Marketing: A Businessman's Perspective," *Journal of Marketing* (October 1974), pp. 2–7; and Roger Kerin and Michael Harvey, "Consumer Legislation: A Proactive or Reactive Response to Consumerism?" *Journal of the Academy of Marketing Science* (Fall 1974), pp. 582–592.
42 Open dating is examined in Prabhaker Nayak and Larry J. Rosenberg, "Does Open Dating of Food Products Benefit the Consumer?" *Journal of Retailing* (Summer 1975), pp. 10–20.

some executive to his secretary that said: "Alice, send this guy the bedbug letter."[43]

A responsible marketing philosophy should encourage consumers to voice their opinions. This can result in significant improvements in the products and services offered by the seller. One company with a responsible attitude toward consumer complaints featured its critics in television advertisements. The critics and the company spokesperson discussed the various issues surrounding the company and its service area. Surveys showed that the public adopted a more favourable attitude toward the company's position on these matters after seeing the advertisements.

Business must include social responsibility as a primary function of the marketing organization. Social and profit goals are compatible, but they require the aggressive implementation of an expanded marketing concept. Explicit criteria for responsible decision-making must be adopted in all companies.[44] This is truly marketing's greatest challenge!

## Summary

At the interface between business and society, the marketer often takes the brunt of criticisms of the operation of the market system. There are many important issues in contemporary marketing's social environment. Marketing's environmental relationships have expanded in scope and importance. The current issues in marketing can be categorized as consumerism, marketing ethics, and social responsibility.

Criticisms of the marketing system are often justified and result from a broad range of ideas about what is ethical and what is not ethical business activity. It is much too easy to point the finger at marketers or at business as the perpetrators of the evils of the system rather than recognizing that the system is *us*. The system is what its members want it to be, and when the system does not respond as we would like it to, the result is government-instituted regulations and controls to correct that situation.

Attempts to make the system more responsive to the desires of society have resulted in increased regulation and the emergence of groups representing consumer interests. Basic consumer rights to choice, to information, to be heard, and to safety and health, and the consumers' interests in maintaining these rights are most commonly ensured by competition in the marketplace. Where the mar-

---

43 A. T. Baker, "Louder!—The Need to Complain More," *Time* (July 3, 1972), p. 33.
44 See for example, Martin L. Bell and C. William Emory, "The Faltering Marketing Concept," *Journal of Marketing* (October 1971), pp. 37–42.

ketplace is inadequate to ensure the consumer rights and interests, governments have responded to public pressure and intervened to improve the situation. Consumer groups have developed to spur business and government in this action and to counteract the natural advantage special interest groups have in representing their interests in the political process at the expense of more broadly based consumer interests.

Increased regulation, better public information, and a more responsible marketing philosophy are possible avenues for resolving these issues. All are expected to play a greater role in the years ahead.

The marketer must recognize that increasingly his or her decisions are made within a highly interactive system. Contemporary marketing decisions must now more than ever regularly involve consideration of the external societal environment. It is difficult to foresee less regulation of the marketplace, and the marketer, at least in the short term, will be facing constraints on activities that have as their aim making the system more responsive to society's needs.

## Key Terms

| | |
|---|---|
| consumerism | ecology |
| consumer rights | planned obsolescence |
| class action suit | pollution |
| marketing ethics | recycling |
| social responsibility | open dating |

## Review Questions

1. Examine Adam Smith's thoughts on competition. How have these views affected the marketing system?
2. Explain the causes of the consumerism movement. Does the rise of consumerism suggest that the marketing concept has failed?
3. Evaluate consumerism's complaints about the operation of the competitive marketing system.
4. Discuss the problems involved in setting up reverse channels of distribution for recycling used packages.
5. Distinguish among individual, organizational, and professional ethics.
6. Describe the ethical problems related to:
   a. marketing research       d. pricing
   b. product management    e. promotional strategy
   c. distribution strategy
7. Describe the main avenues open for the resolution of contemporary issues facing the marketing system.
8. How would you have responded to each of the situations described in the section on ethical problems in marketing research? Explain.

9. Describe the conflict that may exist between the consumer's desire for product durability and the ecology movement.

10. The marketing concept marked the advent of the age of consumerism. Do you agree with this statement? Why or why not?

***Discussion Questions***
***and Exercises***

1. Should Canada ban advertising aimed at children?

2. Some have suggested that the majority of Canadian consumers are consumer illiterates. How would you suggest alleviating this problem?

3. Henry Ford II has argued that in a competitive market system, a firm cannot afford to meet the expense of environmental improvements unless competitors are also legally required to follow the same standards. Discuss.

4. Unit pricing and open dating increase distribution costs and thus prices. Therefore, these policies are undesirable from a consumer's viewpoint. Comment on these statements.

5. Some have suggested a deposit for all beverage containers be made a law in all provinces in an attempt to reduce roadside litter. Do you agree? Why or why not?

# Evaluation and Control

1. To explain the steps in the marketing evaluation and control process.

2. To describe the use of sales analysis and marketing cost analysis.

3. To identify the strengths and limitations of return on investment as an evaluative technique.

4. To describe the major ratios used in evaluating marketing performance.

5. To explain the concept of the market audit and the major steps involved.

The marketing plan at Best Foods called for personal contact by its sales representatives on the individual retail stores, retail chain headquarters, and wholesale accounts selected as its prime target market. Those grocery accounts generate 75 percent of total grocery sales in the country. Marketing managers at Best Foods, whose products range from Skippy peanut butter to Hellmann's mayonnaise, expect each sales representative to make an average of 6.5 daily calls on his or her 100 accounts and to visit each store every seven to 30 days, depending on the store's sales volume. The sales representative is responsible for maintaining good relationships with store personnel, in-store product displays and other promotional activities, and feedback to area managers about changes in the marketplace that might require adjustments in Best Foods' sales-call frequencies. Each sales call costs an average of $25.

How did Best Foods sales managers establish a system of evaluating and controlling the activities of its sales force? The starting point was the establishment of quantifiable standards for account coverage, case sales, number of calls on promising new accounts, and promotional activities, such as building in-store displays. The sales force works in two-month promotion periods, and meetings among the district manager, area managers, and sales representatives establish priorities for each representative prior to each period. Area managers are intimately involved with the goal-setting process for each of their representatives, and they continue to meet informally with each salesperson on a biweekly basis throughout the period.

In order to minimize paperwork, Best Foods managers developed a computerized call reporting system called SCORE (Sales Call Objective Report and Evaluation). After each sales call, the salesperson completes a brief report of sales and promotional activities on a machine-readable form. These are mailed to company headquarters twice a week, where they are read by optical scanners and processed by computer. Within five to seven working days headquarters supplies the sales managers and individual salespersons with a weekly productivity report, and at the end of each promotion period these reports are combined into a bimonthly call summary making such comparisons as scheduled versus actual calls, average number of presentations and success rates, and accounts where no sales have been made during the past four months. Such accounts are candidates for careful study and possible deletion from the customer list. Best Foods sales vice-president Cliff Jennewein is enthusiastic about SCORE as a tool in evaluation and control: "SCORE helps us determine just what (the salesperson) is achieving . . . giving sales reps and managers quantifiable standards of performance and results."[1]

## The Conceptual Framework

The desire of Best Foods marketers to obtain feedback of actual performance and to compare it with expected results is one shared by marketing managers in every organization. Evaluation and control are essential components in the firm's marketing strategy. They determine whether marketing plans are being implemented and whether organizational objectives are being achieved. They are a part of a sequential process that begins with the original analysis of a marketing opportunity. While marketing planning, first discussed in Chapter 3, refers to the establishment of objectives and the development of strategies, **evaluation and control** refer to *the establishment of standards of performance and the comparison of actual results with planned results to determine whether actual performance matches marketing plans.* This chapter examines a number of techniques by which marketing performance may be measured and compared with expectations. Such methods as sales analysis, marketing cost analysis, return on investment, ratio analysis, and marketing audits are important tools in evaluation and control.

## The Need for Evaluation and Control

The evaluation and control phase provides a feedback mechanism that keeps marketing planning and implementation of these plans on track. The control sequence allows marketers to assess whether

---

[1] Sally Scanlon, "Best Foods Knows the Score," *Sales and Marketing Management Sales and Marketing Plans* (New York: Bill Brothers, 1978), p. 30.

corrective actions are needed. In some cases, uncontrollable variables such as technological breakthroughs by a competitor, a recession, a major factory of a customer closing, or the development of a lower priced substitute for the firm's product may adversely affect sales and profits. In such instances, volume or profitability targets will have to be re-evaluated, and new, more realistic goals set. In other situations, the firm's plans may be judged as accurate, but the marketing program may require adjustments. A third possible outcome is that both plans and their implementation may require adjustments. Finally, in instances where the original analysis of the marketing opportunity was faulty, the option may be to abandon the project entirely. Regardless of the final result, the most important contribution of evaluation and control is that it allows the marketer to keep its marketing planning on target.

## The Evaluation and Control Process

Figure 25-1 is a model of the evaluation and control process. Since marketing planning and control are closely related components of an effective marketing program, evaluation and control guide performance to conform to the plan.

A number of elements must be present for evaluation and control to be effective. First, as Figure 25-1 indicates, organizational goals must result in the establishment of standards of performance. Such standards become reference points against which actual performance can be compared. They may take such forms as expected number of sales calls per month, sales, profit, or market-share expectations, or even rankings of consumer awareness.

**Figure 25-1   Steps in the Process of Evaluation and Control**

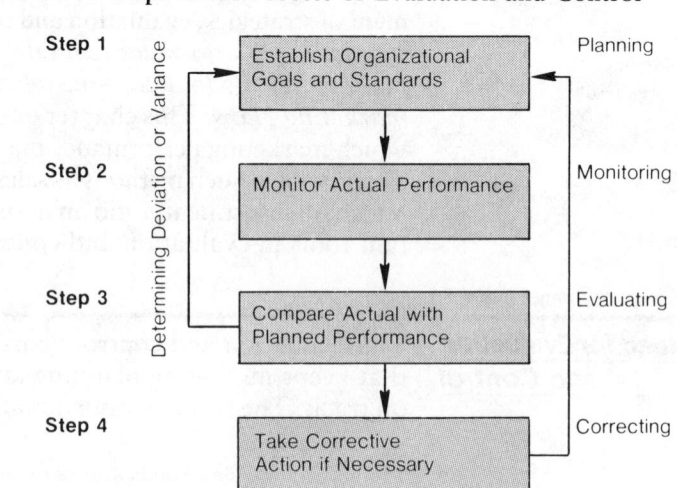

The second step of evaluation and control is monitoring actual performance. Decisions must be made concerning what activities and/or individuals are to be measured and how to measure them. The third step is comparison of actual and planned performance. At this point, decisions must be made about the degree of permissible deviations from standards.

Taking corrective action if significant deviations exist between planned and actual performance is the final step. It consists of two elements: identifying the cause of the deviation and implementing the corrective action.

## Methods of Evaluation and Control

A multitude of evaluative methods exist for measuring marketing performance. Some are based on the use of financial ratios such as return on investment. These calculations are outlined in later sections of this chapter. Other evaluations employ extensive field tests. McDonald's, for example, tested one new sandwich, the McFeast, for two years.[2] Another evaluative favourite is simply hard questioning of executives about organizational achievements. The critical factor is not how it is done, but that the organization does have some procedure for objectively evaluating its marketing plans and programs.

## Using Control Charts

Marketing evaluation and control involves making a comparison of actual performance against some set standard or target. Most organizations set upper and lower control limits on the evaluative standards they employ. Marketers expect some random fluctuations in actual performance; the key to effective control is keeping these variations within the control limits.

Marketers have adapted techniques long used in quality control efforts. For example, **control charts** — *diagrams that plot actual performance against established control limits* — can be easily applied for use in marketing evaluation and control.

Figure 25-2 shows a control chart used to monitor the advertising expense/sales ratio. This control chart has specified that advertising expenditures should constitute 10 percent of sales, but that normal variation can range between 8 and 12 percent. Figure 25-2 indicates that only in time period 15 did the ratio go beyond the acceptable range.

Control charts can be very useful tools. They provide an excellent graphic display of actual against planned performance, and also highlight the need for corrective action.

---

[2] Paul Ingrissia, "McDonald's Fast Track Drops Quinlan into the Hot Seat As Competition Sizzles," *Wall Street Journal* (February 21, 1980), p. 14.

**Figure 25-2   The Standard Control Chart Model**

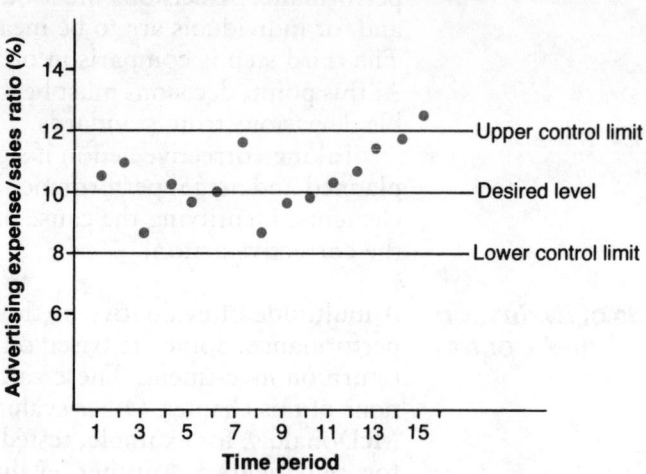

Source: Reprinted from Philip Kotler, *Marketing Decision Making: A Modern Building Approach* (New York: Holt, Rinehart and Winston, 1971), p. 635. Reprinted by permission of the author.

## Assessing Marketing Performance

Standards for marketing performance vary widely. When Coca-Cola entered one new market, it set a 10-year sales volume target of $1 billion.[3] Another firm wants sales to increase at a 20 percent annual rate. But its chairman contends, "We are in business for profit, not primarily for volume."[4] Most marketing objectives and performance standards can be categorized as either volume-oriented or profitability-oriented.

Which type of standard is correct? How should organizations evaluate marketing performance? Typically, most organizations use a combination of evaluative methods to assess marketing performance, such as sales analysis, marketing cost analysis, return on investment, ratio analysis, and marketing audits.

## Sales Analysis

Facts important to evaluation and control are found in the organization's sales records. Analysis of this data can provide a basis for obtaining an overall view of marketing effectiveness.

Basic financial statements are often too broad to be very useful. Where nondetailed accounts are used, their main contribution is that they assist the marketer to raise more specific questions. The

[3] "Coca-Cola: A Spurt into Wine that Is Altering the Industry," *Business Week* (October 15, 1979), pp. 126–131.
[4] Allan F. Hussey, "Philip Morris' Calling," *Barron's* (December 10, 1979), pp. 45, 52–53.

income statement in Figure 25-3 shows that the company earned a profit for the period being considered, and that selling expenses represented approximately 13 percent of sales.

$$\frac{\text{Selling expense}}{\text{Sales}} = \frac{\$\ \ 753\ 000}{\$5\ 783\ 000} = 13\%$$

Comparison of the 13 percent selling expense/sales ratio with previous years may hint at possible problems, but it will not specifically reveal the cause of the variation. To discover the cause, a more detailed breakdown is necessary.

Figure 25-4 shows a typical breakdown of sales by territories. This kind of classification forms part of an overall sales analysis. The purpose of the **sales analysis** — *the in-depth evaluation of a firm's sales*—is to obtain meaningful information from existing data.[5]

**Figure 25-3   Income Statement for XYZ Manufacturing Company**

XYZ Manufacturing Company
Income Statement for the Year Ended December 31, 198__

| | | |
|---|---|---:|
| Sales | | $5 783 000 |
| Cost of goods sold | | 3 291 000 |
| Gross margin | | $2 492 000 |
| Expenses: | | |
| Selling expenses | $753 000 | |
| Other expenses | 301 000 | 1 054 000 |
| Profit before taxes | | $1 438 000 |
| Income taxes | | $ 719 000 |
| Profit after taxes | | $ 719 000 |

**Figure 25-4   Sales and Expense Analysis by Territory**

| District | Average Compensation | Average Expenses | Total Sales Costs | Total Sales | Cost/ Sales Ratio |
|---|---|---|---|---|---|
| 1 | $23 600 | $10 400 | $34 000 | $654 000 | 5.2% |
| 2 | 21 900 | 12 800 | 34 700 | 534 000 | 6.5 |
| 3 | 27 200 | 13 100 | 40 300 | 790 000 | 5.1 |
| 4 | 25 700 | 12 300 | 38 000 | 180 000 | 21.1 |
| 5 | 24 200 | 11 700 | 35 900 | 580 000 | 6.2 |

Easily prepared from company invoices stored on computer tapes, the sales analysis can be quite revealing for the marketing executive. As Figure 25-4 shows, the sales force in District 4 has a

[5] For a classical treatment of sales analysis, see Charles Sevin, *Marketing Productivity Analysis* (New York: McGraw-Hill, 1965).

much higher cost/sales ratio than the sales force in other districts

In order to evaluate the performance of the salespeople in the five districts, the marketing executive must have a standard o comparison. District 4, for example, may be a large area but with relatively few industrial centres. Consequently, the costs involved in obtaining sales there will be higher than for other districts.

The standard by which actual and expected sales are compared typically results from a detailed forecast by territories, products customers, and salespersons. Once the **sales quota**, *the level of expected sales to which actual results are compared*, has been established, it is a simple process to compare the actual results to the expected performance. Figure 25-5 compares actual sales to the quota for each person in District 4.

Even though Shapiro had the smallest amount of sales for the period, her performance was better than expected. However, the district sales manager should investigate Chandler's performance since it resulted for the most part in the district's failure to meet its quota for the period.

**The Iceberg Principle**      The performance of the salespersons in District 4 provides a good illustration of the **iceberg principle**, which suggests that *important evaluative information is often hidden by aggregate data*. The tip of the iceberg represents only one-tenth of its total size. The remaining nine-tenths lies hidden beneath the surface of the water. Summaries of data are useful, but the marketer must ensure that summaries do not actually conceal more than they reveal. If the sales breakdown by salesperson for the district had not been available, Chandler's poor performance would have concealed the unexpectedly high sales performances by Belliveau and Shapiro.

**Figure 25-5   Sales Breakdown by Sales Representatives in District 4**

| Salesperson | Quota | Actual | Performance to Quota |
|---|---|---|---|
| Conti | $136 000 | $128 000 | 94% |
| Belliveau | 228 000 | 253 000 | 111 |
| Shapiro | 118 000 | 125 000 | 106 |
| Chandler | 246 000 | 160 000 | 65 |
| Total | $728 000 | $666 000 | 91% |

**Other Classifications**      Other possible breakdowns for sales analysis include customer type, product, method of sale (mail, telephone, or personal contact), type of order (cash or credit), and size of order. Sales analysis is one of the least expensive and most important sources of marketing information, and any firm with data-processing facilities should include sales analysis as part of its evaluation and control system.

## Marketing Cost Analysis

Marketing cost analysis is *the evaluation of such items as selling costs, billing, warehousing, advertising, and delivery expenses* in order to determine the profitability of particular customers, territories, or product lines.

Marketing cost analysis requires a new way of classifying accounting data. **Functional accounts,** *representing the purpose for which an expenditure is made*, replace the traditional **natural accounts** *used in financial statements.* These natural accounts, such as salary, must be reallocated to the pertinent functional accounts. Portions of the original salary account, for example, will be allocated to selling, inventory control, storage, billing, advertising, and other marketing costs. In the same manner, an account such as supply expenses will be allocated to the functions that utilize supplies.

The costs allocated to the functional accounts equal those in the natural accounts. But instead of showing only total profitability, functional accounts can show the profitability of, say, particular districts, products, customers, salespersons, and order sizes. The most common reallocations are to products, customers, and territories or districts. Figure 25-6 shows how allocations can be made.

### Figure 25-6   Allocation of Marketing Costs

| Marketing Costs | By Customer | | By District | | |
|---|---|---|---|---|---|
| | *Large* | *Small* | *A* | *B* | *C* |
| Advertising | $14 000 | $ 30 000 | $20 000 | $10 000 | $14 000 |
| Selling | 52 000 | 62 000 | 38 000 | 38 000 | 38 000 |
| Physical distribution | 33 000 | 26 000 | 28 000 | 14 000 | 17 000 |
| Credit | 400 | 2 600 | 1 600 | 600 | 800 |
| Total | $99 400 | $120 600 | $87 600 | $62 600 | $69 800 |

The marketing decision-maker can then evaluate the profitability of particular customers and districts on the basis of the sales produced and the costs incurred in producing them.

Figure 25-7 indicates that District B is the most profitable and district A is unprofitable. Attention can now be given to plans for increasing sales or reducing expenses in this problem district to make market coverage of the area a profitable undertaking. Marketing cost analysis is similar to sales analysis in that both pro-

**Figure 25-7    Income Statement for Districts A, B, and C**

|  | District | | | |
|  | A | B | C | Total |
|---|---|---|---|---|
| Sales | $260 000 | $200 000 | $191 000 | $651 000 |
| Cost of sales | 175 000 | 135 000 | 120 000 | 430 000 |
| Gross margin | $ 85 000 | $ 65 000 | $ 71 000 | $221 000 |
| Marketing expenses | 87 600 | 62 600 | 69 800 | 220 000 |
| Contribution of each territory | ($ 2 600) | $ 2 400 | $ 1 200 | $ 1 000 |

vide warning signals of deviations from plans and allow the marketing executive the opportunity to explain and possibly correct the deviations.[6]

### Return on Investment: A Commonly Used Evaluative Technique

Evaluation is one of the most challenging tasks facing the marketing manager. The basic problem is to find an instrument capable of measuring marketing performance, actual and planned. Historically, sales volume was first used in this capacity; later, profitability became the accepted measure. More recently, **return on investment** (ROI) has gained popularity as an effective evaluative device. It is particularly useful in evaluating proposals for alternative courses of action.

ROI is a quantitative tool that seeks to relate the activity or project's profitability to its investment. It is equal to *net income or earnings divided by net profit*. ROI can be calculated as follows:

$$\text{ROI} = \frac{\text{Net income}}{\text{Investment}}$$

A brief example shows how ROI can be used as an evaluative device. Consider a new product idea for which the firm estimates that a $200 000 investment will be required. The company expects to reach $500 000 in sales, with a net profit of $40 000. The proposed project's ROI is calculated in the following manner:

$$\text{ROI} = \frac{\$\ 40\ 000}{\$200\ 000}$$
$$= 20 \text{ percent}$$

Whether or not this expected performance is acceptable depends on the ROI of alternative uses of corporate funds. It would not be viewed favourably at Gould, Inc., for instance. This major indus-

---

[6] An excellent discussion of marketing cost analysis is presented in Patrick M. Dunne and Harry I. Wolk, "Marketing Cost Analysis: A Modularized Contribution Approach," *Journal of Marketing* (July 1977), pp. 83–94.

trial goods manufacturer wants all new products to generate a return on investment of 40 percent before taxes.

ROI is often used in conjunction with other evaluative tools. For example, Gould also specifies that its new products should generate profits on sales of 30 percent before taxes and 15 percent annual sales and profit growth. It also insists on a $20-million sales potential within five years following introduction and a total market potential of about $50 million.[7]

**The Limitations of ROI**   ROI should be used with caution and in conjunction with other evaluative tools in assessing marketing performance. A variety of factors can affect ROI calculations: book value of assets, depreciation, industry conditions, time periods, and transfer pricing. Consider how these factors could affect an attempt to judge the overall effectiveness of different divisions within a large corporation.

Book Value of Assets   If an older division is using assets that have been largely written off, both its current depreciation charges and its investment base will be low. This will make its ROI high in relation to those of newer divisions.

Depreciation   ROI is very sensitive to depreciation policy. If one division is writing off assets at a relatively rapid rate, its annual profits, and hence, its ROI will be reduced.

Industry Conditions   If one division is operating in an industry where conditions are favourable and rates of return are high, whereas another is in an industry suffering from excessive competition, such environmental differences may cause the favoured division to look good and the unfavoured division to look bad, quite apart from any differences in their respective managers. External conditions must be taken into account when appraising ROI performance.

Time Periods   Many projects have long gestation periods — expenditures must be made for research and development, plant construction, market development, and the like; such expenditures will add to the investment base without a commensurate increase in profits for several years. During this period, a division's ROI could be seriously reduced; without proper constraints, its division manager could be improperly penalized.

Transfer Pricing   In most corporations some divisions sell to other divisions. In General Motors, for example, the Fisher Body Division sells to the Chevrolet Division; in such cases the price at which

7 The Gould example is reported in "Industrial Newsletter," *Sales & Marketing Management* (April 3, 1978), p. 32.

goods are transferred between divisions has a fundamental effect on divisional profits. If the transfer price of auto bodies is set relatively high, then Fisher Body will have a relatively high ROI and Chevrolet a relatively low ROI.[8]

**Tying ROI to Profit Centres**

Dresser Industries, a diversified $3.5-billion manufacturer, illustrates how return on investment can be used to evaluate a marketing program. Dresser has a profitability goal of increasing earnings by 10 to 15 percent annually. To stay on target, Dresser has set up 300 separate profit centres worldwide. A **profit centre** is *any administrative unit whose contribution to corporate earnings can be measured.* The company's objective is to make the smallest possible operational unit responsible for its own performance. Dresser requires that each profit centre report operating results to its headquarters by the fourth day of business each month. Any profit centre reporting an annual ROI of less than 25 percent is immediately studied, and corrective action is taken if necessary.[9] ROI is a major evaluative tool at Dresser Industries.

**Ratio Analysis**

In addition to the market share and ROI calculations outlined earlier in this chapter, there are a variety of ratios useful in the evaluation and control process. These ratios are especially helpful in the analysis of specific aspects of marketing performance. The starting place for such analysis is the firm's *income statement* (sometimes referred to as the operating statement or the profit and loss statement) which presents a summary portrait of the firm's revenues and expenses over a period of time, such as a month, quarter, year, or any period selected by the firm's management. The second primary type of financial statement, the *balance sheet*, shows the financial condition of the firm at a specific point in time by examining its assets, liabilities, and net worth. The balance sheet provides a snapshot view of the organization at one moment, while the income statement is similar to a motion picture, showing activities — income and expenditures — over a stretch of time.

The income statement in particular helps marketing decision-makers focus on overall sales and the costs incurred in generating these sales; it indicates both whether a profit or loss was incurred and the amount of this loss or profit. Nonprofit organizations can use the income statement to assess the ability of the organization's

---

[8] This material is excerpted from J. Fred Weston and Eugene F. Brigham, *Essentials of Managerial Finance*, 4th ed. (Hinsdale, Ill.: Dryden Press, 1977), p. 116.

[9] Grover Herman, "Jack James Directs Dresser's Destiny, Texas-Style," *Nations Business* (November 1979), pp. 68–72, 75–76.

revenues and contributions to cover the cost involved in its operation. The income statement provides the basic data required to calculate numerous ratios used by the marketing decision-maker.

Figure 25-8 shows the operating (or income) statement for Ski Alberta, a relatively small Jasper retailer that markets ski equipment, ski clothing, group ski tours, and ski instructions. Note that the income statements for manufacturers and marketing intermediaries (retailers and wholesalers) are similar except that the statement for a retailer or wholesaler contains a net purchases subsection under the cost of goods sold section while the statement for a manufacturer would include a section labelled *cost of goods manufactured* in addition to purchases of raw materials and component parts.

Figure 25-8 may be divided into the following major sections:

| | |
|---|---:|
| Net sales | $110 000 |
| *Minus:* Cost of goods sold | − 54 200 |
| *Equals:* Gross margin | 55 800 |
| *Minus:* Expenses | − 43 300 |
| *Equals:* Net income before taxes | 12 500 |
| *Minus:* Taxes | − 4 000 |
| *Equals:* Net income | $   8 500 |

*Net sales* was calculated by subtracting merchandise returned by customers from total sales revenue. In some cases, overall sales are reduced when the retailer refunds a portion of the sales price (a sales allowance) on an item that is damaged or partially defective. In other instances, returned merchandise must be subtracted from the total sales figure to accurately reflect net sales.

*Cost of goods sold* by Ski Alberta is somewhat more complicated. At the beginning of the operating period, total inventory of $26 000 was on hand. In addition, Ski Alberta managers purchased $52 000 in inventory during 1985 to add to the beginning inventory, but received a purchase discount of $1000 from one firm for quantity purchases. Delivery charges of $1200 for the new purchases resulted in total net delivered purchases of $52 000. When this was added to the cost of beginning inventory, the total cost of products available for sale amounted to $78 200.

At the end of the operating period, some $24 000 was still on hand, indicating that the cost of goods sold during 1985 was $54 200 ($78 200 minus $24 000). Total *gross margin* ($110 000 net sales less $54 200 cost of goods sold) amounted to $55 800.

In order to determine net income for 1985, Ski Alberta managers must deduct the various selling and general expenses incurred from

**Figure 25-8   Ski Alberta Income Statement for Year Ending December 31, 1985**

*Revenues*

| | | |
|---|---:|---:|
| Gross sales | | $112 000 |
| Less: Sales returns and allowances | $ 2 000 | |
| Net sales | | $110 000 |

*Cost of Goods Sold*

| | | |
|---|---:|---:|
| Beginning inventory, January 1 (at cost) | | 26 000 |
| Gross purchases during year | 52 000 | |
| Less: Purchase discounts | 1 000 | |
| Net purchases | 51 000 | |
| Plus: Freight in | 1 200 | |
| Net purchases (total delivered cost) | | 52 200 |
| Cost of goods available for sale | | 78 200 |
| Less: Ending inventory, December 31 (at cost) | | 24 000 |
| Cost of goods sold | | 54 200 |

*Gross Margin*                                                                      55 800

*Expenses*

| | | |
|---|---:|---:|
| Selling expenses | | |
| Sales salaries and commissions | 17 000 | |
| Advertising | 4 500 | |
| Sales supplies | 2 000 | |
| Delivery expenses | 1 000 | |
| Miscellaneous selling expenses | 3 500 | |
| Total selling expenses | | 28 000 |
| General expenses | | |
| Office salaries | 12 000 | |
| Office supplies | 1 000 | |
| Miscellaneous general expenses | 2 300 | |
| Total general expenses | | 15 300 |
| Total expenses | | 43 300 |

| | |
|---|---:|
| *Net Income before Taxes* | 12 500 |
| Taxes | 4 000 |
| *Net Income* | $  8 500 |

the $55 800 gross margin total. *Selling expenses* include salaries and commissions paid to store personnel, advertising, sales supplies, delivery expenses, and such miscellaneous selling expenses as telephone charges, depreciation, insurance, and utilities allocated to sales. *General expenses* include salaries of office personnel; supplies; special services such as consultants, accounting services, or legal fees; insurance; postage; and depreciation. Total expenses for Ski Alberta in 1985 were $43 300.

*Net income before taxes* amounted to $12 500 ($55 800 gross margin less $43 300 total expense). After subtracting $4 000 for taxes, Ski Alberta earned a total *net income* of $8 500 for 1985.

**Analytical Ratios**  By analysing the operating statement shown in Figure 25-8, Ski Alberta can use a number of ratios in evaluating its performance and comparing it with that of previous periods and of similar firms in the industry. Four important analytical ratios are the gross margin percentage, the net profit percentage, the selling expense ratio, and the operating expense ratio.

Gross Margin Percentage  The **gross margin percentage** *is the ratio of gross margin to net sales*. It indicates the percentage of revenues available for covering expenses and earning a profit after the payment of the cost of products sold during the period. The gross margin percentage for Ski Alberta is calculated as follows:

$$\text{Gross Margin Percentage} = \frac{\text{Gross Margin}}{\text{Net Sales}}$$

$$= \frac{\$\ 55\ 800}{\$110\ 000} = 50.7 \text{ percent.}$$

Net Income to Sales  As its name indicates, the **ratio of net income to sales** measures company profitability *by comparing net income and sales*. It is calculated as follows:

$$\text{Ratio of Net Income to Sales} = \frac{\text{Net Income}}{\text{Sales}}$$

$$= \frac{\$\ \ 8\ 500}{\$110\ 000} = 7.7 \text{ percent.}$$

In comparing the 7.7 percent net profit percentage with those of previous periods and of other firms, it is important to note that in this case taxes have been deducted from the net income figure. Other firms may use net income before taxes in their calculations. Obviously, valid comparisons can be made only if the ratios use the same base.

Selling Expense Ratio  The **selling expense ratio** reveals *the relationship between major sales expenses and total net sales*. It is calculated by dividing total selling expenses by net sales.

$$\text{Selling Expense Ratio} = \frac{\text{Total Selling Expenses}}{\text{Net Sales}}$$

$$= \frac{\$\ 28\ 000}{\$110\ 000} = 25.5 \text{ percent.}$$

Operating Expense Ratio   The **operating expense ratio** *combines both selling and general expenses and compares them with overall net sales.* The operating expense ratio for Ski Alberta is calculated as follows:

$$\text{Operating Expense Ratio} = \frac{\text{Total Expenses}}{\text{Net Sales}}$$

$$= \frac{\$\ 43\ 300}{\$110\ 000} = 39.4 \text{ percent.}$$

Whether or not these ratios are considered acceptable depends primarily upon industry averages, the firm's past performances, and the alternatives available to the company. In any case, ratio analysis combined with sales analysis, cost analysis, and return on investment, can be enlightening to marketing management in providing concrete, quantifiable comparisons with actual and expected performances.

## The Marketing Audit

A comprehensive marketing audit can provide a valuable — and sometimes disquieting — perspective on a firm's marketing performance. Consider the pharmaceutical firm that was delighted with an 83 percent awareness rating for an advertising campaign, but shocked upon learning that this yielded an intent-to-buy of only 28 percent. A marketing audit is invaluable not only in identifying the tasks that the organization does well but also in highlighting its failures. Periodic review, criticism, and self-analysis are crucial to the vitality of any organization. They are particularly critical to a function that is as diverse and dynamic as marketing.

Marketing audits are especially valuable in pointing out areas in which managerial perceptions differ sharply from reality. Figure 25-9 reports some of the things that were learned in marketing audits at various pharmaceutical enterprises.

### The Marketing Audit: A Definition

William S. Woodside, the president of American Can Company, has been quoted as saying: "The roughest thing to get rid of is the Persian Messenger Syndrome, where the bearer of bad tidings is beheaded by the king. You should lean over backward to reward the guy who is first with the bad news. Most companies have all kinds of abilities to handle problems, if they only learn about them soon enough."[10]

If the marketing organization is to avoid the Persian Messenger Syndrome, as Woodside calls it, it must not only institute periodic program reviews, but must also be willing to accept the objective results of such evaluations. For most organizations, this means the

---

[10]Quoted in Arthur R. Roolman, "Why Corporations Hate the Future," *MBA* (November 1975), p. 37.

use of a **marketing audit,** *a thorough, objective evaluation of an organization's marketing philosophy, goals, policies, tactics, practices, and results.*[11]

### Figure 25-9   Staff Assumptions Compared with Audit Findings

| Focus | Marketing Staff Assumptions | Audit Findings |
|---|---|---|
| **Personal selling** | | |
| 1. Scale of efforts | 6.5 calls daily | 4.0 calls daily |
| 2. Quality of effort | Full presentation, 100 percent of calls | Full presentation, 70 percent of calls |
| 3. Message integrity | 100 percent accuracy | 65 percent accuracy |
| 4. Communication with sales force | 100 percent readership | 82 percent readership, with 81 percent accuracy |
| **Advertising** | | |
| 1. Ad agency interface | Harmonious | Disharmonious |
| 2. Message integrity | 100 percent accuracy | 62 percent accuracy |
| 3. Message impact | | 83 percent awareness; 28 percent acceptance (intent to buy) |
| **Product** | | |
| 1. Manufacturing cost | No change | 11 percent increase |
| 2. Market growth | 7 percent growth | 2 percent growth |
| 3. Penetration | 45 percent accepting; | 28 percent accepting; |
| | 25 percent neutral; | 57 percent neutral; |
| | 10 percent rejecting | 15 percent rejecting |
| **Intracompany** | | |
| 1. Interface processing | No problems | Communication and co-operation problems |
| 2. Marketing intelligence system | provides adequate information | Unsatisfactory |
| 3. Approval processing | 1–5 working days; average, 3 working days | 3–14 working days; average, 9 working days |

Source: Ed Roseman, "An Audit Can Make the 'Accurate' Difference," *Product Marketing/ Cosmetic & Fragrance Retailing* (August 1979), p. 24. Reprinted by permission.

---

[11] The basis of this section and the next was taken from an excellent discussion of marketing audits appearing in David T. Kollat, Roger D. Blackwell, and James F. Robeson, *Strategic Marketing* (New York: Holt, Rinehart and Winston, 1972), pp. 498–500.

The marketing audit goes beyond the normal control system. The control process for marketing essentially asks: Are we doing things right? The marketing audit extends this question to: Are we also doing the right thing?[12]

---

**Figure 25-10 Marketing Audit Usage by Industry**

| Type of Company | Percentage Conducting Marketing Audits |
|---|---|
| Industrial goods manufacturers | 36 |
| Consumer goods manufacturers | 19 |
| Manufacturers of consumer and industrial goods | 22 |
| Service-related firms | 28 |
| Total of all firms | 28 |

Source: Adapted from Louis R. Capella and William S. Sekely, "The Marketing Audit: Usage and Applications," in *Proceedings of the Southern Marketing Association*, eds. Robert S. Franz, Robert M. Hopkins, and Alfred G. Toma, New Orleans, La. (November 1978), p. 412. Used by permission of the Southern Marketing Association. Copyright © 1978 by the Southern Marketing Association. All rights reserved.

---

Marketing audits are applicable to all organizations — large or small, profitable or profitless, and nonprofit or profit-oriented. Audits are particularly valuable when they are performed for the fist time or after a long absence from the managerial process. Not all organizations have implemented marketing audits, but the number of firms using them is expected to grow. One study found that 28 percent of the firms surveyed had used a marketing audit. Figure 25-10 reflects the use of audits in different industries.

**Selecting the Marketing Auditors**

Selection of the auditors is a critical aspect of conducting a marketing audit. Three potential sources of auditors are regular corporate executives, special marketing audit staffs, and outside marketing consultants.

Some firms prefer to assign selected executives to perform marketing audits on a periodic basis. The difficulties in such an arrangement include the time pressure of the executives' regular duties and the problem of maintaining impartiality. Other organizations set up a separate marketing staff if their size permits such a structure. This arrangement can provide an excellent balance between impartiality and extensive in-house knowledge. Marketing consultants are often recommended for marketing audits because they enter the evaluation with an independent viewpoint that is valuable. Consultants also may be able to offer the most up-to-date evaluation methodology.

---

[12]*Ibid*, p. 500.

***Conducting a*** Marketing audits are probably as diverse as the people who con-
***Marketing Audit*** duct them. Some auditors follow only informal procedures. Others
have formulated elaborate checklists, questionnaires, profiles, tests,
and related research instruments. According to Philip Kotler, all marketing audits follow four major steps regardless of the tools
employed.

1. Securing agreement between the auditor and the organization
   on the audit's objectives and scope
2. Developing a framework for the audit
   a. Studying the company's external environment
   b. Profiling the major elements of the marketing system
   c. Examining the key marketing activities
3. Preparing an audit report with findings and recommendations
4. Presenting the report in a manner that will lead to action[13]

These steps can be implemented in a variety of ways. Certainly
some basic questions can be raised under each topic, and they must
be answered if a proper audit is to be made. For instance, during
the initial stage, the auditor and the organization should agree on
the goals to be achieved by the audit, the audit's coverage and depth,
and the provision of data sources for the audit. Similar vital questions can be raised during each of the other stages of the marketing
audit.

The real value of a marketing audit may not emerge until considerably after the final report has been prepared and presented. As
Kotler has pointed out:

> The marketing audit can function as a catalyst to start management
> discussion as to where the company should be going. The final
> actions taken may vary from those recommended, but the audit has
> served its purpose in starting the needed dialogue about the
> company's marketing strategy.[14]

Such an audit can make a significant contribution to improved
marketing productivity in virtually all organizations. The starting
point, as noted earlier, is to stop beheading the Persian Messenger.

***An Audit of Marketing*** Philip Kotler has devised a checklist to measure marketing
***Effectiveness*** effectiveness. This audit is based on five variables: consumer
philosophy, integrated marketing organization, adequate market-

---

13 This section is adapted from an address by Philip Kotler to the Chicago chapter
of the American Marketing Association. Reported in "Kotler Presents Whys,
Hows of Marketing Audits for Firms, Nonprofit Organizations," *Marketing
News* (March 26, 1976), p. 21.
14 *Ibid.*, p. 21.

ing information, strategic orientation, and operational efficienc
These activities are defined as follows.[15]

1. *Customer philosophy:* Does management acknowledge the pr
   macy of the marketplace and of customer needs and wants i
   shaping company plans and operations?
2. *Integrated marketing organization:* Is the organization staffe
   so that it will be able to carry out marketing analysis, plannin
   and implementation and control?
3. *Adequate marketing information:* Does management receive tl
   kind and quality of information needed to conduct effectiv
   marketing?
4. *Strategic orientation:* Does marketing management generate i
   novative strategies and plans for long-run growth and profi
   ability?
5. *Operational efficiency:* Are marketing plans implemented in
   cost-effective manner, and are the results monitored for rap
   corrective action?

Figure 25-11 presents a suggested marketing effectiveness aud
and a scoring system for assessing overall effectiveness.

---

**Figure 25-11   The Marketing Effectiveness Audit**

**Customer philosophy**

---

*Score* A. *Does management recognize the importance of designing the company to serve the needs and wants of chosen markets?*

0   ☐   Management primarily thinks in terms of selling current and new products to whoever will buy them.

1   ☐   Management thinks in terms of serving a wide range of markets and needs with equal effectiveness.

2   ☐   Management thinks in terms of serving the needs and wants of well-defined markets chosen for their long-run growth and profit potential for the company.

B. *Does management develop different offerings and marketing plans for different segments of the market?*

0   ☐   No.

1   ☐   Somewhat.

2   ☐   To a good extent.

C. *Does management take a whole marketing system view (suppliers, channels, competitors, customers, environment) in planning its business?*

0   ☐   No. Management concentrates on selling and servicing its immediate customers.

1   ☐   Somewhat. Management takes a long view of its channels although the bulk of its effort goes to selling and servicing the immediate customers.

2   ☐   Yes. Management takes a whole marketing systems view, recognizing the threats and opportunities created for the company by changes in any part of the system.

---

*Figure 25-11 continued*

## Integrated marketing organization

**D. Is there high-level marketing integration and control of the major marketing functions?**

☐   No. Sales and other marketing functions are not integrated at the top and there is some unproductive conflict.

☐   Somewhat. There is formal integration and control of the major marketing functions but less than satisfactory co-ordination and cooperation.

☐   Yes. The major marketing funtions are effectively integrated.

**E. Does marketing management work well with management in research, manufacturing, purchasing, physical distribution, and finance?**

☐   No. There are complaints that marketing is unreasonable in the demands and costs it places on other departments.

☐   Somewhat. The relations are amicable although each department pretty much acts to serve its own power interests.

☐   Yes. The departments co-operate effectively and resolve issues in the best interest of the company as a whole.

**F. How well-organized is the new-product development process?**

☐   The system is ill-defined and poorly handled.

☐   The system formally exists but lacks sophistication.

☐   The system is well-structured and professionally staffed.

## Adequate marketing information

**G. When were the latest marketing research studies of customers, buying influences, channels, and competitors conducted?**

0   ☐   Several years ago.

1   ☐   A few years ago.

2   ☐   Recently.

**H. How well does management know the sales potential and profitability of different market segments, customers, territories, products, channels and order sizes?**

0   ☐   Not at all.

1   ☐   Somewhat.

2   ☐   Very well.

**I. What effort is expended to measure the cost-effectiveness of different marketing expenditures?**

0   ☐   Little or no effort.

1   ☐   Some effort.

2   ☐   Substantial effort.

## Strategic orientation

**J. What is the extent of formal marketing planning?**

0   ☐   Management does little or no formal marketing planning.

1   ☐   Management develops an annual marketing plan.

2   ☐   Management develops a detailed annual marketing plan and a careful long-range plan that is updated annually.

**K. What is the quality of the current marketing strategy?**

0   ☐   The current strategy is not clear.

1   ☐   The current strategy is clear and represents a continuation of traditional strategy.

2   ☐   The current strategy is clear, innovative, data-based, and well-reasoned.

**L. What is the extent of contingency thinking and planning?**

0   ☐   Management does little or no contingency thinking.

1   ☐   Management does some contingency thinking, although little formal contingency planning.

2   ☐   Management formally identifies the most important contingencies and develops contingency plans.

*Figure 25-11 continued*

### Operational efficiency

*M. How well is the marketing thinking at the top communicated and implemented down the line?*

0 ☐  Poorly.
1 ☐  Fairly well.
2 ☐  Successfully.

*N. Is management doing an effective job with the marketing resources?*

0 ☐  No. The marketing resources are inadequate for the job to be done.
1 ☐  Somewhat. The marketing resources are adequate, but they are not employed optimally.
2 ☐  Yes. The marketing resources are adequate and are deployed efficiently.

*O. Does management show a good capacity to react quickly and effectively to on-the-spot developments?*

0 ☐  No. Sales and market information is not very current and management reaction time is slow.
1 ☐  Somewhat. Management receives fairly up-to-date sales and market information; management reaction time varies.
2 ☐  Yes. Management has installed systems yielding highly current information and fast reaction time.

### Total score

*Rating marketing effectiveness*
The auditing outline can be used in this way. The auditor collects information as it bears on the 15 questions. The appropriate answer is checked for each question. The scores are added — the total will be somewhere between 0 and 30. The following scale shows the equivalent in marketing effectiveness:

| | |
|---|---|
| 0–5 | None |
| 6–10 | Poor |
| 11–15 | Fair |
| 16–20 | Good |
| 21–25 | Very good |
| 26–30 | Superior |

To illustrate, 15 senior managers in a large building materials company were recently invited to rate their company using the auditing instrument in this exhibit. The resulting overall marketing effectiveness scores ranged from a low of 6 to a high of 15. The median score was 11, with three-fourths of the scores between 9 and 13. Therefore, most of the managers thought their company was at best "fair" at marketing.

Several divisions were also rated. Their median scores ranged from a low of 3 to a high of 19. The higher scoring divisions tended to have higher profitability. However, some of the lower scoring divisions were also profitable. An examination of the latter showed that these divisions were in industries where their competition also operated at a low level of marketing effectiveness. The managers feared that these divisions would be vulnerable as soon as competition began to learn to market more successfully.

An interesting question to speculate on is the distribution of median marketing effectiveness scores for *Fortune* "500" companies. My suspicion is that very few companies in that roster would score above 20 ("very good" or "superior") in marketing effectiveness.

Source: Reprinted with permission from Philip Kotler, "From Sales Obsession to Marketing Effectiveness," *Harvard Business Review* (November-December 1977), pp. 70–71. Copyright © 1977 by the President and Fellows of Harvard College; all rights reserved.

**Summary**   The control process is an important part of marketing. Evaluation and control refers to all the various assessments that marketers employ to determine whether the marketing opportunity analysis, the objectives and the standards set during the marketing planning phase, and/or the implementation of the marketing program itself have been effective. Evaluation and control permits marketers to determine whether corrective actions are needed. Control charts are sometimes used to set both upper and lower control limits for such assessments.

Several techniques or procedures are useful in measuring marketing performances. Sales analysis is an in-depth evaluation of a firm's sales designed to obtain meaningful information from existing data. Marketing cost analysis is the evaluation of such items as selling costs, billing, warehousing, advertising, and delivery expenses in order to determine the profitability of particular customers, territories, or product lines. ROI is a quantitative tool that seeks to relate the activity or project's profitability to its required investment. Also, the calculation of various ratios helps in analysing specific aspects of marketing performance. The marketing audit, which entails a thorough study of a firm's marketing program, is extremely useful in improving overall effectiveness.

**Key Terms**

evaluation and control
control chart
sales analysis
sales quota
iceberg principle
marketing cost analysis
functional accounts
natural accounts

return on investment (ROI)
profit centre
gross margin percentage
ratio of net income to sales
selling expense ratio
operating expense ratio
marketing audit

**Review Questions**

1. Explain the steps in the marketing evaluation and control process.
2. Explain the role of sales quotas in sales analysis.
3. Compare sales analysis and marketing cost analysis.
4. Distinguish between functional accounts and natural acco⸱⸱
5. Identify the primary benefits of return on investm⸱⸱ evaluation and control. What are the maj⸱⸱
6. Identify and briefly explain the major ra⸱ evaluation and control.
7. How would a marketer decide whether the firm are satisfactory?

8. Compare the marketing audit with the typical control system in an organization.
9. Who should conduct the marketing audit?
10. Identify the major steps in a marketing audit.

---

**Discussion Questions and Exercises**

1. If Great Lakes Enterprises had a gross margin of $4 million on net sales of $9 million, what is its gross margin percentage?
2. What is the net profit percentage for a store with a net income of $72 000 on net sales of $900 000?
3. El Paso Industries had total selling expenses of $85 000. The firm's net sales were $440 000. What was the selling expense ratio for El Paso Industries?
4. Bridgeport Standard ($4 million in net sales) had total expenses of $1.6 million. What was the firm's operating expense ratio?
5. A marketing vice-president is considering a new product idea. The firm estimates that a $600 000 investment will be required. The company expects to achieve sales of $3 million with a net profit of $300 000. What is the proposed project's ROI?
6. Outline the probable steps in a marketing audit for a food supermarket. Which would be the most difficult to implement?
7. Develop an evaluation and control system for a dry cleaning firm.

---

**MICROCOMPUTER EXERCISE: Sales Analysis**

Sales analysis — the in-depth evaluation of a firm's sales — uses existing internal data like invoices, purchase orders, and sales-representative reports. It is an invaluable tool in the evaluation and control of a marketing effort (see also Chapter 5).

Directions: Use the Menu Item titled "Sales Analysis" on the Foundations of Marketing disk to solve the following problems.

**1.** Ludlow Industries of Camrose, Alberta organizes its sales force into Eastern, Western, and Headquarter regions. The average salaries in these regions are $36 000, $32 000, and $40 000, respectively. The Eastern Region sales personnel average $660 000 in sales; the Western Region, $600 000; and the Headquarter Region, $750 000. Selling expenses average $20 000 in all regions. Calculate the cost/sales ratios for the three regions.

**2.** The Atlantic division of a major manufacturer is staffed with five sales representatives. All are assigned annual sales quotas of $500 000. Marie Poulet, the division manager, is preparing an analysis of how her people did in 1987. The actual sales results are shown on page 723:

| Adams-Jones | $575 000 |
| Brooks | $550 000 |
| Douglas | $525 000 |
| Morris | $475 000 |
| Peralta | $500 000 |

**a.** Calculate the performance-to-quota ratio for each of the sales representatives in the Atlantic division.

**b.** What is the overall performance-to-quota ratio for the division?

---

***MICROCOMPUTER***
***EXERCISE:***
***Ratio Analysis***

Four major analytical ratios are gross margin percentage; net profit percentage; selling expense ratio; and operating expense ratio. The gross margin percentage is the ratio of gross margin to net sales. Net profit percentage is the ratio of net profit to net sales. The selling expense ratio shows the relationship between sales expenses and total net sales. And the operating expense ratio equals total expenses divided by net sales.

Directions: Use Menu titled "Ratio Analysis" on the Foundations of Marketing disk to solve the following problems.

**1.** If Sudbury Enterprises had a gross margin of $4 million on net sales of $9 million, what is its gross margin percentage?

**2.** What is the net profit percentage for a store with a net income of $72 000 on net sales of $900 000?

**3.** Kamloops Enterprises had total selling expenses of $85 000. The firm's net sales were $440 000. What was the selling ratio for Kamloops Enterprises?

**4.** Federated Enterprises ($4 million in net sales) had total expenses of $1.6 million. What was the firm's operating expense ratio?

# APPENDIX D

# *Careers in Marketing*

The more one knows about business, careers, and employment trends when entering the labour force, the better. Business administration is now one of the most popular programs for university and college students, and completion of one or more marketing courses is a good step toward preparing for the job marketplace.

The marketing of goods and services plays a vital role in our economy. Occupations necessary to get the marketing tasks done constitute a significant and interesting aspect of the overall employment picture. This appendix discusses marketing careers, emphasizing 1) the kinds of positions available, with brief descriptions of the responsibilities attached to each; 2) the necessary academic and other preparation for marketing employment; and 3) marketing employment trends and opportunities.

## Extensive and Varied Career Opportunities

This text has examined the great extent and diversity of the components of the marketing function. The types of marketing occupations required to perform these tasks are just as numerous and diverse. Indeed, with the growth of our industrial society, marketing occupations too have become more complex and specialized. The student intending to pursue a marketing career may be bewildered at the range of employment opportunities in marketing. How does one find one's way through the maze of marketing occupations and concentrate on those possibilities that most match one's interests and talents? Gaining a knowledge of the different positions and the duties required of each is a convenient starting point.

Marketing personnel are described as either sales-force personnel or marketing-staff personnel. Marketing-staff personnel include persons employed in such service and staff functions as advertising, product planning, marketing research, public relations, purchasing, and distribution management. The precise nature of their responsibilities and duties varies from organization to organization and industry to industry. Marketing tasks may be undertaken in-house by the company marketing personnel, or they may be subcontracted to outside sources. Indeed, there is a whole host of agencies available to support the in-house marketing effort. Among them are advertising agencies, public relations firms, and marketing research agencies. Marketing employment is found in a variety of organizations — manufacturing firms, nonprofit organizations such as art galleries, distributive enterprises such as retailers and wholesalers, service suppliers, and advertising and research agencies.

All these organizations have managerial marketing positions. The specific management duties vary with the size of the organization, the nature of its business, and the extent to which marketing operations are departmentalized or centralized. Marketing management jobs generally require the individual to formulate and to assist in the formulation of the organization's marketing policies and to plan, organize, co-ordinate, and control marketing operations and resources. Some of the typical management positions (actual titles or designations may differ) and descriptions of their responsibilities follow.

Source: Universal Press Syndicate.

**The Chief Marketing Executive**   The person who oversees all the marketing activities and is ultimately responsible for the success of the marketing function is the chief marketing executive. All other marketing executives report through channels to this person.

**The Product Manager**   The person in charge of marketing operations for a particular type of product — such as clothing, building materials, or appliances — is the product manager. This person also assumes responsibilities for some or all of the functions described as falling under the chief executive's authority, but only insofar as they pertain to particular products.

**The Brand Manager**   The brand manager has a position similar to the product manager but only with regard to a specific brand. Sometimes the two position titles are used interchangeably.

**The Marketing Research Director**

The marketing research director determines the marketing research needs of the organization, and plans and directs various stages of the marketing research projects: the formulation of the problem, research design, data collection, analysis, and interpretation of results. On the basis of these studies, the director also helps formulate marketing strategies for the organization.

**The Sales Manager**

The sales manager is responsible for managing the sales force. Some of the sales manager's specific duties include establishing sales territories, deploying the sales force, recruiting and hiring the sales force, sales training, and setting sales quotas.

**The Advertising Manager**

The advertising manager plans and arranges for the promotion of the company's products or services. Particular duties encompass formulating advertising policy, selecting advertising agencies, evaluating creative promotional ideas, and setting the advertising budget.

**The Public Relations Officer**

The public relations officer directs all activities required to project and maintain a favourable image for the organization. These may include arranging press conferences, exhibitions, news releases, and the like. Some firms divide the duties of the public relations officer between a customer or consumer affairs officer and a press information officer.

**The Purchasing or Procurement Manager**

The purchasing manager is in control of all purchasing and procurement activities pertaining to the acquisition of merchandise, equipment, and materials for the organization.

**The Retail Buyer**

The retail buyer is responsible for the purchase of merchandise from various sources — like manufacturers, wholesalers, and importers — for resale through retail outlets. Often the buyer also plans and manages the retail selling activities of a department.

**The Wholesale Buyer**

The wholesale buyer buys products from manufacturers, importers, and others for resale through wholesale outlets. Duties are similar to those for the retail buyer but within the specific context of wholesale distribution.

**The Physical Distribution Manager**

All the varied activities of the physical distribution function — transportation, warehousing, inventory control, and so forth — are co-ordinated by the physical distribution manager. The trend for companies to consolidate physical distribution activities under a single managerial hierarchy has resulted in a significant increase in the importance of the position.

The discussion thus far has placed the spotlight on the upper management level. Depending on the company size, there may be several levels of management under any of the categories described above. Also, for every management position, there are several other marketing occupations that involve personnel in the "doing" of the specific tasks that are supervised and controlled by the managers. The exact number of these personnel varies considerably from organization to organization. In the area of marketing research, for instance, employees are engaged in field work, information collection, editing, coding, tabulation, and other statistical analyses of the data.

In advertising, the advertising copywriter gathers information on the products and customers or likely customers, and then writes copy — creating headlines, slogans, and text for the advertisements; the media planner is more often than not a time and space buyer, specializing in determining which advertising media will be most effective; the advertising layout person decides the exact layout of illustrations and copy that make up the finished advertisement.

The majority of people in marketing work in sales. Sales representatives are engaged at the manufacturing, wholesale, or retail level. Their job descriptions vary somewhat with the type of product being sold and the level of distribution being serviced. Sales positions are a common entry point for people desiring promotion to marketing management positions.

## Preparing for a Career in Marketing

What are the educational or other requirements necessary to obtain a marketing job? What are the typical positions in which one might commence a marketing career? What are the usual patterns of progression to a top spot in the marketing function?

Top-ranking executives in the Canadian marketing field state that education and experience are important criteria in corporate hiring for marketing positions. Most large firms now prefer candidates with a college education, and express particular interest in the graduate who holds a degree in business administration or a bachelor of commerce degree with a minor in marketing. Also, community college graduates in business and marketing have an advantage in gaining a position in the marketing field. But business education is not enough. Business graduates must also be well-rounded individuals with good communications skills and an understanding of their society and culture such as may be gained through a knowledge of literature, history, and other more general subjects. This will enable them to be more effective in the long run.

Although companies strongly suggest that academic preparation is significant, any experience the marketing student has or can acquire in the business or specific marketing fields is a decided benefit in launching a career in marketing. But firms also rely on company training programs to equip the individual with a knowledge of the company's products and policies. The entry point for a marketing career is not as clear-cut as for some other business positions. This is partly because marketers do not have to "article" as do many accountants. It is also because there is such a wide variety of marketing positions. This lack of specificity is sometimes confusing. However, virtually all graduates quickly find themselves in challenging and interesting roles. One common starting point is in sales, but movement into marketing staff and managerial positions is common. Moreover, top marketing executive positions can be reached at relatively young age.

## The Marketing Employment Outlook

Canada Employment and Immigration furnishes some data on employment on different occupations. However, with few exceptions, marketing staff positions are not detailed separately but rather are grouped within an overall administrative category.

Experience indicates, however, that the demand for individuals in the categories we have listed is relatively steady, and is a function of the growth and turnover in business in general. There does appear to be an increasing demand for people in marketing research. Furthermore, it is our opinion that there is a small but growing desire on the part of advertising agencies to hire university graduates with marketing training. More and more nonprofit organizations are looking for marketing people as well.

As we have mentioned, a very large entry point for many marketing positions is sales. Many firms wish future managers to have some sales experience. University graduates starting in sales normally find these positions much more interesting and challenging than they had imagined.

## Salaries in the Marketing Profession

Figure D-1 shows the range of salaries of eight middle-management positions on a national basis in Canada. It can be seen that marketing and sales positions compare favourably with other functions. (The graph shows the top end of the salary range for each percentage group; thus 50 percent of top marketing personnel earn $50 000 or less, and 25 percent earn between $50 000 and $61 000.)

Figure D-2 shows the compensation ranges for various top marketing and sales positions. These data illustrate the earnings potential in marketing careers. From the student's viewpoint, starting salary ranges can be estimated from looking at the lower ranges in Figures D-1 and D-2.

Figure D-1    Range of Salaries of Middle Management Positions

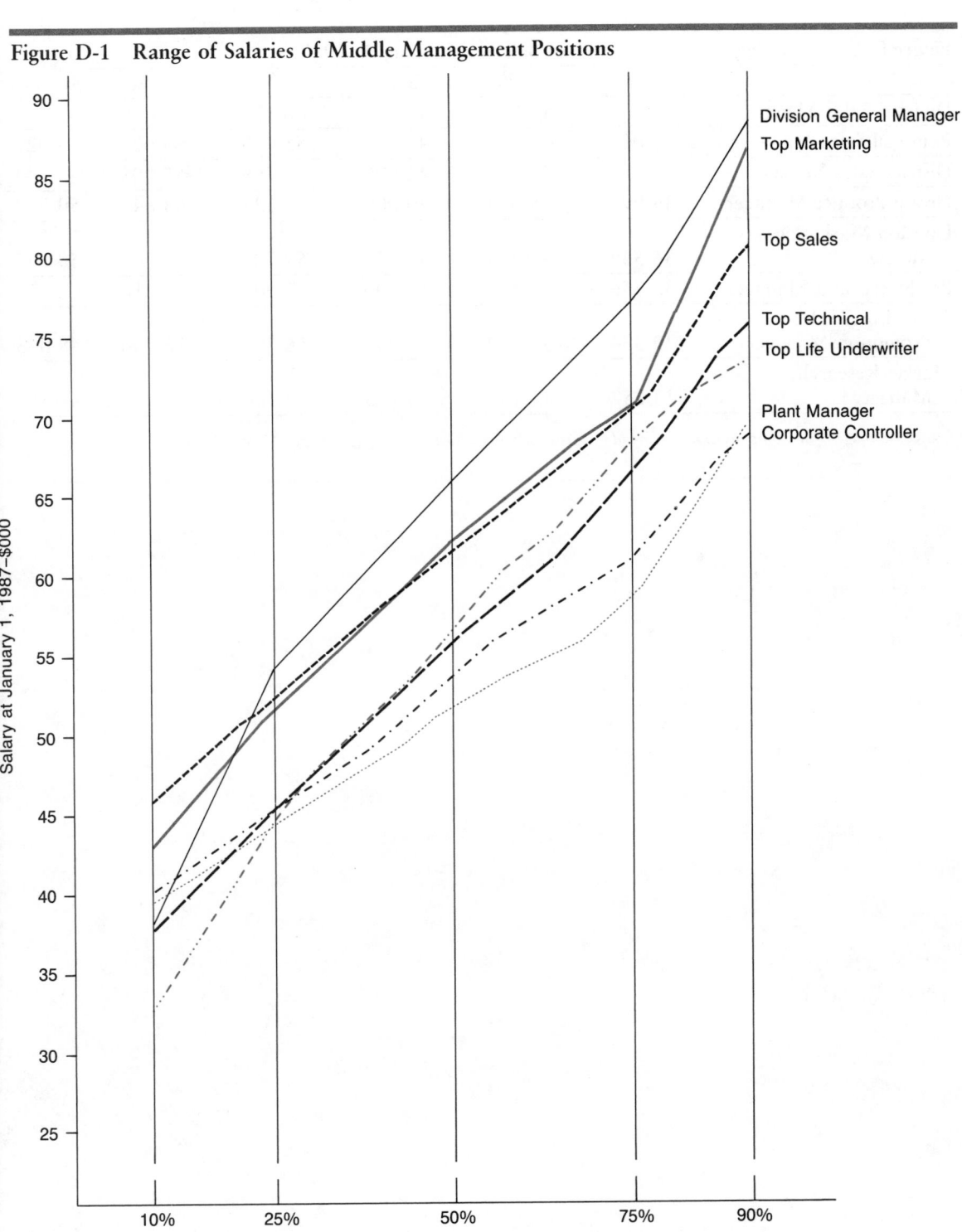

## Figure D-2    Marketing Positions: Range of Salaries, January 1, 1987

|                                   | 10%    | 25%    | 50%    | 75%    | 90%    | Average |
|-----------------------------------|--------|--------|--------|--------|--------|---------|
| Division Sales Manager            | 32 350 | 41 062 | 51 060 | 60 178 | 70 000 | 51 711  |
| Regional Sales Manager            | 36 000 | 41 496 | 47 550 | 55 000 | 63 000 | 49 027  |
| District Sales Manager            | 31 350 | 36 993 | 42 000 | 49 799 | 55 008 | 43 144  |
| Group Product Manager             | 36 996 | 45 024 | 50 000 | 57 125 | 63 647 | 50 952  |
| Division Marketing<br>Manager     | 36 569 | 41 875 | 48 350 | 59 700 | 67 700 | 50 357  |
| Product/Brand Manager             | 32 856 | 37 475 | 41 800 | 47 900 | 51 210 | 42 475  |
| Advertising/Sales<br>Promotion Manager | 29 384 | 37 500 | 45 250 | 56 791 | 72 200 | 48 043  |
| Market Research<br>Manager        | 33 752 | 43 150 | 50 775 | 59 100 | 61 335 | 49 582  |

Source: *Management Compensation in Canada* (Toronto: Sobeco Group Inc., 1987), pp. 47 and 91–132.

# C A S E S

Certalab
*The Left-Handed Market*
*Gillette*
*Worthington Foods*
*Robitussin*
*Sports Equipment Limited*
*Pricing a Sockeye Salmon*
*Holt Renfrew and Co. Ltd.*
*Detyzco, Inc.*
*Active Detergent*
*SPACEMAX*
*Coffeesavr*
*Porta-Broil*
*Jefferson Spark Plug Co. Ltd.*
*Different Strokes*
*Star Electronics*
*Energuide*
*Duradent 1-2-3*
*Leduc Manufacturing*
*Moose Poop*
*Federated Chemicals Ltd.*
*Computron Inc.*
*Time Unlimited Inc.*
*Lucas Foods*
*Tootsizer, Canada*
*Southern Cross, Pty. Ltd.*
*Lime Light Cinema*
*Midland Tools, Ltd.*
*CJUM FM*
*Aylmer Fair*
*Diagnostic Chemicals*

## A Note on the Case Method

What is a case? It is a description of a specific situation or incident, which usually requires a decision. It normally includes more than the bare facts of the situation. Varied opinions of individuals involved in the case and background information to which the real decision-maker in the case might have access are also provided.

A case puts you in the role of the decision-maker. Solving a case is like working with the problems that people in actual business situations encounter.

In some ways, the case method of learning is more difficult than the lecture method. Instead of casting the facts into some suitable semipermanent pedagogical order, the instructor assumes the difficult task of helping students meet new and different problems. The instructor's task becomes one of fostering a facility for approaching and handling new and unstructured situations. The students often find initial difficulties:

Instead of beginning with . . . textbook . . . principles . . . the student is given a pedestrian description of how the Ward Machine Company put a mechanical shaver on the market.

The initial atmosphere of the classroom does little to restore a feeling of certainty. The behavior of the professor is strangely disconcerting. There is an absence of professorial dicta, a surprising lack of "answers" and "cold dope" which the student can record in his notebook; rather he is asked what *he* thinks, what *he* would do, what problems *he* feels are important.[1]

Despite these difficulties, experience indicates some strong arguments in favour of the case method.

First, it challenges you to use and develop your own insight and knowledge in a realistic situation.[2] Second, as you genuinely apply yourself to the analysis of cases, you will develop abilities to deal successfully with new management problems as they occur in the business world. Thus, your transition from the world of formal education will be easier. Third, the case method gives you an opportunity to experiment with various ways of using your knowledge of the basic principles of the field you are studying.[3]

## Preparing a Case

Preparation of a case requires some diligence. It is not enough to skim the case once or twice and then come to class and "shoot from the hip" (or lip), or write down the first solution that comes to mind. Rather, the solution is a progressive process through a methodical and systematic analysis that provides great challenge and interest.

You should read the case several times, starting first with a quick skim to get the overall feel of the situation. Then read it again in more detail as you learn more facts and begin to think about the various aspects of the case. There are several possible approaches to successful case analysis. One alternative is presented below. Use it, but do not try to follow every point slavishly. You are not being asked to "fill in the blanks," but to intelligently analyse the case, fully using your own judgment and analytical skills.

This note is based on M. Dale Beckman, "Evaluating the Case Method," *The Educational Forum* (May 1972), pp. 489–497.

[1] Donald R. Scheen and Philip A. Sprague, "What is the Case Method?" in Malcolm P. McNair (ed.), *The Case Method at the Harvard Business School* (New York: McGraw-Hill, 1954), p. 78.
[2] Charles I. Gragg, "Because Wisdom Can't Be Told," in Malcolm P. McNair, ed. *The Case Method at the Harvard Business School* (New York: McGraw-Hill, 1954), pp. 2–7.
[3] John T. Gullahorn, "Teaching by the Case Method," *School Review* (January 1959), pp. 448–60.

## Suggestions for Development of Case Solutions

A. The development of a case solution should be organized into five parts.
  I. Summary of Important Facts
  II. Problem
  III. Analysis
  IV. Conclusion
  V. Recommendations

B. *Summary of Important Facts*   There are two possible methods of making this summary. You should probably use the first method until you have developed some competence in logically outlining the facts in a case. Then the briefer summary (described in number 2 below) will suffice. The alternative methods are as follows:

1. Outline in logical order the important facts given in the case.
   a. Do not merely list miscellaneous facts in the order given in the case.
   b. Organize your outline in logical fashion under a few main headings. Possible groupings include: nature of the company and its products; competitive situation; market for the product; channels of distribution; pricing policies; organization of sales department; policies relating to management of salespeople, etc.
2. A concise, one-paragraph summary giving a brief picture of the company and the factors that gave rise to the problem to be solved.

II. *Problem*   Clearly and concisely state the problem that is to be solved.

1. This may be an exact restatement of the problem given at the end of a case, or
2. The problem may be given to you by your instructor, or
3. You may have to use your own powers of discernment in order to pick out the main problem, because it is not stated in so many words.

## III. Analysis

1. This is the crucial segment in the development of a case. You should make a detailed analysis, leading to your decision and recommendations. You should organize it in accordance with the basic issues or factors in the case.
2. In your analysis, it is necessary and important to consider the weakness of your decision. Consider and present arguments on both sides of the major issue involved.
3. Analytical arguments should be based upon the facts of the case, as well as upon logical and clear-cut reasoning.
4. State clearly any assumptions you make, and give your reasons for making them.
5. Where possible, "push your pencil" and make use of the data. Make creative use of all possible information in the case.
6. Use an objective, unemotional approach in your analysis. This does not mean that you may not be persuasive in your methods of presentation. In fact, you may do an effective "selling" job in your presentation. A logical grouping of related points will help, as will full development of each point. Give your analysis depth, as well as breadth; substantiate major points with minor points. Be sure that you cover each point adequately by explanation or evidence.

IV. *Conclusion*   The conclusion should summarize briefly the arguments used in the development of the case analysis. In a written report it is inadequate to simply state that "the arguments above warrant . . . ." It is too much to expect the reader to think back and perhaps reread the report to discover what the arguments were.

V. *Recommendations*   State in point form the course of action you believe to be the most sound solution, based on your exhaustive analysis of all alternative possibilities.

B.  Common difficulties encountered in case analysis:

I.  Students at first have a tendency to repeat the statements in the problem book without reorganizing them and relating them to the problem. Thus the report becomes simply a rehash of the problem. To avoid this the student should keep in mind at all times what the problem is and should constantly think, "What has this to do with the problem?" It is wise also to close the book while writing the report, referring to it only in order to get the accurate facts.

II.  Statements of conclusions may be presented without the reasoning that leads to them. So far as the reader is concerned such statements are simply snap judgments and have no more validity than the flipping of a coin. All statements must be *substantiated* by the evidence. A conclusion may be stated at the beginning or at the end of the evidence, but in either case it is necessary to show how the evidence connects with the conclusion. This is done by the use of connectives — "because," "the reason is," and "it follows that."

III.  It is tempting to neglect to present evidence that is adverse to the conclusion in the report. However, since the report is to lead to executive action, both sides must be considered and carefully weighed one against the other. Here again, the proper use of connectives is helpful.

Such connectives as "notwithstanding," "in spite of," and "be that as it may" indicate that the argument given is subordinate to some other.

IV.  Students often fail to carry through the argument to a logical conclusion. This indicates lazy thinking. The careful reader or listener wonders, "So what?" indicating that the analyst has failed to show the pertinence of some statement to the problem solution.

V.  Do not use generalizations when specific statements can be made. Most material in the problems is specific, and applies to this particular problem. There is no point in making it general and thus weakening the argument.

VI.  Do not use your personal attitude as an argument. Statements such as "I firmly believe" or "It is my considered opinion" are pompous excuses for real arguments.

VII.  Students sometimes come up with the conclusion and recommendation that the firm should do the "best thing under the circumstances." Such a recommendation is simply passing the buck and would indicate to the employer a refusal to take responsibility. The reader or listener wants you to decide, not sit on the fence.

Source: R. H. Evans and M. D. Beckman, *Cases in Marketing: A Canadian Perspective* (Toronto: Prentice-Hall, 1972), pp. xi–xiii.

# Case 1 Certalab

When Ron Schiller confides jokingly that he's "a little crazy," it may explain his willingness to tangle a second time with the multinationals of the toothpaste world. Schiller and his two partners in Certalab are still very confident about their chances to succeed in marketing Pressdent, a liquid toothpaste dispensed similarly to liquid soap.[1]

Once again, Certalab is taking on Procter & Gamble Inc. (Crest), Colgate-Palmolive Canada (Colgate), Lever Bros. Ltd. (Aim, Pepsodent), and Beecham Canada Inc. (Aqua-fresh).

Round one went to the Big Four, who last year commanded 90 to 95 percent of the national toothpaste market of $90 million at retail, according to Lever's marketing manager of personal products, Murray Cressell.

In October, 1981, Schiller and his two partners had given the world it first liquid toothpaste, Pressdent. On January 14, only 15 months later, they were forced to appeal to their 75 trade creditors to settle claims of $579 069 at 25 cents on the dollar.

The trade creditors accepted, giving Pressdent a second chance to lock horns with Crest et al. Schiller says he is convinced his dentifrice will now find a permanent place on the grocery and drugstore shelves of the nation. "That is going to be a winner, with a capital W!" he insists, pointing to a re-designed container of Pressdent.

A 33-year-old chartered accountant, Schiller is president and 47 percent owner of Certalab Inc., whose sole product is Pressdent. His partners are Robert Goulet, 36, who holds 37 percent of Certalab and handles

marketing, and Jacques Laland, 36, the company secretary, who owns the remaining 16 percent. The three, plus a secretary, form the entire full-time staff, with spartan offices in the Montreal Suburb of St-Eustache. Manufacturing is handled by an independent company.

To be able to come back and win a second battle it helps to know where you went wrong the first time. "Of course we know why we failed," Schiller snaps, ticking off, in his rapid-fire style of speech, a series of "failures we could not see."

They were failures that an experienced company would almost certainly have uncovered before venturing into the marketplace. Take the dispenser, for example. Pressdent is sold in a pump-action container, similar to liquid soaps. Unlike them, however, toothpaste contains an abrasive, and — in use — this was found to clog the pump. A stronger spring is said to eliminate the trouble.

A second problem concerned waste. As much as 20 percent of the paste could not be pumped up from the bottom of the bottle. The interior of the container has been slanted, and Schiller says waste is now less than 10 percent.

A third obstacle was the listing fees sought for new products by supermarket chains in Quebec and Ontario. They can cost as much as $20 000 for a single retailer, Schiller maintains, and "you either pay or else they don't buy." (He says there are no such fees at drugstores or mass-merchandisers. In the West, grocers ask instead for special discounts or free goods, "which is a little bit more practical.")

The marketing vice-president of Dominion Stores Ltd. of Toronto, Roger Acton, contends there is no fixed formula governing the fee, which he calls "a performance allow-

---

[1] Adapted from Alan D. Gray, "Pressdent takes on Toothpaste Multinationalism — Again," *Financial Times of Canada*, Jan. 31, 1983, pp. 14 & 15.

ance." Rather it is determined "by the potential sales velocity of the product, and what amount of promotion is required to get that product moving." The money is used to help pay for promotions, such as newspaper ads and price reductions, and for the "appropriate shelf allocation" for a new item, Acton says.

Being new at the game, Certalab didn't know "you have to buy shelf space," Schiller says. "It cost us a lot of money," (he won't say how much) "but we learned." At any event, the fee is a one-time outlay that has already been paid—If Pressdent can keep its hold on grocers' shelves.

As serious as those problems were, two others were even more damaging. One stemmed from the size of the container: 225 mL, usually retailing for $3.69 or 1.64 cents a millilitre. A 150 mL tube of Crest, the industry leader, was recently selling at about $2.45 or 1.63 cents a millilitre.

The cost per millilitre comparison was deceiving, however. By virtue of its novel dispenser Pressdent was in fact cheaper per portion than pastes in tubes. According to the magazine Canadian Consumer, the saving was 20%.

But the savings were lost on the public. "You're fighting the $3 price barrier," Schiller notes. "On account of the economy, people are no longer buying the large sizes, even though they are much more economical." So now Pressdent has switched to a 150 mL size, at $2.69.

The second serious problem was undercapitalization. At the outset the partners raised $250 000 cash and borrowed $300 000 from the National Bank of Canada, secured by such things as term certificates and second mortgages on their houses.

But it wasn't enough, and by December there was a deficit of $750 000, including bank loans. Asked how much the owners have drawn from the business, Schiller replies with a bitter laugh: "Don't rub it in. We haven't drawn salaries for the past four months."

Most of the money—about $700 000—was spent on TV advertising. "Maybe it was a little too much," Schiller suggests.

Others in the trade, however, take the opposite view—that Pressdent's biggest trouble was its inability to sustain its ad program.

Howard Martin, president of the sales agency that handles Pressdent in drug and dry goods stores in Ontario, believes advertising is particularly crucial where a new concept is involved, such as a liquid toothpaste, to "educate the public . . . how economical it is." Says a Big Four competitor: "They pumped a lot of money to get it listed, but once they had to stop promoting it people went back to their old brands."

With its balance sheet restored to a semblance of respectability through its arrangement with creditors, Certalab is talking of spending $250 000 this year in TV advertising in each of Quebec and Ontario, and $150 000 in the West. This is about one-third of first-year sales of $2 million—a high percentage. Schiller estimates the Big Four spent $9 million in advertising in 1982, or about 10 percent of their retail sales.

Where the money will come from, though, is something of a mystery.

Along with new money and a less expensive size, there are other plans to stimulate sales. Already a bubble-gum flavour is on the market, aimed at young tastes. Two new adult flavours are being considered. And with gels capturing an increasing market share for the traditional manufacturers, Pressdent is planning its own entry in that field.

All this, however, may be too late. A new barrier—perhaps the toughest of all—must now be crossed: how to eliminate the sour taste left in the retail trade by the dentifrice's initial failure.

Dominon Stores bought 48 000 bottles in the original 225 mL size, according to Schiller. Dominion's Acton says a number remain on the shelves, and have been marked down to half price. "We're literally losing our shirts on it now because there is no movement," he says.

For Pressdent such markdowns have serious implications. Dominion, clearing the 225 mL size at $1.99 (its original price was $3.99), wonders how it can take on the new, 150 mL format, which has a suggested retail of $2.69. "We are frightened," Acton says, ". . . because we have been burned in the first issue."

Distributor Martin worries: "We did a great job getting the 225 mL into the stores, and there's still a lot of it out there — it just isn't moving."

## Discussion Questions

1. Explain the implications of the mistakes listed by Certalab management. Were these their major problems?
2. Should Certalab have been able to foresee these mistakes? Explain.
3. Has the company now taken adequate steps to market Pressdent?

# Case 2    The Left-Handed Market

Though most people probably do not think of them as a distinct minority group, left-handers have throughout history faced the same discriminations other minority groups have: social stigmatism, ostracism, even burnings at the stake. Many organizations have been formed to champion the cause of left-handers. One of these has tried to provide its members greater access to products designed specially for them. At the same time the group would like to persuade manufacturers that left-handers are an overlooked segment of the consumer market.

Dean Campbell is chairman and founder of Lefthanders International (LHI). He maintains that about 10 percent of the population (2.5 million people in Canada) use only their left hands for most things, while another 5 percent use their left hands for some things. The 15 percent figure will likely increase if the stigma attached to left-handedness decreases.

While other left-handed organizations exist, none has concerned itself specifically with trying to make more left-handed products — from scissors to golf clubs — available. Though many people don't realize it, even an automobile is designed for right-handers.

Part of the problem is that even when products are available for left-handers they tend to be found only expensively. For example, a power saw, which would normally cost as little as $25.95, when specially designed to be used ambidextrously costs about $225. Pro shops often sell golf clubs for left-handers, but only in the manufacturers' cheapest and most expensive lines. Even then shops seldom keep left-handed models in stock, so that potential buyers cannot try them out before buying, the way right-handers always can.

Companies that do manufacture left-handed products seldom market them seriously. Campbell tried to fill the gap by printing a catalogue of about 80 products for left-handers, including an iron, playing cards, scissors, and even coffee mugs designed so that their messages face the left-handed drinker.

Campbell insists that the group's main goal is to make manufacturers more aware of the left-handed market, hoping they will then produce more merchandise for it and actually

Source: Adapted from Kevin T. Higgins, "Southpaws Left Out by Marketers," *Marketing News* (August 10, 1985), p. 6.

market the merchandise so that left-handers can find it.

1. Relate the case to each of the steps of the market-segmentation process shown in Figure 5-2.

2. What types of products could be offered to this market segment? How would you suggest that they be advertised? Distributed?

3. Identify ways in which this market is currently being serviced.

4. Which type(s) of market segmentation should prove most effective in reaching this market? Defend your answer.

# Case 3   Gillette

When many people think of marketing they automatically think in terms of the Western world market. But one company—Gillette—has tailored a good deal of its marketing to Third World countries. More than half of all Gillette's sales come from abroad. The company's investment in the Third World has paid off. Since 1969 the proportion of its total sales coming from Africa, Asia, Latin America, and the Middle East has doubled and the dollar volume has increased sevenfold. In that year Gillette first allowed subsidiaries in which the company did not have 100 percent ownership to use their trademarks—the Gillette and Papermate names. The policy was changed largely because Gillette realized it lost precious advertising, for example, on stadium walls when it sponsored televised World Cup soccer matches. And since 1969 the company has built one foreign plant a year in countries such as China, Thailand, Egypt, and India.

In developing countries Gillette first opens a plant that produces razor blades—usually double-edged, which are still popular in the Third World. If these sell well, the company later introduces its shampoos, toothbrushes, pens, and deodorants. Gillette has also introduced products specially designed for Third World consumers, such as Black Silk, a hair relaxer developed for blacks in South Africa and Kenya. But despite Gillette's efforts to diversify its product line, the company's razor

blades still provide a third of its revenue and two-thirds of its pretax profit.

Often Gillette sells its regular line of products but packages them differently, mostly because of the financial condition of Third World consumers. For instance, in Latin America Gillette sells Silkience shampoo in half-ounce plastic bubbles because consumers there cannot afford seven-ounce bottles. In Mexico Gillette markets plastic tubs of shaving cream that sell for half the price of the same product sold in North America in aerosol cans. Similarly, in Brazil Gillette sells deodorant in plastic squeeze bottles because they are cheaper than aerosols.

The more complicated problem is to convince Third World men who might not do so otherwise to shave regularly. Gillette sends portable theatres to villages to show movies and commercials that promote daily shaving. In one, made for a Mexican market, a handsome sheriff chases bandits who have kidnapped a woman. The sheriff stops to shave every day on the trail. He gets the woman. At such demonstrations, or in actual shaving demonstrations, free razors are then given to men. The razor blades, of course, must be bought from store owners.

While these tactics may not gain large

Source: David Wessel, "Gillette Keys Sales to Third World Tastes," *The Wall Street Journal* (January 23, 1986), p. 35.

numbers of converts immediately, the increasing migration of peasants to cities may. In the fields peasants have little reason to shave. Working in an office in the city they do.

## Discussion Questions

1. Why, in your opinion, do Gillette marketers choose to develop a specific marketing strategy for different international markets?

What are the disadvantages of a tailored approach such as that used by Gillette?

2. Recommend methods by which Gillette marketers might use the opinion-leader concept in their international marketing efforts.

3. Is reference-group influence important in the purchase of Gillette products? Defend your answer.

# Case 4   Worthington Foods

Worthington Foods, Inc., a subsidiary of Miles Laboratories, stands as a pioneer and leader in the field of researching and test-marketing vegetable protein meatless meats known as meat analogues. These various analogues closely simulate the taste, texture, and appearance of nearly every meat product now available. A prime market for meat analogues is the institutional field. With the costs of meat soaring, the popularity and acceptance of this economical alternative source of protein are growing in nursing homes, hospitals, schools, and other institutions across the nation.

Worthington Foods was first organized in 1939 under the name Special Foods, Inc., by a group of Seventh-Day Adventist business and professional people to meet the vegetarian needs of their religious group. In 1945 the company was incorporated under the name Worthington Foods, Inc., and in 1970 it merged with and became a subsidiary of Miles Laboratories.

## Product Development

Worthington products are developed primarily from soy and wheat protein. The basic raw ingredients are combined with flavourings, binders (high-protein egg whites), and emulsifiers to produce the meat analogues. They are

strikingly similar in taste, texture, and appearance to beef, pork, and poultry products. No meat, meat derivatives, or preservatives are used in any of these foods.

Although Worthington began manufacturing vegetable protein foods in 1939, the revolution in textured protein products did not come about until 1957. At that time Robert Boyer developed the process that enabled protein from soybeans to be spun into a fibre. Worthington's food technologists could now develop foods that approximated much more closely the fibrous texture of animal protein. With the Boyer process a solution of soy protein isolate is pumped through metal spinnerettes containing thousands of tiny holes, each about 0.1 mm in diameter, and into a bath that causes the extruded solution to coagulate into threadlike fibres. At this point the filaments are essentially colourless, tasteless, and odourless. This bland high-protein substance is then turned into a variety of different foods, first by adding flavours, colours, nutrients, and other ingredients, and then by cutting, cooking, and shaping to produce the final product.

Source: *Contemporary Cases in Marketing* by W. Wayne Talarzyk. Copyright © 1974 by The Dryden Press, a division of Holt, Rinehart and Winston. Adapted by permission of Holt, Rinehart and Winston.

## Product Offerings

Today Worthington offers more than 40 alternative products of meatless versions of ham, beef, corned beef, chicken, turkey, bacon, and even seafood. They are formulated scientifically to provide good nutritional levels of protein, fat, and carbohydrate. They are lower in total fat (with polyunsaturates predominating) and calories than most of their animal meat counterparts.

Many of the products are fortified with vitamins and minerals in accordance with government recommendations. Product quality is precisely controlled to assure consistent nutrition, flavour, and tenderness. Flavourings are derived primarily from natural plant extract and, in some instances, from imitation flavour enhancers.

The vegetable protein foods are precooked, experience little or no shrinkage when prepared, and have no bones, gristle, or excess fat. The price per edible pound of vegetable protein is usually significantly lower than the cost of most animal protein. Products are proportioned to reduce preparation time and waste, and they have a long shelf life.

Worthington has also diversified somewhat to become a supplier of texturized vegetable proteins to other food processors and manufacturers. Among the items marketed are extenders for meat, chicken, and seafood. With meats, these extenders reduce shrinkage. The red-meat extenders comprise a mixture of spun protein fibres, binders, emulsifiers, red colouring, and, in some instances, an added beef-like flavour. It is economical to use such extenders and formulas for the less expensive and higher-fat meat cuts. The extenders can also nutritionally upgrade hamburger, sausage, and patty formulas.

Chicken-type extenders are a mixtures tailored for addition to chicken meat. Extenders also provide an opportunity to retexturize and nutritionally upgrade chicken and turkey by-products.

## The Industry

According to a study by the Standard Research Institute, the sales volume in the vegetable protein industry will possibly climb to as high as $2 billion in the 1980s. Cornell University researchers predict that by 1985 production of soy protein products will reach 66 million kg and will account for 10 percent of all domestic meat and poultry consumption. Even further in the future, volume is forecasted to reach an annual rate of 1.11 billion kg by the year 2000. Worthington Foods is the pioneer in this field, but General Mills, Archer-Daniels-Midland, Swift and Company, Griffith Laboratories, and A. E. Stanley are also becoming involved in vegetable proteins.

## The Institutional Market

The vegetable proteins are used by institutional markets in two basic ways — to extend meat and seafood proteins or as direct replacements for meats and seafoods. For both of these applications the primary institutional markets are public hospitals, colleges and universities, schools, in-plant feeding operations, prisons, and nursing homes. Meat packers and processors are also important markets for the protein extenders.

A key element in the marketing of vegetable proteins is to take the right approach with the right account. For example, cost savings and palatability are important to all potential users. But institutions, especially schools, are concerned with nutritional benefits and convenient preparation, while meat processors are usually more concerned about government labelling requirements and how the average consumer will react upon discovering that there is soy in his or her hamburger.

## Discussion Questions

1. Discuss and evaluate the relative importance of the purchasing motives of the

various institutional and industrial market segments for vegetable protein products.

2. Review the relationships between personal selling and advertising for this type of product category. What level of emphasis should be placed on personal selling as compared to other promotional efforts?

# Case 5    *Robitussin*

## The Company

A. H. Robins, Inc., has evolved from a small community pharmacy opened 1866 in Richmond, Virginia, by Albert Hartley Robins to a diversified multinational corporation operating in more than 100 countries. The research centre opened in 1963 with more than 325 scientists and technicians engaged in research in many product areas.

The A. H. Robins Company is engaged principally in the manufacture of finished-dosage forms of pharmaceutical products. Finished products are manufactured and packaged from raw materials purchased from suppliers of pharmaceutical grade chemicals. The company's principal products are ethical prescription and over-the-counter drug products which are promoted by field representatives to physicians, dentists, and pharmacists.[1] Some of Robins' best-known brand names are Robitussin, a cough and cold syrup; Donnatal, an antispasmodic drug; and Robaxin, a skeletal muscle relaxant.

Robins' products are distributed to drug wholesalers which sell to retail drug stores and to hospitals. This distribution system has proven successful in the past. But, in the current market, drug-store chains turn over more than half the volume of the industry. If these large chains buy direct from a manufacturer (at a lower price), they give those brands in-store marketing support, such as end aisle displays, extra shelf facings, and co-op advertising.

While maintaining its major position as manufacturer and researcher of Pharmaceuticals, A. H. Robins has diversified into consumer products. In 1963, Robins acquired Morton Manufacturing, the producer of Chap Stick lip balm. In 1967, Robins acquired Polk Miller Products, producers of the Sergeant's line of pet care products. These two companies later formed Miller-Morton Company in an effort to consolidate consumer product activities. Robins enjoyed further success in the consumer goods area with the introduction of Lip Quencher, a lipstick utilizing the moisturizing qualities of Chap Stick. In 1967, it continued its entry into the consumer field with the acquisition of Parfums Caron, a leading producer of French fragrance products. Consumer products are advertised nationally and marketed through department stores, specialty shops and drug outlets.

A. H. Robins entered the international market in the 1960s. Subsidiaries in Australia, Brazil, Canada, Colombia, France,

---

[1] Drug industry practice is to classify products as either "ethical" or "proprietary" depending on the marketing method employed. Ethical products are marketed by promotion directly to the medical profession. The ethical classification is further subdivided into those drugs which require prescription and those which can be purchased without a prescription and are called "over-the-counter" (OTC) drugs. Proprietary products are promoted directly to the consumer.

---

Source: Reprinted by permission of Ian Stewart, A. H. Robins, Inc., and Professors Thomas D. Giese and Thomas J. Cosse, University of Richmond.

Mexico, the Philippines, South Africa, the United Kingdom, Venezuela, and West Germany provided a base for the company's growing international operations. In recent years, 33 percent of net sales and 34 percent earning before tax, interest, and amortization expenses have come from international operations.

## The Product

Robitussin, a cough and cold syrup, is marketed in five forms, one of which is a prescribed form; the other four are over-the-counter forms. The product to date has been marketed only through wholesalers and directly to nonproprietary hospitals. Demand is stimulated by detailers who call on members of the medical profession and "detail" the drug — describing its advantages and features so that physicians may either prescribe or recommend the product.

Promotion is complemented by sampling, trade deals, and trade medical profession journal advertising. However, demand for the product is now static as it has reached the mature state in its present market segment.

The cough syrup market has grown 5 percent in the past year. The largest growth has been in food stores, which now account for 24 percent of total sales and are increasing at a faster rate than sales in drug stores. Most drug-store sales are in the chains and large independents who want to purchase directly from the manufacturer rather than through wholesalers in order to gain greater margins for retail outlets.

While the ethical segment of the cough sytrup market is still increasing slightly in dollar terms, the proprietary brands in food and drug outlets exhibit a healthy 10 percent increase compared with a 2 percent increase for the ethical segment.

In unit terms, the cough syrup market is not growing; but within the segments, food store sales are moving up in importance while drug store units are declining. One study has shown that the average homemaker visits the grocery store about three times a week and the drug store twice a month. In the drug stores the ethical brands are holding their share while proprietary brands are declining.

By way of comparison with other cold-remedy products, the cough syrup market is 12 percent larger than the cold-tablet market and more than three times larger than the nasal-spray market.

Cough syrup preparations differ from most categories of cold products since the heaviest users usually do not purchase their own product because half of them are under eighteen years of age. The prime prospects can be described as follows:

- Female head of household 25–49 years old
- Households with children 2–17 years old and with 5 or more persons
- Household annual income of $20 000 or lower
- Less educated

The breakdown of unit sales by brand is as follows: Robitussin has a 21.6 percent share of unit sales in drugstores compared to Vicks' 16 percent. In food and drugstores combined, Robitussin has an estimated 14 percent share to Vicks' 27 percent. Based on an earlier survey, the leading brands of cough syrup used were Formula 44, doctor's prescription, and Nyquil.

Toward the end of the financial year, as the planning stage for the following year is being finalized, George Mancini, Robitussin's product manager, has noted that over the past several years the line had only been growing in the 1 to 2 percent range in comparison with the 6 to 8 percent growth of the overall cough syrup market. Robitussin is becoming a mature product in its present segment of ethical over-the-counter drugs.

## Discussion Questions

1. Relate this case to the product life-cycle concept.
2. What action should A. H. Robins take with respect to Robitussin?

# Case 6  Sports Equipment Limited

Sports Equipment Limited has been recently formed as a wholly owned subsidiary of General Chemical Co. General Chemical is a major producer of chemicals, plastics, and textiles. In recent years the chief executive officer of General Chemical has been very keen to enter the consumer leisure market. As a major shareholder he has met with little resistance to his ideas. Rather than developing its own manufacturing facilities, General Chemical has, in the past 10 months, been quietly buying companies engaged in manufacturing sporting goods equipment in Canada. Most, but not all of these companies, produced better quality items but had suffered from poor marketing. After reorganization, General Chemical wants each company to operate autonomously in terms of production. Sports Equpment Limited has been given the responsibility of marketing and distributing the products across Canada. All products are manufactured in Ontario and are sent to Sports Equipment's distribution warehousing facilities in Mississauga, Ontario. Sports Equipment is well financed and organized but is unfamiliar with marketing these products. It has no existing sales force.

## Product Line Description

*Racquets — Classique Racquets*  A fairly complete medium-to-high-price line of tennis, squash, and racquet ball racquets, with no products at the low-priced end of the market.

*Backpacking Equipment — Back Country*  A full line of internal and external frame bags, including a line of day packs, specialty packs (bicycle panniers, soft camera packs, racquet sport bags, etc.), expedition-sized packs, and medium-sized packs. All these products are of superior quality and appeal to the more serious backpacker/hiker. They are priced accordingly.

*Nordic Skiing Equipment — Les Skis du Nord*  A limited line of skis, poles, and boots. The skis are available in wood, fibreglass wrap, and foam core, generally targeted toward the mid-price-range buyer with little appeal to the serious or competitive cross country skier.

*Cycling Accessories — Spoke*  A very high-quality line of cycling skirts, moleskin-lined pants, gloves, pannier packs, helmets, pumps, water bottles, etc., aimed at the more serious cycling enthusiast. The line does not include bicycles.

*Freeze-Dried Foods — Nutri-lite*  A very complete line of freeze-dried foods including meats, vegetables, stews, omelettes, desserts, etc., competitively priced with other manufacturers.

*Fishing Lures — Catch-all*  A full line of fishing accessories including lines, lures, hooks, sinkers, tackle boxes, bait buckets, etc., with a very general appeal. The line does not include rods or reels.

*Hiking Boots — Country Stride*  A limited line of hiking boots directed toward the casual hiker and those who purchase the product becuse of current fashion trends. Serious backpackers and hikers tend to purchase better quality boots. In the past six months they have developed a new ultralight hiking boot that has been rated as a good-quality boot at an attractive price by a sports magazine. The ultralight boot market is viewed by experts as the future for hiking boots.

When Alice Navarre, Sports Equipment's marketing manager, examined the sales records

Source: T. Goddard, Conestoga College, Kitchener, Ontario.

for these companies, she felt that inadequate channels of distribution were a major problem. She feels that these channels will most likely vary from region to region and will certainly vary according to the line,although certain product lines may be logically grouped. A multichannel approach may be adopted in order to serve all types of retailer.

She decides that a logical process is to first determine the market segment(s) she is trying to reach and the type and intensity of retail distribution she desires, and then work backwards. Obviously, not all products will be distributed to all regions of Canada. Her preliminary research indicates that many retail

sporting goods stores are becoming more specialized in specific sports and activities.

### Discussion Questions

1. How would you advise Alice Navarre? Examine the advantages and disadvantages of various channels of distribution.
2. What physical distribution system would you expect Sports Equipment to use? Prepare a map showing the location and area covered for all wholesalers, sales brochures, and/or warehouses. (In preparing your answer, use available secondary data from the library or other sources.)

## Case 7    *Pricing a Sockeye Salmon*

Pacific waters are the homes of some delicious sockeye salmon. Assume that the fish sell fresh in Vancouver for about $4.99 per pound. Of this total only about $0.85 goes to the boat that actually caught the fish. Figure C7-1 shows how the retail price is determined.

### Discussion Questions

1. Describe the approach used to price sockeye salmon.
2. Relate this example to the text's discussion of cost-oriented pricing.
3. Microcomputer Exercise: What is the fish retailer's markup percentage on cost?

Figure C7-1

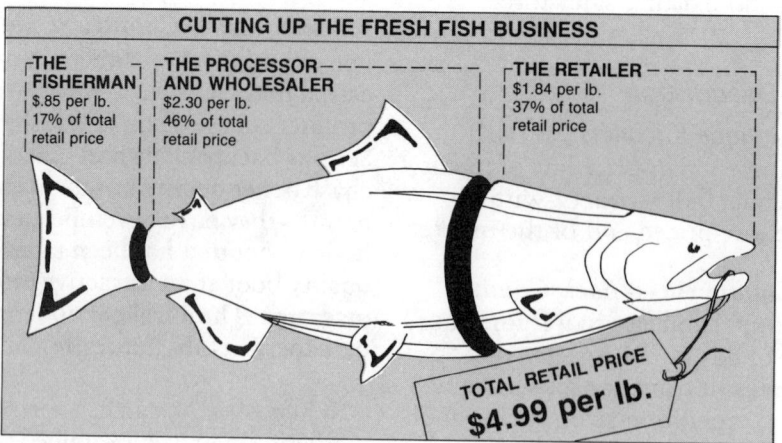

**CUTTING UP THE FRESH FISH BUSINESS**

THE FISHERMAN
$.85 per lb.
17% of total retail price

THE PROCESSOR AND WHOLESALER
$2.30 per lb.
46% of total retail price

THE RETAILER
$1.84 per lb.
37% of total retail price

TOTAL RETAIL PRICE
$4.99 per lb.

Source: Adapted from Steve Bovey, "Upstream Battle," *The Seattle Times* (July 25, 1985), p. D1. Drawing by Robert Massa. Used with permission.

# Case 8   Holt Renfrew and Co. Ltd.

Holt Renfrew and Co. Ltd., the venerable *grande dame* of Canada's retail carriage trade, is expanding its markets beyond its long-established well-heeled clientele.

While Holt is reluctant to relinquish its reputation as a store for the affluent, demographics are creating a rapidly expanding 25-to-45 age bracket which has money to spend and a desire for quality merchandise. The increase in the number of working women has given rise to a large market which Holt wants to tap by providing a wider range of medium-priced merchandise.

Company chairman Lenard Shavick and newly-appointed president Robert Herber hope to double the company's sales within five years. Holt, owned since 1972 by Carter Hawley Hale Stores, Inc., of Los Angeles, keeps its sales and profit figures a closely guarded secret, but Shavick said recently that the five-year sales goal for the company's 18 stores is $100 million. That is about double present volume.

Other merchandisers, from small high-fashion boutiques to major department store chains like The Bay and Eaton's, will be watching Holt's moves closely. If Holt increases its market share it will likely be at the expense of other retailers as the selling environment of the 1980s becomes increasingly competitive.

Attempts to broaden its customer base are only one facet of Holt's new growth strategy. The company has also moved its buying, marketing, and merchandising staff from Montreal to Toronto. Moreover, senior personnel ranks have received an influx of fresh blood, with four of the seven occupants of the executive suite hired from outside the company in the past two years.

Shavick contends the result is a powerful new team. "It's very important to have the stars, and we do now," he declares. Shavick,

who joined the company in 1946 and rose to the position of president and chief executive officer in 1968, has now become the company chairman. Often accused in the past of running a one-man show, he appears to have converted recently to a more flexible team-oriented management style.

Herber, who joined Holt less than a year ago as executive vice-president after eight years with Hudson's Bay Co. and 16 years with Greatermans' Department Stores of South Africa prior to that, is obviously one of Shavick's "stars." Herber will be based in Toronto, while Shavick and the financial, administrative, and personnel departments will remain in Montreal.

"Toronto is the site of our flagship store and the city with the greatest growth opportunities," says an enthusiastic Herber. "We are looking to expand in the west, and Toronto is the logical base. It's a young city, a cosmopolitan city, and it's full of the kind of people who want to shop at Holt's."

The main Toronto store contributed 22 percent of the company's total sales last year while the downtown Montreal store contributed 19 percent. In addition, Holt's studies show the market of households with annual incomes in excess of $40 000 is 39 percent bigger in Toronto than in Montreal. Within three years the spread is expected to reach 45 percent.

A recent company survey in its Ottawa, Vancouver, and Toronto stores found that 75 percent of Holt's shoppers were working, 76 percent had some college or university education, and 60 percent owned their own house or condominium. The median age was

Source: Adapted from "Holts Woos Shoppers From Both Sides Of The Track," *Financial Times*, July 9, 1981.

35 and 85 percent were female. "We are after the market which is well-educated, aware, and prepared to spend money on themselves— the movers and shakers," says Herber.

In broadening its appeal, Holt will concentrate on beefing up merchandise areas such as accessories, women's office wear, and casual clothes for men to augment its suit selection.

But Holt's move to diversify out of an upper-crust market is seen by some observers as a sign that things have not been going as well as they could be in recent years. Specialty boutiques selling exclusive labels are aggressively competing for their share of the high-fashion business, and because of their concentration on a narrower range of merchandise they can often provide greater depth and more personalized service.

To counteract this problem, Holt is experi-menting with a program of clientele development by initiating contact with customers by telephone or letter, letting them know when merchandise in which they are interested has arrived. Sales personnel will also provide the service of keeping a record of customers' sizes and colour and fashion preferences.

"We want to be different from the department stores," says Herber. "Instead of just standing behind a counter and saying 'may I help you?' we want to provide more personalized service."

## Discussion Question

1. Evaluate the plans to respond to the changing competition and the changing demographic profile of the market.

# Case 9   Detyzco, Inc.

"Pet 88 is a nutritionally balanced, frozen dessert for your dog—fortified with vitamins and minerals. Your dog will love it!" are the words used on the package to describe Detyzco's new product aimed at dog lovers. The firm has achieved selected distribution in Southwestern Ontario for its products and would like to attain national market coverage.

## Product Development

About three years ago, Peter DeMarco, a poultry science student working at a pet store, casually asked his employer, "Why isn't there a good nutritional ice cream for dogs?" C. Dale Cook, owner of the Pet Palace, responded that he did not know why, but thought that such an idea might be "just crazy enough to sell." With some interest and mostly curiosity they asked William Tyznik, a recognized animal nutritionist at a local university, about the possibility of such a product.

After many trials and experiments over a period of nine months, Tyznik, working with DeMarco, came up with the basic formula at the laboratory level. Cook, who had formerly worked with a major contract research organization, began to get more involved with the process with the objective of taking the product from the laboratory to the marketplace.

The product was tested and retested on dozens of dogs during most of 1986. It was then necessary to develop the production capability to manufacture and package such a product. In 1987, a patent was sought for the

Source: From *Cases for Analysis in Marketing*, 3rd ed., by W. Wayne Talarzyk, pp. 19–22. Copyright 1985, CBS College Publishing. Reprinted by permission of CBS College Publishing.

roduct and later that year the product was introduced in the market. The three men involved formed Detyzco, a solely owned corporation, to manufacture and market the product. Their joint resources amounted to a modest $75 000.

## roduct Description

et 88 Frozen Dog Dessert is packaged in a x-serving carton. Each individual serving is a four-ounce plastic cup. The product can e served to dogs in its frozen state or thawed n the refrigerator and served as a creamy udding. Additional information about the roduct is provided in Figure C9-1, which hows a handout given to potential customers supermarkets.

## Pricing

The product is currently retail priced at $1.39 per six-pack carton. At this price retailers have a margin of about 25 to 30 percent. Food distributors receive a markup of 15 percent for handling the product from Detyzco to the retailer.

## Promotion

To introduce Pet 88 Frozen Dog Dessert to the market, Detyzco produced a 30-second television advertisement. A brief description of this advertisement is given in Figure C9-2.

A "new business package" consisting of forty 30-second spots and costing a total of $2000 was purchased from a major metropolitan television station. These advertise-

## igure C9-1   Descriptive Product Leaflet

**et 88 Frozen Dog Dessert**

oesn't your dog deserve dessert? Won't you feel better giving ''man's best friend'' — and yours — a treat that is actually *ood* for him?

ET 88 FROZEN DOG DESSERT is a nutritionally complete, well-balanced food made with only the highest quality proteins nd with vitamins and minerals added. And it contains *absolutely no sugar*.

ET 88 FROZEN DOG DESSERT can be fed like ice cream or it can be thawed in the refrigerator and spooned over dry dog ood. And it can be refrozen for your convenience.

an't you just imagine how pleased your pet will be to have a change of taste in its diet after eating the same thing meal after eal?

eed PET 88 FROZEN DOG DESSERT with the confidence that you're feeding the *best*! And have fun watching your pet uly enjoy *a real dessert treat*!

## igure C9-2   Introductory Television Advertisement

| ideo | Audio |
|------|-------|
| ull head shot of dog | Pet 88 is the newest in dog desserts. It's frozen! |
| ull screen of both packages | Now for the first time you can reward your dog with a tasty dessert that's good for him and absolutely unique. It's frozen! |
| oom in on one package with (6) six desserts | Pet 88 is a healthful, nutritious dessert that can be stored easily in your freezer. |
| lodel spooning dessert — dog eating dessert | When your dog is ready for this tasty treat, just spoon it into his bowl or serve it over his favourite dry dog food. |
| ull screen of package | So ask your grocer or pet store for Pet 88 — or call 1-800-279-3922. |
| uperimposed phone number | Because doesn't your dog deserve dessert today! |

ments were "run of schedule," meaning that the station could fit them into its schedule throughout the broadcasting day as space was available.

The primary purpose of this series of advertisements was to provide credibility to the company and its product in order to help convince retailers to carry the product. It was hoped that customers would ask retailers for the product if it was not on display.

Detyzco also developed a point-of-purchase poster for the product along with a counter card to help promote the product. The same graphic logo was used in all promotional materials, including packaging, to provide continuity to the product presentation.

After initial distribution was achieved, the firm utilized a few radio commercials (following the same general theme of the television advertisements). Copy for these radio commercials was read live by the announcers in an attempt to achieve an individual touch with more spontaneity. Sale for the first quarter amounted to $18 000.

### Discussion Questions

1. What are the best ways to expand distribution of the product?
2. How should the product be promoted (i.e., types of advertisements and sales promotions)?
3. Where in the store should the product be displayed—in the frozen-food section, with ice cream, or in a separate area?
4. Should the product line be expanded? If so, how?
5. How would it be possible to keep people from opening the packages to see what is inside?
6. Toward what market target should the product be aimed?
7. Should any marketing research be conducted? If so, what type?

# Case 10   Active Detergent

Will the public purchase a quality product whose manufacturer doesn't advertise and instead passes the savings on to the consumer? Witco Chemical Corporation looked at the detergent market, which is mature, and decided that since a substantial market segment are averse to detergent advertising, they would be willing to choose an unadvertised quality product, if it was cheaper.

So far the answer is "no" for Active, a laundry detergent billed by its maker as a consumer's dream product. However, Witco Chemical Corporation's Ultra division has given itself two years to find out if the faith in consumer buying sharpness will pay off through more active Active Sales.

Active's makers like to point out that it:
- is the only unadvertised manufacturer's brand on the market, according to company officials.

- was judged equal in quality to leading brand-name detergents in two independently conducted tests.
- sells for at least 20 cents less per package than the leading brands.

The detergent market is dominated by three large manufacturers, Procter & Gamble, Leve Brothers, and Colgate-Palmolive. Each of these companies has several individual brands, each aimed at a different market segment. All brands are supported by very large advertising campaigns.

Up to now, sales of Active aren't promising. Although Rusi Patell, the division's consume products manager, estimates sales so far have been 80 per cent of what was first anticipated others aren't so optimistic.

Source: Adapted from William A. Babcock, *The Winnipeg Free Press*, 28 August, 1975.

"Sales are really bad," laments product sales manager James Pifer of the food brokerage firm that sells Active to both wholesale and chain supermarkets. "The product itself has real potential, but the idea of not advertising isn't good. Since they don't advertise, they can't get it across to the consumer that Active is real savings," Mr. Pifer argues.

But Witco's net sales for all products were up 50 percent last year. A manufacturer and marketer of a wide range of specialty chemical and petroleum products for industrial and consumer use, Witco doesn't hinge its future on the failure or success of Active. As a result, the company can afford to give the no-advertising approach plenty of time to catch on.

Although Active isn't advertised in the traditional sense, Witco gets its message across with a combination of supermarket appearances and television interviews by the company's consumer economist, Audrey Clifford. Also, the company president and other company officials plan to make speeches to women's and other consumer groups. In addition, newspaper articles are being sought in public relations campaigns.

Despite Active's less-than-encouraging track record at the moment, Witco representatives have no plans to stray from their no-advertising policy, and eventually expect to introduce the product nationally.

The only exception to the no-advertising policy will be some limited advertising to retailers in trade journals in order to acquaint them with the product, Active's strategy, and the additional margins which retailers would make.

Witco's approach hinges on the intelligent consumer—the buyer who reads labels, compares prices, and decides accordingly. "Our product originates from a consumer need. The time is right for a consumer approach because the days are gone when people would unconsciously pick things up and buy them without reading the packages and comparing prices," a company representative said.

Others, though, don't give shoppers so much credit. "I just don't think consumers are going to spend enough time to do their own research on any product. They're too used to being sold on something and that is the only way they react," contends Neil Engstrom, a buyer for a supermarket chain. "Active sales have been going poorly; homemakers are strongly loyal to national brands, and the competition in this area is tough. If you want to sell your product, you must fight fire with fire and advertise."

### Discussion Questions

1. What are the main features of Witco's marketing mix for Active?
2. What else could Witco do to make its "no-advertising" marketing program more effective?
3. Will Active appeal to a significant segment of consumers?

## Case 11    SPACEMAX

As part of the Entrepreneurialism course in the M.B.A. program at McMaster University, Ashton So, Tony Valaitis, and Kirk Sabo developed a business plan for a new company. Their plan was judged to be the best submitted in the course and on April 10, 1984, they were awarded a $500 prize. The next day, over coffee in the cafeteria, the three Hamilton-area students were trying to decide whether they should pocket the prize money or use it to start a new company.

Source: Marvin Ryder.

## The Company

The three students named their company "SPACEMAX," as the mission of this business was "to provide inexpensive space-saving devices for noncommercial applications." Initially, SPACEMAX was to produce and market only one product—a portable, inexpensive, and easy-to-install locker shelf (called the "Lockermate Shelf"). The primary market for the product was students in high schools, community colleges, and universities. Secondary markets included senior elementary schools and noneducational institutions such as fitness/leisure centres, factories, hospitals, and police stations.

For the remainder of 1984, their plan was to penetrate the school market in the Hamilton–Toronto area. They wanted to earn a before-tax profit of 35 percent of sales and maintain a gross margin of 55 percent. Market coverage was projected to be 3 percent and sales were calculated to be $70 000 in the first year. All these estimates were best guesses. Actual performance could be quite different.

In future years, they felt they could geographically expand the school market while penetrating the nonschool market. They felt that the business could expand by launching one new product each year in the space-saving device field. Further, they projected growth in sales dollars of 90 percent in 1985 and 32 percent in 1986.

The students felt they had a competitive advantage because of: 1) their knowledge of and closeness to the school environment; 2) their emphasis on personal service; and 3) low overhead costs (SPACEMAX would subcontract the manufacture of shelf components). They recognized that the school market was highly seasonal, with over 80 percent of sales expected to occur in September and October; thus, penetration into the nonschool market was essential to smooth out sales during the year.

## The Product

The Lockermate Shelf could be broken down into two components: 1) a single shelf board (12″ × 12″); and 2) a pair of wire legs. The shelf board was made of particle board (½″ thick), finished with a wood veneer on one side, while the legs were made of zinc-plated wire 0.144″ thick. (See Figure C11-1.) When inserted in a locker, the Lockermate Shelf would stand approximately 12″ high. The shelf could be collapsed into a flat unit for ease of packaging and shipping. As well, the shelf would not become a permanent part of the locker, so that the purchaser could reuse the shelf in many different situations.

**Figure C11-1   The Lockermate Shelf**

## INSTALLATION INSTRUCTIONS

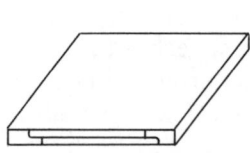

1. The LOCKERMATE shelf folded flat for convenient carrying.

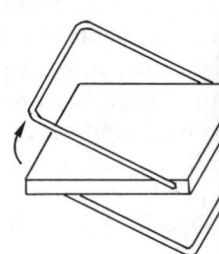

2. Unfold legs.

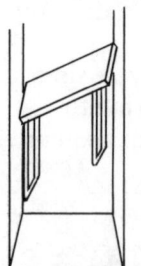

3. Tilt shelf sideways and insert into locker.

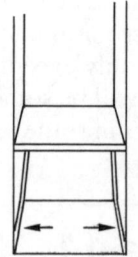

4. Set shelf into bottom locker and press leg up against side wall.

NO SCREWS, BRACKETS or TOOLS are REQUIRED

CAUTION: DO NOT STEP ON THE LOCKERMATE SHELF ONCE INSTALLED.

Before arriving at the final design, the team of students tried ten different prototypes. Wire legs were used with various shelf materials in seven of the designs. Thick corrugated cardboard, Coroplast, sheet metal, moulded plastic, hardwood, and some combinations of these materials were all tested and rejected. Sheet metal and moulded plastic were rejected because they were too expensive. Coroplast and the cardboard were not strong enough. Hardwood had a tendency to warp. The veneer-covered particle board was sturdy enough to take a stack of textbooks, yet cheap enough for production purposes.

Suppliers quoted a cost of $0.80 for the particle board with the holes drilled, and $0.50 for the wire legs. After assembly, shrink wrapping and labelling would cost an additional $0.20. Cardboard boxes for shipping orders of 25 would cost $1.20. Suppliers required cash-on-delivery for all businesses with no previous credit history.

For the first year, the product would be distributed through university and community college bookstores. Distribution to high schools would be obtained through student councils, who would sell the product as part of their fund-raising drives. As well, student-run stores and clubs in high schools could be used as alternative sales outlets. None of these outlets would require any middlemen. Retail stores (such as Coles, Grand & Toy, K-Mart, etc.) would not be approached until 1985, as their purchase deadlines for "back-to-school" merchandise could not be met in 1984.

Market research had indicated that $5.00 appeared to be the upper price limit. To allow markups of 50–55 percent, the planned selling price to the campus bookstores and student councils was to be $3.25. A recommended selling price of $4.95 would allow student councils to make a $1.70 profit per unit.

The promotion plan for community colleges and universities was somewhat different from the approach used for high schools. For the first market, campus bookstores would be contacted to identify the appropriate buyer. That person would be mailed a promotional package that would introduce the product and the company. The mailing would be followed up with a personal sales call. If the bookstore agreed to carry the shelf, SPACEMAX would provide a point-of-purchase display / dump bin unit to stack the shelves. The shelves would be sold on consignment to the bookstore to minimize financial risk. As well, shelves would be delivered to the bookstore in time for the September "rush" when lockers would be issued and bookstore traffic would be the highest.

For high schools, the process began with identifying newly elected student-council presidents. A package introducing the product, the company, and the fund-raising potential of the shelf would be mailed to that person. If possible, personal contact would be made and a presentation given. If the product was accepted, SPACEMAX would provide a point-of-purchase display for the shelves. The shelves would be sold on consignment with free delivery and pickup (if necessary). As well, special record-keeping forms would be given to the student council to ease bookkeeping problems.

## Market and Environmental Analysis

There were approximately 1.4 million lockers in the Canadian school market (high schools, community colleges, and universities). The largest regional markets were Ontario (40 percent) and Quebec (24 percent) and the largest market by school type was represented by the high schools (85 percent). A breakdown of the locker market by region and type of school is shown in Figure C11-2.

The students determined that a standard locker (72″ × 18″ × 12″) was widely used in Canadian schools. The dimensions were obtained by measuring lockers in and around the McMaster University campus. The most prominent weakness of the standard locker was that it offered very limited space and usually had only one shelf, located at the top. The lack of shelving space was an even greater problem when two individuals shared the same locker. As far as SPACEMAX could determine, no company manufactured and sold a portable shelf for use in lockers.

To understand the student purchaser of a Lockermate Shelf, surveys were taken of university, college, and high-school students. The first two groups were surveyed using a face-to-face interview, while the high-school students completed a self-administered survey. The surveys were administered during the first week in February. For this survey "student" referred to a student using a locker. A total of 580 usable responses were obtained from the following sources: McMaster University, 83; Mohawk College, 101; St. Mary's, Lorne Park, Central, Clarkson, and Oakville secondary schools, 396.

Some of the survey results are presented in Figure C11-3.

Finally, the SPACEMAX team measured the intent to purchase the Lockermate Shelf at two price points. Students were made aware of the product (through diagrams and a verbal explanation) before being asked about their purchase intentions. Results of this part of the survey are presented in Figure C11-4.

## The SPACEMAX Team

The three students who developed the SPACEMAX business plan came from different backgrounds. Tony Valaitis was enrolled in the Co-op M.B.A. program at McMaster. His first two work terms were spent with Gulf Canada in the Human Resources Department. His third work term would begin on May 1 and as yet no co-op work placement had been found. Tony had graduated with a B.A. in geography from McMaster in 1978 and had spent three years as the office manager for a Hamilton firm. While pursuing his B.A., Tony had been a member of the varsity basketball team, and he hoped to use his last year of eligibility in the fall while completing his M.B.A.

Kirk Sabo was enrolled as a full-time M.B.A. student. He had come to McMaster after completing a B.B.A. at Wilfrid Laurier University in 1982. His work experience had been limited to summer jobs on the assembly line at the Ford Motor Company plant in Oakville and with pool-cleaning companies as crew chief. Kirk had been a member of the W.L.U. varsity hockey team, but upon being accepted to McMaster he pursued the objective of a career in marketing.

Ashton So was the only married man of the three. His undergraduate degree was a B.A.Sc. in Chemical Engineering, which he

## Figure C11-2 Lockers by Location and School Type[a]

|  | Ontario | Quebec | Rest of Canada | Total |
|---|---|---|---|---|
| High Schools | 485 000 (41%) | 250 000 (21%) | 440 000 (37%) | 1 175 000 (100%) |
| Community Colleges | 40 000 (29%) | 70 000 (51%) | 26 000 (19%) | 136 000 (100%) |
| Universities | 25 000 (42%) | 14 000 (23%) | 21 000 (35%) | 60 000 (100%) |
| TOTAL | 550 000 (40%) | 334 000 (24%) | 487 000 (36%) | 1 371 000 (100%) |

[a] Market size was calculated by multiplying the number of students by a locker-to-student ratio. The ratios were determined to be 15 percent for universities, 50 percent for community colleges, and 75 percent for high schools.

## Figure C11-3  Selected Survey Results

| Do you share a locker? | Yes | No |
|---|---|---|
| University Students | 50% | 50% |
| Community College Students | 67% | 33% |
| High-School Students | 54% | 46% |

(60 percent of people sharing a locker were women.)

| Do you need an extra locker shelf? | | |
|---|---|---|
| University Students | 76% | 24% |
| Community College Students | 73% | 27% |
| High-School Students | 46% | 54% |

(33 percent of high-school students wanted two extra locker shelves.)

| Do you use the bottom of your locker to stack books? | | |
|---|---|---|
| University Students | 77% | 23% |
| Community College Students | 77% | 23% |
| High-School Students | 50% | 50% |

| Do you feel your locker is well organized and well kept? | | |
|---|---|---|
| University Students | 67% | 33% |
| Community College Students | 67% | 33% |
| High-School Students | 50% | 50% |

| Is having a well-organized locker important to you? | | |
|---|---|---|
| University Students | 61% | 39% |
| Community College Students | 65% | 35% |
| High-School Students | 53% | 47% |

| Are you dissatisfied with your current locker facility? | | |
|---|---|---|
| University Students | 14% | 86% |
| Community College Students | 48% | 52% |
| High-School Students | 55% | 45% |

## Figure C11-4  Purchase Intentions at Two Price Points

If the Lockermate Shelf sold for $3.00:

| | Would Definitely Buy | Would Probably Buy | Neutral | Would Probably Not Buy | Would Definitely Not Buy |
|---|---|---|---|---|---|
| University Students | 48% | 19% | 11% | 7% | 15% |
| College Students | 49% | 31% | 11% | 5% | 5% |
| High-School Students | 38% | 29% | 12% | 7% | 14% |

If the Lockermate Shelf sold for $5.00:

| | Would Definitely Buy | Would Probably Buy | Neutral | Would Probably Not Buy | Would Definitely Not Buy |
|---|---|---|---|---|---|
| University Students | 29% | 19% | 16% | 15% | 22% |
| College Students | 25% | 26% | 27% | 13% | 10% |
| High-School Students | 11% | 25% | 29% | 11% | 24% |

had obtained from the University of Waterloo in 1979. He had immediately gone to work for Gulf Canada, working in process engineering to improve the efficiency and energy conservation of the Edmonton and Clarkson refineries. He was now a full-time M.B.A. student.

## The Problem

The $500 that the team won for their business plan was intended to be an incentive for them to start up a new business. They could pocket the money, but they knew the professor of the course would be disappointed if they did not try to sell the Lockermate Shelf.

On the other hand, the preliminary investment would be much more than $500. Because they were students, they knew that banks would probably be wary of giving them a loan. Further, even with all their work on the business plan, they were not sure that they wanted to take a risk and begin a new venture with an untried product. There could be problems with the survey, and they had yet to do any break-even analysis. They did not know what their fixed costs would be, so in any break-even analysis some assumptions would have to be made.

They would need to make a decision soon. The lead time for one production cycle was six weeks. After exams had finished at the end of May, they would not have any shelves in stock until the middle of June. Time was already slipping by if they were to have the Lockermate Shelf in bookstores for the September rush.

## Discussion Question

1. How would you advise the team?

# Case 12   Coffeesavr

In mid-1977 the Shoal Lake Company was operating as a limited company in Beauséjour, Manitoba. Mr. Walter Hagborg, a retired research scientist, was president and sole owner of the company. He had originally formed the company in 1973 to establish a fish farming operation in rural Manitoba. Two years later an apiary was added to enhance the company's profit performance.

In 1976 Mr. Hagborg was approached by his son and a friend with the idea of marketing a new product that could be used as a coffee extender and coffee substitute. He knew of the type of product they described, as people had used roasted cereal grains as a substitute for coffee during the Depression in the 1930s. The idea of developing such a product occurred because of a dramatic increase in world coffee prices. Mr. Hagborg, by utilizing the research skills he had acquired through the years, believed that he could develop an acceptable formula for the proposed coffee extender/substitute.

## The Product

Mr. Hagborg carried out research over a period of several months in order to develop the formula for the new product. The research work, conducted in the basement of Mr. Hagborg's home, was one of trial and error in an effort to determine the best combination of grains and other ingredients. The final formula included rye, barley, caramel, malt, dehydrated alfalfa, and calcium phosphate monobasic. After the formula was developed, the company arranged to have it produced by a large brewing and malting company. Therefore, production and

Source: *Small Business Management*, M. D. Beckman, W. S. Good and Robert G. Wyckham (Toronto: John Wiley and Sons, 1982).

quality could readily be taken care of.

The new product was given the brand name of Coffeesavr. Coffeesavr could be used as either a coffee extender or a coffee substitute. It was expected that consumers would use about one-third Coffeesavr at first, and gradually increase the amount as taste adjusted. The finished product was quite similar in appearance to regular-grind coffee, but it had a faint alfalfa-like aroma.

The company realized that the new product offered several positive features to the consumer, namely, reduced cost of coffee, reduced caffeine intake, reduced bitterness of coffee, and 100 percent natural ingredients. At the same time, there was concern about what were considered to be less attractive features of Coffeesavr, particularly that the coffee flavour was altered, an adding-mixing step was necessary in brewing coffee (if it was combined with coffee), and an additional product (in addition to the coffee) had to be purchased. Also, Coffeesavr was compatible only with regular (brewed) coffee systems, and thus could not be mixed with instant coffee or used as an instant coffee substitute.

## Secondary Market Research

In order to better analyse the market potential for Coffeesavr, Mr. Hagborg decided to carry out some secondary market research. He was able to compile the following information with the help of the local Statistics Canada representatives and the Tea and Coffee Association of Canada located in Don Mills, Ontario.

Canadian coffee consumption among persons ten years of age and older in 1976 was 2.27 cups per person per day (see Figure C12-1). That level represents an overall increase of 0.09 cups, or 4.2 percent from the level of 2.18 cups in 1966. From 1966 to 1976 the consumption of instant coffee had increased almost 73 percent, whereas the consumption of regular coffee had declined approximately 26 percent in that same time period.

About 80 percent of all coffee consumption occurs in the home. Figure C12-2 provides a breakdown of instant versus regular coffee usage in the home. Coffee consumption at restaurants and at work is 4 percent and 16

**Figure C12-1  Canadian Consumption of Regular and Instant Coffee by Persons Age 10 or Over**

| Cups per person per day | 1966 | 1967 | 1970 | 1973 | 1976 | Net Change 1966-1976 Cups | Percent |
|---|---|---|---|---|---|---|---|
| Regular | 1.24 | 1.19 | 0.98 | 0.94 | 0.92 | − 0.32 | − 25.8 |
| Instant | 0.94 | 0.83 | 1.17 | 1.27 | 1.63 | + 0.69 | + 72.9 |
| All coffee | 2.18 | 2.02 | 2.15 | 2.21 | 2.27 | + 0.09 | +  4.2 |

**Figure C12-2  Incidence of Use of Regular and Instant Coffee Among Canadian Households**

| Year | Regular coffee only | Instant coffee only | Both | Total regular | Total instant |
|---|---|---|---|---|---|
| | (Percent of coffee-using households) | | | | |
| 1966 | 22 | 44 | 34 | 56 | 78 |
| 1967 | 24 | 46 | 30 | 54 | 76 |
| 1970 | 20 | 52 | 28 | 48 | 80 |
| 1973 | 18 | 57 | 25 | 43 | 82 |
| 1976 | 17 | 59 | 24 | 41 | 83 |

percent respectively. However, coffee drinking at work, with an increase of more than 63
percent since 1966, has shown a much greater
rate of increase than usage at home and in
eating places (2 percent and 1 percent
respectively). Although the consumption of
regular coffee has declined in general ( − 25.8
percent) over the last ten years, the usage of
regular coffee at work places has increased
approximately 51 percent.

The proportion of the Canadian population ten years of age and older who drink
coffee has remained substantially the same
since 1960 at approximately 64 percent. The
highest average daily consumption is almost
3.3 cups per day, for people in the 30-39 age
group. Within this age group 82 percent of
individuals are coffee consumers. As persons
progress through the life cycle, coffee maintains its popularity, as evidenced by figures of
80 percent, 78 percent, and 76 percent
respectively for the age groups 40-49, 50-59
and over 65.

Persons in the Prairie region of Canada
consume coffee at the highest per capita rate
of 2.9 cups per day. Interestingly enough, it
appears that the coffee drinking rate increases
as Canada is crossed from east to west. The
Maritimes have a per-capita consumption
rate of only 1.4 cups per day.

Persons in the lower-middle income group
appear to be the heaviest users of coffee at
2.5 cups per person per day. However, in
Canada there does not appear to be a high
socio-economic stratification with regard
to the rate of coffee consumption.

There are two coffee-like products currently being sold in Canadian food stores.
They are Postum and Chicoree. Both are used
as coffee substitutes rather than coffee
extenders. There are also a number of other
unadvertised coffee-type products sold in
specialty and health food stores.

Recently, two brands of coffee were introduced to the market by large food companies
that contained added coffee extenders. They
were Mellow Roast (instant or regular coffee
blended with roasted grain) and Encore
(instant coffee with chicory). Both were
offered at a lower price than "pure" coffee
packages of equal weight.

The Canadian coffee industry is subject to
drastic price fluctuations. This has been due
in some instances to frosts affecting coffee
crops in producing countries. For example,
over a ten-week period between February and
April 1977, the green bean price of coffee rose
from approximately $2.20 to $3.40 per
pound, only to fall to a low of about $1.80
per pound in August. The retail price of
coffee is approximately 155 percent of the
green bean price. Any change in the retail
price of coffee is thus a reflection of the
change in the prevailing green bean price.

## Primary Market Research

The Shoal Lake Company conducted a market survey of two main market segments,
restaurants and individual consumers. A third
market segment thought to be less important
by the company was the institutional market
(hospitals, company cafeterias, etc.). No information was gathered on this segment.

The results of the survey are summarized as
follows:

1.  Restaurants: The objective of restaurant
    operators is customer satisfaction. Coffee
    is a basic beverage and is thus an impor-
    tant item on restaurant menus. Their
    prime concern is the coffee's taste. Poor-
    quality coffee (tastewise) was deemed to
    be totally unacceptable in the restaurant
    segment of the market.

2.  Individual consumers: A consumer survey
    was conducted to test the concept of a
    coffee extender. The initial survey was
    conducted with people who did not use a
    coffee extender. Some of the results were
    as follows:

(a) The majority of individuals surveyed drank between one and five cups of coffee per day.

(b) Approximately 50 percent of the respondents bought a particular brand of coffee mainly because of the flavour.

(c) 10 percent of the people said they would try Coffeesavr but only if it did not alter the flavour of the coffee.

(d) People were willing to pay anywhere from $1.50 to $2.50/lb. for Coffeesavr.

A second survey was conducted with users of Coffeesavr. The sample was too small to reach any definite conclusions, but all respondents stated that the coffee extender altered the flavour of the coffee somewhat.

Some information on the effects of the coffee extender on coffee preference and degree of bitterness of regular coffee was obtained from taste tests conducted by the Department of Foods and Nutrition at the University of Manitoba (see Appendix). The study showed that a coffee beverage could be prepared from a mixture of coffee grounds and up to 50 percent Coffeesavr. It was well liked and found to be less bitter.

### Efforts to Market Coffeesavr

A decision was made in January 1977 to produce a limited amount of the new product. In order to minimize capital investment the grains were custom-roasted by the large brewing and malting company (a process that required special equipment and expertise). The company purchased all other necessary processing equipment. Grinding, packaging, and labelling were done in the basement of Mr. Hagborg's home. Initially, 600 pounds of the coffee extender/substitute were produced and packaged in one pound packages.

The product was introduced to the market as Coffeesavr through a café operation in Beauséjour (owned by Mr. Hagborg's son) and Vita Health Stores in Winnipeg. The company did no advertising, mainly because of very limited financial resources, and thus depended solely on word of mouth for product exposure. Sales initially averaged about 100 pounds per month at $1.89 per pound. Essentially all sales of the new product were through the Beauséjour outlet. Mr. Hagborg was not aware of any sales of Coffeesavr at the Vita Health stores. Repeat sales at the restaurant, although slow at first, appeared to be increasing over time.

### Present Situation

The Shoal Lake Company currently has an inventory of 500 pounds of the coffee extender/substitute. Future sales are uncertain, particularly in light of the fact that Mr. Hagborg's son has recently sold his café in Beauséjour.

### Discussion Question

1. What should Mr. Hagborg do next?

### Appendix Coffee Extender Tested

M. Vaisey-Genser and B. Walker of the Department of Foods and Nutrition, The University of Manitoba have conducted extensive tests on the effect of coffee extender on the preference and bitterness taste of regular coffee.

In this experiment regular ground coffee was compared to mixtures of regular coffee with 25 percent, 50 percent, and 75 percent replacement by coffee extender (by weight) for relative preference and bitterness by fifty untrained panelists. The coffee extender (Coffeesavr) was received from W. Hagborg, August, 1977 and was manufactured at Horseshoe Lake Co., Beauséjour, Manitoba. The extender was composed of roasted rye and barley with alfalfa, glucose, and calcium phosphate monobasic. The directions on the package read: "Mix Coffeesavr with coffee to reduce cost and caffeine content, one scoop of Coffeesavr with one or more scoops of coffee."

The coffee samples were prepared identically in a gourmet ocs 100 filter-type commercial coffee machine. The coffee/coffee extender mixture was prepared using 25 percent, 50 percent, and 75 percent by weight regular ground coffee plus 75 percent, 50 percent, 25 percent coffee extender respectively. The regular ground coffee was "Goodhost" coffee from Stuarts' Branded Foods Ltd. Each package had been pre-weighed with approximately 57-58 g coffee. The coffee was prepared and kept hot for a maximum of forty-five minutes on range-top elements before it was poured and served to the panelists.

Sensory evaluation was done by magnitude estimation for both preference and bitterness. The sensory evaluation form used for the test stated these directions:

1. Taste the reference and assign it a score of 10.
2. Taste each coded sample in the order presented and give a magnitude estimate for your preference in relation to the reference. Example: If your preference is 2x that of the reference, assign a score of 20; if less than the reference, assign a

number less than 10. What is your reason for preference for the sample you marked with the highest score?
3. Give a magnitude estimate for bitterness in relation to the reference.
4. Do you normally drink your coffee (a) black, (b) with cream/milk and/or sugar?

Fifty panelists were served five samples of black coffee, the reference being regular coffee. The four coded samples included regular coffee, 25 percent, 50 percent, and 75 percent replacement by coffee extender. The samples were coded and presented in random order in whisky shot glasses which held about 25 ml. The samples were kept hot on a Corning hot plate in each of the sensory booths. Each panelist was paid fifty cents for participating.

The magnitude estimation gives a numerical value for the degree of preference of bitterness of the coded samples in comparison to the reference. The data obtained for sensory evaluation were analysed by Analysis of Variance; Duncan's Multiple Range test was used to compare mean values.

Panelists gave reasons for the most preferred sample as: it was less bitter than the reference or it was more bitter. Comments also indicated that the 50 percent and 75

**Figure C12-3   Calculated Means for Preference of Coffee Samples***

| Sample | 25% extender | Regular Coffee | 50% extender | 75% extender |
|---|---|---|---|---|
| Sample Score | 1.43[a] | 1.18[ab] | 1.14[ab] | 0.94[b] |

*Normalized data, higher score = more preferred N = 50
Value with same alphabetical letter not significantly different

**Figure C12-4   Calculated Means for Bitterness of Coffee Samples***

| Sample | 25% extender | Regular Coffee | 50% extender | 75% extender |
|---|---|---|---|---|
| Sample Score | 1.40[a] | 1.39[a] | 1.04[ab] | 1.00[b] |

*Normalized data, higher score = more bitter
Values with same alphabetical letter are not significantly different

percent was very strong. Some identified this strong sensation as bitterness and some said it was something else, such as meaty, or imitation. There seemed to be some confusion by panelists as to what sensation they were experiencing.

Thirty-two percent of the fifty panelists normally drank their coffee black while 68 percent drank their coffee with cream/milk and/or sugar.

Coffee samples were examined visually with added cream. Those with 25 percent and 50 percent replacement had the same colour as regular coffee, while the 75 percent replacement was much darker or muddier. The 75 percent replacement had a slight amount of white foam on the surface when brewing.

This study shows that a coffee beverage can be successfully prepared from coffee grounds with up to 50 percent replaced by "Coffeesavr." A brew from this mixture was as well liked as regular coffee and tended to be less bitter.

The mean values of fifty judgments indicated that coffee with 25 percent replacement by coffee extender was significantly more preferred than coffee with 75 percent replacement by extender ($p < 0.05$) as shown in Figure C12-3.

The mean values of fifty judgments indicated that regular coffee and coffee with 25 percent replacement by extender were significantly more bitter than the 50 percent replacement ($p < 0.05$) as shown in Figure C12-4.

# Case 13  Porta-Broil

In April 1986, Graham Robson was trying to decide how to market his new product, Porta-Broil. Robson, a young Winnipeg entrepreneur, had purchased the right to this new method of outdoor cooking along with 8000 units of the product. The inventory was stored in a Vancouver warehouse, waiting for Robson to find a market. He needed to get Porta-Broil onto retail shelves in order to cut storage costs and recoup his initial investment.

## The People

Robson had graduated from the University of Manitoba in December 1985, with a B.A. Over the preceding three years he had been involved in various entrepreneurial projects — a landscaping business, a marketing plan for costume jewelry called Twist-A-Bead, and the initial stages of a proposed health club. In the spring of 1986 he was working full-time managing a house-painting franchise, but

had applied to enter the M.B.A. program at the University of Manitoba, training that he felt would be a very good "fit" with his entrepreneurial bent.

Robson first encountered Porta-Broil while working with his older brother Grant in Vancouver. They produced *Mail-Order Marketer*, a publication that listed mail-order advertisements for a variety of products. In September 1985, the Robsons were approached by a fisherman (Jim McKellar), who had developed and tested Porta-Broil, and had arranged to have a firm manufacture it for

Source: This case was prepared by Morva Bowman, M.B.A., under the supervision of Dr. C. Dennis Anderson, as a basis for class discussion rather than to illustrate either effective or ineffective handling of an administrative situation. Copyright © 1986 Case Development Program, Faculty of Management, University of Manitoba. Support for the development of this case was provided by the Canadian Studies Program, Secretary of State, Ottawa; and Management Excellence in Small Business Program, Department of Industry, Trade, and Commerce, Ottawa.

**Figure C13-1    Instructions for Use of Porta-Broil**

# PORTA-BROIL
## A BETTER WAY OF COOKING OUTDOORS

### THIS PACKAGE CONTAINS:

- 6 Impregnated Mattings (12″ × 9″), which act as fuel when ignited.
- 6 Sheets of Aluminum Foil (12″ × 9″), in which you wrap your food.

### GREAT FOR SUMMER OR WINTER OUTDOOR SPORTSMAN:

Light weight: can be tucked away in fisherman's tackle box, carried in a back pack, or stored away in camper or trailer for use when conventional fuels run out. Skiers, hunters, ice-fishermen will appreciate Porta-Broil, as the matting will burn in any kind of weather.

### IDEAL FOR EMERGENCY SITUATIONS:

Lost in bush — no dry wood? Take one impregnated matting and cut into strips. This will dry the wood and ignite.

### BROIL:

Fish, wieners, hamburger patties, steakettes, bacon, breakfast sausage, corn on the cob, green peppers, onions. Food broils in its own juices — a deliciously different taste.

### PREPARATION FOR BROILING:

Wrap two individual servings in one sheet of aluminum foil, airtight. Place the foil-wrapped food in the centre of one sheet of treated matting. Fold the four sides of matting over the aluminum foil and place with flap side in down position on the ground in such a manner that air will circulate around the matting. Use a couple of sticks or small stones underneath; ignite.

Made in Surrey, British Columbia, Canada.

**Figure C13-2  Porta-Broil Package Cover**

him. However, he had no idea how to market
the product, and came to *Mail-Order
Marketer* for advice. The brothers were
intrigued with the new product; they tried
it out, liked it, and decided to purchase
McKellar's entire stock of 8000 units of
Porta-Broil in the hope that they could succeed in turning a profit. Storage for these
units in a Vancouver warehouse was costing
them $15 per month.

## The Product

Porta-Broil was a very simple system for cooking food outdoors. It consisted of sheets of
aluminum foil, in which the food was wrapped,
and sheets of impregnated matting (a burlap
fabric soaked in waxes) that served as fuel.
The product was simple to use: the food was
wrapped in foil, then wrapped in matting,
which was set alight. The flame burned out in
five to eight minutes, cooking the food in its
own juices and providing a unique and very
fresh taste. A variety of foods could be cooked
this way. (See Figure C13-1 for instructions
for use and Figure C13-2 for a picture of the
product in use.)

The Robsons had arranged for Porta-Broil
to be tested by several campers and fishermen;
these users were enthusiastic about it. (See
some of their testimonials, in Figure C13-3.)
A package containing six sheets of foil, six
sheets of matting, and instructions was priced
at $4.95 (suggested retail). The Robsons had
paid $2.00 per unit for their 8000 packages.
They planned to sell the packages to retailers
for $2.75 each.

## Marketing Plans

Grant Robson had initially visited Vancouver
outlets that sold mountain-climbing gear, but
interest was minimal and the brothers felt that
this was probably not the right market. After
discussion with Vancouver retailers, they
decided that Porta-Broil was best suited to
fishermen, hunters, and campers, and that
Manitoba and Northwestern Ontario were
the best places to offer this product.

Because the Robsons were severely limited
in both time and money, they wanted to find
one or more retail outlets that would buy the
product from them in larger order quantities,
and handle any necessary promotion. This
would mean that they only had to arrange
shipping from Vancouver, and while they
were not sure what this would cost, they felt
it would be a simple distribution system
to handle.

Graham Robson approached the owner/
manager of Coughlin's, a Winnipeg-based firm
that is one of North America's largest distributors of camping and hiking accessories;
most of Coughlin's accessory items sold for
less than $2.00. The owner/manager felt that
this product would be of little interest to his
retail customers, and furthermore felt that
the suggested retail price of $4.95 was too
expensive for the end consumer.

Graham next visited Pay-Less Fishing
Tackle, a large fishing equipment specialty
store in Winnipeg, where the owner/manager
seemed somewhat interested. He left a sample
with the owner/manager, and was to check
back in a week's time. Realizing that Pay-Less
might not wish to buy Porta-Broil, or might
take only a small part of his stock, Robson
wondered what his next move should be.

## Discussion Question

1. How would you advise Graham Robson?

## igure C13-3   Testimonials for Porta-Broil

I have used the product known as Porta-Broil and find that it works well. The outdoorsman will recognize the advantages of efficient, light-weight fuel.

As a Scout Leader, I believe that Porta-Broil could be of use to Scouts. A hot meal in any kind of weather is always welcome. Cubs could be introduced to outdoor foil cooking easily and quickly with Porta-Broil.

The product seems to fit very nicely into today's theme of no-trace camping. The idea is a good one and, when used properly, works as stated.

Al Stevenson,
Vancouver, B.C.


On the evening of February 22, we witnessed a demonstration of the Porta-Broil. The foods prepared were fish and wieners. It took approximately 5 minutes for the food to cook. It was then passed around for all of us to have a taste. Everyone was greatly impressed with the taste of the food, which was piping hot and cooked completely.

We are pleased to say this product does everything it states it will. And we all believe the Porta-Broil would be an asset for Boy Scouts to be associated with.

The Ninth East Whalley Group Committee
Vancouver, B.C.


Just a short note to let you know that we did try the sample of Porta-Broil that you gave us last weekend. It really did the trick as far as cooking the meat thoroughly and with a minimum of fuss. Going on the boat as we do, we cannot carry a lot of cooking equipment with us, and are now intending to keep a stock of your product on board.

Thank you again for giving us the opportunity of trying it.

S.J. Pleasant,
Surrey, B.C.


I have used the product Porta-Broil; I cooked fish in it when I was out fishing. It left the juices in and cooked the meat thoroughly. I was well pleased with the product and will continue to use it when I go fishing.

M.E. Williamson
Surrey, B.C.


We have used and are familiar with the product known as Porta-Broil, and find it to be a useful and handy product for the purposes stated. Our teenage son and his friends find it perfect for day and overnight camping and fishing trips. It is particularly suited for our often-wet climate when natural fuel is difficult to ignite.

Shirley Simonson,
Leslie G. Simonson,
Surrey, B.C.

# Case 14 Jefferson Spark Plug Company Limited

During the long period of product development, Rod Jefferson had thought occasionally about the eventual marketing of his new spark plug. As early as 1980, he had discussed the subject with his directors, and a number of alternatives had been considered. By August 1984, with the product having been thoroughly tested and at the point of being put into production, Rod began to devote much of his time to the many decisions that faced him in the marketing of his product.

The Jefferson Spark Plug Company was formed in 1981 in Toronto, Ontario, to develop, produce and market a new spark plug design, several features of which had been patented by one of the founders. The company was a small one, and financial resources were limited. Rod Jefferson, the President and major shareholder, had spent his spare time for several years working on designs, processes and materials for use in the plug.

The chief advantage of the Jefferson Company spark plug was its resistance to fouling, which resulted in easier starting, smoother idling, and much longer life than conventional spark plugs. The relatively long life was especially apparent in stop-and-go driving, and in two-stroke motors such as outboard motors, power mowers and chain saws. In outboards, the improvement in performance was so dramatic that testimonials filled with superlatives were almost invariably offered by people asked to test the plug. Preliminary tests indicated that the average life of a Jefferson Company plug was about four to five times that of conventional plugs, which lasted from 13 000 to 24 000 km, depending on the type of service and condition of the motor.

The superior performance resulted from the use of a very slender centre electrode and insulator. The small, thin insulator heated very rapidly, preventing the condensation of combustion gases. A relatively large and open scavenging chamber promoted the speedy removal of exhaust gases before harmful deposits could condense on the insulator. The thin insulator was cooled rapidly, preventing pre-ignition—i.e., ignition of the gases before the proper point on the compression stroke was reached. The thin insulator was immune to cracking from heat shocks, just as a thin glass cannot readily be broken by boiling water whereas a thick glass will crack easily.

In addition to these patented features, the electrodes were made of more costly material which was more resistant to wear than that used in conventional plugs. In this way, the freedom from fouling could be translated into longer life, even in engines operated continuously and in which fouling takes place very slowly.

Conventional spark plugs had changed very little in the last two decades. They were generally of one quality, with many different sizes to cover the wide variety of internal combustion engines. Because they were usually made on highly automated production lines, large volumes could be produced at a relatively low cost of $0.23 to $0.26 each, Rod Jefferson believed.

Conventional spark plugs operated efficiently within a fairly narrow temperature range. Accordingly, ten or more different conventional plugs were available in each of four thread sizes to accommodate the heat

Source: University of Western Ontario Case Clearing House.
Updated.

nge of different engines. Even in the same
gine, a plug which worked well under
rmal operation would tend to foul up at
ling speed and cause pre-ignition at sus-
ined high speeds in hot weather. Some
anufacturers recommended different plugs
r the same engine, a "hot" plug for city
iving and a "cool" plug for highway driving.
The Jefferson Company's plug had such a
ide temperature range that the company
anned to make only two or three "universal"
ugs for each thread size—one with a
rmal tip and one with an extended tip,
quiring only twelve plugs in all compared to
fty or sixty for competitive makes, and a
naller number for small two stroke engines.
arying the tip of the spark plug was one of
e ways in which the manufacturers varied
e plugs' heat range.

Spark plugs were sold by the manufacturers
original equipment manufacturers, fleet
wners and to individuals for replacement
irposes. The original equipment manufac-
irers (such as Ford and General Motors)
ere estimated to consume about 16 percent of
e total Canadian production of 87 000 000
lugs in 1980. The replacement market, which
onsisted of fleet and individual users, con-
imed the other 84 percent of production.

## he Original Equipment Buyer

he large automobile companies were by far
e most significant purchasers of spark plugs
r original equipment use, but other impor-
nt customers in this category were the
anufacturers of motors for outboard engines,
ower mowers, chain saws, pumps, tractors,
rk lift trucks, and other products which
lied on an internal combustion engine.
lthough the number of these customers was
latively small, their purchases were large.
ompetition for this business was intense,
nd prices of spark plugs for original equip-
ient were extremely low. Such customers
ere usually sold directly by the spark plug

manufacturer on a bid basis covering a specified quantity and period of time.

In the United States, both G.M. and Ford
had purchased their own spark plug manufacturing facilities: General Motors owned AC
Spark Plug and Ford had purchased U.S.
Autolite, but this had not been done in
Canada. Hence these customers were, to all
intents and purposes, closed to the independent spark plug manufacturer.

## The Replacement Plug Buyer

**The Individual User**    The original spark
plugs on an individual's automobile tended to
wear out after 13 000 to 24 000 km of use, or
after about one year's average driving. The
actual useful life varied a great deal depending
on the conditions of use, and spark plugs
could be used even after the point at which
they were operating inefficiently. Spark plug
life in two-cycle motors varied to an even
greater extent, but probably averaged one
year.

Replacement spark plugs were usually purchased by the individual when he was having
repairs or a tune-up done on his car. The
plugs would be obtained from one of the
following: an automobile dealer with a parts
and service business; a gasoline service station,
either chain or independent; an auto repair
specialist; an outlet specializing in the sale of
auto supplies. He might buy plugs which were
identified with the brand of a particular
manufacturer, such as Champion, or he might
buy essentially the same plug bearing the
brand name of the retail outlet (e.g. Canadian
Tire). Retail selling prices of branded plugs
for replacement purposes were usually much
higher than the price of the same plug for
original equipment purposes. The price of
private-brand plugs was often slightly below
the manufacturer-brand plugs.

It was widely believed in the industry that
the individual consumer was largely unaware
of the exact brand of a part used in his car,

and furthermore that he did not care as long as the car ran and the cost of the part was not prohibitive. The consumer was paying for a tune-up, not a set of spark plugs. Moreover, the individual often procrastinated about replacing spark plugs, and a recommendation from the service man was necessary before he would purchase new ones. Private brand outlets, such as the auto supply stores, were believed to cater largely to the "do-it-yourself" customer.

**The Fleet User**   The fleet owner was generally defined as an individual or organization that used one or more vehicles for commercial purposes, either directly or indirectly. Large trucking firms or corporations owning their own trucks constituted the greatest portion of the market, along with taxicabs. These firms generally performed regular maintenance work on their vehicles at prescribed intervals under "preventive maintenance schedules" established by the vehicle's manufacturer and the user's experience. During these overhauls, certain work was done and parts were replaced regardless of the condition of the parts. Thus, spark plugs were changed every 13 000 to 24 000 km, before trouble began. It was cheaper for the trucker to pay for the cost of regular preventive maintenance schedules than to have his expensive vehicle sitting idle at the side of the highway for several hours because a $1.50 spark plug had fouled. Large trucking companies hired their own mechanics and had large overhaul depots. Small companies, on the other hand, might contract their repair work out to a local garage. The switchover point from contracting maintenance work out to hiring a company mechanic appeared to be between 25 and 35 vehicles. The truckers usually purchased their required parts from distributors at 30 percent off retail list, or at the same price as the local gas station purchased its parts. The size of the firm often deter-

mined the purchasing pattern. For instance, large fleets with more than 200 trucks would have a purchasing agent whose job was to obtain the best price discount schedule possible. These companies often stored large quantities of fast-moving replacement items such as spark plugs, filters, tires, etc. The discount available might depend on specific volume of a particular item or the total volume of goods purchased. This discount could be affected by the size and variety of trucks in the fleet or the number of jobbers from whom the trucker bought. It was very seldom that a trucker bought his parts directly from the truck manufacturer or his component supplier; instead he tended to purchase through independent warehouse distributors, company distribution systems of Ford, G.M. and Chrysler, or from local jobbers. Smaller truckers, who had a small one- or two-person repair shop, or contracted their work out, usually purchased their requirements from jobbers. The decision on what to buy and when to buy it was not dictated by the general manager but rather by the man who installed the parts — the shop foreman or manager.

Some of the factors which influenced the buying decision of fleet operators appeared to be: personality of the supplier, discounts offered, speed of service, range of products on hand, or special deals on the items. Generally, the fleet buyer was performance conscious and would not purchase equipment that would not last.

The mileage put on fleet trucks varied considerably, depending upon the use and type of truck. Large diesel tractors could be driven 480 000 km a year, small city vans or taxis perhaps 160 000 to 200 000 km per year. If a company was largely inter-city in its operations, its trucks might be mostly diesels, but if it did a great deal of city work, a large number of gasoline trucks were usually used.

The price structure on conventional spark plugs was roughly as follows:

## Figure C14-1  Price Structure on Conventional Spark Plugs

| | Private Brand at Discount Outlet | Name Brand | Discount off |
|---|---|---|---|
| Retail List Price | 1.40 | 1.50* | |
| Price to Service Stations | | 1.05 | 30% |
| Price to Jobbers | | 0.735 | 30% |
| Price to Independent Warehouse Distributors | | 0.625 to 0.662 | 10–15% |
| Manufacturer's Selling Price to Automobile Manufacturer | | | |
| As original equipment | | 0.10 to 0.20 | |
| For Replacement market | | 0.43 | |
| to Independent Warehouse Distributors | | 0.625 to 0.662 | |
| to Private Branders | 0.625 to 0.662 | | |
| to Large Fleet Buyers | | 1.05 | |
| Average Production Cost | | 0.23 to 0.26 | |

*A $0.40 installation charge was normally added, bringing the total cost to $1.90.

Jefferson Company had spent four years doing extensive technological research in an effort to discover what plastics would work and how to apply them correctly. Much of this work could only be accomplished by methods of trial and error, as there was no previous knowledge to draw from in this particular area of application. For this reason, the company felt it had at least a two-year advantage over any possible competitors who might try to copy the idea by making small changes in the pattern.

In early June, preliminary estimates of company costs were $0.56 per plug, which covered raw material, direct labour, and factory overhead. In addition, management salaries, selling expenses, office and storage space were estimated at $56 000 annually. It was further estimated that these costs would be relatively constant until total company sales exceeded 200 000 units. Between 200 000 and 600 000 units annually, the per-unit manufacturing cost of the plugs was expected to fall to $0.40 per plug, while management salaries and supervision were estimated to rise to $80 000. Between 600 000

and 1 200 000 units annually, the cost of management was expected to be $136 000 annually, whereas direct per-unit manufacturing costs of the plugs were expected to drop to $0.27 per plug.

In trying to determine a price, Rod Jefferson saw two essentially different alternatives. The first was to "skim" the market at a high price, the second to set the price low and penetrate the market. In skimming the market, he speculated about the price-sensitivity of demand in the early stages of market development, when direct product competition would be less likely.

The other strategy, penetration pricing, was essentially a keep-out policy. If the company were to come in at a low price, with much smaller margins, it would go after market share and high volume. Since a number of manufacturers are making similar products with little or no technological or quality differences discernible to the consumer, a strategy of preserving market share through effective pricing, distribution and advertising might be appropriate.

It was also important to settle the question

**Figure C14-2   The Distribution of Spark Plugs in the Automotive Industry**

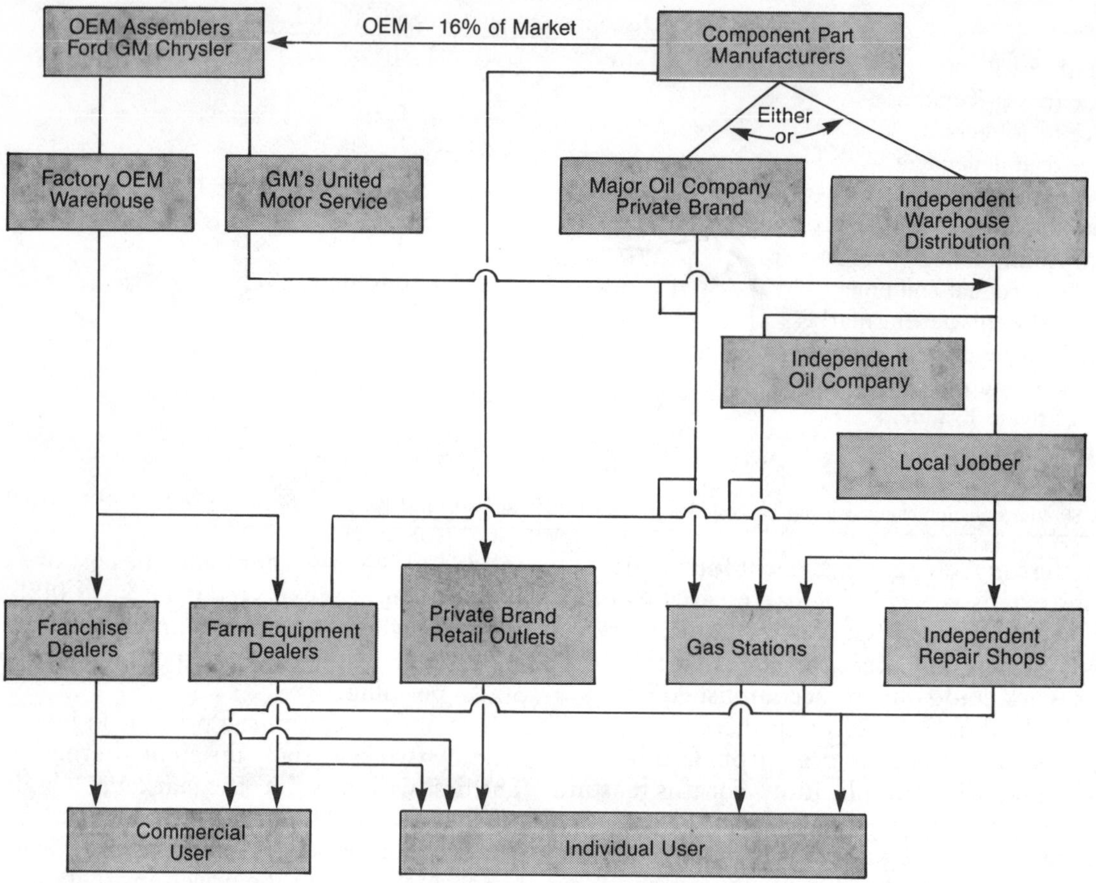

of distribution channels at an early date. The company could sell directly to customers through its own salesmen, or it could sell to distributors and jobbers, or it could use advertising in automotive publications to stimulate mail-in orders.

In determining whether or not to use salespeople, and if so, to whom they should sell, Rod Jefferson made the following assumptions. A salesperson working full time could be expected to make between six and eight calls per day. His or her cost would be roughly twice a salary of $1500 per month. If the

company were to sell to fleets, the sales job would consist of selling the president, purchasing agent, and chief mechanic on Jefferson plugs. The salesperson would have to keep control over the use of the spark plugs, eventually obtaining testimonials from the early users to place in advertisements. On the other hand, if the company sold to independent warehouse distributors or jobbers, or direct private branders, the nature of the selling job would change. There would be little control over the actual use of the plug and it would be difficult to obtain accurate performance data that would be useful in testimonials. The salesperson would be working with these people to show them how to sell and merchandise the Jefferson plug. Under either approach, it was assumed that a large fleet or wholesale account would require one call a month to keep it active.

Another alternative would be to advertise in motor magazines such as *Auto/sport, Carmag* and *Wheelspin News*. This advertising would contain a mail-in coupon requesting a set of plugs. A one-third page advertisement would cost approximately $504, $1325, or $379, respectively, per issue. The circulation for these magazines would cover car enthusiasts across Canada. Direct mail solicitation might also be used, at an estimated cost of $0.60 per mailing piece sent, including postage.

# Case 15  Different Strokes

For some time Keith Deahl, a Winnipeg firefighter and avid golfer, had been considering purchasing and operating a golf course. An 18-hole, par-3 course located on the outskirts of Winnipeg recently came onto the market, and Keith was interested. Two years earlier, he had inherited a considerable amount of money and was just waiting for an appropriate opportunity to acquire a functioning golf course. Deahl had not had a chance to go over the books of the privately owned (but open to the public) Rolling Hills Golf Course, although he understood from discussions with other local businesspeople that a couple of problem areas existed. First, the course was too short to provide a real challenge to "serious" golfers. Second, novice players found that a round took "forever" (hours) to play. And third, it was felt that the present course could not accommodate enough players in a day for the operation to break even. Deahl was not sure how he could solve these problems, until he happened to be leafing through a recent issue of *Golf Digest* and proclaimed, "I think I've found the answer; the Cayman Ball."

## The Cayman Ball

For many years, golf ball manufacturers have been devoting their principal research efforts to the development of a "longer" ball—that is, a golf ball that can be driven farther and still meet Golf Association standards. It came as some surprise, then, when Jack Nicklaus, a living legend in the game of golf, announced the development of a new ball that travelled only *half* as far as a conventional golf ball.

For several years, Nicklaus—a golfer, course designer, and golf equipment manufacturer—had been considering the concept of a golf ball with regular performance characteristics that would travel only half the regular distance. Convincing the MacGregor Company to begin research and development on the project was no problem—Nicklaus owned the company.

The ball was manufactured by a relatively simple process. It consisted of heating a combination of microscopic glass bubbles and surlyn, and injecting this mixture into the cavity of a mold for a one-piece ball. The ball had a variable density—it was lighter in the

Source: Written by Stephen Tax, M.B.A., under the supervision of Professor Walter S. Good, as a basis for classroom discussion rather than to illustrate either effective or ineffective handling of an administrative situation. Copyright © Case Development Program, Faculty of Management, University of Manitoba. Support for the development of this case was provided by the Canadian Studies Program, Secretary of State, Government of Canada.

centre and heavier toward the outside. Its flight and other characteristics closely resembled those of a conventional ball, except for one thing — it floated on water.

The new ball was the same size as a regular ball, 1.68 inches in diameter, but weighed only 40 percent of normal weight, or two-thirds of an ounce. The cost of the ball to the consumer was expected to be similar to that of a conventional ball.

Nicklaus found that using this new ball effectively halved the distance he could normally hit with each of his clubs. This translated into a typical shot of approximately 135 yards with his driver, 100 yards with a 3-iron, and 50 yards with a full wedge. It putted about the same as a regular ball, although on longer putts, he commented, "You [had] to hit it a tad harder."

## Why The New Ball?

The basic question asked by many people was, why would Jack Nicklaus, affectionately known as the Golden Bear and considered by many to be the greatest golfer of all time, want to change the fundamental structure of the game? The answer was simple: a combination of economics and and a desire to introduce new players to the game of golf.

Conventional 18-hole golf courses required a lot of land, could handle relatively few golfers per day, and took what seemed to be an eternity (four hours or more) to play. For example, a typical par-72 municipal golf course might require 150 acres of land, while a similarly designed par-72 "short-ball" course could be constructed on 50 acres. Nicklaus believed that this would be especially appealing in large cities, or countries (such as Japan) where land is expensive or in limited supply and the demand to play golf is very high.

He also believed that a 150-acre municipal course that would normally accommodate 200 people in one day could handle 1600 if it was designed for the short ball. He figured that a foursome could play an 18-hole round of golf in two hours on a short-ball facility. In effect, golf could be played in half the time, on one-third the land, by eight times as many people. People familiar with the concept also felt that the short ball could spawn a number of interesting marketing opportunities for golf entrepreneurs such as lunch-hour golf, backyard golf (MacGregor figured that it could also make a ball that would only travel one-quarter the distance of a normal ball), mixed tournaments in which the man hits the short ball and the woman a conventional ball, and so on. Nicklaus also saw some potential in converting existing par-3 (holes under 250 yards) courses overnight into championship-calibre short-ball courses.

## Critics of the Concept

Detractors of the idea contended that the short ball did not have a chance. They felt that no one seriously wanted to drive a golf ball only 100 yards. In contrast, most golfers were combing sporting goods stores and golf course pro shops for balls they could "send into orbit." One golf course architect believed that golf traditionalists/purists would resist the short ball just as they had resisted Arnold Palmer's ill-fated attempt to introduce 12-hole golf. In addition, this ball was affected more by strong wind conditions than conventional balls. This could be quite frustrating for many golfers, and what golfer needed another source of frustration?

## Introduction of the Idea

Once the ball was well along in its development, Nicklaus and MacGregor had another decision to make — where to introduce the short ball?

In late 1983, an opportunity arose for Nicklaus to design a golf course as part of a new resort development on Grand Cayman Island. Grand Cayman, part of Cayman Islands, a British dependency, consisted of 76 square miles of coral, with a population of about 18 000. It is located in the Caribbean, approximately 480 miles south of Miami. Nicklaus believed that the resort site being developed there by Ellesmere Developments Ltd., of Edmonton, would be perfect for unveiling his new ball.

Despite the fact that only 88 acres were available in Grand Cayman to build a golf course, clubhouse, 240-room hotel, and marina, plus a number of villas and condominium units, Nicklaus was able to design two 18-hole short-ball courses and a conventional par-35, 9-hole course.

The cost for the design, construction, and initial six-month startup period for the Brittania course was about $4 million. The average cost of a conventional 18-hole course was about $2 million. The annual maintenance budget for Brittania was $550 000, double that of most 18-hole courses. However, these high costs were primarily a function of specific site characteristics such as high labour costs, the difficulty in developing water hazards, and import duties for machinery and materials shipped in from Miami, rather than the type of golf ball being used.

On February 17, 1985, with Jack Nicklaus in attendance, the Brittania golf course opened for business. Initial golfer reaction was quite positive, although some players found club selection to be a problem. Nicklaus was very enthusiastic about the future of the short-ball concept.

### Conclusion

The Cayman ball appeared to have the potential to solve many of the problems of the Rolling Hills Golf Course in an interesting and unique fashion. "The course could be more challenging, faster to play, and be accessible to more golfers per day using the short ball," exclaimed Keith Deahl. "Maintenance costs shouldn't change very much either," he thought. Deahl made a note on his calendar to call his lawyer, accountant, and banker to begin negotiations for the purchase of Rolling Hills.

## Case 16   Star Electronics, Inc.

Star Electronics[1] is a medium-size manufacturer of electronic components, tools, and repair kits. It enjoyed a sales volume of $13 million in a recent year and employed 340 persons in all phases of its operation. Star Electronics is headquartered in Ottawa, Ontario. The firm is particularly known for its line of tools, chemicals, and repair kits for the professional and amateur stereo, hi-fi, and television repair people. The amateur or do-it-yourself market appears to be growing in importance.

[1] Names of the corporation and its executives are disguised to protect their identity. The material in the case study, however, consists of information obtained from interviews with company executives.

The professional repair market is reached through several electronics goods wholesalers who call on local electrical supply houses where most repair people and technicians procure their supplies. Up to this point the amateur market has represented less than 10 percent of company sales. This market is reached through retail chain outlets such as Canadian Tire, Sears, and Woolco. Star Electronics sells tools, kits, and chemicals to these stores under its own label and also under the retailers' private brands. Products sold under the two labels are generally identical.

Source: This case was prepared by Professor A. H. Kizilbash, Northern Illinois University, as a basis for class discussion. Reprinted by permission.

Because of the advances made in the design and construction of stereos, hi-fis, and televisions, there is now less need for frequent repairs. When repair is needed, it can be quickly performed by replacing the defective part with a new one, eliminating the need for traditional tools, kits, and chemicals. As a result of these and related developments, Star Electronics sales to the professional repair market has dropped $3 million over the past six years.

Recognizing that the professional repair market was shrinking, management of Star Electronics decided to search for a new product line that could strengthen their position in the consumer market. After a careful study by the New Product Development Department, a line of furniture-style stereo speakers was unveiled. The proposed product line consisted of stereo speakers with cabinets made in various furniture styles, such as contemporary, Pre-Confederation, and Mediterranean. The product developers believed that a majority of stereo speakers sold are of the black box variety and do not blend in well with the decor of a home. They reasoned that furniture-style speakers would therefore appeal to a vast majority of consumers.

Three months before the beginning of full-scale production of the new line of furniture-style stereo speakers, management decided to undertake a marketing study to determine whether a demand for this product existed. David Tanner, a recent college graduate who had been serving as an assistant to the sales manager, was asked to undertake the study. Tanner completed the study in the assigned two months. Excerpts from his report to the management are reproduced here.

## Summary of the Report

*Research Method*   In order to gain insights into consumer motivation, perceptions, and preferences for stereo speakers, this investiga-tion was conducted in two phases. The first phase of research consisted of a focus group session conducted by a trained psychologist with nine women in Toronto. In the second phase 106 personal in-store interviews were conducted with shoppers after demonstrating the product in use. These interviews were conducted in the Toronto area. Two Eatons and one Sears stores were selected for this purpose. Three identical speakers, each encased in a different style of cabinet were chosen. The three cabinet styles selected were 1) Pre-Confederation, 2) Mediterranean, and 3) black box. Interviewers would ask the respondent to listen to their chosen record on the three speakers. Using a switching system, the respondent had the opportunity to hear the same record on all three speakers. Respondents were *not* forewarned about the similarities and dissimilarities of the three speakers. They were asked to rate the three speakers on cabinet style, sound quality, and overall preference and to state the reasons for their choice.

*Focus Group Findings*   The following represents hypotheses generated from the exploratory group discussion with the nine Toronto women, four of whom owned console units and four component stereo units. The statements below are intended to be directional and indicative of possible consumer perceptions and behaviour rather than definitive.

*It would appear that when a family decides to purchase its first stereo set they are young marrieds possibly beginning a family, do not have a great deal of discretionary income, and live in smaller quarters than they anticipate once they begin to establish themselves and earn greater income. Therefore, the first stereo purchase would appear to be a console unit. The console unit, at this point in time, is compact, fits in more appropriately in a small living room, and becomes a piece of furniture.*

The middle-aged women participating in this study appeared to be neophytes in stereo sound reproduction when they purchased their first unit. Neither they nor their husbands had a sophisticated understanding of stereo systems. They relied basically on the salesperson for information and at this time in their life cycle appeared to be looking for a satisfactory sound coupled with a good-looking piece of furniture.

A console unit seems to last indefinitely and therefore does not require replacing until the family moves into larger quarters, children become teenagers, and additional music systems are required in the household. The console then may be kept in the living room as a piece of furniture or moved to another room, and a component stereo system is then considered. At this point in time, especially if there are boys in the family and reaching the teenage years, they become music consultants to their parents. Since these boys are into music, they will more than likely advise their parents to buy a component system and which components to buy.

While the father accepts the responsibility of paying for the system and the mother's input has to do with its acceptability as part of the decor, the son may very well determine the brands and quality of the components. Additional input for upgrading appears to come from listening to the music quality on friends' units, assimilating information from stereo and music magazines, and from visiting music stores.

The comparison between console and component stereo systems seems to be that for consoles you sacrifice sound for style and pay for furniture versus components which offer you much better sound, but not much style.

Two major problems appear to surface when discussing components. One is the difficulty in hiding the wires that run from the amplifier, turntable, etc., to the speakers. While some people tape them along shelving, this does pose an unsightly problem for others. The second problem is that stereo component speakers are not attractive and in some cases are hidden behind furniture or disguised in some way with planters to make them more acceptable as part of the room decor. Therefore, with this frame of reference, the exposure to the test speakers was for the most part quite favourable.

Women perceived the line of speakers as being highly decorative; depending on whether they preferred Pre-Confederation or Mediterranean, these speakers would be much preferred over what they term box speakers. However, it would seem that if these speaker boxes are priced much higher than the plain box speakers there would be resistance to purchasing them simply because they are a necessity and not an addition to the room that the woman makes voluntarily. In other words, speakers are more or less forced on her and she must arrange them in her room to accommodate the sound from a stereo. She apparently does this reluctantly, especially if she feels it interferes with her planned decor.

None of the six speakers presented to this group of women were rejected although the tighter and more heavy grill work seems to be more attractive than the standard type grill work on the market currently. Moreover, they would like to have a choice of colours in the speaker cloth behind the grill work so that they could better integrate it with their colour scheme.

On the whole then, while these speakers are more acceptable than the standard box speakers, women would prefer them to be more functional. The use of stereo speakers as end tables seems to be one possibility that is of interest. They could then use the speakers as a table lamp stand, etc. There also appears to be a feeling for an optimum sized speaker. The 35 × 65 cm speaker seems to approximate a more ideal size than its smaller counterpart but may still be slightly larger than optimum. It also appears that a double door speaker is much preferred over a single door.

From this initial exploration, it should be kept in mind that ideally these women desire stereo component speakers to be invisible. Since this is obviously impossible, they should blend in as much as possible with other decor and be multifunctional.

Younger married or single women probably feel differently about component stereo units as well might men. But for these middle-aged women and their families the above findings appear to be reasonable.

*Survey Findings*

*Demographic Profile*

1. Respondents were about equally divided for age groups above and below 30. An adequate representation of the age group over 30 was essential in view of the findings from the focus group that mature shoppers may be more receptive towards furniture-style speakers.
2. The sample appeared to have a cross-section of various occupational classes, and the distribution of population by sex and marital status was adequate.
3. Both homeowners and apartment dwellers were well represented giving us a good fix on both lifestyles.
4. Fifty-two percent of the sample population had incomes in excess of $25 000, while 30 percent had incomes in excess of $35 000. This suggests that the bulk of our sample was in the middle and upper-income range which is the target population for stereo and speaker products.
5. An overwhelming majority of the respondents were owners of component sets, which is the target population for speakers.
6. Somewhat different from the findings regarding the focus group, owners of all styles of stereo sets generally keep sets in the living room of their home or apartments.

7. Forty-two percent of the respondents owned 25 cm or smaller speakers.
8. Most persons surveyed had contemporary or "mix and match" furniture in the room in which they kept their stereo equipment.
9. Somewhat different from the focus group, a majority of these women did not participate in decisions about stereo purchase. The proportion who did participate— 42 percent — is still significant.
10. Contrary to focus group findings, those women who participated in stereo purchase decisions did not appear to have such influence that cabinet style was selected over sound quality.
11. Subjected to a hypothetical situation ("If you were shopping around for a stereo, which type would you buy?"), a majority (85 percent) would prefer components.
12. Out of the three sizes (25, 30, or 35 cm) being tested, a majority (43 percent) would prefer the 30 cm size.

*Store Test and Interview*  The study also called for an actual product test for sound, quality, and cabinet style. Interviewees were asked to pick their preferred cabinet size from the three speaker styles being tested (Pre-Confederation, Mediterranean, and black box). Each of these three styles were presented in 25, 30, and 35 cm sizes. Once the respondent chose his or her preferred size, the three speaker styles were played in the preferred size. In this way the respondent was listening to music of his or her choice on the same size speaker in each of the three cabinet styles. Respondents were told that the three speakers of a given size were of the same price. Hence, all other variables were kept constant, and the respondents were asked to rank the speakers on the basis of sound quality and cabinet style. Data gained from this product test appear in Figures C16-1 through C16-4.

**Figure C16-1    Preference for Sound Quality in Three Cabinet Styles**

| | Rankings | | |
|---|---|---|---|
| Cabinet Style | First Choice | Second Choice | Third Choice |
| Pre-Confederation | 46 (43%) | 29 (27%) | 29 (27%) |
| Mediterranean | 32 (30%) | 39 (37%) | 33 (31%) |
| Black Box | 30 (28%) | 33 (31%) | 41 (39%) |

Weighted Averages: Pre-Confederation = 1.80
Mediterranean = 1.972   Black Box = 2.066

**Figure C16-2    Preference for Cabinet Style**

| | Rankings | | |
|---|---|---|---|
| Cabinet Style | First Choice | Second Choice | Third Choice |
| Pre-Confederation | 45 (43%) | 35 (33%) | 22 (21%) |
| Mediterranean | 13 (12%) | 40 (38%) | 49 (46%) |
| Black Box | 46 (43%) | 26 (25%) | 32 (30%) |

Weighted Averages: Pre-Confederation = 1.708
Mediterranean = 2.264   Black Box = 1.83

**Figure C16-3    Overall Preference**

| | Rankings | | |
|---|---|---|---|
| Cabinet Style | First Choice | Second Choice | Third Choice |
| Pre-Confederation | 51 (48%) | 23 (22%) | 29 (27%) |
| Mediterranean | 20 (19%) | 40 (38%) | 43 (41%) |
| Black Box | 35 (33%) | 39 (37%) | 32 (30%) |

Weighted Averages: Pre-Confederation = 1.736
Mediterranean = 2.16   Black Box = 1.972

**Figure C16-4    Reasons for First Choice**

| Reason for First Choice | Respondents |
|---|---|
| Sound Quality | 63 (59%) |
| Cabinet Style | 26 (25%) |
| Both Sound and Cabinet | 17 (16%) |

**Discussion Questions**

1. Describe how the stereo speaker market is affected by life-cycle stages of consumers.
2. What recommendations should Tanner make to the Star Electronics marketing manager?

# Case 17   ENERGUIDE

In 1978 the federal government developed a labeling scheme for household appliances that has the potential for significantly affecting electrical appliance product strategy and promotion.[1] The name of the scheme is ENERGUIDE.

ENERGUIDE requires manufacturers to attach a label to major household electrical appliances (refrigerators, freezers, stoves, dishwashers and dryers) stating the kilowatt hours per month of energy consumed by each model under normal use. The ratings are verified by Canadian Standards Association (CSA) tests.

The ENERGUIDE program is an attempt by the Canadian government to ensure a "consumer information environment" whereby modification of consumers' purchase decisions will contribute to substantial savings in residential energy use. (See Figure C17-1.)

The ENERGUIDE program was introduced with considerable publicity, and has been advertised since that time in various media. Consumer response to this program, as well as consumer purchase behaviour has been monitored through several research studies by professors Dennis Anderson and John Claxton. Some highlights of their findings are included in Figures C17-2 through C17-4.

The impact of the program, as well as the possibility of changing consumer criteria for selection of appliances, has great potential significance for affecting the marketing strategy of appliance manufacturers. One observer stated that this "could be the beginning of a bitter, low-energy war among electrical appliance companies."[2]

### Discussion Questions

1. What impact do you feel the provision of this objective information on appliance labels will have on consumers' decision-making?
2. Assume that you are the assistant to the marketing manager of an appliance manufacturing company. On the basis of the information provided, as well as the research results, how much emphasis would you recommend that the company place on the matter of energy-savings in product development and promotion?

---

[1] Adapted from materials developed by C. Dennis Anderson, University of Manitoba.

[2] "Which Fridge is the Energy Guzzler?" *Chatelaine*, August 1978, p. 12.

**Figure C17-1 Exhibit   The EnerGuide Label and Statement by Consumer and Corporate Affairs[3]**

*The following is an excerpt from the
ENERGUIDE Directory, a booklet published
by Consumer and Corporate Affairs Canada.
This is supposed to be made available to
salespeople and customers at the point of sale.
The directory contains information on various specifications of appliances, including
the energy consumption per month. Tables
are also included which show how much this
will actually cost the consumer.*

Consumer and Corporate Affairs Canada would
like to acknowledge the assistance of many energy
conservation-minded groups and organizations
in the development and production of this
ENERGUIDE Directory for refrigerators and
freezers.

This appliance
model    #A209    uses
**72** kWh
of electricity per month when
tested in accordance with CSA standards.

ENER**G**UIDE

Cet appareil de modéle n°    A209
vérifié conformément aux
normes de l'ACNOR, consomme
**72** kWh
d'électricité par mois.

The co-operative efforts by the consumer
associations, major appliance manufacturers
and the many electrical utilities contributed
significantly towards the successful implementation of the department's ENERGUIDE Program.
Their continuing co-operation will ensure that all

Canadians reap the energy conservation benefits
that the energy-labelling program will provide for
years to come.

Beneficial guidance for all Canadians can be
found in the new ENERGUIDE Directory. The
ENERGUIDE Program can provide Canadian
consumers with immediate and long-term
benefits. As energy costs continue to increase,
there will be a corresponding rise in demand from
Canadians for improved appliance energy
efficiency. Consumers will see, in cash dollars,
the savings that can be realized by choosing an
appliance model that consumes less energy. By
looking for the ENERGUIDE label and choosing
wisely, shoppers will save both money and energy.

Retailers can now assist their customers in making
a purchase decision based in part on the energy
characteristics of each appliance model featured in
their store. By using the ENERGUIDE label, they
not only help their customers save money by
conserving energy; they also make a significant
contribution to the development of more efficient,
long-term use of products and energy.

Finally, appliance manufacturers now have a
distinct comparison between the energy
characteristics of their products and those of their
competitors. The energy consumption figures
contained within should act as a positive incentive
and stimulus for manufacturers to continue to
improve the energy efficiency of their products
through research, design and development.

The pursuit of energy conservation consensus
with a minimum of regulation is an activity which
is endorsed by the federal government. The
evolution and application of the ENERGUIDE
program through voluntary co-operative
participation clearly supports that viewpoint.

As Canadians become familiar with the dollar
benefits of this Refrigerator/Freezer ENERGUIDE
Directory, we are confident that energy will
become an increasingly important factor to them
when purchasing a major electrical household
appliance.

3 *1980 ENERGUIDE Directory, Refrigerators and Freezers*, Consumer and Corporate Affairs Canada, p. ifc.

Figure C17-2    Selected Measures of Refrigerator Purchase Criteria and Search Behaviour
(and Trends 1978 vs. 1980)

| MEASURE | 1980 NATIONAL SURVEY | TREND COMPARISON (Western Canada Only) | |
|---|---|---|---|
| | | 1978 | 1980 |
| *Sample Size:* | 235 | 303 | 100[1] |
| *Purchase Criteria (Rank Order of Importance):* | | | |
| • Type of defrost (frost-free or manual) | 1 | 1[2] | 2 |
| • Warranty | 2 | 2 | 3 |
| • Total storage capacity | 3 | 3 | 1 |
| • Number and type of shelves | 4 | 5 | 5 |
| • Colour | 5 | 4 | 4 |
| • Low price | 6 | 7 | 6 |
| • Operating Cost (energy costs) | 7 | 11 | 8 |
| • Dual temperature controls | 8 | 6 | 7 |
| • Brand name | 9 | 10 | 9 |
| • Type of insulation | 10 | 8 | 10 |
| • Interior Wall construction | 11 | 9 | 10 |
| • Thin-wall construction | 12 | 12 | 12 |
| • Ice maker | 13 | 13 | 13 |
| *Search Behaviour:* | | | |
| • Considered no other sizes | 50% | 54% | 51% |
| • Considered manual defrost models | 26% | 21% | 25% |
| • Considered only one or two brands | 42% | 47% | 43% |
| • Considered only one or two stores | 39% | 39% | 39% |
| *Factor Precipitating Search:* | | | |
| • Didn't own one before | 19% | NA | 24% |
| • Product breakdown | 30% | 27% | 26% |
| • Wanted newer/bigger | 27% | 36% | 25% |
| • Wanted smaller size | 3% | NA | 0% |
| • Moved and sold/needed second one | 20% | 29% | 22% |

[1] Because the 1978 study covered only Western Canadian cities, only a sub-sample of the 1980 national survey (N = 100, from corresponding Western Canadian cities) is used for comparison purposes.
[2] In 1978 a total of 19 purchase criteria were rated. Only 13 of the 19 product attributes were common between the 1978 and 1980 research instrument, hence the rank orders for 1978 are adjusted accordingly.

Source: Anderson, C. Dennis, and John D. Claxton, "Marketer and Societal Response to Changes in the Energy Information Environment for Durable Products," *Proceedings of the European Academy for Advanced Research in Marketing* (Copenhagen, Denmark: March 1981).

Figure C17-3   Selected Measures of Salesperson Influence On, and Energy Label Utilization By, Refrigerator Purchasers (and Trends 1978 vs. 1980)

| MEASURE | 1980 NATIONAL SURVEY | TREND COMPARISON (Western Canada Only) | |
|---|---|---|---|
| | | 1978 | 1980 |
| *Sample Size:* | 235 | 303 | 100[1] |
| *Influence Attributed to Salesperson (percent agree or strongly agree):* | | | |
| • Made useful suggestions | 54% | 53% | 53% |
| • Explained differences among models | 60% | 58% | 56% |
| • Provided useful printed information | 42% | 44% | 45% |
| • Advice was very important in my choice | 29% | 29% | 37% |
| *Utilization of Energy Labels:* | | | |
| • Saw labels on models | 72% | 33% (N-237)[2] | 76% |
| • Who brought attention to labels | | | |
| – noticed myself | 81% (N-154) | 82% (N-71) | 82% (N-68) |
| – salesperson pointed out | 19% (N-154) | 18% (N-71) | 18% (N-68) |
| • Labels explained by salesperson | 30% | 12% (N-237) | 29% |
| • Labels were understandable | 61% | 25% (N-237) | 63% |
| • Noticed large or medium differences in kwh ratings (energy consumption) among models | 26% | 20% (N-237) | 24% |
| • Kwh rating was a major factor in model choice | 29% | 10% (N-237) | 21% |
| • Kwh mentioned as main reason for choosing brand (response to open-ended question) | 3% | NA | 2% |

[1]Because the 1978 study covered only Western Canadian cities, only a sub-sample of the 1980 national survey (N-100, from corresponding Western Canadian cities) is used for comparison purposes.
[2]Only 237 of the 303 respondents in the 1978 study bought at stores where energy labels were attached to refrigerators. The remaining 66 respondents bought at control stores where there were no energy label treatments in place.

Source: Anderson, C. Dennis, and John D. Claxton, "Marketer and Societal Response to Changes in the Energy Information Environment for Durable Products," *Proceedings of the European Academy for Advanced Research in Marketing* (Copenhagen, Denmark: March 1981).

**Figure C17-4**

Important-Difference Grid with Ratings for Selected Applicance Attributes[a]: 1976 Study

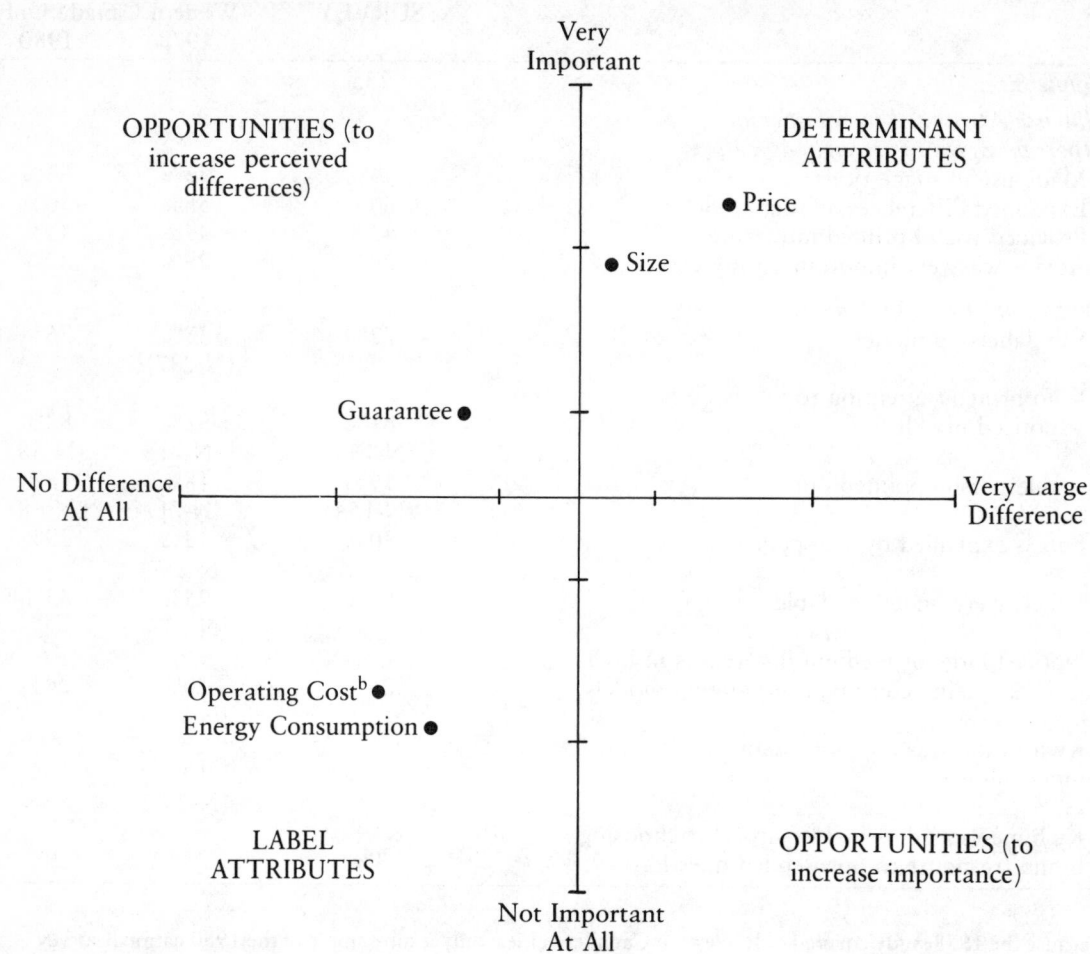

[a] Based on mean ratings for refrigerator and freezer
[b] Example: respondent is saying, "I feel there are a few differences in operating costs among products in the market today, and operating costs are not very important to me."

Source: Anderson, C. Dennis, "Consumer Behaviour and Energy Information Labels for Home Appliances," *Proceedings of the Marketing Division of the Canadian Association of Administrative Sciences* (Fredericton, New Brunswick: June 1977).

# Case 18   Duradent 1-2-3

Twenty-five years ago, Mr. Ringer entered the drugstore business by working in one of his father's stores when he graduated as a pharmacist. Today he manages the store which is located on a major traffic artery in a suburban residential area of Winnipeg and has built it into one of the most successful drugstores in Western Canada. It provided the Ringers with a comfortable and secure livelihood. Mr. Ringer is interested in new business opportunities; however, he is cautious about becoming involved in a venture which would seriously jeopardise his existing base. He has recently been investigating a new product, Duradent 1-2-3, which seems to have significant sales potential if marketed correctly.[1]

As a scientist, Mr. Ringer is very impressed by the technical aspects of Duradent 1-2-3, a colourless, odourless coating for dentures that allows them to adhere more naturally and efficiently. The way it works is difficult to describe, and Mr. Ringer has had mediocre success in market testing the product in his own store. With his limited experience in this type of mass marketing, he is reassessing the opportunity.

Mr. Ringer has Canadian rights to the Duradent process, which was developed in the United States. It duplicates in three simple steps a treatment that previously required elaborate equipment to apply to dentures. The process leaves a long lasting, colourless, odourless, tasteless, and dimension-free hydrophilic (water "loving") layer on the surface of the acrylic plastic from which most complete dentures are made. Essentially, the surface-tension of moisture on the plastic is reduced, improving adherence in the way adherence (or "suction") is created when two

pieces of glass are pressed together with water in between. (Because partial plates usually have clips or straps to hold them in place, Duradent is not useful in retaining them.)

Some common problems experienced by wearers of one or two full plates are:
— the denture slipping laterally
— food becoming caught beneath the denture
— the denture dropping down
— interference and anxiety when speaking
— embarrassment when eating
— odours from decaying food caught in dentures
— food sticking to exposed areas
— anxiety when sneezing, laughing, and so forth

Except for lateral slippage, Duradent has helped to eliminate all of these discomforts, but *only* if the dentures are well fitted (so that the suction can work).

Other products now generally used for denture retention include powders and pastes which are put into the area of contact between the denture and the gums. These relatively messy products require daily use and sometimes make users feel nauseous. Not all people use them. Generally, the poorer fitting the denture, the more the use of such adhesives.

Instead of squeezing a paste or applying a powder onto the denture, the Duradent process requires the painting of the entire denture. Inside the Duradent 1-2-3 box (approximately $5 \times 6 \times 14$ cm) are 3 distinctly labelled vials, a disposable plastic glove, 3 cotton swabs, and an instruction sheet.

The denture must be thoroughly cleaned with detergent and allowed to dry; the plastic glove prevents the skin's oils from soiling the denture. Using a cotton swab, solution (Duraprime) is rubbed lightly but thoroughly over the entire denture. Using fresh swabs, the procedure is repeated with solutions #2

[1] Source: M. D. Beckman and Murray Kawchuk.

(Durabase) and #3 (Durabond). The denture is allowed to dry for 15 minutes. This process should take place in a well ventilated area because the vapours from solutions 2 and 3 are similar to hydrochloric acid.

From then on the denture requires normal cleaning with water and any denture cleaner, soap or detergent. If hard brushes and abrasive cleansers are avoided, the Duradent application will last for about 12 months.

Mr. Ringer explains that the Duradent process makes the denture "less of a foreign object to the body by increasing the hydrophilic characteristics of the acrylic plastic." This gives increased comfort to the wearer and leads him to believe that Duradent can, given the process is correctly performed and the dentures fit well, significantly improve the quality of life for denture wearers. Recently, Mr. Ringer had tested sales of Duradent from an on-the-counter display in his own drugstore. Because of his interest in the product, Mr. Ringer usually personally attended to customers inquiring about Duradent.

Over five months he used several media to promote the Duradent. Mobile trailer signs, window posters and an overhead outdoor neon sign served as advertising to passers-by. Duradent 1-2-3 was featured in a half-page newspaper advertisement and also among other weekly drugstore specials. Mr. Ringer wanted mass, knowledge oriented advertising and, since he had some experience in developing advertising for his store, he wrote and produced two of his own radio ads (see Figure C18-1). Mr. Ringer had done many radio ads for his store, and could deliver such a commercial as well as or better than most professional radio announcers.

Mr. Ringer's promotional efforts yielded very slow sales but feedback was generally positive, though mixed. Before going further, he wants to assess the situation. Mr. Ringer sold Duradent at $14.95 a box, a price taking into consideration the quality arrived at and longevity of the product (see Figure C18-2). Competitive powders and pastes cost approximately $2–$3 a tube, or box, with an annual

---

**Figure C18-1   Radio ads written, produced, and read by Mr. Ringer:**

1. Denture wearers: there's a fabulous new denture adhesive on the market called "Duradent 1-2-3". Treat your dentures with Duradent and a micro-thin layer of moisture will coat your dentures at all times. As a result, less effort is required to hold your dentures in place. Your denture will feel more natural in your mouth, feel more secure when you eat, feel more secure when you cough, feel more secure when you laugh and when you speak. Treat your dentures with easy to use Duradent 1-2-3 and you'll have no need for messy powders and sticky pastes. One treatment with Duradent costs only $14.95 and lasts about a year. Duradent 1-2-3, $14.95 a kit, available only at Ringer's.
2. Denture wearers, at last there's a fabulous new colourless, odourless, tasteless, invisible denture

adhesive on the market called Duradent 1-2-3. Treat your dentures with Duradent and a micro-thin layer of moisture will coat your dentures at all times. As a result, less effort is required to hold your dentures in place. Your denture will feel more natural in your mouth, feel more secure when you eat, feel more secure when you cough and sneeze, feel more secure when you laugh, and when you speak. Treat your dentures with easy to use Duradent 1-2-3 and you'll have no need for messy powders and sticky pastes. One treatment of Duradent lasts about a year. Duradent 1-2-3, $14.95 a kit, only at Ringer's, we guarantee it!

Note: Each ad was 45 seconds long and featured only Mr. Ringer's voice without music or other introduction.

Source: Company records

**Figure C18-2    Duradent: Per Unit Cost Data**

| | |
|---|---|
| Sales Price | $14.95 |
| Retaler's Margin (25%) | 3.74 |
| | 11.21 |
| Wholesaler's Margin (15%) | 1.68 |
| | 9.53 |
| Materials, packaging, displays | 4.00 |
| Contribution Margin | $5.53 |

Source: Company records

cost varying greatly ($3–$20) depending upon the brand used, the frequency of use, and the number of dentures. These were primarily marked by large pharmaceutical companies on a national level.

Data on the Canadian market show that 25.9 percent of all Canadians wear dentures of some type (see Figure C18-3). Although the present growth rate is 5 percent, it is expected that long-term growth may be slowed by water fluoridation and improved dental care. One type of segmentation that Mr. Ringer is considering is depicted in Figure C18-4.

However, problems in dealing with the range of prospects in this potential market might include:
— prospects not entering the market in short run
— consumers failing to perceive benefits
— consumers failing to purchase the product
— consumers rejecting the product
— consumers not understanding the concept

For distribution of Duradent, Mr. Ringer has considered marketing through dental clinics, dentists' offices or through a mass marketing effort. His many years of experience in the retail pharmacy industry have led Mr. Ringer to reject the first two alternatives. He feels that inadequate effort and attention would be given to his product through such channels. Before proceeding to the third alternative

though, he is entertaining the idea of test marketing Duradent in Brandon, a trade area of about 70 000 people. An analysis of associated costs for media coverage is presented in Figure C18-5. A properly executed campaign will cost approximately $100 000, with advertising absorbing most of the funds.

Although he favours it, this approach leaves some concerns with Mr. Ringer. First, the financial commitment will be quite large and he is unsure whether the risk is acceptable. Second, he believes that many denture wearers perceive their problems as incorrectible inconveniences that must be tolerated, which leads to a seemingly different communication task. A final concern is that the benefits of Duradent are not always perceived immediately. Sometimes a month will pass before the user begins to notice them. On the other hand, his experiences suggest that users become aware of the benefits as the treatment began to wear off about a year later.

## Discussion Questions

1. Evaluate the steps taken by Mr. Ringer thus far.
2. Develop a marketing program that would make Duradent 1-2-3 a success.
3. Should Mr. Ringer introduce Duradent 1-2-3 into the market?

## Figure C18-3  Profile of Denture Adhesive Use, Denture Wearers, and Market Share

|  | Percentage of wearers | Percentage of volume of adhesives |
|---|---|---|
| Heavy users of adhesives | 20% | 60% |
| Moderate users of adhesives | 30% | 30% |
| Light users of adhesives | 50% | 10% |
| Full lower & upper plate | 47% of wearers | |
| Lower *or* upper plate | 33% | |
| Partial plate | 20% | |
| Age of wearers | | |
|   65 and over | 20% | |
|   55–64 | 20% | |
|   45–54 | 21% | |
|   35–44 | 19% | |
|   under 35 | 20% | |

Source: Special report prepared for company

*MARKET SHARE:*
| | |
|---|---|
|   Poli-grip | 33% |
|   Fasteeth | 21% |
|   Orafix | 20% |
|   Corega | 12% |
|   Other | 14% |

Source: Data collected by the company from trade sources

## Figure C18-4  Possible Market Segments

Heavy users of adhesives
Moderate users of adhesives
Light users of adhesives
Tried adhesives & rejected them
Some dissatisfaction with dentures
Practical Potential Market
Indifferent
No dissatisfaction with dentures

## Figure C18-5  Media Rates in the Proposed Test Market

*RADIO*

| TIME CLASSIFICATIONS | RATES | |
|---|---|---|
| | 30 Sec. | 60 Sec. |
| AA: 6–10 A.M. | $23.00 | $25.00 |
|  A: 10 A.M.–1 P.M. & 4–7 P.M. | $18.00 | $20.00 |
|  B: 1–4 P.M. & 7–12 P.M. | $16.00 | $18.00 |

**Figure C18-5 continued**

*TELEVISION*

| | RATES | |
|---|---|---|
| | 30 Sec. | 60 Sec. |
| AA: 5–6 P.M. Sun.; 6–11 P.M. Mon. thru Sun. | $60.00 | $85.00 |
| A: 11–12 P.M. Sat. & Sun.; 12 P.M.-S/O Sat. | $50.00 | $75.00 |
| B: S/O–5 P.M. Sun.; 5–6 P.M. Mon. thru Sat.; | | |
|   11–12 P.M. Mon. thru Sat. | $45.00 | $60.00 |
| C: S/O–5 P.M. Mon. thru Sat.; | | |
|   12 P.M.-S/O Sun. thru Fri. | $20.00 | $25.00 |

*NEWSPAPER*

Full Page .... $640.64
1/2 Page .... $320.32
1/4 Page .... $160.16
1/8 Page ..... $ 80.08

Source: Report prepared for company

# Case 19  Leduc Manufacturing Company

On October 3, 1984, William R. Nelson, division manager of Leduc Manufacturing Company and vice-president of its multi-million-dollar conglomerate parent company, has called a meeting of the division's top echelon to expedite the launch of a new line of pipes and tubing. He is chagrined that, according to production manager Ian McMichaels, the scheduled commercialization date of July 1, 1985, cannot be met.

This impatience is shared by Dale N. Schroder, Ph.D. (chemical engineering), director of research and development, who personally contributed much to the new line. Also attending is controller Frank B. Abt, RIA, an enthusiastic advocate of formal planning. The final participant is J. Robertson (Bob) Hellas, sales manager. All of these executives, now in their 50s, have been with the division a long time.

## Sales Department

A major producer of plastic pipes and tubes, Leduc Manufacturing Company has a functional organization. (See Figure C19-1.) In the sales department, executives reporting to Bob Hellas include four regional industrial sales managers (corresponding to Leduc's four factories), an advertising manager, and a consumer-goods product manager. The regional sales managers supervise 35 salespersons. The sales force obtains leads and exhortations from headquarters and from regional sales managers, but, by and large, they make up their own schedules. In addition

Source: This case was prepared by Harold W. Fox, George A. Ball Distinguished Professor in Marketing at Ball State University. Names and data of the co-operating firms have been altered to preserve anonymity. Reprinted by permission.

**Figure C19-1    Organization of Leduc Manufacturing Company**

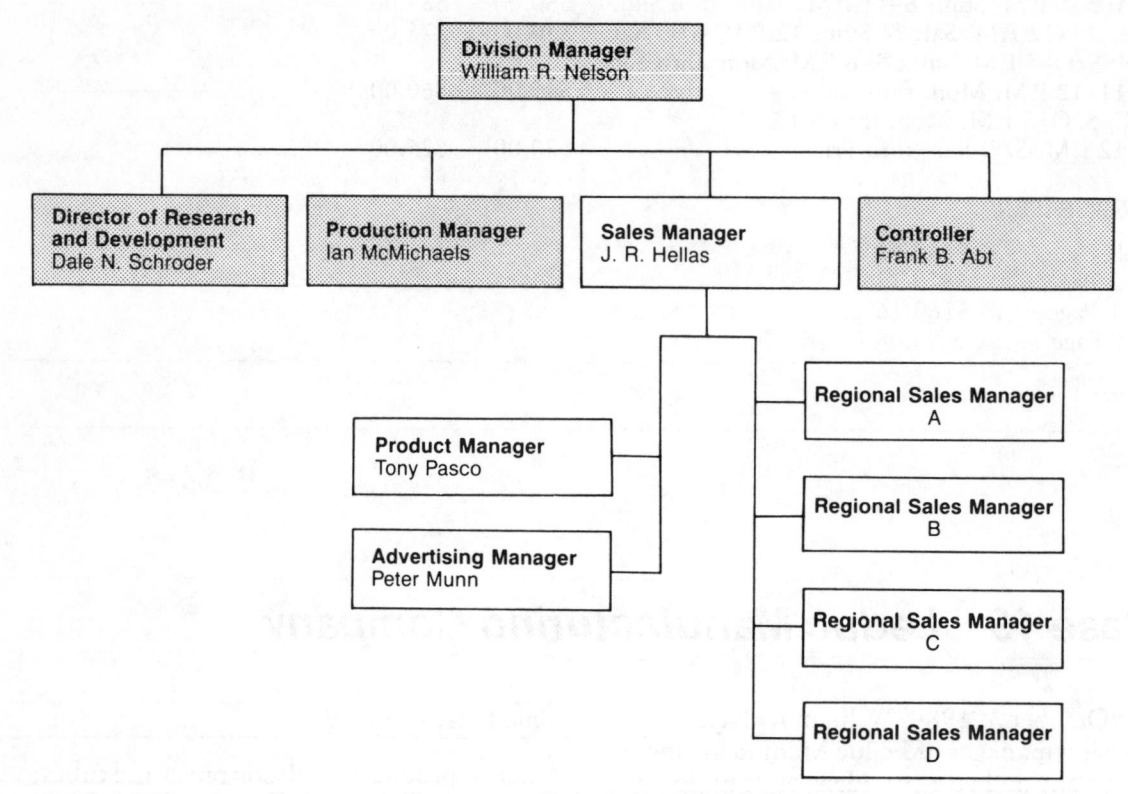

to prospecting for orders, following up customers, and so on, an important part of their job is verifying that distributors are well stocked with Leduc's wares.

Compensation of the sales force is salary plus ten percent commission on total dollar sales above individual quota. On the average, salespersons' earnings derive 50 percent from salary and 50 percent from commission. Leduc also reimburses each salesperson for travel and entertainment expenses in accordance with the company's policy manual.

Leduc confines its industrial advertising to reminder-type messages in specialized industry periodicals serving the division's markets.

An advertising manager, Peter Munn, was hired in 1984. A former public relations officer, he deals with Leduc's industrial advertising agency; plans industrial sales promotion campaigns; designs collateral materials such as catalogues, brochures, point-of-purchase displays, and booklets; reserves space at trade show; releases publicity; and relieves the sales manager of other non-selling promotional tasks.

Consumer goods, mainly garden hose and sprinklers, are under the jurisdiction of Tony Pasco. Determination of consumer goods' brand names, prices, advertisements and sales promotions, and distribution channels is separate from the industrial unit. Hellas is very satisfied with the profit and progress of this subdivision and lets product manager Pasco run it almost autonomously on a modest budget. According to the controller, this business could and should be tripled, even at the risk of losing some component business; i.e., sales of plastic piping and tubing to lawn equipment manufacturers.

## Product Lines

In 1983, sales of Leduc plastic tubes and pipes amounted to $53 million — about the same as in 1982 and 1981. The burgeoning department of consumer goods registered a new high of $340 000 in 1983.

On tubes and pipes up to 30 cm in diameter, plastic resins are in many uses more flexible, more durable, and more economical than conventional materials. The main resins are polyvinyl chloride and styrene. Lately, supply of these resins has occasionally been interrupted or threatened because of shortages of raw materials and dangers to the health of suppliers' employees. The general consensus is that over the next 10 years these supply problems will become worse.

Over the past two years, the research and development department of Leduc Manufacturing Company has developed a patented energy-efficient formulation. Proved workable in the laboratory, this new formulation substitutes readily available synthetics for petroleum-based inputs. Leduc pins its hopes for the future on this forthcoming line to recapture leadership among its established customers and to penetrate hitherto closed markets.

## End Uses

All industrial distributors and most end users of plastic pipe and tubing divide their purchases among several competing vendors. Leduc's market share has slipped from number one to number two.

A major end use of polyvinyl chloride pipes and components is irrigation for farms and turfs. Plastics are superior to metal and open-ditch water transportation systems. Due to consolidations and industrialization, much of agriculture buys on a rational basis. The faster-growing turf irrigation market is comprised of municipal park districts and manufacturers of lawn watering installations.

Another important end use is residential and commercial construction. Sales to large buyers, such as electrical and mechanical contractors and mobile home manufacturers, are direct, often on a bid basis; so are most sales of electrical conduits for the protection and insulation of electric power lines and telephone lines to public utilities and large construction companies. Smaller users buy from various distributors.

Over the past 10 years, acceptance of plastic pipe has been more rapid in public than in private systems. Many local building codes specify copper, aluminum, steel, or iron, thus excluding plastic pipe from home systems. This exclusion has been strongly advocated by plumbing unions, which point to the traditional materials' superior strength and resistance to thermal expansion, melting, and crushing. Where plastic pipe has been allowed, it has proved to generate substantial labour savings because both installation and maintenance are much simpler.

Plastic pipe and tubing are also used in the production operations of various industries. Sales potential seems to be smaller than in the aforementioned uses, but business can be much more profitable.

Technical and commercial services must satisfy the particular needs of these industries. Hi-tech industries, for example, insist on the highest quality and are willing to trade off cost for highest performance. The medical equipment industry is similarly disposed. Leduc Manufacturing Company is still number one in medical equipment. With its effective reliability and quality assurance procedures, Leduc is in a superior position to serve these customers. Electronics manufacturers and mines, on the other hand, are price conscious. In between these extremes are food processors and paper companies. These last two industries are especially concerned about contamination of their raw materials from migrating plastic ingredients.

A recent study ranked growth prospects in the 1980s as follows, from highest to lowest: electronics, medical equipment, hi-tech, mining, food processing, paper manufacture. Leduc Manufacturing Company is very strong with medical equipment, paper mills, and food processors, but relatively weak in the other fields.

Besides price and quality, an important consideration for most buyers is delivery. Except for some specialities, plastic tubes and pipes from different manufacturers are interchangeable. Buyers often switch from one source to another based on earliest availability.

List prices FOB factory on competing plastic pipes and tubes are the same. Even slight price cutting leads to immediate retaliation. Leduc's four geographically dispersed plants have low freight rates and speedy transit to all buyers. This capability is an important competitive advantage.

Altogether, Leduc's success rests largely on the momentum from early aggressive entry into this field, large size, high quality, and excellent physical distribution.

## Physical Status of the New Line

When the top-echelon meeting on the stalled innovation convenes, the discussion turns quickly to the production department. "The new formulation works perfectly in the lab," the R & D director noted. "I see no reason why we don't proceed with full-scale production now."

Ian McMichaels, the production manager, is still irate over the loss of production and the cost of extruder repairs that was charged to his department when R & D personnel experi-

mented with the new formulation on the production floor last month. The new formulation works only within very narrow tolerances. Slight deviations in the mix proportions can clog the dies and cause the electrical system to overheat, and apparently this is what occurred. Nothing like this has ever happened before.

McMichaels explains calmly that factory operations are not controllable to the same extent as laboratory trials. Small batches in the lab are not necessarily indicative of long runs in the plant. Jobs will have to be redesigned and machine surveillance tightened. Quality control has advised him that standard grades of raw material vary more widely than R & D specifications for the new formulation allow. As of now, the new formulation is not producible. Another difficulty is post extrusion bath.

The controller interrupts, "What does the union say about job redesign?"

"That's a good question," replies McMichaels. "As I was saying, the present single bath . . ."

"Hold it!" This time it is Nelson, the division manager, who breaks in. "Rather than go over technical details that we can figure out for ourselves, you may be better served by a systematic approach. I suggest that you and Dale (R & D director) get together this week and work out a practical method for speedy and smooth transition from R & D to production.

"Could the three of us meet on Monday in my office at 10:00 a.m. to discuss your plan? Let's go over all feasible options and your reasons for recommending one particular approach." The two executives nod, signifying acquiescence.

## Marketing Status

"This brings us to the second point," resumes William Nelson, "our entry marketing strategy." Nelson looks at Hellas. The sales manager concedes that he lacks detailed knowledge about the new line. "I guess I've been too busy producing profitable business. No apologies needed for that, eh?"

Somewhat defensively, Hellas explains that the new line does not pose any new marketing problems. When the new formulation has been debugged, Leduc will simply ship it instead of the old. Customers will, of course, receive notice. None are likely to object. No price increase will be necessary, according to the accounting department. And the last he has heard, the R & D department has proved performance of the new is identical with the old.

Schroder, the R & D director, confirms this reasoning. Total discontinuation of the old formulation will be necessary. Changeovers between old and new are too expensive and time consuming. The sensitivity of the new formulation requires perfect purification of the machines before a run starts. This entails first producing scrap from the residues of the old then running an industrial cleanser until

all vestiges are removed. Extra tests are needed to assure that the new formulation is properly balanced. All of this applies only to changes from old to new formulation. There is no difficulty other than minor setup for adjustments *within* either formulation. Product mix changes per se are simple.

In the opinion of Abt, the controller, the unfurling challenges call for formal planning. There are things to be done between now and the time when shipments begin, but this suggestion does not sit well with the other functional managers.

At this point, an urgent telephone call for Nelson from the corporate president requires him to adjourn the meeting. The managers decide to break for lunch and resume the meeting at 2 p.m.

### Discussion Questions

1. What recommendations would you make to the division manager?

## Case 20    Moose Poop

Debbie Gerrits, John McDonald, and Jeff Johnson felt more confident than ever that 1984 would be the year of the moose. The three partners in Concept Enterprises were still basking in the success of the market test of their new fad product, "Genuine Canadian Moose Poop," when they met at John and Jeff's Winnipeg apartment in early February. Their task was to prepare a marketing plan for the full scale introduction of Moose Poop in Canada and the United States. They were particularly concerned with finalizing plans for production and distribution before seeking additional financing.

### Concept Enterprises

Concept Enterprises was a limited partnership formed in August 1983 by Debbie Gerrits, John McDonald, and Jeff Johnson. The three partners were in their mid-twenties and had successful careers in administration, marketing, and accounting. The three had combined their personal assets of $100 000 in Concept Enterprises in order to gain more control over their careers without giving up their flexible lifestyles.

Source: C. Dennis Anderson, University of Manitoba.

Debbie gave up her job to work full-time managing Concept Enterprises' day-to-day operations. John and Jeff worked for Concept Enterprises only on evenings and weekends. John was a marketing representative for an industrial sales company and Jeff was an accountant. Their combined salaried income of $70 000 per year was important because it allowed Concept Enterprises to develop at its own pace rather than rushing to market unprepared. Nevertheless, the partners wanted to minimize their personal investment in Concept Enterprises, and were prepared to use financing.

## Moose Poop

Genuine Canadian Moose Poop was just what its name implied. Concept Enterprises' promotional material described Moose Poop as "a gross natural product" which was "the end result of a moose." Moose Poop was first commercialized by John Smith of Kenora, Ontario. Mr. Smith, a retired Hydro worker, collected moose droppings, dried them, coated them with marine varnish, then strung them on strips of moose hide to make necklaces or glued them to sticks. The resulting products which he called Pet Poops and Poopsie Pops developed a small following in the local area.

Debbie, John, and Jeff discovered these *objets d'art* while attending a wedding in Kenora in October 1983. They decided that the necklaces had potential as a novelty item, and met with Mr. Smith to obtain the right to market the product. Mr. Smith agreed to allow Concept Enterprises to market Moose Poop in North America for a royalty fee of two cents per poop sold. Debbie also applied for copyright protection as a precautionary measure.

## The Market

Fad products are one of the great puzzles in marketing. People have studied the phenomenon for years. They know how a product takes off but no one can predict which product will be next nor how long it might last. Fads seem to come out of nowhere, generating nationwide interest and publicity, only to fade into obscurity once more, although some products, like the yo-yo and the hula hoop, manage a comeback every five to ten years.

The partners in Concept Enterprises felt that Moose Poop had the potential to repeat the Pet Rock craze of the mid 1970s. The Pet Rock was created by Gary Dahl, a former advertising copy writer. Dahl surprised himself by ringing up North American sales in excess of 1.25 million Pet Rocks at $4.00 each. The Pet Rocks came complete with a "training manual" and carrying case. They received coverage in radio, television, and newspapers, without Dahl's having to spend a penny on advertising. Dahl suggested that the Pet Rock was successful because it allowed people to share a little humour after the Vietnam War and Watergate years. John felt that with a creative promotion campaign Moose Poop could also capture the imagination of consumers.[1]

Moose Poop was to be promoted primarily as a gift item, although it also had potential as a tourist gimmick. Debbie found data that suggested most gift purchases were made by women buying for men. Jeff thought that Moose Poop would make a great gift for someone's boss or in-laws.

Total demand was difficult to estimate. The most recent census data listed the Canadian population at over 24 million, and that of the United States at 226 million, with just under three people per household. The population in both countries was divided with approximately 75 percent living in urban areas and 25 percent in rural. Demand in the tourist market was impossible to quantify. In order

---

[1] For more information on the Pet Rock and fad products see "The Fickle Finger of Fads," in *Industry Week* (September 26, 1976), p. 64.

to get a better feel for the market before making a large commitment, the partners decided to conduct a market test in Winnipeg and northwestern Ontario.

## Market Test

The market test of Moose Poop was conducted during November and December 1983. It was designed to determine consumer response to the product (both as a gift and as a tourist item), pricing policy, and the effectiveness of different retail outlets. For the test, Concept Enterprises simply repackaged John Smith's original Pet Poop necklaces into a plain cardboard display unit featuring the slogan "give 'em poop." Moose Poop was distributed to nine outlets in northwestern Ontario and sixty-two in Winnipeg, as well as a craft show. A variety of price points, ranging from $3.00 to $7.00, were tried during the test and sales were closely monitored.

The market test was supported by a low-key "free publicity" campaign. Press releases were issued to local newspapers and radio stations. The resulting coverage included a front-page spot in the Winnipeg Free Press, and over a half-dozen radio interviews, including one with Arthur Black on the CBC national network and another with Stephanie Marks from ABC New York, which were aired on 1800 stations across the United States. Television coverage was actively avoided during the market test, because the partners felt they would have only one chance with TV.

## The Meeting: February 1984

**Debbie:** Let's start off tonight by having John review the market test results, then I'll fill you in on all the production and packaging details.

**John:** Okay. Overall I think we'd agree that the response to Moose Poop was very strong. We sold almost 300 units in northwestern Ontario in the dead of winter, so I think we've got a real winner in the tourist segment. In

Winnipeg, which has a population of 600 000, we sold 700 through only one-thirtieth of the available outlets. With a strong push next year, we could easily sell twenty to thirty times that many. (See Figure C20-1.)

However, on the downside, sales in the twenty-four hour and tobacco stores were pretty slow. I think this was because of the bland displays, and the fact that people just don't shop at these stores for gifts. Even with the redesigned packaging (see Figure C20-3), I don't think these outlets will be viable.

The market test also indicated that a retail price of $5.00 is as high as we can go. Sales really dropped off at anything above that. Out of $5.00, the retailers want half and then we have to pay our agents 10 percent commission and 9 percent federal sales tax. This leaves us with a little over $2.00 per unit in Canada. Debbie, I hope that production and packaging won't eat up the whole $2.00!

**Debbie:** Not quite; our unit costs can vary from 60 to 70 cents, and administration and wages will cost approximately $1500 per month. I've summarized the expenses in table form for you, so I'll just go over the highlights. (See Figure C20-2.) I've managed to secure a supply of poops from a number of trappers, game farms, and biologists. They tell me we could easily get up to 5 million poops on short notice. Our lead time will be about three weeks from the time we place our orders to store delivery, although the initial run for the cardboard outhouse packages and display units will take eight to ten weeks. The critical part in this venture will be keeping close track of sales at the retail level.

**Jeff:** That sounds good, Debbie. Did you get more information on distribution in the U.S.?

**Debbie:** I had another chat with Tom Jackson from ADC. They've got good connections with card and gift shops across the country and should be able to get Moose Poop into a few of the major department stores as well. Tom said that ADC would carry Moose Poop

## Figure C20-1   Summary of Moose Poop Market Test Sales

| Location and store type | Units sold |
|---|---|
| *Northwestern Ontario:* | |
| 6 general stores | 188 |
| 1 gas station | 24 |
| 2 gift stores | 72 |
| Total northwestern Ontario outlets | 284 |
| | |
| *Manitoba:* | |
| 1 craft show | 160 |
| 1 men's store | 48 |
| 1 major department store | 72 |
| 52 24-hour convenience stores | 371 |
| 2 drug stores | 61 |
| 3 card shops | 86 |
| 1 hotel gift shop | 24 |
| 1 tobacco & magazine shop | 9 |
| 1 personal order | 24 |
| Total Manitoba outlets | 855 |
| Orders received through media coverage | 81 |
| | |
| Total test market sales | 1220 |

## Figure C20-2   Moose Poop: Unit Costs, Quantities, and Terms

| Item | Unit cost | Min. qty. | Lead time | Terms |
|---|---|---|---|---|
| Poop | $.10 | — | 7 Days | A.S.A.P. |
| Drying | .05 | — | 3 Days | Net 30 |
| Packaging | .17 | 10 000 | 4 Days | Net 30 |
| Artist | .01 | — | — | Monthly |
| Royalty | .02 | — | — | Monthly |
| Sub Total | $.35 | | | |

| Packaging unit cost | /50 000 | /100 000 | /250 000 | |
|---|---|---|---|---|
| Booklet* | $.08 | $.07 | $.06 | Net 30 |
| Outhouse† | .20 | .16 | .13 | ½ Down, ½ C.O.D. |
| Display† | .06 | .045 | .026 | ½ Down, ½ C.O.D. |
| Total packaging costs/unit | $.34 | $.275 | $.216 | |
| Total unit costs | $.69 | $.625 | $.566 | |

\* 2 weeks' lead time
† 8 – 10 weeks' lead time for first run, 2 weeks on subsequent orders

**Figure C20-3    Product Advertisement**

and handle all customs work and costs if we would sell it to them at $1.10 per unit and grant exclusive rights. He even said he would consider helping us out with a loan to cover half our start-up costs.

One alternative to granting exclusive rights for the whole U.S. market would be to develop an agent network and handle start-up costs, paper work, and duties ourselves. Agents want 30 percent, duty is 10 percent, and the paperwork would be awful.

**Jeff:** It sounds like you want to go with the distributor, ADC. I'll go through a cash flow analysis for our meeting next week and make sure this is the best option from a financial point of view. John, are you still gung-ho on the free publicity?

**John:** I sure am. I think that if Moose Poop is going to make it, free publicity is the only way to go. We have to be creative and capture the public's imagination. We can't afford to spend the big bucks required to make enough noise in the marketplace on our own anyway.

**Debbie:** Why don't we call it a night? Jeff, will you bring in some hard numbers next time, and John, will you work up the framework for a publicity campaign? I want just to sit and listen for a change.

## Discussion Questions

1. Prepare a marketing plan for launching Moose Poop in Canada and the United States.
2. Calculate the annual break-even sales volume in Canada and the United States.
3. Estimate the likely annual sales volume for Moose Poop.
4. Prepare a cash flow statement for Concept Enterprises in 1984, based on your estimate of its likely sales volume.

# Case 21   Federated Chemicals Ltd.

On May 19, 1984, an inquiry was received by the Floor Covering Division of Federated Chemicals Ltd. from a leading passenger plane manufacturer requesting a proposal for a rubber substitute for the conventional cloth rugs used as flooring in commercial planes.

The purchasing agent for the plane manufacturer expressed discontent with the short service life of the cloth rugs then being used. He emphasized that the substitute should not only be attractive but, most important, would have to be fire resistant and able to withstand spillage of food and beverages, vomiting, and normal wear experienced by a flooring material without permanent staining or other damage.

In addition, the substitute rug would have to be competitive in price. Only by possessing features warranting their consideration could the substitute induce customers to pay a higher price.

After considering the customer requirements, the technical department of the Floor Covering Division designed the "AirO Rug." The new product consists of a vinyl-coated glass fibre cemented to a sponge rubber backing material. Extended tests indicate that this new idea is the answer to the manufacturer's needs. The surface material is highly abrasion-resistant and soil-proof and requires very little effort to clean and maintain. The sponge backing, specially treated for fire resistance, imparts a cushioned effect to the foot much like the conventional cloth rug. A variety of colours rivals any offering of the conventional rugs, and estimated service life of the product is five years.

The Floor Covering Division is able to use a top material and sponge that are production items currently being manufactured by the Industrial Products Division of Federated Chemicals Ltd. As per company policy, material costs are transferred at the standard cost rate only; that is, no profit is included in interdivisional finished-goods transfers. The Industrial Products Division also has to maintain quality standards, replacing any material deemed unacceptable and rejected by the Floor Covering Division.

This source of supply results in the receipt of high quality materials at a minimum cost. Then too, the raw materials do not necessitate outlays for facilities to produce them. Because the raw materials are produced in an adjacent building, incoming transportation costs are nonexistent and lead time on materials is to be a maximum of two weeks.

## Elements of Cost

Inquiries reveal that the coated glass fibre costs $4.18 per metre in a 90 cm width, and the sponge $1.17 per metre in the same width. From the test samples, the product engineer calculates that 10 m$^2$ of AirO Rug will need 8.3 L of cement, which costs 80 cents per litre.

Using similar products and manufacturing operations as a bsis for their computations, the Time Study Department estimates 1.84 direct labour hours at the rate of $7.10 per hour to construct 10 m$^2$ of rug.

The Production Department has submitted anticipated manufacturing operations costs. These monthly prorates include: supervision, $1020; inspection, $140; miscellaneous indirect labour, $84; floor space expense, $320; and small tools and expense materials, $30. Three building tables, costing $1320 with a service life of five years, and a material-cutting machine with a service life of 10 years,

costing $480, have to be purchased before beginning the production. Selling and administrative expense are to be $4300 per month, which includes an outlay of $1150 semi-monthly for advertising AirO Rugs in *Aviation Age*, a trade magazine.

## Capacity

The building procedure for AirO Rugs is as follows:

1. Roll out sponge on table and cut to desired length.
2. With paint roller, cement the entire top area of the sponge.
3. Allow cement to tackify (dry slightly) for approximately 15 minutes.
4. Apply top material on sponge and roll with hand roller to ensure adhesion.
5. Trim edges and clean top area with cleaning solvent

While one table is being used for cementing, the other two can be used for laying the top material or final finishing. In short, three building tables are required to keep the assemblers busy and the production process flowing smoothly.

The complete production cycle to build 50 m$^2$ of rug requires an average of 3 hours and 20 minutes. Based on a 173-hour work month, the optimum capacity seems to be 2598 m$^2$ per month. Experience proves, however, that actual capacity in assembly production such as this generally turns out to be about 77 percent of optimum capacity. With this past history as a guide, actual production capacity is deemed to be 2000 m$^2$ per month.

## Cost Reduction Considerations

The requirements of the market prevent AirO Rug from being an off-the-shelf item. The colour selection offered the customers has to equal or surpass that of the competition, the cloth rug. To meet the changing demands of the industry, Federated Chemicals Ltd.

specially tints the vinyl of the top material according to each customer's specification. Because the colour requirements change from time to time for each customer, top material cannot be prepared in advance.

The home office of the Floor Covering Division Sales Department telegraphed the particulars of AirO Rug to the branch sales offices with a request to obtain other potential customers' reactions to the new product. Technical tests, revealing a useful life of five years for the rug, were relayed in detail along with small samples to branch salespeople

From the accumulation of responses, the home office has determined that a conservative estimate indicates a potential of 500 m²

per month. Cloth rugs have an average life of one year, and sell for $11.50 per square metre. Installation costs are not included in the selling price of either rug, but they are estimated at $4.80 per square metre for the cloth, and $5.40 for the AirO Rug.

## Discussion Questions

1. What do you recommend as a base selling price? What would be the break-even point at this price?
2. What considerations other than cost were influential in helping you arrive at this decision?

# Case 22   Computron, Inc.

In July 1978, Mr. Thomas Zimmermann, manager of the European Sales Division of Computron, Inc., was trying to decide what price to submit on his bid to sell a Computron 1000X digital computer to König & Cie., A.G., Germany's largest chemical company. Were Mr. Zimmermann to follow Computron's standard pricing policy of adding a 33⅓ percent markup to factory costs and then including transportation costs and import duty, the bid he would submit would amount to $311 200. Mr. Zimmermann was afraid that a bid of this magnitude would not be low enough to win the contract for computron.

Four other computer manufacturers had been invited by König to submit bids for the contract. Mr. Zimmermann had received information from what he considered to be a "reliable trade source" which indicated that at least one of these four competitors was planning to name a price somewhere in the neighbourhood of $218 000. Computron's normal price of $311 200 would be $93 200 or approximately 43 percent higher than this price. In conversation which he had had with

König's vice-president in charge of purchasing, Mr. Zimmermann had been led to believe that Computron would have a chance of winning the contract only if its bid were no more than 20 percent higher than the bid of the lowest competitor.

Inasmuch as König was Computron's most important German customer, Mr. Zimmermann was particularly concerned over this contract and was wondering what strategy to employ in pricing his bid. Deadline for submission of bids was August 1, 1978.

## Background on Computron and Its Products

Computron, Inc., was an American firm which had, in the winter of 1976, opened a European sales office in Paris with Mr. Zimmermann as its manager. The company's main product, both in the United States and in Europe, was the 1000X computer, a medium-sized digital computer designed specifically for process control applications.

In the mid to late 1970s, the market for digital process control computers was growing quite rapidly. These computers were substantially different from the computers used for data processing and engineering calculations, and were generally produced by specialized companies, not by the manufacturers of office and/or calculation-oriented digital computers nor by the companies which had produced analog process control computers, the traditional units used for process control.

Digital computers were classed as small, medium, or large depending on their size, complexity, and cost. Small computers sold in the price range up to $80 000; medium computers in the price range $80 000–$600 000; and large computers in the $1–$6 million price range.

The Computron 1000X had been designed specifically for process control applications. It was used in chemical and other process industries (oil refining, pulp and paper, food manufacture, etc.) as well as in power plants, particularly nuclear power plants.

In addition to its 1000X computer, Computron manufactured a small line of accessory process control computer equipment. These accessories, however, constituted a relatively insignificant share of the company's overall sales volume.

During the first six months after its opening, the European sales office did only about $1.1 million worth of business. In the 1977–78 fiscal[1] year, however, sales increased sharply, the total for the year being $5 million. Computron's total worldwide sales during that year were roughly $44 million. Of the European countries, Germany constituted one of Computron's most important markets, having contributed $1.2 million, or 24 per-

cent of the European sales total in 1977–78. England and Sweden were also important markets, having contributed 22 percent and 18 percent, respectively, to the 1977–78 total. The remaining 36 percent of sales was spread throughout the rest of Europe.

Computron computers sold to European customers were manufactured and assembled in the United States and shipped to Europe for installation. Because of their external manufacture these computers were subject to an import duty. The amount of this tariff varied from country to country. The German tariff on computers of the type sold by Computron was 17.5 percent of the U.S. sales price.

Prompted primarily by a desire to reduce this importation duty, Computron was constructing a plant in Frankfurt, Germany. This plant, which would serve all of the European Common market, was scheduled to open on September 15, 1978. Initially, it was to be used only for the assembly of 1000X computers. Assembly in Germany would lower the German importation duty from 17.5 percent to 15 percent. Ultimately, the company planned to use the plant for the fabrication of component parts as well. Computers which were completely manufactured in Germany would be entirely free of importation duty.

The new plant was to occupy 1000 m² and would employ 20–30 people in the first year. The initial yearly overhead for this plant was expected to be approximately $300 000. As of July 1978, the European sales office had no contracts on which the new plant could begin work, although it was anticipated that training of employees and the assembly and installation of a pilot model 1000X computer in the new plant could keep the plant busy for two or three months after it opened. Mr. Zimmermann was somewhat concerned about the possible risk that the new plant might have to sit idle after these first two or three months unless Computron could win the present König contract.

---

[1] Computron's fiscal years were July 1 to June 30.

## Company Pricing Policy

Computron had always concentrated on being the quality, "blue-chip" company in its segment of the digital computer industry. The company prided itself on manufacturing what it considered to be the best all-around computer of its kind in terms of precision, dependability, flexibility, and ease of operation.

Computron did not try to sell the 1000X on the basis of price. The price charged by Computron was very often higher than that being charged for competing equipment. In spite of this fact, the superior quality of Computron's computers had, to date, enabled the company to compete successfully both in the United States and Europe.

The European price for the 1000X computer was normally figured as follows:

U.S. "cost"
(Includes factory cost and factory overhead)
*plus*
Markup of 33⅓ percent on "cost"
(To cover profit, research and development allowances, and selling expenses)
Transportation and installation costs
*plus*
Importation duty
Total European price

Prices calculated by this method tended to vary slightly because of the country-to-country difference in tariffs and the difference in components between specific computers[2]. In the case of the present König application, Mr. Zimmermann had calculated that the "normal" price for the 1000X computer should be $311 200. Figure C22-1 shows his calculations.

The 33⅓ percent markup on cost used by the company was designed to provide a before-tax profit margin of 15 percent, a research and development allowance of 10 percent, and a selling and administrative

[2]Depending on the specific application in question, the components of the 1000X varied slightly, so that each machine was somewhat different from the rest.

**Figure C22-1    Calculated "Normal" Price for the 1000X Computer for König**

| | |
|---|---:|
| Factory cost | $192 000 |
| 33⅓% markup on cost | 64 000 |
| U.S. list price | $256 000 |
| Import duty (15% of U.S. list price) | 38 400 |
| Transportation and installation | 16 800 |
| Total "normal" price | $311 200 |

expense allowance of 8 percent. The stated policy of top management was clearly against cutting this markup in order to obtain sales. Management felt that the practice of cutting prices "not only reduced profits, but also reflected unfavourably on the company's 'quality' image." Mr. Zimmermann knew that Computron's president was especially eager not to cut prices at this particular moment, inasmuch as Computron's overall profit before taxes had been only 6 percent of sales in 1977–78 compared to 17 percent in 1976–77. Consequently, the president had stated that he not only wanted to try to maintain the 33⅓ percent markup on cost but was eager to raise it.

In spite of Computron's policy of maintaining prices, Mr. Zimmermann was aware of a few isolated instances when the markup on cost had been dropped to the neighbourhood of 25 percent in order to obtain important orders in the United States. In fact, he was aware of one instance in the United States when the markup had been cut to 20 percent. In the European market, however, Computron had never yet deviated from the policy of maintaining a 33⅓ percent markup on cost.

## The Customer

König & Cie., A.G., was the largest manufacturer and processor of basic chemicals and chemical products in West Germany. It operated a number of chemical plants located throughout the country. To date it had purchased three digital computer process control systems, all from Computron. The three systems had been bought during 1977–78 and had represented $1-million worth of business for Computron. Thus König was Computron's largest German customer and had alone constituted over 80 percent of Computron's 1977–78 sales to Germany.

Mr. Zimmermann felt that the primary reason König had purchased Computron computer systems in the past was because of their proven reputation for flexibility, accuracy, and overall high quality. So far, König officials seemed well pleased with the performance of their Computron computers.

Looking ahead, Mr. Zimmermann felt that König would continue to represent more potential future business than any other single German customer. He estimated that during the next year or two König would have a need for another $1-million worth of digital computer equipment.

The computer on which König was presently inviting bids was to be used in the training of operators for a new chemical plant. The training program was to last for approximately four to five years. At the end of the program the computer would either be scrapped or converted into other uses. The calculations which the computer would be called upon to perform were highly specialized and would require little machine flexibility. In the specifications which had been published along with the invitations to bid, König management had stated that in buying this computer König was interested primarily in dependability and a reasonable price. Machine flexibility and pinpoint accuracy were listed as being of very minor importance, inasmuch as the machine was to be used primarily for training purposes and not for on-line process control.

## Competition

In Germany, approximately nine companies were competing with Computron in the sale of medium-priced digital process control computers. Figure C22-2 shows a breakdown of sales among these companies for one year. As can be seen, four companies accounted for 80 percent of industry-wide sales in 1977–78.

**Figure C22-2  1977–78 Market Shares for Companies Selling Medium-Priced Digital Computers to the German Market**

|  | Sales | |
|---|---|---|
|  | Dollars | Percent |
| Computron, Inc. | $1 200 000 | 30.0 |
| Ruhr Machinenfabrik, A.G. | 800 000 | 20.0 |
| Elecktronische Datenverarbeitung-sanlagen, A.G. | 500 000 | 12.5 |
| Digitex, G.m.b.H. | 700 000 | 17.5 |
| Six other companies (combined) | 800 000 | 20.0 |
| Total | $4 000 000 | 100.0 |

Mr. Zimmermann was concerned primarily with the competition offered by the following companies:

*Ruhr Machinenfabrik*, A.G. A very aggressive German company, which was trying hard to expand its share of the market. Ruhr sold a medium-quality, general-purpose digital computer at a price which was roughly 22½ percent lower than the price which Computron charged for its 1000X computer. Of this price differential, 17.5 percent was attributable to the fact that there was no import duty on the Ruhr machine because it was manufactured entirely in Germany. Although to date Ruhr had sold only general-purpose computers, reliable trade sources indicated that the company was presently developing a special computer in an effort to win the König bid. The price which Ruhr was planning to place on the special-purpose computer was reported to be in the neighbourhood of $218 000.

*Elektronische Datenverarbeitungsanlagen,
A.G.* A relatively new company which had
recently developed a general-purpose computer of comparable quality to that of the
Computron 1000X. Mr. Zimmermann felt that
Elektronische Datenverarbeitungsanlagen presented a real long-range threat to Computron's
position as the "blue-chip" company in the
industry. In order to get a foothold in the
industry, it had sold its first computer "almost
at cost." Since that time, however, it had
undersold Computron only by the amount of
the import duty to which Computron's computers were subject.

*Digitex, G.m.b.H.* A subsidiary of an
American firm, this company has complete
manufacturing facilities in Germany and produced a wide line of computer equipment.
The Digitex computer which competed with
the Computron 1000X was of only fair
quality. Digitex often engaged in price-cutting
tactics and the price which it charged for its
computer had sometimes, in the past, been as
much as 50 percent lower than that charged
by Computron for its 1000X. In spite of this
difference, Computron had usually been able
to compete successfully against Digitex because
of the technical superiority of the 1000X.

Mr. Zimmermann was not overly concerned about the remaining competitors inasmuch as he did not consider them to be
significant factors in Computron's segment
of the computer industry.

## German Market for Medium-Priced Digital Computers

The total estimated German market for
medium-priced digital process control computers of the type manufactured by Computron
was presently running at about $4 million per
year. Mr. Zimmermann thought that this
market could be expected to increase at an
annual rate of about 25 percent for the next
several years. For 1978–79 he already had
positive knowledge of about $1.3-million
worth of specific new business. This new
business was broken down as follows:

| | |
|---|---:|
| König & Cie., A.G. | |
| Frankfurt plant | $1 300 000 |
| Dusseldorf plant | 250 000 |
| Mannheim plant | 150 000 |
| Central German Power | |
| Commission | 440 000 |
| Deutsche Autowerke | 160 000 |
| | $1 300 000 |

The business noted above was in addition
to the computer which König was presently
seeking for its new experimental pilot plant.
None of this already known business was
expected to materialize until late spring or
early summer.

## Deadline for Bids

In light of the various facts and considerations
discussed above, Mr. Zimmermann was wondering what price to bid on the König contract.
Deadline for submission of bids to König was
August 1, 1978. Since this was less than two
weeks away, he knew he would have to reach
a decision sometime during the next few days.

## Discussion Question

1. How would you advise Mr. Zimmermann?

# Case 23   Time Unlimited, Inc.

The Microcomputer Division of Time Unlimited, Inc., manufactures and sells two models of computers. The smallest one, the RAM-64, has 64K internal memory, two double density 5¼" floppy disk drives with 197K bytes each, a detachable full typewriter keyboard, and a 12" video display of 80 columns × 24 rows with scrolling capability. In addition, it includes as standard software a profit plan, a household budget program, a word processing system, and two computer games of the customer's choice. It can be used either as a home computer or in a small business where the data processing needs are not extensive. The other model, the RAM-128, is larger than the RAM-64 and has greater capacity including two 8" double-sided double density disk drives holding over 700K bytes. In addition to the software package offered with the RAM-64, a complete accounting program and a sophisticated statistical analysis package are included as part of the standard software. However, it still is classified as a microcomputer. The RAM-128 is purchased by businesses that want a small computer with the additional data processing capabilities that the smaller model does not offer. Time Unlimited, Inc.'s prices are higher than their competitors because the RAM computers offer processing and programming features not available from competitors, as well as a superior warranty and service program. Time Unlimited usually announces any price changes after the competition has posted theirs for the year.

Late in 1981, the Computer Division managers held a meeting where the following discussion took place. In attendance were:

- Jon Patric — Marketing Manager
- Andrea Suzanne — Chief Accountant
- Ross Edwards — Vice-President of the Computer Division
- Jim Mathews — Production Manager

**Jon Patric:** In a few months we are going to raise the price of the RAM-64 from $1800 to $2000 per unit, while our competition will be raising their prices from $1700 to $1850 per unit. In addition, the price of the RAM-128 will go from $13 500 to $15 000 per unit. By contrast, our competition is planning on raising their prices from $12 500 to $14 000. We project that our microcomputer sales division should sell at least 40 000 units of the RAM-64 at $1800 per unit; at $2000 per unit we should sell at least 20 000 units. Our market studies also indicate that at $13 500 per unit we should sell at least 4000 units of RAM-128 while at $15 000 per unit we project sales of at least 2000 units. I'm very concerned about this decrease in our volume of sales and question the advisability of raising our prices at this time.

**Andrea Suzanne:** The reason we are increasing the prices of the RAM-64 and RAM-128, Jon, is due to the fact that labour and material prices have gone up about 12 percent over the past year. Our increase in price just reflects the cost of inflation. I have finished compiling some current data (see Figure C23-1) through June 1981, if anyone is interested. One idea to decrease costs would be to cut the 10 percent sales commission to 7 or 8 percent. That's all our competitors are paying their sales staff. Also, our service warranty costs have increased from 4 percent to approximately 7 percent of sales. We really need to know the cause of this increase.

**Ross Edwards:** Jon, if we kept both models at the current price, would the competitors keep

Source: This case was prepared by Mary Ziebell and Don T. Deloster, Albers School of Business, Seattle University. Reprinted with permission.

Figure C23-1   Time Unlimited, Inc.
Estimated Cost of RAM-64 at Different Production Volumes Through June 1981

| Volume (no. of units) | 2 000 | 5 000 | 8 000 | 10 000 | 12 000 |
|---|---|---|---|---|---|
| Raw Materials | $ 144 | $ 144 | $ 144 | $ 144 | $ 144 |
| Purchased Parts | 160 | 160 | 160 | 160 | 155 |
| Direct Labour | 510 | 500 | 490 | 485 | 490 |
| Departmental Overhead | | | | | |
| Direct[a] | 35 | 34 | 32 | 33 | 33 |
| Equipment Depreciation | 144 | 72 | 48 | 36 | 29 |
| Indirect[b] | 235 | 120 | 80 | 60 | 48 |
| General Overhead[c] | 127 | 125 | 120 | 122 | 123 |
| Production Costs | $1 355 | $1 155 | $1 074 | $1 040 | $1 022 |
| Marketing & Administration[d] | 677 | 578 | 537 | 520 | 511 |
| Total Costs | $2 032 | $1 733 | $1 611 | $1 560 | $1 533 |

Estimated Cost of RAM-128 at Different Production Volumes Through June 1981

| Volume (no. of units) | 500 | 1 000 | 2 000 | 3 000 | 4 000 |
|---|---|---|---|---|---|
| Raw Materials | $ 1 450 | $ 1 450 | $ 1 450 | $ 1 450 | $ 1 450 |
| Purchased Parts | 1 740 | 1 740 | 1 740 | 1 730 | 1 720 |
| Direct Labour | 4 600 | 4 500 | 4 350 | 4 400 | 4 500 |
| Departmental Overhead | | | | | |
| Direct[a] | 400 | 380 | 373 | 365 | 370 |
| Equipment Depreciation | 870 | 435 | 290 | 218 | 174 |
| Indirect[b] | 1 305 | 652 | 435 | 326 | 261 |
| General Overhead[c] | 1 110 | 1 100 | 1 087 | 1 095 | 1 100 |
| Production Costs | $11 475 | $10 257 | $ 9 725 | $ 9 584 | $ 9 575 |
| Marketing & Administration[d] | 5 738 | 5 129 | 4 858 | 4 793 | 4 788 |
| Total Costs | $17 213 | $15 385 | $14 583 | $14 377 | $14 363 |

[a] Power, supplies, repairs
[b] Supervision, interest, rent, property taxes
[c] Allocated on the basis of 25% of Direct Labour
[d] Allocated on the basis of 50% of Production Costs

their prices at the current level or would they still raise their prices? We really need to know this. Also, it seems from the income statement (see Figure C23-2) that the RAM-128 line is not as profitable as the RAM-64 line. Perhaps we should be concentrating our marketing efforts on the RAM-64. It also seems to me that we should seriously consider Andrea's suggestion on reducing sales commissions.

**Jon Patric:** Our competition would probably raise their prices even if we kept ours the

same, though perhaps not as much as originally planned, Ross. We are currently in a strong market position (see Figure C23-3) and I would not like to see this market share lost. In response to Andrea's suggestion, I am certain that a decrease in the level of commissions would seriously affect our market share because of decreased salespeople's motivation.

**Jim Mathews:** From a product line evaluation standpoint, we are not making much money on the RAM-128. Maybe we should drop it

**Figure C23-2   Time Unlimited, Inc.**
**Income Statement For Year Ending December 31, 1980 (000's)**

|  | RAM-64 | RAM-128 | Total |
|---|---|---|---|
| Gross Sales | $54 000 | $40 500 | $94 500 |
| Expenses: |  |  |  |
| Raw Materials | $ 3 880 | $ 3 915 | $ 7 795 |
| Purchased Parts | 4 320 | 4 698 | 9 018 |
| Direct Labour | 12 960 | 11 745 | 24 705 |
| Direct Overhead | 864 | 980 | 1 844 |
| Equipment Depreciation | 1 440 | 870 | 2 310 |
| Indirect Overhead | 2 160 | 1 174 | 3 334 |
| General Overhead | 3 240 | 2 935 | 6 175 |
| Marketing & Administration | 14 364 | 13 114 | 27 478 |
| Total Expenses | $43 228 | $39 431 | $82 659 |
| Income | $10 772 | $ 1 069 | $11 841 |

Sold in 1980: 30 000 Units of RAM-64
3 000 Units of RAM-128

**Figure C23-3   Time Unlimited, Inc.**

RAM-64: PRICES AND SALES

|  | Sales Volume | | Price (Per Unit) | |
|---|---|---|---|---|
| Selling Year | Industry Totals | Time Unlimited | Competition's Average Price | Time Unlimited |
| 1978 | 40 000 | 5 000 | $ 5 000 | $ 6 000 |
| 1979 | 75 000 | 10 000 | $ 2 500 | $ 2 700 |
| 1980 | 150 000 | 30 000 | $ 1 700 | $ 1 800 |
| 1981 | 200 000 | — | $ 1 850 | $ — |

RAM-128: PRICES AND SALES

|  | Sales Volume | | Price (Per Unit) | |
|---|---|---|---|---|
| Selling Year | Industry Totals | Time Unlimited | Competition's Average Price | Time Unlimited |
| 1978 | 7 500 | 500 | $20 000 | $23 000 |
| 1979 | 15 000 | 1 500 | $15 000 | $16 500 |
| 1980 | 25 000 | 3 000 | $12 500 | $13 500 |
| 1981 | 35 000 | — | $14 000 | — |

and produce only the RAM-64 or develop another model. I realize we cannot transfer all of the equipment that is used in manufacturing the RAM-128 to the manufacture of the RAM-64, but we can transfer the labour that is used to produce the RAM-128 to produce the RAM-64. However, your question on increasing warranty costs, Andrea, is harder to answer. Up through 1980 we have always considered 4 percent of the sales price of both the micros a reasonable estimate of our costs of servicing the computers under the one-year warranty, and this proved accurate in the past. But with the increase in parts and labour costs as well as some small problems in this year's production process, it's not surprising that warranty costs have increased. In fact, I'm rather surprised the increase wasn't more. It is important, given our current marketing strategy, that we maintain the highest possible reputation in this area. At least that's what Jon is always telling me.

**Andrea Suzanne:** To get back to the idea of dropping the RAM-128 line, we really may want to give that further consideration. Our records show that the nontransferable RAM-128 equipment has a book value of $4 350 000. We should be able to sell this equipment for around $2 000 000. This would give us a good cash inflow, enough perhaps to develop a new product line.

**Jim Mathews:** Great idea, Andrea. Our current plant capacity is 50 000 units of the RAM-64 and 5 000 units of the RAM-128. With the cash from the sale of the RAM-128 equipment we could expand our plant capac-ity to 70 000 units of the RAM-64. It would cost about $3 000 000 for an additional build-ing and equipment, give or take a little.

**Ross Edwards:** Well, I can see from our discussion that there are several options open to us. I do have an additional concern. After reviewing the data brought in by Andrea, I'm not exactly sure how much it is costing us to produce and sell either of our models. We really need this piece of information. And while you are thinking about that, please keep one important point in mind. Our divisional goal is an income of 12 percent of sales, so we should consider that when seeking solutions to the questions that were brought up in today's meeting. It is reasonably urgent that we come up with a suitable analysis as soon as possible. We are almost through the year now and must make some decisions for the coming year. I'll see you back here in one week.

## Discussion Questions

1. Evaluate the suggestions offered at the meeting.
2. Relate this case to the material contained in the pricing chapters in this text.

# Case 24    Lucas Foods

Harold Riley was marketing manager of Lucas Foods, a diversified food manufacturing and wholesaling company based in Winnipeg. The company had recently had some success with a new product, Gold Medal Crumpettes. Jerry Lucas, president of Lucas Foods, asked his marketing manager to recommend an appropriate strategy for the new product that would best capture the available opportunity and support the mission of the company.

## The Industry

Lucas Foods was in the food manufacturing and wholesaling business, marketing a broad

Source: Prepared by John Fallows under the direction of Walter S. Good, as a basis for classroom discussion rather than to illustrate either effective or ineffective handling of an administrative situation. Copyright © Case Development Program, Faculty of Management, University of Manitoba. Support for the development of this case was provided by the Canadian Studies Program, Secretary of State, Government of Canada.

product line that included frozen egg products, shortening, flour, baking mixes, spices, and bulk ingredients. Its primary customers were the five major national food wholesalers, with smaller regional wholesalers and independent grocery stores accounting for a smaller portion of their sales.

Gold Medal Crumpettes was a recent entry in Lucas Foods' bakery products group. This product fell into the product class commonly known as *biscuits*. Competitive products in this class included crumpets, scones, English muffins, and tea biscuits. Competition also came from a variety of substitute products such as toast, donuts, and muffins. Biscuit producers included such prominent names as Weston Bakeries and McGavin Foods Ltd. domestically, as well as the American firm of S.B. Thomas, which concentrated on English muffins, and dominated the market for that product.

Lucas Foods estimated that the product life-cycle for specialty bakery goods was from five to seven years. Generally, if a new product was going to be successful, it enjoyed quick acceptance in the marketplace. Introduced in 1984, Gold Medal Crumpettes at first had limited distribution. They had been sold in Manitoba and Saskatchewan, had recently been introduced in Alberta and Minnesota. Safeway was presently the only major chain to carry the product, but sales growth had been steady to date.

## History of Lucas Foods

The company was originally formed under another name over 50 years previously. It specialized at first in frozen egg products, and later diversified into cabbage rolls and frozen meat products. The company was purchased by a major brewery in 1972, but the frozen egg portion of the business was sold back to the original owners six years later. They sold the business to Jerry Lucas in 1979. Since

then sales have doubled to their present annual level of $12 million.

The company followed a "portfolio approach" to its product line, regularly adding or deleting items according to established criteria with respect to the marketing cycle. With the single exception of frozen egg products, no specific product or product family dominated their overall product offering. (An exception was made for frozen egg products because of their unique life-cycle and recession-proof qualities.)

In its business mission statement, Lucas Foods indicated a desire to grow to an annual sales level of $50 million and to become a major national food manufacturer and wholesaler, as well as an exporter. Its major competitive weapons were believed to be its excellent reputation, product knowledge, marketing expertise, and level of customer service.

## Marketing Gold Medal Crumpettes

Lucas Foods believed that the consumption of biscuit products was uniform across age groups, seasons, and geographic locations. It was a mature market. The product itself was targeted toward the "upscale buyer." Package design, pricing policy, and product ingredients positioned Gold Medal as high-priced and high-quality relative to the competition. Therefore, the primary variables for segmenting the market were socio-economic: Gold Medal Crumpettes were a luxury item.

The Crumpettes were designed to incorporate the taste and texture of scones, English muffins, and biscuits. They could be eaten with or without butter, either toasted or untoasted. They were available in four flavours — plain, raisin, cheese, and onion — and the company had plans to add three more flavours, including pizza. The product could be stored frozen. The name, Gold Medal Crumpettes, was specifically selected to imply a connotation of quality.

Since wholesale food distribution in Canada was dominated by relatively few firms, management felt that it had little choice in the distribution of its products. Lucas Foods did not own a large warehouse to store its finished baked goods. It manufactured Gold Medal Crumpettes to order. The merchandise was then transported by common carrier to various customers under net 30 days credit terms.

The goal of the company's promotional efforts was to stimulate and encourage consumer trial of the product. There was some radio advertising when the product was first introduced. Although Lucas suggested the retail price, the distributor, especially in the case of Safeway, did most of the promotion. Typical promotions included:

- hostesses distributing free samples of the product in supermarkets
- crossover coupon promotions with jam companies
- mailout coupons to consumers
- free products to stores
- temporary price reductions for distributors

So far, $50 000 dollars had been spent on the promotion of Gold Medal Crumpettes. To complement these promotional efforts, Lucas Foods had three salespersons, who, along with the marketing manager, regularly called on all major accounts.

Gold Medal's high price was consistent with its positioning, and was arrived at after evaluating consumer surveys and the company's production costs. The expected price sensitivity of the market was also considered. A package of eight biscuits retailed for $1.89. The product was sold to supermarket chains in a case of twelve packages, with a factory price of $12.00 per case. Manufacturing costs, including allocated overhead, were $8.40 per case. This provides a contribution margin of $3.60 per case, or 30 percent. Production capacity was available for up to 16 000 cases per month.

## Capturing the Opportunity

The estimated total potential market for Gold Medal Crumpettes is shown in Figure C24-1. Harold Riley felt that Lucas Foods held a 16 percent share of the Manitoba market.

| Figure C24-1 | Total Potential Market for Gold Medal Crumpettes (Yearly Sales) | |
|---|---|---|
| | Cases | Volume |
| Manitoba | 43 000 | $ 520 000 |
| Canada | 960 000 | $ 11 500 000 |
| United States | 9 600 000 | $115 000 000 |

The Manitoba consumer had been very receptive to the product. However, outside Manitoba, the company had only a limited reputation and was not well known as a wholesale food supplier. This lack of awareness made it more difficult for the product to obtain the acceptance of retailers. Also, the company faced an almost total lack of consumer awareness outside the province.

If Gold Medal succeeded in obtaining quick acceptance in new markets, competitors might view the development of a similar product as an attractive proposition. This could be particularly distressing if the competitor taking such an action was a major producer with an existing broad distribution system. Therefore, the speed with which Gold Medal Crumpettes could be introduced and developed into a dominant market position was very important to the long-term survival and profitability of the product. There was also the question of whether or not the degree of consumer acceptance the product had achieved in Manitoba could be repeated in new markets.

Pricing research conducted by the company indicated that consumers were not prepared to cross the $2.00 price level at retail to purchase the product. If production costs were to rise and force an increase in selling price, sales might decline. Also, while the current exchange rate allowed Lucas to be quite competitive in the U.S. market, a strengthening of the Canadian dollar could damage the company's export position.

## Selecting a Strategy

Harold Riley had to propose a marketing strategy to Jerry Lucas that he felt would best take advantage of the opportunity available to Gold Medal Crumpettes. He was considering three alternatives:

1. Maintain the product's existing market coverage and strategy. This implied limiting distribution of the product and focusing the company's efforts on the Prairie provinces and the state of Minnesota.
2. Phased Expansion. This would involve expanding across Canada, region by region, to become a major force in the Canadian biscuit market and begin selective entry into the U.S. market.
3. Rapid Expansion. This approach would involve an attempt to expand rapidly in both countries, to precede and preferably pre-empt competitive products in all mar-

kets, and to seek a dominant position in the North American biscuit market.

During their early discussions, Jerry had pointed out that the company had the financial capacity to undertake any of these options. It was a question of how best to focus the available resources.

Before evaluating his alternatives, Harold drew up the following list of criteria to guide him in coming to an appropriate decision:

- The alternative should be feasible.
- The alternative should be profitable.
- The market opportunity should be exploited as far as possible while still meeting the first two criteria.
- The alternative should fit into the activities of the company.
- The alternative should be consistent with the mission of the company.
- The alternative should be consistent with Lucas Foods' portfolio management approach concerning return, risk, and diversity.
- There should be early evidence to support the alternative.

# Case 25    Tootsizer Canada

Tootsizer is the only patented plant food in North America. It had never been marketed in Canada when Traff Green became interested in it in 1982. Green, a farm equipment dealer in Winnipeg, heard about Tootsizer from his brother Bruce, who had assisted its inventor while teaching university in Rolla, Missouri, and held the patent and marketing rights for Canada. The two brothers got together because Traff's present business had largely fall and winter sales and Tootsizer, with a spring and summer sales period, would balance the cash flow.

Tootsizer Canada Ltd. seemed to be going well. Despite this, Traff Green, the president, realized that the roof could fall in if Tootsizer's venture into television advertising did not pay off. In 1984 he decided to re-evaluate the total marketing strategy of the firm.

Green hired consultants to study the buying behaviour and media effectiveness for plant food and fertilizer in the Winnipeg market. He hoped that this information would help

Source: M. D. Beckman and R. Lederman

to plan his strategy for the next year. The results of their survey, conducted soon after

Tootsizer's 1984 ad campaign, are summarized in Figure C25-1.

---

**Figure C25-1    Selected Findings from Market Research Study**

The following is a summary of the results of each question based on the number of responses to that particular question.

1. Do you have potted plants in your home?
   Yes   99.0%
   No      1.0%

2. Do you have a garden?
   Yes   80.8%
   No    19.2%

3. Do you use plant food?
   Yes   80.8%
   No    19.2%

4. Do you use a fertilizer?
   Yes   63.6%
   No    36.4%

5. What type of fertilizer(s) or plant food(s) do you use?
   Organic fertilizer   10.3%
   Liquid fertilizer     65.5%
   Powder fertilizer    50.6%

6. How often do you use your plant food?
   More than once a week              0.0%
   Once a week                             6.9%
   Once a month                          27.6%
   Once every two months             33.3%
   Once every six months             14.9%
   Less than once every six months  10.4%

7. Which of the following statements best describes the reason why you use your present fertilizer?
   Recommended by a family member   30.4%
   Recommended by a friend                17.7%
   Recommended by a gardener, florist
      or other knowledgeable person      45.6%
   Radio advertisement                        1.3%
   Newspaper or magazine
      advertisement                              3.7%
   Television advertisement                    1.3%

8. When you purchased your present fertilizer (or plant food), did you know what brand you were going to purchase before you entered the store?
   Yes   46.6%
   No    53.4%

9. When you made your last fertilizer (or plant food) purchase, did you investigate and compare more than one brand?
   Yes   33.0%
   No    67.0%

10. If you answered yes to question number 8, did you purchase the brand you had intended to purchase?
    Yes   93.2%
    No      6.8%

11. How often do you purchase fertilizer (or plant food)?
    Less than once a year          53.9%
    Once a year                         28.1%
    Twice a year                        14.6%
    More than twice a year           3.4%

12. In which months of the year did you make your last fertilizer (or plant food) purchase?
    January-February          11.5%
    March-April                  37.2%
    May-June                     30.8%
    July-August                   5.1%
    September-October         9.0%
    November-December        6.4%

13. Have you seen or heard of Tootsizer Plant Food?
    Yes   71.5%
    No    28.3%

14. If yes, which of the following statements best describes the medium through which you first saw or heard of Tootsizer?
    Saw it in a store                                      40.3%
    Saw it on a television advertisement   4.2%

Saw it in a newspaper or magazine
advertisement 11.1%
Heard it on a radio advertisement 26.4%
Heard about it through a conversation
with some other person 18.0%

15. Through which of the following media have
you seen or heard advertisements for
Tootsizer? Check all applicable.
Television 26.8%
Radio 35.2%
Newspaper 42.3%

Magazine 35.2%
In-store advertising 76.2%

16. Have you ever purchased Tootsizer?
Yes 15.6%
No 84.4%

17. If you have tried Tootsizer, how do you rate
its performance as a fertilizer?
Poor 13.4%
Fair 0.0%
Average 33.3%
Good 33.3%
Excellent 20.2%

## Production

Originally, Bruce Green produced Tootsizer as a one-man operation from his basement, in very limited quantities. When Tootsizer Canada Ltd. was formed in 1983, Traff Green set up a mass-production facility in the garage behind his farm equipment lot. With the welding equipment from his business, he custom-built some of the processing machinery and purchased the bottling line from the United States. These were capable of supplying well in excess of the projected Canadian demand.

In fact, during their first year of mass production, Tootsizer was almost a custom bottler: when they received a large order they would make it up and restock the warehouse. They sold more than 20 000 bottles, which amounted to an average of about six hours' factory production time per week.

The garage consisted of about 230 m² of usable production and storage space. It was leased from the city for $900 rent plus $625 in taxes, heating, and light per month.

## The Product

Tootsizer is a concentrated liquid plant food-fertilizer. The manufacturing process starts with the same basic raw materials as other fertilizers: nitrogen, phosphates, and potash.

Magnesium is added, then the mixture is put through a patented chemical process that duplicates the first stage of food processing that goes on within a plant. Five elements go into the reaction, producing 15 different chemicals.

The theory behind the product is that it enables plants to conserve energy by not having to process their food at this first level and they then apply that saved energy toward manufacturing fibre within their bodies. As a result, they will grow faster and be more productive. There are indications that this could be true. Edgar van Wick in Roland, Manitoba, who grows world-record pumpkins (about 200 kg), uses Tootsizer for his garden. Green claims to have grown 2 m corn stalks at his cottage when none of his neighbours could get plants more than 1 m high. The majority of people who try Tootsizer are convinced of its merits.

In tests of the product under controlled conditions at a company greenhouse and in independent studies conducted at the University of Manitoba, Tootsizer always outperformed competitive plant foods and fertilizer.

Despite these successful results, there were problems with the product. Tootsizer is a concentrate and unless diluted properly will burn the roots of a plant and kill it. Tootsizer has to be mixed with water, in a ratio of 30 g to 4 L water, for optimum results. Adding a drop of Tootsizer to the soil and then watering does not work because the plant food is not spread evenly to all the roots and might burn some roots. On the bottle label, recommended dilution and instructions for use are given, but the dangerous short cut is not mentioned. There are also advantages to the purchaser of a concentrate such as Tootsizer. The product, while quite convenient to use, will treat a great deal of garden area.

Another problem with Tootsizer was that the solids used in the formulation quickly settled to the bottom of the container and it required some effort to get them into suspension again. This made the product less convenient to use and less attractive on the shelf for customers. In the spring of 1983, Green solved one problem with the aid of the Faculty of Pharmacy at the University of Manitoba. He substituted a different suspension fluid, which gave the product a more uniform appearance and required just one or two shakes of the container to put the solids into suspension. This improved product went into production in midsummer 1983, but was not put on the retail shelves until the old stock was sold.

## Price Policy

Green sold Tootsizer at the same price to all customers. One supermarket chain store acknowledged that it was a good product but would not consider buying unless given a 5 percent discount. Greenheld the price and lost the sale that year even though the chain store might have opened up the large eastern market to Tootsizer.

The wholesale selling price was $22.00 per case of twelve 500 mL bottles, with 2 percent–10–net 30 terms. Suggested retail price was $3.29 per cottle, but one chain sold them at $2.79 per bottle. The total cost of packaging and product for one bottle was 41 cents. Another 46 cents per bottle was set aside for advertising.

Compared with other products on the store shelves, Tootsizer appears to offer good value. Each bottle holds 34 percent nutrient value and, when used as directed, should last for about nine months of heavy home use for houseplants.

Competitive plant foods sold for about $1.59 per 500 mL bottle of 3 percent nutrient mixture. However, they are not concentrates. Concentrates are not common on the shelves of grocery stores. Nonetheless, most garden shops do carry most forms of concentrated plant food. Typically, the concentrates cost in the range of $1.39 for 250 mL of concentrate with about 30 percent nutrient value and have dilution instructions similar to Tootsizer's.

## Distribution Strategy

Bruce Green first sold Tootsizer in 1981. It was tough going and he literally sold in the streets to anyone he could convince to try it. He carried a case in the trunk of his car and was ready to bend anyone's ear on the virtues of Tootsizer. He managed only $1200 in sales that year, but the people who tried it returned for more.

After Tootsizer Canada was formed in 1983, Traff Green took over the marketing of the product. He decided to concentrate primarily on large-volume orders. As a single-product manufacturer with no track record, Green was asked to make numerous concessions to the large retailers before they would even consider his product, much less give it shelf space. "Yes, it sounds good, but what can you do for us?" was a typical response. They not only wanted guaranteed advertising expenditures, but also required that people ask for the product before they would order it.

Finally, with the aid of Midway Brokers (a food brokerage firm supplying grocery stores), Green got Tootsizer listed in the Safeway supermarket chain from Manitoba to Thunder Bay. Then the Loblaws chain followed, on the strength of Tootsizer's radio and newspaper advertising. In the meantime, Green personally sold to individual stores and garden and florist shops in and around Winnipeg. This was difficult and slow. Most orders were for one case of 12 bottles. These outlets did not seem to be interested in the product.

At the year-end (1983), sales were $40 000 for the Winnipeg area, including Safeway. People were no interested in Tootsizer. There were re-orders and Safeway kept the product listed for stocking in its Winnipeg warehouse. Green was pleased and wanted to expand his sales area. With the advice of a consultant and his advertising agency, Baker Lovick, he approached other major chain stores again. This time he made more concessions. First, he committed himself to a six-week television ad campaign from mid-May through June of 1984 with banner mentions of the firms that were carrying Tootsizer. Also, in return for pre-ordering, he offered "guaranteed sales" (any goods not sold could be returned for cash).

On this basis, Tootsizer received distribution coverage from Thunder Bay to Alberta. Once Safeway, the biggest chain, had signed up, the rest became interested and eventually Eaton's, The Bay, Simpsons, Gambles, Woolco, Dominion, and Federated Co-Op, all ordered the product. Still, Winnipeg was the only centre where any small stores had been approached. Furthermore, it must be remembered that distribution and stocking for chain stores was controlled by the regional warehouses, not by Tootsizer.

By February 1984, Tootsizer had over $50 000 of sales prebooked. Considering that in 1983 the first half sales had been $21 000, Green was looking for over $100 000 in sales in 1984.

Supplying Tootsizer was no problem. In fact, all the booking orders were shipped before April to the central warehouses for the chain stores. Members of chains ordered from their company warehouses, which handled deliveries, while the stocking and shelf space

decisions were made centrally by company executives. Any sales to individual stores were sent direct from the factory.

## Advertising

In 1982 the advertising was strictly word-of-month, mostly Bruce Green's. When Traff Green took over in 1983, he needed advertising to be able to approach any major outlets and convince them that there was a demand for the product.

The advertising was all consumer-oriented and mainly through Winnipeg radio stations and newspapers. All through the summer, Tootsizer had weekly ads in both Winnipeg dailies stressing its technical merits. Also, Tootsizer ran radio advertising on CJOB, a middle-of-the-road station, and on CKRC, a light rock station, aimed at a younger audience. The ads were produced by the stations and were humorous in nature. In one, plants told the consumer how Tootsizer was the only plant food for them. In another, the outdoor plants went on stroke against a homeowner for more Tootsizer. Green liked the ads; they were fun and brought attention to the Tootsizer name.

At the point of purchase there was no special advertising. Tootsizer is in plain plastics bottles with small stick-on labels giving its name and instructions for use. It is not particularly eye-catching.

One area that paid good dividends was a special promotion to key people in the media. Cases of Tootsizer were sent to the hosts of radio and television garden shows and to the garden columnists for the daily papers asking them to try it and to give their opinions to Tootsizer. One result was that Mike Willis, a garden expert and Tootsizer employee, appeared on a a 26-week garden show on CKND-TV and made guest appearances on CJOB radio's Problem Corner to answer plant questions.

In all, Tootsizer spent $15 000 on advertising in 1983, including $11 000 for radio and the printed media. The sales results were pleasing and Green was anxious to expand Tootsizer sales to Saskatchewan and Alberta.

An advertising agency sold him on a $90 000 TV campaign covering six cities: Thunder Bay, Winnipeg, Regina, Saskatoon, Edmonton, and Calgary. It would run for six weeks in May and June 1984, giving 30-second spots a week on local stations between 5 and 10 p.m. The agency estimated that this would hit about 90 percent of the watching public. Green was worried but the agency convinced him that the idea was sound.

Mr. Green used the promise of this campaign, which included listings of local dealers under each commercial, to sell bookings for Tootsizer to the major chain stores.

The commercial was finished in mid-March, with a production cost of $20 000. It was very professional and technically good but

Green did not like it. But he had no choice; he could not drop the campaign because all his sales were tied to it, and he could not opt for a new commercial because there was not enough time.

## Discussion Questions

1. Describe Tootsizer's overall marketing strategy for new product production.
2. Evaluate the various elements of their marketing mix in light of this strategy.
3. What did the consultant's survey indicate to you about the plant food and fertilizer market in Winnipeg?
4. What problems was Tootsizer facing in 1984? If you were Green, what changes, if any, would you have made in the marketing program?

# Case 26   Southern Cross, Pty. Ltd.

Southern Cross, Pty. Ltd. — one of Australia's leading manufacturers of surface coatings — has grown steadily since its founding in 1912. It now has factories in each of Australia's six states and employs nearly 3000 people. For readers unfamiliar with Australian geography, the country is divided into six states (Victoria, New South Wales, Queensland, South Australia, Western Australia, and Tasmania), the Northern Territory, and the Australian Capital Territory. Australia, with a population of 14.6 million, is about the same geographical size as the continental United States.

While the company has introduced several new products and developed its own chain of outlets in recent years, it is still regarded as a conservative company. Surveys show that its products are considered to be of excellent quality but the firm is not perceived

as progressive compared with its major competitors.

Southern Cross offers a complete range of interior and exterior paints for domestic and commercial use. In addition, it has a wide range of stains and varnishes. The company also markets specialty lines for industrial, automotive, and marine purposes.

Southern Cross products are sold principally through hardware stores and department

Source: This case was prepared by M. J. S. Collins, Principal Lecturer in Marketing at the Chisholm Institute of Technology (Australia); David L. Kurtz, The Thomas F. Gleed Chair in Business and Finance, at Seattle University; and Louis E. Boone, the Ernest Cleverdon Chair of Business and Management, at University of South Alabama, as a basis for class discussion. The original draft of this case was prepared for use at the Chisholm Institute of Technology. This version changes and disguises the data in order to protect the confidentiality of the company.

stores. In recent years, the firm has also let its products be sold by selected discount and chain stores. Southern Cross has also set up a network of company-owned and operated "Southern Cross—The Beautifier" stores, which are both retail and trade outlets.

Southern Cross has a special sales force to run its own outlets and to sell to professional painters. Other specialist sales personnel handle the industrial, automotive, and marine markets. In addition, the company has a separate retail or direct decorative sales force in each state, with responsibility for sales to independent retail outlets.

## General Background

Michael Allen, Southern Cross's direct decorative sales manager for the state of Victoria, was alarmed when he read the latest sales figures. For the third consecutive month his branch had not made budget and he knew the head office would be expecting an explanation and a correction action plan. While an unfavourable economic climate explained the poor growth in demand, several minor companies, particularly the discounters, were showing sales gains. One of these had now

emerged as a major Victorian competitor through aggressive marketing and expansion of its own chain through franchising to which it confined all its sales. Furthermore, the other major competitors were not being hurt as badly as Southern Cross. Allen began to analyse the data he had available.

## The Retail Market in Victoria

Victoria had a population of 4.1 million, or 28 percent of Australia's total population. As Figure C26-1 indicates, Victoria has a relatively small share of Australia's land area (about 3 percent). Its capital is Melbourne, with a population of 2.9 million. Only Sydney, in the state of New South Wales, is larger. An agriculturally rich state, Victoria boasts numerous towns throughout, of which the largest are Geelong (pop. 147 000), Ballarat (pop. 77 500) and Bendigo (pop. 64 000).

The paint market in Victoria was undergoing a pronounced shift. During the past two years the state's market had barely grown; but the smaller paint companies, largely through aggressive discounting practices, had generally gained at the expense of the traditional

## Figure C26-1   Map of Australia

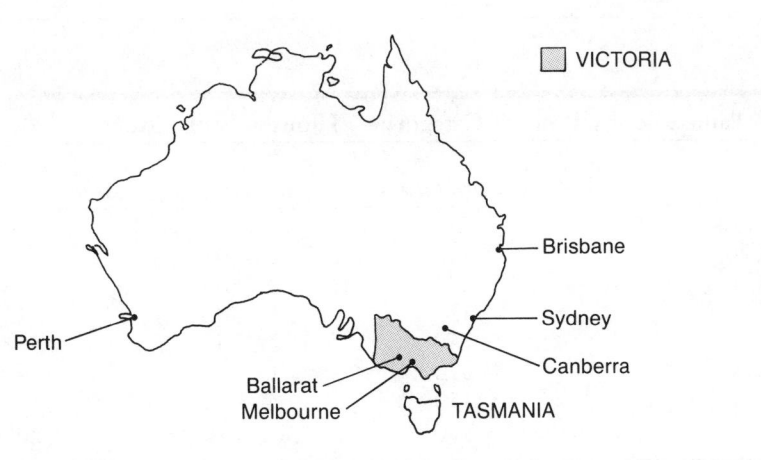

major paint marketers. This not only reflected price discounting but also their more innovative marketing and merchandising (see Figure C26-2).

Southern Cross's sales by main product groupings are shown in Figure C26-3. Overall the average price for paint to retailers was a little under $7 per litre and the better margins were achieved from interior paints and stains. Flat plastics were the most cut-throat segment. The fall in exterior paint reflects the reduction in weatherboard houses or their renovation with coverings that do not require painting.

Paint demand varies somewhat with economic and weather conditions and certain sales peaks such as Easter. But overall sales tend to be spread evenly between quarters.

The retail market represented all sales made through retail outlets, including trade sales as well as sales to the householder. It was estimated that industry retail sales accounted for approximately 40 percent of total paint volume and estimates divided these sales as follows:

|  | 1980 | 1986 |
|---|---|---|
| Hardware Independent Outlets (including Groups) | 45% | 41% |
| Discount Specialist Paint Stores | 10% | 11% |
| Corporate Chains and Department Stores | 20% | 22% |
| Specialist Company owned or Franchised Outlets | 15% | 18% |
| Other | 10% | 8% |
|  | 100% | 100% |

Figure C26-2   The Victorian Paint Market — Millions of Litres

|  | Retail Paint Sales Victoria | | |
|---|---|---|---|
|  | 1985 | 1986 | Year to Date April 1987 |
| Southern Cross | 3.39 | 3.20 | 1.06 |
| Competitor A | 2.40 | 2.48 | 0.83 |
| Competitor B | 2.42 | 2.44 | 0.81 |
| Competitor C | 1.20 | 1.24 | 0.48 |
| Others | 2.93 | 3.14 | 1.09 |
|  | 12.34 | 12.50 | 4.27 |

Figure C26-3   Paint Sales by Product Category — Thousands of Litres

|  | 1985 | | 1986 | |
|---|---|---|---|---|
| Product | Southern Cross | Industry | Southern Cross | Industry |
| Interior Full Gloss | 560 | 2 140 | 585 | 2 250 |
| Exterior Full Gloss | 820 | 2 500 | 735 | 2 375 |
| Interior Semi-Gloss | 525 | 2 550 | 505 | 2 420 |
| Undercoats | 375 | 1 050 | 345 | 1 100 |
| Flat Plastics | 750 | 2 375 | 598 | 2 475 |
| Stains/Varnishes | 210 | 1 725⎤ | 250 | 1 875 |
| Other | 150 | ⎦ | 182 | |
|  | 3 390 | 12 340 | 3 200 | 12 495 |

The remainder is sold direct to professional painters, commercial users and industry.

The corporate chains or mass merchandisers and specialist outlets were gaining market share at the expense of the hardware segment. To battle this trend many hardware stores had banded together to form major buying groups. These groups were increasing in importance and aggressiveness. In particular they were promoting strongly, using cataloguing and advertising, and adopting their own private label paint in some cases. Three major groups, accounting for some 45 percent of the independents, were co-operatives, and the fourth group was controlled by a major wholesaler that had its own field force and claimed a share of 15 percent of the total retail market. Like the corporate chains, these groups bought centrally, but the independents bought individually as well as through their groups according to the deals on offer.

The structure and function of the Direct Decorative field force is indicated in the job description below.

### Job Description — Southern Cross Decorative Sales Representative — Ballarat Territory — Victoria

**Accountability Objective:** Promotes and sells the Southern Cross decorative market range to users and sellers to achieve sales forecast within expense budget.

### Dimensions:

| | |
|---|---|
| Sales Volume | $1 165 000 annually |
| Customers | 170 000 litres annually |
| Distributor/Retailers }<br>Painters | 177 |
| Architects | 5 |
| Government Departments & Local Authorities } | 8 |

**Nature and Scope of Position:** The Direct Decorative force concentrates its activities on

all decorative sales not made through the "Southern Cross — The Beautifier" organization. Direct Decorative sales usually involves selling to the end user through the local reseller, and selling to resellers for stock purposes.

The incumbent is one of seventeen reporting to the Decorative Sales Manager. Eleven are metropolitan representatives who service the Greater Melbourne area. Five are country representatives, of which the incumbent is one, servicing other areas of Southern and Central Victoria in a similar capacity to the metropolitan representatives except that the country representatives usually have a broader function and responsibility. The seventeenth position reporting to the Decorative Sales Manager is the Decorative Market Officer, who provides clerical and office support for the field staff.

The incumbent reports weekly to the Decorative Sales Manager on such items as calls made, mileage, cost/mile, entertainment, competition, and the like.

The incumbent handles all customer complaints in the Ballarat territory. Complaints and problems of a minor nature or those that may require an adjustment of up to four litres of paint for repairs are handled entirely by the incumbent. Difficulties requiring an adjustment of more than that are referred to the Decorative Sales Manager for approval. For problems involving technical factors beyond the representative's technical knowledge, the Decorative Sales Manager will request technical assistance from the laboratories.

The incumbent is required to provide support for company promotions, including point-of-sale materials, merchandising, and the like. Should he or she require special assistance for a promotion, he or she must approach the Decorative Sales Manager to obtain such assistance. The representative can initiate special promotions for a territory and implement these once approval has been obtained.

The incumbent is relatively free in relation

to how to sell the product, providing that such methods are not detrimental to the company's image or policies. Pricing of the product is done according to a chart supplied by the firm. Prices vary according to customer classifications. The representative is not involved with the setting of prices on the chart.

An overall sales budget is set by the Decorative Sales Manager. Sales representatives set their own budget in accordance with this general plan. Before it comes into force, it must be approved by the Decorative Sales Manager, who may make alterations in consultation with the field salesperson. Once the budget is set, it remains current for twelve months. The representative cannot alter the budget.

A company vehicle is supplied to the incumbent. This is replaced after four years or 80 000 business kilometres. The representative notifies the Decorative Sales Manager and the State Accountant when the replacement time is approaching. The salesperson obtains three replacement quotes and recommends which quote should be taken.

The incumbent is required to help resellers with store and layout problems, merchandising stock levels, and the like. He or she is also expected to provide colour schemes and/or product specifications for householders and others who request help. The representative keeps customer record sheets and sales statistics as well as taking note of competitors' activities in the territory.

## Summary of Principal Tasks
- Promotes company image to ensure ready acceptance of products.

- Maintains customer files to provide a reliable history of customers.
- Initiates and implements territorial promotions to maintain sales performance.
- Handles any problems arising from the territory, referring only the larger or difficult problems to the Decorative Sales Manager.
- Controls the costs incurred within the territory so that the sales targets may be reached within budgeted costs.
- Requests special assistance where necessary to maintain amiable customer relations.
- Reports regularly to the Decorative Sales Manager about the conditions within the territory.

The total sales budget set by the marketing plan for 1987 was designed to hold market share and assume an industry growth rate of approximately 4 percent. With inflation running at more than 8 percent, this represented a fall in real growth, reflecting the inroads by nonpaint building materials, the virtually static building construction market, and the impact of more durable paints. The first four months' results for Victoria are shown in Figure C26-4.

Brief sketches of a cross-section of the sales representatives comprising the Victoria field force, and their respective sales performance, are shown in Figures C26-5 through C26-10, as selected by Michael Allen.

**Edwin Chandler:** Chandler was an energetic metropolitan sales representative, aged 28, who had formerly been a junior trainee. He had only been a representative for one year,

### Figure C26-4   Budget Versus Actual Sales: 1987

| Litres | January | February | March | April | Year to Date |
|---|---|---|---|---|---|
| Total Budget ($000) | 1 645 | 1 645 | 1 850 | 2 600 | 7 740 |
| Units (000) | 240 | 240 | 270 | 380 | 1 130 |
| Actual ($000) | 1 650 | 1 489 | 1 702 | 2 353 | 7 194 |
| Units (000) | 245 | 219 | 251 | 345 | 1 060 |

but he compensated for his lack of experience with hard work (see Figure C26-5).

**Ian Bannion:** Bannion was a solid, conscientious representative who had worked the

Bendigo territory for 14 years. Aged 51, Bannion was well known throughout the area and all his resellers spoke highly of him (see Figure C26-6).

**Figure C26-5  Chandler: 1987 Sales Performance**

|  | January | February | March | April | Year to Date |
|---|---|---|---|---|---|
| Budget A$ | 58 250 | 58 250 | 58 250 | 71 900 | A$ 246 650 |
| Units | 8 500 | 8 500 | 8 500 | 10 500 | |
| Actual A$ | 54 675 | 55 640 | 54 400 | 59 425 | A$ 224 140 |
| Units | 8 122 | 8 224 | 7 993 | 8 831 | |

**Figure C26-6  Bannion: 1987 Sales Performance**

|  | January | February | March | April | Year to Date |
|---|---|---|---|---|---|
| Budget A$ | 58 550 | 58 900 | 58 900 | 75 350 | A$ 251 700 |
| Units | 8 550 | 8 600 | 8 600 | 11 000 | |
| Actual A$ | 62 153 | 60 035 | 60 527 | 78 775 | A$ 261 490 |
| Units | 9 014 | 8 703 | 8 911 | 11 523 | |

**Colin Donaldson:** Originally a driver with the company, Donaldson had spent 12 years in sales, 5 of them in his current, western, more industrialized area. He was 44 years old and well liked, but his paperwork had sometimes been criticized (see Figure C26-7).

**Figure C26-7  Donaldson: 1987 Sales Performance**

|  | January | February | March | April | Year to Date |
|---|---|---|---|---|---|
| Budget A$ | 68 500 | 69 850 | 69 850 | 76 750 | A$ 284 950 |
| Units | 10 000 | 10 200 | 10 200 | 11 200 | |
| Actual A$ | 56 674 | 70 219 | 61 758 | 69 388 | A$ 256 039 |
| Units | 8 398 | 10 803 | 9 486 | 10 497 | |

**George Nelson:** Nelson had been promoted to representative just that year, but at 39 he showed mature judgment. He had joined Southern Cross as a junior clerk straight from school and had outstanding procedural and product knowledge. Being new at sales, he had been given one of the smaller, more remote country territories (see Figure C26-8).

**Figure C26-8  Nelson: 1987 Sales Performance**

|  | January | February | March | April | Year to Date |
|---|---|---|---|---|---|
| Budget A$ | 41 000 | 41 000 | 44 500 | 61 500 | A$ 188 000 |
| Units | 6 000 | 6 000 | 6 500 | 9 000 | |
| Actual A$ | 38 088 | 35 365 | 42 164 | 51 348 | A$ 166 965 |
| Units | 5 612 | 5 203 | 6 217 | 7 531 | |

**John Tarry:** Tarry was efficient and experienced. He had originally been with a competitor, but seven years previously, at the age of 34, he had joined Southern Cross as a sales representative; he had had his current metropolitan territory for four years. He had a reputation of always doing whatever was required of him (see Figure C26-9).

**Figure C26-9   Tarry: 1987 Sales Performance**

|  | January | February | March | April | Year to Date |
|---|---|---|---|---|---|
| Budget A$ | 66 450 | 66 450 | 68 500 | 87 000 | A$ 288 400 |
| Units | 9 700 | 9 700 | 10 000 | 12 700 | |
| Actual A$ | 73 247 | 75 121 | 78 738 | 91 915 | A$ 319 021 |
| Units | 10 481 | 10 752 | 11 254 | 13 321 | |

**Robert Holmes:** Holmes was an astute, highly motivated sales representative with an impressive sales record. He was generally regarded as the next sales manager. He had been with Southern Cross for 15 years and was now 38 years old. He had a prime metropolitan area that had reflected excellent growth as a result of population explosion into the outer, more affluent, eastern suburbs of Melbourne. In addition, he had responsibility for one major account, which had a number of outlets in other territories but had all its sales included in this territory's results (see Figure C26-10).

**Figure C26-10   Holmes: 1987 Sales Performance**

|  | January | February | March | April | Year to Date |
|---|---|---|---|---|---|
| Budget A$ | 116 450 | 117 800 | 117 800 | 150 700 | A$ 502 750 |
| Units | 17 000 | 17 200 | 17 200 | 22 000 | |
| Actual A$ | 114 613 | 117 347 | 133 621 | 149 852 | A$ 515 433 |
| Units | 17 112 | 17 479 | 20 041 | 22 490 | |

**Compensation and Evaluation Procedures**

Sales representatives were paid on a straight salary basis. Newly appointed sales personnel were paid A$18 000 per year, and after approximately three years were given a "mature" grading with a range from A$24,000–27,000.[1] A few representatives were given senior sales status, with a higher salary based on service and performance.

Each representative had a car but had to pay for all private mileage at 10 cents per mile. They were also given an advance of A$500 for expenses, and reported actual expenses on a monthly basis. Expenses in metropolitan areas were not expected to exceed A$50 per week. Car running expenses were separate from the above, which were largely used for accommodation, hospitality, and special business purposes.

From time to time, sales representatives were given the opportunity to earn additional rewards through contests. These were used to push a particular product line and generally took the form of cash based on sales over a given quota. Occasionally merchandise was given instead.

In addition to sales and budget figures, representatives were also evaluated against objectives they had set in conjunction with their sales manager. These were normally of a qualitative or descriptive nature, to reflect the

_____

[1] In 1987, the Australian dollar (A$) was worth approximately 0.95 Canadian dollars.

way each representative intends to develop a territory.

1. What actions would you implement to reverse Southern Cross's sales problem?

2. Should Southern Cross modify its compensation system?
3. What is your opinion of Southern Cross's sales organization in the state of Victoria, including the selection and recruitment policies?
4. Should the budgetary system and sales data information be changed?

# Case 27 Lime Light Cinema

In December 1985, after nine months of operation, the Lime Light Cinema of Burloak, Ontario, was still not generating satisfactory revenues. To attract larger audiences, Head Office in Montreal decided on major changes in the programming format and the pricing strategy. Bill Williams, the new manager, was faced with the responsibility for successfully implementing these changes.

## Company History

The theatre had been operated as a sex-film house under the name Cosmopolitan Cinema for 15 years. In January 1985, Celebrity Films of Montreal had purchased the business as part of an expansion plan. To reposition the theatre as a first-run art-film cinema featuring two films per evening, major renovations were undertaken in late February. In March, Celebrity Films had reopened the theatre as the New Cosmopolitan Cinema.

From the beginning, the new cinema encountered problems with image. Even though the concept had changed, association with the previous name still branded the cinema as a place to see sex films. In October, the name had been changed to Lime Light Cinema, and a new marquee was acquired. In November, the owners had fired the manager and promoted Bill Williams, the assistant manager

of four months, to the position. Prior to becoming assistant manager, Williams had worked for five months as one of the theatre's ushers.

## Company Problems

After the name change and under Williams's new management, business had improved slightly. In January and February the average audience size had been about 60 persons per show, well below the 375-seat capacity. Attendance in December was up to 90–100 people per show. Williams remarked, "As we will be receiving an average admittance fee of $2.00 per head, we will pretty well have to pack the place every night to break even."

In Williams's opinion, the theatre had two problems: 1) people did not know much about the theatre; and 2) people did not know much about the films being shown. "People don't know what they are getting when they go to see an art film," stated Williams.

After eight months of operation, Celebrity Films finally realized that Burloak did not have the population size or audience interest to support a first-run art-film cinema. (Cost data are outlined in Figure C27-1.)

Source: Marvin Ryder.

**Figure C27-1    Theatre Cost Information**

| | |
|---|---|
| Film rental per showing | $    75 |
| Estimated management salaries | $20 000 per year |
| Estimated theatre lease (building & utilities) | $  2 000 per month |

Estimated gross margin on candy counter operation — 65%
   ($0.65 of each dollar spent at the candy counter represented profit)

Average staffing per night
1 cashier
1 candy counter attendant (two on Friday and Saturday nights)    } (average of 3.5 hours per person at minimum wage)
2 ushers
1 doorman

plus 1 projectionist (4.5 hours per night at $10.00 per hour)

## Recent Changes

Responding to the low attendance figures, Celebrity changed the theatre's concept again. Beginning in mid-December, Lime Light Cinema became a repertory theatre, featuring two different movies every night (one shown at 7:00 p.m. and the other at 9:15 p.m.). Features would include second-run commercial films (movies shown two to three months after their premiere), occasional premiere films, and first-run art films. Williams explained, "Most of the films shown will have been in Burloak already. People will know the films and that will make our promotion job a lot easier." The variety of films and reduced prices were key elements in the new strategy.

Lime Light would be moving (on January 1, 1986) from a straight admission fee of $3.00 for students and $4.00 for adults to a membership basis. Company management felt that the old prices were not low enough to attract enough people to come to see a film with which they were unfamiliar. Members would pay $5.00 a year to join the cinema and $1.50 per show admission fee. For nonmembers the fee per film would be $2.50. At these prices Lime Light Cinema would be offering lower prices than the other repertory theatre in town, which charged a $4.00 membership fee, and $2.50 and $3.50 for admission to members and nonmembers,

respectively. Initially, Lime Light Cinema had ordered 5000 membership cards.

Williams had increased theatre revenues and profits by making changes in the candy counter operation — adding and deleting products and readjusting prices on soft drinks and popcorn. The average receipt per patron had increased from about $0.50 to $0.75. The theatre would generate a high percentage of any profits from the candy operation, so these changes were important.

## The Theatre Industry

There were eight commercial theatres and one repertory theatre in Burloak. Originally, Lime Light Cinema was not directly competing with either type of theatre. However, with the changes, they would be competing directly with the other repertory theatre in town, which was very well established. Williams expected to have some initial difficulty competing for business, but believed that there was room for two repertory theatres in Burloak.

Besides the other theatres, another source of competition was home videotape machines. By the time second-run commercial films were shown at the Lime Light Cinema, they were available on videocassettes. People could purchase or rent these cassettes for home viewing. Premiere films would not be affected

**Figure C27-2   Typical Newspaper Advertisements**

*Daily Ad in* The Burloak Chronicle

*Weekly Ad in* The Shadow *(Burloak University Newspaper)*

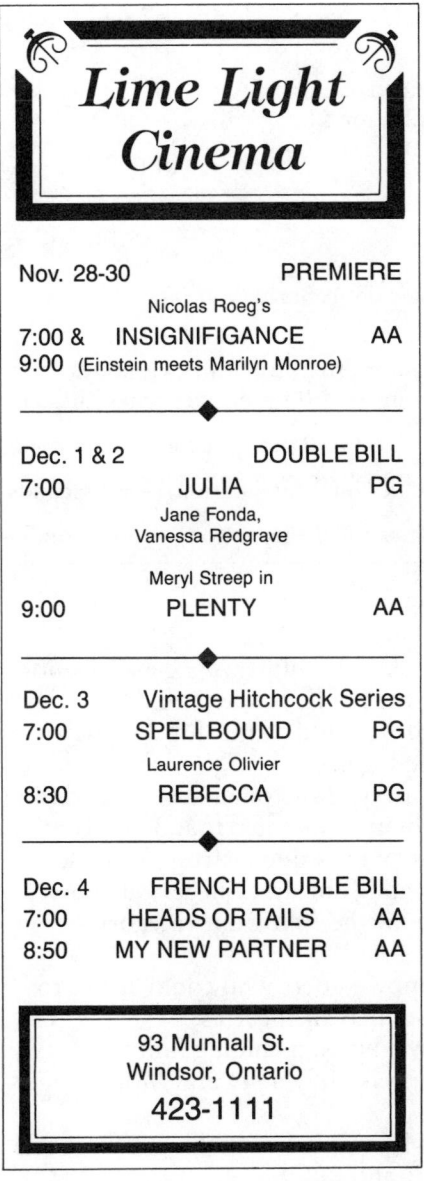

**Lime Light Cinema**

Last Night — Double Bill

Jane Fonda in JULIA (PG) 7:00

Meryl Streep in PLENTY (AA) 9:00

---

**Lime Light Cinema**

| | | |
|---|---|---|
| Nov. 28-30 | | PREMIERE |
| | Nicolas Roeg's | |
| 7:00 & | INSIGNIFIGANCE | AA |
| 9:00 | (Einstein meets Marilyn Monroe) | |

---

| | | |
|---|---|---|
| Dec. 1 & 2 | | DOUBLE BILL |
| 7:00 | JULIA | PG |
| | Jane Fonda, Vanessa Redgrave | |
| | Meryl Streep in | |
| 9:00 | PLENTY | AA |

---

| | | |
|---|---|---|
| Dec. 3 | Vintage Hitchcock Series | |
| 7:00 | SPELLBOUND | PG |
| | Laurence Olivier | |
| 8:30 | REBECCA | PG |

---

| | | |
|---|---|---|
| Dec. 4 | FRENCH DOUBLE BILL | |
| 7:00 | HEADS OR TAILS | AA |
| 8:50 | MY NEW PARTNER | AA |

93 Munhall St.
Windsor, Ontario
**423-1111**

---

## Figure C27-3    Advertising Rates in Burloak

*Print*

|  | Circulation | Line Rate (per column) |
|---|---|---|
| The Burloak Chronicle | 147 448 (total paid daily) | $2.16 |
|  |  | $1.61 (over 10 000 lines per year) |
| TV Facts (Burloak edition) (free distribution) | 26 913 (weekly) | 1/4 page — $105.00/week (26-week schedule) |
| The Shadow | 14 000 (weekly) | $0.62 |
|  |  | $0.48 (weekly contract) |

*Radio*

|  | AAA | AA | A | B |  |
|---|---|---|---|---|---|
| CABC (#1 station in Burloak area) | $55 | $43 | $35 | $28 | 60 seconds |
|  | 45 | 34 | 29 | 23 | 30 seconds |

AAA — 6:00 a.m. to 10:00 a.m. weekdays          AA — 4:00 p.m. to 11:00 p.m. weekdays
A — 10:00 a.m. to 4:00 p.m. weekdays and Saturday     B — all other times

Reach plan     $35.00 per spot for 21 60-second spots consisting of 4 AAA, 6 AA, 6 A, and 5 B spots

CFBU (Burloak University station) — 60 seconds — $2.00

CFMC (Mohican College station) — 60 seconds — $1.00

---

by cassette sales. Art films were generally not available to the public on cassette. Only with concerted effort could some of the exotic art film titles be located.

A wide variety of customers patronized the cinema. Williams estimated that 35 percent of his customers were students from Burloak University and Mohican College. Customers fell into one of the following categories:

1. regular movie-goers who could afford to go to commercial theatres;
2. avid movie buffs, including film students from Burloak University and Mohican College;
3. people who wanted something offbeat and different; and
4. people who were just looking for an inexpensive night out.

He believed they were marketing to everybody.

### Promoting the New Concept

Approximately $17 000 had been allocated to promotion for 1986. In the past, most advertising had been allocated to newspapers. Lime Light Cinema placed a daily ad in *The Burloak Chronicle* and an occasional ad in *The Shadow*, the university student newspaper. (See Figure C27-2 for examples.) Williams felt that radio advertising was generally too expensive, but would use it occasionally to promote premiere features. In addition, bimonthly tabloid-type program schedules were distributed to potential customers through all record stores and donut shops in the city. These schedules were provided by Head Office. (Information on media costs is shown in Figure C27-3.) Williams did not really know if the advertising was effective. He did know that the future promotional strategy for the repertory concept had to be successful or he would be out of a job. (Population information is given in Figure C27-4.)

The objective of the new promotional program was to make people aware of the repertory format, the new prices, and to sell memberships. So far, Williams had purchased a 60-line ad in *The Burloak Chronicle* to announce the opening and had arranged an interview on a CBUR-TV entertainment program to talk about the new concept. He was thinking of trying to arrange a couple of radio interviews as well, but he knew more had to be done.

**Figure C27-4   Population Statistics for Burloak**

Metropolitan Burloak

| | |
|---|---|
| Population | 324 000* |
| Age Groups | |
| Under 14 | 72 380 |
| 15–24 | 61 920 |
| 25–34 | 51 540 |
| 35–44 | 38 045 |
| Over 44 | 84 485 |

*Student population

| | |
|---|---|
| Burloak University | 14 500 |
| Mohican College | 4 000 |

# Case 28   *Midland Tools Ltd.*

Early in 1975, the marketing department of Midland Tools Ltd., England, was still busy finalizing the marketing plan for the year, even though the plan should have been ready nearly three months before. The marketing planning manager was going through the information sent to him from the various departments and was contemplating writing a memo to the marketing director pointing out some of the inadequacies in the information available that were making life difficult for him.

## Background

Midland Tools is a wholly owned subsidiary of Tools International, which produced industrial cutting and hand tools and cutlery. In the early 1970s the group has been trying to break into the power tools market, through setting up a small power tools division and acting as agent for a number of foreign lines. Midland manufactured garden, builder's, carpenter's, and engineer's tools including wrenches, files, hammers, and chisels. In 1974, it accounted for just under half of the group sales of £40 million. The group had been concentrating its efforts in developing overseas operations, primarily through acquiring smaller companies in related product groups and nearly half the trading profits came to be generated overseas. Export sales accounted for 35 percent of Midland's sales, mostly to EEC countries and the U.S.

A characteristic of the industry has been that larger companies try to close product gaps through acquiring smaller companies dominant in the field, rather than investing in new-product development or manufacturing facilities. In most cases, the acquired brand names are retained, although the operations are integrated into one of the principal subsidiaries.

Tools International had been pursuing this strategy, and a recent acquisition was Spanfile Co. Ltd., a well-known manufacturer of engineer's hand tools. Its operation was merged

This case was made possible by the co-operation of the organization concerned. It was prepared by Dr. F. Azim, of the Cranfield School of Management, as a basis for class discussion rather than to illustrate effective or ineffective handling of an administrative situation. Distributed by the Case Clearing House of Great Britain and Ireland, Cranfield Institute of Technology, Bedford, MK43 OAL England.

into Midland's. Some doubts were expressed at the time about the wisdom of this integration, as there were some basic differences in the operation of the two companies. Midland was consumer and user oriented in its marketing approach and provided considerable support for the trade. Its policy was to sell directly to retailers as well as to wholesalers, in roughly equal proportions. In contrast, Spanfile concentrated on industrial and engineering sectors and used wholesalers exclusively for distribution. Both enjoyed a reputation for quality and were at the high-priced end of the market. For about three years after acquisition, the only area of co-ordinated activity had been in overseas selling. No attempt was made by either company to exploit the achievements or contacts of the other. Spanfile had a record of poor delivery performance and the situation had been getting worse during the intervening period.

The integration resulted in extensive rationalization of production and distribution facilities and merging of the sales administration. The two sales forces were combined and the representatives were selling the complete new range. An analysis of Midland's customers showed that 50 percent of the U.K. turnover was accounted for by customers with annual purchases of £15 000 or more. The majority of these customers were wholesalers. The company decided to change its distribution policy to one based on wholesalers while retaining a number of large retail accounts. It was further decided to cut out outlets which did not achieve annual sales of £5000. This nearly halved the total number of outlets serviced by Midland. Changes were made in the discount policy which used to be linked to annual sales. The company now offered a flat rate discount for customers (wholesale and retail) with annual sales exceeding £5000.

Midland was suffering increasingly from the rising cost of raw materials (mainly steel) and finished goods. The situation was worsened by the imbalances caused by the rationalization of selling arrangements and of product range that had resulted in the company producing about 5000 different patterns after integration compared to over 12 000 a few years ago. In the U.K. the recession had hit the engineer's and builder's tools markets (40 percent of U.K. sales) with a resultant decrease in orders in hand and in order intakes. But the larger part of U.K. business is dependent on the do-it-yourself trade, and on home and garden tools, which are less affected by the current economic climate.

The top management has been under pressure to "sell" the recent policy changes to the trade and to reduce the finished goods inventory, especially of the discontinued lines. In terms of capital investment and sales, Midland is among the top three manufacturers in hand and garden tools. In 1973, its market share in most product groups was 25–35 percent. Since then the competitive situation had changed considerably. A major competitor on the hand-tool side, Southern Tools became a contender for the garden-tool market through the acquisition of a smaller company with an extensive range. Another competitor had also been very active in the acquisition field and now offered a product range more comprehensive than Midland's. To complicate matters, a leading power-tool manufacturer entered the hand-tool market with a wide range of tools for the do-it-yourself sector. In addition to this, there was competition from smaller companies with a reputation for service and special discounts, and from Continental manufacturers, especially German.

The Midland management felt that it would be hard pushed to maintain its share of the U.K. market, let alone increase it. It was at a disadvantage in terms of the depth of product range on offer. The investment and time needed to develop a full range in a new-product group constituted too high a risk, and Midland's experience with licensing or acting as an agent has not been fruitful. The company's strategy in acquiring smaller companies has been comparatively unsuccessful and it was now looking more and more to expand its operations in overseas markets.

## Information for Marketing Planning and Control

Midland Tools enjoyed a reputation for aggressive marketing and for the merchandising and promotional support which it provided to the trade. For some time the top management had been worried about the quality and the use of marketing information, collected from internal and external sources, especially after the Spanfile acquisition and integration. It was decided to invite a firm of management consultants to evaluate the sources and uses of information by marketing executives and to recommend improvements. Accordingly, a consultant conducted a number of informal interviews with various marketing executives. Excerpts from the interviews are given below and an organization chart for the marketing division is shown in Figure C28-1. Midland's overseas activities, which are looked after by the overseas sales director, are excluded here.

## Marketing Planning Manager

— *What are your sources of information on market size and trends?*

— For information on total market size and growth trends, we depend largely on publications from the government's Central Statistics Office, such as *Business Monitors* and *Economic Trends*. I am not particularly happy with these statistics as there are some problems with definition and product groupings. The CSO depends on information provided by the manufacturers in reply to questionaires that it sends around, and it is not always clear where a manufacturer should enter each product group,

and where a particular product group fits in their subgroups. But this is the only regular source at the moment and it is very cheap.

— *What are your other sources of information on total market size and trends? The Manufacturers' Associations, for instance?*

— The File Manufacturers' Association releases information on total sales of files, U.K. and export, but the Federation of British Hand Tool Manufacturers does not really compile or release any statistics. The associations do not provide anything on market shares. Some information is available on garden-tool ownership through a biannual survey carried out by Contimart, and we subscribe to this. It relies very much on the memory of the respondents, going back, say, five years, but it does give you a guide to changing ownership. We've had some problems with information on files and wrenches and had to commission special surveys to be carried out by outside market research organizations. As you can imagine, these were expensive.

— *How do you obtain information on competitive brand shares?*

— Until '73 we used to get continuous audit and distribution data from Retail Audits Ltd., which covered all the product groups. This used to cost about £5000–7000 per annum. We've since discontinued this, because it is too expensive and we were not making full use of the information. I feel that we did not have a marketing function strong and flexible enough to react to or use the data. We looked at the feasibility of setting up our own audit panel and my report on this is still under consideration. It will certainly be more flexible than Retail Audit and the information will be specific to our requirements. It will cost less, especially if we can interest one or two other manufacturers in sharing the data. We are exploring the possibilities now. As you know, we've recently changed our distribution policy; so I expect the proposals for setting up our own panel will need to be revised.

— *So what about market-share data for 1974?*

— Unfortunately, we do not have any and have to rely on data up to '73 and our estimates. Earlier in the year, I prepared a number of detailed reports on U.K. markets for various product groups, which dealt with our position with respect to competition. But for the coming plan, we are having to depend on estimates. We do get some qualitative information on competitive activity through the trade press. Unfortunately, this is not a regular source and we don't train our sales force specifically to look for information on competitors, be it special deals or promotions, new products, and so on. There is no systematic collection of regular feedback from the sales force. I used to prepare a brief report for the marketing director on the basis of Retail Audit data pointing out problem areas, such as declining market share, overstocking, and so forth, and suggesting what action I thought was necessary. Obviously, I have not prepared any such report for a while. Another use of the Audit data on market shares was that it allowed us to calculate the total market size, changes, and so on more accurately.

— *Perhaps we could now talk about internal sales data?*

— Yes, they are quite extensive at the moment. I shall let you have copies of these reports, which are available on a monthly basis. (See Figures C28-2 through C28-4.) I think they are adequate from planning and control points of view. They allow us to

calculate sales and contribution by product group, brand, area, sales reps, and so on. A monthly summary of these reports is prepared for the marketing director.

— *I notice you are responsible for pricing.*

— This has become rather confused at the moment. We are in fact changing or prices every three months to keep up with inflation. Our management accountants work out the effects of rising production costs and apply to the government for price increases. Once the increase has been sanctioned, we sit down and adjust the prices, mostly in line with competitive prices and the sales volume of the brand or pattern. We are the top end of the market and have to keep a keen eye on what our major competitors are doing.

## Advertising and Promotion Manager

— We have recently changed our advertising agency. The detailed brief is yet to be settled. The marketing director is handling this himself, and he will be able to give you a better picture. The agency will be responsible for setting up and maintaining an information and intelligence service on competitor activity, including details of advertising and promotional expenditure, breakdown of media, and an evaluation of advertising strategy. At the moment, we don't have reliable information on spending by the competition. We get some qualitative information through the press, but this is not collected in a systematic way.

— *What about background information for developing your advertising strategy?*

— We had a consumer brand-awareness survey carried out in '73, which showed Midland Tools is well known as one of the top three manufacturers of hand and garden tools. The brand awareness in all the product group was high. The survey gave a good idea of regional variation in awareness and showed where our strengths and weaknesses lay. Unfortunately, Spanfile brands fared rather poorly. Of course, as you are probably aware, the competitive situation has changed considerably. We have had major competitors trying to break into new product groups, through massive advertising and promotional campaigns. We had hoped to have a similar survey done last year to keep track of any changes and assess the effectiveness of our own campaigns in various regions. This did not come off.

We do not have any formal procedure for assessing the impact of our advertising and promotional efforts. This is very important with merchandising units and other point-of-sale material, on which we spend the major share of the advertising and promotional budget.

The budget, by the way, is usually based on previous years' figures and is roughly 2–3 percent of sales. The appropriations under various sections are modified from year to year.

We used to prepare a regular monthly progress report on the activities of this section so that the rest of the marketing group and the sales force were kept informed of what was happening on our fronts. But we have fallen behind with this.

step procedure in new-product development, from the collection of ideas to the product launch. This will delineate the responsibility of the various departments involved; in this case marketing, product development, and engineering. We can then prepare standard documentations for the control of the program. We have to liaise very closely with engineering, and at the moment, the exchange of information on ongoing projects takes place on an informal, ad hoc basis.

I prepare a monthly progress report for the marketing director. The engineering and marketing directors meet on a monthly basis to co-ordinate and control the activities of the respective teams. A quarterly progress report is prepared for the managing director.

— *What about information for evaluating the marketing feasibility of new-product ideas?*

— We have fairly elaborate data on our own sales of various brands, sizes, patterns. I can easily lay my hands on this data when I need to. The problem starts when we want some information on sales of competitive products. The market research people do help out, but as you know, we stopped taking the Retail Audit data and don't have any other source at present. The provision is there for carrying out special studies on market feasibility of particular products. I have not had an occasion to do this yet.

## Product Development Manager

— The emphasis in this area has been on improving existing products or on filling up gaps in a particular product group with respect to the competition. Ideas are generated within marketing and engineering and usually involve the improvement of design and quality of a product or some cost savings in its manufacture. We are at present trying to lay down a formal step-by-

## Customer Services Manager

— This post has only been created recently. I am responsible for the sales office and for co-ordinating the informational inputs from manufacturing, distribution, and credit control. We have to ensure that our sales force and the distributors are kept informed of delivery schedules, lead times, etc., especially on the large-volume products. We deal with customer complaints.

I have to sign the credit notes, which we issue for faulty and damaged goods. So I am aware of the types of complaints, who they are coming from, and so on. The quality control manager used to prepare a monthly "faulty tools report" for the different manufacturing units, but he has not prepared any report in recent months. In any case, the format of the report needs to be changed, as it does not mention brand names or the value of the tools returned.

These are early days for this section. We have yet to decide on a formal procedure for monitoring the activities here — things like back-order status, "key customer" service level, and so on. I report to the marketing director on an informal basis, mostly when problems arise.

## Marketing Director

— I'll deal with our relationship with the advertising agency first. They will carry out a monitoring function for us in two ways — one is a check and an estimate of expenditure and the amount of effort which competitors are putting in; the second is an evaluation of their creative and copy strategy, probably through press cuttings and samples of competitors' promotional literature. Our own people on this side will supplement their efforts. We are now instituting a system for the formal collection and analysis of feedback from the sales force. They will be required to fill in a standardized report on competitive promotions, pricing, discounts, new products, merchandising, and so forth. The market research people will be responsible for putting these reports together and for ensuring that the relevant information reaches the executives concerned on a regular basis. The agency will prepare a quarterly report.

They will also undertake "before" and "after" consumer-image checks for a particular campaign. You're probably aware that at the moment we are rather short of up-to-date and reliable information on our consumers. Most of our stuff is fairly dated and we don't have very much on the Spanfile side. The market planning people will carry out a distribution survey to check on the level of our coverage of the outlets against competition. This will help in deciding on where to direct our advertising and promotional efforts.

— *What about information on the impact of the campaign?*

— The agency will supply this type of information — be it opportunities to see the campaign, total recall, viewing figures, etc. We have not decided on the type of data and the frequency of reports yet. I would like to mention here that we are engaging a market research agency to provide us information about the impact of our booth in the Annual Trades Fair. We spend about 5 percent of the promotional budget on the exhibition.

— *Perhaps we could talk about sales management?*

— Well, as you know, we don't have a national sales manager at the moment. A number of changes are taking place in this area. We've recently changed our distribution policy and cut out a lot of accounts. After the integration of Spanfile, sales territories have been redefined. There has been a considerable rationalization of the combined product range. We are now operating under a special sales plan: firstly to shift the old product lines; and secondly to inform the trade of the changes that are taking place. This is partly the reason why

**Figure C28-1   Midland Tools Ltd. — Marketing Division**

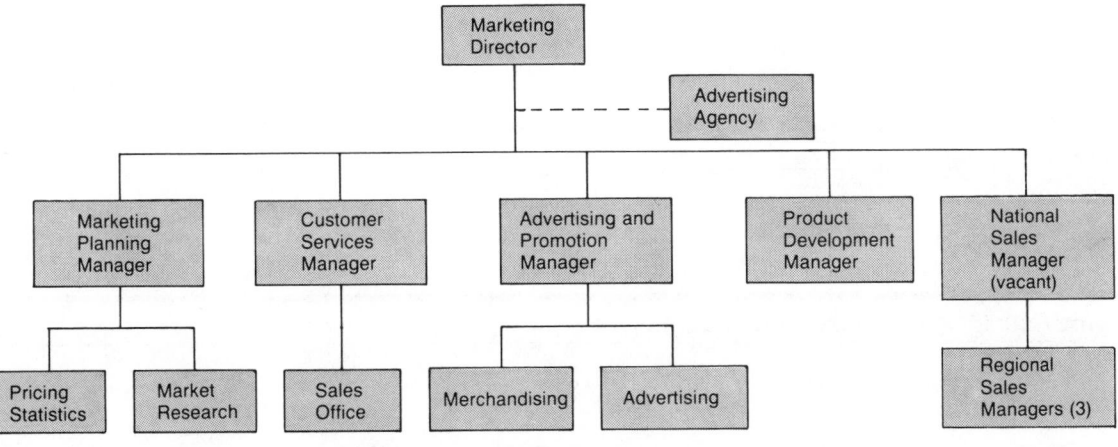

the marketing plan is behind schedule. We had to take this emergency plan up on an ad hoc basis. I would like future sales plans to be broken down on the basis of key national customers — to build up customer profiles — present order intake from them and potential order level, what they are buying from our competitors, what their promotional needs are, and so forth. The sales forecasts will be broken down on this basis and also on the basis of territory, so that the sales management have a target to aim for and we can keep track of whether things are going according to plan. All this will obviously take some time.

At the moment, I receive a monthly summary of the various sales statistics from market planning, which draws my attention to the exceptions, the problems. As I said, I would like dossiers to be gradually built up on our major customers and would like to be able to consult the dossiers for problem diagnosis, and so on. The regional managers will obviously pay detailed attention to this on a regular basis and should have the answers for me when required.

The regional managers now send me a monthly report on sales force activities and expenditure. Sales expenditure is controlled as a total against a budget. Again, this is because of the changes and the current emergency sales plan. We shall be preparing territorial expenditure budgets and discussing this with the sales reps. A lot of work has to be done on this as well.

— *I had a chat with the customer services manager, but I would like your comments on this area.*

— We have been worried about customer services for some time. Our parent company had a trade attitude survey done last year. It showed that Midland was well known as one of the top three in terms of quality, product range, brand loyalty. Where we tend to fall down is on customer services — mainly our delivery performance. This is particularly true of Spanfile. This was one of the reasons why we decided to create the post of customer services manager, who can be responsible for order processing, keeping the customers informed

## Figure C28-2   Selling Report by Item

| | This Month | | | | | Year to Date | | | | |
|---|---|---|---|---|---|---|---|---|---|---|
| Product Code | Invoiced Sales | | | Orders recd. Value | Orders on hand | | Invoiced Sales | | Actual/ Budget % | Orders recd. Value |
| Product Group | Budget | Actual | Actual/Budget % | | This month | Last month | Budget | Actual | | |
| Sub-product group | Value | Qty | Value | Qty | | | | Value | Qty | Value | Qty | | |
| Patterns | | | | | | | | | | | | |

## Figure C28-3   Rep. Sales/Contribution Report

Representative:                          Area code:                          Month:

| | | | | | | | | | Year to date | | | |
|---|---|---|---|---|---|---|---|---|---|---|---|---|
| Product Code | Invoiced Sales | | | Orders received | | Contribution | | Invoiced Sales | | | |
| Product Group Sub-product group Patterns | Budget | Actual | Actual/Budget % | Value | Qty | Budget | Actual | Budget | Actual | Actual/Budget % | |
| | Value | Qty | Value | Qty | | | | | | Value | Qty | Value | Qty | |

## Figure C28-4   Customer Analysis

| | Sales classification | | This year | | | | Last year | | | |
|---|---|---|---|---|---|---|---|---|---|---|
| Account Code | Representative Code | Delivery Name & Address | Year to Date | | | | Year to Date | | | |
| | | | Orders received | | Invoiced Sales | | Orders Received | | Invoiced Sales | |
| Account Branch | | | Value | Qty | Value | Qty | Value | Qty | Value | Qty |

about deliveries, customer complaints, and so on. We don't have any formal statement of the work-load of this section — turn-around time, how many orders outstanding at the end of the week, how many complaints, type of complaints, etc. Complaints could arise from two sources — technical ones that will involve the lab and engineering, or clerical errors. But I am more concerned about the actual process by which a faulty tool is returned to us and a replacement or a credit note given. The reps usually arrange for the faulty tools to be collected by our transport from various customers. We have to check whether the complaints were genuine — whether the tool has been used properly. We would like to ensure, at the same time, that the whole process — from receiving to replacement — does not involve a long time-lag.

— *Any comments on product development?*

— What is being done there is that a standard

procedure will be agreed on between marketing and engineering. This will show the various decision points beyond which the project will not proceed unless it has been checked for marketing or technical feasibility. This in fact will be covered by simple authorization slips or forms. I think we have a problem of tying together the engineering and marketing sides. One can easily end up in a situation where the things just get behind schedule and it's nobody's fault. At the moment, the engineering people, their dates are their own. I think it's much better if it rests in marketing. As for the control of ongoing projects, I have monthly meetings with the engineering director and some of the other directors too, depending on what is happening at the time.

## Discussion Questions

1. What are the opportunities and problems faced by Midland?
2. As the consultant, what is your assessment of the information situation?
3. What other questions should have been asked by the consultant?
4. What is the next step?

# Case 29   CJUM-FM

In February 1979, Mike Crutch, the business manager for the University of Manitoba's Student Union (UMSU), had several difficult decisions to make. He had just taken direct control of the management of CJUM-FM, an on-campus radio station which was principally funded by UMSU, and he realized that the station was in a critical financial situation. The station had a large accounts payable balance and a payroll of $13 000 which had to be met by the week's end. Its cash balance was $5000. In addition the station had an accumulated deficit of over $100 000.

It was obvious that CJUM-FM was in an extremely difficult financial position. However, Mike was confident that he could obtain a $25 000 line of credit from UMSU which would alleviate immediate cash-flow problems. He was much more concerned about the long-term viability of the radio station. Although CJUM was originally designed to support six staff, the station presently had 11 full-time employees and an operating budget of $150 000, of which $100 000 was dedicated to salaries and commissions. UMSU had set up an annual operating grant of $60 000 for CJUM. At the present budgeted level of expenditures the station had to generate an additional $90 000, either through advertising sales (see Figure C29-1 for advertising rates), which were limited by the Canadian Radio-television and Telecommunications Commission (CRTC), or by fund raising. Donations to CJUM-FM were tax deductible. To put his thoughts in perspective Mike reviewed the history of CJUM.

CJUM-FM began broadcasting in October 1975 as a limited-advertising community radio station. The idea of station had been a central issue in several student elections. UMSU first applied for an FM broadcasting licence to operate a commercial nonprofit radio station in 1973. The CRTC rejected the initial application and recommended that the student union reapply for a noncommercial licence.

Prepared by John M. Rigby and M. Dale Beckman, University of Manitoba.

The noncommerical licence, which UMSU was eventually granted, allowed four minutes of advertising per clock hour (i.e., advertising time could not be accumulated) and a maximum of six interruptions per hour. As well as the amount of advertising which CJUM was permitted to sell, the type of message was restricted. The CRTC ruling read, in part:

Such statements must not contain language which attempts to promote particular services or products, for example, such statements may not refer to price, quality, convenience, durability or contain other comparative [statements].

Despite these restrictions, UMSU felt that enough advertising could be sold to put CJUM in a break-even position within three years.

Capital costs for the radio station of $125 000 were covered by a bank loan secured by the University of Manitoba. It soon became evident, however, that more funding would be necessary if CJUM was to be launched successfully. The student union, therefore, granted the station $150 000 to be disbursed in varying amounts over a five-year period. In 1976, the station received $31 893 from UMSU. In 1977, it received $60 000 and was to receive decreasing amounts each year thereafter until 1981, at which time the station was expected to be self-sufficient. Despite these operating grants the station continued to operate at a deficit. Hoping to stabilize the situation, UMSU granted CJUM a $60 000 annual operating budget in 1978. Nevertheless, the station continued to experience serious financial difficulty, which led to UMSU's decision in 1979 to instal Mike Crutch as acting manager.

As Mike reviewed CJUM's problems, he became convinced that his most difficult task would be to formulate a marketing plan for the station that would include details of how CJUM could capture a reasonable portion of the FM listening audience and a fair percent-age of radio advertising dollars or suggest alternate ways to raise funds.

CJUM was regulated by the CRTC in that the station was required to run a variety of alternative program types; that is, programming that would not normally be carried by commercial stations. The station played jazz, classical music, reggae, and progressive and mainstream rock. In addition the station ran a relatively high percentage of foreground programming, which required the audience's active attention. These included talk shows, literary readings, and children's programs. The CRTC did not regulate the scheduling of these programs. When Mike assumed his role as station manager, much of CJUM's prime time was devoted to jazz, classical, and alternative programming. In fact, the station was exceeding the CRTC's alternative programming requirements.

CJUM's advertising campaigns stressed the variety of programming. Recognizing that different listeners would be interested in different aspects of their total programming, CJUM published a monthly program guide. The guide was intended to foster selective listening habits among CJUM's audience, with people tuning in to those programs which were attractive to them, personally. Mike noted, however, that the program guide was actually being published much less frequently than the original monthly schedule.

Despite the problems facing him, Mike was encouraged by the results of a listener survey conducted by a second-year statistics class. The class had 600 people, 400 of whom were university students, complete a questionnaire entitled "CJUM-FM Listener Survey." Of the total, 32.6 percent indicated that they listened to CJUM-FM frequently. However, Mike was not certain what use to make of the information and he was somewhat concerned about the actual validity of the survey. He also had at his disposal a second survey of 150 university and college students indicating their music-listening preferences (see Figure C29-2). This second survey seemed to indicate that in order to appeal to the general student population, CJUM-FM would have to revise its program format to some degree.

Mike was concerned about potential negative reactions from the large number of volunteers who worked at the station to possible changes that he might have to make in CJUM's programming format. CJUM needed volunteers to aid in its daily operation and presently had approximately 100 people donating some of their time. Of these, 80 volunteers were from the Winnipeg community. Many were former students of the university who continued to work at CJUM even though they no longer took courses on campus. The volunteers had had a strong voice in the management of CJUM in the past, and earlier this year a policy paper had been prepared by the former management which largely reflected the volunteers' views of the direction CJUM should take. This paper argued in part that commercials must not be allowed to detract from the "sound" or image of CJUM. The community volunteers had very strong views about the content of CJUM's programming, arguing that as much time as possible should be devoted to alternative and serious music. They considered CJUM to be a unique station offering a unique product to its listeners.

Although Mike had assumed his duties as manager of CJUM just recently, he was aware that the UMSU council would soon want his assessment of the viability of the station and his planned course of action. Mike was still not certain how he would respond to the council.

## Discussion Questions

1. Analyse the situation and develop a complete set of recommendations for Mike Crutch.
2. What should be Mike's next step?

---

**Figure C29-1   Advertising Rates**

General Advertising:
A rotation of best available time from 6:00 a.m.–2:00 a.m.

|  | Number of spots per year | |
|---|---|---|
|  | 10–300 | Over 300 |
| 60 seconds | $7.00 per spot | $6.00 per spot |
| 30 seconds | $6.00 | $5.00 |

Preferred Audience Plan:
Guaranteed placement with the music format and audience of the advertiser's choice. Minimum of six spots per week.

|  | 2–12 weeks | over 12 weeks |
|---|---|---|
| 60 seconds | $9.00 per spot | $7.00 per spot |
| 30 seconds | $8.00 | $6.00 |

Exclusive Sponsorship:
each hour   $24.00

## Figure C29-2  Preference of Listeners

|  | New Wave | Country | Disco | Blue-grass | Jazz | Rock | Classical | Folk | Easy Listening |
|---|---|---|---|---|---|---|---|---|---|
| Dislike | 19.0 | 38.8 | 40.8 | 36.1 | 26.5 | 4.1 | 34.7 | 29.9 | 17.0 |
| Dislike somewhat | 9.5 | 21.8 | 11.6 | 16.3 | 14.3 | 5.4 | 13.6 | 18.4 | 12.2 |
| Neutral | 19.0 | 15.0 | 21.1 | 20.4 | 23.8 | 14.3 | 21.8 | 17.0 | 19.0 |
| Like somewhat | 22.4 | 8.8 | 11.6 | 10.9 | 14.3 | 10.9 | 10.9 | 18.4 | 17.7 |
| Like | 21.1 | 8.8 | 12.2 | 9.5 | 15.6 | 62.6 | 12.9 | 11.6 | 29.3 |

## Figure C29-3  CJUM-FM Incorporated Balance Sheet

*Assets*

Current:

| Term Deposits | $ 15 000 |
|---|---|
| Accounts Receivable — net | 23 307 |
| Prepaid Expenses | 84 |
| | 38 391 |
| Fixed | 129 055 |
| Equipment | 14 532 |
| Set-up Costs | 143 587 |
| Less Accumulated Depreciation and Amortization | 23 244 |
| | 120 343 |
| Total Assets | $158 734 |

*Liabilities*

Current:

| Bank Overdraft | $  2 078 |
|---|---|
| Accounts Payable | 23 445 |
| Advances from University of Manitoba | 52 761 |
| Loan — UMSU | 1 000 |
| Deferred Revenue | — |
| | 79 284 |

Long term:

| Bank Loan | 100 047 |
|---|---|
| University of Manitoba Students' Union | 80 146 |
| | 180 193 |
| Total Liabilities | 259 477 |
| Deficit | (100 743) |
| Total Liabilities & Deficit | $158 734 |

**Figure C29-4   CJUM-FM Incorporated Statement of Income & Deficit
For the 10 Months Ended January 31st, 1979**

|  | Budget Year to Date | Actual Ten Months Jan. 31/79 | Total Budget 1978–79 |
|---|---|---|---|
| *Revenue* | | | |
| Advertising on Air | $ 68 246 | $ 80 000 | $ 54 000 |
| Advertising on Air-Contra | 1 749 | 10 000 | 2 757 |
| Advertising-Program Guide | 4 625 | 9 000 | 2 863 |
| Other | 1 216 | 3 000 | 2 328 |
|  | $ 75 836 | $102 000 | $ 61 948 |
|  | | | |
| *Expenses* | | | |
| Programming: | | | |
| Salaries & Benefits | $ 43 187 | $ 52 600 | $ 45 722 |
| Honorariums | 2 186 | 2 700 | 3 019 |
| Tapes | 2 082 | 1 800 | 1 278 |
| News Machine | 2 683 | 3 700 | 3 376 |
| Records | 1 280 | 1 700 | 1 309 |
| Syndicated Programs | 250 | 500 | 500 |
| Program Guide | 8 267 | 9 000 | 4 736 |
| Miscellaneous | 641 | 500 | 730 |
|  | $ 60 576 | $ 72 500 | $ 60 670 |
|  | | | |
| Technical: | | | |
| Salaries & Benefits | $ 11 850 | $ 14 600 | $  8 500 |
| Contract Maintenance | 2 819 | 3 600 | 2 675 |
| Technical Supplies | 1 678 | 1 500 | 2 096 |
| Remote Line Charges | 335 | 500 | 400 |
|  | $ 16 682 | $ 20 200 | $ 13 671 |
|  | | | |
| Sales & Promotions: | | | |
| Salaries & Benefits | $ 13 628 | $ 15 800 | $ 12 000 |
| Commission | 10 841 | 16 000 | 14 476 |
| Promotion | 1 273 | 2 000 | 1 028 |
| Funding Expense | 925 | 1 000 | 0 |
| Miscellaneous | 847 | 300 | 200 |
|  | $ 27 514 | $ 35 100 | $ 27 704 |

Figure C29-4   CJUM-FM Incorporated Statement of Income & Deficit
For the 10 Months Ended January 31st, 1979 (continued)

|  | Budget Year to Date | Actual Ten Months Jan. 31/79 | Total Budget 1978–79 |
|---|---|---|---|
| Administration: | | | |
| Salaries & Benefits | $ 18 346 | $ 22 500 | $ 19 500 |
| Telephone | 2 619 | 2 800 | 3 546 |
| Postage | 498 | 600 | 578 |
| Xerox | 290 | 300 | 363 |
| Office Supplies | 821 | 1 000 | 1 069 |
| Insurance | 1 701 | 1 200 | 1 137 |
| Accounting & Audit | 875 | 1 500 | 1 514 |
| Legal | 128 | 0 | 0 |
| Bad Debt Expense | 3 265 | 3 000 | 5 267 |
| Miscellaneous | 749 | 500 | 900 |
| Depreciation | 5 983 | 7 200 | 7 200 |
| Printing | 56 | 300 | 300 |
| Interest | 9 052 | 10 000 | 10 623 |
| Honorariums | 1 470 | 300 | 600 |
|  | $ 45 853 | $ 51 200 | $ 52 597 |
| | | | |
| *Total Expenses* | $150 625 | $179 00 | $154 642 |
| Net Loss on Operations | $ 74 789 | $ 77 000 | |
| | | | |
| *Non-Operating Revenue* | | | |
| Grants — UMSU | $ 30 000 | $ 30 000 | $ 40 000 |
| Grants — Other | 3 400 | 40 000 | 37 853 |
| Donations | 5 349 | 3 000 | 3 064 |
| Special Project Grants | (818) | 0 | 295 |
| Special Projects | | | |
| — Fund Raising | 17 160 | 4 000 | 724 |
|  | $ 55 091 | $ 77 000 | $ 81 936 |
| | | | |
| Net Surplus (Deficit) for Period | $(19 698) | 0 | $ 10 758 |
| | | | |
| Deficit Balance, Beginning | $ 81 045 | $ 81 045 | |
| Deficit Balance, Ending | $100 743 | $ 81 045 | |

# Case 30   Aylmer Fair

John White, president of the Aylmer and East Elgin Agricultural Society, was sifting through a marketing report prepared by an external consultant. It was March 1985 and White was beginning to plan for the August 1985 edition of Aylmer Fair. The consultant indicated that the fair's advertising was not as effective as it could be, but White was unsure as to what specific changes the fair should undertake.

Source: Marvin Ryder.

## The Fair Industry in Ontario

Almost all the fairs in Ontario are organized by agricultural societies like the one in Aylmer. Each society relies on a large team of volunteers to organize the fair. Each fair has an executive consisting of a past president, a president, first and second vice-presidents, a secretary, and a treasurer. Operating under the executive is a series of committees responsible for the activities that form a fair, such as the Cattle Committee, the Reception Committee, the Poultry Committee, the Advertising Committee, etc.

For purposes of scheduling, societies are grouped into 15 districts spanning the province; within these districts, fairs are given a classification of A, B, or C. In 1984, there were 30 A fairs (including the C.N.E., Rockton's World Fair, the Ancaster Fair, and the Western Fair), 60 B fairs (such as the Binbrook Fair), and 142 C fairs (such as the Ohsweken Fair and the Burford Fair).

Though as many as 26 fairs can be scheduled at the same time, they do not directly compete with each other because of geographic dispersion. Instead, the major competition to the industry comes from other entertainment sources like television, movies, theatre, pageants, festivals, and attractions like Canada's Wonderland.

## Aylmer Fair History

First held in 1853, Aylmer Fair has been organized annually by the Aylmer and East Elgin Agricultural Society. Aylmer is a small southwestern Ontario town (pop. 5500) located 16 km north of Lake Erie, between St. Thomas (pop. 15 000) and Tillsonburg (pop. 9000), and 40 km south-east of London (pop. 300 000). (See Figure C30-1.) Though originally a one-day spring event, the Aylmer Fair was by now five days long and was scheduled for the third week of August. The Aylmer Fair was classified as a B fair.

Figure C30-1   Map of Southwestern Ontario

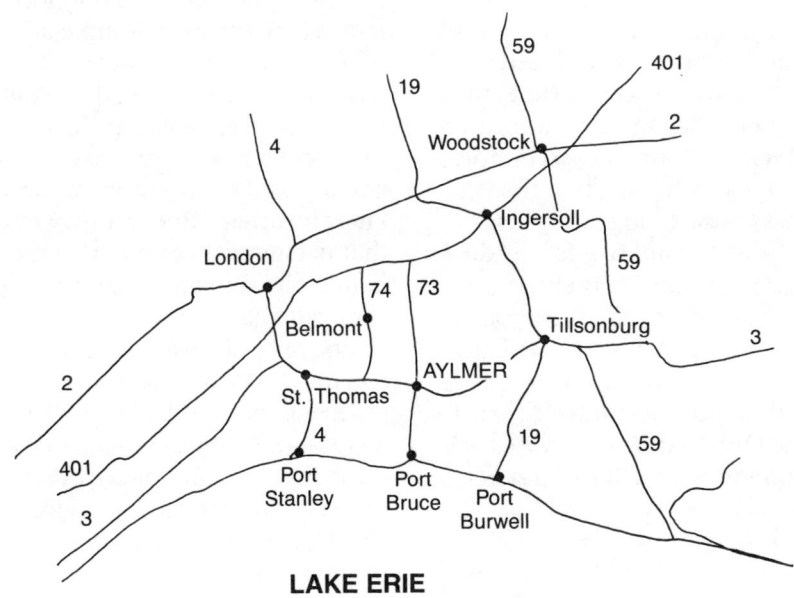

LAKE ERIE

The hours of operation for the fair varied from day to day: Wednesday 4:00 p.m. to 10:00 p.m.; Thursday to Saturday 10:00 a.m. to 10:00 p.m.; and Sunday 12:00 noon to 6:00 p.m. The exhibit buildings opened at noon each day and closed with the fair, while the midway did not start up until 1:00 p.m., and operated past midnight.

In addition to the midway, there was lots to see and do at the fair. There were judged exhibits of work done in high schools (woodwork, metalwork, typing, etc.) and elementary schools (writing, printing, drawing, etc.); ladies' baking, preserves, and handicrafts; vegetable, flower, tobacco, 4-H, and grain displays; and a poultry show. While these exhibits did not change on a day-to-day basis, the cattle and horse shows varied over the duration of the fair (e.g., Holstein, Jersey, Guernsey, Ayrshire, and Hereford cattle shows).

Many of the events at the fair were aimed specifically at children. Sunday was Family Day; children under 12 were admitted free, and the midway had a special all-day ride passport for sale. Sunday also had a Baby Show, in which more than 135 babies competed for prizes while accompanied by proud parents and grandparents. On Wednesday, Chidren's Day, there were special events for the children to enter, ranging from decorated tricycles and bicycles to foot races to bubble-gum blowing. Thursday highlighted the Pet Show with classes for cats, dogs, rabbits, gerbils, and in 1984, a minnow-eating duck.

At night, the drawing card was entertainment in front of the grandstand. Wednesday brought the crowning of "Miss Aylmer Fair," the Official Fair Opening by a celebrity (in 1984, Bobby Hull), and a motorcycle thrill show called "The Death Riders," whose highlight was the "Human Bomb." On Thursday, rock and roll sounds were generated by a group such as "Teenage Head," while on Friday, the roar of a Mini-Tractor Pull drew throngs. Saturday night offered the "Chicago

Knockers," a troupe of swimsuit-clad female mud wrestlers. On Sunday afternoon, the crowd cheered for the Semi-Truck Pull. (Pulls consisted of a vehicle dragging a load that became heavier the farther it was pulled. The vehicle that could drag the load the farthest, usually 100–200 metres, was declared the winner.) Entertainment highlights of recent years had included the "Hell Drivers" (an automobile thrill show), a local talent show, and such varied entertainers as Wilf Carter, Sylvia Tyson, and Cheryl and Robbie Rae.

One other feature of the fair was commercial exhibits on view in the arena. These were displays of household wares by local merchants. Some commercial exhibitors included Tate's Home Furnishings, Gulf Farm Service, the *London Free Press*, the Elgin Co-operative, and Fanshawe College.

Admission charges were levied each day of the fair. Adults paid $3.00 at all times, but children, who usually paid $1.00, were admitted free on Wednesday until 6:00 p.m. and all day on Sunday. No distinction was made in admission rates for senior citizens or students. Six weeks prior to the fair opening, people had the opportunity to purchase a pass to the fair, which offered multiple admissions for $5.00. Passes were valid on any day but could only be used for three admissions in total. At no time was parking, at the rate of $1.00 per car, included with the pass. Should any person need to leave the fair and return at a later time that same day (say to get a sweater), that person was stamped on the back of the hand. The stamp design and colour were changed each day.

The midway also contributed to the fair's revenues. Midway operations were conducted independently of the fair by Conklin's Amusements — the largest supplier of amusements in Canada. Conklin's operated many travelling midways in Ontario to service the fair trade. For Alymer Fair, the large trucks of equipment usually arrived on the Sunday prior to the fair. The rides and concession stands were set up on Monday and Tuesday; these provided some advance publicity, as they were quite visible to anyone passing through town on Highway 3 (one of the two Ontario highways that intersect at Aylmer).

## Finances and Promotion at the Fair

The fair generated money in four ways:

1) admission charges and parking fees; 2) rentals paid by commercial exhibitors and midway operators; 3) entry fees from exhibitors; and 4) grants and donations. This money was used to pay for: 1) prize money; 2) entertainment; 3) operating expenses; 4) administrative expenses; and 5) advertising. Comparative figures are given in Figures C30-2 and C30-3.

**Figure C30-2    Attendance and Admission Charges 1979–84**

|  | 1979 | 1980 | 1981[a] | 1982 | 1983 | 1984 |
|---|---|---|---|---|---|---|
| Paid Attendance: |  |  |  |  |  |  |
| Adults | 13 373 | 13 185 | 10 592 | 12 175 | 11 903 | 11 575 |
| Children | 2 744 | 3 213 | 2 088 | 2 223 | 1 681 | 1 597 |
| Cars Parked | 1 855 | 1 765 | 1 751 | 2 004 | 1 689 | 1 960 |
| Memberships Sold | 1 540 | 1 348 | 1 180 | 1 090 | 1 026 | 689 |
| Price: Adults | $2.00 | $2.50 | $2.50 | $2.50 | $2.50 | $3.00 |
| Children | 0.50 | 1.00 | 1.00 | 1.00 | 1.00 | 1.00 |
| Parking | 1.00 | 1.00 | 1.00 | 1.00 | 1.00 | 1.00 |
| Memberships | 4.00 | 5.00 | 5.00 | 5.00 | 5.00 | 5.00 |

[a]In 1981, Aylmer Fair experienced three days of intermittent rainstorms.

**Figure C30-3    Selected Financial Data 1979-84**

|  | 1979 | 1980 | 1981[a] | 1982 | 1983 | 1984 |
|---|---|---|---|---|---|---|
| Revenues: |  |  |  |  |  |  |
| Admission Charges & Parking | 36 132 | 43 742 | 36 740 | 41 377 | 38 263 | 42 287 |
| Midway & Commercial Rentals | 13 062 | 15 585 | 16 596 | 18 832 | 20 110 | 18 094 |
| Exhibitor Entry Fees | 3 084 | 4 152 | 3 391 | 3 488 | 3 870 | 4 166 |
| Grants and Donations | 10 121 | 10 764 | 10 846 | 13 734 | 12 090 | 12 934 |
| Total Revenues | $62 409 | $74 213 | $67 513 | $77 431 | $74 333 | $77 481 |
| Expenses: |  |  |  |  |  |  |
| Prize Money | 17 381 | 17 117 | 16 825 | 15 647 | 17 333 | 16 682 |
| Entertainment | 13 330 | 13 264 | 13 728 | 12 998 | 10 566 | 16 288 |
| Operating Expenses | 15 216 | 11 668 | 12 373 | 20 045 | 23 415 | 23 600 |
| Administration Expenses | 16 900 | 17 192 | 20 167 | 16 995 | 18 020 | 15 275 |
| Advertising | 2 811 | 4 050 | 4 911 | 5 067 | 5 496 | 6 970 |
| Total Expenses | $65 638 | $63 291 | $67 996 | $70 752 | $74 830 | $78 815 |
| Profit (Loss) on Operations | $ (3 229) | $10 922 | $ (423) | $ 6 679 | $ (497) | $ (1 334) |

[a]In 1981, Aylmer Fair experienced three days of intermittent rainstorms.

In recent years, many directors had been dissatisfied with the performance of Aylmer Fair. Though the fair had built a new cattle barn in 1968, a new secretary's office in 1973, and a new curling club in 1980, financial performance over the past few years had been spotty. The fair had been operating around the break-even point, showing minimal profits and losses, and many wondered how the fair board would be able to pay back the $15 000 bank loan it had needed for the construction of the curling club.

The fair board felt that its position in the people's minds was changing, so Aylmer Fair responded with increased promotion. Two examples are given here. The first was designed to increase the purchase of membership passes. Starting four weeks before the fair, a draw was made on Friday night at the town corners, from all the passes sold to that point in time. Each week, six names were drawn and those lucky people won five dollars. As well, each night of the fair, one ticket was drawn for a $50 cash prize. If that person was at the fair, they would win double the money — $100!

A second facet of the promotional effort was advertising. Ten years previously, the Aylmer Fair had advertised through three vehicles — *The Aylmer Express*, posters, and word-of-mouth. Some free publicity also was generated by the TV, radio, and newspaper reporters sent to cover the fair as a news item.

In recent years, the attitude toward advertising had changed. Advertising had been directed not only to Aylmer, but to the larger markets of London and St. Thomas through a host of media: BX-93, a country-and-western FM station in London; CJBK, a pop/rock AM station in London; CFPL-TV, the closest TV station — located in London; CHLO, a middle-of-the-road AM station in St. Thomas; CKOT, a middle-of-the-road AM station in Tillsonburg; the *Elgin County Market*, a free paper distributed to the doorstep of every Elgin County household; and the original

three — *The Aylmer Express* (the local Wednesday weekly newspaper), posters, and word-of-mouth. In the past five years, advertising expenses have more than doubled. (See Appendix C30-A for samples of poster, newspaper, and radio advertising.)

Radio and television advertising began the week before the fair and continued until the last day of the fair. Ads in the two weekly papers appeared on the Wednesday before the fair and on the opening day. Posters went up two weeks before the fair. There was not enough money in the budget to take advantage of all the media alternatives. Newspapers in Tillsonburg and St. Thomas, along with many other London radio stations, were not used.

## The Consultant's Report

To help the fair improve its performance, an external consultant had been hired to review the fair's operations and suggest areas for improvements. Though the report covered all the facets of the fair, two parts of the document related directly to advertising.

During the 1984 Aylmer Fair, the consultant conducted some market research in the form of a self-administered survey. The questionnaire was camouflaged as an opportunity for people to enter a free draw. Everyone who passed through one of the four admission gates was given the survey, which was printed on both sides of card stock (about the size and thickness of a post card). None of the seven questions asked were open-ended (other than name and address) and all could be answered with a checkmark or a circle.

The survey was co-sponsored by the St. Thomas AM radio station, CHLO. They had a display in the arena along with the other commercial exhibitors and they provided a drum in which people deposited their cards. A draw was made daily at 10:00 p.m. from the cards for $25 in cash or a $50 gift certificate from one of the commercial exhibitors. Once the draw was completed, the remaining cards were removed from the drum so that responses could be compared by day of attendance. The survey card is shown in Figure C30-4.

Of the approximately 10 000 cards given out, 2915 were returned during the five fair days; the 29 percent response rate was considered to be fairly good for this type of survey. In coding the surveys for analysis on the computer, the sex of the respondent was determined from his or her name, the address indicated the respondent's location, and the day of attendance was noted. The results of the survey are summarized in Figure C30-5.

The consultant was also able to assign costs to the media vehicles used for promotion. Figure C30-6 presents a cost breakdown of the advertising dollars spent for the Aylmer Fair.

---

**Figure C30-4    The Survey Card (Front and Back)**

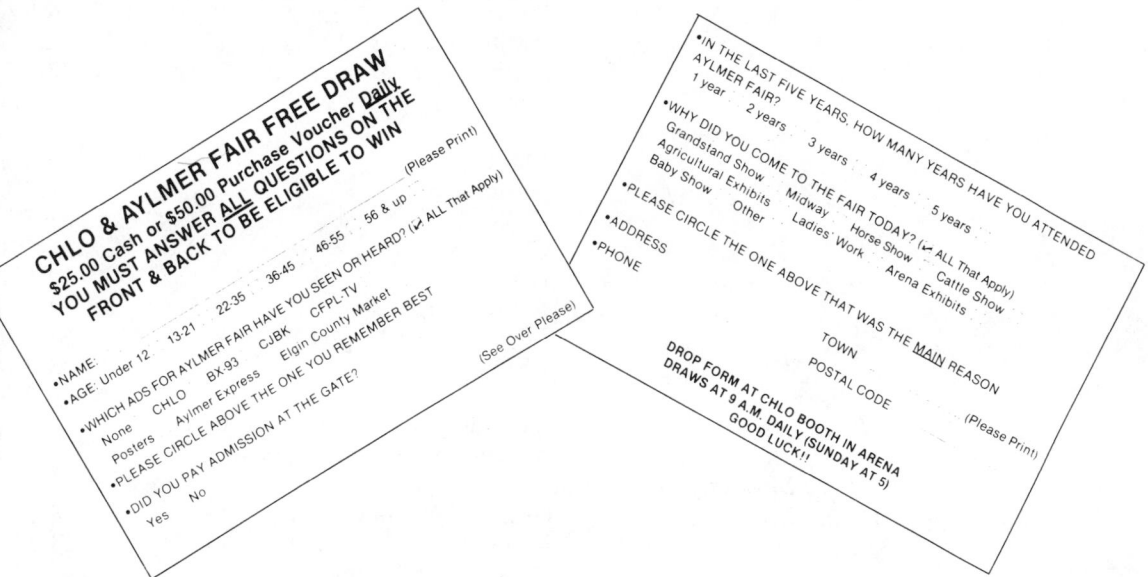

---

### The Problem

Given the various pieces of information he had in front of him, John White was uncertain what steps should be taken to improve the advertising for 1985. After all, White was a volunteer on the fair board. The rest of the time, he operated a successful farm operation and raised Jersey cattle.

Should the advertising budget be increased, decreased, or left at the same level? Should the distribution of the advertising dollars be changed and, if so, in what manner? Should any medium be dropped? Perhaps money was not an issue. Maybe the ads themselves were to blame. White thought the ads were effective, but he had no business experience with advertising.

He needed to know the answers to these questions. The Aylmer Fair board wanted a profit in 1985.

**Figure C30-5   Summary of Survey Results**

| Sex: | Male | 42.2% |
|---|---|---|
| | Female | 57.8% |
| Age: | 12 & Under | 8.9% |
| | 13–21 | 20.3% |
| | 22–35 | 32.3% |
| | 36–45 | 15.0% |
| | 46–55 | 8.4% |
| | 56 & Over | 15.0% |
| Most-remembered ad: | | |
| | CHLO | 13.1% |
| | BX-93 | 11.7% |
| | CJBK | 7.9% |
| | CFPL-TV | 8.2% |
| | Posters | 6.8% |
| | *Aylmer Express* | 22.1% |
| | *Elgin County Market* | 22.2% |
| | CKOT | 7.1% |
| Ads seen/heard: | | |
| | CHLO | 35.0% |
| | BX-93 | 32.5% |
| | CJBK | 23.7% |
| | CFPL-TV | 26.7% |
| | Posters | 30.1% |
| | *Aylmer Express* | 44.9% |
| | *Elgin County Market* | 51.6% |
| | CKOT | 23.9% |
| | None | 10.0% |
| | (Percentages do not add to 100% because of multiple responses.) | |
| Most important attraction: | | |
| | Grandstand Show | 38.0% |
| | Midway | 23.2% |
| | Agricultural Exhibit | 5.8% |
| | Horse Show | 5.1% |
| | Cattle Show | 4.3% |
| | Ladies' Work | 8.0% |
| | Commercial Exhibits | 12.2% |
| | Baby Show | 3.3% |
| Attractions that they came to see: | | |
| | Grandstand Show | 58.0% |
| | Midway | 47.3% |
| | Agricultural Exhibit | 30.9% |
| | Horse Show | 16.3% |
| | Cattle Show | 14.5% |
| | Ladies' Work | 28.0% |
| | Commercial Exhibits | 44.4% |
| | Baby Show | 9.6% |
| | (Percentages do not add to 100% because of multiple responses.) | |

## Figure 30-5   Summary of Survey Results — continued

Respondents' location:

|  |  |
|---|---|
| Urban Aylmer | 21.7% |
| Rural Aylmer | 18.8% |
| St. Thomas | 16.1% |
| Elgin Other | 14.5% |
| London | 10.1% |
| Middlesex-Oxford | 10.3% |
| Other | 8.4% |

## Figure C30-6   Advertising Dollar Breakdown for 1984

| Media Used | | Cost |
|---|---|---|
| Radio: | CJBK | $ 384 |
|  | CHLO | 1179 |
|  | CKOT | 780 |
|  | BX-93 | 1160 |
| Television: | CFPL | 1414 |
| Print: | Aylmer Express | 1099 |
|  | Elgin County Market | 653 |
| Posters: |  | 301 |
| Total |  | $6970 |

## Figure C30-7   Map of the Fairgrounds

**Location Key**
HR — Horse Ring
P — Poultry Building
GE — General Exhibits Building
ST — Stage
S — Secretary's Office
HE — Horticultural Exhibits
G — Admission Gates

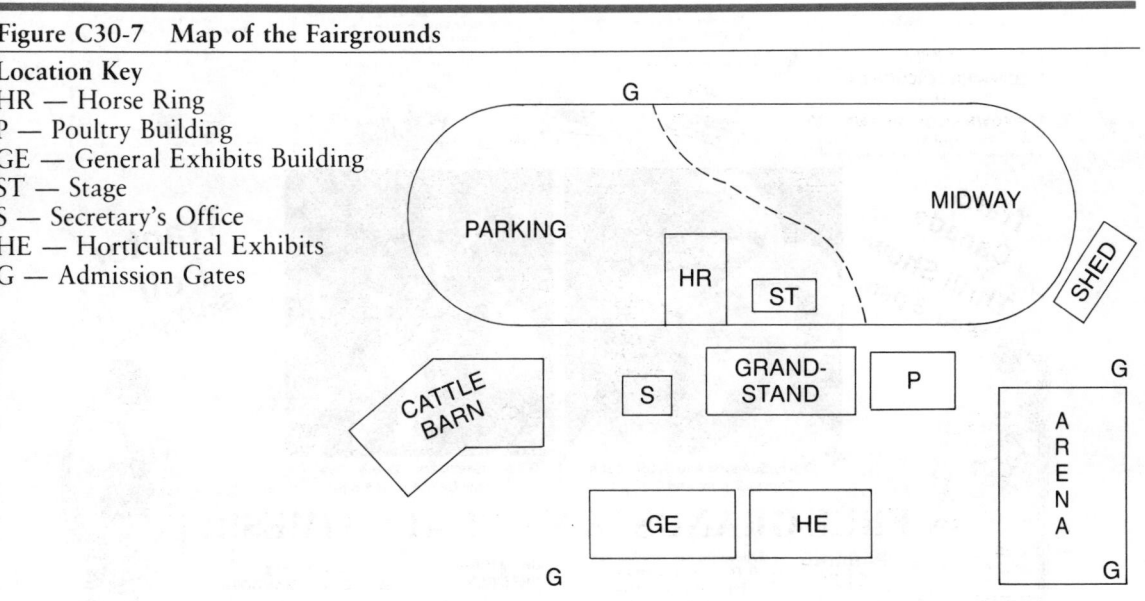

## Appendix C30-A   Sample Advertisements for Aylmer Fair

Elgin County Market *Advertisement*

Wed., August 11, 1982—AYLMER EXPRESS—PAGE 9

# AYLMER FAIR

**ELGIN'S COUNTY FAIR**
**1846-1982**

Conklin's
Magic
Midway

**General Admission $2.50**
12 and Under $1.00
**Children's Day (Wednesday, Only Til 6 p.m.) FREE!**
Admisssion $1.00 After 6 p.m.
Buy a $5.00 Advance Sale Ticket. Admits Owner to Grounds
for the 4 Fair Days. Also eligible for $50 draw each night —
$100 if person in attendance.

### WEDNESDAY, AUGUST 18

**CHILDREN'S DAY**

**FREE**
**GRANDSTAND AT ALL TIMES**
ELGIN COUNTY HOLSTEIN SHOW
Judging at 11 a.m.

PONY AND JUNIOR SHOW
12 p.m.

CHILDREN'S SPECIAL EVENTS
1 p.m.

EAST ELGIN 4-H HORSEMANSHIP
CLUB ACHIEVEMENT DAY
10 a.m.

**GENERAL EXHIBITS BLDG. NO. 2**
''The Hat Story''
''Where did you get that hat?''
Presented by Mrs. Barbara Fisher, St. Thomas
2:30-3 p.m.
7:30-8 p.m.

FLOWER SHOW GEN. EXHIBITS BLDG. NO. 1

HOME COOKED MEALS UPSTAIRS IN ARENA

JERSEY CATTLE SHOW—7 p.m.

**7 p.m.**

**OPENING CEREMONIES**
**AND**
**CROWNING OF THE FAIR**
**QUEEN**

### THURSDAY, AUGUST 19

**AGRICULTURAL DAY**

**GRANDSTAND FREE**

**Daytime**
ARABIAN SHOW — Starting at 9 a.m.
WESTERN SHOW — Beginning at 10 a.m.

**Cattle Barn**
GUERNSEY SHOW
1 p.m.

PET SHOW
1 p.m. In Front of Grandstand

JUNIOR CAKE BAKING CONTEST
2 p.m.

**EXHIBITS BUILDING NO. 2**
''Calling Cards''
Presented by Mrs. Pat Zimmer, Aylmer Museum
2:30-3 p.m.

**Weaving Demonstration**
Presented by Mrs. Bill Bontje
Black Creek Pioneer Village
7-7:30 p.m.

**Cattle Barn**
AYRSHIRE SHOW — 7 p.m.
POULTRY SHOW EVERY DAY

### FRIDAY, AUGUST 20

**AYLMER DAY**

HUNTER AND JUMPER PERMIT SHOW
9:00 a.m.

ANGUS AND HEREFORD CATTLE SHOW
12:30 p.m.

**GENERAL EXHIBITS BLDG. NO. 1**
FLOWER SHOW

**Afternoon**
**GENERAL EXHIBITS BLDG. NO. 2**

''The Gloom Chasers''
A Senior Citizen's Band
2:30-3 p.m.

''The History of Make-Up''
Presented by Mrs. Eileen Maloney
7-7:30 p.m.

**LOG SPLITTING CONTEST**
In Front Of The Grandstand
Beginning at 6 p.m.

EAST ELGIN 4-H DAIRY GOAT CLUB
ACHIEVEMENT DAY EXERCISES — 6 p.m.
EAST ELGIN 4-H PORK PRODUCERS
CLUB ACHIEVEMENT DAY EXERCISES — 7 p.m.

### SATURDAY, AUGUST 21

**INDUSTRIAL DAY**

**GRANDSTAND**
**FREE ADMISSION**

REGISTERED QUARTER HORSE SHOW
9:00 a.m.

**Cattle Barn**
EAST ELGIN 4-H DAIRY CALF CLUB
ACHIEVEMENT DAY EXERCISES — 9 a.m.
CORINTH 4-H DAIRY CALF CLUB
ACHIEVEMENT DAY EXERCISES — 10 a.m.
BELMONT DAIRY CALF CLUB
ACHIEVEMENT DAY EXERCISES — 11 a.m.
ELGIN 4-H INTER-CLUB DAIRY CLASSES
1:30 p.m.

BABY SHOW
General Exhibits Bldg. No. 2
Weighing and Measuring — 1 p.m.
Judging to commerce at 2 p.m.

**Also In General Exhibits Bldg. No. 2**
''Butter Making''
Presented by Anne Williams and
Janice Auckland, Elgin Museum
2-2:30 p.m.
4-4:30 p.m.

**Trans Canada Thrill Show**
**Wed. 8 p.m.**

**Tractor Pull**
**Sat. 7 p.m.**

**Terry Sumsion and Stagecoach**
Thurs.  7 p.m. and 8:30 p.m.

**Great Pretenders**   Zaneville, Ohio
1 Show Only, Fri. at 8 p.m.

# FREE GRANDSTAND AT ALL TIMES!!!

**PARKING**
**$1.00**

While At The Fair  Buy Your Copy
Of The ''History of the Aylmer
Fair 1846-1982''  $5.00

**Bruce Howe**
PRESIDENT

**Jack Harvey**
SECRETARY-MANAGER

# COLOSSAL!

## 1983 AYLMER FAIR
### ELGIN'S COUNTY FAIR

## FREE GRANDSTAND
# ENTERTAINMENT

Your $2.50 Adult Gate Admission Gets You On The Grandstand For All 5 Shows ★ FREE OF CHARGE! ★ Children, 12 Years & Under $1 Parking Is Available for $1.00 Per Car

**THURSDAY, AUGUST 18**
*THE CHICAGO KNOCKERS! This all girl world famous mud-wrestling team will present a wild evening of family fun in their 80 minutes of mud-slinging entertainment. Show time 8 p.m.*

**WEDNESDAY, AUGUST 17**
*TRANS CANADA HELL DRIVERS! Now in their 18th season. Show time 8 p.m. Wednesday is also KIDS DAY! Children admitted FREE until 6 p.m. Special KIDS DAY MIDWAY PRICES on Conklin's Magic Midway until 6 p.m. Come early to see the Opening Ceremonies and the crowning of Miss Aylmer Fair, beginning at 7 p.m.*

**SATURDAY, AUGUST 20**
*MINI TRACTOR PULL! Roar with the excitement as these mini tractors go through their paces in several events. Come early to get a front row seat. You won't be disappointed. Pull starts at 7 p.m.*

SOUTHWESTERN ONTARIO YOUTH TALENT SEARCH

**SUNDAY AFTERNOON, AUGUST 21: FAMILY DAY**
*Let yourself be royally entertained by the 15 finalists in the Southwestern Ontario Youth Talent Search (all from Elgin County) as they compete for $1000 in prize money. Winners will go on to Western Fair where they will try to go on to Memphis, Tennessee. MARY GARFAL of CFPL TV will be the Master of Ceremonies, beginning at 1:00 p.m. in front of the grandstand.*

*Watch your favourite youngster (3 to 24 months) compete in the ALL NEW BABY SHOW beginning at 1 p.m. upstairs in the Arena. FREE DRAW for Baby Show Contestants only (a large plush animal courtesy of Conklin's Magic Midway). Mothers! Please remember to pre-register your child.*

*RIDE THE MIDWAY ALL AFTERNOON FOR JUST $5.00! Yes, the complete Conklin Midway will be in full swing all afternoon. Here's your chance to ride, ride, ride! For those of you who like just one or two rides, regular rates are still available.*

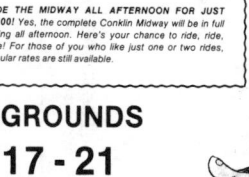

## AYLMER FAIRGROUNDS
# AUGUST 17 - 21
### AYLMER, ONT.

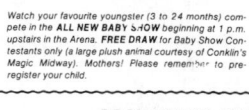

**FRIDAY, AUGUST 19**
*TUG-O'-WAR, LOG-SAWING, SQUARE DANCERS and NICKEL PLATE ROAD! Join the action in front of the grandstand beginning at 5:30 for an interesting programme of local talent. Watch your friends compete in skill and strength and relax to the sound of Nickel Plate Road during breaks.*

Radio Ads for Aylmer Fair

# CONTINUITY

CLIENT    AYLMER FAIR

START    AUG. 15    END AUG. 15 TILL 7 PM

UNIT LENGTH    30

WRITER    JACKIE CAMERON

CART NUMBER

WHAT'S THE 1983 AYLMER FAIR GOT IN STORE FOR YOU?
LOTS OF THINGS! AND ALL FOR JUST $2.50 A PERSON
INCLUDING FREE GRANDSTAND ENTERTAINMENT. THIS
WEDNESDAY NIGHT — TAKE THE KIDS TO SEE THE
TRANS CANADA HELL DRIVERS. KIDS GET IN FREE TILL
SIX. THERE'LL BE SPECIAL KIDS MIDWAY PRICES TOO —
PLUS THE CROWNING OF MISS AYLMER FAIR AT SEVEN.
THE AYLMER FAIR WILL HAVE DISPLAYS AND EXHIBITS
FOR EVERYONE TOO AND ON SATURDAY IT'S THE FAMOUS
MINI-TRACTOR PULL. THE 1983 AYLMER FAIR—THIS
WEDNESDAY THROUGH SUNDAY AT THE AYLMER
FAIRGROUNDS. IT'S COLOSSAL!

---

# KOT

## 1510 AM
19 000 WATTS
"Community Information Radio"

## Stereo 101 FM
50 000 WATTS

"The Sound of Music Station"

LIVELY FAIR-TYPE MUSIC!

TILLSONBURG, ONTARIO, CANADA  N4G 4H3
Information: Tel. 519-842-4281

Start: Aug. 10-16/83

Instructions
AM-C
FM-C

Co-op

Date Written: Aug. 9/83

Writer: Valerie Carter

Salesman: George
D'Ambrose

1 . . 25 sec.

| | |
|---|---|
| 10 Sec | COLOSSAL ENTERTAINMENT IS COMING YOUR WAY! |
| | WEDNESDAY AUGUST SEVENTEENTH TO SUNDAY AUGUST |
| 15 Sec | TWENTY FIRST . . . IT'S FAIR TIME IN AYLMER! FIVE BIG |
| | DAYS . . . FIVE BIG GRANDSTAND EXTRAVAGANZAS . . . ALL |
| 20 Sec | YOURS WITH YOUR GATE ADMISSION . . . ADULTS TWO |
| | FIFTY . . . CHILDREN ONE DOLLAR. SEE THE TRANS CANADA |
| 30 Sec | HELL DRIVERS . . . THE CHICAGO KNOCKERS ALL-GIRL MUD |
| | WRESTLING TEAM, THERE'S THE MINI TRACTOR PULL, |
| | TUG O WAR, LOG-SAWING, SQUARE DANCERS, THE |
| 40 Sec | SOUTHWESTERN ONTARIO YOUTH TALENT SEARCH AND |
| | MORE! . . . ALL AT AYLMER FAIR, BE THERE! |
| 50 Sec | |

| DATE-TIME | ANNCR | DATE-TIME | ANNCR | DATE-TIME | ANNCR |
|---|---|---|---|---|---|
| | | | | | |
| | | | | | |
| | | | | | |
| | | | | | |
| | | | | | |

# Case 31   Diagnostic Chemicals Ltd.

A recent visit to your physician may have included taking blood and urine samples for routine biochemical tests or even a complete "profile" involving six to twelve tests. In each test reagents are employed to produce a chemical reaction that leads to diagnosis. These tests are performed in hospitals and private laboratories on a manual, semi-automated, or automated basis.

According to Regis Duffy, Ph.D., president of Diagnostic Chemicals Ltd. (DCL), the new breed of physician is reluctant to diagnose the simplest of ailments without the benefit of diagnostic tests. In the last decade diagnostic medicine has experienced dramatic technological advances, with hundreds of new product introductions, some of which have created entirely new industries.

Dr. Duffy points out that research and development is ongoing, and any product has a maximum life of five years before a substitute or better procedure is introduced. In addition, the health-care industry is always looking for new specialty products such as enzyme reagents. In the United States, malpractice actions are accelerating the growth of diagnostic medicine.

In 1982, DCL was the sole Canadian manufacturer of biochemical diagnostic reagents, although a few other Canadian firms were involved in other segments of the laboratory reagent industry. The industry is dominated by large multinational companies based in Europe and the United States that are the leaders in health-care technology and produce and distribute a full line of laboratory reagents and related equipment world wide. Dr. Duffy suggests that DCL's impact in Canada or elsewhere is insigificant — a mosquito among giants.

In May of 1982, Dr. Duffy found he had to decide how to improve the firm's sales growth. DCL employed a sales representative locally in the Atlantic region, and had a number of distributorship arrangements in Canada, Europe, the Pacific Rim, and the United States. None of these arrangements were successful in either increasing sales significantly, or securing a strong market position for the firm.

## Company Background

DCL was founded in 1970, while Dr. Duffy was Chemistry Professor and Dean of Science at the University of Prince Edward Island. By 1975, DCL moved from its downtown garage to the West Royalty Industrial Park, which offered low-cost floor space and financing of capital assets.

Initially, the firm produced only "fine" chemicals and solvents, which were used in the production of diagnostic reagents. However, Dr. Duffy realized that diagnostic reagents themselves represented the greatest potential for the firm.

He secured grants from the National Science and Engineering Research Council and Industry, Trade and Commerce Canada to assist in covering research and development costs. The grants, which were received over a period of five years, amounted to $465 000, and Dr. Duffy estimated that they covered 60 percent of the total cost of launching the production of reagents.

In 1978 the firm began work on the production of enzyme reagents under similar funding. By 1982 the firm had developed its own successful production processes and was able to produce $2500 worth of materials from 100 kg of beef liver. All in all, DCL now had sales approaching $1.25 million annually and produced a full line of biochemi-

Source: Professor T. E. Carroll, University of Prince Edward Island.

cal reagents along with fine chemicals and enzymes.

## The Market

In 1982, the total Canadian market for seven categories of laboratory reagents was estimated at $87 million. Biochemical reagents are the largest product group at $22 million. Canada imported 90–95 percent of its requirements. By the year 2000, the laboratory reagent bill for Canada was projected at $540 million if imports were to remain above the 90 percent level. In the United States, considered the richest health-care market in the world, the biochemical reagents market was estimated at $750 million, or 30 percent of the total world market.

In Canada, the market was 87 percent hospitals and 13 percent private labs. In the United States, the market was 65 percent hospitals (mostly private) and 35 percent private labs.

Further differences in the two markets were highlighted in the degree of concentration of suppliers. A recent market survey sponsored by DREE reported that three multinational companies (Technicon, Abbot, and BMC) each held a 10 percent or greater share of the market in Canada. In contrast, one U.S. report estimated that the top 25 companies in that market each had market shares of 1–5.6 percent.

A 1980 survey of purchasing agents in Canada listed the following factors as influencing brand selection: quality, ease of use, price, and service. Dr. Duffy stressed that offering comparable or improved products was not enough to capture markets. The market, in his view, was very conservative.

Hospitals, in particular, were very reluctant to change unless a glaring problem occurred with their existing supplier. The other problem perceived by Dr. Duffy was that in the complex bureaucracy of the hospital it was often difficult to identify the person who made the purchase decision. Depending on size, budget restrictions, or even less rational reasons, the decision might rest with anyone from a lab technician to the chief administrator.

The recent squeeze on health-care costs in Canada and the U.S. had led to some harsh competitive realities for DCL. Canada, in Dr. Duffy's opinion, was a convenient and unrestricted dumping ground, particularly for U.S.-based firms. Some of the more aggressive firms were now offering hospitals long-term agreements on price. In many hospitals, capital budgets had been frozen since 1980. Some reagent firms who produced lab equipment were offering new reagent hardware at no charge. Costs were recovered through the sale of reagents, according to Dr. Duffy.

All of the major companies in the reagent business employed sales representatives who were both sales oriented and technically knowledgeable in the use of reagents. They were actively calling on hospitals and labs and attending health-care conventions and conferences. Many of the schools where lab technicians were trained were provided with free samples from the major companies.

DCL encountered major difficulty obtaining information on production processes and the market. DCL's research and development on a product usually started from square one. Without knowing what equipment was in use or even what tests were being demanded, the researchers were required to develop processes and procedures themselves, since the journals studied by Dr. Duffy and his professional staff contained very little information on these aspects of the market. The task, therefore, was to develop a good kit which was better than or comparable to anything available and then set about introducing the product to the market. Dr. Duffy estimated that his ongoing cost of research and development to stay competitive was approximately $130 000 per year.

Margins and markups in the industry reflected the high cost of research and development. Dr. Duffy estimated that a reagent or reagent kit, which costs $12–30 to produce (exclusive of research and development cost), listed anywhere from $50–150 per unit. The markup was at least 100 percent of cost, while some product lines returned double or even triple that markup.

## Marketing at DCL

Dr. Duffy described his present distribution network as a collection of arrangements picked up along the way with no particular strategy in mind. He paid very little attention to the distributors and exercised almost no control over them in terms of price or sales activities.

DCL Marketing in Toronto, which was operated by a business associate of Dr. Duffy, contributed approximately $180 000 a year to DCL's total sales. The cost of this operation, which concentrated on private labs in the Toronto area, amounted to approximately $60 000 per year.

All other distributors contributed on an individual basis anywhere from $20 000 to $70 000 per year, with their return averaging approximately 30 percent of DCL's list price. Growth in sales among distributors had generally not exceeded more than 5 percent annually.

The largest market for DCL was serviced by their own sales representative, who covered the Atlantic region. Her sales amounted to approximately 20 percent of total sales at an annual cost of $50 000 per year. These sales were accounted for by several small accounts as well as the large hospitals in Halifax.

In 1980, Fisher Scientific, an American-based producer of clinical chemistry hardware, decided to distribute reagents produced by DCL under private label. Dr. Duffy indicated that the results from this arrangement were encouraging in terms of recent sales growth of more than 40 percent per annum.

DCL's promotion activities were very limited. They included production and distribution of 3500 full-colour booklets, which outlined DCL's operations, products, and prices (see Figure C31-1). Dr. Duffy reported that there was limited sales response to this effort. The firm also participated to a limited extent in health-care conferences and conventions. Dr. Duffy felt that the cost associated with DCL's selling arrangements was too high.

## Conclusion

"DCL has never failed to show some profit each year. Sales grew from $10 000 in the first year to almost $1.25 million in 1982. We have developed excellent R & D and production departments. We have achieved full-line manufacturing capability this year, including the production of enzymes. The market penetration we experienced is only a fraction of the potential that exists or will open up in the future, particularly in the United States."

"My concern," continued Dr. Duffy, "is that sales and profits must grow at an accelerated rate if we are to finance the research and development necessary to stay competitive. I feel that a well-managed marketing program is necessary for DCL to realize its potential."

## Discussion Questions

1. Evaluate the marketing efforts of DCL up to now.
2. What opportunities and problems does the company face?
3. Develop an integrated marketing plan for the next three years.

Figure C31-1   Diagnostic Chemical Limited

# dcl

## Canadian Manufacturer of Diagnostic Reagents Fine Chemicals and Enzymes

## Chemical Manufacturing

The chemical manufacturing facility is equipped with glass lined Pfaudier reactors with a temperature range of −20°C to +50°C, distillation systems, vacuum drying ovens, vacuum pumps, filtering equipment and cold rooms. Quality control equipment available include gas chromatographs and UV-Visible spectrophotometers. We also have access to infrared and nuclear magnetic resonance spectrophotometers. Fine chemicals currently being produced include p-nitrophenylphosphate salts, glutamyl-p-nitroanilide, PDT disulfonate (Ferrozine), thiothreitol (DTT), dithioerythritol (DTE), phosphoenolpyruvate, monocyclohexylamine salt, Ferene™ a superior novel iron reagent, (3-(2-pyridyl)-5,6-bis(2-(5-furyl sulfonic acid))-1,2,4 azine, disodium salt), and Fast Red PDC salt.

## Diagnostic Reagents for Clinical Chemistry

The company manufactures chemical diagnostic reagent systems suitable for use on manual or automated systems such as centrifugal analyzers. Standards in S.I. units and specialty solutions are also manufactured. Equipment available for diagnostic production and quality control includes freeze driers, automatic dispensers, and several spectrophotometers.

## Enzymes

Several enzymes are currently isolated including GLDH, Urease, Cholesterol Esterase, Glycerol phosphate dehydrogenase and peroxidase. The isolation of several other enzymes is currently under investigation. Pilot plant facilities available include freeze dryers, fraction collectors, chromatographic equipment, centrifuges, plate coolers, filter presses and jacketed tank facilities to 400 litres.

## Contract Projects

We are interested in contract work in the area of clinical diagnostics, fine chemicals or enzymes and invite your inquiries.

## Personnel

The President of the Company is J. Regis Duffy, Ph.D., Professor of Chemistry at the University of Prince Edward Island and former Dean of the Faculty of Science. The Vice-President for research and development is D. J. Hennessy, Ph.D., Professor Emeritus of Chemistry, Fordham University, New York. The plant manager in charge of chemical manufacturing is Gary Reid, Ph.D., a graduate of the University of New Brunswick. Julien Gaudin, Ph.D. (Waterloo), is Director of diagnostic manufacturing. Praful Patel, Ph.D., (University of Saskatchewan) is head of the Enzyme Division.

---

**Figure C31-2    Excerpts from a 1980 DREE-Sponsored Investigation into the Laboratory Reagent Market in Canada**

## Current Canadian Market

The total Canadian market for laboratory reagents is estimated at $66.5 million, broken down by discipline, as follows:

| | |
|---|---|
| Biochemistry | $17 100 000 |
| Bacteriology | 11 531 000 |
| Radio-immunoassay | 9 827 000 |
| Hematology | 8 092 000 |
| Blood Bank | 4 835 000 |
| Urinalysis | 3 785 000 |
| Serology | 3 287 000 |
| Virology | 2 992 000 |
| Blood Coagulation | 2 891 000 |
| Immunology | 2 175 000 |
| Total | $66 515 000 |

The largest market is biochemistry, accounting for approximately 25 percent of the total expenditure.

The second largest field is bacteriology, with approximately 17 percent of the market, followed by radio-immunoassay, blood bank, urinalysis, serology, etc., accounting for respectively 15, 12, 7, 6, and 5 percent of total expenditure.

In general, the largest market for these products is in hospitals of 401 to 700 beds and 701 beds and over, as well as private and government laboratories.

Ontario is the largest consumer of laboratory reagents, accounting for 34–39 percent of the total market, followed by Quebec, which is 29–32 percent of the total market, depending on the discipline. Expenditures in B.C. and the Prairies vary from 10–18 percent. The Maritimes represent the smallest market, accounting for 4–9 percent of the total market.

## Biochemistry

Biochemistry is the chemistry of living organisms and of vital processes.

The biochemistry or clinical chemistry laboratory is probaby the biggest and the busiest of all laboratories performing tests to detect general chemical pathologies. Depending on the size of the hospital, the laboratory may perform these tests

by manual, semi-automated, or fully automated methods. Biochemical reagents are, therefore, designed for either manual, semi-automated, or fully automated methods.

The most important tests are albumin, acid phosphatase, alkaline phosphatase, amylase, bilirubin, blood gas, BUN, calcium total, $CO_2$, chloride, cholesterol, CPK, creatinine, glucose, SGOT, SGPT, iron, LDH, phosphorus, potassium, sodium, triglycerides, total protein, uric acid, and control and standards. There are reagents for each of the above tests for the three methods. The manual test reagents are usually in a more expensive kit form, while the automated test reagents can often be bought in bulk.

Biochemistry is a highly automated field. Laboratories often have more than one chemistry analyser. Some of these analysers are small, with only one channel, while some are multichanneled and computer-controlled.

Biochemistry is the largest segment of the diagnostic market. Most of the suppliers are subsidiaries of U.S. companies. There are a few European and one or two Canadian companies.

The most important suppliers are Abbott, Technicon, BMC (Beohringer-Mannheim Corporation), Worthington, Calbiochem (Hoechst), SKI (Smith Klein & Instrument), BDH, General Diagnostics, Hyland, Ortho, Dade, Pharmacia, and American Monitor. Diagnostic Chemicals, a Canadian manufacturer, is based in the Maritimes.

## Market Environment

The Canadian diagnostic market is dominated by large multinational companies. The top 30 diagnostic companies, which share about 80 to 85 percent of the market, are all subsidiaries of large, foreign-owned multinational corporations. Generally, the Canadian market is characterized by:
— extensive price and product competition
— improvement in efficiency in both manufacturing and marketing
— low expenditure in research and development

## Demand Projection

The total expenditures in Canada on laboratory

reagents will be of the order of $66.5 million in 1980. Based on the consultant's estimate, the total expenditure by 1985 will be of the order of $113 million. Assuming the same annual average rate of growth between 1986 and 2000, total expenditure in the year 2000 will be of the order of $585 million.

If the local manufacturing content of the above expenditures is maintained at between 5 and 10 percent, Canada will import laboratory reagents by the year 2000 of the order of $540 million.

The fastest growing segments of the laboratory reagent market are: bacteriology and biochemistry (13 percent per annum) and immunology (12 percent per annum).

The requirements for success for manufacturing concerns in Canada can be summarized as follows:
— establishment of a well-planned marketing strategy
— optimum selection of product mix, in the area recommended above
— competitive product or product line in quality, price, service, ease of use, availability, etc.
— because of the economy of scale and heavy research cost, the plant capacity should be sized for an international vocation
— a substantial budget for the penetration of national and international markets should be foreseen
— establishment of a well-planned territory coverage (either through direct or indirect selling practices), etc.

It should, however, be pointed out that the identification of opportunities for Canadian manufacturing can be approached in two ways:
— by identifying a number of potential products in a few areas, as recommended above
— by evaluating the potential for the creation of a Canadian laboratory reagent manufacturing industry with a vocation for national and international markets, and with the collaboration of the existing Canadian manufacturers.

## Potential for the creation of a Canadian laboratory reagent manufacturing industry.

The above recommendation is based on the following arguments:

— A number of small Canadian firms operate successfully in this area but a high growth rate in the individual companies is unlikely.
— The Canadian market is very attractive to foreign firms.
— The aging Canadian population will require higher health-care expenditures.
— If products are accepted by the Canadian market, they will be accepted in the international market.
— This would be a project of national pride.
— It would decrease the use of foreign currency, improve the balance of payments, and generally reduce dependence on foreign manufacturing.
— Canada has all the human resources to build and operate this project.
— Canada possesses the general technology required for research, implementation, and operation of a project of this magnitude.

Figure C31-3   Diagnostic Chemicals Limited Statement of Earnings for the Year Ended August 31, 1980 and 1981

|  | 1981 | 1980 |
|---|---|---|
| Sales | $680 925 | $510 578 |
| Cost of Sales: |  |  |
| Inventory — beginning of year | 109 749 | 83 590 |
| Purchases and freight | 275 892 | 207 873 |
|  | 385 641 | 291 463 |
| Inventory — end of year | 141 973 | 109 749 |
|  | 243 668 | 181 714 |
| Gross Profit | 437 257 | 328 864 |
| Expenses: |  |  |
| Wages and wage levies | 271 861 | 164 652 |
| Grants received | 149 763 | 81 950 |
|  | 122 098 | 82 702 |
| Commissions | 36 112 | — |
| Other operating expenses | 105 846 | 87 906 |
| Bank charges and interest | 2 179 | 6 791 |
| Interest on long-term debt | 19 278 | 8 201 |
| Travel and promotion | 17 035 | 12 339 |
| Depreciation and amortization | 54 554 | 47 137 |
| Total Operating Expenses | 360 842 | 252 658 |
| Net Operating Income | $ 76 415 | $ 76 206 |

# Glossary

*Note: Number in parentheses indicates chapter where term first appears.*

**Absolute advantage** (22) In international marketing, the relative position of a nation that is the sole producer of a product or that produces the product more cheaply than other nations can.

**Accelerator principle** (9) The disproportionate impact that changes in consumer demand has upon industrial market demand.

**Accessory equipment** (10) Capital items such as typewriters, hand tools, small lathes, and adding machines. They are usually less expensive and shorter-lived than installations.

**Active exporting** (22) In international marketing, the activities of a firm that has made a commitment to seek export business.

**Administered vertical marketing system** (15) A VMS in which channel co-ordination is achieved through the exercise of economic and political power by the dominant member. *See also* Channel captain.

**Adoption process** (9) The various decisions a consumer makes about a new product. The consumer adoption process has several identifiable stages: awareness, interest, evaluation, trial, and adoption.

**Advertising** (19, 20) A nonpersonal sales presentation usually directed to a large number of potential customers.

**Advertising agency** (20) Independent businesses used to assist advertisers in planning and implementing advertising programs.

**Advocacy advertising** (20) A paid public communication or message that presents information or a point of view bearing on a publicly recognized controversial issue.

**Agent wholesaling middleman** (15, 16) A middleman who performs wholesaling functions but does not take title to the products handled. Sometimes called *agent*.

**AIO statements** (4) *See* Psychographics.

**Approach** (21) The step in the sales process that involves the initial contact between seller and buyer.

**Area sampling** (18) Used when population lists are unavailable for sampling. Blocks instead of individuals are selected at random. Then everyone on the selected block is interviewed or, in some cases, respondents are randomly selected from each designated block.

**Asch phenomenon** (7) An occurrence first documented by the psychologist S. E. Asch, which illustrates the effect of the reference group on individual decision-making.

**Aspirational group** (7) A sub-category of a reference group where the member desires to associate with a group.

**Attitude** (8) One's enduring favourable or unfavourable evaluations, emotional feelings, or pro or con action tendencies.

**Auction house** (16) An agent wholesaling middleman who brings buyers and sellers of such products as used cars, livestock, antiques, and tobacco together in one location and allows potential buyers to inspect the merchandise physically before purchasing.

**Average cost** (13, 14) Obtained by dividing total cost by the quantity associated with these costs.

**Average fixed cost** (13, 14) Determined by dividing total fixed costs by the related quantity.

**Average revenue** (13, 14) Obtained by dividing total revenue by the related quantity. The average revenue line is actually the demand curve facing the firm.

**Average variable cost** (13, 14) The total variable costs divided by the related quantity.

**Balance of payments** (22) The money flow into or out of a country.

**Balance of trade** (22) The relationship between a nation's exports and imports.

**Bartering** (22) The exchange of one product for another instead of for money.

**Benefit segmentation** (4) Dividing a population into homogenous groups based on the benefits the consumer expects to derive from the product.

**Bid** (9) In the industrial market, a written sales proposal from a vendor to a firm that wants to purchase a good or service.

**Bottom line** (23) Business jargon referring to the overall profitability measure of performance.

**Brand** (11) A name, term, sign, symbol, design, or some combination used to identify the products of one firm and to differentiate them from competitive offerings.

**Brand insistence** (11) The ultimate stage in brand acceptance when consumers will accept no alternatives and will search extensively for the product.

**Brand name** (11) That part of the brand consisting of words or letters making up a name used to identify and distinguish the firm's offerings from those of competitors. The brand name is that part of the brand that may be vocalized.

**Brand preference** (11) The second stage of brand acceptance. Based on previous experience with the product, consumers will choose it rather than a competitor's — if it is available.

**Brand recognition** (11) The first stage of brand acceptance, when the consumer is able to identify a specific brand.

**Break-bulk centre** (18) A central warehouse where economical carload and truckload shipments are disassembled and then redistributed to numerous customers over shorter distances at the higher less-than-carload or -truckload rates.

**Break-even analysis** (13) A tool for assessing the profit consequences of alternative prices. The *break-even point* (in units) equals total fixed cost divided by the per-unit contribution to fixed cost.

**Broadening concept** (23) An idea introduced by Philip Kotler and Sidney J. Levy, suggesting that marketing is a generic function to be performed by all organizations.

**Broker** (16) An agent wholesaling middleman who facilitates marketing operations by bringing together small, geographically dispersed sellers and buyers.

**Buyer's market** (1) A market with an abundance of goods and services.

**Buying centre** (9) Refers to everyone who participates—in some fashion — in an industrial buying action.

**Canadian Transport Commission** (18) Established by the National Transportation Act, it is responsible for the air, rail, pipeline, and water components of the transportation industry.

**Canned approach** (21) A memorized sales presentation used to ensure uniform coverage of the points deemed important by management.

**Cannibalizing** (11) A product that takes sales from another offering in a product line. Marketing research should

take steps to see that cannibalizing is minimized or at least anticipated.

**Capital items** (9) Long-lived business assets that must be depreciated over time.

**Cartel** (22) A monopolistic organization of firms.

**Cash-and-carry wholesaler** (16) A merchant wholesaler who does not offer credit and delivery services.

**Cash discount** (14) Deduction from list price that is given for prompt payment of a bill.

**Casual exporting** (22) The activities of a firm that takes a passive level of involvement in international marketing.

**Catalogue retailer** (17) A merchant who operates from a showroom displaying samples of the product line. Customers order from the store's catalogue and orders are filled from a warehouse, usually on the premises.

**Census** (6) Collection of marketing data from all possible sources.

**Chain stores** (17) Groups of retail stores centrally owned and managed, and handling the same lines of products.

**Channel captain** (15) The dominant member of each channel, who assumes the responsibility for obtaining co-operation among the individual channel members.

**Channel conflict** (15) Competition between channel members.

**Channels of distribution** (15) *See* Marketing channels.

**Charter** (10) A document drawn up by a manufacturing firm specifically defining the functions, operating procedures, and other guidelines for a venture team. Also known as a *venture team charter*.

**Class action** (24) A legal suit brought by private citizens on behalf of a group of consumers for damages caused by unfair business practices.

**Closed sales territories** (15) Restricted geographic selling regions ordered by a manufacturer for its distributors.

**Closing** (21) The step in the sales process when the salesperson actually asks the prospect for an order.

**Cluster sample** (6) A sampling technique where areas or clusters are selected, then all or a sample within them become respondents.

**Cognitions** (8) An individual's knowledge, beliefs, and attitudes about certain events.

**Cognitive dissonance** (8) The postpurchase anxiety that occurs when an imbalance exists among a person's cognitions (knowledge, beliefs, and attitudes).

**Cold canvassing** (21) Unsolicited sales calls upon a random group of people; the prospecting and qualifying effort is minimal.

ombination plan (21) A method of compensating sales rsonnel by using a base salary along with a commission centive.

ombines Investigation Act (2) Canada's major legislation gulating business relationships (e.g. monopolies) and busi-ss practices. It deals with pricing, advertising, exclusive aling, and other practices.

ommission (21) Payment directly tied to the sales or profits hieved by a salesperson.

ommission merchant (16) An agent wholesaling middle-an who exercises physical control over and negotiates e sale of goods that he or she handles.

ommodity rate (18) Sometimes called a special rate, since it given by carriers to shippers as a reward for either regu-r use or large quantity shipments.

ommon carrier (18) A regulated carrier who offers trans-ortation services to all shippers.

ommon market (22) In international marketing, a for-at for multinational economic integration involving a ustoms union and continuing efforts to standardize trade gulations of all governments. See also Customs union.

ommunications (19) The transmission of a message from sender (or source) to a receiver (or recipient).

ommunity shopping centre (17) A group of 15 to 50 tail stores, often including a branch of a department ore as the primary tenant. This type of centre typically rves 20 000 to 100 000 persons within a radius of a few lometres.

omparative advantage (22) In international marketing, e relative position of a nation that can produce one articular product more efficiently than it can produce ternative products.

omparative advertising (20) A type of persuasive prod-ct advertising that makes direct comparisons with com-etitive brands.

ompetitive bidding (14) A process by which buyers re-uest potential suppliers to make price quotations on a roposed purchase or contract.

ompetitive environment (2) The interactive process that ccurs in the marketplace.

omponent parts and materials (10) In the industrial arket, the finished industrial goods that actually become art of the final product.

oncentrated marketing (5) An extreme form of differen-ated marketing, where a firm selects one segment of the otal market and devotes all of its marketing resources to atisfying this single segment.

Concept testing (11) The evaluation of a product idea prior to the actual development of the physical product in the new-product development process.

Consumer behaviour (7, 8) The acts and decision pro-cesses involved in obtaining and using goods and services.

Consumer goods (4, 9) Products destined for use by the ultimate consumer and not intended for resale or further use in producing other goods.

Consumer innovator (10) The first purchaser of new prod-ucts and services.

Consumer market (9) Individuals who purchase goods and services for personal use.

Consumer rights (24) The rights to safety, to be informed, to choose, and to be heard.

Consumerism (24) A demand that marketers give greater attention to consumer wants and desires in making their decisions.

Containerization (18) The combination of several unitized loads of products into a single load, facilitating inter-transport changes in transportation modes.

Contract carrier (18) A carrier that establishes specific contracts with a few customers and does not offer its services to the general public.

Contractual vertical marketing system (15) A VMS where channel co-ordination is achieved through formal agree-ments between channel members. The three types of con-tractual systems are wholesaler-sponsored voluntary chains, retail co-operatives, and franchise organizations.

Control charts (25) Diagrams that plot a firm's actual per-formance against established limits.

Convenience goods (10) Those items the consumer wants to purchase frequently, immediately, and with little effort, such as milk, bread, and gasoline. Convenience goods are usually branded and are low-priced.

Convenience retailer (17) One who sells to the ultimate consumer and focusses chiefly on a central location, long store hours, rapid checkout, and adequate parking facilities.

Convenience sample (6) A nonprobability sample based on the selection of readily available respondents.

Co-operative advertising (20) A program in which adver-tising costs are shared between retailers and the manufac-turer or vendor.

Corporate vertical marketing system (15) A VMS created through single ownership of each stage in the marketing channel.

**Cost-plus pricing** (13) An approach to price determination using cost as the base to which a profit factor is added. There are two cost-plus pricing procedures: *full-cost* pricing, which uses all relevant variable costs in setting a product's price, and the *incremental approach*, which considers only those costs directly attributable to a specific output.

**Cost trade-offs** (18) The "total system" approach to physical distribution, whereby some functional areas of the firm will experience cost increases while others will have cost reductions, but the result will be that *total* physical distribution costs will be minimized.

**Coupon** (20) A sales promotion technique that offers a discount from the next purchase of a product.

**Creative selling** (21) A basic sales task that characterizes purchases involving a considerable degree of analytical decision-making on the part of the consumer.

**Cues** (8) Any objects existing in the environment that determine the nature of the response to a drive.

**Culture** (7) A learned way of life including values, ideas, and attitudes that influence consumer behaviour.

**Customary pricing** (13) Price-setting by custom or tradition in the marketplace.

**Customer service standards** (18) The quality of service that the firm's customers will receive.

**Customs union** (22) In international marketing, a format for multinational economic integration that sets up a free trade area for member nations and a uniform tariff for nonmember nations.

**Decoding** (19) The consumer's interpretation of the sender's message.

**Demand curve** (13) A schedule relating the quantity demanded to specific prices. It is the average revenue line.

**Demand variability** (11) In the industrial market, the impact of derived demand on the demand for interrelated products used in producing consumer goods.

**Demarketing** (2) The process of cutting consumer demand for a product back to a level that can reasonably be supplied by the firm.

**Demographics** (10) The characteristics of potential buyers; for example, age, sex, and income level.

**Demographic segmentation** (7) Dividing a population into homogeneous groups based on characteristics such as age, sex, and income level.

**Demonstration** (21) The step in the selling process when the salesperson actually involves the prospect in the pres-

entation by allowing him or her to use, test, or expe ment with the product.

**Department store** (17) A large retailer organized into se rate departments for purposes of promotion, service, a control. A department store typically stocks a wide vari of shopping and specialty goods, including women's rea to-wear and accessories, men's and boys' wear, piece goo and home furnishings.

**Depreciation** (9) The accounting concept of charting a p tion of a capital item as a deduction against the compan annual revenue for purposes of determining its net incom

**Derived demand** (9) In the industrial market, the dema for an industrial product that is linked to demand for consumer good.

**Detailers** (21) Special representatives of firms in the healt care industry, who familiarize physicians and hospita with the firms' products.

**Devaluation** (22) When a nation reduces the value of currency in relation to gold or some other currency.

**Differentiated marketing** (5) The development of differe marketing programs for each segment of the total mark

**Diffusion process** (10) The way in which new products a adopted by customers in a particular community or soc system.

**Direct-sales results test** (19) A tool for measuring the effe tiveness of promotional expenditures, by ascertaining t increase in revenue per dollar spent.

**Disassociative group** (7) A sub-category of a referen group, one in which an individual does not want to identified with by others.

**Discount house** (17) A retail operation that competes the basis of price appeal by operating on a relatively lo markup and minimal customer services.

**Discretionary income** (6) That part of total income th remains after expenditures for necessities.

**Distribution channel** (15) Refers to the various marketir institutions and their interrelationships responsible f the physical and title flow of goods and services from pr ducer to consumer or industrial user.

**Distribution strategy** (1) An element of marketing decisio making dealing with the physical handling of goods an the selection of marketing channels.

**Distribution warehouse** (18) A place to assemble and the redistribute products. The objective of the distribution war house is to facilitate rapid movement of products to th purchasers rather than to serve as a storage facility.

**Distributor** *See* Wholesaler.

**Drive** (8) Any strong stimulus that impels action.

**Drop shipper** (16) A merchant wholesaler who sells for delivery by the producer direct to the buyer. The shipper usually does not carry inventories but consolidates orders to be filled by several producers.

**Dumping** (22) Situations where products are sold at significantly lower prices in a foreign market than in a nation's own domestic market.

**Ecology** (24) The relationship between people and their environment.

**Economic environment** (2) A setting of complex and dynamic business fluctuations that historically tended to follow a four-stage pattern: 1) recession, 2) depression, 3) recovery, and 4) prosperity.

**Economic order quantity (EOQ)** (18) The optimum order quantity of each product. The optimum point is determined by balancing the costs of holding inventory and the costs involved in placing orders.

**Ecumene** (6) Inhabited space; in Canada, this is mainly the East-West strip of land adjacent to the American border.

**Elasticity** (13) A measure of responsiveness of purchasers and suppliers to a change in price.

**Embargo** (22) A complete ban of certain products.

**Encoding** (19) Translating a message into terms understandable to a receiver.

**Engel's Laws** (4) An early spending behaviour study published by a German statistician, Ernst Engel. He advanced three generalizations about the spending resulting from increases in family income: 1) a smaller percentage of expenditures would go for food; 2) the percentage spent on housing and household operations and clothing will remain constant; and 3) the percentage spent on other items will increase.

**EOQ** *See* Economic Order Quantity.

**Escalator clause** (14) In pricing, part of many bids allowing the seller to adjust the final price, based upon changes in the costs of the product's ingredients, between the placement of the order and the completion of construction or delivery of the product.

**Ethics** (24) *See* Marketing ethics.

**Evaluation and control** (25) The various assessments that marketers employ to determine whether all phases of a marketing program have been effective.

**Evaluative criteria** (8) In consumer decision-making, the features considered in a consumer's choice of alternatives.

**Evoked set** (8) In consumer decision-making, the number of brands that a consumer actually considers before making a purchase decision.

**Exchange control** (22) When firms gaining foreign exchange by exporting must sell their foreign exchange to a control authority, while importers must buy foreign exchange from the same organization. Exchange control is a method of regulating foreign trade.

**Exchange process** (1) The process by which two or more parties give something of value to one another to satisfy felt needs.

**Exchange rate** (22) The rate at which a nation's currency can be exchanged for other currencies or gold.

**Exclusive dealing** (15) A contract prohibiting a middleman from handling competing products. Such a contract is legal except in those cases where it has the effect of "substantially lessening competition or tending to create a monopoly."

**Exclusive distribution** (15) An extreme form of selective distribution wherein the manufacturer grants exclusive rights to a wholesaler or retailer to sell in a geographic region.

**Expected net profit** (14) A concept employed in competitive bidding strategy. Expected net profit equals the probability of the buyer accepting the bid *times* the bid price *minus* related costs.

**Expense item** (9) Industrial products and services that are used within a short period of time.

**Experience curve** (25) The idea that higher market shares reduce costs because of factors like learning advantages, increased specialization, higher investment, and economies of scale.

**Experiment** (6) A scientific investigation in which a researcher controls or manipulates a test group or groups and compares the results with that of a control group that did not receive the controls or manipulations.

**Exploratory research** (6) Research designed to give the researcher an intelligent understanding of the problem area and some insights into its causes and effects.

**Exporting** (22) Selling goods and services abroad.

**External data** (8) In marketing research, the type of secondary data that comes from sources outside a firm.

**Fabricated parts and materials** (11) Industrial goods that actually become a part of the final product.

**Facilitating agencies** (15) Institutions, such as insurance companies, banks, and transportation companies, that provide specialized assistance to channel members in moving the product from producer to consumer.

**Fads** (10) Fashions with abbreviated life cycles. Examples include disco, punk, and new wave.

**Family brand** (11) A brand name that is used for several products made by the same firm, such as General Electric or Johnson & Johnson.

**Family life cycle** (4) The process of family formulation and dissolution. The stages of the cycle include the bachelor stage, young married couples with no children, young married couples with children, older married couples with dependent children, older married couples with no children at home, and solitary survivors.

**Fashions** (10) Currently popular products that tend to follow recurring life cycles.

**FCN treaties** (22) Friendship, commerce, and navigation treaties that include many aspects of world marketing.

**Feedback** (19) Information about receiver response to messages. This data is returned to the sender.

**Fiscal policy** (2) The use of taxation and government spending as a means of controlling the economy.

**Fixed costs** (13) Costs that do not vary with differences in output, such as depreciation and insurance.

**Fixed sum per unit** (19) A budget allocation method under which a predetermined promotional amount is allocated, either on an historical or forecasted basis.

**Flanker brands** (11) The introduction of new products into the market in which the company has established positions in an attempt to increase overall market share. For example, Butcher's Blend Dry Dog Food is Ralston Purina's flanker to their Dog Chow line.

**Flexible pricing** (14) A pricing policy allowing variable prices.

**F.O.B. plant** (14) A price quotation that does not include any shipping charges. The abbreviation refers to Free on Board. The buyer must pay all freight charges. Also called *F.O.B. origin*.

**F.O.B. plant with freight allowed** (14) A price quotation where the seller permits the buyer to deduct transportation expenses from the invoice.

**Focus group interview** (6) A marketing research information-gathering procedure that typically brings eight to 12 individuals together in one location to discuss a given subject.

**Follow-up** (21) The step in the sales process that concerns postsales activities.

**Foreign freight forwarders** (18) Transportation middlemen who specialize in physical distribution outside Canada.

**Foreign licensing** (22) In international marketing, an agreement between a firm and a foreign company, whereby the foreign company produces and distributes the firm's goods in the foreign country.

**Form utility** (1) Created when raw materials are converted into finished products.

**Franchise** (15) An agreement whereby dealers (franchisees) agree to meet the operating requirements of a manufacturer or other franchiser.

**Free trade area** (22) In international marketing, economic integration among participating nations, without any tariff or trade restrictions.

**Freight absorption** (14) A pricing system under which the buyer of goods may deduct shipping expenses from the cost of the goods.

**Freight forwarder** (18) A wholesaling middleman who consolidates shipments from several shippers to enable them to achieve the cost savings of truckload or carload shipments.

**Full-cost pricing** (13) A pricing procedure in which all costs are considered in setting a price, allowing the firm to recover all of its costs and realize a profit.

**Full-function merchant wholesaler** (16) A wholesaling middleman who provides a complete assortment of services for retail customers, including storage, regular contacts through a sales force, delivery, credit, returns privileges, and market information.

**Full service research supplier** (6) An independent marketing research firm that contracts with a client to conduct the complete marketing research project. They define the problem or conceptual stage; work through the research, design, data collection, and analysis stages; and prepare the final report to management.

**Functional accounts** (25) Income statement expense categories representing the purpose for which an expenditure is made.

**GATT** *See* General Agreement on Tariffs and Trade.

**General Agreement on Tariffs and Trade (GATT)** (22) An international trade accord that has sponsored various tariff negotiations.

**General merchandise retailer** (17) A retail store that cars a wide variety of product lines, all of which are stocked some depth. General merchandise retailers would inude department stores, variety stores, and many discount ouses.

**eneric name** (11) A commonly used word that is descrip/e of a particular type of product, such as cola or nylon.

**eneric product** (11) A food or household item characterd by plain labels, little or no advertising, and no brand me.

**eographic segmentation** (4) Dividing a population into omogeneous groups on the basis of location.

**oods – services continuum** (12) A method of presenting le differences and similarities among goods and services.

**ross margin percentage** (25) An evaluative technique in-cating the percentage of revenues available for covering xpenses and earning a profit after the payment of the roduction costs of products sold during a certain time eriod.

**louse-to-house retailing** (17) Direct contact between the tailer-seller and the customer at the home of the customer.

**ypermarket** (17) A giant mass-merchandising retail out-t that operates on a low-price, is self-service, and carries nes of soft goods and groceries. Also called *hypermarché*.

**ypothesis** (6) A tentative explanation about some spe-ific event. A hypothesis is a statement about the relation-hip between variables and carries clear implications for sting this relationship.

**ceberg principle** (25) A theory that suggests that impor-ant evaluative information is often hidden by collected ata when it exists in a summary format.

**dea marketing** (23) The identification and marketing of a ause to chosen consumer segments.

**mporting** (22) Purchasing foreign goods and raw materials.

**mport quota** (22) A restriction on the amount of goods in specific product category that may enter a country.

**mpulse goods** (10) Products for which the consumer spends ittle time in conscious deliberation in making a purchase lecision. Such products are often displayed near cash egisters in retail stores to induce spur-of-the-moment onsumer purchases.

**ncremental-cost pricing** (13) A pricing procedure in which nly the costs directly attributable to a specific output are onsidered in setting a price.

**Individual brand** (11) The strategy of giving each item in a product line its own brand name, rather than identifying it by a single named used for all products in the line. An example would be the many detergents marketed by Procter & Gamble — Tide, Cheer, Oxydol, and so on. *See also* Family brand.

**Individual offerings** (11) One of the primary components of a product mix, it consists of single products.

**Industrial distributor** (10) A wholesaling middleman who operates in the industrial goods market and typically handles small accessory equipment and operating supplies.

**Industrial goods** (4, 9) Products that are used directly or indirectly in producing other goods for resale.

**Industrial goods market** (9) A marketplace made up of customers who purchase goods and services for use in producing other products for resale. Examples include manufacturers, utilities, government agencies, retailers, wholesalers, contractors, mining firms, insurance and real estate firms, and institutions, such as schools and hospitals.

**Inflation** (2) A generally rising price level resulting in reduced purchasing power for the consumer.

**Informative institutional advertising** (20) Advertising intended to increase public knowledge of a concept, idea, philosophy, industry, or company.

**Informative product advertising** (20) Advertising intended to develop initial demand for a product.

**Input-output models** (3) Quantitative forecasting techniques first developed by Wassily Leontif which show the impact on supplier industries of production changes in a given industry and which can be utilized in measuring the impact of changing demand in any industry throughout an economy.

**Installations** (10) A firm's major capital assets such as factories and heavy mahinery. They are relatively long-lived and are expensive. Their purchase represents a major decision for a company.

**Institutional advertising** (20) Promoting a concept, idea, philosophy, or goodwill of an industry, company, or organization.

**Intangible products** (9, 12) Products best illustrated by services such as legal advice or a medical examination.

**Intensive distribution** (15) Practised by marketers of convenience goods who attempt to provide saturation coverage of a given market with their products.

**Intermediary** (15) A business firm operating between the producer and the consumer or industrial purchaser. Both wholesaler and retailer are included in the definition of intermediary.

**Internal secondary data** (6) In marketing research, the type of information that is found in records of sales, product performances, sales force activities, and marketing costs.

**Inventory adjustments** (11) Changes in the amounts of raw materials or goods in process a manufacturer keeps on hand.

**Inventory turnover** (25) An evaluative figure showing how many times the average value of a firm's stock of merchandise is sold in a year.

**Jobber** (15) *See* Wholesaler.

**Job-order production** (15) A production system in which products are manufactured to fill customers' orders.

**Joint demand** (9) In the industrial market, the demand for an industrial good as related to the demand for another industrial good that is necessary for the use of the first item.

**Joint venture** (22) A foreign enterprise jointly held with a national of the country involved.

**Judgement sample** (6) A nonprobability sample of people with a specific attribute.

**Jury of executive opinion** (3) A qualitative sales forecasting method which combines and averages the outlook of top executives from such functional areas as finance, production, marketing, and purchasing.

**Just price** (13) A concept held by the early philosophers. Essentially, they believed that there was one fair price for each good or service.

**Label** (11) The descriptive part of the package, which usually contains the brand name or symbol, name and address of the manufacturer or distributor, product composition and size, and recommended uses of the product.

**Law of retail gravitation** (17) Sets the retail trade area of a potential site on the basis of mileage between alternative locations and relative populations.

**Learning** (8) Any change in behaviour as a result of experience.

**Life-cycle costing** (9) In the industrial market, the cost of using a product over its lifetime.

**Lifestyle** (4) The mode of living of consumers.

**Limited-function merchant wholesaler** (16) A wholesaling middleman who reduces the number of services provided to retail customers and also reduces the costs of servicing such customers.

**Limited-line store** (17) A retail store that competes w larger stores by offering a complete selection of a narr line of merchandise such as clothing, hardware, shoes, sporting goods.

**Line extension** (11) A new product that is closely related existing product lines.

**List price** (14) The rate that is normally quoted to pote tial buyers. It is the basis upon which most price structu are built.

**Local-content law** (22) In international marketing, la specifying the portion of a product that must come fr domestic sources.

**Loss leader** (14) A good priced at less than cost in order attract customers who may then buy other regularly pri merchandise.

**Mail order wholesaler** (16) Limited-function mercha wholesalers who utilize catalogues instead of a sales fo to contact their customers in an attempt to reduce oper ing expense.

**Make-bulk centre** (18) A central warehouse where in vidual small shipments of products are shipped small d tances at high freight rates, reassembled into economi carload or truckload quantities, and then shipped ov longer distances to a large customer or to a storage war house.

**Manufacturers' agent** (16) An agent wholesaling middl man who markets a line of related but noncompeting pro ucts for a number of manufacturers. The agent usua operates on a contractual basis and covers a limited territor

**Marginal analysis** (13, 19) A budgeting procedure, t objective of which is to allocate the same amount for expenditure (such as promotion) that the expenditure w generate in profits.

**Marginal cost** (13) The change in total cost that resu from producing an additional unit of output.

**Marginal revenue** (13, 19) The change in total reven that results from selling an additional unit of output.

**Markdown** (13) A reduction in the price of an item.

**Market** (4) Customers who possess purchasing power a both the willingness and the authority to buy.

**Market price** (14) The amount a consumer or middlem pays for a product.

**Market segmentation** (4, 7) Companies producing nume ous separate products and designing different marketi mixes to satisfy smaller homogeneous segments of the to market.

**.rket share** (25) The percentage of a submarket con-
.lled by a particular seller. The attainment of a specific
.rket share is a common primary objective advocated by
.ny companies.

**.rket share objective** (13) Pricing objective linked to
.ieving and maintaining a stated percentage of the mar-
. for a firm's product or service.

**.rket target** (5) A specific segment of the overall poten-
. market that has been analysed and selected by the
.n. The firm's marketing mix will be directed toward
.isfying this chosen consumer segment.

**.rket target decision analysis** (5) The evaluation of
.ential market segments by dividing the overall market
.o homogeneous groupings. Cross-classifications may
.based on such variables as type of market, geographic
.ation, use frequency, and demographic characteristics.

**.rketing** (1) The development and efficient distribution
.goods, services, ideas, issues, and concepts for chosen
.isumer segments.

**.rketing audit** (25) A thorough, objective evaluation of
. organization's marketing philosophy, goals, policies,
.ocedures, practices, and results.

**.rketing channels** (1, 15) The path a good or service
.lows from producer to final consumer.

**.rketing communications** (19) Messages that deal with
.yer–seller relationships.

**.rketing concept** (1) A managerial philosophy of con-
.ner orientation. The marketing concept holds that all
.nning begins with an analysis of the consumer and that
. company decisions are based upon profitable satisfac-
.n of consumer wants.

**.rketing cost analysis** (25) The evaluation of such items
.selling costs, billing, warehousing, advertising, and de-
.ry expenses, to determine the profitability of particu-
. customers, territories, and product lines. It involves
.ssifying accounting data into *functional* accounts (by
. purpose for which each expenditure was made) rather
.n the traditional *natural* accounts, such as salaries
.d supplies.

**.rketing ethics** (24) The marketer's standards of conduct
.d moral values.

**.rketing functions** (1) Buying, selling, transporting,
.ring, grading, financing, entrepreneurial risk-taking,
.d marketing information.

**.rketing Information System (MIS)** (6) A systematic ap-
.ach to providing relevant information to decision-makers
. a continual basis.

**.rketing institutions** (15) Include such middlemen as
.ailers and wholesalers.

**Marketing mix** (1) The blending of the elements of product planning, price, distribution strategy, and promotion
to satisfy chosen consumer segments.

**Marketing myopia** (1, 12) A term coined by Theodore
Levitt that identifies his thesis that top executives in many
industries have failed to recognize the scope of their businesses. Levitt argues that they lack a marketing orientation.

**Marketing planning** (3) The implementation of planning
activity as it relates to the achievement of marketing
objectives.

**Marketing research** (6) The systematic gathering, recording,
and analysing of data about problems relating to the marketing of goods and services.

**Marketing strategy** (3) The overall company program for
selecting a particular market segment and then satisfying
the segment through the careful use of the elements of the
marketing mix.

**Mark-on** (13) Markup compared against cost of a product,
expressed as a percentage.

**Markup** (13) The amount that is added to cost to determine the selling price.

**Maslow's hierarchy** (8) A classification of needs whereby
priority is assigned to the basic needs that must be at least
partially satisfied before proceeding to the next order of
needs. The hierarchy proceeds from physiological needs
to safety to social needs to esteem to self-actualization.

**Mass merchandisers** (17) Retailers stocking a wider line of
products than department stores, but in less depth.

**Materials handling** (18) All the activities associated in moving products among the manufacturer's plants, warehouses,
and transportation company terminals.

**Membership groups** (7) A sub-category for a reference
group, where the members of the reference group belong
to, say, a country club.

**Merchandise mart** (16) A permanent exhibition facility
where manufacturers rent showcases for their product offerings and display them for visiting retail and wholesale
buyers.

**Merchant wholesaler** (16) A wholesaler middleman who
takes *title* to products.

**Message** (19) Information transmitted by a (marketing)
communication system.

**Middleman** (15) A business firm operating between the
producer and the consumer or industrial purchaser. Both
wholesaler and retailer are included in the definition of
middleman.

**Misleading advertising** (2) A false statement of any kind
made to the public about products or services.

**Missionary sales** (21) A basic sales task. It is an indirect type of selling that can be subclassified into selling the goodwill of a firm and providing the customer with technical or operational assistance.

**Missionary salesperson** (15) A manufacturer's representative who assists wholesalers and retailers in becoming more familiar with the firm's products and aids in store displays and promotional planning.

**Modified breakeven analysis** (13) A pricing technique that combines the traditional breakeven analysis model with an evaluation of consumer demand.

**Modified rebuy** (9) A situation where industrial purchasers are willing to re-evaluate their available options in a repurchase of the same product or service. Lower prices, faster delivery, or higher quality may be buyer desires in this type of purchase situation.

**Monetary policy** (2) Various techniques used by the Bank of Canada to control the money supply and interest rates as a means of controlling the economy.

**Monopolistic competition** (13) A market situation where a large number of sellers offer a heterogeneous product. The existence of product differentiation allows the marketer some degree of control over price. This situation is characteristic of most retailing.

**Monopoly** (13) A market situation with only one seller of a product with no close substitutes. Anti-combines legislation has attempted to eliminate all but *temporary* monopolies, such as those provided by patent protection, and *regulated* monopolies, such as the public service companies.

**Motive** (8) An internal tension state that directs individuals toward the goal of satisfying a felt need.

**MRO items** (10) Supplies for an industrial firm, so called because they can be categorized as maintenance items, repair items, or operating supplies.

**Multinational corporation** (22) A firm that operates in several countries and literally views the world as its market.

**National brands** (11) Those offered by manufacturers. In fact, they are sometimes called *manufacturer's brands*.

**National Transportation Act** (18) Defines transportation policy in Canada.

**Natural accounts** (25) Expense categories traditionally listed on an organization's income statement. An example is salary expenses.

**Need** (8) The lack of something useful; a discrepancy between a desired state and the actual state.

**Negotiated contract** (11) Sometimes used in industrial a governmental purchases when there is only one availa supplier and/or contracts requiring extensive research a development work.

**Neighbourhood shopping centre** (17) A geographi cluster of stores, usually consisting of a supermarket a about 5 to 15 smaller stores. The centre provides con nient shopping for 5 000 to 15 000 shoppers in its vicin

**Net profit percentage** (25) An evaluative technique refl ing the ratio of net profits to net sales for an organizati

**New product committee** (11) An inter-disciplinary gr on temporary assignment that works through functio departments. Its basic task is to coordinate and integr the work of these functional departments on some spec project.

**New-product department** (10) A separate, formally org ized division that is involved with new-product devel ment on a permanent, full-time basis.

**New task buying** (9) Refers to first time or unique ind trial purchase situations that require considerable eff on the part of the decision makers.

**Noise** (19) Interruptions in a communications system.

**Nonprobability sample** (6) Sample chosen in an arbitr fashion in which each member of the population does have a representative chance of being selected.

**Nonprofit organization** (23) A firm whose primary ob tive is something other than the return of a profit to owners.

**Observational study** (6) Conducted by actually view (either by visual observation or through mechanical me such as hidden cameras) the overt actions of the responde

**Odd pricing** (14) A type of psychological pricing that u prices with odd endings, such as $16.99, $17.95, a $18.98. Originally, odd pricing was initiated to force cle to make change, thus serving as a cash control device wit the firm.

**Oligopoly** (13) A market situation with relatively few sell such as in the automobile, steel, tobacco, and petroleu refining industries. There are significant entry barriers new competition due to high start-up costs.

**Open dating** (24) Shows the last possible date that a peri able or semiperishable food item may be sold.

**Operarating expense ratio** (25) An evaluative technic that combines both selling and general expenses and co pares them with overall net sales.

**pinion leader** (7) An individual in any group who is the endsetter. The opinion of such individuals is respected, d they are often sought out for advice. Opinion leaders rve as information sources about new products.

**rder processing** (21) Selling at the wholesale and retail vels; specifically, identifying customer needs, pointing t the need to the customer, and completing the order.

**rganization marketing** (23) Marketing by *mutual bene- organizations* (churches, labour unions, and political rties), *service organizations* (colleges, universities, hos- tals, museums), and *government organizations* (military rvices, police and fire departments, post office) that seeks influence others to accept the goals of, receive the ser- ces of, or contribute in some way to that organization.

**wnership utility** (1, 15) Created by marketers when *title* products is transferred to the consumer at the time of rchase.

**rty-plan selling** (17) A distribution strategy under which company's representative makes a presentation of the oduct(s) in a party setting. Orders are taken and the host hostess receives a commission or gift based on the amount sales.

**netration pricing** (14) A new-product pricing policy that es an entry price lower than what is believed to be the ng-term price. The premise is that an initially lower price ll help secure market acceptance.

**rception** (8) The meaning we attribute to stimuli coming rough our five senses.

**rceptual screen** (8) The perceptual filter through which essages must pass.

**rson marketing** (23) Marketing efforts designed to culti- te the attention, interest, and preference of a market rget toward a person. Person marketing is typically em- oyed by political candidates and celebrities.

**rsonal selling** (19, 21) A seller's promotional presenta- n conducted on a person-to-person basis with the buyer.

**rsuasive institutional advertising** (20) Used to advance e interests of a particular institution within a competi- e environment.

**rsuasive product advertising** (20) A competitive type of vertising that attempts to develop demand for a particu- r product or brand.

**antom freight** (14) In a uniform delivered price system, e amount by which the average transportation charge ceeds the actual cost of shipping for customers near the pply source.

**Physical distribution** (18) Activities concerned with effi- cient movement of finished products from the producer to the consumer. These activities include freight transportation, warehousing, materials handling, protective packaging, inventory control, order processing, plant and warehouse site selection, market forecasting, and customer service. Also known as logistics.

**PIMS study** (13) Acronym for Profit Impact of Market Strategies, a project that discovered that market share and return-on-investment figures are closely linked.

**Place utility** (1, 15) Created by marketers having products available *where* the consumer wants to buy.

**Planned obsolescence** (24) A policy of producing products with only a limited life span. This can occur where the producer uses materials of lower cost without any com- pensating benefits to the consumer such as lower prices or better performance characteristics.

**Planned shopping centre** (17) A group of retail stores owned, co-ordinated, and marketed as a unit.

**Planning** (3) The process of anticipating the future and determining the course of action to achieve company objectives.

**Point-of-purchase advertising** (20) Displays and demon- strations that seek to promote the product at a time and place closely associated with the actual decision to buy.

**Political and legal environment** (2) Component of the mar- keting environment consisting of laws and interpretation of laws that require firms to operate under competitive conditions and to protect consumer rights.

**Pollution** (24) A broad term that is usually defined as "making unclean"; it can be categorized as either *environ- mental* (water and air) or *cultural* (aesthetic and intellectual) pollution.

**Population** (6) The total group that the researcher wants to study. For a political campaign, the population would be eligible voters.

**Positioning** (5) A marketing strategy that concentrates on particular market segments rather than attempting a broader appeal. It attempts to introduce the product into the mind of the potential customer by relating it to competitive products, as exemplified by 7-Up's "Uncola" campaign, relating 7-Up as an alternative to cola beverages.

**Possession utility** (1, 15) *See* Ownership utility.

**Posttesting** (20) The assessment of an advertisement after it has been used.

**Posttransactional phase** (4) The time span after the actual sale.

**Premium** (20) A bonus item given free with the purchase of another product.

**Presentation** (21) The step in the sales process when the salesperson gives the sales message. Typically, the representative describes the product's major characteristics, points out its advantages, and concludes by citing examples of customer satisfaction.

**Prestige goals** (13) In pricing policy, adopting relatively high prices so as to maintain a prestige or quality image with consumers.

**Pretesting** (20) The assessment of an advertisement's effectiveness before it is actually used.

**Pretransactional period** (4) The time span prior to the actual sale.

**Price** (13) The exchange value of a good or service.

**Price elasticity of demand** (13) A measure of responsiveness of purchasers to changes in price; calculated as the percentage change in the quantity of a product or service demanded divided by the percentage change in its price.

**Price elasticity of supply** (14) A measure of responsiveness of suppliers to changes in price; calculated as the percentage change in the quantity of a product or service supplied divided by the percentage change in price.

**Price flexibility** (14) The policy of maintaining a variable price for a product in the market.

**Price limits** (13) A concept that consumers have a price range within which product quality perception varies directly with price. A price below the lower limit is regarded as "too cheap," while one above the higher limit means it is "too expensive."

**Price lining** (14) The practice of marketing merchandise at a limited number of prices.

**Pricing objectives** (13, 14) The goals a company seeks to reach through implementation of its pricing strategy.

**Pricing policy** (14) A general guideline based upon pricing objectives and intended for use in specific pricing decisions.

**Pricing strategy** (1) An element of marketing decision-making dealing with the methods of setting profitable and justified prices.

**Primary data** (6) Data collected for the first time during a marketing research study.

**Private brand** (11) A line of merchandise offered by a wholesaler or retailer under its own label such as Eaton's Birkdale, Eatonia, and Tecomaster brands.

**Private carrier** (18) A freight carrier who only transports products for the firm's use and who cannot legally solic the transportation business of anyone else.

**Probability sample** (6) A sample in which every member the population has an equal chance of being selected.

**Producers** (9) Industrial customers who purchase goo and services for the production of other goods and service

**Product** (10) A bundle of physical, service, and syr bolic characteristics designed to produce consumer wa satisfaction.

**Product advertising** (20) The nonpersonal selling of a pa ticular good or service.

**Product deletion** (10) The elimination of marginal item from a firm's product line.

**Product life cycle** (10) The path of a product from intr duction to deletion. The stages of the product life cyc include introduction, growth, maturity, and decline.

**Product line** (11) A series of related products.

**Product manager** (11) The management officer assigne to one product or product line with complete responsib ity for determining objectives and establishing marketi strategies.

**Product mix** (11, 5) The assortment of product lines a individual offerings available from a marketer.

**Product positioning** (11) Refers to the consumer's perce tion of a product's attributes, use, quality, and advantag and disadvantages.

**Product strategy** (1) An element of marketing decisio making comprising package design, branding, trademark warranties, guarantees, product life cycles, and new-produ development.

**Profit centre** (14, 25) Any part of an organization to whi revenue and controllable costs can be assigned.

**Profit Impact of Market Strategies** (13) *See* PIMS study

**Profit margin on sales** (25) An evaluative figure showir the percentage of each sales dollar that remains after cos and taxes.

**Profit maximization** (13) The traditional pricing objecti of classical economic theory. The assumption is that a firms need to maximize their gains or minimize their losse In actual practice, few, if any, firms meet this goal.

**Promotion** (19) The function of informing, persuadin and influencing the consumer's purchase decision.

**Promotional allowance** (14) An advertising or sales prom tional grant by a manufacturer to other channel membe an attempt to integrate promotional strategy within the channel.

**romotional mix** (19) The blending of personal selling and onpersonal selling (including advertising, sales promotion, nd public relations) by marketers in an attempt to accomlish promotional objectives.

**romotional price** (14) A price that is used as a part of a rm's selling strategy.

**romotional strategy** (1) An element of marketing strategy volving personal selling, advertising, and sales promoon tools.

**rospecting** (21) The step in the selling process that involves identification of potential customers.

**sychographics** (4) Behavioural profiles of consumers, deeloped from analysis of activities, interests, opinions, and festyles, that may be used to segment consumer markets.

**sychological pricing** (14) The belief that certain prices or rice ranges are more appealing to buyers than others.

**sychophysics** (8) The relationship between the actual physial stimulus and the corresponding sensation produced in he individual.

**ublic relations** (19, 20) A firm's communications and elationships with its various publics, including customers, uppliers, stockholders, employees, the government, and he society in which it operates.

**ublic responsibility committee** (24) A permanent group within the board of directors of a firm that considers matters f corporate social responsibility.

**ublic warehouse** (16) An independently owned storage acility that will store and ship products for a rental fee.

**ublicity** (19, 20) The segment of public relations directly elated to promoting a company's products or services.

**ulling strategy** (19) A promotional effort by the seller to timulate final user demand, which then exerts pressure on he distribution channel. The plan is to build consumer lemand for the product that is recognizable to channel members, who will then seek to fill this void.

**ure competition** (13) A market situation in which there is uch a large number of buyers and sellers that no one of hem has a significant influence on price. Other characterstics include a homogeneous product and ease of entry for ellers resulting from low start-up costs. The closest examles exist in the agricultural sector.

**ushing strategy** (19) A promotional effort directed toward the members of the marketing channel. This can be lone through co-operative advertising allowances, trade liscounts, personal selling, and other dealer support.

**Qualifying** (21) The step in the sales process that seeks to determine whether a prospect can become a customer. In most cases financial resources are a determining factor.

**Quantity discount** (14) A price reduction granted because of large purchases. Such a discount can be either *cumulative* (based on purchases over a stated period of time) or *noncumulative* (one-time reduction in list price).

**Quota** (21) A specified sales or profit target that a salesperson is expected to achieve.

**Quota sample** (6) A nonprobability sample that is divided so that different segments or groups are represented in the total sample.

**Rack jobber** (16) A wholesaler who markets specialized lines of merchandise to retail stores and provides the services of merchandising and arrangement, maintenance, and stocking of display racks.

**Rate of return on common equity** (25) An evaluative figure showing how successful a firm has been in earning returns on stockholders' investments.

**Rate of return on total assets** (25) An evaluative figure showing the firm's net profit after taxes as measured against the total assets.

**Raw materials** (10) Industrial goods used in producing the final products such as *farm* products (wheat, cotton, milk) or *natural* products (copper, iron ore, and coal). Since most raw materials are graded, the purchaser is assured of a standardized product with uniform quality.

**Rebate** (14) A refund of a portion of the purchase price, usually granted by the manufacturer of a product.

**Receiver** (19) The person(s) a message is directed toward in a communications system.

**Reciprocity** (9) The practice of giving favourable consideration to suppliers who are also purchasers of the firm's products.

**Recycling** (24) The re-use of such items as packaging materials. Recycling provides a new source of raw materials and alleviates a major factor in environmental pollution. The major problem in recycling is getting the used materials from the consumer back to the manufacturer.

**Reference groups** (7) Groups with which a person identifies and to which his or her behaviour patterns are oriented.

**Referral sample** (6) Referred to as the Snowball Sample. It is a sample which is done in waves as more respondents with the requisite characteristics are identified.

**Regional shopping centre** (17) The largest type of planned cluster of retail stores, usually involving one or more major department stores and as many as 200 other stores. A centre of this size is typically located in an area with at least 250 000 people within 30 minutes driving time of the centre.

**Reinforcement** (8) The reduction in drive that results from a proper response.

**Reminder-oriented institutional advertising** (20) Used to reinforce previous promotional activity on the behalf of an institution, concept, idea, philosophy, industry, or company.

**Reminder-oriented product advertising** (20) Used to reinforce previous promotional activity by keeping the name of the product in front of the public.

**Research design** (6) A comprehensive plan for performing a marketing research study.

**Response** (8) The consumer's reaction to cues and drive.

**Retail advertising** (20) All nonpersonal selling by stores that offer goods or services directly to the consuming public.

**Retail co-operative** (15) A contractual agreement between a group of retailers where, in order to compete with chain operations, each retailer purchases stock in a retail-owned wholesaling operation and agrees to purchase a minimum percentage of supplies from the operation.

**Retail image** (17) Refers to the consumer's perception of a store and the shopping experience it provides.

**Retail life cycle** (17) The concept that retail institutions pass through a series of stages in their existence — introduction, growth, maturity, and decline.

**Retail trade area analysis** (17) Refers to studies that assess the relative drawing power of alternative retail locations.

**Retailer** (15) A middleman who sells products that are purchased by persons for their own use and not for resale.

**Retailing** (17) The activities of persons and firms selling to the ultimate consumer.

**Return on investment (ROI)** (14, 16, 25) The rate of profit (net profit/sales) multiplied by turnover (sales/investment).

**Revaluation** (22) When a nation adjusts its currency upward relative to gold or some other currency.

**Reverse channel** (15) The path goods follow from consumer to manufacturer, in an effort to recycle used products or by-products. *See also* Recycling.

**Reverse reciprocity** (9) The practice of extending supply privileges to firms that provide needed supplies.

**ROI** *See* Return on investment.

**Role** (7) The rights and duties expected by other members of the group of the individual in a certain position in the group.

**Safety stock** (18) In inventory control, a certain quantity of merchandise kept on hand to protect a firm from fluctuations in demand and to prevent depletion of inventory.

**Salary** (21) Fixed payment made on a periodic basis to employees, including salespersons.

**Sales analysis** (25) The study of internal sales data. It involves breaking aggregate data down into its component parts in order to obtain more meaningful information.

**Sales branch** (16) An establishment maintained by a manufacturer that serves as a warehouse for a particular sales territory, thereby duplicating the services of independent wholesalers.

**Sales force composite** (3) A qualitative sales forecasting method in which sales estimates are based upon the combined estimates of the firm's sales force.

**Sales forecast** (3) An estimate of sales, in dollars or physical units, for a specified future period under a proposed marketing plan or program and under an assumed set of economic and other forces outside the unit for which the forecast is made. The forecast may be for a specified item of merchandise or for an entire line.

**Sales management** (21) Management effort exerted in the direction of securing, maintaining, motivating, supervising, evaluating, and controlling an effective sales force.

**Sales maximization** (13) The pricing philosophy analysed by William J. Baumol, an economist. Baumol believes that many firms attempt to maximize sales within a profit constraint.

**Sales office** (16) An establishment maintained by a manufacturer that serves as a regional office for salespersons. The sales office, unlike the sales branch, does not carry inventory.

**Sales promotion** (19, 21) Assorted, one-time, and somewhat extraordinary nonpersonal selling activities (other than advertising).

**Sales quota** (25) A standard of comparison used in sales analysis. It is the level of expected performance by which actual results are compared.

**Sample** (8) A representative group.

**Sampling** (20) Free distribution of a product in an attempt to secure consumer acceptance resulting in future purchases.

**Scrambled merchandising** (17) The attempts of retailers to satisfy consumer demands for convenient one-stop shopping by carrying a variety of seemingly unrelated products; for example, antifreeze in supermarkets.

**Secondary data** (6) Information that has been published previously.

**Selective distribution** (15) The use of a small number of retailers to handle the firm's product or product line.

**Selective perception** (8) People's awareness of only those incoming stimuli they wish to perceive.

**Self-concept** (8) The way people picture themselves, which influences the manner in which they act as consumers.

**Seller's market** (1) A market with a shortage of goods and services.

**Selling agent** (16) An agent wholesaling middleman who markets the products of a manufacturer. The selling agent has full authority over pricing decisions and promotional outlays and often provides financing for the manufacturer.

**Selling expense ratio** (25) An evaluative technique revealing the relationship between selling expenses and total net sales.

**Selling up** (21) The technique of convincing a customer to buy a higher-priced item than he or she originally intended. The practice of selling up should always be used within the constraints of the customer's real needs.

**Semantic differential** (8) An attitude-scaling device that uses a number of bipolar adjectives, such as hot and cold.

**Sender** (19) The source of a message in a communications system.

**Services** (12) Intangible products such as tax advice, management consulting, and hair care. Services are included in the marketing definition of products.

**Shaping** (8) The process of applying a series of rewards and reinforcement so that more complex behaviour can evolve over time.

**Shopping centre** (17) A geographical cluster of retail stores, collectively handling a varied assortment of goods designed to satisfy purchase needs of consumers within the area of the centre.

**Shopping goods** (10) Products purchased by the consumer only after he or she has made comparison of competing goods on such bases as price, quality, style, and colour. Shopping goods may be classified as either *homogeneous* (where the consumer views them as essentially the same) or *heterogeneous* (where the consumer sees significant differences in quality and styling).

**SIC codes** *See* Standard Industrial Classifications.

**Simple random sample** (8) A sample chosen in such a way that every member of the group has an equal chance of being selected.

**Single-line store** *See* Limited-line store.

**Skimming price** (14) A new-product pricing policy that uses a relatively high entry price.

**Social and ethical considerations** (13) A pricing objective based on certain factors of society and ethics. A sliding-scale fee schedule is an example.

**Social class** (7) The relatively permanent divisions in a society into which individuals or families are categorized based on prestige and community status.

**Social responsibility** (24) The duty of business to be concerned with the quality of life as well as its quantity.

**Societal–cultural environment** (2) A marketer's relationship with society in general.

**Sorting** (15) The contribution of distribution channels in securing a balanced stock of goods available to match the needs of customers. It consists of accumulating, allocating, assorting, and sorting out goods.

**Specialty advertising** (20) A sales promotion medium that utilizes useful articles carrying the advertiser's name, address, and advertising message. These include calendars, pens, and matchbooks.

**Specialty goods** (10) Products that possess unique characteristics so as to cause the consumer to make a special effort to obtain them. Specialty goods are typically high-priced and frequently are branded.

**Specialty retailer** (17) One who provides a combination of product lines, service, and/or reputation in an attempt to attract customer preference.

**Specialty store** (17) A retail store that handles only part of a single line of products such as a meat market, a men's shoe store, or a millinery shop.

**Specifications** (9) In the industrial market, a written description of a product or a service needed by a firm. Prospective bidders use this description initially to determine whether they can manufacture the product or deliver the service, and subsequently to prepare a bid.

**Speculative production** (15) A production system based on management's estimate of future demand for its products. Products are produced in advance of orders for them.

**SSWD** (4) Market segment composed of single, separated, widowed, and divorced people.

**Stagflation** (2) A situation where an economy has high unemployment and a rising price level at the same time.

**Standard Industrial Classification (SIC)** (9) A series of industrial classifications developed by the federal government for use in collecting detailed statistics for each industry. These classifications are called *SIC codes*.

**Status** (7) An individual's relative position in a group.

**Status quo objectives** (13) In pricing strategy, goals based on the maintenance of stable prices.

**Stock out** (18) An item that is not available for shipment.

**Stock turnover** (13) The number of times the average inventory is sold annually.

**Storage warehouse** (18) The traditional warehouse where products are stored prior to shipment. Often storage warehouses are used to balance supply and demand problems of the producing firm.

**Straight rebuy** (9) A recurring industrial purchase decision where an item that has performed satisfactorily is purchased again by a customer.

**Strategic business units (SBU)** (3) Related product groupings or classifications within a multi-product firm, so structured for optimal planning purposes.

**Strategic planning** (3) The process of determining an organization's primary objectives, and allocating funds and proceeding on a course of action to achieve those objectives.

**Strategic window** (3) The limited periods during which the "fit" between the key requirements of a market and the particular competencies of a firm is at an optimum.

**Stratified sample** (6) A probability sample that is constructed so that randomly selected sub-samples of different groups are represented in the total sample.

**Subculture** (7) A separate and distinct segment of the prevailing culture.

**Subliminal perception** (8) Communication at the subconscious level of awareness.

**Suboptimization** (18) A condition where individual objectives are accomplished at the cost of accomplishing the broader objectives of the total organization.

**Suggestion selling** (21) Broadening the customer's original purchase with related items, special promotions, and/or holiday and seasonal merchandise.

**Supermarket** (17) A large-scale, departmentalized retail store offering a large variety of food products, such as meats, produce, dairy, canned goods, and frozen foods. It operates on a self-service basis and emphasizes price and adequate parking facilities.

**Supplies** (11) Industrial goods that are considered regular expense items necessary in the daily operation of a firm, but that do not become part of the final product. Supplies include *maintenance, repair,* and *operating* items.

**Supply curve** (18) A schedule relating the quantity offered for sale to specific prices. It is the marginal cost curve above its intersection with the average variable cost curve.

**Survey study** (8) Asks respondents to answer questions in order to obtain information on attitudes, motives, and opinions. There are three types of surveys: telephone, mail, and personal interview.

**Syndicated service** (6) An organization that offers to provide a standardized set of data on a regular basis to all who wish to buy it.

**System** (18) An organized group of parts or components linked together according to a plan to achieve specific objectives.

**Systematic sample** (6) A probability sample that takes every Nth item on a list.

**Tactical planning** (3) The implementation of activities necessary in the achievement of a firm's objectives

**Tangible products** (9) Goods (rather than services, such as legal advice or a medical examination).

**Target return objectives** (13) Either short-run or long-run, they are the profit goals a firm seeks to reach. Typically, they are stated as a percentage of sales or investment.

**Tariffs** (18, 22) Official publications listing the rates for shipping various commodities. This term is also used to identify taxes on imports.

**Task objective method** (19) A sequential approach to allocating promotional budgets. The organization must 1) define the particular goals that it wants the promotional mix to accomplish and 2) determine the amount (as well as type) of promotional activity required to accomplish each of the objectives that have been set.

**Technological environment** (2) The applications of knowledge based upon discoveries in science, inventions, and innovations to marketing.

**Teleshopping** (17) A new type of shopping made possible by cable television whereby the shopper can order merchandise that has been displayed on his or her television set.

**Tertiary industries** (12) A term that has been used to identify the service industries.

**Test marketing** (6, 11) Selection of a specific city or area considered reasonably typical of the total market and the introduction of a new product in this area complete with a

otal promotional campaign. The results of such a program largely determine whether the product will be introduced on a larger scale.

**Tied selling** (15) An agreement requiring a middleman
who wishes to become the exclusive dealer for a manufacturer's products to also carry other of the manufacturer's products in inventory. The legality of a tying contract
is based on whether it restricts competitors from major
markets.

**Time utility** (1, 15) Created by marketers having products
available *when* the consumer wants to buy.

**Tokyo Round** (22) A series of international trade negotiations intended to reduce the amount of tariffs throughout
the world.

**Total-cost approach** (18) This approach to physical distribution advocates considering all distribution-related
factors as a whole, rather than by individual cost item.

**Trade discount** (14) A payment to a channel member
or buyer for performing some marketing function normally required of the manufacturer. Also called *functional
discount*.

**Trade fair or trade exhibition** (16) A periodic show where
manufacturers in a particular industry display their wares
for visiting retail and wholesale buyers.

**Trade-in** (14) An allowance often used in selling durable
goods such as automobiles. A trade-in permits a price
reduction without altering the basic list price.

**Trade industries** (9) Organizations such as retailers and
wholesalers who purchase for resale to others.

**Trademark** (11) A brand that has been given legal protection and has been granted solely to its owner. Thus the
trademark includes not only pictorial design but also the
brand name.

**Trade show** *See* Trade fairs and trade exhibitions.

**Trading stamps** (20) Sales promotion premiums offered by
some retailers. These stamps may be exchanged for items
of value at specified redemption centres.

**Transactional phase** (4) The point in time when a sale is
actually closed.

**Transfer mechanism** (19) In marketing communications,
the means of delivering a message.

**Transfer pricing** (14) Charges for goods sent from one
profit centre to another within the same company.

**Trend analysis** (3) A quantitative sales forecasting method
in which estimates of future sales are determined through
statistical analyses of historical sales patterns.

**Trigger pricing system** (22) In international marketing, a
protective measure taken by a country to combat the practice of dumping. When a price level for a commodity dips
below a preordained figure, it sets off an immediate investigation by a government agency. *See also* Dumping.

**Truck wholesaler** (16) A wholesaler who specializes in the
marketing of perishable food items and making regular
deliveries to retail stores. Also called *trade jobber*.

**Turnover** (13) The number of times the average inventory
is sold annually. The turnover rate is often frequently used
as a sales efficiency measure.

**Tying agreement** (15) An understanding between a dealer
and a manufacturer that requires the dealer to carry the
manufacturer's full product line in exchange for an exclusive dealership.

**Undifferentiated marketing** (5) When firms produce only
one product and attempt to match it to their consumers
with a single marketing mix.

**Uniform delivered price** (14) The same price (including
transportation expenses) quoted to all buyers. The price
that is quoted includes an "average transportation charge"
per customer. This is sometimes called *postage stamp
pricing*.

**Unitizing** (18) The combination of smaller packages into
a single load, often on a pallet. It requires less labour in
materials handling, promotes faster product movement,
and reduces damage and pilferage.

**Unit pricing** (14) Pricing items in terms of some recognized
unit of measurement, such as kilogram, litre, or standard
numerical count.

**Unit trains** (18) A time- and money-saving service provided by railroads to large-volume customers, in which a
train is loaded with the shipments of only one company
and transports solely for that customer.

**Universal product code** (11) Special codes on packages
that can be read by optical scanners. The scanner can print
the item and its price on a sales receipt and simultaneously
maintain a sales and inventory record for the retailer or
shipper.

**Utility** (1) The want-satisfying power of a good or service.

**Value added by manufacturing** (11) The difference between the price charged for a manufactured good and the
cost of the raw materials and other inputs.

**Variable costs** (13) Costs that change when the level of
production is altered, such as raw materials and the wages
paid to operative employees.

**Venture team** (11) An organizational arrangement combining representatives from marketing, engineering, and financial accounting who are responsible for development of new products and services. The venture team is physically separated from the permanent organization and is linked directly with top management for high-level support.

**Vertical Marketing Systems** (**VMS**) (15) Networks that are professionally managed, centrally programmed, and pre-engineered in order to attain operating economies and maximum impact in the channel.

**Voluntary chains** *See* Wholesaler-sponsored voluntary chain.

**Want satisfaction** (9) A state of mind achieved when a consumer's needs have been met as the result of a purchase.

**Warranty** (10) A guarantee to the buyer that the manufacturer or retailer will replace a defective product or refund its purchase price during a specified period of time.

**Weber's Law** (8) The proposition that the higher the initial intensity of a stimulus, the greater the amount of the change in intensity that is necessary in order for a difference to be noticed.

**Wheel-of-retailing** (17) A hypothesis by Malcolm McNair to explain changes in retailing. McNair contended that new types of retailers enter the marketplace by offering lower prices and fewer services and gradually increase the number of services and prices, thereby becoming vulnerable to new types of low-price retailers.

**Wholesaler** (16) A wholesaling middleman who takes title to the goods that he or she handles. The terms *jobber* and *distributor* are synonymous with wholesaler.

**Wholesaler-sponsored voluntary chain** (15) A contractual agreement between a group of retailers and a wholesaler to enable the retailers to compete with chain operations.

**Wholesaling** (15) The activities of firms selling to retailers, other wholesalers, and industrial users, but who do not sell to the ultimate consumer.

**Wholesaling middleman** (16) A broad term that includes wholesalers (those wholesaling middlemen who take title to the products they handle) and also the agents and brokers who perform wholesaling activities but do not take title to the goods.

**Zone pricing** (14) A uniform delivered price quoted by geographical regions.

# Name Index

# Subject Index

## To the Owner of this Book

We are interested in your reaction to M. Dale Beckman's *Foundations of Marketing, Fourth Canadian Edition.* Through feedback from you, we may be able to improve this book in future editions.

1. What was your reason for using this book?

   _____ college course

   _____ university course

   _____ continuing education

   _____ other (please specify)

2. If you used this text for a program, what was the name of that program?

3. Which chapters or sections were omitted from your course?

4. Have you any suggestions for improving this text?

**Fold here**

**Tape shut**